An atlas and index of the
tithe files of mid-nineteenth-century
England and Wales

'Clerical Anticipation'. Cartoon by Cruikshank, published by Allen & Co., London, 1797 (see pp. 1–2).

An atlas and index of the tithe files of mid-nineteenth-century England and Wales

ROGER J. P. KAIN
Senior Lecturer, University of Exeter

in association with
RODNEY E. J. FRY (*cartography*)
HARRIET M. E. HOLT (*research assistant*)

a sequel to
ROGER J. P. KAIN and HUGH C. PRINCE
The tithe surveys of England and Wales

CAMBRIDGE UNIVERSITY PRESS
Cambridge
London   New York   New Rochelle
Melbourne   Sydney

CAMBRIDGE UNIVERSITY PRESS
Cambridge, New York, Melbourne, Madrid, Cape Town, Singapore,
São Paulo, Delhi, Dubai, Tokyo, Mexico City

Cambridge University Press
The Edinburgh Building, Cambridge CB2 8RU, UK

Published in the United States of America by Cambridge University Press, New York

www.cambridge.org
Information on this title: www.cambridge.org/9780521071543

© Cambridge University Press 1986

This publication is in copyright. Subject to statutory exception
and to the provisions of relevant collective licensing agreements,
no reproduction of any part may take place without the written
permission of Cambridge University Press.

First published 1986
First paperback edition 2010

A catalogue record for this publication is available from the British Library

Library of Congress Cataloguing in Publication Data

Kain, R.J.P. (Roger J. P.)
An atlas and index of the tithe files of midnineteenth-
century England and Wales.
Sequel to: The tithe surveys of England and Wales.
Bibliography: p.
Includes indexes.
1. Tithes - England - History - Maps. 2. Tithes -
Wales - History - Maps. I. Fry, Rodney E. J.
II. Holt, Harriet M. E. III. Title
G1816.E423K3 1986   912'.13362   85-675541

ISBN 978-0-0521-25716-9 Hardback
ISBN 978-0-0521-07154-3 Paperback

Cambridge University Press has no responsibility for the persistence or
accuracy of URLs for external or third-party internet websites referred to in
this publication, and does not guarantee that any content on such websites is,
or will remain, accurate or appropriate.

*For Annmaree and my mother
and in memory of Peter Kain, my father*

Preface

The tithe surveys of the early Victorian Age, after the great Domesday Book of the eleventh century, represent the most detailed and important national inventory to be taken before our own times. While tithe surveys have been used in a great number of local studies, this is the first reconstruction deriving a national picture from their data. It is a happy coincidence that this book is published in the year which celebrates both the 900th anniversary of Domesday Book and the 150th anniversary of the Tithe Commutation Act which bequeathed the tithe surveys of England and Wales.

In *The tithe surveys of England and Wales* (Cambridge, Cambridge University Press, 1985), Hugh Prince and I provide an up-to-date guide and work of reference for users of tithe surveys. That book was also conceived as a general introduction to the detailed material which forms the basis of this present work. It is hoped that together these studies will lead to a broader understanding and deeper appreciation of the nation's rural landscapes and agriculture in the middle years of the nineteenth century.

The objects of this *Atlas and index of the tithe files of mid-nineteenth-century England and Wales* are twofold. First, it communicates some of the wealth of quantitative data on mid-nineteenth-century landscapes and farming to be found in the tithe files. To this end, some elements of mid-nineteenth-century landscapes and agricultural systems are reconstructed cartographically, by a set of computer-generated maps, and statistically, by a series of tables in which parish and township data are aggregated, first to counties and then for the whole of England and Wales. Secondly, this work endeavours to reveal some of the richness and variety of written evidence contained in the whole body of 14,829 tithe files. This task is accomplished by means of analytical place and subject indexes arranged county-by-county and by brief essays in which themes commonly encountered in the tithe file papers of each county are described and some flavour of their authors' attitudes is provided by selected quotations. These sections of the work are intended as a research tool to draw attention to source material discussed in tithe files and to assist future scholars to exploit these documents.

This *Atlas and index* represents the principal fruits of a research project financed by the Economic and Social Research Council whose support over a period of more than four years is gratefully acknowledged. Financial help for this work has also been provided by the Leverhulme Trust and the University of Exeter. The assistance of two of my Exeter colleagues is recorded on the Title Page of this work. Harriet Holt helped search the tithe files and extracted information on the nature of tithes and the making of tithe surveys, transcribed statistical data from the files, and listed topics discussed in their papers. I am extremely grateful for the careful way in which she undertood all these tasks. Rodney Fry has directed cartographic procedures, compiled all the base maps needed for computer mapping, and all the hand-drawn maps in this book are his work. Other colleagues at Exeter have also been especially helpful in practical ways. John Buckett modified the GIMMS computer mapping packing for the Exeter computer system and adapted it to the special requirements of this project. Gill Skinner and Raymond Burnley wrote the computer programs to compile the indexes (Oxford University Computing Service's help in typesetting these by LASERCOMP is also gratefully acknowledged); Hilary Collett managed the day-to-day tasks of computer mapping; Andrew Teed produced most of the final photographic prints which Terry Bacon made up into camera-ready pages. I am delighted to record my thanks to these individuals and to everyone else who gave of their time. Professor William Ravenhill as my Head of Department for most of the period of this project granted me generous use of departmental resources and has encouraged this work from the very beginning, as have H. C. Darby, W. R. Mead, Hugh Prince and my Exeter colleague, Brian Harley.

Contents

Preface	*page* vii
List of figures and maps	xiii
List of tables	xxv

INTRODUCTION	1
Tithe, tithe commutation, tithe surveys	1
Reconstructing nineteenth-century landscapes and farming patterns using tithe surveys	1
Tithe files	4
Quantitative data on farming in reports on tithe agreements	16
Transcribing data from tithe files	19
Compiling an atlas of maps	20
Texts and tables	22
Compiling Place and Subject Indexes	23

EASTERN COUNTIES ('arable' format reports on tithe agreements)	26

Essex, p. 27; Suffolk, p. 41; Cambridgeshire, p. 55; Norfolk, p. 69; Lincolnshire, p. 84; Huntingdonshire, p. 99

SOUTHERN COUNTIES ('arable' format reports on tithe agreements)	101

Sussex, p. 102; Kent, p. 112; Hertfordshire, p. 126; Berkshire, p. 137; Hampshire, p. 151; Surrey, p. 165; Middlesex, p. 179

SOUTH-WESTERN COUNTIES ('pastoral' format reports on tithe agreements)	181

Somerset, p. 182; Wiltshire, p. 192; Dorset, p. 201; Devon, p. 211; Cornwall, p. 221

WESTERN COUNTIES ('pastoral' format reports on tithe agreements)	231

Gloucestershire, p. 232; Herefordshire, p. 242; Worcestershire, p. 250; Monmouthshire, p. 260

NORTH-WESTERN COUNTIES ('arable' format reports on tithe agreements)	262

Lancashire, p. 263; Cheshire, p. 272; Staffordshire, p. 283; Shropshire, p. 297; Cumberland, p. 312; Westmorland, p. 314

NORTHERN COUNTIES
('arable' format reports on tithe agreements) 316

Northumberland, p. 317; Durham, p. 329; Yorkshire, North Riding, p. 341; Derbyshire, p. 355; Nottinghamshire, p. 367; York City and Ainsty, p. 369; Yorkshire, East Riding, p. 370; Yorkshire, West Riding, p. 373

MIDLAND COUNTIES
('arable' format reports on tithe agreements) 376

Rutland, p. 377; Warwickshire, p. 384; Oxfordshire, p. 397; Buckinghamshire, p. 411; Bedfordshire, p. 425; Leicestershire, p. 427; Northamptonshire, p. 428

WALES
('pastoral' format reports on tithe agreements) 430

Anglesey, p. 431; Brecon, p. 433; Caernarvonshire, p. 435; Cardiganshire, p. 438; Carmarthenshire, p. 440; Denbighshire, p. 442; Flintshire, p. 445; Glamorgan, p. 447; Merionethshire, p. 449; Montgomeryshire, p. 451; Pembrokeshire, p. 453; Radnorshire, p. 455

ENGLAND AND WALES 457
Arable and grass 458
Crop relativities 458
Crop yields and patterns of output 461

PLACE INDEX 468

England: Bedfordshire, p. 470; Berkshire, p. 470; Buckinghamshire, p. 471; Cambridgeshire, p. 472; Cheshire, p. 473; Cornwall, p. 476; Cumberland, p. 477; Derbyshire, p. 478; Devon, p. 480; Dorset, p. 482; Durham, p. 484; Essex, p. 486; Gloucestershire, p. 488; Hampshire, p. 490; Herefordshire, p. 491; Hertfordshire, p. 493; Huntingdonshire, p. 494; Kent, p. 494; Lancashire, p. 496; Leicestershire, p. 499; Lincolnshire, p. 501; Middlesex, p. 505; Monmouthshire, p. 505; Norfolk, p. 506; Northamptonshire, p. 510; Northumberland, p. 512; Nottinghamshire, p. 514; Oxfordshire, p. 516; Rutland, p. 517; Shropshire, p. 518; Somerset, p. 520; Staffordshire, p. 523; Suffolk, p. 524; Surrey, p. 527; Sussex, p. 528; Warwickshire, p. 530; Westmorland, p. 531; Wiltshire, p. 531; Worcestershire, p. 533; York City and Ainsty, p. 534; Yorkshire, East Riding, p. 535; Yorkshire, North Riding, p. 536; Yorkshire, West Riding, p. 539;

Wales: Anglesey, p. 543; Brecon, p. 543; Caernarvonshire, p. 543; Cardiganshire, p. 544; Carmarthenshire, p. 544; Denbighshire, p. 545; Flintshire, p. 545; Glamorgan, p. 545; Merionethshire, p. 546; Montgomeryshire, p. 546; Pembrokeshire, p. 547; Radnorshire, p. 548;

SUBJECT INDEX 549

England: Bedfordshire, p. 562; Berkshire, p. 562; Buckinghamshire, p. 564; Cambridgeshire, p. 565; Cheshire, p. 567; Cornwall, p. 569; Cumberland, p. 570; Derbyshire, p. 571; Devon, p. 572; Dorset, p. 575; Durham, p. 576; Essex, p. 578; Gloucestershire, p. 580; Hampshire, p. 582; Herefordshire, p. 584; Hertfordshire, p. 585; Huntingdonshire, p. 587; Kent, p. 588; Lancashire, p. 589; Leicestershire, p. 591; Lincolnshire, p. 592; Middlesex, p. 595;

Monmouthshire, p. 596; Norfolk, p. 597; Northamptonshire, p. 601;
Northumberland, p. 602; Nottinghamshire, p. 604; Oxfordshire, p. 605;
Rutland, p. 607; Shropshire, p. 607; Somerset, p. 610; Staffordshire, p. 613;
Suffolk, p. 614; Surrey, p. 617; Sussex, p. 619; Warwickshire, p. 620;
Westmorland, p. 622; Wiltshire, p. 622; Worcestershire, p. 624;
York City and Ainsty, p. 625; Yorkshire, East Riding, p. 625;
Yorkshire, North Riding, p. 627; Yorkshire, West Riding, p. 629;

Wales: Anglesey, p. 631; Brecon, p. 632; Caernarvonshire, p. 633;
Cardiganshire, p. 634; Carmarthenshire, p. 634; Denbighshire, p. 635;
Flintshire, p. 637; Glamorgan, p. 637; Merionethshire, p. 638;
Montgomeryshire, p. 639; Pembrokeshire, p. 640; Radnorshire, p. 641

EPILOGUE 643

Appendix Data held in E.S.R.C. Survey Archive, University of Essex 644

References 649

Figures and maps

Frontispiece 'Clerical Anticipation'. Cartoon by Cruikshank, published by Allen & Co., London, 1797.
Map The coverage of England and Wales by this
Atlas and index of the tithe files   *page* xxviii

1	'The Vicar': a political satire (after Woodward) published by W. Holland, London, 1790	2
2	The tithe files of England and Wales	6
3	'Description of the parish . . .' from the report on the agreement for the commutation of tithes at Castle Camps, Cambridgeshire, 1840 ('arable' format)	7
4a, 4b and 4c	Report on the agreement for the commutation of tithes at Mamhead, Devon, 1838 ('pastoral' format)	8
5	'Rough estimate of the titheable produce' from the report on the agreement for the commutation of tithes at Coveney, Cambridgeshire, 1841 ('arable' format)	17
6	Assistant commissioners' and local tithe agents' appraisals of soil type and quality in Norfolk, Cheshire and Somerset	24
7	Essex: Tithe district key map	30
8	Essex: Reference map	30
9	Essex: Arable as a percentage of tithe district area	31
10	Essex: Pasture as a percentage of tithe district area	31
11	Essex: Woodland as a percentage of tithe district area	32
12	Essex: Common as a percentage of tithe district area	32
13	Essex: Wheat as a percentage of arable	33
14	Essex: Barley as a percentage of arable	33
15	Essex: Oats as a percentage of arable	34
16	Essex: Pulse crops as a percentage of arable	34
17	Essex: Turnips as a percentage of arable	35
18	Essex: Clover and seeds as a percentage of arable	35
19	Essex: Dead fallow as a percentage of arable	36
20	Essex: Yield of wheat in bushels per acre	37
21	Essex: Yield of barley in bushels per acre	37
22	Essex: Yield of oats in bushels per acre	38
23	Essex: Yield of pulse crops in bushels per acre	38
24	Essex: Yield of turnips in £s per acre	39
25	Essex: Yield of clover and seeds in cwts per acre	39
26	Essex: Yield of meadow in cwts per acre	40
27	Essex: Yield of pasture in shillings per acre	40
28	Suffolk: Tithe district key map	44
29	Suffolk: Reference map	44
30	Suffolk: Arable as a percentage of tithe district area	45

xiv   List of figures and maps

31 Suffolk: Pasture as a percentage of tithe district area	45
32 Suffolk: Woodland as a percentage of tithe district area	46
33 Suffolk: Common as a percentage of tithe district area	46
34 Suffolk: Wheat as a percentage of arable	47
35 Suffolk: Barley as a percentage of arable	47
36 Suffolk: Oats as a percentage of arable	48
37 Suffolk: Pulse crops as a percentage of arable	48
38 Suffolk: Turnips as a percentage of arable	49
39 Suffolk: Clover and seeds as a percentage of arable	49
40 Suffolk: Dead fallow as a percentage of arable	50
41 Suffolk: Yield of wheat in bushels per acre	51
42 Suffolk: Yield of barley in bushels per acre	51
43 Suffolk: Yield of oats in bushels per acre	52
44 Suffolk: Yield of pulse crops in bushels per acre	52
45 Suffolk: Yield of turnips in £s per acre	53
46 Suffolk: Yield of clover and seeds in cwts per acre	53
47 Suffolk: Yield of meadow in cwts per acre	54
48 Suffolk: Yield of pasture in shillings per acre	54
49 Cambridgeshire: Tithe district key map	58
50 Cambridgeshire: Reference map	58
51 Cambridgeshire: Arable as a percentage of tithe district area	59
52 Cambridgeshire: Pasture as a percentage of tithe district area	59
53 Cambridgeshire: Woodland as a percentage of tithe district area	60
54 Cambridgeshire: Common as a percentage of tithe district area	60
55 Cambridgeshire: Wheat as a percentage of arable	61
56 Cambridgeshire: Barley as a percentage of arable	61
57 Cambridgeshire: Oats as a percentage of arable	62
58 Cambridgeshire: Pulse crops as a percentage of arable	62
59 Cambridgeshire: Turnips as a percentage of arable	63
60 Cambridgeshire: Clover and seeds as a percentage of arable	63
61 Cambridgeshire: Dead fallow as a percentage of arable	64
62 Cambridgeshire: Yield of wheat in bushels per acre	65
63 Cambridgeshire: Yield of barley in bushels per acre	65
64 Cambridgeshire: Yield of oats in bushels per acre	66
65 Cambridgeshire: Yield of pulse crops in bushels per acre	66
66 Cambridgeshire: Yield of turnips in £s per acre	67
67 Cambridgeshire: Yield of clover and seeds in cwts per acre	67
68 Cambridgeshire: Yield of meadow in cwts per acre	68
69 Cambridgeshire: Yield of pasture in shillings per acre	68
70 Norfolk: Tithe district key map	73
71 Norfolk: Reference map	73
72 Norfolk: Arable as a percentage of tithe district area	74
73 Norfolk: Pasture as a percentage of tithe district area	74
74 Norfolk: Woodland as a percentage of tithe district area	75
75 Norfolk: Common as a percentage of tithe district area	75
76 Norfolk: Wheat as a percentage of arable	76
77 Norfolk: Barley as a percentage of arable	76
78 Norfolk: Oats as a percentage of arable	77
79 Norfolk: Pulse crops as a percentage of arable	77
80 Norfolk: Turnips as a percentage of arable	78
81 Norfolk: Clover and seeds as a percentage of arable	78

82	Norfolk: Dead fallow as a percentage of arable	79
83	Norfolk: Yield of wheat in bushels per acre	80
84	Norfolk: Yield of barley in bushels per acre	80
85	Norfolk: Yield of oats in bushels per acre	81
86	Norfolk: Yield of pulse crops in bushels per acre	81
87	Norfolk: Yield of turnips in £s per acre	82
88	Norfolk: Yield of clover and seeds in cwts per acre	82
89	Norfolk: Yield of meadow in cwts per acre	83
90	Norfolk: Yield of pasture in shillings per acre	83
91	Lincolnshire: Tithe district key map	88
92	Lincolnshire: Reference map	88
93	Lincolnshire: Arable as a percentage of tithe district area	89
94	Lincolnshire: Pasture as a percentage of tithe district area	89
95	Lincolnshire: Woodland as a percentage of tithe district area	90
96	Lincolnshire: Common as a percentage of tithe district area	90
97	Lincolnshire: Wheat as a percentage of arable	91
98	Lincolnshire: Barley as a percentage of arable	91
99	Lincolnshire: Oats as a percentage of arable	92
100	Lincolnshire: Pulse crops as a percentage of arable	92
101	Lincolnshire: Turnips as a percentage of arable	93
102	Lincolnshire: Clover and seeds as a percentage of arable	93
103	Lincolnshire: Dead fallow as a percentage of arable	94
104	Lincolnshire: Yield of wheat in bushels per acre	95
105	Lincolnshire: Yield of barley in bushels per acre	95
106	Lincolnshire: Yield of oats in bushels per acre	96
107	Lincolnshire: Yield of pulse crops in bushels per acre	96
108	Lincolnshire: Yield of turnips in £s per acre	97
109	Lincolnshire: Yield of clover and seeds in cwts per acre	97
110	Lincolnshire: Yield of meadow in cwts per acre	98
111	Lincolnshire: Yield of pasture in shillings per acre	98
112	Sussex: Tithe district key map	105
113	Sussex: Reference map	105
114	Sussex: Arable as a percentage of tithe district area	106
115	Sussex: Pasture as a percentage of tithe district area	106
116	Sussex: Woodland as a percentage of tithe district area	106
117	Sussex: Common as a percentage of tithe district area	107
118	Sussex: Wheat as a percentage of arable	107
119	Sussex: Barley as a percentage of arable	108
120	Sussex: Oats as a percentage of arable	108
121	Sussex: Pulse crops as a percentage of arable	108
122	Sussex: Turnips as a percentage of arable	109
123	Sussex: Clover and seeds as a percentage of arable	109
124	Sussex: Dead fallow as a percentage of arable	109
125	Sussex: Yield of wheat in bushels per acre	110
126	Sussex: Yield of barley in bushels per acre	110
127	Sussex: Yield of oats in bushels per acre	110
128	Sussex: Yield of pulse crops in bushels per acre	111
129	Sussex: Yield of turnips in £s per acre	111
130	Kent: Tithe district key map	115
131	Kent: Reference map	115
132	Kent: Arable as a percentage of tithe district area	116

133 Kent: Pasture as a percentage of tithe district area	116
134 Kent: Woodland as a percentage of tithe district area	117
135 Kent: Orchards and fruit as a percentage of tithe district area	117
136 Kent: Hops as a percentage of tithe district area	118
137 Kent: Wheat as a percentage of arable	118
138 Kent: Barley as a percentage of arable	119
139 Kent: Oats as a percentage of arable	119
140 Kent: Pulse crops as a percentage of arable	120
141 Kent: Turnips as a percentage of arable	120
142 Kent: Clover and seeds as a percentage of arable	121
143 Kent: Dead fallow as a percentage of arable	121
144 Kent: Yield of wheat in bushels per acre	122
145 Kent: Yield of barley in bushels per acre	122
146 Kent: Yield of oats in bushels per acre	123
147 Kent: Yield of pulse crops in bushels per acre	123
148 Kent: Yield of turnips in £s per acre	124
149 Kent: Yield of clover and seeds in cwts per acre	124
150 Kent: Yield of meadow in cwts per acre	125
151 Kent: Yield of pasture in shillings per acre	125
152 Hertfordshire: Tithe district key map	129
153 Hertfordshire: Reference map	129
154 Hertfordshire: Arable as a percentage of tithe district area	130
155 Hertfordshire: Pasture as a percentage of tithe district area	130
156 Hertfordshire: Woodland as a percentage of tithe district area	130
157 Hertfordshire: Common as a percentage of tithe district area	131
158 Hertfordshire: Wheat as a percentage of arable	131
159 Hertfordshire: Barley as a percentage of arable	131
160 Hertfordshire: Oats as a percentage of arable	132
161 Hertfordshire: Pulse crops as a percentage of arable	132
162 Hertfordshire: Turnips as a percentage of arable	132
163 Hertfordshire: Clover and seeds as a percentage of arable	133
164 Hertfordshire: Dead fallow as a percentage of arable	133
165 Hertfordshire: Yield of wheat in bushels per acre	133
166 Hertfordshire: Yield of barley in bushels per acre	134
167 Hertfordshire: Yield of oats in bushels per acre	134
168 Hertfordshire: Yield of pulse crops in bushels per acre	134
169 Hertfordshire: Yield of turnips in £s per acre	135
170 Hertfordshire: Yield of clover and seeds in cwts per acre	135
171 Hertfordshire: Yield of meadow in cwts per acre	135
172 Hertfordshire: Yield of pasture in shillings per acre	136
173 Berkshire: Tithe district key map	140
174 Berkshire: Reference map	140
175 Berkshire: Arable as a percentage of tithe district area	141
176 Berkshire: Pasture as a percentage of tithe district area	141
177 Berkshire: Woodland as a percentage of tithe district area	142
178 Berkshire: Common as a percentage of tithe district area	142
179 Berkshire: Wheat as a percentage of arable	143
180 Berkshire: Barley as a percentage of arable	143
181 Berkshire: Oats as a percentage of arable	144
182 Berkshire: Pulse crops as a percentage of arable	144
183 Berkshire: Turnips as a percentage of arable	145

List of figures and maps xvii

184	Berkshire: Clover and seeds as a percentage of arable	145
185	Berkshire: Dead fallow as a percentage of arable	146
186	Berkshire: Yield of wheat in bushels per acre	147
187	Berkshire: Yield of barley in bushels per acre	147
188	Berkshire: Yield of oats in bushels per acre	148
189	Berkshire: Yield of pulse crops in bushels per acre	148
190	Berkshire: Yield of turnips in £s per acre	149
191	Berkshire: Yield of clover and seeds in cwts per acre	149
192	Berkshire: Yield of meadow in cwts per acre	150
193	Berkshire: Yield of pasture in shillings per acre	150
194	Hampshire: Tithe district key map	154
195	Hampshire: Reference map	154
196	Hampshire: Arable as a percentage of tithe district area	155
197	Hampshire: Pasture as a percentage of tithe district area	155
198	Hampshire: Woodland as a percentage of tithe district area	156
199	Hampshire: Common as a percentage of tithe district area	156
200	Hampshire: Hops as a percentage of tithe district area	157
201	Hampshire: Wheat as a percentage of arable	157
202	Hampshire: Barley as a percentage of arable	158
203	Hampshire: Oats as a percentage of arable	158
204	Hampshire: Pulse crops as a percentage of arable	159
205	Hampshire: Turnips as a percentage of arable	159
206	Hampshire: Clover and seeds as a percentage of arable	160
207	Hampshire: Dead fallow as a percentage of arable	160
208	Hampshire: Yield of wheat in bushels per acre	161
209	Hampshire: Yield of barley in bushels per acre	161
210	Hampshire: Yield of oats in bushels per acre	162
211	Hampshire: Yield of pulse crops in bushels per acre	162
212	Hampshire: Yield of turnips in £s per acre	163
213	Hampshire: Yield of clover and seeds in cwts per acre	163
214	Hampshire: Yield of meadow in cwts per acre	164
215	Hampshire: Yield of pasture in shillings per acre	164
216	Surrey: Tithe district key map	168
217	Surrey: Reference map	168
218	Surrey: Arable as a percentage of tithe district area	169
219	Surrey: Pasture as a percentage of tithe district area	169
220	Surrey: Woodland as a percentage of tithe district area	170
221	Surrey: Common as a percentage of tithe district area	170
222	Surrey: Hops as a percentage of tithe district area	171
223	Surrey: Wheat as a percentage of arable	171
224	Surrey: Barley as a percentage of arable	172
225	Surrey: Oats as a percentage of arable	172
226	Surrey: Pulse crops as a percentage of arable	173
227	Surrey: Turnips as a percentage of arable	173
228	Surrey: Clover and seeds as a percentage of arable	174
229	Surrey: Dead fallow as a percentage of arable	174
230	Surrey: Yield of wheat in bushels per acre	175
231	Surrey: Yield of barley in bushels per acre	175
232	Surrey: Yield of oats in bushels per acre	176
233	Surrey: Yield of pulse crops in bushels per acre	176
234	Surrey: Yield of turnips in £s per acre	177

235	Surrey: Yield of clover and seeds in cwts per acre	177
236	Surrey: Yield of meadow in cwts per acre	178
237	Surrey: Yield of pasture in shillings per acre	178
238	Somerset: Tithe district key map	185
239	Somerset: Reference map	185
240	Somerset: Arable as a percentage of tithe district area	186
241	Somerset: Pasture as a percentage of tithe district area	186
242	Somerset: Woodland as a percentage of tithe district area	187
243	Somerset: Common as a percentage of tithe district area	187
244	Somerset: Wheat as a percentage of arable	188
245	Somerset: Barley as a percentage of arable	188
246	Somerset: Oats as a percentage of arable	189
247	Somerset: Pulse crops as a percentage of arable	189
248	Somerset: Yield of wheat in bushels per acre	190
249	Somerset: Yield of barley in bushels per acre	190
250	Somerset: Yield of oats in bushels per acre	191
251	Somerset: Yield of pulse crops in bushels per acre	191
252	Wiltshire: Tithe district key map	194
253	Wiltshire: Reference map	194
254	Wiltshire: Arable as a percentage of tithe district area	195
255	Wiltshire: Pasture as a percentage of tithe district area	195
256	Wiltshire: Woodland as a percentage of tithe district area	196
257	Wiltshire: Common as a percentage of tithe district area	196
258	Wiltshire: Wheat as a percentage of arable	197
259	Wiltshire: Barley as a percentage of arable	197
260	Wiltshire: Oats as a percentage of arable	198
261	Wiltshire: Pulse crops as a percentage of arable	198
262	Wiltshire: Yield of wheat in bushels per acre	199
263	Wiltshire: Yield of barley in bushels per acre	200
264	Wiltshire: Yield of oats in bushels per acre	200
265	Dorset: Tithe district key map	204
266	Dorset: Reference map	204
267	Dorset: Arable as a percentage of tithe district area	205
268	Dorset: Pasture as a percentage of tithe district area	205
269	Dorset: Woodland as a percentage of tithe district area	206
270	Dorset: Common as a percentage of tithe district area	206
271	Dorset: Orchards and fruit as a percentage of tithe district area	207
272	Dorset: Wheat as a percentage of arable	207
273	Dorset: Barley as a percentage of arable	208
274	Dorset: Oats as a percentage of arable	208
275	Dorset: Yield of wheat in bushels per acre	209
276	Dorset: Yield of barley in bushels per acre	209
277	Dorset: Yield of oats in bushels per acre	210
278	Devon: Tithe district key map	214
279	Devon: Reference map	214
280	Devon: Arable as a percentage of tithe district area	215
281	Devon: Pasture as a percentage of tithe district area	215
282	Devon: Woodland as a percentage of tithe district area	216
283	Devon: Common as a percentage of tithe district area	216
284	Devon: Orchards and fruit as a percentage of tithe district area	217
285	Devon: Wheat as a percentage of arable	217

List of figures and maps

286	Devon: Barley as a percentage of arable	218
287	Devon: Oats as a percentage of arable	218
288	Devon: Yield of wheat in bushels per acre	219
289	Devon: Yield of barley in bushels per acre	219
290	Devon: Yield of oats in bushels per acre	220
291	Cornwall: Tithe district key map	224
292	Cornwall: Reference map	224
293	Cornwall: Arable as a percentage of tithe district area	225
294	Cornwall: Pasture as a percentage of tithe district area	225
295	Cornwall: Woodland as a percentage of tithe district area	226
296	Cornwall: Common as a percentage of tithe district area	226
297	Cornwall: Orchards and fruit as a percentage of tithe district area	227
298	Cornwall: Wheat as a percentage of arable	227
299	Cornwall: Barley as a percentage of arable	228
300	Cornwall: Oats as a percentage of arable	228
301	Cornwall: Yield of wheat in bushels per acre	229
302	Cornwall: Yield of barley in bushels per acre	229
303	Cornwall: Yield of oats in bushels per acre	230
304	Gloucestershire: Tithe district key map	235
305	Gloucestershire: Reference map	235
306	Gloucestershire: Arable as a percentage of tithe district area	236
307	Gloucestershire: Pasture as a percentage of tithe district area	236
308	Gloucestershire: Common as a percentage of tithe district area	237
309	Gloucestershire: Wheat as a percentage of arable	238
310	Gloucestershire: Barley as a percentage of arable	238
311	Gloucestershire: Oats as a percentage of arable	239
312	Gloucestershire: Pulse crops as a percentage of arable	239
313	Gloucestershire: Yield of wheat in bushels per acre	240
314	Gloucestershire: Yield of barley in bushels per acre	240
315	Gloucestershire: Yield of oats in bushels per acre	241
316	Gloucestershire: Yield of pulse crops in bushels per acre	241
317	Herefordshire: Tithe district key map	245
318	Herefordshire: Reference map	245
319	Herefordshire: Arable as a percentage of tithe district area	246
320	Herefordshire: Pasture as a percentage of tithe district area	246
321	Herefordshire: Woodland as a percentage of tithe district area	247
322	Herefordshire: Common as a percentage of tithe district area	247
323	Herefordshire: Wheat as a percentage of arable	248
324	Herefordshire: Barley as a percentage of arable	248
325	Herefordshire: Oats as a percentage of arable	249
326	Herefordshire: Pulse crops as a percentage of arable	249
327	Worcestershire: Tithe district key map	253
328	Worcestershire: Reference map	253
329	Worcestershire: Arable as a percentage of tithe district area	254
330	Worcestershire: Pasture as a percentage of tithe district area	254
331	Worcestershire: Woodland as a percentage of tithe district area	255
332	Worcestershire: Common as a percentage of tithe district area	255
333	Worcestershire: Wheat as a percentage of arable	256
334	Worcestershire: Barley as a percentage of arable	256
335	Worcestershire: Oats as a percentage of arable	257
336	Worcestershire: Pulse crops as a percentage of arable	257

337	Worcestershire: Yield of wheat in bushels per acre	258
338	Worcestershire: Yield of barley in bushels per acre	258
339	Worcestershire: Yield of oats in bushels per acre	259
340	Worcestershire: Yield of pulse crops in bushels per acre	259
341	Lancashire: Tithe district key map	266
342	Lancashire: Reference map	266
343	Lancashire: Arable as a percentage of tithe district area	267
344	Lancashire: Pasture as a percentage of tithe district area	267
345	Lancashire: Wheat as a percentage of arable	268
346	Lancashire: Barley as a percentage of arable	268
347	Lancashire: Oats as a percentage of arable	269
348	Lancashire: Pulse crops as a percentage of arable	269
349	Lancashire: Yield of wheat in bushels per acre	270
350	Lancashire: Yield of barley in bushels per acre	270
351	Lancashire: Yield of oats in bushels per acre	271
352	Lancashire: Yield of pulse crops in bushels per acre	271
353	Cheshire: Tithe district key map	275
354	Cheshire: Reference map	275
355	Cheshire: Arable as a percentage of tithe district area	276
356	Cheshire: Pasture as a percentage of tithe district area	276
357	Cheshire: Common as a percentage of tithe district area	277
358	Cheshire: Wheat as a percentage of arable	277
359	Cheshire: Barley as a percentage of arable	278
360	Cheshire: Oats as a percentage of arable	278
361	Cheshire: Turnips as a percentage of arable	279
362	Cheshire: Dead fallow as a percentage of arable	279
363	Cheshire: Yield of wheat in bushels per acre	280
364	Cheshire: Yield of barley in bushels per acre	280
365	Cheshire: Yield of oats in bushels per acre	281
366	Cheshire: Yield of turnips in £s per acre	281
367	Cheshire: Yield of meadow in cwts per acre	282
368	Staffordshire: Tithe district key map	286
369	Staffordshire: Reference map	286
370	Staffordshire: Arable as a percentage of tithe district area	287
371	Staffordshire: Pasture as a percentage of tithe district area	287
372	Staffordshire: Woodland as a percentage of tithe district area	288
373	Staffordshire: Common as a percentage of tithe district area	288
374	Staffordshire: Wheat as a percentage of arable	289
375	Staffordshire: Barley as a percentage of arable	289
376	Staffordshire: Oats as a percentage of arable	290
377	Staffordshire: Pulse crops as a percentage of arable	290
378	Staffordshire: Turnips as a percentage of arable	291
379	Staffordshire: Clover and seeds as a percentage of arable	291
380	Staffordshire: Dead fallow as a percentage of arable	292
381	Staffordshire: Yield of wheat in bushels per acre	293
382	Staffordshire: Yield of barley in bushels per acre	293
383	Staffordshire: Yield of oats in bushels per acre	294
384	Staffordshire: Yield of pulse crops in bushels per acre	294
385	Staffordshire: Yield of turnips in £s per acre	295
386	Staffordshire: Yield of clover and seeds in cwts per acre	295
387	Staffordshire: Yield of meadow in cwts per acre	296

388	Staffordshire: Yield of pasture in shillings per acre	296
389	Shropshire: Tithe district key map	301
390	Shropshire: Reference map	301
391	Shropshire: Arable as a percentage of tithe district area	302
392	Shropshire: Pasture as a percentage of tithe district area	302
393	Shropshire: Woodland as a percentage of tithe district area	303
394	Shropshire: Common as a percentage of tithe district area	303
395	Shropshire: Wheat as a percentage of arable	304
396	Shropshire: Barley as a percentage of arable	304
397	Shropshire: Oats as a percentage of arable	305
398	Shropshire: Pulse crops as a percentage of arable	305
399	Shropshire: Turnips as a percentage of arable	306
400	Shropshire: Clover and seeds as a percentage of arable	306
401	Shropshire: Dead fallow as a percentage of arable	307
402	Shropshire: Yield of wheat in bushels per acre	308
403	Shropshire: Yield of barley in bushels per acre	308
404	Shropshire: Yield of oats in bushels per acre	309
405	Shropshire: Yield of pulse crops in bushels per acre	309
406	Shropshire: Yield of turnips in £s per acre	310
407	Shropshire: Yield of clover and seeds in cwts per acre	310
408	Shropshire: Yield of meadow in cwts per acre	311
409	Shropshire: Yield of pasture in shillings per acre	311
410	Northumberland: Tithe district key map	320
411	Northumberland: Reference map	320
412	Northumberland: Arable as a percentage of tithe district area	321
413	Northumberland: Pasture as a percentage of tithe district area	321
414	Northumberland: Woodland as a percentage of tithe district area	322
415	Northumberland: Wheat as a percentage of arable	322
416	Northumberland: Barley as a percentage of arable	323
417	Northumberland: Oats as a percentage of arable	323
418	Northumberland: Pulse crops as a percentage of arable	324
419	Northumberland: Turnips as a percentage of arable	324
420	Northumberland: Clover and seeds as a percentage of arable	325
421	Northumberland: Dead fallow as a percentage of arable	325
422	Northumberland: Yield of wheat in bushels per acre	326
423	Northumberland: Yield of barley in bushels per acre	326
424	Northumberland: Yield of oats in bushels per acre	327
425	Northumberland: Yield of pulse crops in bushels per acre	327
426	Northumberland: Yield of turnips in £s per acre	328
427	Durham: Tithe district key map	332
428	Durham: Reference map	332
429	Durham: Arable as a percentage of tithe district area	333
430	Durham: Pasture as a percentage of tithe district area	333
431	Durham: Woodland as a percentage of tithe district area	334
432	Durham: Wheat as a percentage of arable	334
433	Durham: Barley as a percentage of arable	335
434	Durham: Oats as a percentage of arable	335
435	Durham: Pulse crops as a percentage of arable	336
436	Durham: Turnips as a percentage of arable	336
437	Durham: Clover and seeds as a percentage of arable	337
438	Durham: Dead fallow as a percentage of arable	337

439 Durham: Yield of wheat in bushels per acre — 338
440 Durham: Yield of barley in bushels per acre — 338
441 Durham: Yield of oats in bushels per acre — 339
442 Durham: Yield of pulse crops in bushels per acre — 339
443 Durham: Yield of turnips in £s per acre — 340
444 Yorkshire, North Riding: Tithe district key map — 345
445 Yorkshire, North Riding: Reference map — 345
446 Yorkshire, North Riding: Arable as a percentage of tithe district area — 346
447 Yorkshire, North Riding: Pasture as a percentage of tithe district area — 346
448 Yorkshire, North Riding: Wheat as a percentage of arable — 347
449 Yorkshire, North Riding: Barley as a percentage of arable — 347
450 Yorkshire, North Riding: Oats as a percentage of arable — 348
451 Yorkshire, North Riding: Pulse crops as a percentage of arable — 348
452 Yorkshire, North Riding: Turnips as a percentage of arable — 349
453 Yorkshire, North Riding: Clover and seeds as a percentage of arable — 349
454 Yorkshire, North Riding: Dead fallow as a percentage of arable — 350
455 Yorkshire, North Riding: Yield of wheat in bushels per acre — 350
456 Yorkshire, North Riding: Yield of barley in bushels per acre — 351
457 Yorkshire, North Riding: Yield of oats in bushels per acre — 351
458 Yorkshire, North Riding: Yield of pulse crops in bushels per acre — 352
459 Yorkshire, North Riding: Yield of turnips in £s per acre — 352
460 Yorkshire, North Riding: Yield of clover and seeds in cwts per acre — 353
461 Yorkshire, North Riding: Yield of meadow in cwts per acre — 353
462 Yorkshire, North Riding: Yield of pasture in shillings per acre — 354
463 Derbyshire: Tithe district key map — 358
464 Derbyshire: Reference map — 358
465 Derbyshire: Arable as a percentage of tithe district area — 359
466 Derbyshire: Pasture as a percentage of tithe district area — 359
467 Derbyshire: Woodland as a percentage of tithe district area — 360
468 Derbyshire: Wheat as a percentage of arable — 360
469 Derbyshire: Barley as a percentage of arable — 361
470 Derbyshire: Oats as a percentage of arable — 361
471 Derbyshire: Pulse crops as a percentage of arable — 362
472 Derbyshire: Turnips as a percentage of arable — 362
473 Derbyshire: Clover and seeds as a percentage of arable — 363
474 Derbyshire: Dead fallow as a percentage of arable — 363
475 Derbyshire: Yield of wheat in bushels per acre — 364
476 Derbyshire: Yield of barley in bushels per acre — 364
477 Derbyshire: Yield of oats in bushels per acre — 365
478 Derbyshire: Yield of pulse crops in bushels per acre — 365
479 Derbyshire: Yield of meadow in cwts per acre — 366
480 Rutland: Tithe district key map — 379
481 Rutland: Reference map — 379
482 Rutland: Arable as a percentage of tithe district area — 380
483 Rutland: Pasture as a percentage of tithe district area — 380
484 Rutland: Woodland as a percentage of tithe district area — 380
485 Rutland: Common as a percentage of tithe district area — 380
486 Rutland: Wheat as a percentage of arable — 380
487 Rutland: Barley as a percentage of arable — 380
488 Rutland: Oats as a percentage of arable — 381
489 Rutland: Pulse crops as a percentage of arable — 381

490	Rutland: Turnips as a percentage of arable	381
491	Rutland: Clover and seeds as a percentage of arable	381
492	Rutland: Dead fallow as a percentage of arable	381
493	Rutland: Yield of wheat in bushels per acre	382
494	Rutland: Yield of barley in bushels per acre	382
495	Rutland: Yield of oats in bushels per acre	382
496	Rutland: Yield of pulse crops in bushels per acre	382
497	Rutland: Yield of turnips in £s per acre	382
498	Rutland: Yield of clover and seeds in cwts per acre	383
499	Rutland: Yield of meadow in cwts per acre	383
500	Rutland: Yield of pasture in shillings per acre	383
501	Warwickshire: Tithe district key map	387
502	Warwickshire: Reference map	387
503	Warwickshire: Arable as a percentage of tithe district area	388
504	Warwickshire: Pasture as a percentage of tithe district area	388
505	Warwickshire: Woodland as a percentage of tithe district area	389
506	Warwickshire: Wheat as a percentage of arable	389
507	Warwickshire: Barley as a percentage of arable	390
508	Warwickshire: Oats as a percentage of arable	390
509	Warwickshire: Pulse crops as a percentage of arable	391
510	Warwickshire: Turnips as a percentage of arable	391
511	Warwickshire: Clover and seeds as a percentage of arable	392
512	Warwickshire: Dead fallow as a percentage of arable	392
513	Warwickshire: Yield of wheat in bushels per acre	393
514	Warwickshire: Yield of barley in bushels per acre	393
515	Warwickshire: Yield of oats in bushels per acre	394
516	Warwickshire: Yield of pulse crops in bushels per acre	394
517	Warwickshire: Yield of turnips in £s per acre	395
518	Warwickshire: Yield of clover and seeds in cwts per acre	395
519	Warwickshire: Yield of meadow in cwts per acre	396
520	Warwickshire: Yield of pasture in shillings per acre	396
521	Oxfordshire: Tithe district key map	400
522	Oxfordshire: Reference map	400
523	Oxfordshire: Arable as a percentage of tithe district area	401
524	Oxfordshire: Pasture as a percentage of tithe district area	401
525	Oxfordshire: Woodland as a percentage of tithe district area	402
526	Oxfordshire: Common as a percentage of tithe district area	402
527	Oxfordshire: Wheat as a percentage of arable	403
528	Oxfordshire: Barley as a percentage of arable	403
529	Oxfordshire: Oats as a percentage of arable	404
530	Oxfordshire: Pulse crops as a percentage of arable	404
531	Oxfordshire: Turnips as a percentage of arable	405
532	Oxfordshire: Clover and seeds as a percentage of arable	405
533	Oxfordshire: Dead fallow as a percentage of arable	406
534	Oxfordshire: Yield of wheat in bushels per acre	407
535	Oxfordshire: Yield of barley in bushels per acre	407
536	Oxfordshire: Yield of oats in bushels per acre	408
537	Oxfordshire: Yield of pulse crops in bushels per acre	408
538	Oxfordshire: Yield of turnips in £s per acre	409
539	Oxfordshire: Yield of clover and seeds in cwts per acre	409
540	Oxfordshire: Yield of meadow in cwts per acre	410

541	Oxfordshire: Yield of pasture in shillings per acre	410
542	Buckinghamshire: Tithe district key map	414
543	Buckinghamshire: Reference map	414
544	Buckinghamshire: Arable as a percentage of tithe district area	415
545	Buckinghamshire: Pasture as a percentage of tithe district area	415
546	Buckinghamshire: Woodland as a percentage of tithe district area	416
547	Buckinghamshire: Common as a percentage of tithe district area	416
548	Buckinghamshire: Wheat as a percentage of arable	417
549	Buckinghamshire: Barley as a percentage of arable	417
550	Buckinghamshire: Oats as a percentage of arable	418
551	Buckinghamshire: Pulse crops as a percentage of arable	418
552	Buckinghamshire: Turnips as a percentage of arable	419
553	Buckinghamshire: Clover and seeds as a percentage of arable	419
554	Buckinghamshire: Dead fallow as a percentage of arable	420
555	Buckinghamshire: Yield of wheat in bushels per acre	421
556	Buckinghamshire: Yield of barley in bushels per acre	421
557	Buckinghamshire: Yield of oats in bushels per acre	422
558	Buckinghamshire: Yield of pulse crops in bushels per acre	422
559	Buckinghamshire: Yield of turnips in £s per acre	423
560	Buckinghamshire: Yield of clover and seeds in cwts per acre	423
561	Buckinghamshire: Yield of meadow in cwts per acre	424
562	Buckinghamshire: Yield of pasture in shillings per acre	424
563	England and Wales: Arable as a percentage of total county area	462
564	England and Wales: Pasture as a percentage of total county area	462
565	England and Wales: Ratio of arable to pasture	462
566	England and Wales: Wheat as a percentage of arable	463
567	England and Wales: Barley as a percentage of arable	463
568	England and Wales: Oats as a percentage of arable	463
569	England and Wales: Pulse crops as a percentage of arable	463
570	England and Wales: Turnips as a percentage of arable	464
571	England and Wales: Clover and seeds as a percentage of arable	464
572	England and Wales: Dead fallow as a percentage of arable	464
573	England and Wales: Yield of wheat in bushels per acre	465
574	England and Wales: Yield of barley in bushels per acre	465
575	England and Wales: Yield of oats in bushels per acre	465
576	England and Wales: Yield of pulse crops in bushels per acre	465
577	England and Wales: Yield of turnips in £s per acre	466
578	England and Wales: Yield of clover and seeds in cwts per acre	466
579	England and Wales: Gross output of wheat in five regions	467
580	England and Wales: Gross output of barley in five regions	467
581	England and Wales: Gross output of oats in five regions	467
582	England and Wales: Gross output of all grains in five regions	467

Tables

1	Assistant tithe commissioners/local tithe agents and their reports on agreements for commutation of tithes in England and Wales	*page* 11
2	Reports on agreements for commutation of tithes in Essex	29
3	Land use, crops and yields in Essex *c.* 1836	29
4	Reports on agreements for commutation of tithes in Suffolk	43
5	Land use, crops and yields in Suffolk *c.* 1836	43
6	Reports on agreements for commutation of tithes in Cambridgeshire	57
7	Land use, crops and yields in Cambridgeshire *c.* 1836	57
8	Reports on agreements for commutation of tithes in Norfolk	72
9	Land use, crops and yields in Norfolk *c.* 1836	72
10	Reports on agreements for commutation of tithes in Lincolnshire	87
11	Land use, crops and yields in Lincolnshire *c.* 1836	87
12	Reports on agreements for commutation of tithes in Huntingdonshire	100
13	Land use, crops and yields in Huntingdonshire *c.* 1836	100
14	Reports on agreements for commutation of tithes in Sussex	104
15	Land use, crops and yields in Sussex *c.* 1836	104
16	Reports on agreements for commutation of tithes in Kent	114
17	Land use, crops and yields in Kent *c.* 1836	114
18	Reports on agreements for commutation of tithes in Hertfordshire	128
19	Land use, crops and yields in Hertfordshire *c.* 1836	128
20	Reports on agreements for commutation of tithes in Berkshire	139
21	Land use, crops and yields in Berkshire *c.* 1836	139
22	Reports on agreements for commutation of tithes in Hampshire	153
23	Land use, crops and yields in Hampshire *c.* 1836	153
24	Reports on agreements for commutation of tithes in Surrey	167
25	Land use, crops and yields in Surrey *c.* 1836	167
26	Reports on agreements for commutation of tithes in Middlesex	180
27	Reports on agreements for commutation of tithes in Somerset	184
28	Land use, crops and yields in Somerset *c.* 1836	184
29	Reports on agreements for commutation of tithes in Wiltshire	193
30	Land use, crops and yields in Wiltshire *c.* 1836	193
31	Reports on agreements for commutation of tithes in Dorset	203
32	Land use, crops and yields in Dorset *c.* 1836	203
33	Reports on agreements for commutation of tithes in Devon	213
34	Land use, crops and yields in Devon *c.* 1836	213
35	Reports on agreements for commutation of tithes in Cornwall	223
36	Land use, crops and yields in Cornwall *c.* 1836	223
37	Reports on agreements for commutation of tithes in Gloucestershire	234
38	Land use, crops and yields in Gloucestershire *c.* 1836	234

39	Reports on agreements for commutation of tithes in Herefordshire	244
40	Land use and crops in Herefordshire c. 1836	244
41	Reports on agreements for commutation of tithes in Worcestershire	252
42	Land use, crops and yields in Worcestershire c. 1836	252
43	Reports on agreements for commutation of tithes in Monmouthshire	261
44	Land use in Monmouthshire c. 1836	261
45	Reports on agreements for commutation of tithes in Lancashire	265
46	Land use, crops and yields in Lancashire c. 1836	265
47	Reports on agreements for commutation of tithes in Cheshire	274
48	Land use, crops and yields in Cheshire c. 1836	274
49	Reports on agreements for commutation of tithes in Staffordshire	285
50	Land use, crops and yields in Staffordshire c. 1836	285
51	Reports on agreements for commutation of tithes in Shropshire	300
52	Land use, crops and yields in Shropshire c. 1836	300
53	Reports on agreements for commutation of tithes in Cumberland	313
54	Reports on agreements for commutation of tithes in Westmorland	315
55	Reports on agreements for commutation of tithes in Northumberland	319
56	Land use, crops and yields in Northumberland c. 1836	319
57	Reports on agreements for commutation of tithes in Durham	331
58	Land use, crops and yields in Durham c. 1836	331
59	Reports on agreements for commutation of tithes in Yorkshire, North Riding	344
60	Land use, crops and yields in Yorkshire, North Riding, c. 1836	344
61	Reports on agreements for commutation of tithes in Derbyshire	357
62	Land use, crops and yields in Derbyshire c. 1836	357
63	Reports on agreements for commutation of tithes in Nottinghamshire	368
64	Reports on agreements for commutation of tithes in York City and Ainsty	369
65	Reports on agreements for commutation of tithes in Yorkshire, East Riding	372
66	Land use, crops and yields in Yorkshire, East Riding, c. 1836	372
67	Reports on agreements for commutation of tithes in Yorkshire, West Riding	375
68	Land use, crops and yields in Yorkshire, West Riding, c. 1836	375
69	Reports on agreements for commutation of tithes in Rutland	378
70	Land use, crops and yields in Rutland c. 1836	378
71	Reports on agreements for commutation of tithes in Warwickshire	386
72	Land use, crops and yields in Warwickshire c. 1836	386
73	Reports on agreements for commutation of tithes in Oxfordshire	399
74	Land use, crops and yields in Oxfordshire c. 1836	399
75	Reports on agreements for commutation of tithes in Buckinghamshire	413
76	Land use, crops and yields in Buckinghamshire c. 1836	413
77	Reports on agreements for commutation of tithes in Bedfordshire	426
78	Land use, crops and yields in Bedfordshire c. 1836	426
79	Reports on agreements for commutation of tithes in Leicestershire	427
80	Reports on agreements for commutation of tithes in Northamptonshire	429
81	Reports on agreements for commutation of tithes in Anglesey	432
82	Land use and crops in Anglesey c. 1836	432
83	Reports on agreements for commutation of tithes in Brecon	434
84	Land use in Brecon c. 1836	434
85	Reports on agreements for commutation of tithes in Caernarvonshire	437
86	Land use in Caernarvonshire c. 1836	437
87	Reports on agreements for commutation of tithes in Cardiganshire	439
88	Land use in Cardiganshire c. 1836	439
89	Reports on agreements for commutation of tithes in Carmarthenshire	441

90	Land use in Carmarthenshire c. 1836	441
91	Reports on agreements for commutation of tithes in Denbighshire	444
92	Land use, crops and yields in Denbighshire c. 1836	444
93	Reports on agreements for commutation of tithes in Flintshire	446
94	Land use and crops in Flintshire c. 1836	446
95	Reports on agreements for commutation of tithes in Glamorgan	448
96	Land use in Glamorgan c. 1836	448
97	Reports on agreements for commutation of tithes in Merionethshire	450
98	Land use and crops in Merionethshire c. 1836	450
99	Reports on agreements for commutation of tithes in Montgomeryshire	452
100	Land use and crops in Montgomeryshire c. 1836	452
101	Reports on agreements for commutation of tithes in Pembrokeshire	454
102	Land use in Pembrokeshire c. 1836	454
103	Reports on agreements for commutation of tithes in Radnorshire	456
104	Land use in Radnorshire c. 1836	456
105	Area of arable, meadow and pasture in England and Wales 1801–72	459
106	Grain and pulse crops in England c. 1836	460
107	Clover, seeds, roots and fallows in England c. 1836	460
108	Gross per annum output of grain crops in England c. 1836	460

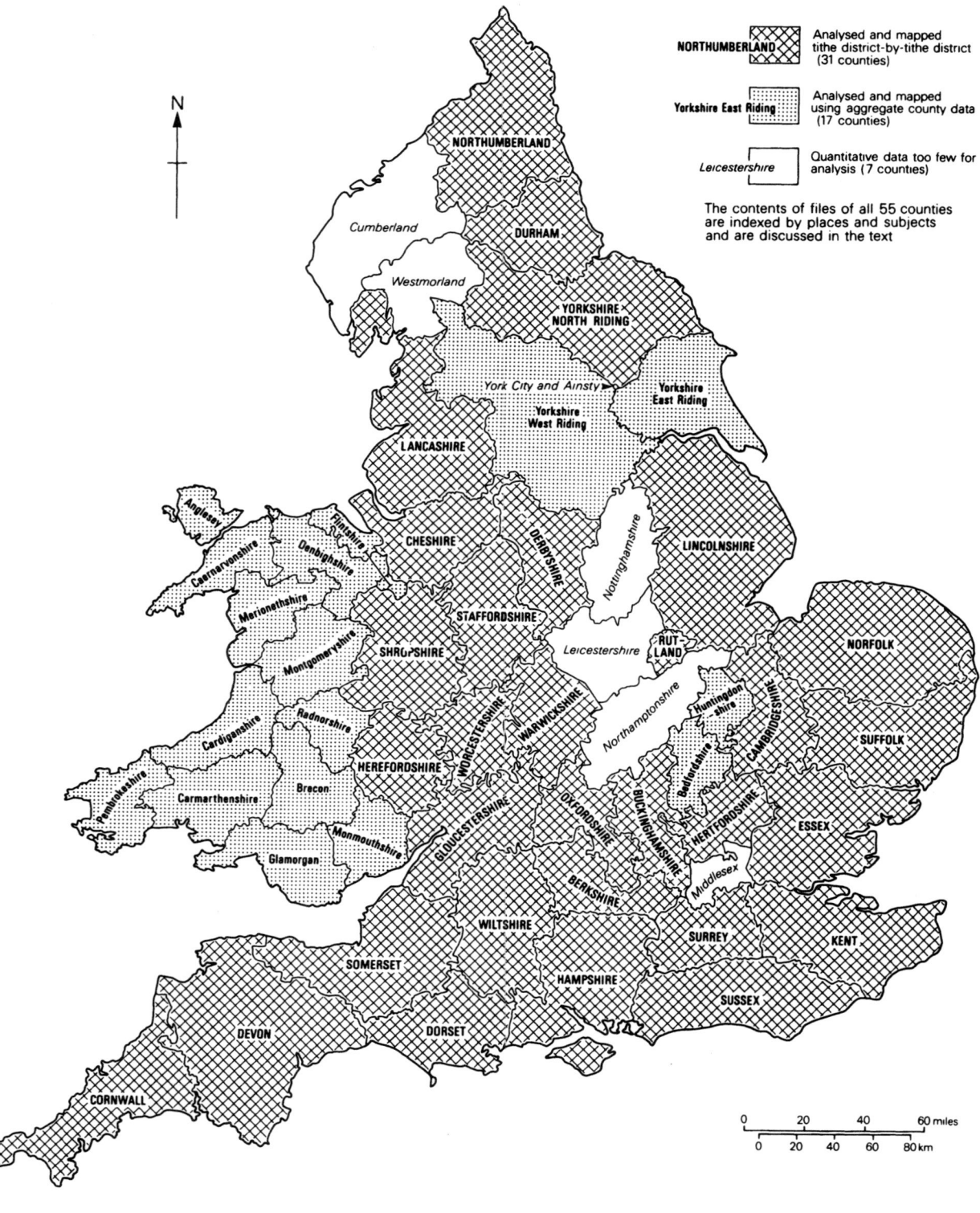

The coverage of England and Wales by this *Atlas and index of the tithe files*

INTRODUCTION

Tithe, tithe commutation, tithe surveys

Traditionally farmers were required to give a proportion, usually about a tenth, of the gross annual produce from their land for the support of the Church (Evans, 1976). This method of financing the Church was popular with few in the parishes of England and Wales, was liable to abuse by both oppressive claims of tithe owners and flagrant evasions by tithe payers and it fomented rural unrest. Moreover, by the end of the eighteenth century, the rural base of tithe collection was becoming both anachronistic and unfair as increasing proportions of the nation's wealth were generated by industries which had no obligation to pay tithe. Furthermore, those farmers who invested in expensive agricultural improvements to produce more crops and livestock had to pay more tithe than their less enterprising neighbours. The Church was a sleeping partner in these capital improvements, took none of the risks but nonetheless received its tenth of the profits. Local parsons were caricatured as avaricious, grasping capitalists, more concerned with amassing wealth than with saving souls (Fig. 1).

The Tithe Commutation Act of 1836, one of a number of great reforms enacted by Parliament during the 1830s, commuted tithe to a fluctuating money payment based on an average of the actual value of tithes paid in each parish or township over the previous five years. This sum was then apportioned among the properties of each district according to the land use of each field or farm. Inquiries were conducted under the Act in 14,829 separate tithe districts (usually a parish in southern England and a township in the north) which revealed that some tithe remained to be commuted in more than 12,000 tithe districts in England and Wales. In most of these (some 11,800 districts) commutation was effected by map and schedule of apportionment. Together these constitute what is commonly known as the 'parish tithe survey'. The nature of tithes, the process of commutation and the characteristics of tithe documents are discussed in Chapters 1–4 of *The tithe surveys of England and Wales*.

Reconstructing nineteenth-century landscape and farming patterns using tithe surveys

The value of tithe surveys as sources of information for historical inquiries has been long appreciated; they were being used by agricultural commentators within a few years of their compilation and have since been employed in many hundreds of historical studies of past

1 'The Vicar': a political satire (after Woodward) published by W. Holland, London, 1790. Beneath the picture is etched:
   Then the Vicar
   Full of fees customary, with his burying gloves;
   Jealous of his rights, and apt to quarrel;
   Claiming his paltry penny farthing tithes
   E'en at the Lawyers price

land use, field systems, farming and land tenure. Many of these contributions to our understanding of nineteenth-century England and Wales are reviewed in Chapters 5–8 of *The tithe surveys of England and Wales*.

In a short prospective section in the concluding chapter of that book, Hugh Prince and I set out the following brief rationale for reconstructing mid-nineteenth-century rural landscapes of England and Wales. We noted that the middle years of the nineteenth century have been acclaimed as a period of capital intensive or high farming (Perry, 1981). These decades, we said, have been considered to mark the culmination of two centuries or more of great technical improvement in agriculture, of improvements made possible by the introduction of new farm implements, of improved breeds of livestock and of new methods of conserving and increasing soil fertility by adopting new crop rotations and applying new kinds of fertilisers. Changes in farming technique were accompanied by an intensification of farming on land already occupied, and by an extension of cultivation to land that was formerly waste. At the beginning of Queen Victoria's reign, the new husbandry was very much an accomplished fact. In most parts of England, communal grazing on the fallow field and on the stubble after harvest had disappeared as the exchange and consolidation of scattered holdings in open fields was nearing completion. At the same time, the reclamation of many tracts of heath, waste and unimproved grazings was approaching its furthest limits; draining and embanking were proceeding in the remaining waterlogged areas; while in parks and on land of little value for agriculture, hundreds of acres of woodland were being planted every year.

Soon after the tithe survey of England and Wales was effectively completed, fresh stimuli to agricultural change appeared. From about 1840 onwards, for example, a number of developments improved the competitive position of clay land farmers and began to mask the previously marked distinction between the cold, heavy clay lands and the warmer light soil areas of the country. Really effective drainage, the only feasible technical solution to the expense, uncertainty and inefficiency of the old three-course clay land arable system, was made possible with the production of cheap tile drains and the availability of financial assistance. Also, in the middle years of the nineteenth century, a sound scientific base for agriculture was being developed and the increasing use of bone meal, the importation of guano and the purchase of feedstuffs showed that the farmer was beginning to heed the advice so readily made available to him in contemporary didactic literature. Wheat yields, which had remained fairly level during the first three decades of the century, rose markedly after about 1840 (Healy and Jones, 1962). Finally, the extension of the railway network after 1840 had far-reaching effects on the agriculture of this country. Markets for products were widened and regional specialisation was facilitated, whilst manures and fertilisers could be more efficiently and cheaply distributed.

The tithe surveys picture the nation's rural landscape just before these later transformations occurred, at a time early in the expansion of the urban–industrial food market and before the great Victorian extension of the urban area over the countryside. Indeed, the post-1840 advance in agriculture was in no small measure assisted by the Tithe Commutation Act which removed an iniquitous tax on the produce of land and so dismantled a further barrier to improvement. Tithe surveys tell us little, however, about the people who lived and worked in these landscapes. Nor do they contain much information on the demand side of the production equation, or on the flows of working and investment capital which sustained agricultural activities. Tithe surveys provide an essentially static picture, a characterisation of the consequences of a myriad of unknown, individual management decisions.

In a retrospective commentary on *An historical geography of England before A.D. 1800* (Cambridge, 1936), Professor H. C. Darby wrote: 'a second group of sources that cry aloud for attention is the body of Tithe Surveys made on a parish basis in the years around 1840' (Darby, 1960, p. 154). He reviewed a number of pioneer analyses of the tithe documents and declared 'well would it be if such work could be extended to give us as complete a map of England about 1840 as possible' (Darby, 1960, p. 154). A principal contention of this *Atlas and index* is that without such a map the geography of nineteenth-century England and Wales can be only partially understood. Since 1960 considerable advances have been made with this source and indeed the *New historical geography of England* (Cambridge, 1973) contains a number of maps based upon tithe survey evidence (Harley, 1973). At the commencement of this project in 1978, sufficient work had been completed to enable broad regional contrasts in agriculture at mid-century to be recognised but the greater part of England and Wales still awaited detailed investigation to establish more precisely the patterns of farming and the characteristics of rural landscapes. A majority of these previous studies (reviewed in *The tithe surveys of England and Wales*, Chapters 6 and 7) have plotted land use field-by-field from tithe apportionments and maps mainly for East Anglia, the Home Counties and southern England. This concentration of activity reflects both the good coverage of tithe surveys in these areas and also the interests of the Department of Geography at University College, London, where many of these students were based. In total these forty and more workers have prepared land use maps of some six million acres and it is contended that the point has been reached beyond which the repetition of such studies of the detailed interdigitations of land use decline in usefulness (Kain, 1979a). On the other hand, data in the tithe files discussed in the following section of this Introduction are at once sufficiently detailed to produce a vivid picture of the rural landscape of England and can also throw more light on the nature of farming at mid-century than a field-by-field map of arable land. The files are also the most neglected of tithe survey documents. Although one fifth of them had been examined for various purposes at the commencement of this project, fully 85 per cent of the farming data awaited transcription and analysis when we began work to collect information on the nature of tithes and the process of tithe commutation for *The tithe surveys of England and Wales* and to compile this *Atlas and index*.

Tithe files

A separate tithe file was opened for each of the 14,829 districts where inquiries were made under the Tithe Commutation Act. All the files are now in the custody of the Public Record Office at Class IR18 and it is these which provide data for the set of maps published in this volume and it is their contents which are the subject of the two indexes printed in this book. Tithe files are described in greater detail in *The tithe surveys of England and Wales*, pp. 103–12 and 141–5. In outline the files contain a record of the process of commutation as it was effected in each tithe district, the papers and correspondence that were generated,

Introduction 5

minutes of meetings that were held, records of inquiries that were conducted, drafts of and reports on agreements for tithe commutation, notes relating to the imposition of a compulsory award if agreement could not be achieved and papers concerning the apportionment of rent-charge once its amount had been confirmed. Not all these categories of papers were generated at every place or still remain in every file. All tithe files have been weeded, many in the two years of 1911 and 1912, but without any obvious rationale. In a few places the weeding has been quite savage; some Shropshire files, for example, are quite empty and bear an enigmatic note on the outside cover that all papers were 'valueless' and have, therefore, been discarded. On the other hand some Somerset files contain scores of closely written pages describing disputed customary modus payments in lieu of tithes.

On the basis of their general contents, the whole body of tithe files can be divided into three broad categories:

> *Category 1:* files for 2,096 districts where tithe was no longer payable in 1836 or was redeemed or about to be redeemed by direct merger in the land.
>
> *Category 2:* files for 5,993 districts where tithe was commuted by compulsory award.
>
> *Category 3:* files for 6,740 districts where tithe owners and tithe payers entered into a voluntary agreement for commutation by apportionment. These agreements were usually confirmed by the Tithe Commission but in about 400 places they were replaced by compulsory awards.

One of the commonest reasons for tithe exemption (category 1 files) was the extinction of tithe under the terms of an earlier parliamentary enclosure act. The files for these places usually contain only a copy of this act or a summary of its provisions concerning tithe commutation. In districts where tithe owners and tithe payers could not reach an agreement (category 2 files), tithe was commuted by an award drawn up by an assistant commissioner. Files for these places usually contain a draft of the award, a record of the commissioner's inquiries, minutes of evidence presented at meetings he may have attended to hear cases put by disputing parties and evidence of witnesses brought to him under oath. Sometimes tithe payers and tithe owners had been deadlocked in dispute for years, but often there was nothing more sinister than the fact that amounts of tithe remaining to be commuted were so small that there was little incentive to initiate the voluntary process. Generally speaking, the more complex problems were, the more likely it is that extensive records were generated. But assistant commissioners' interpretations of what they were expected to do prior to framing an award varied greatly as does the detail with which they set down their decision.

When tithe owners and tithe payers entered into a voluntary agreement for commutation (category 3 files) and decided to apportion rather than merge the rent-charge, the Tithe Commission instructed one of its local tithe agents or assistant commissioners to visit the district to write a report advising whether the agreement was fair to all parties and should be confirmed and then apportioned. From November 1837, local agents were issued with printed forms to help focus their inquiries and to standardise their answers. These reports contain descriptions of local landscapes and farming practices written by local tithe agents or assistant commissioners in support of their judgement of the fairness or otherwise of an agreed rent-charge. Their answers were written on one of only two types of form provided by the Tithe Commission depending on its officers' perception of a county as one characterised by arable or pastoral farming (Fig. 2). Figures 3 and 4c indicate the difference in the breadth of information required by these two types of questionnaire forms, a fact which is reflected in the length and content of the answers, though, as with the compulsory awards, information provided does vary according to the predilections of individual local tithe agents and assistant commissioners (Holt, 1984). Assistant tithe commissioners and local agents who worked in England and Wales are listed in Table 1 which also specifies the total number of reports compiled by each man, the counties in which they worked, the number of reports for each county written by each man and the number completed in each year. In any one county, one agent reported on a clear majority of districts and, therefore, the value of the descriptive material can vary from one part of the country to another in line with the

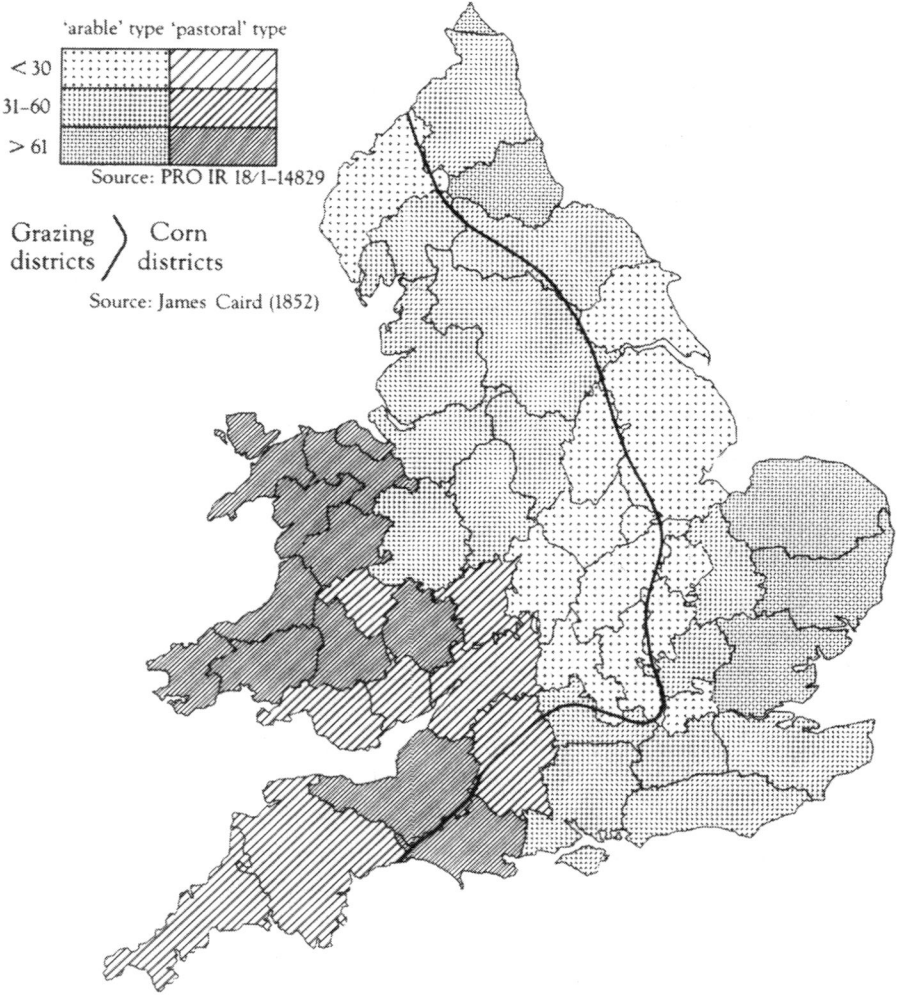

2 The tithe files of England and Wales

3 'Description of the parish . . .' from the report on the agreement for the commutation of tithes at Castle Camps, Cambridgeshire, 1840 ('arable' format)

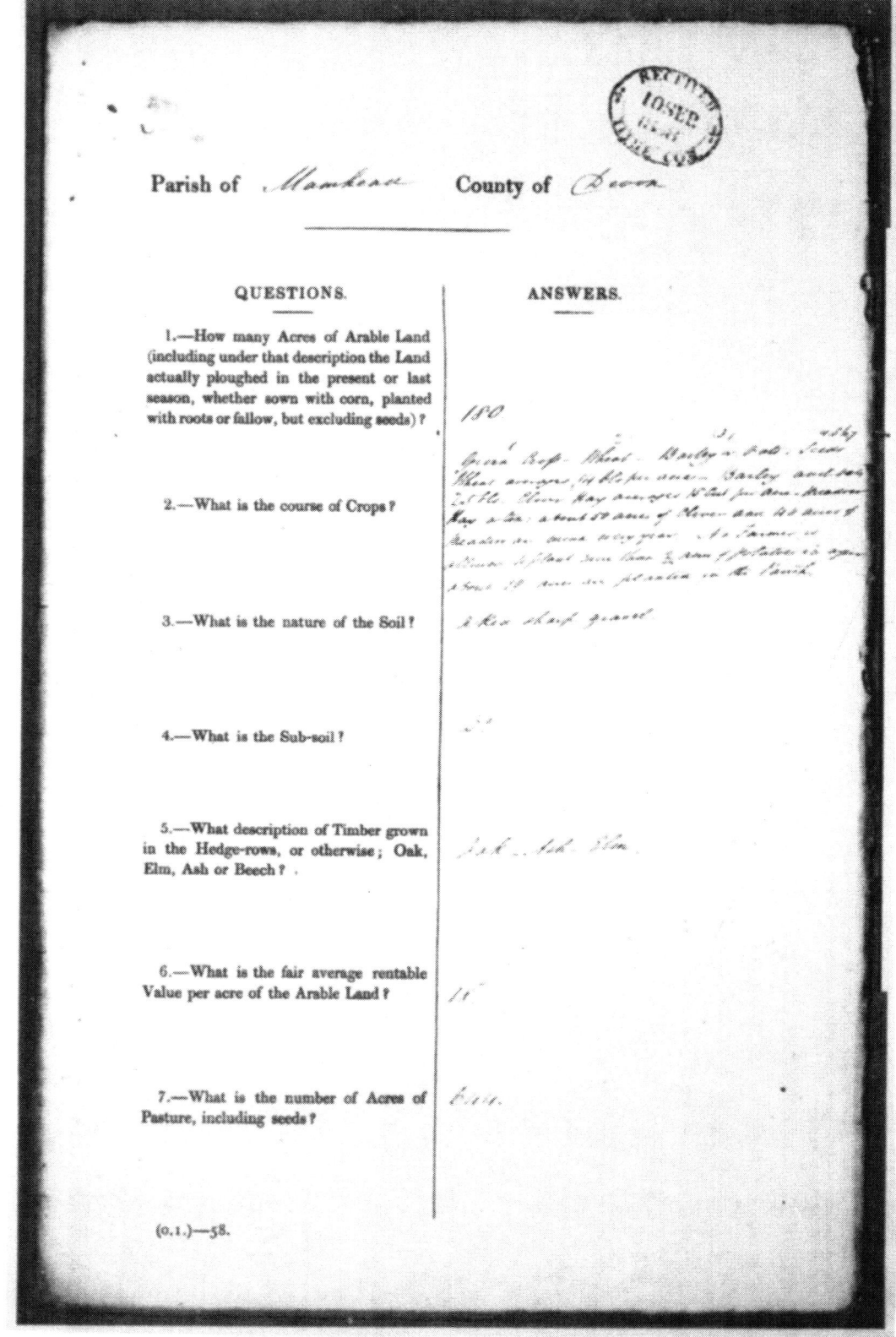

4a, 4b and 4c Report on the agreement for the commutation of tithes at Mamhead, Devon, 1838 ('pastoral' format)

(2)

QUESTIONS.	ANSWERS.
8.—What is the nature of the Soil?	Middle Gravel
9.—What is the Sub-soil?	Do.
10.—What description of Timber?	Elm – Oak
11.—What is the number of Acres of Common?	30
12.—Stock: Number of Cows? Ditto - Bullocks? Ditto - Horses? Ditto - Sheep?	20 55 25 240 } For actual Number
13.—What is the fair average rentable Value of the Pasture?	2–
14.—Ditto, of the Common?	1
15.—Average Composition on the seven years previous to Christmas 1835	£. s. d. 136. 9. 6
Add average amount of Rates, if paid by the Occupiers or Landowners for the Tithe-owner	3. 9. 22 139. 18. 12

(3)

VALUATION.

		£. s. d.
One-fifth of the Arable, at	15 per Acre	32. 8. 0
One-eighth of the Pasture, at	27 per Acre	108. 13. 6
One-eighth of the Common, at	1 per Acre	0. 3. 9

Total	£. 141. 5. 3
Total Rent-charge, exclusive of Glebe	145. 0. 0
Difference	£. 3. 14. 9

Remarks, stating the peculiar circumstances of the Parish, which may affect the value of the Tithe.

The Course of Husbandry, which Mr Robert Newman has adopted, tends very much to improve the Parish: but as much of the arable land is being converted into Pasture, the present value of the Tithes is not likely to be much enhanced. However the great improvements now carrying on into effect in the rough lands of the parish will very probably prevent the Tithes from considerably diminishing in Value.

Sept. 8th 1838.

Introduction

Table 1 *Assistant tithe commissioners/local tithe agents and their reports on agreements for commutation of tithes in England and Wales**

Assistant commissioner/ local tithe agent	Total number of reports	Counties and number of reports				Year and number of reports			
George Ashdown	61	Shropshire	42			1839	24	1842	7
		Staffordshire	19			1838	12	1841	6
						1840	12		
Richard Atkinson	1	Cumberland	1			1837	1		
A. O. Baker	51	Hampshire	46	Sussex	1	1839	23	1837	9
		Kent	4			1838	13	1840	6
Arthur Biddell	22	Suffolk	21			1838	15	1837	3
		Essex	1			1839	4		
George Bolls	327	Wiltshire	144	Herefordshire	16	1839	117	1841	28
		Dorset	116	Worcestershire	13	1838	116	1837	17
		Gloucestershire	37	Radnorshire	1	1840	40	1842	9
F. Browne Browne	139	Buckinghamshire	19	Warwickshire	8	1839	64		
		Hampshire	18	Northamptonshire	7	1840	41		
		Essex	16	Surrey	7	1841	18		
		Suffolk	13	Bedfordshire	4	1838	16		
		Berkshire	10	Hertfordshire	4				
		Cambridgeshire	10	Middlesex	3				
		Kent	10	Huntingdonshire	1				
		Oxfordshire	9						
John Coldridge	2	Devon	2			1838	1	1839	1
Henry Dixon	11	Essex	7	Cambridgeshire	1	1837	8		
		Somerset	2	Suffolk	1	1836	3		
William Downes	11	Essex	10	Suffolk	1	1838	7	1837	4
John Farncombe	169	Sussex	158			1839	58	1842	20
		Hampshire	9			1838	28	1843	6
		Kent	2			1841	28	1844	1
						1840	27	1845	1
John Fenton	192	Caernarvonshire	50	Flintshire	8	1840	71	1842	29
		Denbighshire	43	Merionethshire	8	1841	43	1843	9
		Anglesey	42	Pembrokeshire	1	1839	40		
		Montgomeryshire	40						
Henry Gilbert	13	Kent	13			1839	9	1840	2
						1838	2		
William Glasson	44	Cornwall	44			1839	24	1840	9
						1838	11		
Edward Greathed	48	Hertfordshire	8	Lincolnshire	4	1838	43		
		Derbyshire	7	Essex	3	1837	3		
		Rutland	6	Bedfordshire	1	1839	2		
		Staffordshire	6	Middlesex	1				
		Warwickshire	6	Surrey	1				
		Leicestershire	5						
Henry Bertram Gunning	214	Norfolk	109			1839	89	1838	14
		Suffolk	86			1840	52	1843	8
		Cambridgeshire	17			1841	27	1845	2
		Huntingdonshire	2			1842	19	1846	2
Edward Young Hancock	34	Essex	34			1839	18	1838	16
Robert Hart	22	Yorkshire, N.R.	10	Yorkshire, W.R.	5	1840	12		
		Yorkshire, E.R.	6	Nottinghamshire	1	1839	10		

Table 1 (cont.)

Assistant commissioner/ local tithe agent	Total number of reports	Counties and number of reports				Year and number of reports			
William Heard	175	Essex	49	Surrey	3	1839	44	1845	10
		Hertfordshire	37	Bedfordshire	2	1842	31	1844	7
		Suffolk	35	Huntingdonshire	2	1840	27	1846	2
		Norfolk	20	Oxfordshire	2	1843	24	1848	2
		Cambridgeshire	11	Middlesex	1	1838	15	1847	1
		Hampshire	9	Warwickshire	1	1841	12		
		Berkshire	3						
Thomas P. Hilder	39	Kent	39			1839	23	1838	7
						1840	9		
James Hodsen	1	Sussex	1			1838	1		
John Holder	173	Cheshire	132	Shropshire	11	1839	55	1841	23
		Staffordshire	17	Nottinghamshire	1	1838	41	1842	16
		Derbyshire	12			1840	32	1843	6
Thomas Hoskins	538	Herefordshire	103	Carmarthenshire	29	1839	203		
		Monmouthshire	56	Gloucestershire	27	1840	125		
		Pembrokeshire	55	Radnorshire	20	1838	100		
		Brecon	52	Yorkshire, W.R.	16	1841	58		
		Worcestershire	43	Cheshire	10	1842	33		
		Cardiganshire	42	Shropshire	9	1843	15		
		Glamorgan	38	Staffordshire	5	1837	2		
		Yorkshire, N.R.	31	Lincolnshire	2	1844	2		
Charles Howard	303	Yorkshire, N.R.	75	York, City and Ainsty	7	1839	149		
		Yorkshire, W.R.	71	Cheshire	6	1838	117		
		Yorkshire, E.R.	43	Staffordshire	5	1837	27		
		Durham	41	Cumberland	3	1840	6		
		Lincolnshire	27	Nottinghamshire	2	1845	2		
		Lancashire	11	Rutland	2	1844	1		
		Shropshire	8	Westmorland	2	1846	1		
Anthony Jackson	4	Cambridgeshire	3	Hertfordshire	1	1838	3	1837	1
Henry Jemmett	20	Oxfordshire	13	Buckinghamshire	2	1839	12		
		Berkshire	5			1838	8		
James Jerwood	214	Devon	122	Somerset	7	1838	59	1842	16
		Cornwall	61	Wiltshire	2	1839	53	1843	8
		Dorset	22			1840	49	1844	6
						1841	22	1845	1
John Johnes	132	Pembrokeshire	37	Flintshire	4	1838	81		
		Carmarthenshire	26	Denbighshire	3	1837	38		
		Glamorgan	14	Herefordshire	2	1839	10		
		Monmouthshire	12	Wiltshire	2	1836	2		
		Cardiganshire	11	Montgomeryshire	2	1846	1		
		Radnorshire	10	Worcestershire	1				
		Brecon	8						
Roger Kynaston	207	Essex	63	Cambridgeshire	2	1839	101		
		Suffolk	49	Middlesex	2	1838	50		
		Kent	27	Staffordshire	2	1840	46		
		Hampshire	23	Bedfordshire	1	1841	9		
		Berkshire	10	Buckinghamshire	1	1836	1		
		Derbyshire	8	Hertfordshire	1				
		Norfolk	6	Surrey	1				
		Oxfordshire	6	Warwickshire	1				
		Warwickshire	4						

Introduction

Table 1 (cont.)

Assistant commissioner/ local tithe agent	Total number of reports	Counties and number of reports				Year and number of reports			
Frederick Leigh	75	Devon	73			1840	31	1841	14
		Cornwall	2			1839	25	1842	5
George Louis	31	Dorset	17	Cornwall	2	1838	26		
		Gloucestershire	4	Durham	1	1842	3		
		Devon	3	Somerset	1	1843	2		
		Lincolnshire	3						
Thomas Martin	132	Lancashire	82	Westmorland	6	1839	48	1842	9
		Derbyshire	20	Yorkshire, W.R.	6	1840	26	1844	7
		Cheshire	12			1838	20	1841	5
		Cumberland	6			1843	15	1845	2
John Mee Mathew	167	Essex	45	Middlesex	4	1838	73		
		Suffolk	19	Buckinghamshire	3	1839	66		
		Kent	16	Cambridgeshire	3	1840	15		
		Staffordshire	16	Hertfordshire	3	1837	9		
		Hampshire	13	Westmorland	3	1841	3		
		Norfolk	9	Oxfordshire	2	1842	1		
		Shropshire	9	Warwickshire	2				
		Surrey	7	Cheshire	1				
		Berkshire	6	Cumberland	1				
		Nottinghamshire	5						
? Mears	91	Norfolk	80	Cambridgeshire	4	1838	41	1840	15
		Suffolk	5	Huntingdonshire	2	1839	31	1841	4
James Drage Merest	232	Norfolk	161	Essex	1	1838	111	1840	6
		Suffolk	64	Lincolnshire	1	1839	63	1842	2
		Staffordshire	4	Shropshire	1	1837	50		
Horace William Meteyard	156	Norfolk	42	Yorkshire, W.R.	5	1838	71		
		Kent	28	Buckinghamshire	4	1839	60		
		Suffolk	12	Derbyshire	4	1840	11		
		Surrey	12	Middlesex	3	1841	9		
		Shropshire	11	Oxfordshire	3	1842	2		
		Hampshire	9	Cambridgeshire	2	1843	2		
		Berkshire	7	Nottinghamshire	2	1844	1		
		Essex	5	Cheshire	1				
		Warwickshire	5	Leicestershire	1				
N. S. Meryweather	16	Worcestershire	9	Staffordshire	2	1838	15		
		Shropshire	5			1839	1		
John Milner	8	Dorset	7			1837	8		
		Somerset	1						
John B. Neal	6	Durham	3			1840	6		
		Northumberland	3						
Thomas Neve	1	Kent	1			1837	1		
Charles Osborn	26	Hampshire	22			1838	11	1840	6
		Sussex	4			1839	7	1837	2
Aneurin Owen	145	Denbighshire	47	Caernarvonshire	7	1838	38	1848	4
		Flintshire	18	Dorset	5	1839	38	1841	2
		Wiltshire	17	Devon	2	1843	23	1846	1
		Montgomeryshire	17	Somerset	1	1844	20		
		Merionethshire	16	Cardiganshire	1	1845	15		
		Anglesey	13	Pembrokeshire	1	1840	4		
Robert Page	334	Somerset	284	Herefordshire	6	1838	119	1837	14

Table 1 (cont.)

Assistant commissioner/local tithe agent	Total number of reports	Counties and number of reports				Year and number of reports			
		Gloucestershire	23	Wiltshire	4	1839	102	1842	13
		Devon	9			1840	54	1843	10
		Dorset	8			1841	21	1844	1
Thomas Clements Parr	69	Berkshire	35	Hampshire	6	1840	45	1839	3
		Oxfordshire	28			1841	19	1842	2
John Story Penleaze	18	Durham	13	Yorkshire, E.R.	2	1839	18		
		Yorkshire, N.R.	3						
John Penny	65	Lancashire	30	Yorkshire, E.R.	4	1839	39		
		Cheshire	11	Northumberland	2	1840	14		
		Durham	4	Staffordshire	2	1841	12		
		Lincolnshire	4	Yorkshire, N.R.	2				
		Shropshire	4	Yorkshire, W.R.	2				
Richard Burton Phillipson	340	Yorkshire, W.R.	53	Derbyshire	21	1840	93		
		Cheshire	43	Lincolnshire	14	1841	62		
		Yorkshire, N.R.	40	Yorkshire, E.R.	8	1839	51		
		Northumberland	38	Nottinghamshire	7	1842	51		
		Shropshire	30	Leicestershire	3	1843	39		
		Durham	27	Westmorland	3	1844	24		
		Staffordshire	26	Rutland	2	1845	16		
		Lancashire	24	Cumberland	1	1846	4		
Thomas Phippard	4	Hampshire	3	Dorset	1	1839	3	1838	1
John Pickering	277	Lincolnshire	63	Berkshire	5	1839	119		
		Surrey	29	Cambridgeshire	5	1838	61		
		Suffolk	24	Kent	4	1840	56		
		Essex	20	Northamptonshire	4	1841	26		
		Yorkshire, W.R.	18	Rutland	4	1842	11		
		Leicestershire	17	Buckinghamshire	3	1843	4		
		Nottinghamshire	17	Hertfordshire	3				
		Derbyshire	12	Huntingdonshire	3				
		Shropshire	10	Norfolk	3				
		Staffordshire	8	Yorkshire, E.R.	3				
		Warwickshire	7	Oxfordshire	2				
		Hampshire	6	Middlesex	1				
		Bedfordshire	5	Sussex	1				
Henry Pilkington	422	Northumberland	173	Cheshire	8	1838	140	1845	4
		Durham	101	Staffordshire	8	1839	136	1846	2
		Lancashire	32	Essex	5	1840	35		
		Yorkshire, N.R.	23	Yorkshire, E.R.	4	1837	32		
		Shropshire	20	Northamptonshire	3	1843	30		
		Yorkshire, W.R.	16	Leicestershire	2	1842	26		
		Cumberland	13	Lincolnshire	2	1844	11		
		Westmorland	11	Derbyshire	1	1841	6		
Charles Pym	163	Somerset	37	Monmouthshire	3	1837	76	1841	1
		Gloucestershire	31	Oxfordshire	2	1838	61	1846	1
		Herefordshire	27	Staffordshire	2	1844	5		
		Worcestershire	17	Berkshire	1	1839	4		
		Wiltshire	12	Lincolnshire	1	1842	4		
		Devon	11	Middlesex	1	1843	4		
		Cornwall	6	Yorkshire, E.R.	1	1845	4		
		Shropshire	5	Denbighshire	1	1840	2		
		Essex	4	Flintshire	1	1836	1		

Introduction

Table 1 (cont.)

Assistant commissioner/ local tithe agent	Total number of reports	Counties and number of reports				Year and number of reports					
John Job Rawlinson	106	Cumberland	24	Yorkshire, W.R.	7	1838	64				
		Lancashire	18	Lincolnshire	5	1839	28				
		Westmorland	16	Derbyshire	4	1840	7				
		Yorkshire, N.R.	14	Nottinghamshire	3	1841	5				
		Durham	7	Leicestershire	1	1842	1				
		Northumberland	7			1844	1				
William Richards	1	Cornwall	1			1839	1				
Morris Sayer	1	Carmarthenshire	1			1838	1				
John S. Donaldson Selby	65	Northumberland	51	Lancashire	1	1839	26	1841	2		
		Durham	5	Lincolnshire	1	1838	20	1840	1		
		Yorkshire, N.R.	4	Westmorland	1	1837	5	1845	1		
		Cumberland	2			1842	4	1846	1		
						1843	4	1847	1		
Job Smalepiece	2	Sussex	2			1837	2				
John Smith	1	Sussex	1			1838	1				
Thomas Sudworth	74	Cheshire	54	Derbyshire	1	1838	56				
		Staffordshire	7	Lincolnshire	1	1837	15				
		Shropshire	5	Norfolk	1	1839	3				
		Lancashire	2	Warwickshire	1						
		Yorkshire, W.R.	2								
Thomas Sutton	38	Norfolk	31	Essex	1	1838	21	1839	5		
		Suffolk	6			1837	12				
Gelinger C. Symons	38	Shropshire	34			1839	37				
		Staffordshire	4			1838	1				
Thomas James Tatham	8	Essex	6	Surrey	1	1837	6	1842	1		
		Middlesex	1			1838	1				
Joseph Townsend	104	Essex	17	Cambridgeshire	3	1838	55				
		Hampshire	15	Bedfordshire	2	1837	32				
		Buckinghamshire	13	Yorkshire, E.R.	2	1840	10				
		Hertfordshire	13	Kent	1	1844	3				
		Berkshire	10	Leicestershire	1	1839	1				
		Sussex	8	Lincolnshire	1	1841	1				
		Oxfordshire	6	Rutland	1	1846	1				
		Huntingdonshire	5	Norfolk	1	1848	1				
		Surrey	4	Northamptonshire	1						
Thomas Turner	12	Suffolk	7			1837	7				
		Norfolk	5			1838	5				
Charles Warner	4	Shropshire	4			1837	4				
John West	33	Northamptonshire	16	Buckinghamshire	5	1838	15	1837	2		
		Huntingdonshire	9	Bedfordshire	3	1839	14	1840	2		
Charles Wilson	6	Kent	5			1837	3				
		Sussex	1			1838	3				

Table 1 (cont.)

Assistant commissioner/ local tithe agent	Total number of reports	Counties and number of reports				Year and number of reports			
Thomas Smith Woolley**	258	Lincolnshire	47	Hertfordshire	7	1838	73		
		Kent	46	Cambridgeshire	6	1837	68		
		Warwickshire	26	Derbyshire	5	1839	35		
		Norfolk	14	Huntingdonshire	5	1841	29		
		Suffolk	12	Bedfordshire	4	1842	27		
		Leicestershire	13	Berkshire	4	1840	11		
		Nottinghamshire	11	Staffordshire	4	1843	10		
		Sussex	11	Surrey	4	1844	4		
		Buckinghamshire	9	Hampshire	1				
		Hampshire	9	Wiltshire	1				
		Northamptonshire	9	Worcestershire	1				
		Essex	8	Yorkshire, E.R.	1				
Thomas Smith Woolley Jr**	42	Lincolnshire	11	Hertfordshire	2	1842	15	1844	1
		Warwickshire	9	Huntingdonshire	2	1841	13		
		Oxfordshire	7	Bedfordshire	1	1843	8		
		Berkshire	5	Essex	1	1845	4		
		Surrey	3	Nottinghamshire	1	1840	1		

Notes
* The table includes both early (1836–7) manuscript reports and later (1837 onwards) printed reports.
** It is likely that some of the reports entered under Thomas Smith Woolley were written by his son, Thomas Smith Woolley Junior. Entries under the son's name in this table are reports which can be ascribed to him with certainty; he appears not to have been employed by the Tithe Commission before 1840 so only the authorship of that minority of reports post-dating 1840 and entered under his father's name is in doubt. In the set of tables accompanying county-by-county analyses, the two men's reports are entered under one name.

approaches of particular commissioners. The nature of some of these variations are discussed in the county texts below and in Holt (1984) and in Kain (1984). Some make do with cryptic one or two sentence answers on 'arable' forms, while others greatly exceeded the limited brief of 'pastoral' type questions. The nature of this descriptive material is discussed further on pp. 23–5 where the procedure followed for compiling the Place and Subject Indexes is described.

Quantitative data on farming in reports on tithe agreements

To help assistant commissioners and local tithe agents judge whether agreements were fair to all parties, they were required to value the titheable produce of each district. 'Arable' format reports asked for a 'description and rough estimate of the titheable produce' (Fig. 5). These valuations usually set out the titheable acreage of a district and the amounts of arable, meadow and pasture, woodland, common, orchards, gardens and hops. In a separate table after these land use data, the acreages of crops grown on the arable are provided together with the yields and prices used to calculate the gross produce of the arable.

On 'pastoral' format report forms, local agents were asked to estimate the acreage of arable defined as 'land actually ploughed in the present or last season, whether sown with

5 'Rough estimate of the titheable produce' from the report on the agreement for the commutation of tithes at Coveney, Cambridgeshire, 1841 ('arable' format)

corn, planted with roots or fallow, but excluding seeds' (Fig. 4a). They were asked to state separately the number of acres of pasture including seeds. In these reports the acreage of crops is not asked for but rather Question 2 says: 'what is the course of crops?'. It is possible to derive estimates of the acreages of individual crops by dividing the acreage of the arable by the number of courses (excluding the seeds courses) in the rotation. In fact this is exactly the method by which most tithe agents produced their 'rough estimate of the titheable produce' for 'arable' format report forms. However, for a number of reasons it is not possible to derive acreages of all crops in this way. First, more than one rotation might be stated without any indication of that proportion of the district to which each applied. Secondly, rotations are sometimes less than perfectly described; at Marham Church in Cornwall, William Glasson recorded a rotation of 'wheat, barley or oats – part potatoes and a small quantity of turnips'. Further variations in the practice of valuing land on 'pastoral' forms are detailed in Chapter 3 of *The tithe surveys of England and Wales* but in short, data on land use and crops in 'pastoral' format reports are not as comprehensive or consistently recorded as in 'arable' format reports. This fact is reflected in the fewer maps which it is possible to construct for counties where these forms were employed.

Crop yield figures quoted in both types of reports on tithe agreements were not always those obtained in the harvest previous to the report. For the purposes of tithe commutation, a fair par rent-charge over the 'years of average', 1829–35, was required and to assess this, average yields could be fairer and more appropriate than those relating to one specific season. These average yields were the basis of compulsory commutations but it is evident that some assistant tithe commissioners also ascertained yields over a similar run of years when examining the fairness of agreed rent-charges. Equally certain is the fact that yet others did obtain estimates of actual yields in the year prior to their visit, i.e. in a majority of instances, in 1837 or 1838. Therefore, the effective span of dates for these tithe file derived data runs from the early to the late 1830s. Thus in both the text and tables in this *Atlas and index* such information is referred to a date of *circa* 1836 rather than to the usual median date of tithe apportionments at *circa* 1840.

Some of the problems faced by Tithe Commission agents in obtaining yield figures are reviewed in *The tithe surveys of England and Wales*, pp. 141–3. The Tithe Commission's representatives depended very much on figures provided by local farmers but the tithe owner was always there in the background poised ready to protest at any flagrant under-statement of gross produce.

In 'pastoral' reports, the titheable produce of grassland was assessed on the basis of the number of livestock kept rather than by reference to the agistment value of pasture and the yield of mown meadow hay as in 'arable' format reports (Fig. 4b). While references in tithe files by assistant tithe commissioners and local agents to conscious attempts by farmers to deceive them about crop acreages and yields are rare, they do report many instances of their being intentionally misled by landowners about the number of stock kept on farms. For this reason, and because of the general difficulties of estimating reliably the number of stock kept in a parish discussed in *The tithe surveys of England and Wales*, pp. 143–5, the tithe file livestock data have been transcribed and archived in machine-readable form (see Appendix) but are not used in this study.

Introduction

Transcribing data from the files

The tithe files are stored in the Public Record Office's Kew repository where the catalogue follows the same county-by-county system used by the Tithe Commission for organising commutation. The county units of the Tithe Commission have been retained in this study not merely for convenience but because first, the quantitative data are formatted in reports on tithe agreements according to the Tithe Commission's perceptions of the 'arable' or 'pastoral' agricultural character of each county, and secondly, because the content of written reports also varies on a county-by-county basis. Every one of the 14,829 tithe files has been searched for reports on tithe agreements and all the papers in each file have been indexed (see below: 'Compiling Place and Subject indexes', pp. 23–5). Statistics on land use, crop acreages and yields, and numbers of livestock were transcribed from all reports on tithe agreements and then subjected to a series of tests to determine whether data from a particular tithe district should be used in subsequent cartographic and tabular analyses. Broadly speaking, these tests checked the potential representativeness of the data in terms of the proportion of a tithe district to which they relate, and the completeness with which all categories of land and types of crops are enumerated.

Most agreements for commutation cover the whole of a tithe district. Even where a part was tithe free, the produce of the whole district is commonly enumerated. Data covering less than 90 per cent of tithe district total acreage are rejected from subsequent analyses. Corroboration of the percentage of a tithe district enumerated in each report was obtained either by internal checks with the articles of agreement for commutation where these are extant in the file (about 80 per cent of cases) or with acreages stated in the published volumes of the 1851 census of population which were themselves derived from tithe maps. For a small residue of places the area covered by the report on tithe agreement could only be ascertained by consulting the original tithe map and apportionment.

Many rejected tithe districts were eliminated, not because their data relate only to titheable land, but because either it is not possible to obtain a complete listing of all land uses, or because some but not all crops are enumerated. In upland Cornish parishes, for instance, the value of tithes was very small and rotations long and complex with seeds pastured for upwards of ten years. In such circumstances, assistant commissioners and local tithe agents did not think it necessary to value each crop or every field, but rather they calculated a rent-charge on an acreage basis for comparison with the sum agreed by tithe owners and payers. On the other hand, in Midland counties such as Buckinghamshire, the reports usually enumerate crops very carefully so that, although the number of reports is quite small (for reasons of commutation at the time of parliamentary enclosure), their data are almost all usable. At the other end of the spectrum are counties such as Norfolk with both good coverage in terms of number of reports and with a high proportion of these with complete data. For the country as a whole about 54 per cent of tithe districts have data which pass our tests of representativeness.

Data were transferred to prepared coding forms in the Public Record Office using a combination of fixed and free formats. County and tithe district reference numbers, names of tithe districts, accuracy codes and numerical data on land use, crops and livestock are entered in fixed fields. Index data were entered format-free and a code number for each topic was recorded in the sequence in which it was encountered as the file was searched. The topics used to form the entries in the index were derived from a content analysis of a number of contemporary and modern writings on nineteenth-century agriculture and rural history, and a sample of tithe files. The derivation of these headings is discussed further below (pp. 23–5). A set of computer programs was devised to assist with checking for and editing of transcription errors before analysis commenced. All the numerical data and all the original index codes as recorded during initial transcription have been deposited with the Economic and Social Research Council Survey Archive at the University of Essex and can be accessed on request to its Director. Precise details on the organisation of these data files and the key to data coding are provided in the Appendix.

Compiling an atlas of maps

The idea of a 'tithe atlas' has been mooted in the past but computerised data processing and cartographic techniques have rendered it no longer a pipe-dream. Data quality does restrict the range of appropriate analytical and cartographic techniques and was a major influence in our decision to employ choropleth methods of mapping. A particular weakness of tithe file data is that the land use statistics, crop acreages and yields are often estimates, albeit estimates made by experienced valuers. Reducing the data to ratios and a limited number of classes for mapping does not eliminate errors resulting from inaccurate estimation but at least avoids our investing the data with unwarranted precision. The great strength of the tithe surveys on the other hand is their comprehensiveness and consistency of format. Furthermore, all tithe survey data gain in strength when the data for one tithe district are ranged alongside that of its neighbours; maps enable the immediate communication of such conjunctions and permit one place to be seen in the context of its neighbours. However, as it is intended that our maps should fulfil a reference purpose as well as contributing to a synthetic picture of agrarian landscapes c. 1836, we have not used contouring or other interpolation techniques to produce a continuous mapped surface from the extant sample of data. It is considered important that readers of the maps should be able to identify precisely the area to which each tithe survey refers, and, conversely, those areas for which data are absent. A major task was thus obtaining and digitising the boundaries of parishes and townships for those counties for which mapping was to proceed at a tithe district scale. Cartographic analysis at this scale has been conducted for thirty-one counties where more than 18 per cent (a significant break in the frequency distribution) of tithe districts possess data acceptable by the criteria discussed in the previous section. Of Welsh counties, only Denbighshire and Flintshire have any potentially reliable and fairly complete data so Wales has been omitted entirely from analysis at this scale. In England, this cut-off percentage places Buckinghamshire at the foot of a ranked list of mapped counties and Norfolk at its head.

Introduction

i. Constructing base maps

All the base maps used as source maps for digitising and published here as key maps for tithe district identification, were compiled by Rodney Fry. On these maps, tithe districts are identified by PRO reference numbers placed within their boundaries; tie-lines and bracketed numbers are used for very small districts (see Maps 7, 28, 49, etc.). Place names can be obtained by referring these reference numbers to county Place Indexes (pp. 470–521). The maps are provided with both areal and linear scales. Parish and township boundaries have been obtained from the special edition of the Ordnance Survey Old Series one-inch maps known as the 'Index to the Tithe Survey' for places south of the line from Hull to Preston, the area for which these maps are extant. For counties north of this line, boundaries are taken from the index keys to the first edition of the Ordnance Survey six-inch maps.

The 'Index to the Tithe Survey' maps purport to show the boundaries of tithe districts as plotted in the London Tithe Office from original tithe maps. The record is, however, far from perfect. Some districts are missing entirely and for others sections of boundaries are omitted. In these circumstances the tithe maps themselves were consulted to ensure the maximum possible accuracy of representation on our maps. For most counties only a few places had to be checked in this way, though for Lancashire it was as many as thirty-eight. Greater difficulties were encountered in those northern counties for which only the six-inch Ordnance Survey key sheets are available. Some tithe districts are not townships or parishes but are places which enjoy status solely for tithe commutation purposes and so their boundaries are not plotted by the Ordnance Survey. Further problems arise as in the North Riding of Yorkshire where tithe maps are inconsistent in their portrayal of tithe district boundaries. Sometimes moorland is included within the boundary; at other places, tithe maps represent enclosed lands only, regardless of whether or not moorland was titheable.

ii. Computer mapping

Computer mapping was conducted using the GIMMS-IV system developed by Dr T. C. Waugh of the University of Edinburgh (Waugh, 1977) and modified for the specific requirements of this project by Dr John Buckett of the University of Exeter. Working copies of maps for design development and checking were produced on a graph plotter and camera-ready maps were obtained by plotting on high resolution negative microfilm at the University of London Computer Centre. Our objectives are not those of cartographic innovation but rather the application of established computer mapping techniques to a project of landscape reconstruction, the scale of which has previously defeated the traditional, manual mapping techniques of the historical geographer.

Once the decision to employ a choropleth technique had been made and the GIMMS mapping system adopted, we addressed the question of selecting class intervals. A prime criterion introduced at this stage was the requirement that readers be able to make direct comparisons of maps of one county with those of another; it is thought important that, when maps from counties with contrasting agricultural systems are juxtaposed, the agrarian differences between them should be communicated clearly. Secondly, the mapping system had to be sensitive enough to highlight important differences at a sub-regional scale within counties, as between the markedly different soil regions of Kent, for example. Thus systems based, for instance, on standard deviations calculated county-by-county were ruled out because they would produce different class intervals for each county and thus militate against between-county comparisons. On the other hand, a consequence of employing uniform levels across the country is that differentiation obtained within counties is sub-optimal, as, for example, when no values fall within a number of the nationally derived data classes. However, at least three intervals appear on most of the maps in the sections which follow and provide a reasonable degree of sub-regional differentiation.

As computer mapping had to be conducted for logistical reasons in parallel with data transcription, it was not possible to calculate overall statistical measures for establishing the national set of class intervals. As we have mapped direct agricultural parameters rather than derived or constructed indices or statistical surfaces, it has been possible to class data by assigning exogenous levels which had some meaning to the nineteenth-century farmer. Intervals of one third, one quarter, or one fifth of arable sown to particular crops have a real meaning in terms of crop rotation and are not the arbitrary divisions that at first sight they may appear. Yield intervals were chosen in a similar way; fewer than 2 quarters (16 bushels) an acre for wheat was thought a miserable return, 3 quarters seems to have been an average in the minds of assistant tithe commissioners and local agents, 4 was considered good and more than 4 quarters an acre was exceptional *c.* 1836. The symbols for 'no quantities' on crop maps indicate places where a crop was grown but a precise acreage is not stated in the tithe file.

Texts and tables

In this section, conventions employed in the brief essays written for each county and the manner of calculating aggregate land use, crop acreage and yield tables are described.

Though reference is made to some of each county's maps in the essays, lengthy verbal description of map patterns is not undertaken; the maps themselves are the chosen media for communicating this information. The object of these texts is first to summarise some facts concerning the compilation of each county's tithe surveys and tithe files, such as the number of tithe districts exempt from tithe payment, principal reasons for exemption and compilers of tithe file reports on tithe agreements (further summarised in a table for each county). A second object is to highlight the principal themes and topics which are the subject of comment in tithe file papers; in this respect the short essays amplify and extend the Place and Subject Indexes. Thirdly, and related to the previous point, some flavour of the source material is provided by direct quotations from the documents, principally from assistant commissioners' and local tithe agents' 'parish descriptions' written in reports on agreements for the commutation of tithes.

Place names noted in the essays are rendered in modern spelling wherever possible. Public Record Office press marks are not cited but as each quotation is accompanied by a place name, PRO reference numbers can be ascertained from the Place Index.

Land use, crop acreage and crop yield tables for each county have been compiled by aggregating data from all the reports on tithe agreements for that county. The estimates of land use acreages have been obtained by multiplying the total acreage enumerated in tithe file reports on agreements by a weighting factor equivalent to the ratio of county area: sample area. County areas are those calculated under the direction of R. K. Dawson from tithe maps and recorded in the published tables of the 1851 census of population. A similar method employing weighting factors calculated for individual crops was used to obtain estimates of the acreage of crops in each county. In detail, the aggregate acreages for each crop do not total exactly to the county arable figure, nor do the percentages of land under the different crops add up exactly to 100 per cent due to variation in sample sizes and thus of the weighting factors used. Also, some crops which occupied minor proportions of the arable were omitted when the documents were originally compiled. Mean crop yields are calculated from figures cited at each tithe district.

These county aggregate figures are also the source of data used for compiling the set of maps of England and Wales on a county basis (Maps 563–82) and the summary tables of land use, crop acreages and outputs in England and Wales *c*. 1836 (Tables 105–8).

Compiling Place and Subject Indexes

As a body, the 14,829 tithe files contain a wealth of source material on the nature of local landscapes, farming practices and the history of tithes and Church incomes. This is information of great value to historians and historical geographers working on the nineteenth century and much of it is unequalled in its wealth of detail at any other period in the nation's history. But information on particular topics is to be found scattered throughout many hundreds or even thousands of files so that most researchers are unable to devote the time necessary for its search and retrieval. It is intended that these indexes, which describe and list the main contents of each tithe file under a number of standardised headings and contain some 200,000 entries, will answer both the needs of historians who require direction to files with information on particular topics and local historians concerned with finding information on a particular place. Each of the fifty-five counties of England and Wales has been indexed separately and the index for each county consists of two parts. The first is a Place Index which lists all a county's files in numerical order of their Public Record Office reference numbers and records the main classes of papers which each file contains. The second part is a Subject Index which lists those files which provide information on 182 topics of concern to students of nineteenth-century rural economies and landscapes.

An initial set of some 250 subject headings was obtained by a content analysis of a sample of 400 tithe files and a number of land management textbooks and commentaries, agrarian histories and glossaries (Cobbett, 1912 edition; Caird, 1852; Prothero, 1961 edition; Orwin and Whetham, 1964; Chambers and Mingay, 1966; Adams, 1976). Each heading was assigned a number and the contents of each file classified as it was searched in the Public Record Office by recording as many index numbers as its contents warranted. A few further headings were added in the light of experience gained when coding the first files, while during computer analysis prior to printing the index pages some redundant headings were eliminated and others amalgamated under more general categories. These last relate to topics which our content analysis of both contemporary tracts and modern histories revealed to be matters of interest among commentators on the nineteenth century, but

24 Introduction

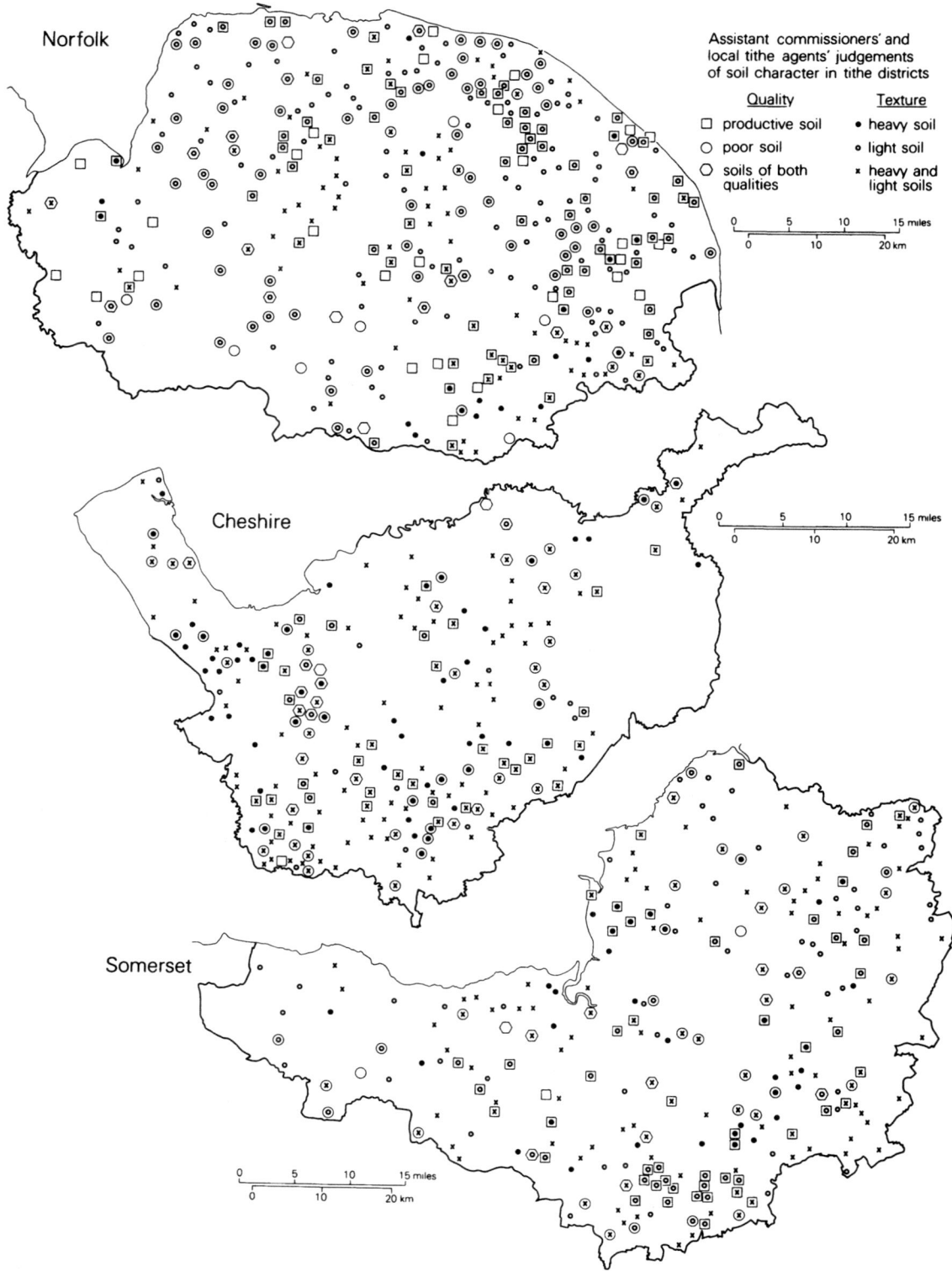

6 Assistant commissioners' and local tithe agents' appraisals of soil type and quality in Norfolk, Cheshire and Somerset

which are not matters of detailed comment in tithe files. Topics on which tithe files are rather quiet, if not entirely silent, are:
1. The form of man-made structures – the architecture of rural buildings, types of field boundary, the layout of parks and gardens.
2. Rural society – including the social status of landowners, property sizes (see tithe apportionments for these) and matters concerning the rural labour force.
3. Inputs to agriculture in terms of capital and labour and machinery used.

These apart, tithe files contain information on an impressive array of topics and are particularly strong on the output of agriculture and on local factors that might influence its level. This reflects the main concern of the Tithe Commission's agents which was to ascertain the gross output of local agriculture in order to judge the fairness of a commutation agreement or to assess the level of a just award.

The Subject Index of each county is organised under three broad headings:
1. The Church and the tithe system.
2. Rural landscapes.
3. Agriculture.

The 'rural landscapes' section is divided into further sub-sections: topographic descriptions, settlements, fields, woodland, unfarmed land. Likewise under 'agriculture' there are sub-sections on environmental influences (including soils), transport and marketing, management, change and improvement, arable farming (including rotations and crops), livestock farming and, finally, fruit, vegetable and industrial crops. Some index headings are of a broad nature, for example, that of 'local topography' subsumes a wide variety of descriptive comments found in tithe files about local landscape, scenery and the general visual appearance of the countryside. Others are much more specific. Some are specifications of precise numbers of courses in a generally adopted rotation or describe the character of local soils. The degree of specificity reflects in large measure how central a particular topic was to the main concerns of the Tithe Commission's agents.

In the course of their inquiries, local tithe agents and assistant commissioners made and recorded a number of value judgements on matters relating to tithe commutation as, for example, when calculating what proportion of gross tithe ought to be deducted from a rentcharge in lieu of costs of collection that a tithe owner would have borne under the unreformed tithe system. So, local roads are judged as good or poor, markets near or distant, farmland accessible or difficult of access. These contemporary appraisals are recorded in the Subject Index as are similar judgements on the quality of soils, pasture, woodland and so on. As a result, the Subject Index can also be viewed as a source of data as well as a guide to the contents of this source. It is possible, for example, to map places with entries under particular categories. Figure 6 illustrates contemporary appraisals of soil type and quality in the counties of Norfolk, Cheshire and Somerset. Where local agents mention the presence of particular systems of cultivation or the occurrence of particular activities, we have no reason to doubt that they were recording what they believed to be true. However, it is not possible to argue the reverse; it does not necessarily follow that because a particular practice, such as underdraining arable or pasture land, is not remarked upon, that it was not practised.

EASTERN COUNTIES

Essex　　　　　　　Norfolk
Suffolk　　　　　　Lincolnshire
Cambridgeshire　　Huntingdonshire*

The 'arable' type of printed form used for reporting on tithe agreements in these counties requires a 'description and rough estimate of the titheable produce' and asks assistant tithe commissioners and local tithe agents to 'describe the parish and the quality of the lands, the system of farming, and whether the quality of the produce has been affected by any extraordinary instances of high or low farming'.

*Data for Huntingdonshire are too few to warrant compiling maps tithe district-by-tithe district.

Essex

418 tithe districts
296 reports on tithe agreements

Elwyn Cox's thesis (1963) which analyses the agricultural geography of the million acres of the county of Essex *c.* 1840 set a new scale for exploiting tithe survey data. Cox compiled maps of arable, pasture, wood and common by plotting state of cultivation data field-by-field from tithe apportionments and maps and constructed a further series of maps of the distribution of wheat, barley, oats, green crops, beans and peas, turnips and dead fallow from tithe files. Two of these latter maps are published in Cox and Dittmer (1965). Cox's study also includes a full analysis of the written evidence on agriculture in Essex files so this short note does no more than highlight some of the topics most frequently encountered while indexing Essex files. Additionally, D. W. Gramolt (1961) and R. Allison (1966) have mapped land use from tithe surveys for the eastern coastal and Thames marshes respectively.

Only seventeen Essex parishes were entirely free of tithes in 1836. A few early commutations were associated with parliamentary enclosure in the north-west, whilst several small urban parishes generated no titheable produce or, as at Colchester, were exempt as former abbey lands. Almost three-quarters of Essex commutations were effected by voluntary agreements, one of the highest proportions in any English county. The potentially litigious practice of tithe collection in kind is discussed in thirty-two tithe districts but at most of these places it related to the Essex practice of exacting wood tithe in kind. At North Shoebury a bitter dispute resulted in farmers growing seeds instead of corn to escape great tithes but surviving papers in tithe files suggest that such avoidances and the invidious practice of collecting tithes of corn in kind were exceptional in Essex. Certainly, voluntary commutation commenced very early in Essex and was all but completed by 1840 (Table 2). Two agreements were assessed in the same year as the Tithe Commutation Act, forty had been examined by the beginning of 1838, well before the Tithe Commission was effectively regulating the system of reporting by supplying printed forms for its agents' use, and 184 agreements (62 per cent) were examined in the two years 1838 and 1839. No fewer than eighteen assistant commissioners and local tithe agents worked on agreement assessments. With so many reporters and a number of very detailed reports in manuscript, the documents vary very much in content and scope. Only Henry Dixon and Thomas James Tatham set out valuations in such a way that coding crops and yields is completely precluded. William Downes usually amalgamated individual crops into combinations such as 'clover, peas and beans' and 'barley and oats' but Horace William Meteyard, on the other hand, valued the produce of each quality and type of soil in a tithe district separately, thus providing an exceptionally detailed set of data on which to base his assessment of tithe agreements. Many Essex reports, especially the early ones, contain quite lengthy descriptions of parish landscapes, particularly of settlements and topography (see Subject Index). These include, for instance, accounts of villa developments close to London, country mansions in the vicinity of Colchester and Chelmsford and the growth of holiday resorts as at Walton.

Table 3 and Maps 9–12 reveal the overwhelming dominance of arable land in Essex at the time of the tithe surveys. In all but seven parishes where tithe was commuted by agreement, and these all in the south-west of the county close to London and in the Lea Valley and Thames marshes, arable acreages exceeded those of grass; in 86 per cent of districts the ratio of arable to grass was greater than 1.5 to 1. Livestock farming did not occasion very much comment in Essex files beyond discussion of marsh pastures (very variable, but in general not held in such high esteem as those of Kent by assistant commissioners who worked in both counties) and general statements about cattle breeding and 'the buying of Scotch cattle and feeding them for the London markets'.

Assistant commissioners employed in Essex were very conscious of the contrasts in arable farming on light and heavy soils, a contrast confirmed by Maps 13–19. The problems of clay soil farming were given especial attention, with commissioners noting at very many places (see Subject Index) how their cultivation, in the words of one of their number, Roger Kynaston, 'has been wonderfully improved'. Recurring comments concern high and increasing yields (see Maps 20–5) as a result of underdrainage, liming and chalking, growing mangolds, swedes and tares on fallows and the increasing numbers of sheep kept. All these themes are discussed in detail in the files and are considered by Cox (1963). The following extracts are illustrative of the kind of comments to be found. At Broxted in 1839, Roger Kynaston reported that

> till within a very few years, the system of cultivation in this and neighbouring parishes was crop and fallow; by means however of a little more expense in husbandry, they are now enabled to adopt the 4 course tilth, which, from all that I could learn from the farmers, with whom I conversed, is likely to be much improved from the general spirit of improvement, which now prevails in the parish, and from the increased quantity of stock of which each farm can now boast, in comparison with former times.

In the same year, Edward Young Hancock wrote of Little Dunmow: 'the soil throughout is of a poor thin staple upon a marl bottom. There has been a gradual improvement within these last thirty years in the system of farming, and a partial change from the old Roothing system of crop and fallow alternately to the four course system.' On lighter loams, four-course turnip systems were widely adopted, extended in some places, as at Latchingdon for example, to a six-course with two crops of wheat and one of beans of which William Heard wrote: 'it is the opinion of some of the occupiers (which I fully concurred in) that on the four course system more would be produced'. Close to London, farmers were able to purchase manure easily and cultivate their land with less regard to rotation. Market gardening is a topic much discussed in south-west Essex files. At Dagenham, Roger Kynaston reported that 'there is a good deal of high farming in the parish, amongst those of the farmers, who grow different kinds of vegetables for the London market, and in consequence, as in other parishes in the immediate neighbourhood of London, there is no predominant system of cultivation'. At East Ham, Joseph Townsend commented: 'from the close vicinity of London the land of the parish has always under the stimulus of manure been kept in a high state of cultivation, its produce being those of the garden rather than the farm and the succession of crops being without intermission'.

Table 2 *Reports on agreements for commutation of tithes in Essex*

Assistant commissioner/ local tithe agent	1836	1837	1838	1839	1840	1841	1842	1843	1844	1845	1846	1847	Totals
Roger Kynaston	1		11	19	25	7							63
William Heard			2	22	3	2	12	1	2	4		1	49
John Mee Mathew		9	20	14	2								45
Edward Young Hancock			16	18									34
John Pickering			9	3		8							20
Joseph Townsend		2	15										17
F. Browne Browne			9	6		1							16
William Downes		4	6										10
Thomas Smith Woolley		4		1		1	3						9
Henry Dixon	1	6											7
Thomas James Tatham		6											6
Henry Pilkington		3	2										5
Horace William Meteyard			5										5
Charles Pym		4											4
Edward Greathed			3										3
Arthur Biddell			1										1
James Drage Merest			1										1
Thomas Sutton			1										1
Totals	2	38	101	83	30	19	15	1	2	4		1	296

Table 3 *Land use, crops and yields in Essex c. 1836*

	A Land use	Percentage of total land area enumerated in reports on tithe agreements	Estimated acreage in whole county
	Arable	72.4	768,156
	Grass	19.7	209,162
	Wood	4.1	43,662
	Common	1.2	12,176

	B Crop	Mean percentage of arable	Mean yield per acre	Estimated acreage in whole county
	Wheat	25.6	24.6 bushels	196,605
	Barley	18.5	34.5 bushels	142,298
	Oats	6.2	41.1 bushels	47,763
	Pulses	8.8	25.8 bushels	67,311
	Turnips	7.3	£3.18	55,934
	Seeds	17.9	22.8 cwts	137,713
	Fallows	15.5	—	118,795

Eastern counties

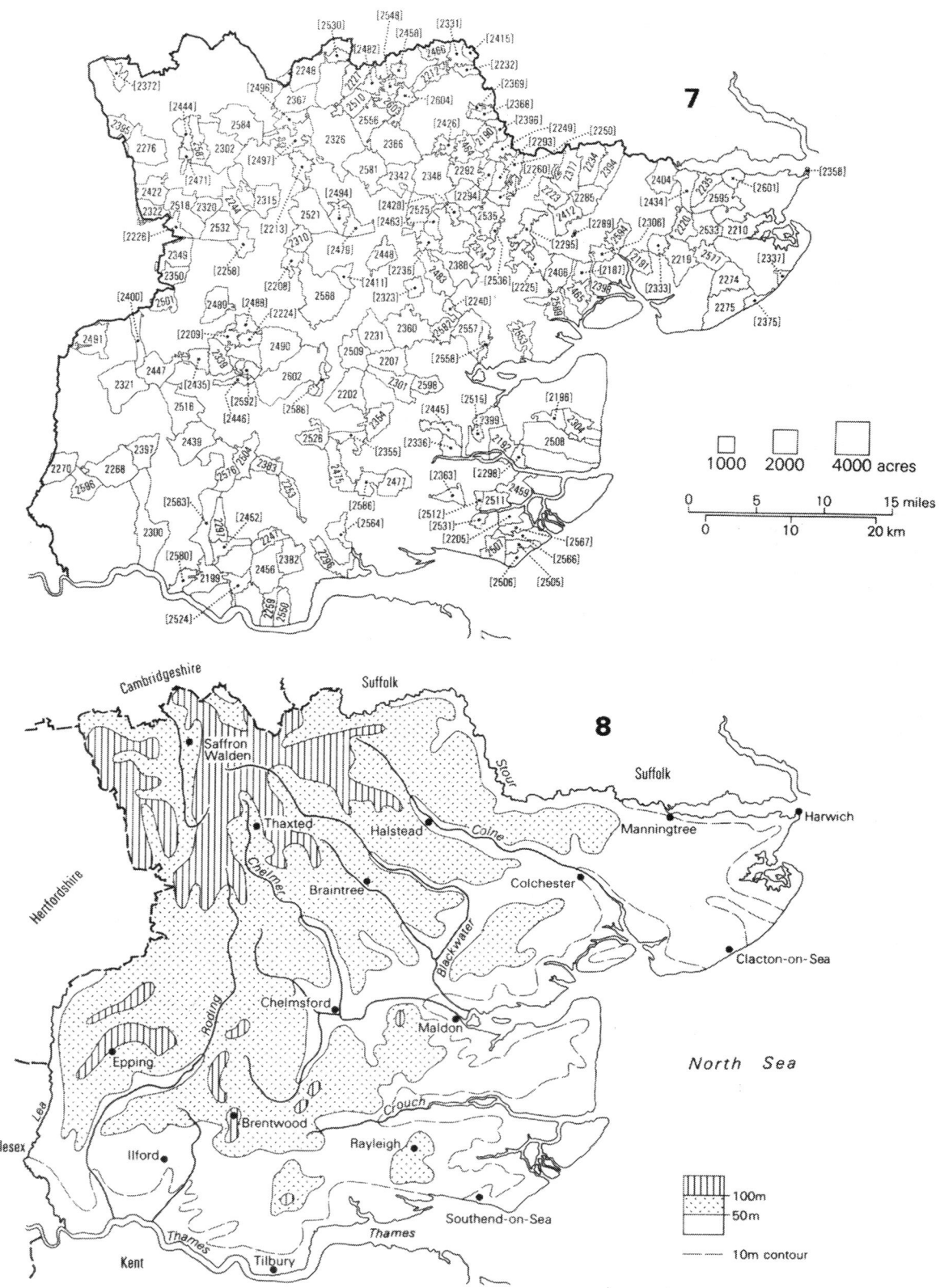

Essex 31

9 Arable as a percentage of tithe district area

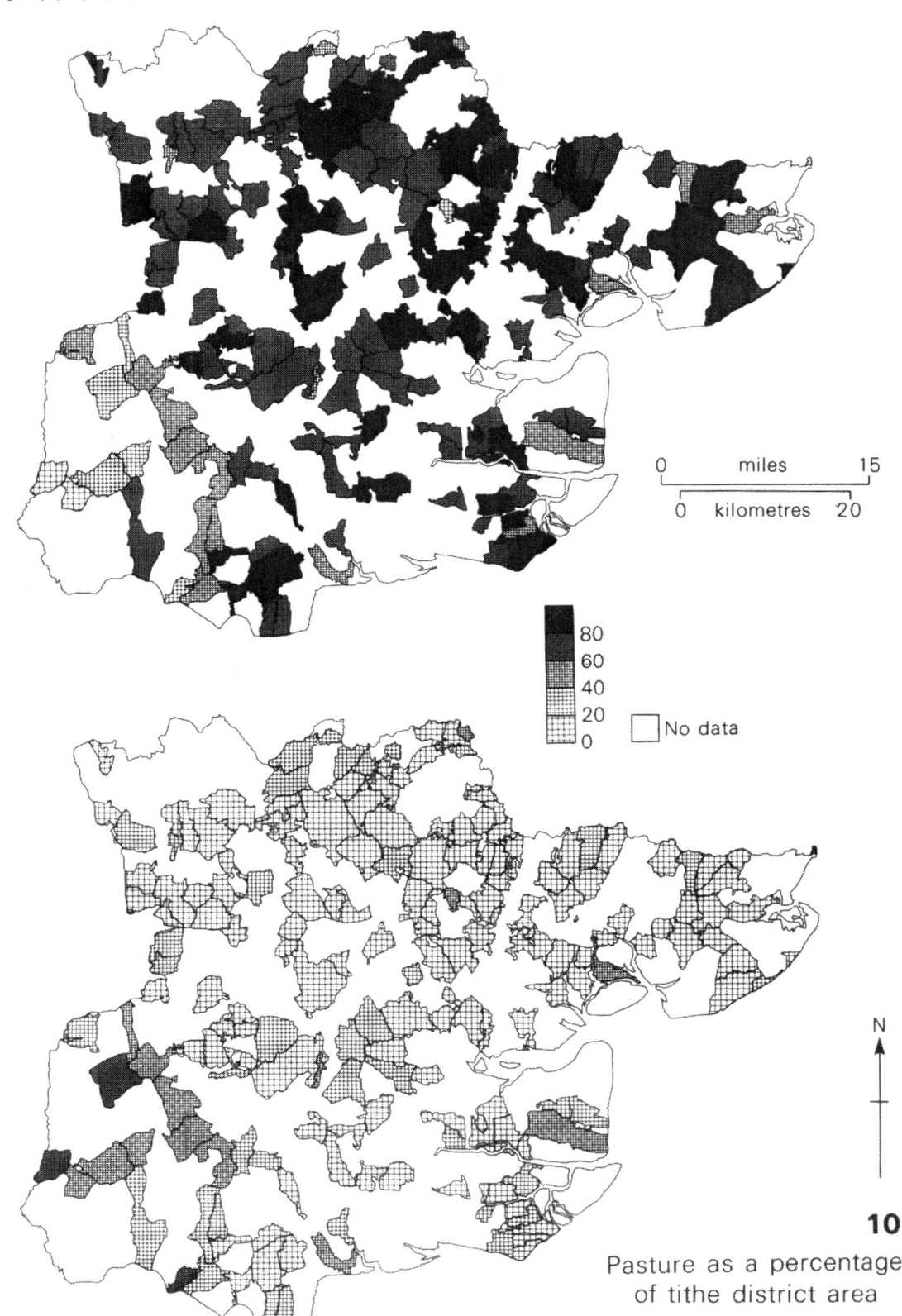

10 Pasture as a percentage of tithe district area

32 Eastern counties

11 Woodland as a percentage of tithe district area

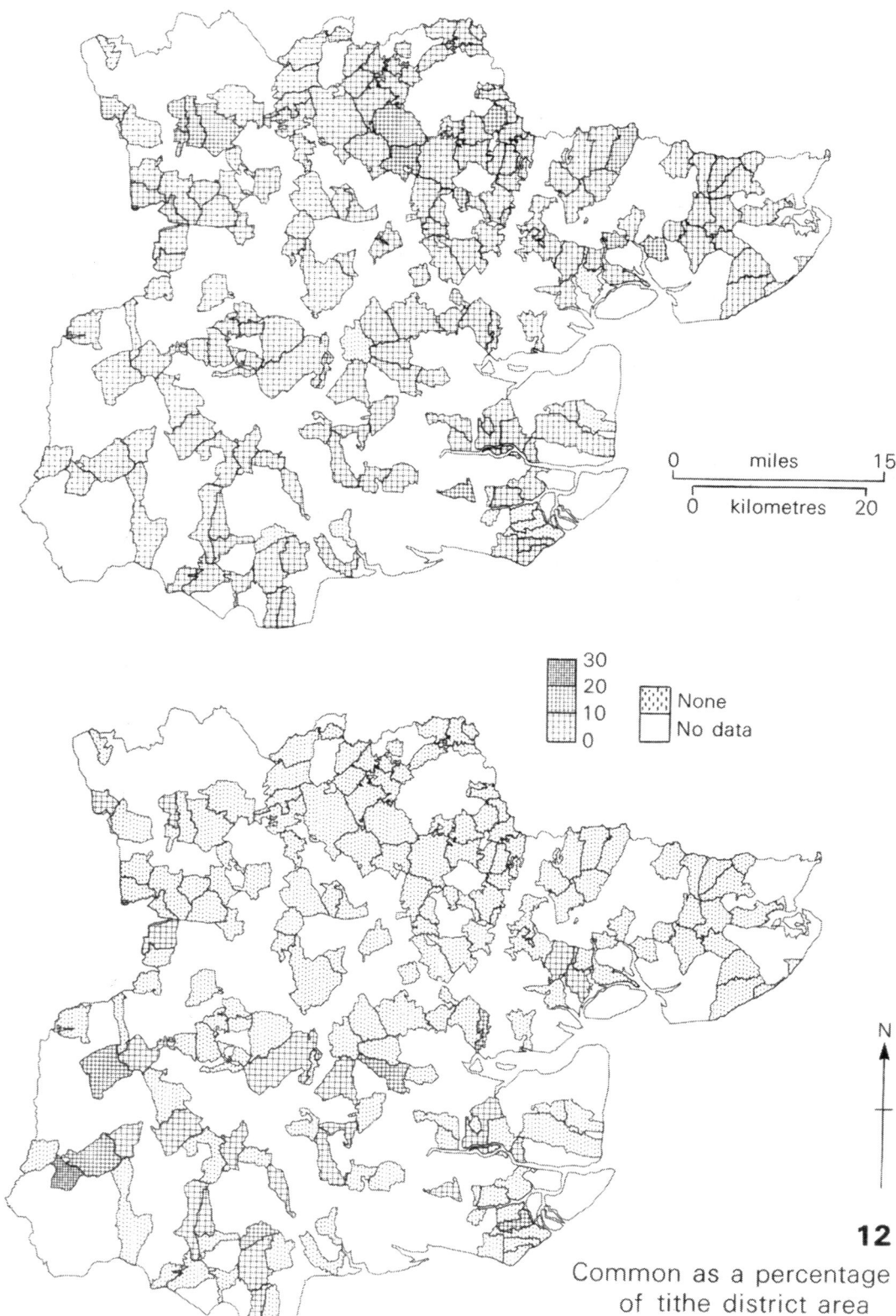

12 Common as a percentage of tithe district area

Essex

13 Wheat as a percentage of arable

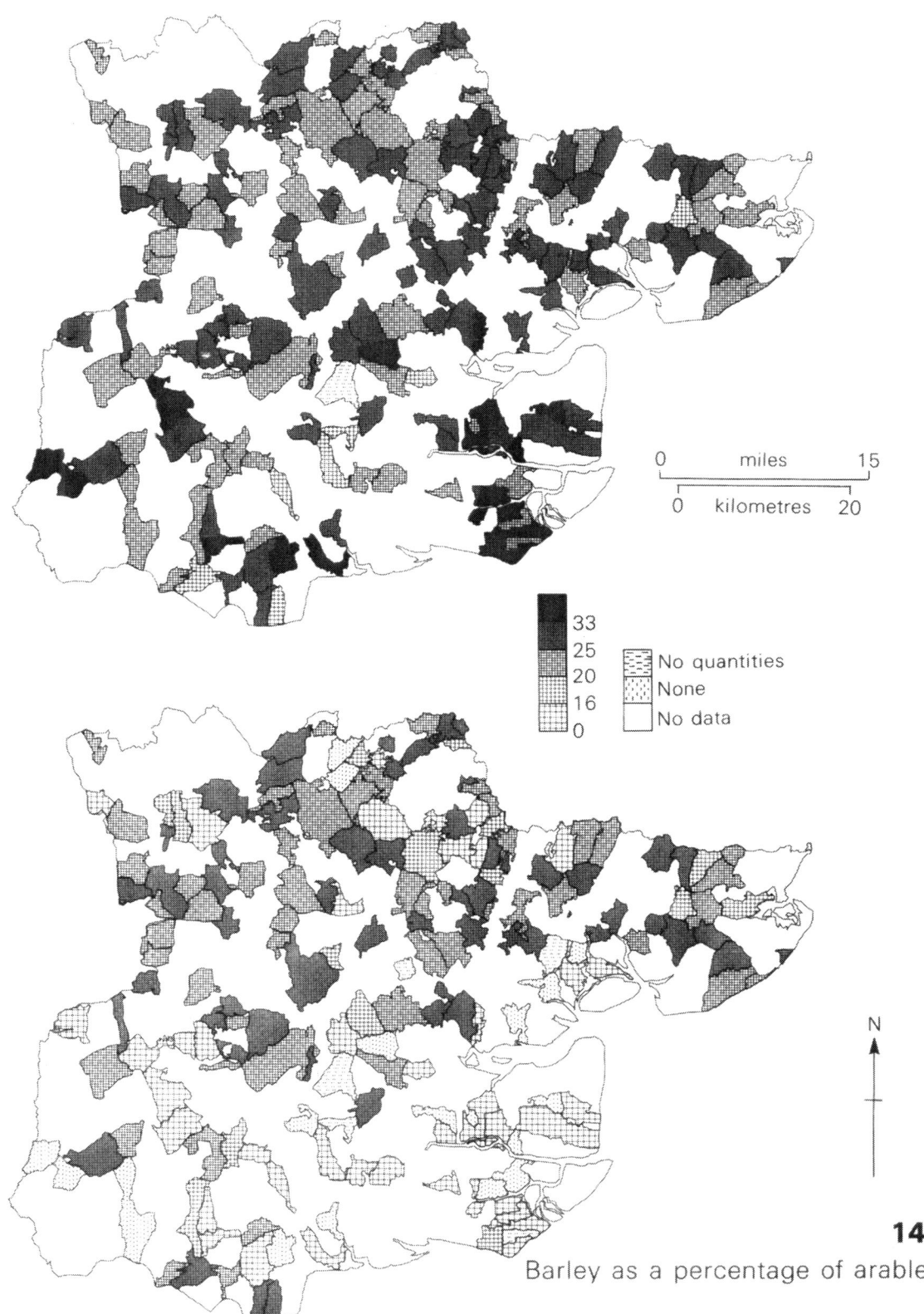

14 Barley as a percentage of arable

34 Eastern counties

15 Oats as a percentage of arable

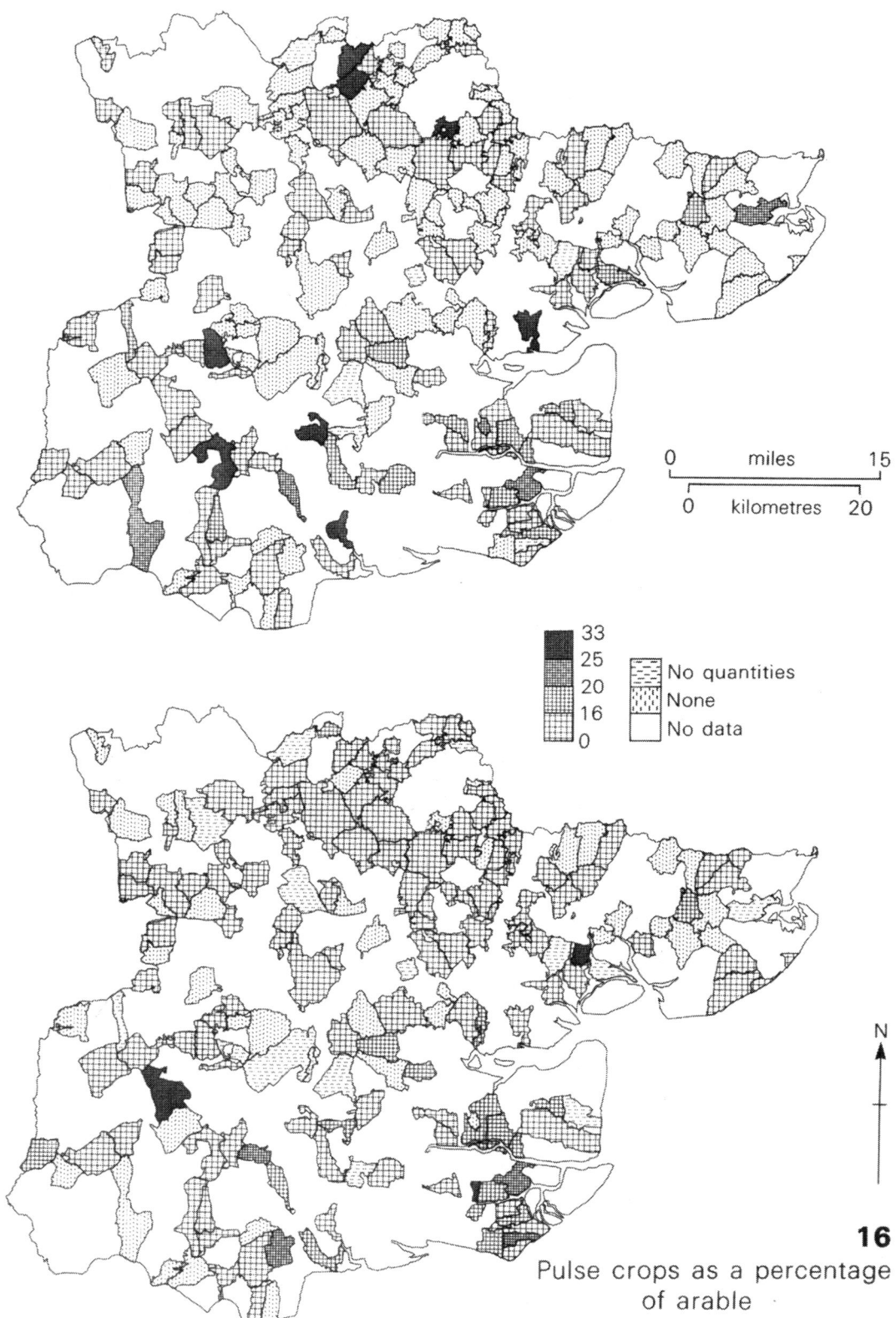

16 Pulse crops as a percentage of arable

Essex

17 Turnips as a percentage of arable

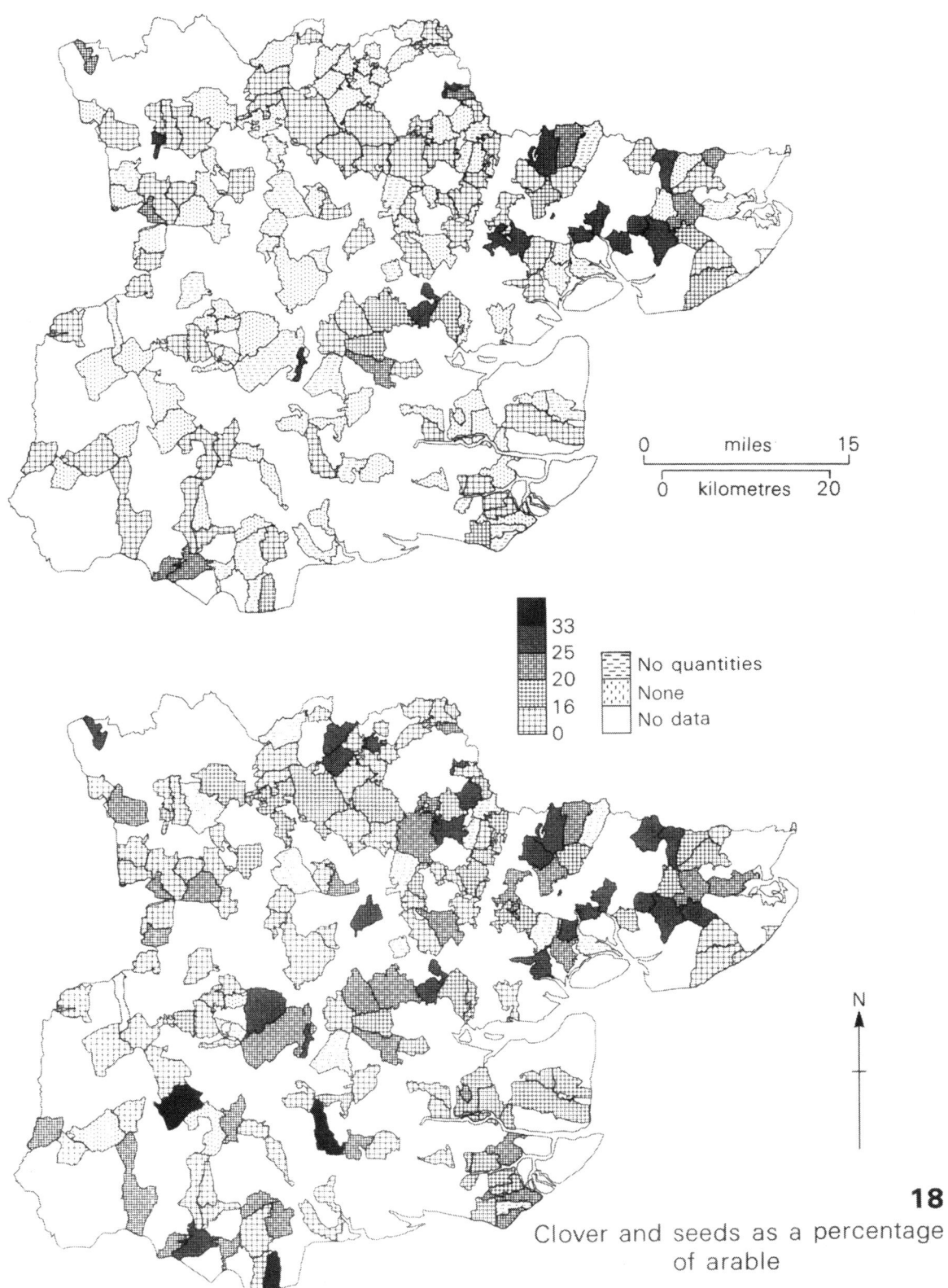

18 Clover and seeds as a percentage of arable

19 Dead fallow as a percentage of arable

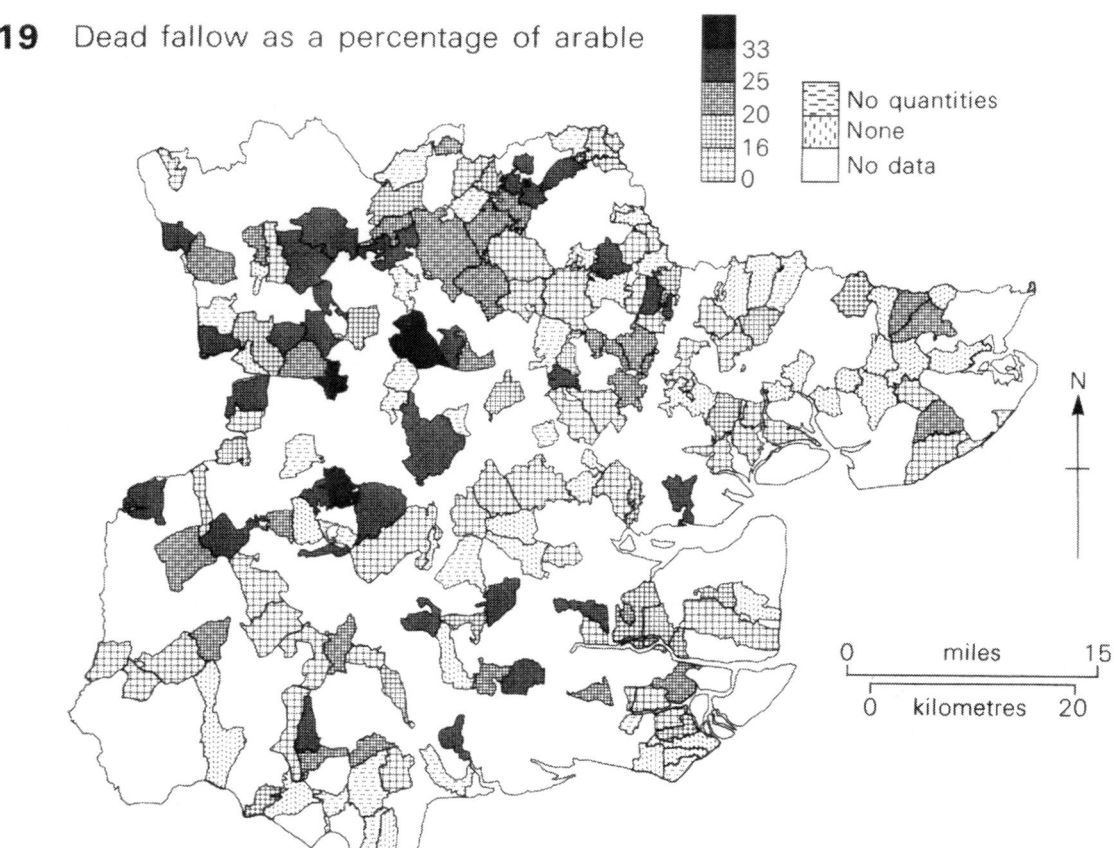

Essex 37

20 Yield of wheat in bushels per acre

21 Yield of barley in bushels per acre

38 Eastern counties

22 Yield of oats in bushels per acre

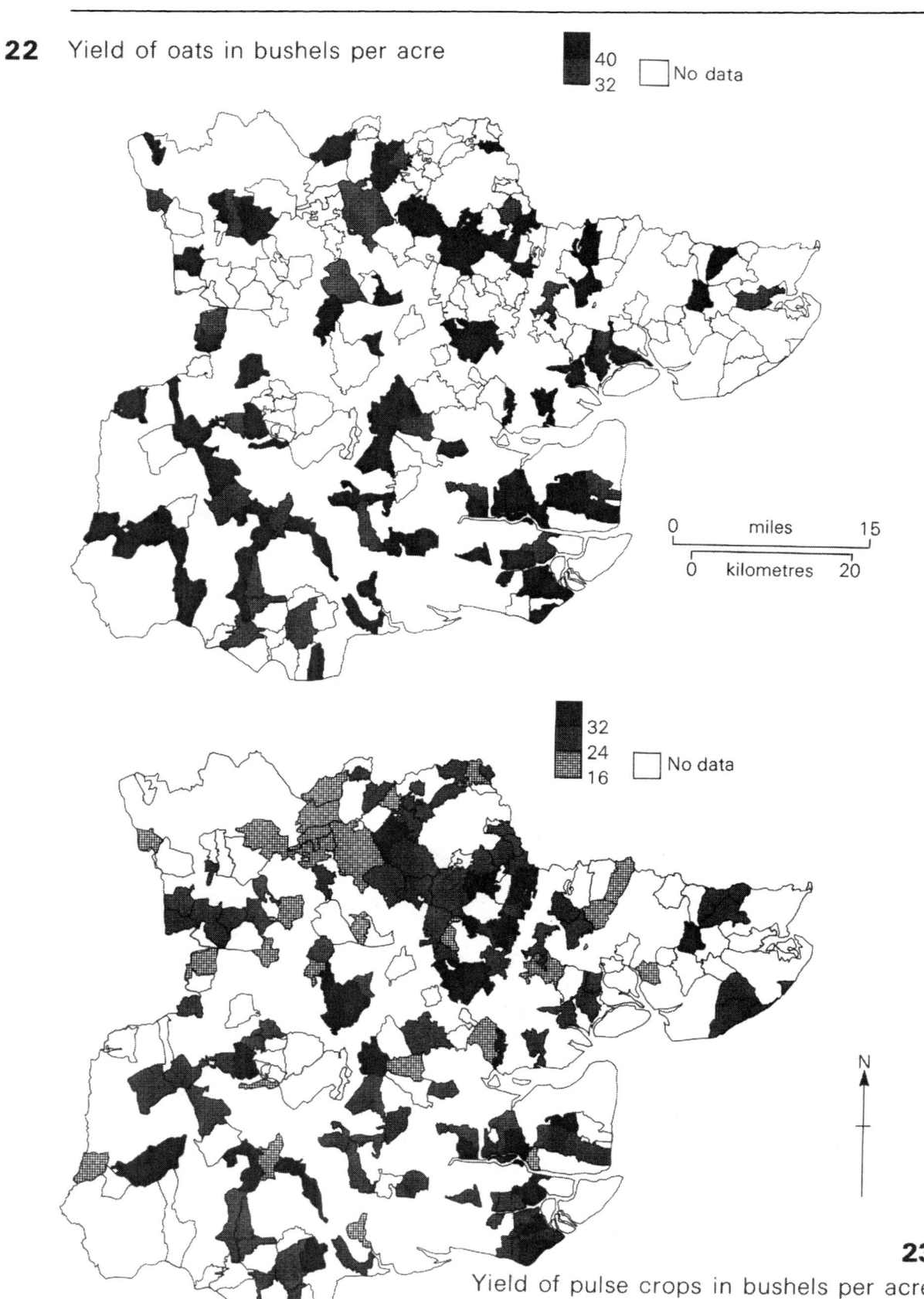

23 Yield of pulse crops in bushels per acre

24 Yield of turnips in £'s per acre

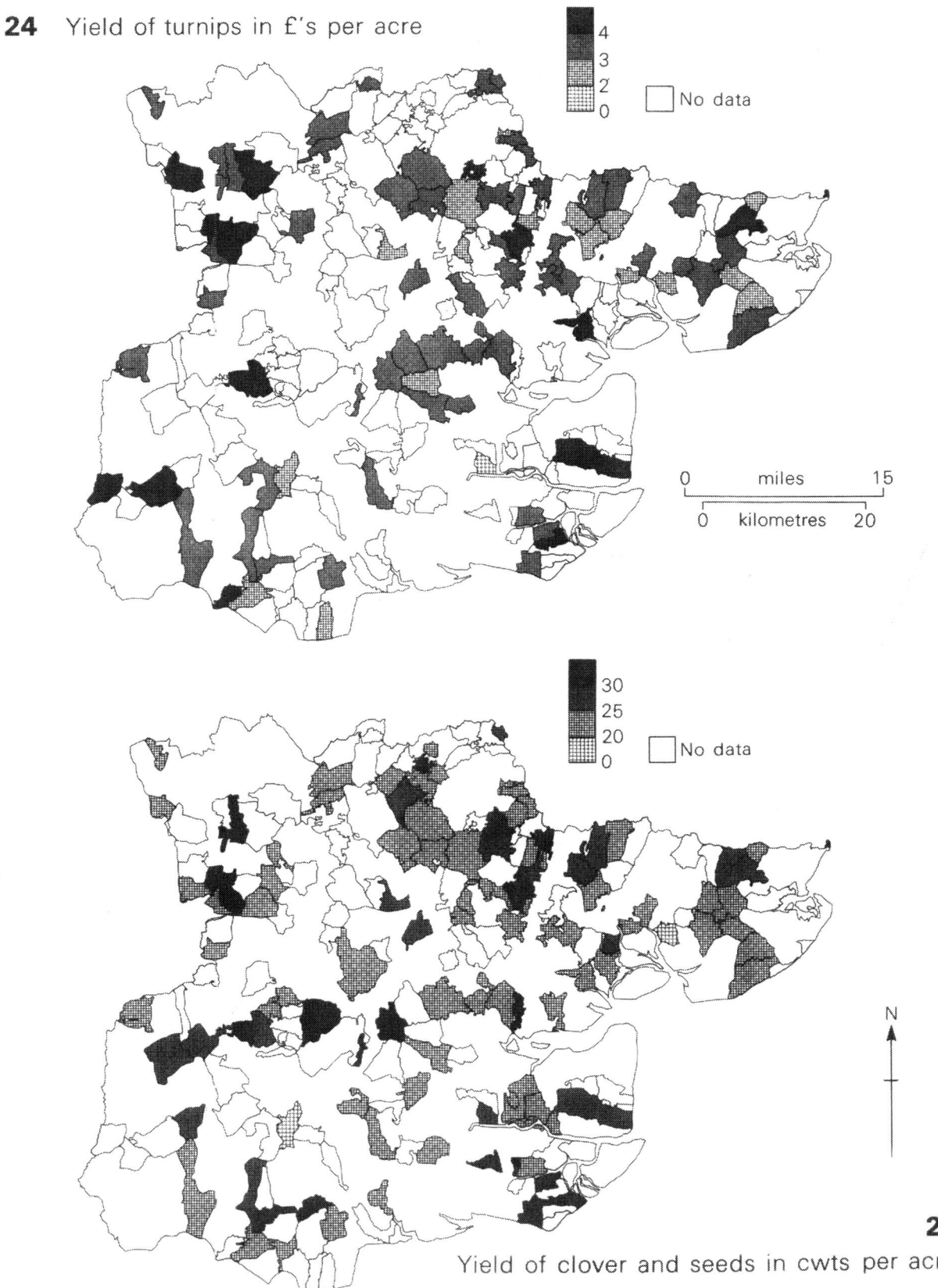

25 Yield of clover and seeds in cwts per acre

40 Eastern counties

26 Yield of meadow in cwts per acre

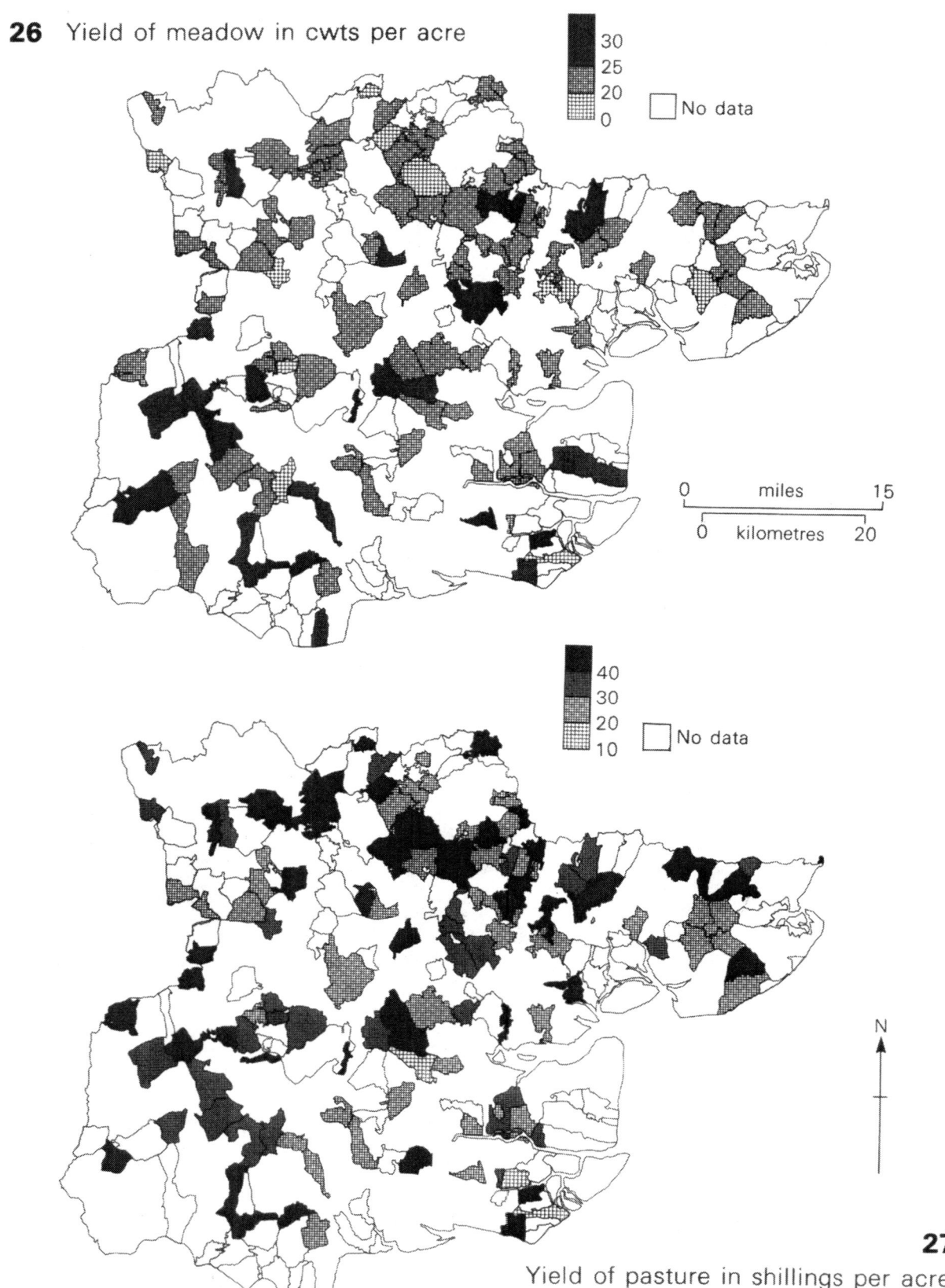

27 Yield of pasture in shillings per acre

Suffolk

522 tithe districts
355 reports on tithe agreements

Some elements of the agricultural geography of Suffolk revealed by an analysis of data from tithe files are discussed in a paper by H. M. E. Holt and R. J. P. Kain (1982). Elizabeth Burrell (1960) and Malcolm Postgate (1961) have mapped land use from tithe apportionments for Sandling parishes of east Suffolk and for 400 square miles of the Breckland respectively.

Only twenty-five Suffolk parishes were entirely tithe free in 1836 and the high ratio of commutation agreements to compulsory awards (more than 2 to 1) is well above the national average (Table 4). As early as the end of 1840, some 70 per cent of voluntary commutations had been agreed. Most assistant commissioners and local tithe agents who worked in Suffolk also worked in Norfolk and were very much aware of agricultural improvements taking place in eastern England. Instances of high farming rarely escaped their notice and are recorded in their notes (see Subject Index). Henry Bertram Gunning who completed the largest number of reports (24 per cent of the total) worked extensively in East Anglia (Table 1 in the Introduction) and his parish descriptions are particularly full and informative.

Maps of Suffolk land use and aggregate county data in Table 5 reveal that at least 85 per cent of parishes with extant tithe file data had more than 60 per cent of their land under the plough; in all but a very few parishes the ratio of arable to pasture was greater than 1.5 to 1. Only 9 per cent of parishes had more than one third of their area under permanent meadow or pasture. Unfarmed land occupied but a very small proportion of most Suffolk parishes.

Wheat was the grain most extensively grown in mid-nineteenth century Suffolk (Maps 34–6 and Table 5). It averaged 24 per cent of arable in those parishes with extant tithe file data. Barley was almost as important, averaging 23 per cent of arable, but oats were little grown in the county, occupying less than 2 per cent of arable acreage. The pattern of yields for each of these grain crops is similar (Maps 41–3 and Table 5); yields were lowest in the Breckland where less than 16 bushels per acre for wheat and 24 bushels for barley are recorded for some places. The highest yields were obtained in the central, eastern and northern clay land parishes where yields of 32 bushels and more for wheat and 40 and more for barley were achieved. Pulses were an integral part of the agricultural system on heavy soils but were unimportant in very light soil parishes. In many Breckland tithe districts, artificial grasses and green crops were important arable crops in terms of acreage occupied. Ryegrass was common and coleseed and sainfoin were being tried (see Subject Index). Conversely, on heavier soils, seed crops occupied less than 20 per cent of arable. Evidence in tithe files suggests that bare fallowing was decreasing in Suffolk and Map 40 shows that it was absent from all but heavy land parishes by *c.* 1836. The map of turnips (Map 38) is largely a mirror-image of that of fallow; where there was little bare fallow, turnips and other root crops occupied between 25 and 33 per cent of the arable.

Assistant commissioners and local agents reported that the system of agriculture based on sheep rearing practised on the very lightest soils, i.e. in the Breckland, was very different from that in other parts of the county where the produce of the arable was all important and where livestock, though an integral part of the agricultural system, were really a means of increasing productivity of arable (see Subject Index). At Wickham Skeith, Henry Bertram Gunning noted that 'the custom is extending here of fattening beasts upon oil cake, corn, hay and turnips; one of the most important improvements in Agriculture as far as regards the immense benefit which the manure so produced, is of to the land'. Recent improvements in the claylands such as the more widespread cultivation of root crops, more livestock and better manuring meant that in many heavy land parishes a four-course rotation similar to that adopted on the light soils of Suffolk could be practised. At the clay land parish of Athelington, James Drage Merest reported that 'it is farmed upon the four-course system generally followed in this county, and which is by far the best that can be adopted on this description of land'. Many tenants were obliged by covenants in their leases to adopt the four-course rotation (see Subject Index). Other improvements in the cultivation of heavy lands had not, however, been so widely adopted by *c.* 1840. For example, despite the recognised importance of underdrainage, assistant commissioners remarked in many places that this practice was much neglected; underdrainage is discussed in eighty Suffolk tithe files.

Table 4 *Reports on agreements for commutation of tithes in Suffolk*

Assistant commissioner/ local tithe agent	1837	1838	1839	1840	1841	1842	1843	1844	1845	1846	Totals
Henry Bertram Gunning			27	37	14	4	1	1		2	86
James Drage Merest	22	25	13	2		2					64
Roger Kynaston		8	40	1							49
William Heard				12		11	10		2		35
John Pickering		9		10	3	2					24
Arthur Biddell	3	14	4								21
John Mee Mathew		19									19
F. Browne Browne		1		6	6						13
Horace William Meteyard		12									12
Thomas Smith Woolley	12										12
Thomas Turner	6	1									7
Thomas Sutton	1	3	2								6
? Mears		4			1						5
Henry Dixon	1										1
William Downes		1									1
Totals	45	97	104	57	17	19	11	1	2	2	355

Table 5 *Land use, crops and yields in Suffolk c. 1836*

A	Land use	Percentage of total land area enumerated in reports on tithe agreements	Estimated acreage in whole county
	Arable	70.3	665,716
	Grass	20.4	193,240
	Wood	3.6	34,306
	Common	4.2	40,146

B	Crop	Mean percentage of arable	Mean yield per acre	Estimated acreage in whole county
	Wheat	23.9	23.2 bushels	158,910
	Barley	23.3	32.4 bushels	154,918
	Oats	1.6	36.9 bushels	10,818
	Pulses	5.9	25.1 bushels	39,568
	Turnips	14.0	£2.68	92,908
	Seeds	19.4	21.9 cwts	129,303
	Fallows	9.8	—	65,037

Eastern counties

Suffolk

30 Arable as a percentage of tithe district area

31 Pasture as a percentage of tithe district area

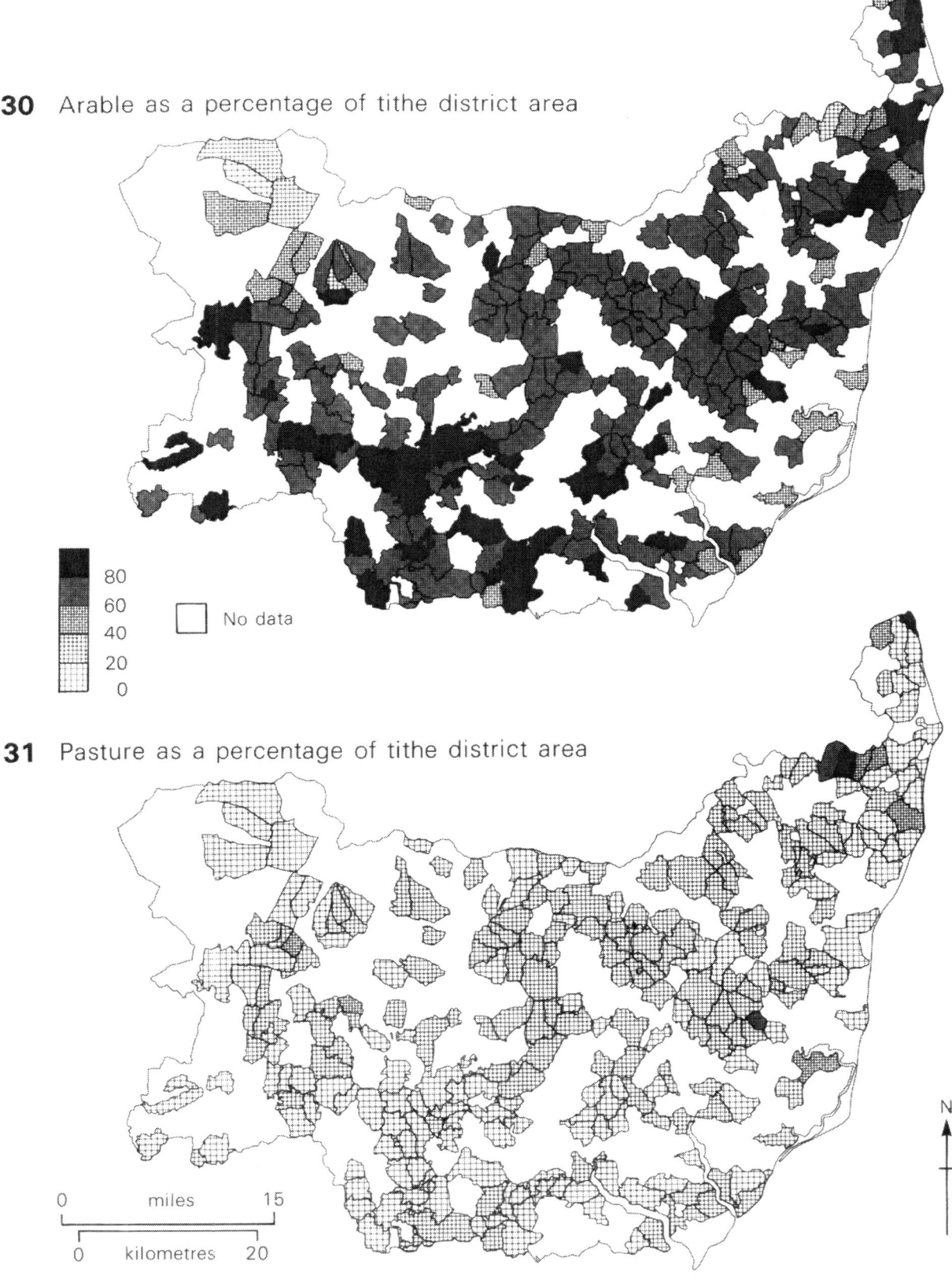

Eastern counties

32 Woodland as a percentage of tithe district area

33 Common as a percentage of tithe district area

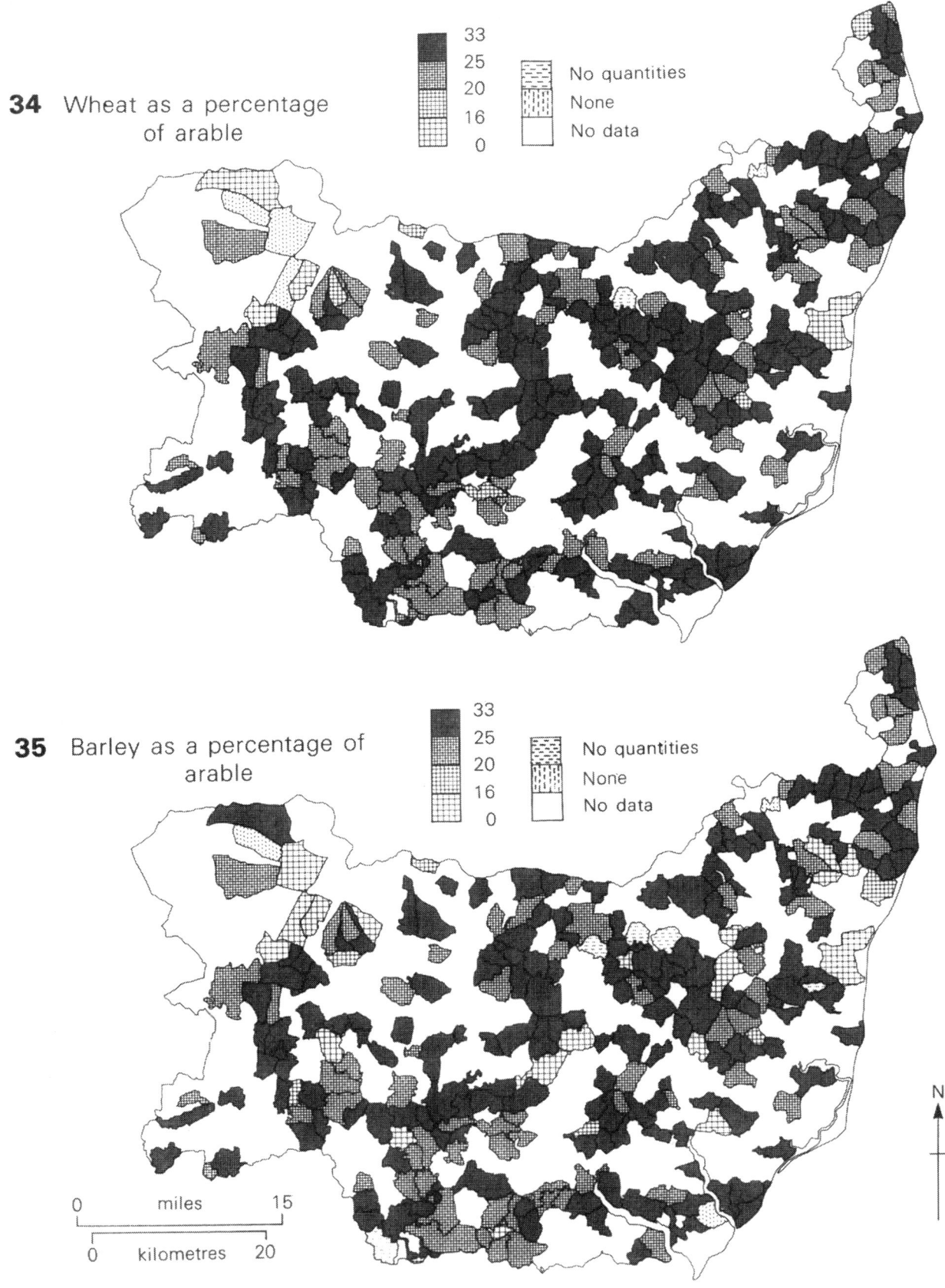

34 Wheat as a percentage of arable

35 Barley as a percentage of arable

48 Eastern counties

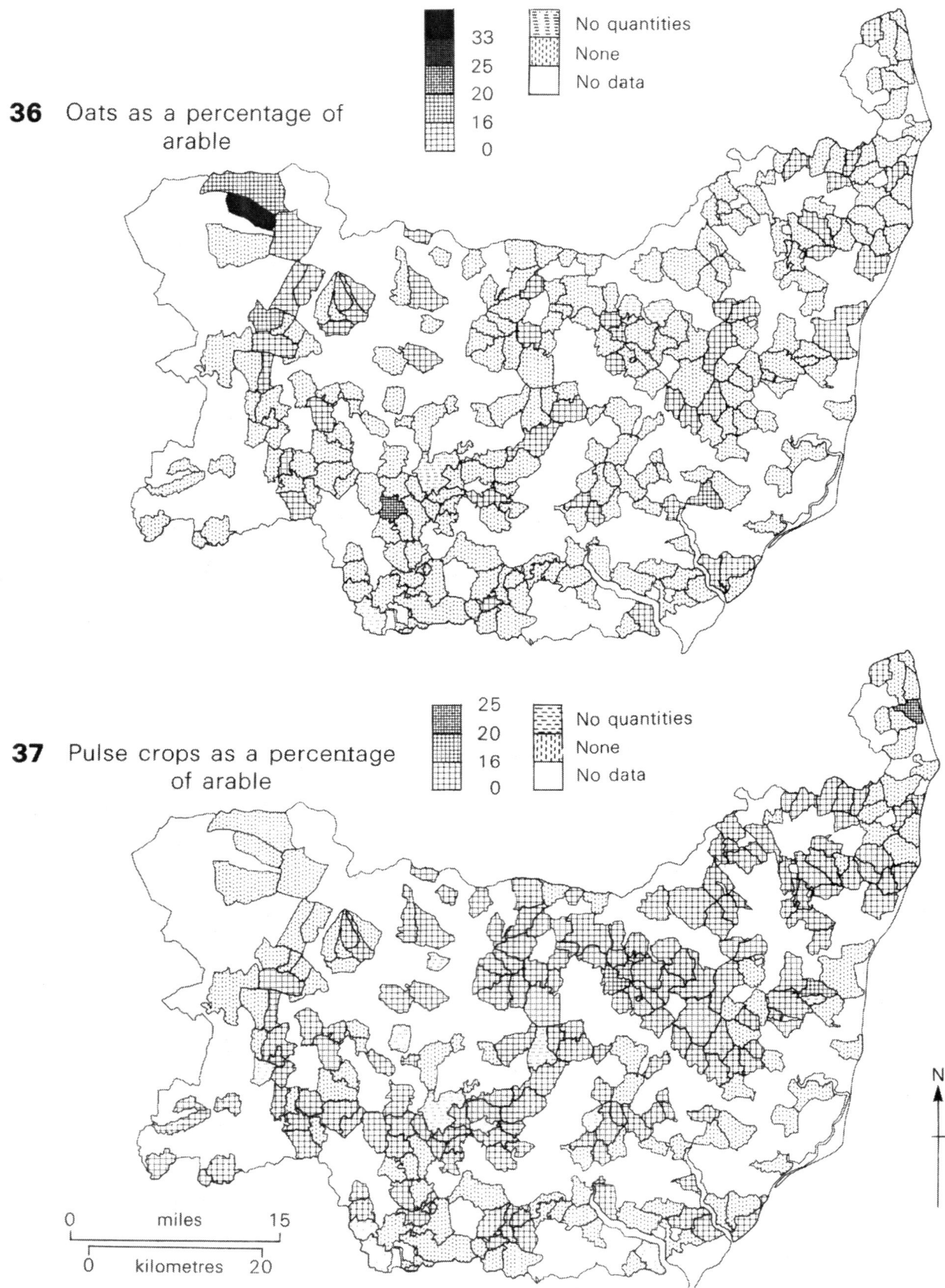

36 Oats as a percentage of arable

37 Pulse crops as a percentage of arable

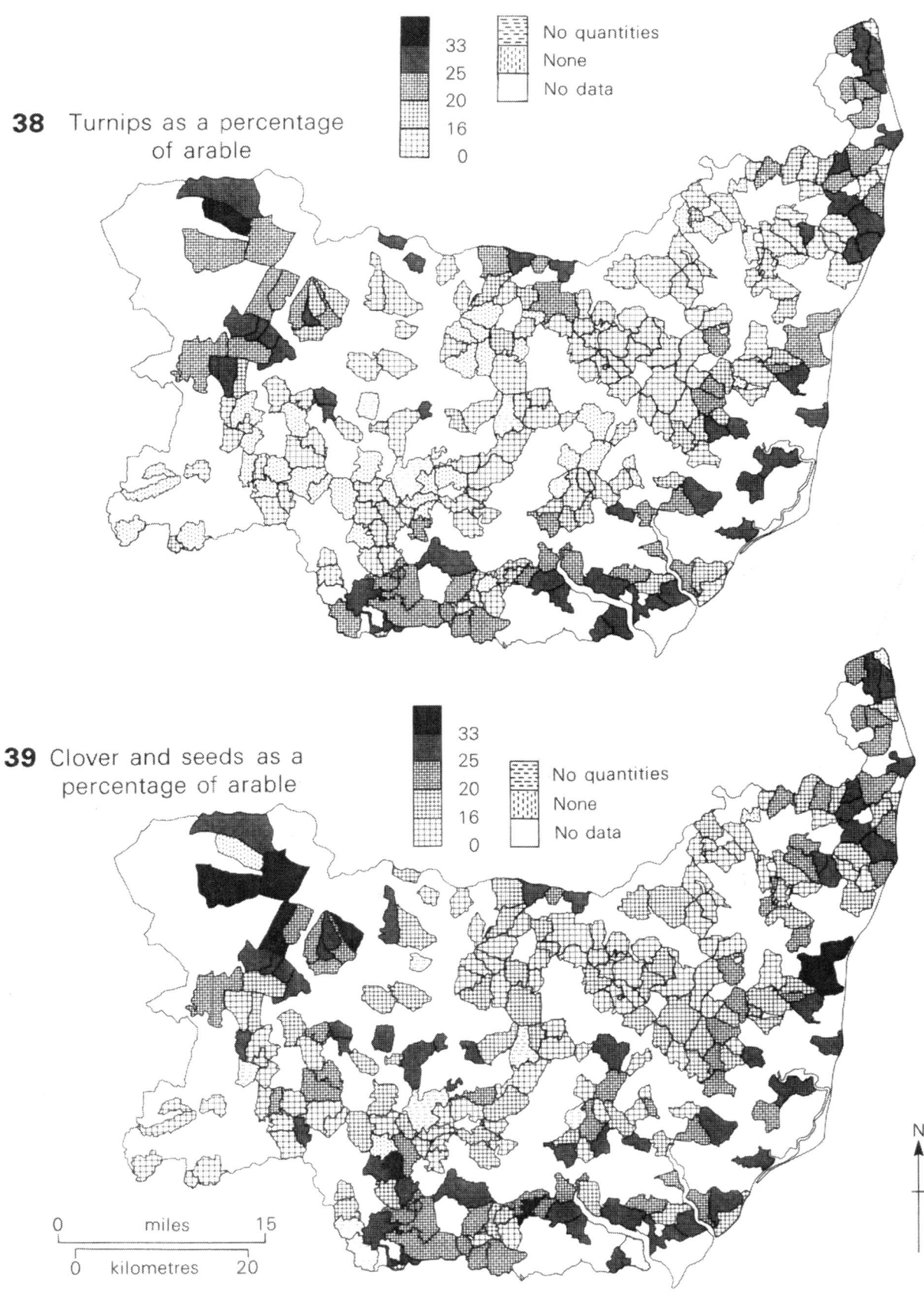

38 Turnips as a percentage of arable

39 Clover and seeds as a percentage of arable

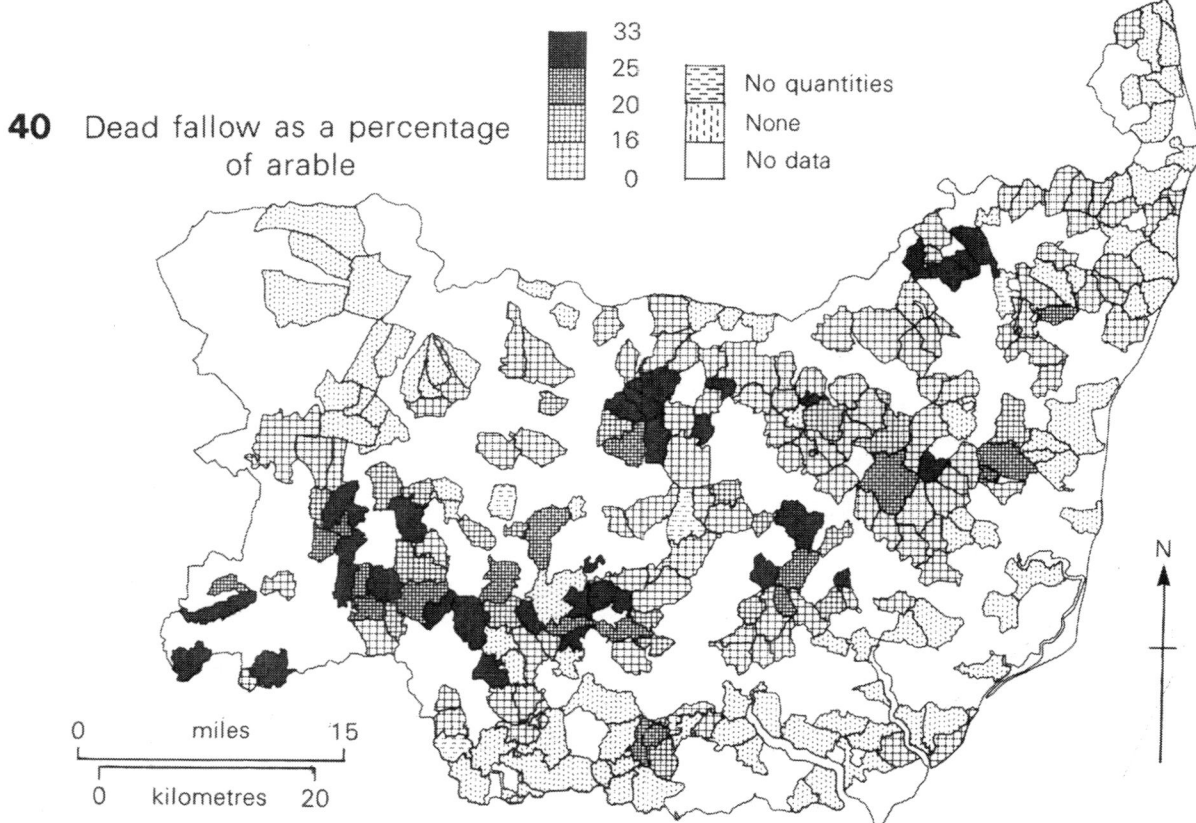

40 Dead fallow as a percentage of arable

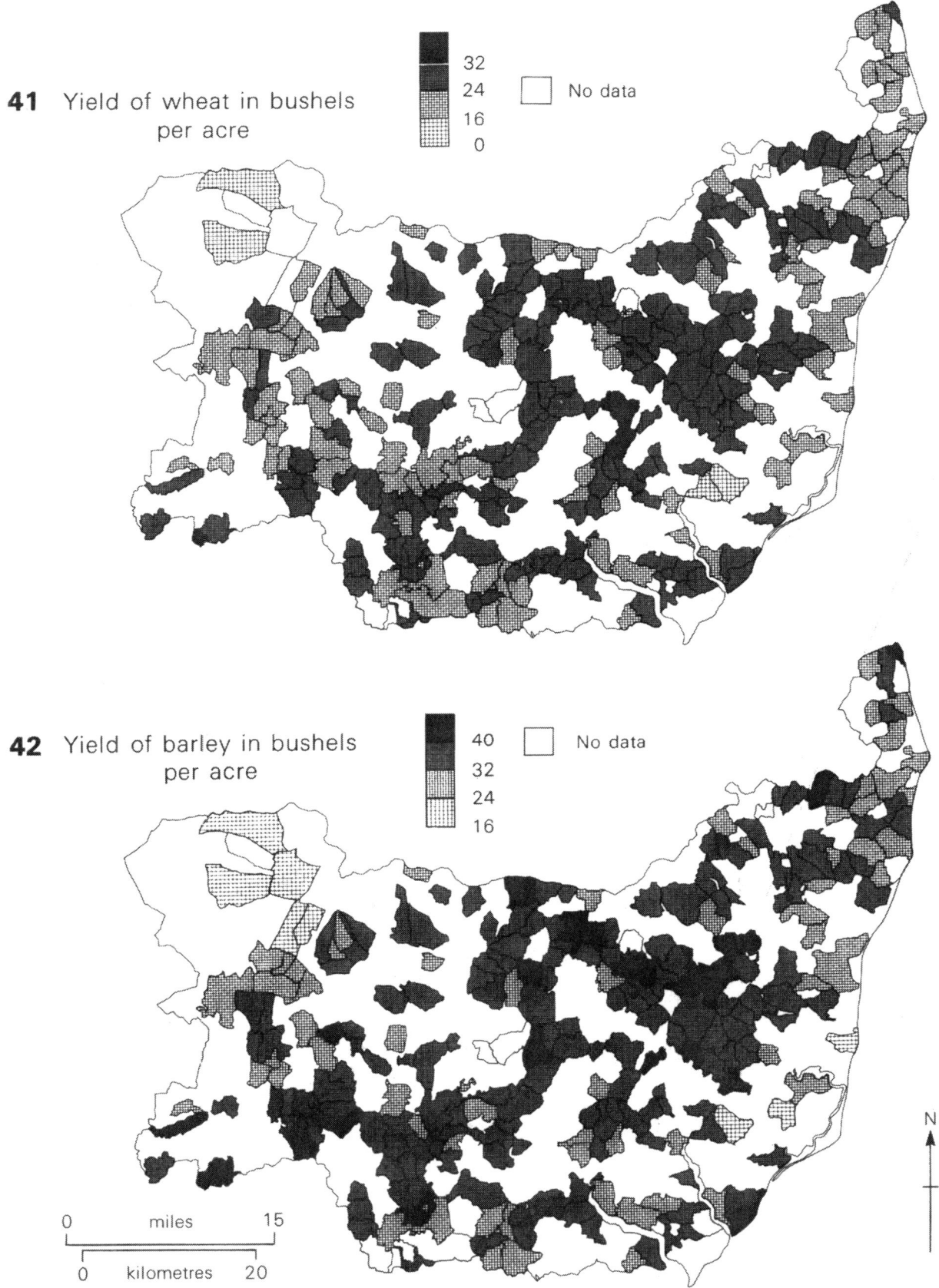

41 Yield of wheat in bushels per acre

42 Yield of barley in bushels per acre

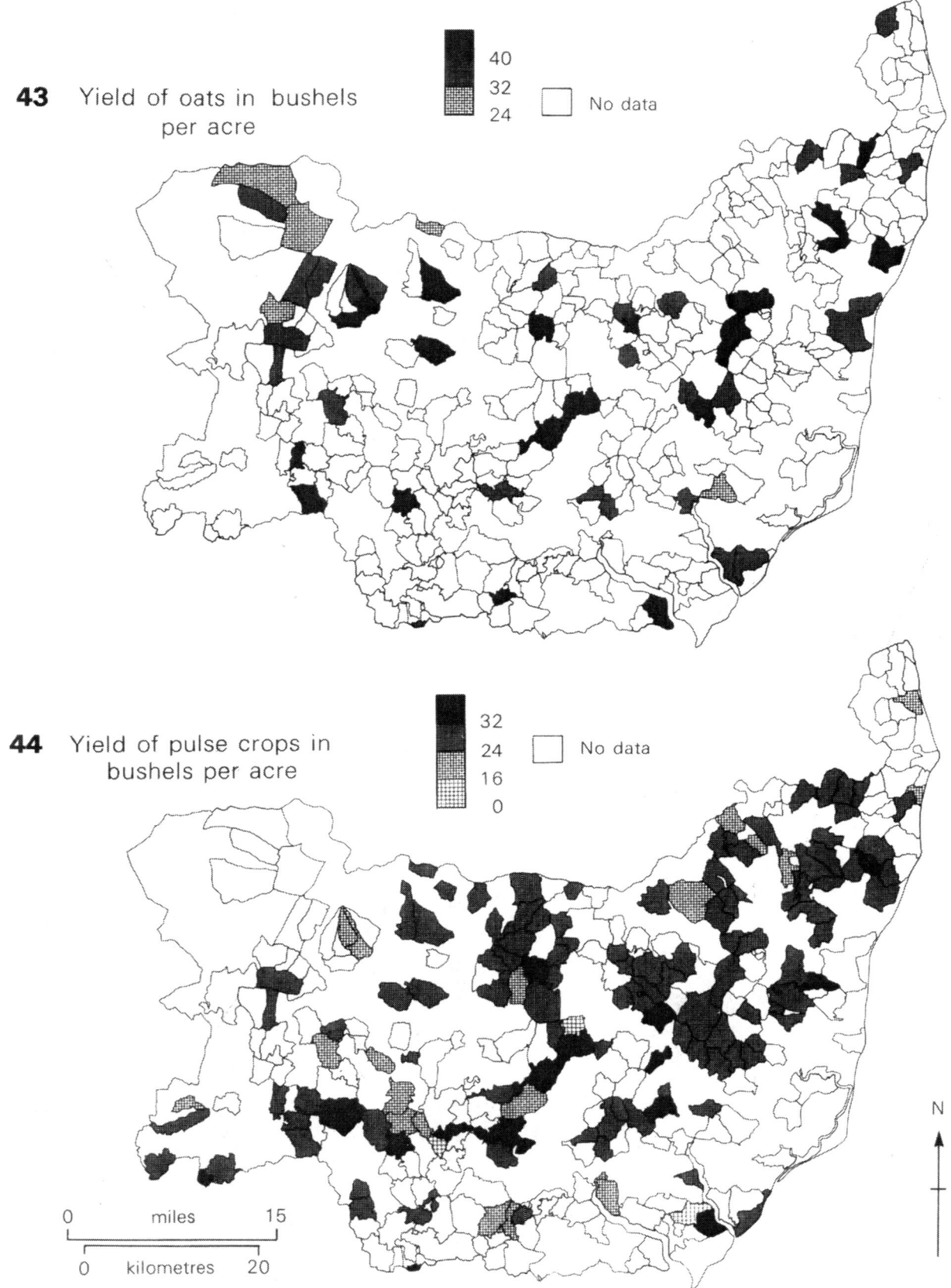

43 Yield of oats in bushels per acre

44 Yield of pulse crops in bushels per acre

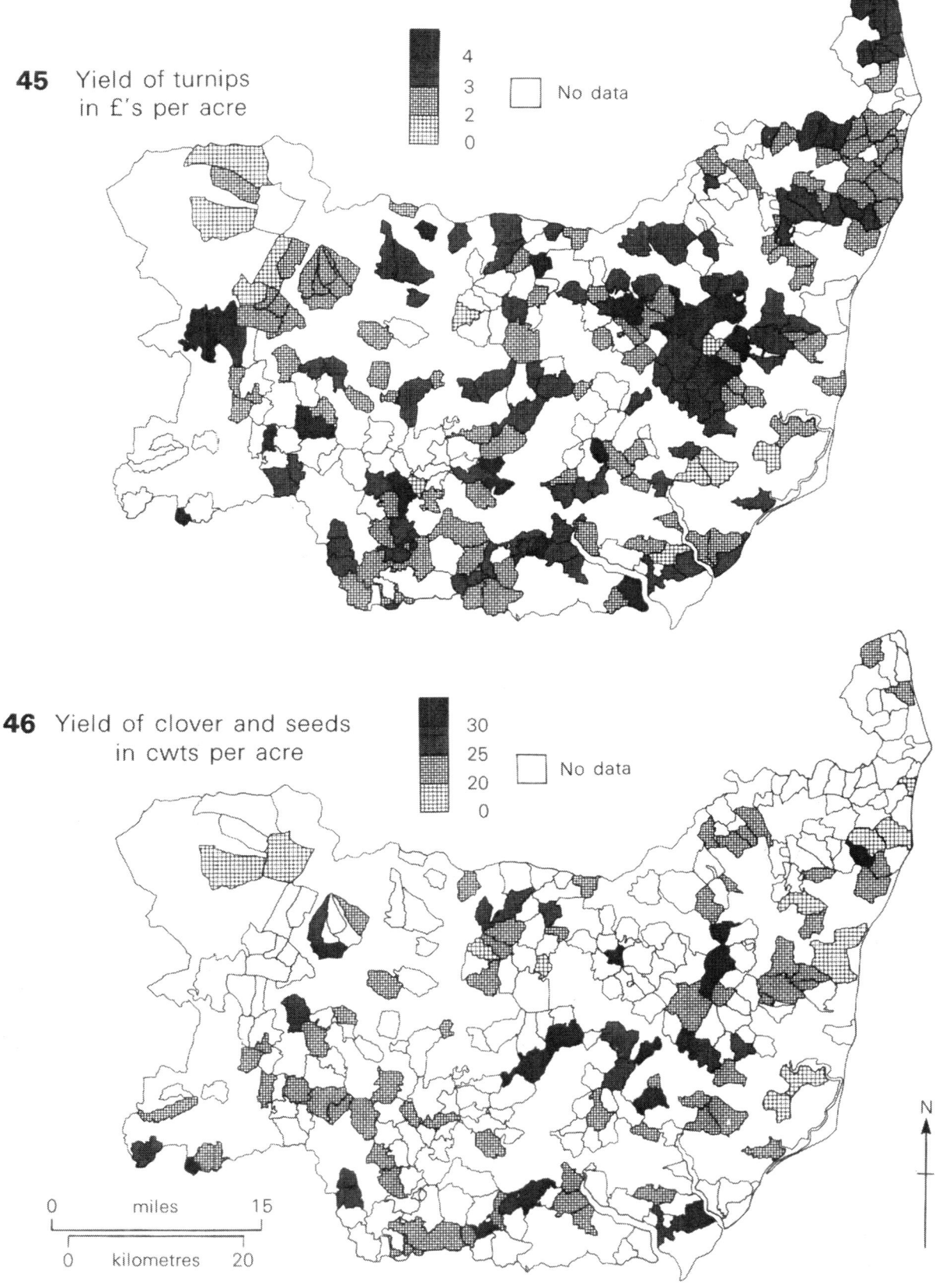

45 Yield of turnips in £'s per acre

46 Yield of clover and seeds in cwts per acre

54 Eastern counties

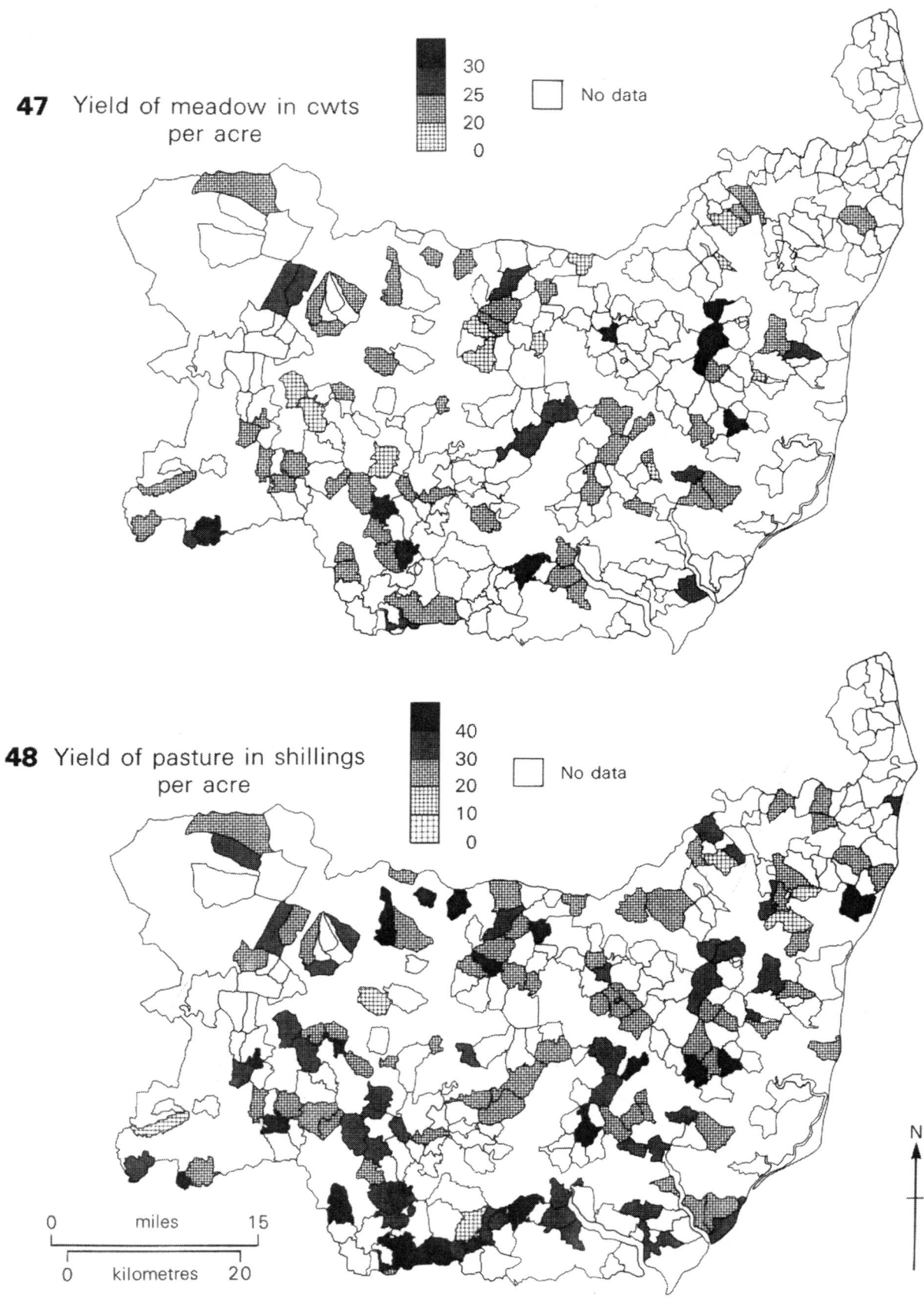

47 Yield of meadow in cwts per acre

48 Yield of pasture in shillings per acre

Cambridgeshire

177 tithe districts
67 reports on tithe agreements

Although only about a third of Cambridgeshire parishes have tithe file reports on agreements with complete farming data, these are fairly evenly distributed across the county with the exception of that tract of country enclosed by Cambridge, Newmarket and Ely where very many parishes had been exonerated from tithes at the time of parliamentary enclosure (Map 49). The process of voluntary tithe commutation commenced early in Cambridgeshire; almost two-thirds of agreements had been inspected and assessed by the end of 1839. Indeed, many reports were completed before printed questionnaire forms came into general use during 1838 but these manuscript documents contain the same categories of information as later printed forms. An unusually large number of assistant commissioners and local tithe agents worked in Cambridgeshire (Table 6). Henry Bertram Gunning worked extensively in other East Anglian counties as well as in Cambridgeshire and wrote some of the longest and fullest accounts of local conditions of all the many assistants employed by the Tithe Commission in England and Wales. Although his descriptions are comprehensive, i.e. he mentions soils, rotations, farms, drainage, manures, transport and so on, they are not stereotyped. He was clearly closely acquainted with a parish by the time he came to write his report and describes in detail those improvements taking place in local agriculture. Most valuably, he sets one parish in the comparative context of its neighbours drawing out similarities and differences in landscape and farming practices. By contrast, the reports of F. Browne Browne who worked extensively in Midland counties are rather stereotyped and dull, as are those of William Heard, most of whose work for the Tithe Commission was in the neighbouring counties of Hertfordshire, Essex and Suffolk. These three men together completed 57 per cent of Cambridgeshire reports.

The evidence of extant tithe file reports on agreements reveals that Cambridgeshire was an overwhelmingly arable county c. 1840 (Table 7 and Maps 51–4); in only seven tithe districts was the ratio of arable to pasture less than 1.5 to 1. In many parishes no woodland was recorded and the files contain little discussion of coppice, plantations or hedgerow timber (see Subject Index). The category 'common' in Table 7 and on Map 54 does not include unenclosed arable or meadows with common grazing rights. 'Sheepwalks' caused some assistant commissioners difficulties of classification and there is evidence of their confusion at some places between rights of sheepwalk over common fields at certain times of the year and sheepwalk as a type of rough pasture.

Assistant commissioners found it difficult to generalise about crop rotations on the arable as many different systems were used. The major distinctions were between the practices of open and enclosed parishes and highland and fenland districts. Many open fields were still farmed on the old four-course of two corn crops and a fallow. At Hildersham in south Cambridgeshire, Joseph Townsend found in 1837 that 'the arable lands are almost entirely in the open fields, the ordinary course of husbandry is two crops and a fallow. It is only by sufferance and the agreement of the occupiers that the culture of clover and turnips is permitted.' On heavy land at Rampton north-west of Cambridge, Henry Bertram Gunning described a commonly found Cambridgeshire variant of the four-course:

> one fourth has been entirely fallow, without any artificial grasses or grain crops of any kind. Wheat has followed the fallow instead of following the beans and barley has succeeded the wheat instead of coming after the summer fallow. This and the circumstances of the lands being without under-drains, gave but a low average of the corn, more especially as regards the barley crop.

On poorer peat lowlands it was common to find a six-course rotation with corn being planted for one or two years after paring and burning and then the land was laid down to seeds. Assistant commissioners found that the fens presented widely different states of productivity depending on the extent to which improvements had been effected. Cambridgeshire tithe files contain a number of detailed descriptions of the costs and processes of fen drainage and of improvement of peat soils by marling with clay (see Subject Index).

For the county as a whole, approximately equal acreages of wheat and spring grains were sown, though clover and seeds occupied the greatest acreage of any crop (Table 7 and Maps 55–61). Henry Bertram Gunning remarked that 'the cultivation of rye except as sheep feed, is nearly exploded; formerly large breadths were grown, and eaten by the labourers. Potatoes and wheaten bread form better and more grateful food.' Generally, the quality of corn crops was higher on the highland, though some peat lands recorded exceptionally high yields (Table 7 and Maps 62–7). The potato is a crop which receives very little notice in tithe file reports but Cambridgeshire is one of the few counties for which acreages of this crop are reported in some parishes. Two hundred acres at March, eighty at Wimblington, and ten to fifty acres at Outwell, Croydon-cum-Clapton and Doddington indicate the extent of culture of this crop and underline the contribution potatoes must have made to total agricultural production in this part of England.

Table 6 *Reports on agreements for commutation of tithes in Cambridgeshire*

Assistant commissioner/ local tithe agent	1837	1838	1839	1840	1841	1842	1843	1844	1845	Totals
Henry Bertram Gunning		1	14	1		1				17
William Heard			1		6	2	1		1	11
F. Browne Browne		1	1	6	2					10
Thomas Smith Woolley	2	4								6
John Pickering		3	2							5
? Mears		4								4
Anthony Jackson	1	2								3
Joseph Townsend	3									3
John Mee Mathew		1		2						3
Horace William Meteyard			2							2
Roger Kynaston		2								2
Henry Dixon	1									1
Totals	7	18	20	9	8	3	1		1	67

Table 7 *Land use, crops and yields in Cambridgeshire c. 1836*

A	Land use	Percentage of total land area enumerated in reports on tithe agreements	Estimated acreage in whole county
	Arable	70.1	367,370
	Grass	25.4	133,282
	Wood	1.4	7,579
	Common	1.5	6,028

B	Crop	Mean percentage of arable	Mean yield per acre	Estimated acreage in whole county
	Wheat	23.1	22.4 bushels	84,885
	Barley	10.8	30.0 bushels	39,526
	Oats	13.6	39.6 bushels	50,032
	Pulses	5.5	23.9 bushels	20,399
	Turnips	5.0	£3.35	18,417
	Seeds	28.2	21.5 cwts	103,471
	Fallows	10.8	—	39,612

Eastern counties

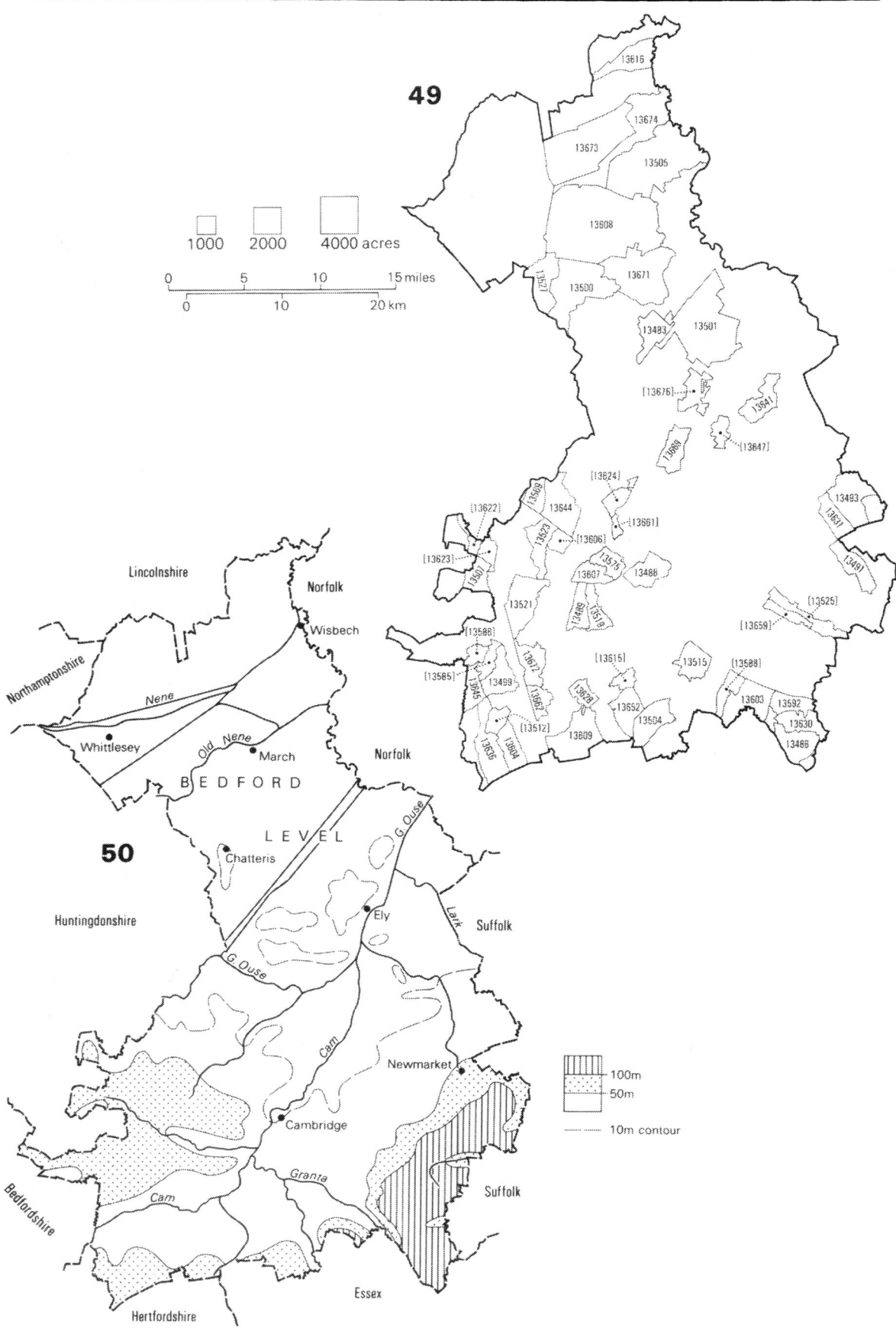

Cambridgeshire

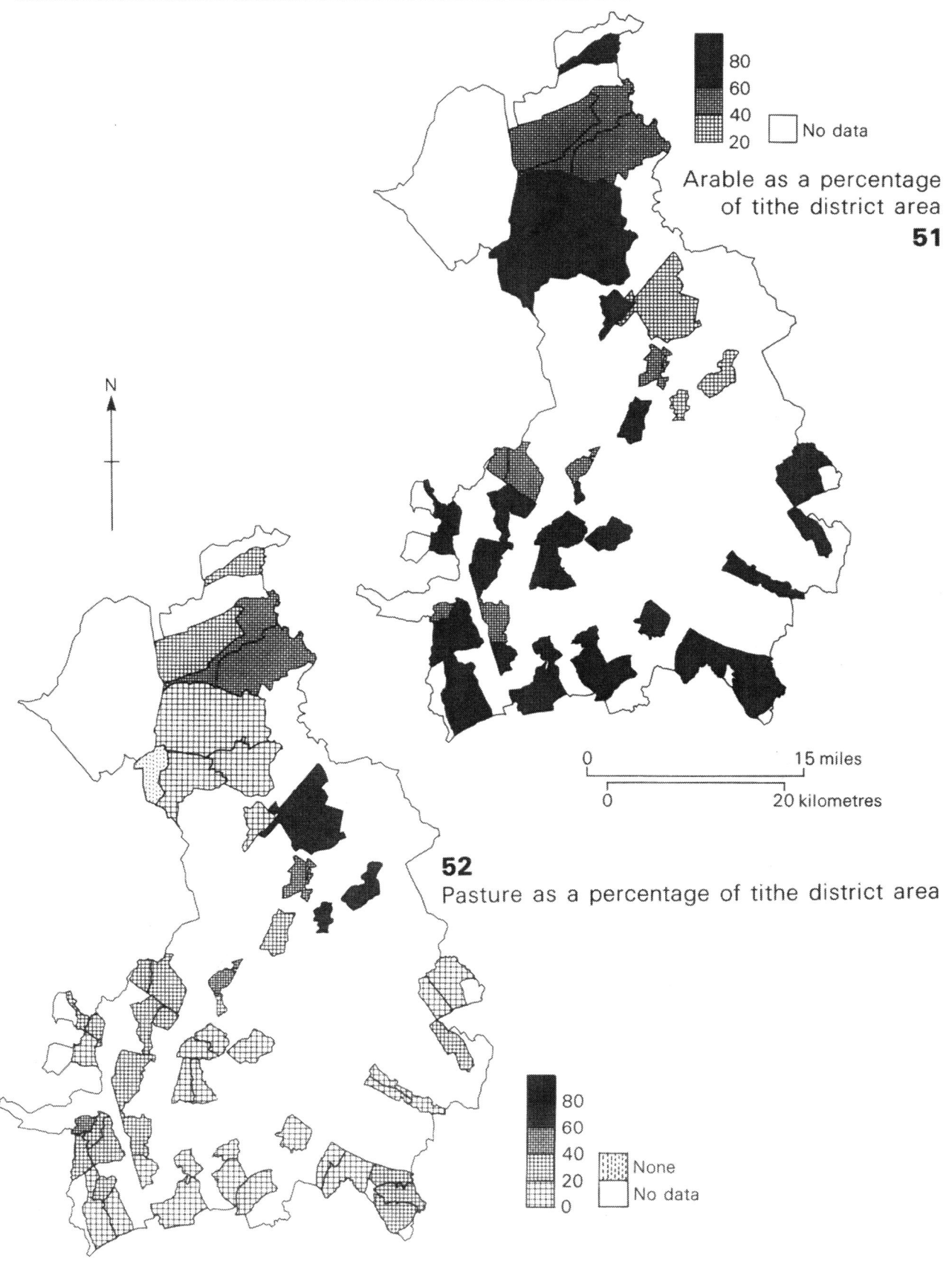

51 Arable as a percentage of tithe district area

52 Pasture as a percentage of tithe district area

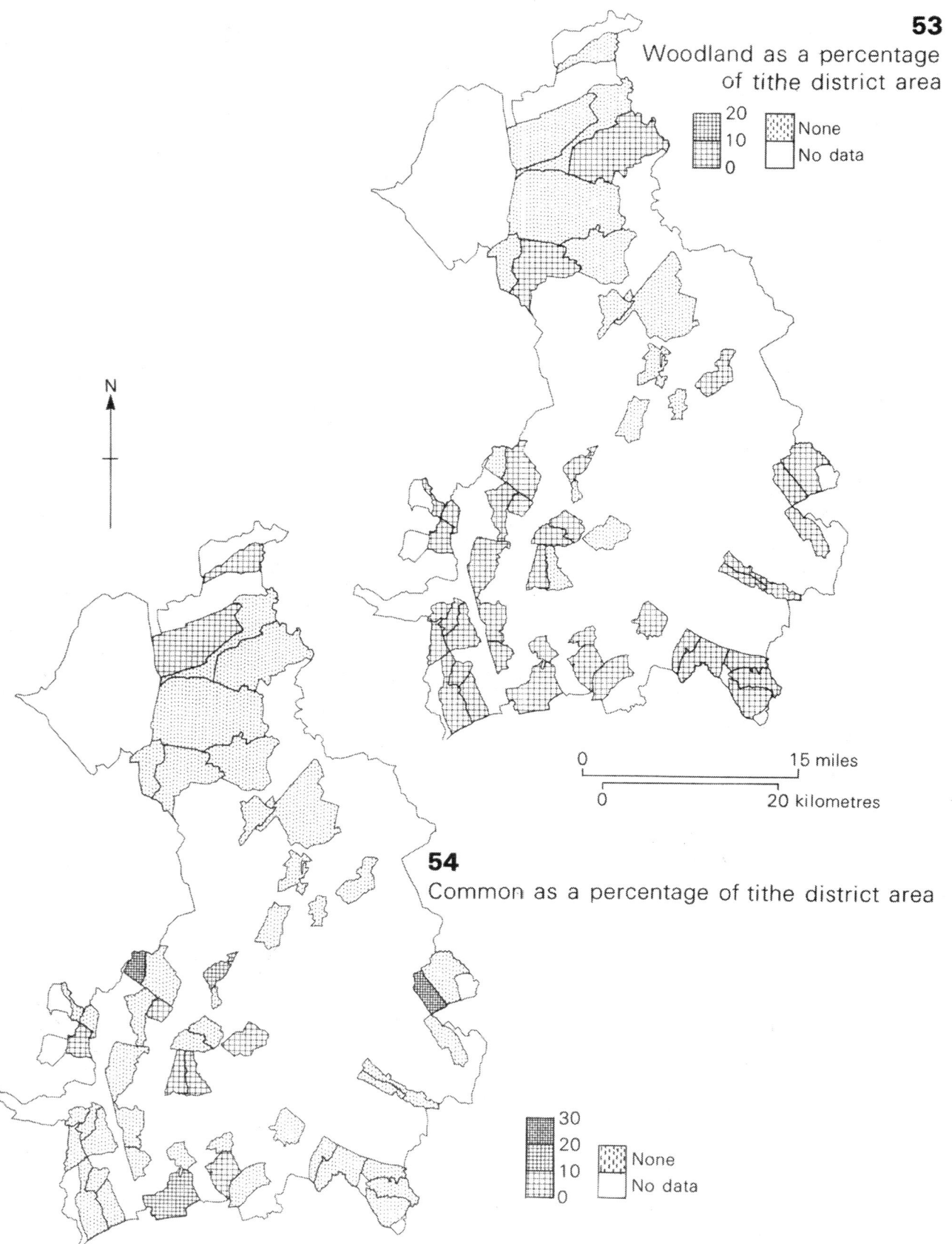

53 Woodland as a percentage of tithe district area

54 Common as a percentage of tithe district area

Cambridgeshire

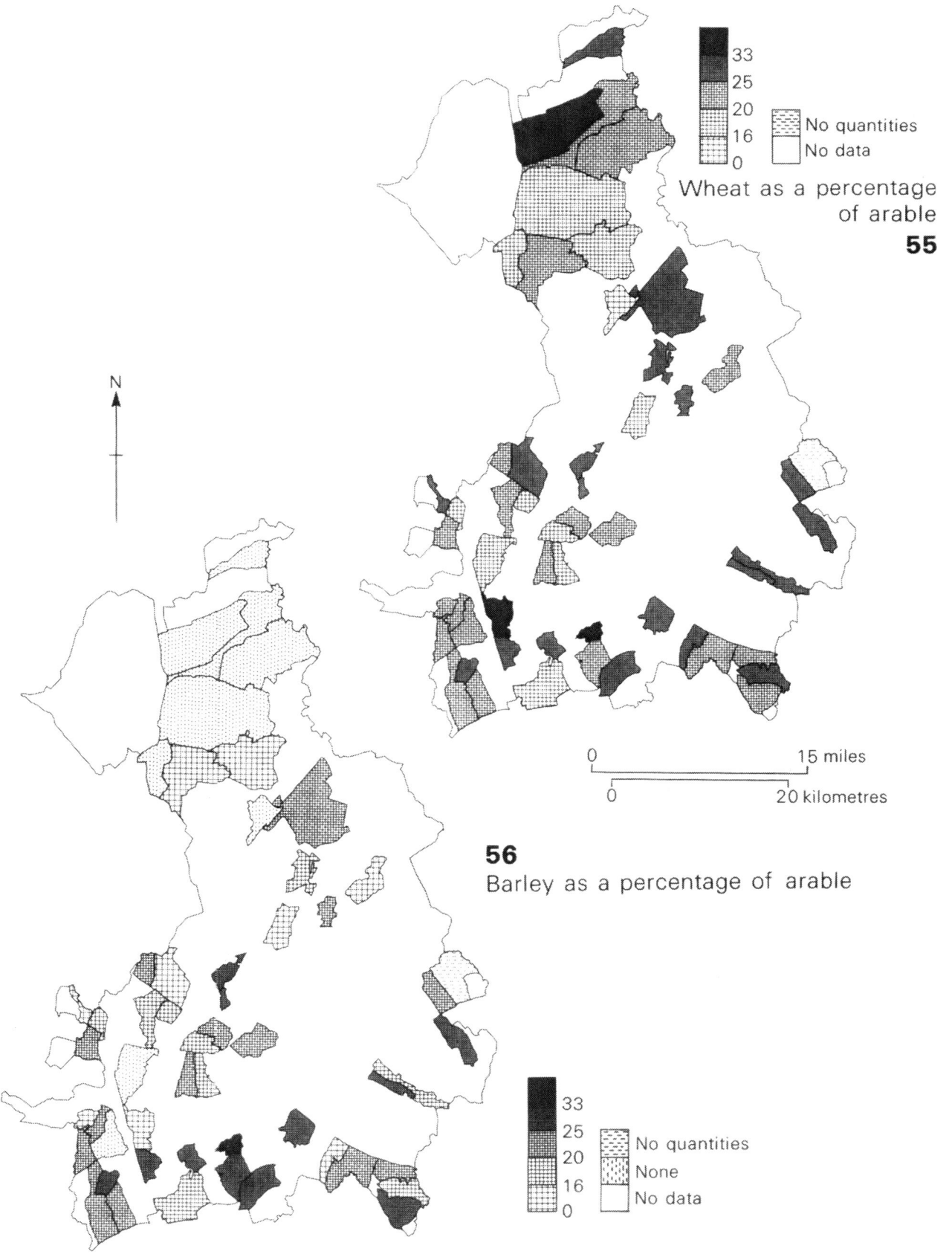

55 Wheat as a percentage of arable

56 Barley as a percentage of arable

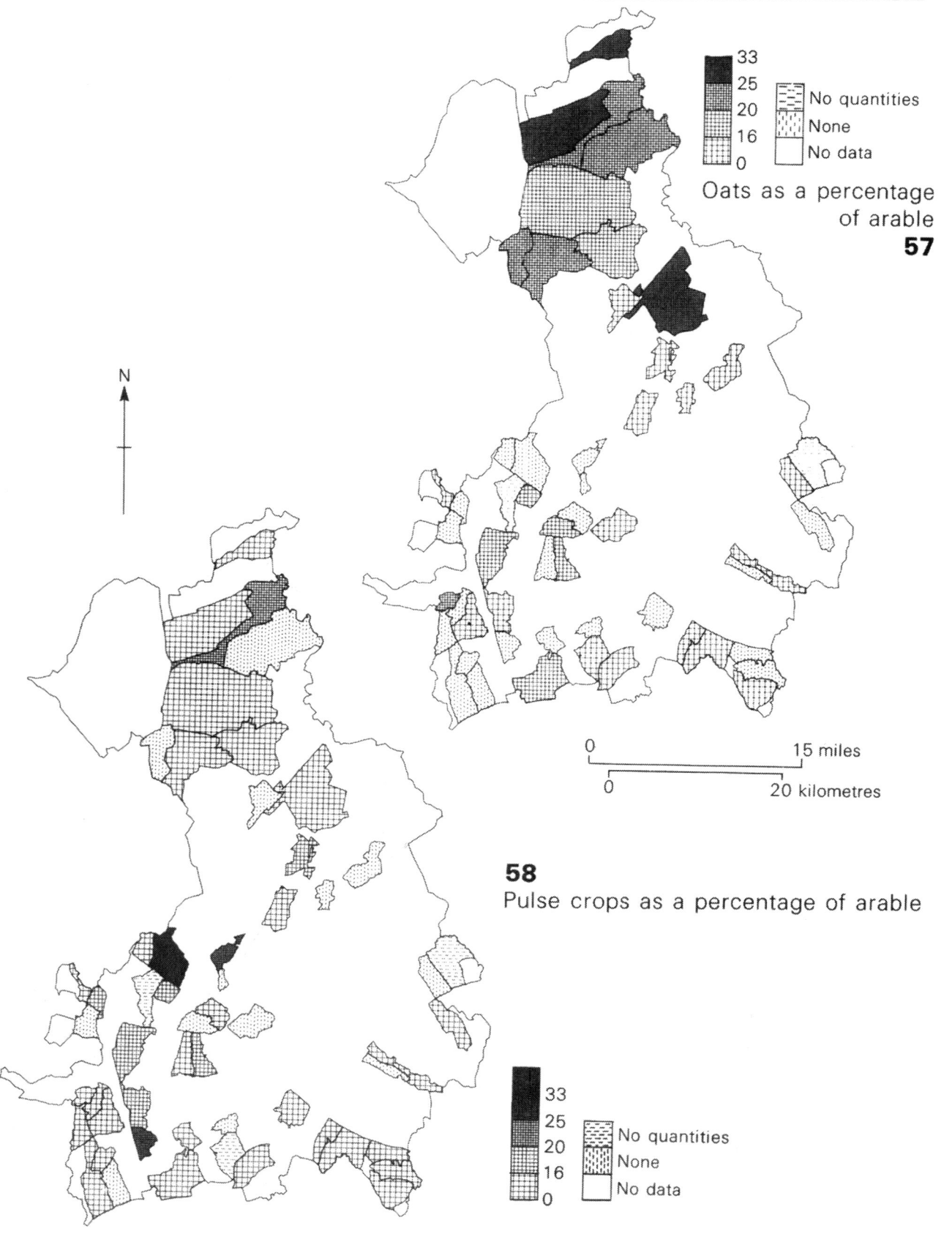

57 Oats as a percentage of arable

58 Pulse crops as a percentage of arable

Cambridgeshire

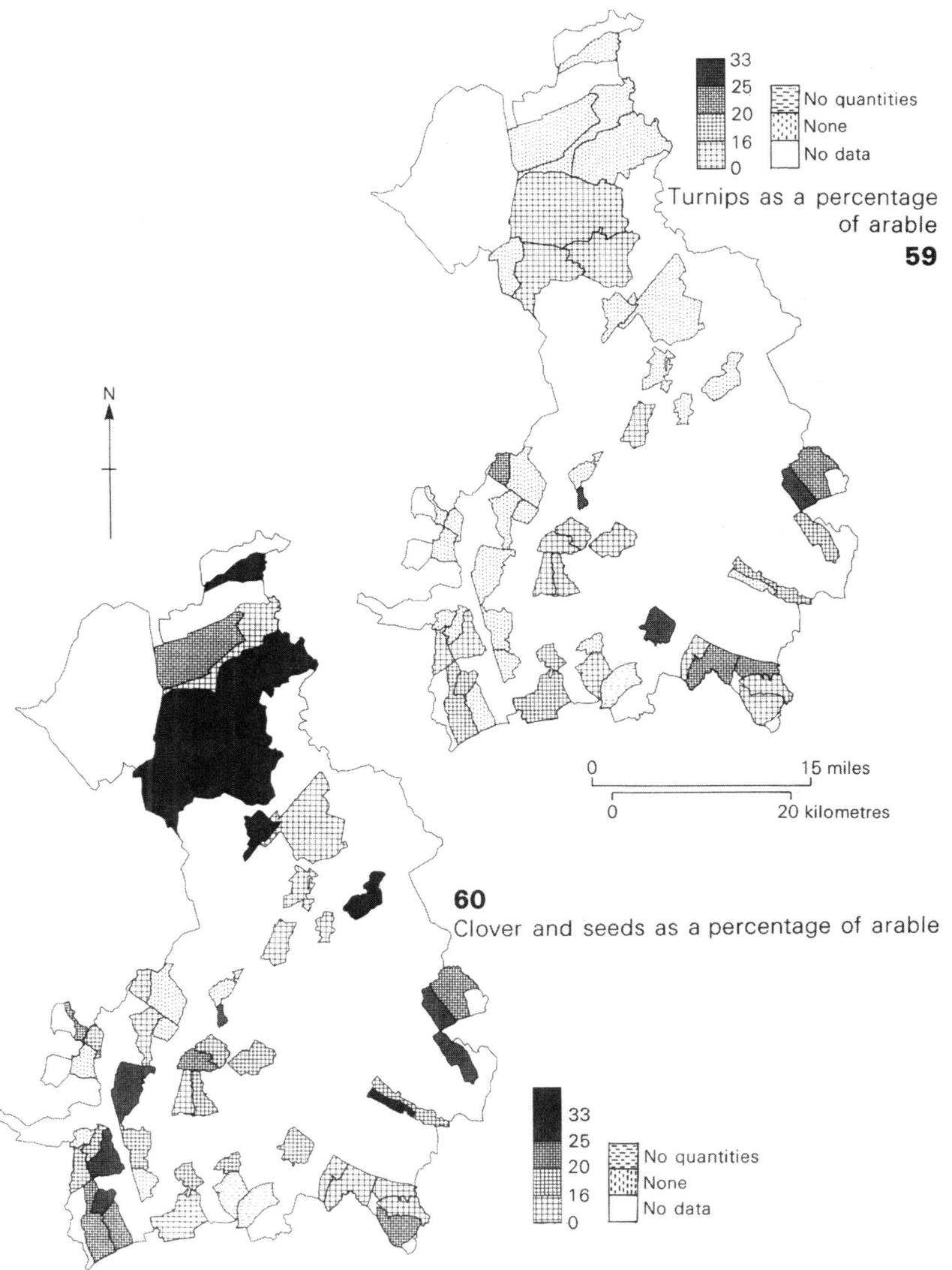

Turnips as a percentage of arable
59

60
Clover and seeds as a percentage of arable

Eastern counties

61
Dead fallow as a percentage of arable

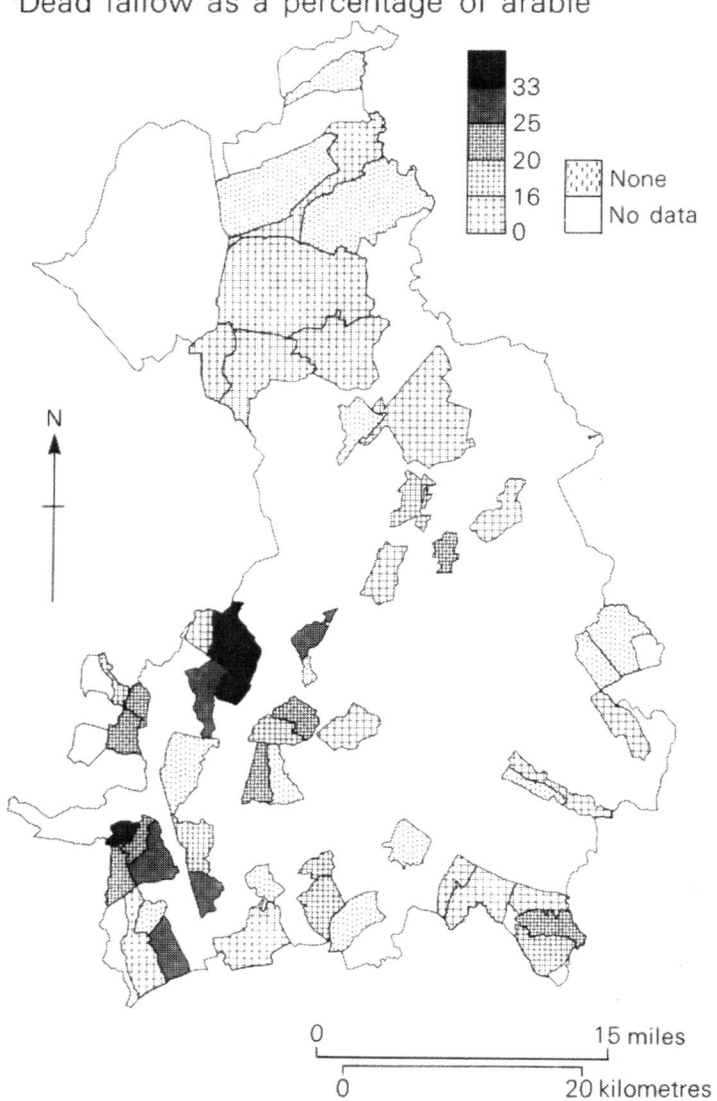

Cambridgeshire

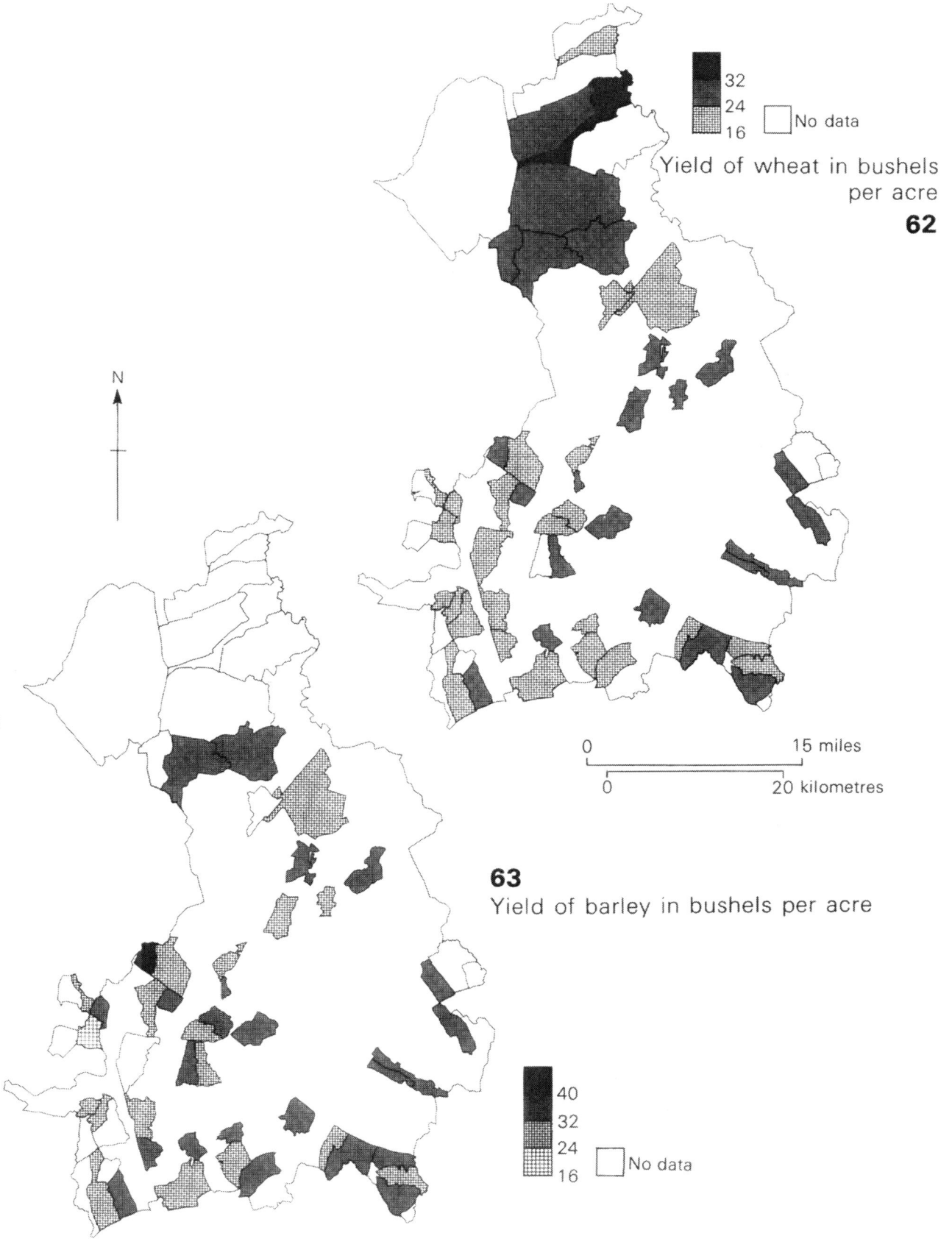

62 Yield of wheat in bushels per acre

63 Yield of barley in bushels per acre

66 Eastern counties

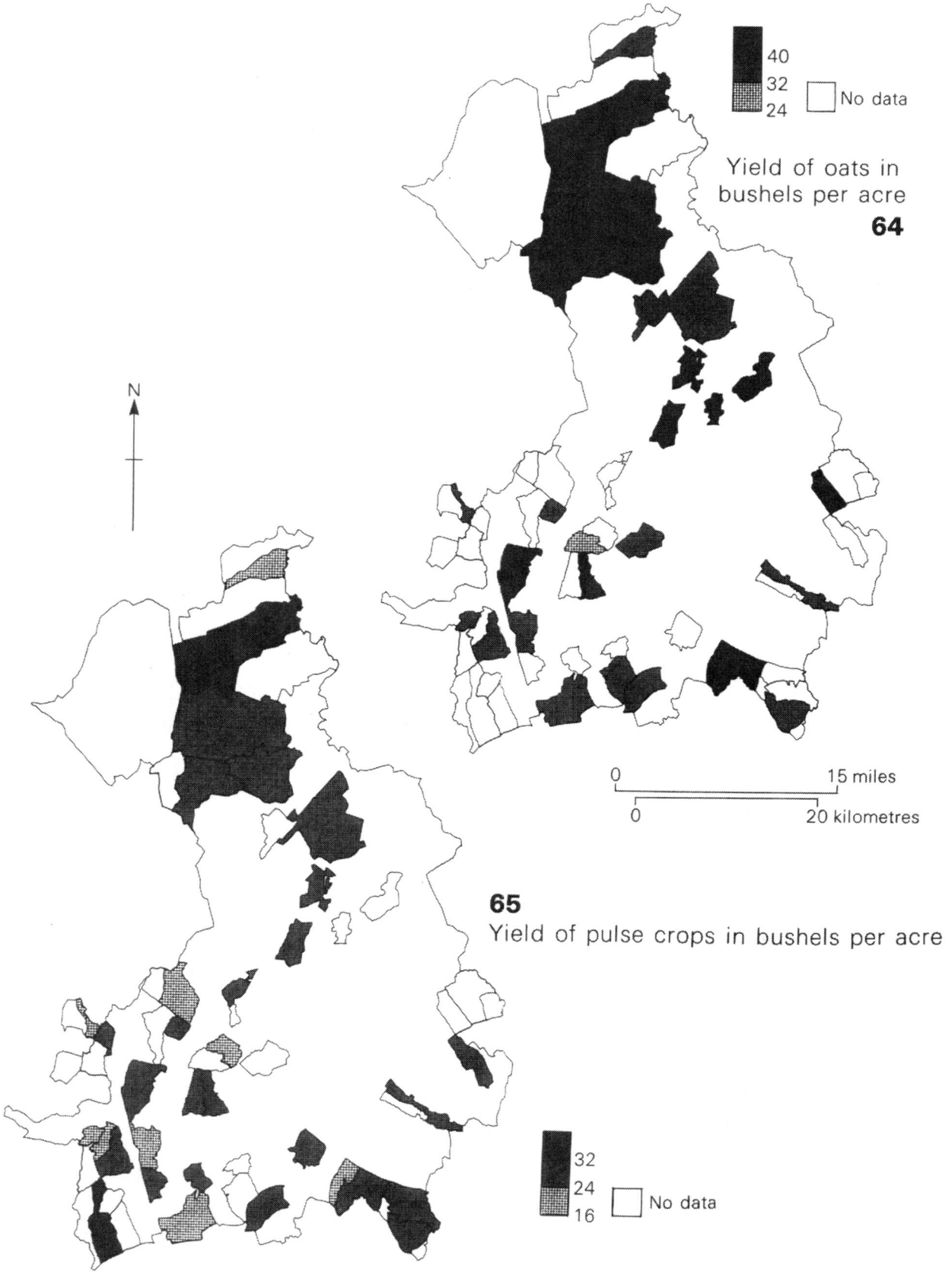

64 Yield of oats in bushels per acre

65 Yield of pulse crops in bushels per acre

Cambridgeshire 67

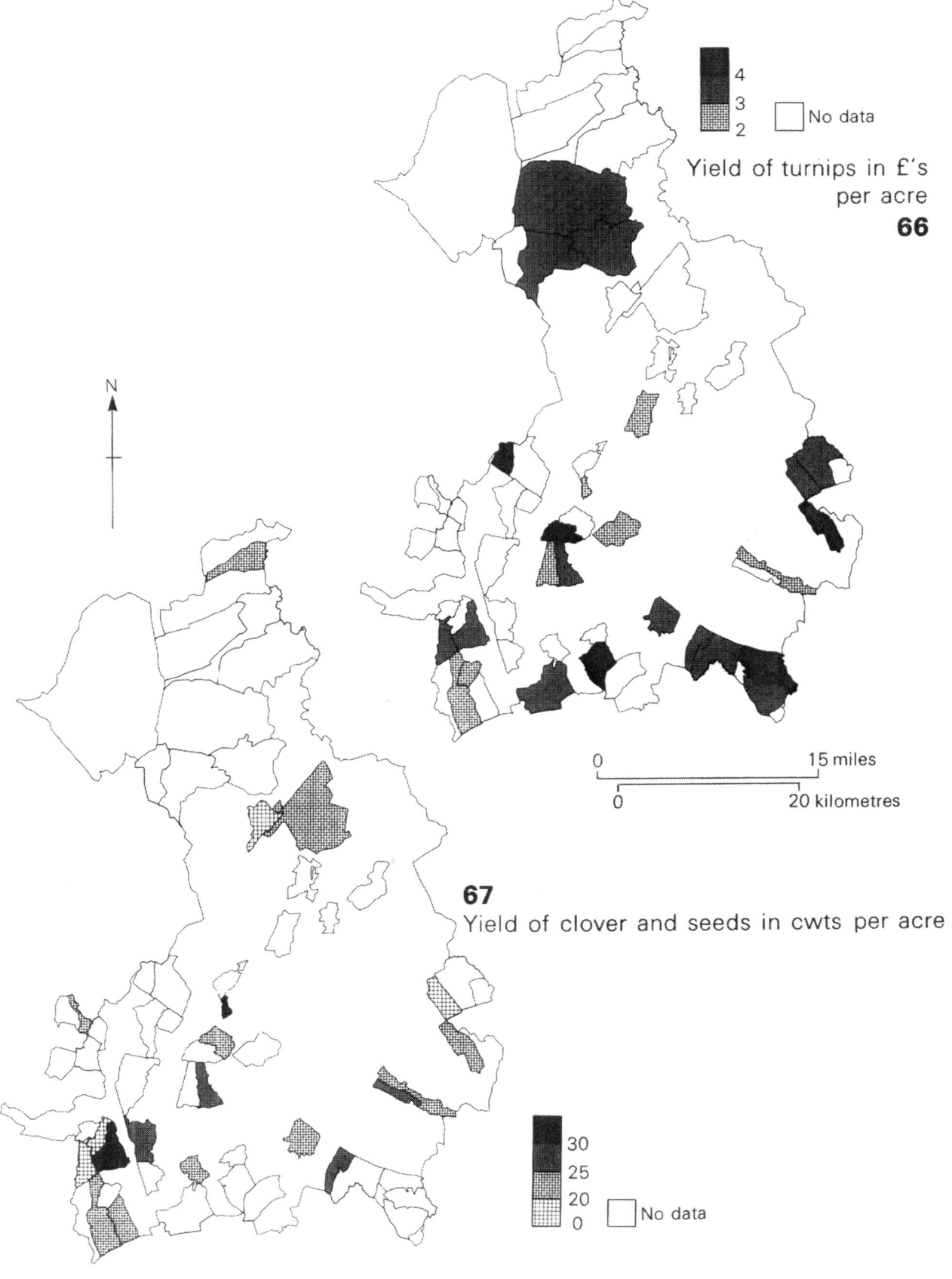

66 Yield of turnips in £'s per acre

67 Yield of clover and seeds in cwts per acre

Eastern counties

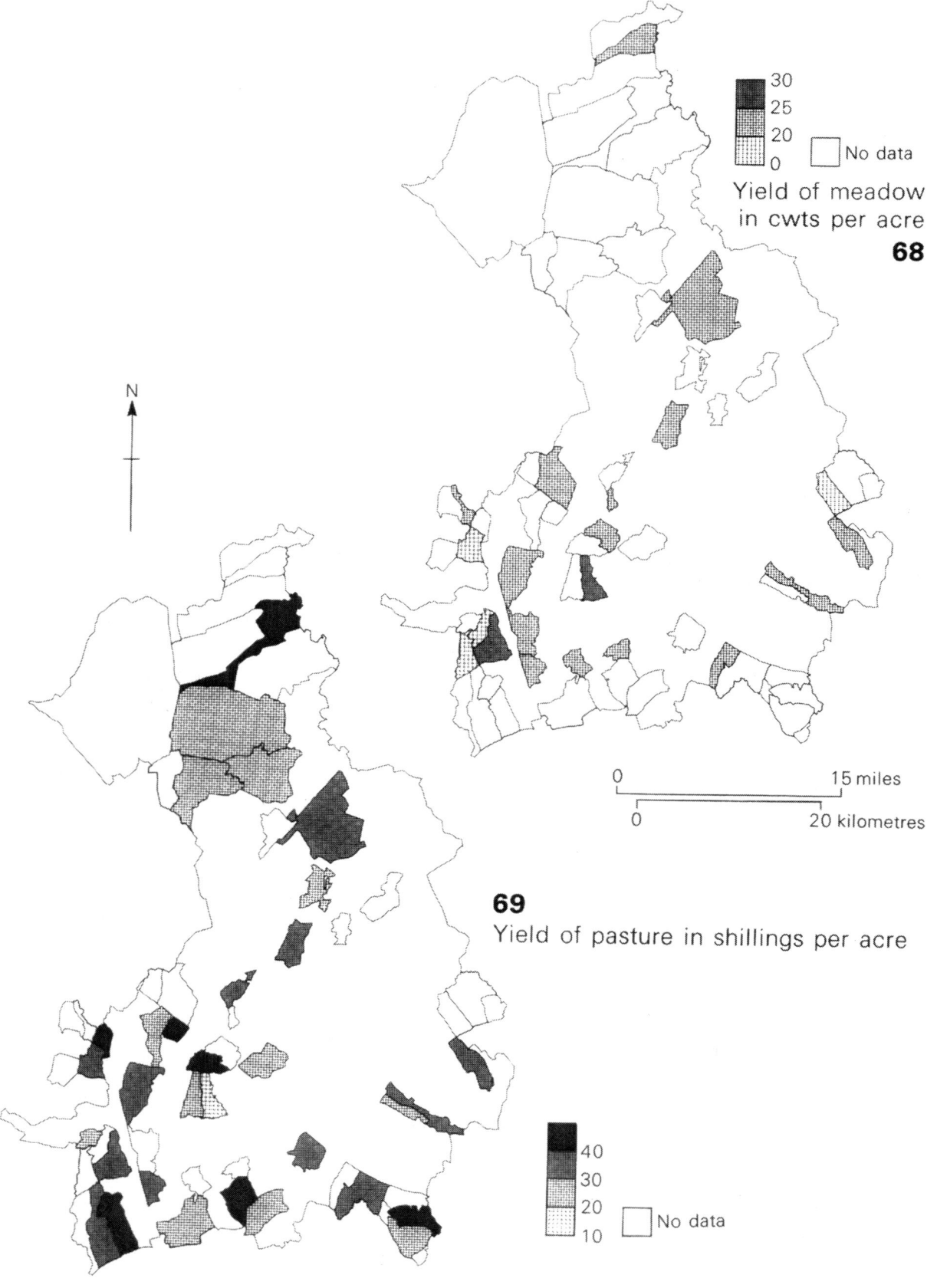

68 Yield of meadow in cwts per acre

69 Yield of pasture in shillings per acre

Norfolk

732 tithe districts
483 reports on tithe agreements

The publication in 1938 of J. E. G. Mosby's report on the findings of the First Land Utilisation Survey of Norfolk marked an important advance in the exploitation of tithe survey information on mid-nineteenth-century land use and farming. Mosby mapped arable land field-by-field for the extensive Good Sand Region of north Norfolk, mapped changes in land utilisation, 1840–1935, by comparing acreages in schedules of tithe agreements and awards with parish statistics collected by the Ministry of Agriculture for 1935, assessed the former extent of infield–outfield by plotting all 'breck' field and place names recorded in tithe apportionments and reconstructed patterns of field boundaries and land use on sample farms and estates. The existence and value of the tithe files were unknown to historians at that time. Those for the Breckland have since been consulted by Malcolm Postgate (1961), whilst J. P. Dodd (1976) cites some of Mosby's tithe-derived statistics in support of those he obtained from the 1854 agricultural statistics for Norfolk.

Norfolk is exceptionally well provided with tithe file data. Its 483 reports on agreements set it at the head of all counties in absolute numbers, whilst its 66 per cent of tithe districts with reports places Norfolk in the leading group of counties in terms of completeness of cover. Voluntaryism was the norm in Norfolk; in over 70 per cent of districts where tithe remained to be commuted, voluntary agreements were achieved and more than three-quarters of these were ready for assessment by the end of 1839 (Table 8). Only fifty-three parishes were entirely tithe free in 1836 but in many others some categories of land were exempt, notably woodland of more than twenty years growth, recently reclaimed marshland, 'new' crops such as coleseed, and enclosed commons, heaths, and wastes where allotments of land had been given in lieu of tithes. Where marshland was not completely exempt, it often paid only a nominal modus. Heathland, unimproved fenland and sheepwalks generated very little titheable produce and were normally classified as 'common' by assistant commissioners in this county; hence the high figure of 11.2 per cent of the total county classified as common in Table 9.

It is clear from the descriptions of parish farming given by assistant commissioners and local tithe agents listed in Table 8, that some were much more familiar with Norfolk farming than others. Henry Bertram Gunning's Norfolk reports are the most informative and rank among the best in the whole body of English and Welsh tithe files. They are normally two foolscap pages in length and for most districts contain detailed remarks on the nature and quality of different types of land, rotations, summer fallows and root crops, yields, the state of drainage, pasture and meadowland, the kinds of stock kept, wasteland and woodland, and accessibility of markets. At the other extreme, reports by Horace William Meteyard consist mainly of a chronicle of local events from 1066 to 1836, or such of these as he could discover. He admits to taking much information directly from farmers and where these were uncooperative or just plain ignorant, his parish descriptions are in consequence rather thin. James Drage Merest, who compiled exactly one third of Norfolk reports, did not enumerate individual crop acreages but rather stated the total arable acreage, the usual rotation and the yield and price of crops. It is necessary, therefore, to divide his total arable by the number of courses in the rotation to obtain estimates for individual crops.

It is very clear from the tithe files that Norfolk farmers focussed most of their attention on their arable lands. The overall proportion of arable to grass was 3 to 1; only in Broadland, on the alluvial strip along the north coast and in low-lying parishes around King's Lynn, was pasture at all significant in terms of the area it occupied (Maps 72–3). Most assistant commissioners accepted that the Norfolk four-course system was that most usually adopted in this county. In some poor soil parishes, Felbrigg was one, farmers were bound by covenants to the six-course

> which has some advantages and several disadvantages. On the one hand, the longer period which intervenes between the return of the same crops prevents this inferior description of land from tiring of them; on the other hand, the artificial grasses lying two years renders the land liable to be over-run with the miserable weed called spear-grass.

The very best land was considered strong enough to produce a crop every year; no regular system applied, and fallows interspersed only once in eight to ten years. Bare fallows still existed on heavy soils (Map 82) but were decreasing according to local tithe agents (see Subject Index). Turnips were grown wherever possible, and where they were not successful, winter tares were being planted, obviating the need for long summer fallows. These changes were recognised by Henry Bertram Gunning in his report on the tithe agreement at Buckenham in south Norfolk:

> winter tares also are sown in some considerable quantity and are fed off by sheep early in the spring; this is practised upon those lands which are too heavy for turnips or other roots. This is a system of husbandry which seems on the increase, rendered almost necessary by the increase in the number of sheep kept; and is superseding the somewhat disheartening system of long summer fallows as a preparation for barley.

Eighty instances of high farming arable systems are recorded in Norfolk files and as a result naturally light and poor soils could produce corn crops at the level of yields recorded on Maps 83–8. Seaweed, fish, saltpetre, oil dust, rape cake, oil cake, soda and bone dust are among the manures, artificial fertilisers and feedstuffs mentioned frequently in tithe files (see Subject Index). A sentence from Horace William Meteyard's report on Barford, west of Norwich, encapsulates the essence of a system discussed similarly at many other places: 'artificial manures are used; linseed cake with the mangel pulled for the bullocks makes an excellent yard heap and rape cake, salt petre, soil from Norwich, lime and soot are applied in quantities as dressings; pea and bean meal, corn, barley meal, beet, salt and oil cake are

Norfolk

given to the stock'. Assistant commissioners considered that the purpose of such practices was to 'artificially force a crop'. If fertilisers and feeds were reduced, so gross titheable produce would fall. The Tithe Commission required that some allowance in the level of rent-charge be made for instances of extraordinarily high farming. On the other hand, claying of light soils and underdraining of heavy soils effected more permanent improvement. Straw, stones, ling, gorse and, increasingly, tiles were used to fill drains. A farmer with 600 acres at South Runcton 'has during a long tenancy, dug and carted upon his land the surprising quantity of 79,462 loads of clay, each load containing 32 bushels . . . The blowing sand of which a part of the parish consists, has been much changed and improved.'

On the whole, assistant commissioners and local tithe agents considered pasture in Norfolk not nearly as productive as arable; references to 'poor quality pastures' in the Subject Index outnumber those judged 'good quality' by almost 2 to 1. Much grassland was considered only of feeding not fattening quality. On light soils, pastures were liable to burn in dry seasons and most parishes had only small quantities of mown meadows. The largest areas of permanent pastures in this county were the marshes (Map 73). Undrained, these provided only poor summer sheepwalks; there was much room for improvement. At Potter Heigham in Broadland, James Drage Merest considered that

> the system of drainage here is as bad as in some other cases in Norfolk upon which I have made observations. There are only 2 or 3 small mills of weak power, and consequently it not infrequently appears that this extent of low land is inundated at a period of the year when it is the utmost consequence that the water should be taken off. I have no hesitation in saying that if the power of steam were applied this whole extent might be converted into good grazing ground.

Table 8 *Reports on agreements for commutation of tithes in Norfolk*

Assistant commissioner/local tithe agent	1837	1838	1839	1840	1841	1842	1843	1844	1845	1846	Totals
James Drage Merest	22	85	50	4							161
Henry Bertram Gunning		13	46	14	13	14	7		2		109
? Mears			31	31	15	4					81
Horace William Meteyard			36	5				1			42
Thomas Sutton	11	17	3								31
William Heard					15		2	2		1	20
Thomas Smith Woolley	4					9	1				14
John Mee Mathew			5	4							9
Roger Kynaston			6								6
Thomas Turner	1	4									5
John Pickering					2	1					3
Thomas Sudworth	1										1
Joseph Townsend					1						1
Totals	39	186	146	52	20	24	10	3	2	1	483

Table 9 *Land use, crops and yields in Norfolk c. 1836*

A	Land use	Percentage of total land area enumerated in reports on tithe agreements	Estimated acreage in whole county
	Arable	63.8	864,264
	Grass	21.1	146,646
	Wood	3.7	25,880
	Common	11.2	77,870

B	Crop	Mean percentage of arable	Mean yield per acre	Estimated acreage in whole county
	Wheat	23.5	23.3 bushels	203,102
	Barley	22.3	31.5 bushels	192,730
	Oats	2.8	35.7 bushels	25,858
	Pulses	1.9	26.5 bushels	16,421
	Turnips	24.2	£2.80	209,497
	Seeds	24.9	23.1 cwts	212,523
	Fallows	2.1	—	18,149

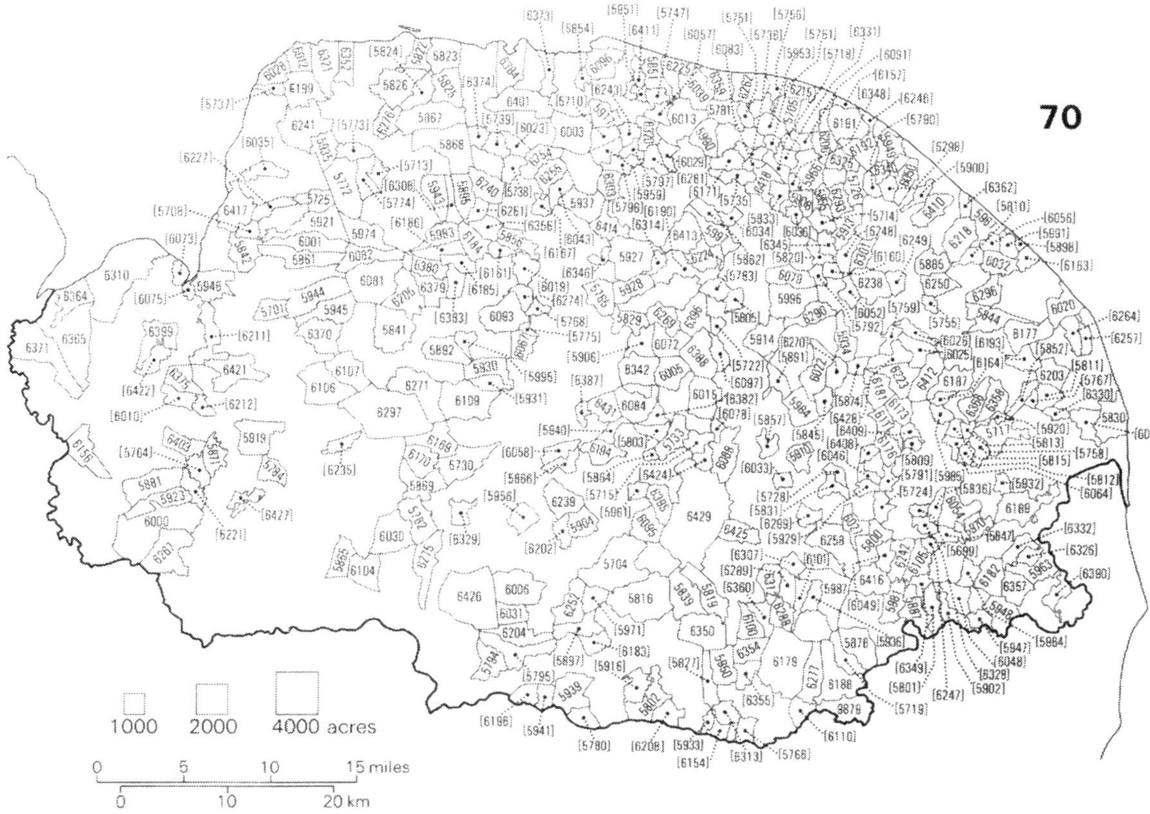

Norfolk

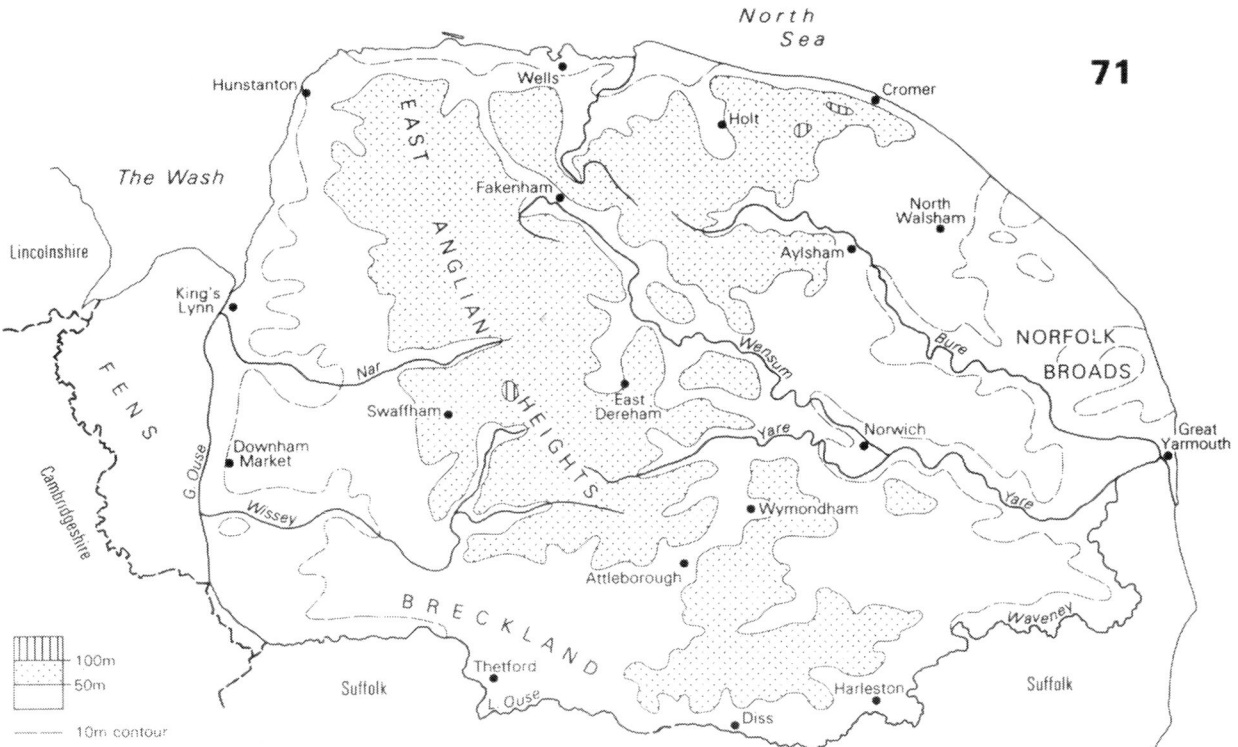

70

71

72
Arable as a percentage of tithe district area

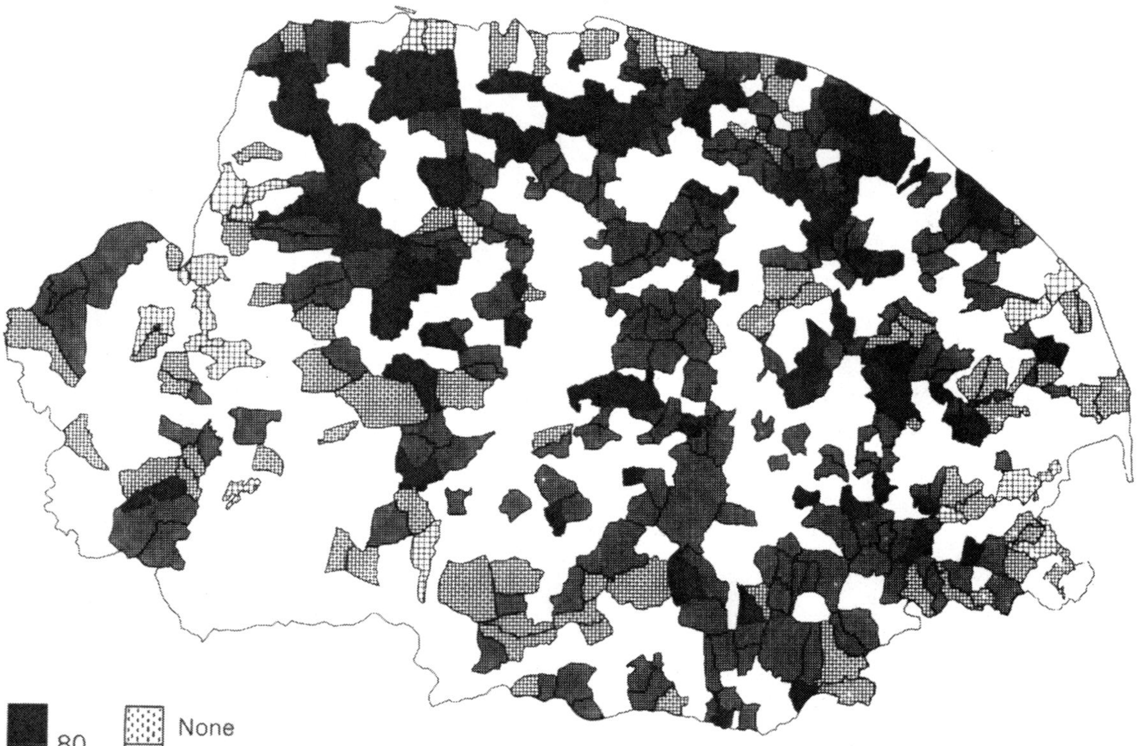

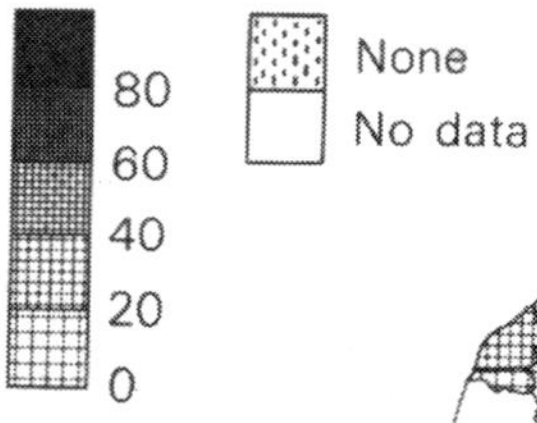

73
Pasture as a percentage of tithe district area

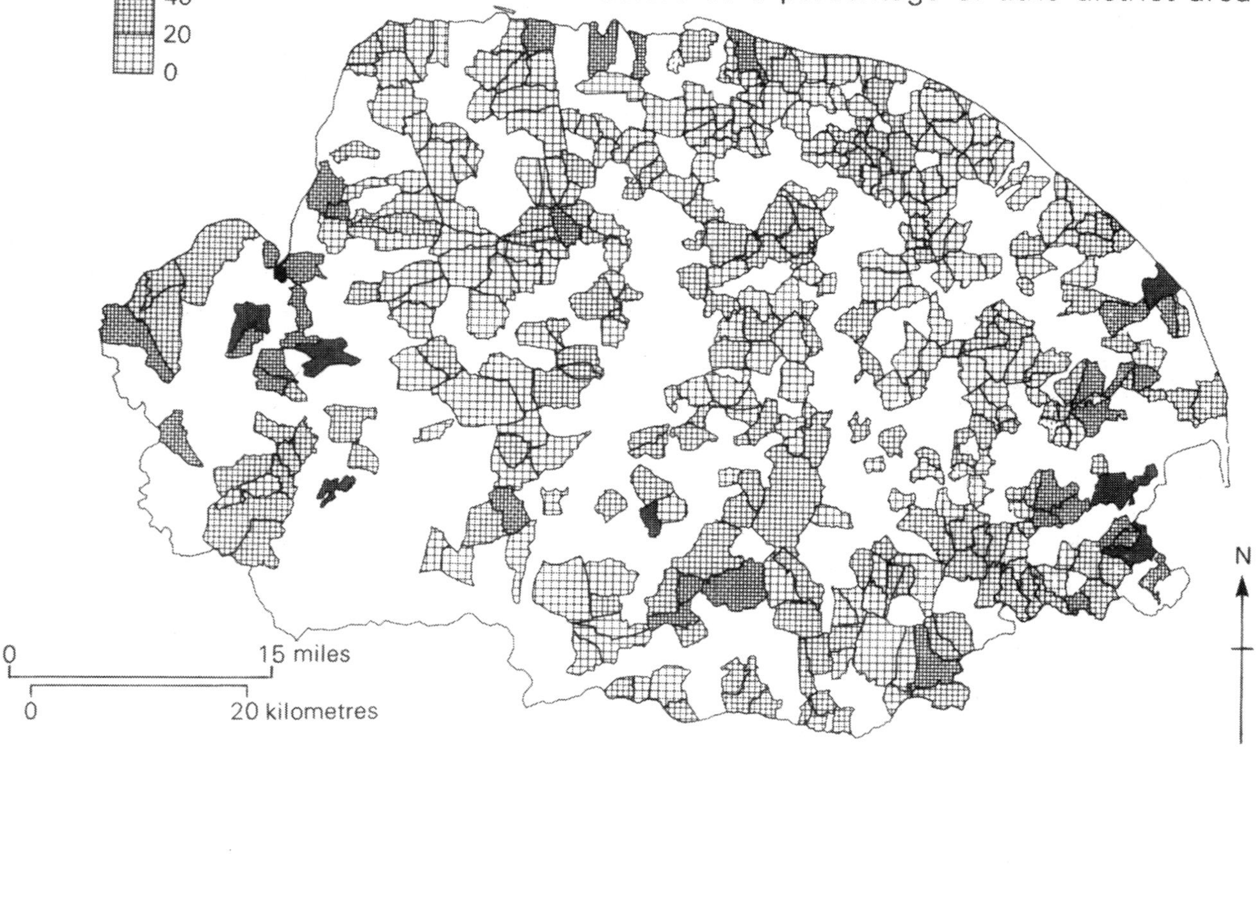

Norfolk

74
Woodland as a percentage of tithe district area

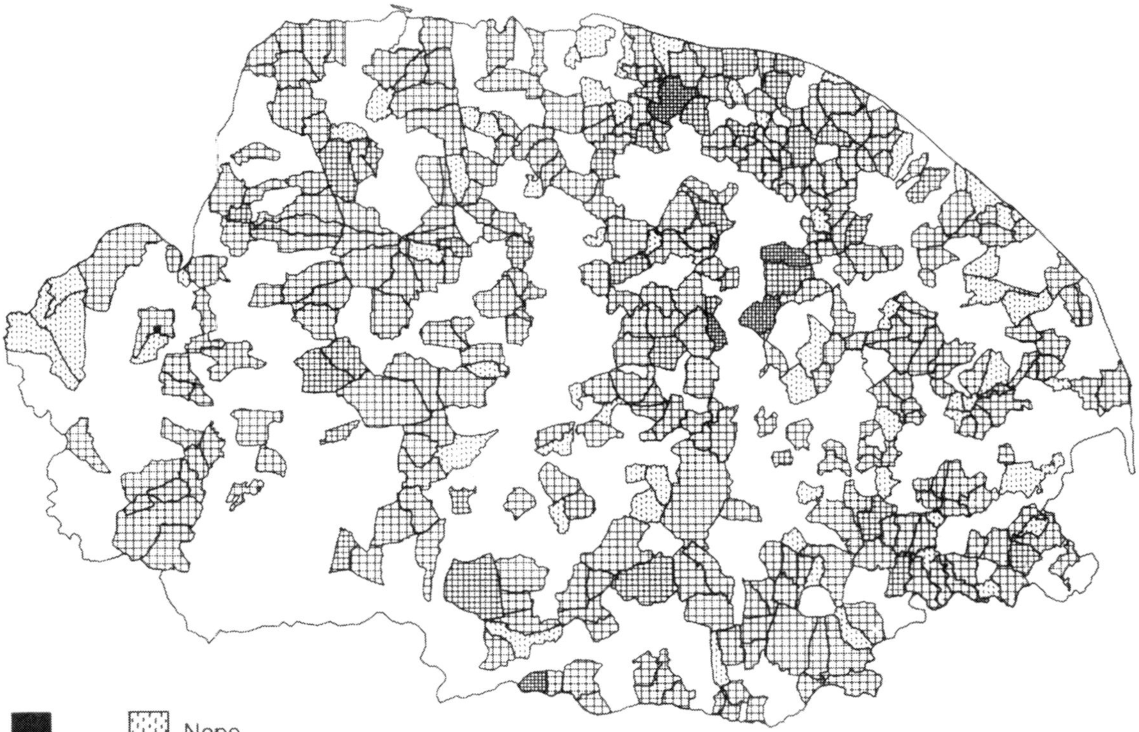

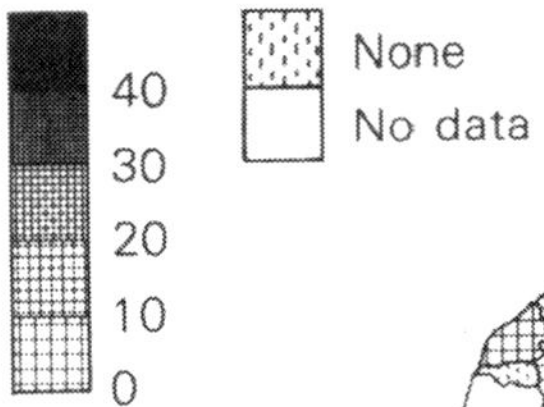

75
Common as a percentage of tithe district area

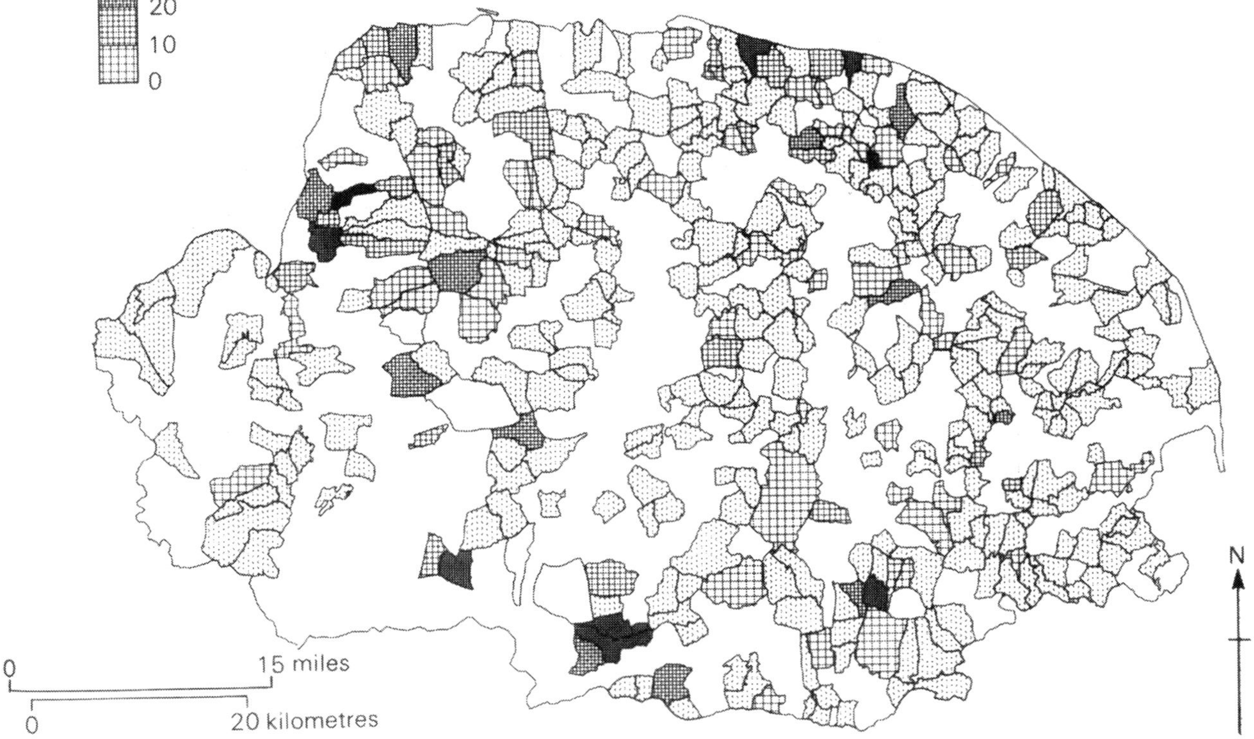

76 Eastern counties

76
Wheat as a percentage of arable

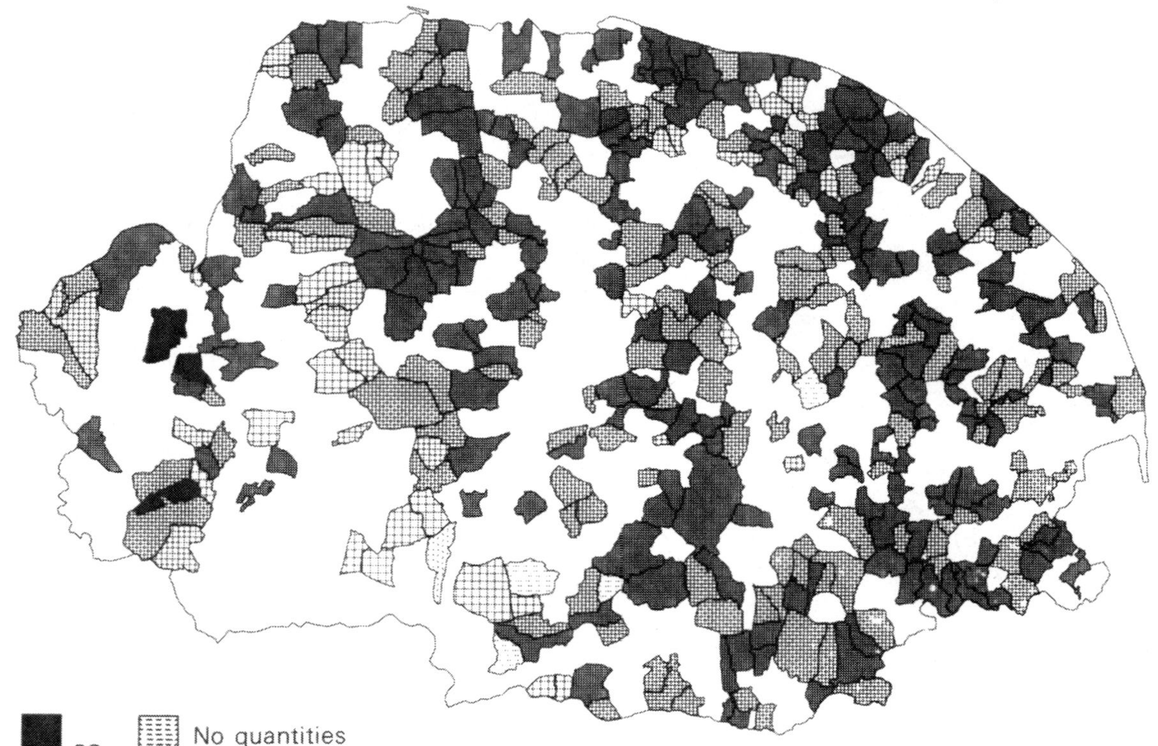

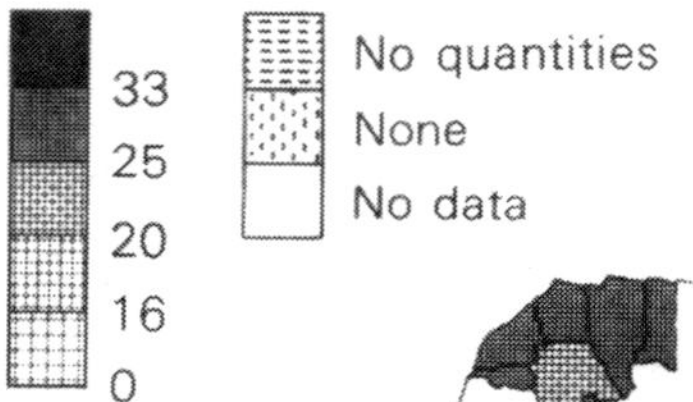

77
Barley as a percentage of arable

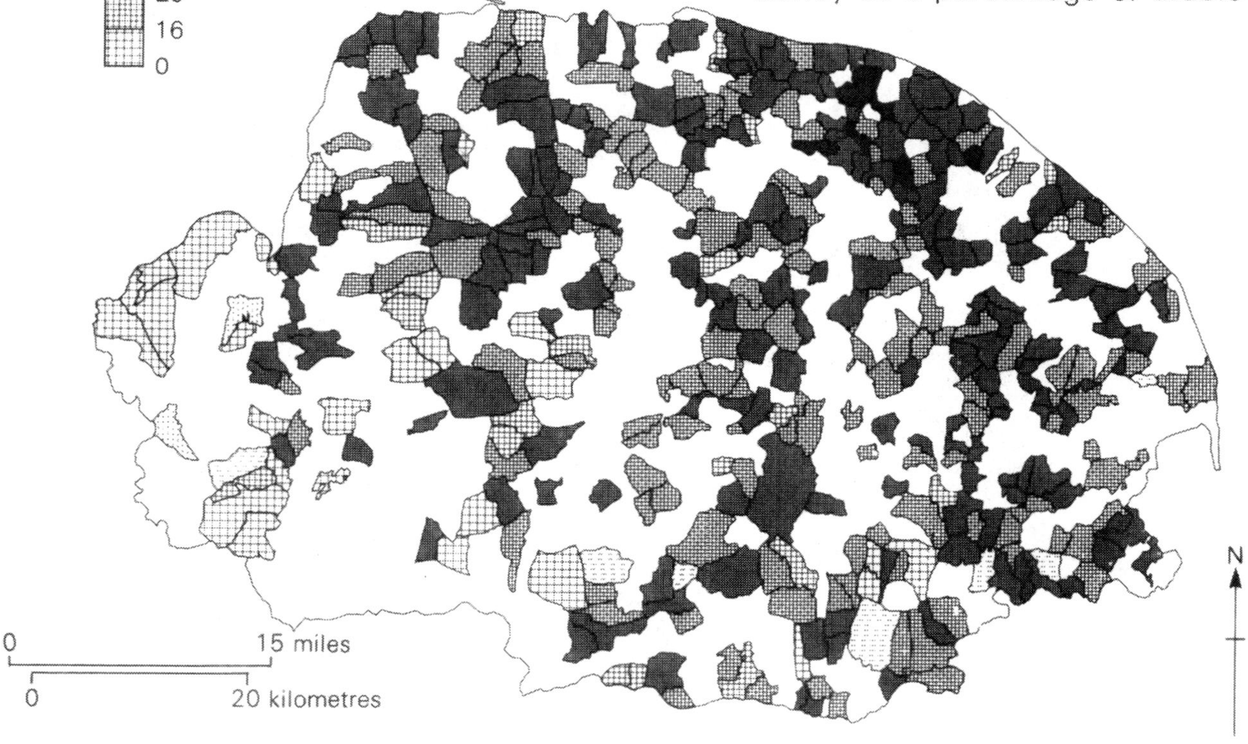

Norfolk

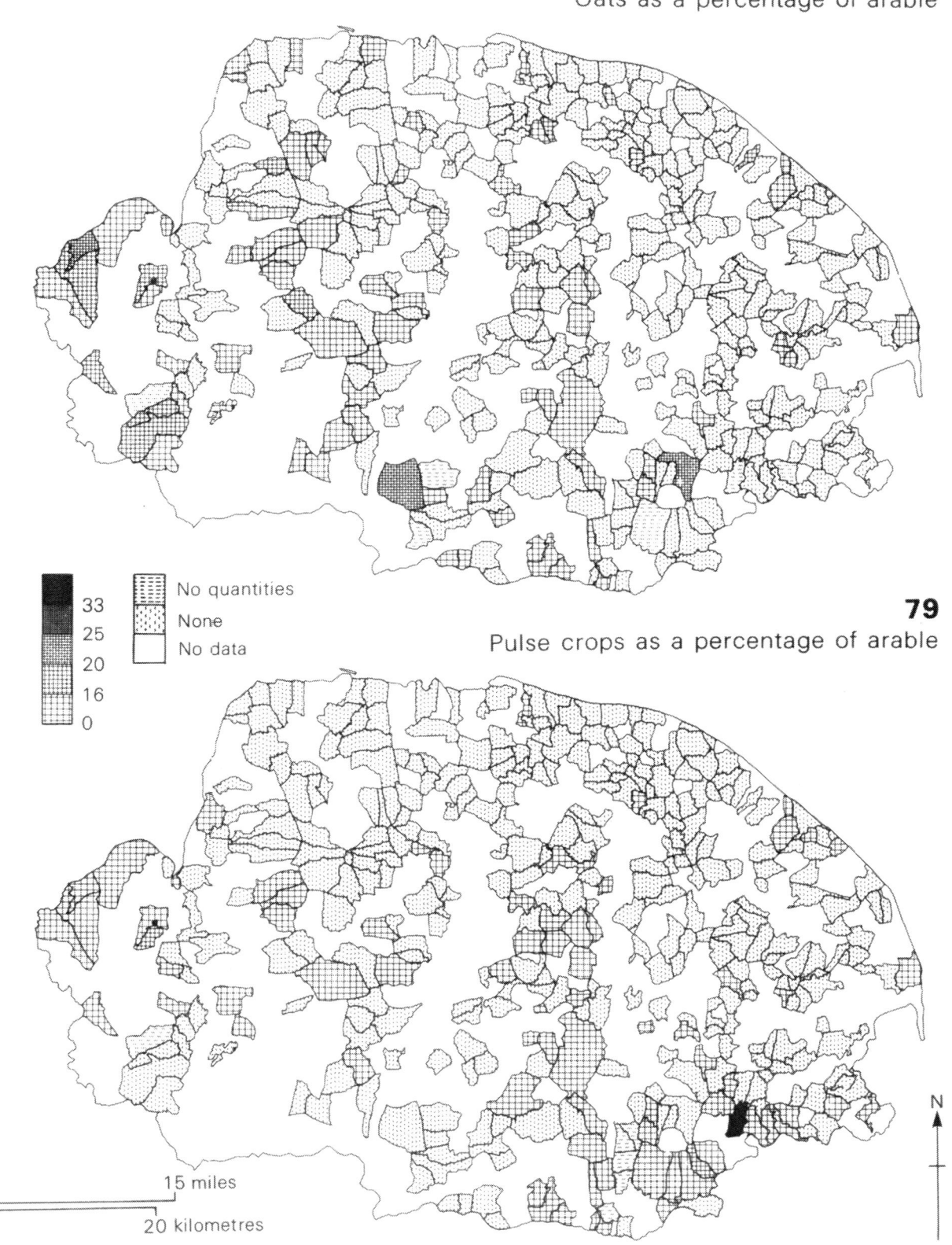

78 Oats as a percentage of arable

79 Pulse crops as a percentage of arable

80
Turnips as a percentage of arable

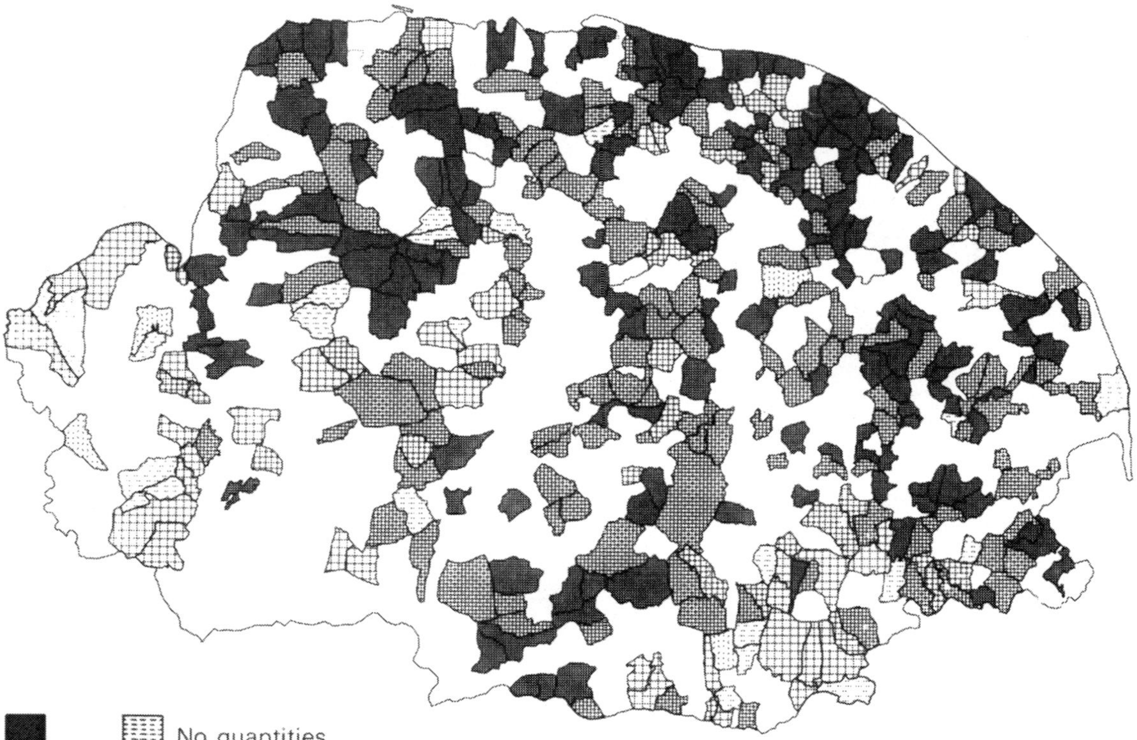

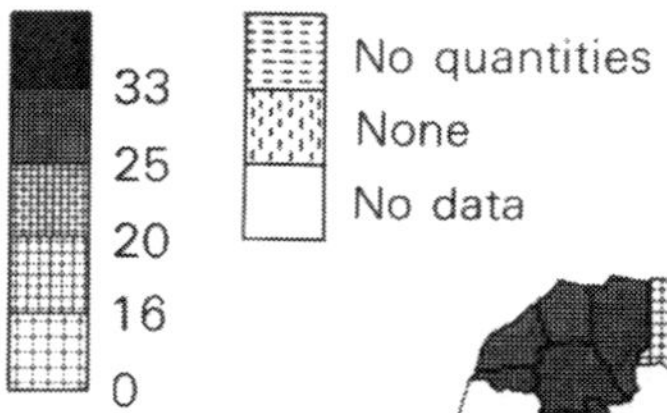

81
Clover and seeds as a percentage of arable

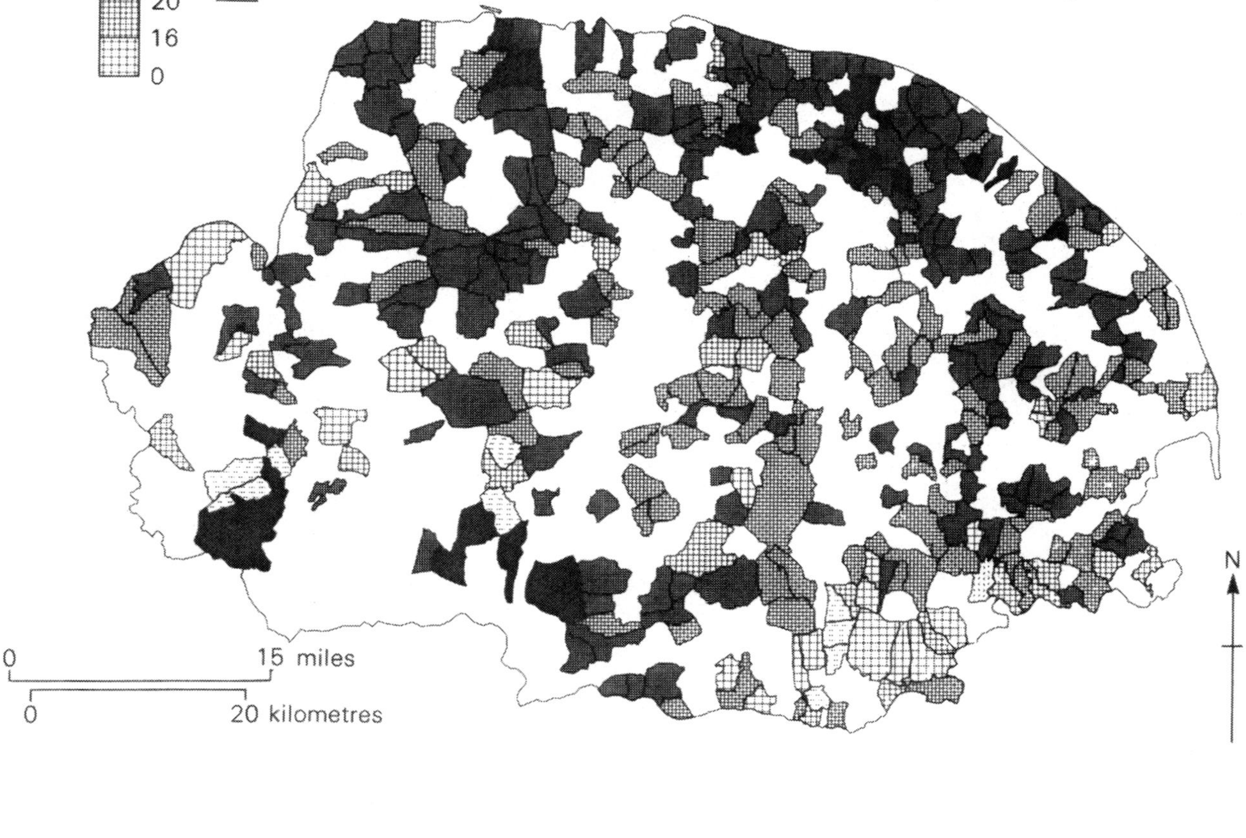

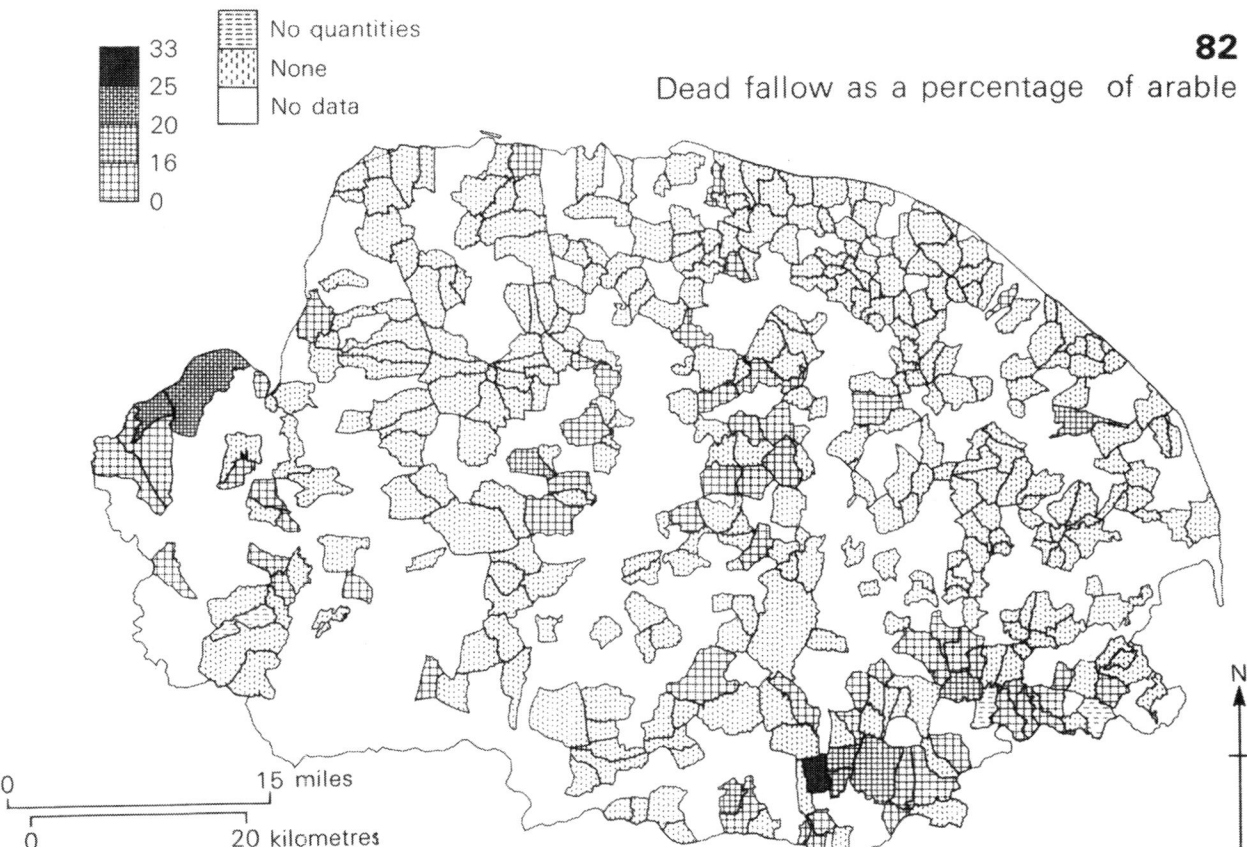

82 Dead fallow as a percentage of arable

80 Eastern counties

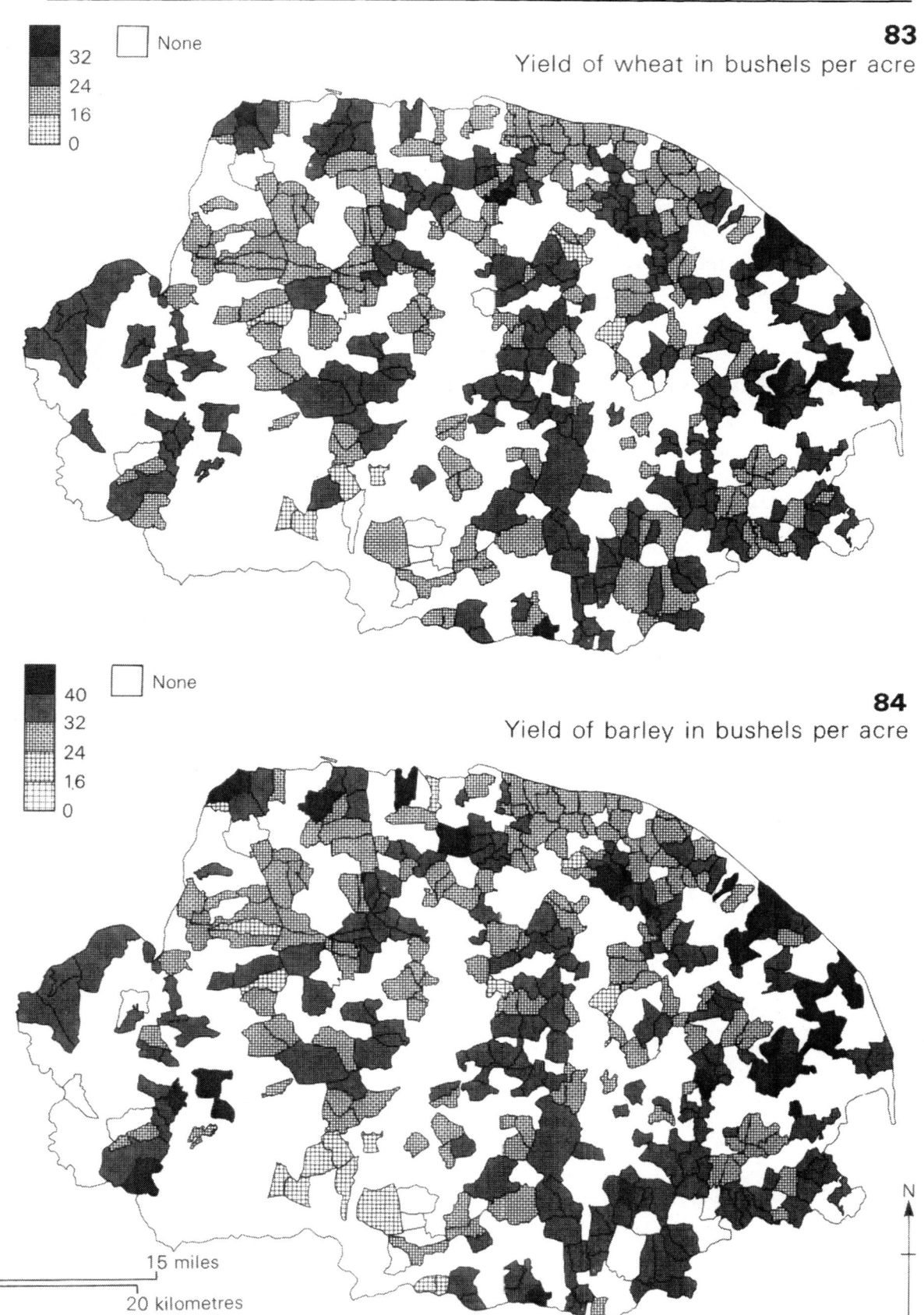

83
Yield of wheat in bushels per acre

84
Yield of barley in bushels per acre

Norfolk   81

85
Yield of oats in bushels per acre

86
Yield of pulse crops in bushels per acre

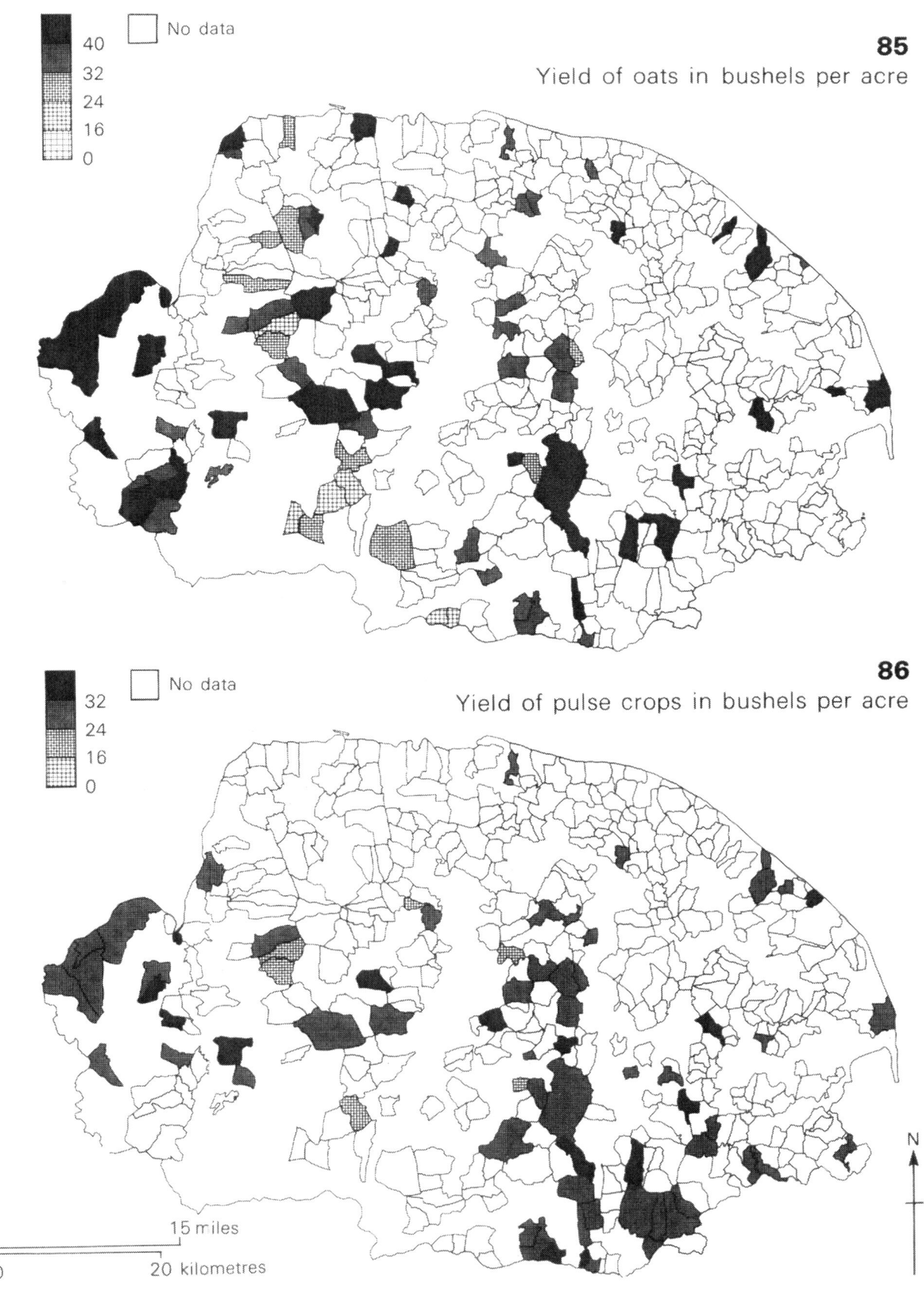

82 Eastern counties

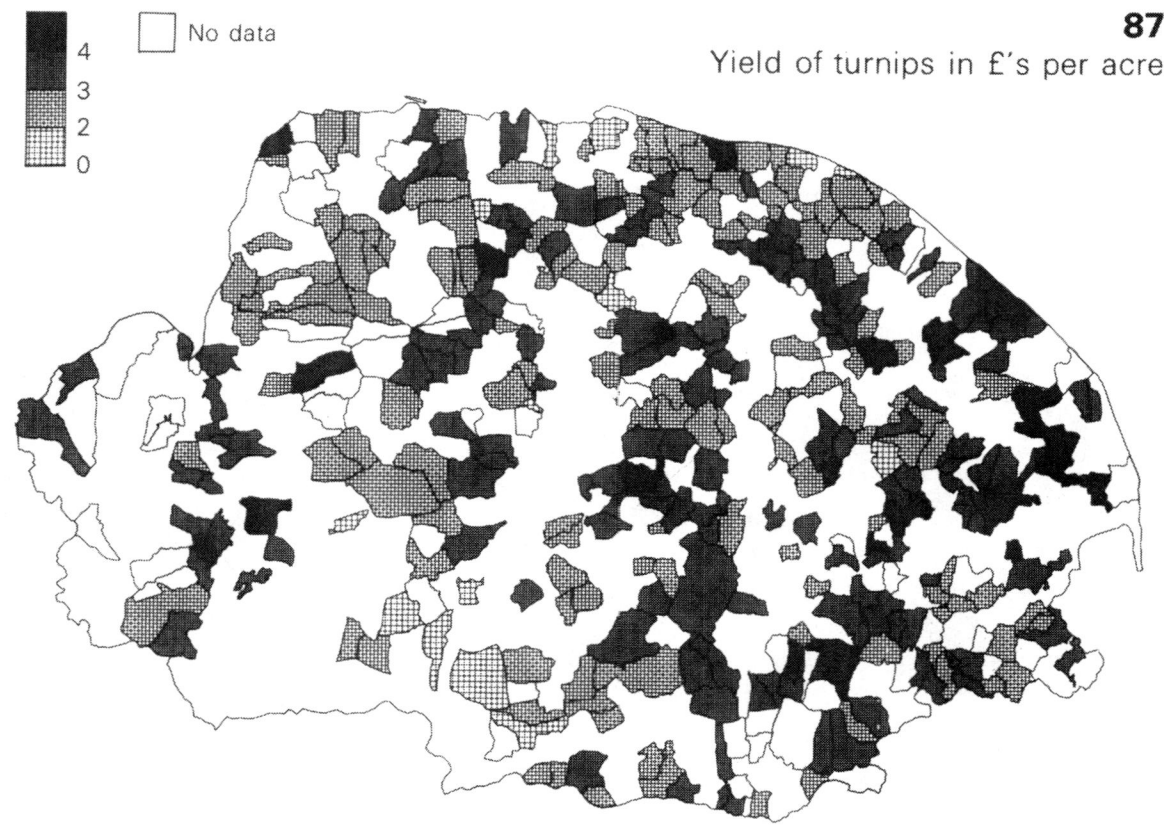

87 Yield of turnips in £'s per acre

88 Yield of clover and seeds in cwts per acre

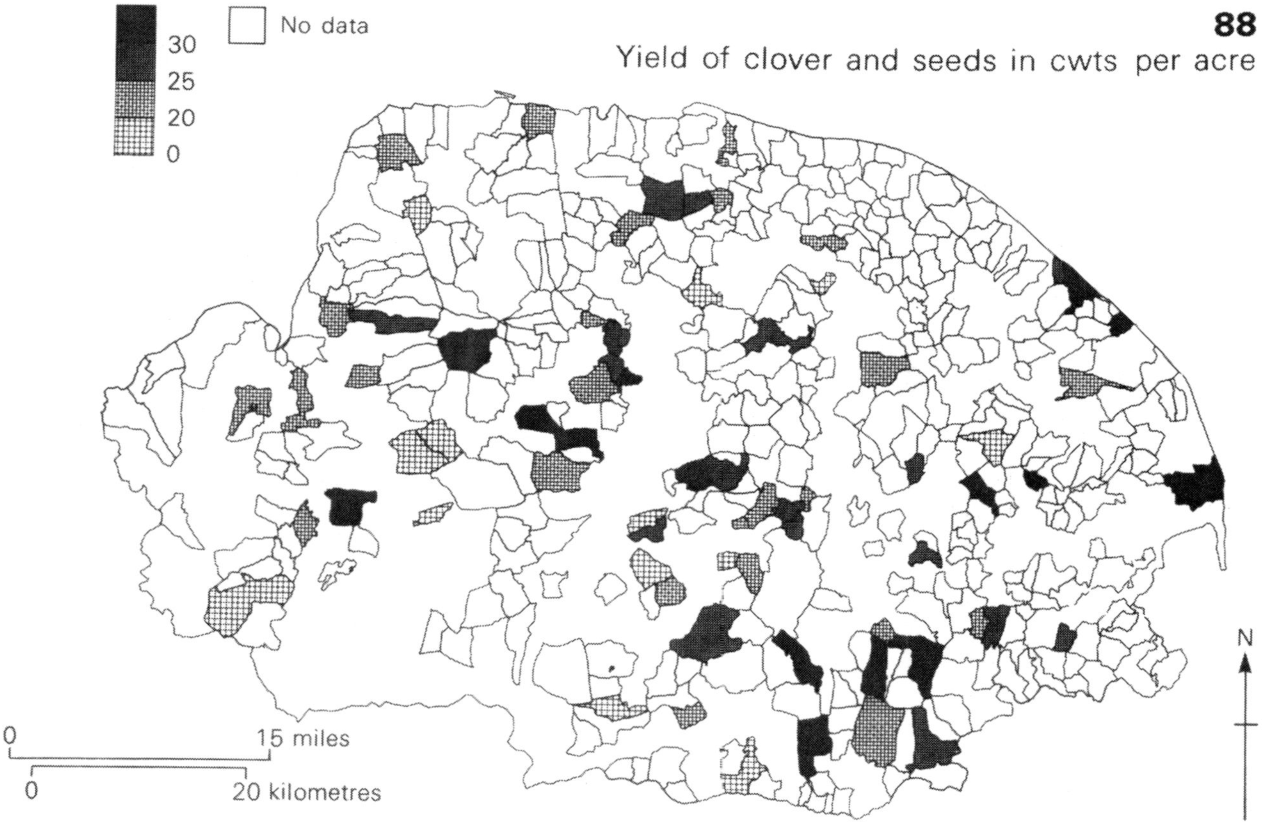

Norfolk

89
Yield of meadow in cwts per acre

90
Yield of pasture in shillings per acre

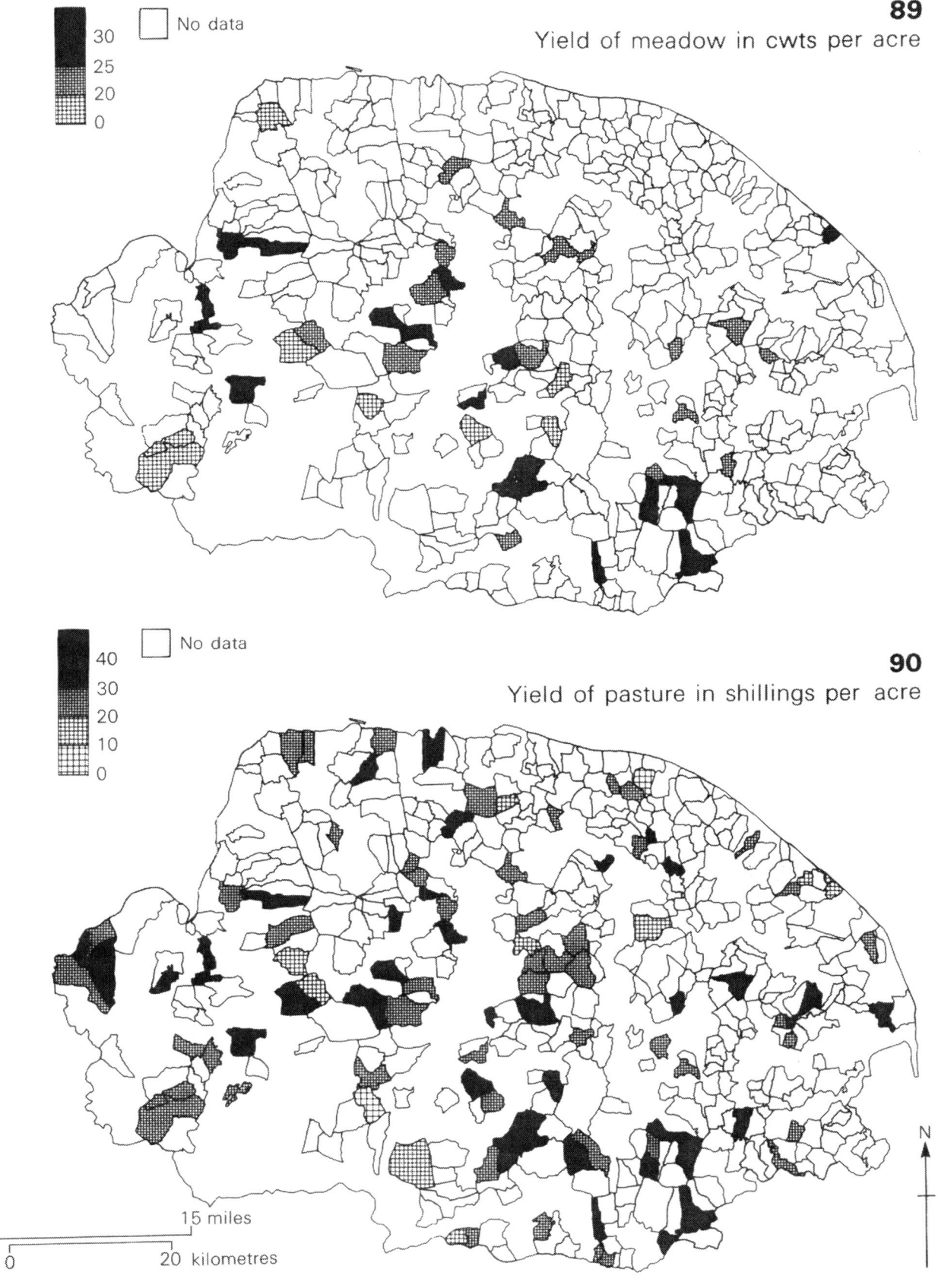

Lincolnshire

757 tithe districts
187 reports on tithe agreements

In his critical review of evidence for an agricultural revolution in south Lincolnshire, David Grigg (1966) draws extensively on land use data in tithe apportionments.

Lincolnshire's 757 tithe districts containing in total some 1.8 million acres represent the largest area retained as a single administrative unit by the Tithe Commission. By 1836, the tithes of more than a third of Lincolnshire districts had already been extinguished when open fields, fens and heaths were enclosed under the terms of enclosure acts. In those parishes where enclosure was in progress or had been effected during the years of average, effects on the quantity of titheable produce are closely analysed in tithe files. Thus these are a source of detailed accounts of enclosure of meadows and 'ings', as at Saltfleetby St Peter; heath, as at Doddington; and of open field arable, as at Alford where, in 1838, 'a large proportion is open land now in the course of inclosure by which it will be vastly improved – it has hitherto been farmed on the system of two crops and a fallow'. Enclosure acts often left small amounts of tithe payable on items such as mills and on old established closes. The Tithe Commission usually had to invoke the compulsory clauses of the 1836 Act to clear up these outstanding tithe liabilities and Lincolnshire was no exception in this respect. Here compulsory commutations outnumber voluntary agreements by more than 2.5 to 1. The 25 per cent of districts where agreements were reached are not evenly spread over the county, being particularly sparse in a large tract of south-east Lincolnshire, including much of Kesteven (Map 91). A good number of Wolds parishes have land use and crop data, and for eastern Holland coverage is fairly complete.

Fifteen assistant commissioners and local tithe agents worked on Lincolnshire tithe agreements but more than 85 per cent were investigated by just four men. Some reports by Charles Howard which pre-date the use of printed pro-formas do not have detailed breakdowns of crop acreages; some of the later reports listed in Table 10 under the name of Thomas Smith Woolley are undoubtedly the work of his son, Thomas Smith Woolley Junior – at Reepham there is confirmation that both father and son worked for the Tithe Commission in Lincolnshire. John Pickering encountered some difficulties in obtaining what he considered to be accurate accounts of crops. At Sutton, for example, 'some evidence taken by Mr Woolley in the neighbouring parish of St James has induced me to rather lower my estimate of the growth of wheat and to raise that of oats. In parts of the parish a considerable extent of potatoes is grown but an exact proportion cannot be safely fixed.'

On the other hand, for a few parishes some exceptionally detailed crop records are extant. The file for North Ormsby, for example, contains a ten chain to an inch map indicating crops growing in each field in 1840; for Aisthorpe and Dunholme the produce of each crop in every field is listed in valuations made by John Pickering and Richard Burton Phillipson respectively.

Table 11 indicates that arable and pasture were just about balanced in acreage terms in Lincolnshire c. 1840, though within the county, parish scale maps indicate a considerable range of proportions between fen, Wold, heavy soil and light soil areas (Maps 93–4). A topic of frequent note in this county's files relates to the conversion of pasture to arable, both in the recent past and as a possible future consequence of achieving a fair commutation of tithes. Of the former situation, Thomas Smith Woolley remarked at Northorpe in 1839 that 'the produce of corn has been little less than doubled since 1829. A large proportion of the second rate grassland having been converted into tillage and made very productive.' At Cadney, south-east of Brigg, John Mee Mathew sets out the land use in 1810, 1828, 1835 and 1844, during which time 2,012 acres of grassland were converted to arable. As to the future, at Skidbrooke, Charles Howard thought that arable 'will probably be naturally increased now that the drawback of one tenth of the produce is removed'. There was very little woodland in Lincolnshire at this date (Table 11 and Map 95), though recently established plantations elicited some comment as at Kirmond le Mire north-east of Market Rasen where Thomas Smith Woolley found that 'the woodland consists entirely of plantations of recent part, ash and other poles, cut periodically but principally firs and other trees yielding no tithe'. Common land is not much discussed in Lincolnshire tithe files.

Comments on the nature of rotations and the quality of farming in the county are, by contrast, very numerous. Dead fallowing was reportedly still quite common at this date (see Map 103); where the old three-course flourished, bare fallows were the norm. At one of these places, the parish of Great Steeping, 'the system of farming on the old inclosed land was two crops and a fallow – on the open land the course was 1st year fallow, 2nd year wheat, 3rd *land laid waste or thistles* as it is usually very appropriately called and 4th beans, it will be gathered from this that the style of farming was by no means first rate'. Fenland three-course shifts were quite different with rape, coleseed, turnips or potatoes in place of the dead fallow and then wheat or oats. Coleseed and rape were considered well suited to alluvial and peaty soils; at Tydd St Mary there was 'an alluvial soil excellently adapted for wheat, beans and oats – though generally speaking too tenacious for turnips grows good crops of cole or rape for sheep pasture in lieu of them'. Four- or five-course rotations were usual on lighter soils with the four-course normally a standard Norfolk shift and the five-course with an extra year of seeds. On the very poorest, lightest soils, some rye was grown instead of wheat – 152 acres at Bucknall, for example. At the other extreme, prodigious corn yields were obtained in some fen parishes – 32 bushels of wheat and 48 of oats at Saltfleetby, for instance.

Though high farming is noticed at twenty-three places (see Subject Index), the overall impression of Lincolnshire farming that comes across from tithe files is not an entirely favourable one. 'Overploughing' and the need of enclosure and drainage are topics of frequent comment (see Subject Index). By contrast, assistant commissioners did encounter some instances of exceptionally high farming, particularly on light soils near Lincoln. One such place, West Firsby, presented to John Penny 'one of the finest specimens of artificial farming that I have seen in any part of England, the natural soil is of a very poor description'. Marling of light soils and chalking of heavy lands are both matters of comment, though local agents were not always convinced of the sense. At Linwood, John Pickering found that 'the heathland is very irregularly cultivated. The application of clay to these weak sands is practised at an expense which seems almost unlikely to be compensated.' At Little Cawthorpe, south-east of Louth, Charles Howard ascribed the 'principal means of effecting these improvements' to 'the "chalking" of the strong soil, which is done at a considerable expense by carting and spreading over the land about 100 tons of chalk per acre'. The use of bone dust and artificial fertilisers is recorded as well. Files such as those for Broxholme, Wainfleet St Mary, Scotton and others, itemised in the Subject Index, provide information on other improvements, notably on processes of fen drainage and warping.

Local tithe agents identified two major categories of grassland in Lincolnshire. Upland pastures they considered sound enough for stock but not sufficiently good for fattening unless used in conjunction with turnips. At Digby where the 'grassland of the parish is of an average quality, and is generally employed in the breeding and rearing of store cattle the system like that of a considerable part of the intermediate grassland of Lincolnshire, being to rear cattle 3 years old, after which they are generally sold to the richer districts'. Receiving parishes were such as Saltfleetby where 'cattle and sheep are purchased from the wolds and districts of inferior grass to be fattened in the parish'.

Table 10 *Reports on agreements for commutation of tithes in Lincolnshire*

Assistant commissioner/ local tithe agent	1837	1838	1839	1840	1841	1842	1843	1844	1845	1846	Totals
John Pickering		11	49	1	2						63
Thomas Smith Woolley	3	34	9	2	7	3					58
Charles Howard	9	18									27
Richard Burton Phillipson				4	1	2	2	4	1		14
John Job Rawlinson			3	2							5
Edward Greathed	1	3									4
John Penny				4							4
George Louis						3					3
Thomas Hoskins	2										2
Henry Pilkington							2				2
James Drage Merest	1										1
Charles Pym	1										1
John S. Donaldson Selby				1							1
Thomas Sudworth	1										1
Joseph Townsend										1	1
Totals	18	66	61	14	10	8	4	4	1	1	187

Table 11 *Land use, crops and yields in Lincolnshire c. 1836*

A	Land use	Percentage of total land area enumerated in reports on tithe agreements	Estimated acreage in whole county
	Arable	48.7	865,678
	Grass	45.8	814,514
	Wood	2.5	44,676
	Common	1.9	34,334

B	Crop	Mean percentage of arable	Mean yield per acre	Estimated acreage in whole county
	Wheat	24.9	22.9 bushels	215,616
	Barley	10.3	31.1 bushels	88,751
	Oats	13.8	38.0 bushels	119,587
	Pulses	5.6	22.7 bushels	48,021
	Turnips	12.2	£2.47	105,242
	Seeds	24.2	22.5 cwts	209,776
	Fallows	7.7	—	66,243

Eastern counties

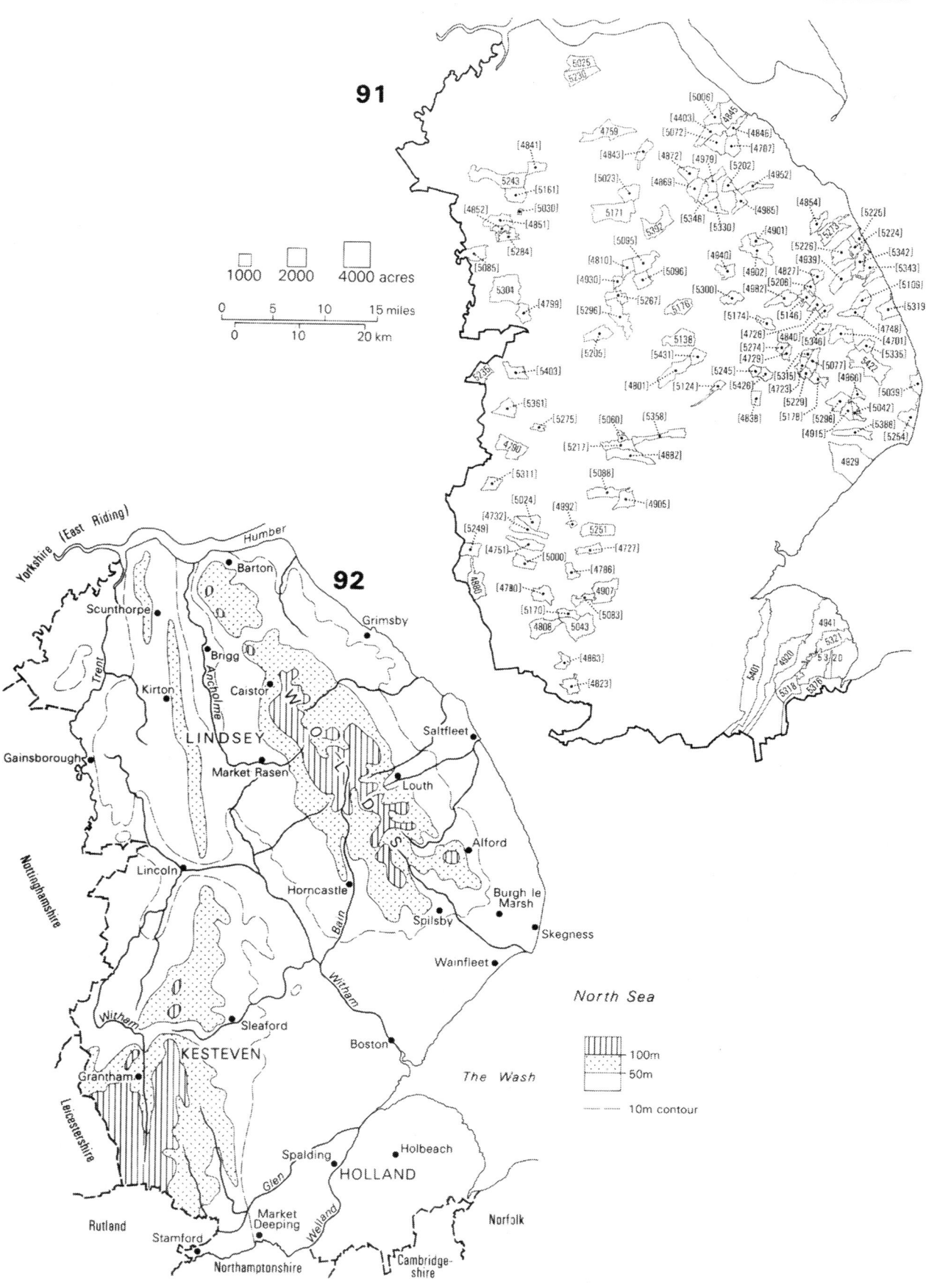

93 Arable as a percentage of tithe district area

94 Pasture as a percentage of tithe district area

95 Woodland as a percentage of tithe district area

96 Common as a percentage of tithe district area

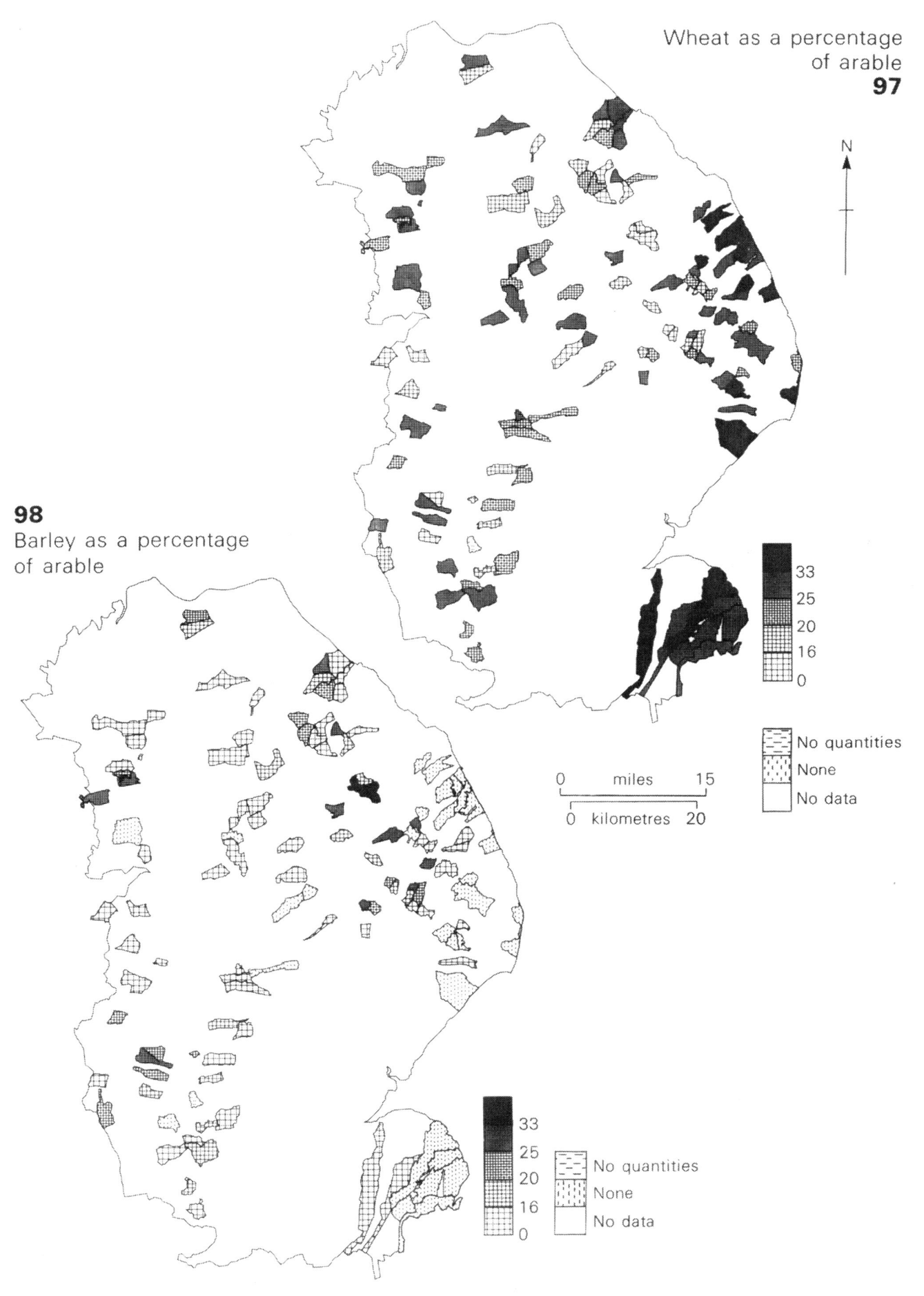

97 Wheat as a percentage of arable

98 Barley as a percentage of arable

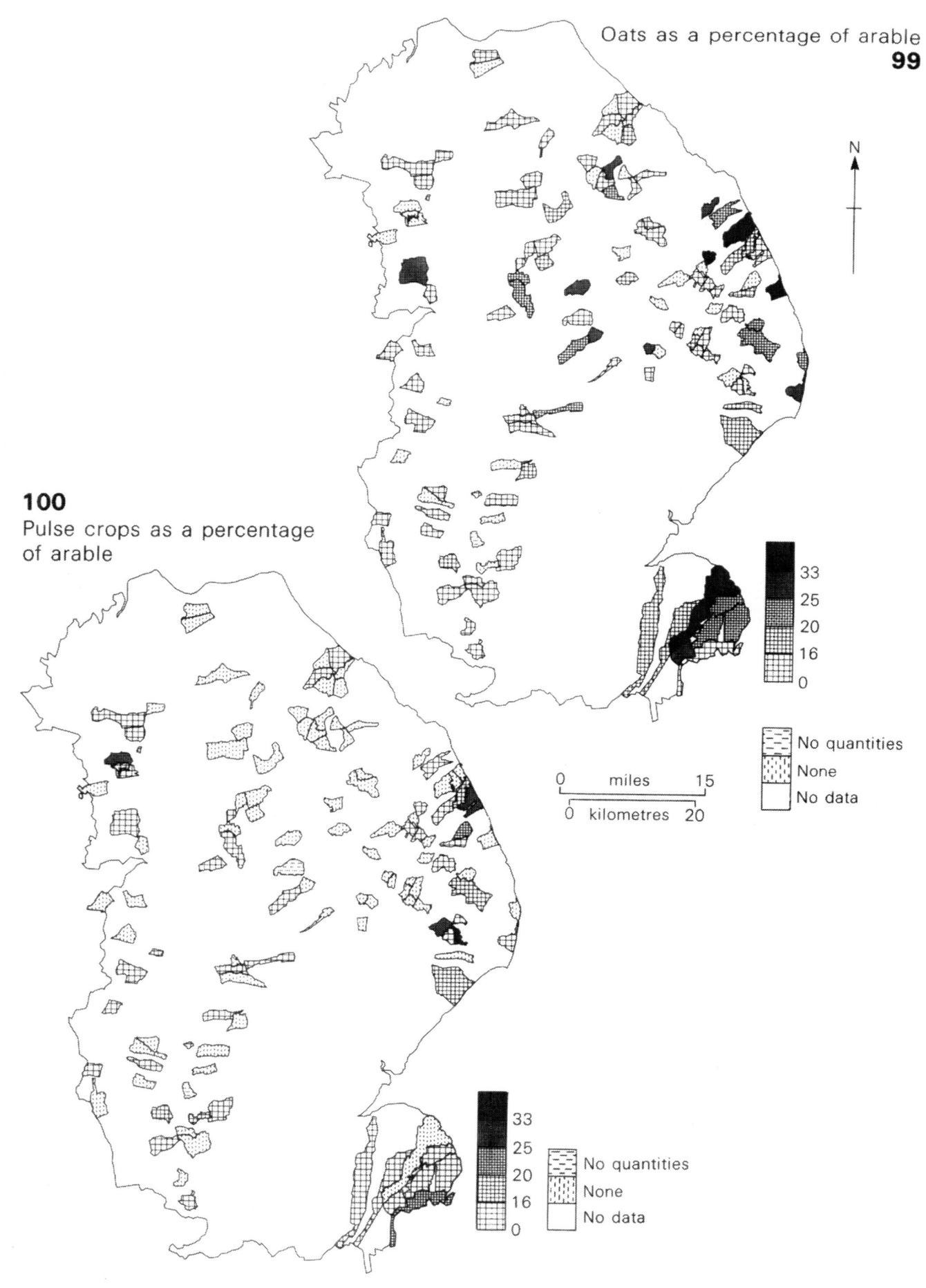

99 Oats as a percentage of arable

100 Pulse crops as a percentage of arable

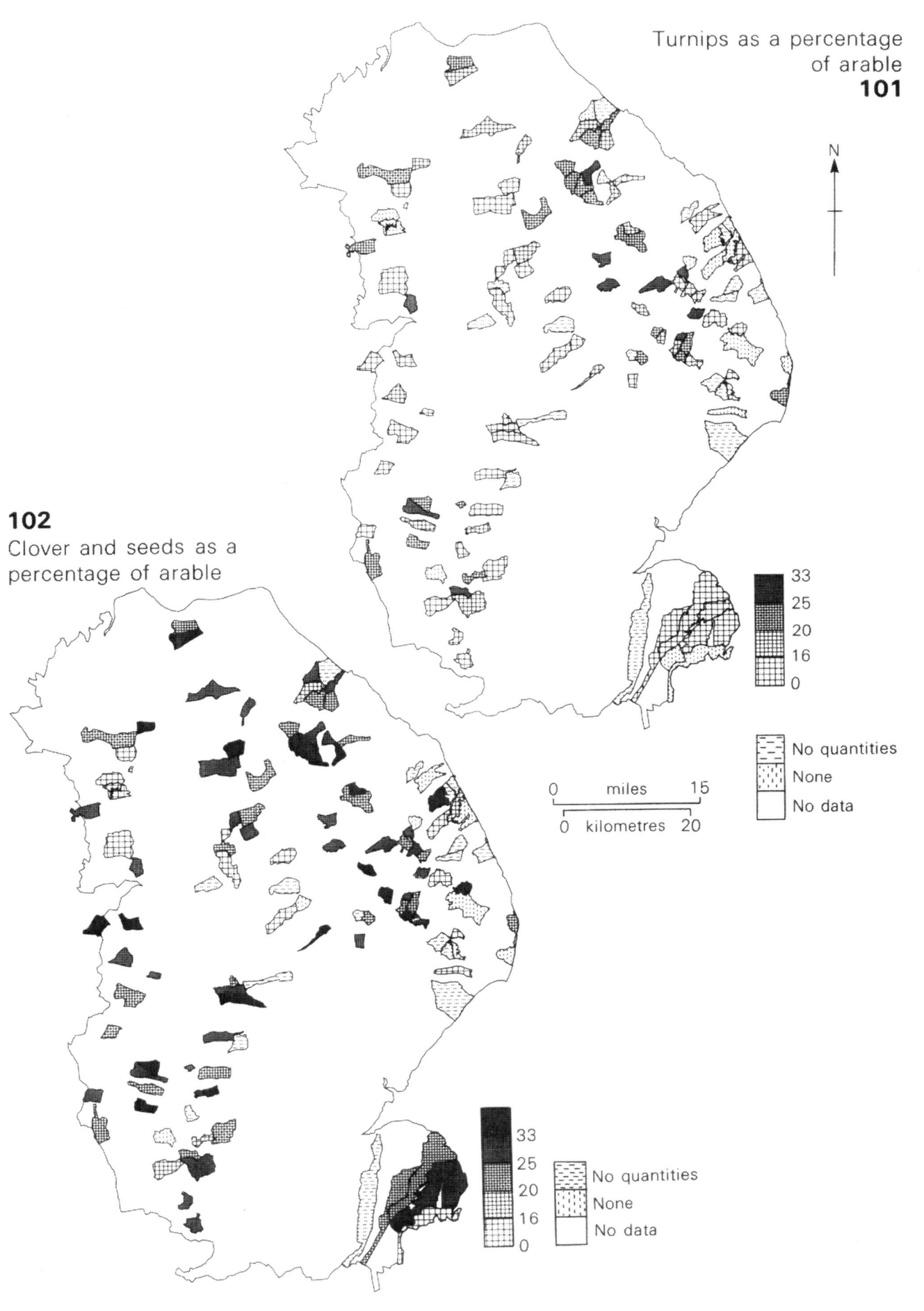

Eastern counties

Dead fallow as a percentage of arable
103

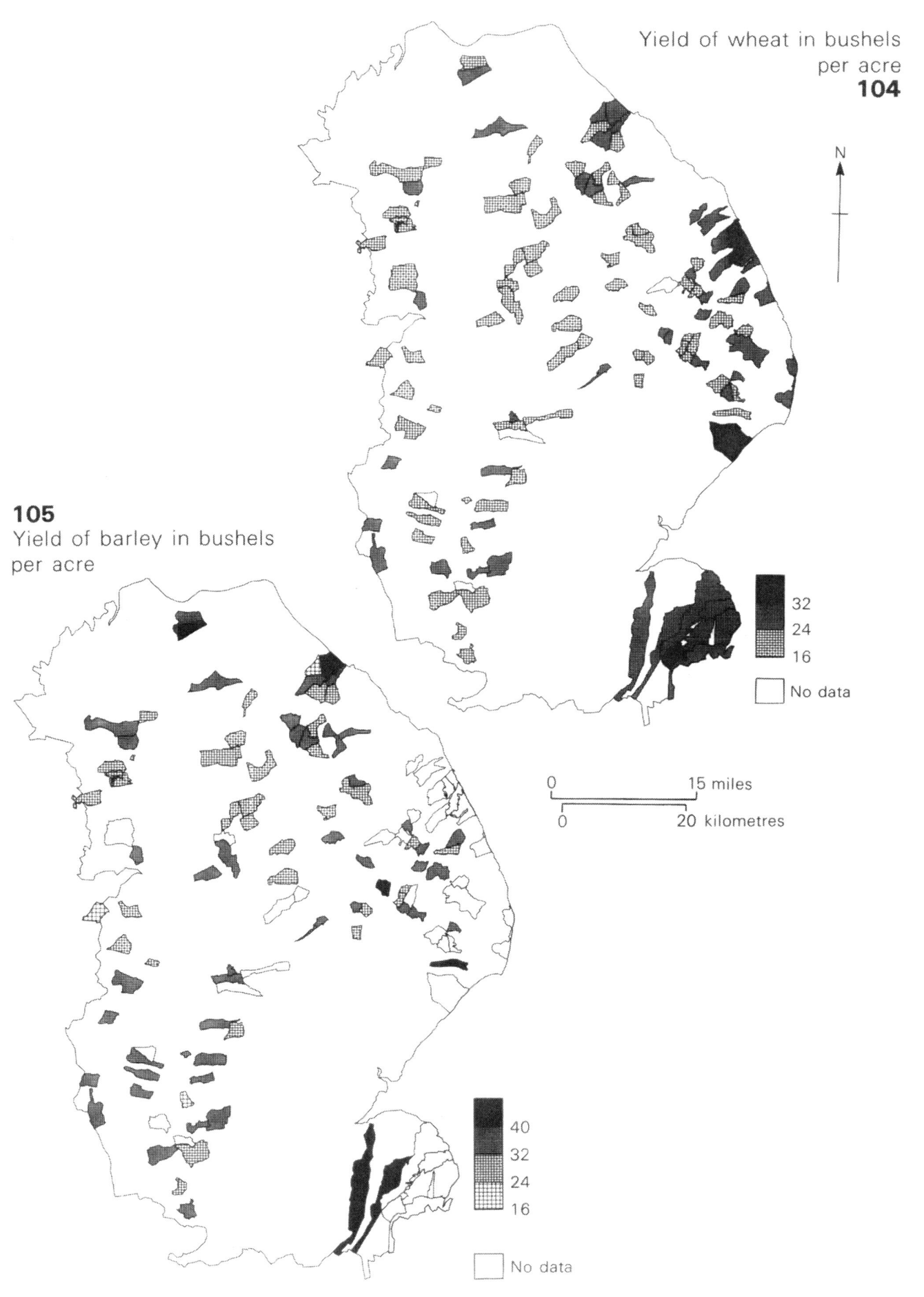

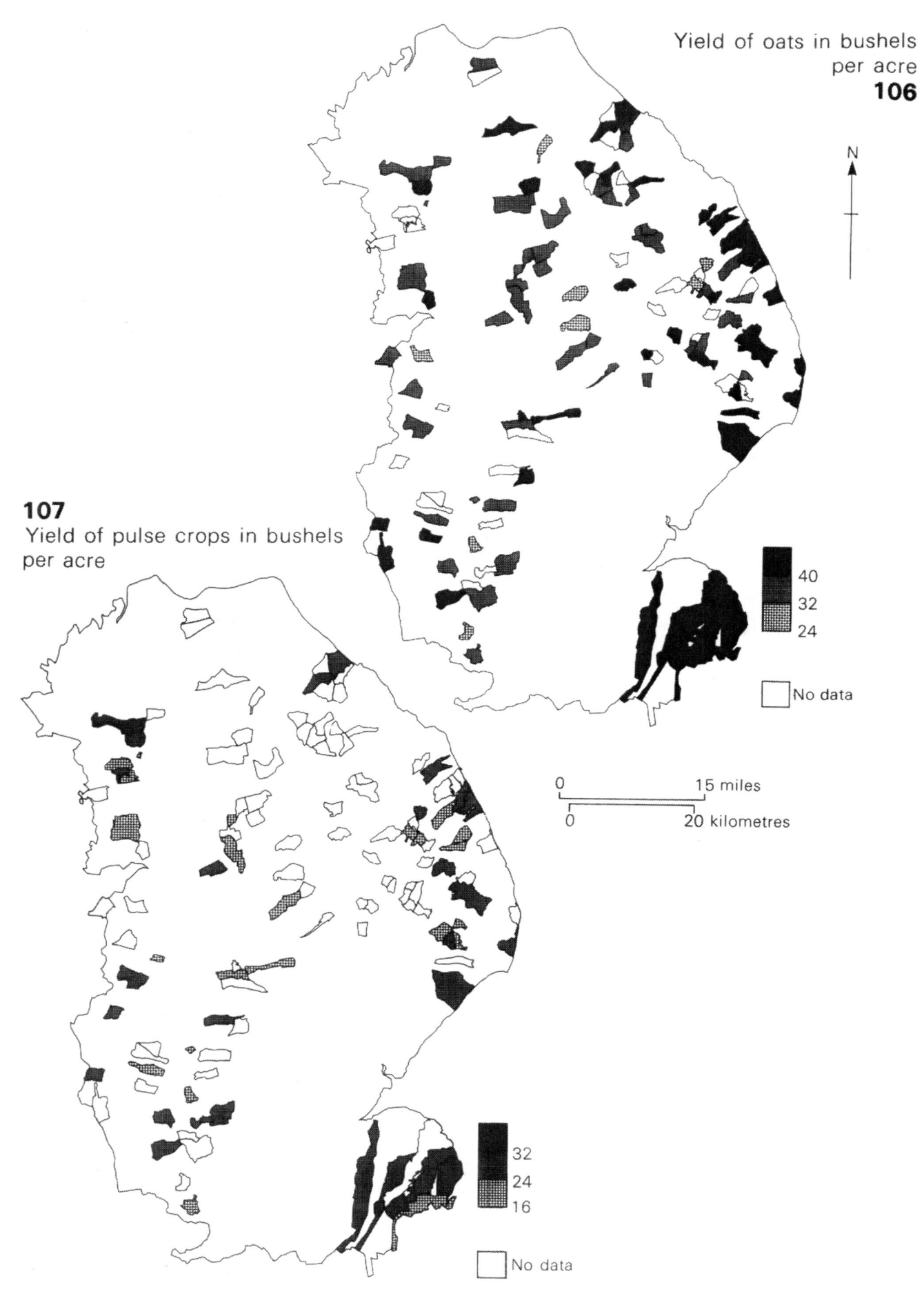

106 Yield of oats in bushels per acre

107 Yield of pulse crops in bushels per acre

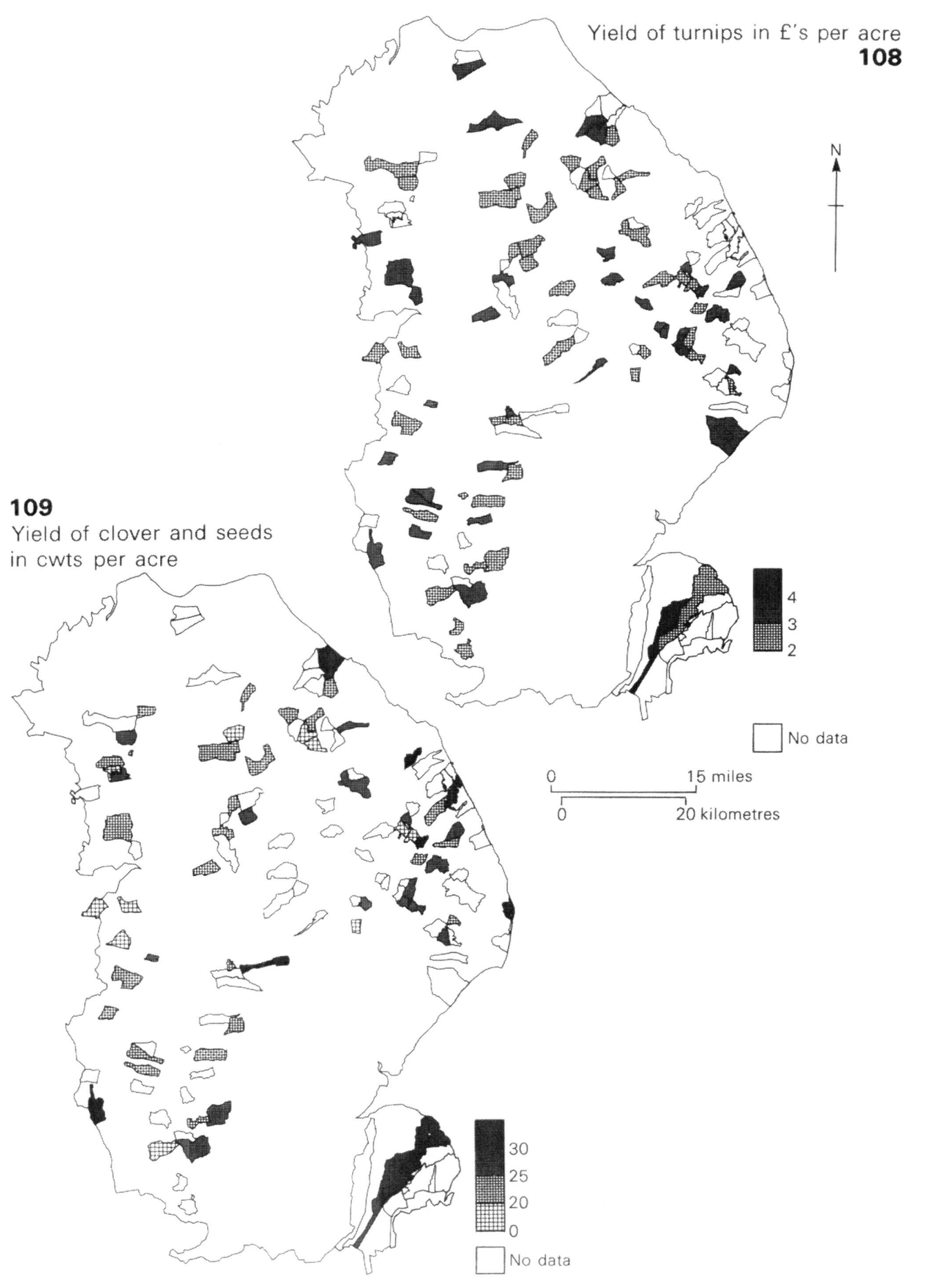

108 Yield of turnips in £'s per acre

109 Yield of clover and seeds in cwts per acre

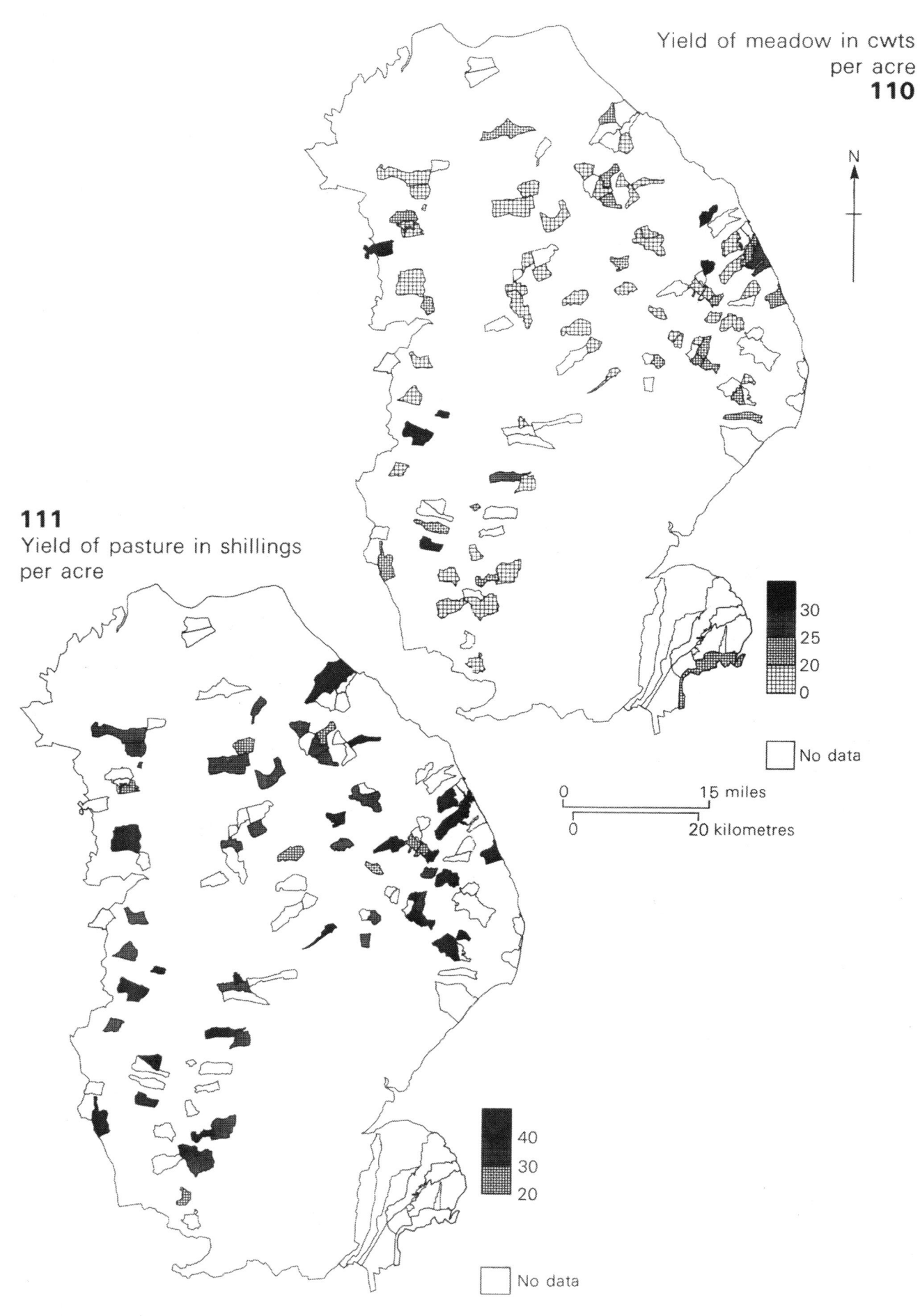

Huntingdonshire

112 tithe districts
31 reports on tithe agreements

Exoneration at the time of parliamentary enclosure explains the existence of forty-eight tithe free parishes in Huntingdonshire *c*. 1840. Moreover, in very many of the remainder, only a small proportion of land was still titheable by this date. In only seventeen of the thirty-one parishes where tithe was commuted by agreement did land still titheable exceed 90 per cent of parish area.

Parish descriptions in reports on tithe agreements are not very illuminating in this county. Neither John West nor Joseph Townsend, who together compiled 45 per cent of these (Table 12), wrote more than a few sentences each. Thomas Smith Woolley's reports are the most comprehensive and contain detailed discussion of different soils and related management practices. His comments, albeit at only a small sample of places, suggest that farming on clay soils was especially backward and still followed a two-crop and bare fallow system. Ridge-and-furrow on these soils is remarked upon; at Hilton, near St Ives 'the land lies in high backs with balks. Often there is a small open drain in the centre of the balk. It can be utilised in underdrainage and materially lessens the expense. The best farmers are using tiles which can be purchased 4 miles distant.' By contrast, in light soil parishes, 'the system of digging clay where the fens afford it and laying a thick coating on the surface which has been introduced of later years has done much for the improvement of the lighter fen land and must have had considerable effect in increasing their productive qualities'.

Table 12 *Reports on agreements for commutation of tithes in Huntingdonshire*

Assistant commissioner/ local tithe agent	1837	1838	1839	1840	1841	1842	Totals
John West		5	2	2			9
Thomas Smith Woolley	3		2		1	1	7
Joseph Townsend	1	4					5
John Pickering		2	1				3
Henry Bertram Gunning			2				2
William Heard					1	1	2
? Mears		2					2
F. Browne Browne			1				1
Totals	4	13	8	2	2	2	31

Table 13 *Land use, crops and yields in Huntingdonshire c. 1836*

A	Land use	Percentage of total land area enumerated in reports on tithe agreements	Estimated acreage in whole county
	Arable	49.8	114,986
	Grass	42.3	97,614
	Wood	2.9	6,618

B	Crop	Mean percentage of arable	Mean yield per acre	Estimated acreage in whole county
	Wheat	23.7	22.0 bushels	27,275
	Barley	16.6	31.4 bushels	19,110
	Oats	6.0	35.1 bushels	6,868
	Pulses	11.3	22.8 bushels	12,978
	Turnips	2.7	£2.60	3,149
	Seeds	15.8	22.5 cwts	18,199
	Fallows	21.1	—	24,281

SOUTHERN COUNTIES

Sussex   Hampshire
Kent   Surrey
Hertfordshire Middlesex*
Berkshire

The 'arable' type of printed form used for reporting on tithe agreements in these counties requires a 'description and rough estimate of the titheable produce' and asks assistant tithe commissioners and local tithe agents to 'describe the parish and the quality of the lands, the system of farming, and whether the quality of the produce has been affected by any extraordinary instances of high or low farming'.

---

*Data for Middlesex are too few to warrant constructing maps of land use and crops tithe district-by-tithe district, and the sample of tithe districts with extant data are too small to justify compiling county aggregate figures of land use and crop acreages and yields.

Sussex

323 tithe districts
188 reports on tithe agreements

H. C. K. Henderson (1936) reconstructed the pattern of arable land *c.* 1840 in the Adur basin of Sussex using evidence from tithe apportionments and maps. His study pioneered the method of plotting tithe survey data for tracts of contiguous parishes.

In Sussex, a full 84 per cent of the 188 reports on tithe agreements were the work of one man, John Farncombe, a local tithe agent whose work was confined almost entirely to Sussex (Tables 1 and 14). He is also the author of this county's Royal Agricultural Society of England *Prize Essay* which was published in volume 11 of the Society's journal in 1850. His familiarity with Sussex farming does not entirely compensate, however, for the very brief and rather stereotyped reports on tithe agreements that he wrote for the Tithe Commission. These contain at most a few sentences on soils, rotations and markets. He did, though, inquire more carefully than most local tithe agents into the accuracy of land use acreages stated in schedules of tithe agreement. Even small differences between estimated acreages accepted as a basis for agreement and those obtained when new maps were being made for apportionment elicited the comment 'inaccurate'. Differences though, were usually small. At East Grinstead, for example, he commented in 1842 that 'the schedule to the agreement is made by estimation . . . it appears to be more than the accurate admeasurement from the enclosed statement . . . the total acreage of this parish is 15,040 according to the survey made by Mr Dixon this year being 32a, 3r, 38p less than that in 1828 upon which the rent charge has been fixed'.

All but eight Sussex parishes contained some titheable land *c.* 1840 and voluntary commutation was begun early and was achieved in three-fifths of titheable districts. Traditionally one of the hearths of tithing in kind, this method of collection had virtually ceased by 1836 (six references in the Subject Index). Where it was still employed, as at Northiam in east Sussex, a lengthy series of meetings was held, out of all proportion to the monetary equivalent at dispute. Woodland in the Weald was exempt from tithe but Farncombe recorded woodland acreages in his reports, though he did not set out hay or seeds yields consistently enough for these to be mapped. Hop gardens occasioned written comment at thirty places but again acreages are not recorded consistently in valuations.

On clay soils, a four-course of wheat, oats, seeds, fallow – either bare or with some tares or beans is the rotation most frequently listed. On better, lighter loams, four-course turnip husbandry was employed whilst on the lightest, poorest soils, seeds were allowed to lie for two or three years. At Framfield, east of Uckfield, John Farncombe found 'the soil is partly of clay and partly of sandy gravel. The system of farming (generally) 4 courses as described in my rough estimate, some small portions are used in thirds, viz with wheat, oats, seeds and tares for wheat on the coldest clay.' Joseph Townsend reports that high chalk tracts of Stanmer 'are frequently allowed to lay down a second and sometimes a third year to grass seeds before they are again subjected to the plough. Sainfoin is less cultivated than might be expected, and does not enter into regular rotations.' As in Kent, criticism frequently voiced in Sussex tithe files concerns hop cultivation. At Rotherfield, Baker commented that 'there are but few instances of high farming except as regards hoplands to maintain which other cultivation is much neglected. Almost the whole of the farmyard manure is absorbed by them.'

Meadow, pasture and livestock farming did not elicit detailed comment in Sussex files. Sheep breeding is discussed in the files of thirty-three parishes, mostly those with downland pasture. At Burpham, for example, 'breeding of sheep is the general system on the Downs which are not very productive of grass'. At Ninfield, John Farncombe expanded a little to say that 'a considerable number of Sussex bred stock are raised, and a few sheep are bred for folding, but the greater proportion of sheep raised are fatted in the adjoining marshes of Pevensey'. Developing resort towns such as Brighton and Eastbourne provided ready markets for dairy products. The parish of Hove was 'advantageously situated for raising vegetable matter and milk having good grass pastures, a great quantity of cows are kept to supply milk to Brighton and its own population which is considerable. The arable land is much improved by this system it producing without much expense an increase of good manure.' Similarly at Ovingdean 'much local benefit is derived from its vicinity to Brighton in interchange of the produce of straw for manure and also in the supply of vegetable matter, green food, clover, tares etc, and milk'.

Table 14 *Reports on agreements for commutation of tithes in Sussex*

Assistant commissioner/ local tithe agent	1836	1837	1838	1839	1840	1841	1842	1843	1844	1845	Totals
John Farncombe			23	57	27	28	15	6	1	1	158
Thomas Smith Woolley	1	6		1	1	2					11
Joseph Townsend		3	5								8
Charles Osborn		2	1	1							4
Job Smalepiece		2									2
A. O. Baker			1								1
James Hodsen			1								1
John Pickering				1							1
John Smith			1								1
Charles Wilson			1								1
Totals	1	13	33	60	28	30	15	6	1	1	188

Table 15 *Land use, crops and yields in Sussex c. 1836*

A	Land use	Percentage of total land area enumerated in reports on tithe agreements	Estimated acreage in whole county
	Arable	43.8	409,633
	Grass	34.9	326,541
	Wood	15.1	140,785
	Common	2.8	26,276

B	Crop	Mean percentage of arable	Mean yield per acre	Estimated acreage in whole county
	Wheat	22.6	25.6 bushels	104,835
	Barley	6.1	34.4 bushels	24,782
	Oats	18.7	35.6 bushels	76,388
	Pulses	1.8	26.0 bushels	7,285
	Turnips	7.4	£2.60	30,381
	Seeds	24.8	—	101,396
	Fallows	13.5	—	55,456

Sussex

112

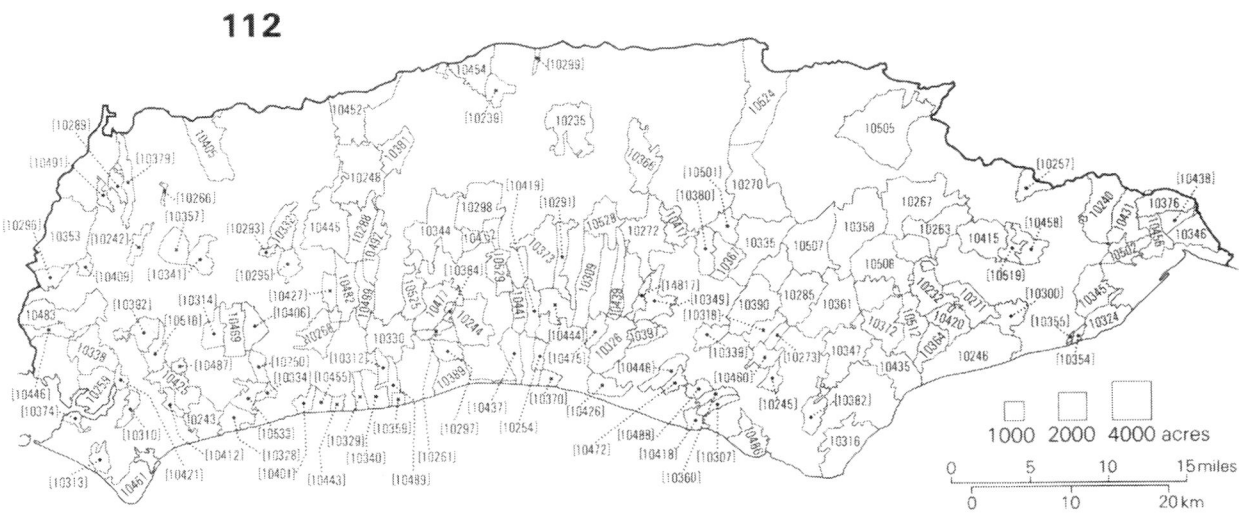

113

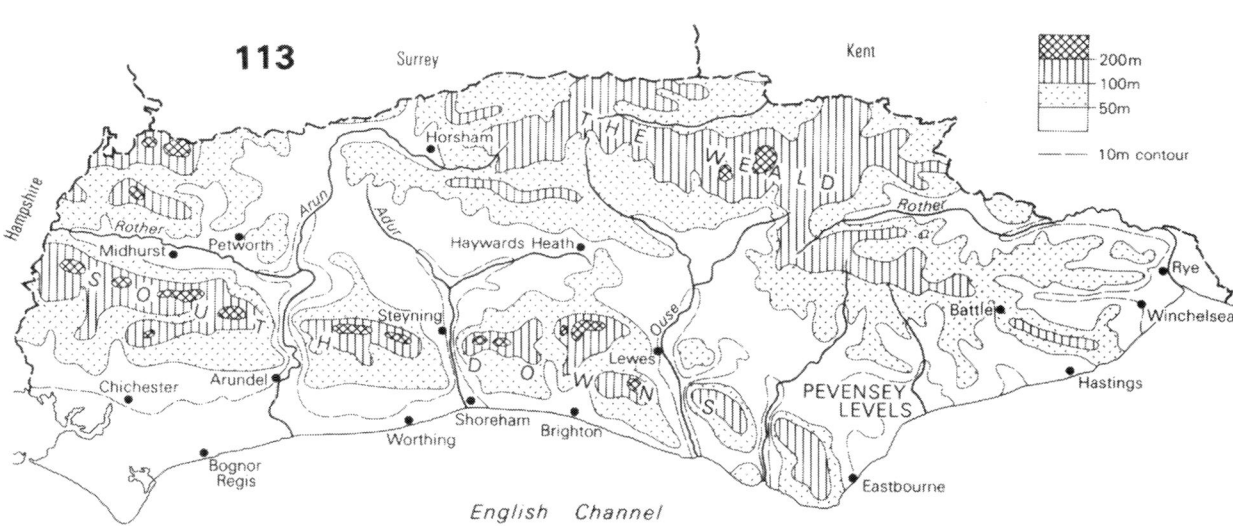

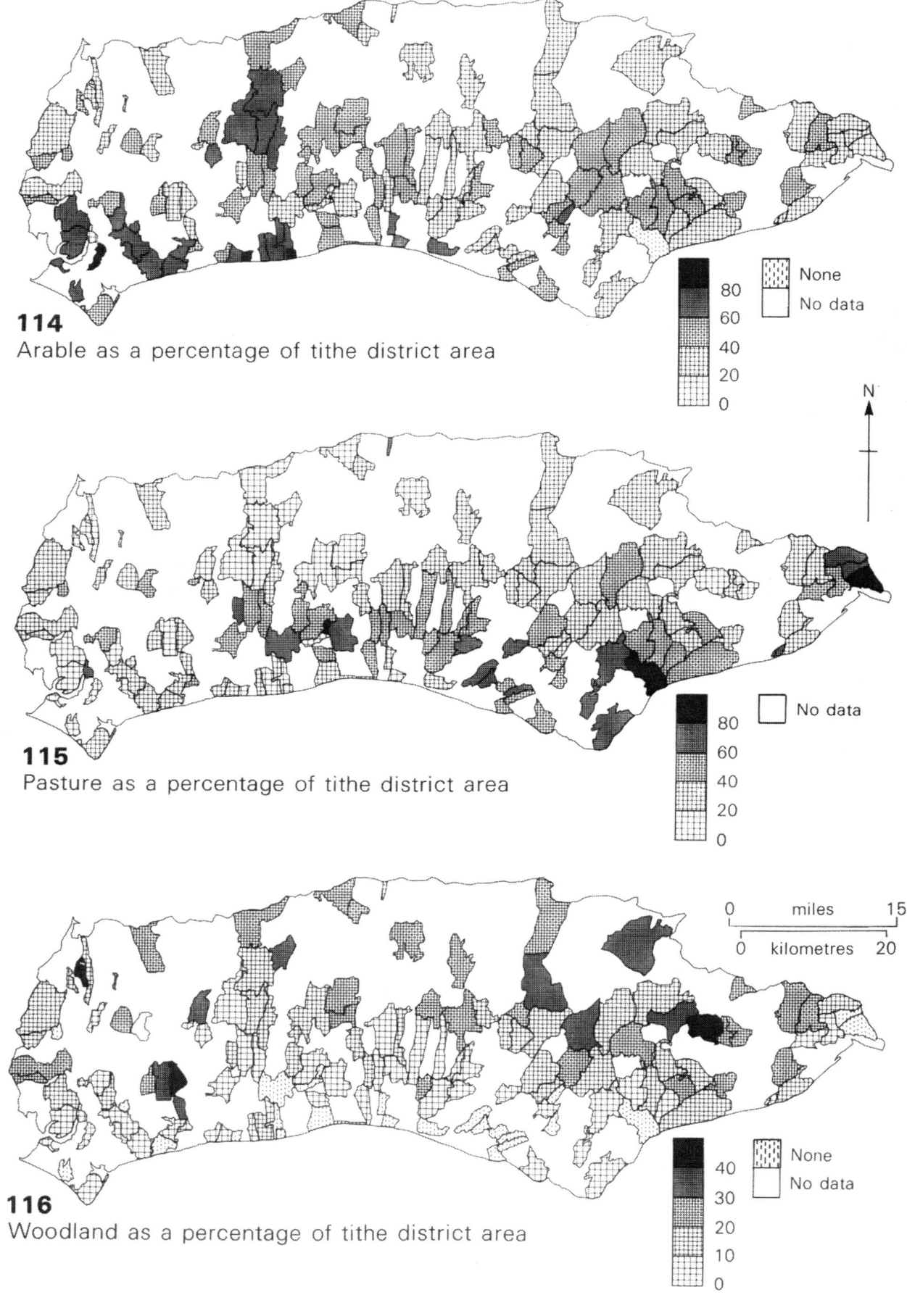

114 Arable as a percentage of tithe district area

115 Pasture as a percentage of tithe district area

116 Woodland as a percentage of tithe district area

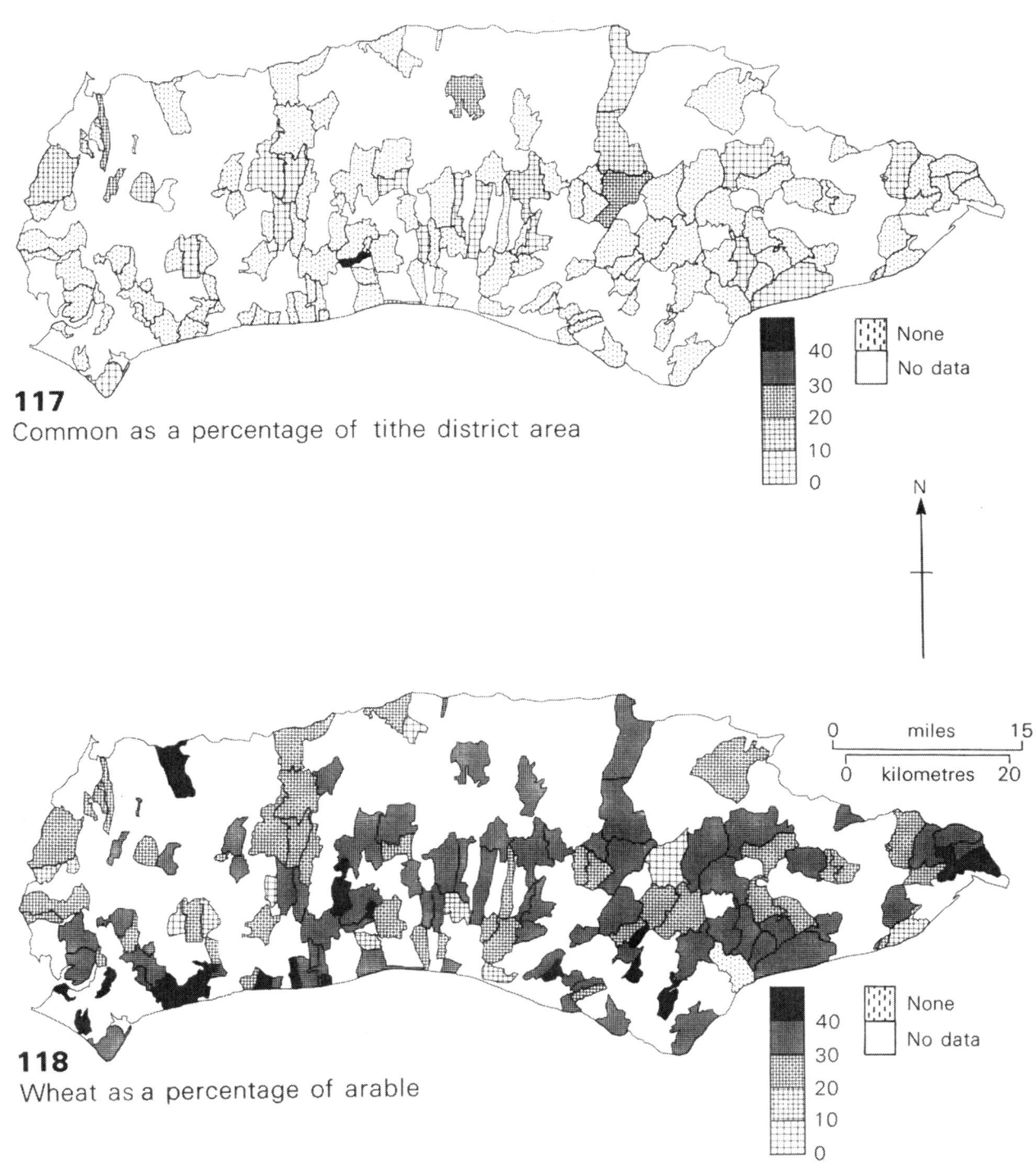

117 Common as a percentage of tithe district area

118 Wheat as a percentage of arable

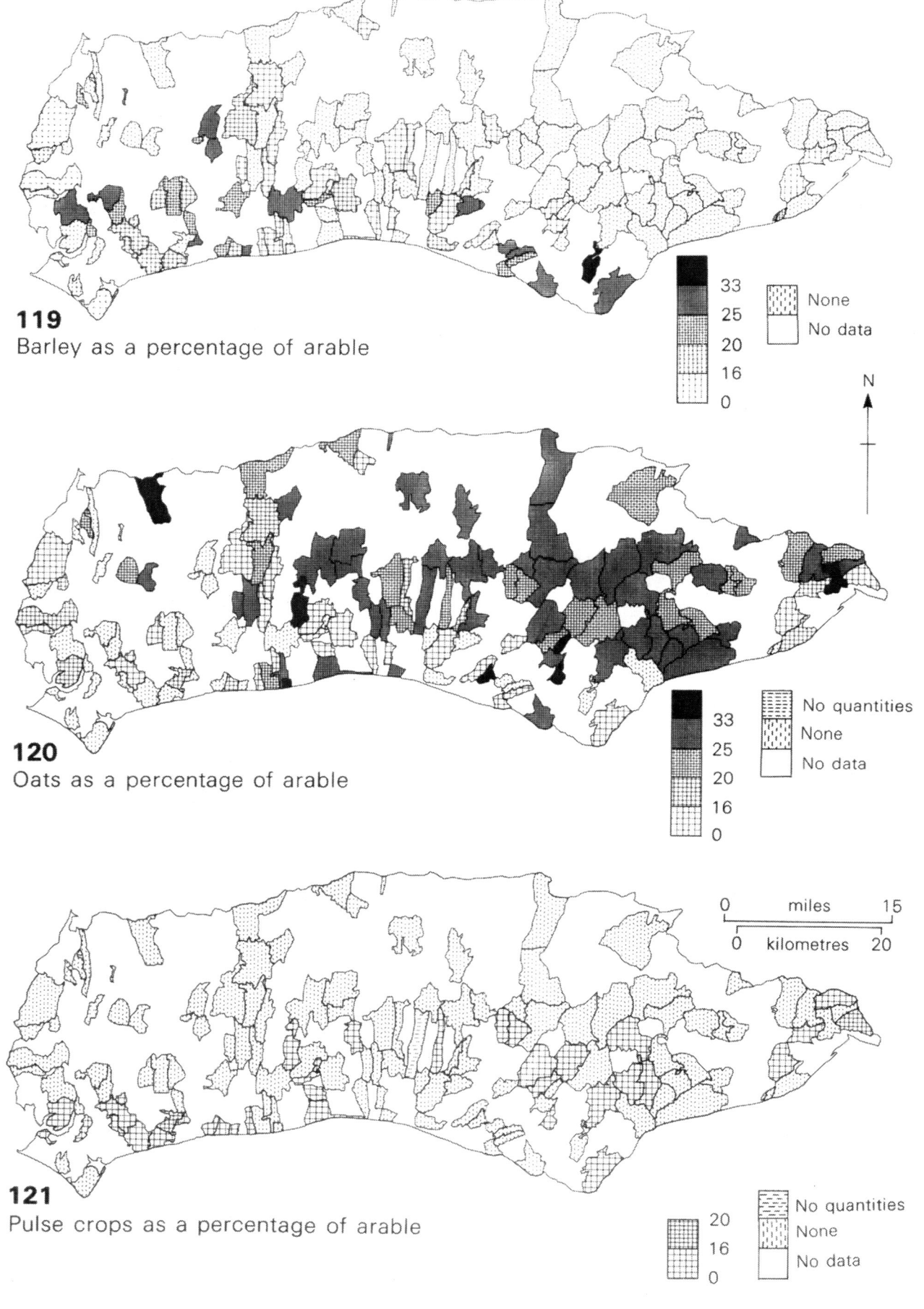

119 Barley as a percentage of arable

120 Oats as a percentage of arable

121 Pulse crops as a percentage of arable

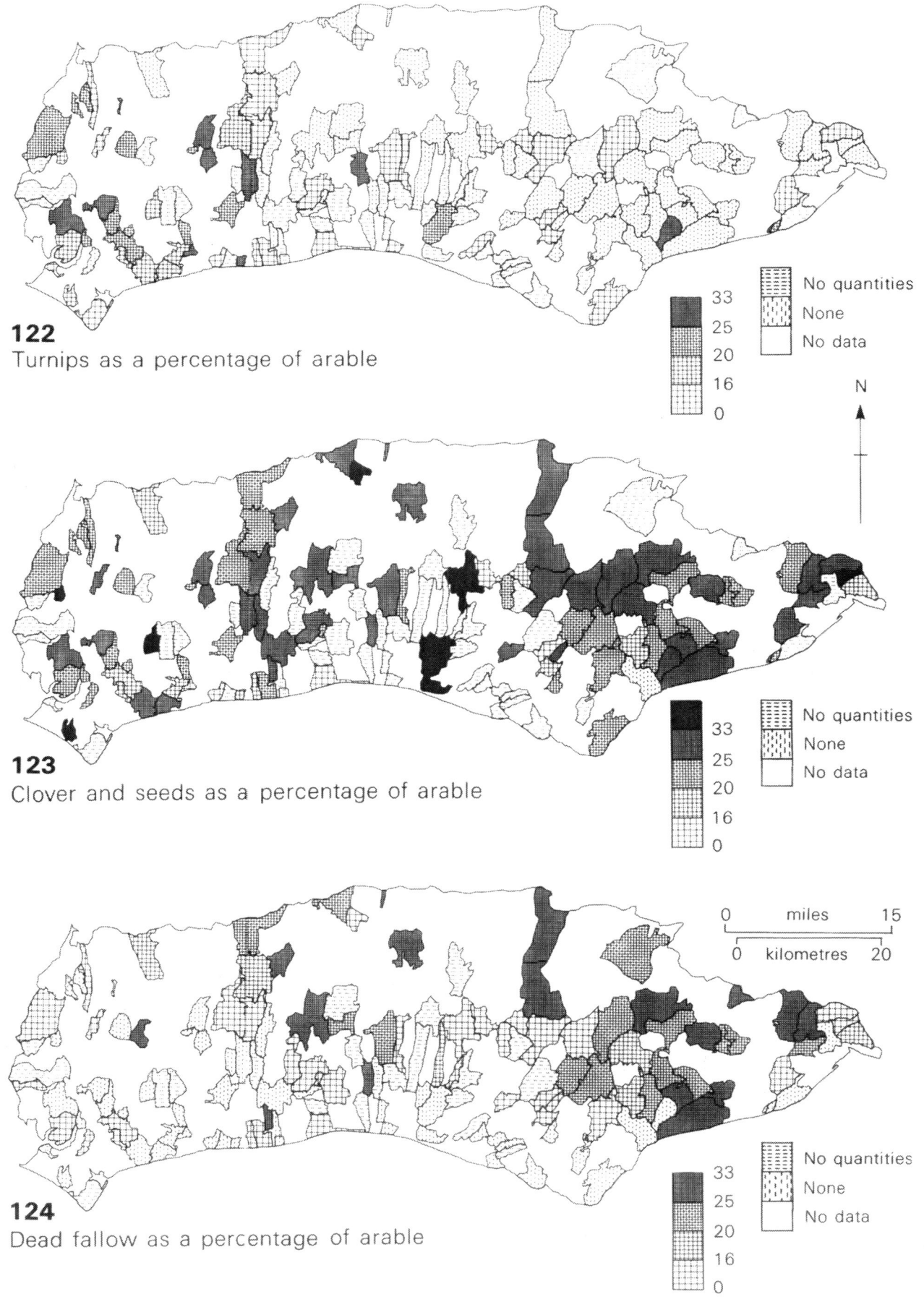

122 Turnips as a percentage of arable

123 Clover and seeds as a percentage of arable

124 Dead fallow as a percentage of arable

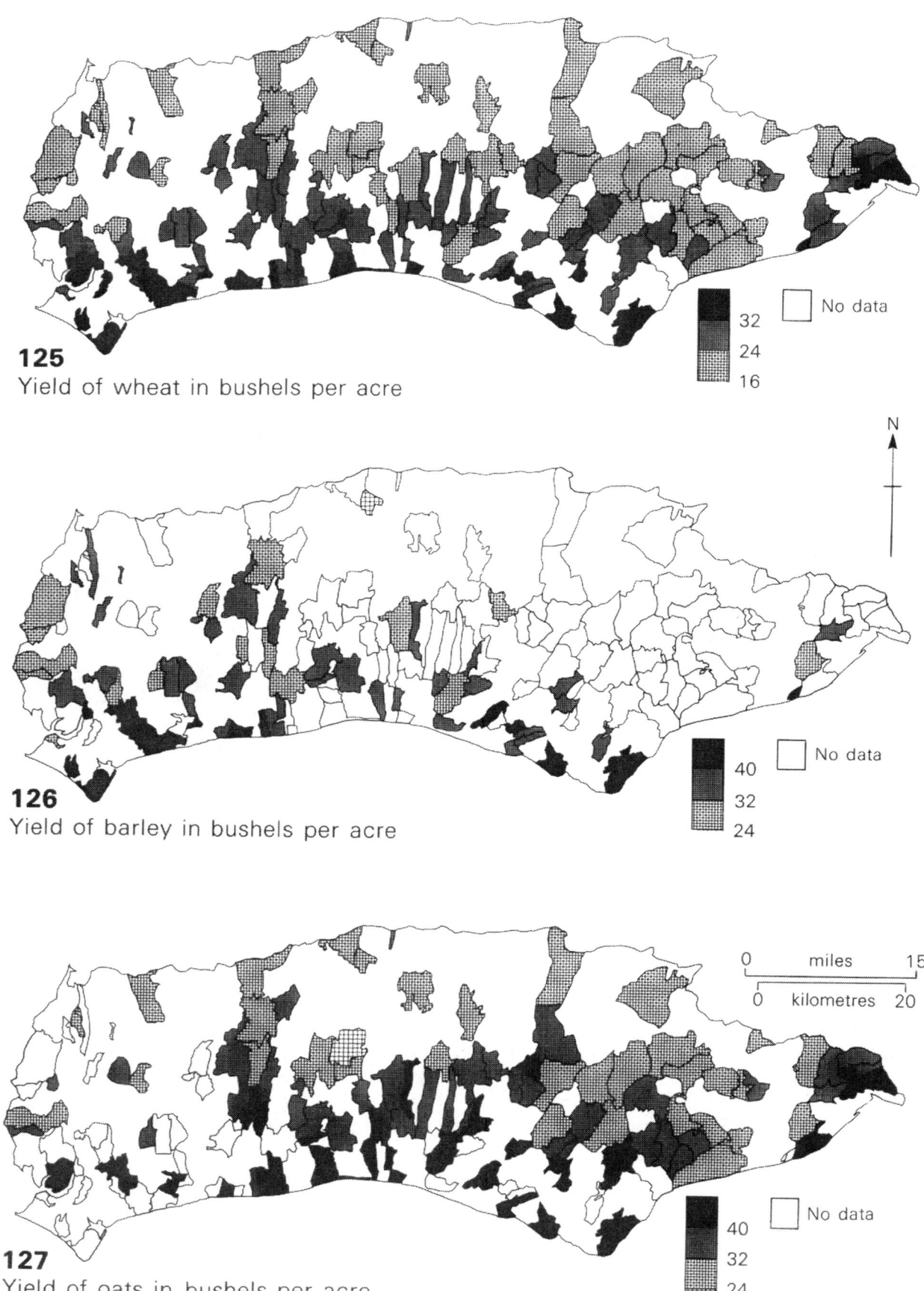

125 Yield of wheat in bushels per acre

126 Yield of barley in bushels per acre

127 Yield of oats in bushels per acre

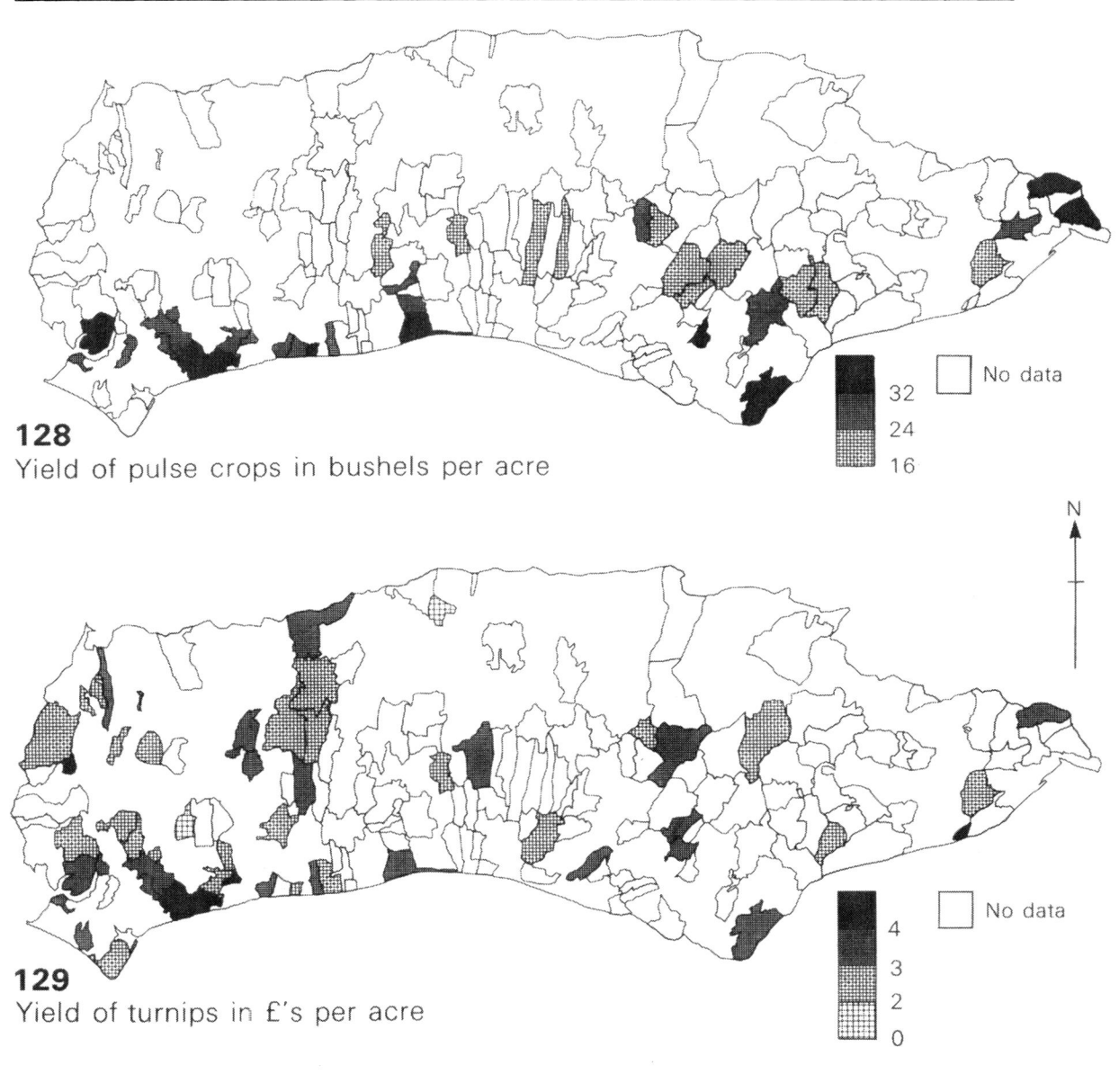

128 Yield of pulse crops in bushels per acre

129 Yield of turnips in £'s per acre

Kent

417 tithe districts
196 reports on tithe agreements

The tithe maps and apportionments of Kent have been described by the present author (1974a) and have been used to reconstruct aspects of the rural landscape and agricultural systems of the county *c.* 1840 (Kain 1973, 1974a and b, 1975). D. W. Harvey (1961, 1963, 1964) has also used tithe maps and apportionments in his studies of fruit and hop growing in Kent.

All but eleven Kent parishes were subject to tithe payment in 1836; just 10,000 acres lay in districts excluded from the tithe survey. But 159 parishes contained some land other than small amounts of glebe in the occupation of parsons, and roads and waste that was tithe free. In particular, all woodland in the Weald of Kent was exempt from tithe by prescription. Tithe was commuted by voluntary agreement in half of Kent parishes. Although about 90 per cent of reports on these agreements were compiled during the four years, 1838-41 (Table 16), the work of the Tithe Commission got off to a slower start in this county compared with other Home Counties, such as Essex. This contrast was due in large part to the continuing practice of collecting some tithe in kind in Kent.

Just under half the land of Kent was ploughed *c.* 1840 (Table 17). The largest tracts of arable were to be found in the Isle of Thanet and north-west Kent, while parishes with smallest proportions of arable were situated in the marshland fringes of Thameside, Medway and Sheppey, and the Stour and Romney marshes (Maps 132–3). Grazing in Kent was traditionally divided into 'upland' and 'marsh' pastures. Upland pastures were usually considered inferior and of lesser value and were often scattered among arable fields. In north-west Kent all pastures were highly prized, though as Horace William Meteyard pointed out at Hayes and Kidbrooke, they were intrinsically poor but 'given a fictitious value by their proximity to the metropolis'. Romney Marsh was the most extensive and renowned area of marshland in the county. Some parts of marsh parishes had been in arable cultivation for many years prior to 1836 and there is much speculation and debate in the tithe files about whether more land would be broken up after tithe commutation. At the time of tithe commutation, however, Romney Marsh was essentially a pasture region. Its breeding grassland could support two or three ewes per acre in winter and about twice that number in summer. Fattening land, though it varied greatly in quality, could carry and fatten at least four or five sheep per acre. Some files record instances of much greater numbers being kept; Horace William Meteyard considered the fattening land of Ruckinge parish equal to any in England.

All assistant commissioners and local tithe agents found it difficult to identify the normal crop rotation of many Kent parishes because of the wide variety of soil types and agricultural practices to be found within a single tithe district. At Shoreham, north of Sevenoaks, Thomas Smith Woolley wrote, 'scarcely two farmers can be found who follow the same course of husbandry'; at Sutton Valence on the Downs the Dean and Chapter of Canterbury 'had formed their estimate on the opinion as to the most proper course to pursue though they did not consider it had been generally adopted nor indeed any regular system'. If there was a particular 'Kentish rotation' in the 1840s it was the six-course: turnips, barley or oats, clover and seeds, wheat, beans or peas, wheat. This was widely adopted in north and east Kent on those soils well adapted to sheep/corn husbandry, but it could not be sustained on heavier or poorer Wealden soils. On heavy but drained clays at at Woodchurch, for example, a five-course of wheat, oats, clover, beans, and summer fallow was employed. Similarly at Bethersden, 'it does not do to sow wheat on a clover fallow as no turnips can be grown, a summer fallow with a few beans is the best preparation for the wheat crop'. Evidence in the tithe files suggests that by about 1840, the extension of drainage had occasioned the virtual disappearance of the traditional Wealden three-course of wheat, beans, fallow. At the other extreme, on the richest soils of the county seven- and eight-course rotations were practised; at Sittingbourne, arable was put out to turnip fallow only once in every ten years. These extended rotations provoked Woolley to comment at Elmstone in east Kent that 'the parish as a whole is very well-farmed, though here as in Kent generally, a west country farmer would be rather astonished at the large proportion in corn'. In mid-Kent, all assistant commissioners considered that the arable as a whole would be better managed and probably more profitable in the long run if agriculture was not focussed so much on the cultivation of hops which starved the rest of the arable of manure.

Table 16 *Reports on agreements for commutation of tithes in Kent*

Assistant commissioner/ local tithe agent	1837	1838	1839	1840	1841	1842	1843	1844	Totals
Thomas Smith Woolley	3			6	20	9	7	1	46
Thomas P. Hilder		7	23	9					39
Horace William Meteyard		9	15	3	1				28
Roger Kynaston		2	5	18	2				27
John Mee Mathew		7	7	2					16
Henry Gilbert		2	9	2					13
F. Browne Browne		1	3	6					10
Charles Wilson	3	2							5
A. O. Baker		2	2						4
John Pickering		3	1						4
John Farncombe		1	1						2
Thomas Neve	1								1
Joseph Townsend		1							1
Totals	7	37	66	46	23	9	7	1	196

Table 17 *Land use, crops and yields in Kent c. 1836*

A	Land use	Percentage of total land area enumerated in reports on tithe agreements	Estimated acreage in whole county
	Arable	48.5	505,030
	Grass	31.6	329,343
	Wood	13.6	141,878
	Common	3.4	3,583

B	Crop	Mean percentage of arable	Mean yield per acre	Estimated acreage in whole county
	Wheat	27.6	25.6 bushels	139,121
	Barley	13.3	33.7 bushels	67,060
	Oats	10.6	39.1 bushels	53,419
	Pulses	11.0	26.2 bushels	55,476
	Turnips	12.0	£2.95	60,617
	Seeds	19.2	22.1 cwts	96,986
	Fallows	5.7	—	28,609

Kent

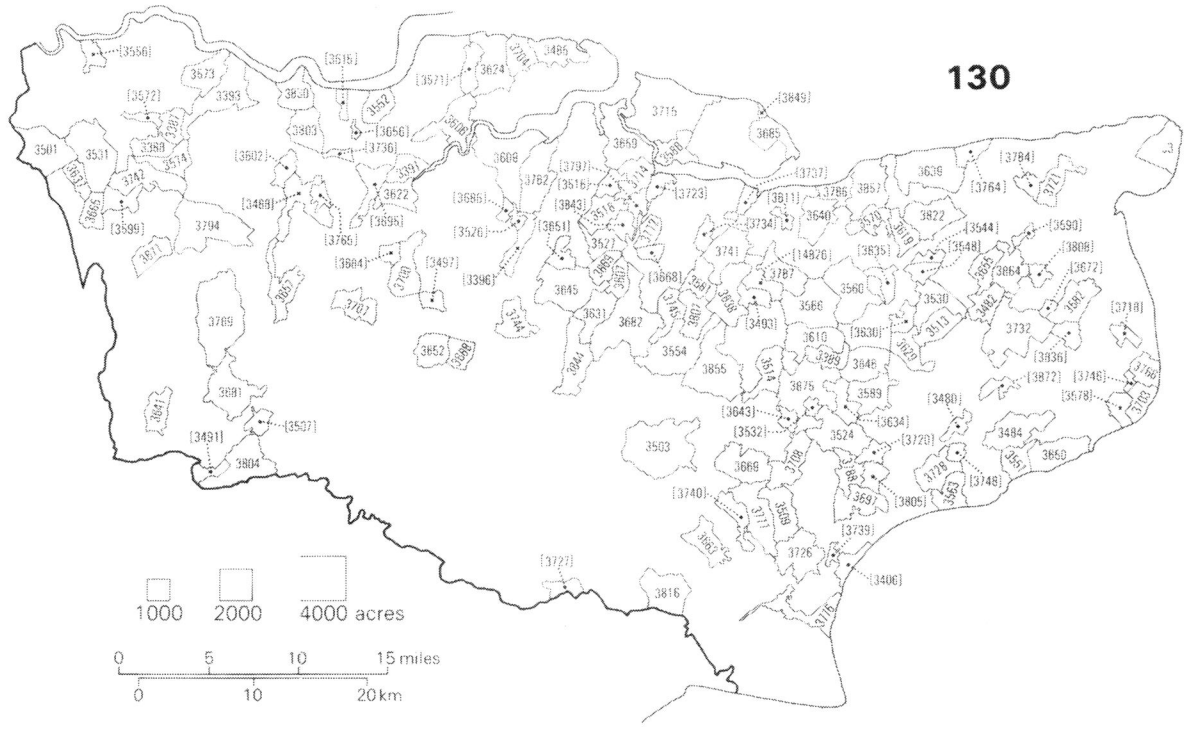

130

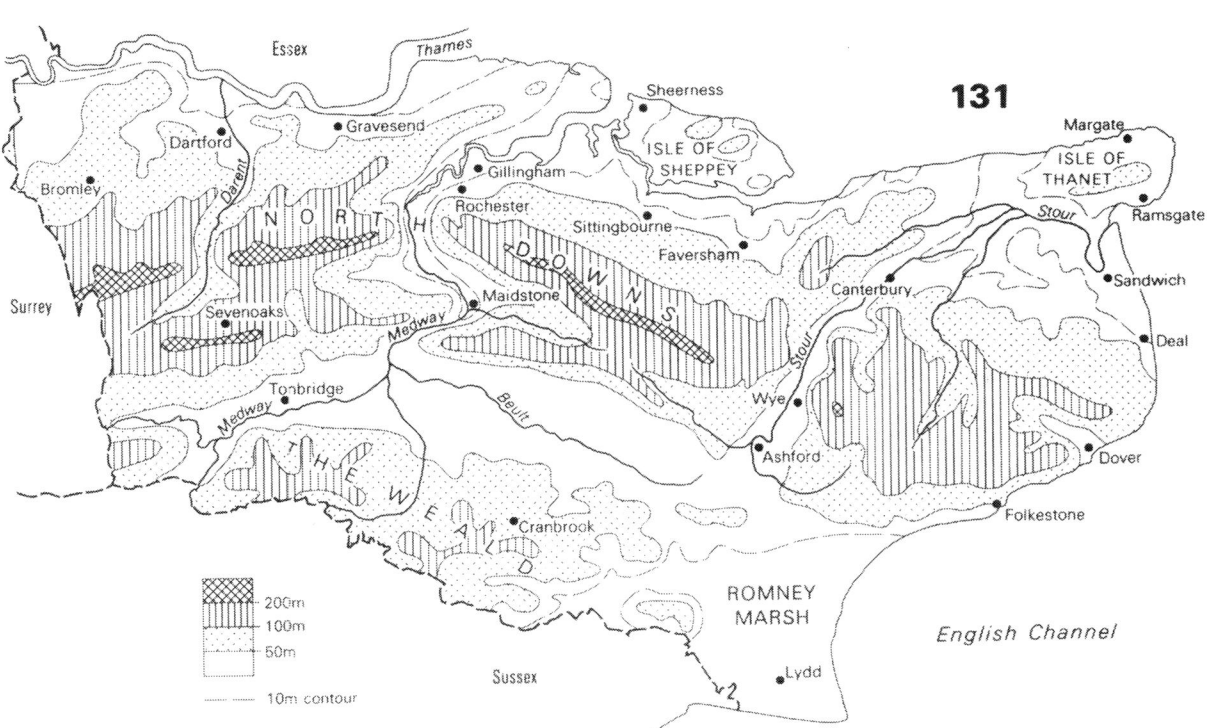

131

116 Southern counties

132 Arable as a percentage of tithe district area

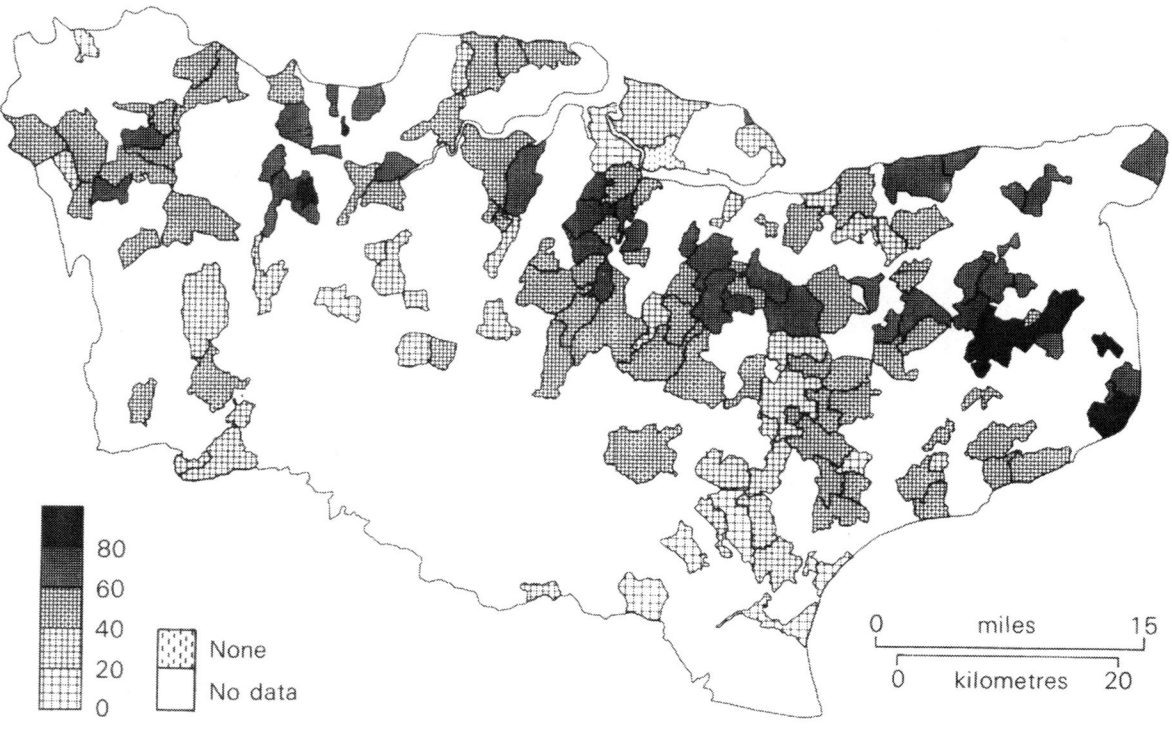

133 Pasture as a percentage of tithe district area

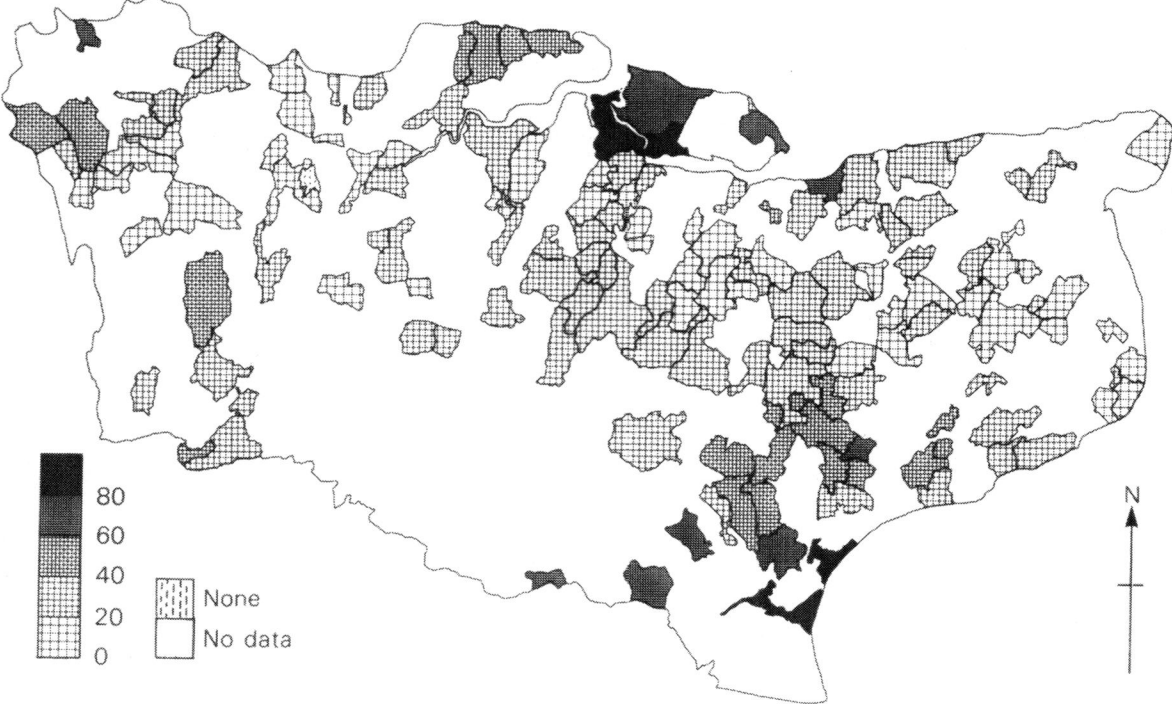

Kent

134 Woodland as a percentage of tithe district area

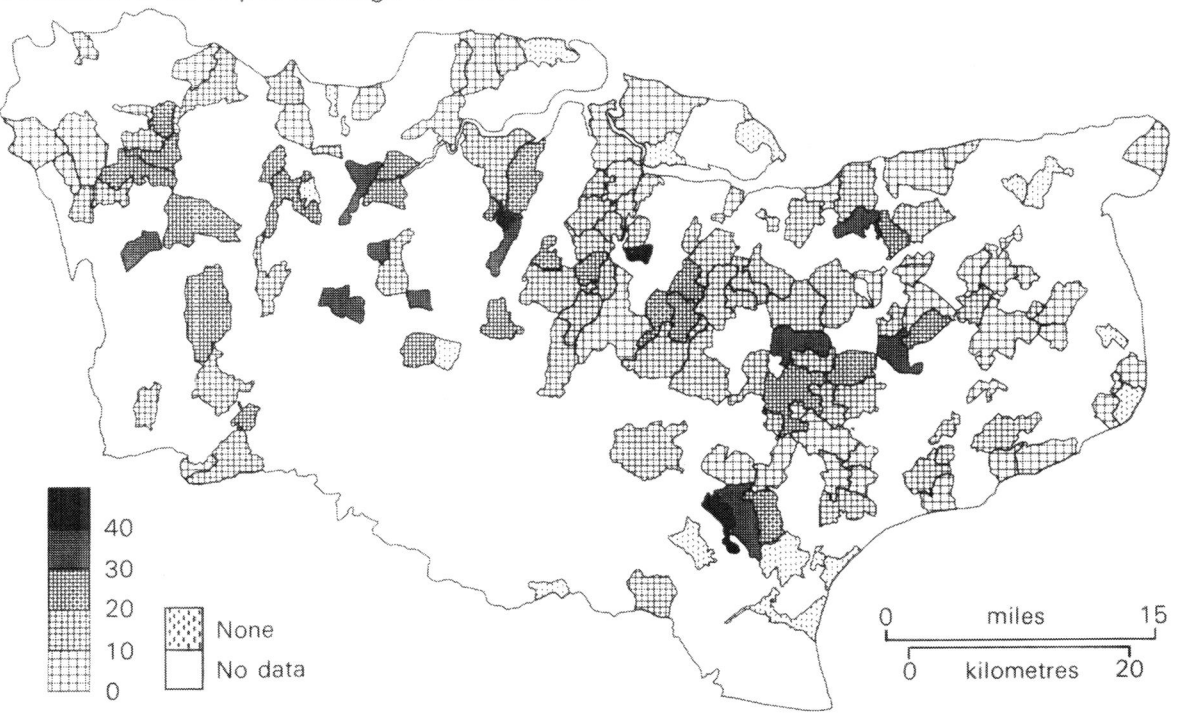

135 Orchards and fruit as a percentage of tithe district area

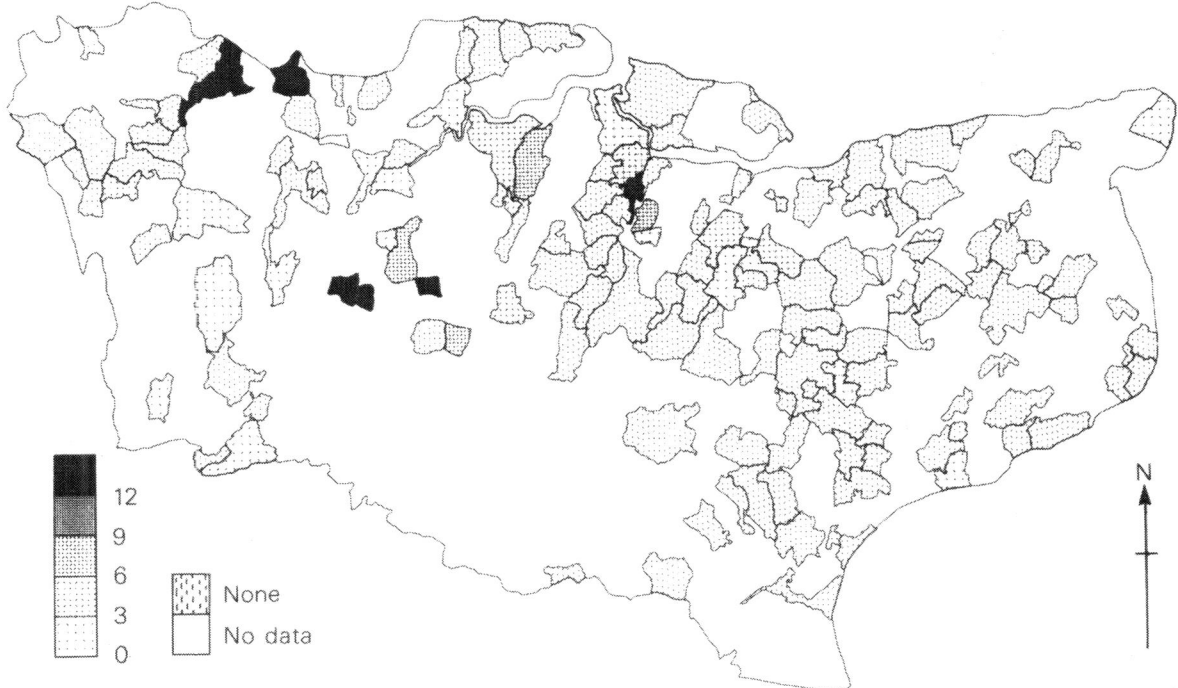

136 Hops as a percentage of tithe district area

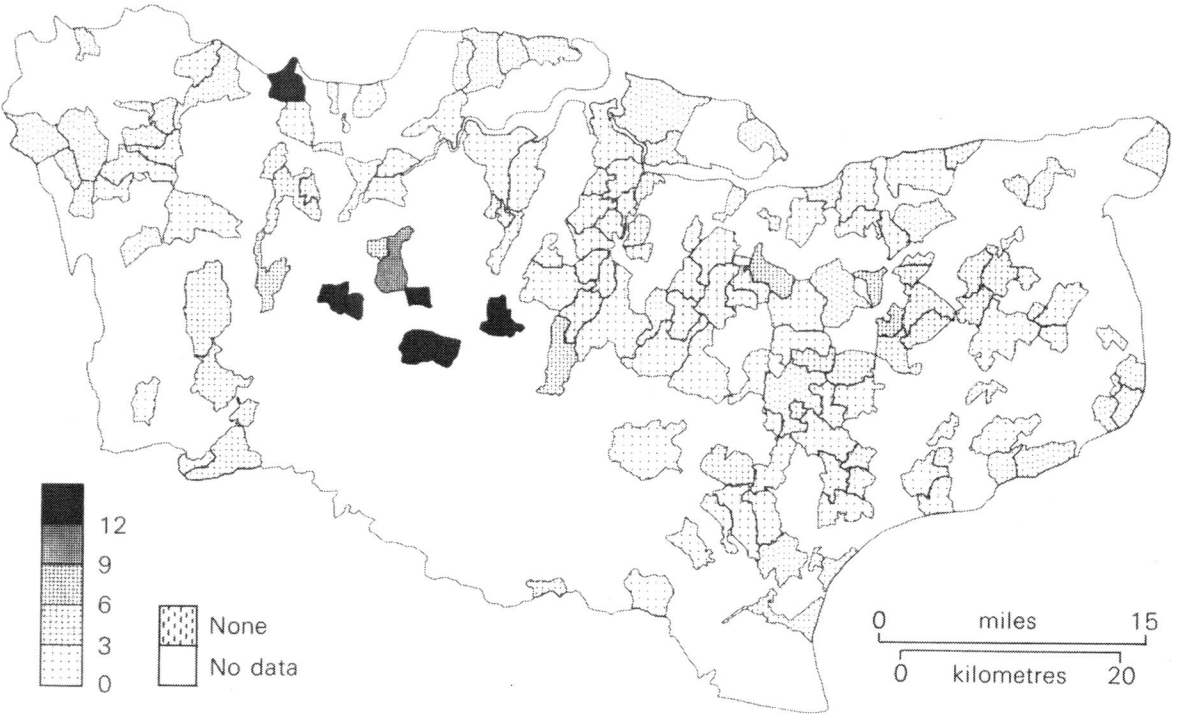

137 Wheat as a percentage of arable

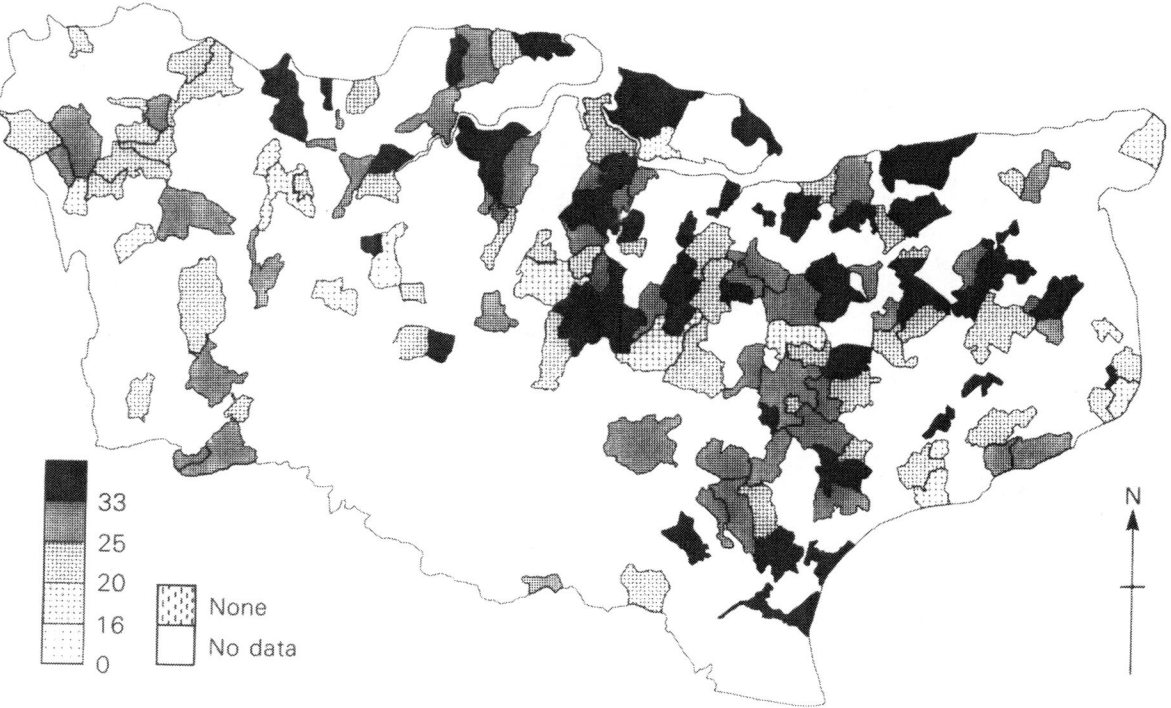

138 Barley as a percentage of arable

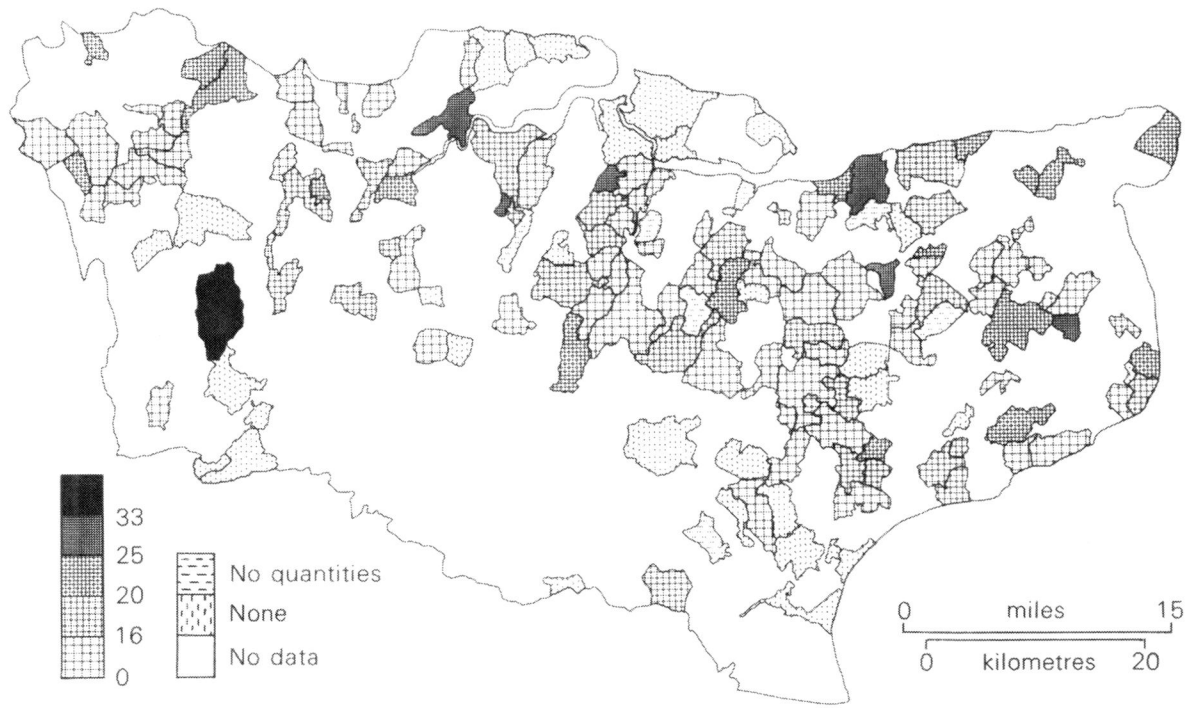

139 Oats as a percentage of arable

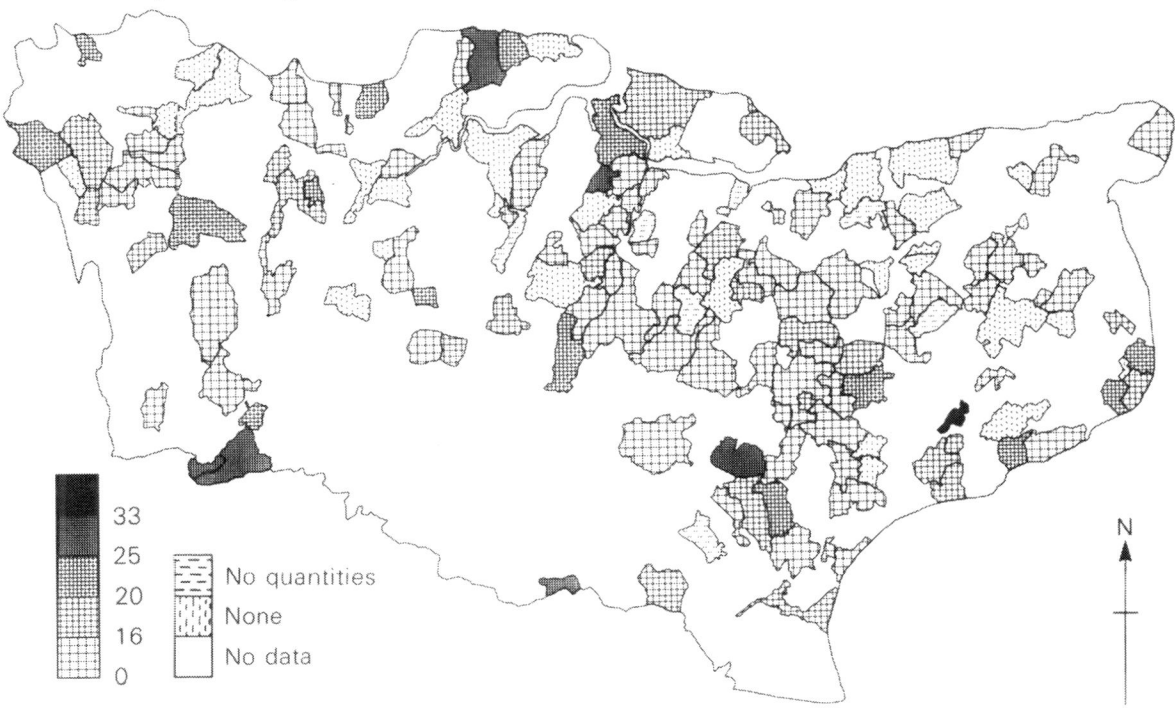

140 Pulse crops as a percentage of arable

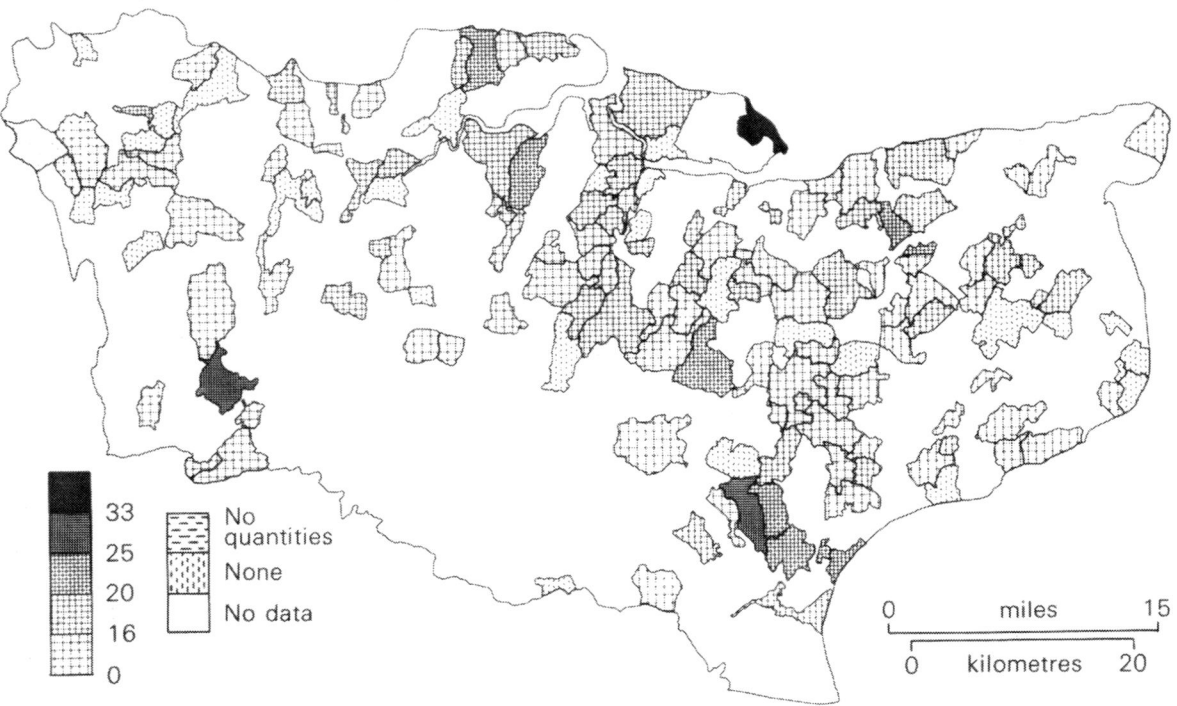

141 Turnips as a percentage of arable

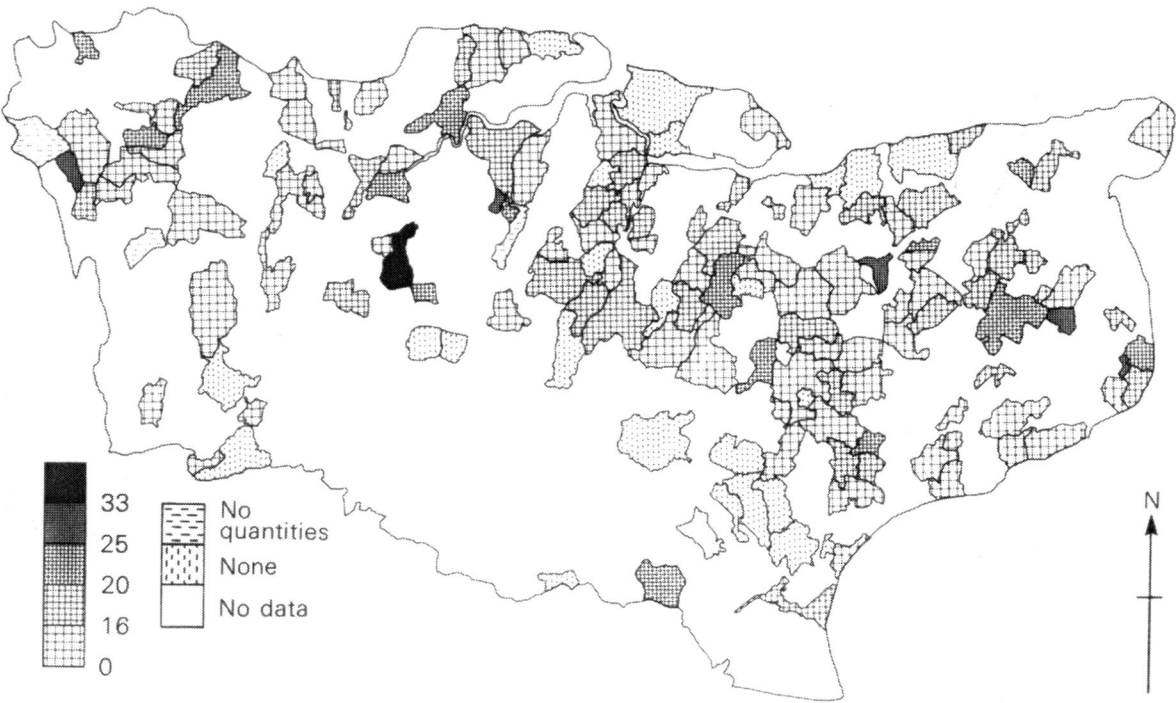

142 Clover and seeds as a percentage of arable

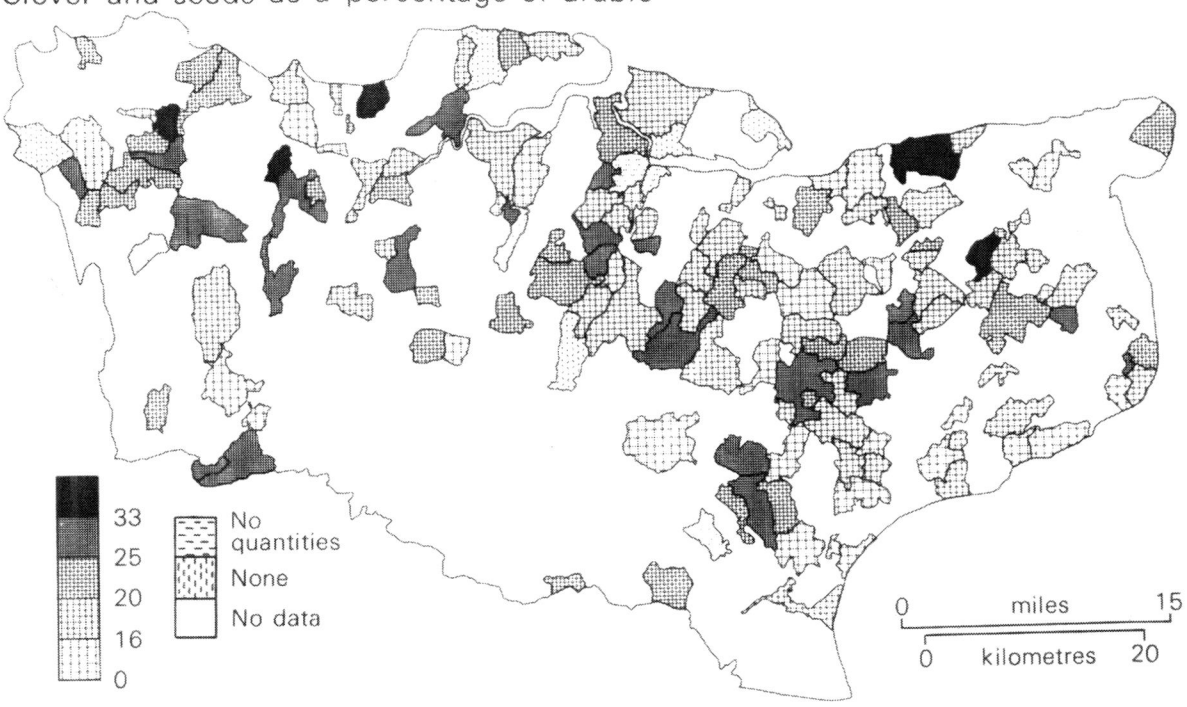

143 Dead fallow as a percentage of arable

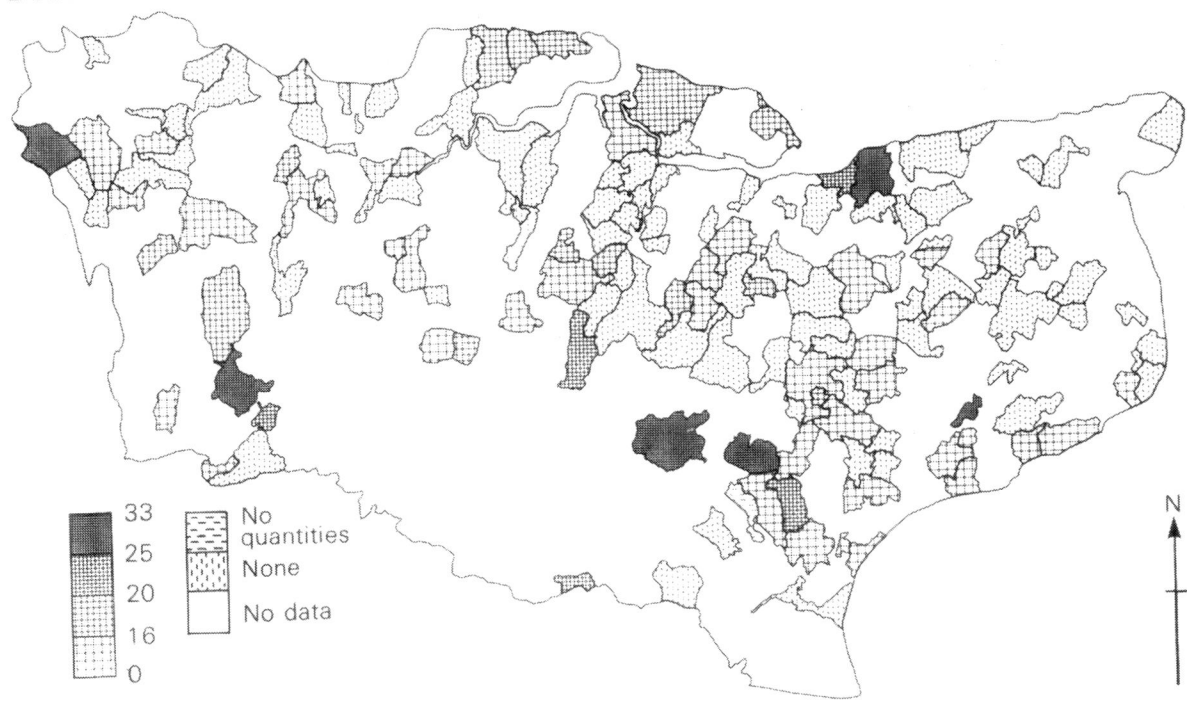

144 Yield of wheat in bushels per acre

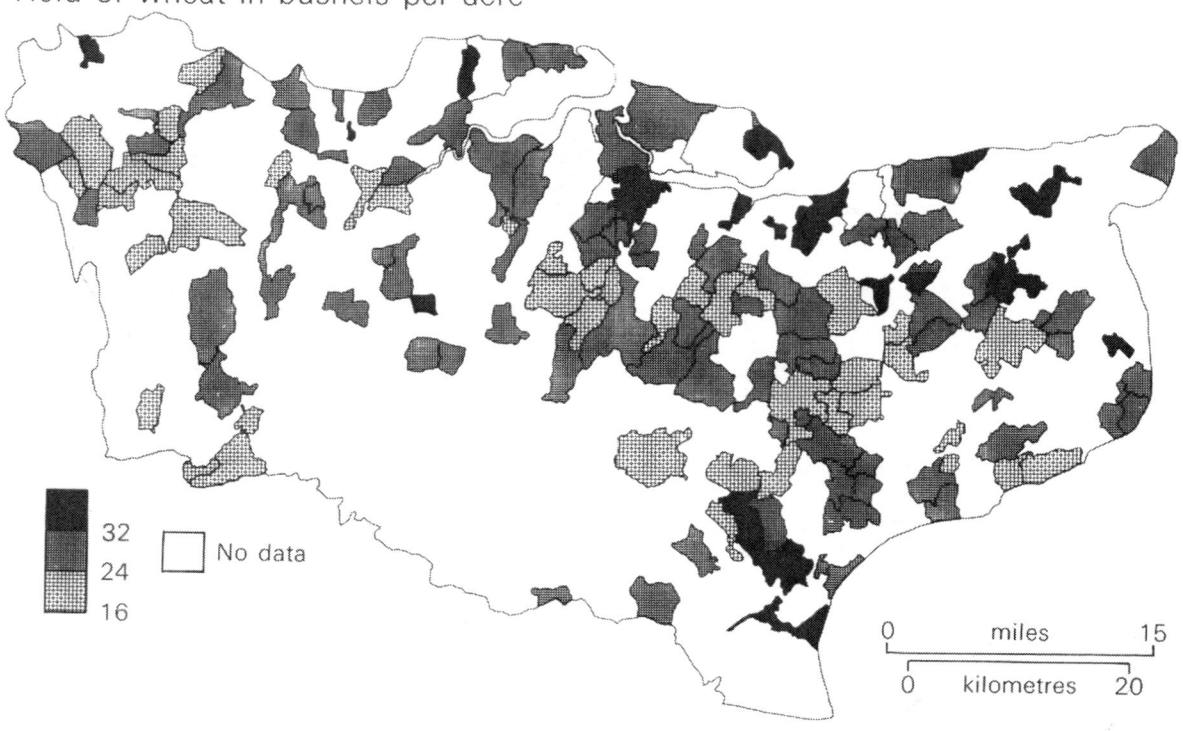

145 Yield of barley in bushels per acre

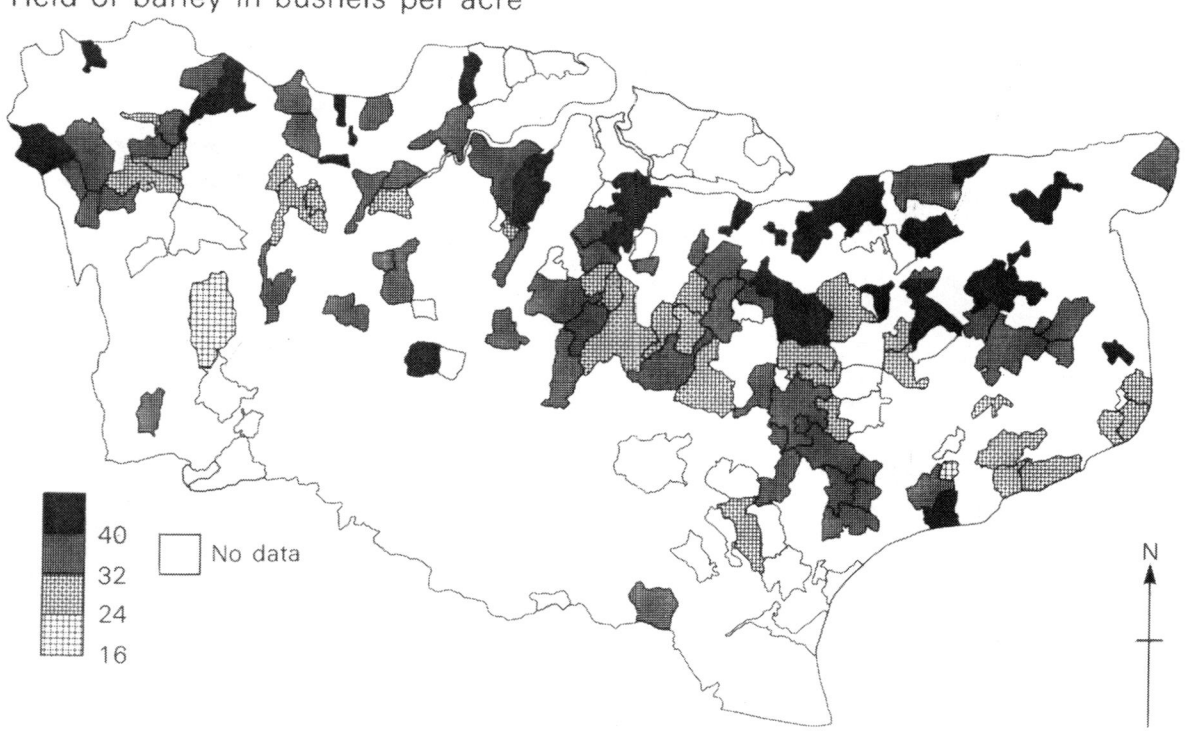

Kent

146 Yield of oats in bushels per acre

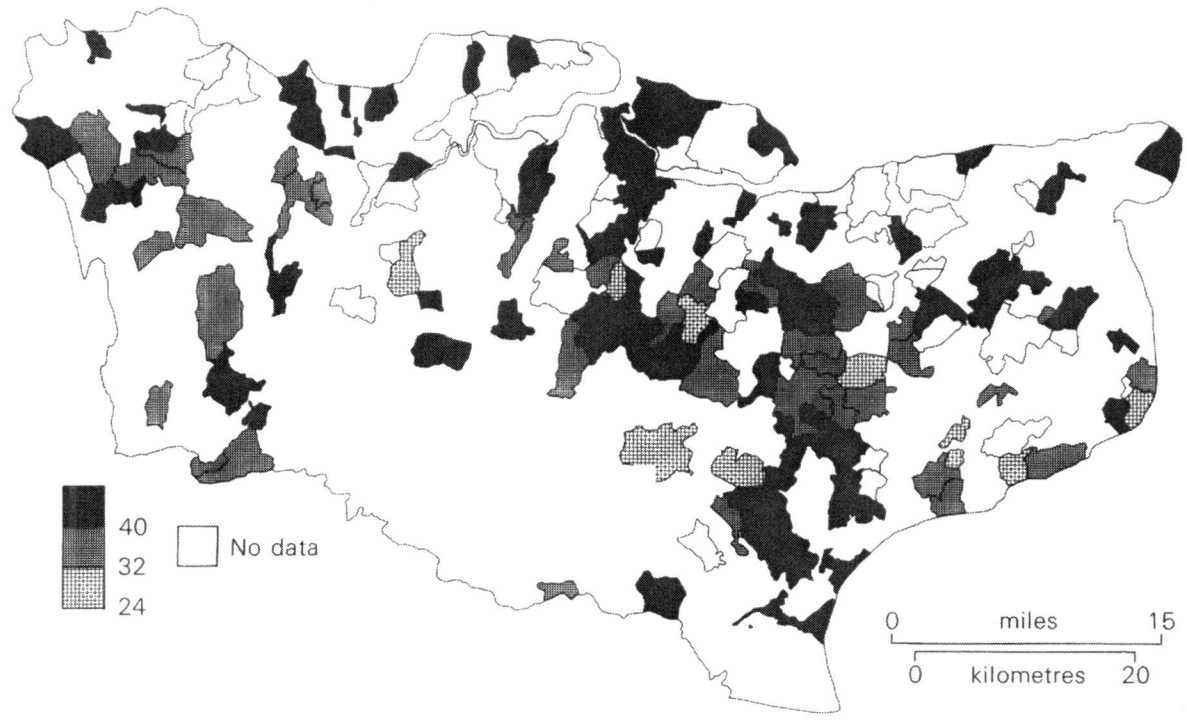

147 Yield of pulse crops in bushels per acre

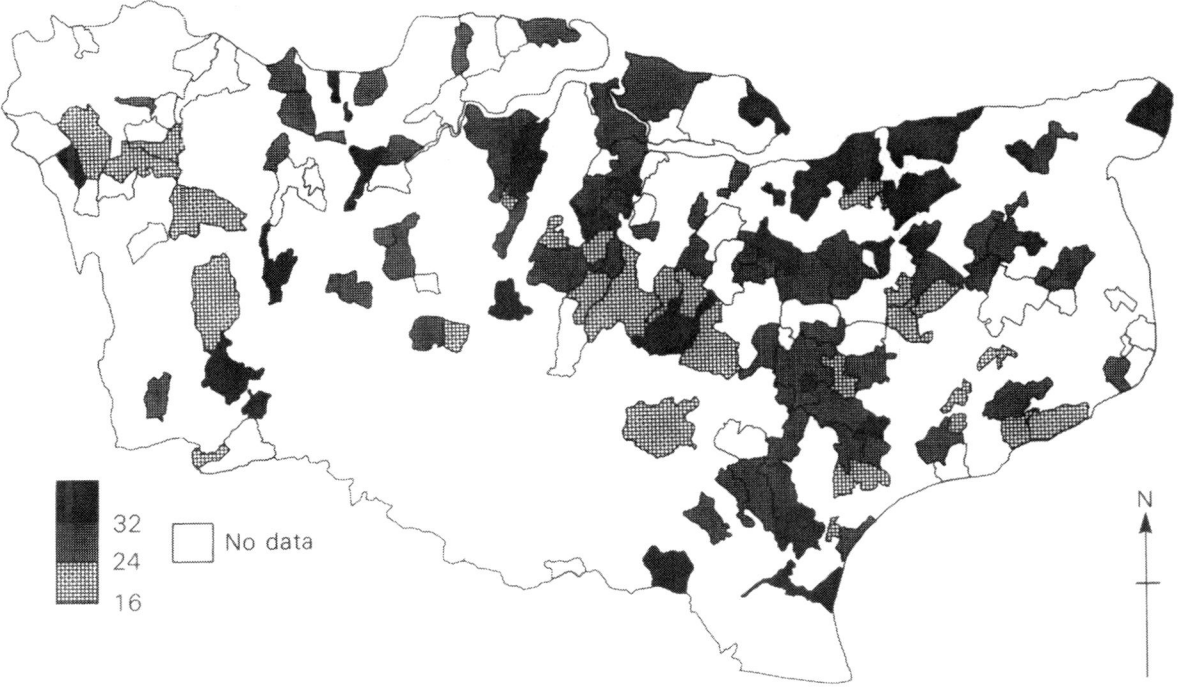

148 Yield of turnips in £'s per acre

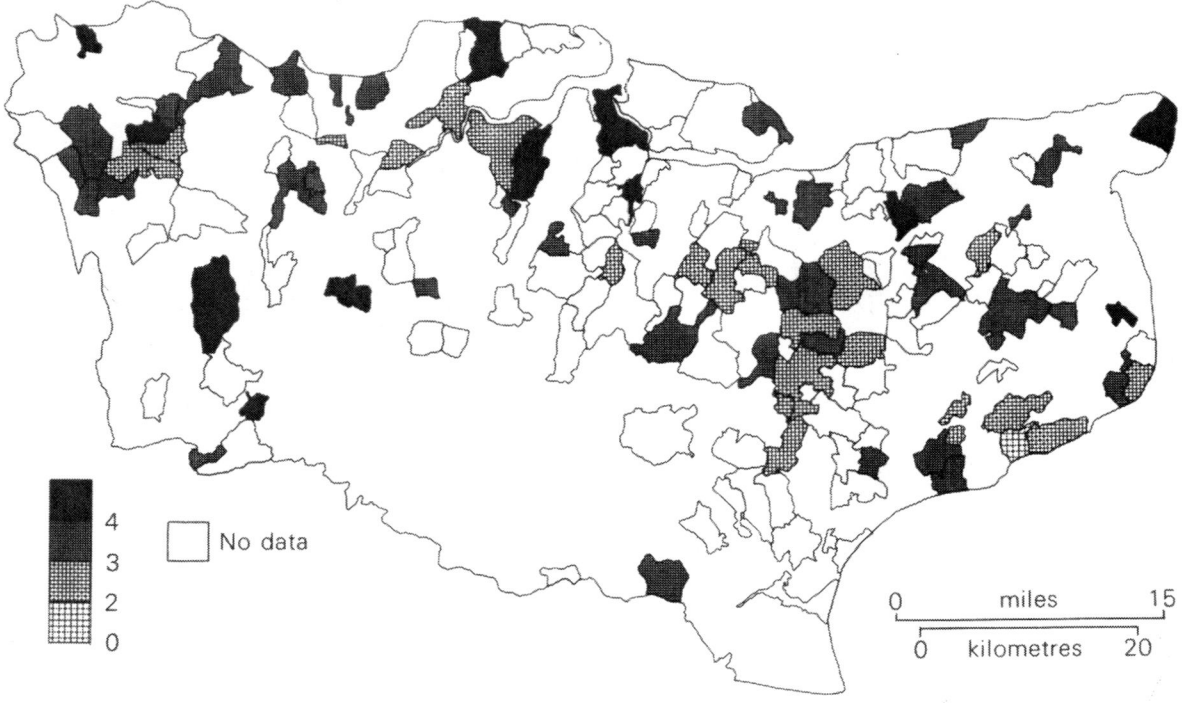

149 Yield of clover and seeds in cwts per acre

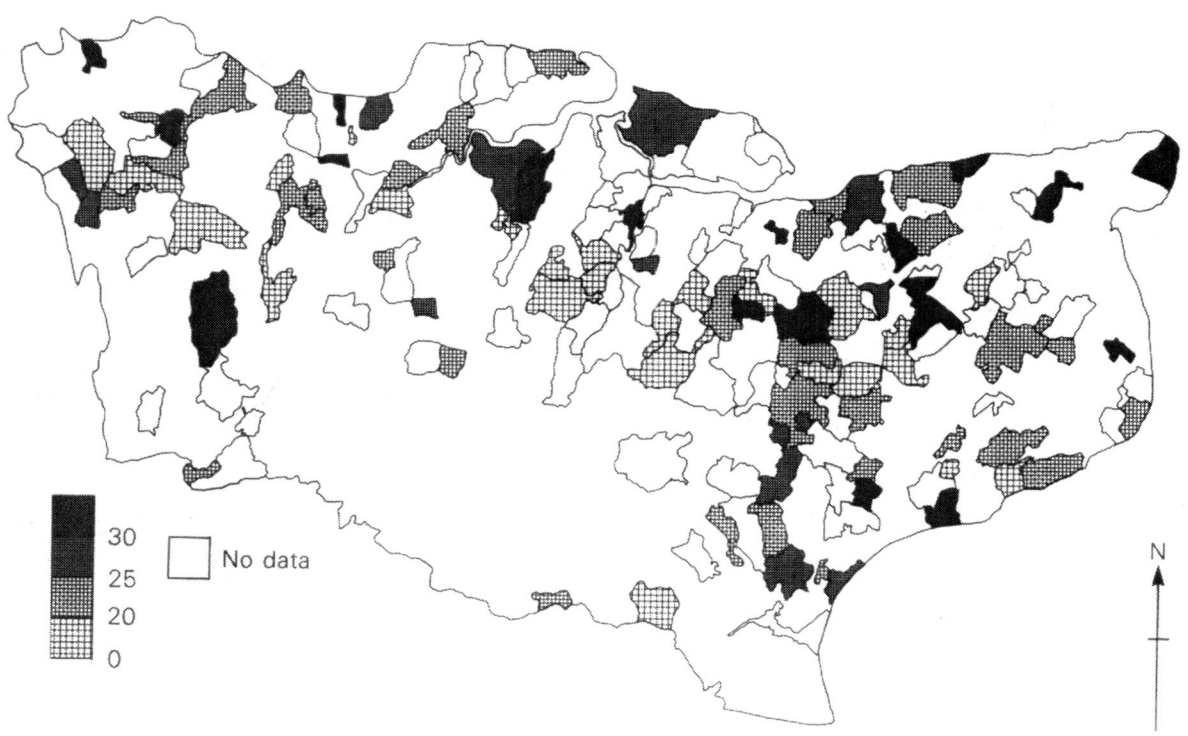

150 Yield of meadow in cwts per acre

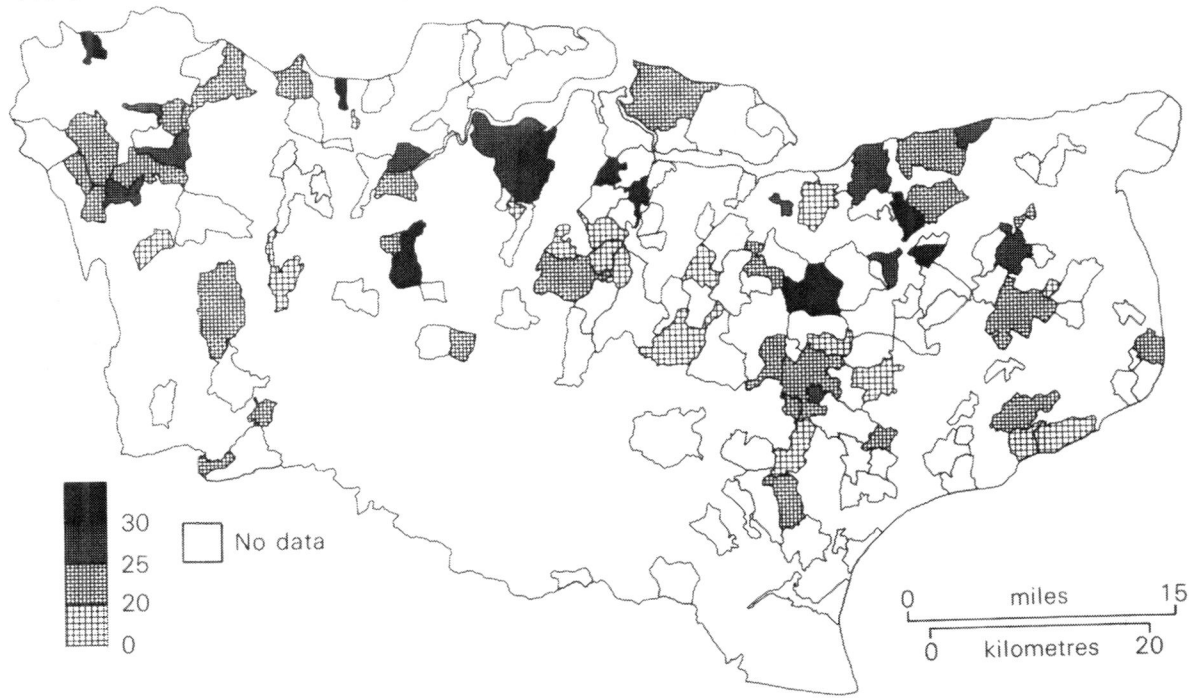

151 Yield of pasture in shillings per acre

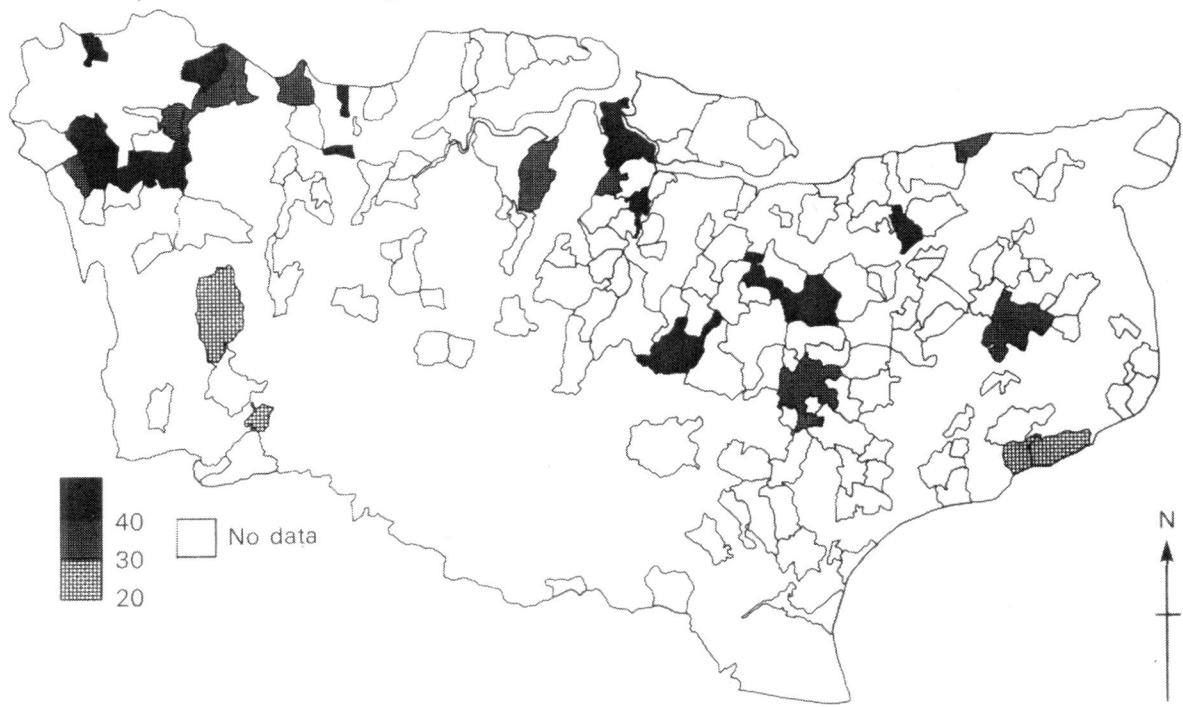

Hertfordshire

138 tithe districts
79 reports on tithe agreements

L. G. Cameron (1941) includes a map of arable land in 156 square miles of south-east Hertfordshire plotted from tithe surveys in his report on the Land Utilisation Survey of Great Britain, and Aileen Carpenter (1965) has abstracted land use data for a block of fourteen parishes. In the first of a series of post-war higher degree theses which examine regional land use and agricultural history, F. D. Hartley (1953) used tithe apportionments and maps to reconstruct the pattern of land use in Chiltern Hertfordshire.

Most of the nineteen tithe free parishes in Hertfordshire had extinguished their tithes when their open fields were enclosed, but in 1836 there was still a considerable area of open field arable and lammas meadows in the county, and the effects of this on agricultural practices and amounts of titheable produce are discussed in some thirty tithe files (see Subject Index). Chiltern beechwoods were tithe free and in nineteen other parishes where tithe was commuted by agreement, there were tracts of tithe free land or non-enumerated modus land amounting to more than 10 per cent of total parish acreage. Nine assistant tithe commissioners and local tithe agents worked in Hertfordshire but one man, William Heard, assessed about half the agreements (Table 18). His invariable method of obtaining crop acreages was to divide total arable acreage by the number of rotation courses. Thomas Smith Woolley used a slightly more refined version of this same technique by first deducting the area of hedges and balks from total arable after which he valued areas of different soil and general land quality separately. For a local man, assistant commissioner Joseph Townsend gives very uninformative, stereotyped descriptions of parish farming which often consist of just a bald statement of soil type and crop rotation.

In terms of land use, mid-nineteenth-century Hertfordshire was an overwhelmingly arable county (Maps 154–7 and Table 19). In lighter soil, particularly Chiltern chalk parishes, arable occupied more than 80 per cent of total enumerated area. In only seven tithe districts with data in reports on tithe agreements was the ratio of arable to grass less than 1.5 to 1, and these were on clay soils and in the south-east, closest to London. William Heard reported at Totteridge in 1840 that 'the natural character of the land is clay and gravel on a clay subsoil very cold and difficult to manage if cultivated under the plough, it has however been for a long period cultivated as pasture and from its nearness to the metropolis been universally mown for hay'. Assistant commissioners and local tithe agents identified two main types of grassland in Hertfordshire: lowland meadows which were mown for hay twice a year and yielded 20–5 cwts an acre, and upland grasslands which were grazed and varied very much in quality; on gravelly soils such pastures were liable to be scorched in dry seasons. Grassland situated in landscape parks is discussed in about a dozen files. Few tithe districts where tithe commutation was effected by agreement retained large commons, but many were well-wooded; more than 7 per cent of the whole county was covered with woods. The tithe files record the presence of some good coppices but there are many comments about the heavily timbered nature of Hertfordshire woods resulting in slow and thin growth of titheable underwood and also about the detrimental effect on arable and pasture occasioned by shading of heavily timbered hedgerows. Thomas Smith Woolley noted both these facts at Stapleford near Hertford on his visit in 1840:

> woods of various extent are intermixed with the other lands, in all parts of the parish. They are generally full of timber, some large and good. The underwood is chiefly hornbeam and hazel and would be good if there were less timber ... the lands adjoining to which are poor and cold much shaded and injured by the woods and hedgerow timber.

In the opinions of Hertfordshire assistant commissioners and local tithe agents, the type of crop rotation employed at a particular place was related to whether arable was open or enclosed and whether soil was light or heavy. Three-course rotations were restricted almost entirely by 1836 to heavy soils and especially those open field clay lands which still required draining. They considered that the Norfolk four-course rotation was most widely adopted on enclosed fields, with perhaps oats substituted for barley and some variations induced by nearness to London. At East Barnet and High Barnet, F. Browne Browne commented that 'the course of cultivation on the arable land is potatoes or turnips, wheat, oats, and clover, but in the neighbourhood of London I believe the four course system is seldom strictly observed'. Where five-course rotations were practised in Hertfordshire, they did not meet with William Heard's approval. At Ayot St Peter the system was 'wheat, barley, clover, oats or peas, turnips ... not only very injurious to the land but to the interests of the cultivator who by such continued cropping so exhausts the soil that the produce cannot possibly repay him for the expenses particularly as so little stock appear to be kept'. Comments such as the following made at Wormley in 1838 suggest that potatoes were a very important part of the system of cropping but as is usual in tithe files, there is no consistent record of their acreages:

> potatoes have the last few years been grown on the fallow land previous to wheat which has answered the expectations of the grower as the quality of the wheat is far superior than after a dead fallow and with the aid of town manure good crops can be produced but without any extraordinary outlay 6 tons an acre can be grown in the average of seasons.

London, both as a market and source of manure is a theme of sometimes extended comment in Hertfordshire tithe files of which the following short extracts are illustrative. At Berkhamstead, John Mee Mathew noted that 'the introduction of the London and Birmingham railway, thro' the parish has given the farmers an increased facility to the London market'. At Totteridge, William Heard considered that 'the produce is in some degree increased by being repeatedly manured with London manure the custom being to return a load of manure for every load of hay conveyed to market'. On the other hand, Thomas Smith Woolley found that the parish of Ware 'is not in a high state of cultivation

– too much of the straw and other produce finding its way to London from whence the distance is too great to allow of manure being brought in return'.

Table 18 *Reports on agreements for commutation of tithes in Hertfordshire*

Assistant commissioner/ local tithe agent	1837	1838	1839	1840	1841	1842	1843	1844	1845	Totals
William Heard		13	8	8	3	3			2	37
Joseph Townsend	8	5								13
Thomas Smith Woolley	6				1				2	9
Edward Greathed	2	6								8
F. Browne Browne			4							4
John Mee Mathew		2	1							3
John Pickering			2		1					3
Anthony Jackson		1								1
Roger Kynaston			1							1
Totals	16	27	16	8	5	3			4	79

Table 19 *Land use, crops and yields in Hertfordshire c. 1836*

A	Land use	Percentage of total land area enumerated in reports on tithe agreements	Estimated acreage in whole county
	Arable	66.6	260,638
	Grass	22.0	85,933
	Wood	7.2	28,198
	Common	0.9	3,508

B	Crop	Mean percentage of arable	Mean yield per acre	Estimated acreage in whole county
	Wheat	23.4	21.6 bushels	60,958
	Barley	20.1	29.4 bushels	52,390
	Oats	6.7	33.6 bushels	17,460
	Pulses	5.3	22.2 bushels	13,794
	Turnips	13.1	£2.45	34,239
	Seeds	19.6	21.0 cwts	50,961
	Fallows	11.9	—	30,885

Hertfordshire

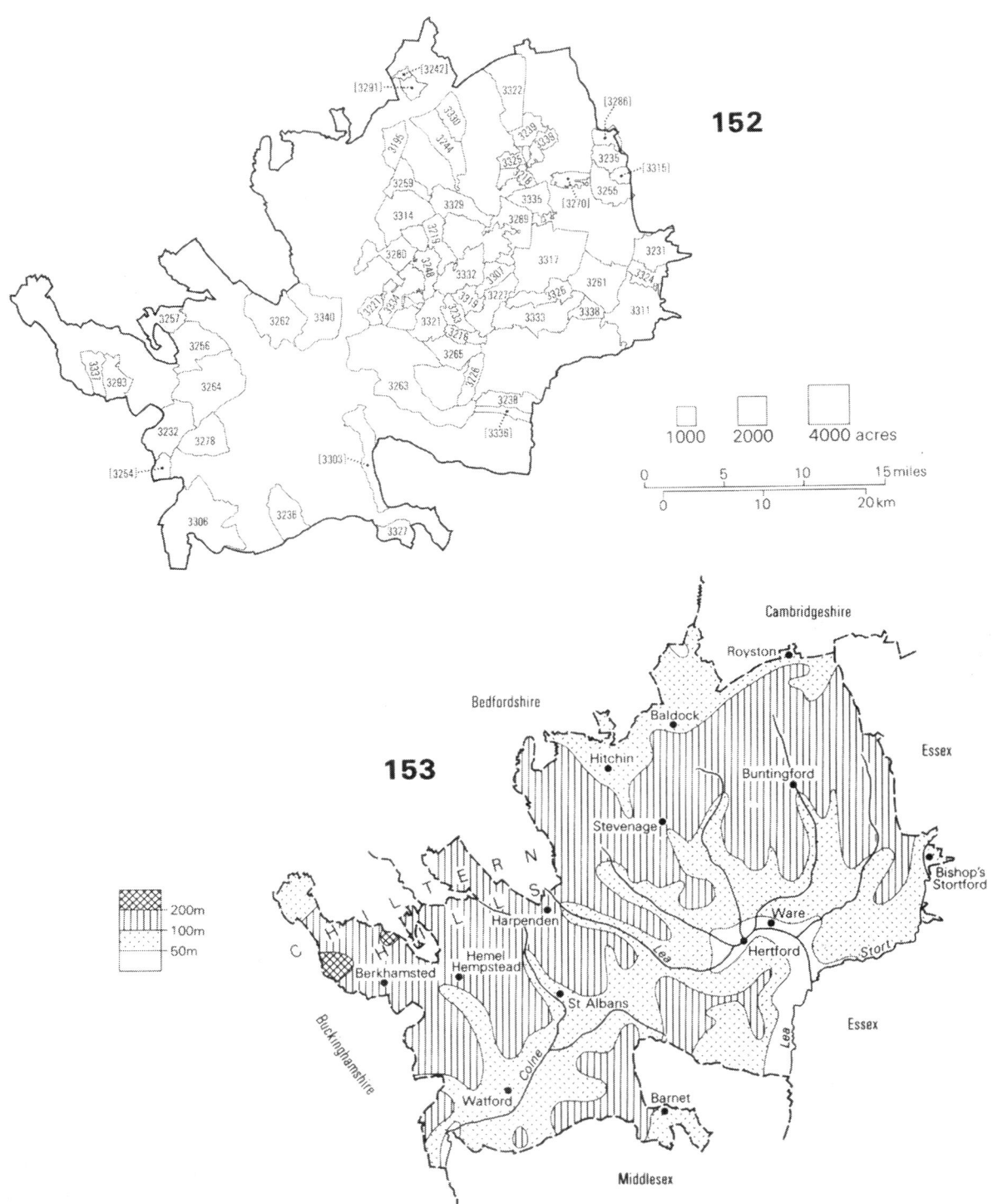

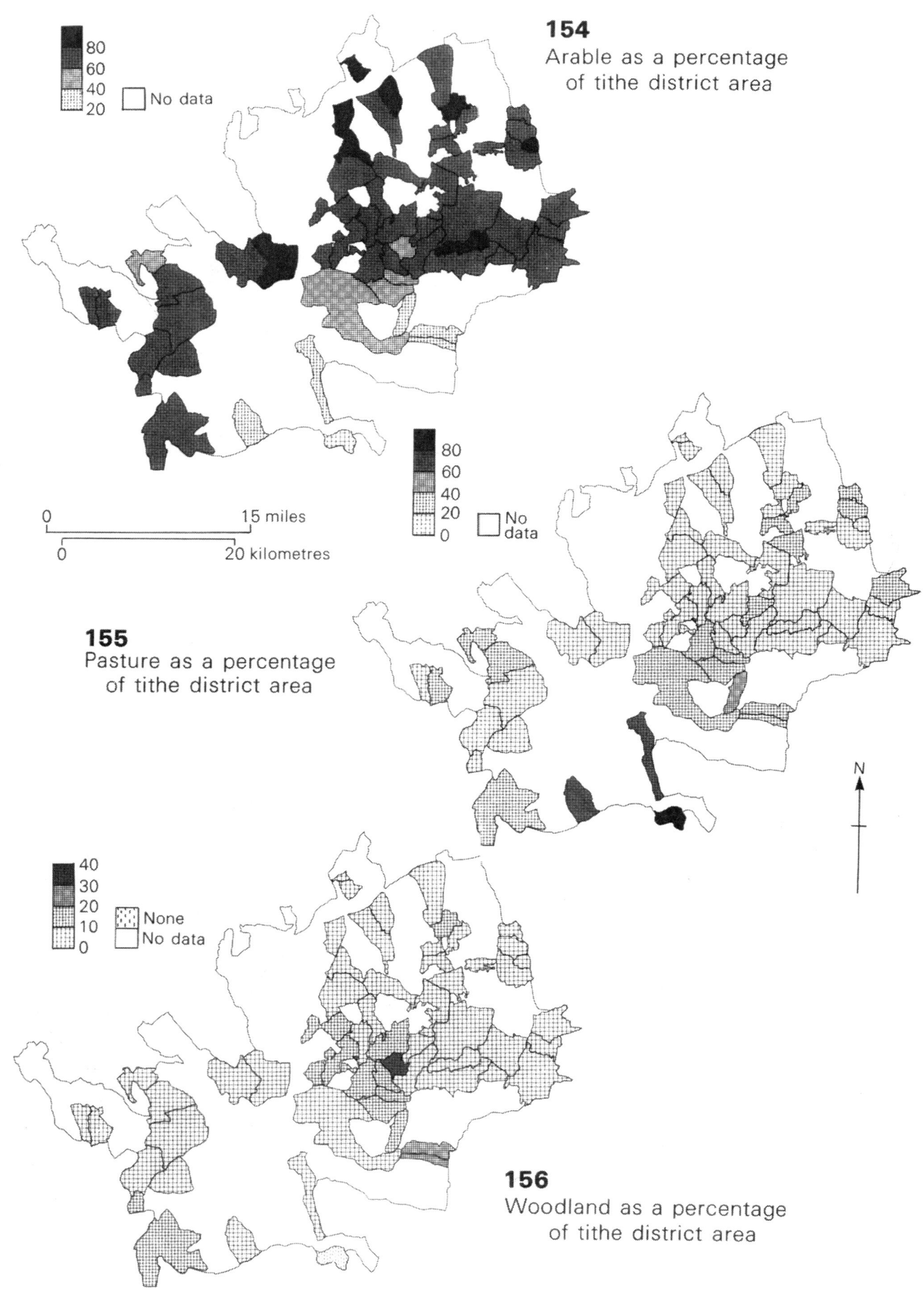

154 Arable as a percentage of tithe district area

155 Pasture as a percentage of tithe district area

156 Woodland as a percentage of tithe district area

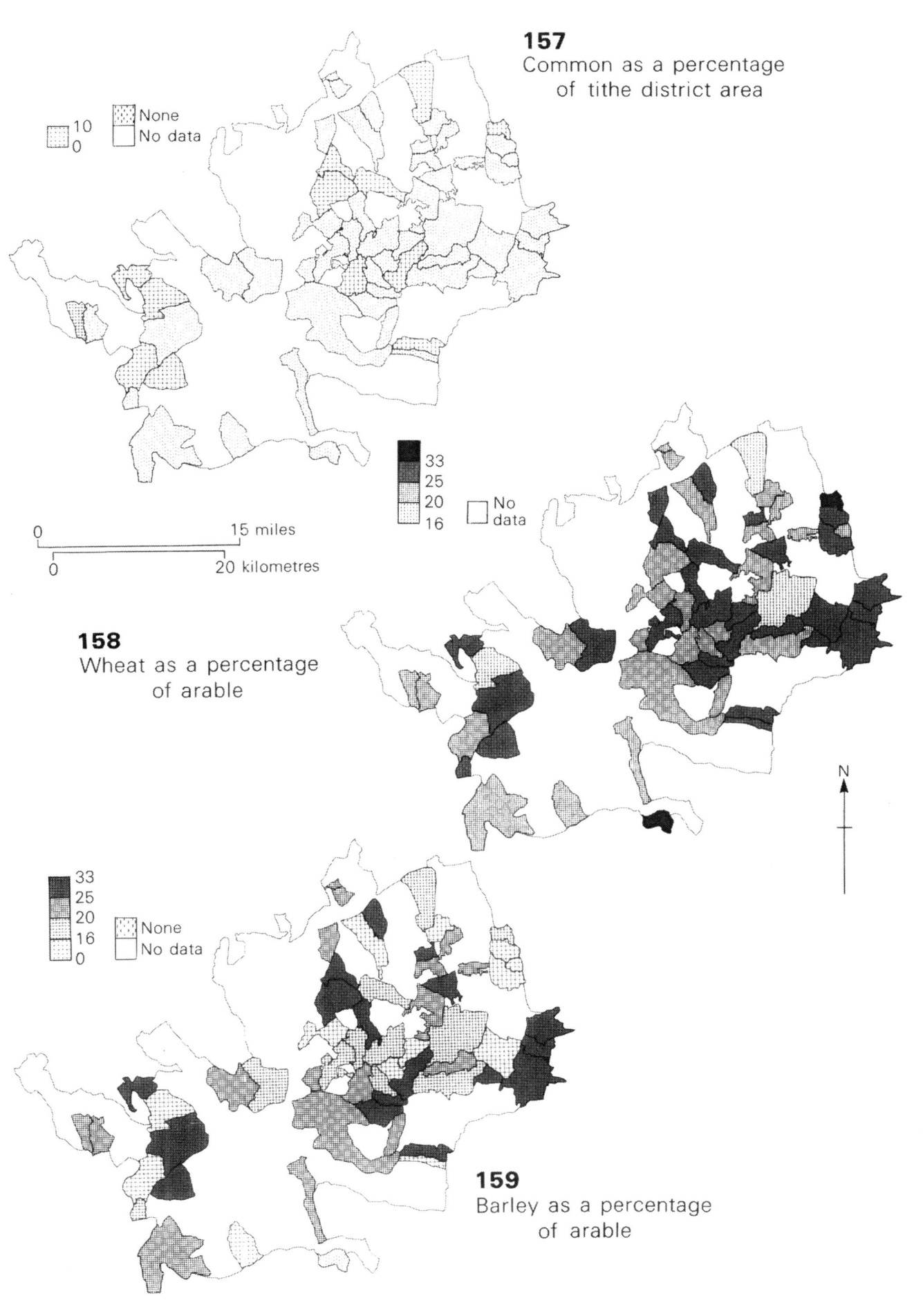

157 Common as a percentage of tithe district area

158 Wheat as a percentage of arable

159 Barley as a percentage of arable

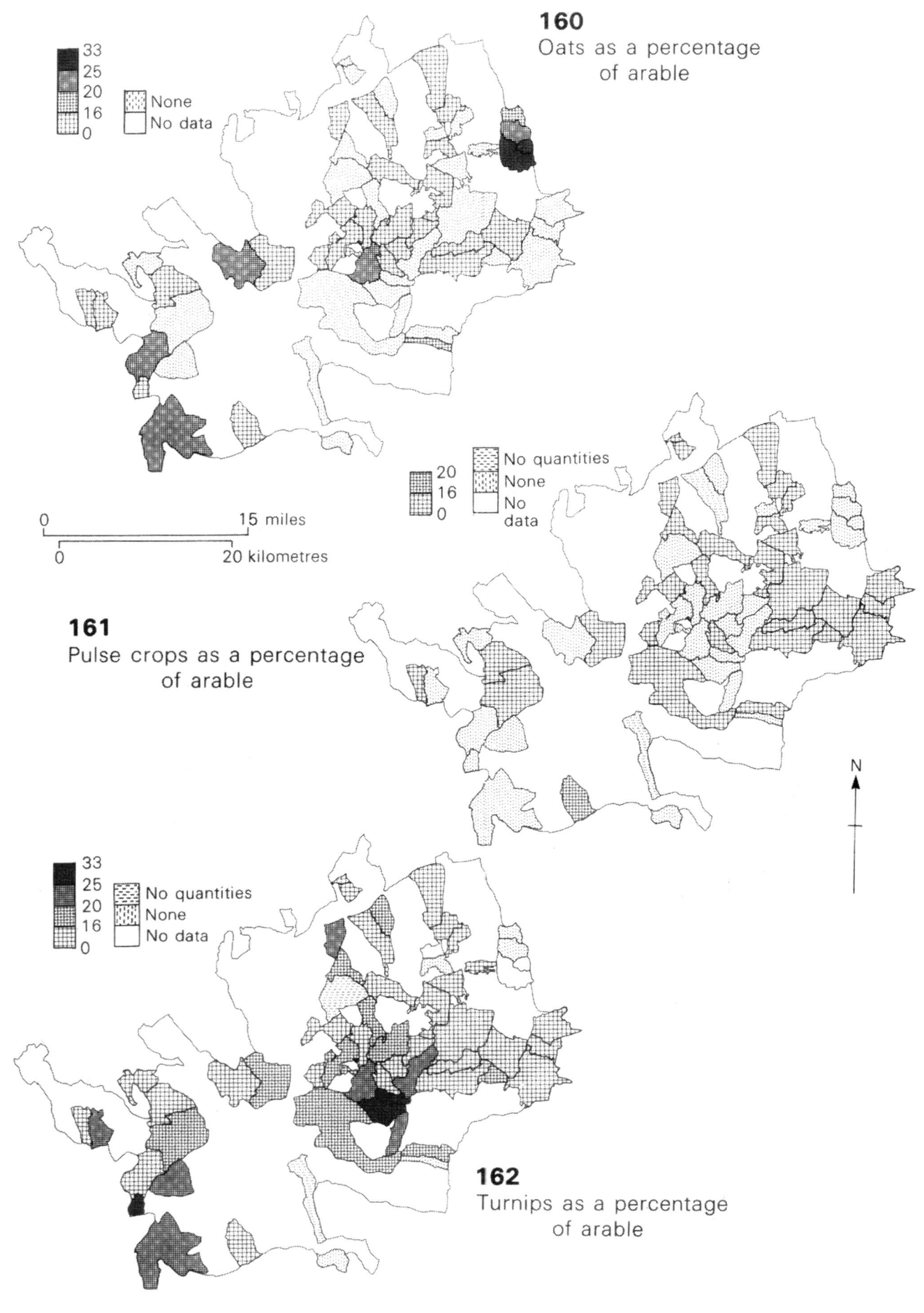

160 Oats as a percentage of arable

161 Pulse crops as a percentage of arable

162 Turnips as a percentage of arable

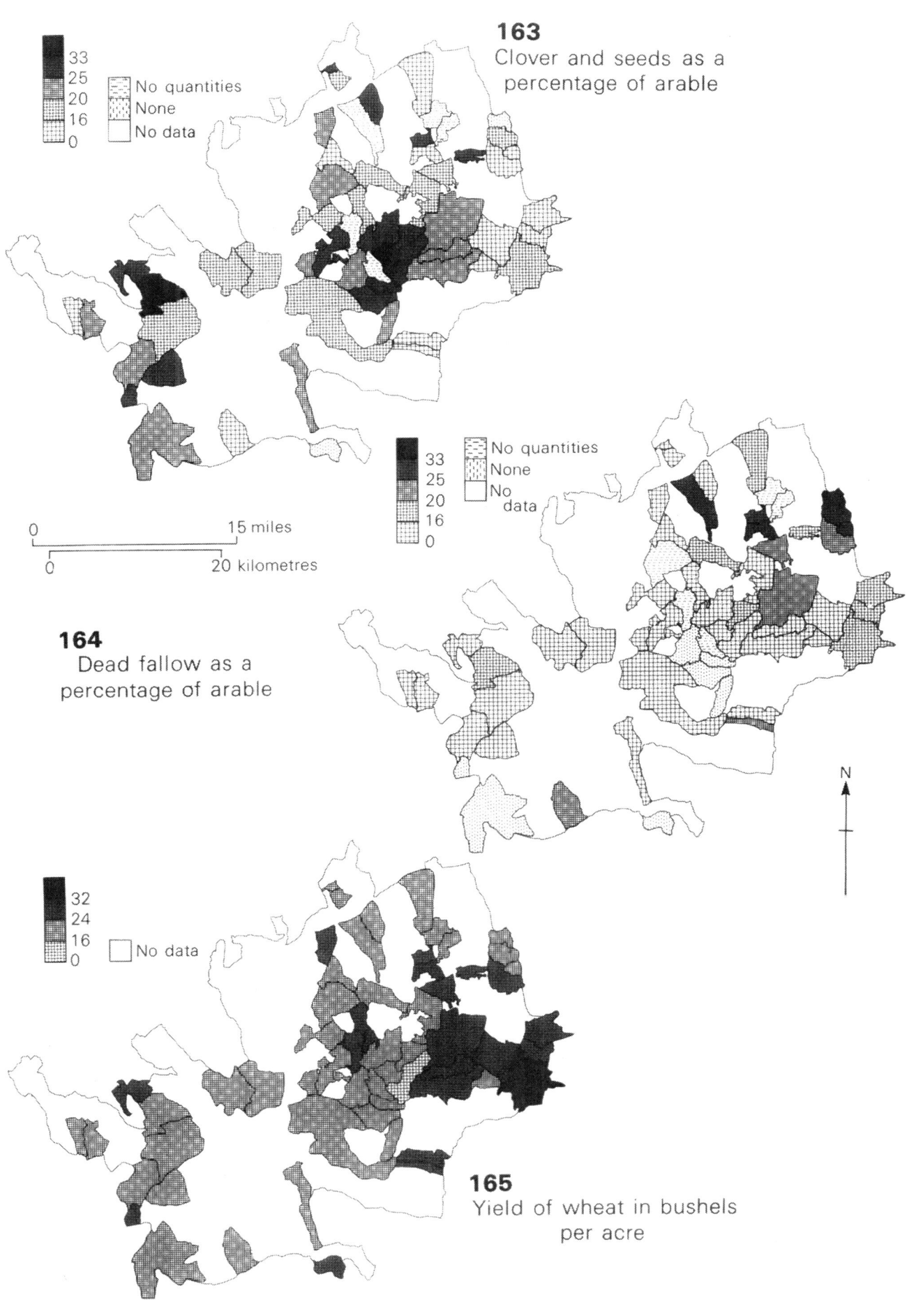

163 Clover and seeds as a percentage of arable

164 Dead fallow as a percentage of arable

165 Yield of wheat in bushels per acre

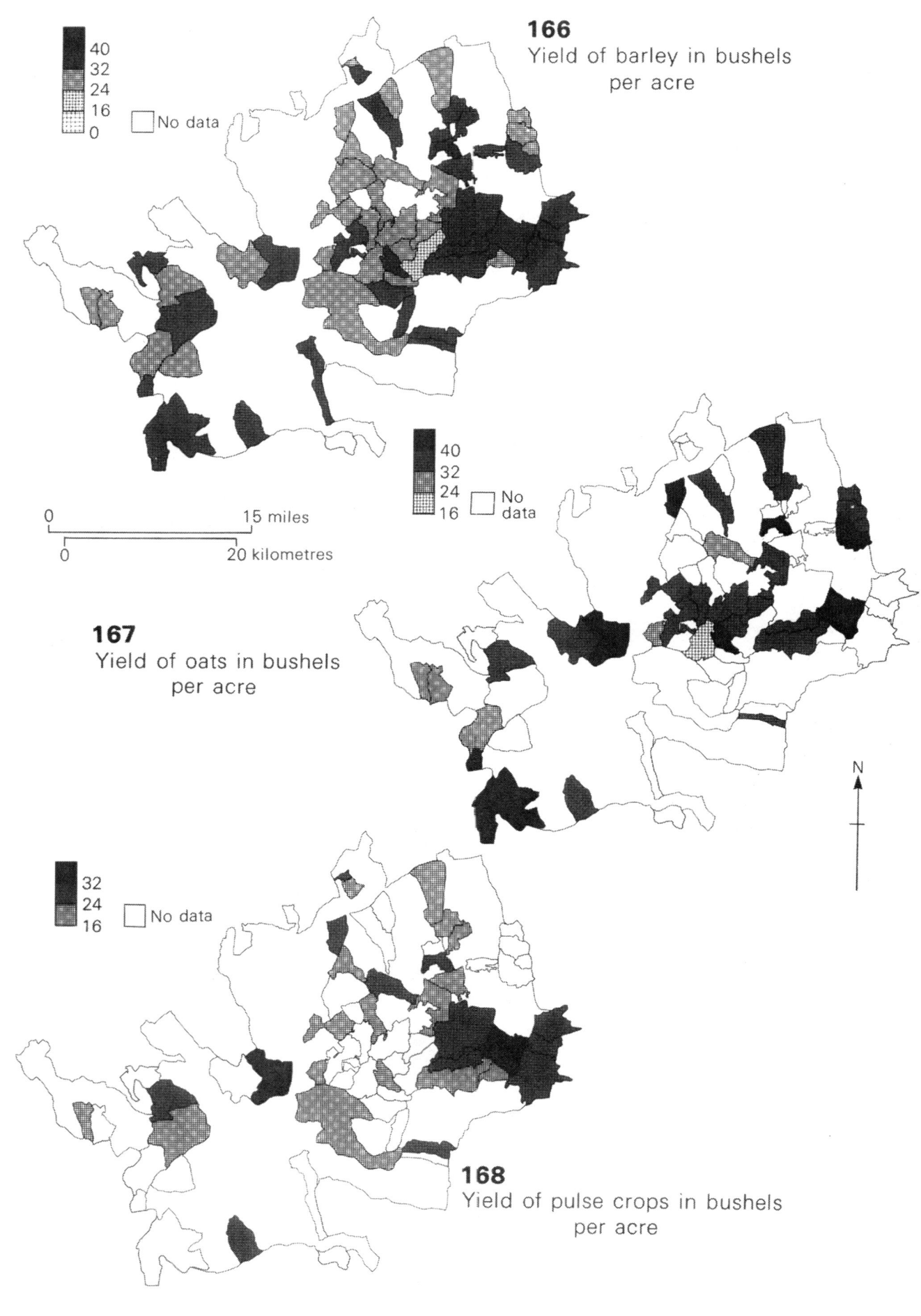

166 Yield of barley in bushels per acre

167 Yield of oats in bushels per acre

168 Yield of pulse crops in bushels per acre

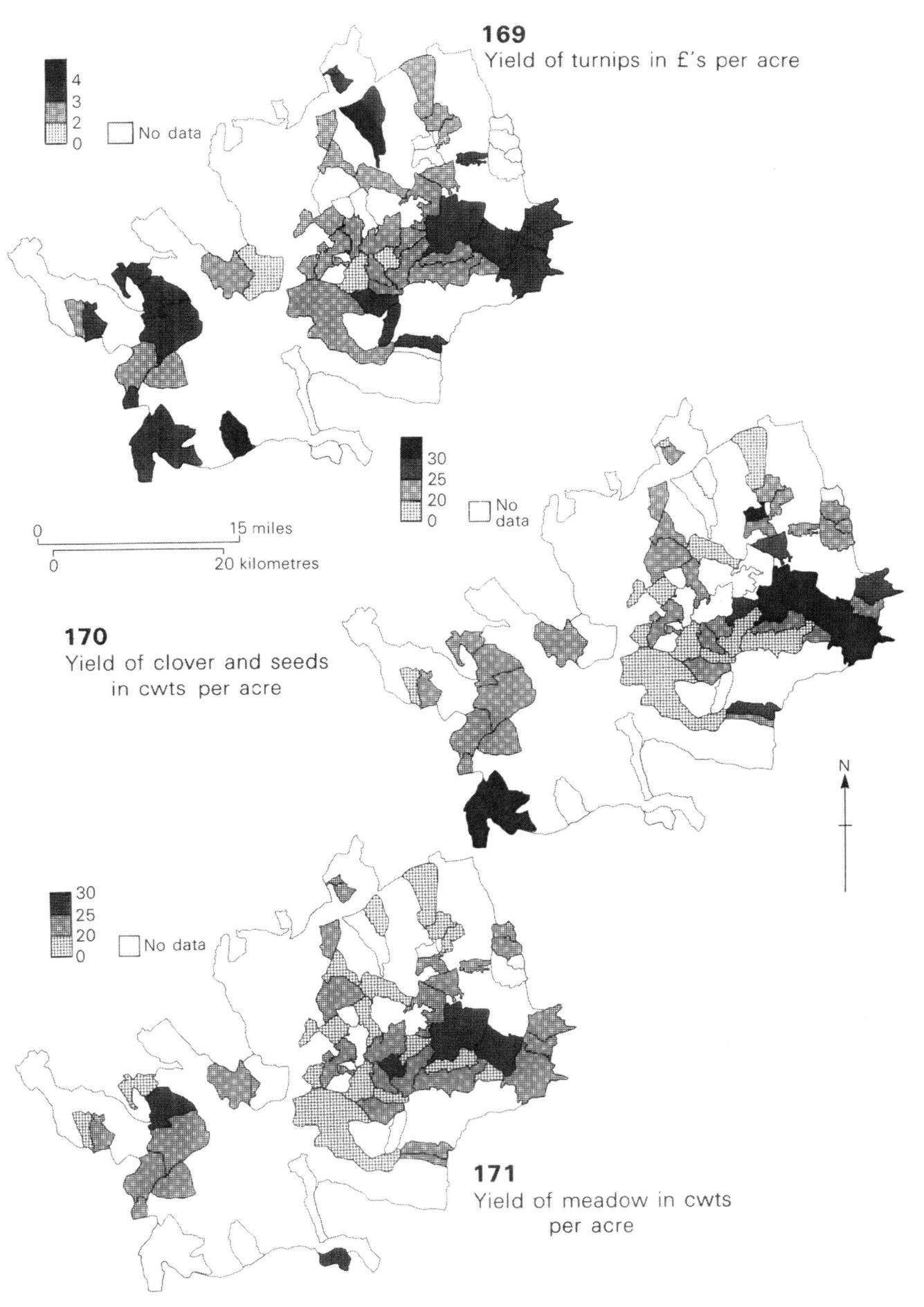

169 Yield of turnips in £'s per acre

170 Yield of clover and seeds in cwts per acre

171 Yield of meadow in cwts per acre

136   **Southern counties**

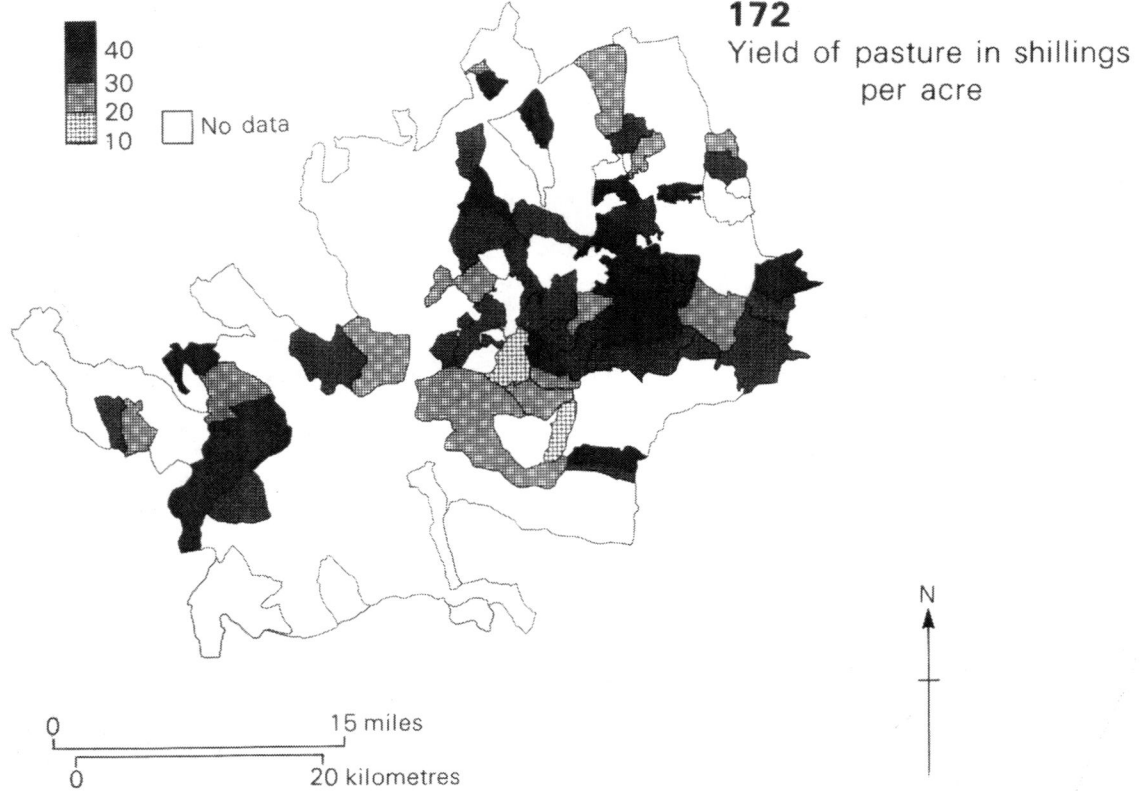

172
Yield of pasture in shillings per acre

Berkshire

188 tithe districts
101 reports on tithe agreements

F. D. Hartley (1953) has constructed field-by-field maps of arable, grass and wood for Chiltern Berkshire parishes from tithe apportionments and maps.

Many Berkshire parishes remained in open field at the time of tithe commutation and in seventeen tithe districts local agents commented similarly to John Mee Mathew at Shinfield, south of Reading, that 'the quantity of produce would be greatly increased if the common fields were inclosed and brought into a state of equal cultivation with other lands in the parish'. A number of parishes on the Berkshire Downs had been affected by parliamentary enclosure with the result that this area stands out on Map 173 as the major area in the county lacking tithe file data (thirty-one districts in the county were tithe free). Table 20 shows that for a county of the small size of Berkshire, its reports on tithe agreements were compiled by a relatively large number of agents; Thomas Clements Parr completed three and a half times as many as any other individual but only 35 per cent of the total. His work for the Tithe Commission was restricted almost entirely to this county and his reports are not particularly full. His usual practice was to extrapolate parish conditions from those that he observed at its largest farm. Of Berkshire reports, 86 per cent were compiled in the four years 1838–41 inclusive.

Table 21 and Maps 175–8 indicate that Berkshire was an essentially arable county c. 1840; only in parts of the western clay lands, the eastern sandy heathlands and in a few places in the Thames valley were arable percentages of less than 40 and grassland percentages of more than 60 to be found. In only seventeen districts was the ratio of arable to grass less than 1.5 to 1. Almost all the downland parishes north of Newbury were more than 60 per cent arable and many were more than 80 per cent ploughed. Downland as a category of land use was not consistently classified by assistant commissioners and local agents. Where it was not separately enumerated, it is not clear whether it had been subsumed in common or grassland in parish statistics. Water meadows were enumerated in many parishes, particularly those traversing the valleys of the rivers Kennet, Lambourn and Thames. These were generally reckoned highly productive with ewes and lambs being depastured on them during April when there was little other pasture after which the meadows would be cut twice for hay. Beech woodland was exempt from tithe in Berkshire and Map 177 and the total figure of 37,749 acres of wood in the whole county relate only to titheable underwood. A common complaint in those files where woodland management is discussed is the shortage of good underwood and the high demand for it for hurdles and firewood so that it was rarely allowed to stand for more than seven years before cutting.

Table 21 and Maps 179–85 reflect the general adoption of four-course rotations in Berkshire, if not always strict Norfolk four-courses. On heavy clay soils west of Wallingford a variation was wheat, beans, barley or oats, fallow with vetches, clover or turnips; on rich sandy soils in the Vale of White Horse: wheat, beans, barley, clover. On lighter soils and especially on the poorest chalk soils, longer rotations were used with perhaps only two or three corn crops in eight years when, as Parr noted at Chaddleworth, north-west of Newbury, 'in the more hilly district of the parish a large proportion of the arable is allowed to remain for six or seven years in sainfoin and is thus taken out of the ordinary course of cropping'. Near to Windsor and Reading, arable land was not worked under a normal rotation, instead much land was given over to the cultivation of vegetable and fodder crops. Similarly around Newbury, John Pickering found 'there is no *system* of farming; a comparatively large extent of cabbage seed and potatoes are grown and to these the general agriculture of the parish appears to me to be sacrificed'. Industrial crops, particularly ozwiers, were cultivated around Reading; 'cultivation of these eyotts is attended with great expense and a large quantity of oziers are cut in consequence'.

The high average yield figures in Table 21, and particularly the distribution of parish yield figures in Maps 186–91, are reflections as much of the prodigious natural fertility of the soil in some parts of the county as of especially high farming. Comments such as 'this district contains some of the most productive land in the kingdom, the soil is a rich sandy loam . . . ' are met with frequently in valley parish descriptions. There is only repeated mention of high farming as such in districts near Reading; poor farming is much more frequently commented upon. In some light land parishes it was considered that farmers overcropped the land, in others that heavy land was in dire need of drainage. Lighter lands could be made to carry more stock in the opinion of the Tithe Commission's agents and would thus be better manured and produce more corn. At Brightwaltham, north of Newbury, assistant commissioner Roger Kynaston was struck by the recent improvement in the system of agriculture and noted that here at least 'the farmers are convinced . . . no stock, no corn'. Some places were of course favourably located for the import of manures. Horace William Meteyard commented at Aldermaston that rape and oil cake were obtained from Reading by the Kennet navigation, although tolls were too high to allow other less costly manures to be conveyed. The Kennet and Avon Canal which connected with the Thames at Reading did, though, offer a great facility for conveying produce to the London market.

Table 20 *Reports on agreements for commutation of tithes in Berkshire*

Assistant commissioner local tithe agent	1837	1838	1839	1840	1841	1842	1843	Totals
Thomas Clements Parr				22	13			35
Joseph Townsend	2	7		1				10
F. Browne Browne			10					10
Roger Kynaston		8	2					10
Thomas Smith Woolley	2				1	1	5	9
Horace William Meteyard		1	6					7
John Mee Mathew		4	2					6
Henry Jemmett		1	4					5
John Pickering			5					5
William Heard						2	1	3
Charles Pym	1							1
Totals	5	21	29	23	14	3	6	101

Table 21 *Land use, crops and yields in Berkshire c. 1836*

A	Land use	Percentage of total land area enumerated in reports on tithe agreements	Estimated acreage in whole county
	Arable	58.5	263,956
	Grass	24.9	112,097
	Wood	8.4	37,749
	Common	5.9	26,813

B	Crop	Mean percentage of arable	Mean yield per acre	Estimated acreage in whole county
	Wheat	24.0	24.2 bushels	63,425
	Barley	15.6	34.7 bushels	41,210
	Oats	8.4	40.3 bushels	22,032
	Pulses	5.7	29.4 bushels	15,122
	Turnips	17.7	£2.74	46,687
	Seeds	23.3	22.7 cwts	61,488
	Fallows	5.0	—	13,240

140 Southern counties

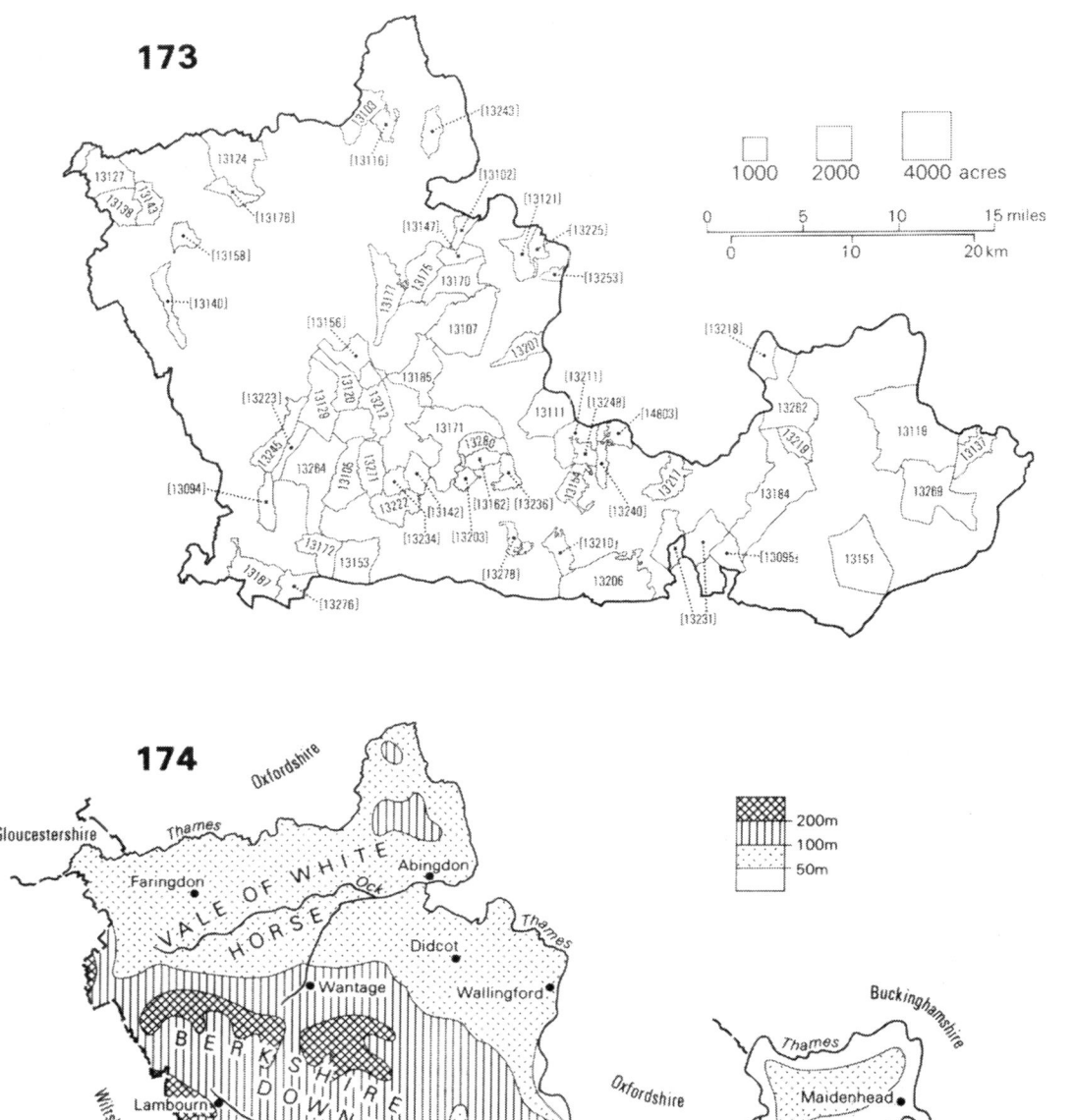

Berkshire

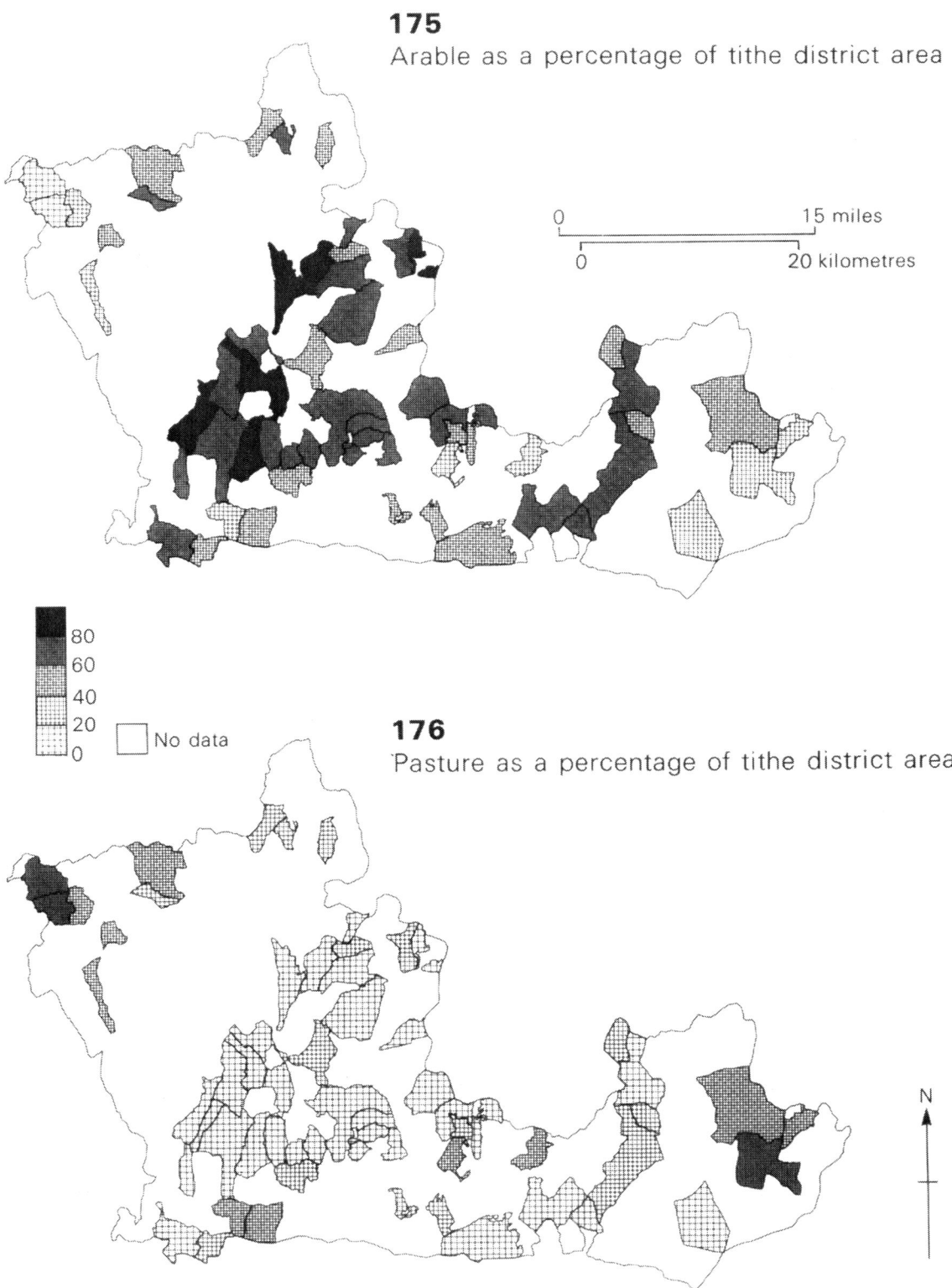

175 Arable as a percentage of tithe district area

176 Pasture as a percentage of tithe district area

Southern counties

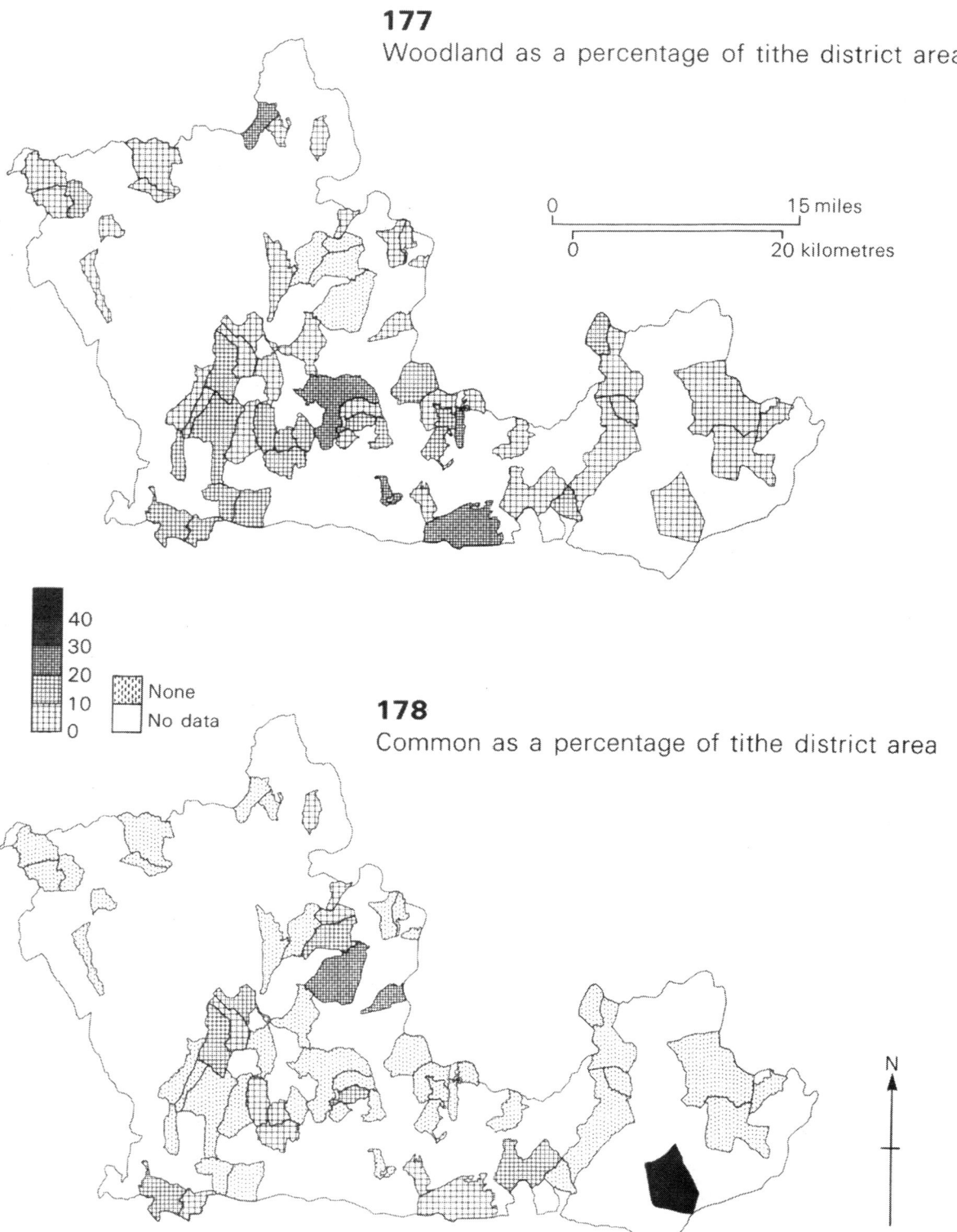

177 Woodland as a percentage of tithe district area

178 Common as a percentage of tithe district area

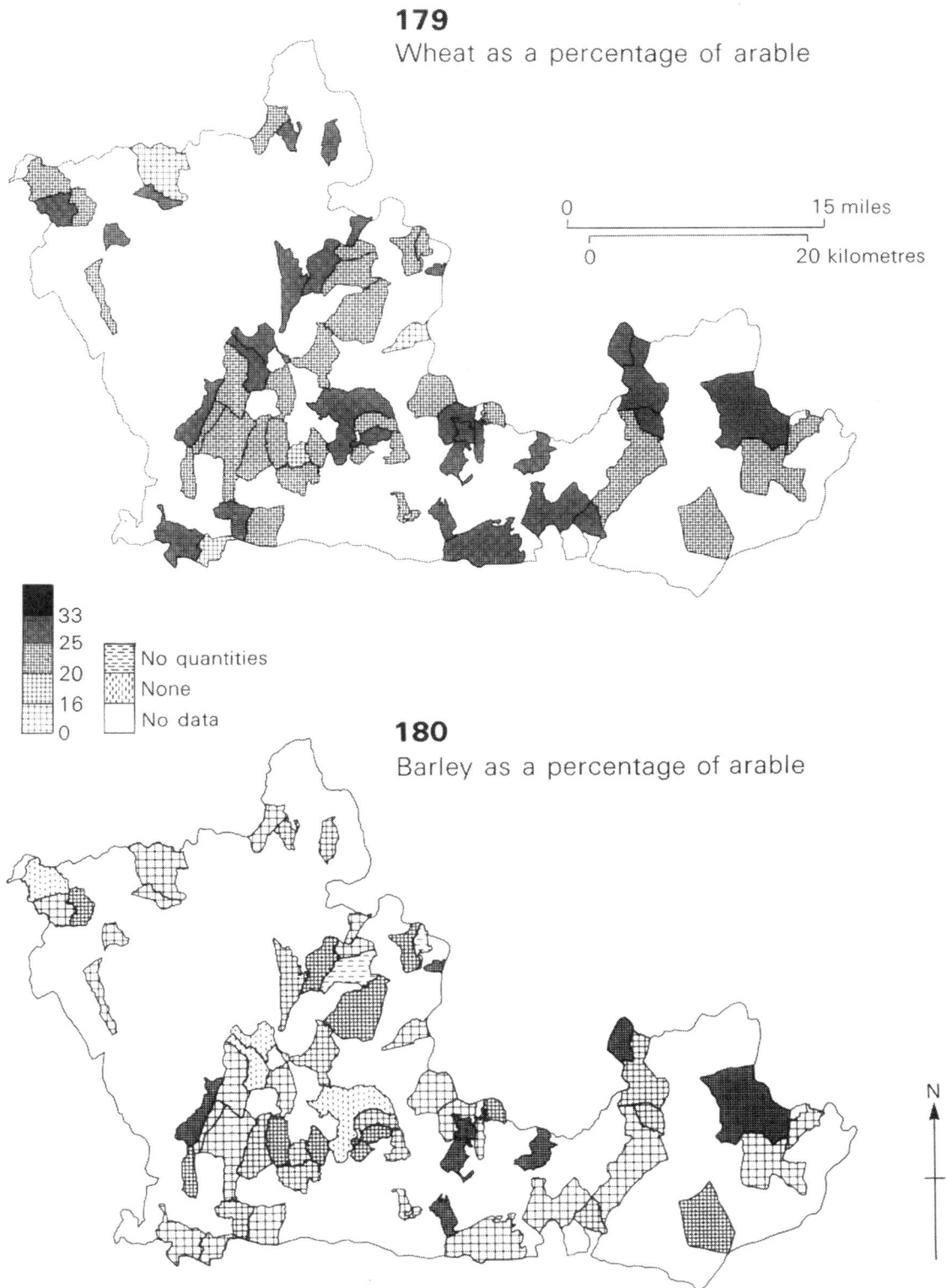

179 Wheat as a percentage of arable

180 Barley as a percentage of arable

144 Southern counties

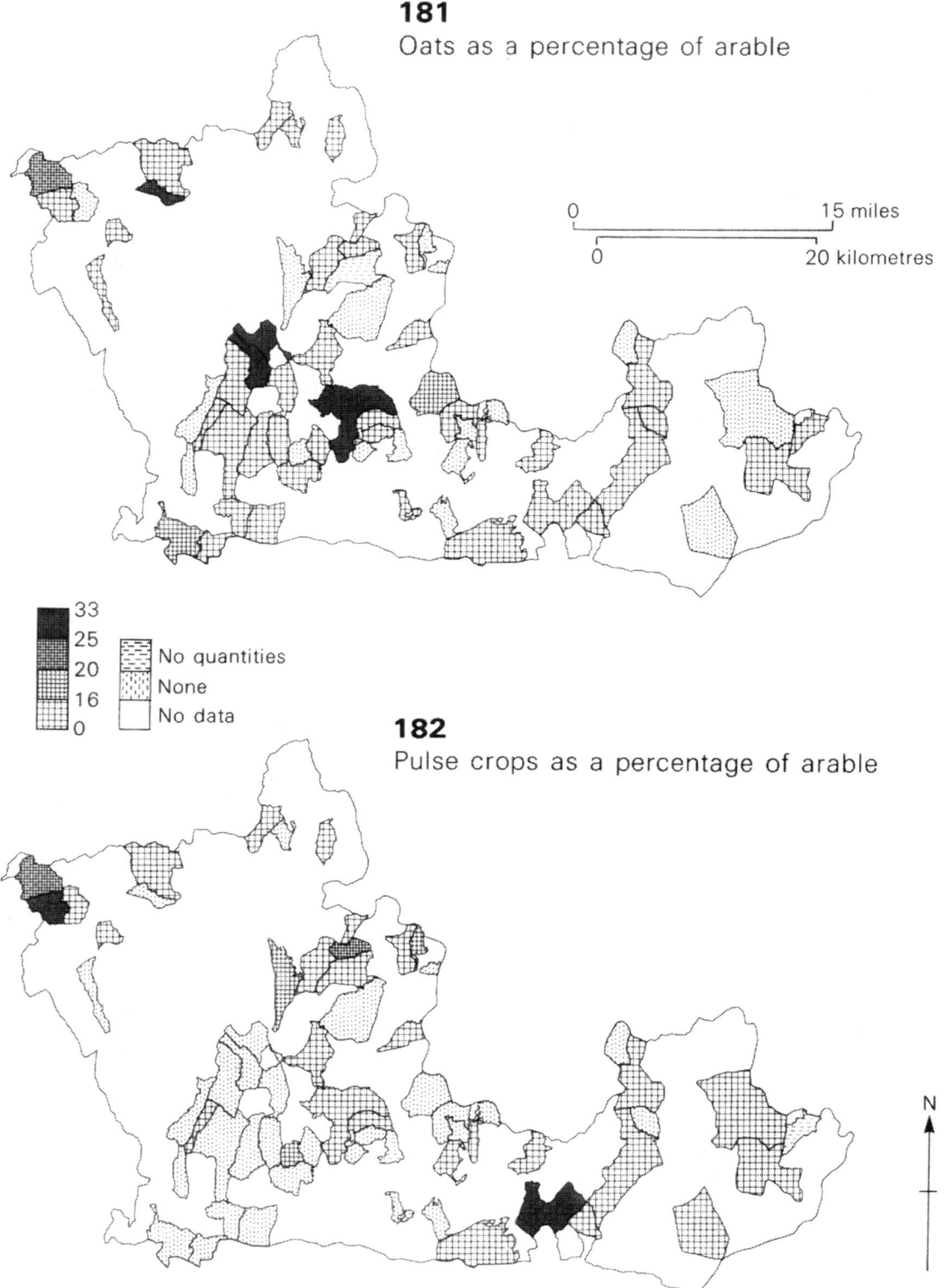

181
Oats as a percentage of arable

182
Pulse crops as a percentage of arable

Berkshire

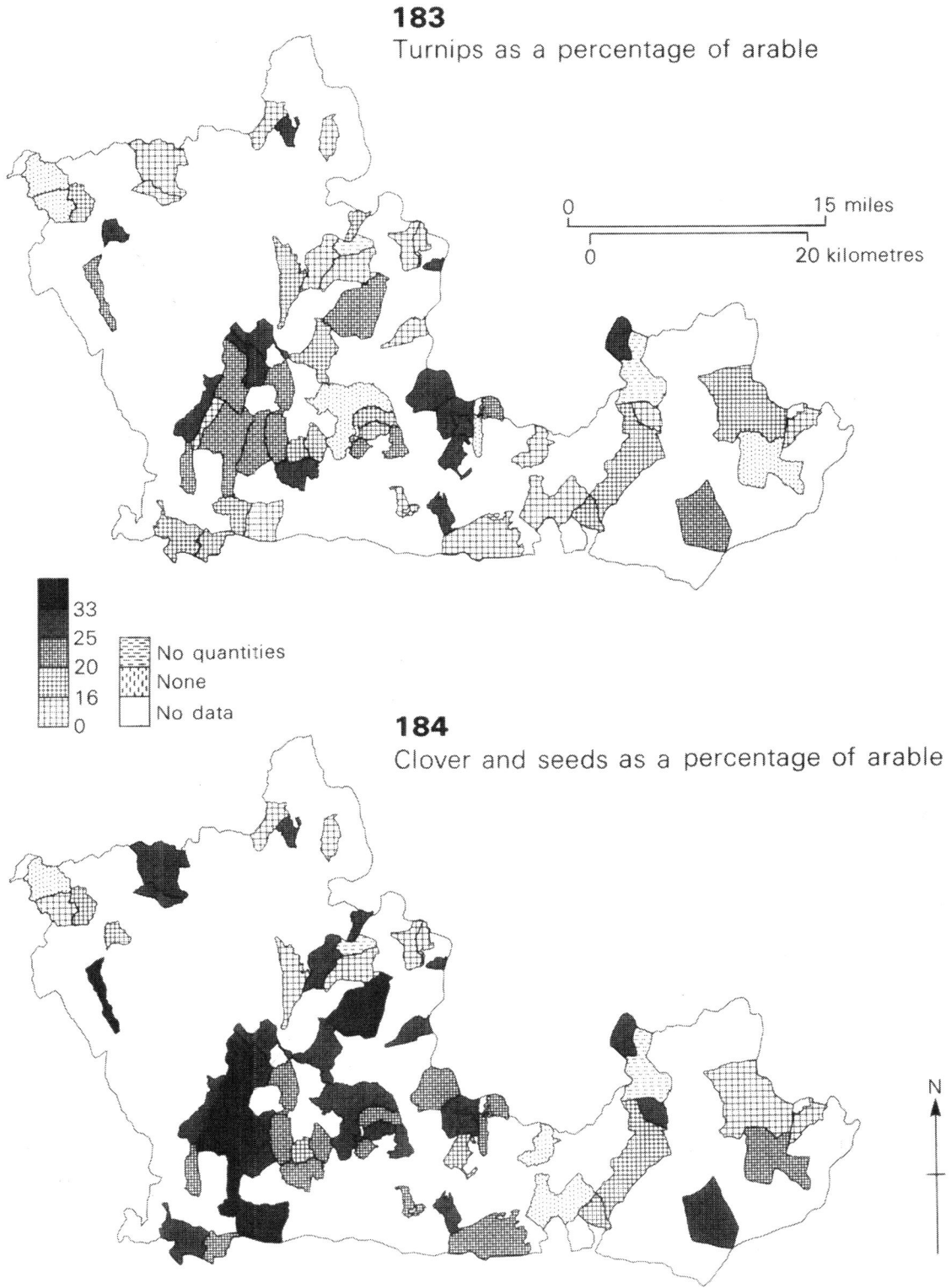

183 Turnips as a percentage of arable

184 Clover and seeds as a percentage of arable

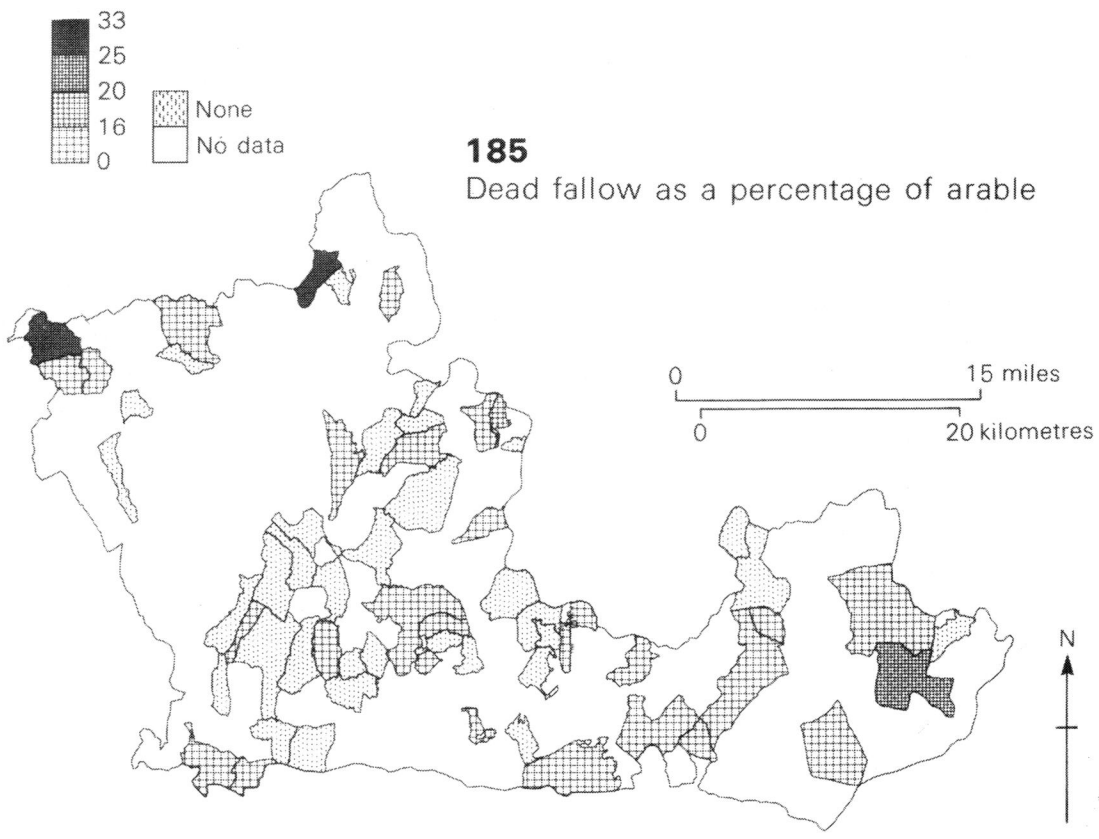

185
Dead fallow as a percentage of arable

Berkshire

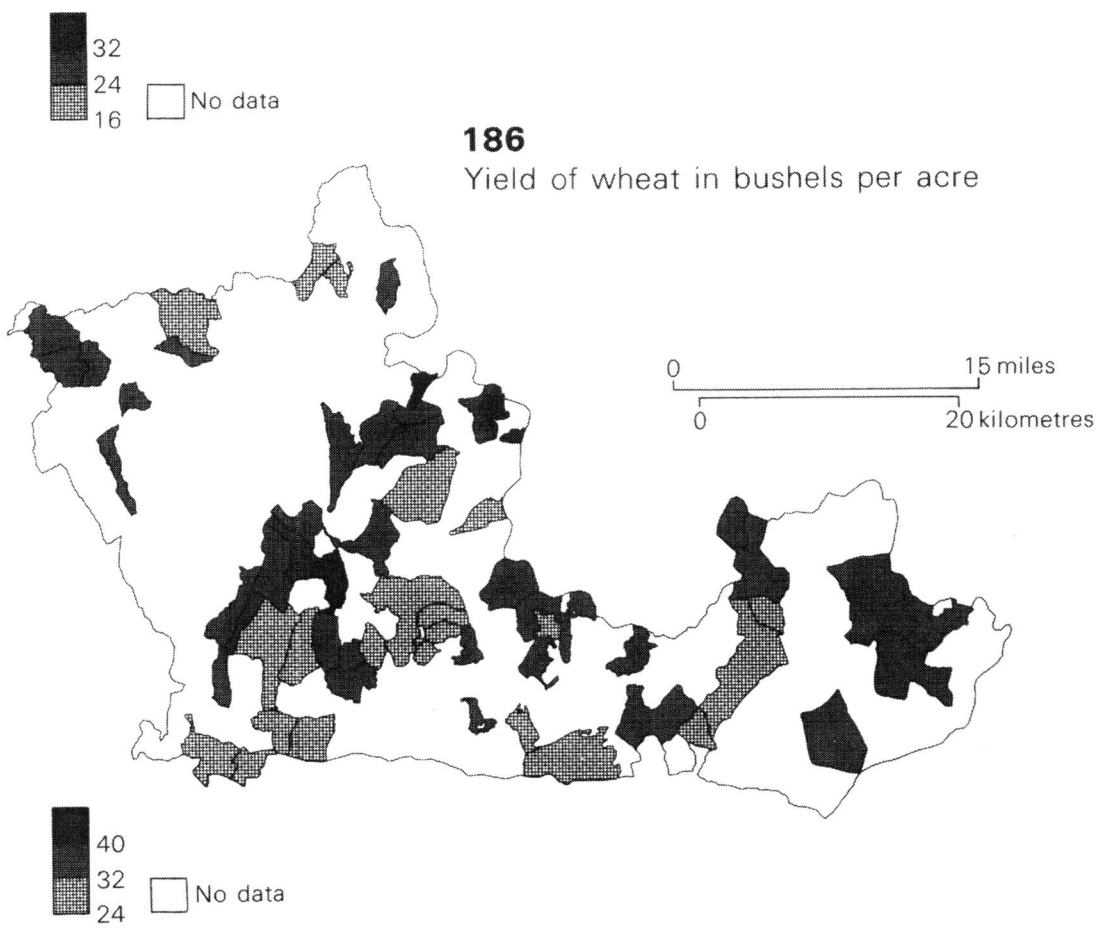

186 Yield of wheat in bushels per acre

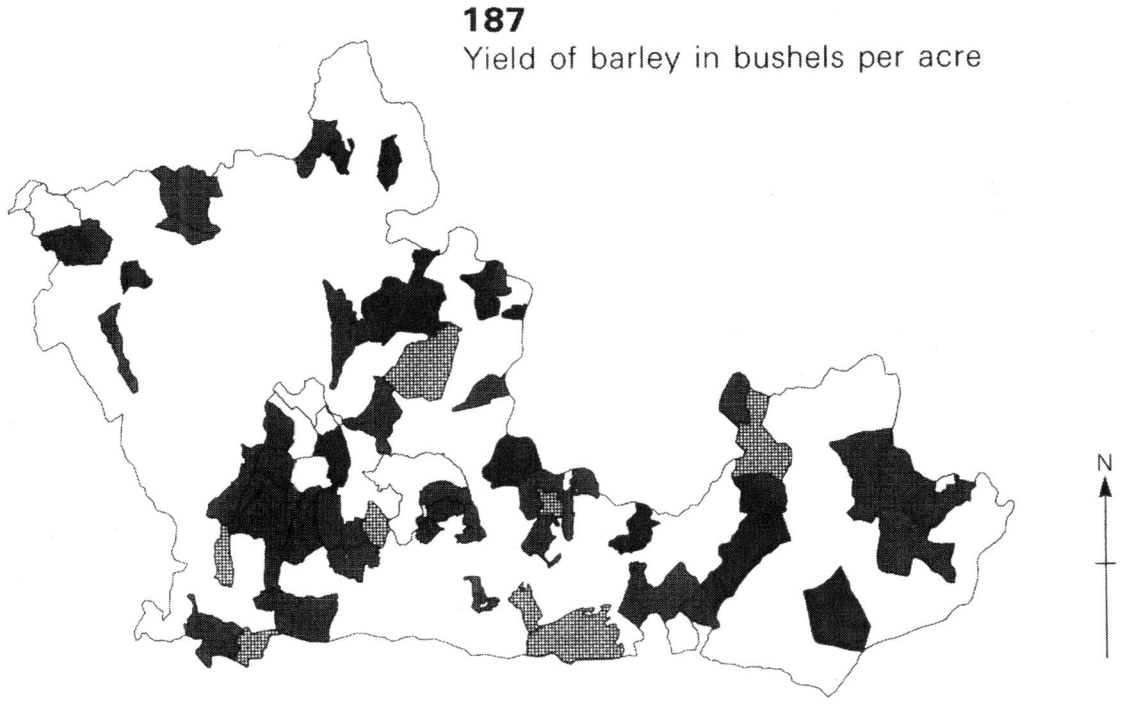

187 Yield of barley in bushels per acre

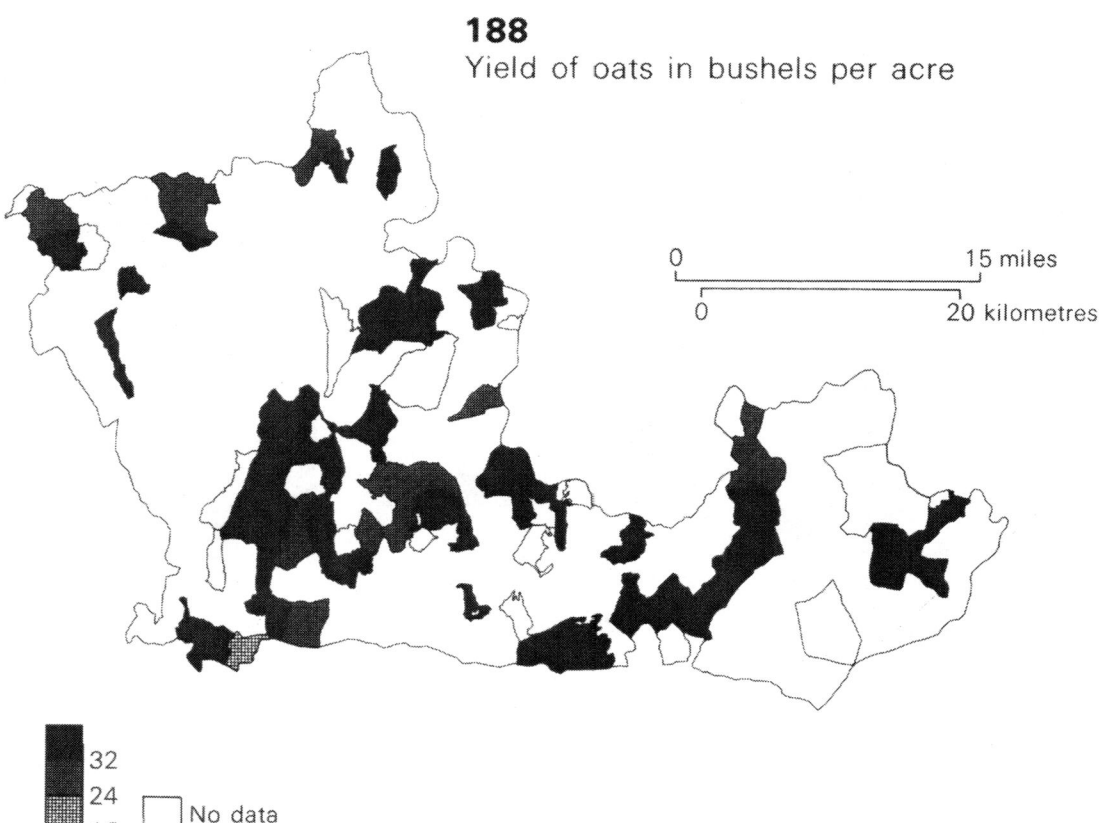

188 Yield of oats in bushels per acre

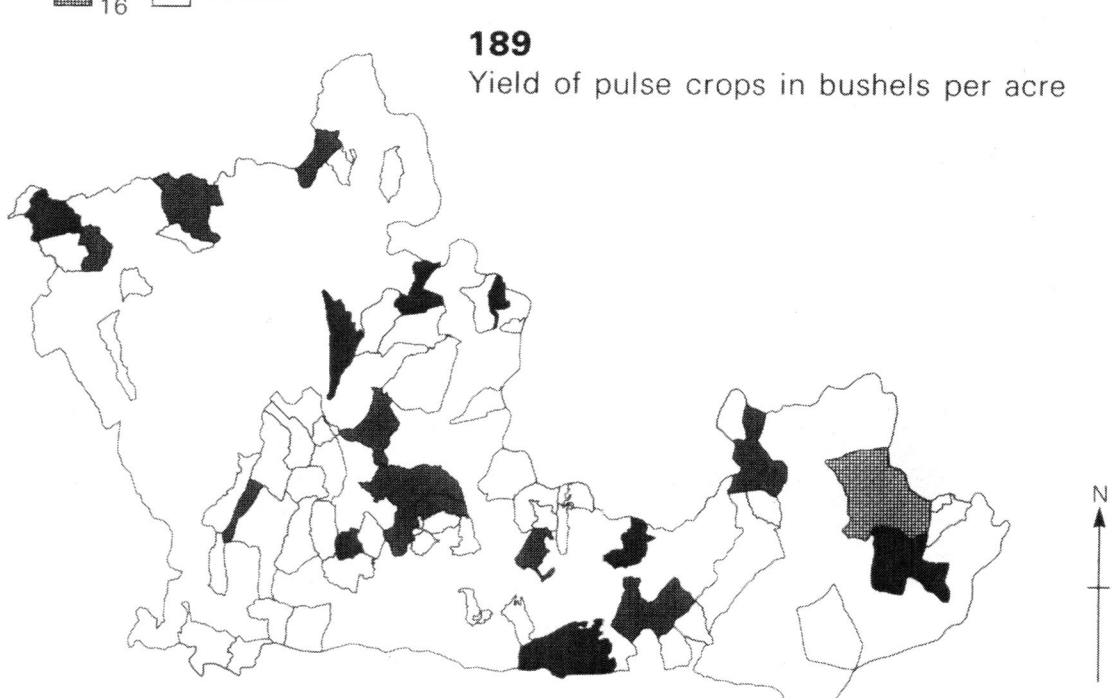

189 Yield of pulse crops in bushels per acre

Berkshire

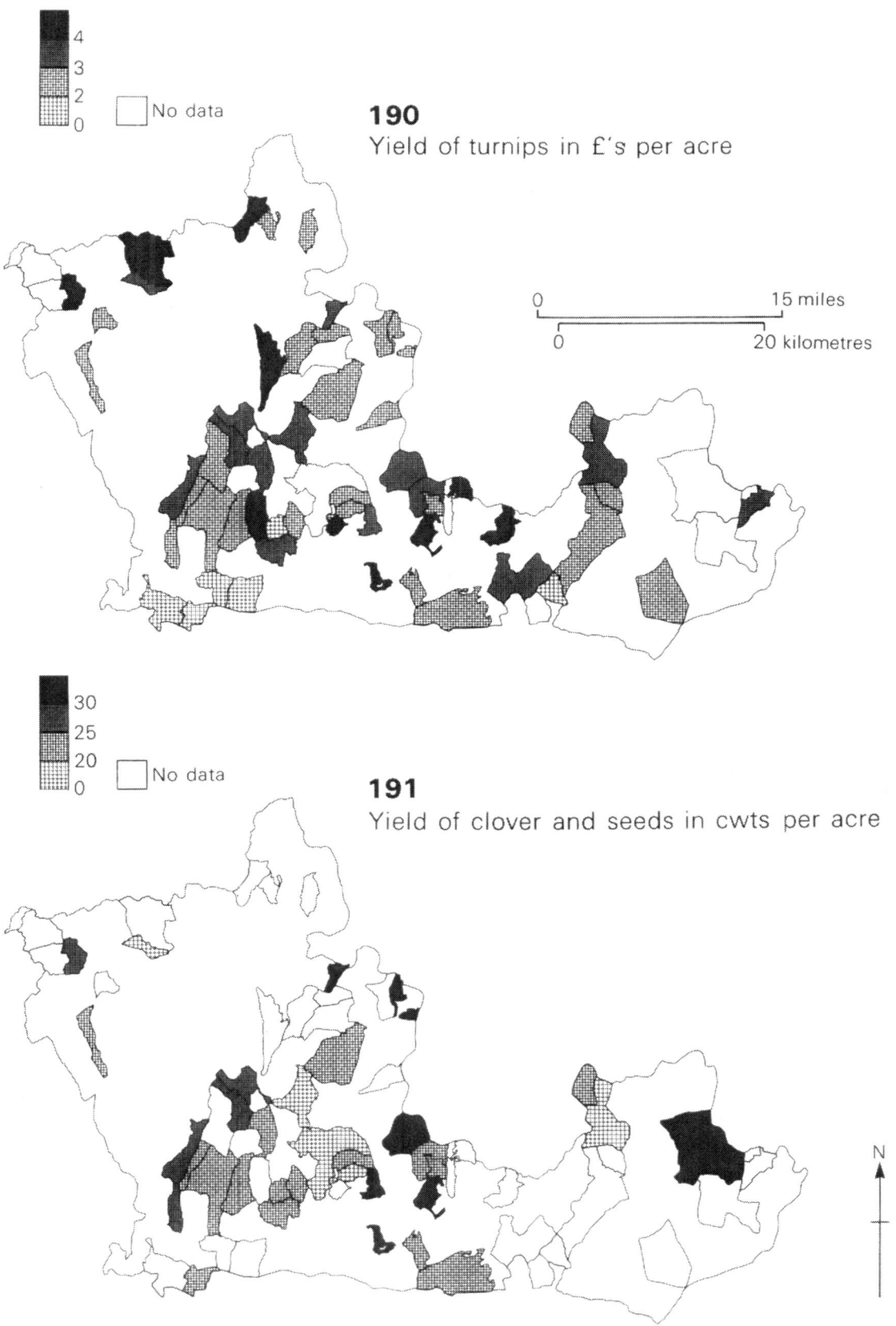

190
Yield of turnips in £'s per acre

191
Yield of clover and seeds in cwts per acre

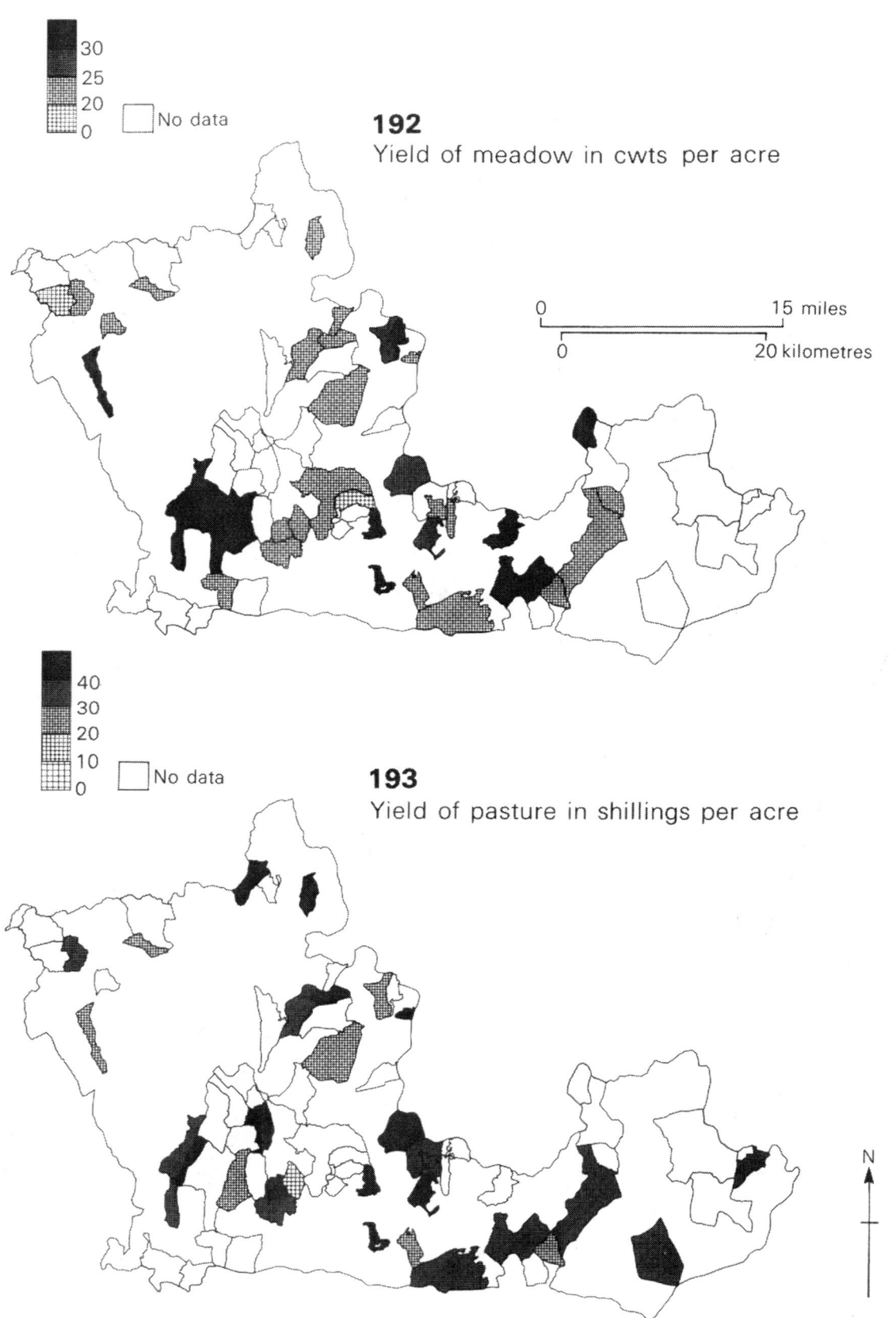

192 Yield of meadow in cwts per acre

193 Yield of pasture in shillings per acre

Hampshire

354 tithe districts
189 reports on tithe agreements

Tithe maps, apportionments and files are used extensively by M. C. Naish (1961) in his thesis on agricultural change on the Hampshire chalklands, and J. Philip Dodd (1979a) has employed descriptive material from tithe files to support evidence from the 1854 agricultural statistics in his study of Hampshire agriculture in the mid-nineteenth century.

In 60 per cent of Hampshire parishes tithe commutation was effected by voluntary agreement. The New Forest was the main area tithe free (by virtue of its status as crown land); thirty-eight parishes were totally exempt in Hampshire but in many others only vicarial tithes remained payable by 1836. In these districts, assistant commissioners, with the exception of William Heard, did not enumerate corn crops as great tithes had been extinguished. As in Dorset, the presence of large tracts of open downland occasioned indecision and inconsistency of recording – sometimes as pasture, alternatively as common. A. O. Baker and Charles Osborn wrote about a third of all Hampshire reports on tithe agreements (Table 22). As a body, Hampshire tithe files are not particularly illuminating on farming practices; some commissioners spend as much space describing landscape – 'the bare, unenclosed chalk hills' of F. Browne Browne – parks, country houses and settlements as they do the system of farming. John Mee Mathew saw 'the great attraction of Farnborough as the tout ensemble of its locality – within 30 miles of the metropolis and contiguous to the Royal haunts of Bagshot – it is studded with villas and diversity of plantations'.

Evidence from the tithe files summarised in the Tables, Maps and Subject Index, points to the overwhelming areal dominance of arable land in Hampshire c. 1840. In chalkland parishes more than 80 per cent of all land was ploughed and in only five tithe districts, all on clay soils, was the ratio of arable to pasture less than 1.4 to 1. On light soils, five- and six-course rotations are usually recorded; at Blendworth, adjoining Horndean, Horace William Meteyard defined the Hampshire system adopted there as 'a five-shift, turnips, barley, 2 years ley and wheat with about one fifth of the entire arable in sainfoin'. At Buckholt, high on the chalk and six miles from Salisbury, 'the system of cropping, from the great difference in the depth and quality of the soil, is necessarily irregular, wheat being taken in some instances at four, and in others at only seven years'. On some of the very poorest soils, as in parts of Liss parish, rye was grown in place of wheat but cut green for use as a fodder crop. Sainfoin might be planted on land that was too light and poor to produce corn and so enable a larger flock of sheep to be kept. On the heaviest, undrained clays, dead fallows were still quite widespread. Pulse crops are not much discussed in this county but small acreages were grown in a few parishes. Hops were an important component of arable farming in parishes bordering on Sussex and focussing on Farnham as a centre. Files of places such as Bentley contain a wealth of detail on the cultivation of this crop which yielded an average of 6 cwts an acre.

In light soil parishes, many of which had extensive tracts of downland, sheep rearing was a vital ingredient of the farming system. At Iwield, William Heard recorded in 1844 that

> there appears to be a good number of sheep kept for which the dryness of the soil is well adapted and without which but little produce could reasonably be expected. Light artificial manures such as guano and bone dust are extensively used for the turnip crop to enable the cultivator to keep more sheep to enrich the soil which in moist seasons repays him for the capital.

At Longstock, on the river Test, and other similarly sited valley parishes, 'very little sainfoin is grown, the water meadows chiefly supplying the sheep with hay'.

Towns such as Portsmouth could furnish 'immense supplies of manure' while at Michelmersh, near Romsey, 'there are chalk pits in the southern part of the parish and much use is made of this as manure'. Chalking went hand-in-hand with draining heavy soils. Although a number of tithe agents reported such attempts at improvement, their comments about poor, backward farming and the natural poverty of many light soils outweigh those of high farming or highly productive crops in this county (see Subject Index). Horace William Meteyard's comments at Hursley are by no means unique in Hampshire tithe files: 'it would surprise anyone that had seen only the turnip crops in the north of England or in Norfolk or Suffolk, to see the miserable thin produce of this shift, often yards apart between each turnip and these of the smallest size'.

Table 22 *Reports on agreements for commutation of tithes in Hampshire*

Assistant commissioner/ local tithe agent	1837	1838	1839	1840	1841	1842	1843	1844	1845	Totals
A. O. Baker	9	10	21	6						46
Roger Kynaston		7	15	1						23
Charles Osborn		10	6	6						22
F. Browne Browne			3	2	13					18
Joseph Townsend	4	4		7						15
John Mee Mathew		8	3	2						13
Thomas Smith Woolley	7		1		2					10
Horace William Meteyard			3	6						9
John Farncombe		4					5			9
William Heard							6	2	1	9
Thomas Clements Parr			3	3						6
John Pickering							6			6
Thomas Phippard			3							3
Totals	20	43	58	33	15	5	12	2	1	189

Table 23 *Land use, crops and yields in Hampshire c. 1836*

A	Land use	Percentage of total land area enumerated in reports on tithe agreements	Estimated acreage in whole county
	Arable	64.3	688,576
	Grass	15.5	165,603
	Wood	11.3	121,067
	Common	6.7	72,477

B	Crop	Mean percentage of arable	Mean yield per acre	Estimated acreage in whole county
	Wheat	20.6	21.5 bushels	141,700
	Barley	15.2	27.9 bushels	104,831
	Oats	5.7	35.0 bushels	39,238
	Pulses	2.2	24.3 bushels	15,207
	Turnips	16.4	£2.53	112,773
	Seeds	33.8	17.6 cwts	232,532
	Fallows	4.4	—	30,105

154   Southern counties

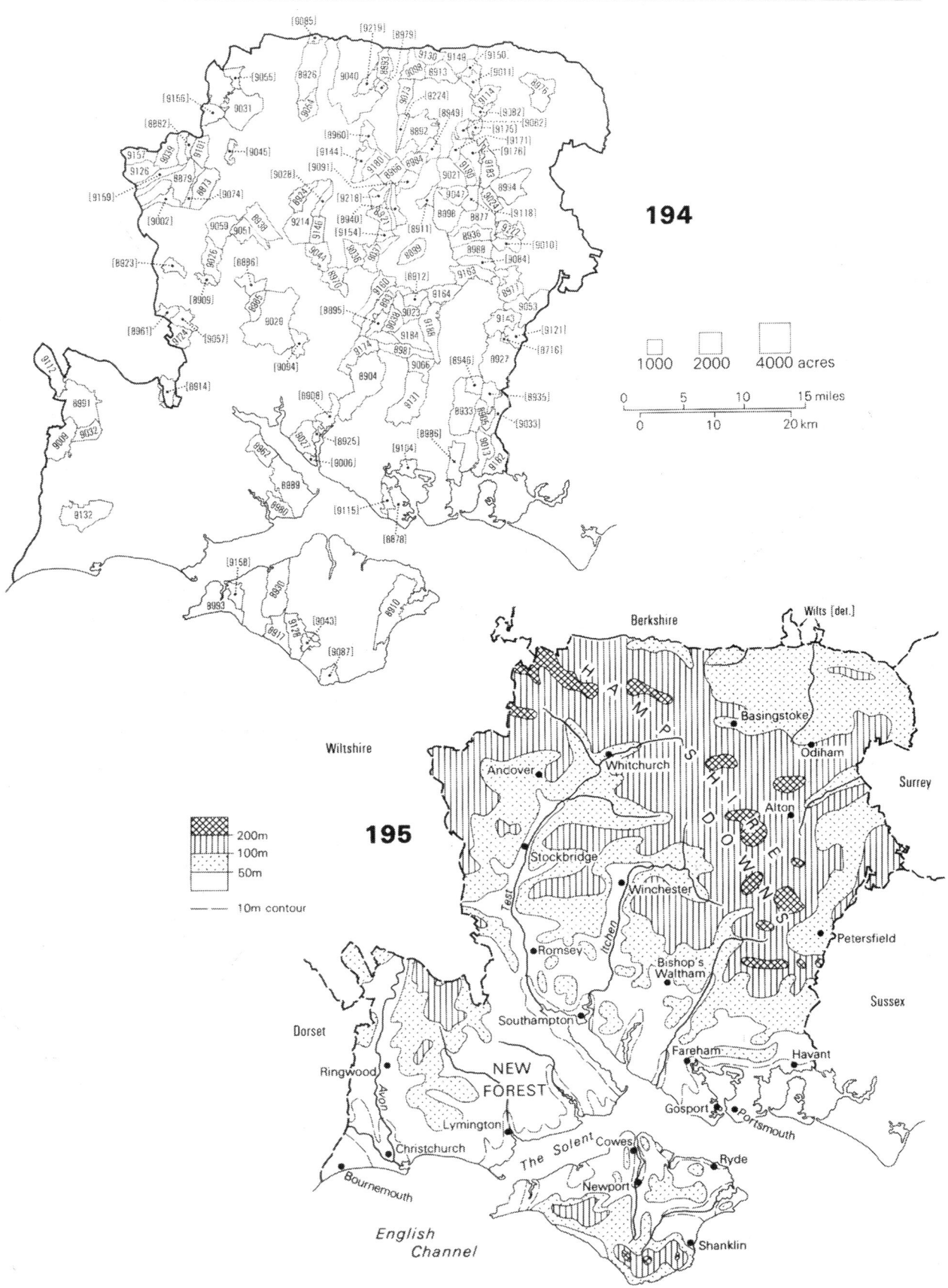

Hampshire

Arable as a percentage of tithe district area
196

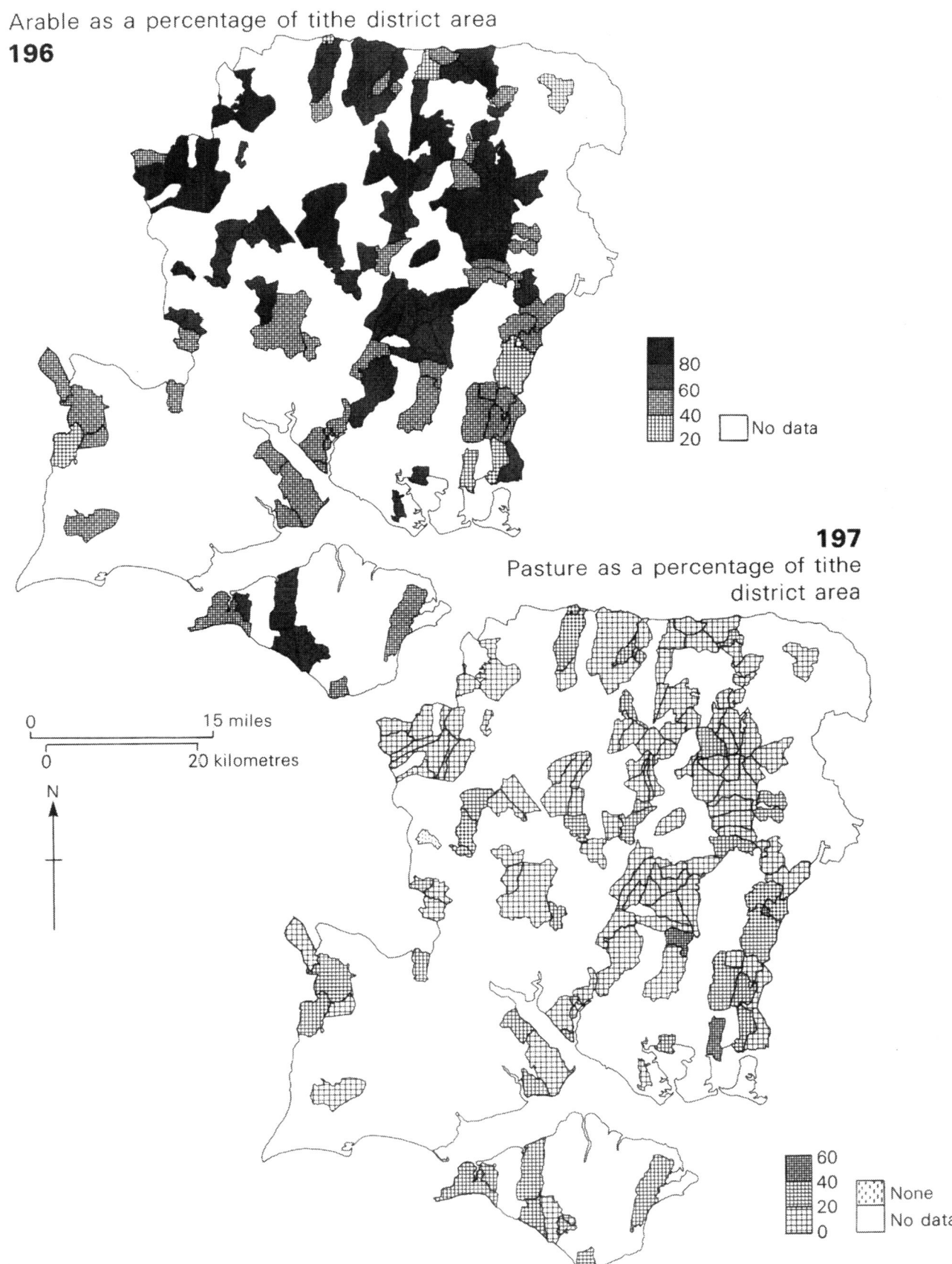

197
Pasture as a percentage of tithe district area

Woodland as a percentage of tithe district area
198

199
Common as a percentage of tithe district area

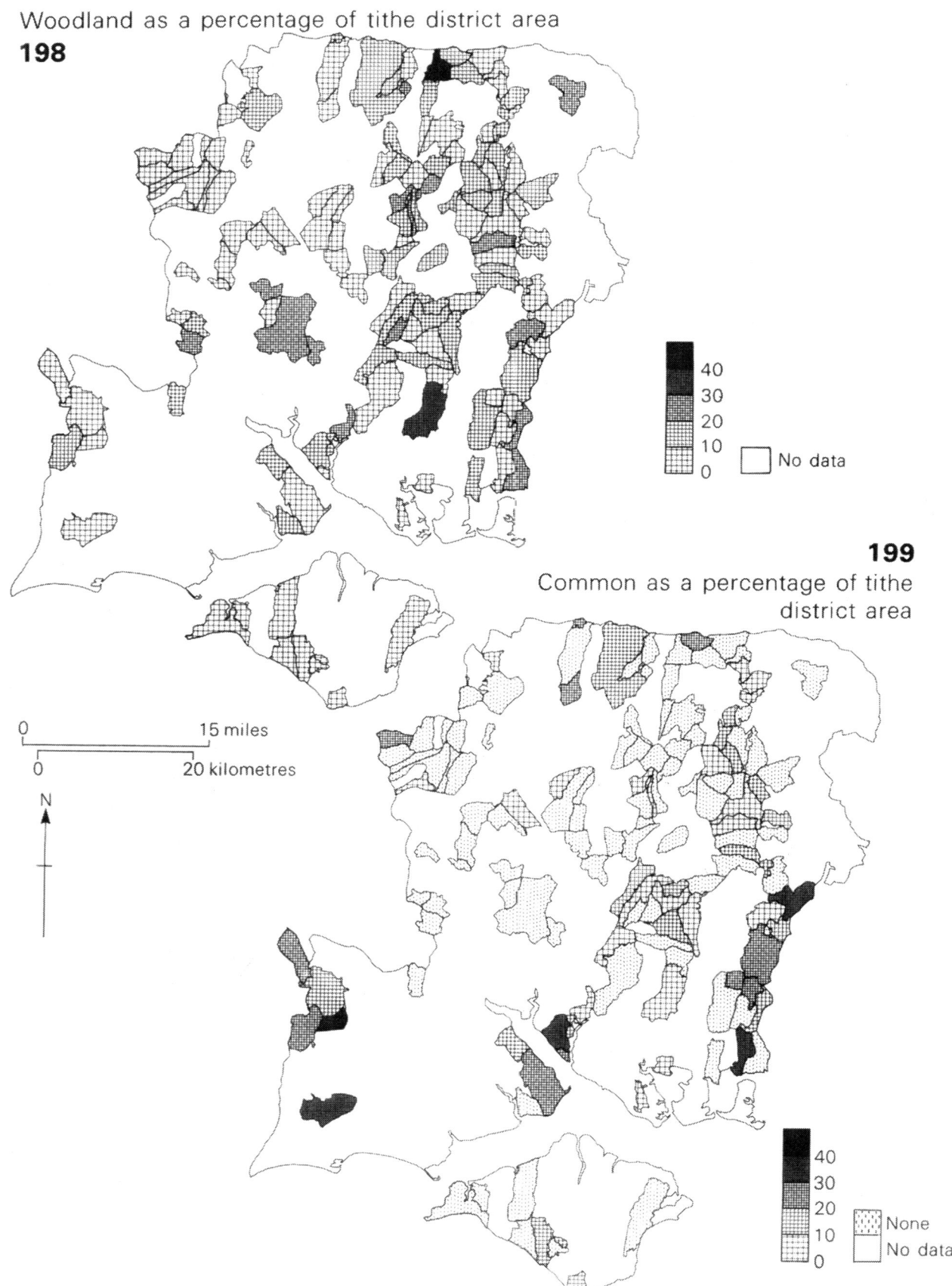

Hampshire

Hops as a percentage of tithe district area
200

201
Wheat as a percentage of arable

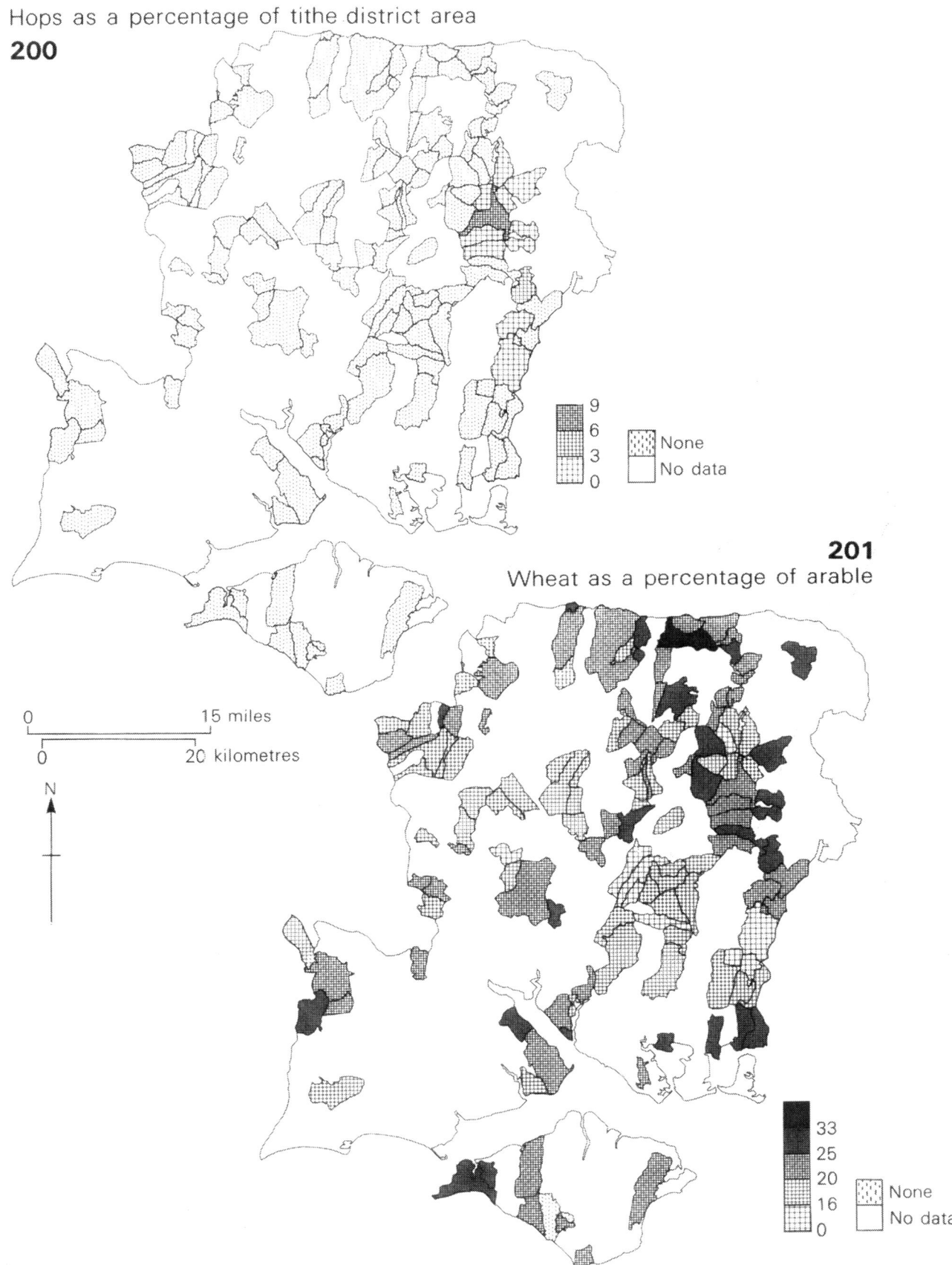

Barley as a percentage of arable
202

203
Oats as a percentage of arable

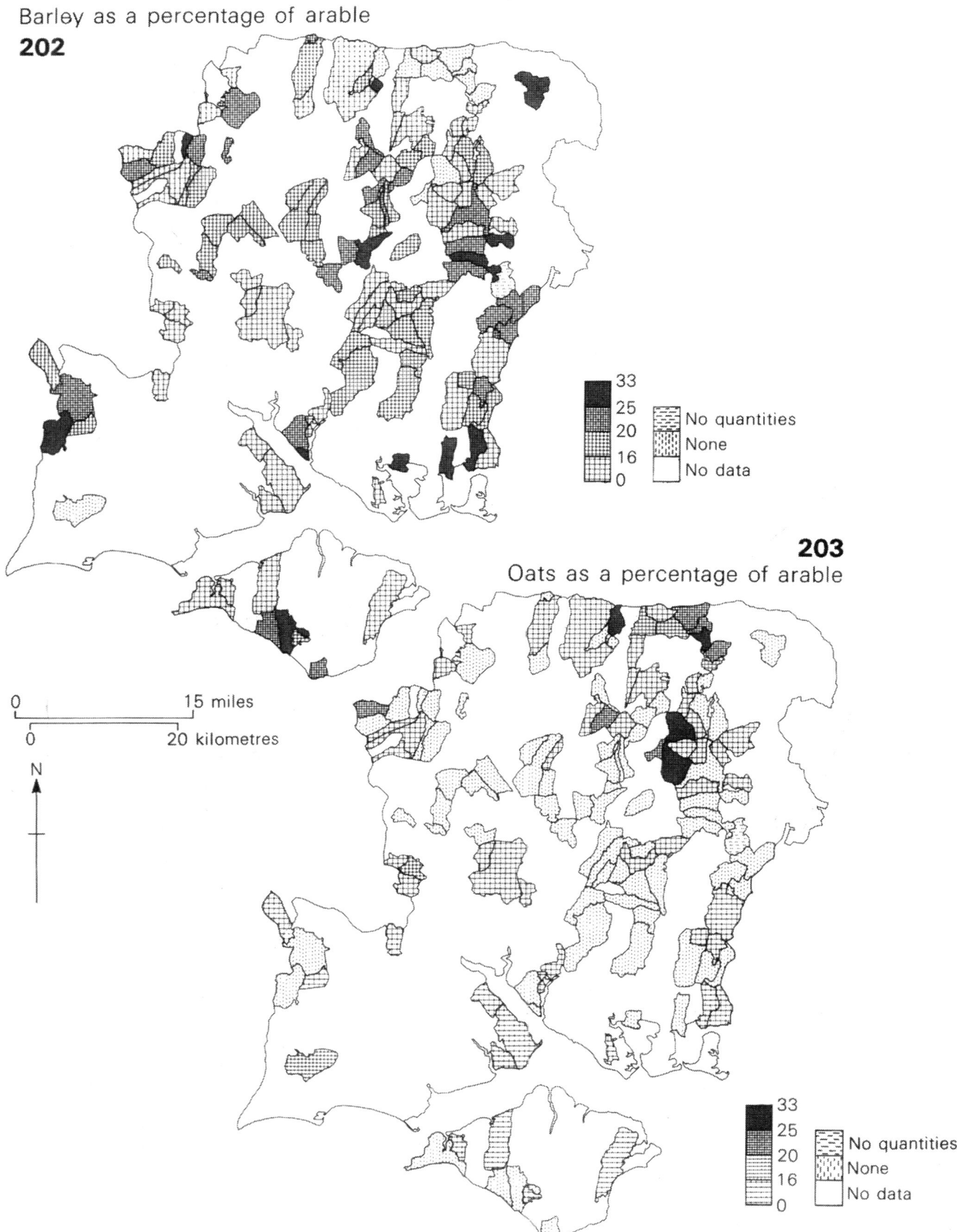

Pulse crops as a percentage of arable
204

205
Turnips as a percentage of arable

206 Clover and seeds as a percentage of arable

207 Dead fallow as a percentage of arable

Hampshire

Yield of wheat in bushels per acre
208

209
Yield of barley in bushels per acre

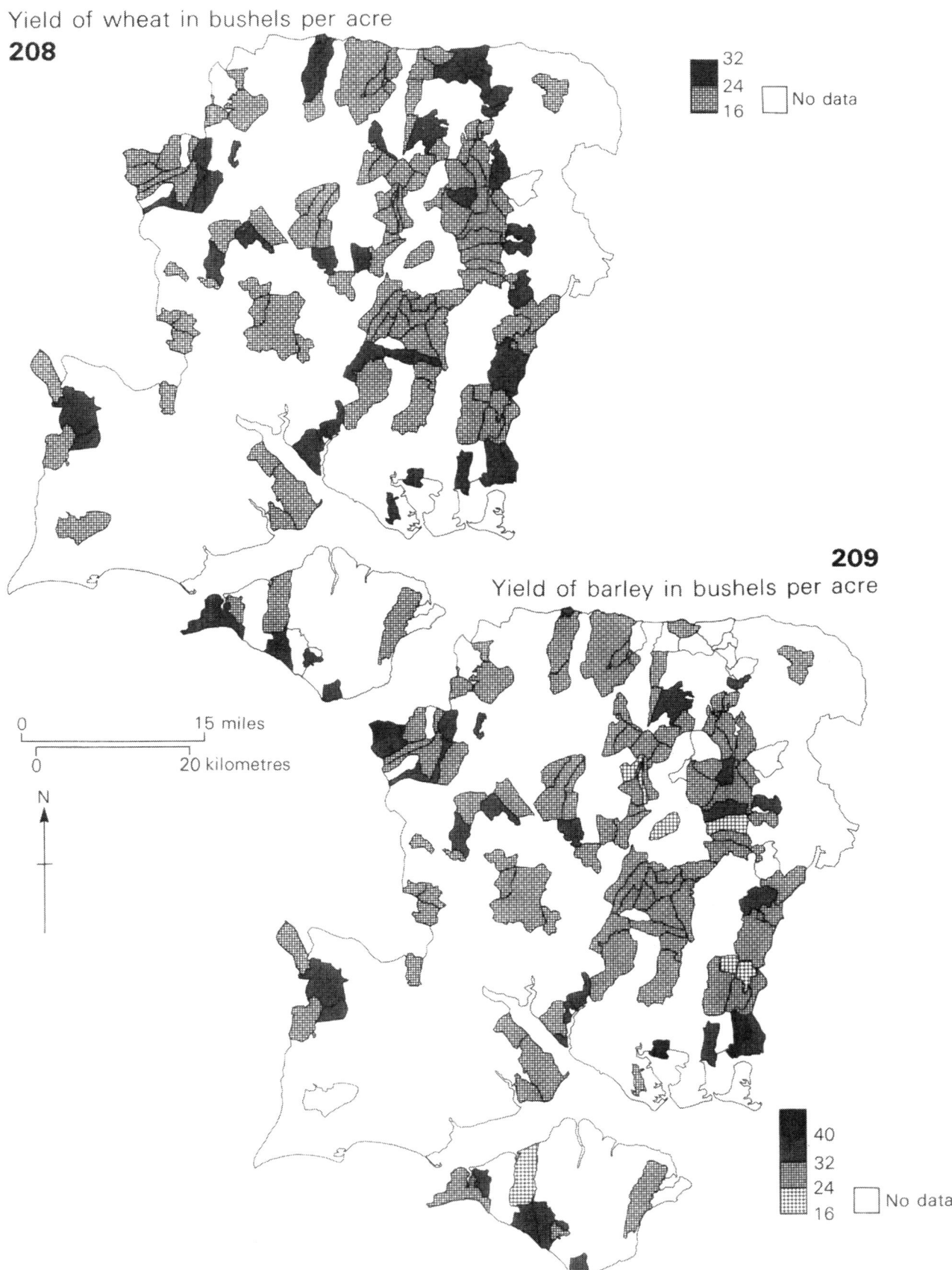

162 Southern counties

Yield of oats in bushels per acre
210

211
Yield of pulse crops in bushels per acre

Hampshire

Yield of turnips in £'s per acre
212

213
Yield of clover and seeds in cwts per acre

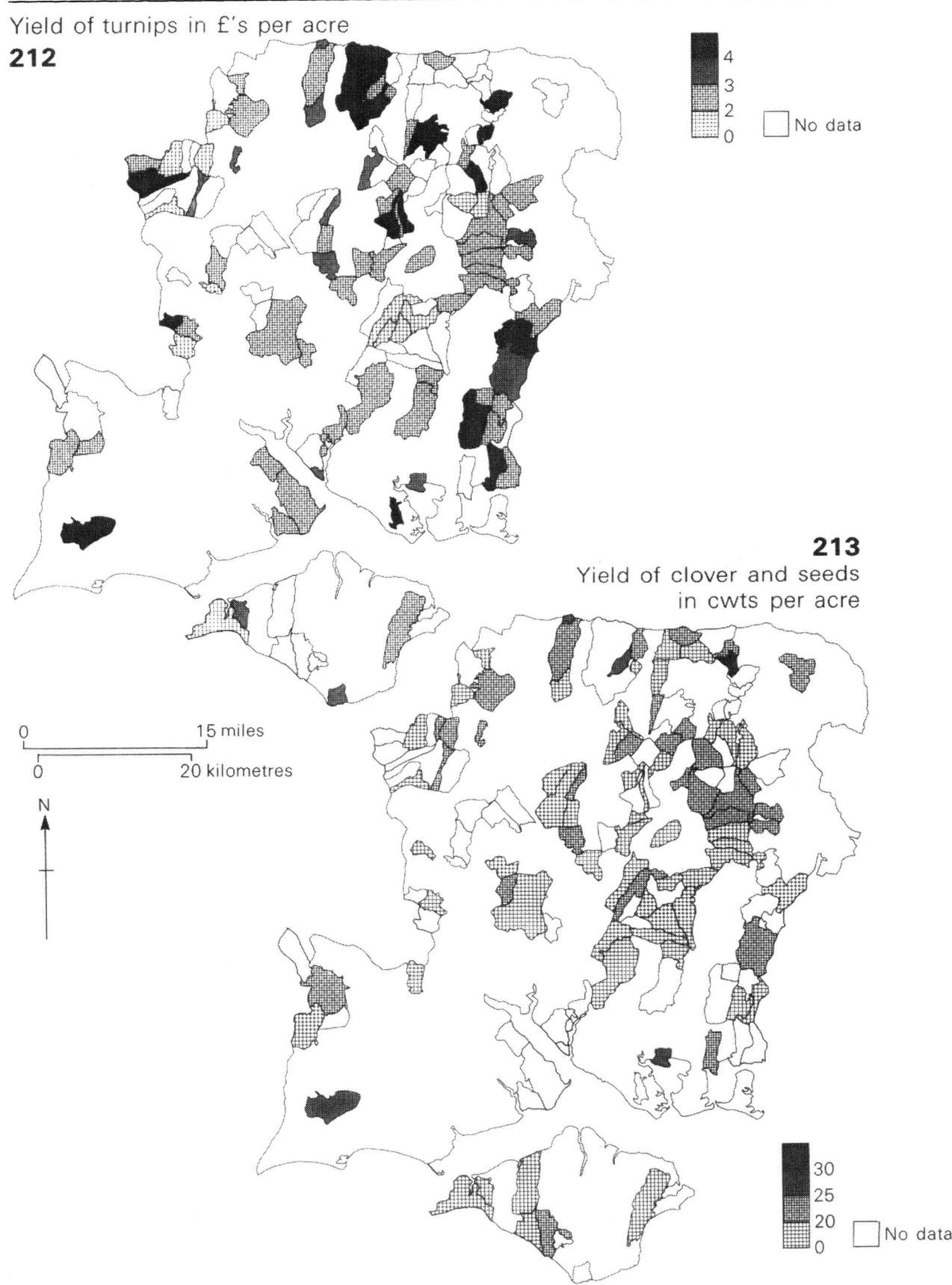

Southern counties

214
Yield of meadow in cwts per acre

215
Yield of pasture in shillings per acre

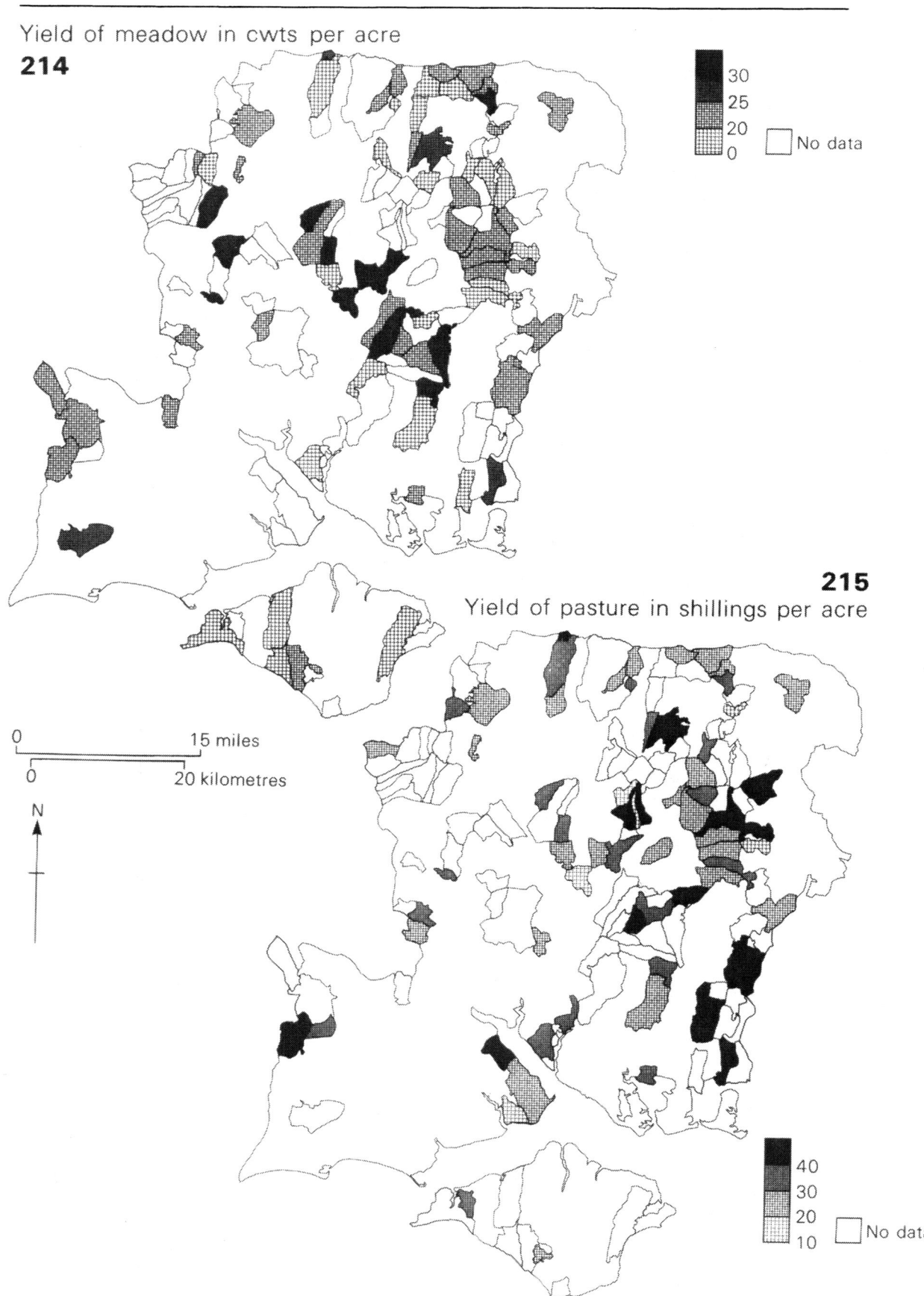

Surrey

150 tithe districts
72 reports on tithe agreements

E. C. Willatts (1933) selected the two Surrey parishes of Ashtead and Headley for his pioneering work on land use mapping from tithe apportionments and maps. These studies were incorporated and extended in his report on the Land Utilisation Survey of Britain for Middlesex and the London Region (Willatts, 1937). Surrey tithe apportionments and files were consulted by Alan Parton (1973) for his thesis 'Town and country in Surrey c. 1800–1870: A study in historical geography'. This includes maps of land use and crop combinations and his chapters on agricultural change draw extensively on written comments in tithe files. Land use has been plotted field-by-field by D. W. Shave (1941) and M. J. Frost (1964) for the basins of the rivers Wey and Mole respectively.

Only ten Surrey parishes were completely tithe free in 1836. Voluntary commutation began early and six agreements were examined during 1837 (Table 24). A number of difficulties, among them the need to fix extraordinary rent-charges on hops at some places, meant that tithe commutation was rather more long drawn-out in Surrey than usual; almost half the reports on tithe agreements are dated 1840 or after. In several parishes near London, assistant commissioners and local tithe agents found it impossible to calculate rent-charge of tilled land by their usual method of ascertaining a normal rotation as large areas were cultivated for fodder or as market gardens. The produce of these last was very varied and changed frequently according to season and demand. Joseph Townsend put the problem neatly in his report for Clapham, where 'the capricious changes constantly in progress in suburban parishes render it impossible to present an estimate of produce at all to be relied on. I have therefore not attempted it.' Most downland pasture was recorded as common in Surrey reports and this depresses the acreages of grassland (Table 25). Oak and elm woodlands in the Weald were generally tithe free by long-standing custom. Coppice wood was titheable but often so overshadowed by timber that it was not very productive (see Subject Index). The chalk hills were also well-wooded and on the Weald clay, as at Chiddingfold, 'the cultivated ground is surrounded to a considerable extent by large hedgerows and much overshadowed by hedgerow timber. It harvests late.' Indeed, Surrey was an especially well wooded county at the time of the tithe surveys (Table 25 and map 220).

Pen-pictures of local landscapes are found in more Surrey reports than usual; there are long descriptions of 'romantic' and 'picturesque' scenery, particularly by local agents visiting North Downs parishes. Mickleham, John Pickering said, 'is distinguished by beautifully diversified and romantic scenery, being much broken by hill and dale'. John Mee Mathew declared that 'the country around Banstead is proverbial for its pleasing variety of scenery, and the views from the downs are commanding and diversified, whilst the lower slopes and vallies are crowned with a rich overhanging foliage'. Horace William Meteyard considered that 'Aldbury is a parish beautifully situated on the declivities of some hills of the chalk formation, is highly undulating and picturesque, and contains many beautiful houses erected by Mr Drummond the banker . . . '.

In the suburbs of London there was very little arable land, most land not occupied by buildings being used for market gardens. At Mortlake, for instance,

> the real wealth of the parish is the market garden amounting to half its extent. The crops are asparagus, cabbages, celery, turnips, late potatoes, some lavender, onions, peas, and early potatoes etc.; a produce as various as possible and one very difficult to draw up in a schedule and even then most unsatisfactory from the great variety in price with the various seasons.

Further from London, parishes contained much more arable land, but if still within easy reach of the metropolis, farmers were able to obtain plentiful supplies of manure and could avoid the necessity of regular crop rotation and instead grew large quantities of fodder crops, including rye cut green, hay and straw for the London market. At New Malden, for example,

> the mode of husbandry on the arable land is scarcely reducible to a system. The easy distance of this parish from London leads to an entire dependence on London dung for manure, and the cultivation is adapted in an excessive degree to the demands of the vicinity for hay and straw, almost the whole of which descriptions of produce are sold from the farms.

Systematic cultivation of arable was found in parishes with less easy access to London or to the other main market at Guildford (listed in Subject Index). On heavy clay soils a three- or four-course rotation was followed, both including a wheat and a bare fallow year. Oats or beans intervened and were followed in the four-course with a fodder or seed crop. On lighter soils four- or five-course turnip shifts were adopted; on the very weakest chalk soils there might be periods of several years when land was in sainfoin ley, and on poor sands as at Pirbright north-west of Guildford 'rye is more grown than wheat'. A few acres of hops were grown in many Surrey parishes and in a few, most notably Farnham, to such an extent that an extraordinary rent-charge had to be imposed. Though there is little comment on high farming as such in Surrey files (five references), recorded crop yields, as Maps 230–5 and Table 25 indicate, were a little above average.

Grassland in Surrey varied from that at Kingston and similarly situated districts where 'meadows contiguous to the river Thames cut 2 tons of hay to the acre and are very advantageous to feeding', to downland which 'burnt' in summer, or common at Pirbright which produced 'nothing but heath, frequently not even a blade of grass is to be seen'. Young cattle were considered best for wetter pastures. Few sheep could be over-wintered in clayland parishes but where, as at Effingham, turnips, seeds and fodder were available in quantity from 'upwards of one thousand acres of the arable being turnip lands, of course a considerable number of sheep are kept . . . They are chiefly "dry flocks" i.e. not breeding flocks.'

Surrey

Table 24 *Reports on agreements for commutation of tithes in Surrey*

Assistant commissioner/ local tithe agent	1837	1838	1839	1840	1841	1842	1843	1844	1848	Totals
John Pickering		5	4	9	7	1	3			29
Horace William Meteyard		4	7	1						12
F. Browne Browne			4	1	2					7
John Mee Mathew			5	2						7
Thomas Smith Woolley	3					3		1		7
Joseph Townsend	3	1								4
William Heard							1	1	1	3
Edward Greathed		1								1
Roger Kynaston				1						1
Thomas James Tatham		1								1
Totals	6	12	20	14	9	4	4	2	1	72

Table 25 *Land use, crops and yields in Surrey c. 1836*

A	Land use	Percentage of total land area enumerated in reports on tithe agreements	Estimated acreage in whole county
	Arable	48.8	233,401
	Grass	18.2	86,895
	Wood	12.2	58,389
	Common	9.9	47,277

B	Crop	Mean percentage of arable	Mean yield per acre	Estimated acreage in whole county
	Wheat	23.2	20.9 bushels	54,116
	Barley	9.2	31.6 bushels	21,375
	Oats	14.3	35.6 bushels	33,451
	Pulses	5.0	22.9 bushels	11,575
	Turnips	9.3	£2.81	21,599
	Seeds	25.2	20.7 cwts	58,802
	Fallows	12.7	—	29,706

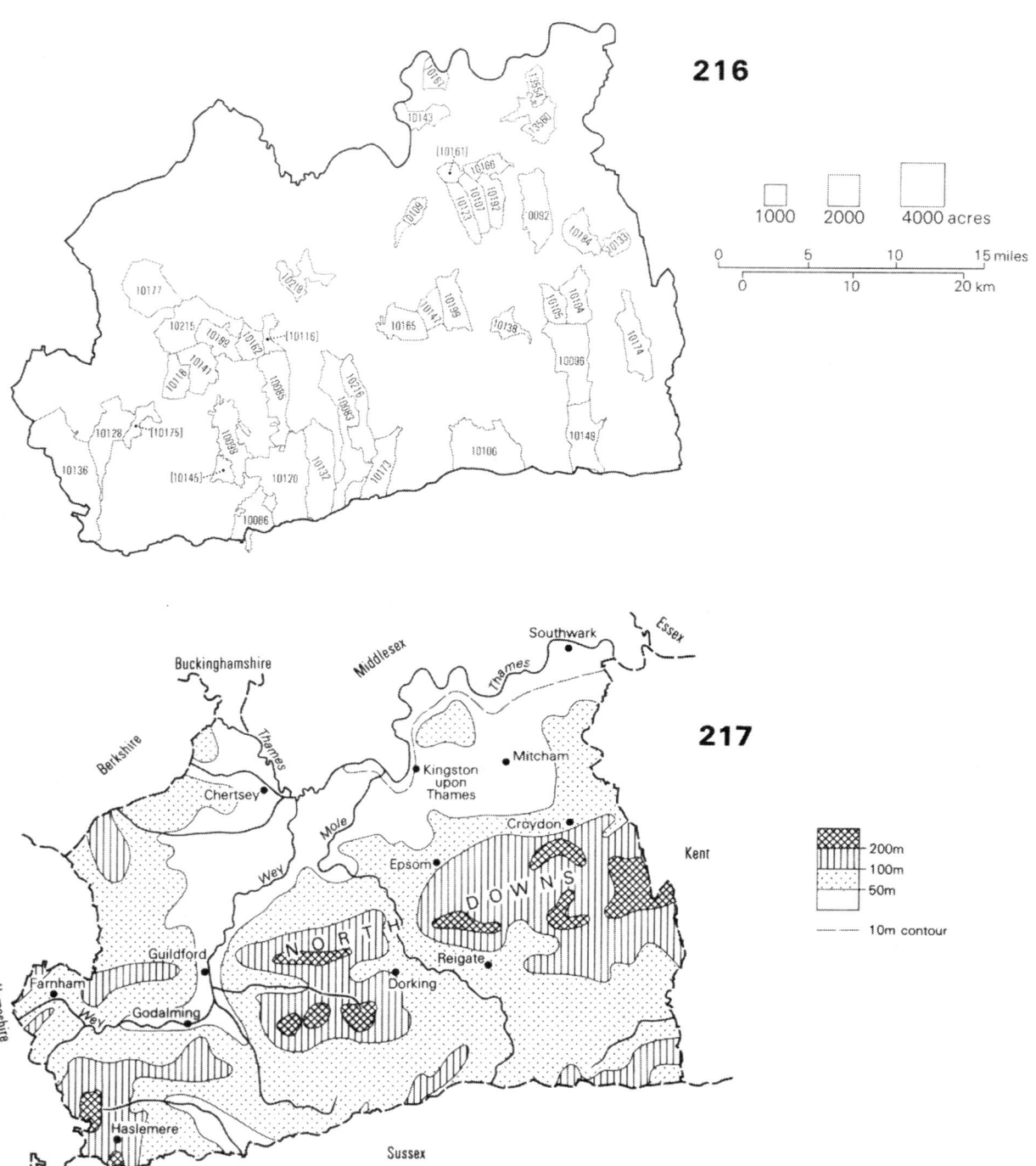

Surrey

218
Arable as a percentage of tithe district area

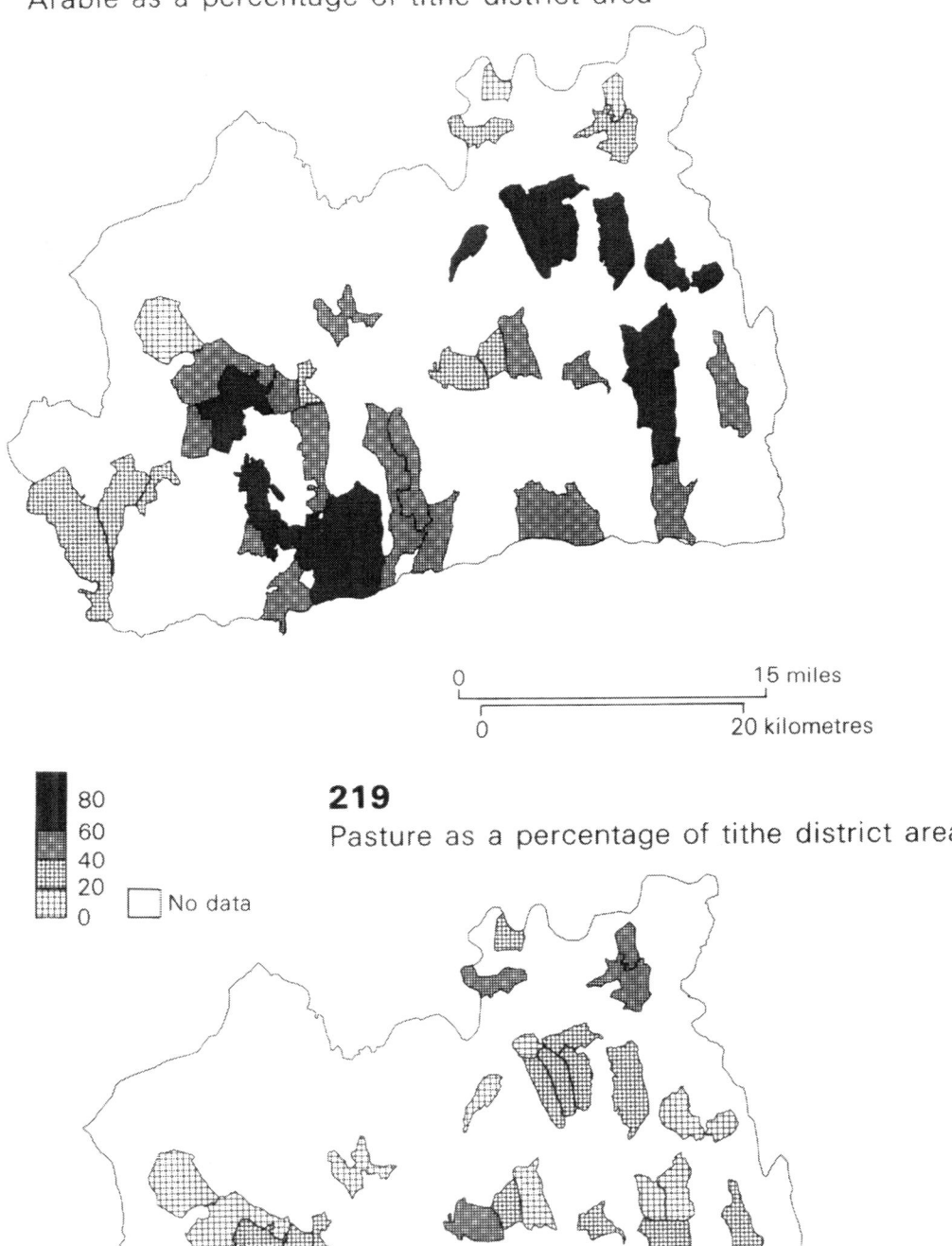

219
Pasture as a percentage of tithe district area

Southern counties

220
Woodland as a percentage of tithe district area

221
Common as a percentage of tithe district area

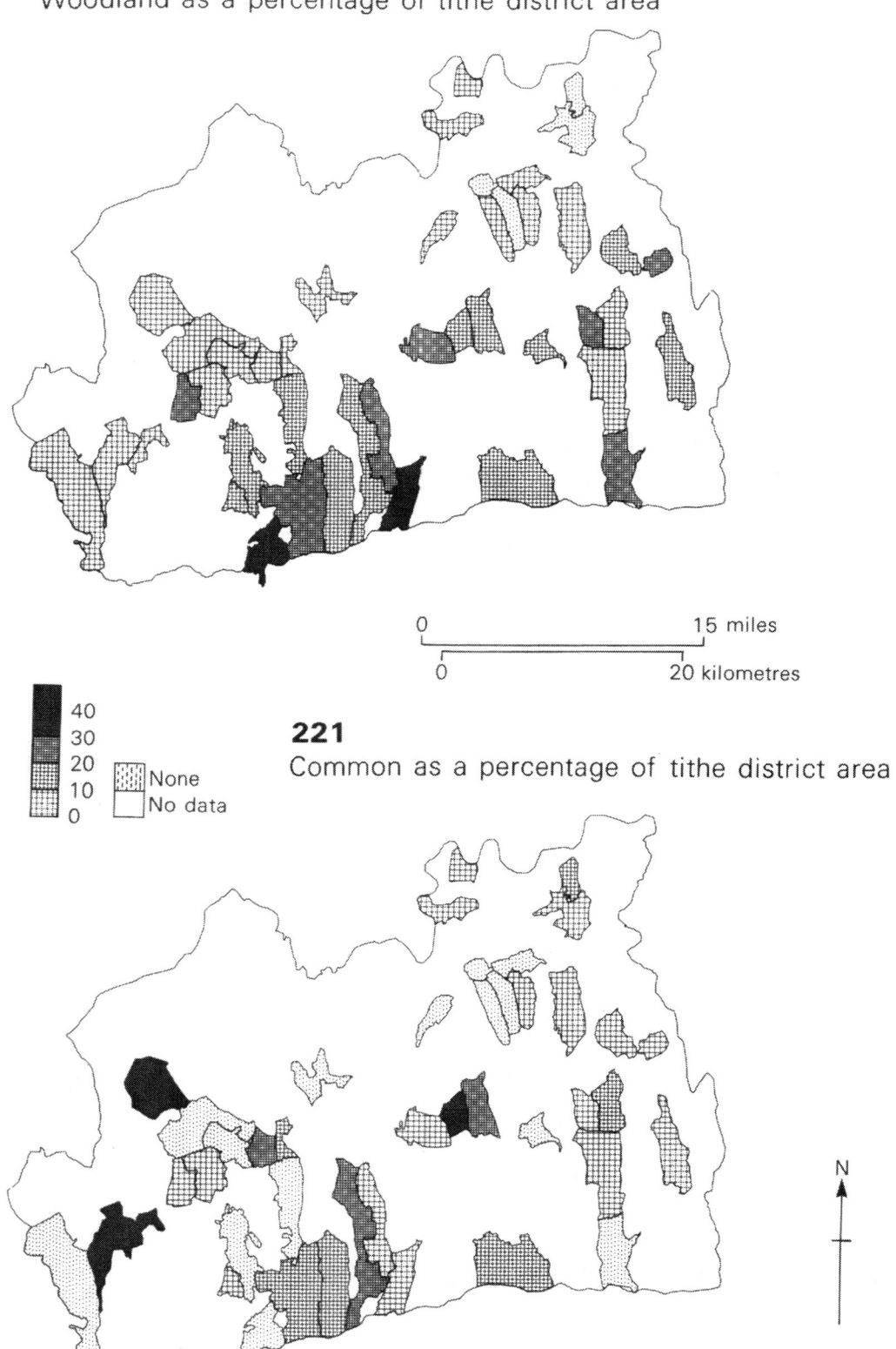

222
Hops as a percentage of tithe district area

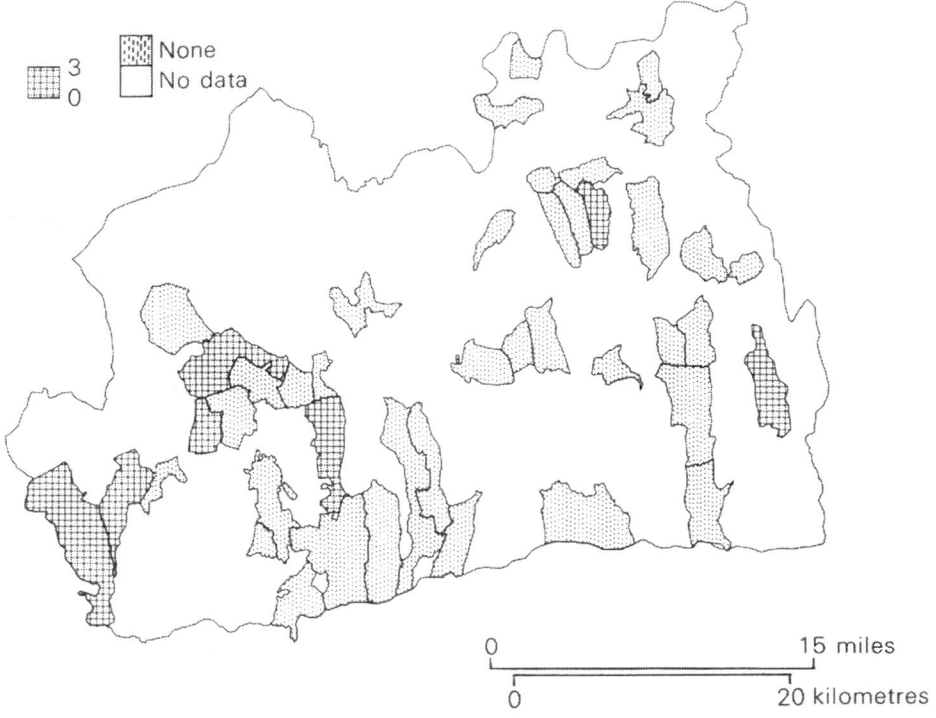

223
Wheat as a percentage of arable

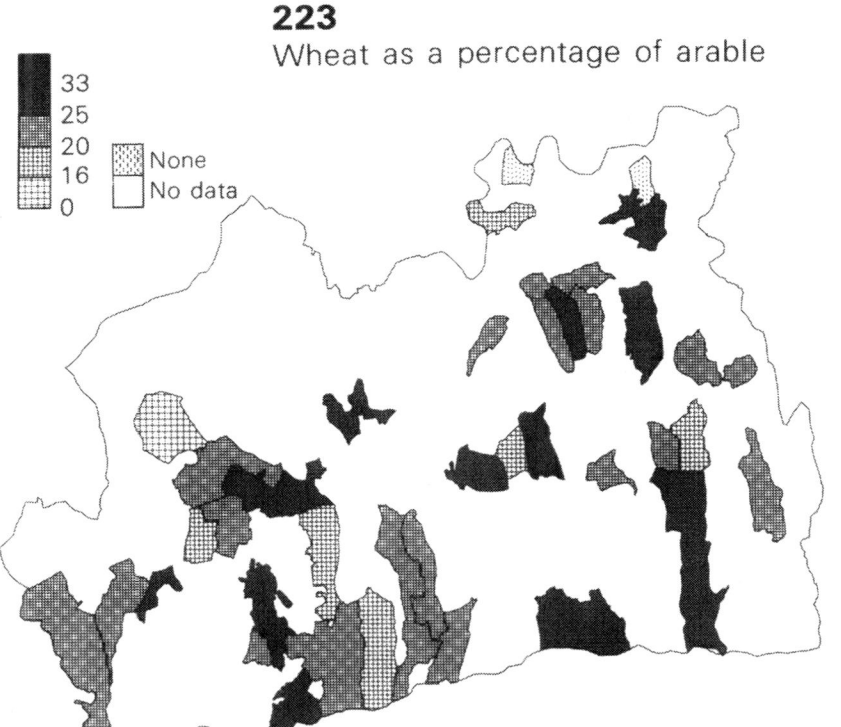

224
Barley as a percentage of arable

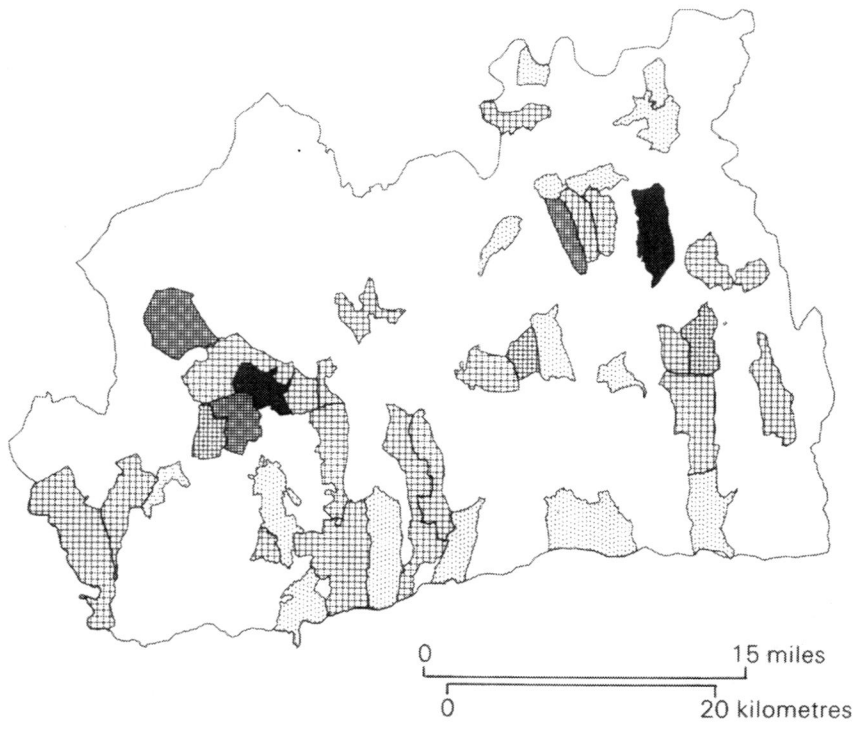

33
25
20
16
0

No quantities
None
No data

225
Oats as a percentage of arable

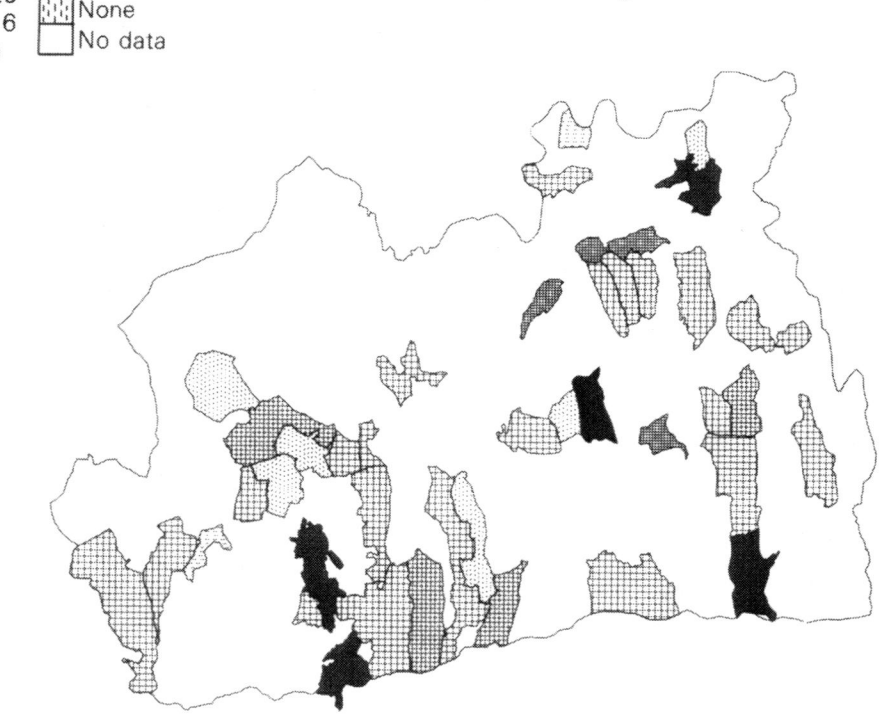

226
Pulse crops as a percentage of arable

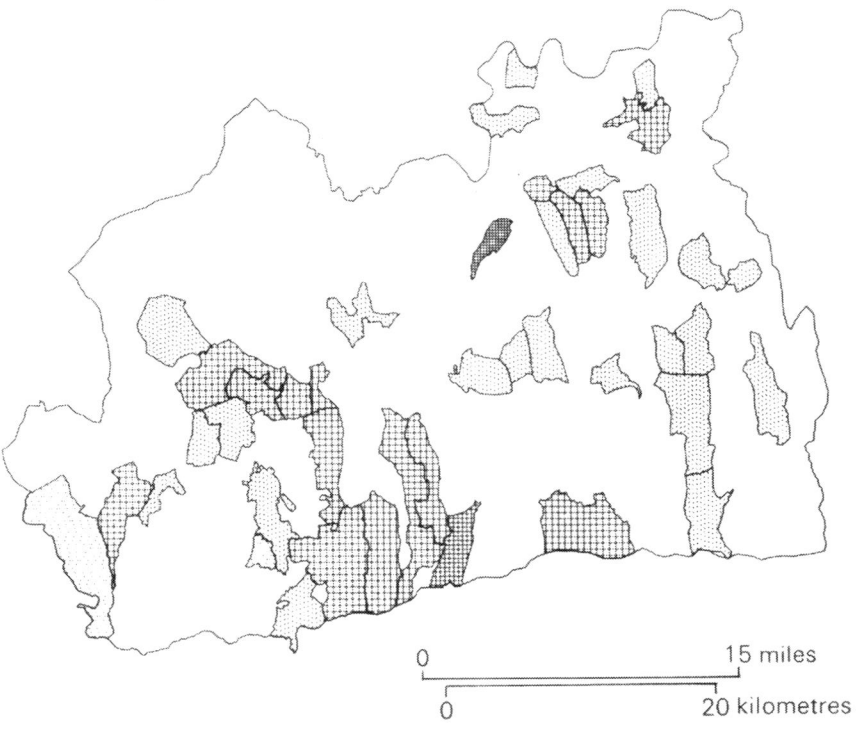

227
Turnips as a percentage of arable

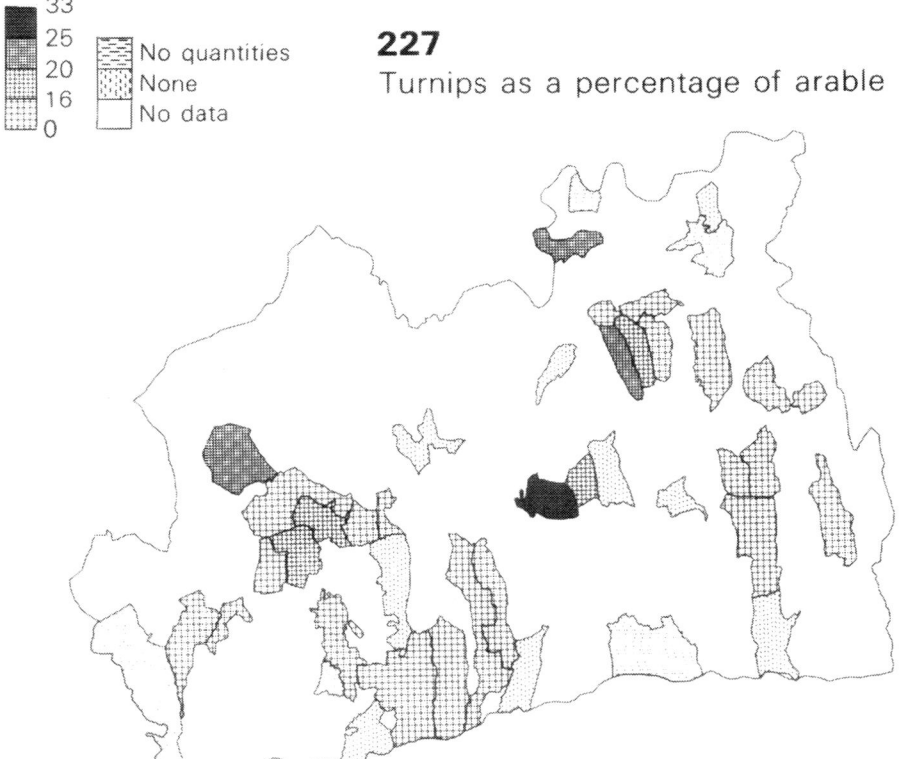

228
Clover and seeds as a percentage of arable

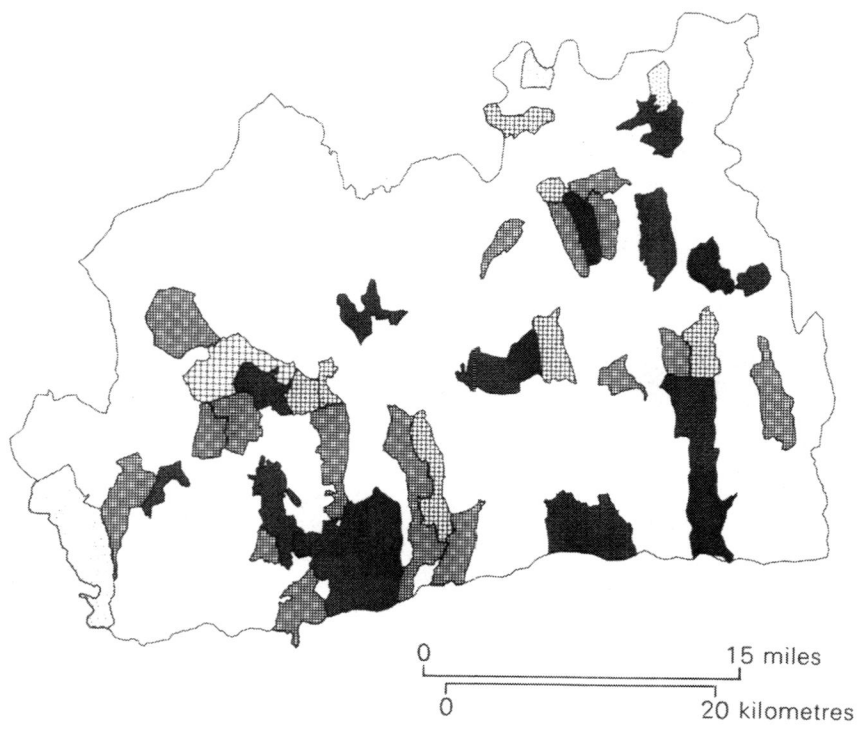

229
Dead fallow as a percentage of arable

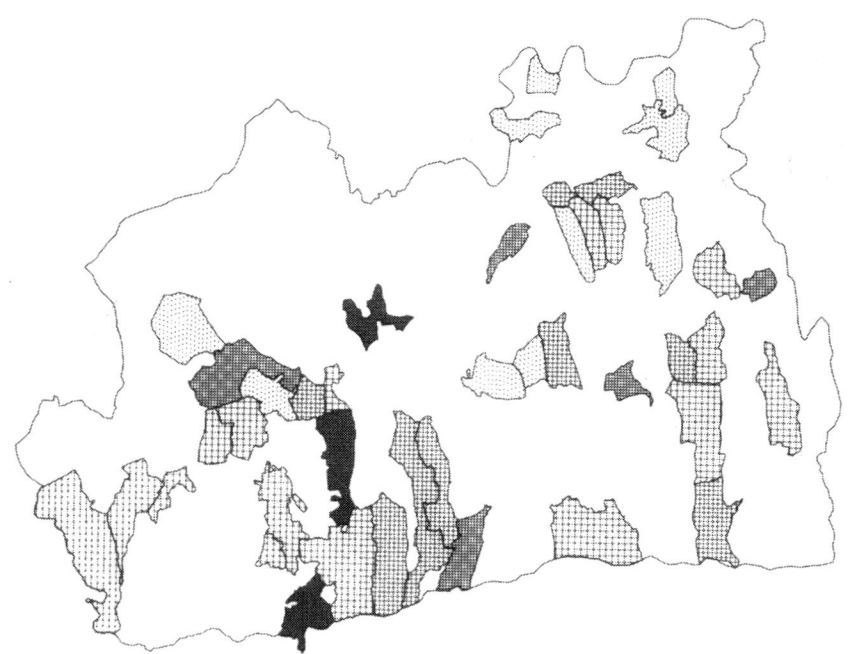

230
Yield of wheat in bushels per acre

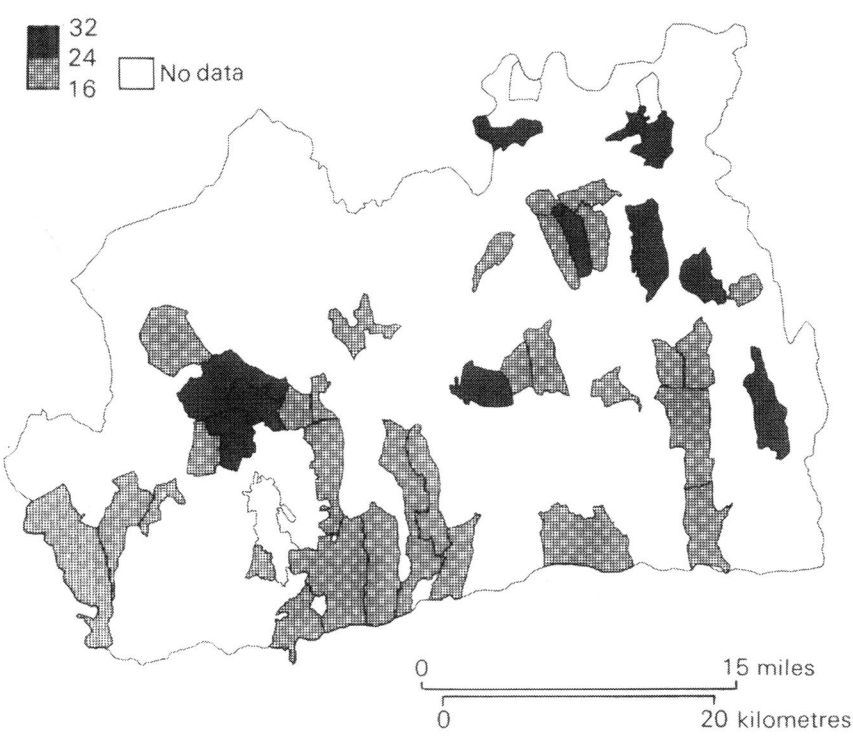

231
Yield of barley in bushels per acre

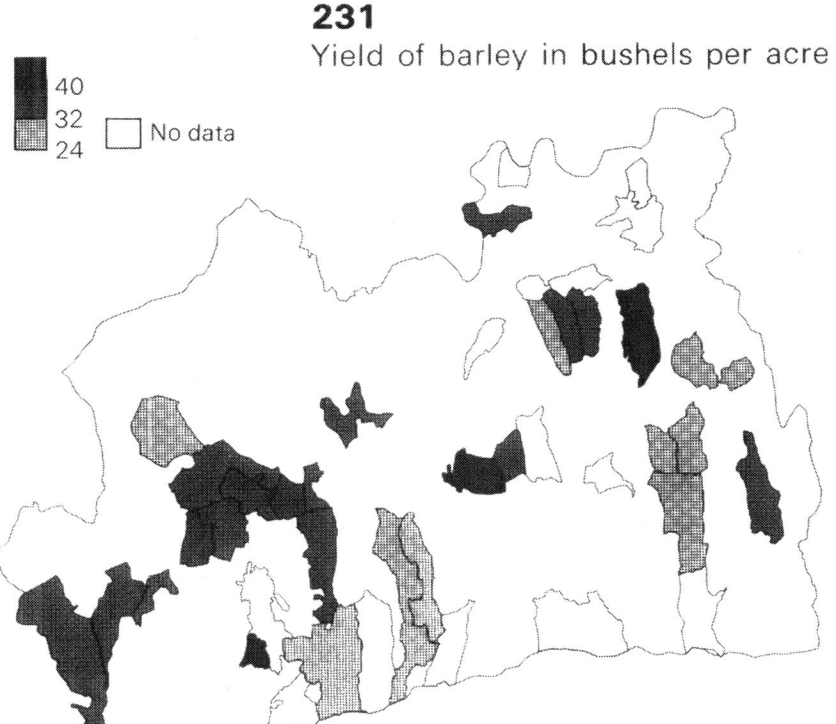

232
Yield of oats in bushels per acre

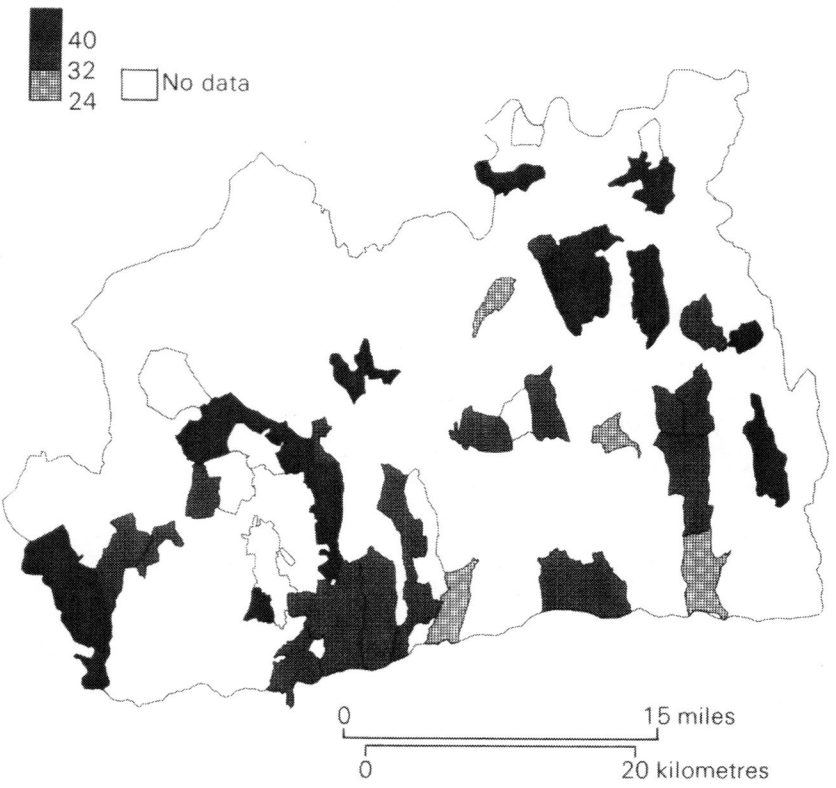

233
Yield of pulse crops in bushels per acre

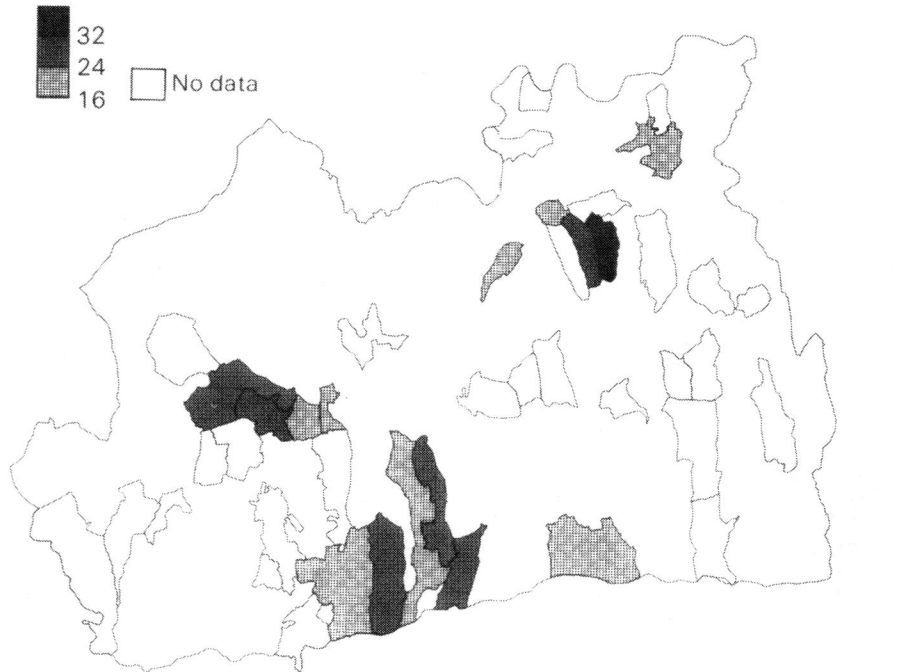

Surrey

234
Yield of turnips in £'s per acre

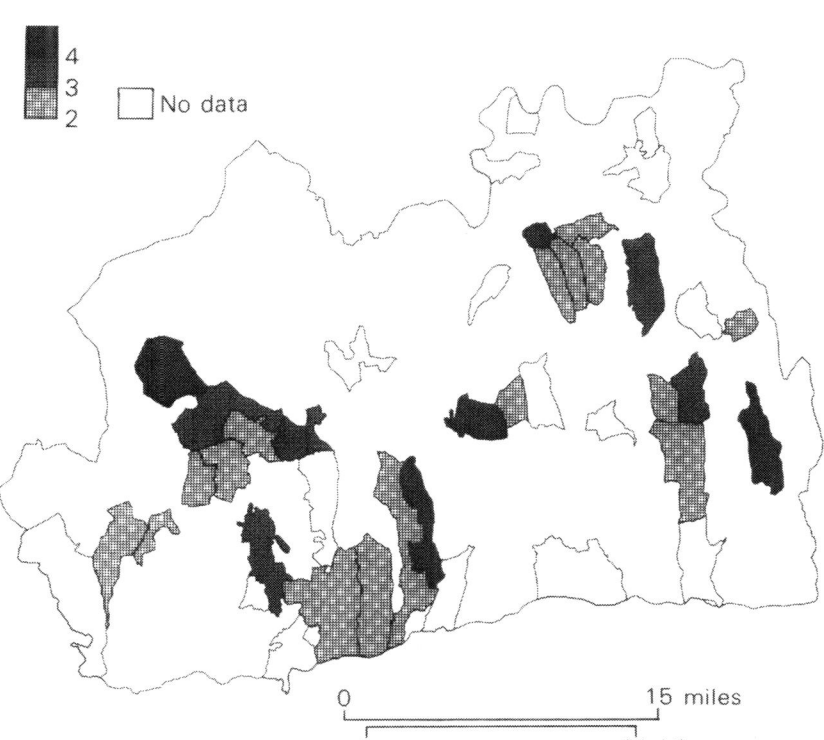

235
Yield of clover and seeds in cwts per acre

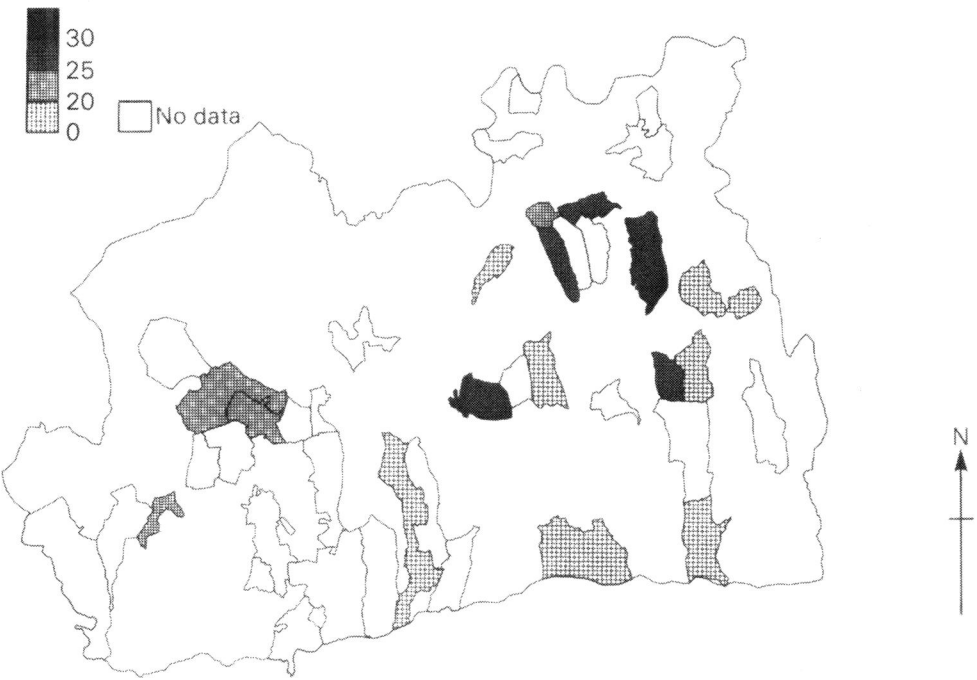

178 Southern counties

236
Yield of meadow in cwts per acre

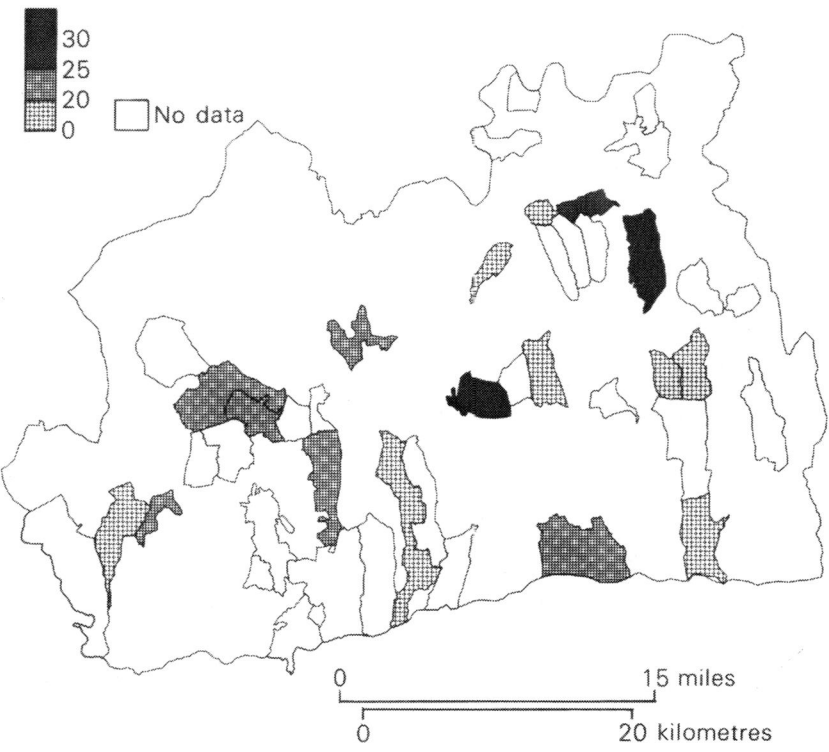

237
Yield of pasture in shillings per acre

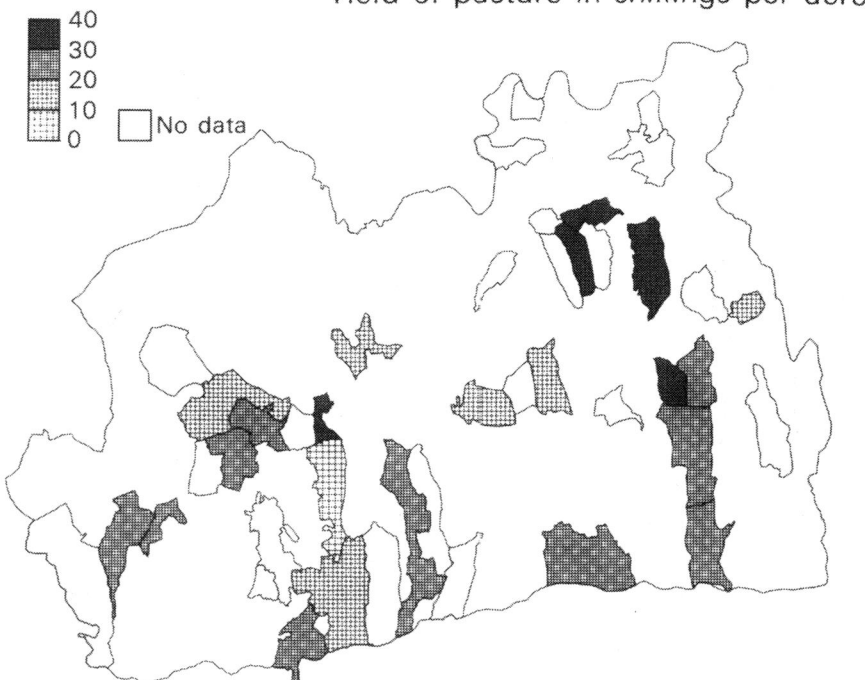

Middlesex

102 tithe districts
17 reports on tithe agreements

E. C. Willatts (1937) mapped land use field-by-field for four Middlesex parishes to illustrate the Middlesex and London Region report of the Land Utilisation Survey of Great Britain.

A number of factors in combination account for the small proportion of districts with reports on tithe agreements in Middlesex. First, in a number of metropolitan parishes such as Bloomsbury and St George-in-the-East, no tithe had accrued during the seven years of average and no claim of tithes or payments in lieu thereof was made. Parliamentary enclosure had exonerated much tithe (see Subject Index) and in the eighty-six parishes where some tithe remained to be commuted in 1836, agreements were reached in only 20 per cent of places. This low figure for voluntary commutation did not reflect a widespread bitterness over tithe payment in Middlesex, but rather the facts that first, titheable land was often small in extent relative to the whole of a parish so tithe was unlikely to be a great burden or local issue, and secondly, because of technical difficulties of commuting tithe of market garden produce which varied so much from season to season. The net result is that there are reliable data on land use and crops for fewer than ten tithe districts, a sample too small to permit either cartographic analysis or compilation of aggregate figures of land use and cropping for the county as a whole. Middlesex files are not completely worthless, however, as in many of those relating to places where awards were imposed there are detailed discussions of farming practices (see Subject Index). Some files also contain papers relating to urban developments such as the laying out of Finsbury Park and the lighting and cleansing of streets in Bethnal Green (see 'topographic descriptions' in Subject Index).

Discussions of farming practices in Middlesex files underline the marked distinction which existed at that time between agricultural systems on heavy clay soils and on light, gravelly loams. The former were primarily devoted to the production of hay, tares and spring rye for the London fodder market. At Little Stanmore in 1838,

> The principal product of the soil is hay, which is of good quality and for which the land is well manured with dung and London soil, the compost being put on the heavy clay land in the autumn after the stock is taken off... the arable land amounts to but 62 acres and is strong clay land farmed not so much according to any system as the wants or caprice of the farmer. Wheat, tares, beans, spring rye and potatoes or oats are what is chiefly produced. The tares and spring rye being cut as green food and sent in bundles to the London

market. Last year 5 acres of winter tares on account of the backward spring fetched £12 an acre.

By contrast, at Harlington, 'the soil is of the most luxuriant and fertile property in the highest state of cultivation and being composed of a fine rich deep loam on marl and such is its productiveness that a wheat crop is grown every third year, without the necessity of a dead fallow'; and at Ealing, 'the mode of cultivation of the arable land is not reducible to a system. By the high manuring which its contiguity to London permits, a perpetual succession of crops is maintained.' Market gardening is a topic of some comment in seven tithe files, not only because of its areal dominance in Thames alluvium parishes, but also because of the difficulties of commuting tithes of such varied and valuable produce. Rents were high, but so were yields: £20 per acre is recorded at Isleworth.

Table 26 *Reports on agreements for commutation of tithes in Middlesex*

Assistant commissioner/ local tithe agent	1836	1837	1838	1839	1840	1841	1842	1843	Totals
John Mee Mathew			1	3					4
F. Browne Browne				2	1				3
Horace William Meteyard			3						3
Roger Kynaston				2					2
Edward Greathed			1						1
William Heard								1	1
John Pickering					1				1
Charles Pym	1								1
Thomas James Tatham							1		1
Totals	1		5	7	2		1	1	17

SOUTH-WESTERN COUNTIES

Somerset   Devon
Wiltshire   Cornwall
Dorset

The 'pastoral' type of printed form used for reporting on tithe agreements in these counties requires estimates of land uses, the course of crops and the number of stock, and asks assistant commissioners and local tithe agents for their 'remarks, stating the peculiar circumstances of the parish which may affect the value of the tithe'.

Somerset

501 tithe districts
333 reports on tithe agreements

Tithe was commuted by agreement in two thirds of Somerset tithe districts and as a result, Somerset has the fullest coverage of reports on tithe agreements of all south-western counties. Only eleven districts were entirely tithe free in 1838. Robert Page wrote 85 per cent of Somerset agreement reports, compiling no fewer than 112 in 1838 alone (Table 27). His normal practice was to write detailed parish descriptions in manuscript reports which he sent to the Tithe Office in addition to printed questionnaire forms. Information available on soils, agriculture, commons, woodland, etc., for Somerset is much greater than for any English or Welsh county where 'pastoral' type report forms were employed. Moreover, for reasons that are unknown, Somerset files have been less heavily weeded than those of any other county which means that in those districts where commutation awards were imposed, there is often a great quantity of papers still extant relating to matters affecting the level of tithe. At the two districts of Broadway Old and New Enclosures, for example, long debates among witnesses on crop rotations, yields and farming practices are summarised in reports by assistant commissioner Charles Pym of twenty-three and forty-nine pages respectively. At Winsford, Robert Page wrote at considerable length on Exmoor farming and the paring and burning, liming, and sheep rearing practised to improve land productivity. For St Cuthbert parish there is a similarly detailed account of Mendip agriculture. Papers recording disputes over modus payments are found in files of very many English and Welsh tithe districts but none approaches the three-inch thick dossier for Bridgwater which documents *in extenso* the claims and counter-claims which were eventually resolved by court actions in 1845.

Moduses did materially affect the value of tithes in many Somerset parishes and were commonly paid on hay, grazing land and cows, and sometimes on milk, sheep, wood, orchards and gardens. Where orchards were not subject to a special modus, they were tithed as pasture and so it is not possible to distinguish these separately. Modus arrangements encouraged farmers to keep grazing and dairy cattle on land covered by a modus and certainly put arable farming at a tithe disadvantage. The consequences of tithe commutation for the extension of arable farming is not, however, a much debated issue in Somerset tithe files.

Where there was only a small amount of arable land in a district, a regular rotation was not adopted generally. Robert Page commented as follows at Dulverton where his observations required him to alter the agreement schedule:

> From the apparently small amount of rectorial rent-charge my attention was directed to the mode of cultivation on the arable and I found on inquiry that not a fifth part of the land denominated arable is annually kept in a state of tillage, out of 3357 acres described in the schedule as arable not more than 610 acres are this year cultivated with grain producing rectorial tithe. By way of illustration I might mention that the largest farm in the parish, 460 acres with the usual admixture of grass and arable, has this year only 31a of wheat, 21a of barley, 12a or oats, 3a of turnips, and 2a of potatoes.

Where assistant commissioners and local tithe agents were able to identify a normal rotation, on clay soils it was most often a three-course of wheat, beans and bare fallow, and on lighter stone-brash or sandy soils a four-course turnip system with in some places flax and potatoes substituted for clover and turnips. At Shepton Beauchamp, both 'flax and hemp are much grown' and at Seavington St Michael, 'the land is kept in a high state of cultivation by the aid of the sheep fold, bone dust and rags. Crop succeeds crop, and it is no uncommon occurrence to have two wheat crops in three years, with flax and turnips in the interim.' Such comments on productive arable husbandry are outweighed in Somerset by the opposite; farmers who over-cropped their arable came in for much criticism and yields on the whole were unexceptional or low.

A preponderance of comments in Somerset files tends to confirm that the breeding, keeping and fattening of livestock and dairying were much more important than the cultivation of arable (see Subject Index). The presence of some good meadow or pasture land is attested in almost all districts with the exception of those on high Mendip and Exmoor where there was still much poor, unenclosed grass used as summer sheepwalk. At Exford,

> the commons consist of an extensive tract of barren heath, or moor, which afford a very valuable sheep walk for a flock of upwards of 4000, from the month of May to November. The system is to place the ewe flock out to keep during the winter, when the spring advances they are with the lambs and wethers driven to the hills.

The wetness of some parts of the Levels also occasioned comment, particularly at places in Sedgemoor where grass was best fed in summer by young cattle, it being considered unhealthy for sheep. Much more characteristic of the county as a whole, though, are the following two extracts describing grassland in reports by Robert Page. At Combe Florey, he found 'the meadows watered by the springs brought from the Quantock Hills, which renders them very fertile, they are fed late, with ewes and lambs, and afterwards mown, producing an average of a ton of hay an acre'. At Lyncombe, near Bath, the meadow land was 'of excellent quality, equally calculated for grazing or the Dairy, the principal occupiers are publicans and cow keepers, the butchers also have their share, they find it convenient to bring their fat cattle from distant markets to the lands they rent at high prices in this parish'. Cattle and sheep breeds, dairying, rearing of oxen and droving of animals to market all receive attention in the exceptionally rich tithe files of Somerset (see Subject Index).

Table 27 *Reports on agreements for commutation of tithes in Somerset*

Assistant commissioner/ local tithe agent	1836	1837	1838	1839	1840	1841	1842	1843	1844	1845	Totals
Robert Page		13	112	90	46	13	9		1		284
Charles Pym		24	7	3		1			1	1	37
James Jerwood				7							7
Henry Dixon	2										2
George Louis			1								1
John Milner		1									1
Aneurin Owen										1	1
Totals	2	38	120	100	46	14	9		2	2	333

Table 28 *Land use, crops and yields in Somerset c. 1836*

A	Land use	Percentage of total land area enumerated in reports on tithe agreements	Estimated acreage in whole county
	Arable	24.4	255,943
	Grass	62.8	657,465
	Wood	4.0	41,829
	Common	7.1	74,194

B	Crop	Mean percentage of arable	Mean yield per acre	Estimated acreage in whole county
	Wheat	34.1	21.0 bushels	87,177
	Barley	17.3	31.3 bushels	44,162
	Oats	2.7	30.8 bushels	6,794
	Pulses	6.2	29.6 bushels	15,798

Somerset

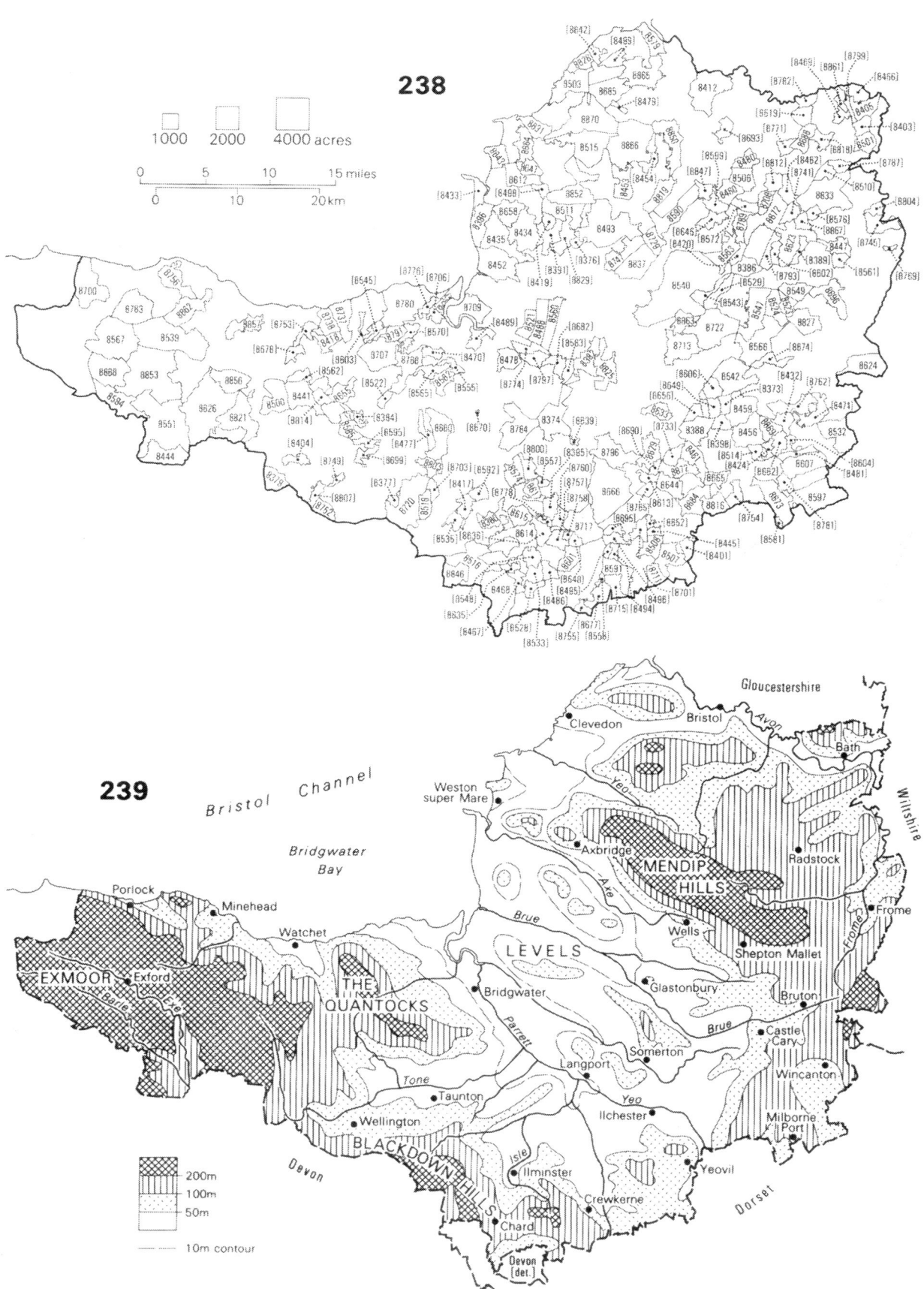

240 Arable as a percentage of tithe district area

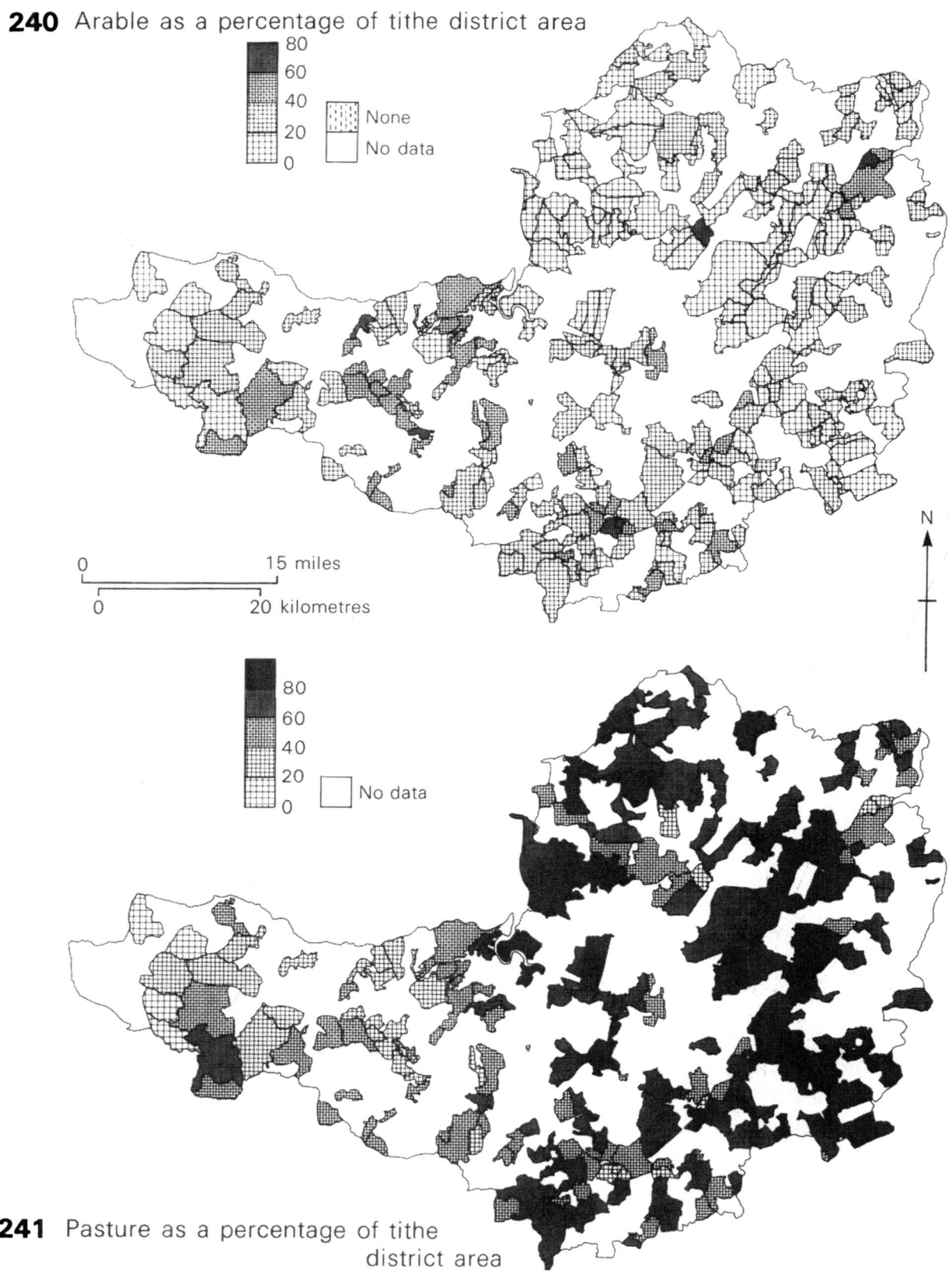

241 Pasture as a percentage of tithe district area

242 Woodland as a percentage of tithe district area

243 Common as a percentage of tithe district area

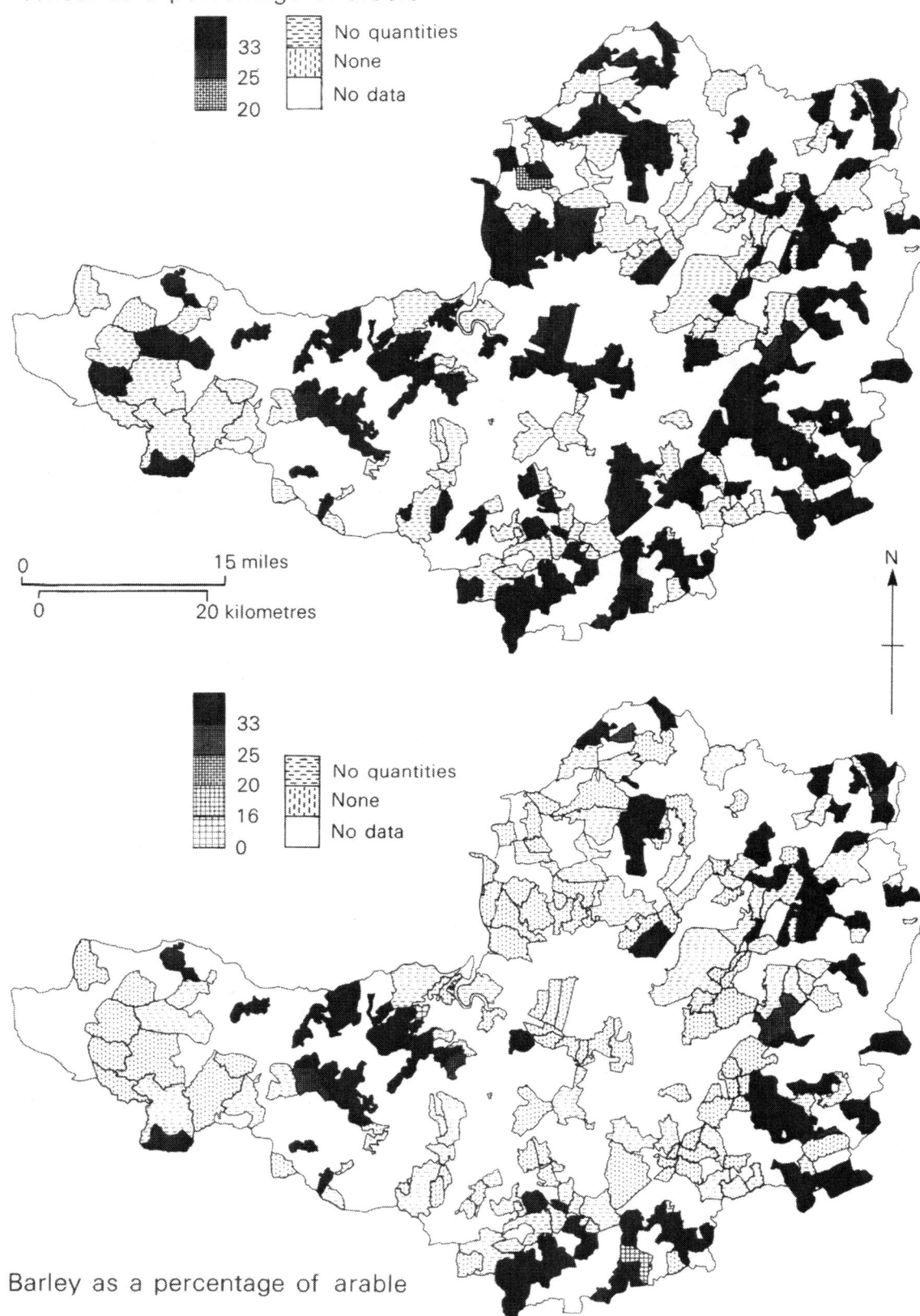

244 Wheat as a percentage of arable

245 Barley as a percentage of arable

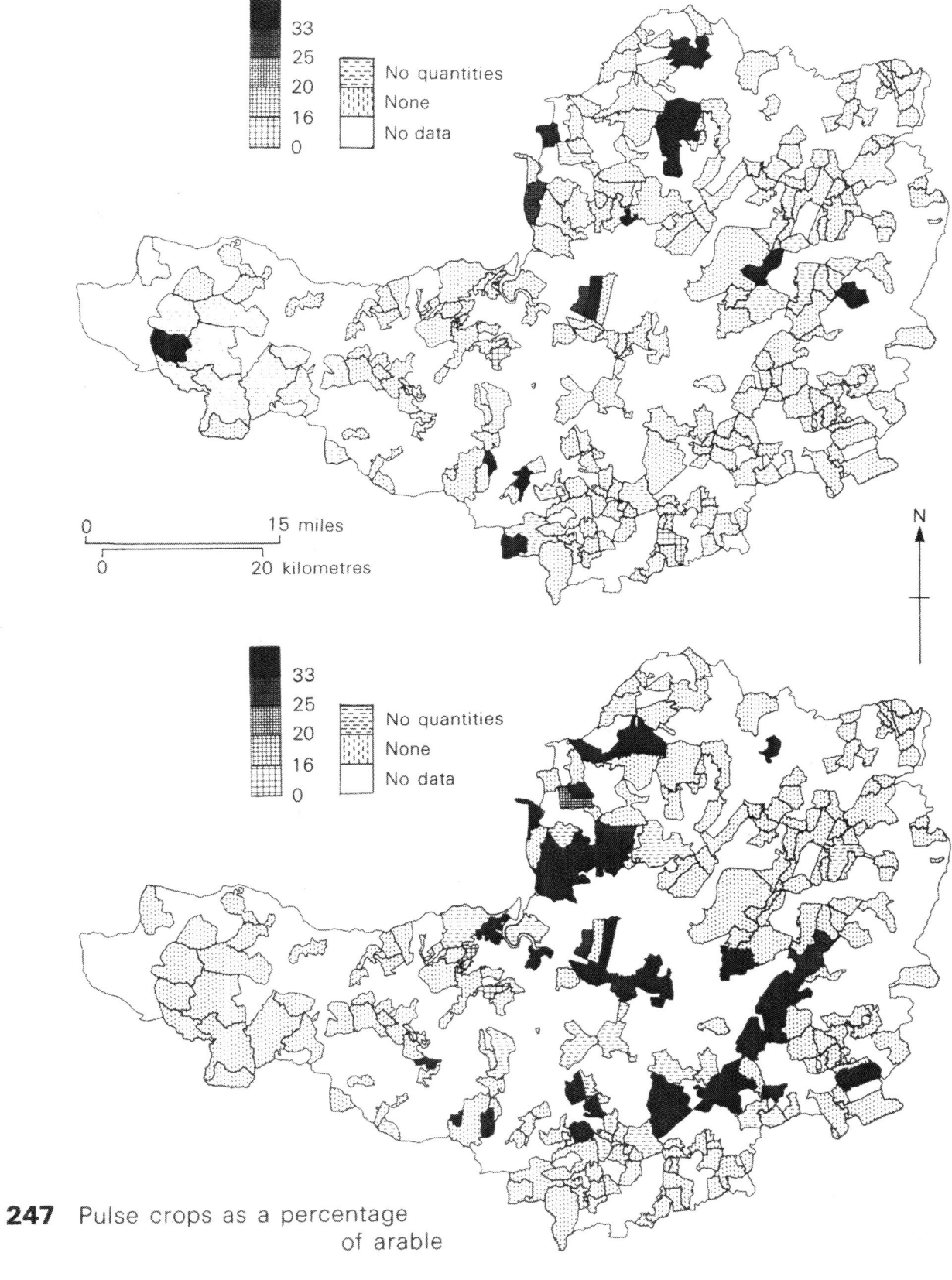

246 Oats as a percentage of arable

247 Pulse crops as a percentage of arable

190 South-western counties

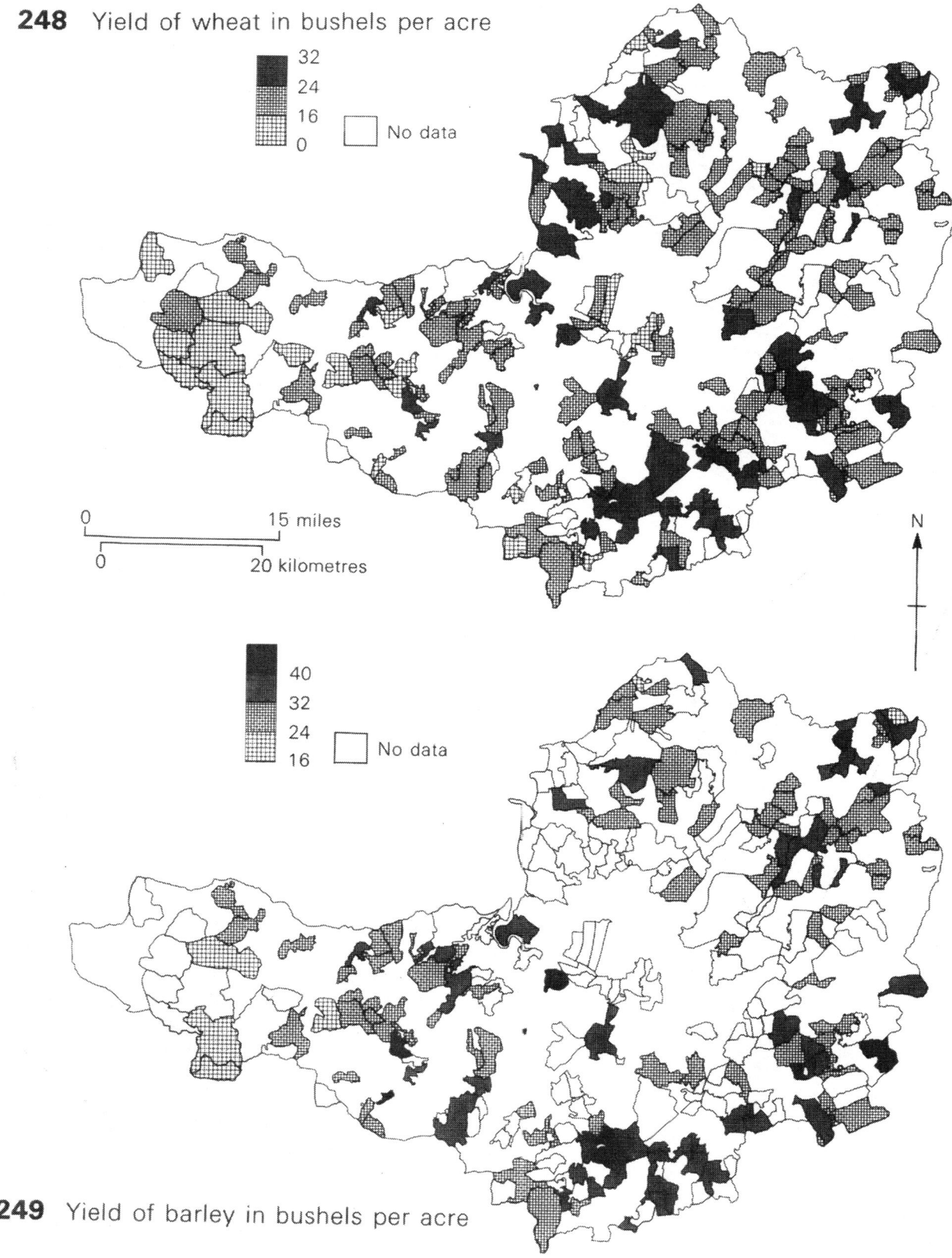

248 Yield of wheat in bushels per acre

249 Yield of barley in bushels per acre

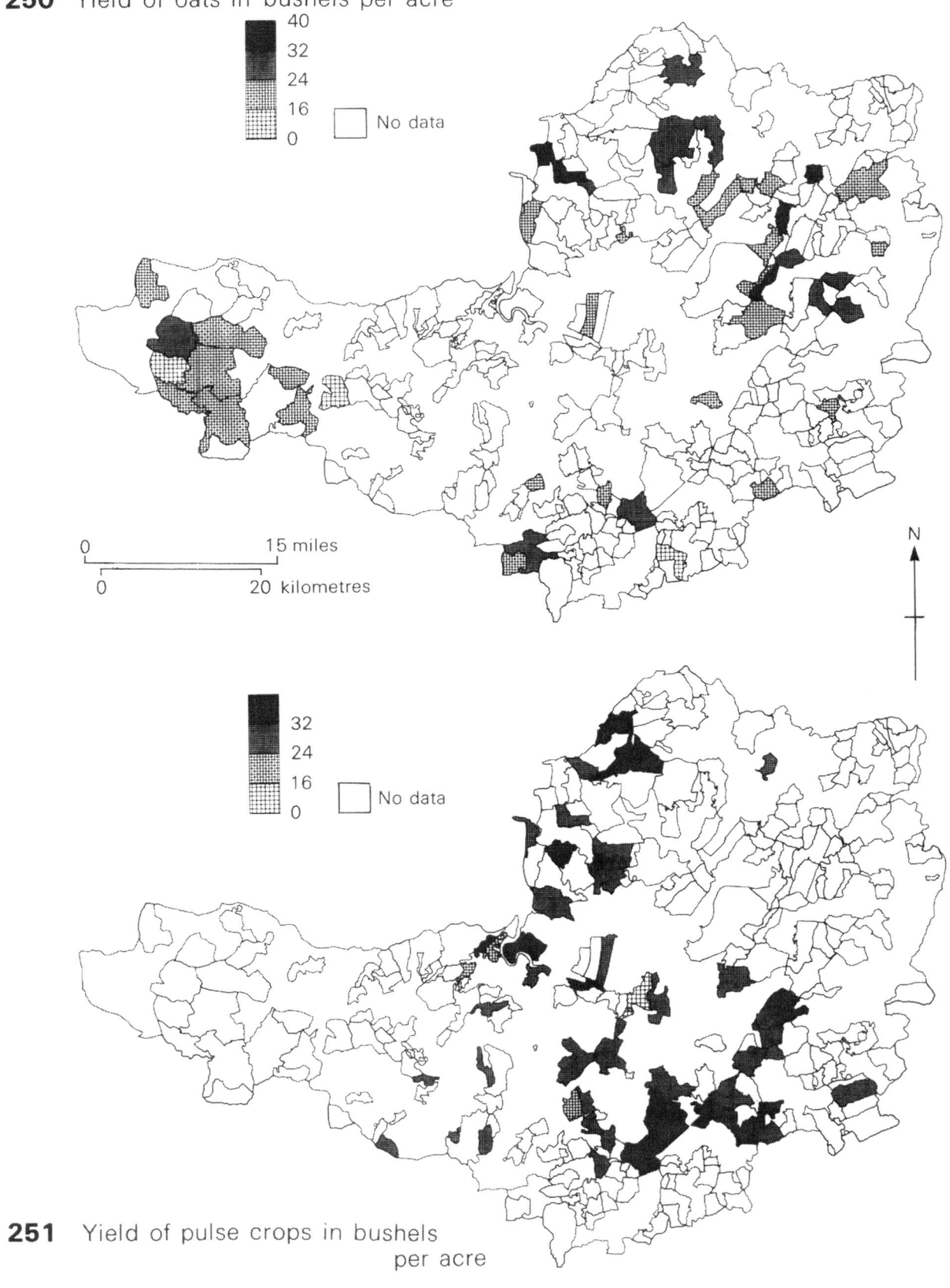

250 Yield of oats in bushels per acre

251 Yield of pulse crops in bushels per acre

Wiltshire

336 tithe districts
182 reports on tithe agreements

Tithe maps, apportionments and files of the mainly clayland parishes of north-west Wiltshire were thoroughly examined by B. R. Dittmer (1963) during research for his M.A. thesis on agricultural change. Wiltshire tithe files are also referred to in the article he co-authored with Elwyn Cox to draw attention of agricultural historians to the value of tithe files as a source of evidence (Cox and Dittmer, 1965). Summary data on land use and landownership have been transcribed from all Wiltshire tithe apportionments by R. E. Sandell (1975) and J. P. Dodd (1982) has aggregated these for comparison with the 1854 agricultural statistics collected on a Poor Law Union basis.

Overall, Wiltshire tithe files are not an especially rich source of information on agriculture and rural landscapes. This is principally because some 80 per cent of reports on agreements were compiled by commissioner George Bolls (Table 29) who assiduously commented on the accuracy of schedules of agreement, estimated acreages of arable, pasture, coppice, down and common, the yields of corn and pulse crops, noted soil type and rotations but said very little on landscapes or agricultural practices.

Most of the thirty-eight tithe free parishes in 1836 were exonerated from payments by allotments of land at the time of parliamentary enclosure. In addition, moduses on hay and cows were widespread and usually plantations as well as timber trees were exempt leaving coppice as the only form of titheable woodland. At a number of places where only part of a parish had been rendered tithe free by enclosure, it is reported that farmers specifically adapted their management practices to take advantage of this situation. At Sherston, for example

> the composition for the Great Tithes has been low, in consequence of there being upwards of 1100 acres of land tithe free, under an Act of Parliament for inclosing the commons and open fields, lands being awarded to the appropriators in lieu of the tithes. These lands are intermixed with the titheable and the occupiers having an opportunity of sowing the principal part of their corn on the tithe free lands and feeding the other for which there is a trifling modus payable to the Vicar.

On chalk and stone-brash soils, a Norfolk four-course (sometimes with clover left for two years) is the rotation most frequently recorded (116 entries in Subject Index). On some heavy clay soils, a traditional three-course wheat, beans, fallow system was still followed. In Wiltshire parishes where there were distinctly different types of land, assistant commissioners stated a rotation for each. At Fovant, for example, it was four-course 'in the vale' and six-course 'on the hills'; at Ham, three-course in 'the clay vale' and four-course 'on the chalk hills'.

Grassland management and livestock husbandry receive even scantier notice than arable farming in Wiltshire tithe files (see Subject Index). Water meadows were exceptionally valuable but receive little comment. Downland was included under the 'pasture' heading at some places but more often open downland is entered as 'common' in tithe file land use schedules. Cattle breeding and fattening are hardly mentioned; the number of cows kept is usually recorded on the printed forms but there are few other details of dairying. Sheep were kept in most parishes and were considered the most important livestock by Wiltshire local tithe agents. Depasturing on Salisbury Plain in summer is discussed as is the complementary practice of taking in tegs for over-wintering in parishes with adequate supplies of feed.

Table 29 *Reports on agreements for commutation of tithes in Wiltshire*

Assistant commissioner/ local tithe agent	1836	1837	1838	1839	1840	1841	1842	1843	1844	1845	1848	Totals
George Bolls		7	47	48	25	14	3					144
Aneurin Owen			4	4	2				2	4	1	17
Charles Pym		4	8									12
Robert Page								4				4
James Jerwood						2						2
John Johnes	2											2
Thomas Smith Woolley		1										1
Totals	2	12	59	52	29	14	3	4	2	4	1	182

Table 30 *Land use, crops and yields in Wiltshire, c. 1836*

A	Land use	Percentage of total land area enumerated in reports on tithe agreements	Estimated acreage in whole county
	Arable	35.1	303,833
	Grass	50.9	440,522
	Wood	6.2	53,479
	Common	7.5	65,085
B	Crop	Mean percentage of arable	Mean yield per acre	Estimated acreage in whole county
	Wheat	34.5	22.0 bushels	104,741
	Barley	28.1	30.2 bushels	85,270
	Oats	5.0	28.9 bushels	15,298
	Pulses	2.5	28.7 bushels	7,496

194 South-western counties

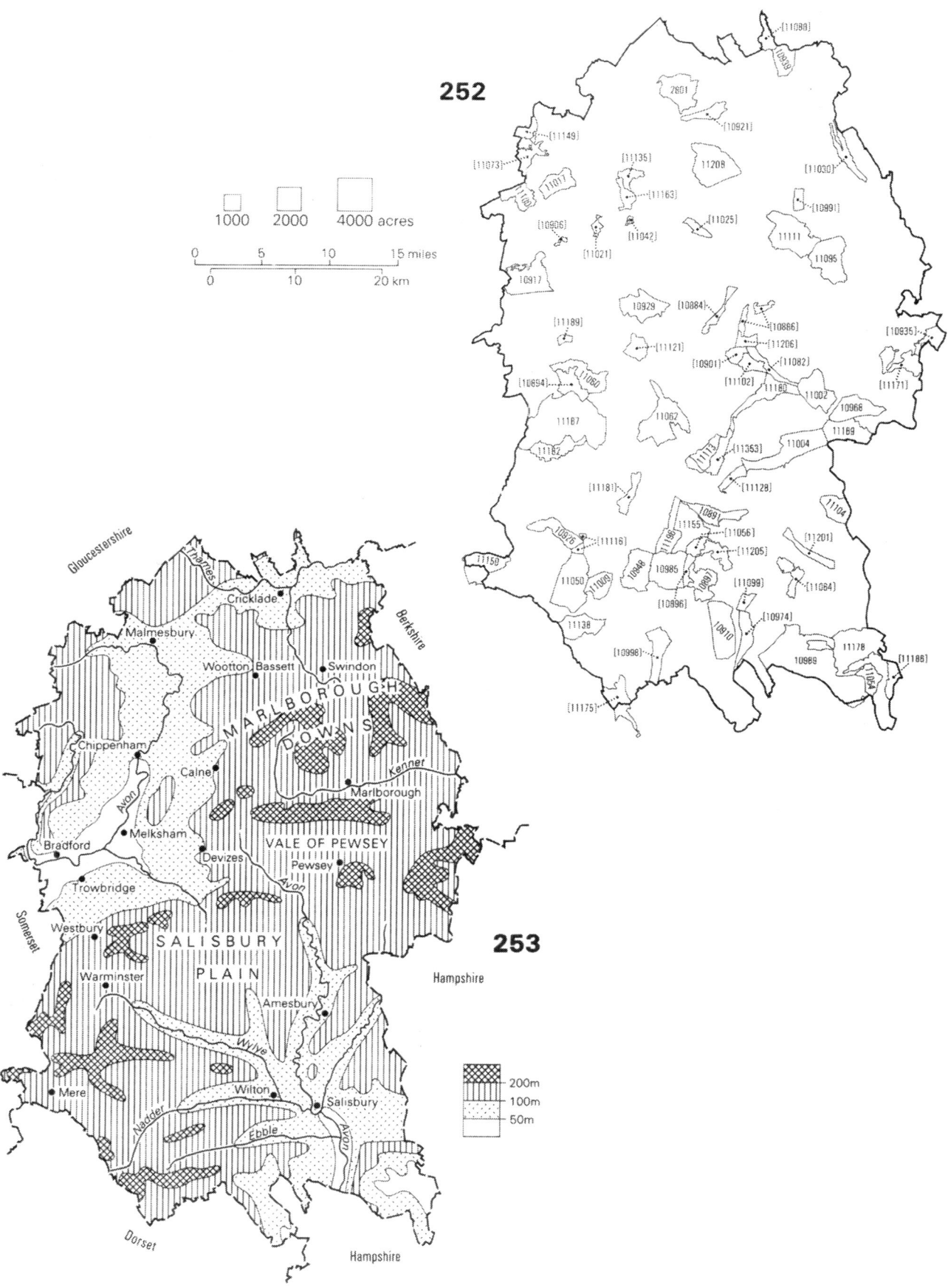

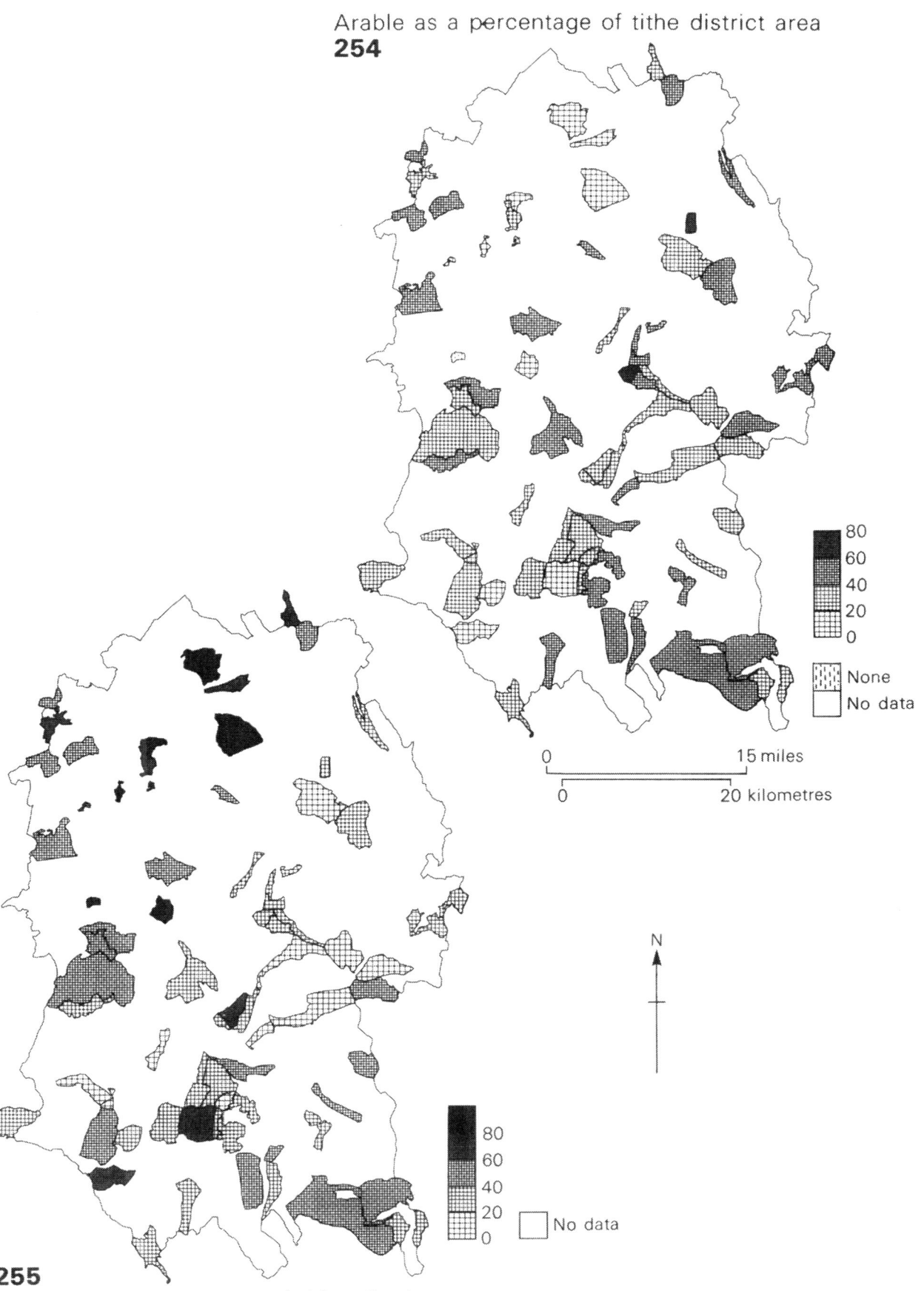

254 Arable as a percentage of tithe district area

255 Pasture as a percentage of tithe district area

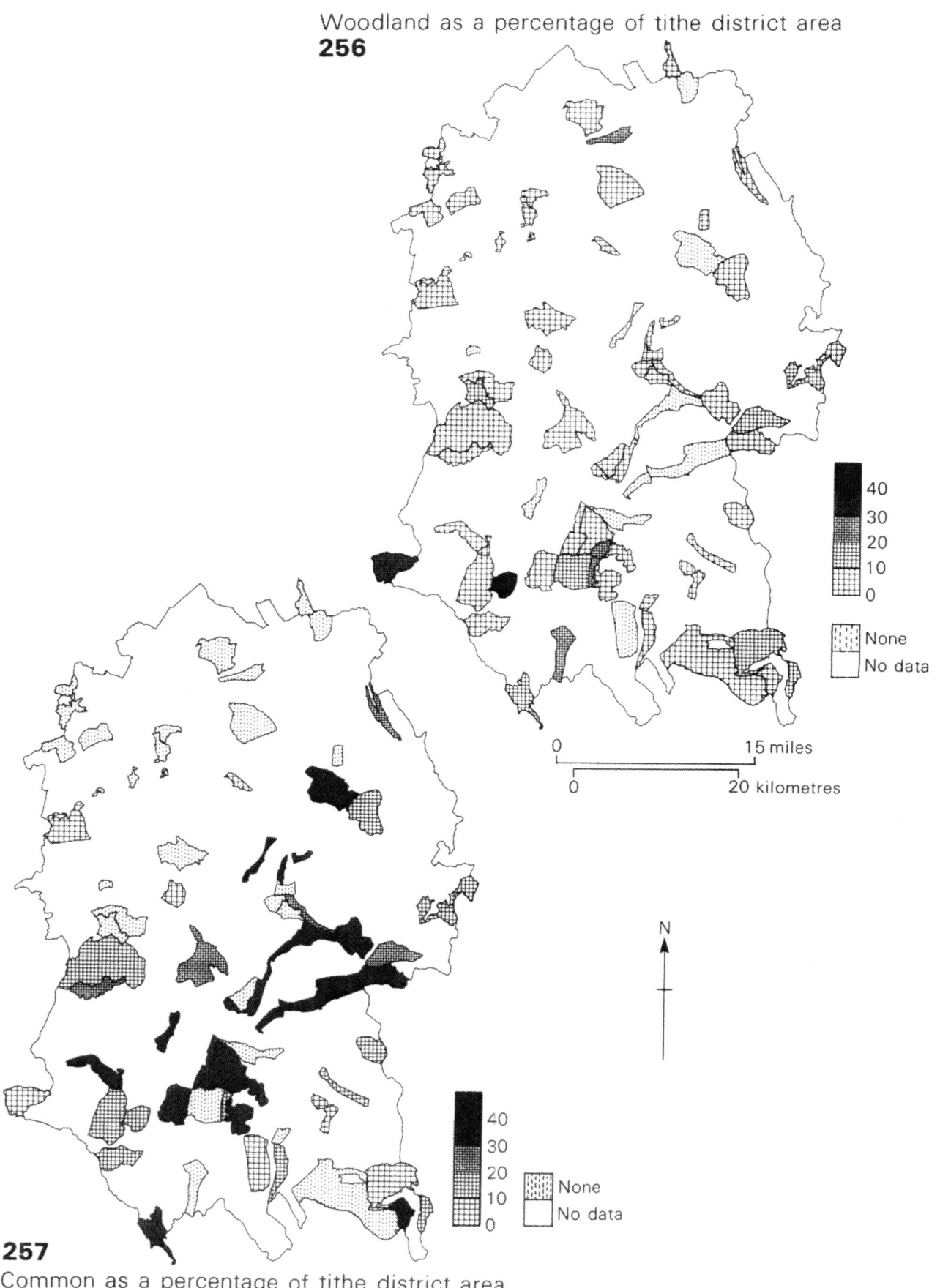

256 Woodland as a percentage of tithe district area

257 Common as a percentage of tithe district area

258 Wheat as a percentage of arable

259 Barley as a percentage of arable

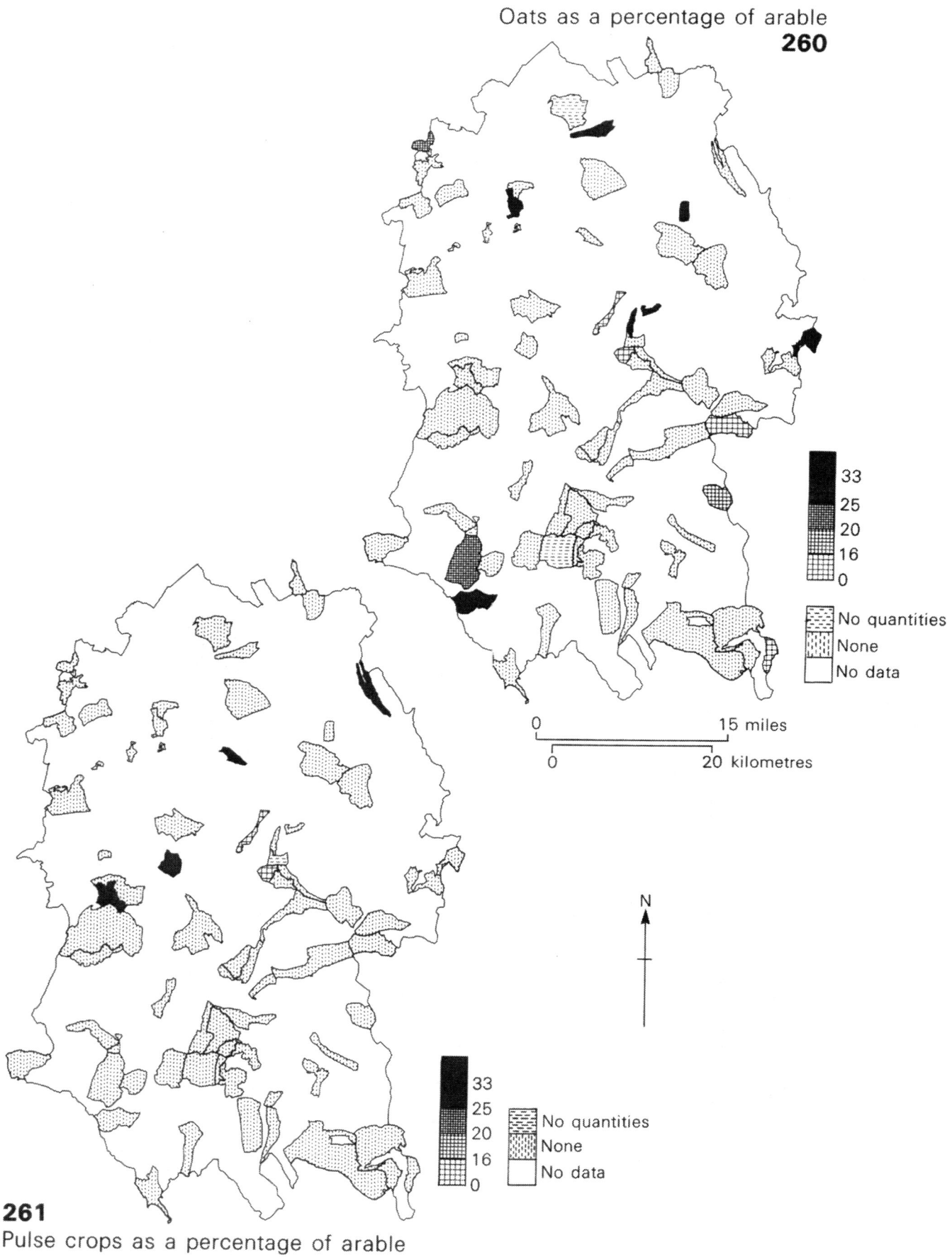

260 Oats as a percentage of arable

261 Pulse crops as a percentage of arable

Wiltshire

Yield of wheat in bushels per acre
262

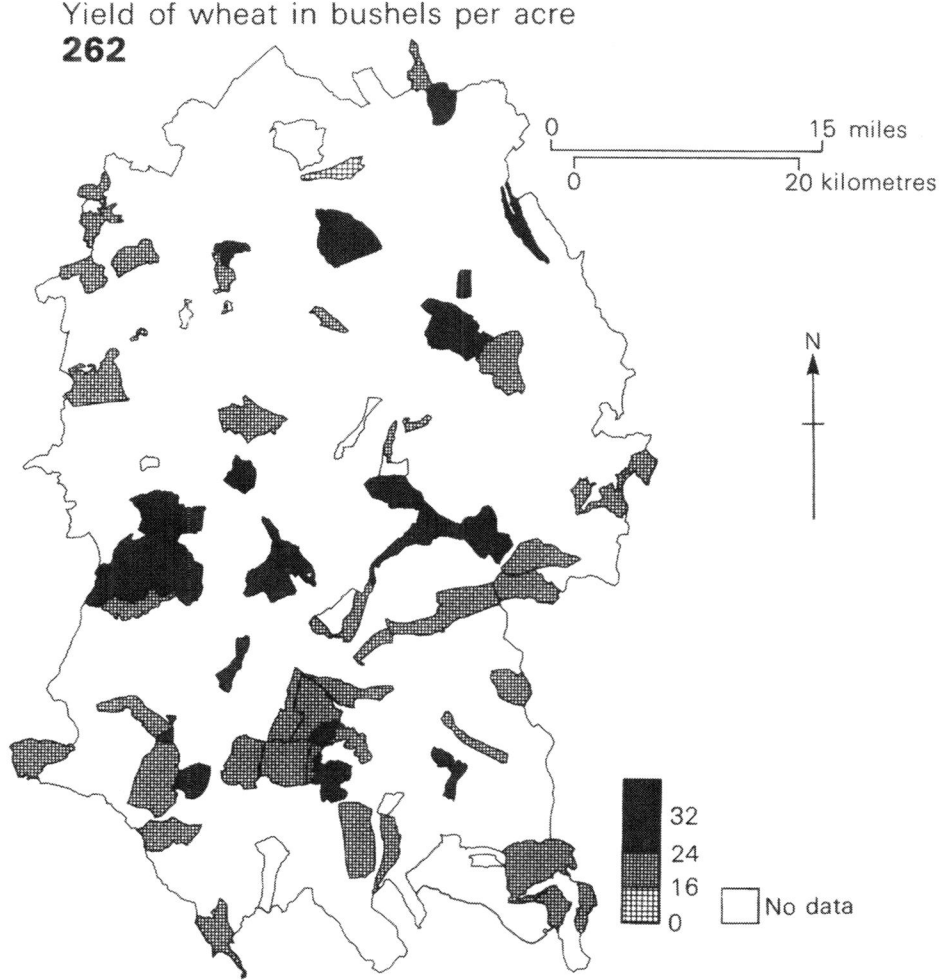

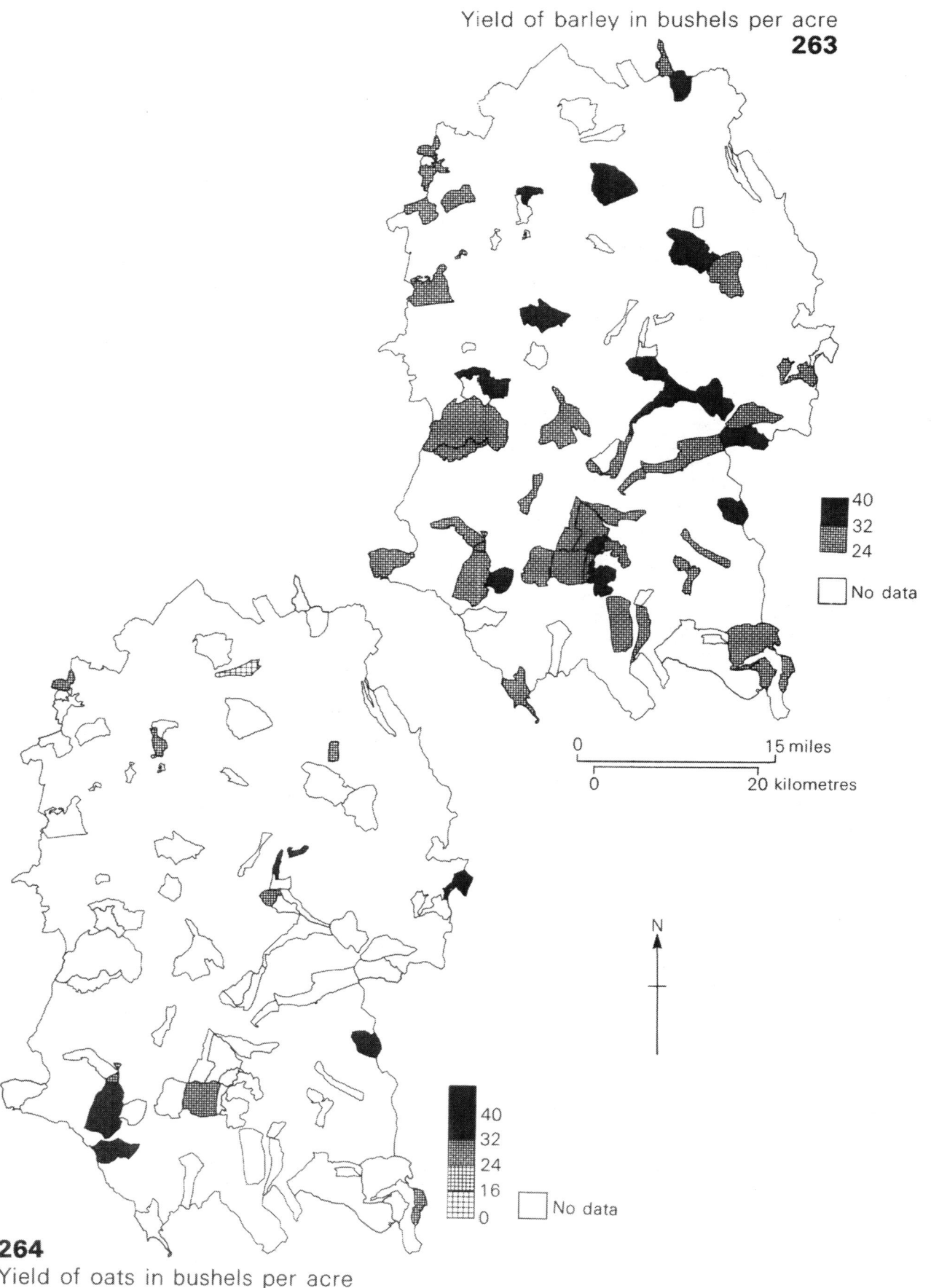

263 Yield of barley in bushels per acre

264 Yield of oats in bushels per acre

Dorset

283 tithe districts
176 reports on tithe agreements

Tithes were commuted by voluntary agreement in about two-thirds of Dorset parishes but for only 112 of these districts are quantitative data in agreement schedules complete in the sense defined in the Introduction, pp. 19–20. Land use and crop statistics are absent for those parishes visited before printed report forms came into general use during 1838, a number of parishes were partially enclosed and had abolished some tithes at the time of enclosure, and assistant commissioners/local tithe agents George Louis, Robert Page and John Milner rarely specify crop rotations in ways which enable estimates of grain crops to be calculated. George Bolls who completed exactly two-thirds of Dorset reports on tithe agreements does not describe local agricultural practices in either his written reports or on printed forms (Table 31). In combination, these factors mean that the body of Dorset tithe files is flawed as a source for reconstructing agriculture and farming practices. The entries for Dorset in the Subject Index are among the fewest for a county of this size. G. L. Cunningham (1974) has used tithe surveys in his reconstruction of the rural landscape of the heathlands of south-east Dorset as has R. F. J. Chiplen (1969) for his study of the Vale of Blackmoor. Reference can be made to these for further details on Dorset tithe surveys and evidence that they contain on agricultural improvement.

Table 32 and Maps 267–8 indicate the quantitative importance of grassland compared with arable in Dorset at the time of tithe commutation, this was particularly the case in the north of the county and the Vale of Blackmoor where Aneurin Owen recorded in 1839 that 'the parish of Stoke Wake is situated upon the south side of the Vale of Blackmore, and is composed partly of declivities which are here steep, and which constitute the arable portion of the lands, and partly of an expanse of a cold ungenial clayey soil, which forms the meadow and pasture lands'. The surface area of arable exceeded that of pasture in only a few parishes on the Dorset downs. The open downland of Dorset occasioned considerable comment in the files mostly about whether it should be classed as pasture or common for purposes of assessing rent-charge. George Bolls' usual practice was to strike out 'common' on printed report forms substituting 'downland' instead. At Chilfrome north-west of Maiden Newton 'there was also great debate as to the amount of arable lands, occasioned by some poor downland having been converted into tillage for a few years and again laid down to grass'. Large acreages of heathland were recorded as common in south-eastern parishes; the parish of Studland, for example, consisted 'principally of a low tract of an infertile silicious soil covered for the most part with heather and stunted furze, and appears to be incapable of improvement but at a great expense'.

Table 32 and Maps 272–7 summarise the quantities and distribution of arable crops and their yields. Four- and five-course rotations were most common especially on lighter soils; on poor soils seeds might lie for three years being mown for the first and fed for the remainder. At Melbury Osmond south of Yeovil, James Jerwood found 'wheat^1, turnips^2, barley^3, clover^{4,5} (best land) and wheat^1, oats^2, clover^{4,5,6} (inferior)'. Where there were still open fields, as at Stratton near Dorchester, for example, a three-course rotation was often practised, otherwise the distinction drawn by assistant commissioners/local tithe agents was always between heavy and light land systems. At Burton Bradstock, a coastal parish, 'it was stated at the meeting that not more than 300 acres of arable land was in tillage in any one year, the greater portion being a strong clay and but seldom ploughed. When the land will not bear grass any longer, they then plough it up, take a crop or two and sow it down to grass again.' By contrast Robert Page remarked in 1843 that 'the parish of West Knighton is situated within four miles of Dorchester, the soil is a light sand, on chalk and gravel, it is easily tilled on the four-field system, and produces good crops of turnips and barley'. Assistant commissioners did not come across many such places; corn yields were not very large particularly on hill lands (Table 32 and Maps 275–7).

Dorset

Table 31 *Reports on agreements for commutation of tithes in Dorset*

Assistant commissioner/ local tithe agent	1837	1838	1839	1840	1841	1842	1843	1844	1845	Totals
George Bolls	10	36	36	15	13	6				116
James Jerwood		6	12	4						22
George Louis		17								17
Robert Page	1	2					5			8
John Milner	7									7
Aneurin Owen			3					1	1	5
Thomas Phippard		1								1
Totals	18	62	51	19	13	6	5	1	1	176

Table 32 *Land use, crops and yields in Dorset c. 1836*

A	Land use	Percentage of total land area enumerated in reports on tithe agreements	Estimated acreage in whole county
	Arable	21.5	135,599
	Grass	66.6	421,157
	Wood	4.5	28,225
	Common	5.3	33,473

B	Crop	Mean percentage of arable	Mean yield per acre	Estimated acreage in whole county
	Wheat	34.0	20.4 bushels	46,036
	Barley	25.1	29.7 bushels	33,978
	Oats	11.0	32.8 bushels	14,869

204 South-western counties

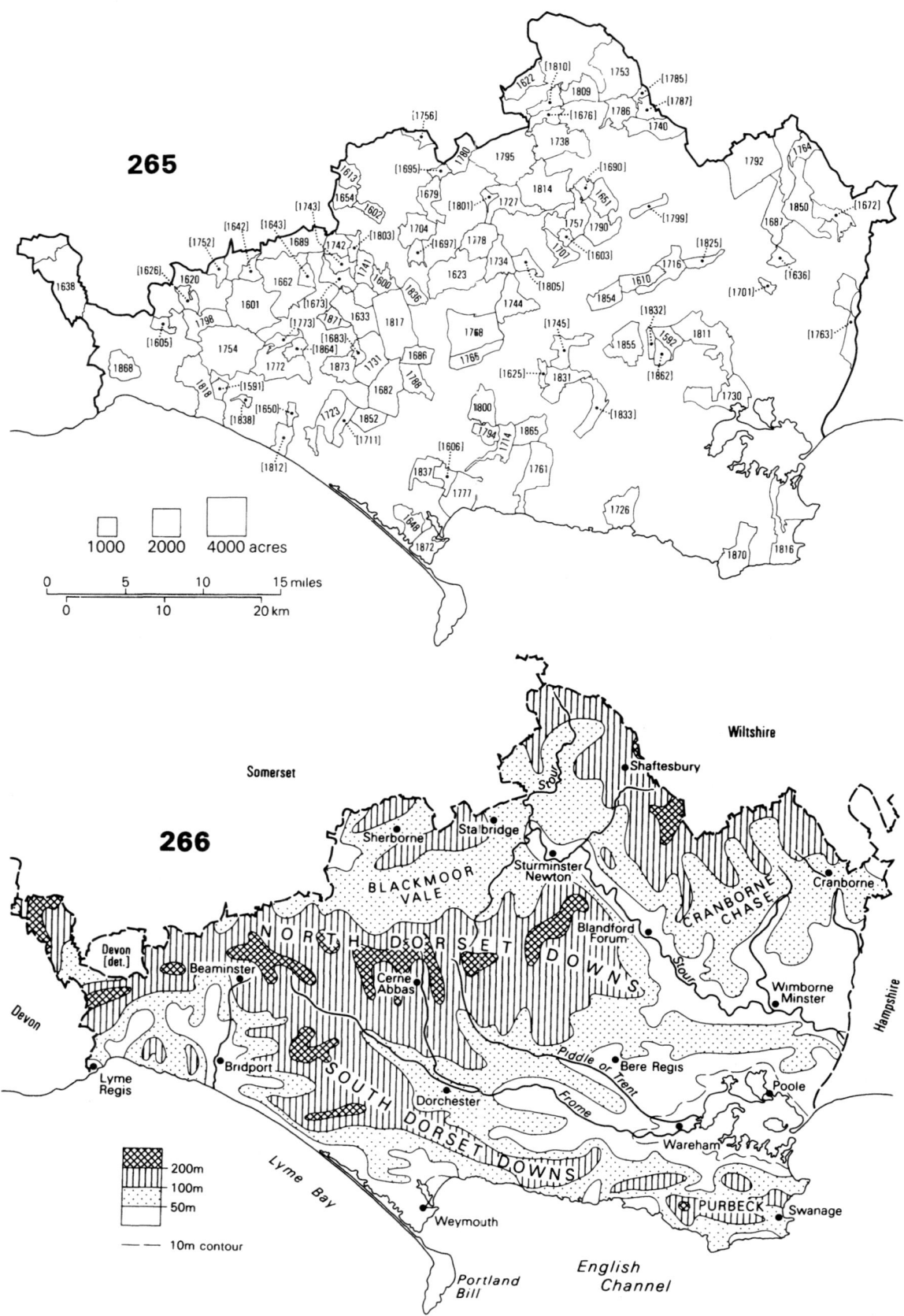

267 Arable as a percentage of tithe district area

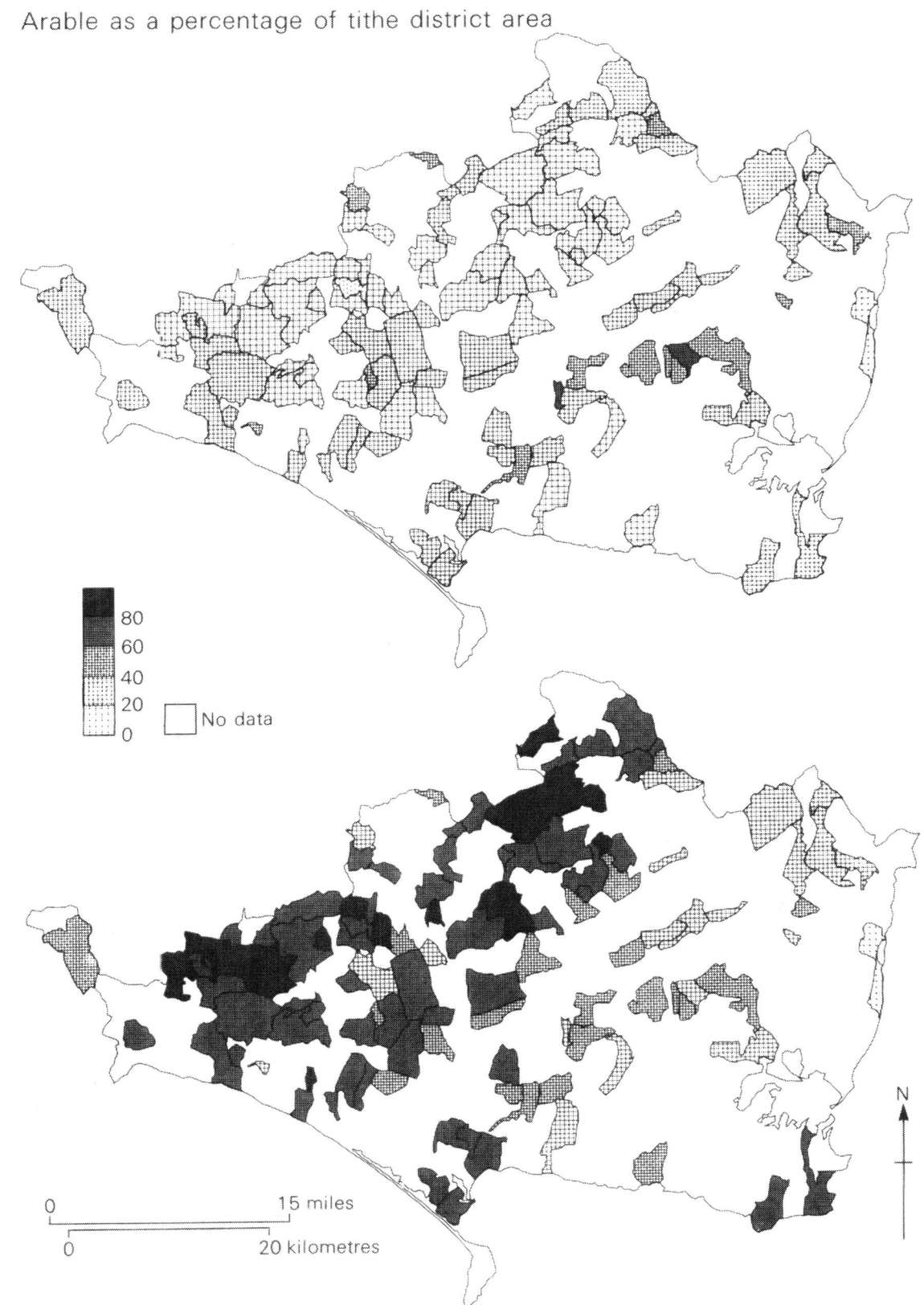

268 Pasture as a percentage of tithe district area

206 South-western counties

269 Woodland as a percentage of tithe district area

270 Common as a percentage of tithe district area

Dorset

271 Orchards and fruit as a percentage of tithe district area

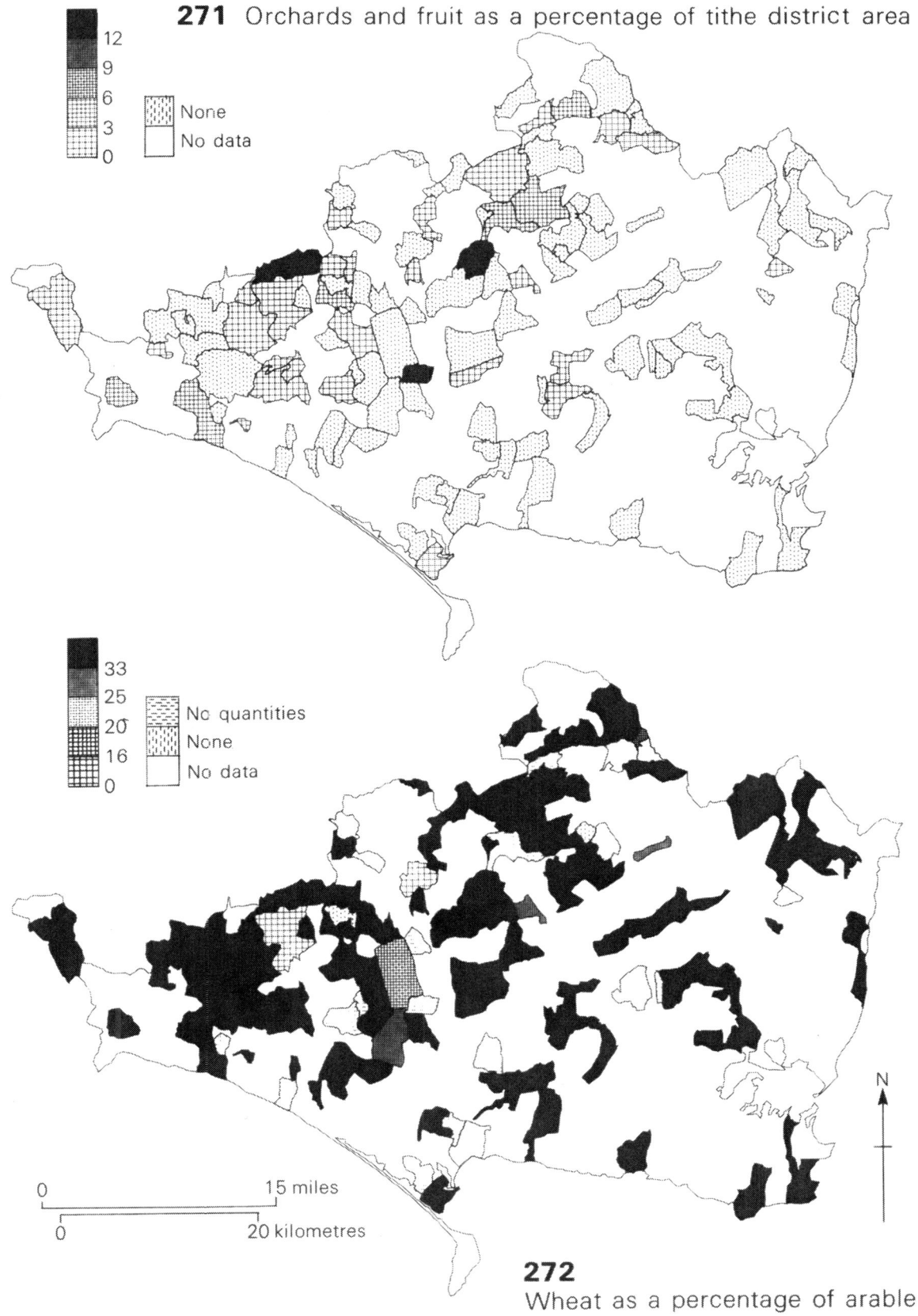

272 Wheat as a percentage of arable

273 Barley as a percentage of arable

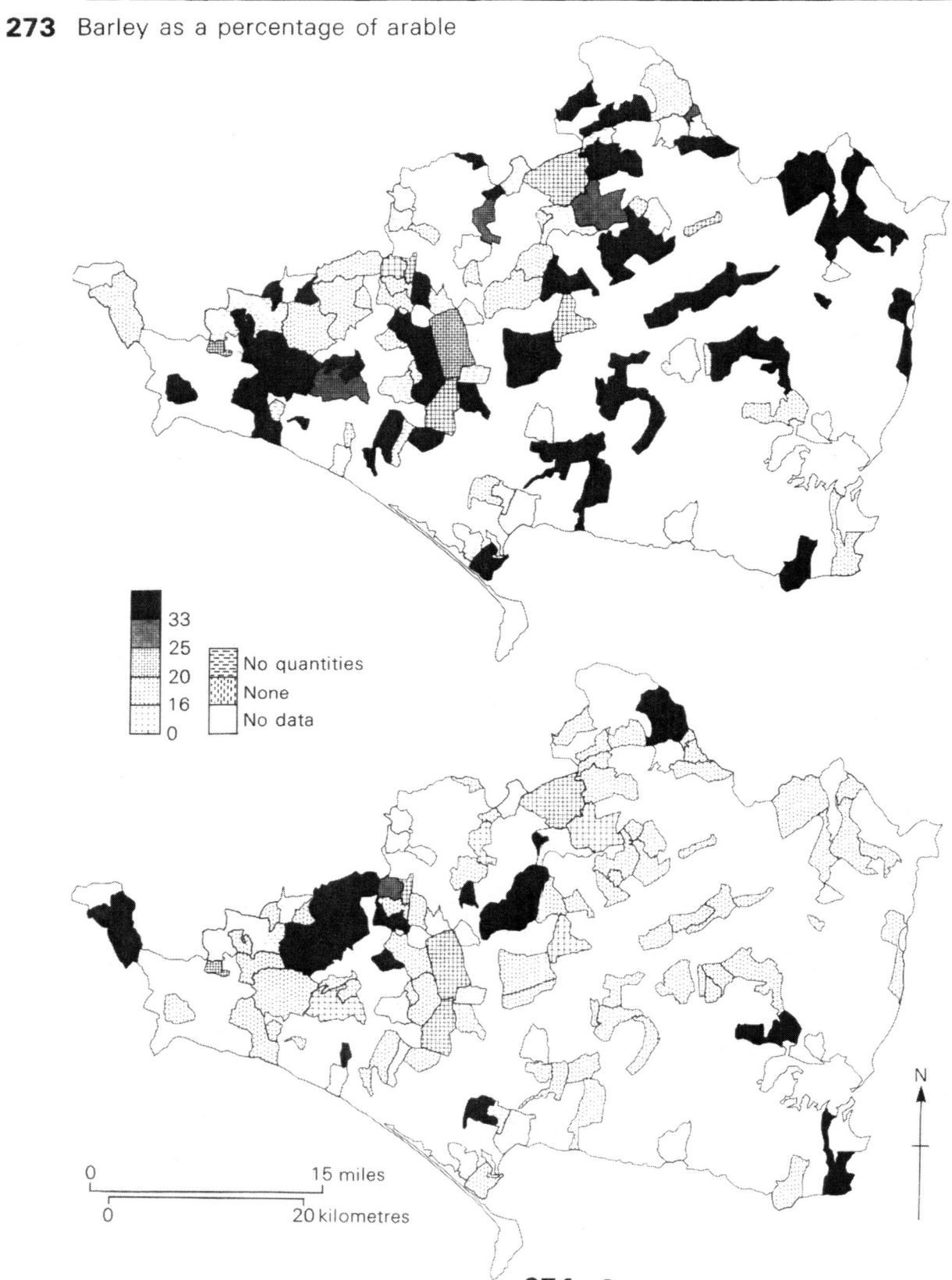

274 Oats as a percentage of arable

275 Yield of wheat in bushels per acre

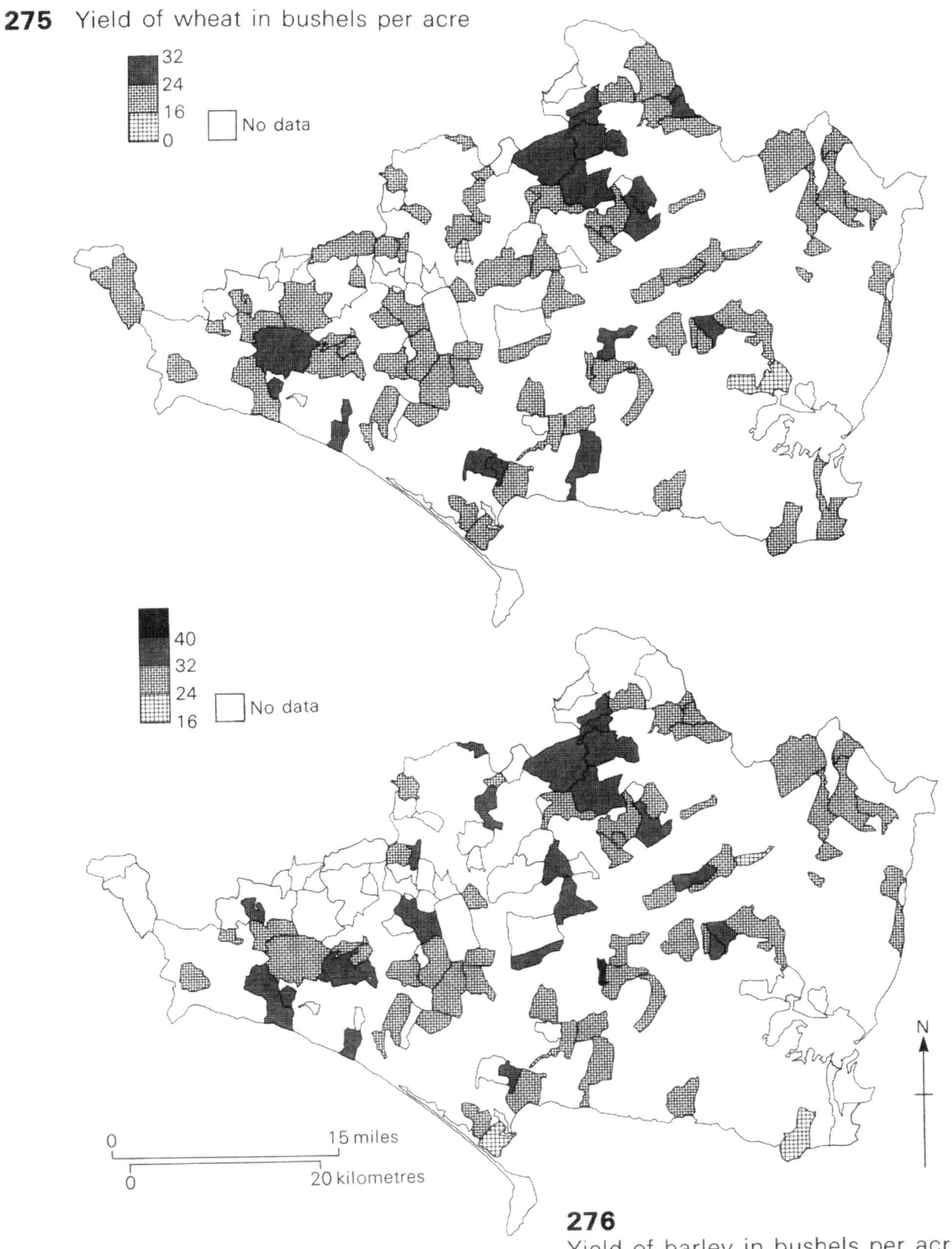

276 Yield of barley in bushels per acre

277 Yield of oats in bushels per acre

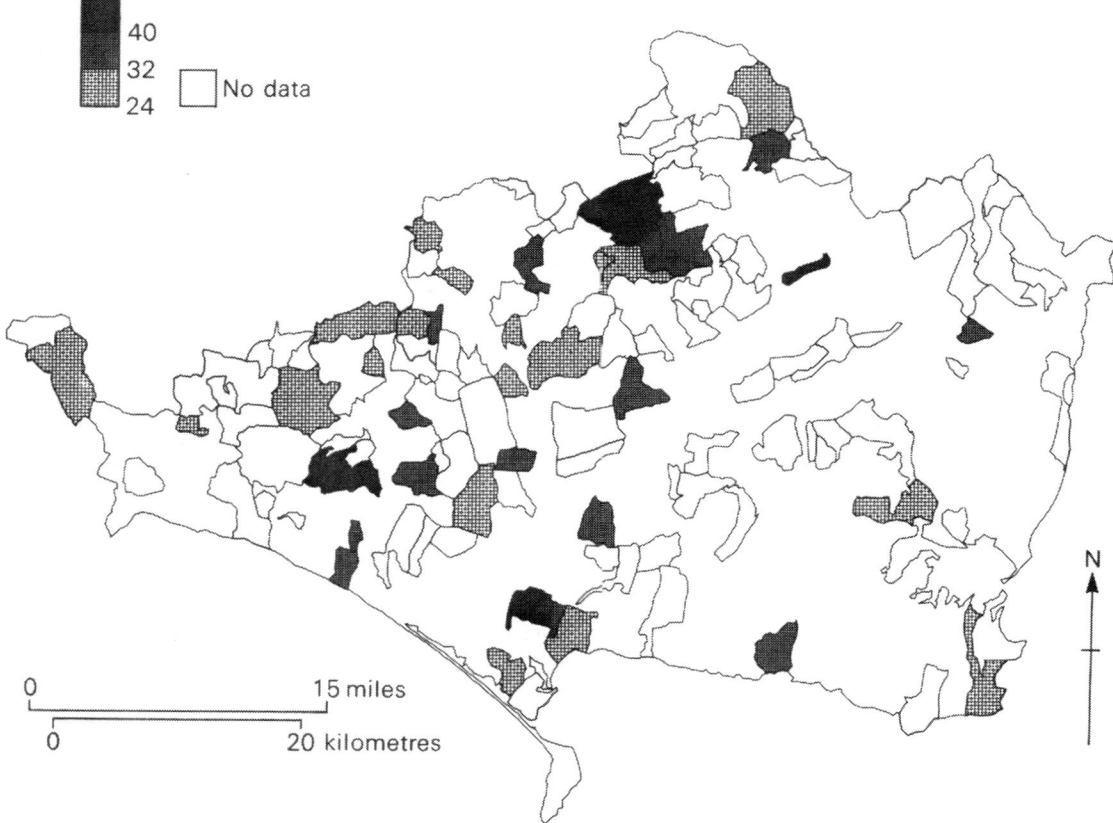

Devon

478 tithe districts
222 reports on tithe agreements

James Jerwood and Frederick Leigh completed 88 per cent of Devon reports on tithe agreements (Table 33); Leigh worked only in Devon and Jerwood only in south-western counties. Both men sent supplementary handwritten reports to the Tithe Commission in addition to printed 'pastoral' type report forms from each parish. Jerwood's reports are particularly full and informative.

There was relatively little land (only ten districts) entirely tithe free in Devon in 1836, the largest tract being the Forest of Dartmoor. In most parishes coppice was the only category of woodland titheable; plantations (usually fir) were invariably tithe free while acreages of commons and furzelands which generated very little titheable produce were only very approximately estimated. At Clannaborough, James Jerwood reported that 'the moorland is still Moss and would produce no tithes worth having and the 32 acres of woodland is filled with timber producing no tithes whatever. In this view of the parish, which I consider to be a correct one, all the lands except the arable would pay the tithe owner a very small sum indeed.' At Holne, Jerwood took issue with the tithe owner's high opinion of the natural productivity of the common 'unless stones and sterility be valuable. The common is a continuation of Dartmoor . . . it is quite noted for its wild, romantic scenery, but the scenery alone will not feed cattle.'

Land use in Devon is summarised in Table 34 and distributions of particular categories of land are presented in Maps 280–3. The system of farming practised in Devon was closely related to the nature of soils as local agent John Coldridge recognised at Crediton in south Devon, where 'on the best arable lands the crops are wheat, turnips, barley, and seeds alternately on the 4-course system of husbandry – and from the 4-course the system gradually declines to the 8-course on some of the most sterile clays'. In Devon and other western counties the term 'seeds' meant something very different from that in the east of England. In Devon it was quite usual for arable land to be laid down to seeds for three or four years after two or three corn crops and it was by no means uncommon for land to be seeded out for seven or eight years before paring and burning prior to another two years in corn (see Subject Index). At Thornbury near Holsworthy in north Devon, Jerwood found that 'much of the 1200 acres called "meadow and pasture" is broken up once in about 20 years'. These extreme practices and even the more common three-year leys were condemned by assistant commissioners, by both those whose main experience was rooted in western farming systems and those whose tithe survey employment had taken them to other parts of the country. Of the wheat, oats or barley, three years' seeds, cropping system of Pyworthy, an exasperated James Jerwood commented that 'their course of crops is the very worse than can be devised – could they be induced to alter it – the change must be an improvement'. He found the general appearance and land quality of Huntshaw 'as rough as the most ardent admirer of moor, bog and bramble-land, could wish to put his foot in'. Charles Pym's commissions took him across the whole breadth of the country (Table 1 in the Introduction) and he remarked of East Buckland, north-west of South Molton, that 'the whole of the hill district in this parish is adapted to turnips and sheep farming but owing to the small size of farms, the want of capital and skill among the occupiers ... the neighbourhood appears doomed not to participate in the improvement which has taken place during the last 25 years in the Midland counties of England'. The maps of crop yields (Maps 288–90) and Table 34 provide some quantitative support for such evaluations of Devon farming. Wheat was sown most extensively but yielded very poorly – as little as 7 bushels in some places; only in south and east Devon were yields comparable to the national average obtained. Barley and oats are distinguished separately in only about a half of the tithe files with extant crop data; a common entry was 'barley or oats' or 'barley and oats'. Rye was not grown and pulse crops not mentioned. Turnips and potatoes were cultivated in many parishes (eighty-six entries for potatoes in the Subject Index) but it is not possible to obtain a set of adequate data for these or other fallow crops for mapping. Where their cultivation is described in tithe files, this is entered in the Subject Index.

Devon

Table 33 *Reports on agreements for commutation of tithes in Devon*

Assistant commissioner/ local tithe agent	1837	1838	1839	1840	1841	1842	1843	1844	Totals
James Jerwood		53	33	19	3	7	4	3	122
Frederick Leigh			25	29	14	5			73
Charles Pym	9	2							11
Robert Page		5	2		2				9
George Louis		3							3
John Coldridge		1	1						2
Aneurin Owen								2	2
Totals	9	64	61	48	19	12	4	5	222

Table 34 *Land use, crops and yields in Devon c. 1836*

A	Land use	Percentage of total land area enumerated in reports on tithe agreements	Estimated acreage in whole county
	Arable	22.5	373,120
	Grass	47.2	782,083
	Wood	4.3	71,948
	Common	23.3	386,397
B	Crop	Mean percentage of arable	Mean yield per acre	Estimated acreage in whole county
	Wheat	34.2	15.6 bushels	127,678
	Barley	23.8	25.9 bushels	88,951
	Oats	12.4	28.3 bushels	46,084

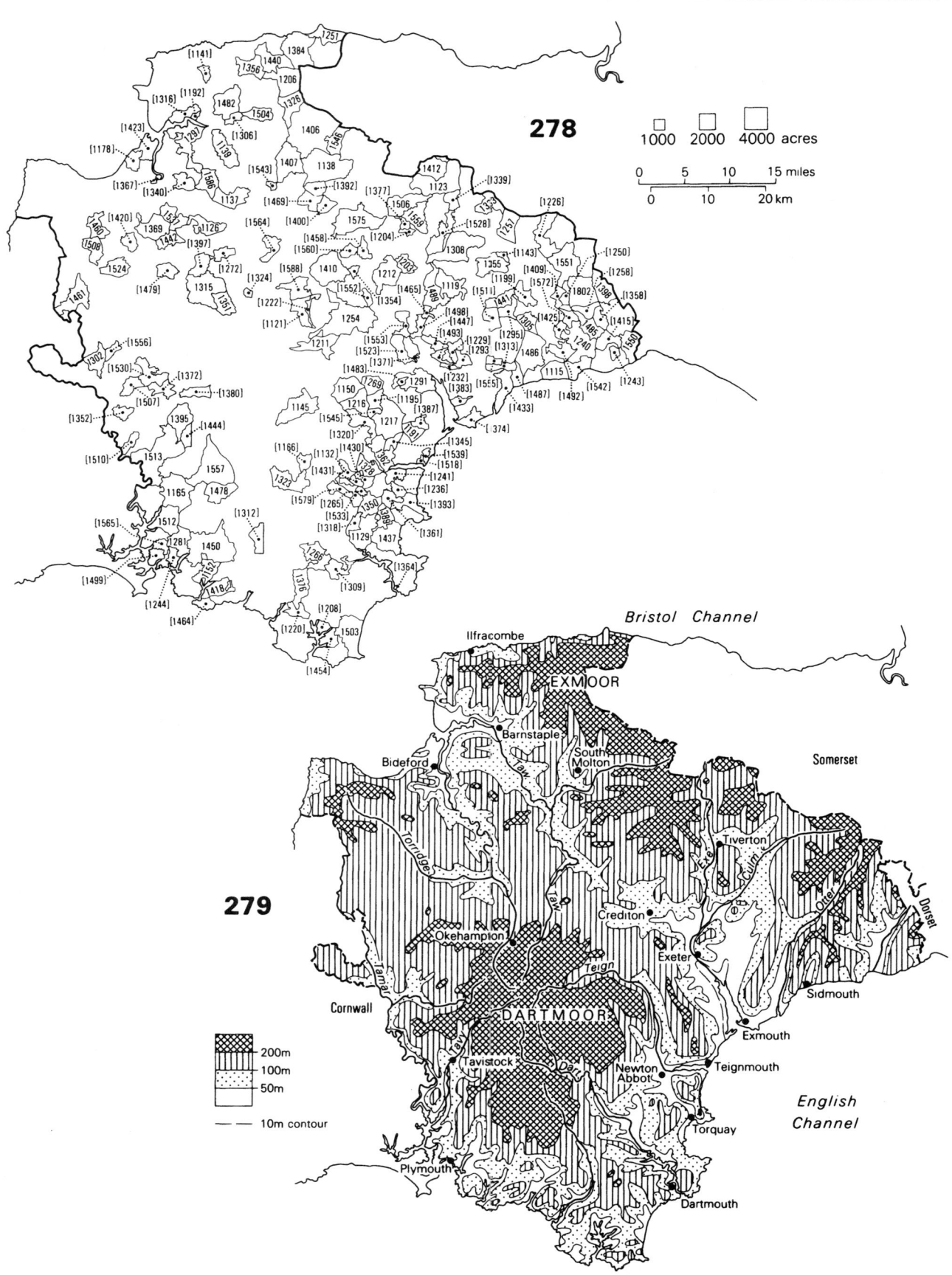

Devon

280 Arable as a percentage of tithe district area

281 Pasture as a percentage of tithe district area

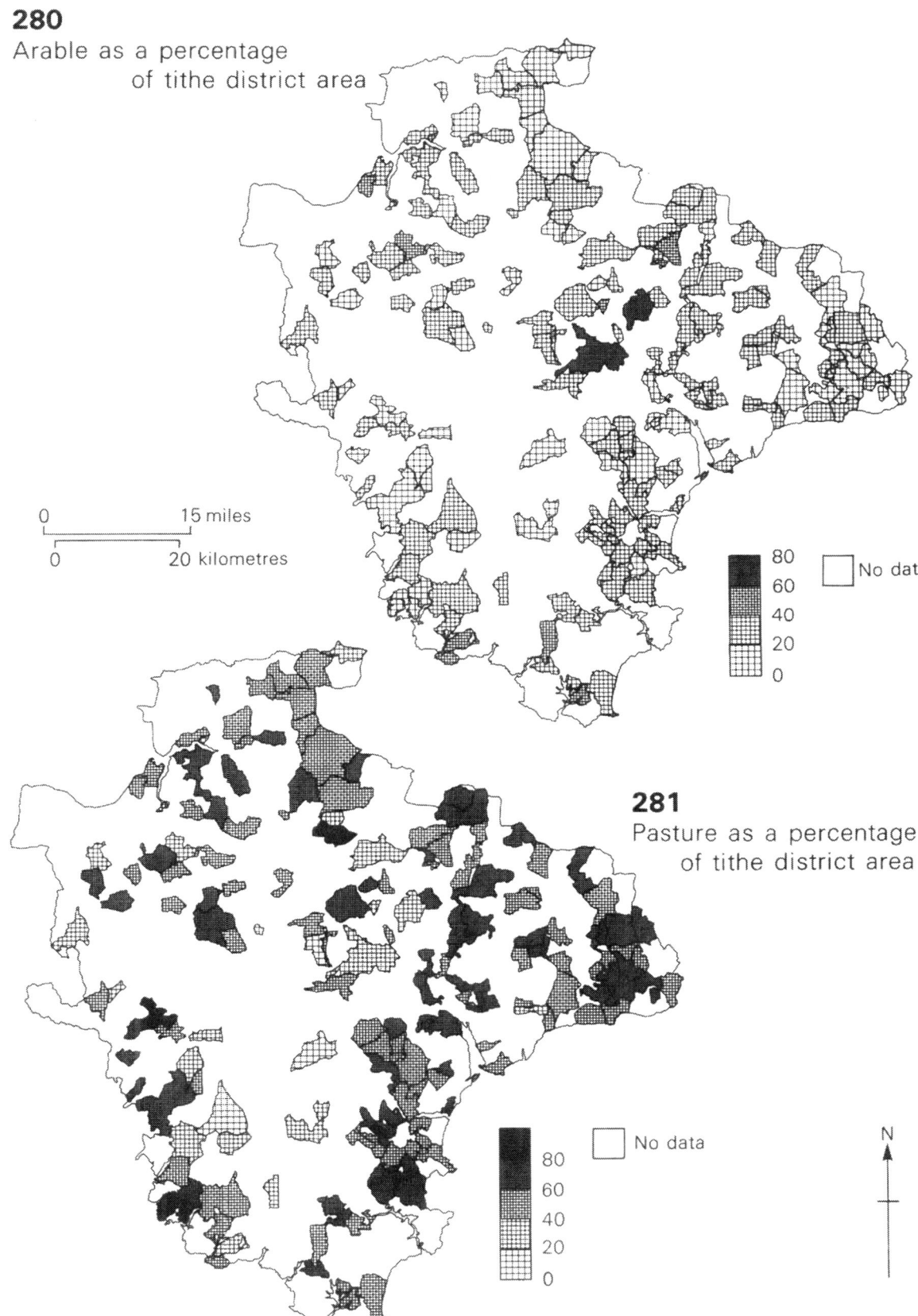

South-western counties

282 Woodland as a percentage of tithe district area

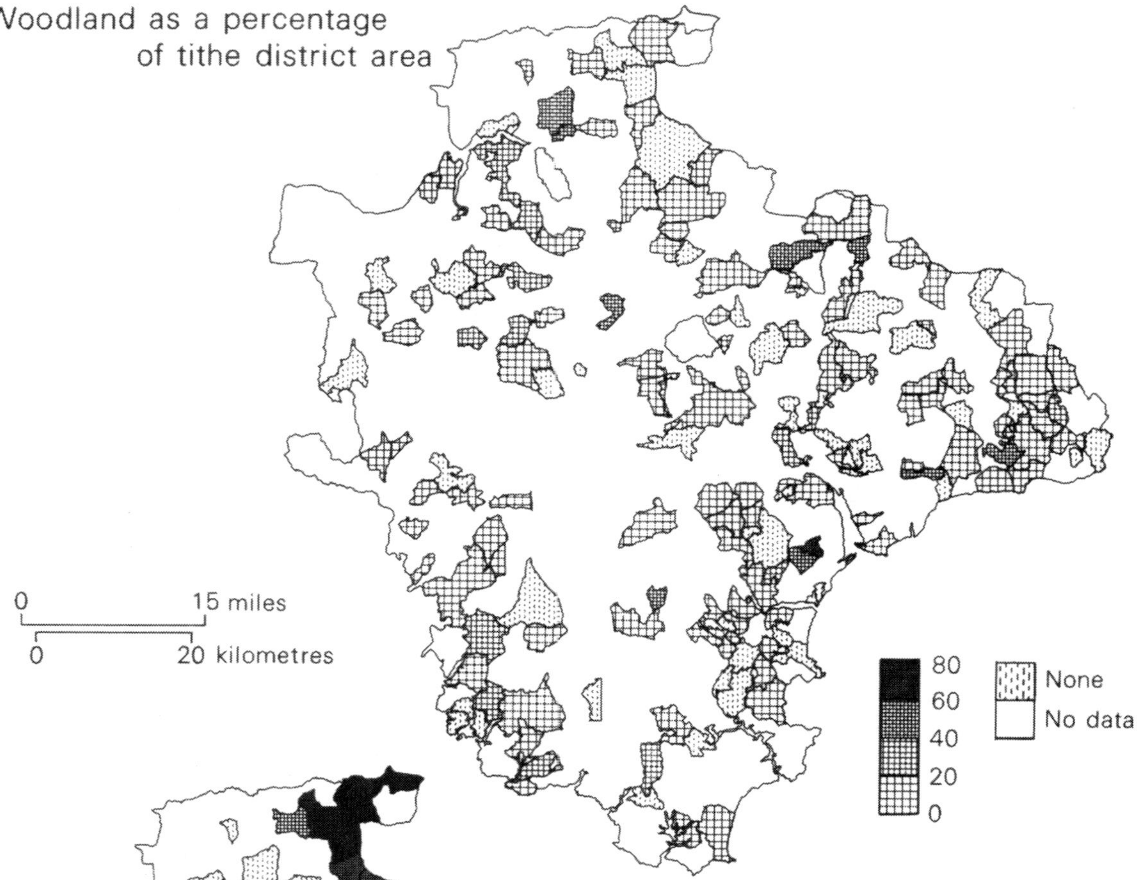

283 Common as a percentage of tithe district area

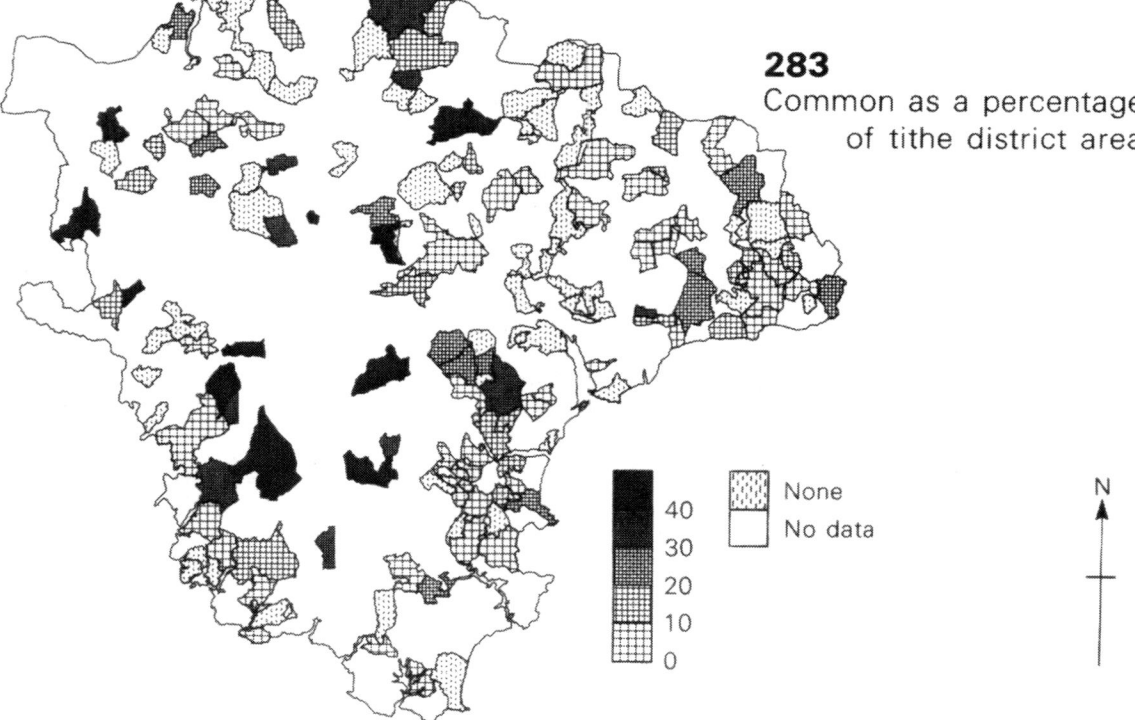

284
Orchards and fruit as a percentage of arable

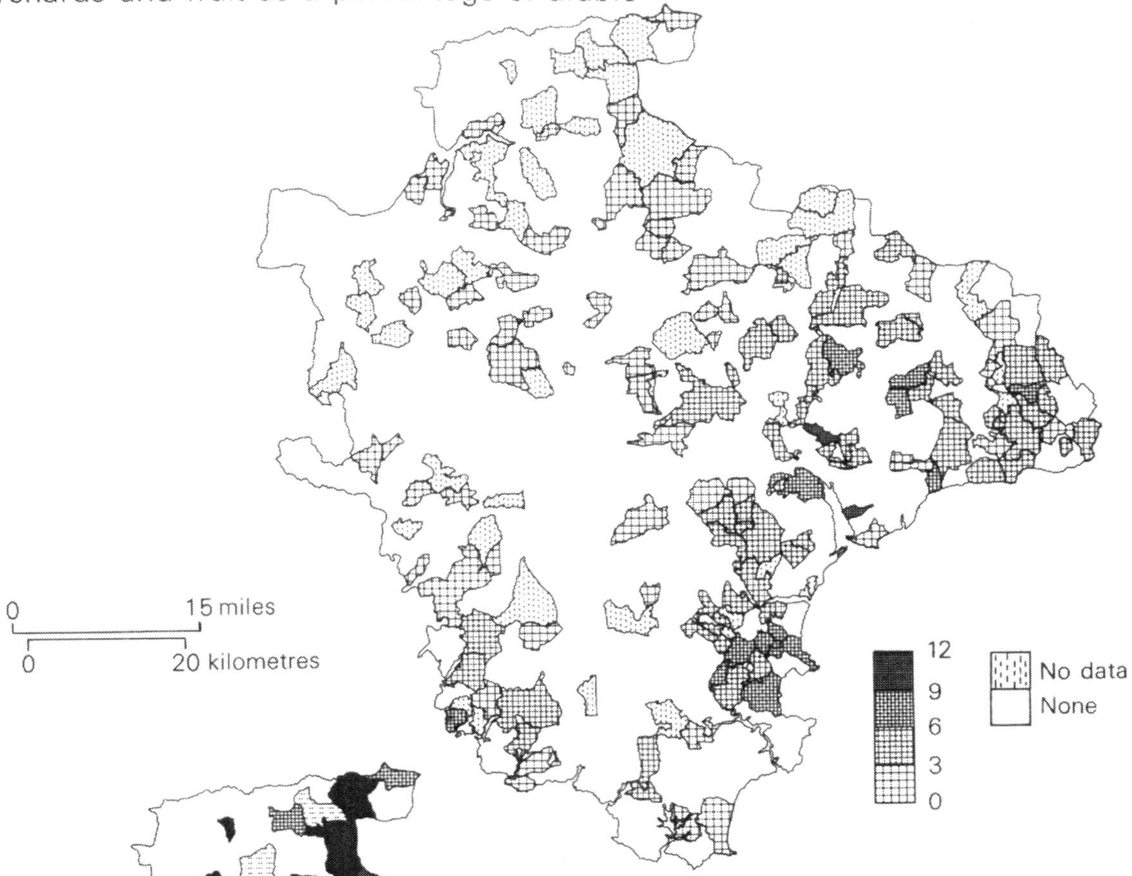

285
Wheat as a percentage of arable

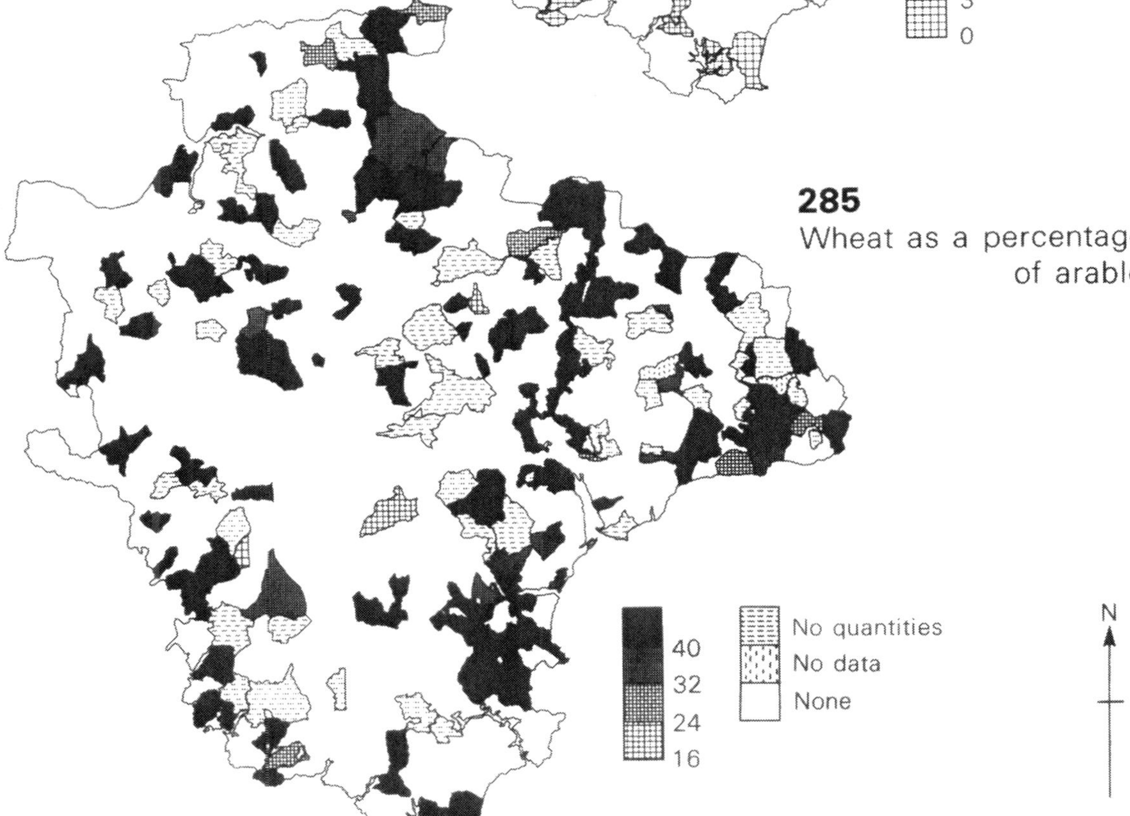

286
Barley as a percentage of arable

287
Oats as a percentage of arable

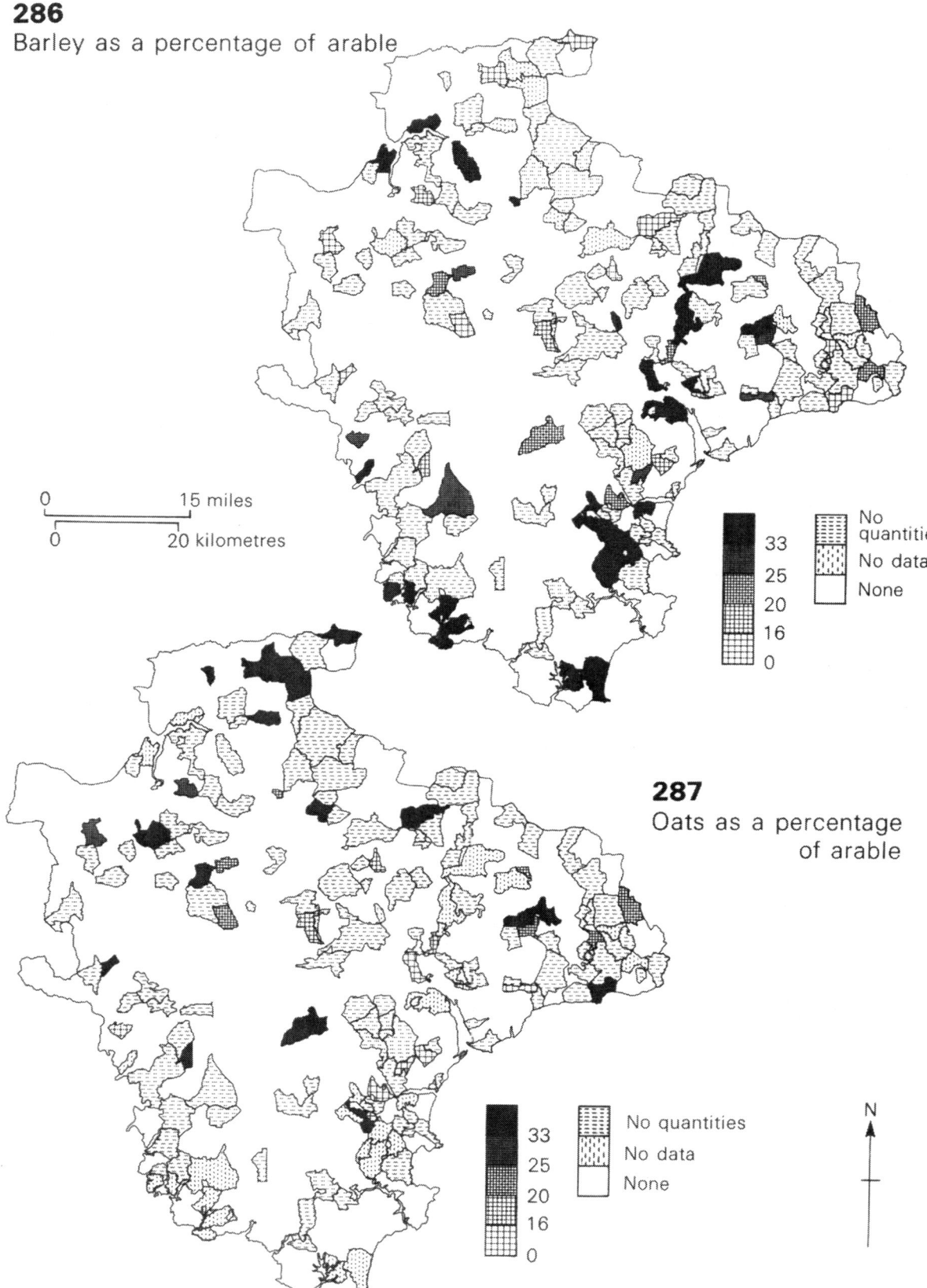

288
Yield of wheat in bushels per acre

289
Yield of barley in bushels per acre

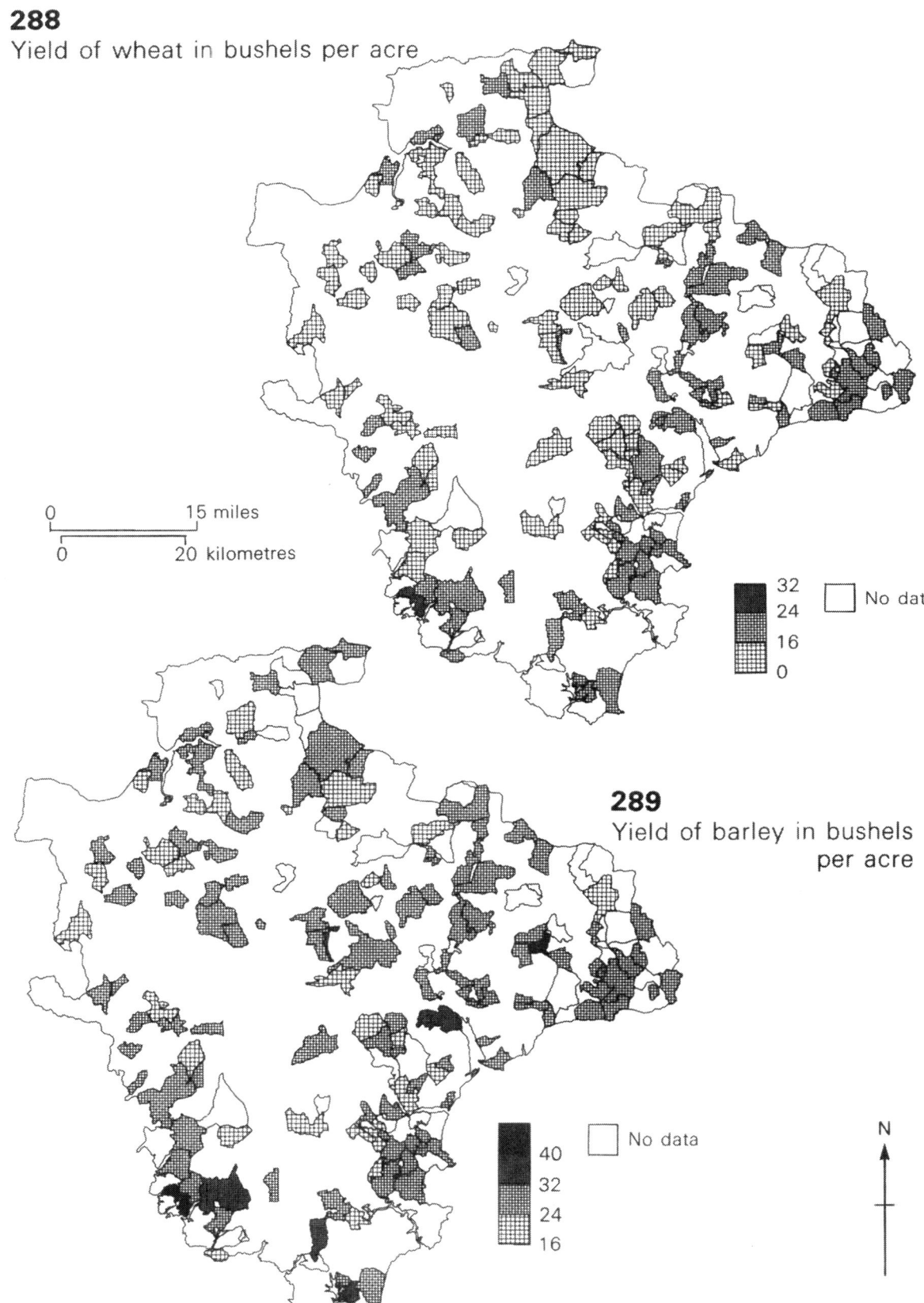

290
Yield of oats in bushels per acre

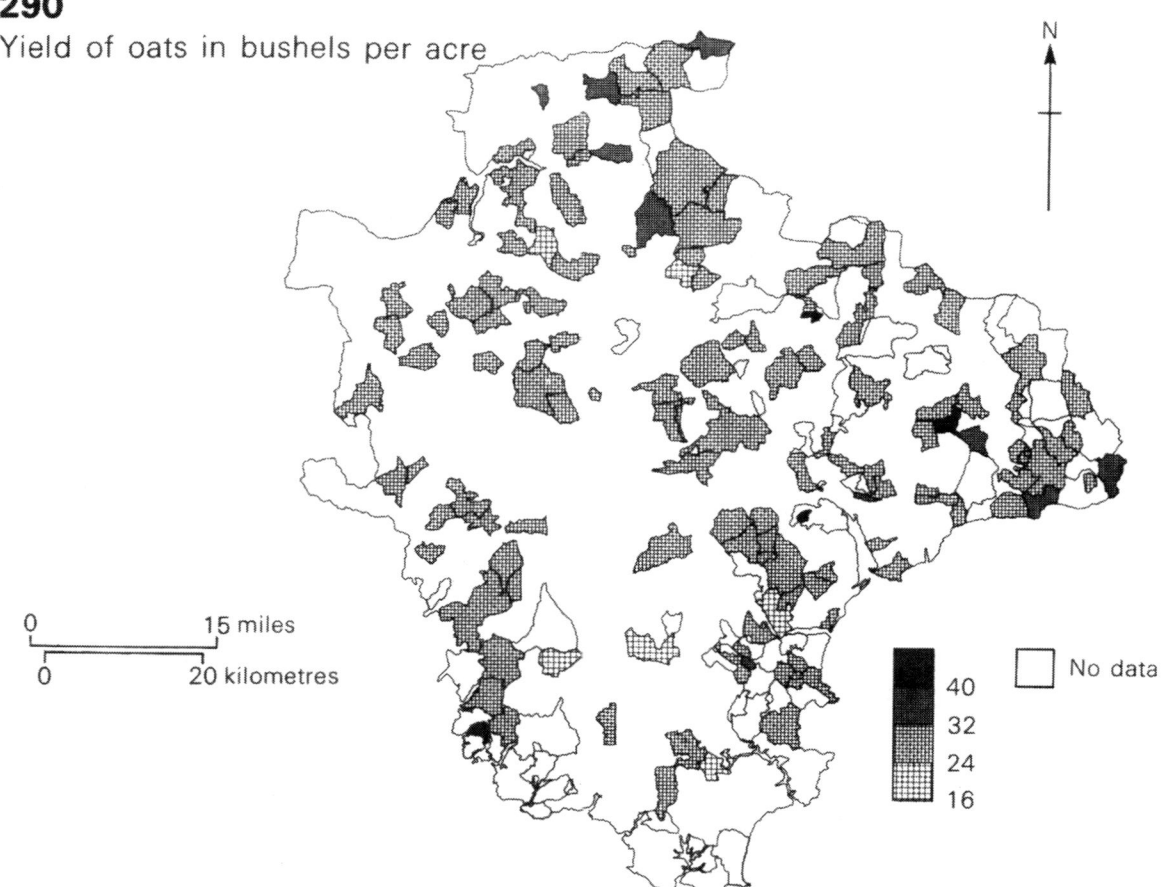

Cornwall

212 tithe districts
116 reports on tithe agreements

T. R. B. Dicks (1964) consulted the estimates of land use in schedules to tithe apportionments for Cornish parishes in his comparative study of farming in Pembrokeshire and the south-west peninsula of England. Land use data from tithe apportionments can be misleading in western counties (see *The tithe surveys of England and Wales*, pp. 193–6), particularly in respect of the proportion of arable to pasture. A study of agriculture and land use in Cornwall revealed by an analysis of tithe file derived data has been published by R. J. P. Kain and H. M. E. Holt (1981) and the following brief account is based on this paper.

No parish in Cornwall was entirely tithe free, although some contained tithe free estates or particular categories of land exempt from tithe payment or land covered by moduses. Table 35 indicates that two assistant commissioners, James Jerwood and William Glasson, completed almost all the Cornish reports (Jerwood 53 per cent; Glasson 38 per cent), and that 83 per cent were compiled in the four years 1838–41 inclusive. Both Jerwood and Glasson worked extensively in Devon as well and, as in that county, they wrote short manuscript reports to supplement the Tithe Office's printed questionnaire form. Their answers in Cornwall are not, however, as full or as useful as those for Devon. Jerwood often states two contrasting crop rotations and so for these parishes it is not possible to deduce the acreages of different crops, in particular, to separate the spring corns – oats and barley, and green and root crops on the fallows. Hence the small number of places which appear on some crop maps (Maps 298–300) compared with the land use maps (Maps 293–7). Furthermore, it is obvious that Glasson has relied on information provided by landowners rather than extensive personal inquiry when completing his reports, which contain little information on topics outside a narrow focus on soil type and crop rotations.

In all but one Cornish parish with extant tithe file data, arable land accounted for less than 40 per cent of parish area *c*. 1840 and for many this figure is less than 20 per cent (Table 36 and Map 293). Parishes on the Hartland Plateau and on Bodmin Moor had particularly low proportions of arable to pasture. There was, though, no great extent of natural meadows, a deficiency that was made up largely by the practice of laying down arable with artificial grasses. Hay was then cut from both meadows and ley pastures which in the extreme south-west produced yields of more than 30 cwts per acre, among the very best in the country at this time. Woodland was almost absent in extreme south-western parishes and covered less than 10 per cent of the surface area in most other places. Commons, many of them described as very poor, were quite extensive in Cornwall (17.4 per cent of county area) and provided rough grazing in summer for livestock. These grazings, known locally as 'crofts', were occasionally fenced for a couple of years and ploughed for one or two corn crops.

Table 36 summarises the average quantities of various crops sown on the arable and Maps 298–300 indicate their distribution and yields throughout the county. Wheat was the leading crop followed closely by barley; relative to the rest of England barley yielded better in Cornwall than did wheat. In only three parishes for which data are extant was more than a third sown with oats and these were all places on granite upland soils. The tithe files reveal that pulses were a rarity in Cornwall at this date. The remainder of the arable was sown with a variety of green crops and root crops including potatoes but none of these is enumerated sufficiently consistently in the files to be mapped or incorporated in Table 36.

Associated with the low arable acreages recorded in Cornwall were exceptionally long rotations; the four-course typical of eastern counties was found in only a very few Cornish parishes (nine references in Subject Index). The traditional Devon and Cornwall system of paring and burning old grassland, manuring it with sea-sand, lime, seaweed or fish, depending on availability, and then growing several crops of corn, the last being undersown with grass seed, was still being followed by many farmers. Rotations of five to eight years are the most frequently recorded (see Subject Index), the variation in length being a matter of how long a piece of land was allowed to lie in seeds.

Cornwall

Table 35 *Reports on agreements for commutation of tithes in Cornwall*

Assistant commissioner/ local tithe agent	1837	1838	1839	1840	1841	1842	1843	1844	1845	Totals
James Jerwood			1	24	19	9	4	3	1	61
William Glasson		11	24	9						44
Charles Pym	2	4								6
Frederick Leigh					2					2
George Louis		1					1			2
William Richards			1							1
Totals	2	16	26	35	19	9	5	3	1	116

Table 36 *Land use, crops and yields in Cornwall c. 1836*

A	Land use	Percentage of total land area enumerated in reports on tithe agreements	Estimated acreage in whole county
	Arable	23.8	206,896
	Grass	54.9	476,244
	Wood	3.3	28,510
	Common	17.4	150,806
	Orchards	0.7	6,032

B	Crop	Mean percentage of arable	Mean yield per acre	Estimated acreage in whole county
	Wheat	32.7	17.9 bushels	67,410
	Barley	29.5	28.2 bushels	60,751
	Oats	10.2	31.0 bushels	21,073

South-western counties

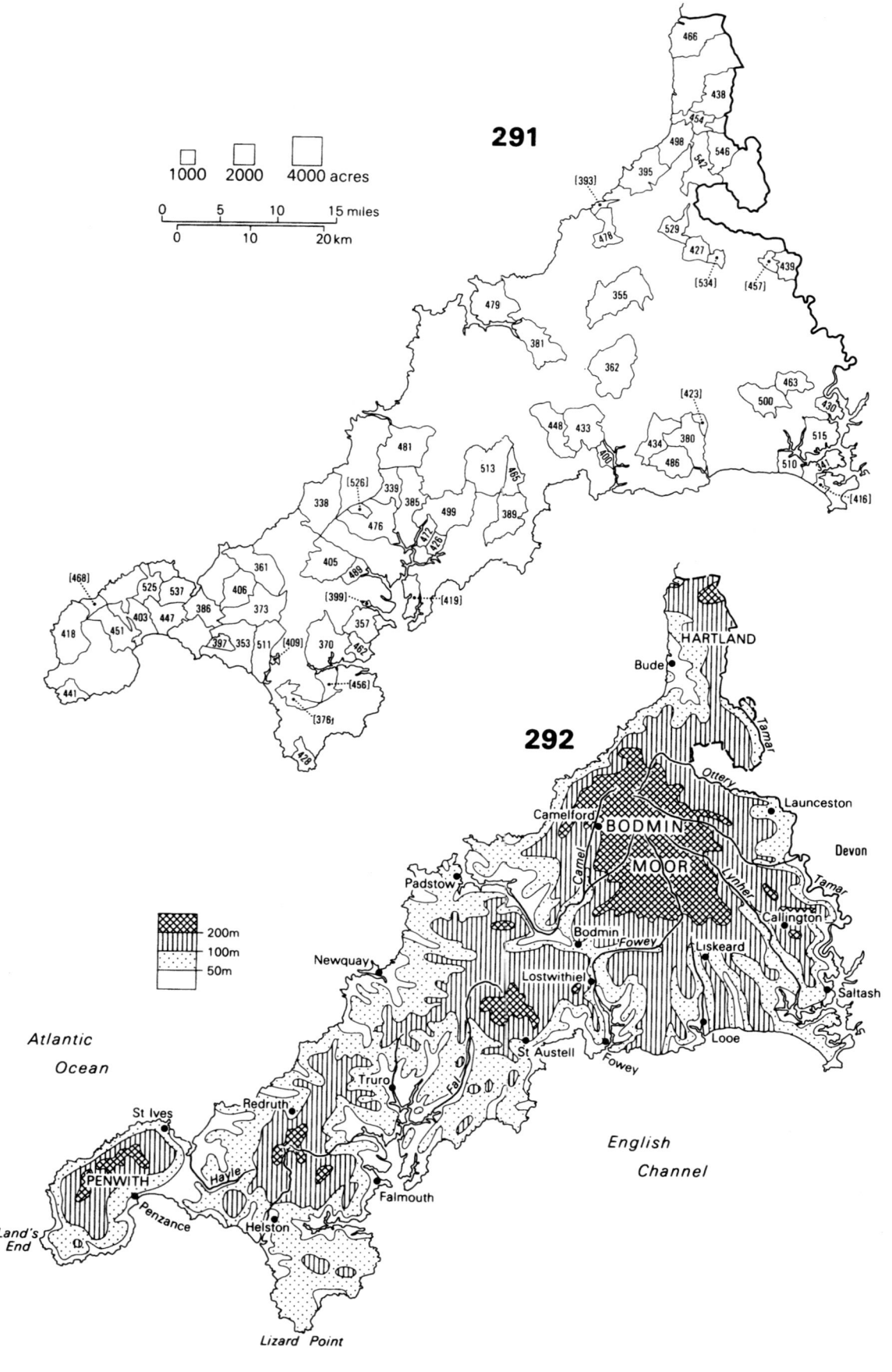

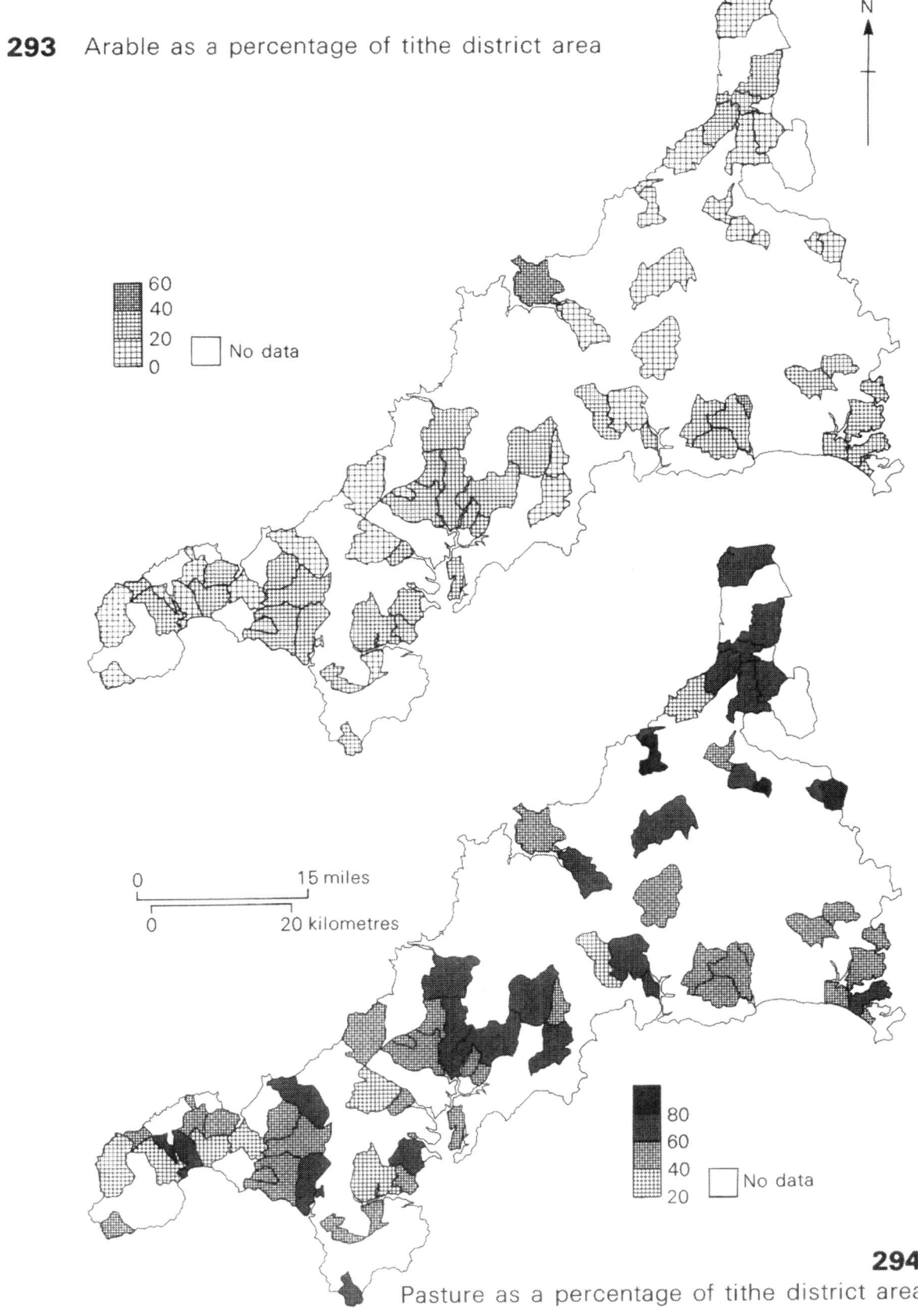

293 Arable as a percentage of tithe district area

294 Pasture as a percentage of tithe district area

226 South-western counties

295 Woodland as a percentage of tithe district area

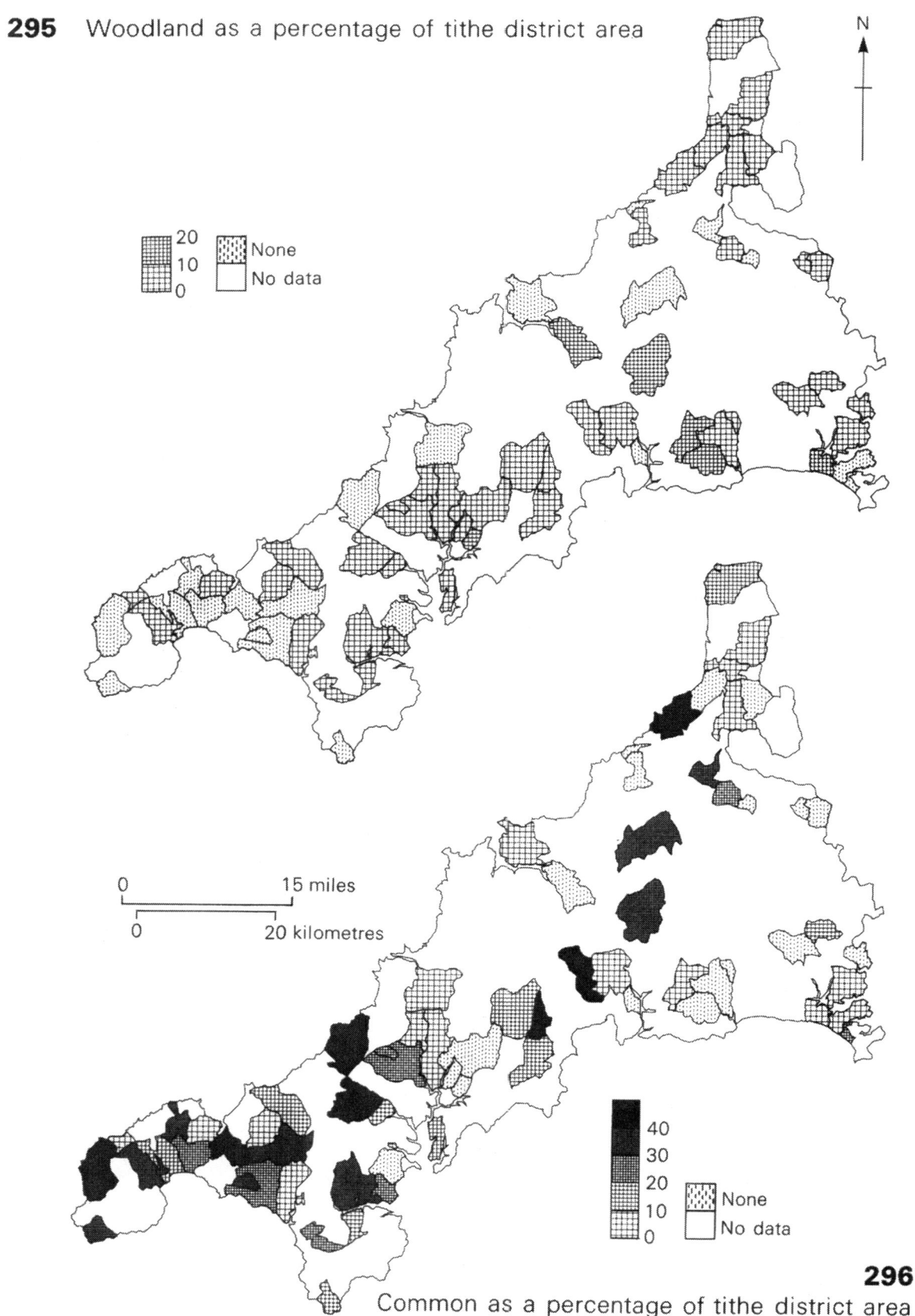

296 Common as a percentage of tithe district area

Cornwall

297 Orchards and fruit as a percentage of tithe district area

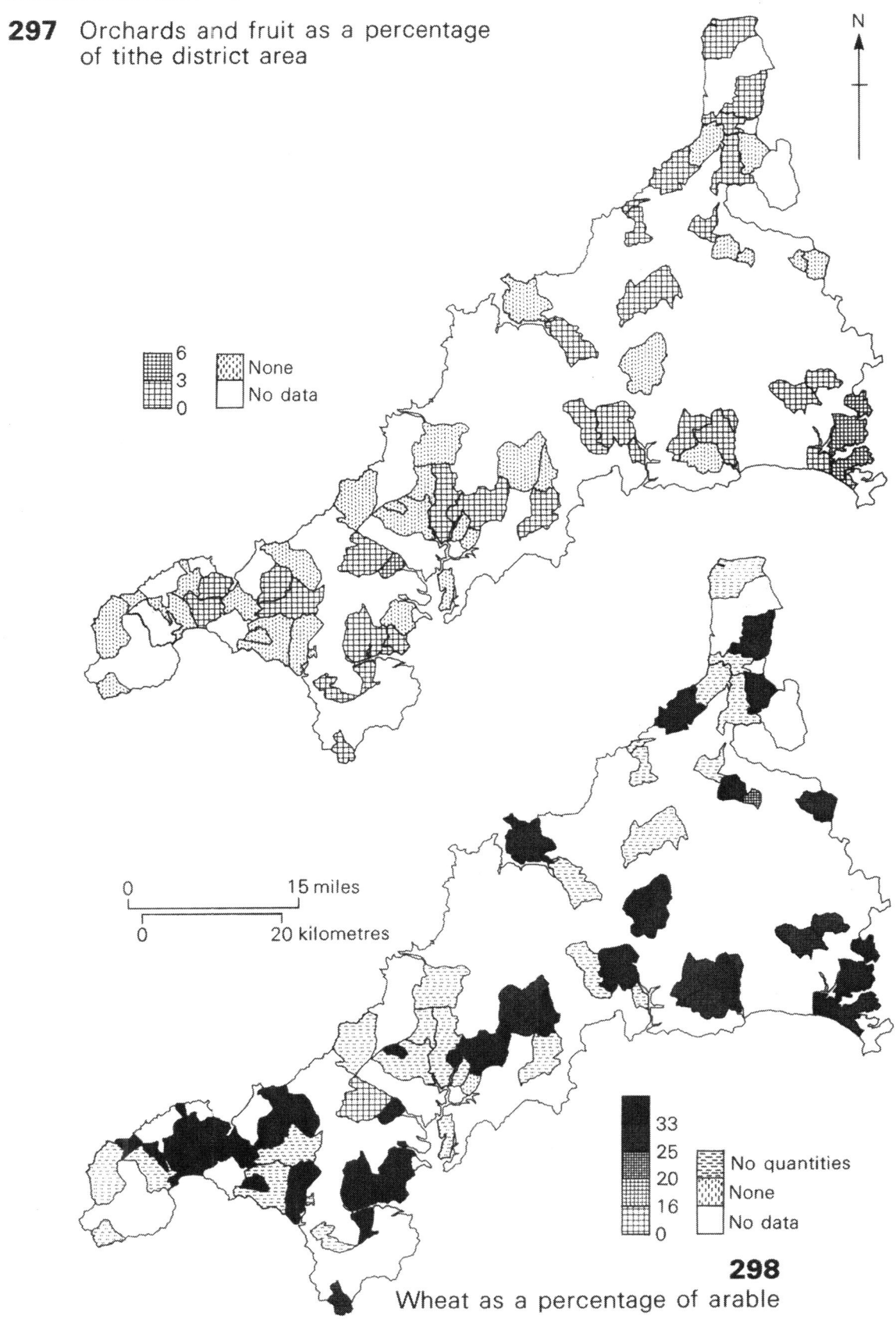

298 Wheat as a percentage of arable

299 Barley as a percentage of arable

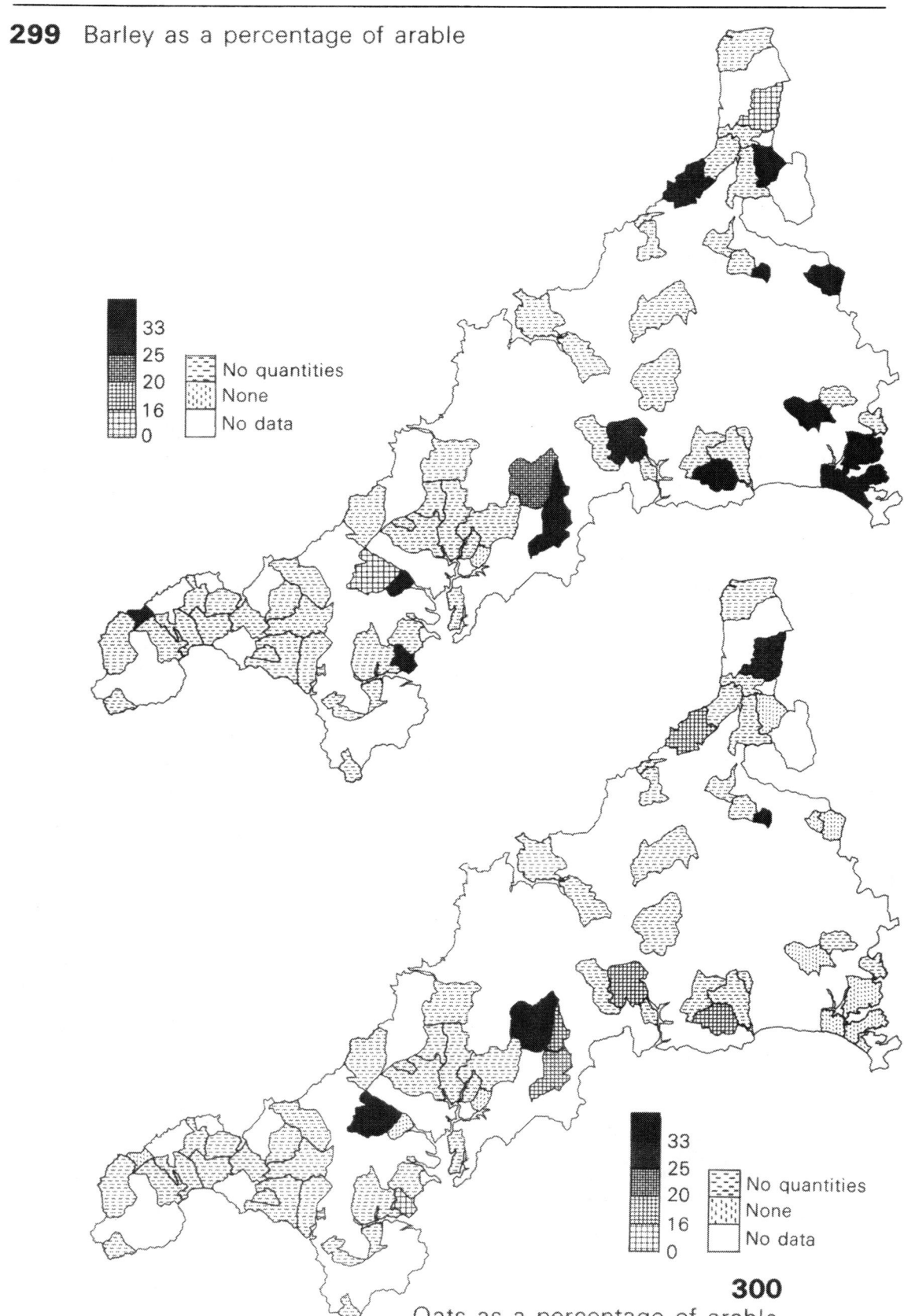

300
Oats as a percentage of arable

Cornwall

301 Yield of wheat in bushels per acre

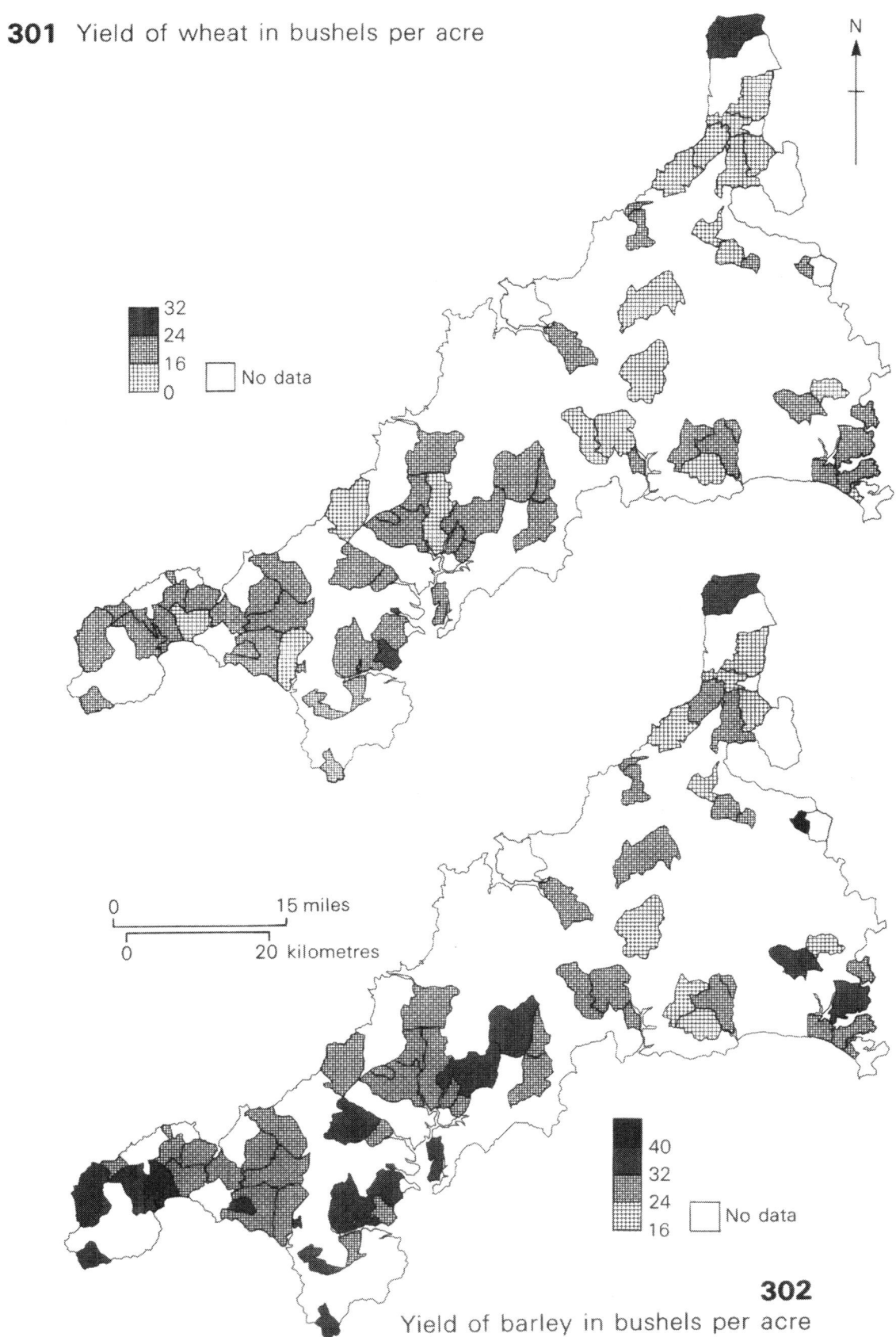

302 Yield of barley in bushels per acre

303 Yield of oats in bushels per acre

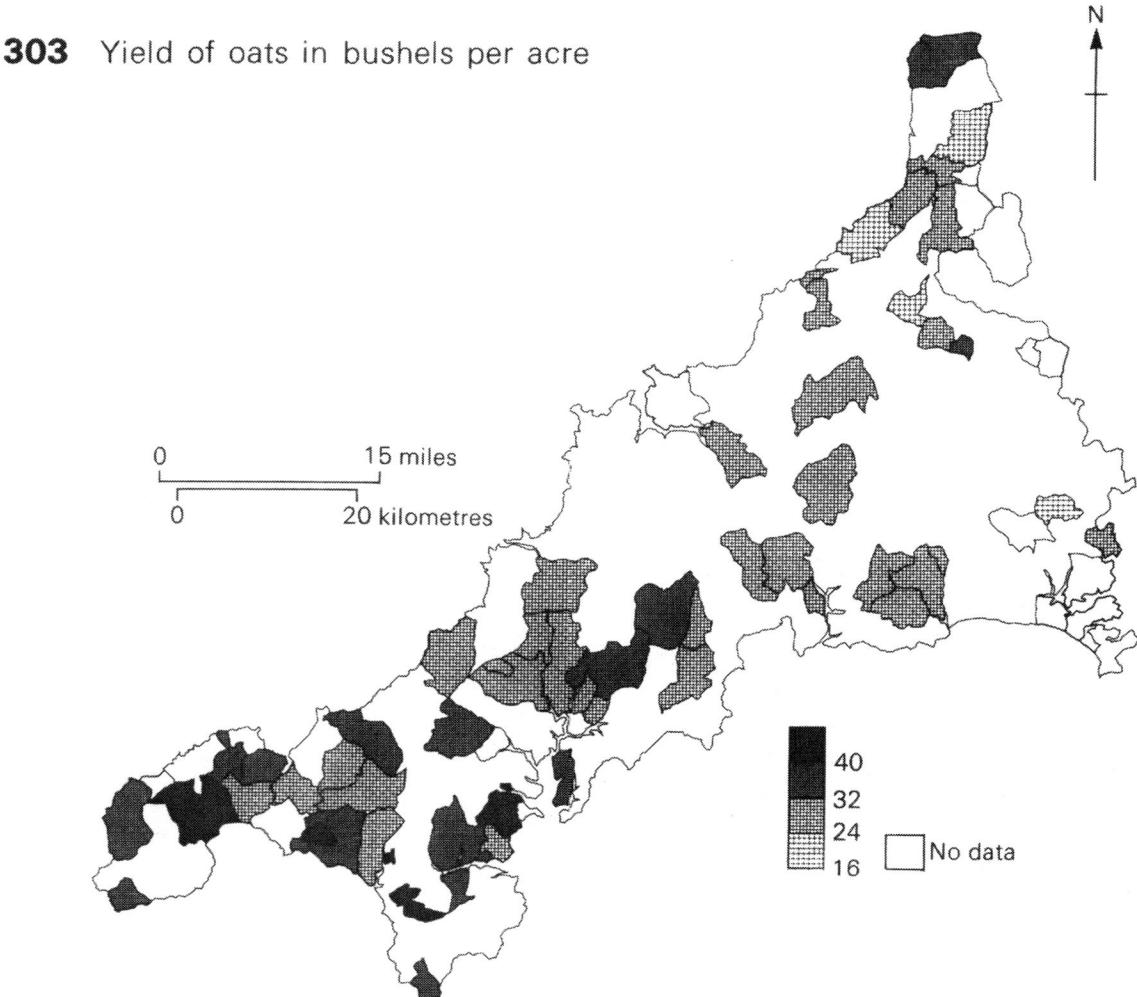

WESTERN COUNTIES

Gloucestershire   Worcestershire
Herefordshire   Monmouthshire*

The 'pastoral' type of printed form used for reporting on tithe agreements in these counties requires estimates of land uses, the course of crops and the number of stock and asks assistant commissioners and local tithe agents for their 'remarks, stating the peculiar circumstances of the parish which may affect the value of the tithe'.

---

* Maps are not compiled for Monmouthshire as useable crop data are extant for only four parishes.

Gloucestershire

349 tithe districts
122 reports on tithe agreements

J. P. Dodd (1979b) has examined agrarian change in Gloucestershire between 1801 and 1854. His analysis is based mainly on evidence from the 1801 Crop Return and 1854 agricultural statistics but he has also extracted data from tithe surveys, particularly for the Severn Vale area for which 1854 agricultural statistics are not extant.

Almost a third (109) of Gloucestershire tithe districts had been exonerated from tithe payment by 1836, mostly as a result of parliamentary enclosure. The main areas of the county for which tithe file data are scanty are the north-east, the southern lowlands and the Forest of Dean (Map 304). More than 80 per cent of Gloucestershire reports on tithe agreements were completed in the three years, 1838–40, and the work was divided fairly evenly among four assistant commissioners and local tithe agents (Table 37). Robert Page is the only man who provides some description of parish farming in his reports but even these are rather stereotyped pieces. Thomas Hoskins, who completed the greatest number of reports of any commissioner in England and Wales, wrote nothing in his Gloucestershire reports, although in North Wales tithe districts he appended a descriptive commentary for some parishes. Each commissioner employed in Gloucestershire constructed his valuation in a rather different manner and this complicates the derivation of crop acreages today. A particular difficulty surrounds the separation of corn crop acreages from those of seeds and fallows and obtaining acreages of individual crops. George Bolls and Thomas Hoskins provide figures for both arable including seed crops and arable minus seeds, so corn and seed acreages can be calculated. A similar calculation can be made for most of Charles Pym's reports. Bolls and Pym usually state the normal rotation followed in a parish in such a way that it is possible to estimate acreages of each of the main corn crops and pulses. Hoskins commonly lists alternative rotations with no indication of what proportion of the arable each refers to or else he states alternative crops within one or more courses of a rotation, both of which practices preclude calculation of crop acreages. Page provides no breakdown of the valuation of individual crops and rarely specifies a rotation so his reports contribute little to Table 38 and Maps 309–16. Neither Hoskins nor Pym provides data on the yield of crops. Few reports contain figures for the acreage of woodland so this land use does not enter calculations in Table 38, nor is its distribution mapped.

Table 38 indicates the areal dominance of grassland over arable for the county as a whole *c.* 1840. These figures mask, however, the traditional and continuing contrast between Vale and Cotswold Gloucestershire which is clearly apparent on Maps 306–7. In a number of Vale parishes grass accounted for more than 80 per cent of titheable area *c.* 1840 while at many places on the Cotswolds the ratio of arable to grass was more than 1.5 to 1. A three-course rotation with beans was commonly adopted on heavy clay soils in the Vales (see Subject Index); at Kempley, Robert Page remarked in 1840 that 'the soil is of a heavy character, being a stiff tenacious clay, expensive to cultivate, and the produce very uncertain, in wet seasons the seed is sown with difficulty, the three field system is usually adopted'. On stone-brash soils four- or five-course systems were practised with wheat, turnips, barley and then seeds for one or two years. At Horsley, 'the arable land is easily tilled on the five field system and produces good crops of turnips, and artificials, enabling the occupiers to keep large flocks of sheep, without which the arable land would be unproductive'. Sainfoin had been introduced into the rotation of a number of light soil parishes and many Gloucestershire farmers cultivated considerable quantities of potatoes but the precise acreage grown is rarely specified in tithe files. Rotations apart, there is little discussion of the cultivation of arable in Gloucestershire tithe files. Yields on the whole were rather low (Table 38). Sheep breeding and feeding, and breeds and their management, receive some brief comment at a number of places (see Subject Index).

Table 37 *Reports on agreements for commutation of tithes in Gloucestershire*

Assistant commissioner/ local tithe agent	1837	1838	1839	1840	1841	1842	1843	Totals
George Bolls		23	13		1			37
Charles Pym	10	19	1	1				31
Thomas Hoskins		8	7	9	3			27
Robert Page			10	6	2	4	1	23
George Louis		4						4
Totals	10	54	31	16	6	4	1	122

Table 38 *Land use, crops and yields in Gloucestershire c. 1836*

A	Land use	Percentage of total land area enumerated in reports on tithe agreements	Estimated acreage in whole county
	Arable	32.0	257,805
	Grass	56.7	456,489
	Common	2.6	20,916

B	Crop	Mean percentage of arable	Mean yield per acre	Estimated acreage in whole county
	Wheat	31.6	19.6 bushels	81,572
	Barley	20.5	27.1 bushels	52,832
	Oats	1.2	27.5 bushels	3,046
	Pulses	6.4	23.2 bushels	16,500

Gloucestershire

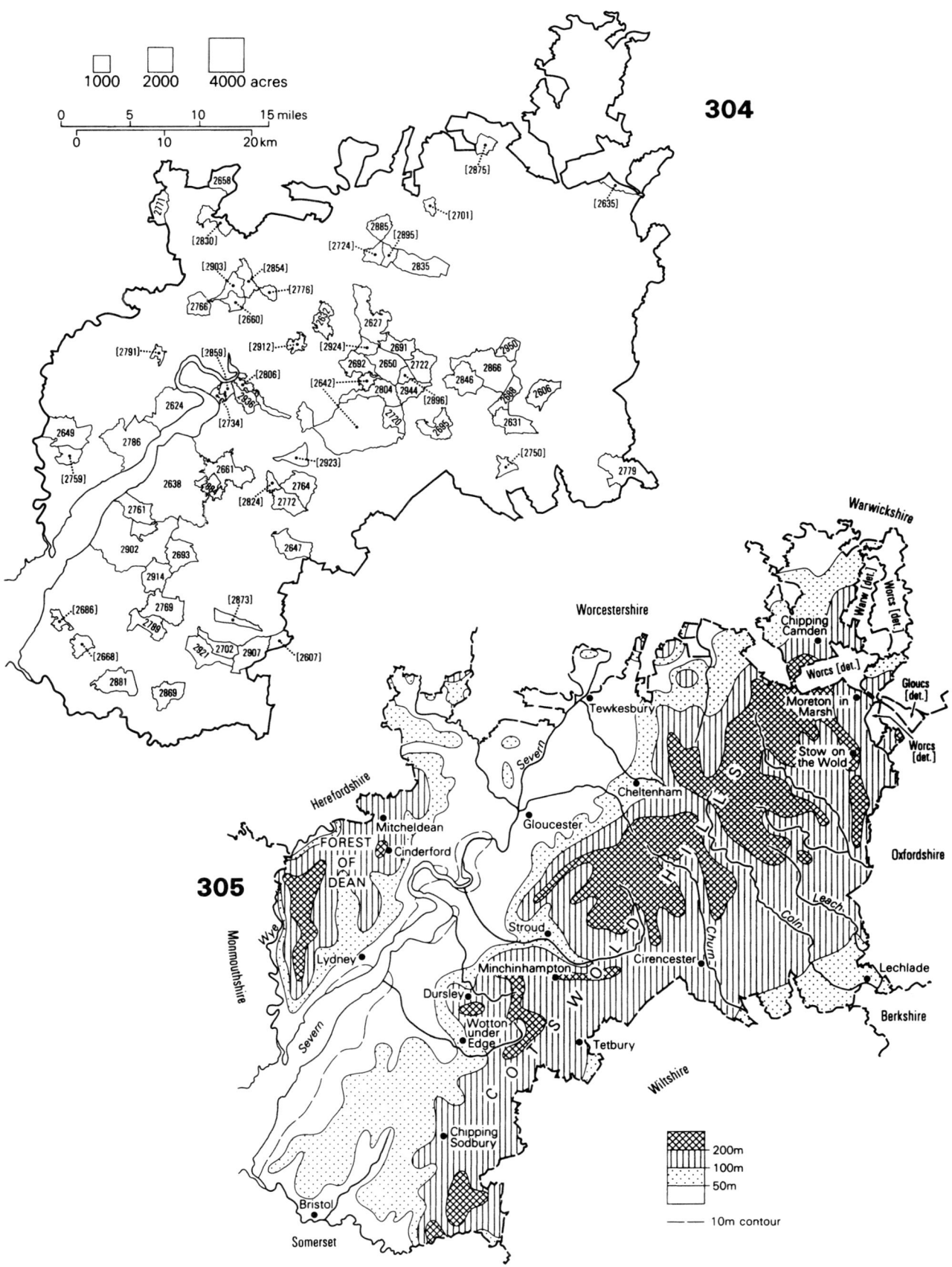

Western counties

306 Arable as a percentage of tithe district area

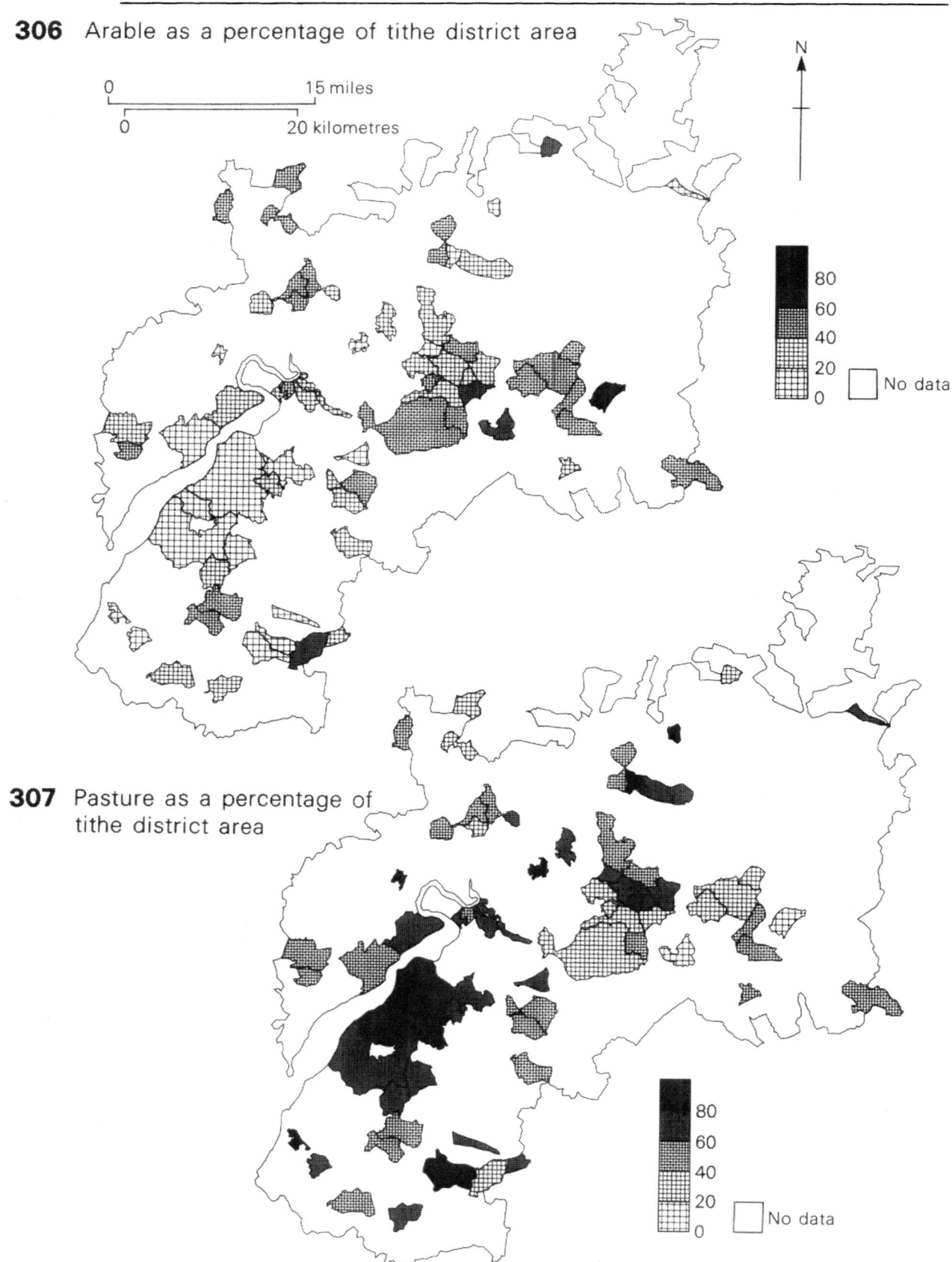

307 Pasture as a percentage of tithe district area

308 Common as a percentage of tithe district area

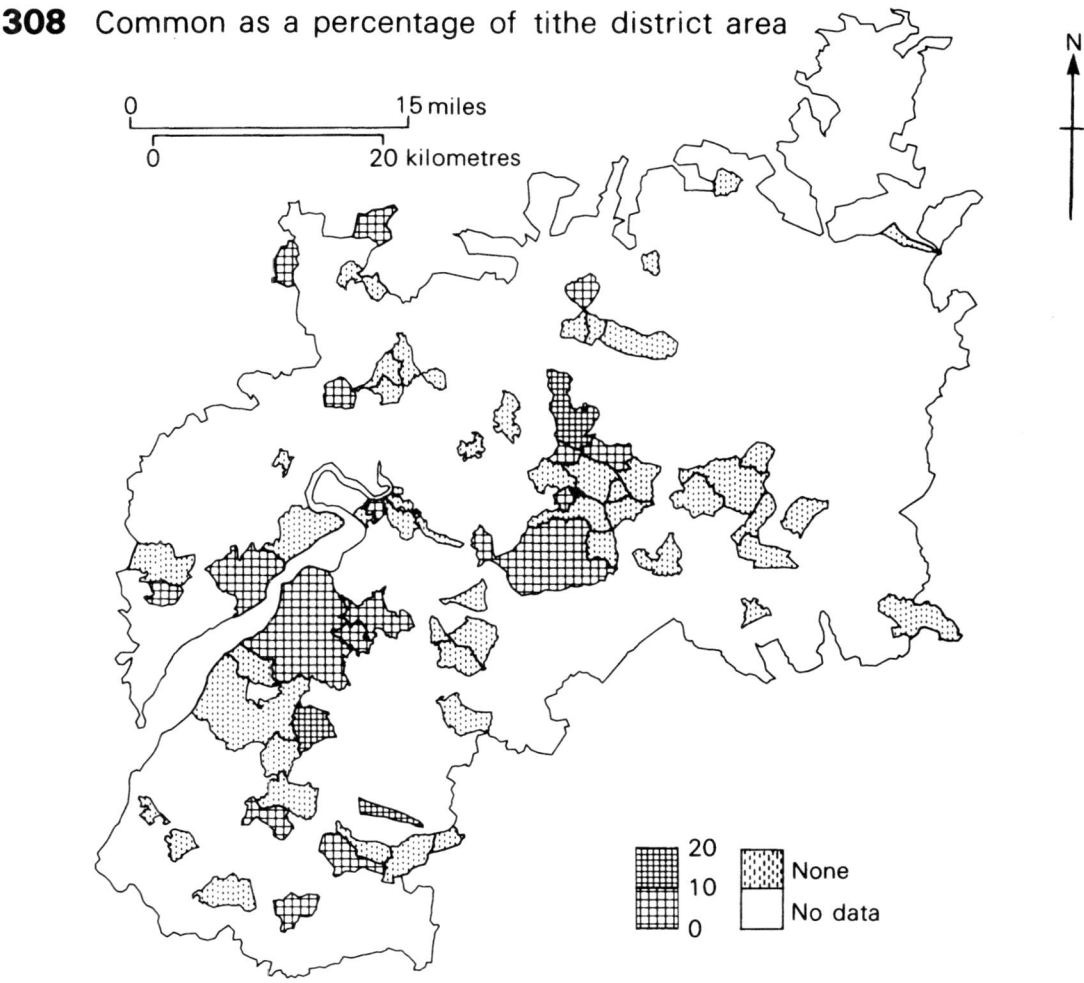

238 Western counties

309 Wheat as a percentage of arable

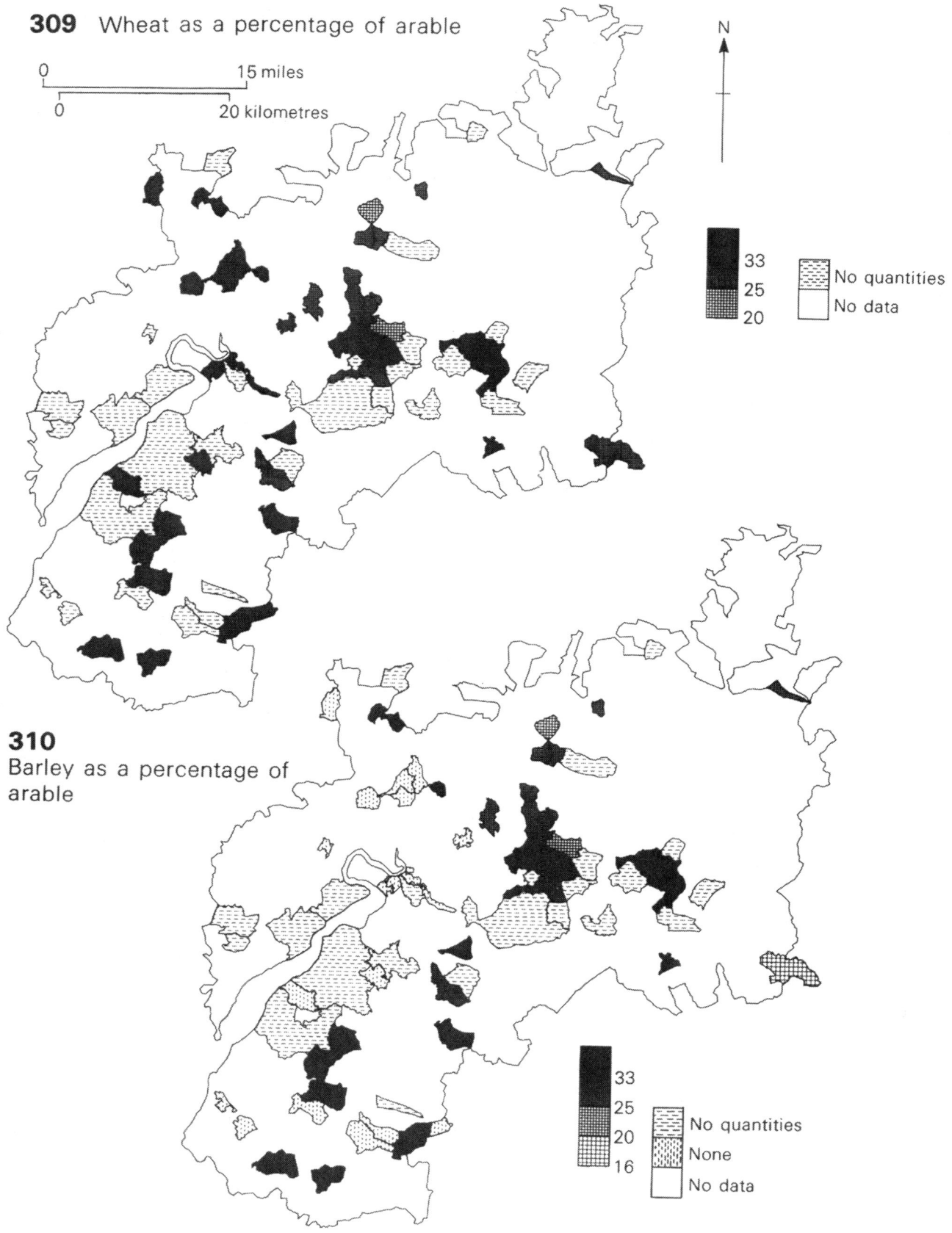

310 Barley as a percentage of arable

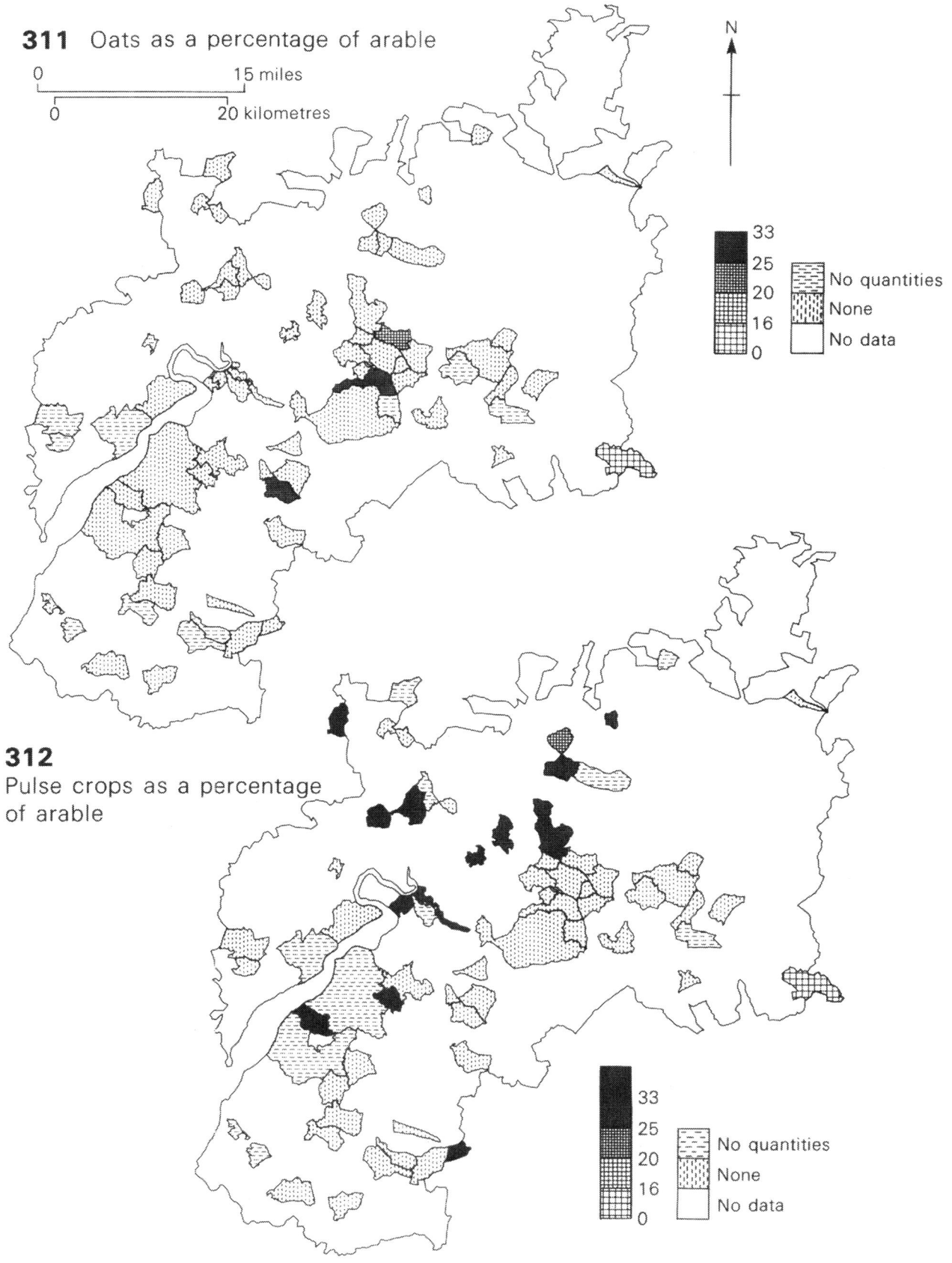

311 Oats as a percentage of arable

312 Pulse crops as a percentage of arable

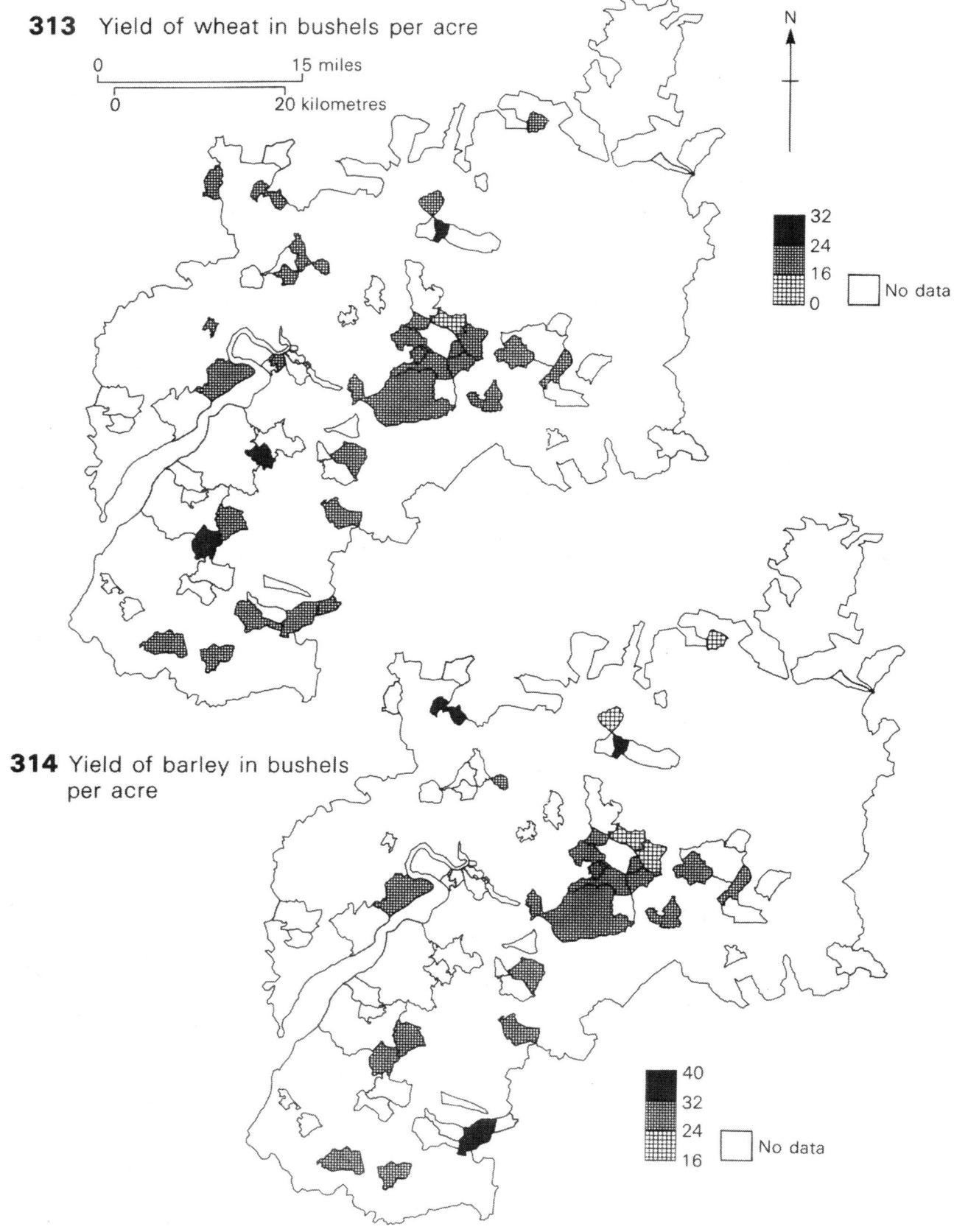

313 Yield of wheat in bushels per acre

314 Yield of barley in bushels per acre

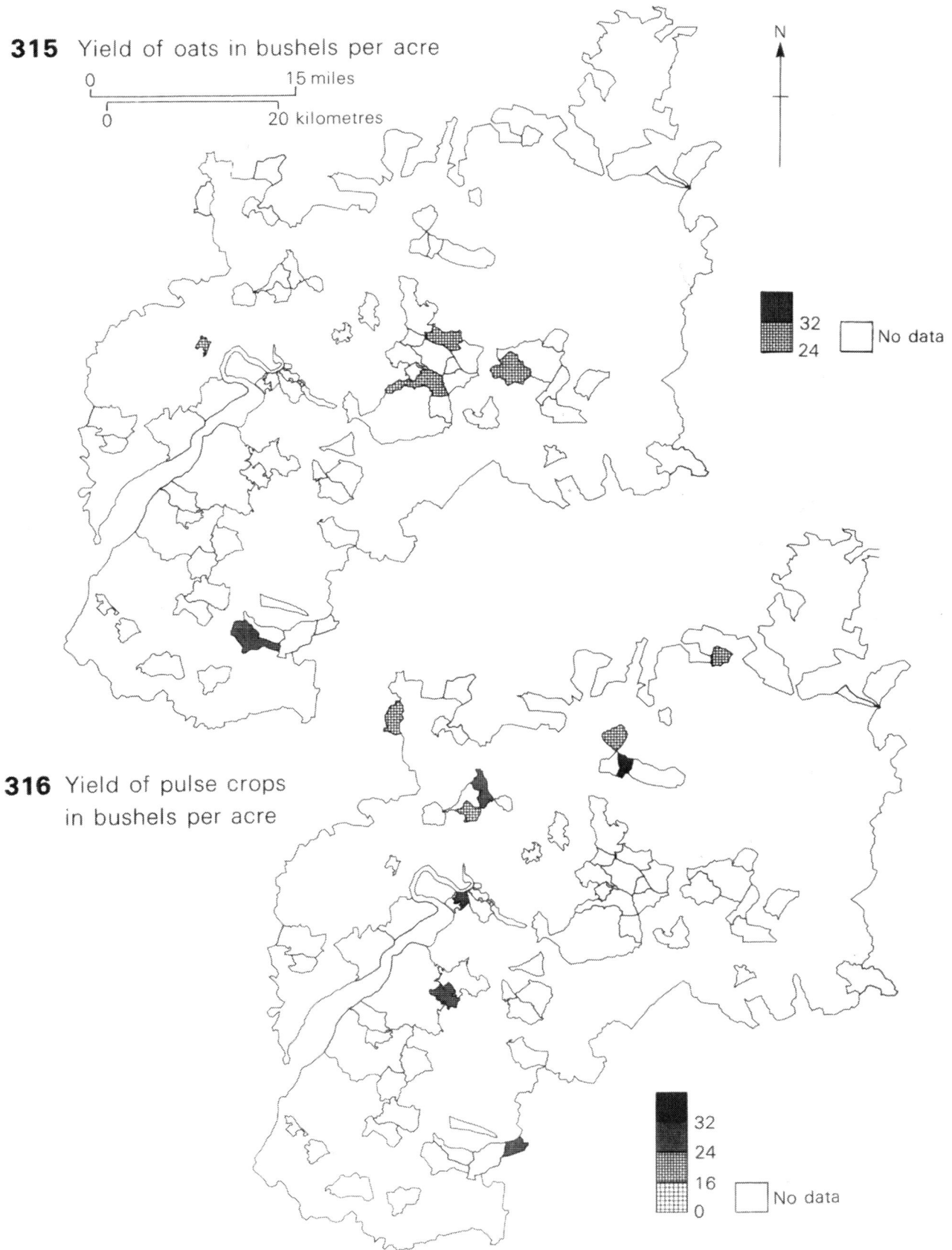

315 Yield of oats in bushels per acre

316 Yield of pulse crops in bushels per acre

Herefordshire

252 tithe districts
154 reports on tithe agreements

A. D. M. Phillips (1979) has published an account of agricultural land use in Herefordshire *c*. 1840 in which he reconstructs patterns of land use from parish summaries in preambles to tithe apportionments. The mean county percentages which he calculates from this source compare very closely with those obtained from the smaller sample of tithe files analysed in this study and presented in Table 40. J. P. Dodd (1980) in his study of Herefordshire agriculture in the mid-nineteenth century notes (p. 205) that the 'tithe apportionments of the 1840s provide a second source of statistics embracing most parishes and these enable one to determine regional changes in the acreage in arable and grass'.

Very few Herefordshire parishes were affected by parliamentary enclosure, a fact that is reflected in the small number of ten completely tithe free parishes. Voluntary agreements account for a high (61 per cent) proportion of all commutations and two-thirds of these were examined and assessed by just one man, Thomas Hoskins. In fact, 95 per cent of all Herefordshire reports were compiled by three men, which makes for consistency and ease of comparison between districts. Unfortunately, as Hoskins always omits to state crop yields in his valuations, it also means that the record is somewhat flawed; no yield maps are presented below and the mean county yields for wheat, barley, oats and pulses are omitted from Table 40 as they can be derived from data relating to only eighteen, seven, four and six tithe districts respectively.

Arable covered just 40 per cent of total land area in Herefordshire *c*. 1836. It was especially extensive in the south and east of the county where a number of parishes had arable to pasture ratios of more than 1.5 to 1; in much of central Herefordshire arable and pasture was fairly evenly balanced but in the north and west pasture was most extensive, as it was for the county as a whole at this date (Table 40). As Phillips (1979) concludes, this pattern of land use can be related to soil conditions. The area of sandy soils in the south was dominated by arable, whilst pasture was most extensive on clay soils. Phillips places the change from arable domination to a grassland dominated county at some time between 1800 and 1840. Later nineteenth-century sources reveal a continued diminution of the arable acreage.

In clay soil districts, bare fallowing was still commonplace with either three-course rotations of wheat, beans, fallow or a four-course of wheat, peas or oats, clover, fallow. On loamier soils, the Norfolk four-course was employed perhaps extended to a five-course with a second wheat crop, viz. wheat, barley, clover, wheat, fallow with some turnips. Long rotations, such as the wheat, barley, oats and seeds, six or seven years, at Fwddog, so typical of south-western counties and of Wales, were encountered in only a relatively small number (fifteen in Subject Index) of Herefordshire tithe districts. Some potatoes were grown in most parishes but acreages are not often recorded as the crop was either not titheable or subject to small tithes and subsumed within the general category of fallow crops. Hops were an important arable crop but despite the frequent levy of an extraordinary rent-charge by reason of the exceptional value of this product, their acreages are not recorded with any consistency in tithe file reports on agreements. A number of reports suggest that hop acreage was in decline. At Canon Pyon in 1842, Thomas Hoskins explained that he was recommending a rent-charge much lower than the pre-1839 hop composition 'in consequence of hop lands having been considerably reduced in quantity since the average of the 7 years ending 1835 and also because the tithes have been considered to be very high'.

Sheep breeding and fattening are reported as important in Herefordshire but assistant commissioners and local tithe agents provide few details of the system of management. Herefordshire was also an important cattle breeding county in the middle of the nineteenth century and livestock husbandry is discussed in the files, but the accuracy of livestock numbers cited in Herefordshire reports is as conjectural as whenever 'pastoral' type report forms were used. At Kings Caple in 1838, George Bolls declaimed, 'with regards to the quantity of stock, I will not vouch for its correctness as I find it almost impossible to ascertain the exact number of stock from the farmers in Hereford'. Robert Page described fattening Herefordshire cattle in his report at Kinnersley: 'the system is to keep the cattle until half fat, then sold to the London dealers, and their grazing finished in Buckinghamshire, or the vicinity of the London markets'.

Table 39 *Reports on agreements for commutation of tithes in Herefordshire*

Assistant commissioner/ local tithe agent	1837	1838	1839	1840	1841	1842	1843	1844	1845	1846	Totals
Thomas Hoskins		5	34	36	11	17					103
Charles Pym	9	12					1	2	3		27
George Bolls		10	6								16
Robert Page				2	4						6
John Johnes			1							1	2
Totals	9	27	41	38	15	17	1	2	3	1	154

Table 40 *Land use and crops in Herefordshire c. 1836*

A	Land use	Percentage of total land area enumerated in reports on tithe agreements	Estimated acreage in whole county
	Arable	39.7	212,456
	Grass	48.8	260,917
	Wood	7.2	38,567
	Common	2.4	12,572
B	Crop	Mean percentage of arable	Estimated acreage in whole county
	Wheat	33.8	71,714
	Barley	15.7	33,286
	Oats	1.1	2,412
	Pulses	8.0	16,999

Herefordshire

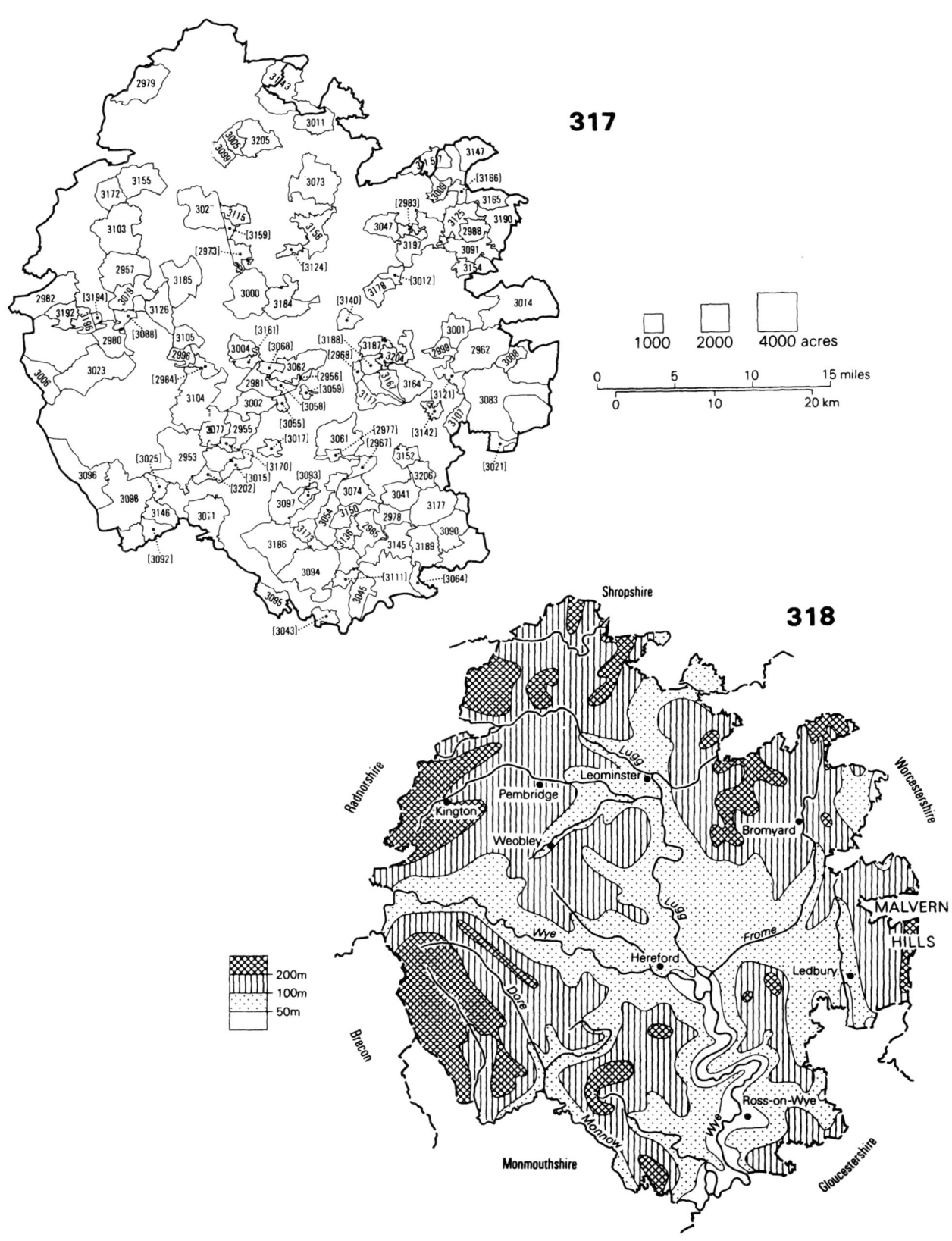

Western counties

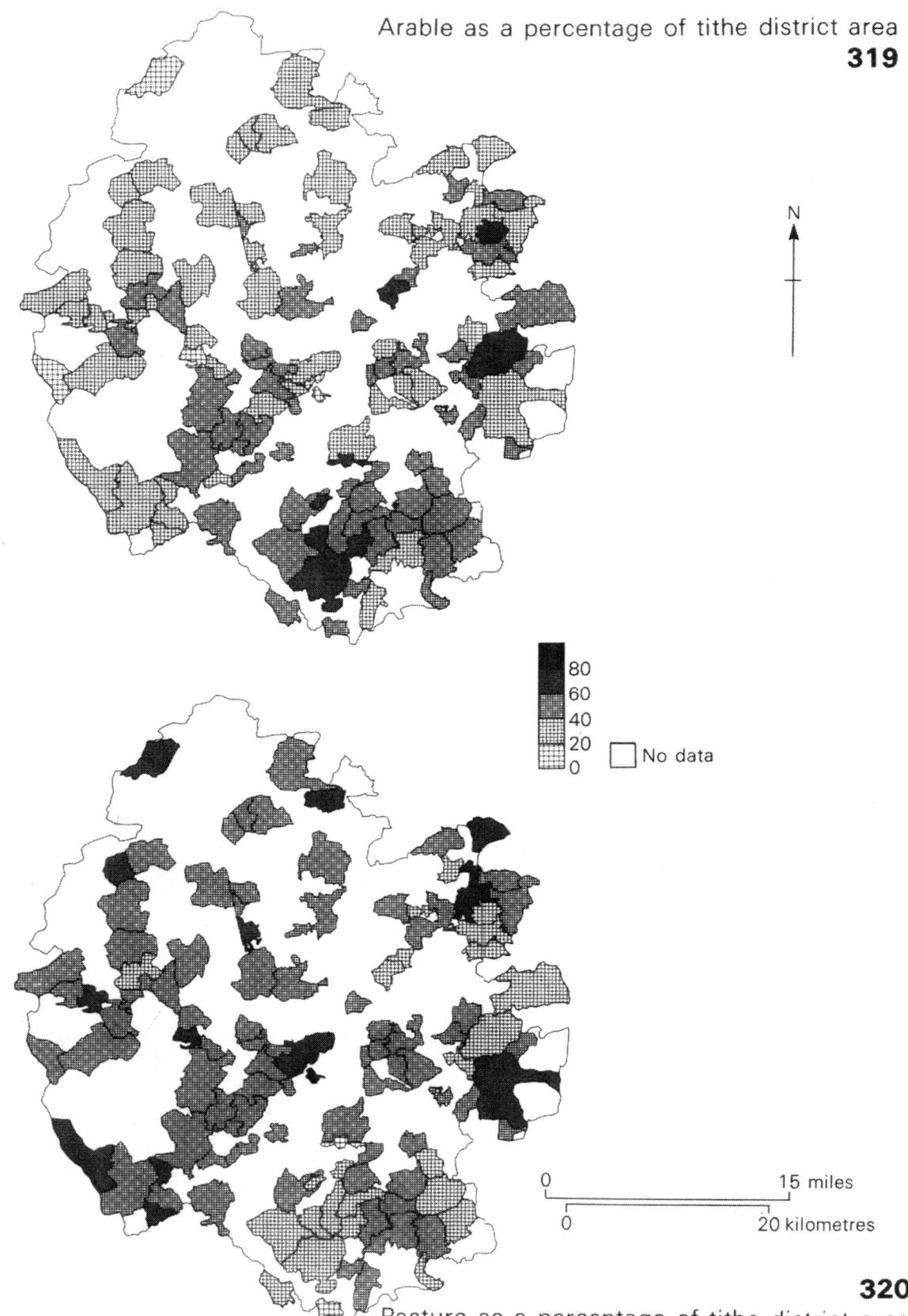

Arable as a percentage of tithe district area
319

320
Pasture as a percentage of tithe district area

Herefordshire

321 Woodland as a percentage of tithe district area

322 Common as a percentage of tithe district area

248 Western counties

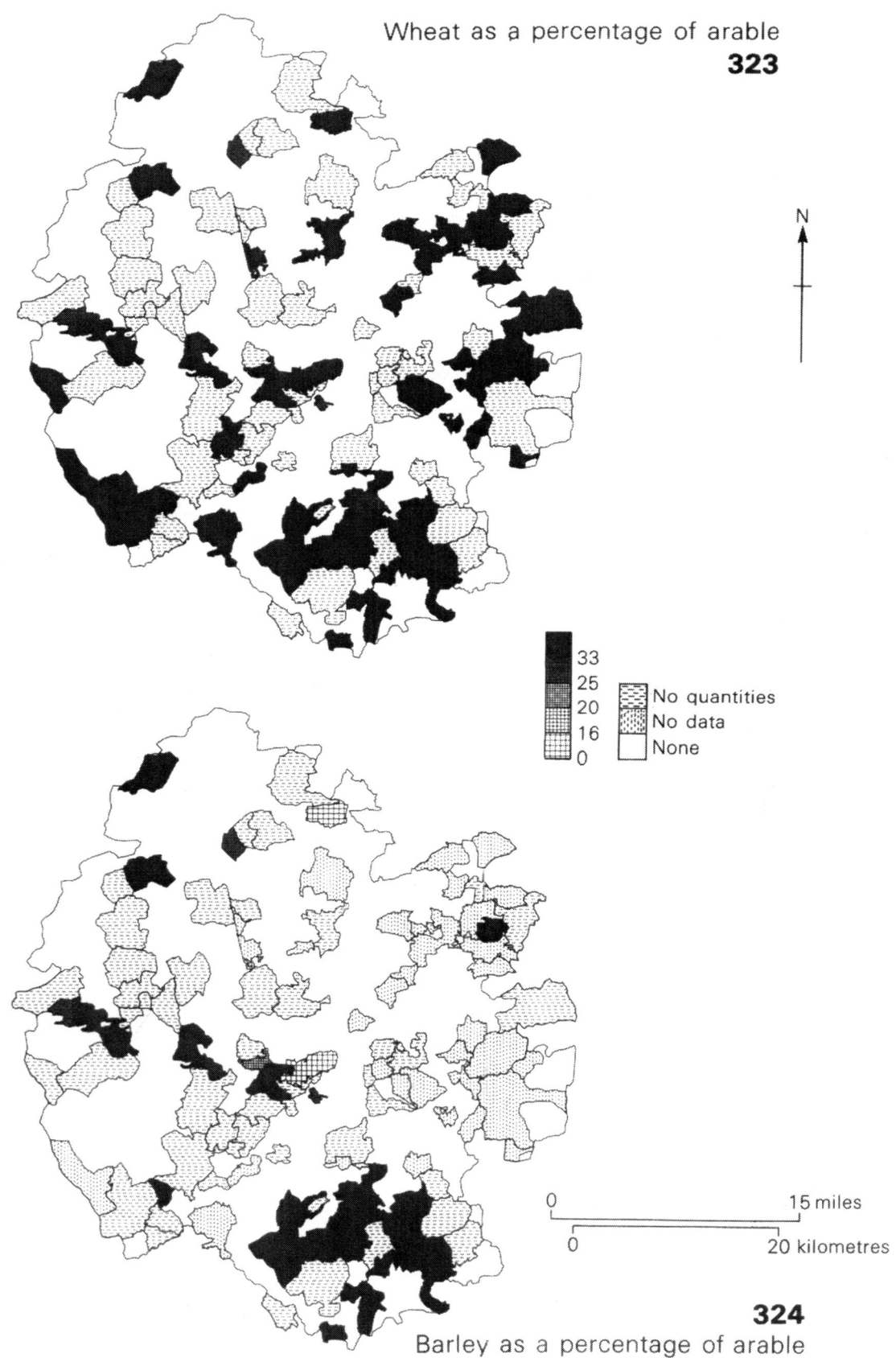

323 Wheat as a percentage of arable

324 Barley as a percentage of arable

Herefordshire

325 Oats as a percentage of arable

326 Pulse crops as a percentage of arable

Worcestershire

208 tithe districts
84 reports on tithe agreements

Exoneration of tithes at the time of enclosure is the reason for a quarter of Worcestershire districts being tithe free in 1836; copies of enclosure awards are preserved in several files. In common with other western counties, moduses were numerous and affected in particular the produce of grassland. At King's Norton, for example

> the vicarial tithes of the parish are greatly affected by the existence of a modus in lieu of the tithes of milk and of cow stock depastured in the parish – there are eight hundred cows kept and from its contiguity to the populous town and neighbourhood of Birmingham they would have been valuable to the tithe owner but for the existence of this modus. There is also a modus of three pence per acre in lieu of the tithe of hay.

At 53 per cent of places where tithe remained to be commuted, tithe owners and tithe payers succeeded in agreeing a rent-charge. These districts are far from evenly distributed across the county (Map 327). Coverage of the western uplands from the Malverns, through the Suckley Hills to Wyre Forest is good as is that of the Clent and Lickey Hills in the east. But there are few reports on tithe agreements relating to the Worcestershire Plain and none at all for the Vale of Evesham. The parish of Evesham itself

> extends altogether over about five hundred acres of land. It comprises a tract of excellent arable, meadow and market garden ground occupied for the most part in the production of fruit and vegetables for the Birmingham market. The excellence of the soil, the genial climate, and freedom from tithes, render it peculiarly eligible for the purposes to which the district has been for a long time past devoted.

Assistant commissioners working in Worcestershire paid particular attention to the nature of soils when investigating agreed rent-charges; very often they encountered both strong and light soils in the same parish and these are valued individually. Thomas Hoskins is particularly careful about this and records separate rotations for each. However, he does not usually assign these to specific proportions of the arable so it is impossible to calculate crop acreages; hence the large number of places on the crop distribution maps with the symbol for 'no quantities'.

Hoskins is very impressed with the productive qualities of soil in Worcestershire Plain parishes, though his perception was no doubt coloured by his numerous commissions in poor Welsh parishes. At Ombersley he exclaimed 'this is *altogether* one of the *finest* and best parishes I have ever met with. It is a very fine rich soil throughout and I could not see a bad acre of land amongst the whole seven thousand acres, altho' I walked over it from one end to the other.'

The arable rotations recorded in reports on agreements certainly demonstrate a close association with soil type. On really heavy clay lands a three-course of fallow, wheat, beans or oats or vetches was still quite common (see Subject Index). On lighter red clay loams, as at Kempsey on the river Severn, for instance, farmers used a type of four-course: fallow, wheat, clover, beans, occasionally substituting peas or oats for beans. In a few places, Lindridge was one, farmers attempted to get two crops of wheat in four years with a system of fallow, wheat, clover, wheat. More often, however, they took two crops of corn in five years adopting rotations as at Kyre, south-east of Tenbury, of fallow, wheat, clover, beans, oats or wheat, or at Inkberrow, of wheat, beans, fallow, wheat, clover. On light sandy loams, the Norfolk four-course is noted most frequently. Unfortunately, Hoskins who completed almost exactly half the reports and Charles Pym who wrote another fifth, did not state crop yields. As a result, there are none at all for the Worcestershire Plain and very few elsewhere.

For the county as a whole, grassland was a little more extensive than arable (Table 42) but there is not much comment on its nature or on livestock husbandry in Worcestershire files. The prevalence of moduses on small tithes obviated detailed valuation.

Table 41 *Reports on agreements for commutation of tithes in Worcestershire*

Assistant commissioner/ local tithe agent	1837	1838	1839	1840	1841	1842	1843	1844	Totals
Thomas Hoskins		7	15	13	7	1			43
Charles Pym	1	8		1		4	1	2	17
George Bolls			13						13
N. S. Meryweather		9							9
John Johnes		1							1
Thomas Smith Woolley	1								1
Totals	2	25	28	14	7	5	1	2	84

Table 42 *Land use, crops and yields in Worcestershire c. 1836*

	A Land use	Percentage of total land area enumerated in reports on tithe agreements	Estimated acreage in whole county
	Arable	42.7	201,722
	Grass	46.6	219,784
	Wood	6.5	30,450
	Common	2.1	9,844

	B Crop	Mean percentage of arable	Mean yield per acre	Estimated acreage in whole county
	Wheat	36.2	22.5 bushels	72,933
	Barley	9.5	34.0 bushels	19,127
	Oats	1.7	32.0 bushels	3,476
	Pulses	14.8	19.0 bushels	29,927

Worcestershire

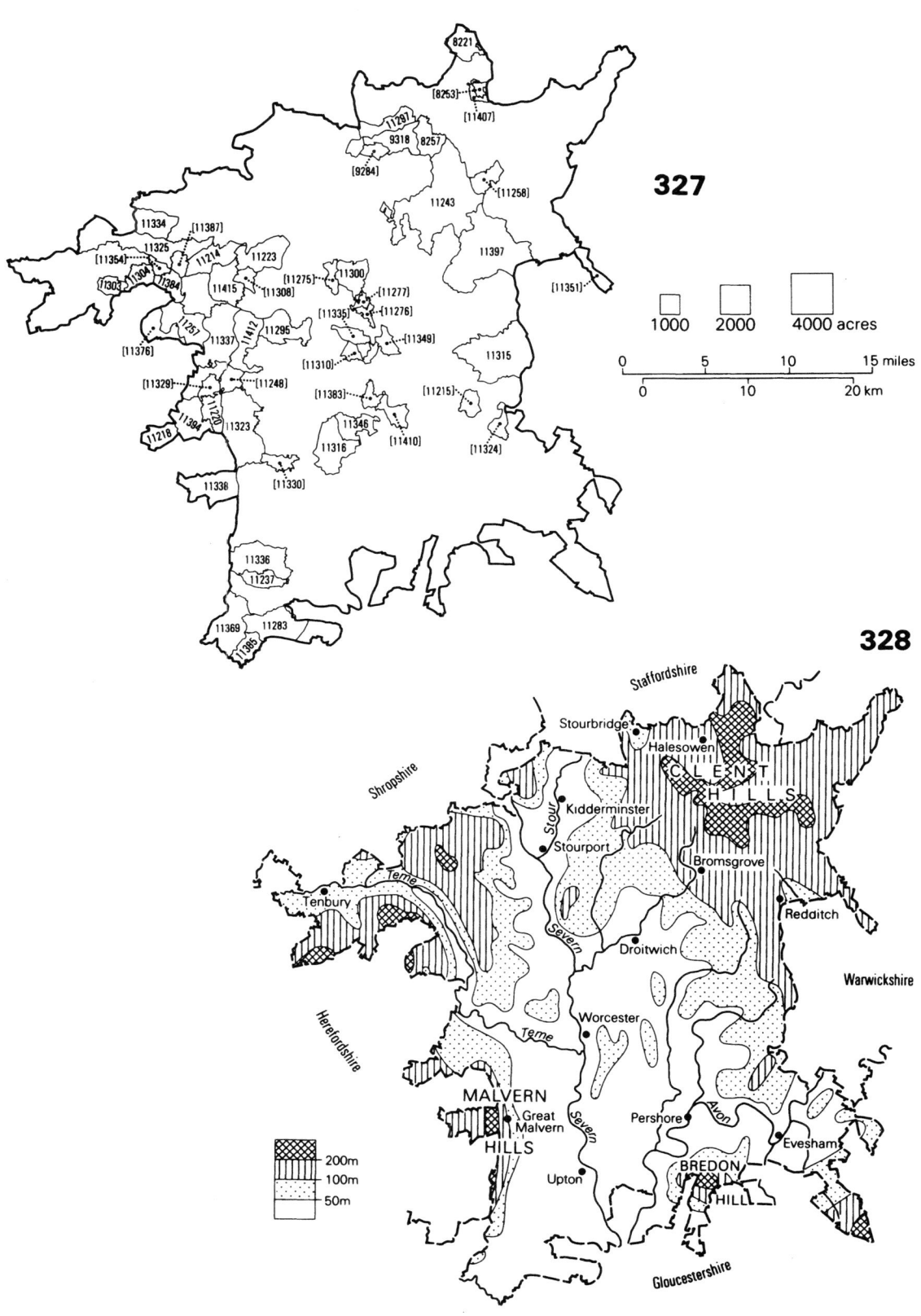

329 Arable as a percentage of tithe district area

Pasture as a percentage of tithe district area
330

Worcestershire

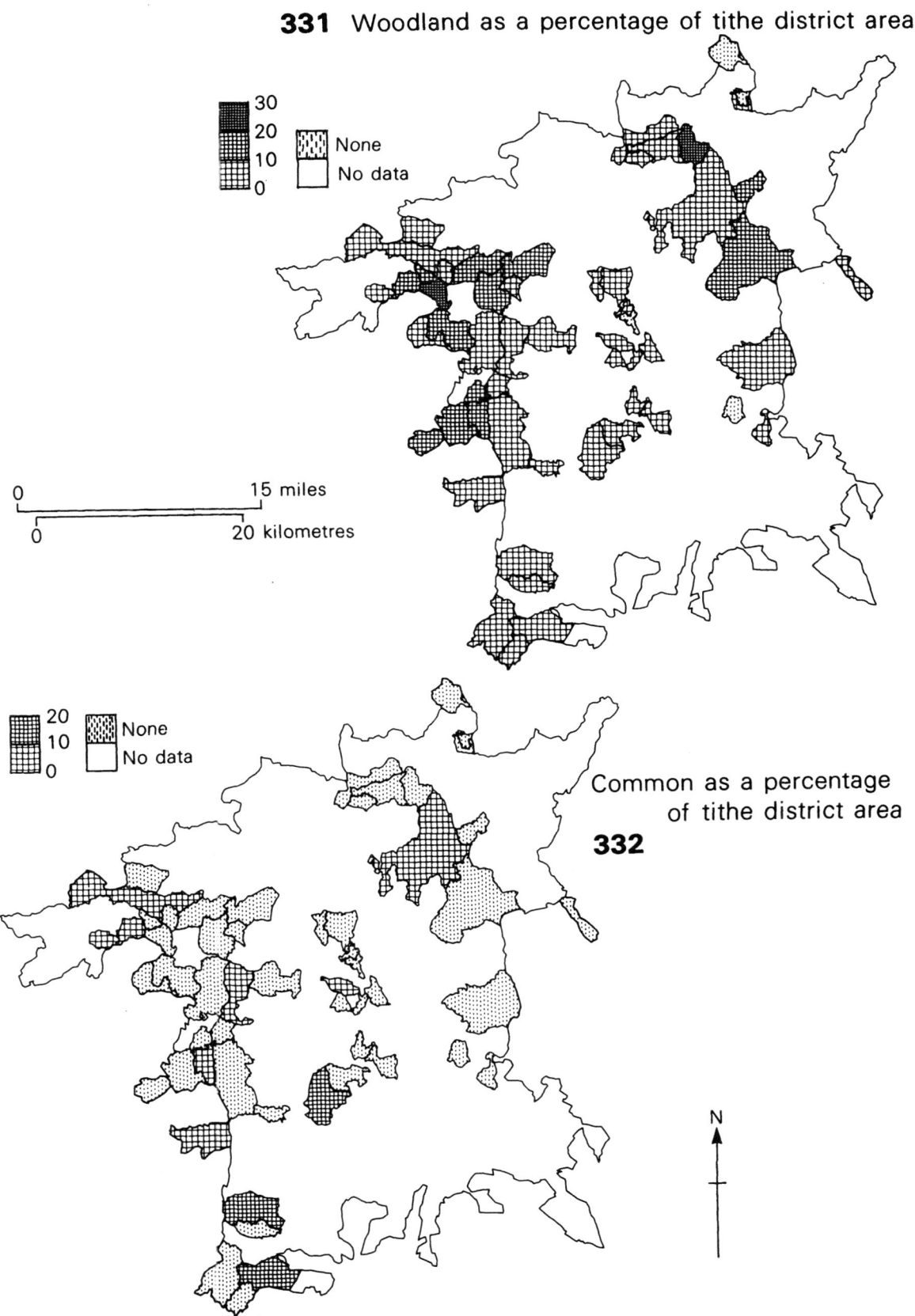

331 Woodland as a percentage of tithe district area

Common as a percentage of tithe district area
332

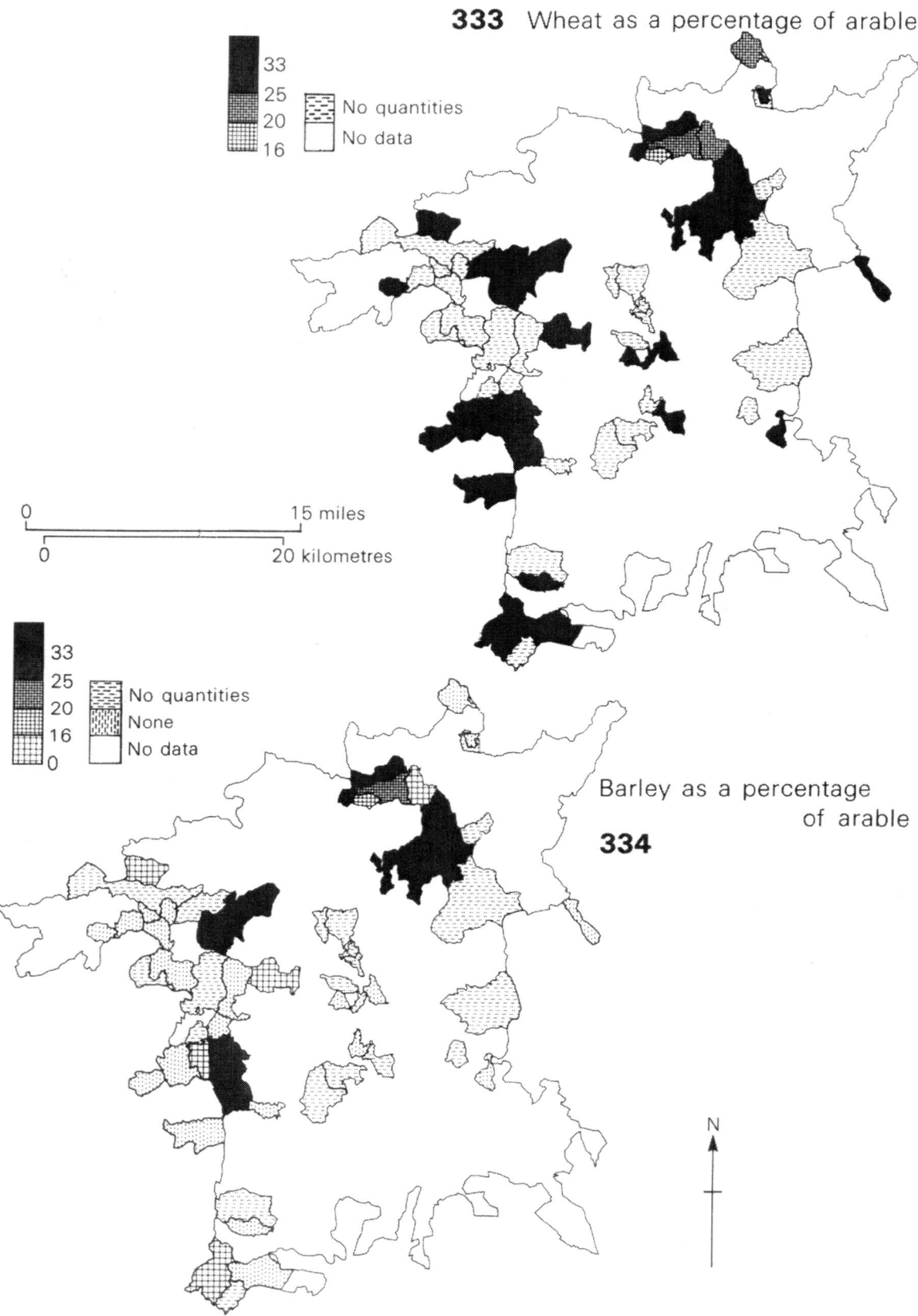

333 Wheat as a percentage of arable

Barley as a percentage of arable **334**

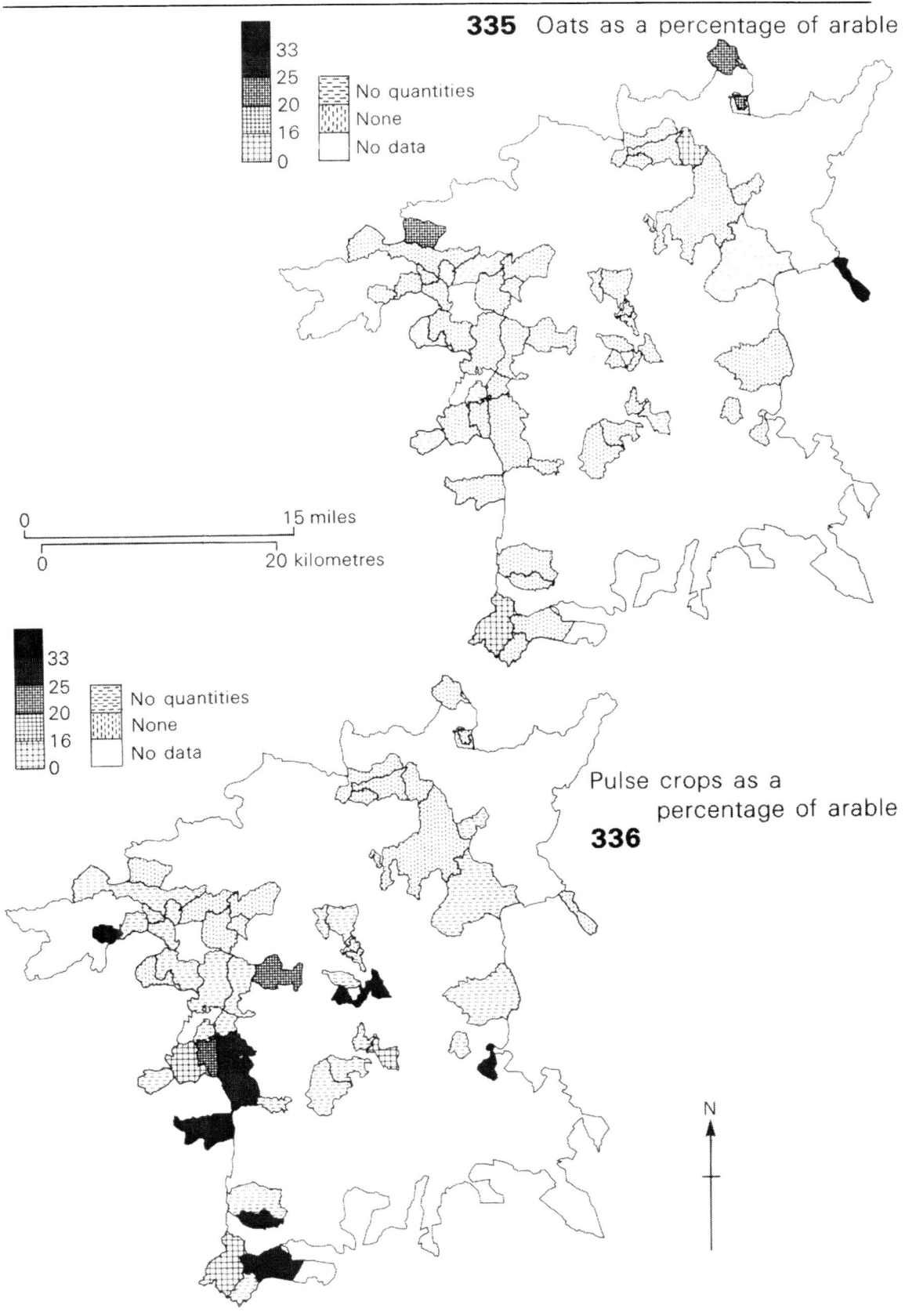

335 Oats as a percentage of arable

336 Pulse crops as a percentage of arable

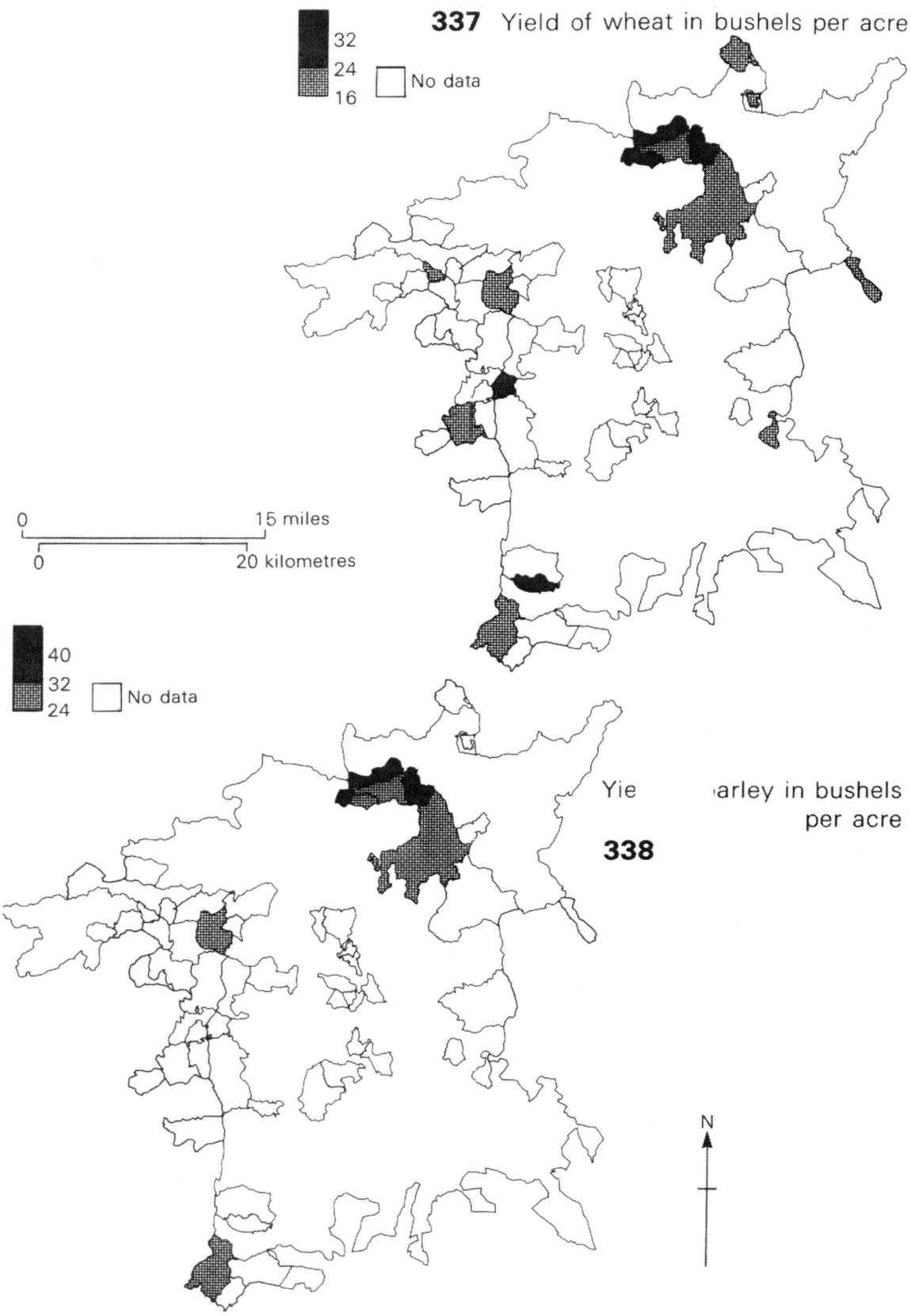

337 Yield of wheat in bushels per acre

338 Yield of barley in bushels per acre

Worcestershire

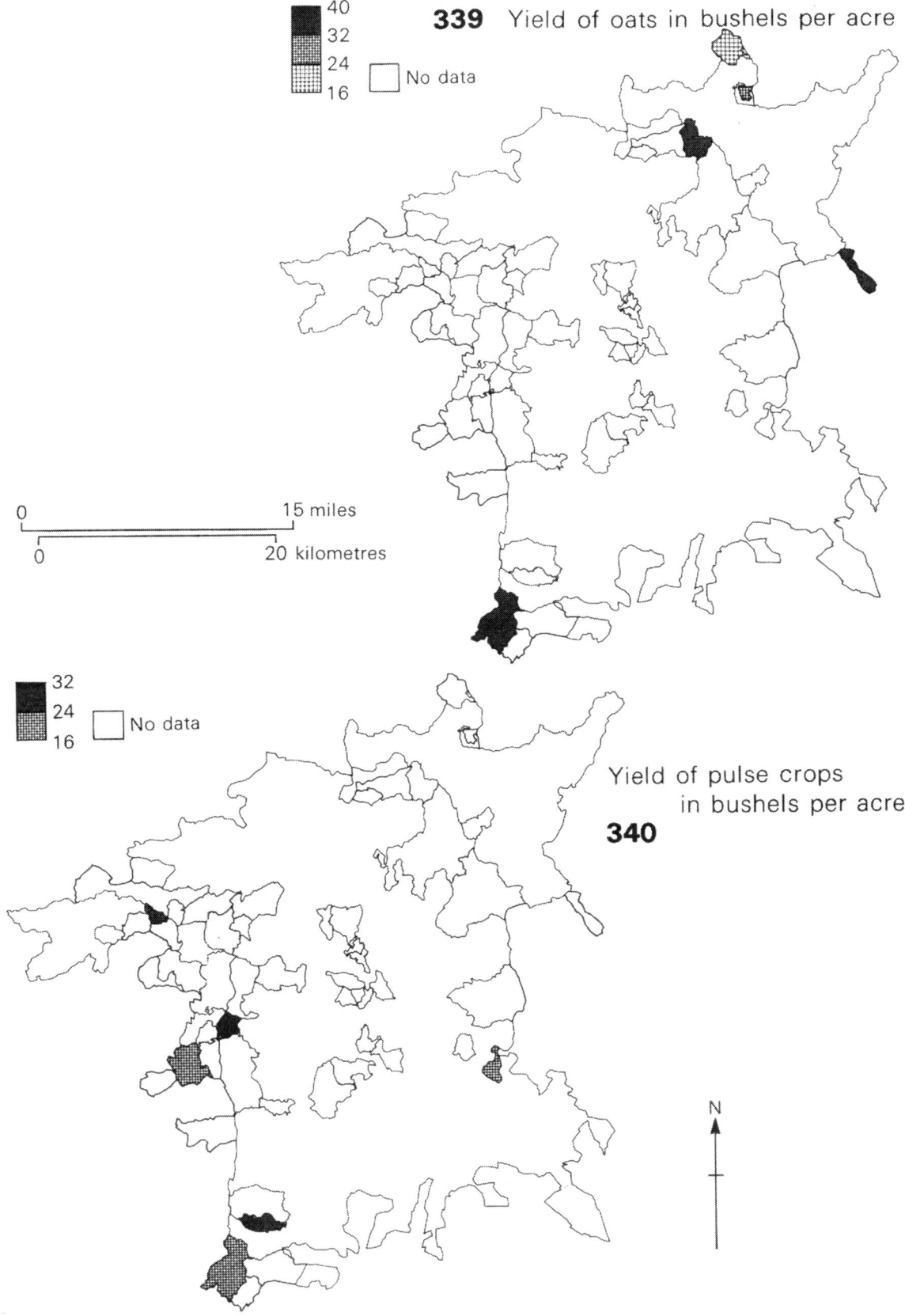

339 Yield of oats in bushels per acre

Yield of pulse crops in bushels per acre
340

Monmouthshire

144 tithe districts
71 reports on tithe agreements

Dr John Chapman (1973) has analysed estimates of parish land use from schedules to tithe apportionments in his study of the changing extent of moorland in Monmouthshire. He considers that these data, despite their imperfections, are the best available basis for constructing a datum line against which change may be measured.

Some 80 per cent of Monmouthshire reports on agreements were compiled by Thomas Hoskins and are seriously flawed as he does not specify individual crop acreages and provides only vague indications of crop rotations so that figures cannot be derived by relating these to total arable acres. In fact, there are useable crop acreages for only four parishes so no cartographic analysis or aggregate figures for crops or yields are compiled. Written comments on farming practices are equally meagre. In those instances where it is possible to be fairly certain about the length of rotations they are of five years or more with corn or root crops grown for three years and then clover sown and the land laid down to grass for anything up to five years. On the very best land, rotations were not dissimilar to those adopted in the east of England, for example, the wheat, turnips, barley, clover system at Welsh Bicknor, but more often oats formed an important part of the rotation and occasionally, as at Aberystruth, they were the only crop grown – 'oats, oats, oats – and lay down several years in the natural grass'. The cultivation of turnips received comment at a number of places but summer fallowing was also widespread (see Subject Index). There is no mention of high farming and surprisingly only one comment on low farming, at Goytre, where Charles Pym reported that 'the small size of the holdings, the poverty of the occupiers, the scourging course of crops all combine to depreciate the quality and rent of a naturally poor soil'. Little or no notice is given in this county's files to grassland (with the exception of meadows alongside the river Severn), to livestock (apart from comments on difficulties of obtaining numbers), to woodland (save hedgerows) or to commons (see Subject Index).

Table 43 *Reports on agreements for commutation of tithes in Monmouthshire*

Assistant commissioner/ local tithe agent	1837	1838	1839	1840	1841	1842	1843	Totals
Thomas Hoskins		8	19	18	5	6		56
John Johnes	3	8	1					12
Charles Pym		1					2	3
Totals	3	17	20	18	5	6	2	71

Table 44 *Land use in Monmouthshire c. 1836*

Land use	Percentage of total land area enumerated in reports on tithe agreements	Estimated acreage in whole county
Arable	28.8	106,217
Grass	49.5	182,393
Wood	11.5	42,353
Common	9.5	34,798

NORTH-WESTERN COUNTIES

Lancashire   Shropshire
Cheshire   Cumberland*
Staffordshire Westmorland*

The 'arable' type of printed form used for reporting on tithe agreements in these counties requires a 'description and rough estimate of the titheable produce' and asks assistant tithe commissioners and local tithe agents to 'describe the parish and the quality of the lands, the system of farming, and whether the quality of the produce has been affected by any extraordinary instances of high or low farming'.

---

* Data for Cumberland and Westmorland are seriously flawed (see *The tithe surveys of England and Wales*, pp. 138–9); they are not mapped and county aggregate figures of land use and crop acreages and yields are not compiled.

Lancashire

469 tithe districts
200 reports on tithe agreements

About 45 per cent of Lancashire tithe districts achieved voluntary agreements for commutation of tithe but these townships are not evenly distributed across the county – the Furness, Pennine and Bowland uplands have little or no coverage (Map 341). By contrast, a good proportion of townships on the Lancashire Plain have extant tithe file data. Woodland was mostly exempt from tithe, and commons were also exempt or covered by moduses. Acreages of both these categories of land are inconsistently recorded in tithe agreement reports. At Lathon, for example, 'the specifications of the titheable land in the schedule, do not agree with the total titheable nor are the woodland and the common excepted in the way they should have been'. Woodland and common data have not been mapped nor have county figures for these categories been aggregated in Table 46. At some places, crops of recent introduction, such as clover, were not tithed. Little tithe was still collected in kind in Lancashire (only five references in the Subject Index) most was paid c. 1836 by compositions. At Cronton, there was a rare instance of the continued collection of personal tithes; each of sixty married couples paid 5d, five widowers and seven widows paid 3d and 2d each respectively.

Assistant tithe commissioner Thomas Martin was responsible for just over 40 per cent of Lancashire reports, a task which accounted for the bulk of his work for the Tithe Commission. Four other commissioners also compiled significant numbers of reports (Table 45) so that Lancashire files display considerable variety in content. Martin's parish descriptions rarely run for more than three or four sentences; Henry Pilkington provides a lot more detail, especially for places where he encountered what he considered to be particularly low farming; John Penny often sets his parishes into a comparative context, though sometimes his metaphors are a little fanciful. At Windle, for example, 'the preparation of nitroil and chemical acids have struck a deadly blight upon the face of nature for several miles around so that the aspect in the brightest summer day is as the cheerless wilds of Siberia in the most uncongenial season'. More realistic are his comparisons of what he encountered in northern England with what he was used to in the south of the country. He likened land at Hoole, for instance, to 'the reclaimed bog lands of Somerset . . . but the contrast in the cultivation was astounding to my southern notion of agriculture. The land is undoubtedly capable of very great improvement.'

An agricultural practice still common in mid-nineteenth-century Lancashire was the cropping of a piece of land continuously for several years until it was exhausted, when it was laid down to grass and used for pasture until ceasing to produce reasonable herbage. At Greenhalgh, for example, John Job Rawlinson reported that the

> system is to continue ploughing the arable land in a three year course of fallow, wheat and oats as long as the land will produce any crop that will yield something more than the seed and labour. When it will no longer do so, it is laid down to rest in pasture for 8, 10, or perhaps 20 years, and this is the kind of land which in the agreement is enumerated as pasture.

If all such land was valued as arable, the rent-charge would have been greatly increased. On the other hand, it was patently unfair to the tithe owner that all intermittently ploughed lands be classified as grass so assistant commissioners carefully investigated the acreages of arable and pasture set down in commutation agreements. At Eccleston, for example, Thomas Martin wrote:

> the only exception to correctness is the very usual one in Lancashire, the proportion of arable and of meadow or pasture. The arable, I am convinced, is much under the reality. It is acknowledged to be too little in the township of Heskin, and my observation with respect to that of Eccleston, applies to another four townships, though in a less degree.

He changed arable from 522 to 694 acres and grass from 1,304 to 1,045 acres. The need for such changes would have been avoided if the Tithe Commission had supplied 'pastoral' rather than 'arable' type forms for use in Lancashire.

A frequent comment made by all assistant commissioners and local tithe agents is the absence of regular crop rotations in Lancashire. An exasperated Henry Pilkington wrote at Langho, 'strictly speaking there is no such thing as a rotation in Lancashire, the farmers hardly knowing what the word means'. At Ightenhill,

> there are only 44a., 0r., 22p. of arable land in the township. There is no grain grown but oats, and they are grown more for the sake of refreshing the worn out grass, than for the value of the corn. With this crop grass seeds are sown again; from 40 to 50 acres being actually ploughed up in this manner.

For the county as a whole, oats were the leading crop in terms of acreage. Assistant commissioners also considered that the general small size of holdings made it difficult to identify the average rotation. At Newton-within-Mackerfield, Henry Pilkington

> never saw land sown in a more foul state, twitch or couch (Triticum repens) being abundant everywhere in the ploughed lands. There is no rotation in the township, or indeed in the parish, nor any attempt at any – and this may be the more readily conceived when I state that there are 49 farms and only 655 acres of arable land in the township.

Where regular rotations were encountered, they were not well thought of. The three-course with a bare fallow was still common. Rotations which elicited more favourable comment were similar to that described by John Penny at Rufford where the course was oats, barley, beans, artificial grass, wheat, potatoes. Low farming was common (twenty specific references in the Subject Index). Characteristic of Lancashire low farming townships were the small quantities of seeds or turnips grown, that no sheep were kept and many fewer cattle than could be raised if available pasture was properly managed. Assistant commissioners commented that often soils were suitable for growing barley (see Subject Index) and that on similar soils elsewhere in England this crop would have been grown in large quantities, though they also accepted that with the food demand from urban manufacturing centres it might be thought more profitable to maximise the output of wheat and potatoes. Immediately around manufacturing towns dairying was one of the most important farming activities. At Newton-within-Mackerfield, 'the farmer mainly relies upon his dairy for paying his rent and supporting his family; its products, also, being here, as nearly everywhere else in the same county, protected from the tithing-man by prescriptive payments'.

Table 45 *Reports on agreements for commutation of tithes in Lancashire*

Assistant commissioner/ local tithe agent	1837	1838	1839	1840	1841	1842	1843	1844	1845	Totals
Thomas Martin		11	38	11	5	4	9	2	2	82
Henry Pilkington		32								32
John Penny			28		2					30
Richard Burton Phillipson			5		1	8	6		4	24
John Job Rawlinson		13	3	1		1				18
Charles Howard	2	9								11
Thomas Sudworth	1	1								2
John S. Donaldson Selby	1									1
Totals	4	66	74	12	8	13	15	2	6	200

Table 46 *Land use, crops and yields in Lancashire c. 1836*

	A Land use	Percentage of total land area enumerated in reports on tithe agreements	Estimated acreage in whole county
	Arable	27.1	330,290
	Grass	65.7	801,347

	B Crop	Mean percentage of arable	Mean yield per acre	Estimated acreage in whole county
	Wheat	26.8	22.9 bushels	88,564
	Barley	2.2	28.3 bushels	7,111
	Oats	27.5	30.6 bushels	90,699
	Pulses	2.6	24.0 bushels	8,417

266 North-western counties

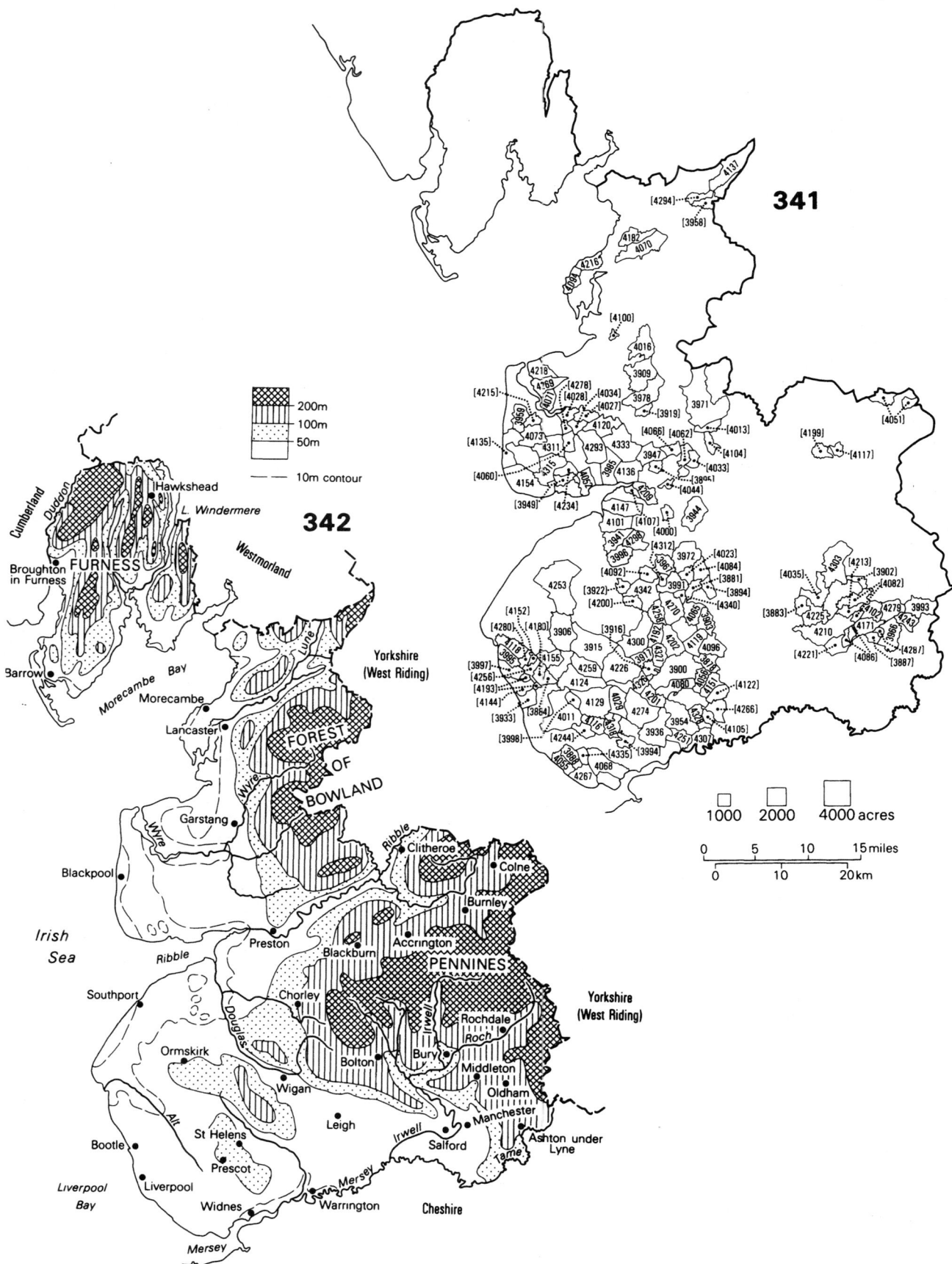

Lancashire

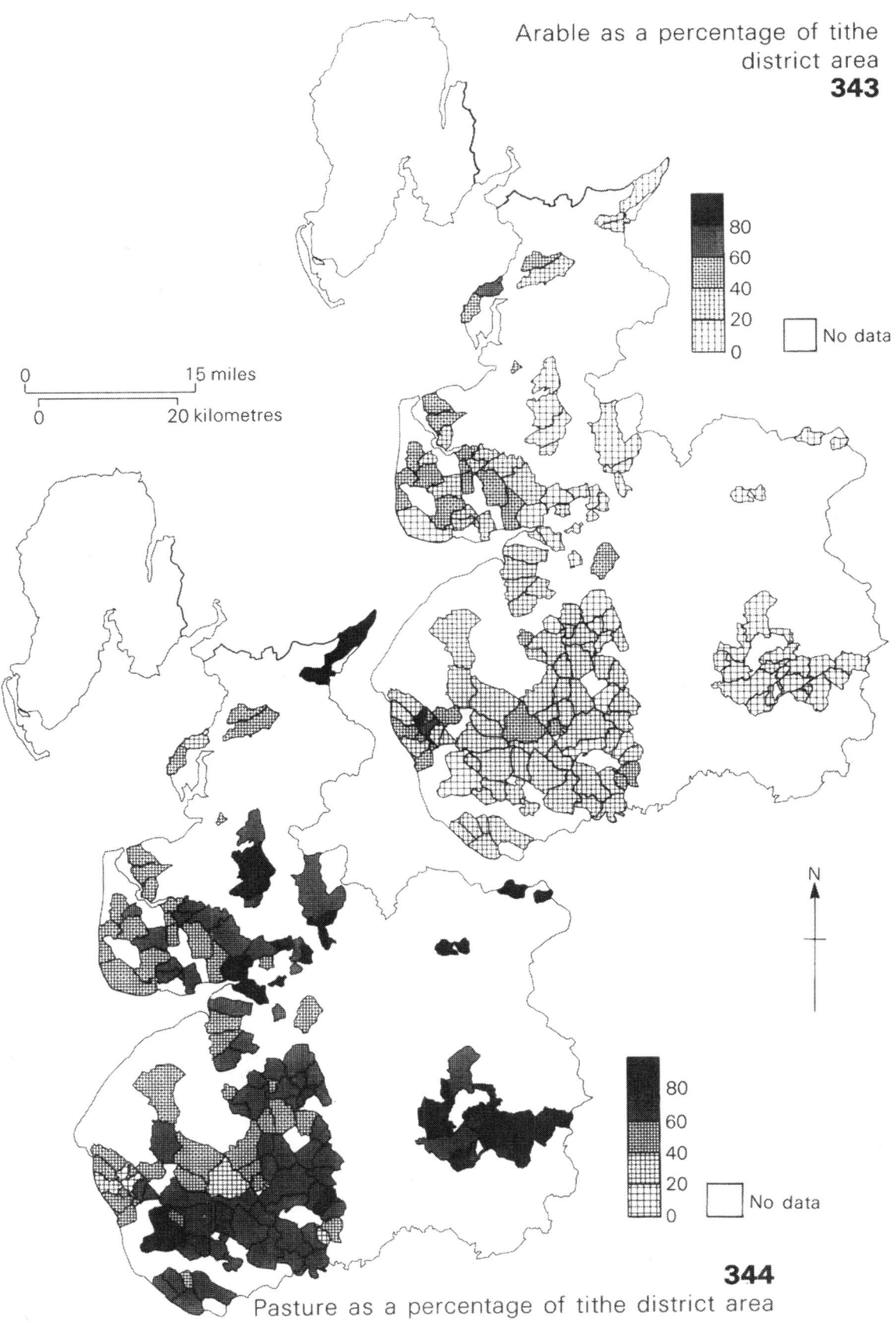

343 Arable as a percentage of tithe district area

344 Pasture as a percentage of tithe district area

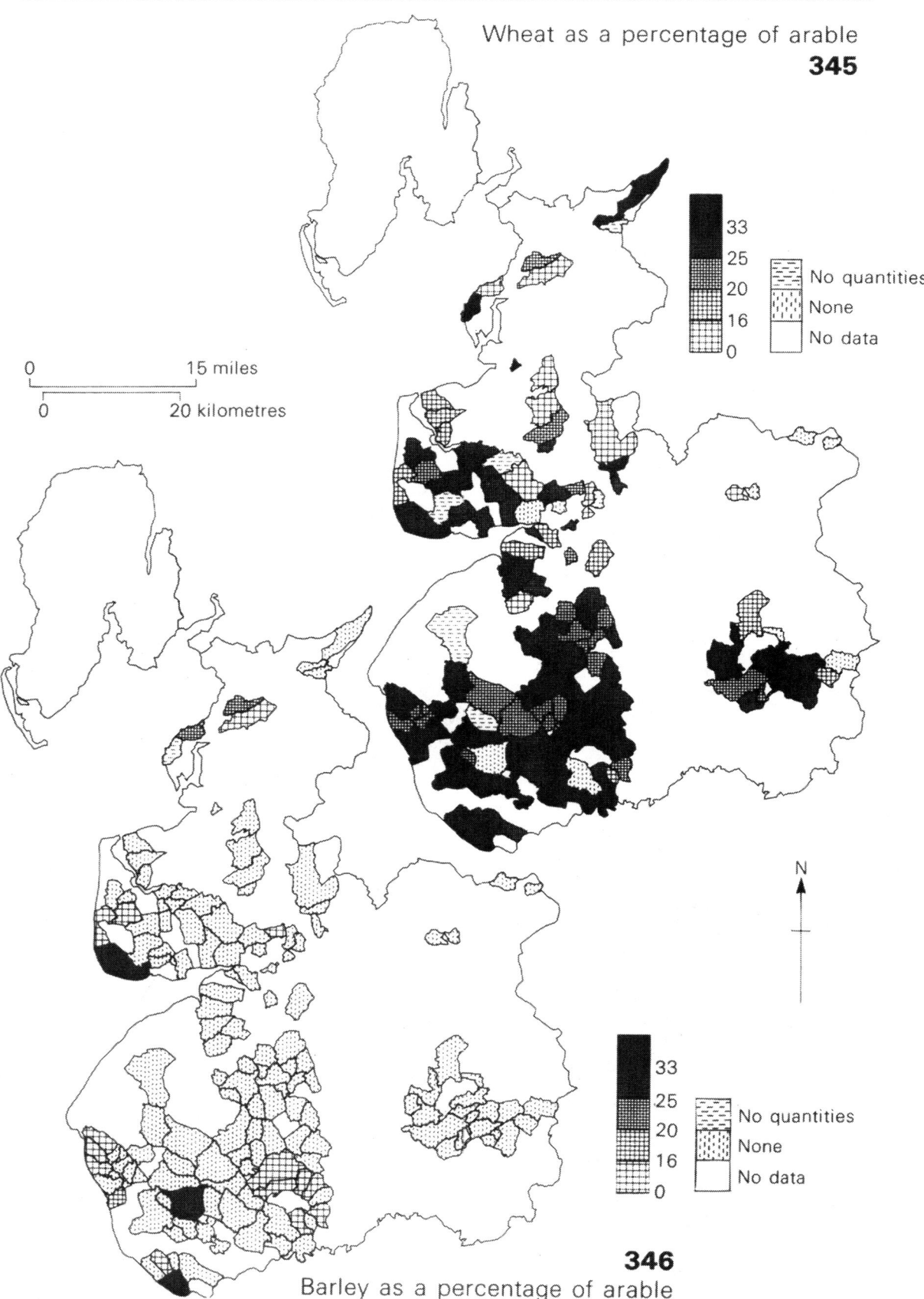

345 Wheat as a percentage of arable

346 Barley as a percentage of arable

Lancashire

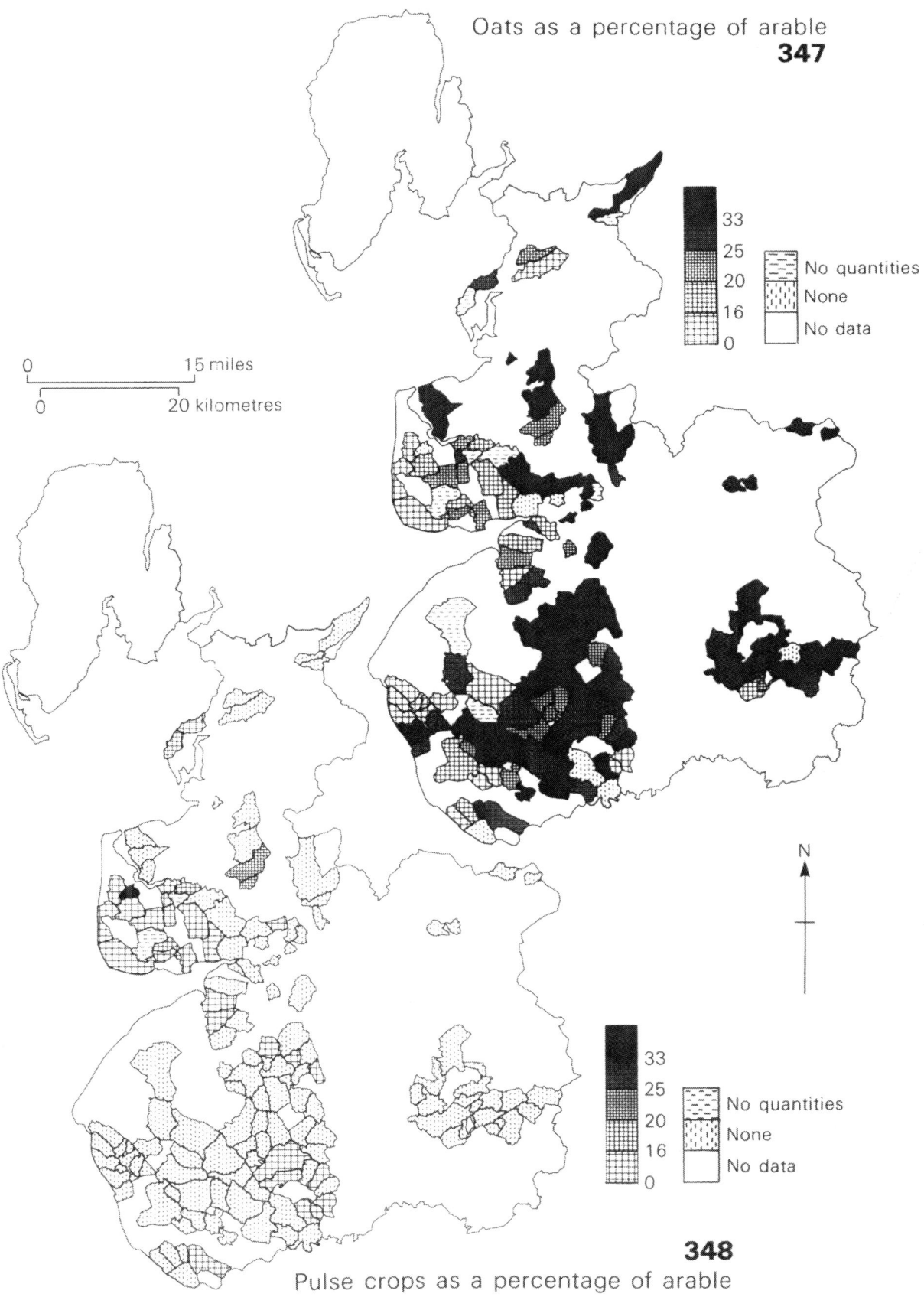

347 Oats as a percentage of arable

348 Pulse crops as a percentage of arable

North-western counties

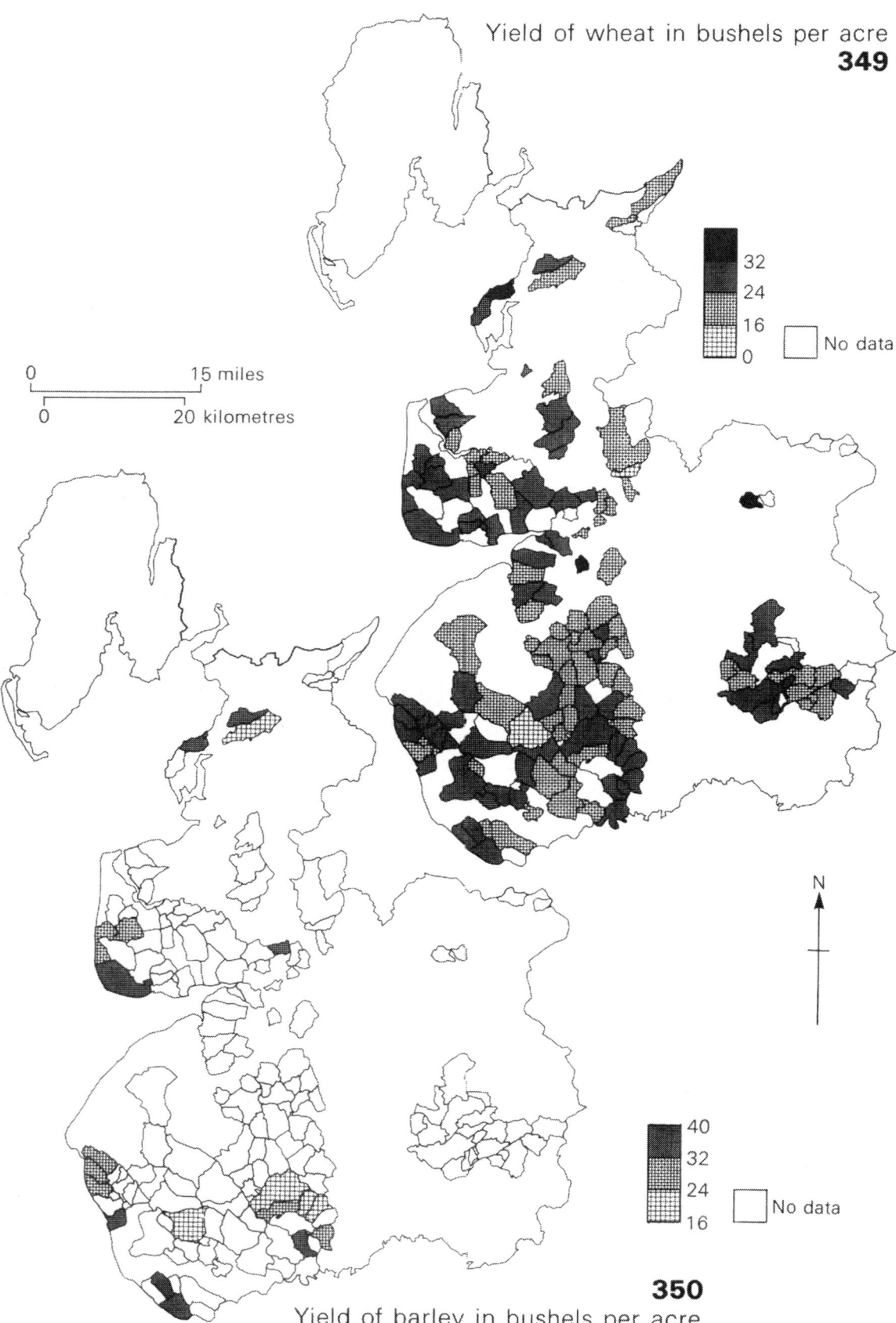

Yield of wheat in bushels per acre
349

350
Yield of barley in bushels per acre

Lancashire

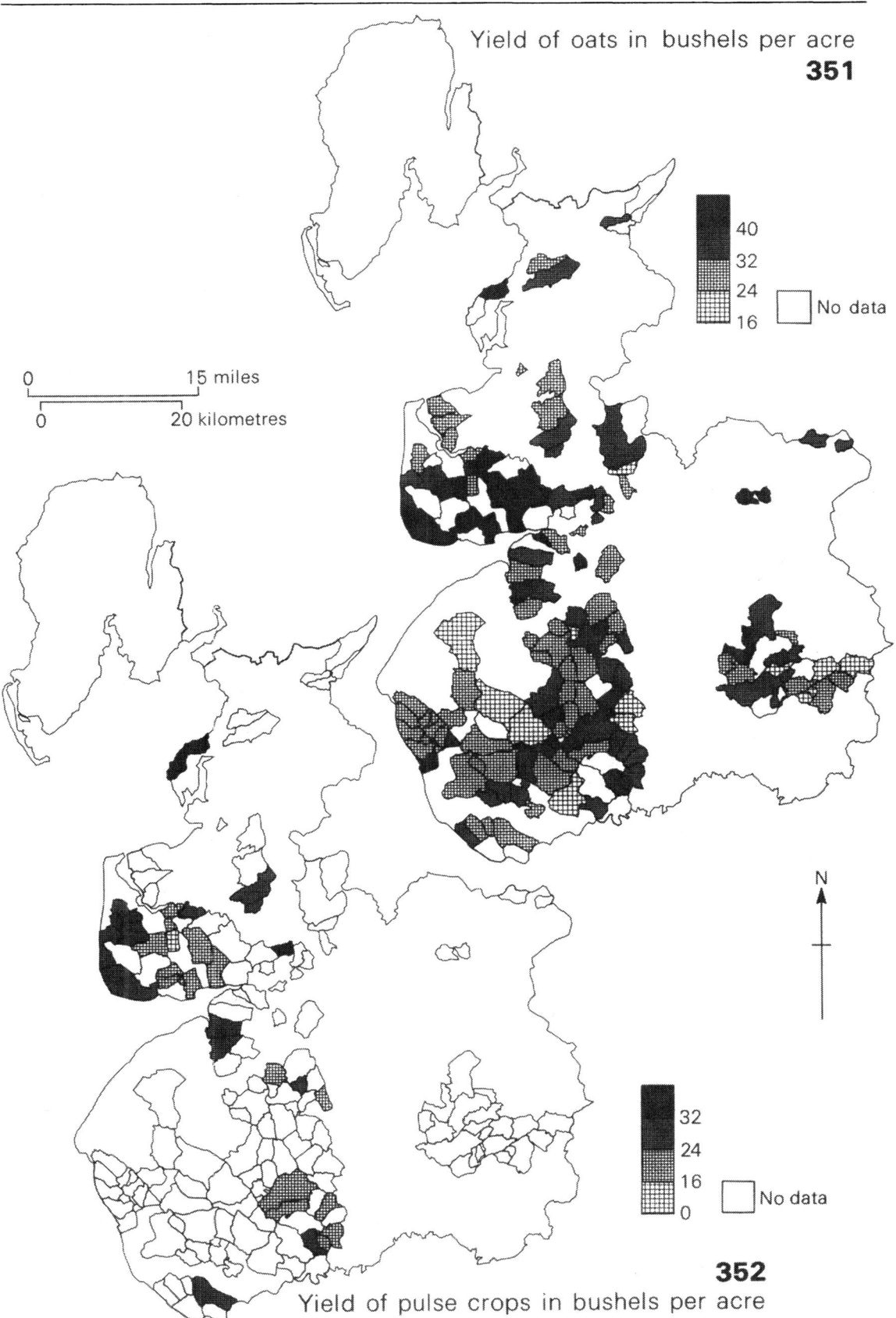

Yield of oats in bushels per acre
351

Yield of pulse crops in bushels per acre
352

Cheshire

477 tithe districts
278 reports on tithe agreements

A reconstruction of farming in Cheshire c. 1840 based on an analysis of tithe files has been published by R. J. P. Kain and Harriet M. E. Holt (1983); the county's tithe files were also consulted by Regina E. Porter (1974) for her study of agricultural change in Cheshire in the nineteenth century.

Evidence in the tithe files suggests that in Cheshire both landowners and tithe owners were anxious for a speedy commutation of tithe under the 1836 Act. Voluntary agreements were reached in 278 of the 477 Cheshire tithe districts and two-thirds of these were reached within three years of the Act. It is somewhat surprising that commutation proceeded at such a pace as Cheshire was very much a dairying county at this date and in many townships moduses were paid on cows, calves and hay. Elsewhere, the existence of such customary payments often complicated and lengthened the process of agreeing a rent-charge. In view of the long tradition of dairying and grassland farming in this county it might be expected that 'pastoral' type questionnaire forms would have been supplied to assistant commissioners and local tithe agents for their reports, but for reasons that are not known, the 'arable' type were used throughout Cheshire, as they were in Lancashire. It is unfortunate that the two assistant commissioners responsible for two-thirds of the reports, John Holder and Thomas Sudworth, wrote some of the briefest and least perceptive accounts of farming to be found in tithe files. This deficiency is made good to some extent by the very full descriptions of agriculture compiled by Richard Burton Phillipson. All Cheshire reporters found it difficult to accommodate data on the county's long ley systems of farming within the format of an 'arable' type of report. Particular problems related to the classification of clover and seeds. Fortunately, Holder, Sudworth and Phillipson, who between them completed more than 80 per cent of Cheshire reports, all used the same definition of arable as land excluding seed crops.

Table 48 and Maps 355–7 summarise the quantity and distribution of various categories of land. Woodland was usually exempt from tithe in Cheshire and acreages are not recorded consistently in the county's tithe files; acreages of this category of land are not tabulated or mapped. Soils of the Cheshire Plain were well adapted to pasture and meadow and the presence of large urban markets encouraged a dairy system; in very many Cheshire Plain townships grassland covered more than 80 per cent of the land surface c. 1840. At Agden, John Holder remarked that 'the dairy is chiefly attended to and no more ploughed than is requisite to provide bread and malt corn for the family and straw for the cattle in winter'. The traditional Cheshire system of cultivating arable land in dairying districts was to plough up a piece of pasture when it would no longer produce good grass, and sow a crop of oats. After this the land would be fallowed and then sown with wheat. Finally, a crop of oats might be taken again and the land then laid down with grass seeds. Though the tithe files indicate that important alterations were under way, this rotation, if such it can be called, was still the most prevalent at the time of tithe commutation. Table 48 and Maps 358–62 testify to the persistence of this old system of cultivating the land. Wheat, oats and bare fallow together account for some 80 per cent of the arable; barley and turnips less than 10 per cent; and pulses were recorded as a field crop in only four townships.

There are many comments in the files about the poor standard of arable farming encountered in Cheshire. At Newton, John Holder remarked that 'the farming in this township as respects the arable is very low and the produce quite stationary'. Even close to manufacturing towns from which manure could be purchased easily, farming was 'below what it ought to be'. Improvements, particularly the adoption of four-course rotations with turnips or potatoes were more prevalent on sandy soils than on clays. At Little Leigh, for example, 'on the sand and loam the farming is improving and the crops consequently; on the clay which is the higher side of the township the land is poor and the farming indifferent'. Notwithstanding such changes and some draining of clay soils, corn yields throughout the county were low; wheat averaged just over 20 bushels per acre, barley less than 30 bushels and oats, 26 bushels. Assistant commissioners' reports lack details of the varieties of corn crops grown and the precise methods of cultivation but it is clear that c. 1840 in Cheshire dairying districts, i.e. over most of the county, corn was grown principally to provide straw for cattle.

Table 47 *Reports on agreements for commutation of tithes in Cheshire*

Assistant commissioner/ local tithe agent	1837	1838	1839	1840	1841	1842	1843	1844	1845	1846	Totals
John Holder		25	55	31	13	8					132
Thomas Sudworth	3	50	1								54
Richard Burton Phillipson			15	4		10	6	2	3	3	43
Thomas Martin		4	2			3	2	1			12
John Penny			11								11
Thomas Hoskins		10									10
Henry Pilkington	8										8
Charles Howard		6									6
John Mee Mathew		1									1
Horace William Meteyard						1					1
Totals	11	96	84	35	13	22	8	3	3	3	278

Table 48 *Land use, crops and yields in Cheshire c. 1836*

	A Land use	Percentage of total land area enumerated in reports on tithe agreements		Estimated acreage in whole county
	Arable	25.5		180,344
	Grass	70.4		497,581
	Common	1.4		9,909
B	Crop	Mean percentage of arable	Mean yield per acre	Estimated acreage in whole county
	Wheat	31.4	20.6 bushels	55,185
	Barley	3.6	29.4 bushels	6,492
	Oats	32.1	26.2 bushels	57,890
	Turnips	2.5	£2.68	4,509
	Seeds	8.8	—	15,870
	Fallows	16.4	—	29,576

Cheshire

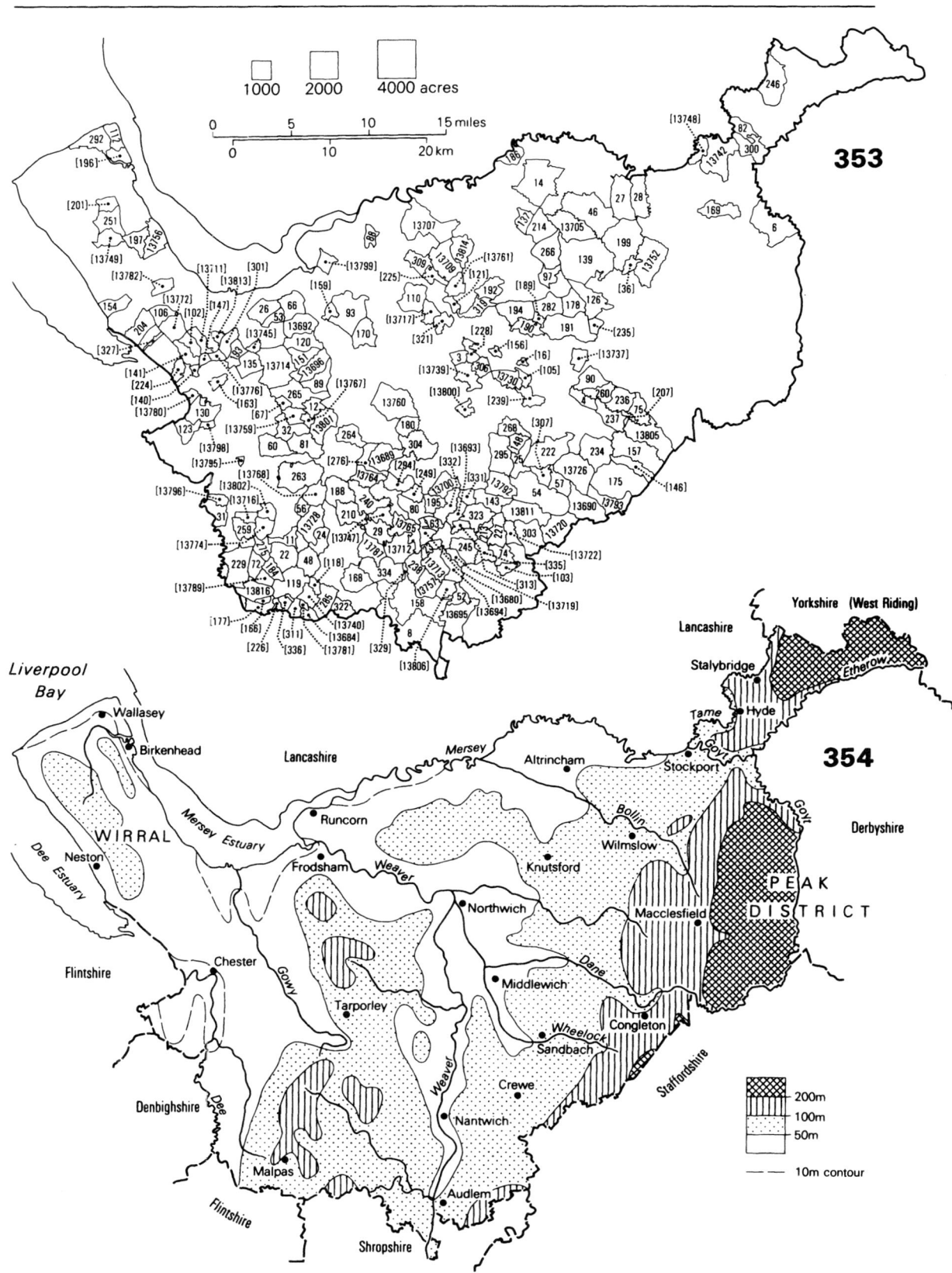

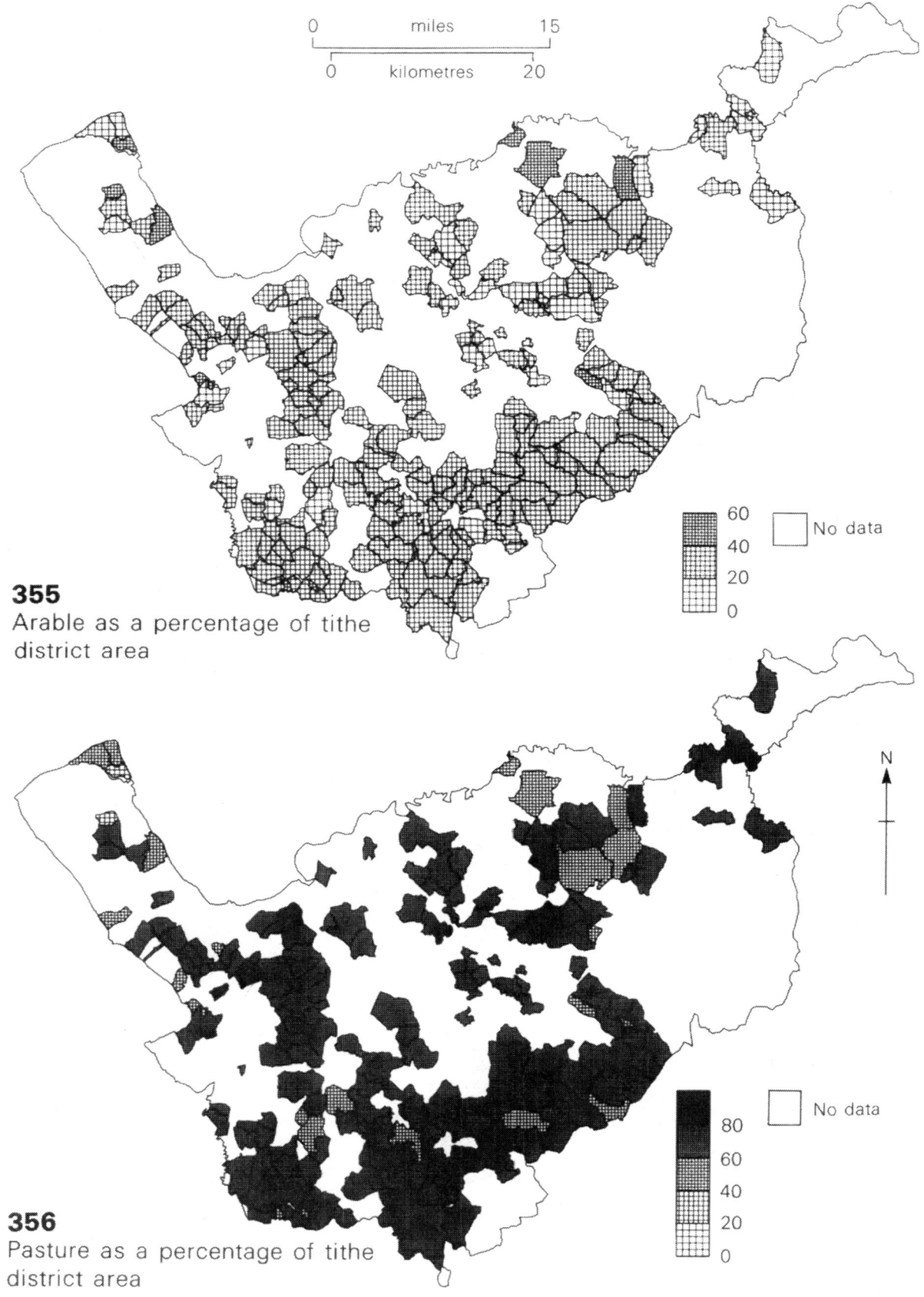

355 Arable as a percentage of tithe district area

356 Pasture as a percentage of tithe district area

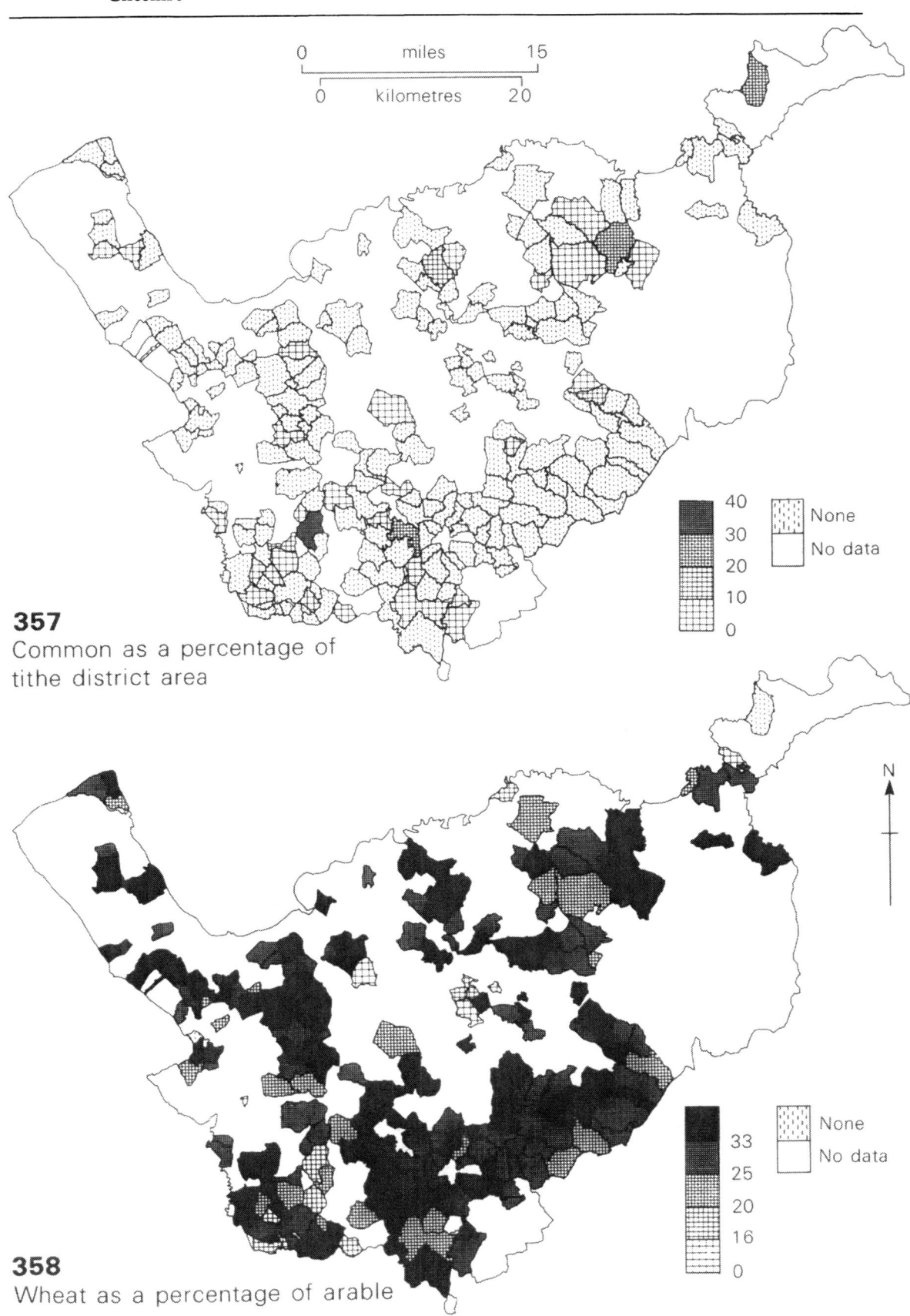

357 Common as a percentage of tithe district area

358 Wheat as a percentage of arable

278 North-western counties

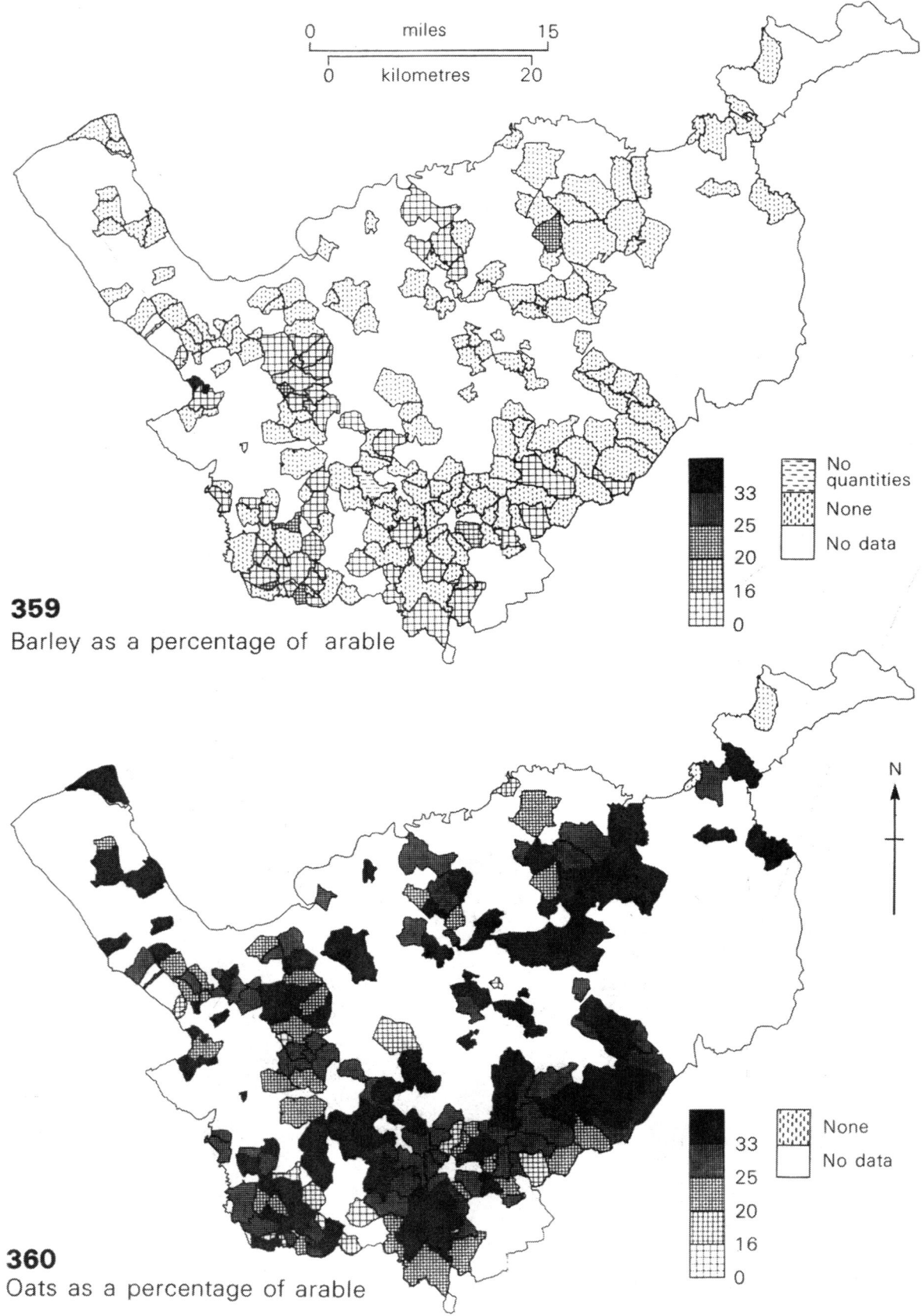

359
Barley as a percentage of arable

360
Oats as a percentage of arable

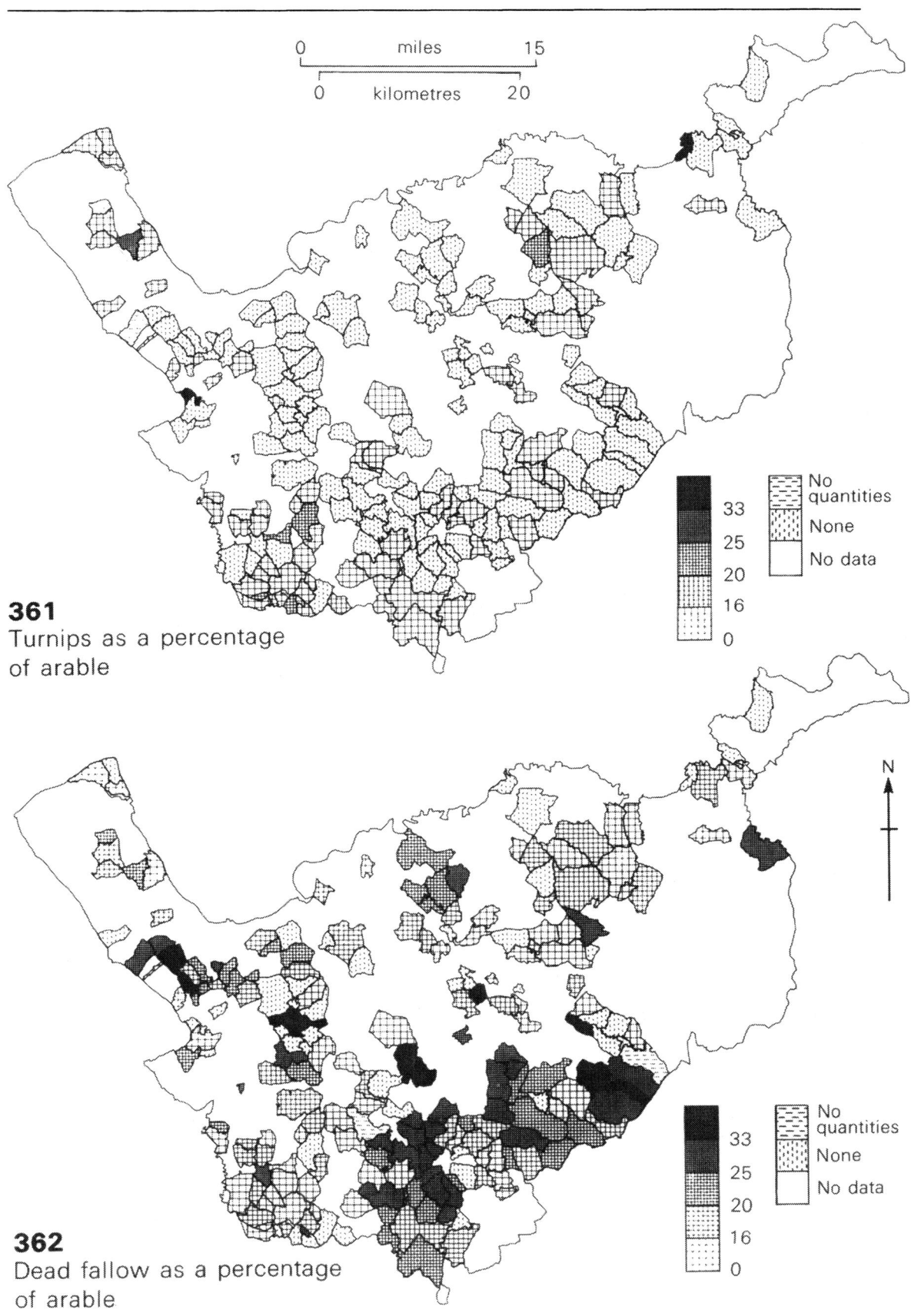

361 Turnips as a percentage of arable

362 Dead fallow as a percentage of arable

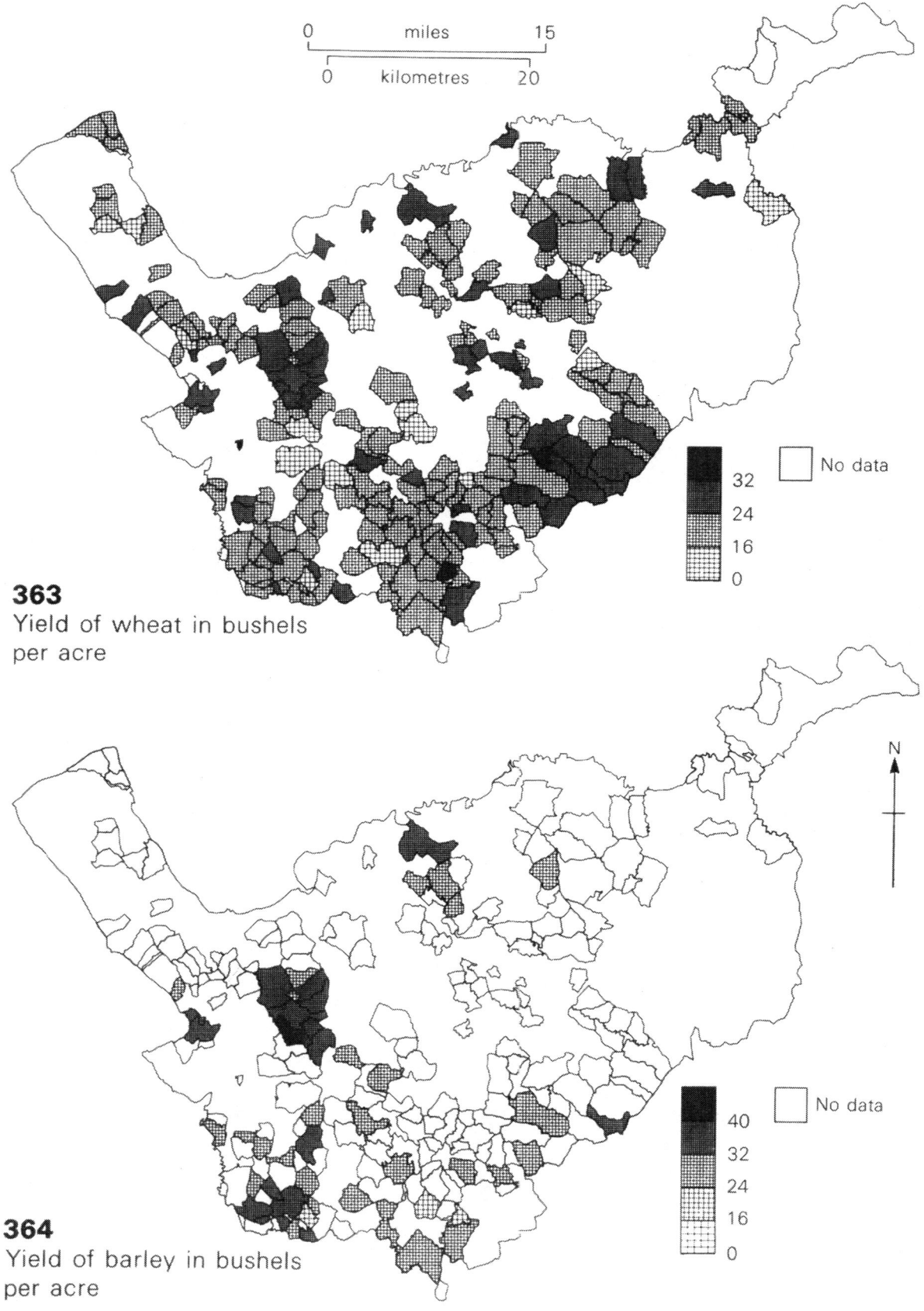

363 Yield of wheat in bushels per acre

364 Yield of barley in bushels per acre

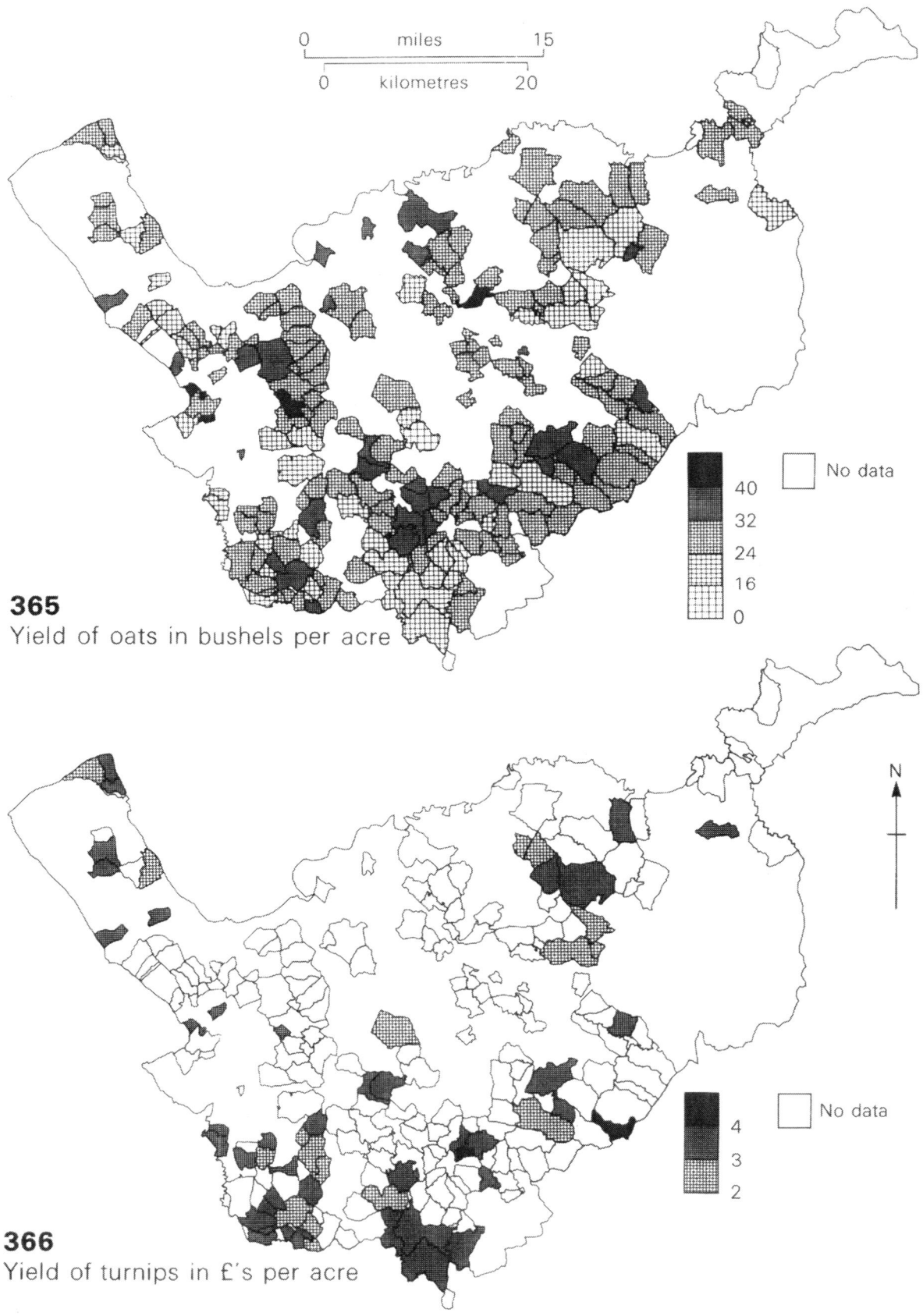

365 Yield of oats in bushels per acre

366 Yield of turnips in £'s per acre

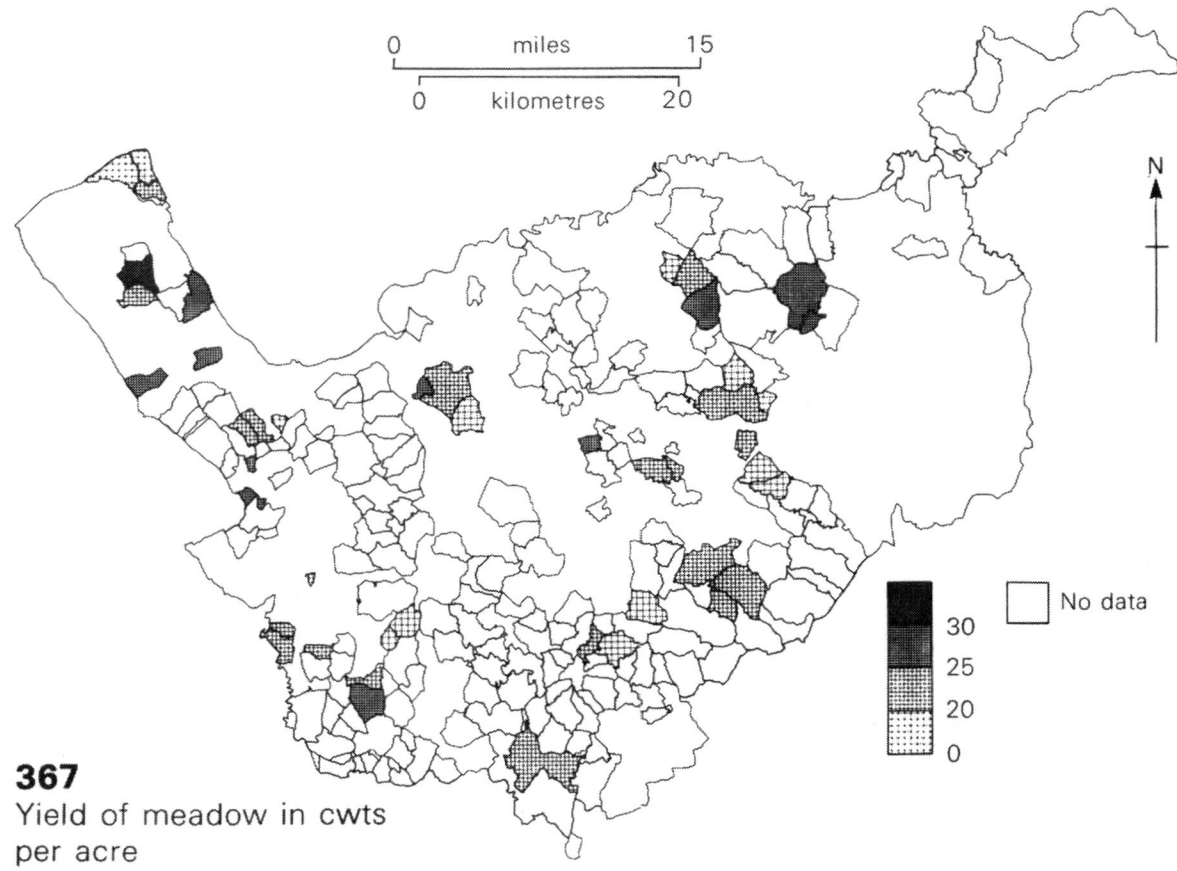

367
Yield of meadow in cwts per acre

Staffordshire

332 tithe districts
137 reports on tithe agreements

Tithe apportionments and tithe files are the primary source material for A. D. M. Phillips' study (1973) of farming practices and soil types in Staffordshire around 1840. He has compiled maps of land use, crops and yields, and discusses distributions and rotations. His analysis of these tithe survey data demonstrates that *c.* 1840 there was a profound distinction between farming on light and heavy soils in this north-western county.

Voluntary commutation was a long-drawn-out process in Staffordshire by comparison with most other counties (Table 49). Although work began early with fifteen reports submitted in the pre-printed questionnaire period, almost 40 per cent are dated 1840 or after. Staffordshire has one of the largest number of assistant commissioners and local tithe agents in proportion to the number of voluntary commutations effected of any county. The forty-five reports filed in the peak year of 1838, for example, were compiled by no fewer than twelve individuals. Not surprisingly they all had very different backgrounds (see Table 1 in the Introduction). The previous experience of some, such as Thomas Hoskins, was mostly in Wales; others like James Drage Merest and Thomas Sudworth worked principally in East Anglia, or, like Roger Kynaston, in southern England. Henry Pilkington and Richard Burton Phillipson were probably most closely acquainted with northern farming. Only John Holder, George Ashdown and John Mee Mathew seemed particularly familiar with Staffordshire agriculture. James Drage Merest's comments suggest that he had little understanding of west of England rotational systems. Only eighteen parishes were entirely tithe free (for some of these the tithe file is completely empty) but woodland in north Staffordshire was usually exempt.

From his extensive analysis of land use and crop statistics in Staffordshire tithe files, A. D. M. Phillips concludes (1973, p. 49) that the

> light lands were more productive: they produced higher yields of wheat, presented higher stocking densities and were more intensively used with little fallowing and a large area devoted to green cropping. Mixed farming practices had been widely adopted, mainly concentrating on cereals although with livestock activities being in some cases important. The heavy lands revealed many of the features that had been attributed to them in this period. Arable occupied a large part of the cultivated area; wheat was the main cereal crop; fallows persisted and were areally significant; and traditional rotations were maintained.

The following extracts from tithe file reports indicate the kind of written material in the tithe files which supports such conclusions (see Subject Index). At Forton near Newport, John Holder reported in 1838 that 'the sandy portion appears to have been well farmed and the produce increased about ten per cent within the last ten years. The strong land is capable of improvement by draining.' At Enville in the same year, Charles Howard wrote: 'the mode of management of course varies in an equal degree, – on the lighter land – turnips, barley, pasture, wheat, whilst on the strong soils, – fallow, wheat, oats or beans with the occasional introduction of clover is the usual course'. Haslour, north of Tamworth, 'contains about 593 acres of which a great part is clay, on marle some clay of depth and some loam on which swede turnips are grown. The system of tillage is fallow for turnips on the loam and dead fallow on the clay then wheat and oats, barley or beans as best adapted and clovered down.' The dairy industry, however, tended to transcend such soil divisions. Cows were fed on both permanent pastures and also on turnips and leys. At Dunstall, James Drage Merest commented that 'the dairy appears the only part of farming that is here understood'. In John Pickering's opinion, 'cheese making may be stated as the staple of the grasslands, but in this township [Bishops Offley] owing to the tendency of the soil to suffer from drought it is not so successfully nor so extensively practised as in other parts of the neighbourhood'. There was of course also a considerable demand for dairy products and especially for fresh milk from towns such as Birmingham and Wolverhampton; the urban food market is a topic much discussed in Staffordshire files as it affected the nature of farm production and level of tithe. Such demand factors introduce local distortions of a soil-based model.

Table 49 *Reports on agreements for commutation of tithes in Staffordshire*

Assistant commissioner/ local tithe agent	1837	1838	1839	1840	1841	1842	1843	1844	1845	1846	Totals
Richard Burton Phillipson			4	10	2	5	4	1			26
George Ashdown		4	5	7	1	2					19
John Holder		5		1	2	6	3				17
John Mee Mathew		7	9								16
John Pickering			1	7							8
Henry Pilkington	5	3									8
Thomas Sudworth	5	2									7
Edward Greathed		6									6
Thomas Hoskins		5									5
Charles Howard		5									5
James Drage Merest	4										4
Gelinger C. Symons		1	3								4
Thomas Smith Woolley		4									4
Roger Kynaston		2									2
N. S. Meryweather		1	1								2
John Penny				2							2
Charles Pym	1									1	2
Totals	15	45	23	27	5	13	7	1		1	137

Table 50 *Land use, crops and yields in Staffordshire c. 1836*

A	Land use	Percentage of total land area enumerated in reports on tithe agreements	Estimated acreage in whole county
	Arable	44.8	326,252
	Grass	44.6	325,070
	Wood	4.8	34,867
	Common	4.1	29,758

B	Crop	Mean percentage of arable	Mean yield per acre	Estimated acreage in whole county
	Wheat	21.9	21.3 bushels	71,323
	Barley	12.7	28.8 bushels	41,300
	Oats	13.0	27.9 bushels	42,503
	Pulses	1.3	23.3 bushels	4,263
	Turnips	12.1	£2.60	39,305
	Seeds	27.7	21.9 cwts	90,248
	Fallows	9.9	—	32,310

286 North-western counties

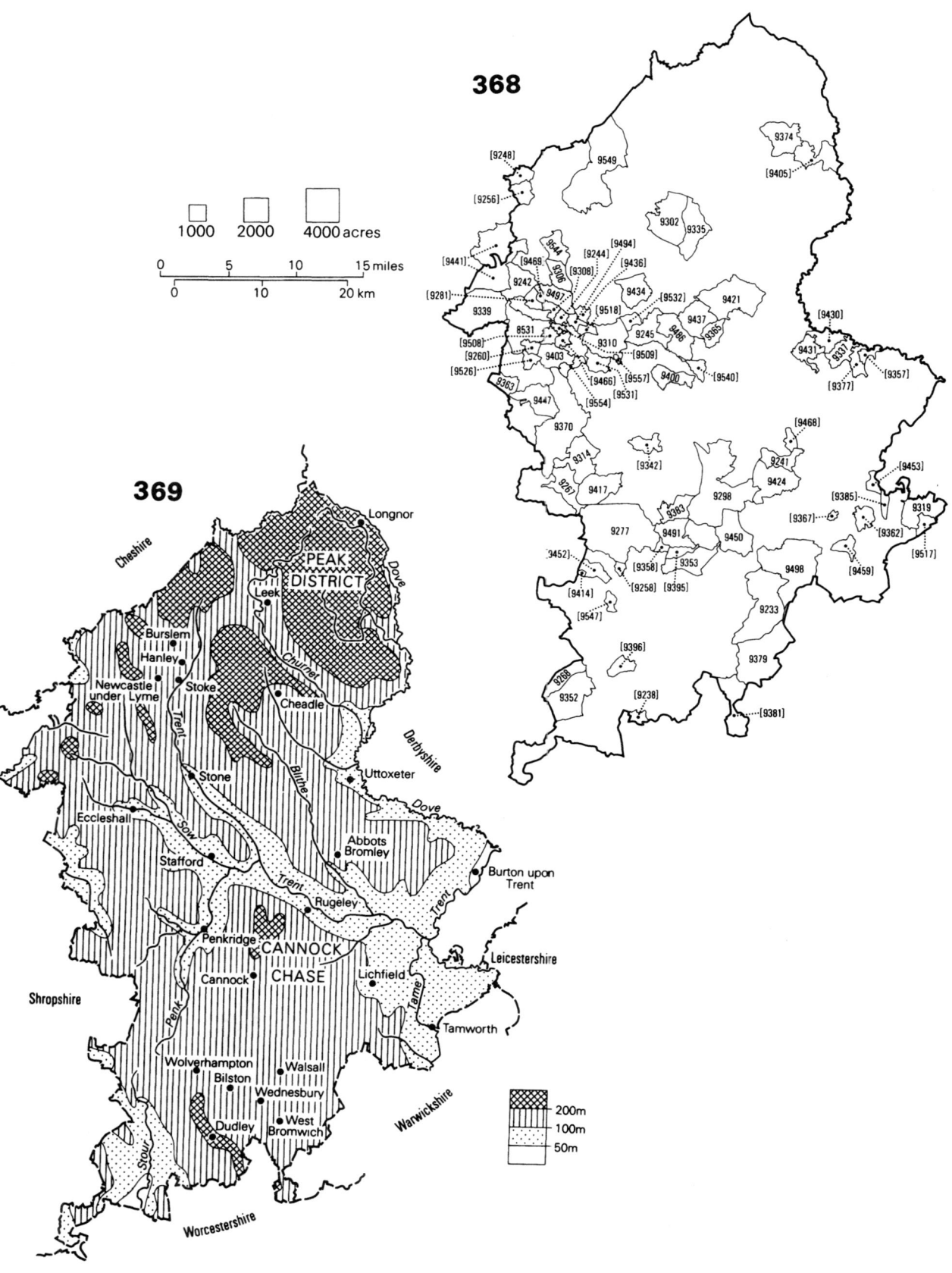

Staffordshire

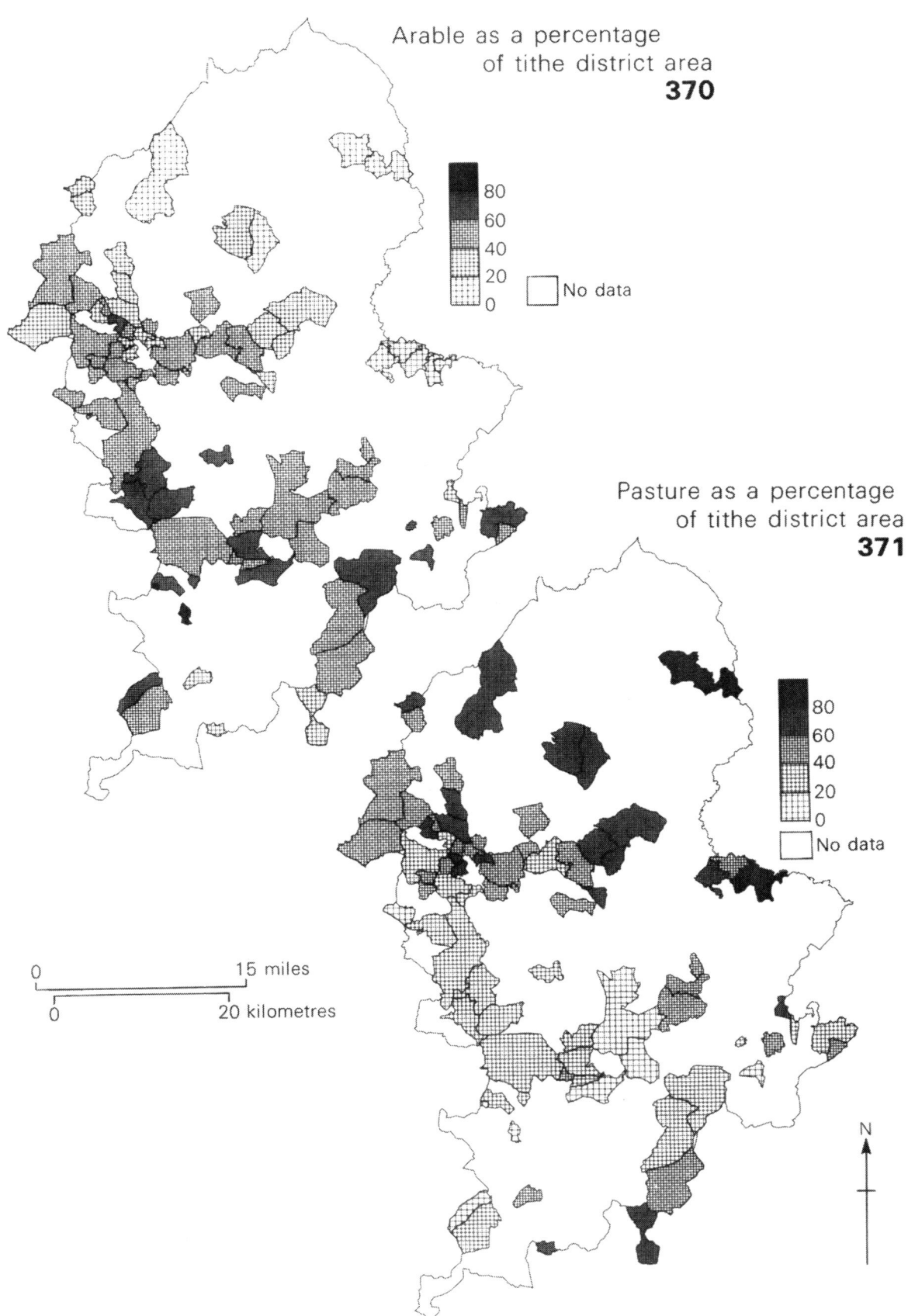

Arable as a percentage of tithe district area
370

Pasture as a percentage of tithe district area
371

288 North-western counties

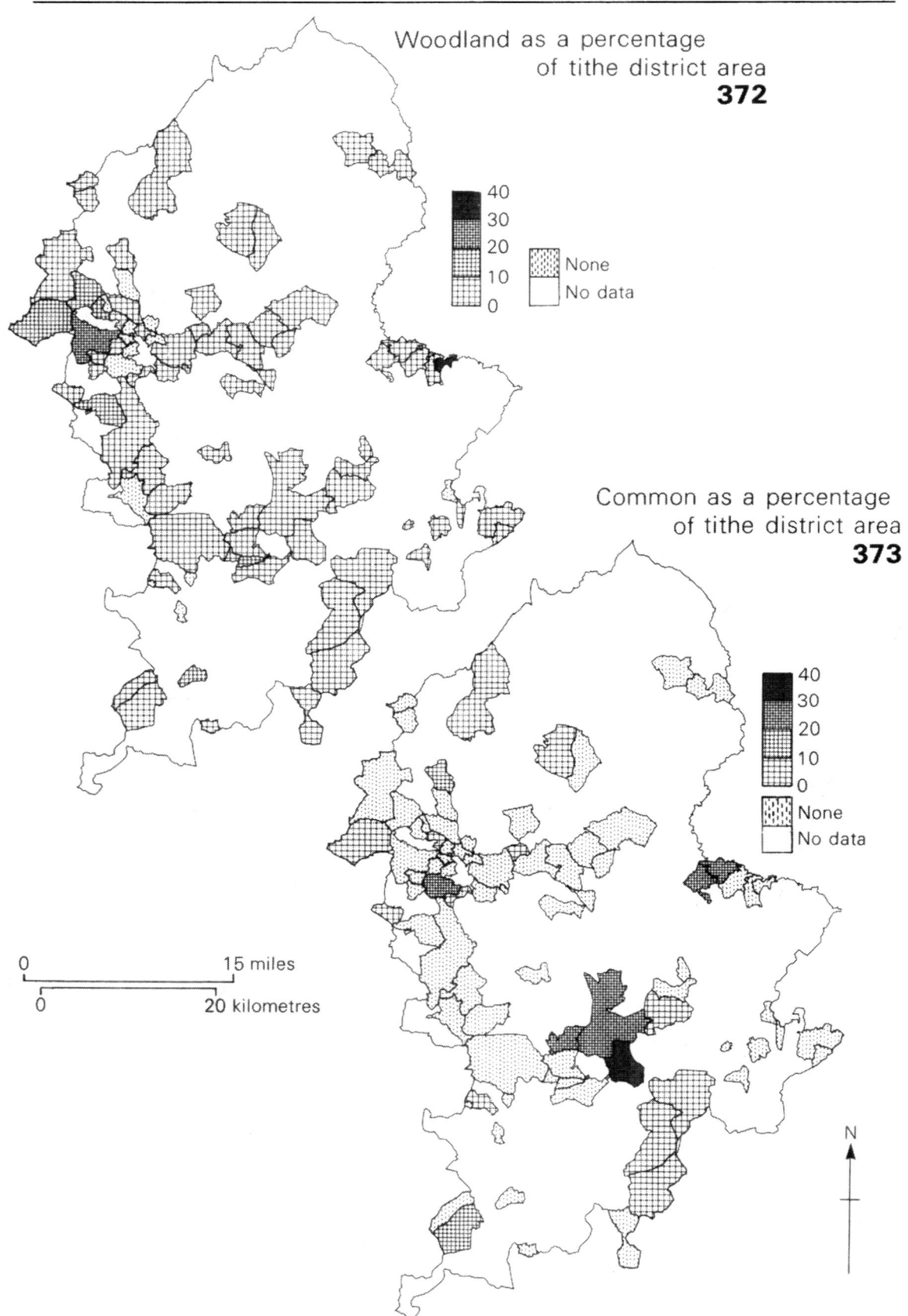

Woodland as a percentage of tithe district area
372

Common as a percentage of tithe district area
373

Staffordshire

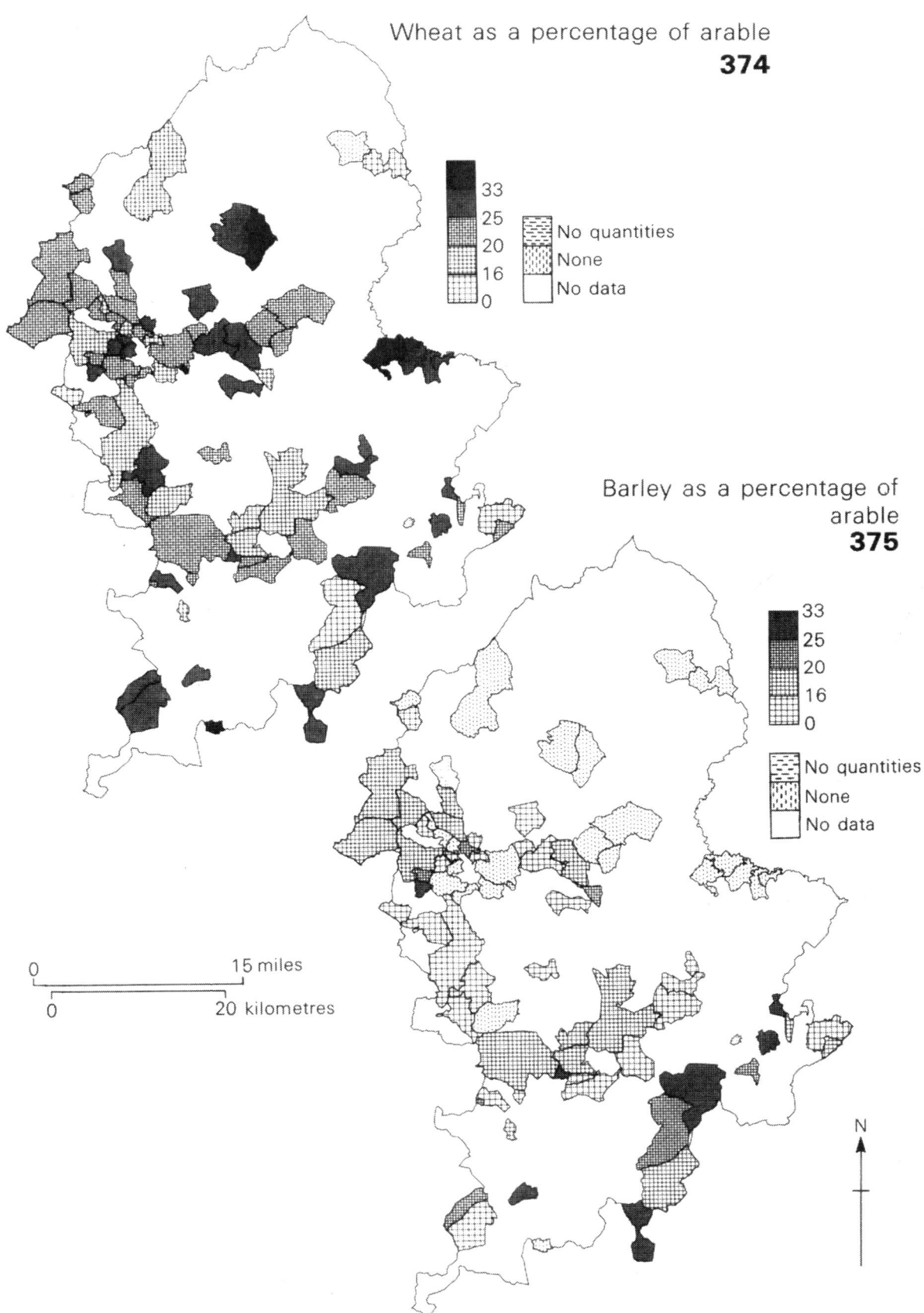

North-western counties

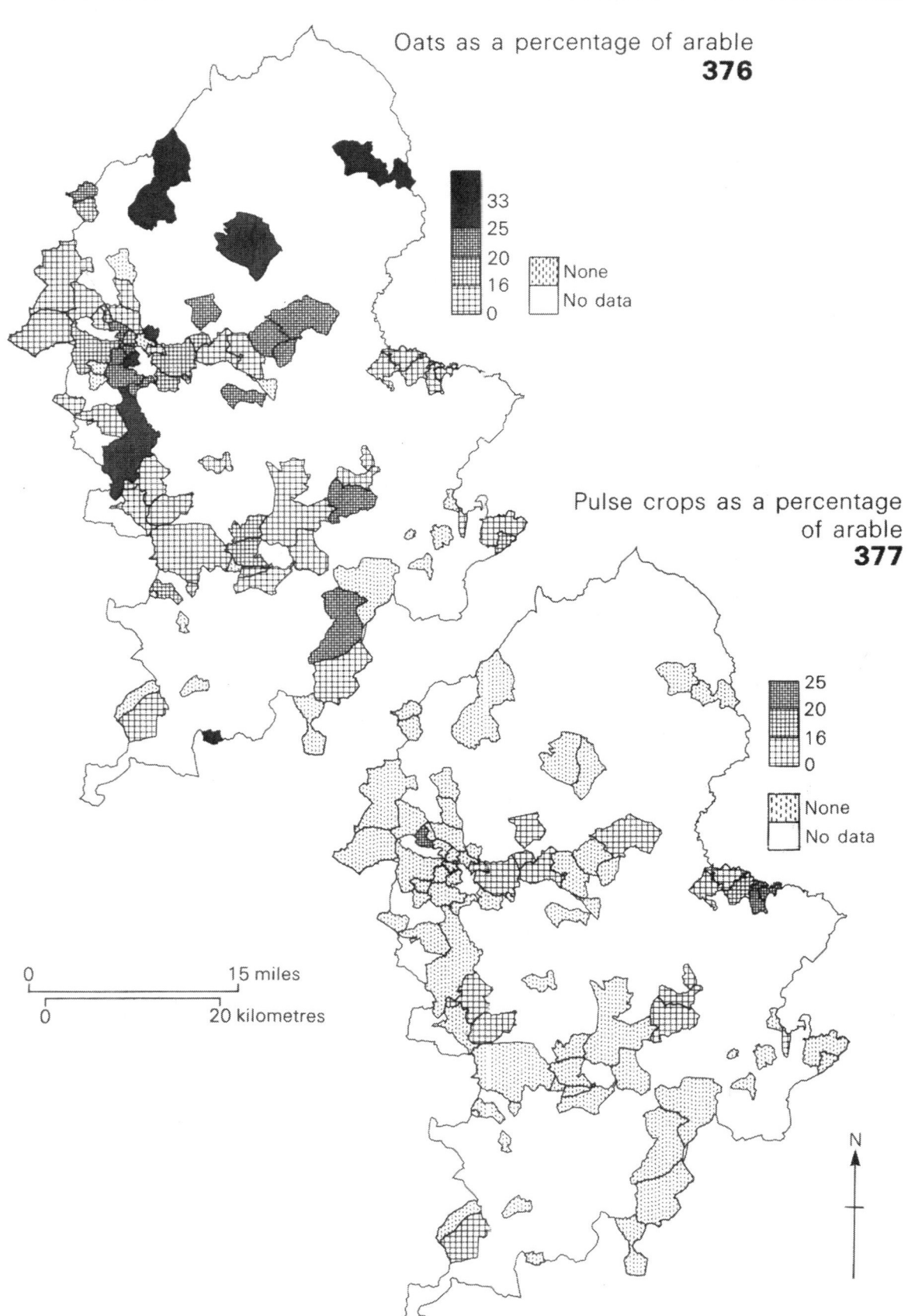

Staffordshire

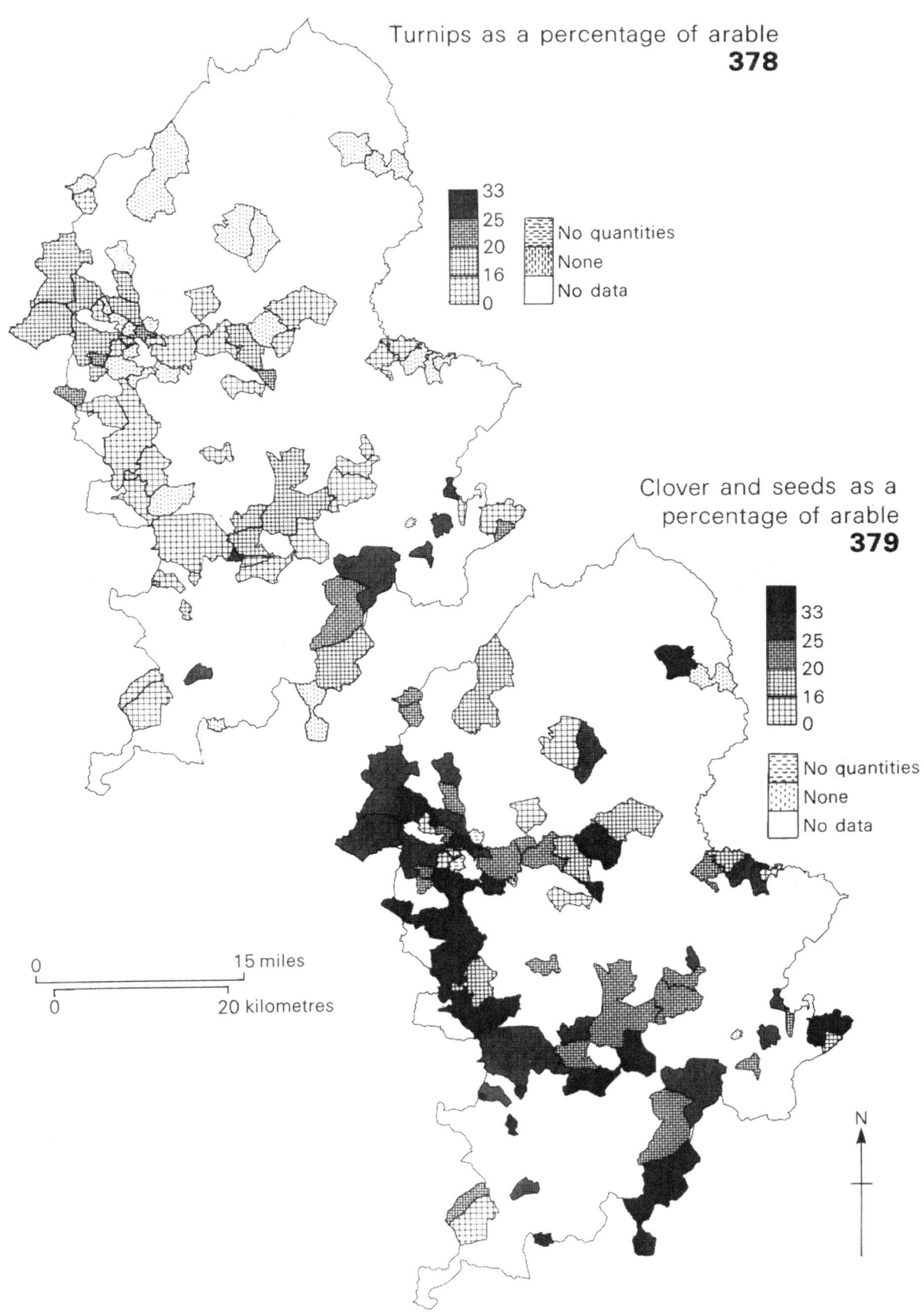

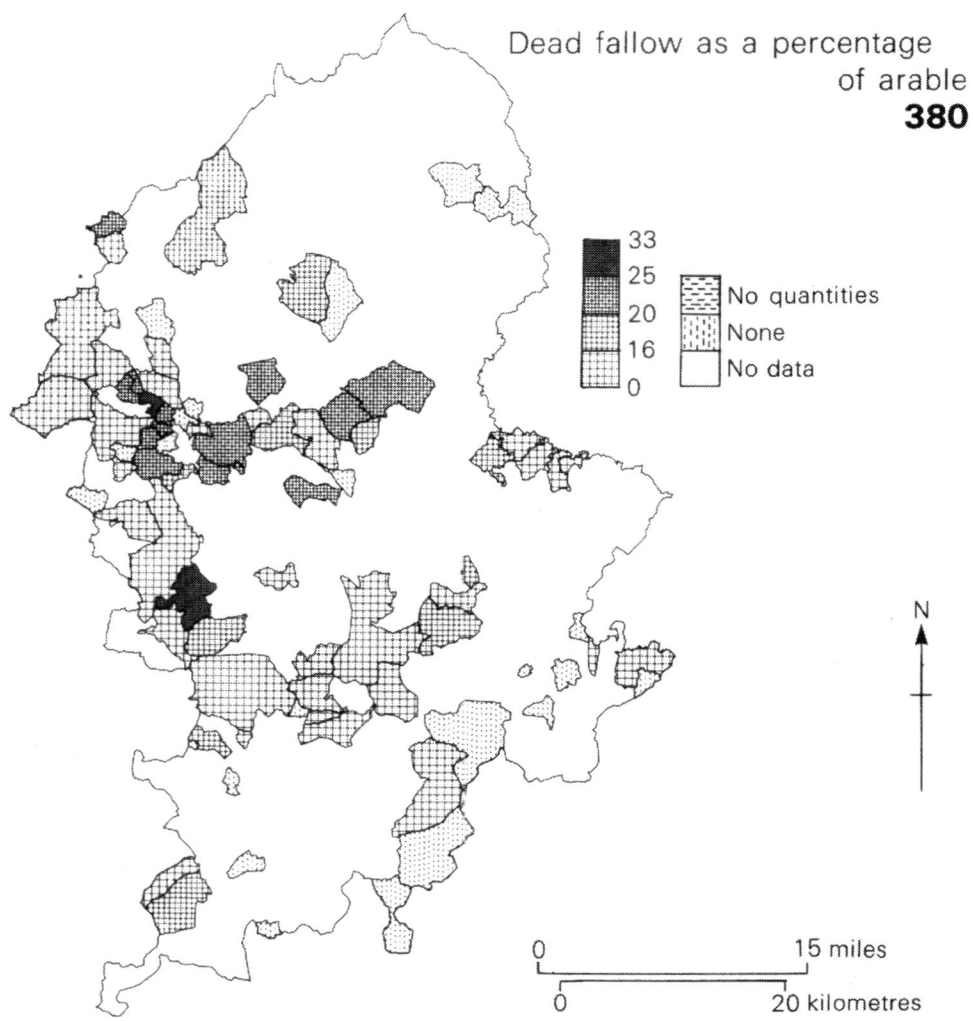

Staffordshire

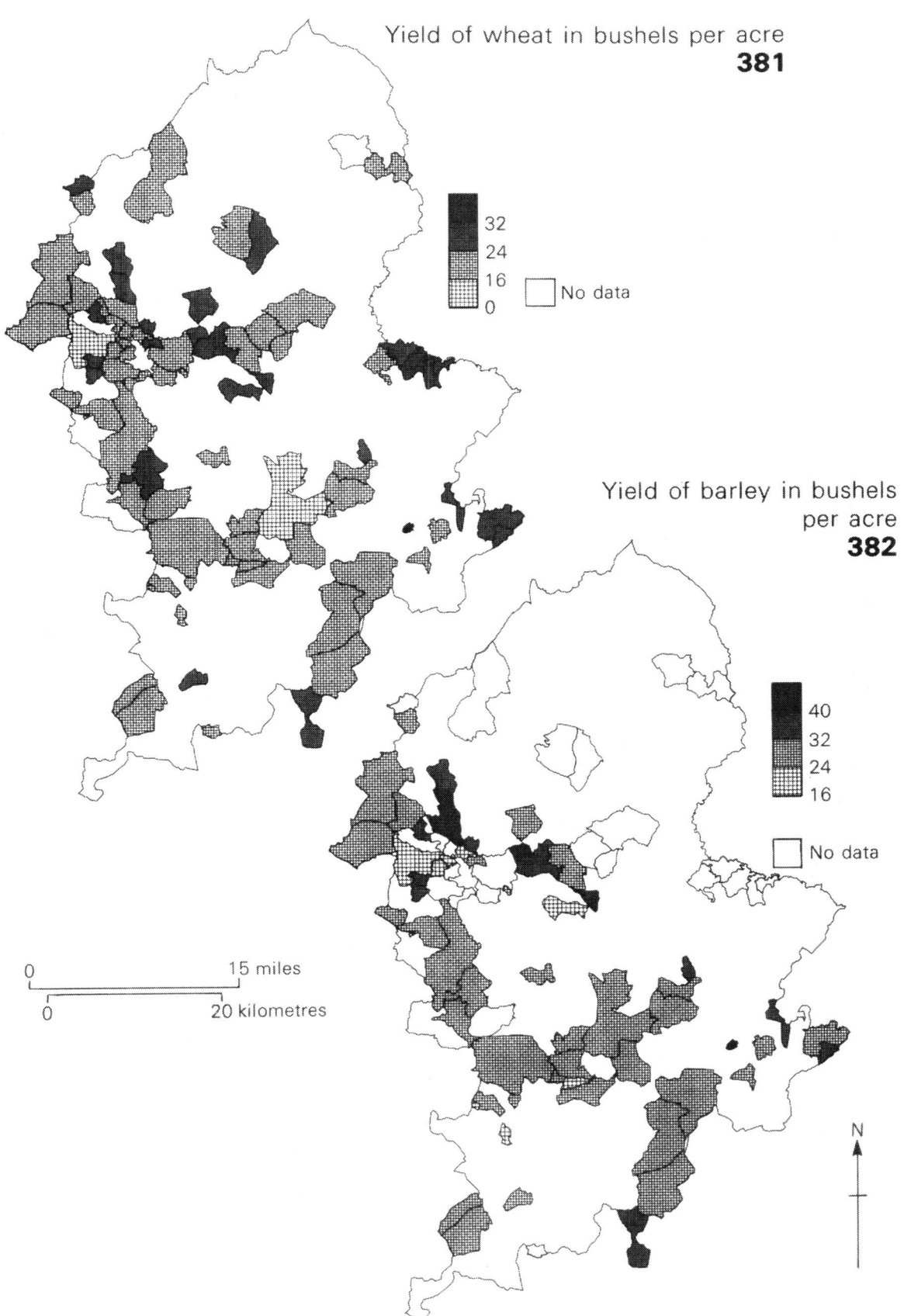

Yield of wheat in bushels per acre
381

Yield of barley in bushels per acre
382

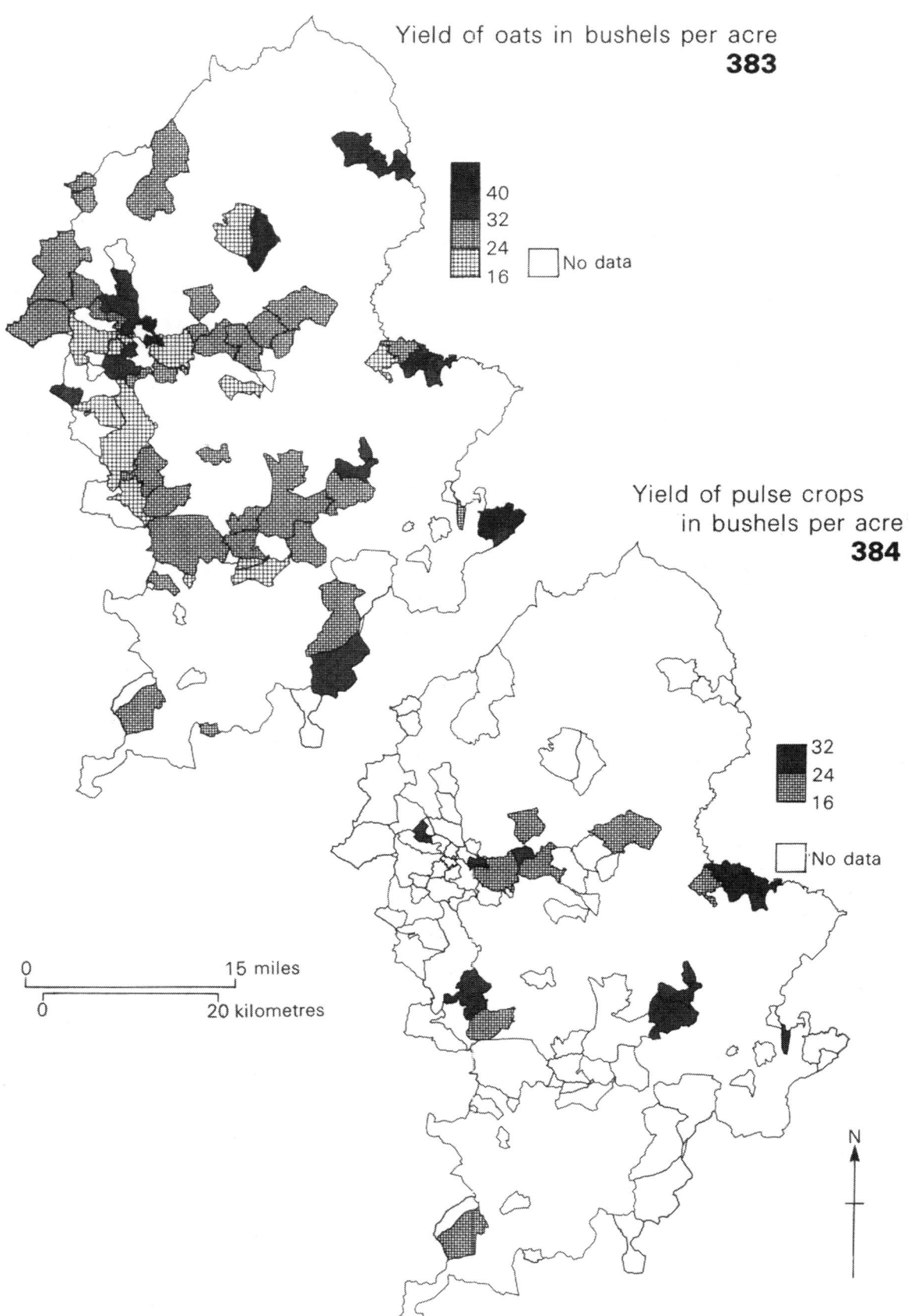

Yield of oats in bushels per acre **383**

Yield of pulse crops in bushels per acre **384**

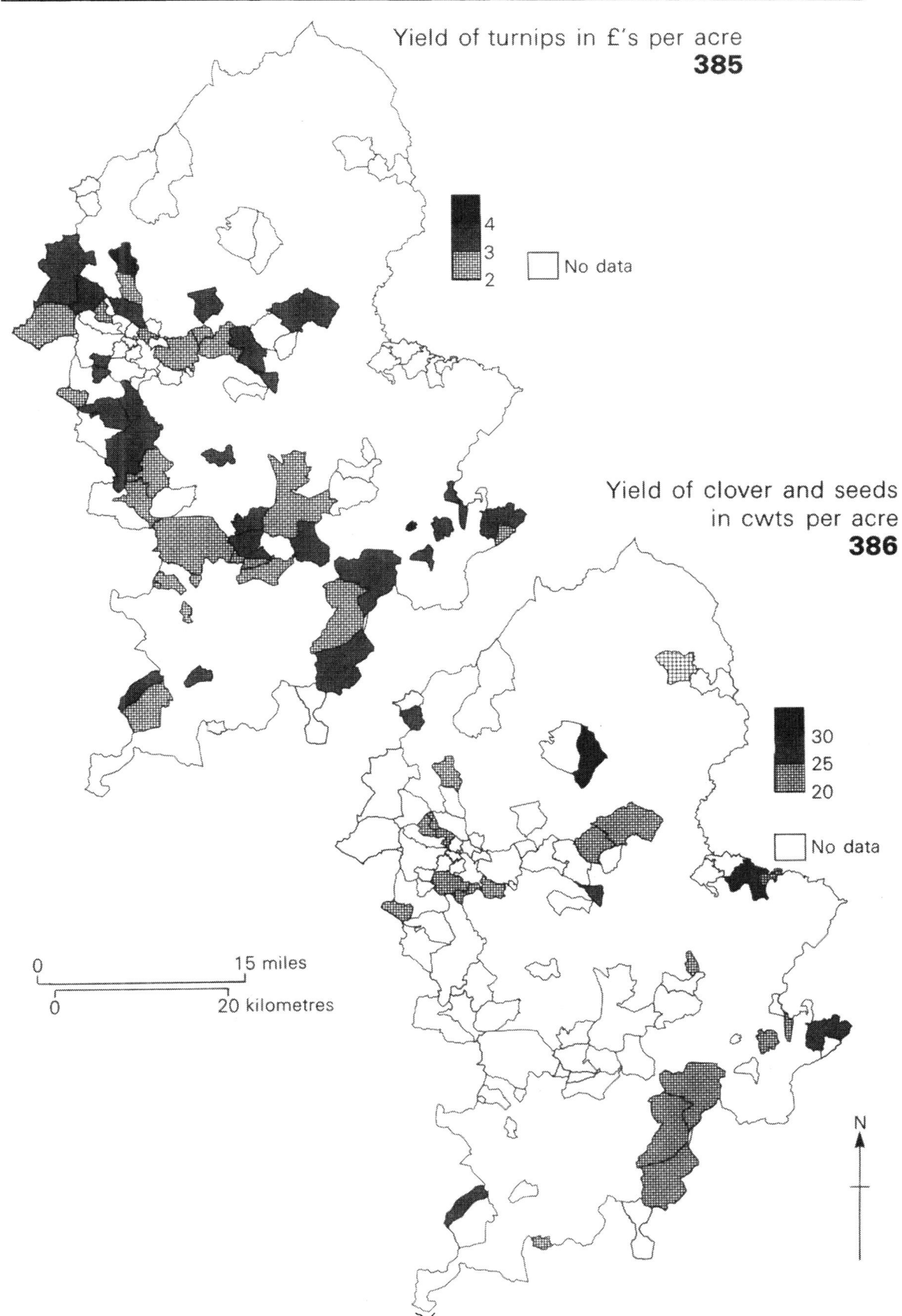

Yield of turnips in £'s per acre
385

Yield of clover and seeds in cwts per acre
386

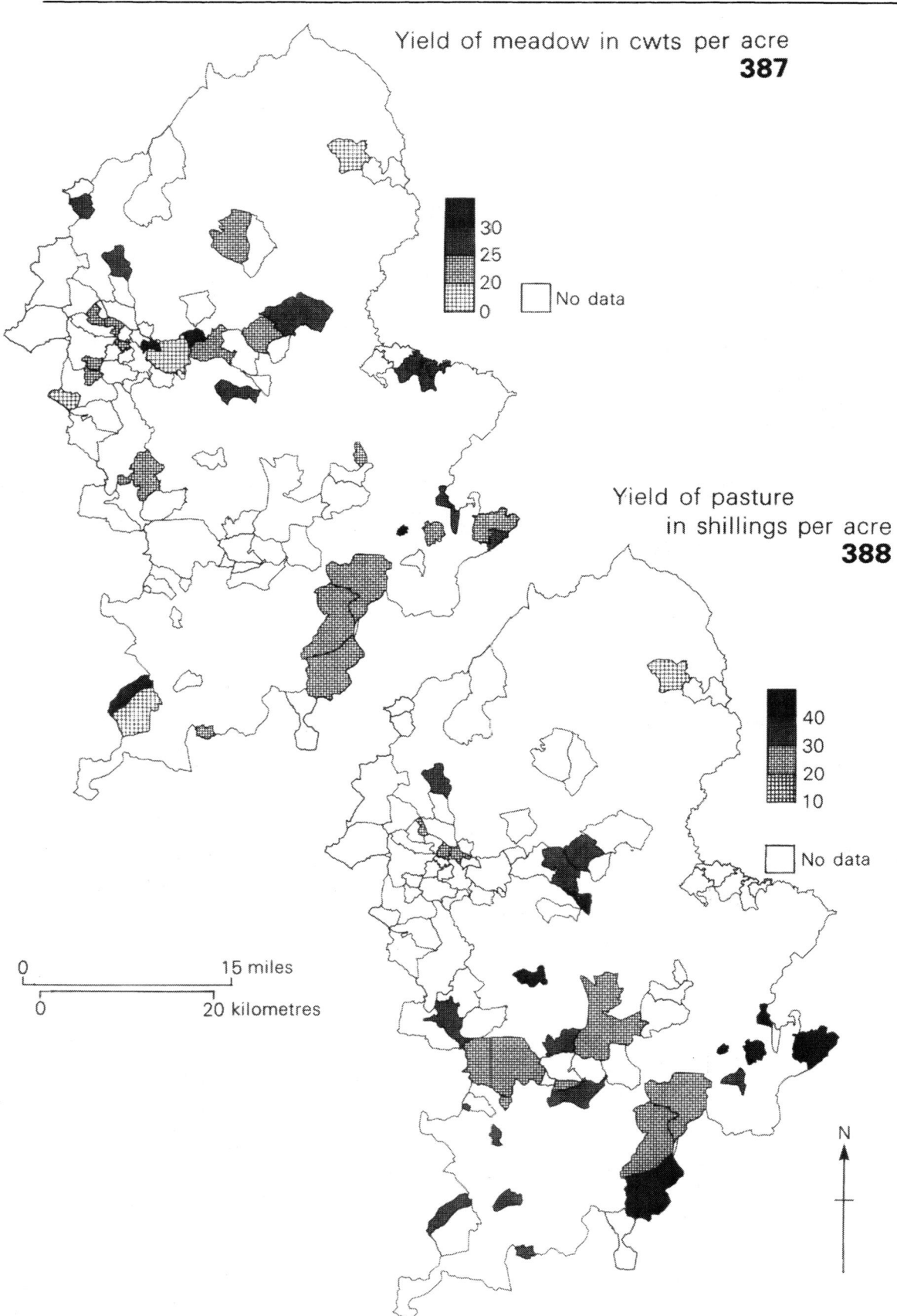

Shropshire

454 tithe districts
208 reports on tithe agreements

The files of eighteen Shropshire tithe districts contain specific information about exemption from tithe payment. Those for another fifty-one districts are quite empty and bear a note from the Edwardian weeder on the outside leaf that he considered all papers worthless and had discarded them. In Shropshire, 369 tithe districts have tithe maps and apportionments which suggests that most of the places with empty files were also tithe free or were about to enroll deeds of merger. In the Place Index, these districts are listed as 'tithe exempt' and where 'type of place' is not obvious from the outside of the file, they are recorded simply as 'tithe district'.

Agreements and awards for tithe commutation are approximately equal in number in Shropshire. Places with agreements are fairly evenly distributed over the county with, if anything, proportionately greater coverage in the Welsh borderland than in the east (Map 389). Shropshire is the western-most county in which 'arable' type report forms were provided. All but Thomas Hoskins and Charles Pym of the no fewer than sixteen Shropshire assistant commissioners and local agents had worked only in counties where this method of assessing the fairness of an agreement was employed. They were not, though, as Table 51 indicates, all working in Shropshire at the same time. George Ashdown inspected agreements from 1838 to 1842 but Gelinger C. Symons' thirty-four agreements were all assessed in 1839 and John Holder's all in 1838. Henry Pilkington travelled in Shropshire before going north to Cumberland and his native Northumberland where he made a substantial contribution to the work of the Tithe Commission. Richard Burton Phillipson assessed most of the delayed agreements ratified between 1841 and 1845. There is also a much more equitable division of the workload than usual between each of the Tithe Commission's agents. Seven men worked in ten or more places each; George Ashdown wrote the largest number of reports but they amount to only 20 per cent of the total. He was a local man 'I have known this parish [Bromfield] upwards of 30 years . . . ; in 1790 my father introduced turnips into this district [Hopesay in south Shropshire], and erected the first threshing machine'. His reports suggest that he was quite familiar with farming in different parts of the county and keenly reported evidence of recent changes which might affect the gross product of land. He was impressed by the importance of soil as a factor affecting agricultural output and drew up separate valuations for light and heavy soils if these were both present in a tithe district.

In Shropshire as a whole, the area of arable exceeded that of grassland c. 1840 but within the county there are marked regional variations in proportions. North and east of the river Severn, arable exceeded pasture in all but a few valley bottom tithe districts and in most the ratio of arable to pasture was greater than 1.5 to 1. By contrast, in most districts in the uplands of south Shropshire, more land was in grass than in arable (Maps 391–2).

The traditional system of farming arable lands in Shropshire was as described by Charles Warner at Adderley: 'fallow limed, wheat, oats, clover to lay two or sometimes more years and so round'. On lighter loam soils, assistant tithe commissioners report use of four-course Norfolk or five-course Northumberland systems. At Middle, near Shrewsbury, for example, Henry Pilkington reported that 'there are some good farmers in the parish, and I saw some fields of swede turnips, drilled on the Northumberland system, very fine and clean'. At Tibberton and Cherrington in the east near Newport, George Ashdown found that 'the soil is a light rich loam, on sand and gravel subsoil, adapted to the Norfolk husbandry and is so cultivated. It is only fair to remark that no part of Shropshire is farmed better, or to greater advantage, than this immediate neighbourhood.' On heavy soils where turnips did not succeed there is less evidence of improvement. On such soils rotations were either a three-course of two crops and a fallow or a traditional Shropshire four- to six-course. Beans were grown in fewer than twenty districts with reports on agreements which is surprising in view of the amount of heavy soil in this county.

Shropshire files contain more comments on the quality of arable farming and on crop yields than those of most other counties; there were marked regional variations. Local tithe agents considered that the best farming and the greatest improvement were to be found in the district around Shrewsbury. Here they considered the Norfolk system the norm with turnips fed off by sheep or used for fattening cattle during the winter. At Ercall,

> there has been a good deal of expensive farming here since 1835 but not much prior to that year. They are improving the heavy lands immensely by the use of the sub soil plough, which costs apart from the teams about £8 per acre, requiring for the two ploughs ten horses. I saw some land producing 30 of the large bushels (customary here of 39 quarts) of wheat per acre which previously did not average 16.

Comments on low farming, however, outnumber those on good farming in eastern, lowland clay parishes where drainage was needed before production could be increased; at one place, Kemberton, George Ashdown suggests that productivity had even decreased for want of drainage.

In dairying districts in the north of the county, as at Hodnet,

> everything appears sacrificed to the maintenance of the dairy which is the staple production of the parish. The grassland and the seeds so far as they are fed, are chiefly depastured by cows for cheese making. Upwards of a thousand cows are so employed. There are probably not more sheep than cows kept in the parish and those in general of an inferior kind.

Similarly, at Whitchurch, 'the grassland is universally the best land of the district, as this is the land of dairies and everything gives way to the cheese press, even corn is a secondary consideration'.

All reporters considered Welsh border parishes the most backward in the county; at Bryn, Gelinger C. Symons found 'the farming very inferior and no means appear to be taken

Shropshire

to improve the land. In most of the border parishes they are greatly behind those further removed from Wales.' At Kevencalonog, Ashdown thought 'the farming miserably bad, and roads almost impassable, not the slightest improvement has taken place to my knowledge these last thirty years'. The upland parishes of Kenley and Loughton were two of the most inaccessible that Henry Pilkington ever visited.

> The parish of Kenley [he said] is almost cut off from the rest of the world. The road to it being nearly impassable. I visited it in a gig but could only proceed at a foot pace for two miles before I arrived at the village, and even then was compelled to get out twice, nearly up to my knees in mud to prevent the carriage sticking fast.

Similarly, at Loughton, 'the roads are only apologies for roads, the bed of a mountain stream frequently affording the best'. In these higher parts of the county, sheep were fed on the common land of Clun Forest and similar areas during the summer but since there was not enough valley pasture to support them during the winter, they were 'tacked out'. At Mainstone, John Pickering describes the practice of sending sheep to winter in Herefordshire. There is also much discussion in the files of these places about the potential for ploughing up some Clun sheepwalks if the Forest were to be enclosed (see Subject Index).

Table 51 *Reports on agreements for commutation of tithes in Shropshire*

Assistant commissioner/ local tithe agent	1837	1838	1839	1840	1841	1842	1843	1844	1845	Totals
George Ashdown		8	19	5	5	5				42
Gelinger C. Symons			34							34
Richard Burton Phillipson				3	1	13	10	2	1	30
Henry Pilkington	16	4								20
John Holder		11								11
Horace William Meteyard						8	1	2		11
John Pickering				10						10
Thomas Hoskins		5	4							9
John Mee Mathew			8	1						9
Charles Howard		8								8
N. S. Meryweather			5							5
Charles Pym	5									5
Thomas Sudworth	3	2								5
John Penny				4						4
Charles Warner	4									4
James Drage Merest	1									1
Totals	29	43	65	23	14	19	12	2	1	208

Table 52 *Land use, crops and yields in Shropshire c. 1836*

A	Land use	Percentage of total land area enumerated in reports on tithe agreements	Estimated acreage in whole county
	Arable	47.0	388,386
	Grass	38.1	314,422
	Wood	5.6	46,521
	Common	7.9	65,626

B	Crop	Mean percentage of arable	Mean yield per acre	Estimated acreage in whole county
	Wheat	23.6	19.5 bushels	91,694
	Barley	9.9	26.4 bushels	38,314
	Oats	14.7	25.7 bushels	57,054
	Pulses	0.8	21.1 bushels	3,187
	Turnips	9.7	£2.64	37,553
	Seeds	24.1	20.8 cwts	93,555
	Fallows	14.4	—	56,047

Shropshire

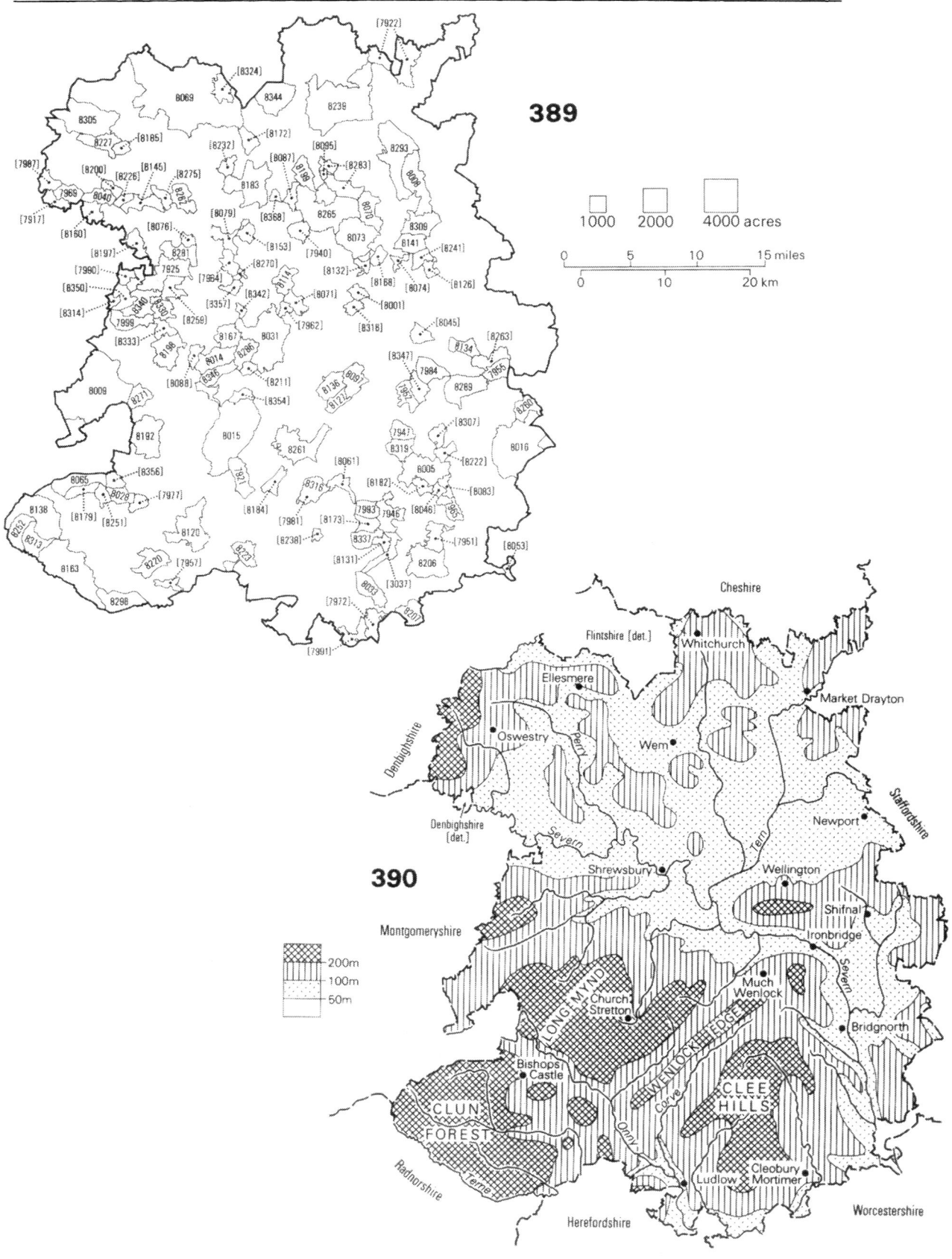

389

390

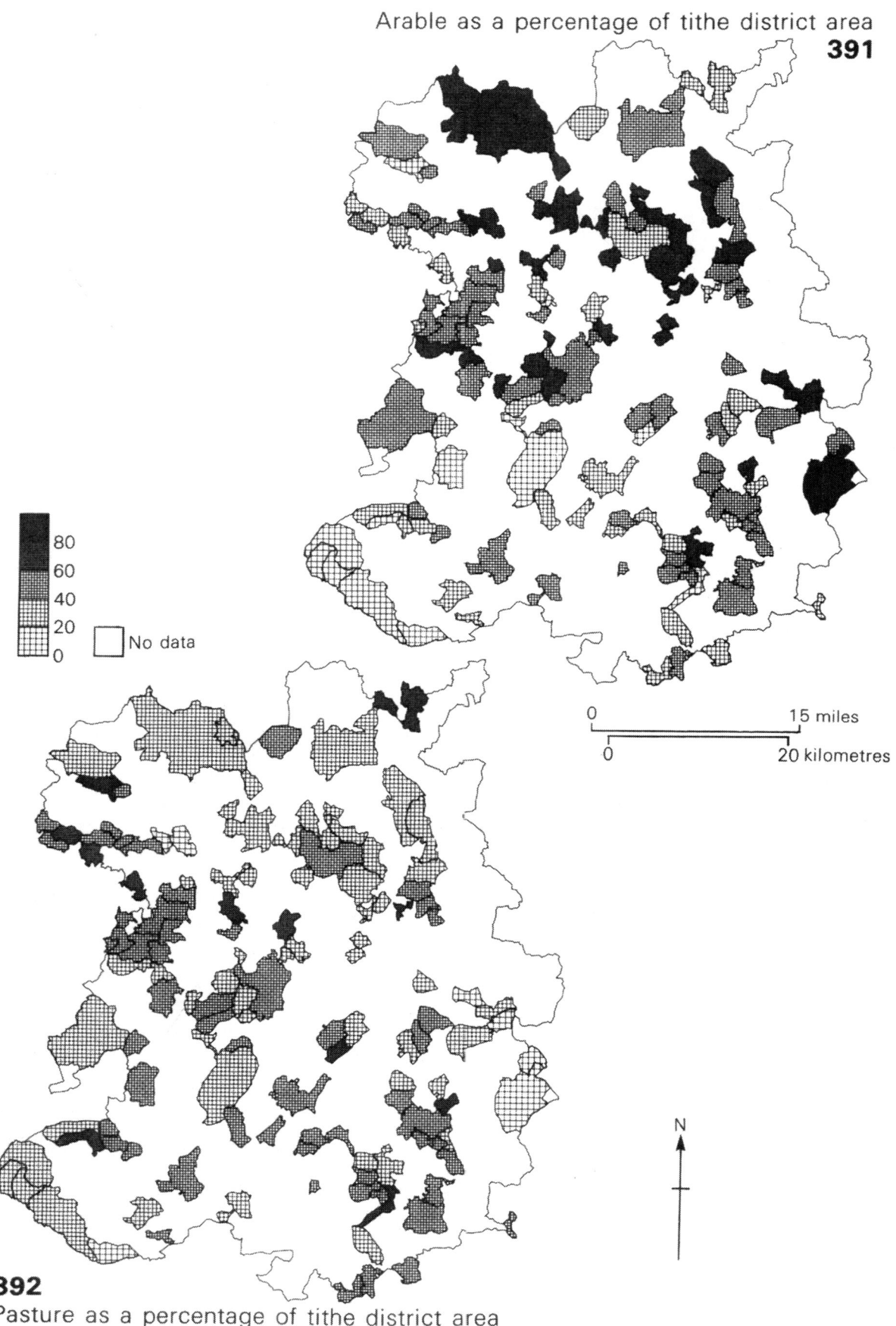

391 Arable as a percentage of tithe district area

392 Pasture as a percentage of tithe district area

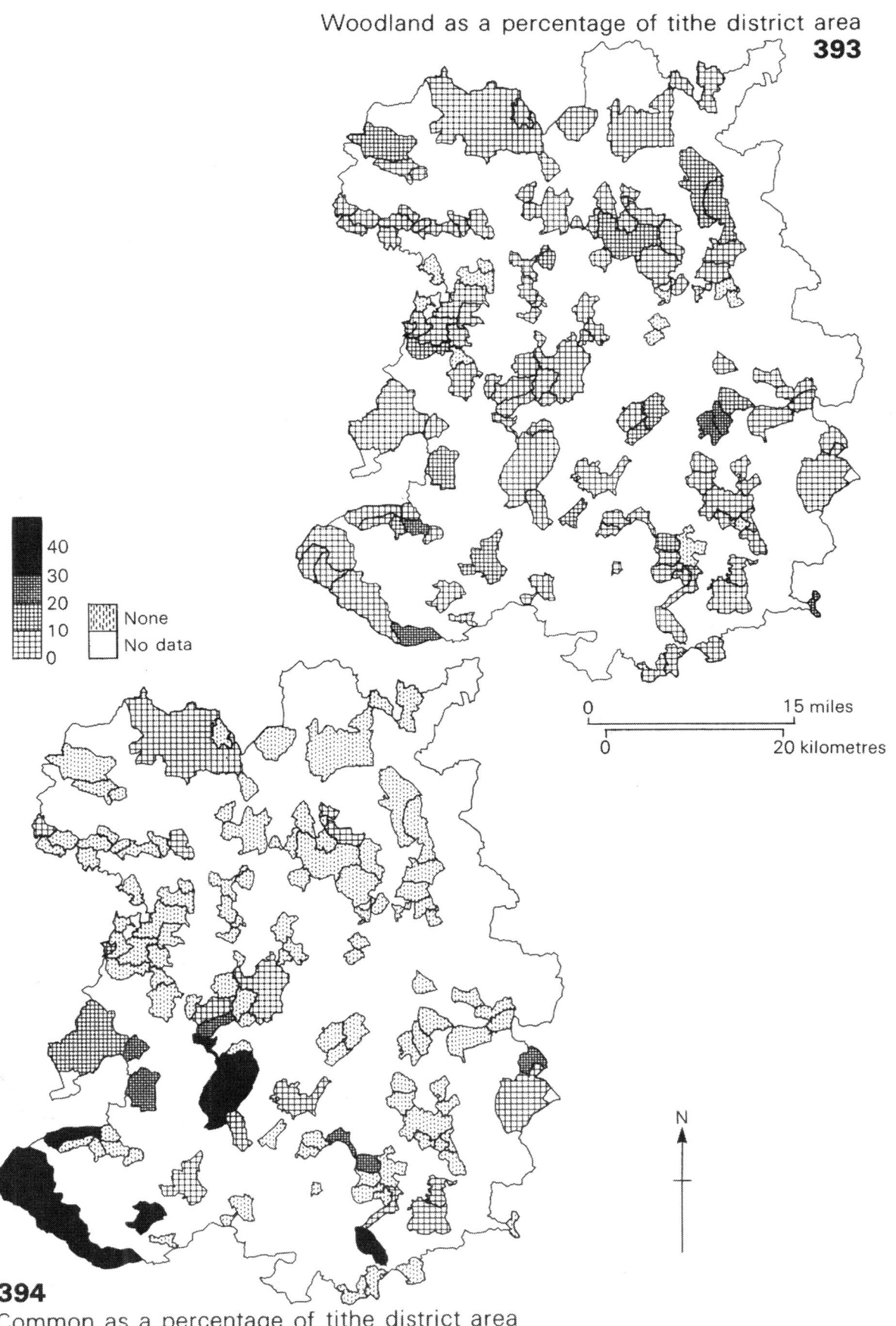

393 Woodland as a percentage of tithe district area

394 Common as a percentage of tithe district area

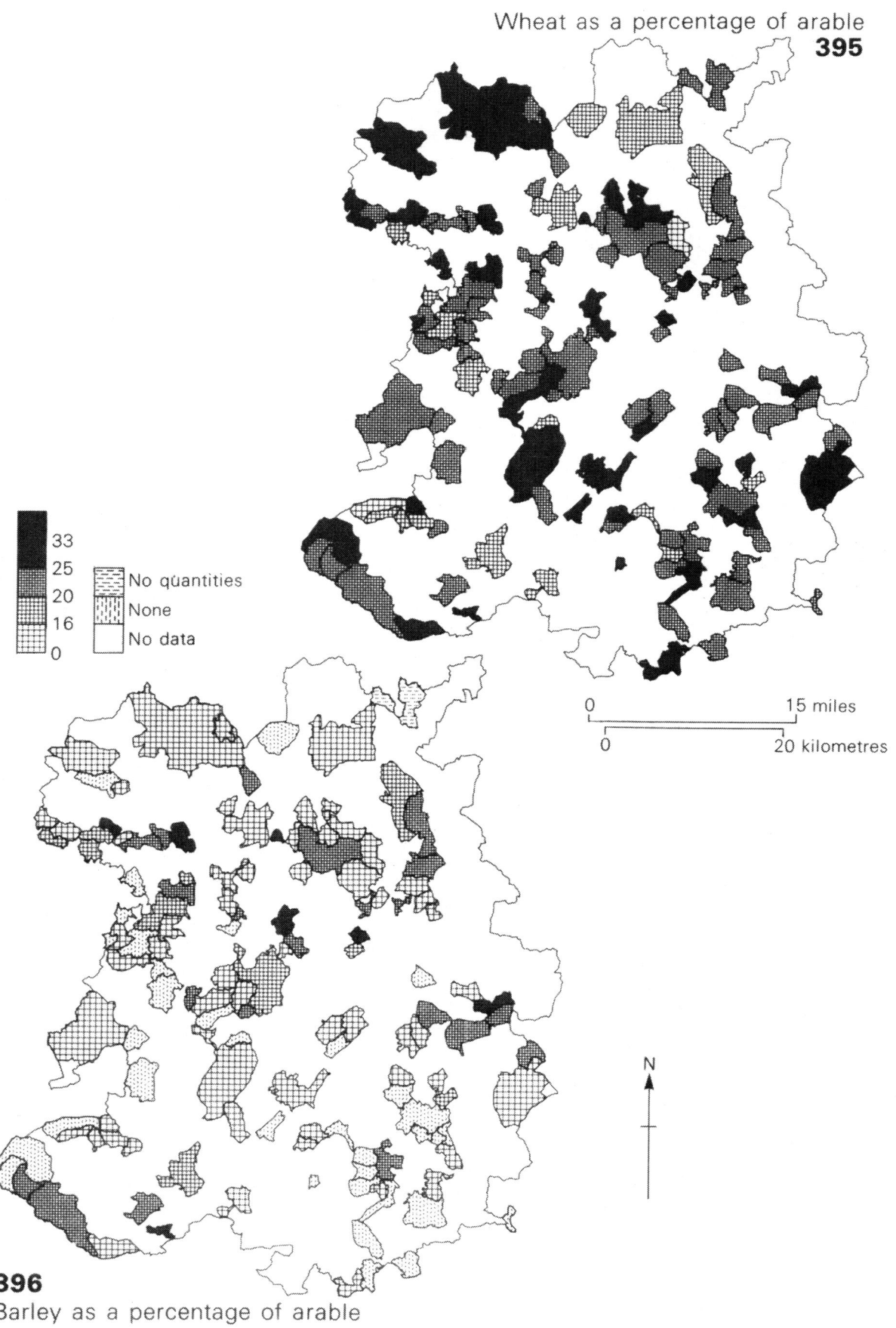

395 Wheat as a percentage of arable

396 Barley as a percentage of arable

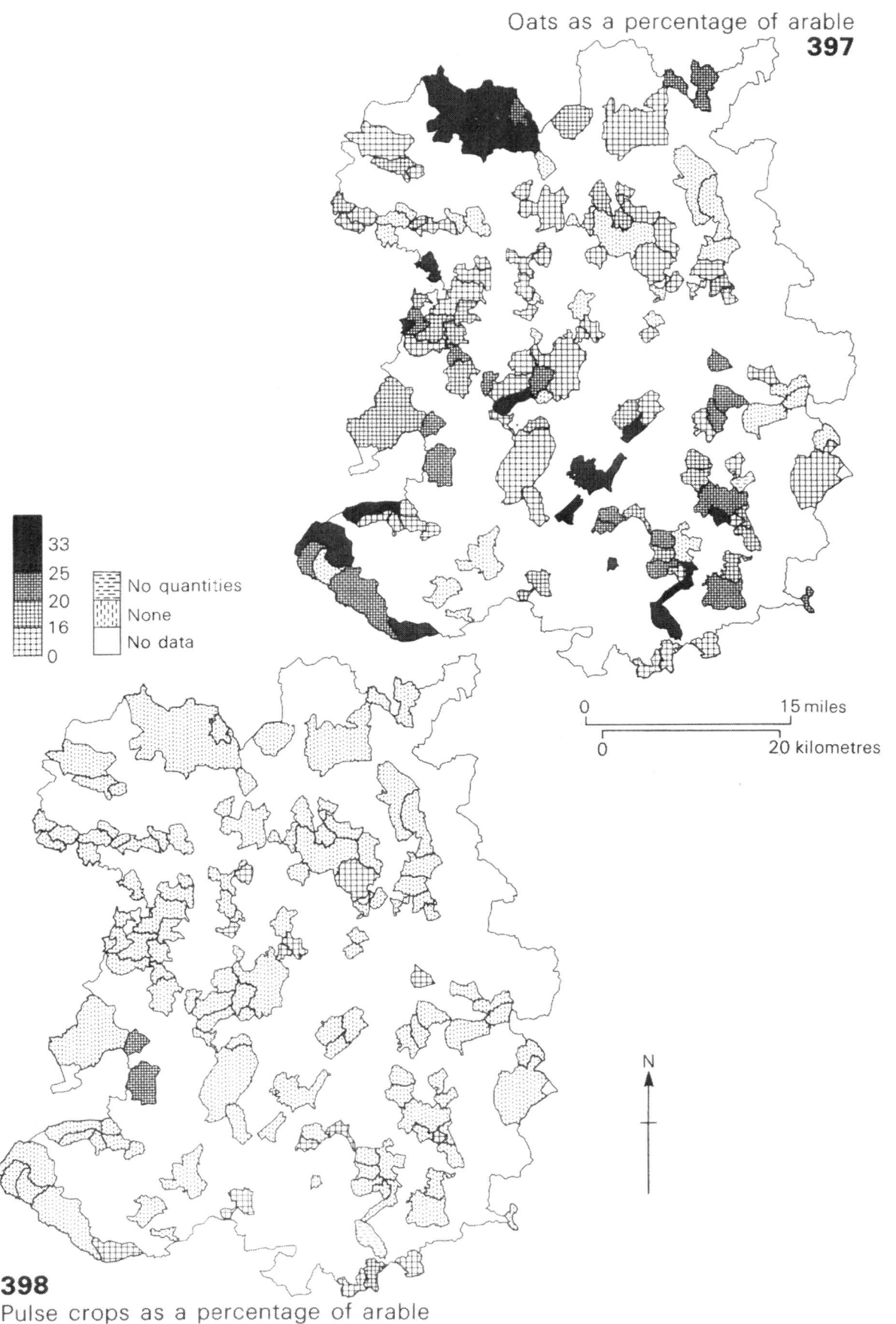

397 Oats as a percentage of arable

398 Pulse crops as a percentage of arable

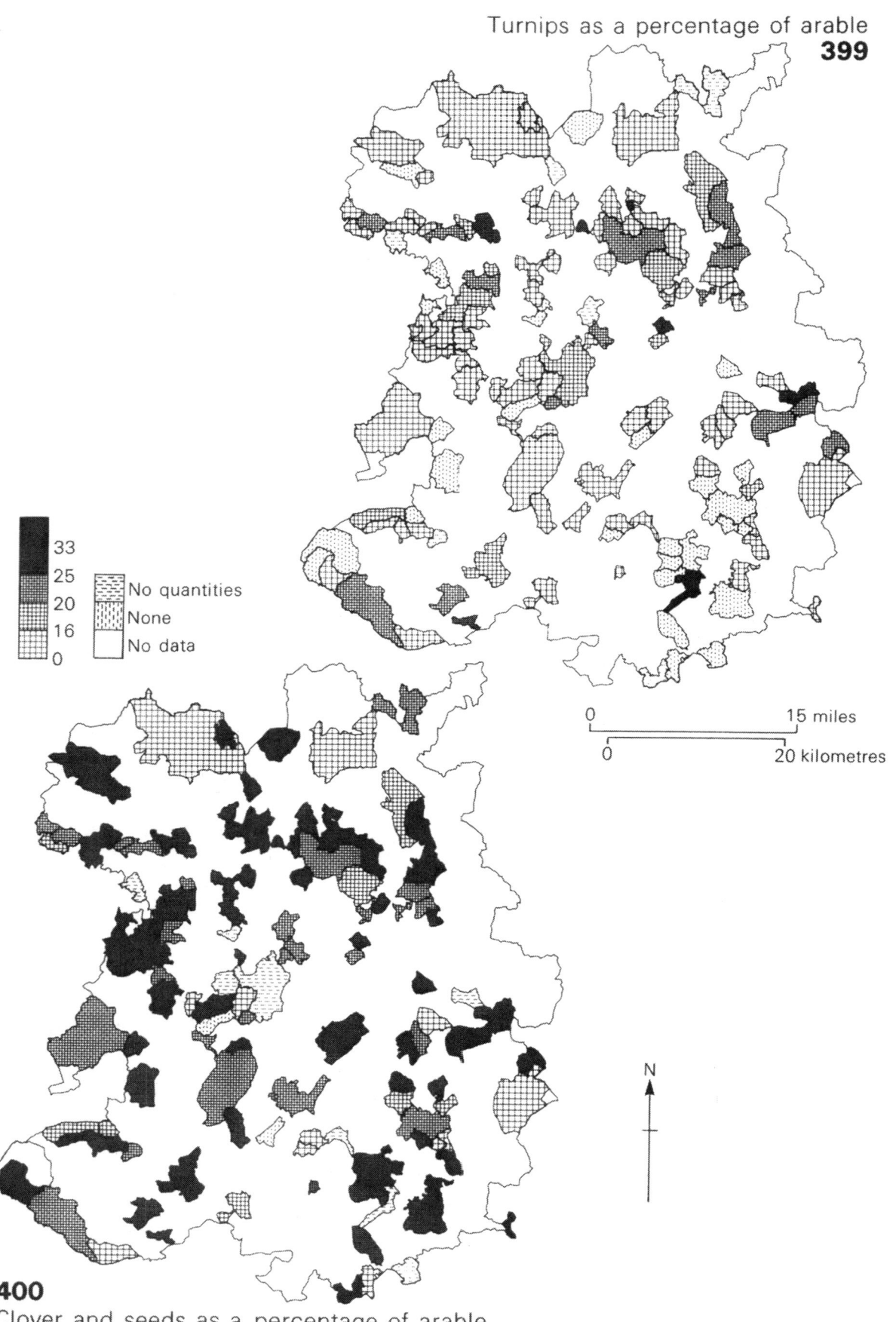

399 Turnips as a percentage of arable

400 Clover and seeds as a percentage of arable

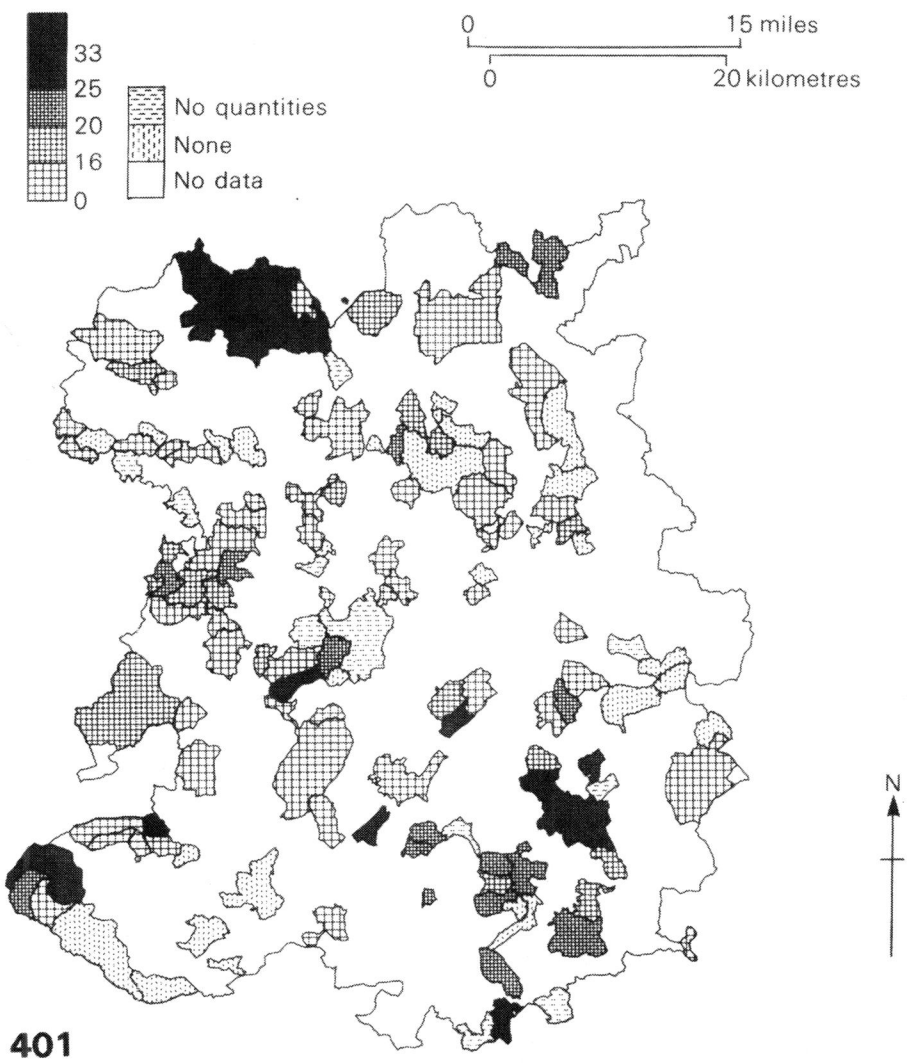

401
Dead fallow as a percentage of arable

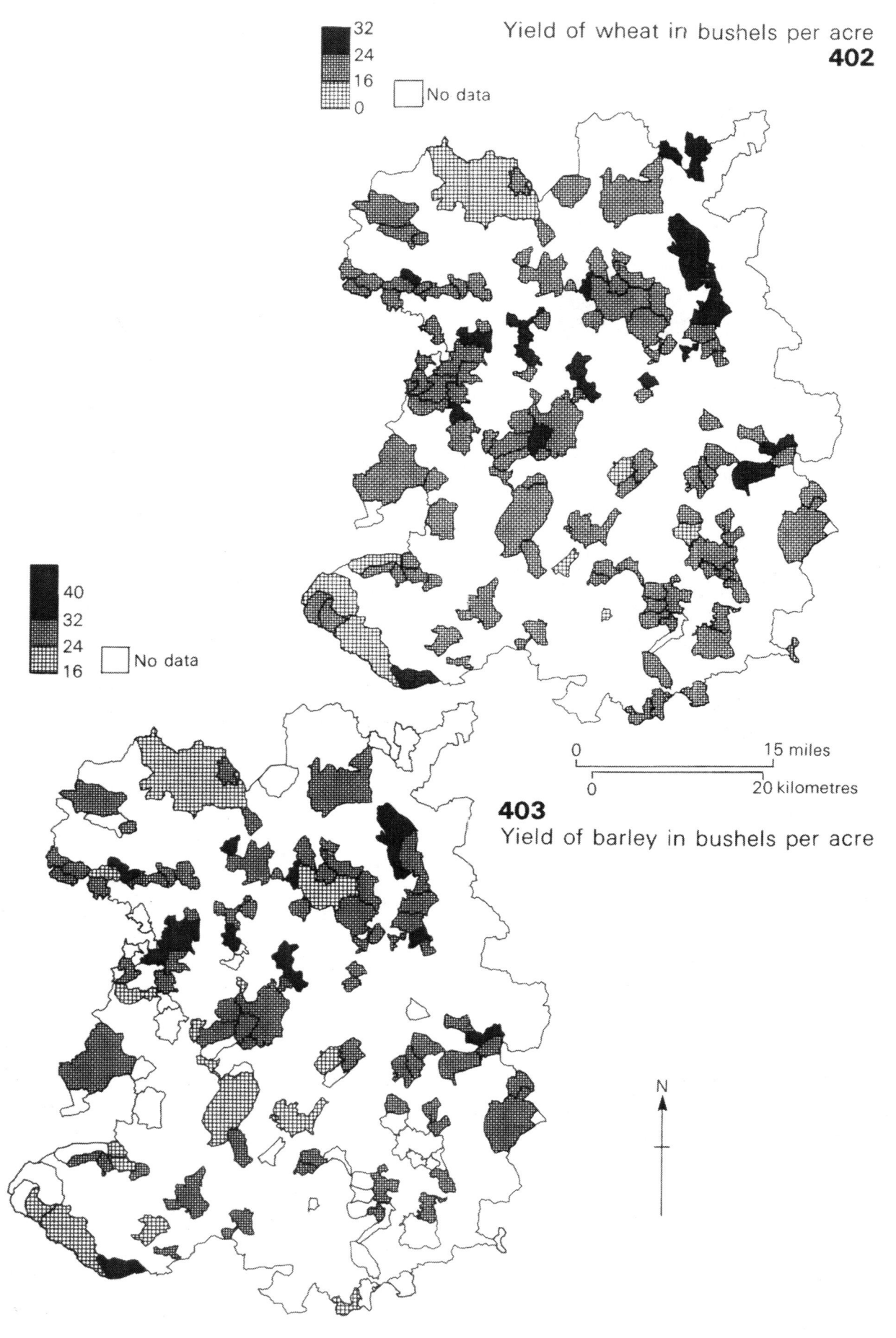

402 Yield of wheat in bushels per acre

403 Yield of barley in bushels per acre

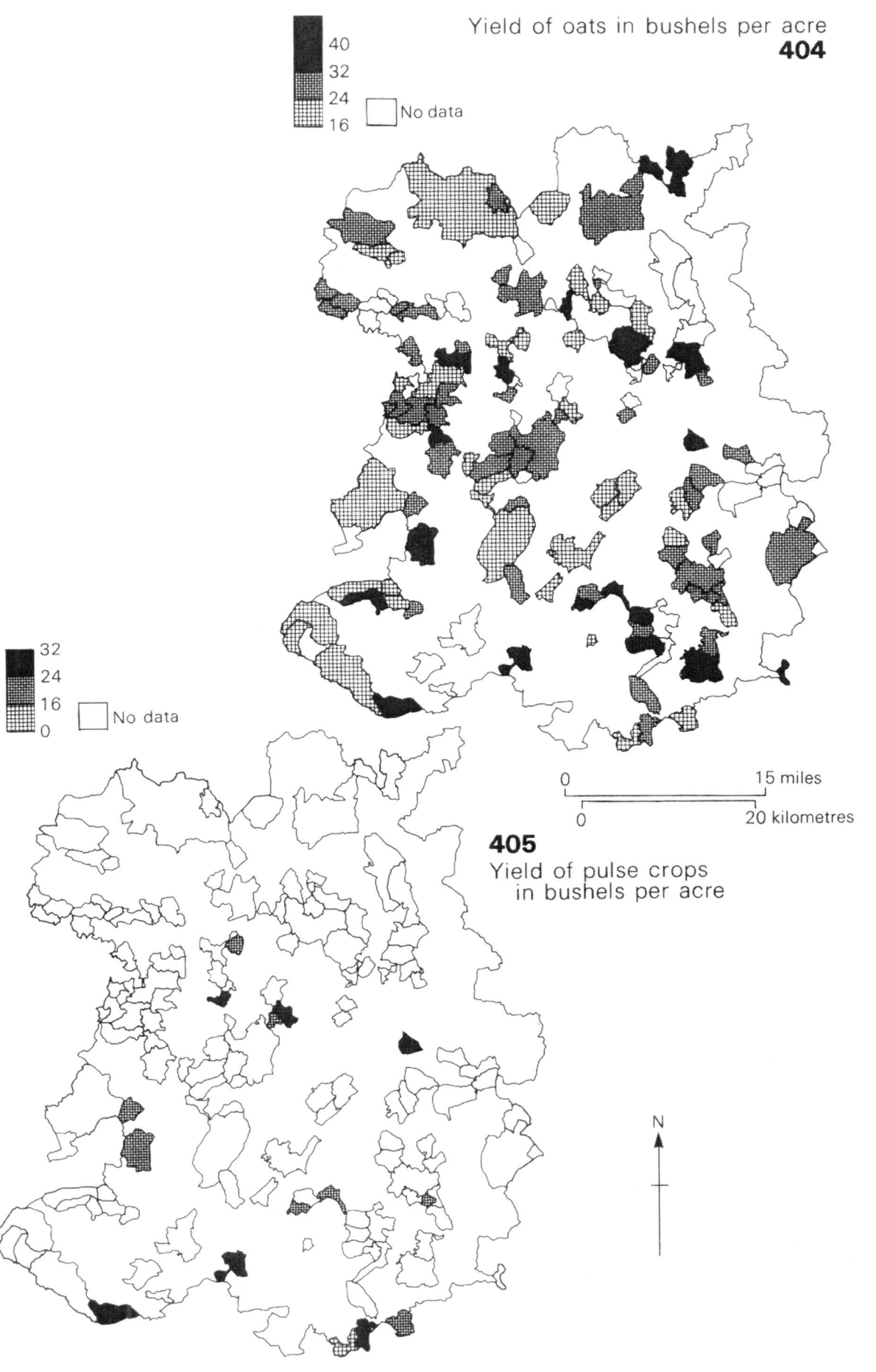

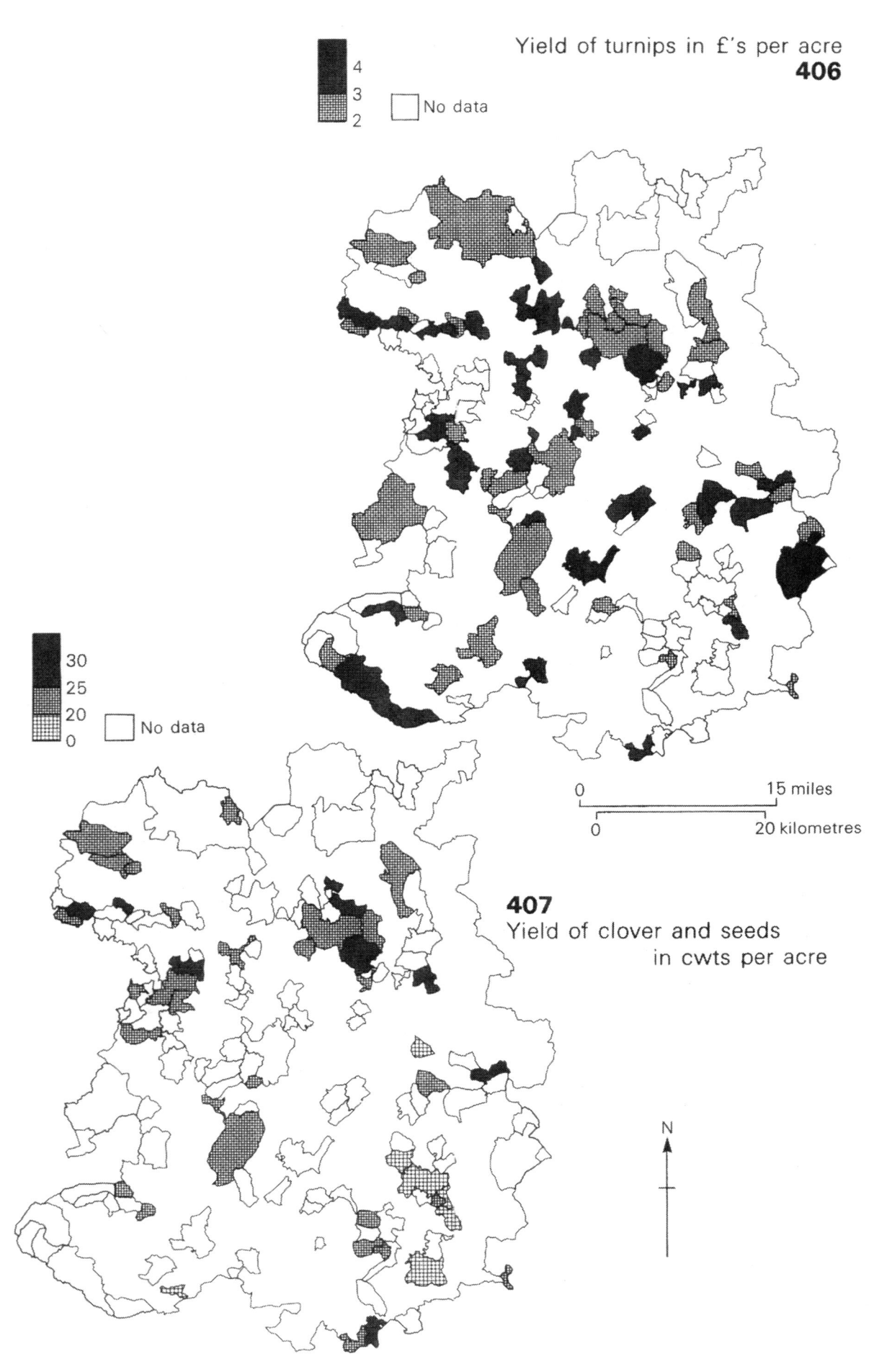

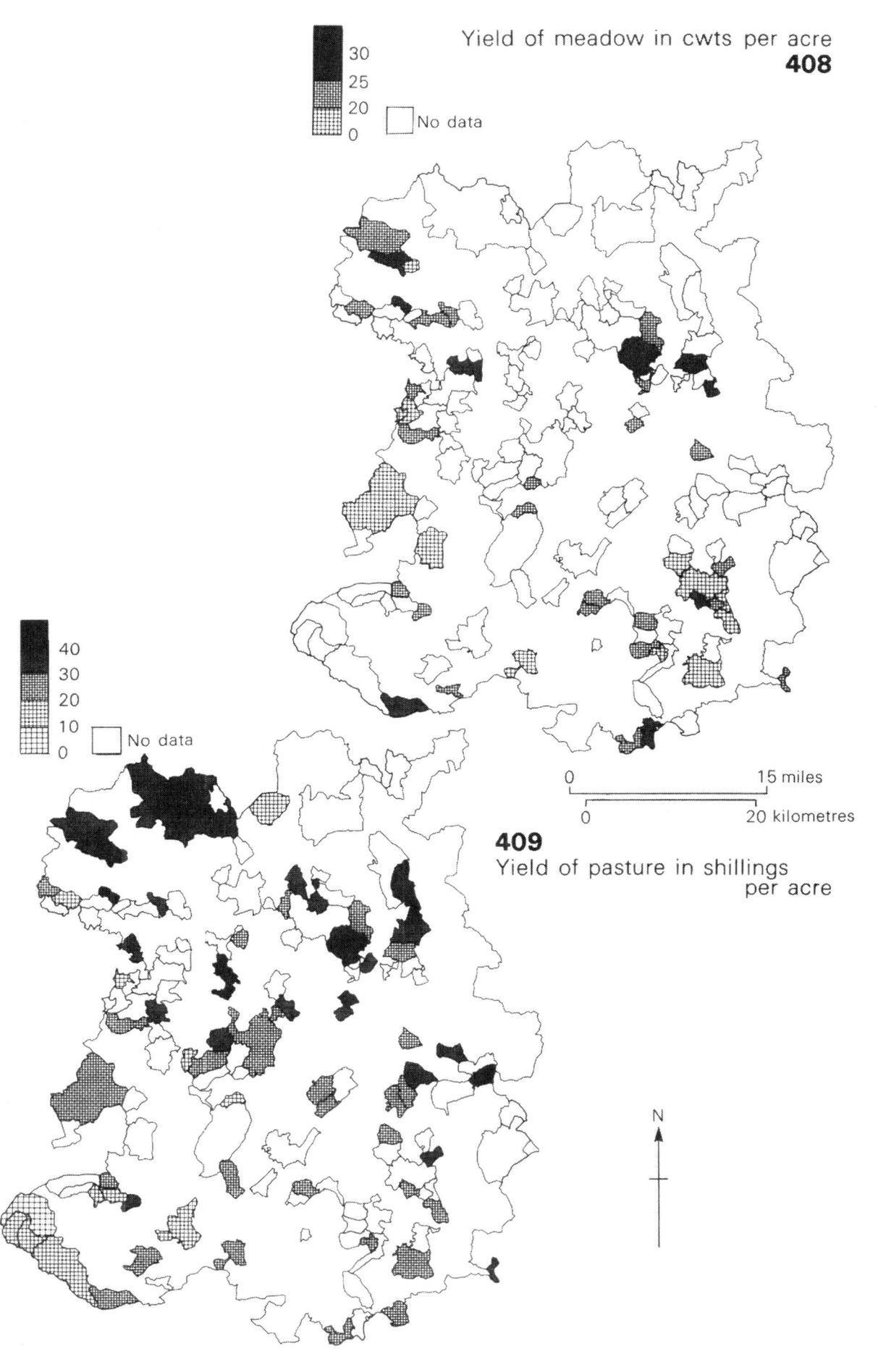

Cumberland

247 tithe districts
51 reports on tithe agreements

There are probably fewer reliable data on land use and cropping for Cumberland than for any other English or Welsh county. Some fifty tithe districts had been completely exonerated from tithe by parliamentary enclosure and in at least 109 parishes where some tithe was still paid, old enclosures were covered by moduses and only new enclosures rendered tithe in kind or by composition. In fact, only two of the fifty-one reports on tithe agreements contain crop data for more than 90 per cent of a tithe district. Assistant commissioners and local tithe agents were highly critical of the accuracy of schedules to tithe agreements in Cumberland (see *The tithe surveys of England and Wales*, pp. 138–9), a fact which further devalues the already meagre quantitative record.

The body of descriptive material which the files contain is somewhat better. John Job Rawlinson who wrote half the reports had worked in other north-western counties and seems familiar with changes that had been taking place in farming even if he did not have such a detailed knowledge of farming practices here as he did of those in his home county of Westmorland. Henry Pilkington worked in Cumberland in 1839, the same year in which he carried out ninety-seven commissions in Northumberland. These two men together compiled about three-quarters of Cumberland reports and wrote perceptively at each place they visited.

Two topics dominate their discussions: modus payments in lieu of tithes, and contrasts between farming on old and new enclosures. On old enclosures, moduses were commonly paid in lieu of great tithes (including hay), milk and cattle, and tithe was not usually paid on potatoes or turnips. Rawlinson commented in his report for Frizington that

> the tithe of hay is payable in kind in very few places in this part of the country, the cause of which I apprehend has been that from the lateness of the hay harvest, and the extreme wetness of the climate it was found in very early times that the tithe of hay was subject to so many casualties in the collection as to be nearly valueless.

Thus in most parishes in Cumberland only the tithe of lambs and wool were of any real value and there were exceptions even to this. At Kirkbampton, 'all the Great Tithes are covered by a modus, very few sheep are kept in the township and milk is by the custom of the country not titheable so that very few sources remain from which tithe of any kind can be drawn'. Occasionally new enclosures of former common land were rendered tithe free but more usually they were liable to tithes in kind. At Embleton, for example, farmers erroneously assumed that their new enclosures would be covered by the same modus as the old, but the courts established that they were liable to tithe in kind.

In general, the Tithe Commission's agents associated old enclosures with the best and most productive loam soils, while new intakes from common or waste were of a much poorer description. At Frizington, Rawlinson considered 'the lands which have been inclosed by virtue of a private Act of Parliament are poor wet lands and in a high and exposed situation. Many of the fields are entirely covered with rushes.' The system of farming old enclosures at Bootle described by Rawlinson in 1838 is repeated by himself and others elsewhere:

> The ordinary course of cultivation is to break up the high ground with oats which is followed (sometimes however with another intervening crop of oats) by a crop of potatoes, turnips, or a naked fallow according to the nature of the soil and of the quantity of manure which the farmer has at command. Then comes a crop of barley or wheat after which the land is laid down again in grass for a period varying from 2 to 7 or 8 years.

'The system of management upon the newly inclosed part of the township', Rawlinson commented at Dearham and again repeated elsewhere

> appears to have been to get as many grain crops off it as the land would bear and then to lay it down to rest in pasture. The professed system however, is 1. oats, 2. fallow, 3. wheat, and then to have grass seeds. I think that at present one half of the arable land of the township may be in grain.

Assistant commissioners comment on the over-cropping of such newly enclosed lands. Farmers attempted to take three grain crops in succession, ploughed up their leys too soon and rarely put sufficient manure on the land to restore its fertility.

Table 53 *Reports on agreements for commutation of tithes in Cumberland*

Assistant commissioner/ local tithe agent	1837	1838	1839	1840	1841	1842	Totals
John Job Rawlinson		13	8	2	1		24
Henry Pilkington			12			1	13
Thomas Martin				6			6
Charles Howard		1		2			3
John S. Donaldson Selby	2						2
Richard Atkinson	1						1
John Mee Mathew						1	1
Richard Burton Phillipson					1		1
Totals	3	14	20	10	2	2	51

Westmorland

98 tithe districts
42 reports on tithe agreements

Although only nine townships were entirely tithe free in 1836 and 47 per cent of all those districts subject to tithes achieved voluntary agreements for commutation, only a handful of reports contain quantitative data which are in any sense reliable. In a large number of districts, assistant commissioners and local tithe agents made no valuation of the various types of land. Reasons for this omission varied. At some places, no great tithes were paid with only wool, pigs and geese titheable; at others, large tracts were exempt or covered by moduses; at yet other districts, it was expected that tithe would be merged with the land as the landowner and tithe owner was one and the same person. The net result is that in Westmorland, as in Cumberland, the amount of land use and crop data is disappointingly small. However, written accounts of local farming practices made by John Job Rawlinson of Milbeck in Westmorland are very full and compensate to some extent for the poor quantitative data. All the Tithe Commission's local representatives were acutely aware that acreages stated in many agreement schedules were little more than notional. At Winton in 1839, an exasperated Henry Pilkington remarked that 'the boundary of the common is "disputed ground" as the boundaries of most of the commons in this part of the kingdom are'. But, accuracy of acreage measurements was of no great consequence for assessing a fair rent-charge when, as was so common in this county, only agistment tithe was payable. In high fell districts even this tithe was difficult to measure. At Hartsop and Patterdale, the 'lands are mountainous rugged, barren, wild and desolate . . . No person, except one who for a long time has kept sheep upon them, could have any idea as to the number of sheep such pastures would maintain.'

In most parishes only a small proportion of land was devoted to arable purposes. At Firbank, for example, John Mee Mathew commented that 'the township may be considered perhaps more in the nature of a sheep walk, than of a cultivated district – there being only 318 acres of arable land whilst the township comprises upwards of 3000 acres'. Assistant commissioners record that a traditional Westmorland system was to take three grain crops in succession and then to allow land to recover for five to nine years before ploughing again. Two crops of oats would have been taken in succession and then the land manured for barley. By the 1830s, the Tithe Commission's representatives found that potatoes and turnips were more commonly grown instead of the second crop of oats. The other main change recorded was enclosure of common land, a process described as follows by

Rawlinson at Great Strickland:

> The common lands within the township were inclosed under a private Act of Parliament which received the Royal Assent on 29 May 1830. As soon after as it could be inclosed it was pared and burned and crops of grain taken in most cases for 3 years in succession, it was then fallowed and in many fields I saw the 4th crop of grain in the 5th year of its cultivation. Some of Lord Lonsdale's allotments were in tillage in 1833 but the bulk of the common was not in cultivation till 1834 . . . Since the inclosure of the common less grain has been grown on the infield land, but the absolute quantity of grain grown in the whole township has been very much increased.

In the Lake District in general, the amount of fell attached to a township largely determined the number of sheep it was possible to keep. A common practice was to send lambs bred on the fells to over-winter on lower pastures. They were brought back before clipping time (see Subject Index).

Table 54 *Reports on agreements for commutation of tithes in Westmorland*

Assistant commissioner/ local tithe agent	1837	1838	1839	1840	1841	1842	1843	Totals
John Job Rawlinson		13	2	1				16
Henry Pilkington		1	10					11
Thomas Martin			6					6
John Mee Mathew					3			3
Richard Burton Phillipson				1		1	1	3
Charles Howard		2						2
John S. Donaldson Selby	1							1
Totals	1	16	18	2	3	1	1	42

NORTHERN COUNTIES

Northumberland
Durham
Yorkshire, North Riding
Derbyshire

Nottinghamshire*
York City and Ainsty*
Yorkshire, East Riding*
Yorkshire, West Riding*

The 'arable' type of printed form used for reporting on tithe agreements in these counties requires a 'description and rough estimate of the titheable produce' and asks assistant tithe commissioners and local tithe agents to 'describe the parish and the quality of the lands, the system of farming, and whether the quality of the produce has been affected by any extraordinary instances of high or low farming'.

*Data for Nottinghamshire, York City and Ainsty, and the East and West Ridings of Yorkshire are too few to warrant constructing maps of land use and crops tithe district-by-tithe district, and for Nottinghamshire and York City and Ainsty the samples of tithe districts with extant data are too small to justify compiling county aggregate figures of land use and crop acreages and yields.

Northumberland

548 tithe districts
274 reports on tithe agreements

Evidence from Northumberland tithe files is used by Harriet M. E. Holt (1985) in her thesis on upland farming in the nineteenth century.

Exactly half of Northumberland files contain reports on tithe agreements and about half of these again were produced in the year 1839 (Table 55). Cheviot and Pennine Northumberland are both under-represented in this sample of places (Map 410). Both Henry Pilkington and John S. Donaldson Selby were given exceptionally heavy work loads in Northumberland. Pilkington visited ninety-four places in this county in 1839 and wrote reports on three others without a visit. At two of these places the tithe owner was also a substantial landowner, so he accepted that the likelihood was that the agreement would be fair to both parties. While on his way to the third, Lyham township, his gig was overturned and subsequent bad weather, he said, prevented him reaching this place. In fact, correspondence in the tithe files suggests that both men tried to find reasons for not visiting a township and for cutting proceedings in the field as short as possible. John S. Donaldson Selby's farming descriptions are brief in the extreme, sometimes non-existent. John Job Rawlinson provides far and away the most detailed district reports but unfortunately he officiated in only seven townships; he did not adhere rigidly to a set of pre-determined headings as did the other assistant commissioners.

Only twenty-nine districts were entirely tithe free in 1836, not many farms or estates were totally exempt from tithes within titheable townships, but large parts of some townships are omitted from agreement enumerations because of moduses. Hay was often covered by a modus and so no value of its gross produce was provided; in fact Pilkington rarely cited yields of hay or clover or value of pasture, and overall there are insufficient places with yield data for cartographic or tabular analysis. Woodland was generally exempt from tithe payment but is enumerated nonetheless. Pilkington did not list moorland separately from improved pasture; for example, at Greystead, a township containing 15,055 acres, he enumerates 14,649 acres of pasture and then in his written description says the place is 'a wild tract of moorland'. Rarely is the category 'common' used as such in Northumberland files, though much moorland was commonable (see Subject Index). Although the Tithe Commission gave instructions to its representatives to ensure that statute measure was used in tithe commutation calculations, local measures and terms are found in quite a number of Northumberland reports. Yields of corn are sometimes expressed in 'bolls'; at Chathill, wheat was '21 bolls of 6 imperial bushels'.

Taking all those townships where tithe was commuted by agreement together, arable and pasture land were in overall balance *c.* 1836. Arable rotations were mainly four- and five-course, there are very few references in Northumberland files to three-course rotations. The Durham four-course is that most frequently recorded. This was fallow (either bare or with turnips or potatoes depending on the soil and location), wheat or barley (again the choice affected by soil characteristics), clover (occasionally replaced by some peas or beans) and oats. Assistant commissioners were not much impressed with this system, but thought better of farmers who extended it into five- or six-courses by allowing seeds to remain for two or three years. In yet other, mainly high grassland, townships, it is recorded that no regular rotation was practised. On such few acres of arable as these farmers cultivated, corn, usually only oats, was all that was grown on small patches of occasionally broken land.

The net result of all these practices is describes in Table 56 and on Maps 415–26. Oats were the leading corn crop in terms of acreage but clover and seeds occupied a greater proportion of the arable than any other individual crop. There were large amounts of bare fallow and only small acreages of barley and turnips; crop yields were at best only moderate. The exception to this last was the turnip crop. There was a good market for turnips in the large towns; farmers in townships near Newcastle, for example, grew turnips to sell to cow keepers in that city. They considered it more profitable to do this and to bring back cheap manure than to keep sheep for the same purpose. At Morpeth, which had a weekly cattle market, turnips fetched £6 an acre, at Byker near Newcastle, £8 an acre.

All assistant tithe commissioners, even those who were relatively unfamiliar with the region's agriculture, recognised the importance of sheep rearing in the Northumberland agrarian economy at this time. John Job Rawlinson, a native of Westmorland, commented thus at Corsenside:

> sheep feeding is what is principally looked to in the parish and the sheep are almost exclusively Cheviots, tho' a few black faced sheep, and only a few, were to be seen. That part of the moor which is covered with coarse grass seemed to me much fitter for pasturing black cattle than sheep. Sheep however are the fashion.

Breeding flocks were to be found throughout the county and, in the judgement of Harriet M. E. Holt (1985), in places where stocking densities were low and virtually no land ploughed, the sheep flock was the prime regulator of rents and tithes. There is much discussion in the tithe files of the respective merits of different breeds in particular circumstances. Cattle breeding was also important (see Subject Index).

Northumberland

Table 55 *Reports on agreements for commutation of tithes in Northumberland*

Assistant commissioner/ local tithe agent	1838	1839	1840	1841	1842	1843	1844	1845	1846	Totals
Henry Pilkington	13	97	29	3	6	16	6	3		173
John S. Donaldson Selby	16	23		2	4	4		1	1	51
Richard Burton Phillipson		13	3	22						38
John Job Rawlinson	6	1								7
John B. Neal			3							3
John Penny				2						2
Totals	35	134	35	29	10	20	6	4	1	274

Table 56 *Land use, crops and yields in Northumberland c. 1836*

A	Land use	Percentage of total land area enumerated in reports on tithe agreements	Estimated acreage in whole county
	Arable	46.5	580,264
	Grass	47.5	592,932
	Wood	3.8	47,800

B	Crop	Mean percentage of arable	Mean yield per acre	Estimated acreage in whole county
	Wheat	19.3	19.5 bushels	111,852
	Barley	4.9	30.7 bushels	28,629
	Oats	22.6	31.7 bushels	131,308
	Pulses	1.6	26.4 bushels	9,193
	Turnips	6.4	£3.08	37,108
	Seeds	26.3	—	152,413
	Fallows	16.9	—	98,207

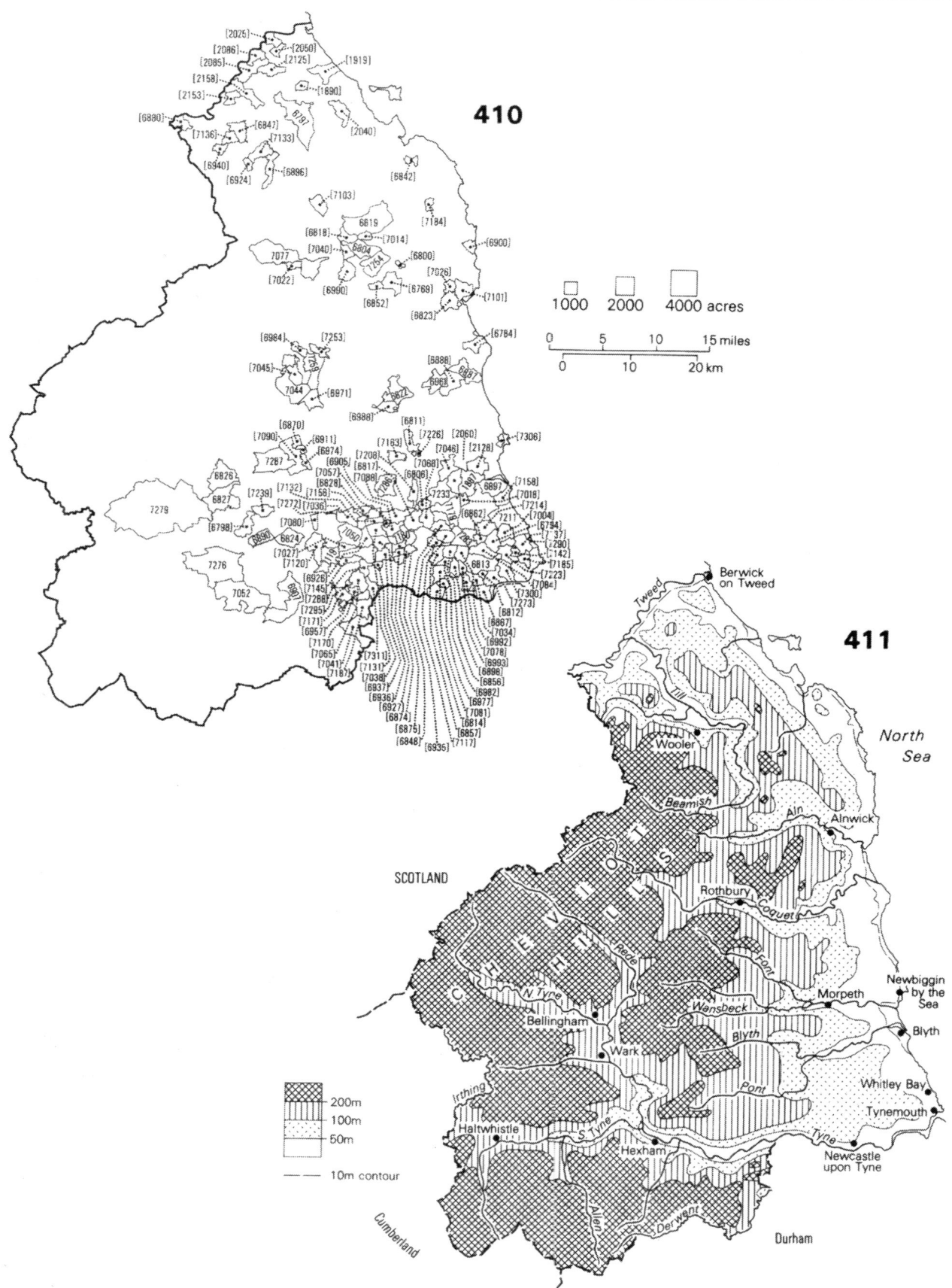

Northumberland

Arable as a percentage of tithe district area
412

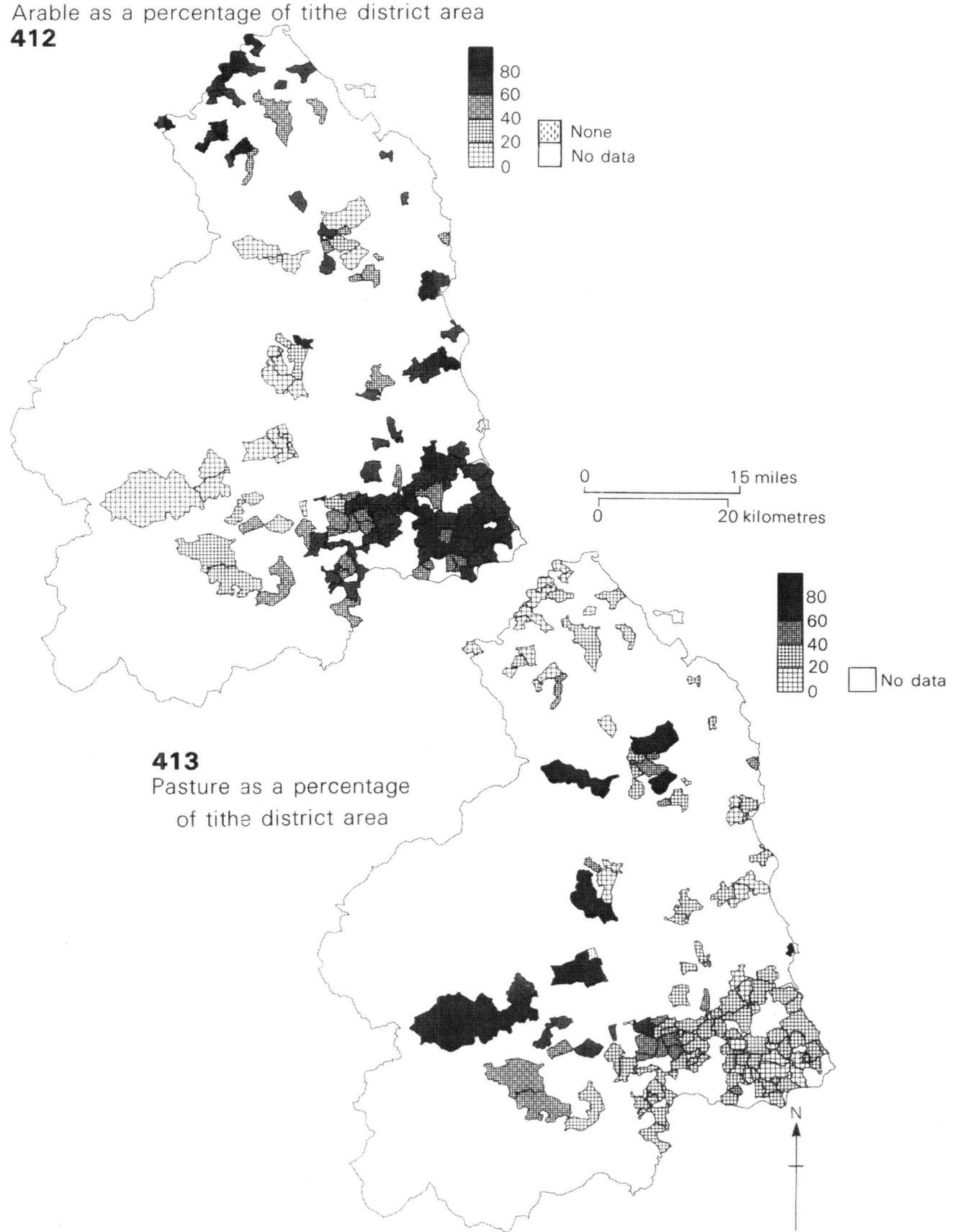

413
Pasture as a percentage of tithe district area

Woodland as a percentage of tithe district area
414

415
Wheat as a percentage of arable

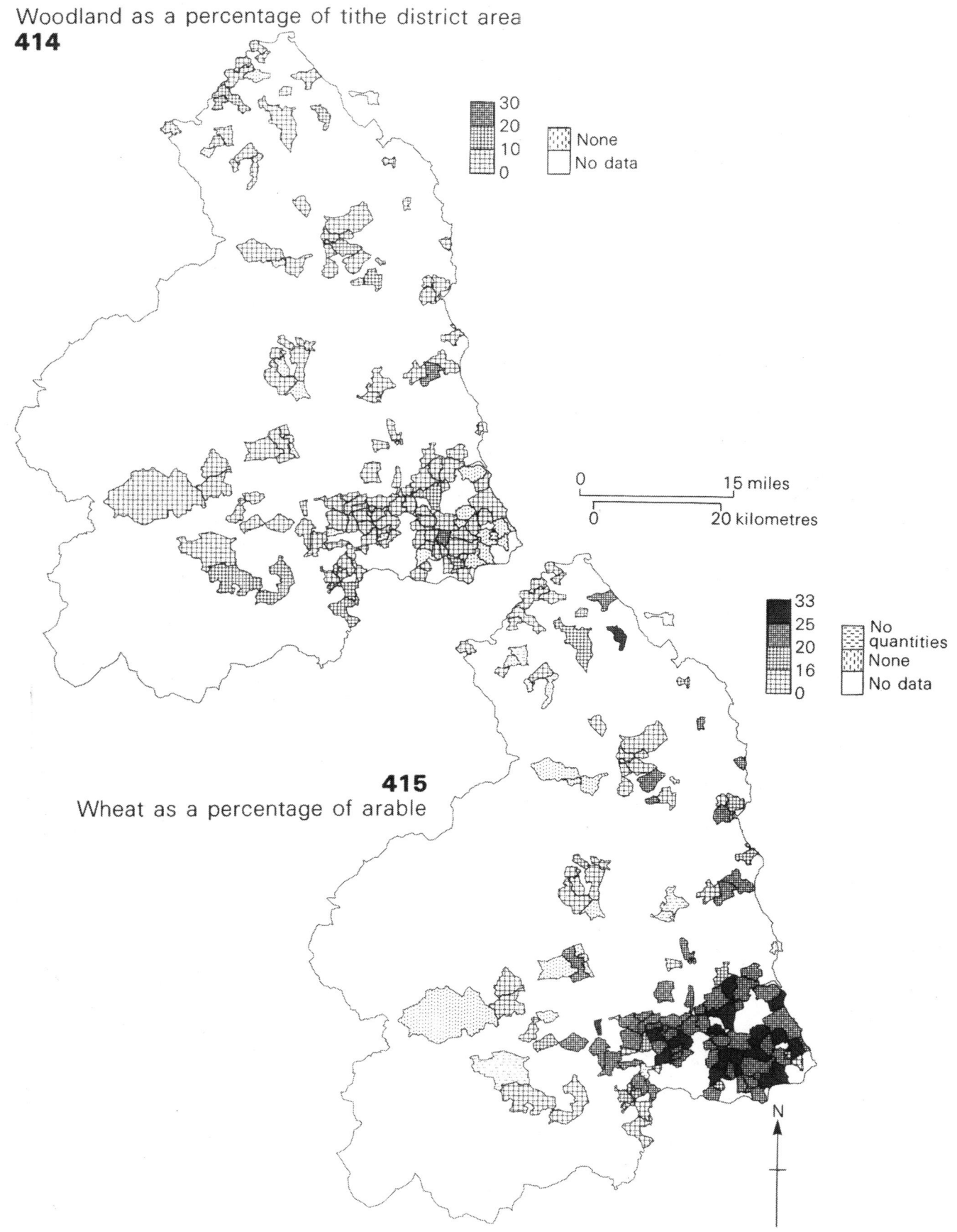

Northumberland

Barley as a percentage of arable
416

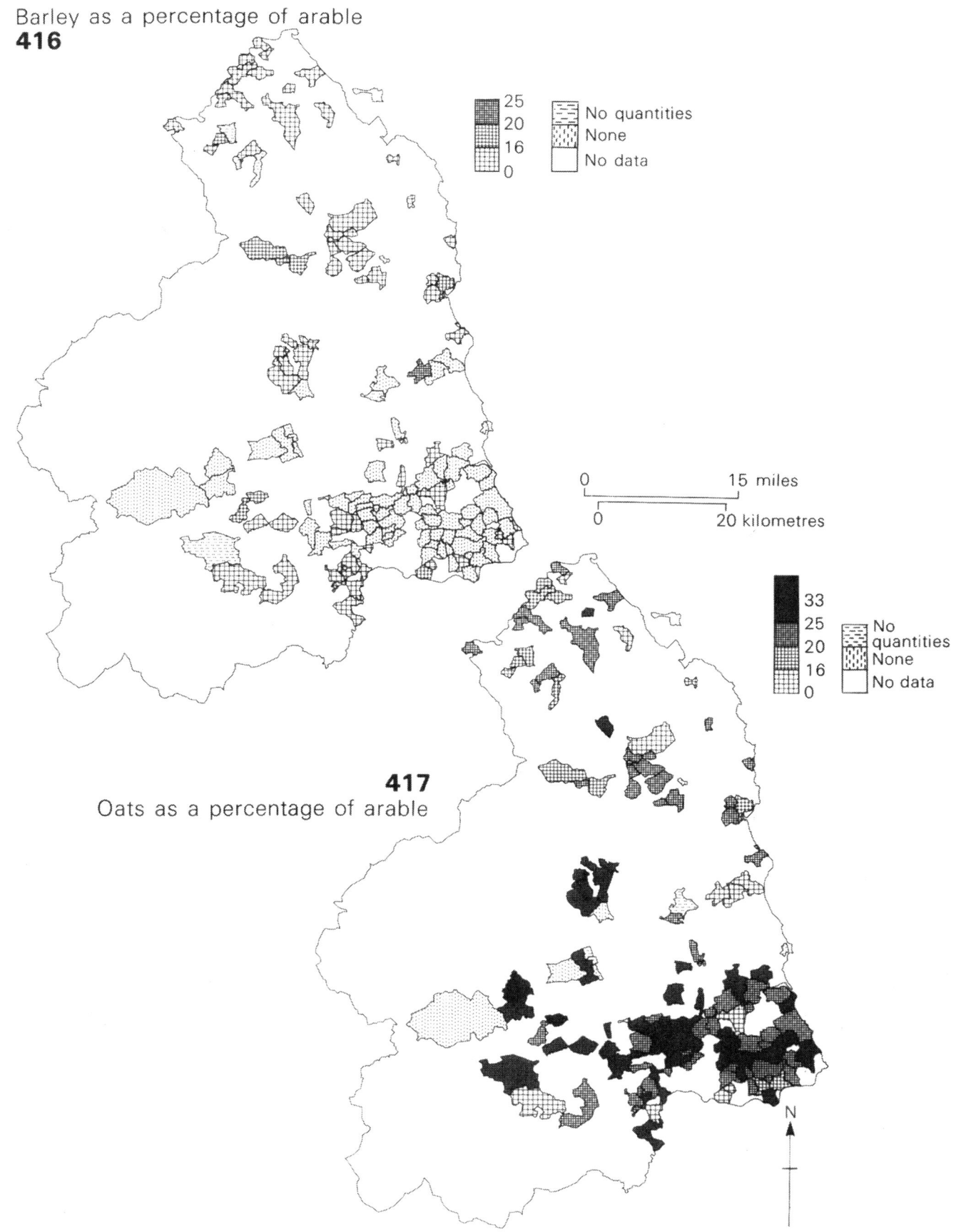

417
Oats as a percentage of arable

324 Northern counties

Pulse crops as a percentage of arable
418

419
Turnips as a percentage of arable

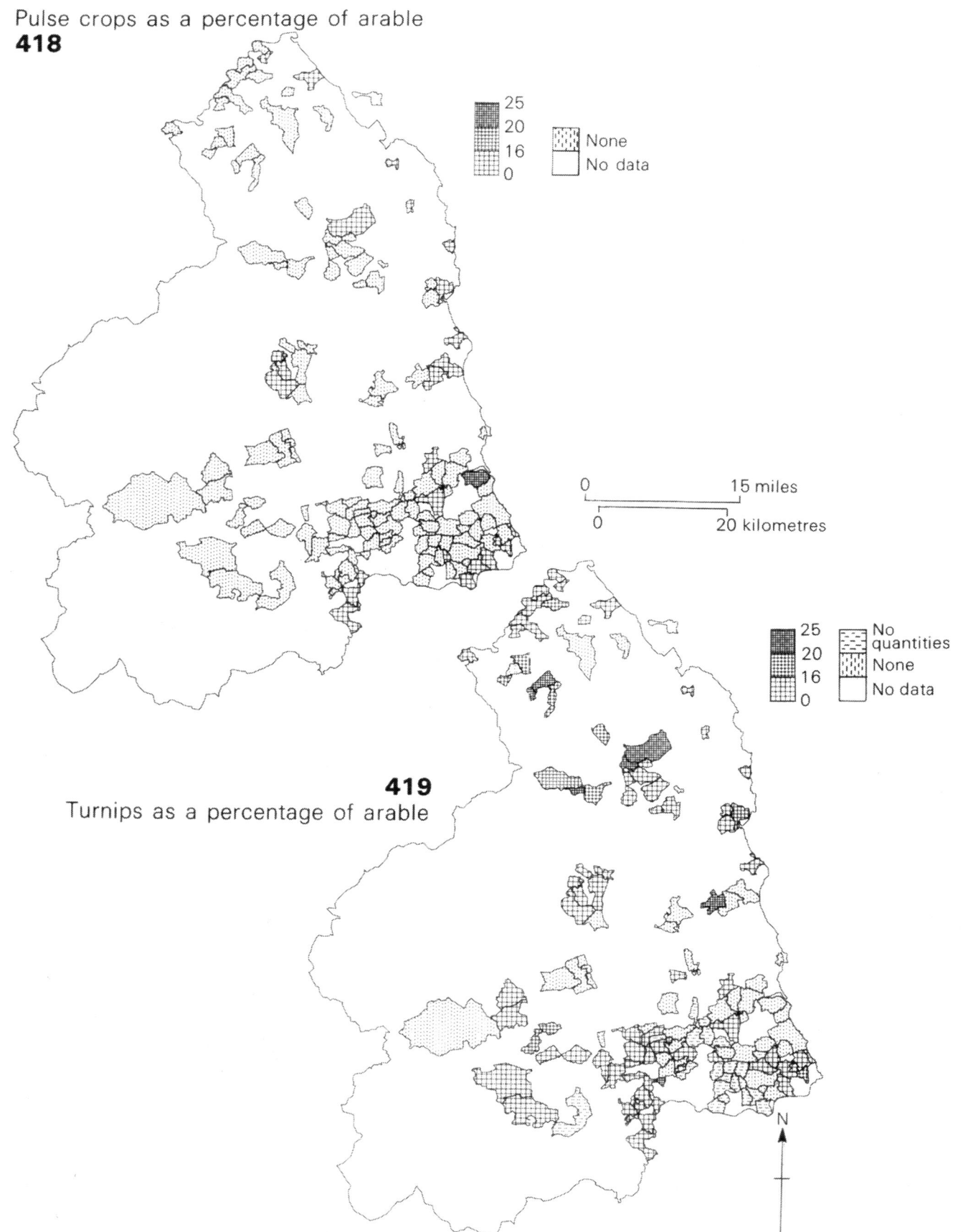

Clover and seeds as a percentage of arable
420

421
Dead fallow as a percentage of arable

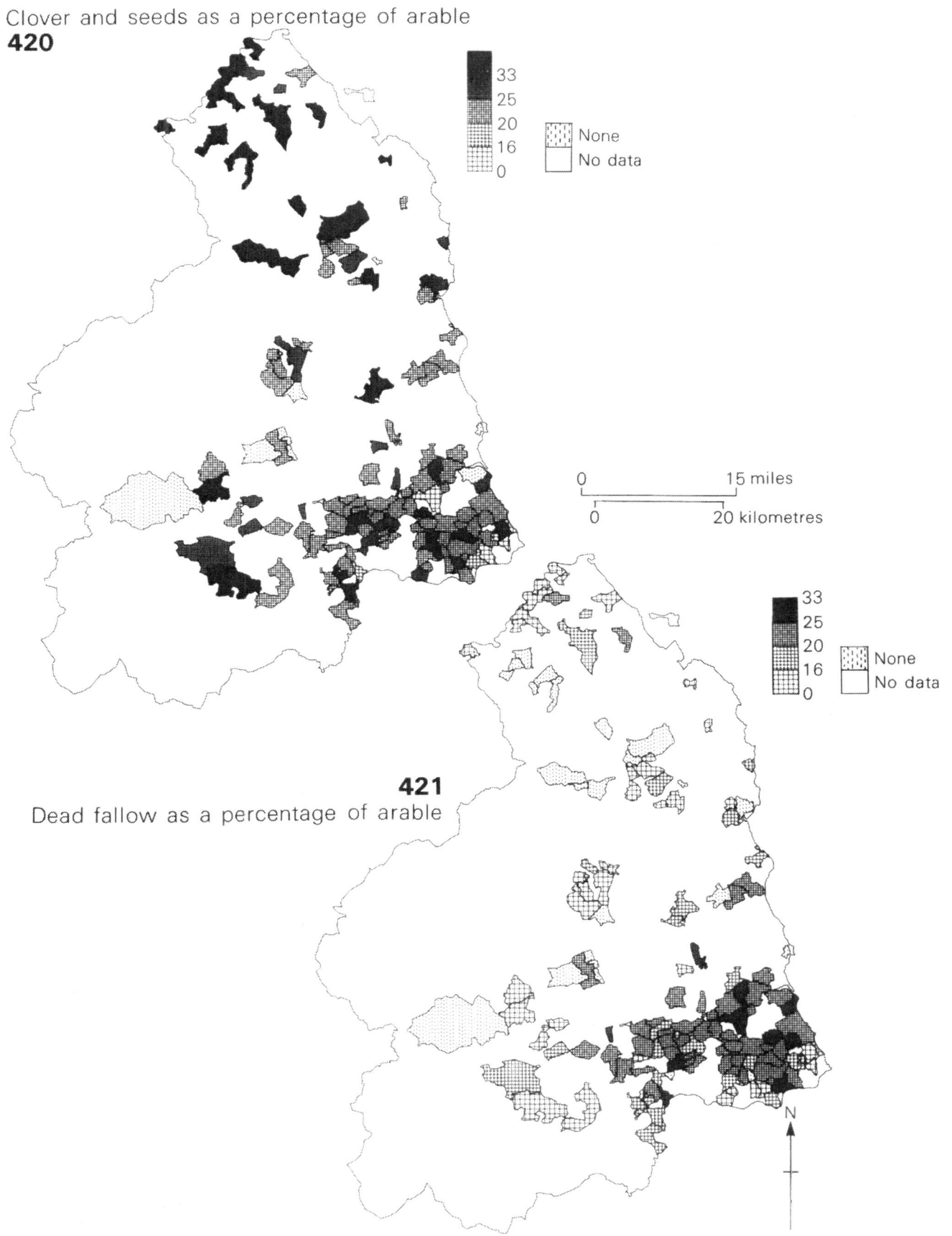

Yield of wheat in bushels per acre
422

423
Yield of barley in bushels per acre

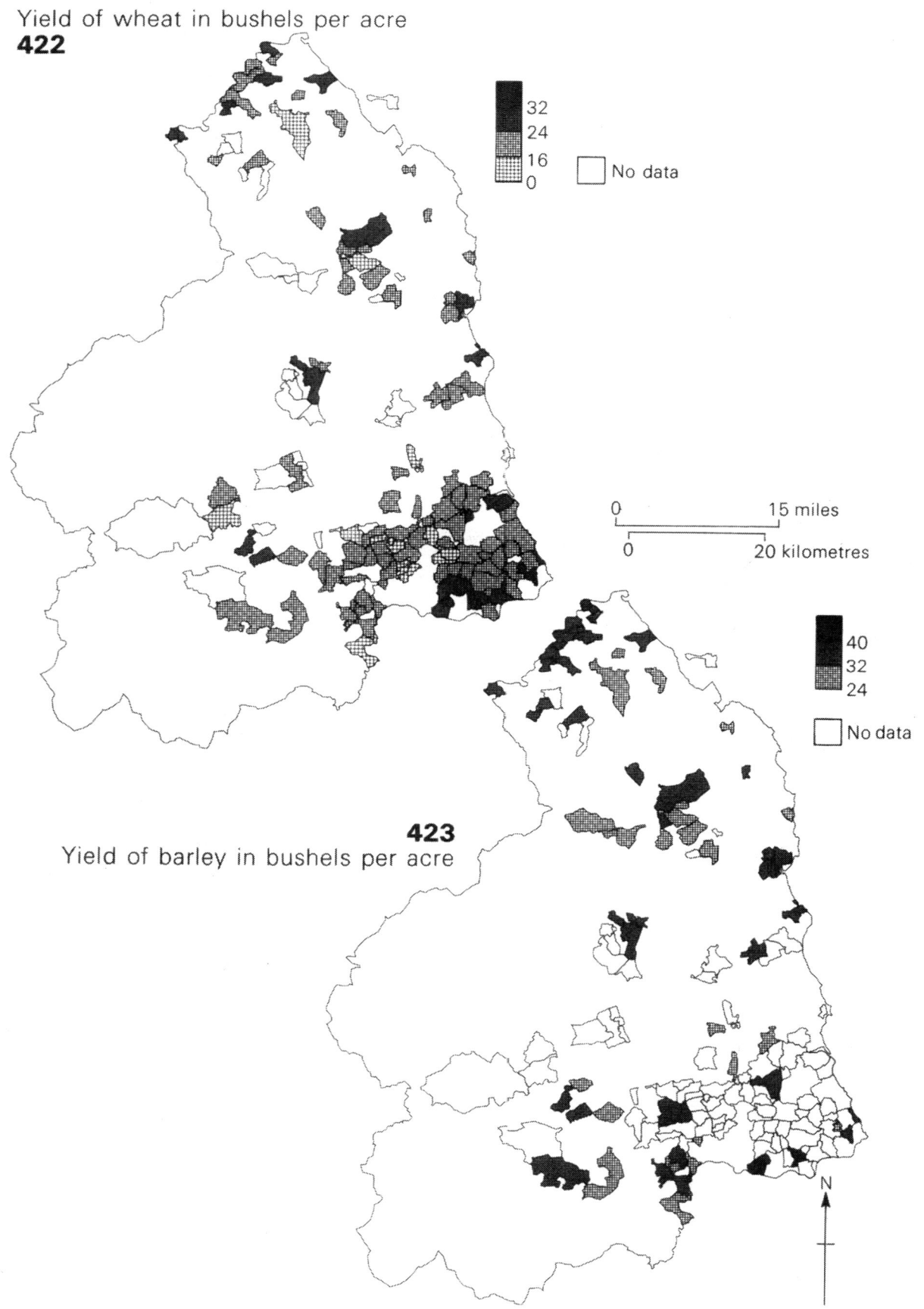

Northumberland

Yield of oats in bushels per acre
424

425
Yield of pulse crops in bushels per acre

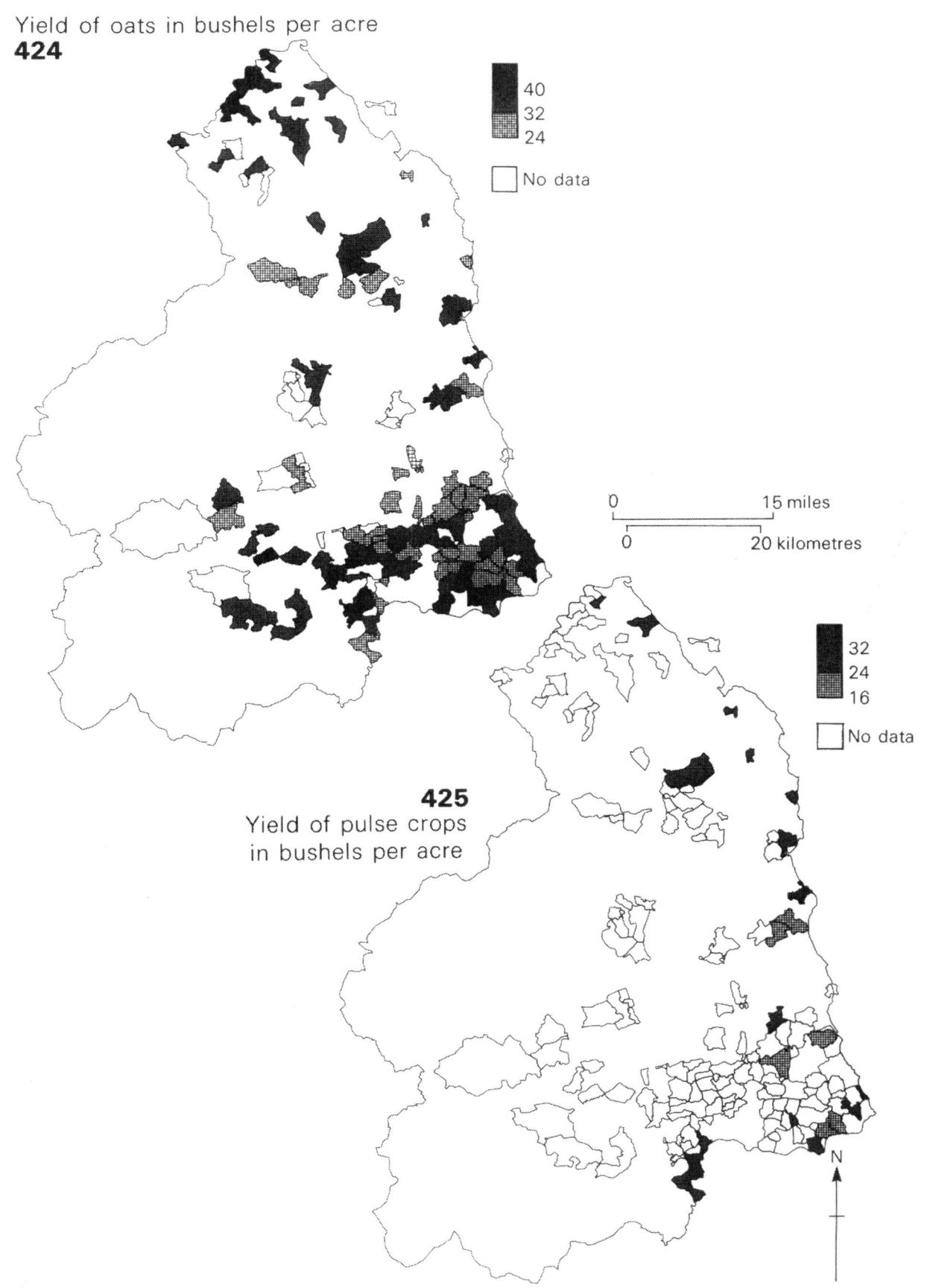

426 Yield of turnips in £'s per acre

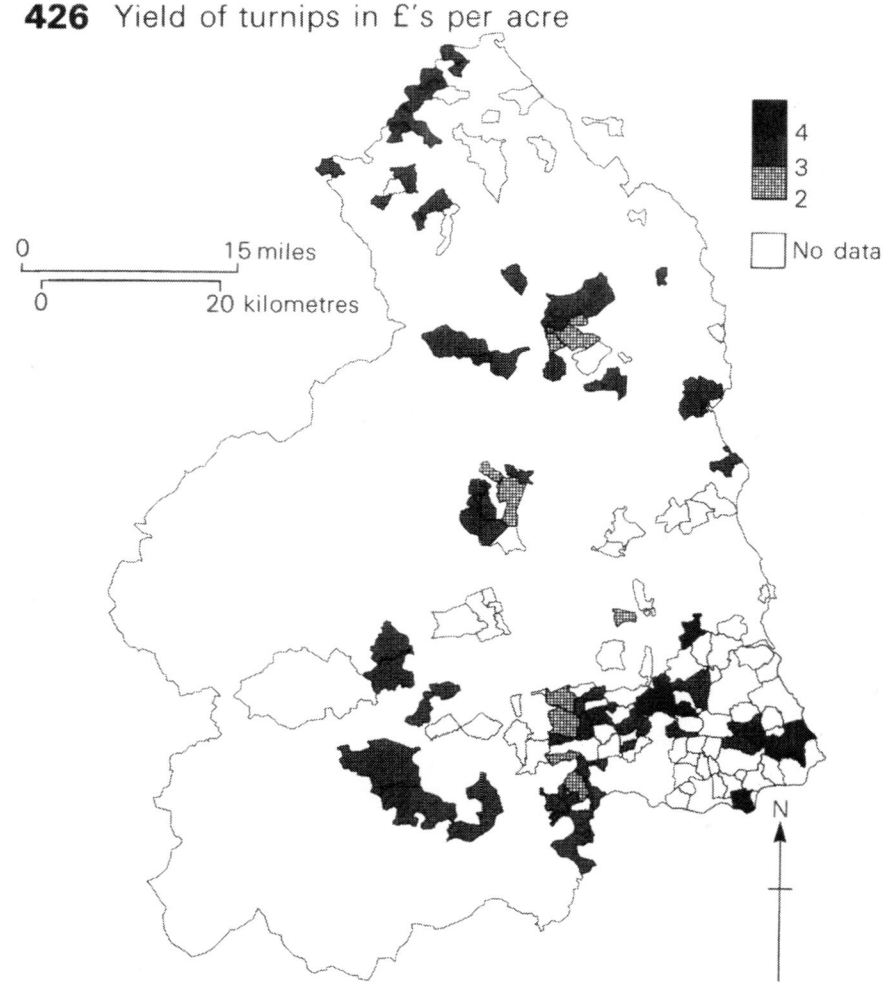

Durham

313 tithe districts
202 reports on tithe agreements

Dr Michael Sill has made extensive use of east Durham tithe surveys to reconstruct the agrarian cadastre upon which a landscape of mineral exploitation was superimposed in the first half of the nineteenth century (Sill, 1982).

Just three of the Tithe Commission's agents wrote 84 per cent of Durham reports on agreements (Table 57); one man, Henry Pilkington, completed exactly half the Durham total himself, visiting no fewer than sixty-six places in the county during the single year, 1838 (Holt, 1984). Very few districts were completely tithe free but moduses on products such as hay and milk were very common and as a result grassland and its products are not much discussed in Durham files. In most of Pennine Durham, tithe commutation was effected by compulsory award rather than by voluntary agreement so this area possesses very few tithe file crop data and much of the discussion in the following two paragraphs refers to the eastern and southern half of the county (Map 427). By 1836, little tithe was still collected in kind as the usual arrangement was for tithes to be valued annually and let on a composition. At Burdon, Charles Howard remarked that 'the annual valuation of these tithes may probably have been an impediment to its improvement'. Similarly at Boldon, John S. Donaldson Selby anticipated the beneficial effects that tithe commutation might bring to local agriculture. On the other hand, remoteness and inaccessibility of many farms could count to the farmers' benefit. Henry Pilkington noted at Emelden in 1838 that 'the township is at great distance from the tithe barn, and so expensive is the collection of tithes considered by the titheowner that his valuer informed me that his directions were, always, to close with the best offer for composition which he could get, but never run the risk of taking in kind if possible'.

Table 58 and Maps 429–31 summarise the acreages and distribution of arable, grass and wood in Durham. The Tithe Commission's representatives encountered great difficulty in obtaining acreages of common in Durham. Where such land was not actually exempt, its contribution to gross tithe revenue was very small and in all but two townships which enter the cartographic analysis its acreage was ignored entirely. Table 58 and Maps 432–43 present data which Durham tithe files contain on acreages and yields of crops and fallows. Yields of wheat and oats were mostly very low, in some places scarcely returning seed. On heavy clay soils the old Durham three-course fallow, wheat, oats system was still widespread. Almost a quarter of the total arable of the county was sown with oats c. 1836 and more than a fifth was bare fallowed each year. In some townships the Durham system had been extended to a four-course with either clover or beans grown between the wheat and oats courses. On some lighter soils assistant commissioners and local tithe agents found a five-course Northumberland system of wheat, turnips, barley and two years of seeds, but bare fallows were still much more common than turnip or potato fallows, even on the lighter soils. At Framwellgate, a township with sandy loam soils, Henry Pilkington remarked that 'the low grade of agricultural skill of Durham farmers prevents that advantage being taken of such soils which might naturally be looked for. In this township the cultivation of barley and turnips is the exception rather than the rule, and the experiment rather than the regular rotation.' Poor farming is the dominant image received by local agents in those 200 townships they visited to report on agreements. Admittedly farmers did labour under difficulties of a harsh climate and in many places heavy, wet soils (see Subject Index). In this respect Henry Pilkington's description of Cold Pig Hill is not atypical: 'the surface is hilly, the climate cold, raw, wet and very backward, the corn in many parts of it in some years hardly ripening at all. The occupation roads about it are very bad, the farmsteads in a dilapidated condition and altogether it presents a poor barren aspect.' But the lack of skill among the 'afternoon farmers' encountered at places like Framwellgate was by no means unique. Recurrent complaints about agriculture recorded in Durham tithe files are over-cropping of arable, keeping too few sheep, lack of manure (despite loads of London manure and Plymouth limestone carried by returning colliers), late sowing of corn, absence of green crops and neglect of drainage (see Subject Index).

Table 57 *Reports on agreements for commutation of tithes in Durham*

Assistant commissioner/ local tithe agent	1837	1838	1839	1840	1841	1842	1843	1844	Totals
Henry Pilkington		66	14	6	2	6	6	1	101
Charles Howard	5	13	23						41
Richard Burton Phillipson			7	15	5				27
John Story Penleaze			13						13
John Job Rawlinson		7							7
John S. Donaldson Selby		4	1						5
John Penny						4			4
John B. Neal					3				3
George Louis							1		1
Totals	5	90	58	24	11	6	7	1	202

Table 58 *Land use, crops and yields in Durham c. 1836*

A	Land use	Percentage of total land area enumerated in reports on tithe agreements	Estimated acreage in whole county
	Arable	54.9	341,828
	Grass	36.4	226,567
	Wood	4.1	25,530
	Common	2.8	17,634

B	Crop	Mean percentage of arable	Mean yield per acre	Estimated acreage in whole county
	Wheat	22.4	17.1 bushels	76,508
	Barley	4.6	27.3 bushels	15,852
	Oats	22.3	26.7 bushels	76,215
	Pulses	2.5	20.4 bushels	8,452
	Turnips	5.1	£3.10	17,277
	Seeds	21.8	19.0 cwts	74,497
	Fallows	20.8	—	71,139

332 Northern counties

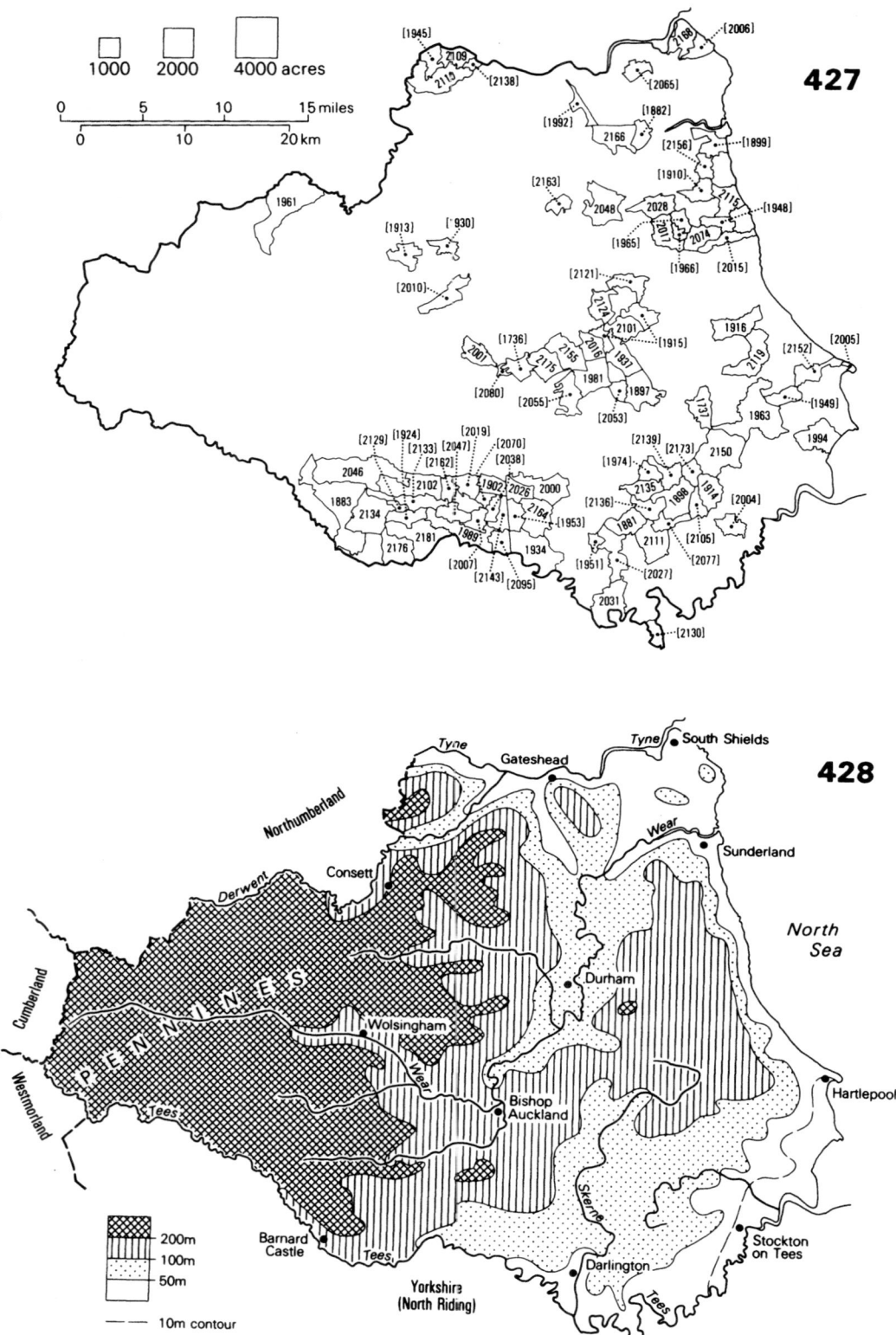

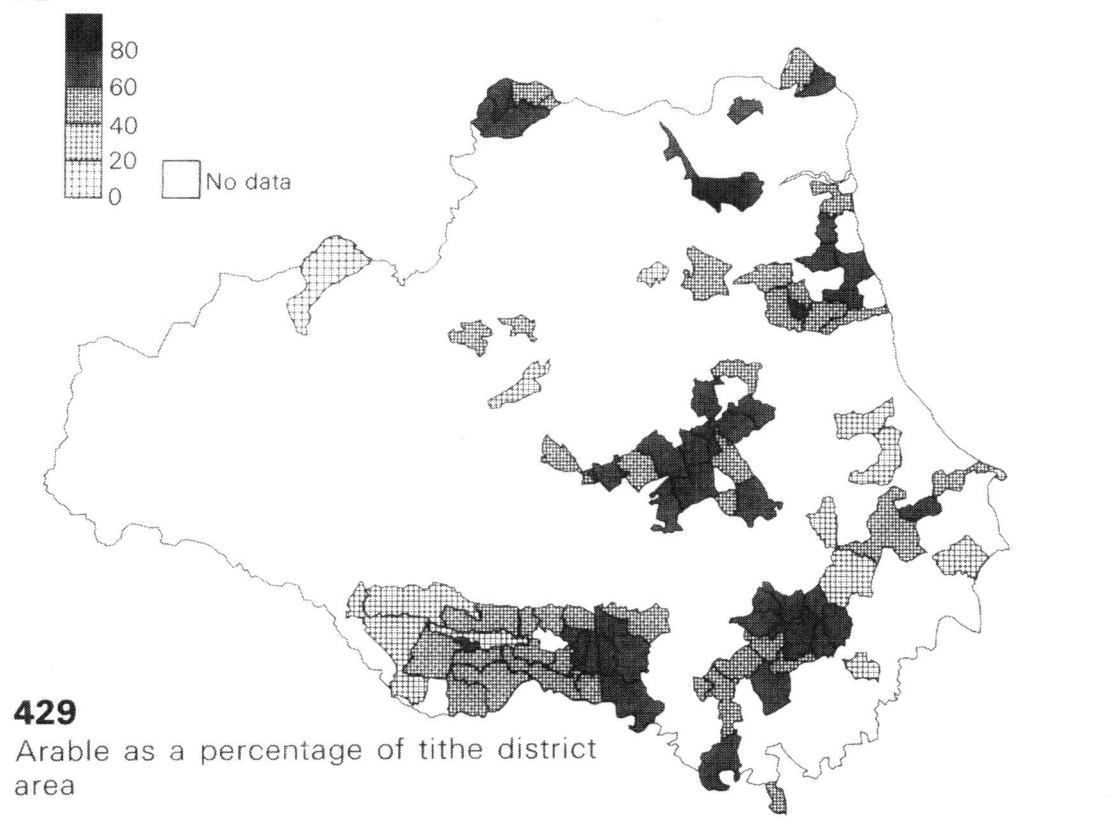

429
Arable as a percentage of tithe district area

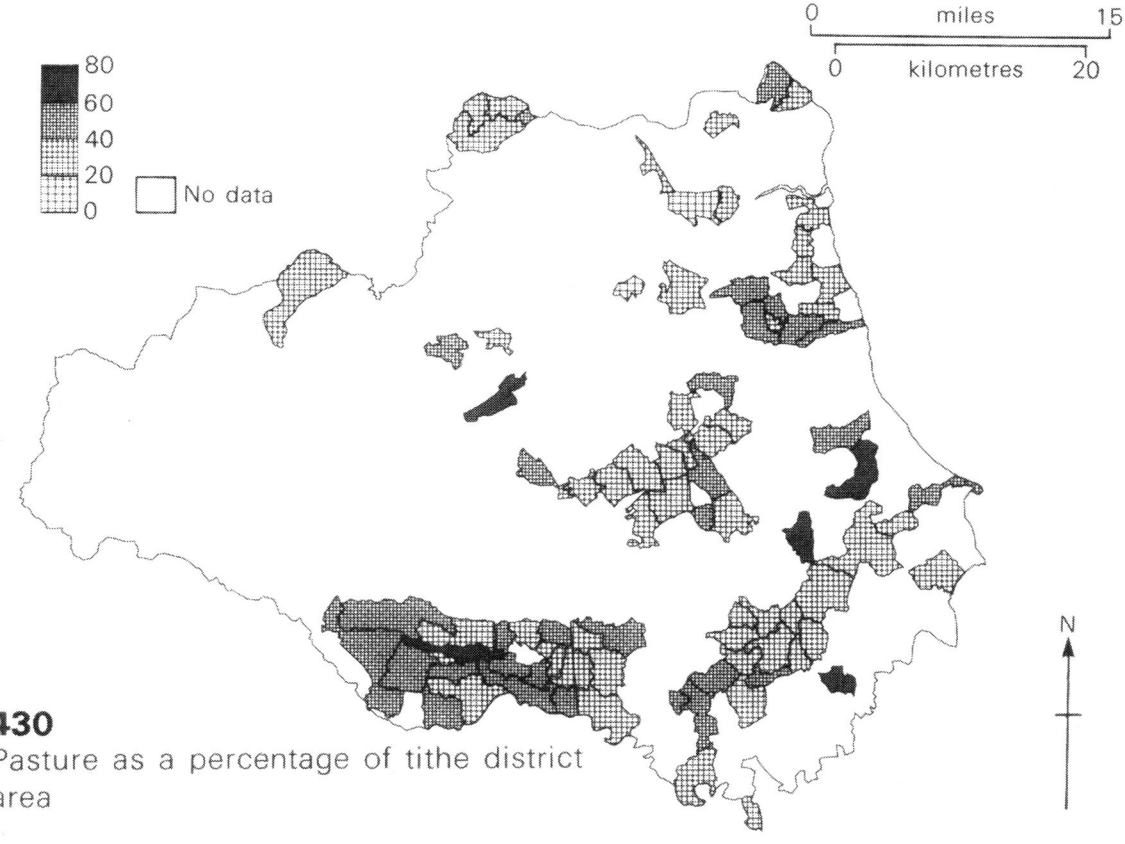

430
Pasture as a percentage of tithe district area

334 Northern counties

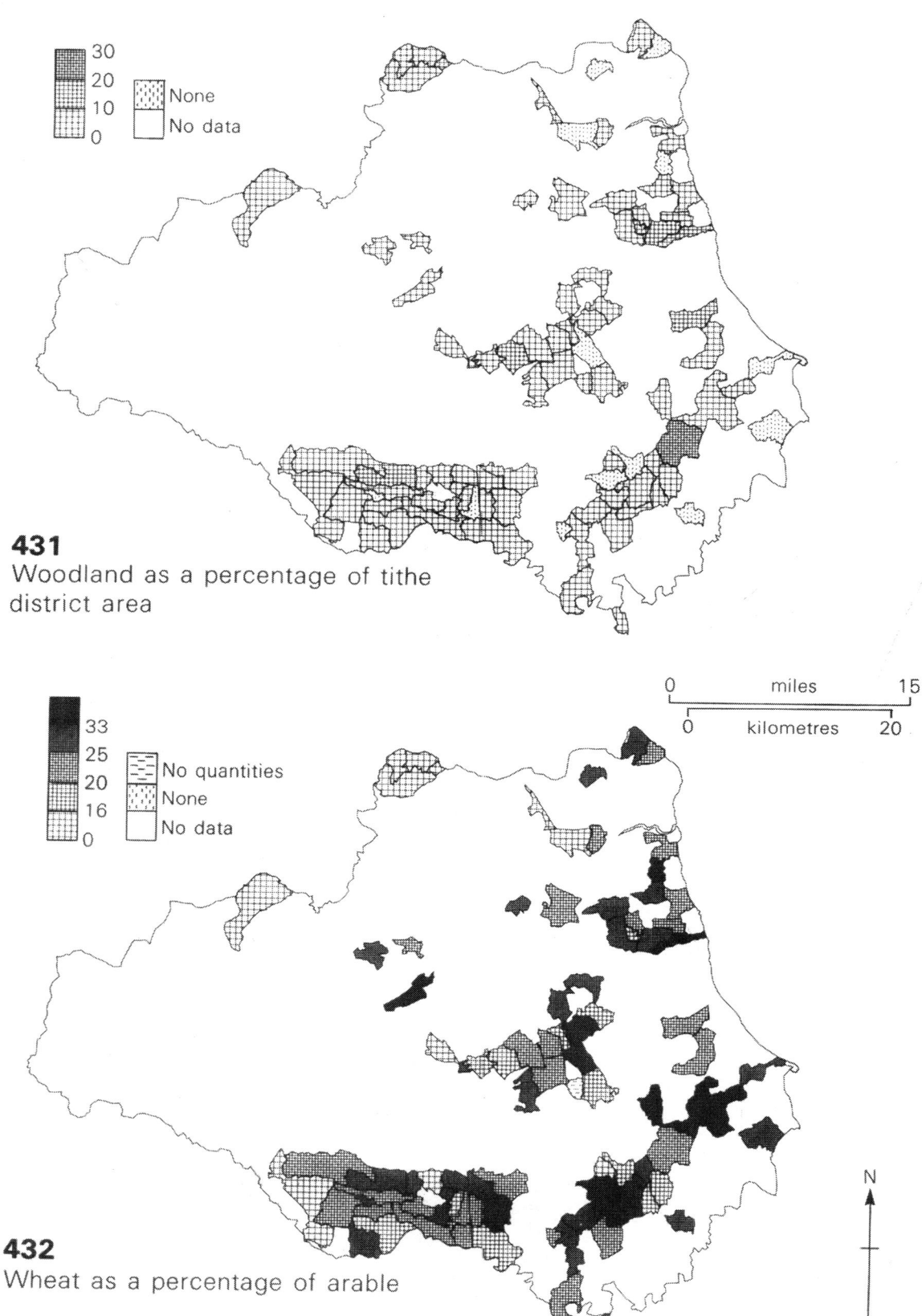

431 Woodland as a percentage of tithe district area

432 Wheat as a percentage of arable

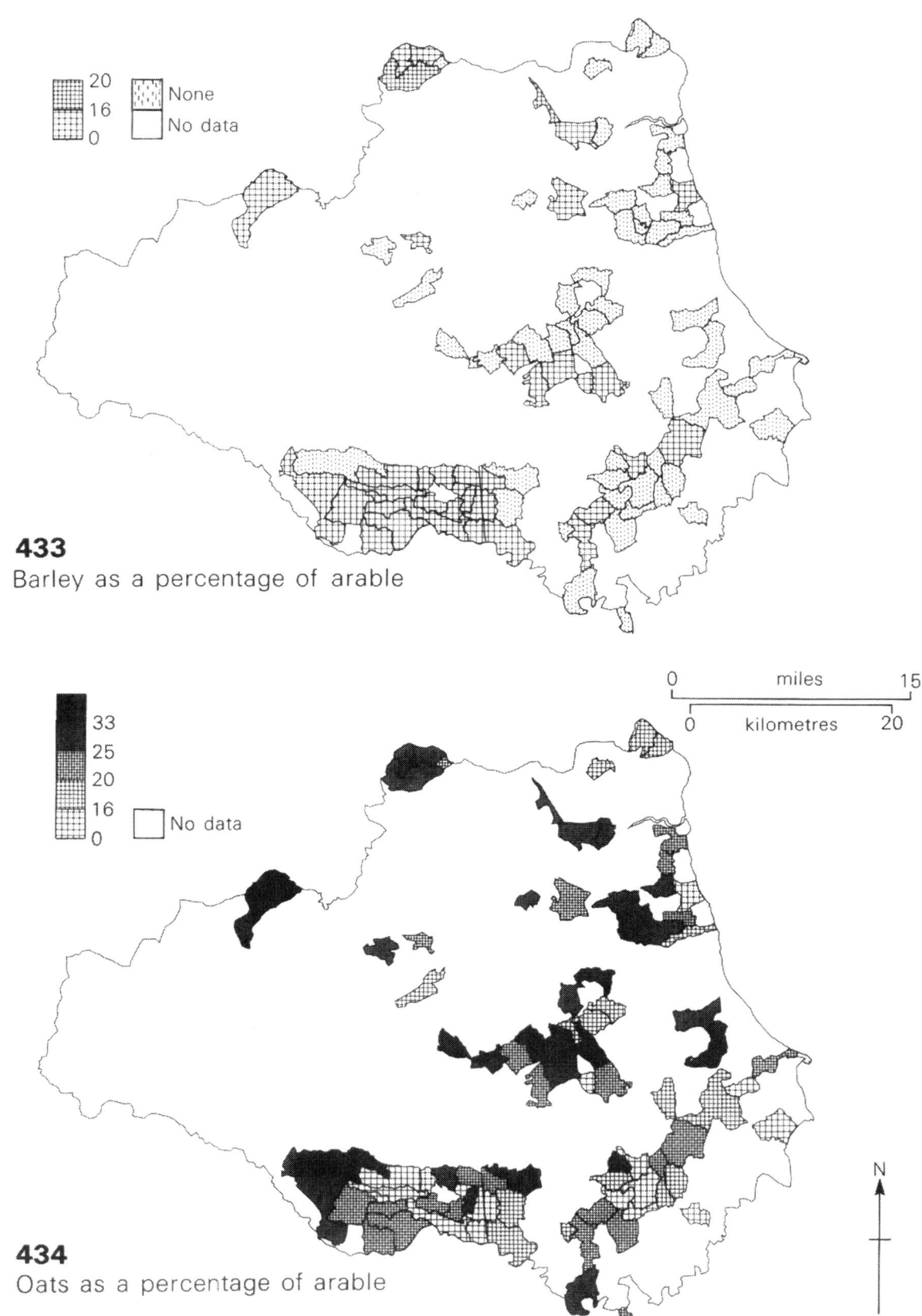

433 Barley as a percentage of arable

434 Oats as a percentage of arable

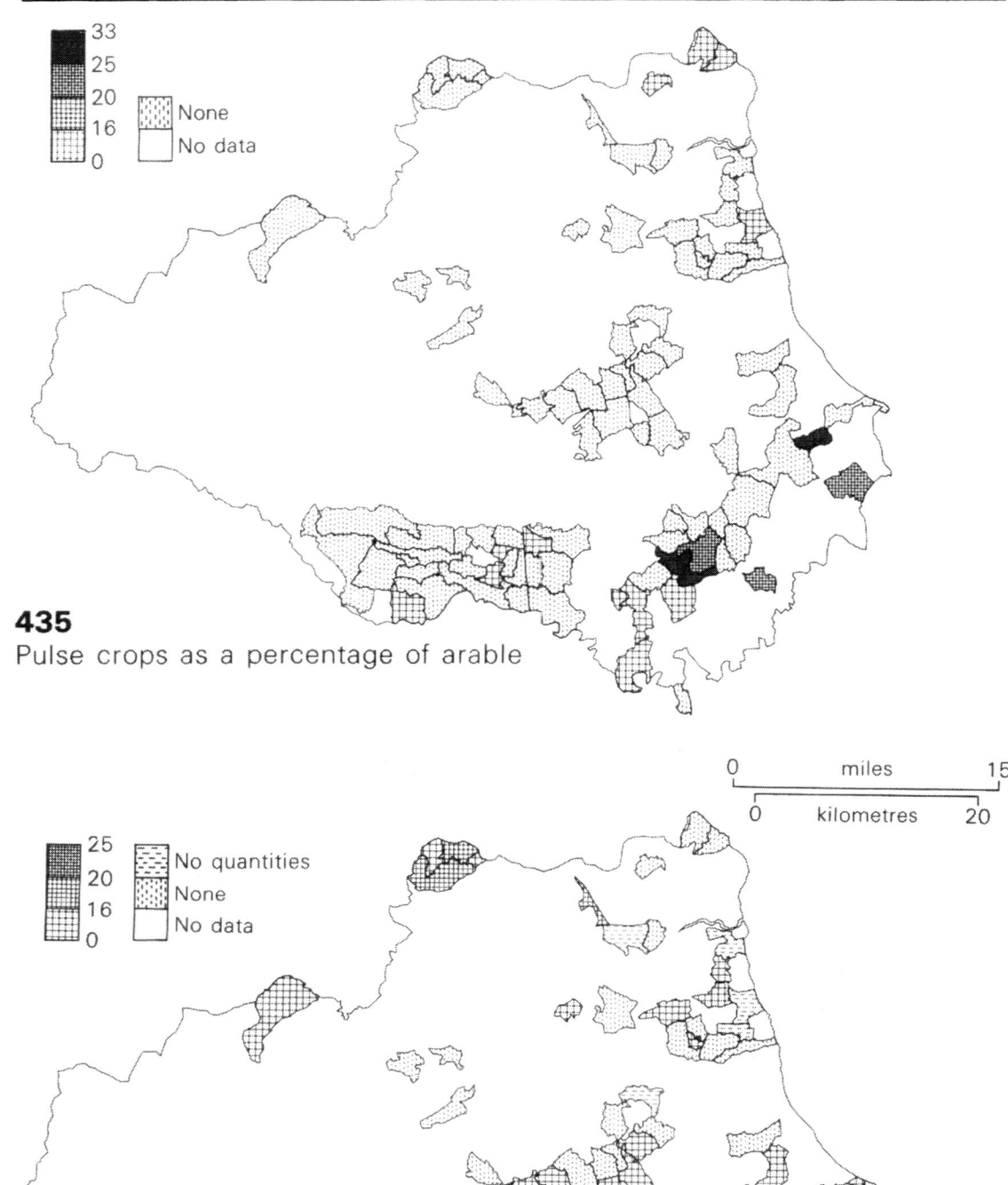

435 Pulse crops as a percentage of arable

436 Turnips as a percentage of arable

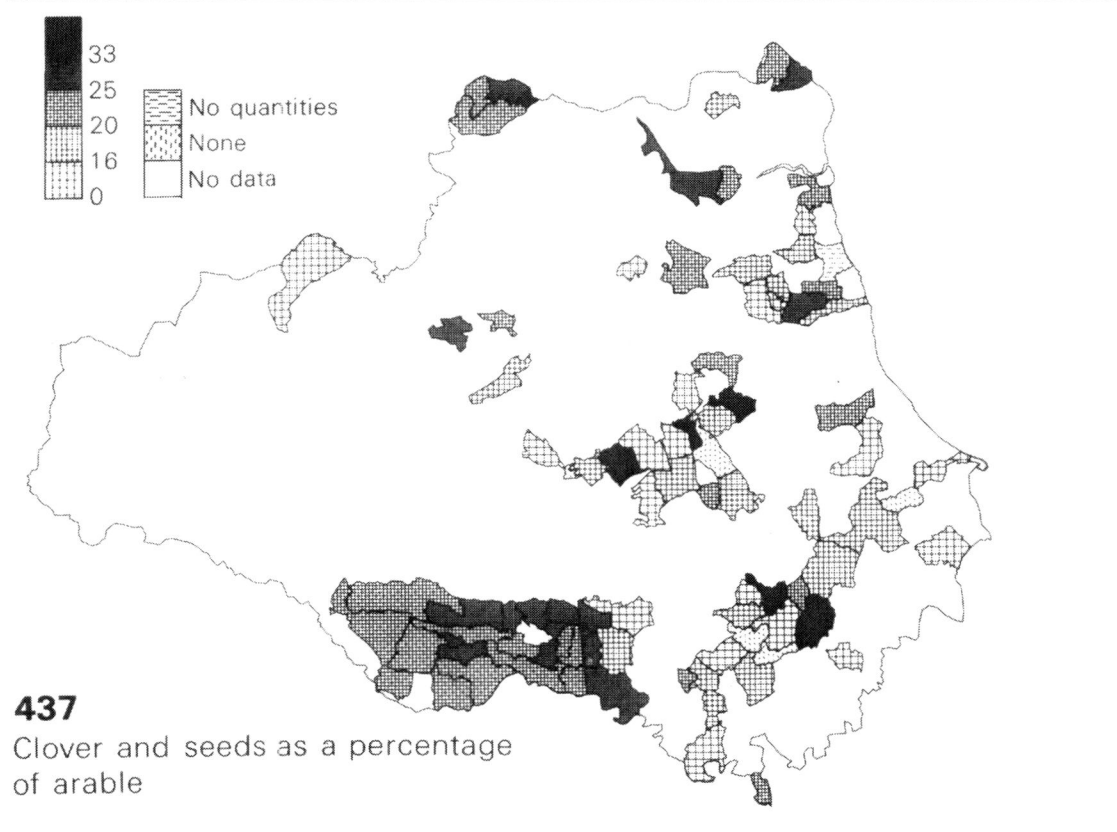

437
Clover and seeds as a percentage of arable

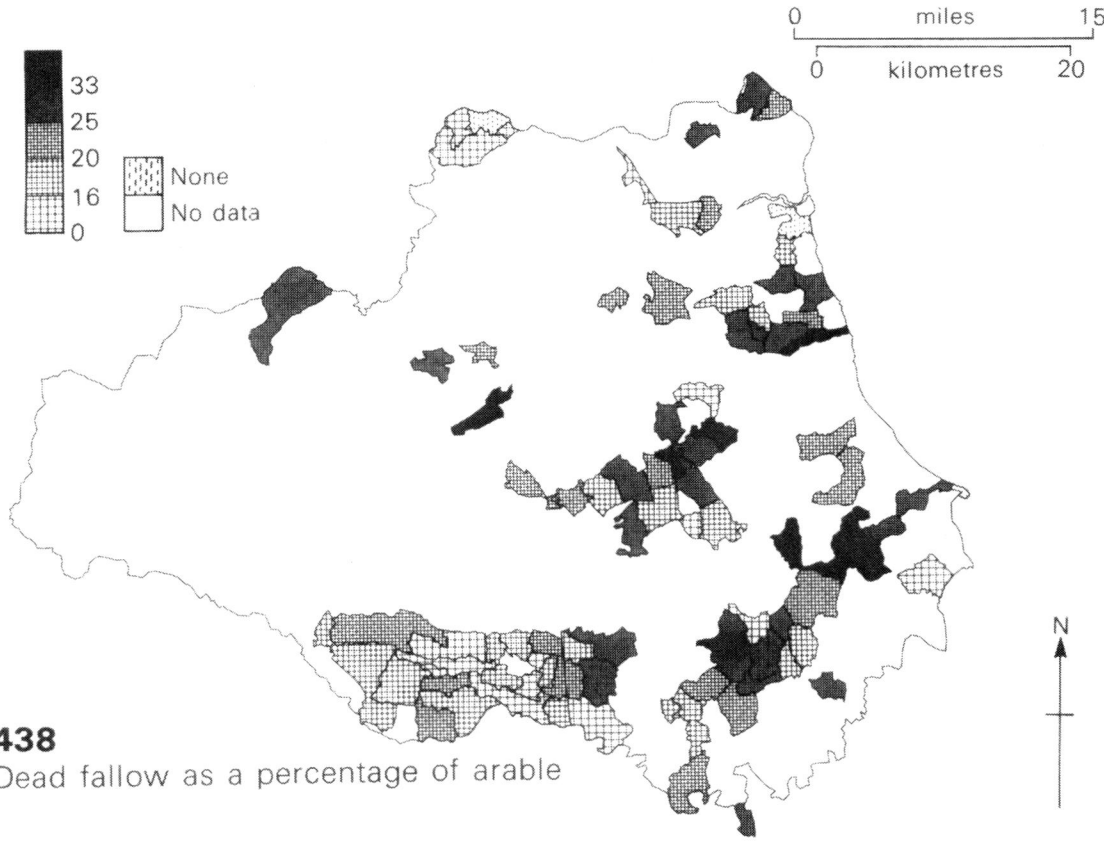

438
Dead fallow as a percentage of arable

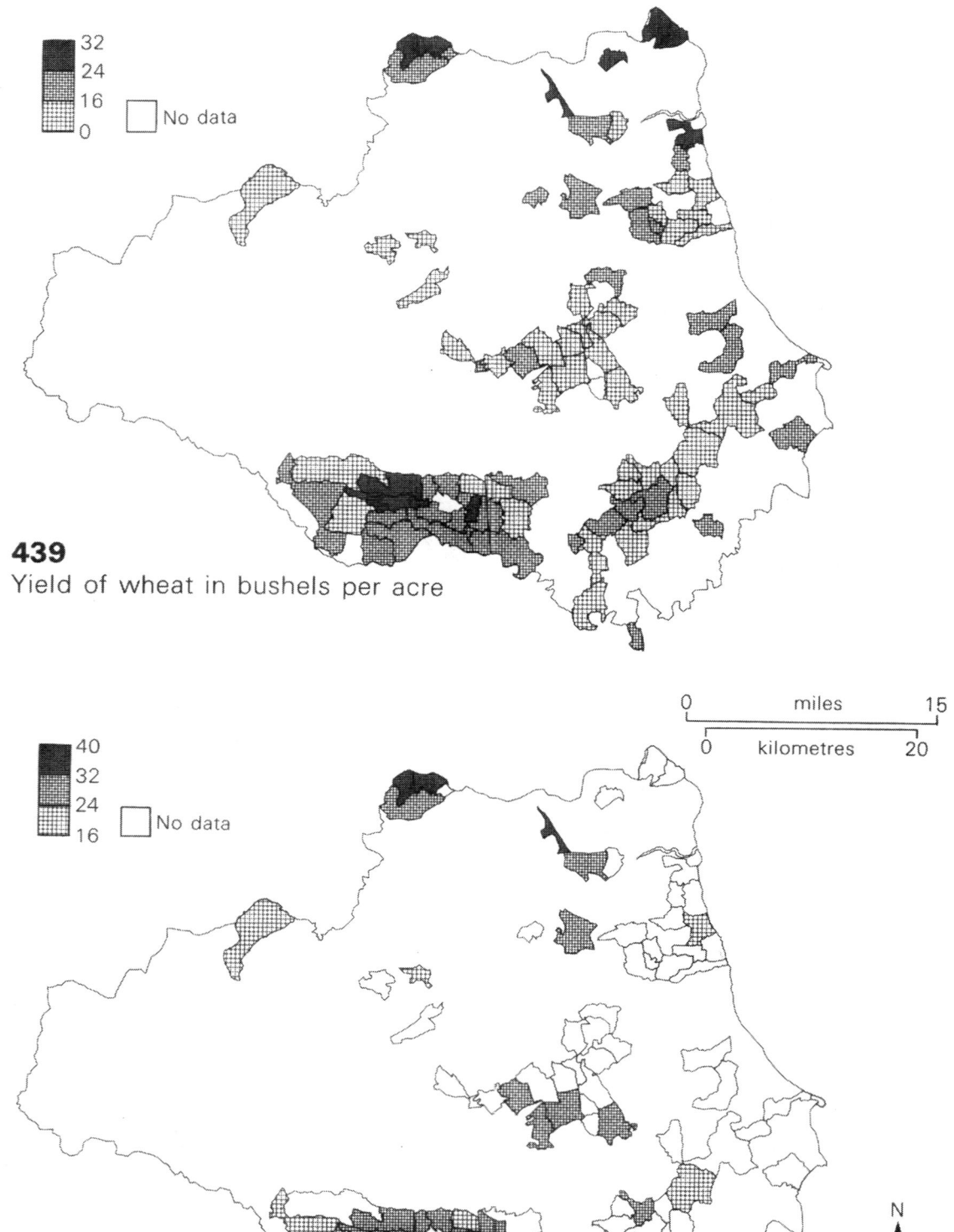

439 Yield of wheat in bushels per acre

440 Yield of barley in bushels per acre

Durham

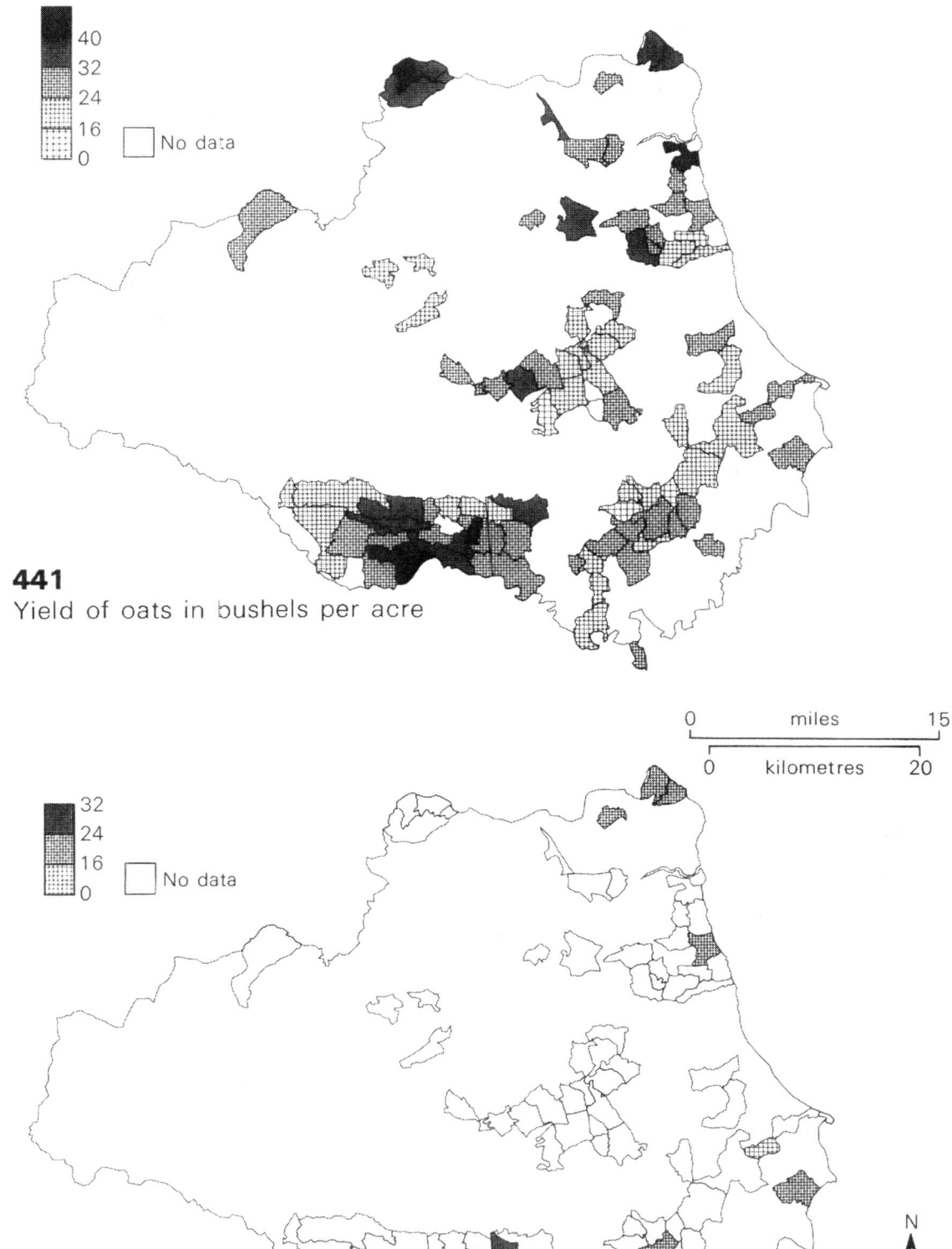

441 Yield of oats in bushels per acre

442 Yield of pulse crops in bushels per acre

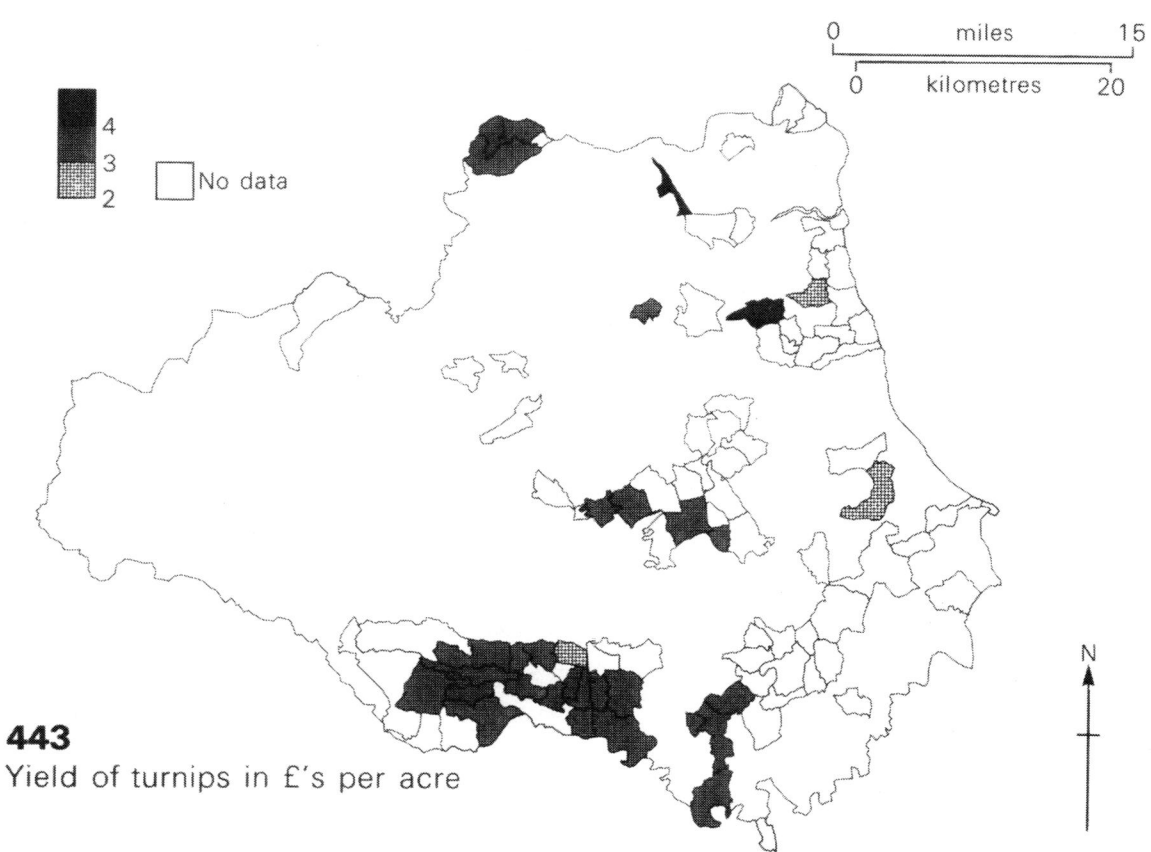

443 Yield of turnips in £'s per acre

Yorkshire, North Riding

520 tithe districts
203 reports on tithe agreements

Dr John Chapman (1961) has utilised evidence from tithe maps and apportionments in his study of the changing moorland edge in North Yorkshire. Maps, apportionments and files of West Cleveland are an important source for P. K. Mitchell's (1965) study of land use in this area. He was one of the first workers outside University College, London, to use tithe files in this way.

North Yorkshire files contain an especially rich body of evidence particularly concerning the nature of upland farming close to the margins of cultivation. In many North Riding townships and parishes, moorland and woodland were exempt from tithes and the often tiny acreages of corn were covered by moduses. Where parliamentary enclosure had exonerated tithe (sixty-two places) or left only old enclosures titheable, it was a common practice to merge these tithes in the land and so obviate the expense of mapping and apportionment. Mergers were recommended at places like Thorpfield where 'the sole occupier of the lands is also the lessee of the tithes, consequently the tithes have always been taken in kind and mixed with the produce of the farm without any separate accounts of their value being kept'. In upland parts of the county, the large size and inaccessibility of townships and frequent bad weather made an assistant commissioner's task well nigh impossible within the limited time at his disposal. Comments such as the following made by Charles Howard at Gatenby are found quite frequently: 'when in the country the snow was too deep and the frost too severe to admit of a personal inspection of the land but I am well acquainted with it and it is similar to the adjoining parish of Pickhill which I had previously inspected'. The extent of common was particularly difficult to ascertain where boundaries were unsure or disputed. John Job Rawlinson reported at Arkendale in 1838 that 'the number of acres of the common of the parish cannot possibly be known as there is a dispute at present pending between this parish and that of Bowes as to their respective limits. The dispute extends over 4 or 5 miles in length and from a 1/4 to a 1/2 mile in breadth.' During their inquiries into disputed parish and township boundaries in the 1850s, the Ordnance Survey contacted the Tithe Commission. Some files of these places contain copy tracings of the boundary at question taken from tithe maps.

North Riding files are a rich source of landscape descriptions as topography was undoubtedly an important influence on farming in this area; wildness, height, steepness and exposure were all qualities which evinced comment (see Subject Index). Charles Howard, for example, described the township of Westerdale south of Guisborough on the flanks of the North York Moors as

> steep and mountainous and though the cultivated land is in a tolerably level valley, it is very difficult of access from the want of roads especially from the south. The arable land appears to be well adapted for the growth of turnips and is evidently a fertile soil, but from situation and climate it is unfavourable for the growth of corn and subject to much loss in backward seasons.

Bilsdale nearby

> lies in a narrow dale through which the River Rye takes its course, in the range of hills called the Hambleton Hills and the enclosed land which is only about one third of the extent of the parish extends from 2 to 5 fields breadth, on each side of the river in most parts ... The soil is generally good near the river but as it increases in altitude becomes of less value and productiveness and the moorland (about 1200 acres) is only fit for pasturage for the small black-faced sheep, and will not carry horned beasts.

The agricultural potential of lower ground was quite different. At Hornby, in the Vale of York, Robert Hart considered that

> the general aspect of the land is remarkably good, scarcely inferior to any in that extensive county – more than two thirds comprise some fine arable lands well adapted to the growth of turnips and barley (and to which they are successfully devoted) together with some rich and very productive pastures and meadow lands.

The upland/lowland distinction is a recurrent theme in local tithe agents' descriptions. Where land was high and exposed, the proportion of arable to pasture was small and farmers relied on stockbreeding. In fact both Richard Burton Phillipson and John Story Penleaze record numbers of stock, a rare occurrence in tithe districts for which 'arable' report forms were issued. Low farming is mentioned more often than high farming (see Subject Index) – the over-ploughing of limited areas of arable is a common complaint. Where high farming is noted, the credit is generally given to the landlord whose example was 'so fine'.

On heavy clay soils, a three-course rotation was general: summer fallow, wheat and oats, which could be extended where soil and drainage permitted by including a year or two of clover between the wheat and oats. At Cowesby, 'the system of farming is bad, a summer fallow, succeeded by meagre crops of 14 bush. wheat and 24 bush. oats, is slowly giving place to turnips, barley, pasture, wheat or oats'. Norfolk four-course systems were encountered on light soils but dead fallows were by no means uncommon in North Yorkshire even on such land so that only one corn crop would be obtained in the shift: corn, turnips, seeds, bare fallow. In areas of harshest climate and poorest soils, oats were the main grain crop but even these would not always ripen: at New Forest in the eastern Pennines, 'the arable land is exceedingly cold – and altho' sown with oats every second year they frequently are obliged to be cut up for the cattle without ripening'. Barley was not much grown; most of the comments on turnips (see Subject Index) bemoan the fact that so few were grown. Table 60 and the yield maps indicate the meagre returns obtained both overall and especially in higher districts. Only small acreages of potatoes were raised and these were generally for home consumption.

Cattle breeding was of particular significance in the uplands; Scotch, Irish and Durhams are the breeds recorded and the system of cattle raising is discussed at a number of places (see Subject Index). At Wensley, for example,

> the occupiers principally depend on pasturing and feeding stock viz, Scotch, Irish and native beasts, of which they generally buy two lots in the year, the first lot in the spring which is sold off at fall of the year fat, the second lot is purchased when these go off and are kept until the next spring.

Butter and cheese were the most important dairy products. Sheep breeding and sheep breeds are also topics which receive especial note in this county's files. Black-faced Scotch sheep were considered best able to survive the rigorous moorland conditions and sometimes they were crossed with Leicesters. On good lowland pastures Leicester and Tees Water sheep were bred. Lambs were either sold before winter or, if there was sufficient feed, some might be wintered and sold before clipping the following year.

Table 59 *Reports on agreements for commutation of tithes in Yorkshire, North Riding*

Assistant commissioner/ local tithe agent	1837	1838	1839	1840	1841	1842	1843	1844	1845	1846	1847	Totals
Charles Howard	2	19	53	1						1		76
Richard Burton Phillipson				19	13	3	2		3			40
Thomas Hoskins		31										31
Henry Pilkington		11			1	6	2	2	1			23
John Job Rawlinson		8	5		1							14
Robert Hart			4	6								10
John S. Donaldson Selby	1		2								1	4
John Story Penleaze			3									3
John Penny					2							2
Totals	3	69	67	26	17	9	4	2	4	1	1	203

Table 60 *Land use, crops and yields in Yorkshire, North Riding, c. 1836*

A	Land use	Percentage of total land area enumerated in reports on tithe agreements	Estimated acreage in whole county
	Arable	32.2	434,768
	Grass	48.2	650,770
	Wood	2.9	39,311
	Common	16.0	216,021

B	Crop	Mean percentage of arable	Mean yield per acre	Estimated acreage in whole county
	Wheat	23.6	19.4 bushels	102,668
	Barley	7.5	30.4 bushels	32,463
	Oats	17.0	29.4 bushels	74,010
	Pulses	4.8	18.6 bushels	20,995
	Turnips	9.1	£2.85	39,561
	Seeds	19.0	23.6 cwts	82,723
	Fallows	16.9	—	73,492

Yorkshire, North Riding

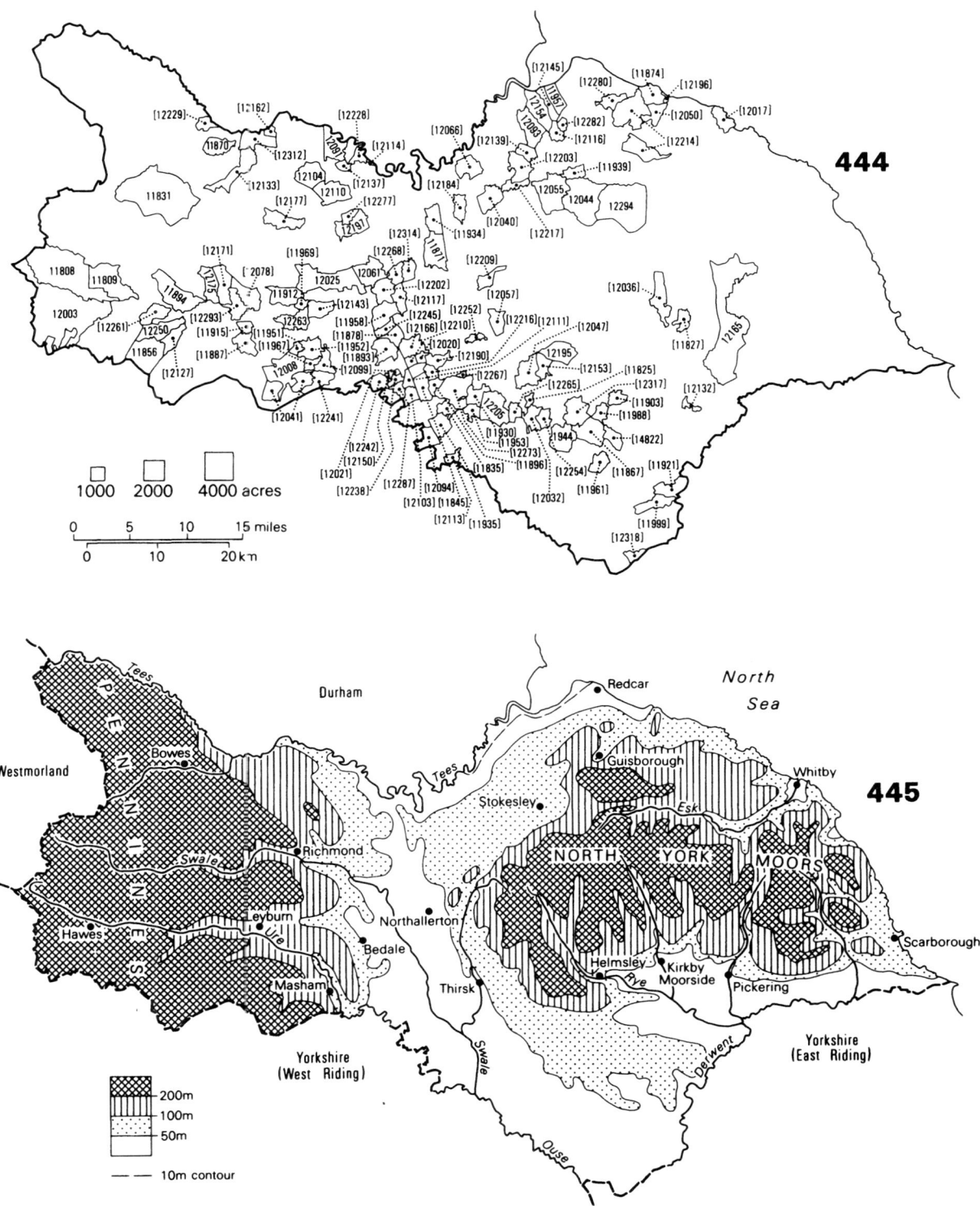

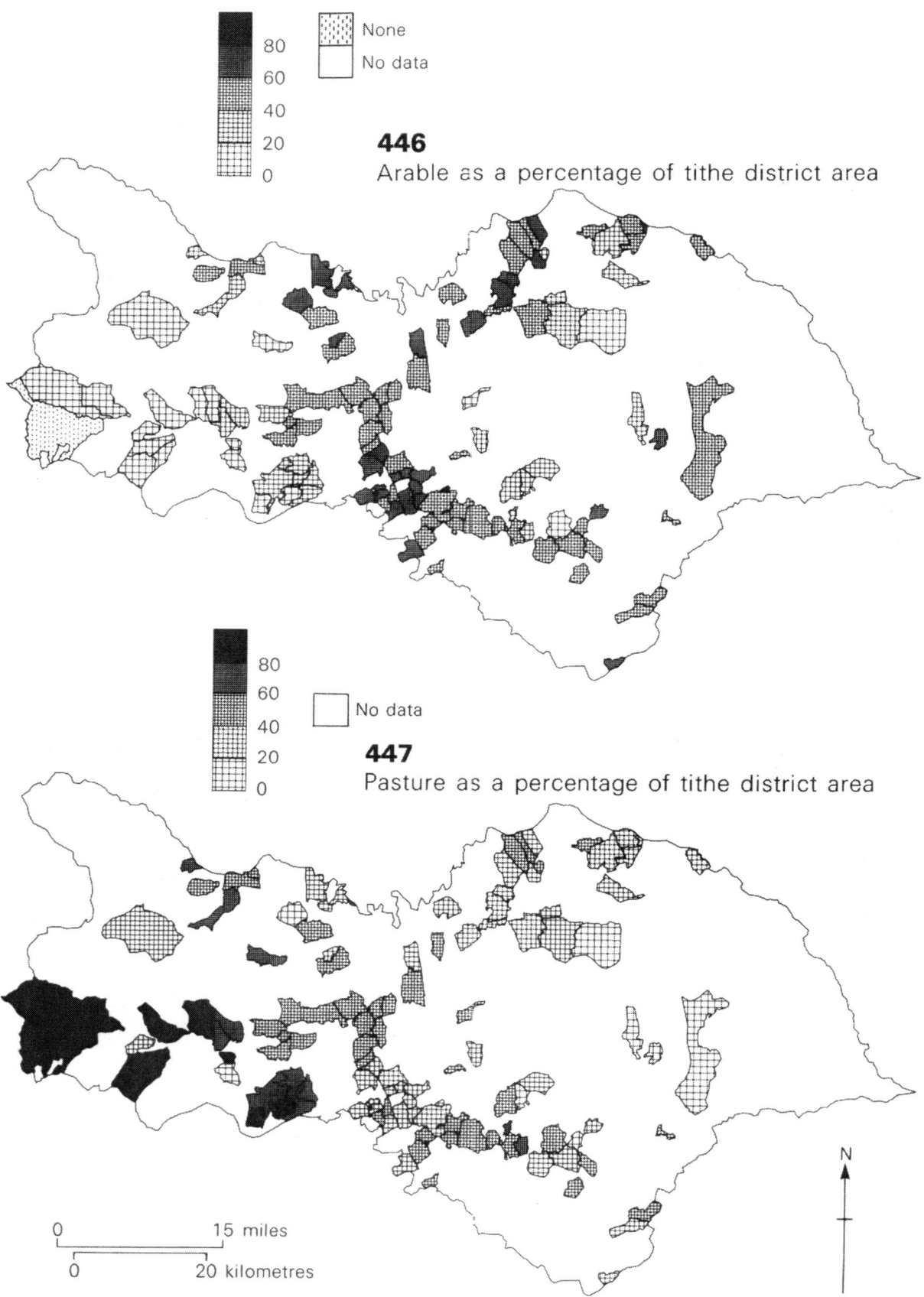

446 Arable as a percentage of tithe district area

447 Pasture as a percentage of tithe district area

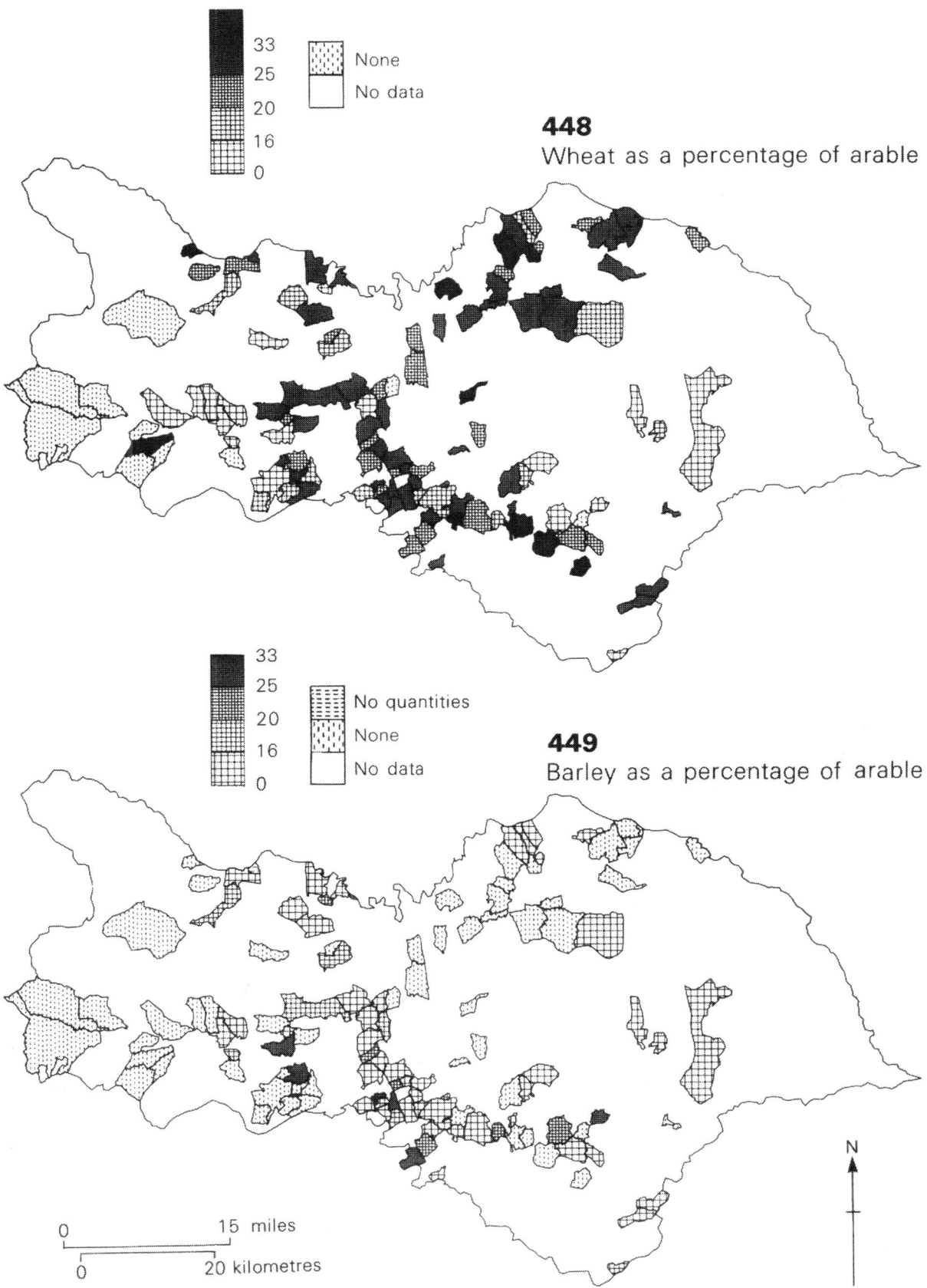

448 Wheat as a percentage of arable

449 Barley as a percentage of arable

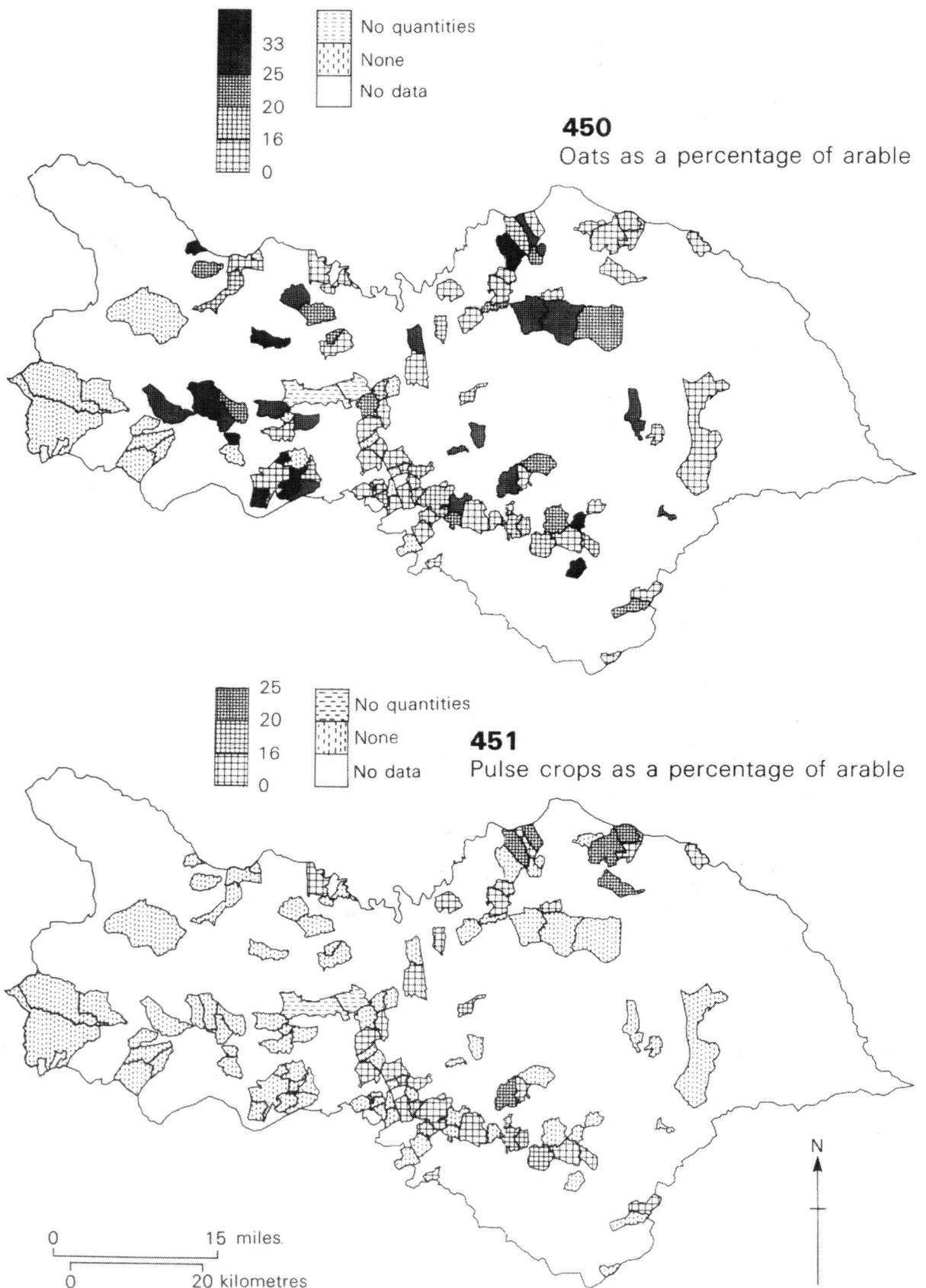

450 Oats as a percentage of arable

451 Pulse crops as a percentage of arable

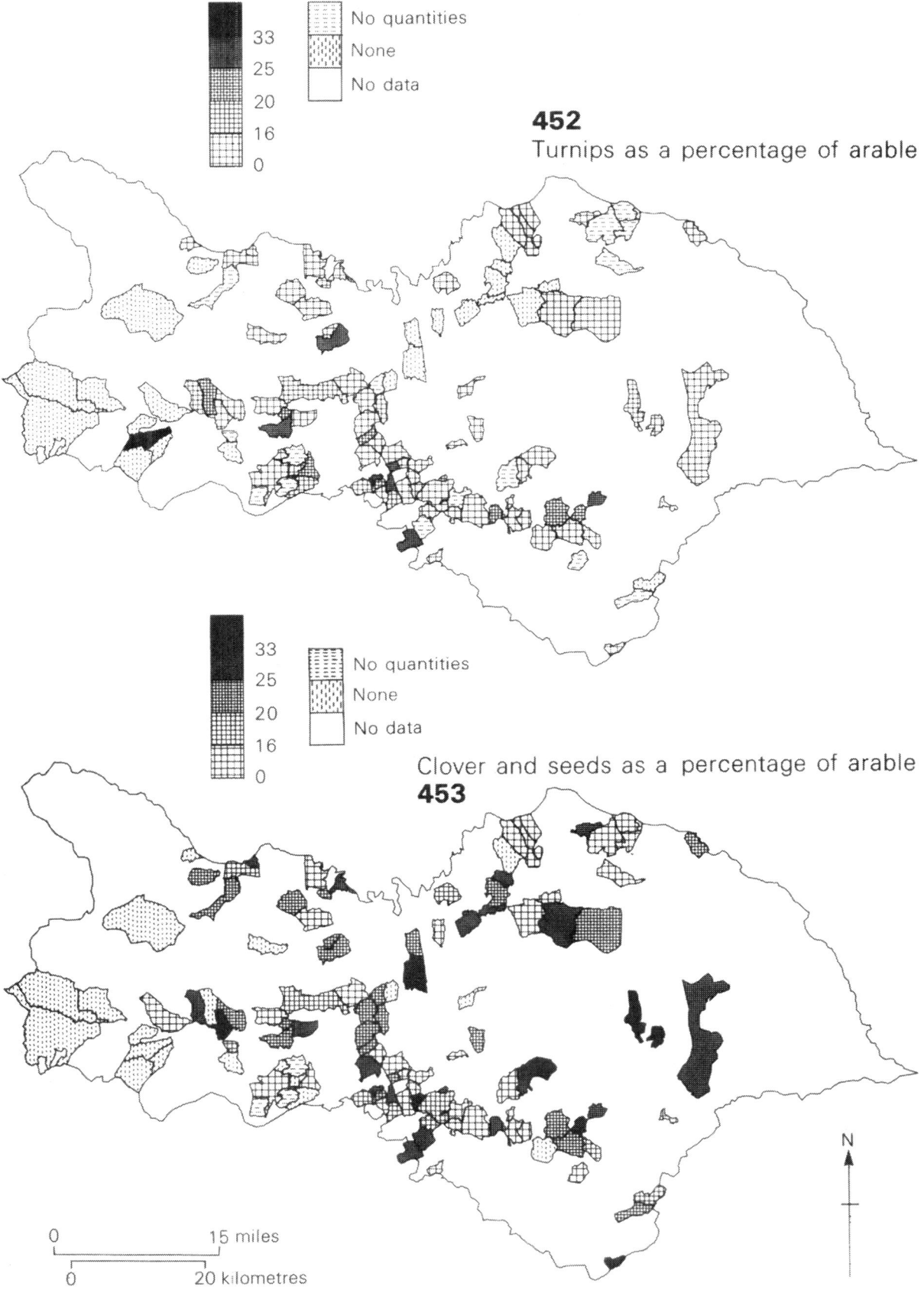

452 Turnips as a percentage of arable

453 Clover and seeds as a percentage of arable

Northern counties

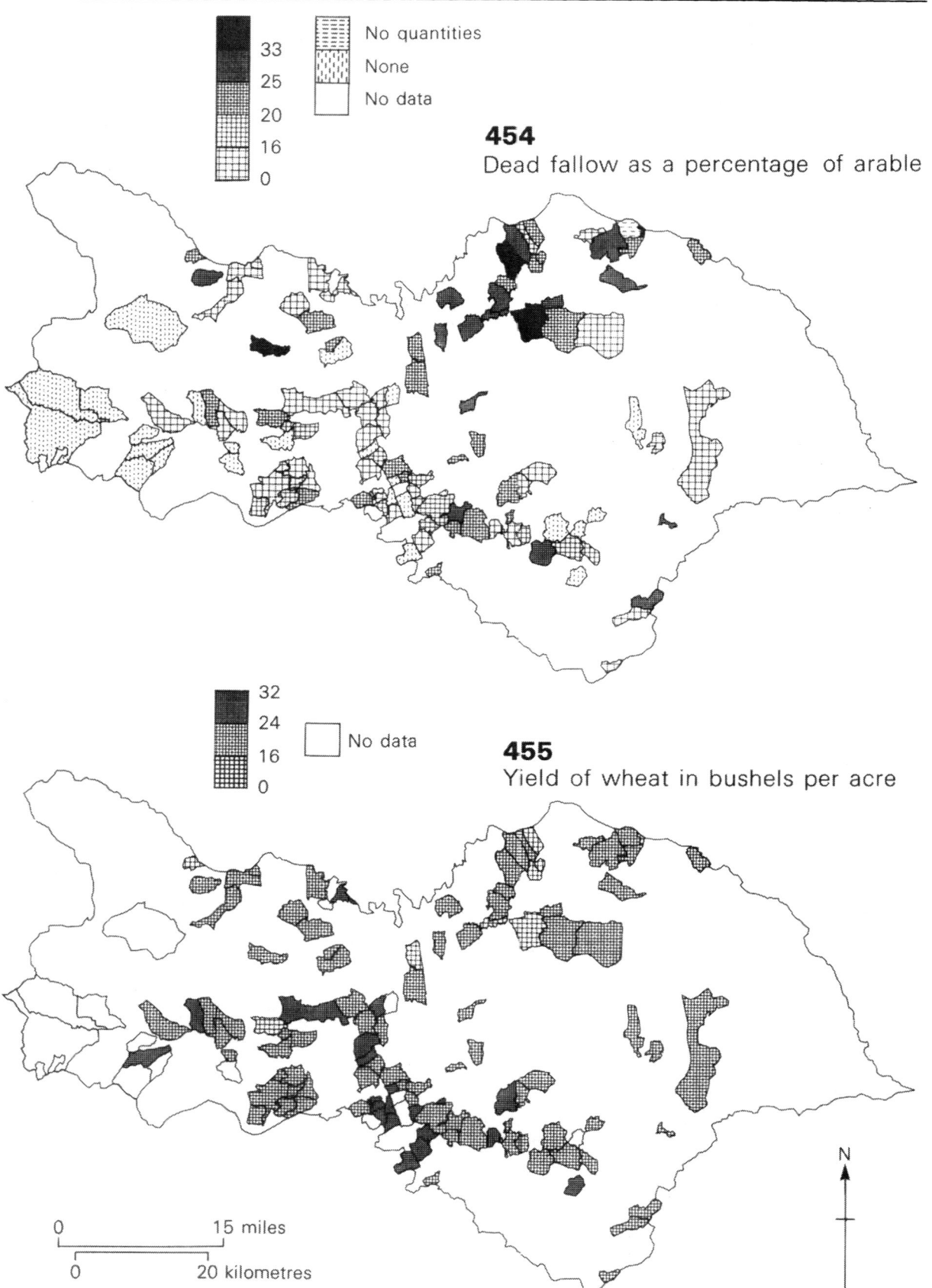

454 Dead fallow as a percentage of arable

455 Yield of wheat in bushels per acre

Yorkshire, North Riding

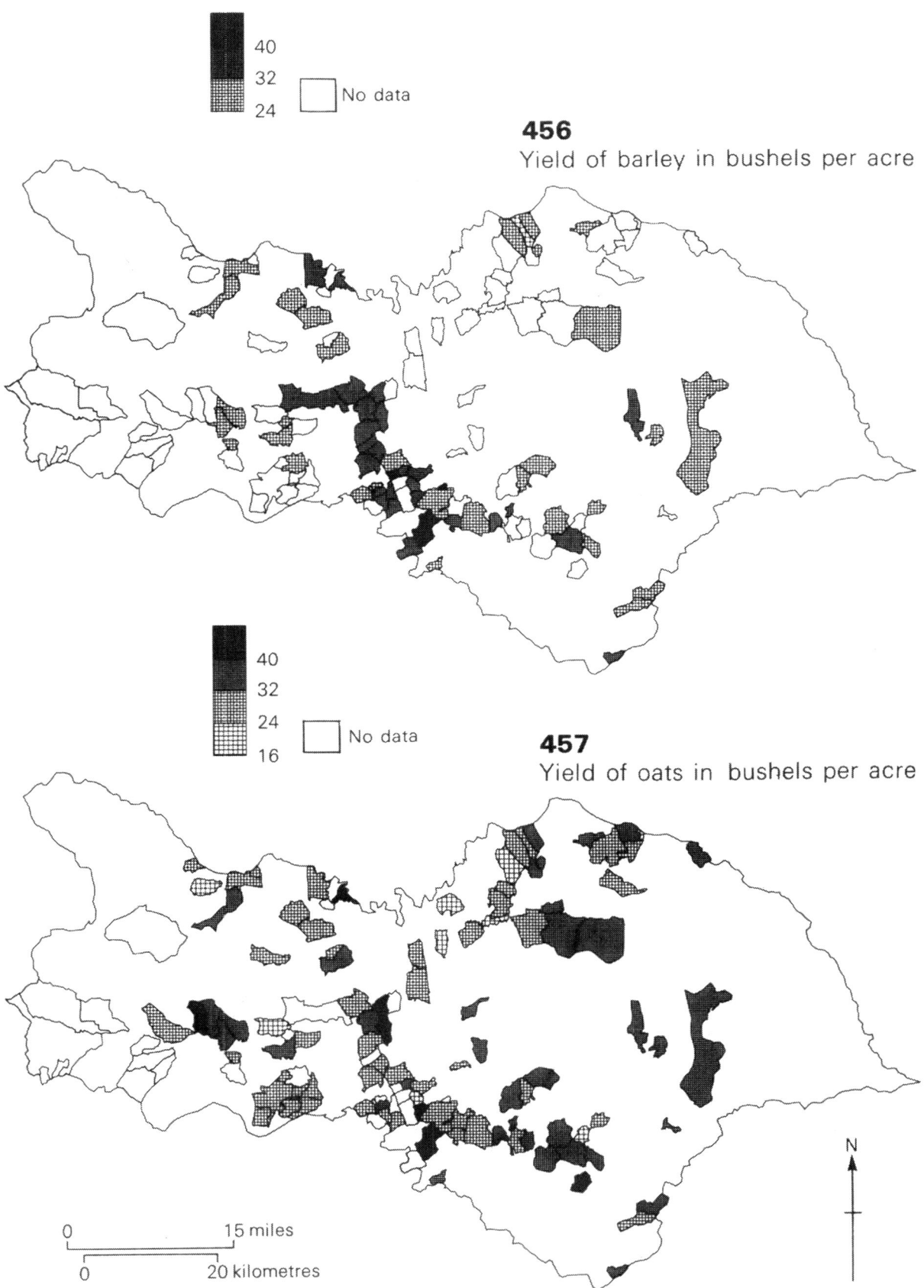

456 Yield of barley in bushels per acre

457 Yield of oats in bushels per acre

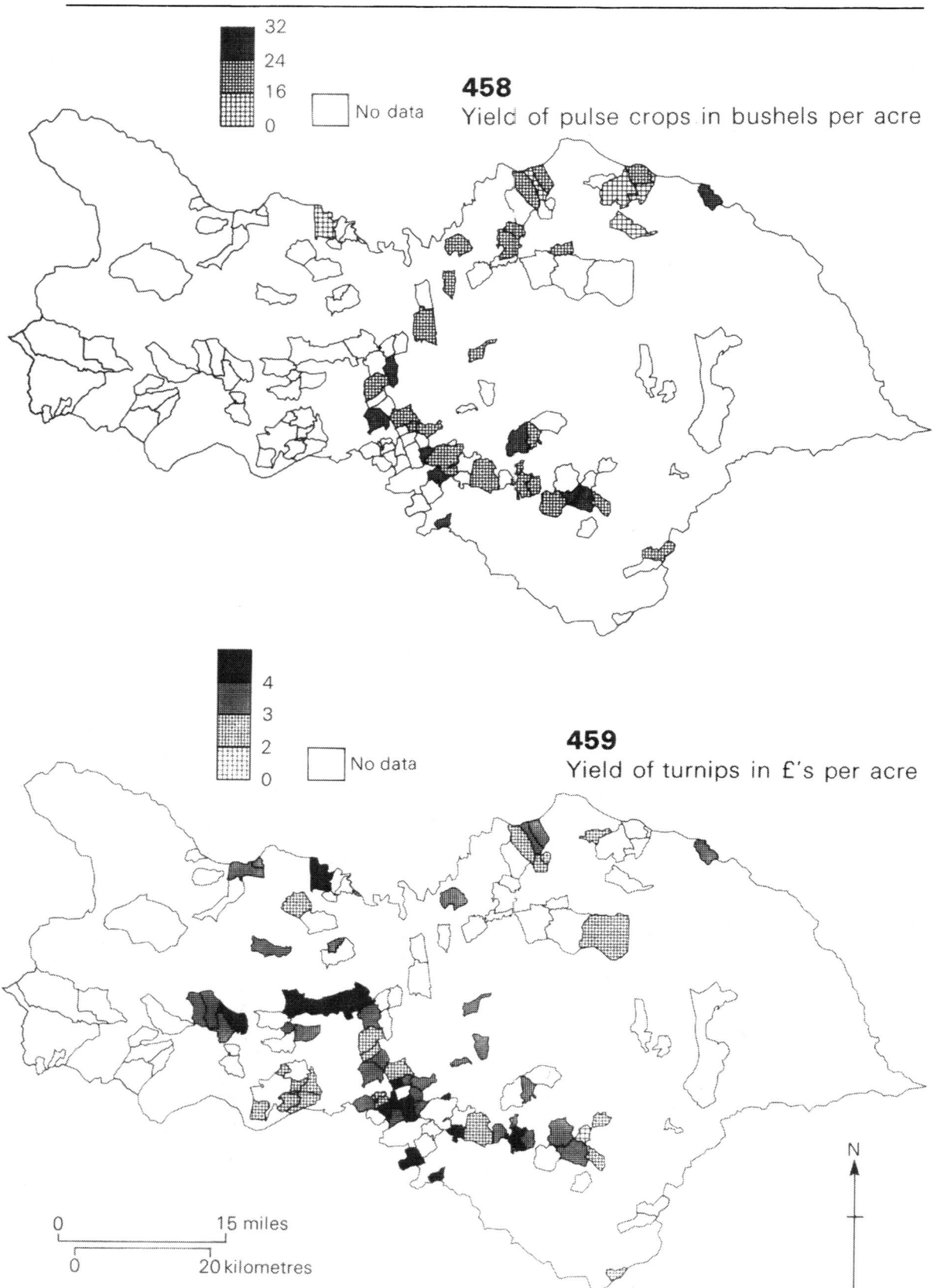

458 Yield of pulse crops in bushels per acre

459 Yield of turnips in £'s per acre

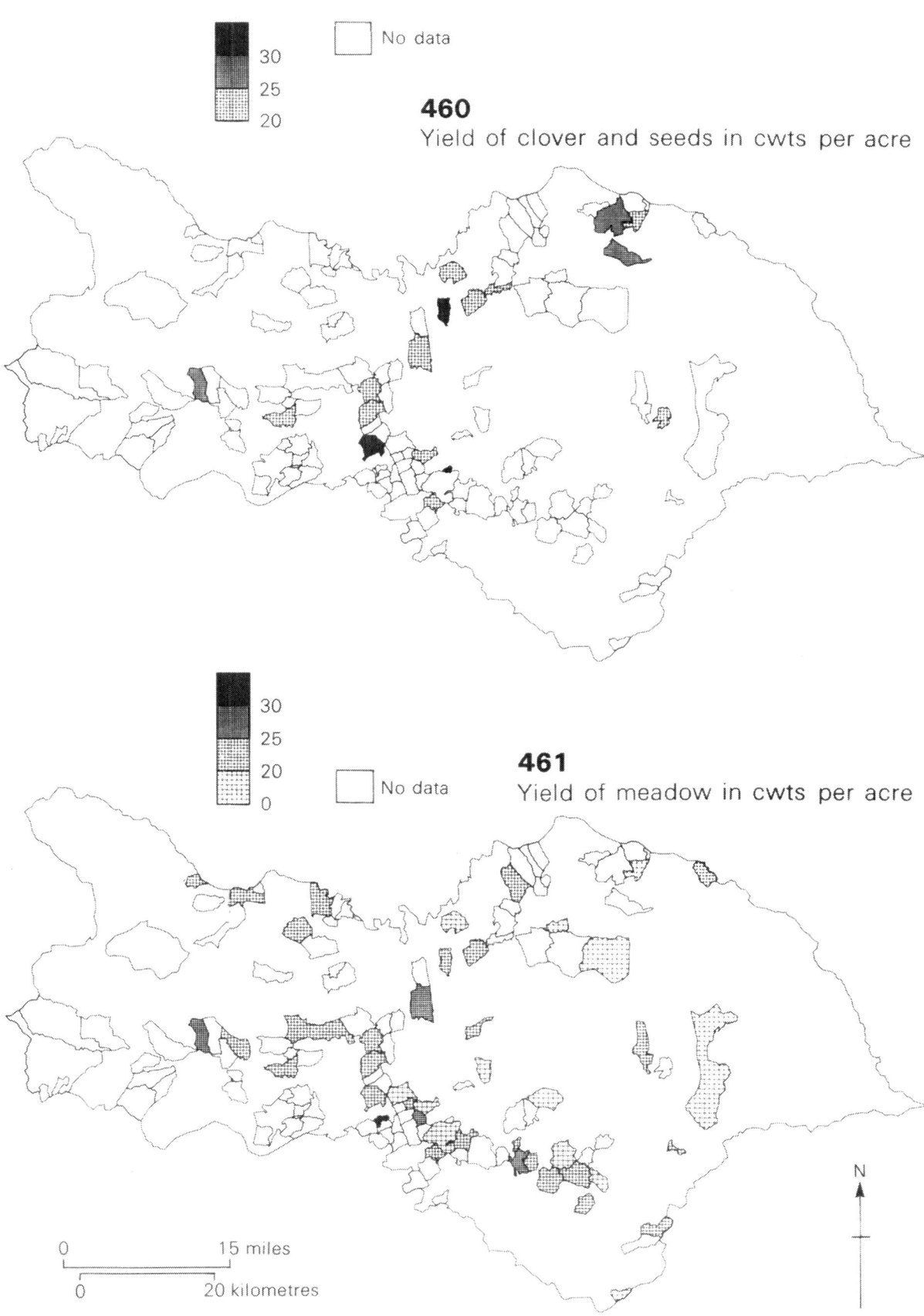

460 Yield of clover and seeds in cwts per acre

461 Yield of meadow in cwts per acre

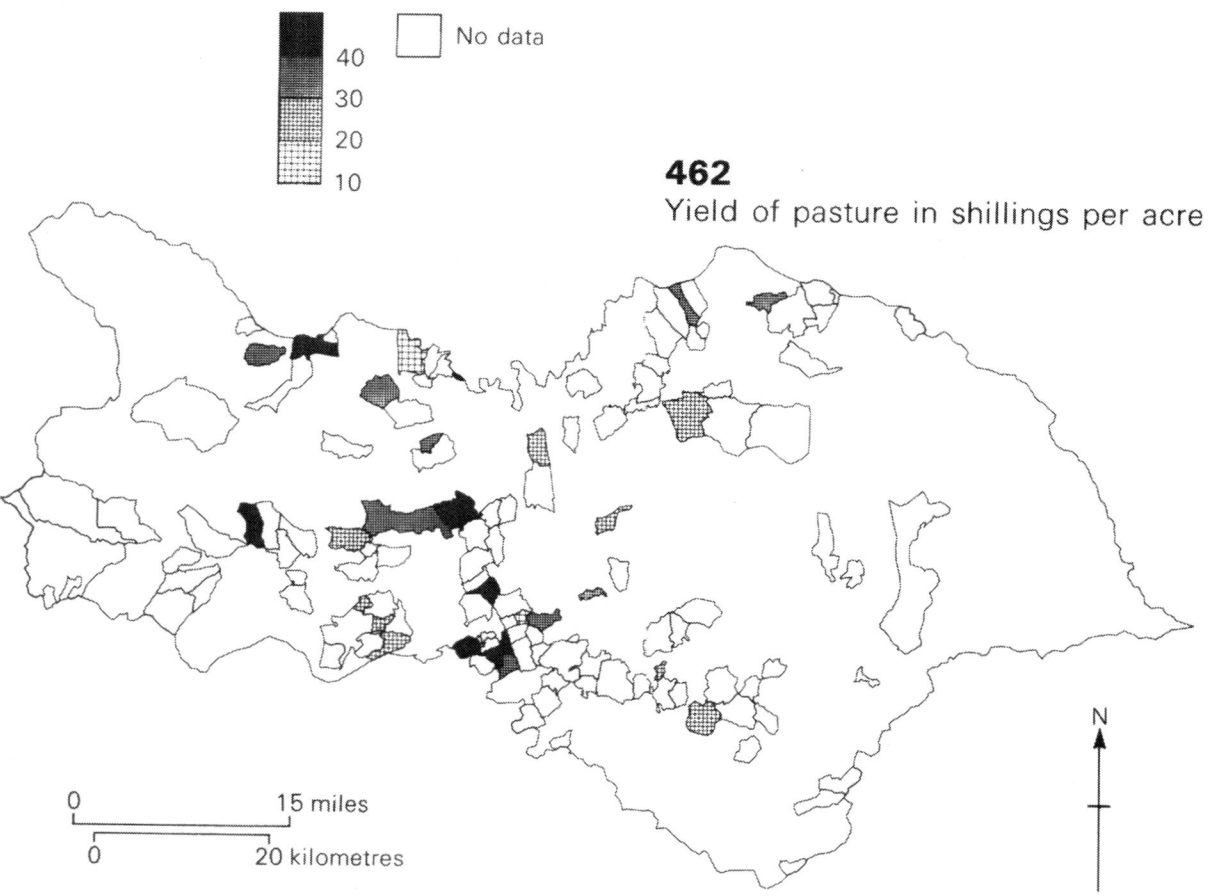

462
Yield of pasture in shillings per acre

Derbyshire

316 tithe districts
95 reports on tithe agreements

The distribution of arable land in a sample transect across Derbyshire has been plotted from tithe maps and apportionments by H. C. K. Henderson (1941) in connection with his Land Utilisation Survey report for this county.

Extinction of tithes, in many cases for land, at the time of parliamentary enclosure accounts for most of the forty-seven tithe free districts in Derbyshire in 1836. Fewer than a third of post-1836 commutations were effected by voluntary agreement and the process of voluntary commutation was also long-drawn-out in this county; 27 per cent of agreements were not reached until after 1840, and the last township was not assessed until 1846. The presence of moduses in lieu of arable tithes, hay and milking cows, claims of personal tithes on wives and housekeepers in some townships, and impending merger of tithe and land are the principal reasons for the need of compulsion and the length of the process. As in some other counties with large tracts of open upland moors, acreages of common land with perhaps trifling contributions to gross titheable produce are frequently absent in tithe valuations. This category of land is thus omitted from the maps and tables below, as are data on yields of turnips, clover and seeds, and pasture which are recorded for only nine, nineteen and one districts respectively.

Table 62 and the land use maps indicate the predominance of grassland in Derbyshire *c.* 1840, particularly in the Peak District where township after township is recorded with more than 80 per cent of titheable land in grass. The files contain very many descriptions of these upland landscapes and their meagre farming potential. John Pickering found the hamlet of Eyam Woodlands 'of a very rude and mountainous character but contains a few spots of fertile meadow and pasture'. At Stony Middleton, 'a considerable part of this township is so full of rock, that though highly favourable to a picturesque scenery, it is not of any value for other purposes – not even for planting'. Only in the lower parts of the county, particularly in the border areas east of Chesterfield and south of Burton-upon-Trent did the arable/pasture ratio rise above 1 to 1. The upland pastures supported a regular transhumance of cattle, a process described as follows by commissioner Richard Burton Phillipson at Castleton: 'it is the custom here, as in the whole neighbouring district, for the occupiers to take in great quantities of cattle to ley from May to November, from Yorkshire, Lancashire and other counties'. The best pastures and those close to mining settlements were used for dairying, but local tithe agents encountered fewer sheep than they expected in Derbyshire.

In those many townships with only small amounts of arable land, regular crop rotations were not encountered. At Staveley, 'crop after crop is taken till the land begins to appear exhausted and then it is laid down to grass for a number of years and fresh land is brought into tillage'. At Stony Middleton, there was 'no corn but oats, and these sown with such inattention to system, that the crops of them generally follow for two successive years in addition to the first – then fallow with turnips for the cattle chiefly; potatoes insignificant, and those for the family use'. At Carsington, 'the main object being the dairy, only a small portion is permitted to be ploughed, and this has the peculiarity of being sown, year by year, with the same corn – oats'. For Derbyshire as a whole, wheat and oats were grown to almost equal extent; yields of both were fairly low on the whole, for wheat the climate in the Peak 'being too cold to ripen it to a good sample'. Very little barley was sown and only a dozen or so townships grew peas or beans and these only in very small quantities (Maps 468–74). Bare fallows were still very common; at Holbrook south-east of Belper, Thomas Martin remarked: 'the fallows are almost wholly without turnips etc. – too generally the custom in Derbyshire'. At Longford, Roger Kynaston, a commissioner of mainly East Anglian and Home Counties commutation experience, 'did not observe any tares growing on their fallow; and to my surprise, the person who accompanied me told me that they were never grown'. In fact assistant commissioners and local tithe agents were much struck by the general backwardness of much Derbyshire farming. They found little to remark on by way of improvement; very many townships seemed on the whole self-sufficient in crops, producing just enough corn and potatoes for their own consumption. Instances of low farming outnumber those of high farming; the sentiments of Thomas Martin's observation at Beard, Ollersett, Whittle and Thornsett are by no means unique in Derbyshire tithe files: 'nothing seems to be known of the science of farming. Land once ploughed is usually ploughed as long as it will bear it.'

Derbyshire

Table 61 *Reports on agreements for commutation of tithes in Derbyshire*

Assistant commissioner/ local tithe agent	1837	1838	1839	1840	1841	1842	1843	1844	1845	1846	Totals
Richard Burton Phillipson			7	4		4	2	3		1	21
Thomas Martin		5	2	9		1	3				20
John Holder					7	2	3				12
John Pickering			10	2							12
Roger Kynaston		8									8
Edward Greathed		7									7
Thomas Smith Woolley	1	2	2								5
Horace William Meteyard			4								4
John Job Rawlinson			4								4
Henry Pilkington		1									1
Thomas Sudworth		1									1
Totals	1	24	29	15	7	7	8	3		1	95

Table 62 *Land use, crops and yields in Derbyshire c. 1836*

A	Land use	Percentage of total land area enumerated in reports on tithe agreements	Estimated acreage in whole county
	Arable	25.3	166,426
	Grass	62.0	408,587
	Wood	7.1	46,649

B	Crop	Mean percentage of arable	Mean yield per acre	Estimated acreage in whole county
	Wheat	24.4	22.3 bushels	40,653
	Barley	6.4	29.4 bushels	10,619
	Oats	24.2	30.6 bushels	40,235
	Pulses	2.3	27.6 bushels	3,782
	Turnips	6.7	£3.22	11,188
	Seeds	21.1	24.6 cwts	35,109
	Fallows	14.3	—	23,763

Northern counties

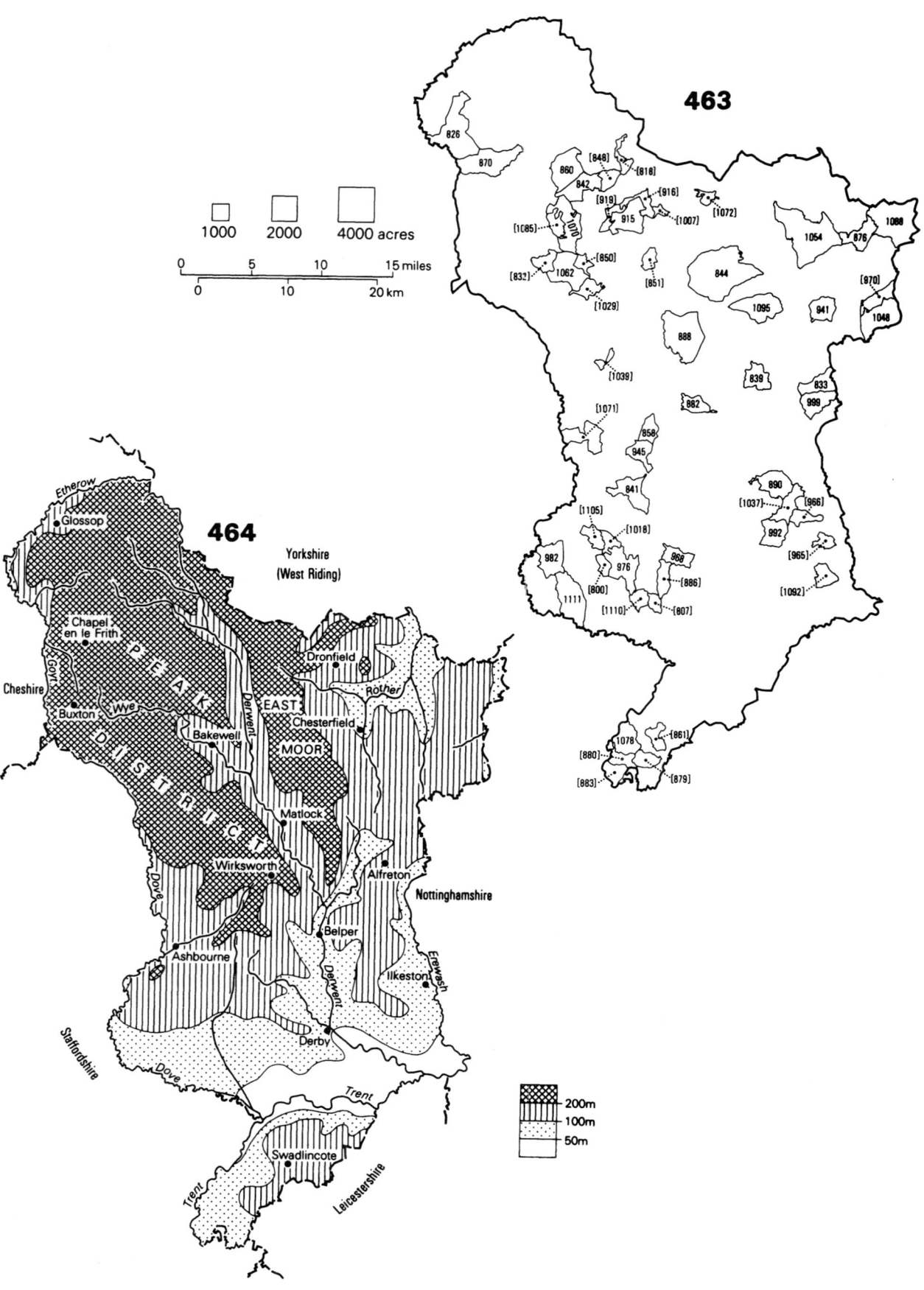

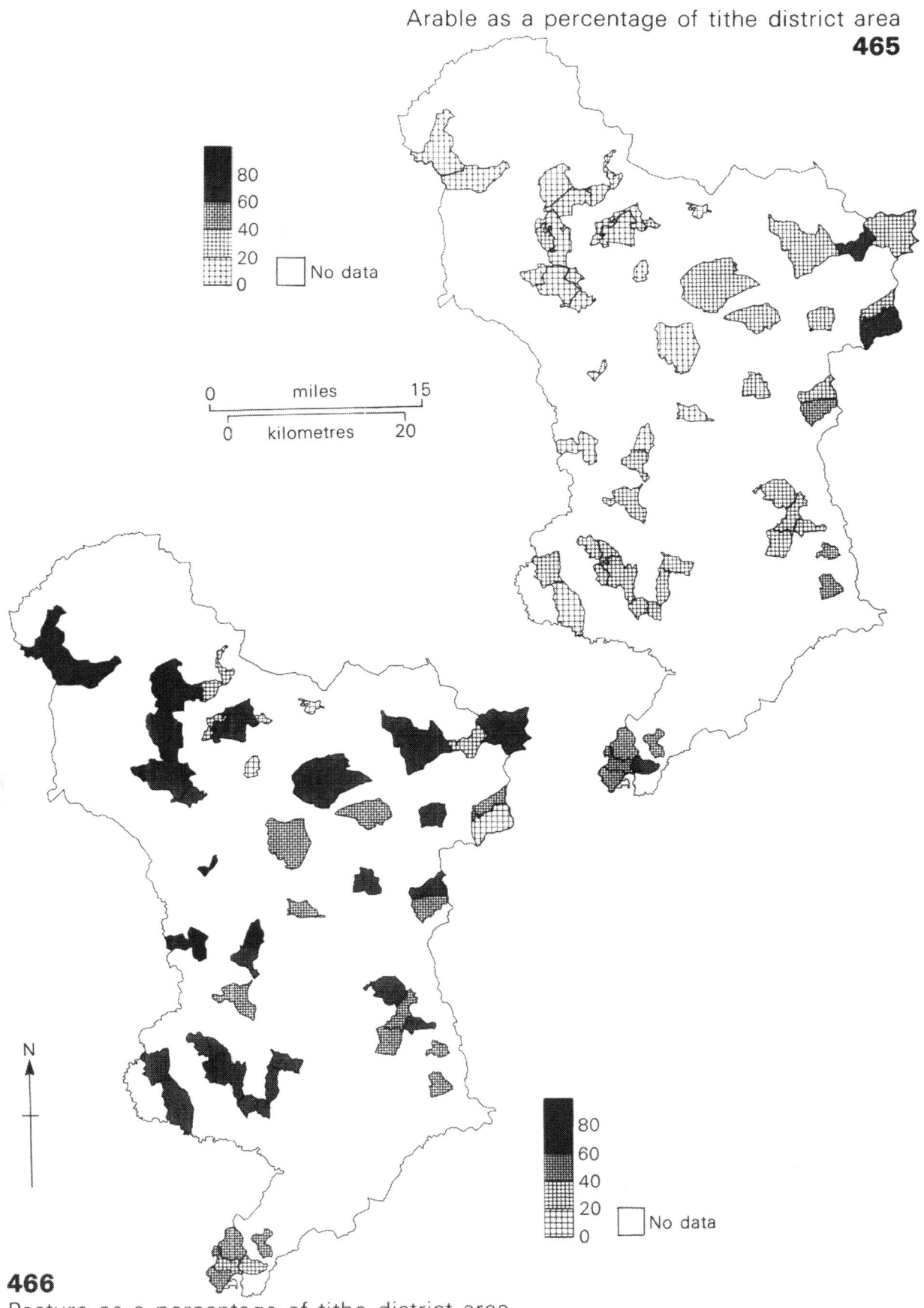

465 Arable as a percentage of tithe district area

466 Pasture as a percentage of tithe district area

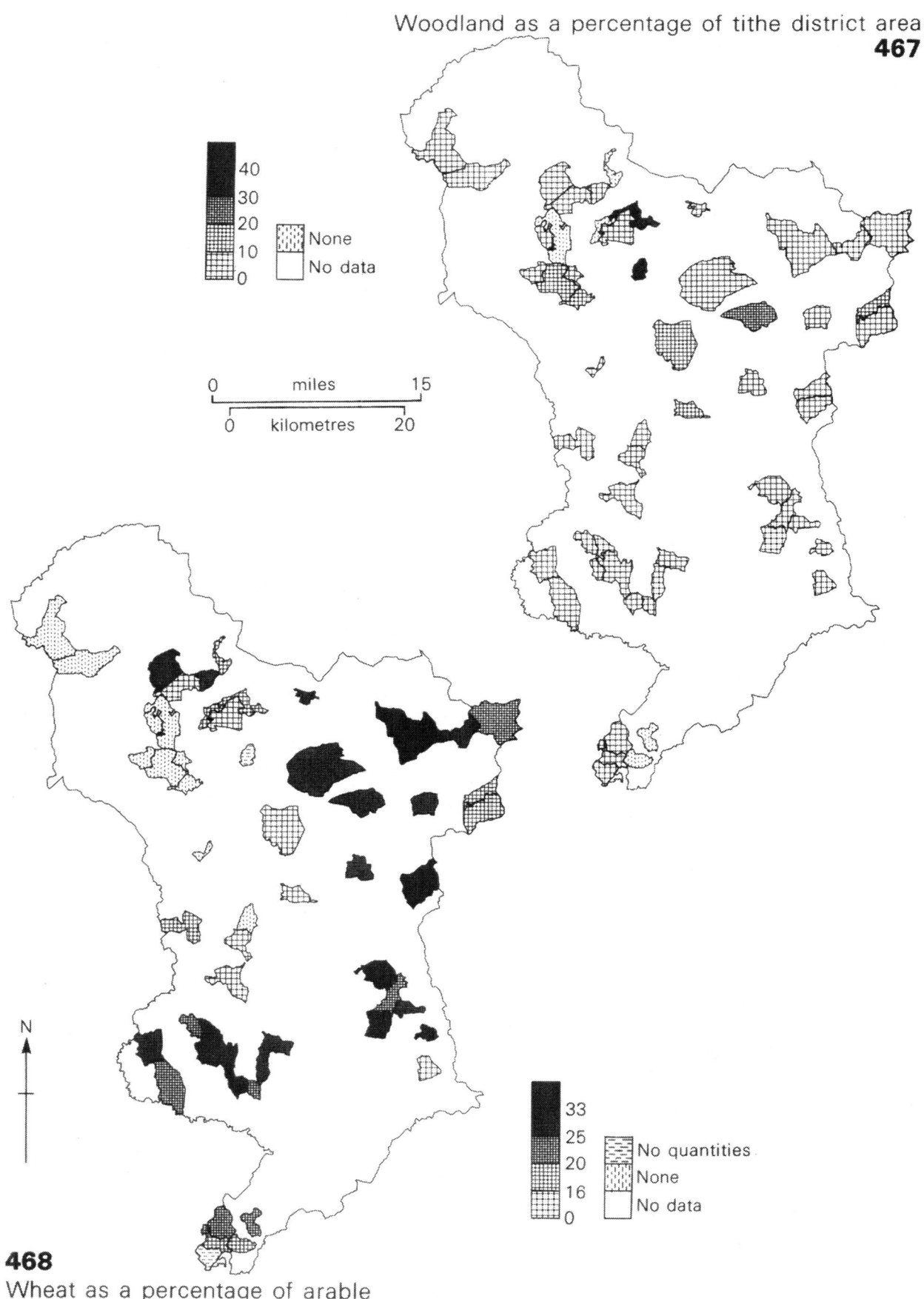

467 Woodland as a percentage of tithe district area

468 Wheat as a percentage of arable

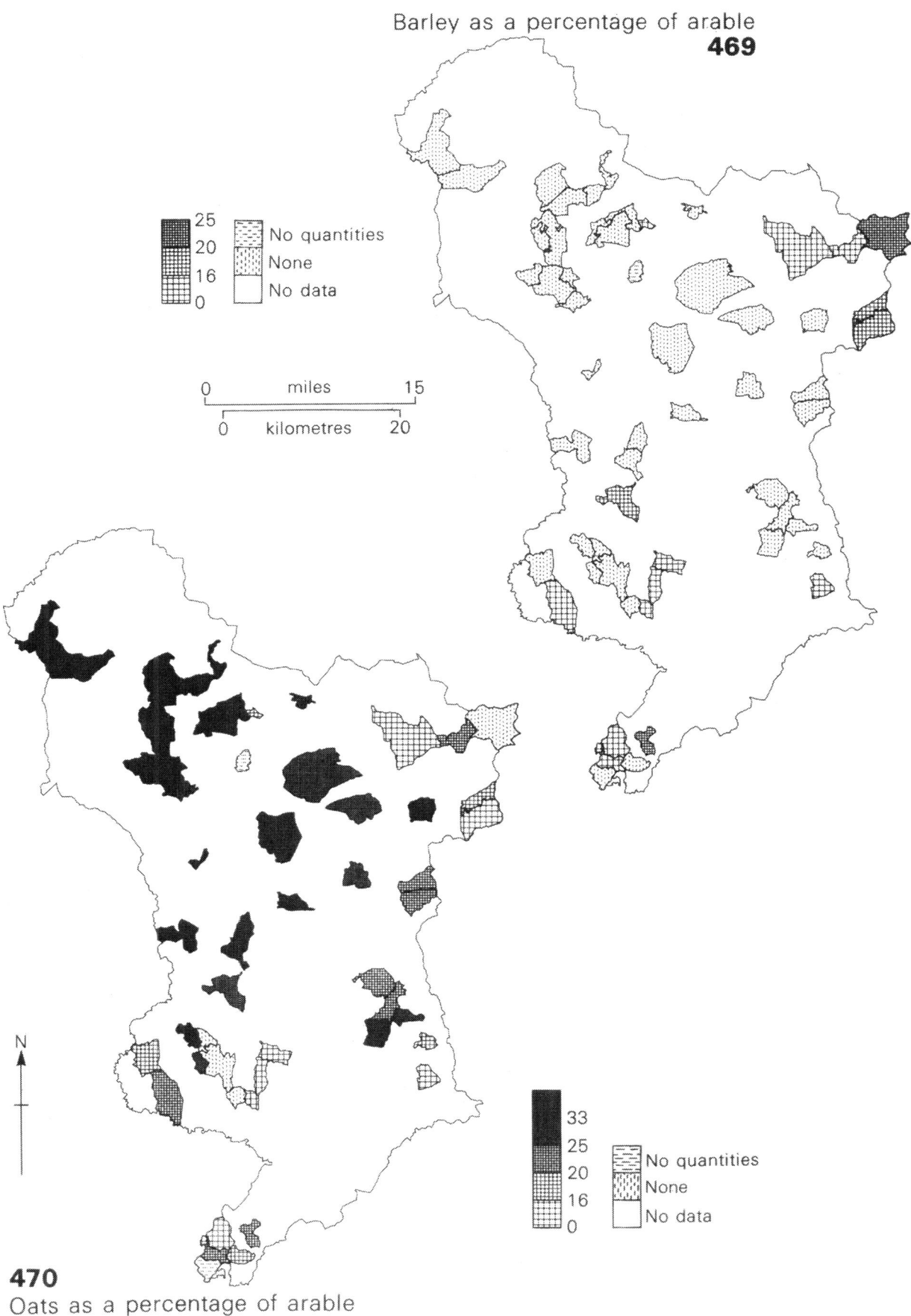

469 Barley as a percentage of arable

470 Oats as a percentage of arable

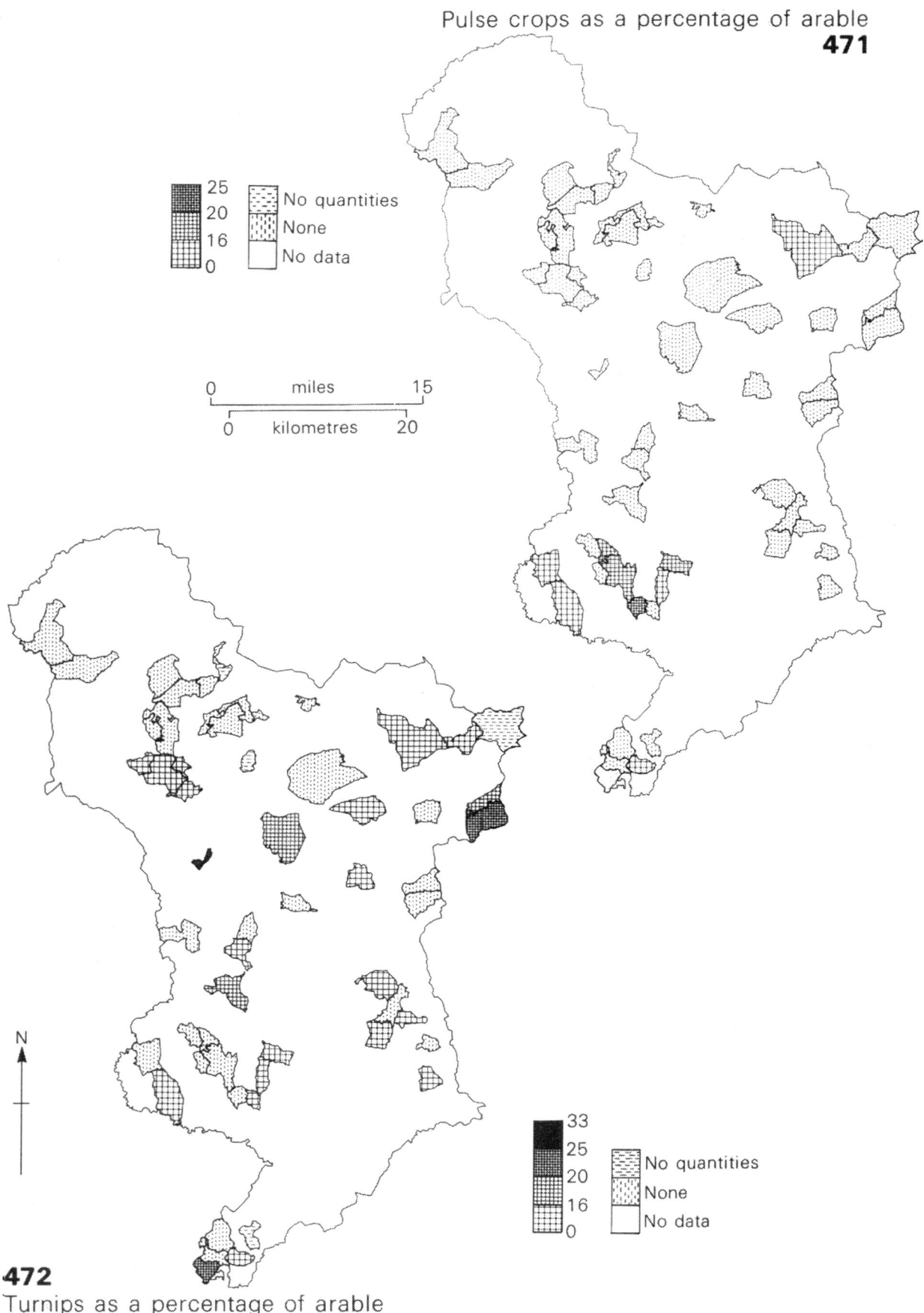

471 Pulse crops as a percentage of arable

472 Turnips as a percentage of arable

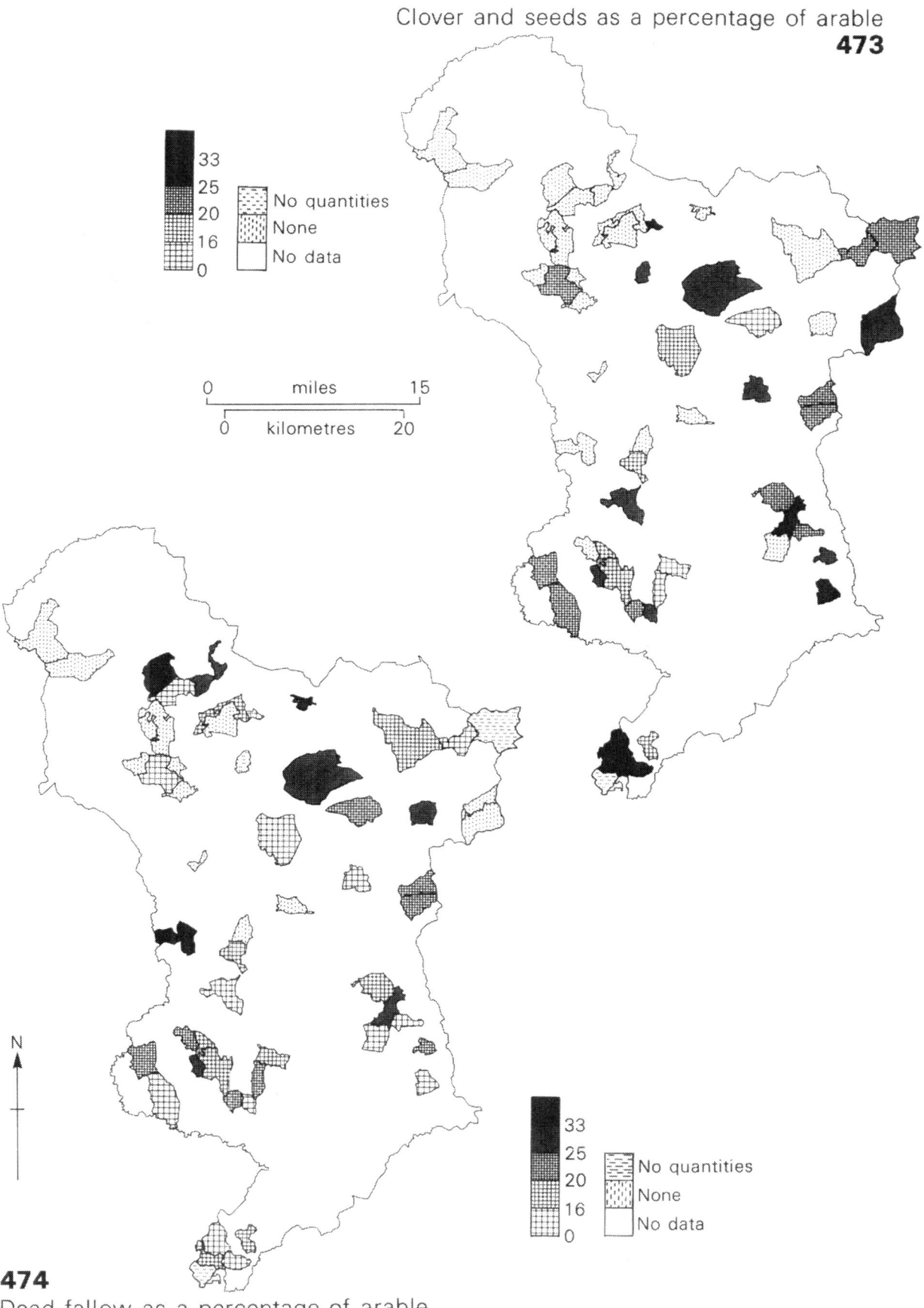

473 Clover and seeds as a percentage of arable

474 Dead fallow as a percentage of arable

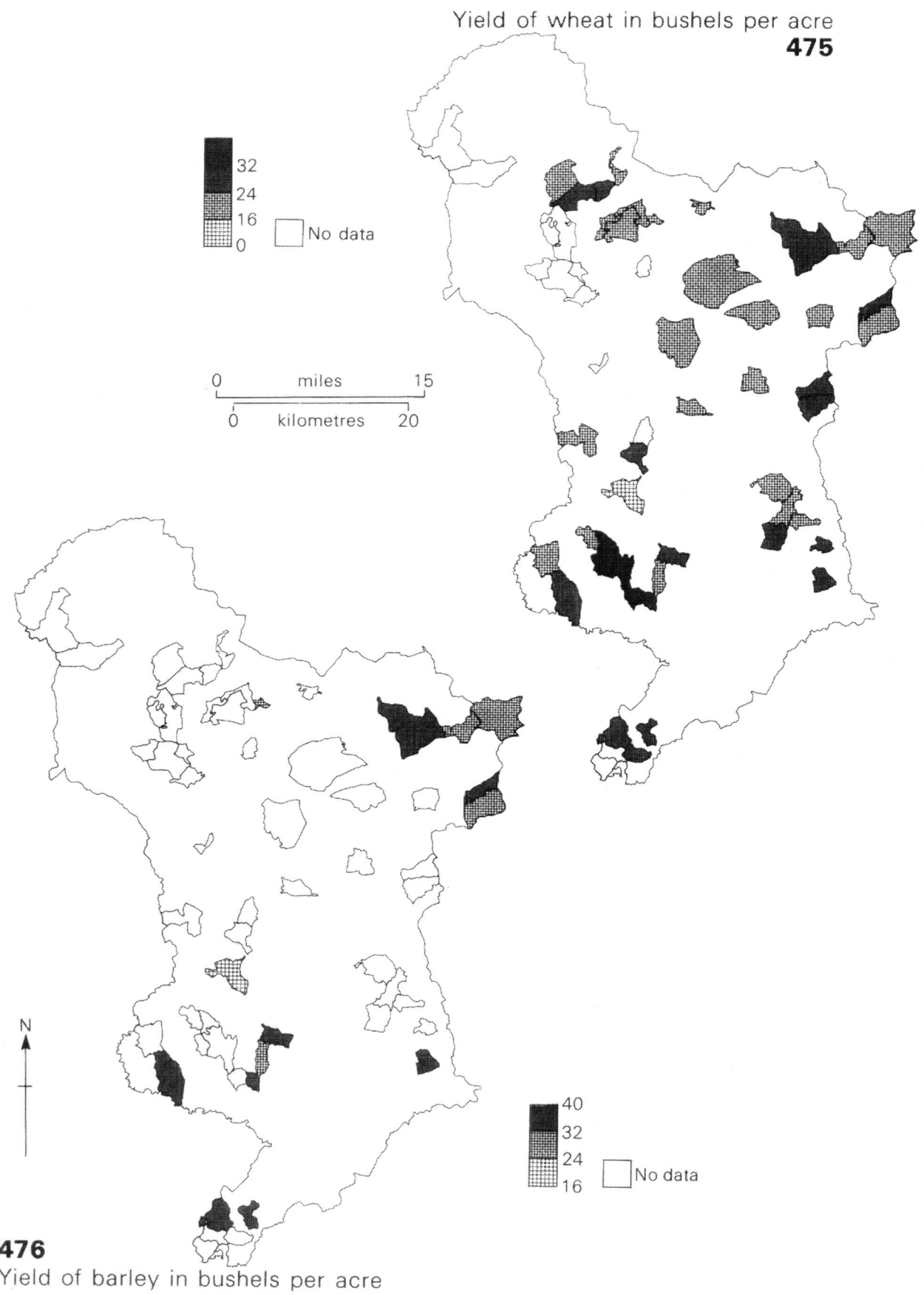

475 Yield of wheat in bushels per acre

476 Yield of barley in bushels per acre

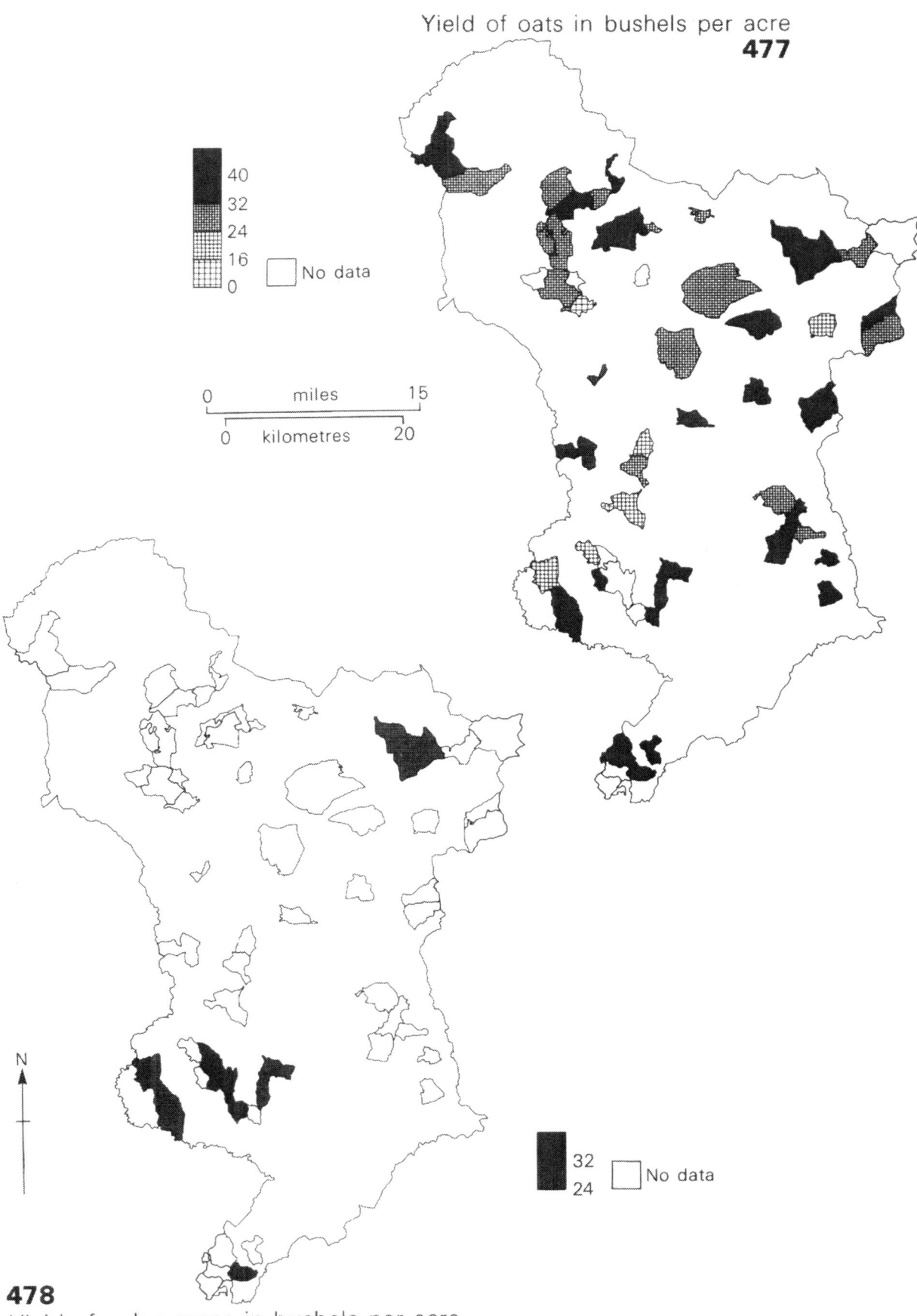

477 Yield of oats in bushels per acre

478 Yield of pulse crops in bushels per acre

479
Yield of meadow in cwts per acre

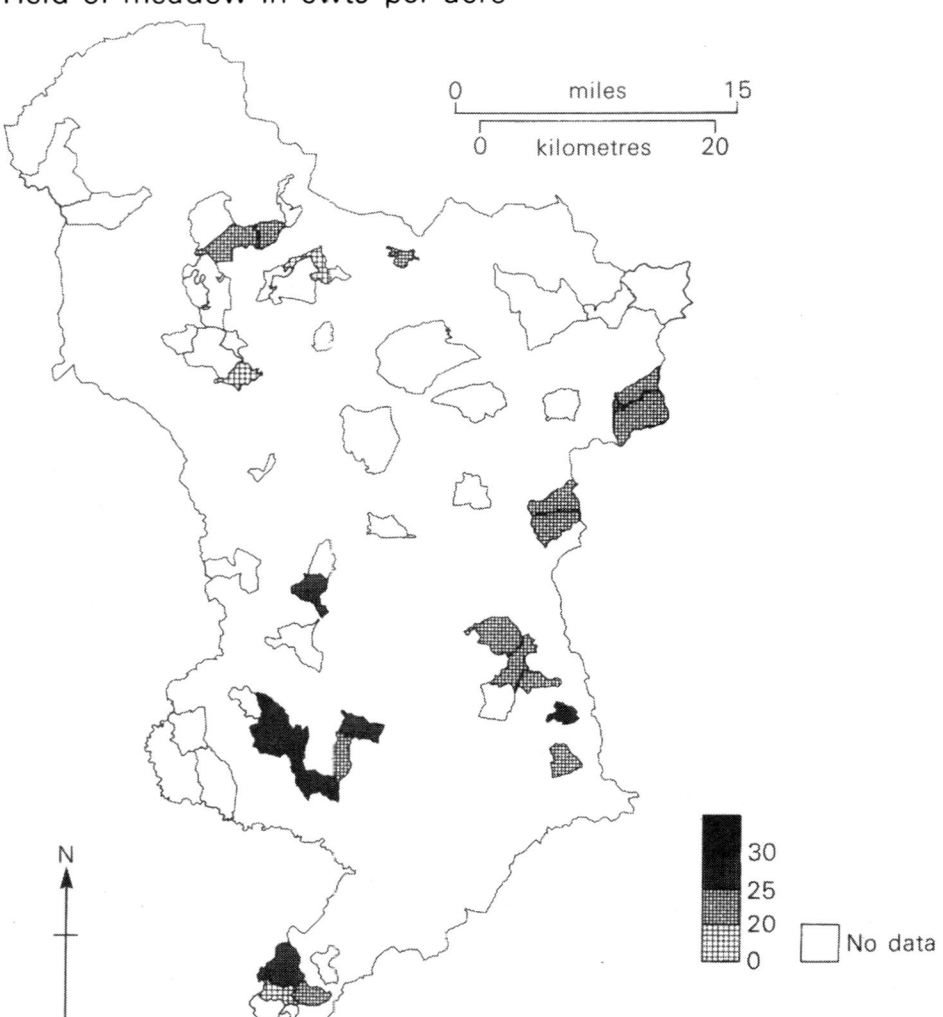

Nottinghamshire

278 tithe districts
50 reports on tithe agreements

Tithe had been extinguished by enclosure acts in 120 Nottinghamshire parishes by 1836. Copies of these acts are preserved in some tithe files but more usually there are summary minutes of inquiries made by assistant tithe commissioners to ascertain that tithes were no longer due (see Place Index). Nottinghamshire files appear to have been more heavily weeded than in most other counties; that for Clayworth contains the articles of a tithe agreement but no report is extant. Only twenty-five reports with cropping data cover at least 90 per cent of tithe district total area. Furthermore, this 9 per cent sample is heavily biased in favour of those still unenclosed parishes. These data are not, therefore, aggregated to produce county-wide estimates, nor are they mapped. A. D. M. Phillips' (1976) study of agricultural land use and soil types in Nottinghamshire extends this very limited tithe file data base by exploiting parish land use estimates in tithe apportionments.

The written record of farming preserved in Nottinghamshire files is much richer than the coverage of statistical data. Files for a number of parishes where Richard Burton Phillipson drafted compulsory awards contain valuations of crops and lengthy discussions of farming practices (see Place Index). In the body of written evidence as a whole (see Subject Index), comments on high farming outnumber those on low farming; on open arable land, three-course rotations of wheat, beans and fallow are most frequently reported; the Norfolk four-course is the rotation numerically most discussed; and in enclosed parishes on both heavy and light soils this might be extended to a five-course by allowing seeds to remain for two years.

The file for Cuckney, south-west of Worksop, contains one of the fullest discussions of woodland management encountered anywhere in the country. Underwood was generally productive in Nottinghamshire; John Pickering records values of 30–40 shillings per year's cut, although a decline in hop growing was resulting in a decreased demand for wood. Of industrial crops, ozier beds were titheable in Nottinghamshire and their management receives extended comment in the files of Rolleston and Thorpe tithe districts.

Table 63 *Reports on agreements for commutation of tithes in Nottinghamshire*

Assistant commissioner/ local tithe agent	1837	1838	1839	1840	1841	1842	1843	1844	1845	Totals
John Pickering		11	6							17
Thomas Smith Woolley	1	10			1					12
Richard Burton Phillipson				1	1	2	1		2	7
John Mee Mathew			5							5
John Job Rawlinson					3					3
Charles Howard		2								2
Horace William Meteyard			2							2
Robert Hart				1						1
John Holder					1					1
Totals	1	23	13	2	6	2	1		2	50

York City and Ainsty

36 tithe districts
7 reports on tithe agreements

Parishes within the city of York and a further six townships in this, the smallest 'county' unit used by the Tithe Commission for administering tithe commutation, were tithe free. Compulsory commutations were required in three-quarters of titheable districts.

Table 64 *Reports on agreements for commutation of tithes in York City and Ainsty*

Assistant commissioner/ local tithe agent	1837	1838	1839	1845	Total
Charles Howard	1	3	2	1	7

Yorkshire, East Riding

352 tithe districts
74 reports on tithe agreements

In his seminal study of rural landscape changes in the East Riding of Yorkshire, Alan Harris (1961) carefully analysed tithe apportionment land use estimates and constructed a map of arable and grass acreages in Holderness.

Almost a third of East Riding tithe districts had been exonerated from tithes under the terms of enclosure acts. After 1836, voluntary commutation was achieved in only 30 per cent of remaining titheable districts. A high incidence of compulsory commutation is not unusual in counties much affected by parliamentary enclosure as in many tithe districts, and here the East Riding was no exception; only small patches of early enclosed land remained subject to tithes. In such instances, there was rarely any great incentive for either party to come together to commute an inconsequential liability. However, evidence in the files suggests that the effect of such understandable reticence was compounded by the fact that the process of commutation once started did not always run smoothly in the East Riding. Both George Louis and Richard Burton Phillipson comment on the high value of tithes claimed in many districts which they visited (see especially their discussions of contestations at Aldbrough and Kirkby Grindalyth) and the huge bulk of minutes from some award meetings, Waghen (Wawne) is a good example, testify to jealously guarded rights. Here no fewer than three of the Tithe Commission's men were involved. First John Thompson at the Tithe Office in London questioned the valuation of impropriate and vicarial tithes made by a Mr Atkinson. Robert Page inspected this, criticised the valuation in detail and reported. There was then an appeal and the matter was not settled until Thomas Smith Woolley went to Waghen to decide what, if any, benefit should accrue to the tithe owner from Holderness drainage. Besides the existence of complicated cases such as the above, there is plenty of evidence of long-standing bitterness as well. At Owborough, Charles Howard recounted his personal experience:

> many years ago more than one half of this small township was in the hands of the reporter (as a trustee), the lay titheowner had been accustomed to draw the tithes in kind for the advantage of his own estate and refuses to let them on composition; in consequence of which refusal the reporter laid down the whole estate to grass and let the lands to a tenant occupying a tithe free farm under the same proprietor, consequently the tithe was nominal for 8 or 10 years.

When reports for districts with large tracts of tithe free land and those where Charles

Howard neglected to state acreages are eliminated, the number of districts with useable data falls to only thirty-six or just 10 per cent of all districts. Thus the figures in Table 66 should be treated with some caution and should be viewed only as indicators of the general balance of land use and of the rank order of crops.

East Riding files contain much descriptive comment on farming practices. On light soils, four- and five-course rotations are recorded most often, usually these were: wheat or oats, turnips, barley and then seeds for either one or two years to complete the course. On strong soils, rotations were of three- or four-courses as at Menethorpe where 'the usual course of farming is summer fallow, wheat, oats or beans; – clover being sometimes introduced after the wheat. This mode of husbandry is the general practice of the neighbourhood on similar soils.' Low farming was noted in several tithe districts (see Subject Index) especially where open fields remained and land needed draining. In addition to enclosure and drainage, three other areas of improvement caught the attention of Tithe Commission reporters in the East Riding. On chalk soils, as at Wharram-le-Street, 'the farming is a fair average of the Yorkshire Wolds. It has been much improved within the last 20 years, since the introduction of the Swedish turnip and bones, and it is one of those soils on which the efficiency of bones (which are here very extensively used) is most visible.' On sandy soils, as at Sutton on Derwent, 'though there is nothing very high in the farming the produce has been much increased within a few years by the cultivation of the heath land which was principally barren or rabbit warren, the principal produce is rye and wheat mixed and oats'. But most spectacular and occasioning much dispute about tithe liability (see above) was draining and warping in the Humber and Ouse valleys. Characteristic of assistant tithe commissioners' comments are Charles Howard's at Blacktoft in 1837:

> A part of the land has been rendered highly and permanently valuable by a process known as 'warping', that is by repeatedly admitting the muddy water from the Ouse to flow over and settle its sediment upon it, thus forming a new surface of extremely rich soil to the depth of from six to twelve inches. The whole of Blacktoft is capable of this improvement but the expense of it is very considerable, not infrequently exceeding £20 per acre.

Neither grassland and livestock management nor woodland and other land uses occasioned much comment in East Riding files (see Subject Index).

Table 65 *Reports on agreements for commutation of tithes in Yorkshire, East Riding*

Assistant commissioner/local tithe agent	1837	1838	1839	1840	1841	1842	1843	1844	Totals
Charles Howard	4	17	21					1	43
Richard Burton Phillipson				2	3	1	1	1	8
Robert Hart			4	2					6
John Penny				3	1				4
Henry Pilkington						4			4
John Pickering			3						3
John Story Penleaze			2						2
Joseph Townsend								2	2
Charles Pym	1								1
Thomas Smith Woolley		1							1
Totals	5	18	30	7	4	5	1	4	74

Table 66 *Land use, crops and yields in Yorkshire, East Riding, c. 1836*

A	Land use	Percentage of total land area enumerated in reports on tithe agreements	Estimated acreage in whole county
	Arable	65.6	503,821
	Grass	28.5	218,765
	Wood	3.2	24,810
	Common	1.8	7,713

B	Crop	Mean percentage of arable	Mean yield per acre	Estimated acreage in whole county
	Wheat	22.0	18.6 bushels	110,629
	Barley	10.4	28.0 bushels	52,472
	Oats	16.6	32.5 bushels	83,819
	Pulses	5.5	19.6 bushels	27,696
	Turnips	10.3	£2.74	52,087
	Seeds	21.2	20.9 cwts	106,794
	Fallows	13.6	—	68,259

Yorkshire, West Riding

642 tithe districts
201 reports on tithe agreements

The West Riding was one of those counties adopted for the 1854 pilot scheme to examine the feasibility of collecting national agricultural statistics and J. P. Dodd (1979c) has analysed these returns but in this particular investigation he does not undertake comparisons with tithe surveys. Though the 1854 returns emphasise the broad differences in land use and farming which existed in the Pennine north and the lowland south, they conceal very great variations which obtained within each of the large Poor Law districts on which their collection was based.

Although there are reports on tithe agreements for almost a third of West Riding tithe districts, the body of useful statistical data is much less than this figure might suggest. Parliamentary enclosure left only parts of many townships titheable, moduses were usual (see Subject Index) and Charles Howard, as in other counties where he worked, was not consistent in the way he presented data to support his calculations. A total of some 110 townships with acceptable data permits, though, aggregation of data to county level (Table 68).

At the time of tithe commutation, boundaries between a number of adjacent tithe districts were uncertain and much disputed, especially where they cut through open moorland. With such large areas of moorland (Table 68), and boundaries so uncertain, errors in the total acreages cited for tithe districts are inevitable and were acknowledged by assistant tithe commissioners. At Sedbergh, Charles Howard commented in 1839 that 'a survey is now being made of the enclosed lands which are well defined; the Fells will be inserted on estimation and there may be some doubt as to their *exact* boundaries but no rent charge is intended to be apportioned upon them'.

J. P. Dodd has discussed regional variations in West Riding land use and farming at this date so that it is intended here only to highlight a number of themes much discussed by Tithe Commission representatives as factors that they considered specifically affected gross value of tithes in the West Riding. First, there is the general question of the effect of tithes and tithe payments themselves on agricultural production, in particular effects on improvement and on changes likely to take place after a final settlement of the tithe question (see Subject Index). It is clear that in this county assistant commissioners and local tithe agents were convinced that the tithe system did have an effect, both in encouraging evasive practices and as a mulct on improvement. At Silkstone, John Pickering declared: 'the circumstances of the lands being free from the tithe of hay and small tithes has no doubt contributed much to put and keep the lands in grass. I think them generally much better adapted to the growth of corn, and have no doubt that when the tithes are commuted corn husbandry will be extended.' As discussed in *The tithe surveys of England and Wales* (pp. 19–20), farmers in the West Riding were adept at managing their enterprises to reduce as much as possible the amount of tithe they would have to pay. At Nidd, farmers took their ewes out of the parish immediately before lambing and again before shearing expressly to deprive the vicar of his tithe of lamb and wool. The occupier of a farm in Stutton township lived in the township of Hazlewood where a modus was paid in lieu of all small tithes. He milked his cows, clipped his sheep and maintained his meadows in Hazlewood with the result that his Stutton pastures paid only agistment tithes.

A second theme of frequent comment is variation in farming with altitude. Richard Burton Phillipson commented that

> the low lands which are of very small extent compared with the magnitude of the township are of good quality for meadow and pasture purposes, though subject to flood, but the lands decrease in fertility as they ascend in height, and they attain here an elevation said to be as great as any in England or Wales. The low lands would let for 50s per acre, but the moor land tract is not worth 6d per acre.

In complete contrast were the low warp lands of the Ouse, for example, which were celebrated 'for the growth of excellent potatoes and the facility afforded of procuring manure for them and exporting the crop directly to London renders that a profitable and consequently a favourite crop'. The quality of farming in the West Riding seems also to have mirrored the quality of the soil. At Beal, east of Pontefract, 'the four course or Norfolk shift is followed, – wheat, turnips, barley and seeds and the farming is good clean husbandry. There were all the concomitants of good tillage, excellent Durham stock, prime sheep, the farm buildings in good order', whereas at Kirk Deighton, north of Wetherby, 'there are several instances of extraordinary low farming, tho' perhaps the words in the order of the query are better adapted to the state of these lands – there are certainly *extraordinary instances* of low farming'.

As well as an upland/lowland dichotomy, assistant tithe commissioners also reported a great difference in farming close to and distant from the growing urban markets for food. At Ripon, Thomas Hoskins found that 'there is no particular system of farming surrounding as it does a large and populous market town; the land is rented at good prices and is in very many hands, each pursuing his own mode of farming and the produce is in general very good'. The contiguity of Barrowby township to Leeds 'gives a high relative value to some species of product' while Lingards township was 'chiefly in grass for keeping cows to supply milk for a manufacturing population and horses to do the manufacturers work'.

Though farm size is noted occasionally as a factor affecting titheable produce elsewhere in England and Wales, nowhere is it a matter of such frequent comment as in West Riding files where very small farms were a distinctive feature of many townships, the only exception being the relatively few large hill farms on the highest land. In the township of Cowling, near Skipton, for example, Richard Burton Phillipson found that 'the lands with very little exception are divided into small holdings of from 3 acres to 100. The majority varying from

20 to 40 acres, and the tenants are principally weavers, carders or combers, who consume the produce of perhaps one arable field, and dispose of their surplus milk or butter.'

Dairying, sheep rearing and enclosure of common moorland to improve livestock husbandry are all topics debated in commutation meetings and recorded in tithe files.

Table 67 *Reports on agreements for commutation of tithes in Yorkshire, West Riding*

Assistant commissioner/ local tithe agent	1837	1838	1839	1840	1841	1842	1843	1844	1845	1846	Totals
Charles Howard	2	14	51	3					1		71
Richard Burton Phillipson				27	10		4	10	2		53
John Pickering		5	10	3							18
Thomas Hoskins		16									16
Henry Pilkington		7				3	2	2		2	16
John Job Rawlinson		4	2					1			7
Thomas Martin						1	1	4			6
Robert Hart			2	3							5
Horace William Meteyard			5								5
John Penny				1	1						2
Thomas Sudworth			2								2
Totals	2	46	72	37	11	4	7	17	3	2	201

Table 68 *Land use, crops and yields in Yorkshire, West Riding, c. 1836*

A	Land use	Percentage of total land area enumerated in reports on tithe agreements	Estimated acreage in whole county
	Arable	30.0	512,276
	Grass	46.6	796,747
	Wood	3.8	64,035
	Common	17.4	296,988

B	Crop	Mean percentage of arable	Mean yield per acre	Estimated acreage in whole county
	Wheat	22.6	21.0 bushels	115,533
	Barley	13.6	30.5 bushels	69,711
	Oats	12.1	33.2 bushels	62,066
	Pulses	2.9	22.3 bushels	14,672
	Turnips	12.5	£2.9	64,091
	Seeds	22.2	21.1 cwts	113,886
	Fallows	11.5	—	59,081

MIDLAND COUNTIES

Rutland
Warwickshire
Oxfordshire
Buckinghamshire

Bedfordshire*
Leicestershire*
Northamptonshire*

The 'arable' type of printed form used for reporting on tithe agreements in these counties requires a 'description and rough estimate of the titheable produce' and asks assistant tithe commissioners and local tithe agents to 'describe the parish and the quality of the lands, the system of farming, and whether the quality of the produce has been affected by any extraordinary instances of high or low farming'.

---

* Data for Bedfordshire, Leicestershire and Northamptonshire are too few to warrant constructing maps of land use and crops tithe district-by-tithe district and for Leicestershire and Northamptonshire the sample of tithe districts with extant data are too small to justify compiling county aggregate figures of land use and crop acreages and yields.

Rutland

59 tithe districts
15 reports on tithe agreements

Rutland with just fifty-nine tithe districts and fewer than 100,000 acres is one of the smallest single administrative units retained by the Tithe Commission. In twenty Rutland tithe districts, tithe had been extinguished at enclosure and in a quarter of districts tithe was commuted after 1836 by voluntary agreement. Thus the representativeness of the sample of reports is far from perfect as it is composed of districts of early enclosure and those still remaining in open fields.

In the mid-nineteenth century, grass exceeded pasture in all but three tithe districts with extant information in tithe files. Rotations on the arable were four-, five- and six-course, with bare fallows at a third of these places. The six-course retained the old open field ratio of two courses to a fallow as John Pickering described at Morcott:

> the system of husbandry is rather peculiar to this neighbourhood which consists chiefly of open fields. The course is 1 turnips, 2 and 3 barley, 4 seeds, 5 wheat, 6 peas or beans. The rotation is kept up for the sake of adhering to the old open field course of two crops and a fallow, the seeds being substituted for the alternative fallow season. On the whole this severe course of cropping is better sustained than might be expected; the crop of turnips is pretty well secured by the application of the manure from 4 crops, and the sheep are folded for the wheat crop.

Table 69 *Reports on agreements for commutation of tithes in Rutland*

Assistant commissioner/ local tithe agent	1837	1838	1839	1840	1841	1842	1843	1844	Totals
Edward Greathed		6							6
John Pickering			3	1					4
Charles Howard	2								2
Richard Burton Phillipson					1	1			2
Joseph Townsend								1	1
Totals	2	6	3	1	1	1		1	15

Table 70 *Land use, crops and yields in Rutland c. 1836*

A	Land use	Percentage of total land area enumerated in reports on tithe agreements	Estimated acreage in whole county
	Arable	38.2	36,610
	Grass	54.0	51,724
	Wood	3.4	3,219
	Common	2.7	2,619

B	Crop	Mean percentage of arable	Mean yield per acre	Estimated acreage in whole county
	Wheat	19.5	23.5 bushels	7,141
	Barley	19.2	33.6 bushels	7,037
	Oats	6.0	40.0 bushels	2,198
	Pulses	10.7	22.0 bushels	3,907
	Turnips	13.0	£2.50	4,758
	Seeds	23.1	23.8 cwts	8,439
	Fallows	—	—	3,037

Rutland

480
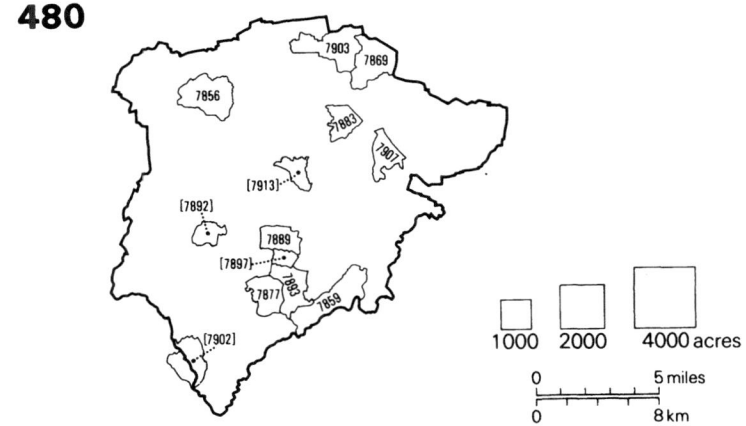

481
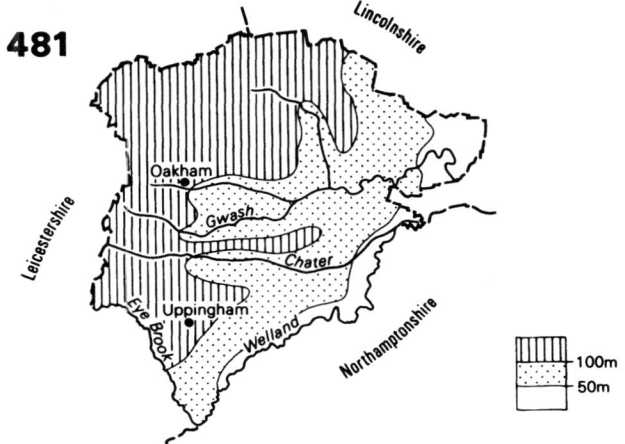

482
Arable as a percentage of tithe district area

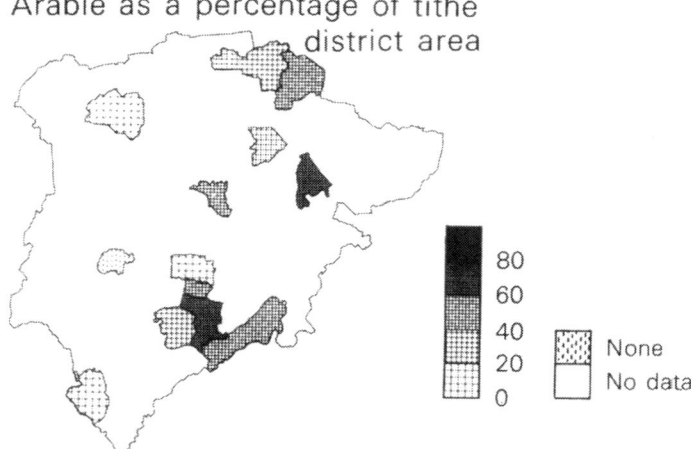

483
Pasture as a percentage of tithe district area

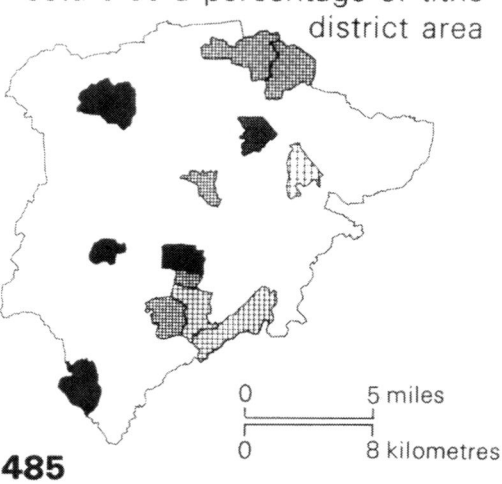

484
Woodland as a percentage of tithe district area

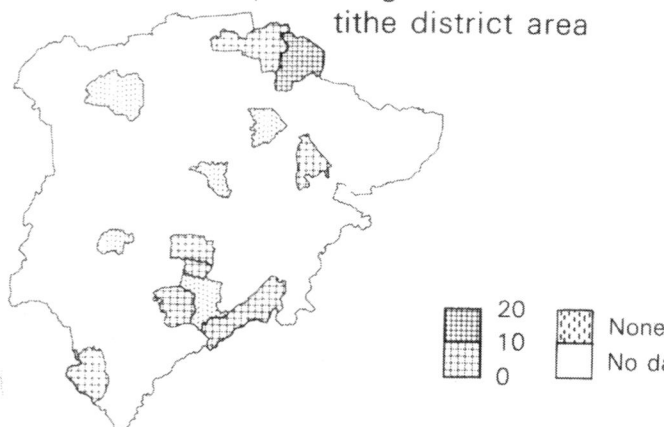

485
Common as a percentage of tithe district area

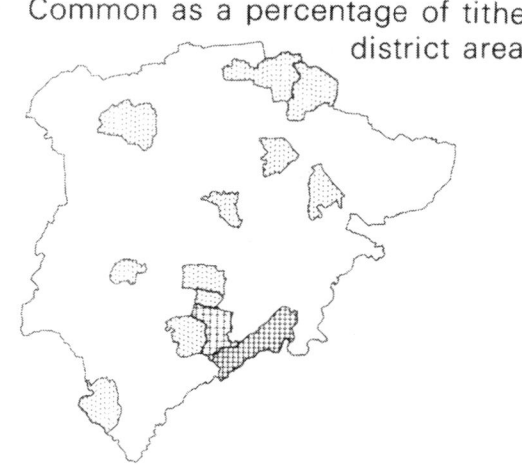

486
Wheat as a percentage of arable

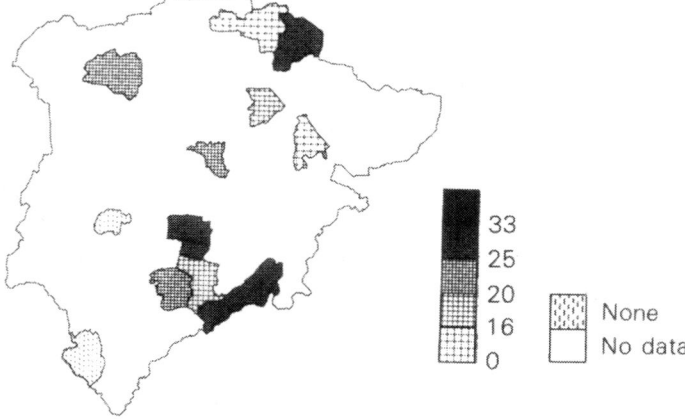

487
Barley as a percentage of arable

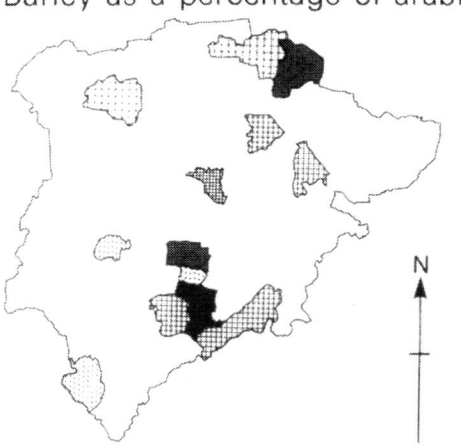

Rutland

488
Oats as a percentage of arable

489
Pulse crops as a percentage of arable

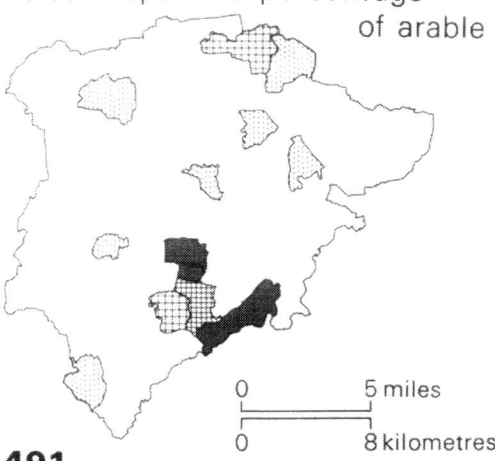

490
Turnips as a percentage of arable

491
Clover and seeds as a percentage of arable

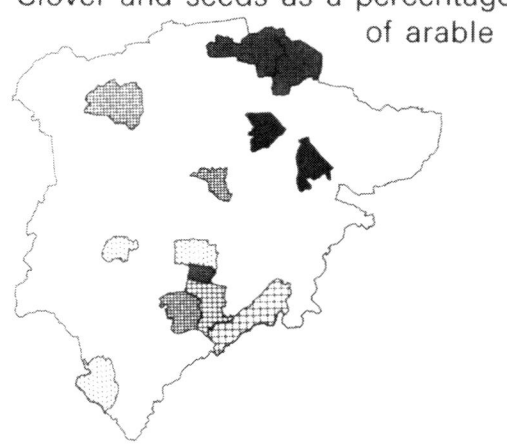

492
Dead fallow as a percentage of arable

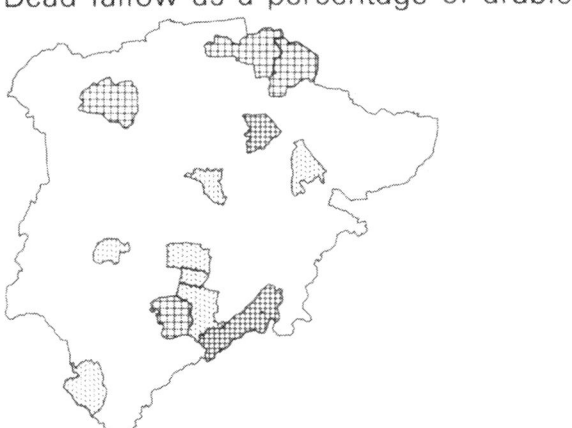

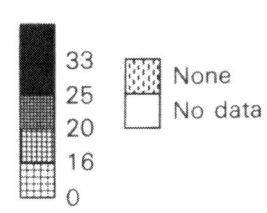

493
Yield of wheat in bushels per acre

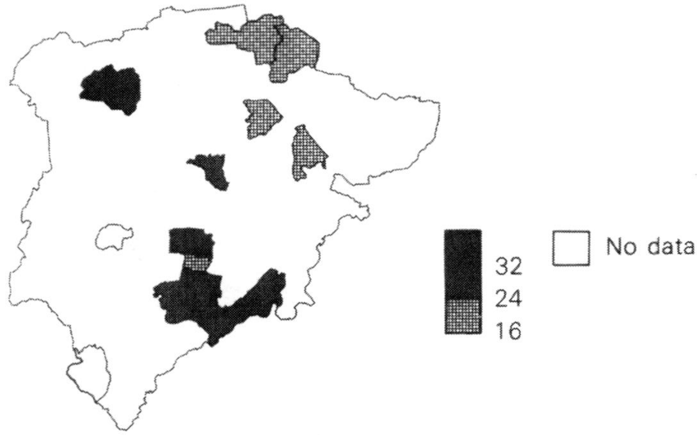

496
Yield of pulse crops in bushels per acre

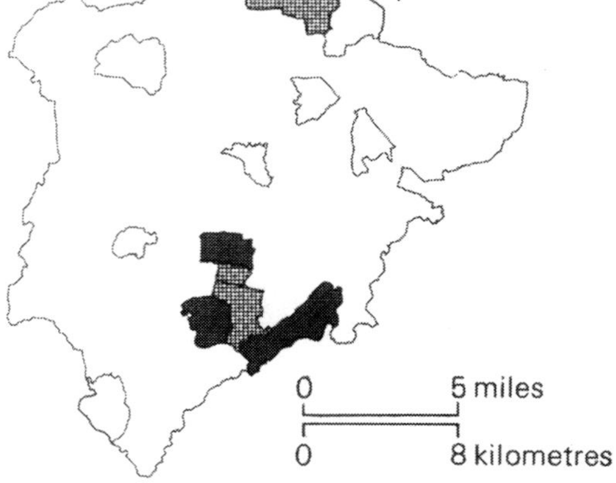

494
Yield of barley in bushels per acre

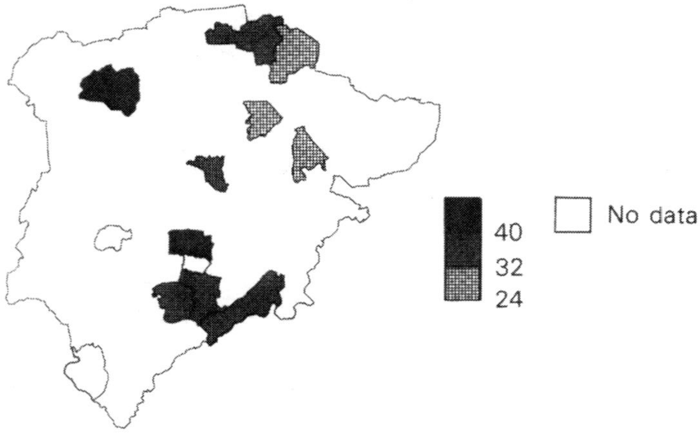

495
Yield of oats in bushels per acre

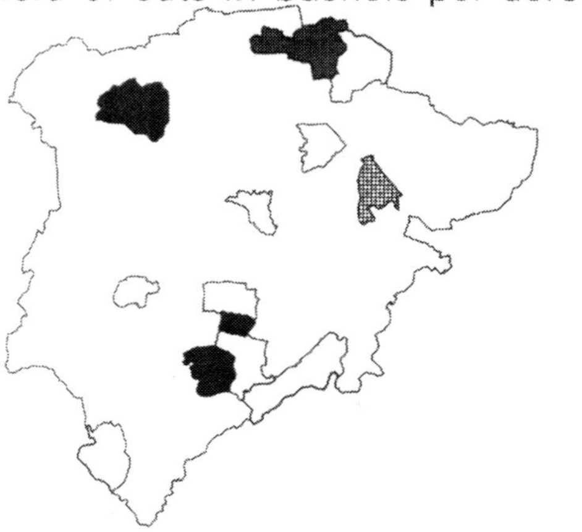

497
Yield of turnips in £'s per acre

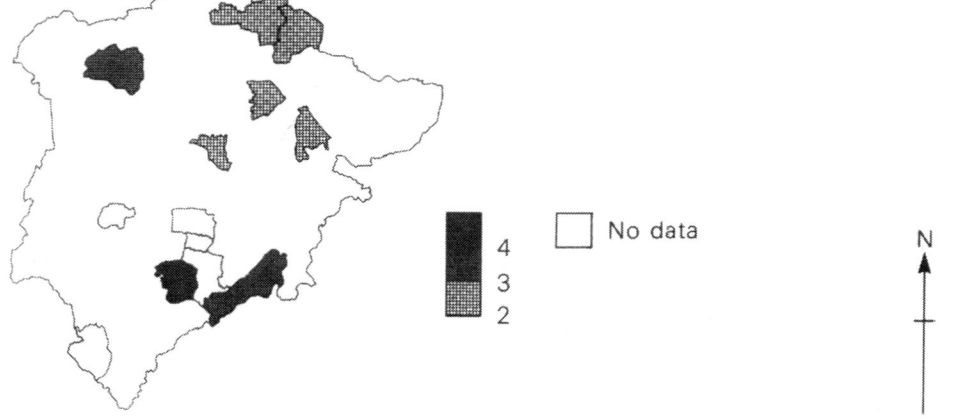

498
Yield of clover and seeds in cwts per acre

499
Yield of meadow in cwts per acre

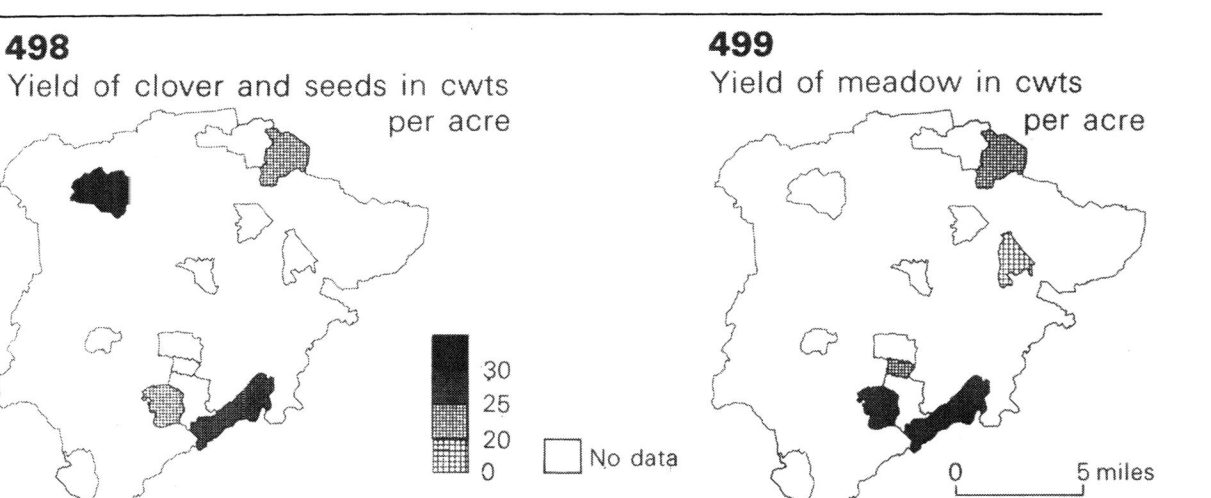

500
Yield of pasture in shillings per acre

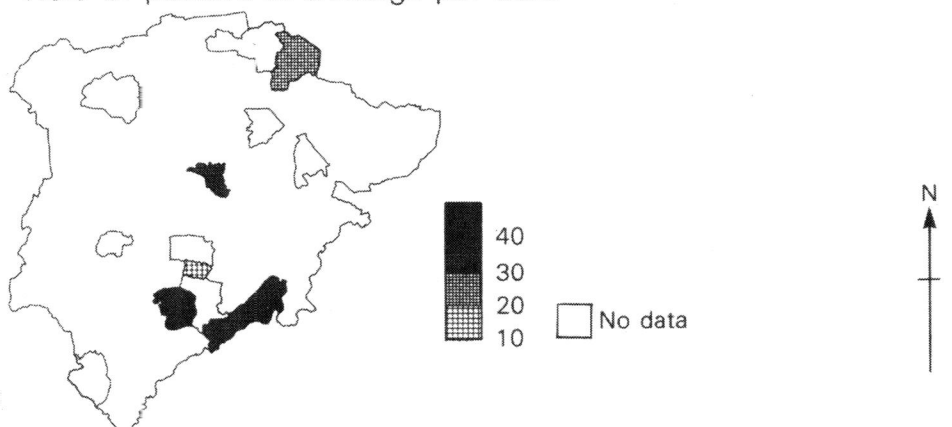

Warwickshire

248 tithe districts
70 reports on tithe agreements

As in other Midland counties, a considerable number of Warwickshire tithe districts (some 23 per cent) were entirely tithe free at the time of the Tithe Commission's inquiries as they had been exonerated at enclosure. There are more compulsory awards than voluntary agreements which is also characteristic of counties where tithe at many places remained payable on only a few, usually early enclosed, fields so that there was little real incentive for parties to initiate commutation themselves. Where titheable and tithe free land interdigitated in open fields, assistant commissioners found assessing a fair rent-charge very difficult. At Wootton Wawen in 1838, Thomas Smith Woolley commented that 'the schedules are made from actual survey – but the extraordinary way in which the lands liable to tithes are intermixed with the lands exonerated renders it difficult to ascertan them'. A quarter of the seventy voluntary commutations concerned less than 90 per cent of a parish total area. This fact, together with the large proportion of the county either tithe free or commuted compulsorily, means that Warwickshire sits above Buckinghamshire at the threshold of data density below which parish-by-parish mapping of extant data is considered unprofitable in this study.

All local agents condemned the persistence of open field farming whenever they encountered it. Thomas Smith Woolley wrote of Whitchurch:

> I should think the style of farming it now is a very fair sample of the system of cultivation three hundred years ago . . . all the 'lands' are separated by wide 'balks' half as wide as the lands . . . in the higher and more distant parts they bear a still larger proportion to the part actually under the plough and are overrun with thorns, briars and brushwood – so that as may be imagined the aspect of the thing is very peculiar . . . there are almost no roads and the manure cart very rarely finds it way up the hills.

High farming was encountered in only six parishes (see Subject Index) but bad if not actual low farming was commonplace. As Thomas Smith Woolley commented at Ipsley: 'like most parishes in which the Dairy is the principal object, it is very closely cropped and in other respects ill managed'. The best arable farming was found on the better soils of the red marls; Woolley's comments at Radford Semele are typical of others made in this part of the county. 'The parish', he said in 1841, 'is altogether one of the best I have been into – at least it contains a less proportion of bad land – it wants, however, some more good grassland.' On heavy land, three- or four-course rotations of wheat, beans, fallow – or wheat, beans, wheat, fallow – are identified by local agents. Beans, though, were avoided in parishes on higher land (Arley was one such place where this received lengthy comment) because they harvested so late and as a consequence it was not possible to prepare land for a winter-sown wheat crop. Oats were substituted instead. The Norfolk four-course is recorded on light soils, as are long ley courses. That described by Edward Greathed at Shustoke is typical of these last:

> Oats off 4 years old ley; wheat – the land ploughed lightly and then deeper; turnips – what is provincially called brushed in; barley; 1 seeds; 2 seeds; 3 seeds; 4 seeds. During the 4 years the leys are well fed and manured – the clover disappears after the first season – but there then comes up a fine coat of grass and natural white clover.

Some landlords insisted that seeds were left for at least two years in an effort to stop overcropping with corn.

As with arable husbandry, the general impression of grassland and livestock management conveyed by the whole body of Warwickshire files is not especially favourable. On really heavy soils, as at Willington, the parish was 'principally in pasture from the expence attendant on the cultivation of such strong land particularly where the husbandry is neither good nor the farmers wealthy or intelligent'. Thomas Smith Woolley considered that many such areas of pasture would be prime targets for conversion to arable when tithes were settled. Cattle fattening and especially dairying receive frequent comment in the tithe files for this county (see Subject Index).

Table 71 *Reports on agreements for commutation of tithes in Warwickshire*

Assistant commissioner/ local tithe agent	1837	1838	1839	1840	1841	1842	1843	1844	1845	Totals
Thomas Smith Woolley	6	9	8	2	3	3	2	1	1	35
F. Browne Browne			2	6						8
John Pickering			1	6						7
Edward Greathed		4	2							6
Roger Kynaston			5							5
Horace William Meteyard			5							5
John Mee Mathew		2								2
William Heard					1					1
Thomas Sudworth	1									1
Totals	7	15	23	15	3	3	2	1	1	70

Table 72 *Land use, crops and yields in Warwickshire c. 1836*

A	Land use	Percentage of total land area enumerated in reports on tithe agreements	Estimated acreage in whole county
	Arable	47.5	268,049
	Grass	46.0	259,391
	Wood	3.9	22,031
	Common	1.0	6,085

B	Crop	Mean percentage of arable	Mean yield per acre	Estimated acreage in whole county
	Wheat	22.4	23.1 bushels	59,977
	Barley	12.0	32.6 bushels	32,111
	Oats	10.3	37.4 bushels	27,715
	Pulses	7.4	24.3 bushels	19,763
	Turnips	7.7	£3.0	20,505
	Seeds	26.6	22.8 cwts	71,259
	Fallows	12.8	—	34,188

Warwickshire

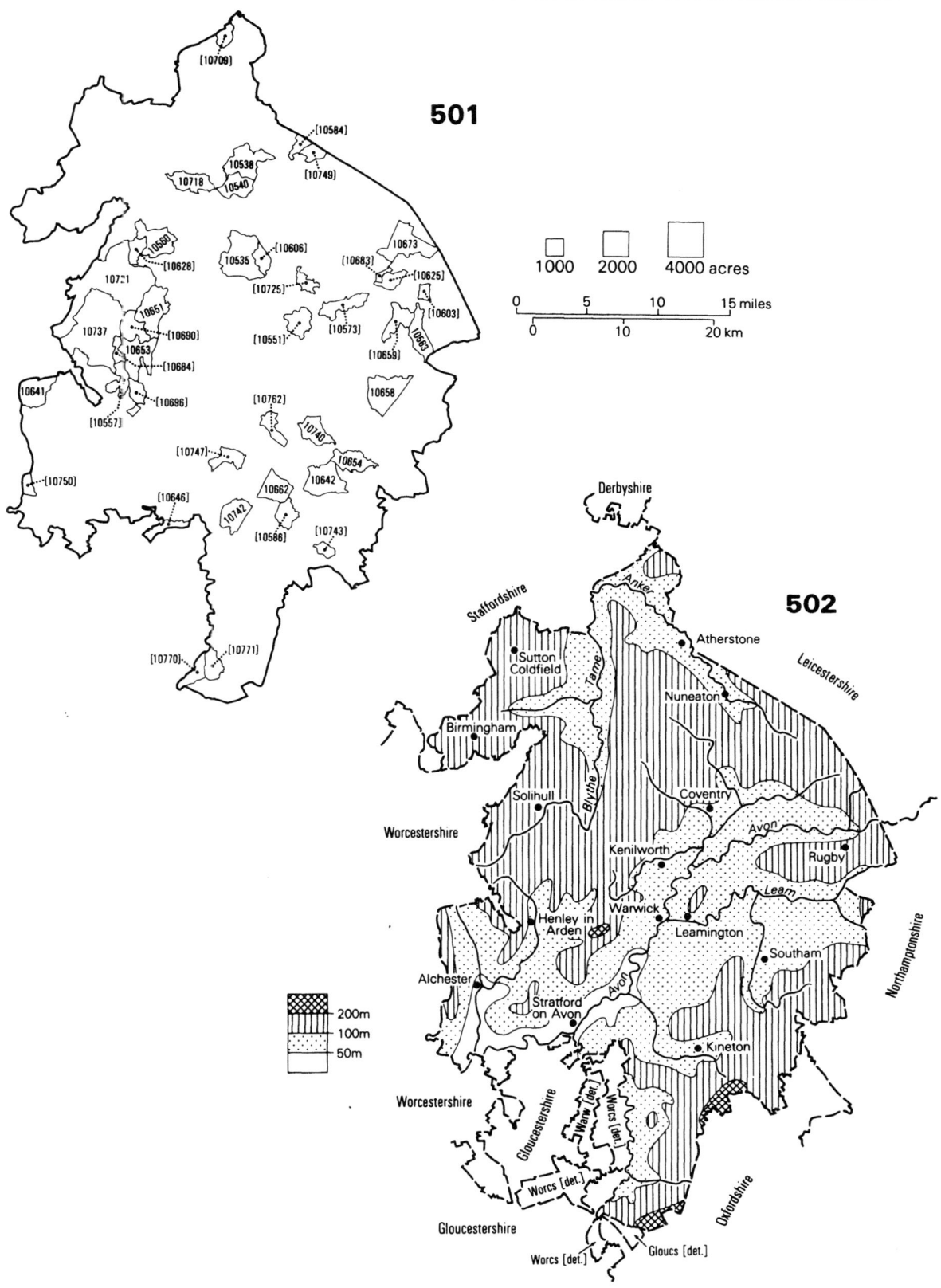

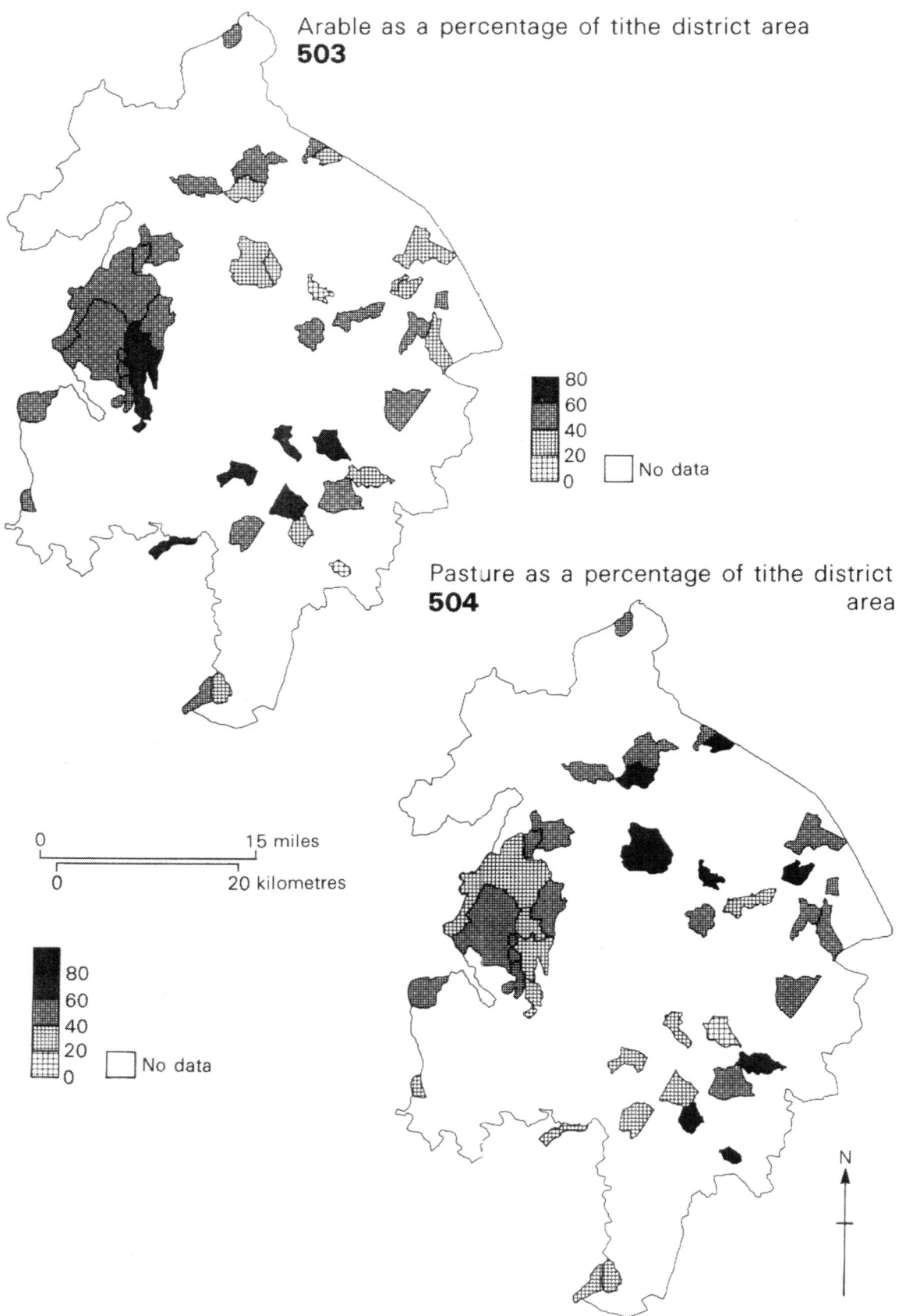

503 Arable as a percentage of tithe district area

504 Pasture as a percentage of tithe district area

Warwickshire

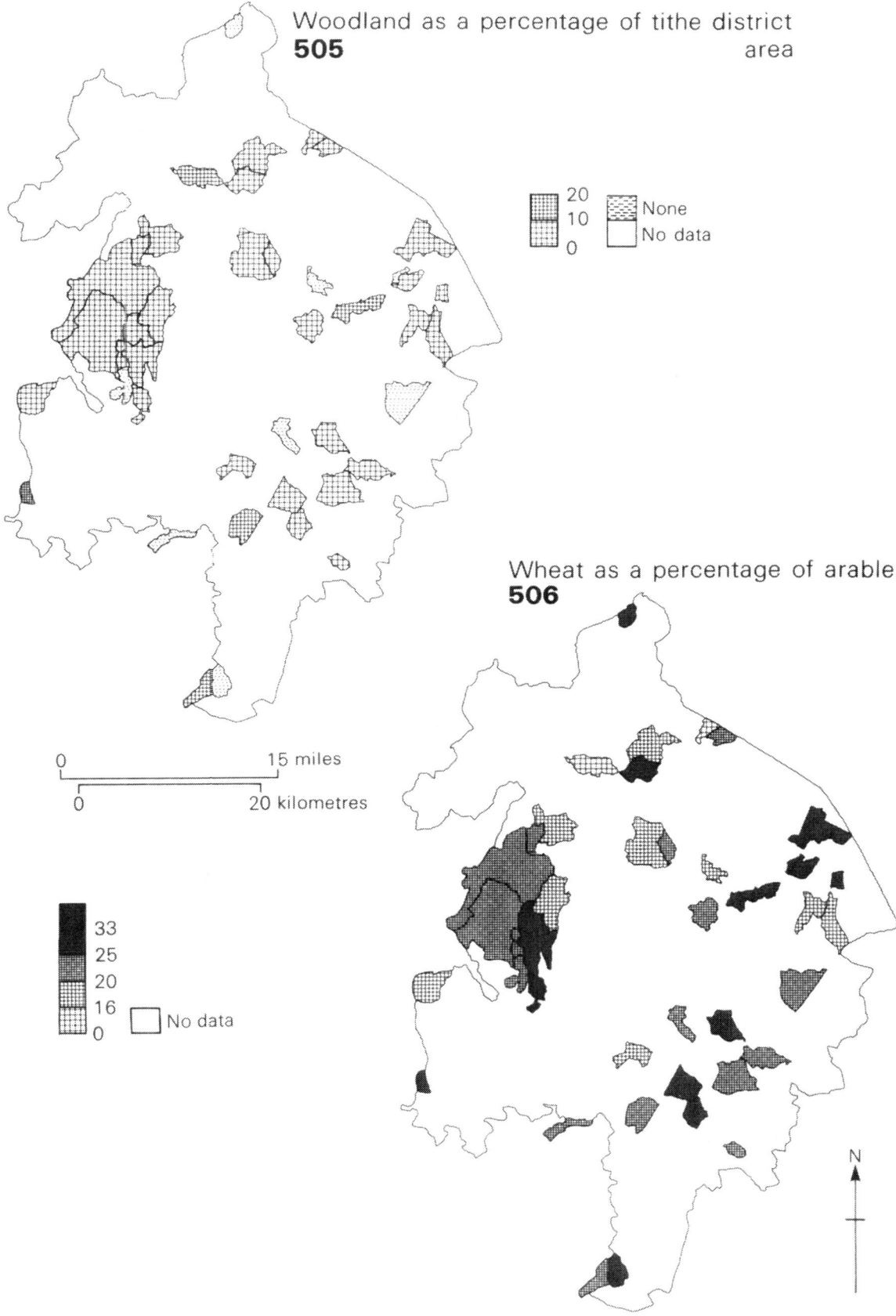

505 Woodland as a percentage of tithe district area

506 Wheat as a percentage of arable

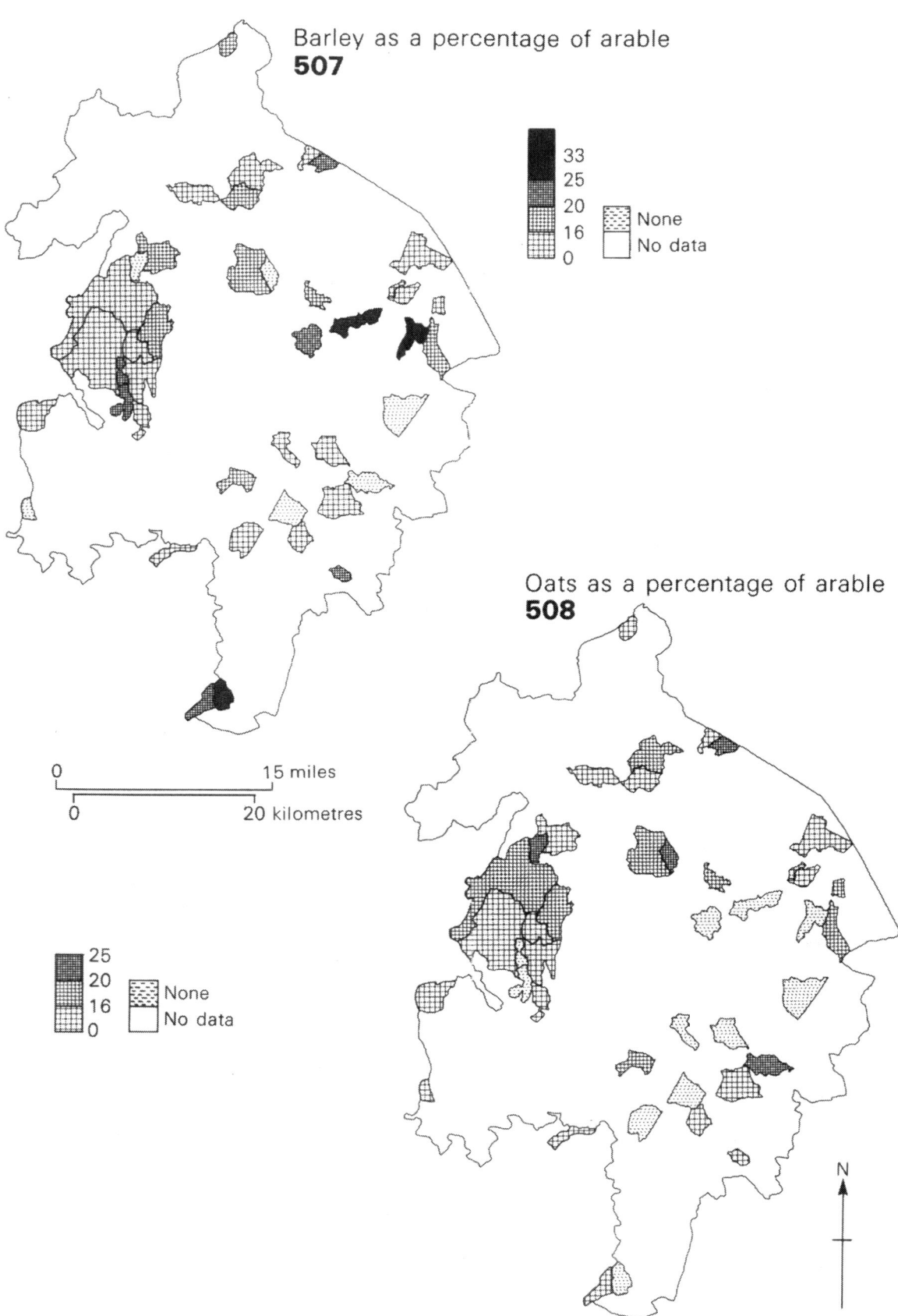

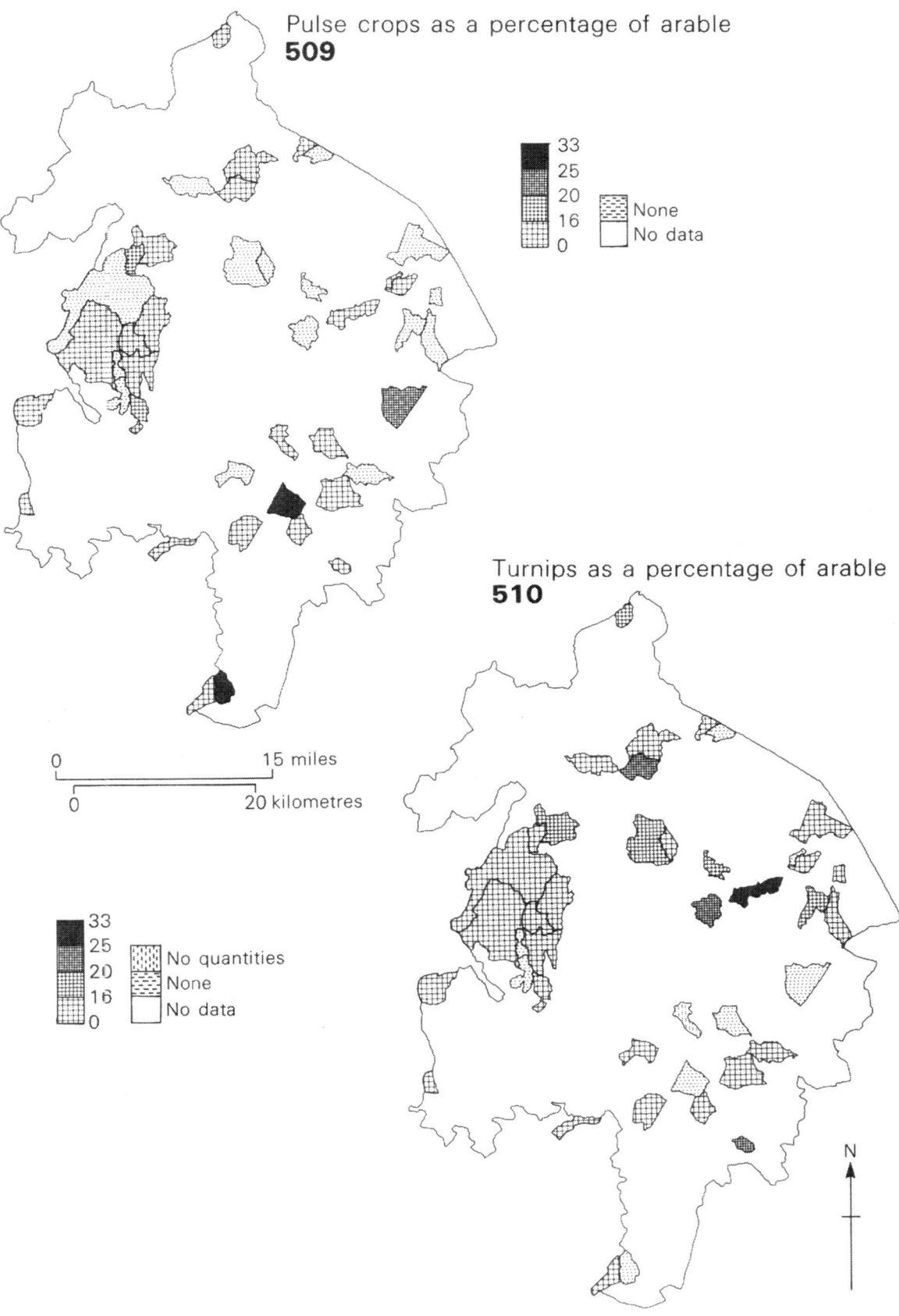

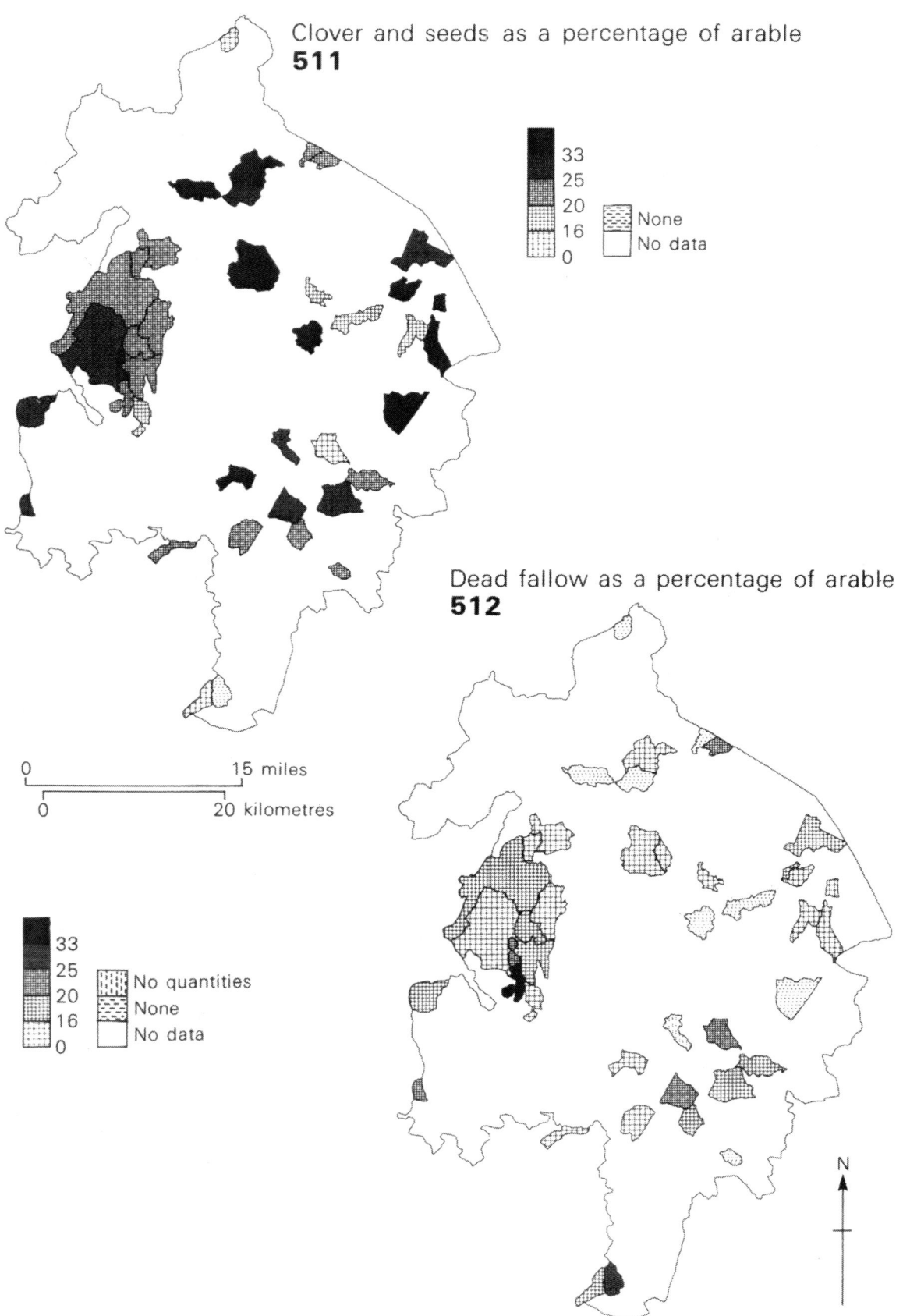

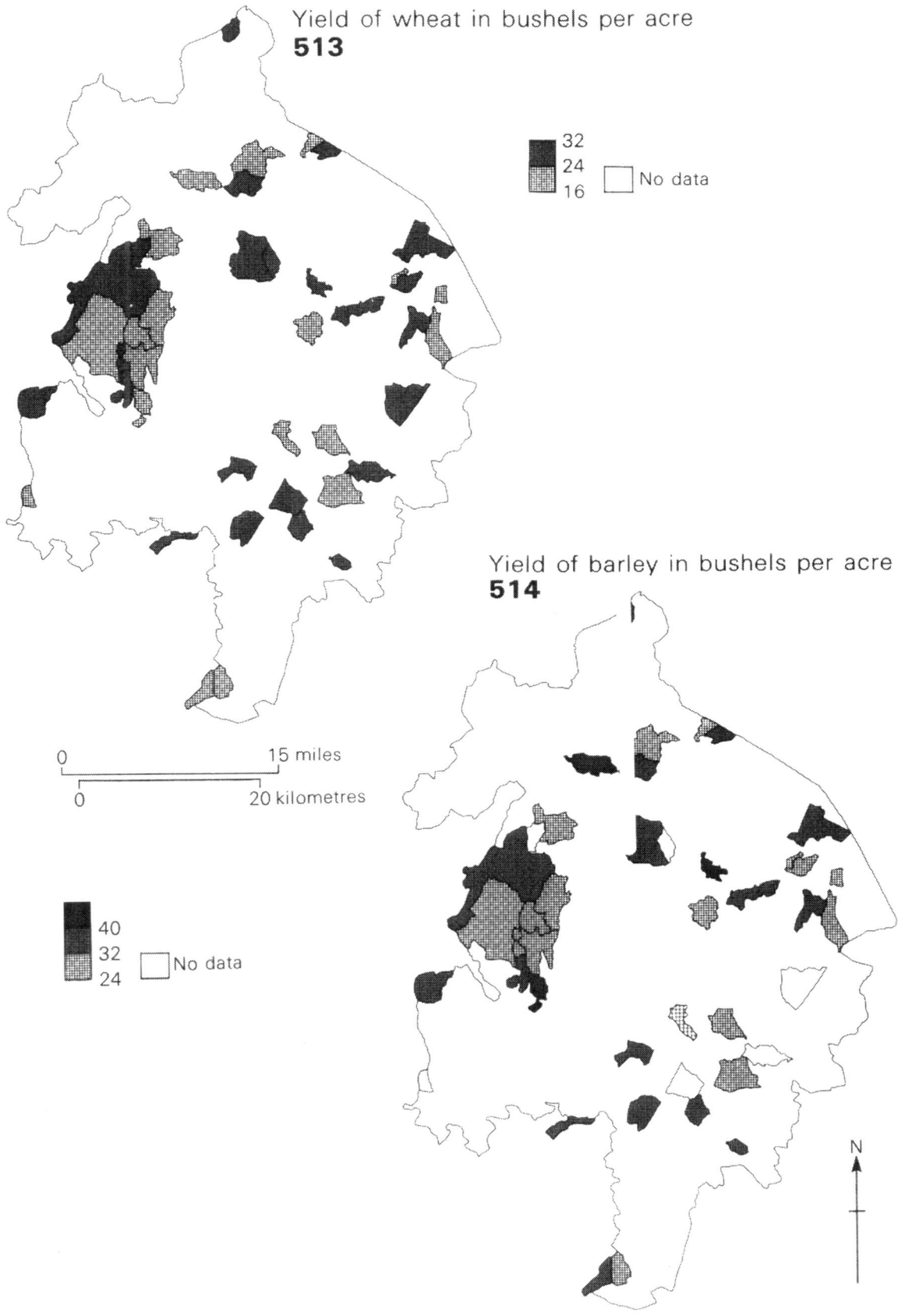

Yield of wheat in bushels per acre
513

Yield of barley in bushels per acre
514

Midland counties

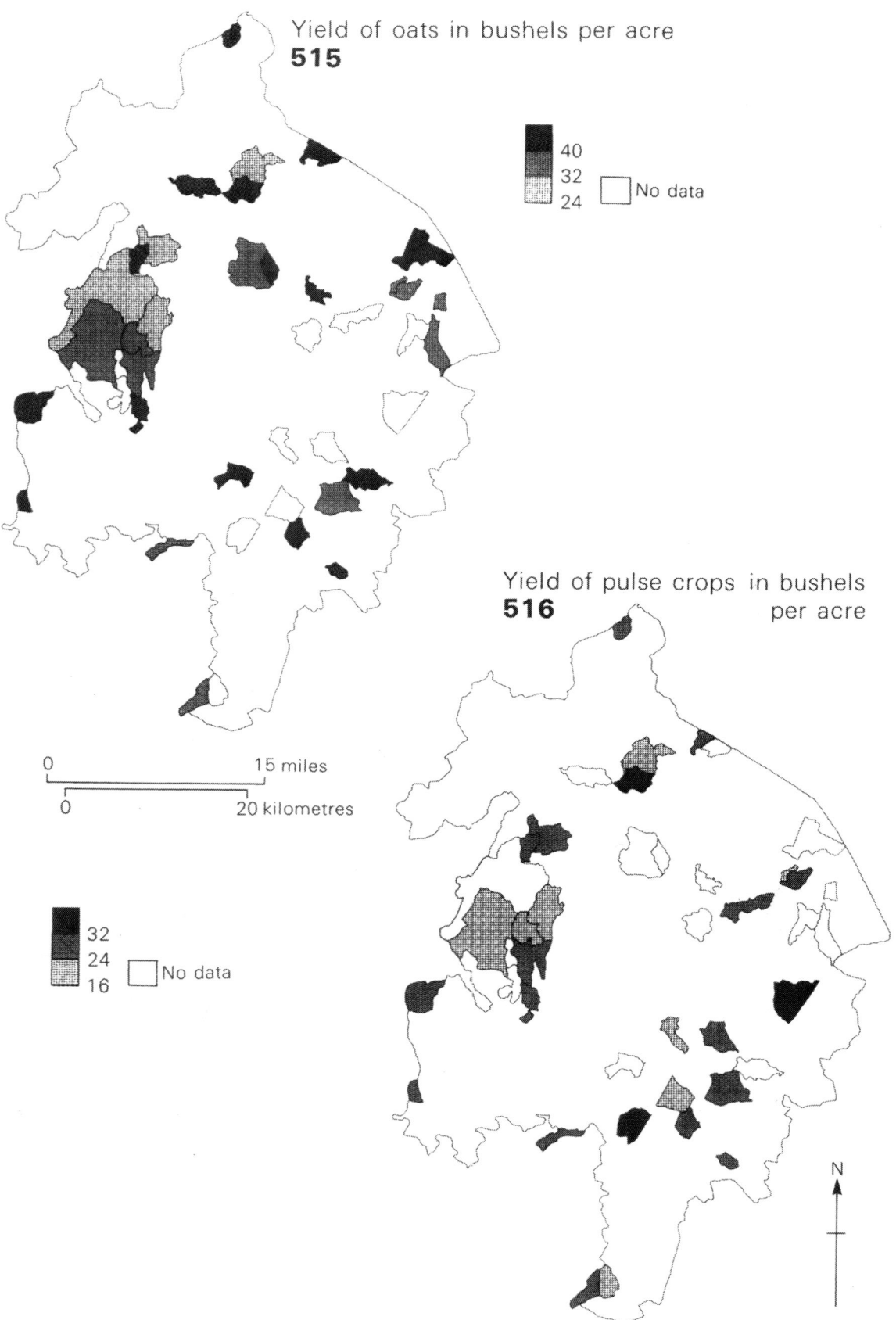

515 Yield of oats in bushels per acre

516 Yield of pulse crops in bushels per acre

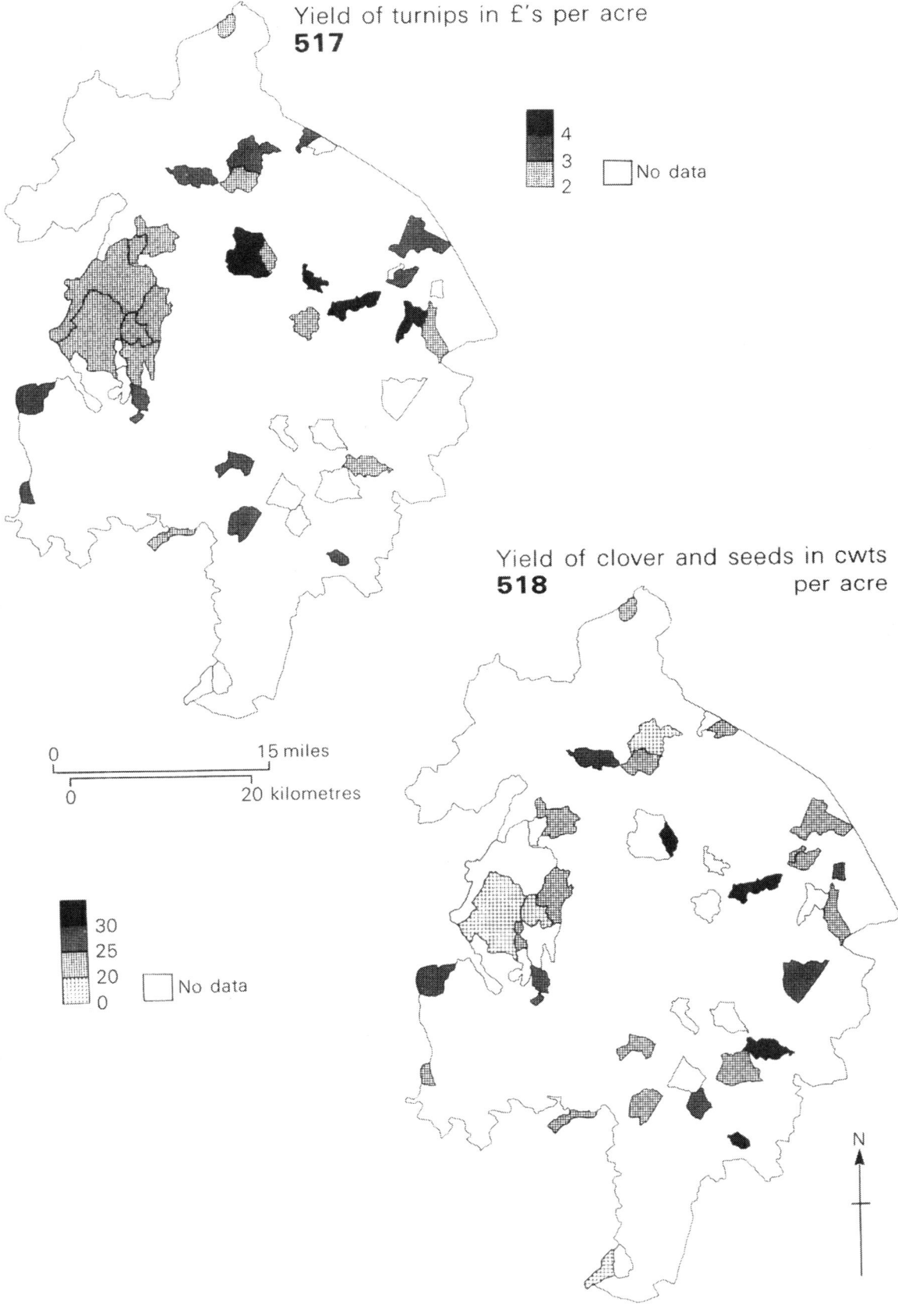

396 Midland counties

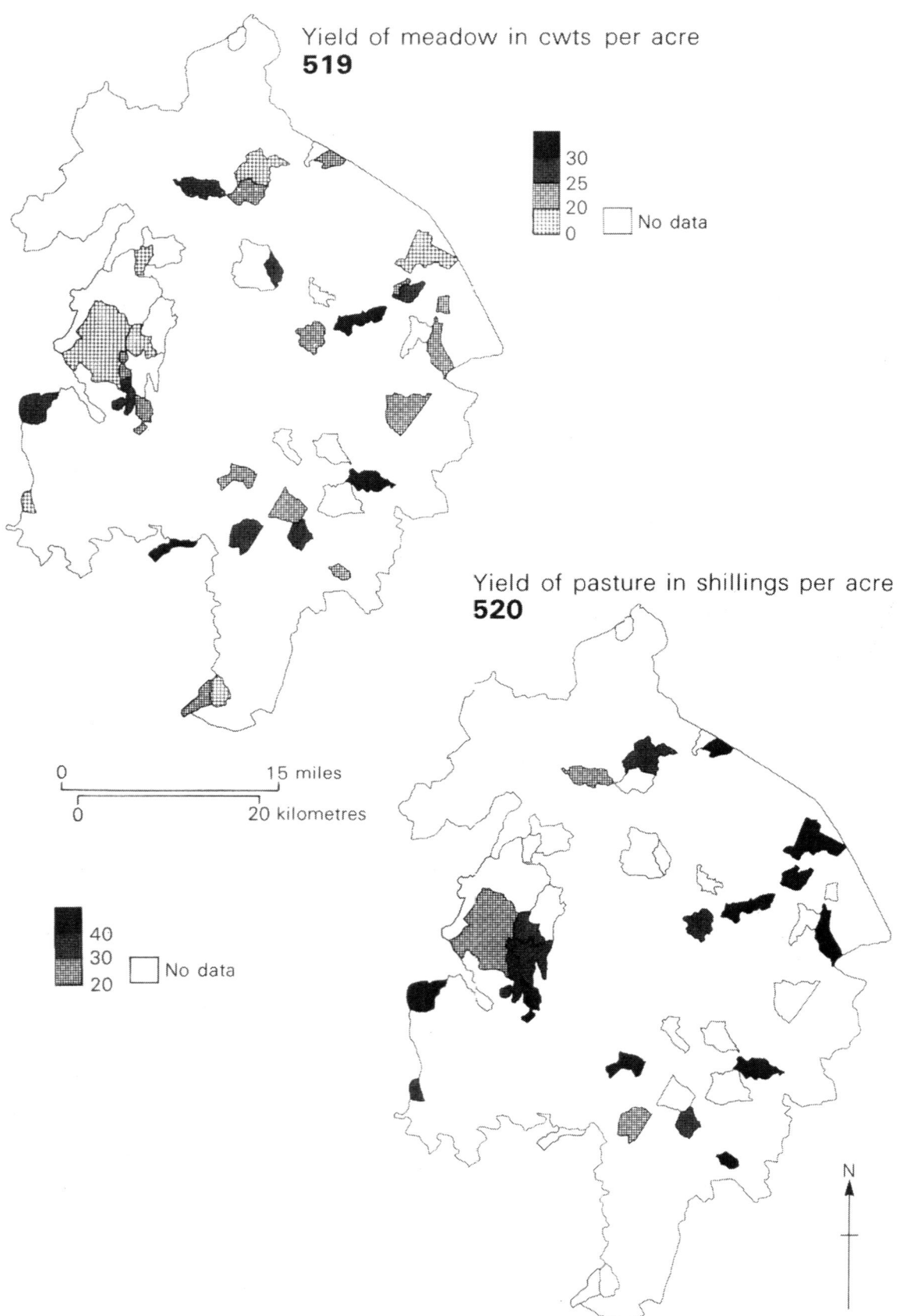

Yield of meadow in cwts per acre
519

Yield of pasture in shillings per acre
520

Oxfordshire

267 tithe districts
80 reports on tithe agreements

More than a third of Oxfordshire parishes were entirely tithe free by 1836 as a result of redemption of tithe for cash or, more usually, allotments of land at the time of parliamentary enclosure. Half of the commutations effected by the 1836 Tithe Act in Oxfordshire were by agreement, and in very many of these districts, tithe was payable on at least 90 per cent of total land area. In total, Oxfordshire has a reasonable 30 per cent cover of tithe agreement reports, rather more than its position in the belt of Midland enclosure might suggest. But, while Chiltern Oxfordshire has good cover, the Cotswold country has very little; practically no data are extant for the tract of land lying between the rivers Windrush and Cherwell (Map 521). This spatial skew in conjunction with the fact that almost all recently enclosed parishes are excluded from the tithe surveys means that Oxfordshire tithe file evidence is rather less representative than might elsewhere be the case, with 30 per cent overall cover. In detail, Chiltern beechwoods were exempt from tithe but the tithe surveys do set out woodland acreages in this county. Many parishes in Cotswold and Chiltern Oxfordshire also had large acreages of common; and 'the occupiers of Leafield, in common with those of 15 other parishes or districts, have the privilege of turning into Wychwood Forest during the summer, as much stock as they can keep through the winter previous'. This was a facility which, to assistant commissioner F. Browne Browne, seemed 'a sort of permanent charity, which operates as a check upon individual exertion'! In fact, a wide variety of attitudes to mid-nineteenth-century rural economy and society are represented in Oxfordshire tithe files as although one man, Thomas Clements Parr, compiled more than twice as many reports as any other individual, 65 per cent of the total number were written by ten other assistant commissioners and local tithe agents (Table 73).

Arable exceeded pasture in all Oxfordshire parishes save those along the Thames valley and on heavy clay soils south of Oxford (Maps 523–4). Rotations were also related closely to soil type. Assistant commissioners considered that chalk land was kept in arable because it produced very poor herbage if in grass; at Checkendon, west of Henley-on-Thames, 'the system of husbandry is a rotation of four crops. Turnips, barley or oats, clover or sainfoin, and wheat. The sainfoin is allowed to remain occasionally for 5 years, without being ploughed up. It is tough and stringy, and apparently much less nutritious than clover, but greater quantities of it can be grown on the chalky soils.' Such evidence as the files contain on Cotswold practices suggests that here rotations were usually five- or six-course. At

Crawley, it was barley, clover, wheat, oats and turnips; at Broughton Poggs, the arable 'is farmed, as is usual on the Cotswold hills upon the five-field system viz: turnips, barley, seeds, wheat, beans or oats, and sainfoin'. In dairying districts, particularly those parishes close to the borders of north Buckinghamshire, local tithe agents comment that arable was rather neglected and rotations irregular. At Shelswell, for example, Thomas Smith Woolley commented that 'the style of farming is far from first rate – there is very little adherence to any regular rotation of crops and a great deal of the land is foul and out of condition. This as far as my experience goes is generally more or less the case in dairying counties'. On clay soils, both three- and four-course rotations were encountered but a consensus of local agents considered, as at Easington, for example, that the three-course was being abandoned in favour of four-course shifts. Few turnips were grown in those districts where there was still a lot of bare fallow with occasional crops of tares or vetches for summer feed. At Stoke Talmage, for example, 'the usual course of husbandry is wheat, beans, and fallow, but clover or vetches are occasionally grown in place of the fallow', and at Berrick Salome, 'they adopt what is called a three course tilth, that is they have wheat every 3 years, and in the last year of the two courses of three years each, they fallow, with or without tares, as the condition of the lands may permit. There is no turnip land in the parish.' The quality of arable farming in still open field parishes was the butt of much criticism, especially by Thomas Clements Parr and Joseph Townsend. Townsend commented at Great Milton, south-east of Oxford, that

> the arbitrary and antiquated customs of open field husbandry present here as they do universally a bar to improved cultivation and check the enterprise of the farmer. The routine of two crops and a fallow is adhered to on the strong open lands but the occupiers on the lighter soils venture upon the innovations of turnip and artificial grasses. They do so however on sufferance as the nonconformity of any one of the open field farmers would place them in peril of a return to the old course of crops.

By comparison with national average figures, meadow and pasture yields in Oxfordshire were quite good. Exceptions were the chalk grasslands of the Chilterns discussed earlier and wet, low-lying grassland in need of drainage. That of Standhill, for example, drove Horace William Meteyard to exceptional heights of hyperbole; 'the land might be made fine rich pasture and support large dairies. But it is in miserable condition – no underdraining. The fields covered with rushes – the roads next to impassable and parts of the pasture so full of anthills that a person could walk from one end of a field to the other upon the tops of them'! Dairying was important around Oxford, Buckingham and Thame with butter and cheese being made for Oxford and London markets (see Subject Index). At Denton, for instance, there was only one farm with some arable, 'the other farms are exclusively dairy farms, and the value of the produce is much increased by the vicinity of the parish to the town of Oxford'.

Table 73 *Reports on agreements for commutation of tithes in Oxfordshire*

Assistant commissioner/ local tithe agent	1837	1838	1839	1840	1841	1842	1843	1844	1845	1846	Totals
Thomas Clements Parr				20	6	2					28
Henry Jemmett		7	6								13
F. Browne Browne		3	6								9
Thomas Smith Woolley						3	3		1		7
Roger Kynaston		1	5								6
Joseph Townsend	1	3	1	1							6
Horace William Meteyard		1	2								3
William Heard										2	2
John Mee Mathew			2								2
John Pickering			2								2
Charles Pym	2										2
Totals	3	15	24	21	6	5	3		1	2	80

Table 74 *Land use, crops and yields in Oxfordshire, c. 1836*

A	Land use	Percentage of total land area enumerated in reports on tithe agreements	Estimated acreage in whole county
	Arable	55.8	264,041
	Grass	29.7	140,339
	Wood	7.9	37,603
	Common	3.8	17,985

B	Crop	Mean percentage of arable	Mean yield per acre	Estimated acreage in whole county
	Wheat	24.0	22.9 bushels	63,468
	Barley	17.2	33.3 bushels	45,404
	Oats	6.6	38.7 bushels	17,521
	Pulses	7.0	30.0 bushels	18,562
	Turnips	13.9	£2.45	36,787
	Seeds	23.9	21.3 cwts	63,039
	Fallows	7.1	—	18,653

400　Midland counties

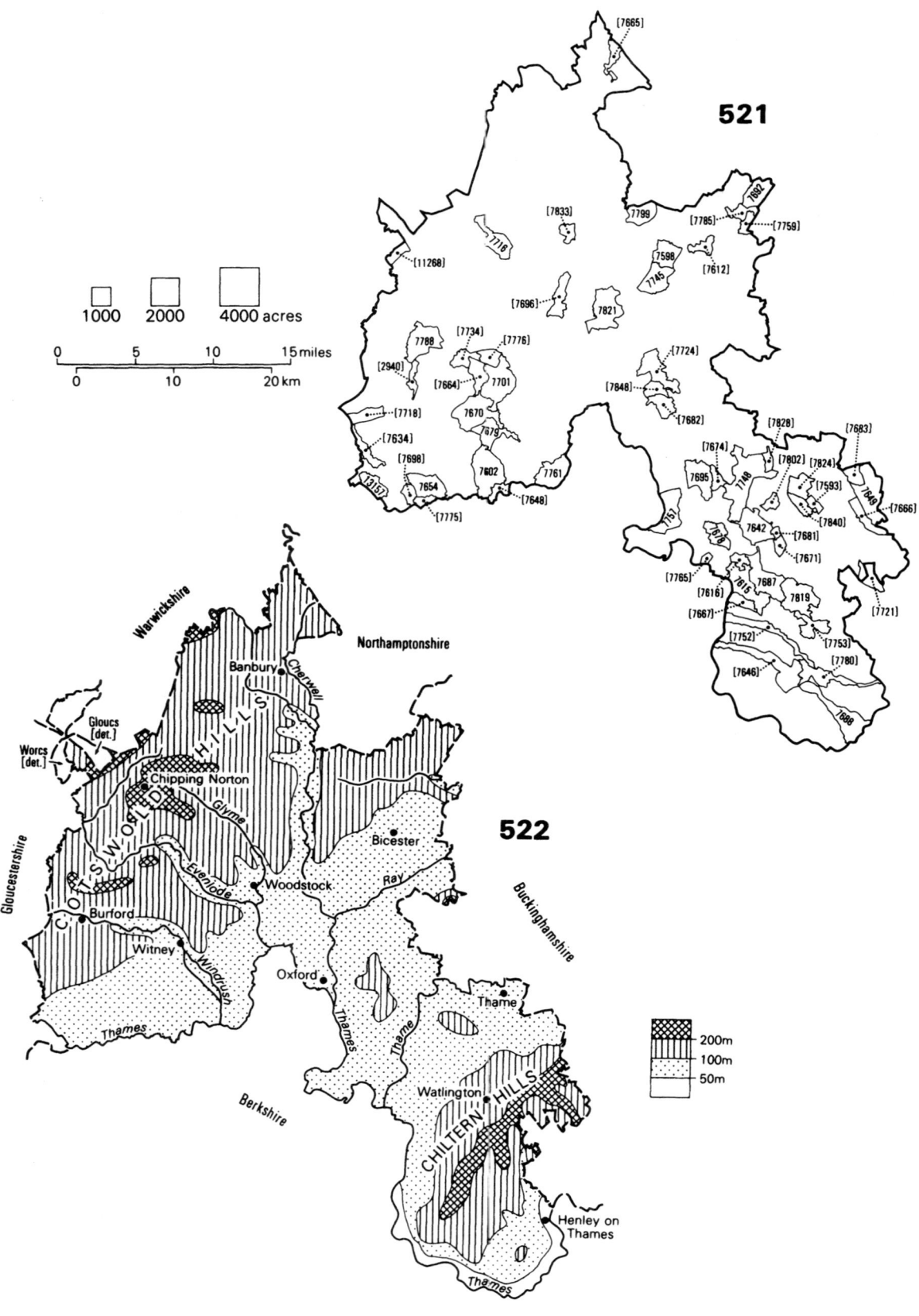

Oxfordshire

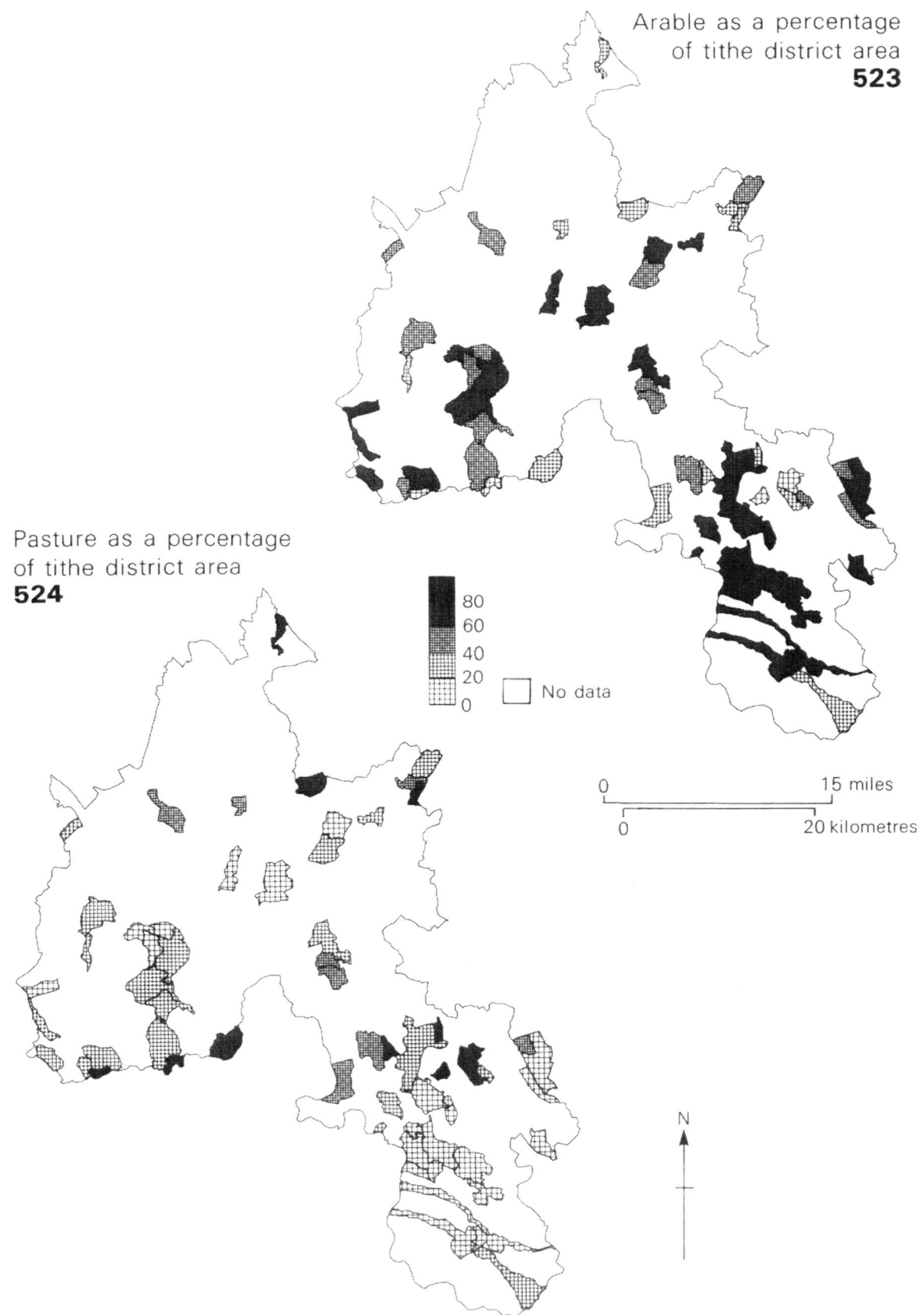

Arable as a percentage of tithe district area
523

Pasture as a percentage of tithe district area
524

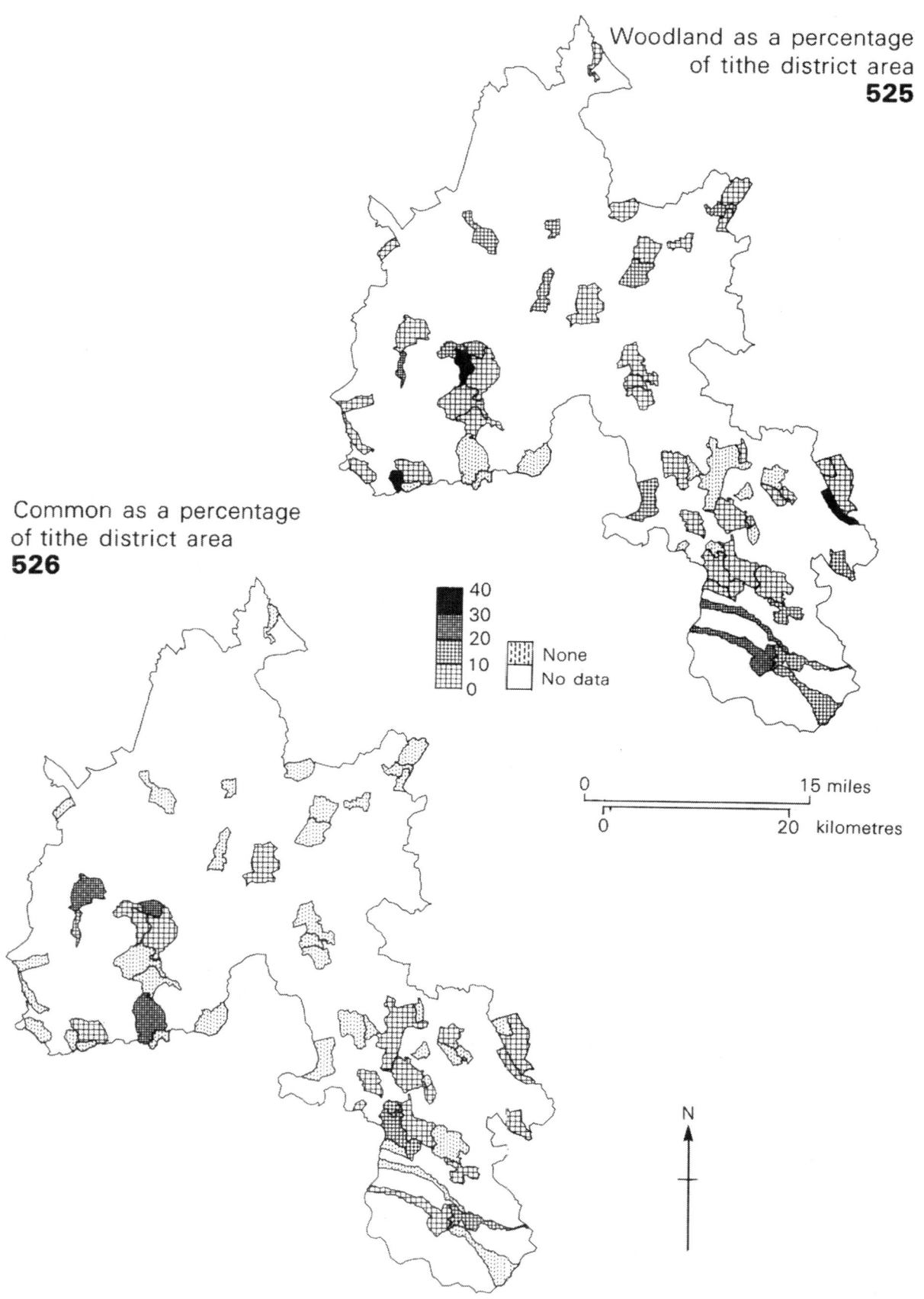

Woodland as a percentage of tithe district area
525

Common as a percentage of tithe district area
526

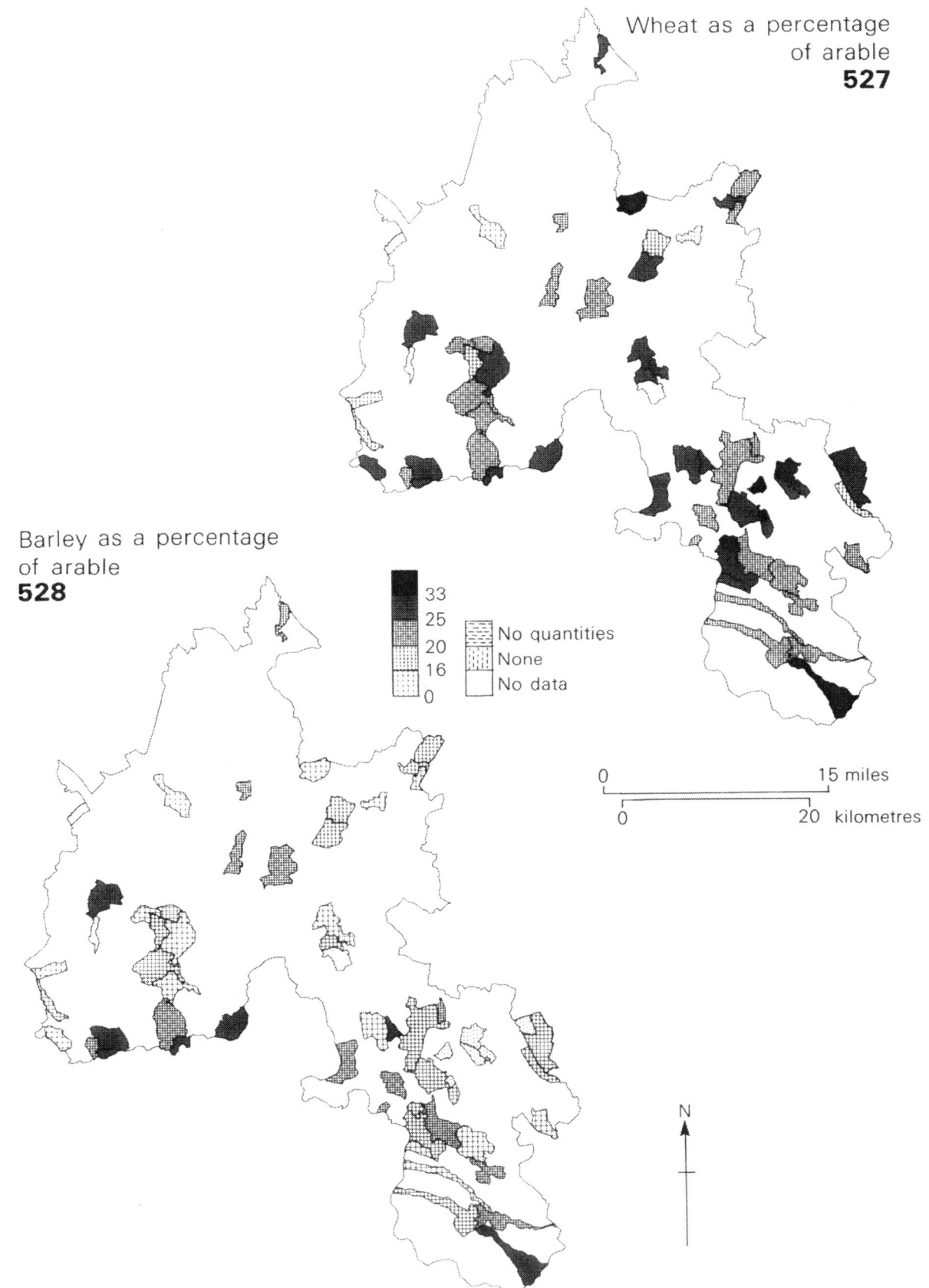

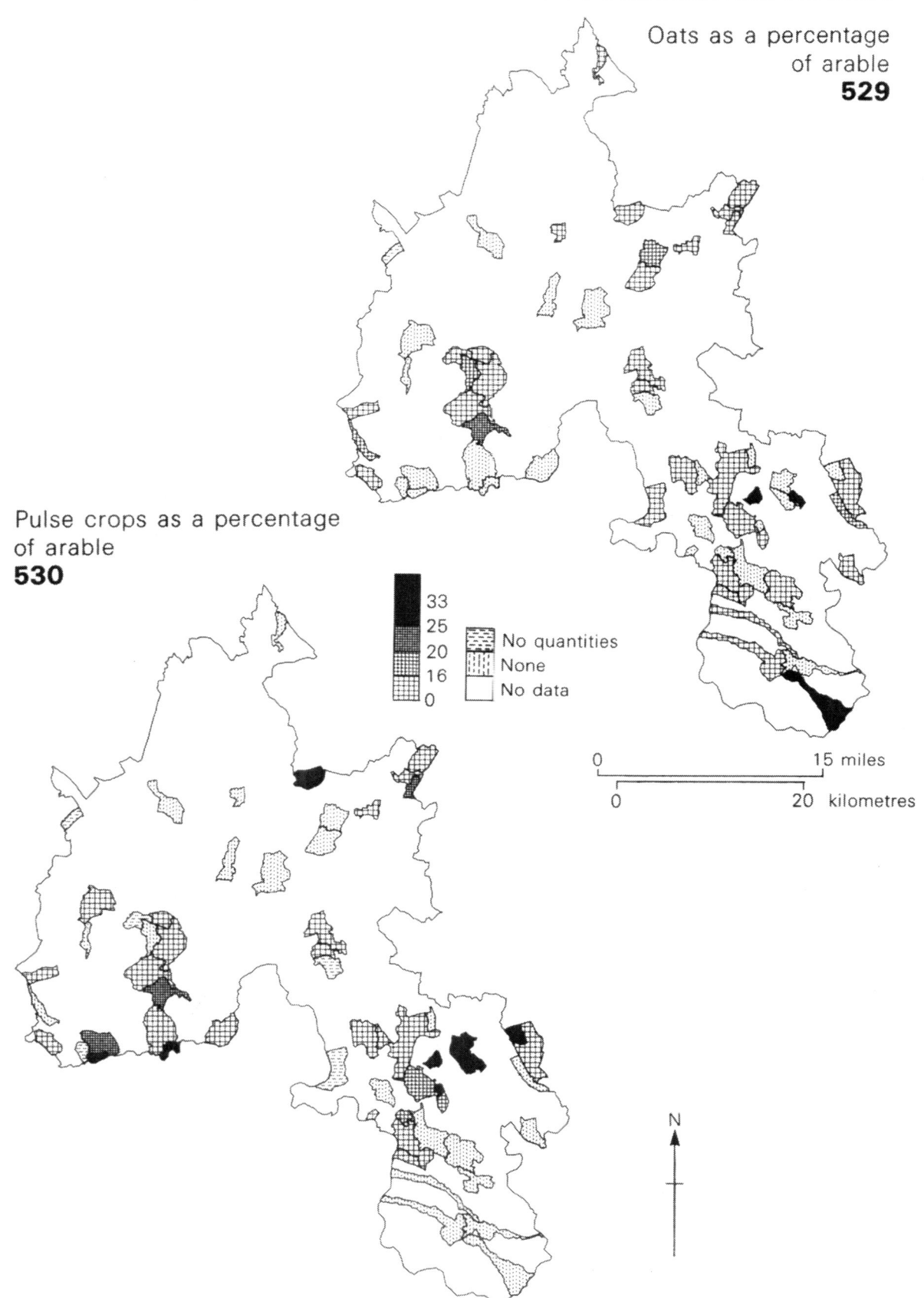

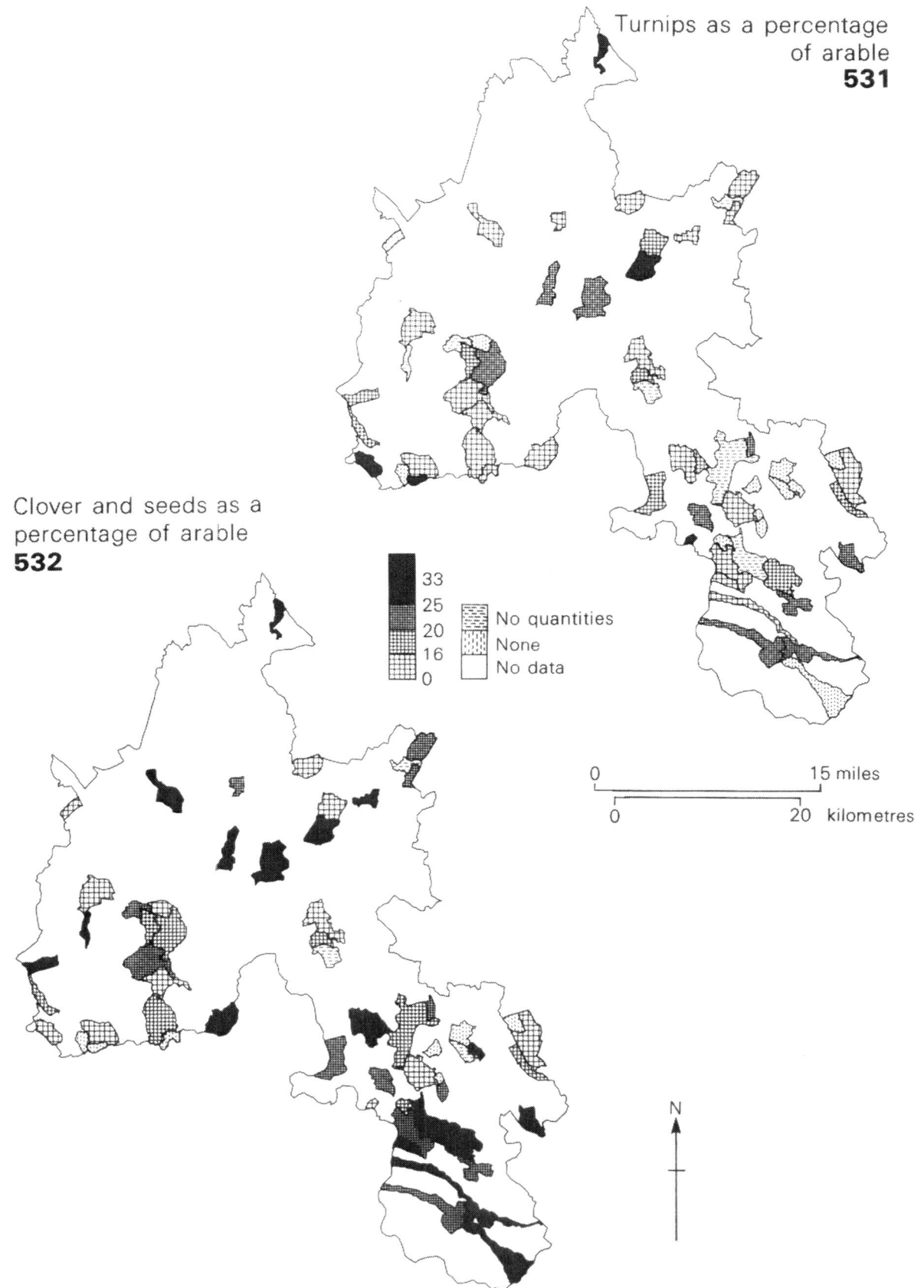

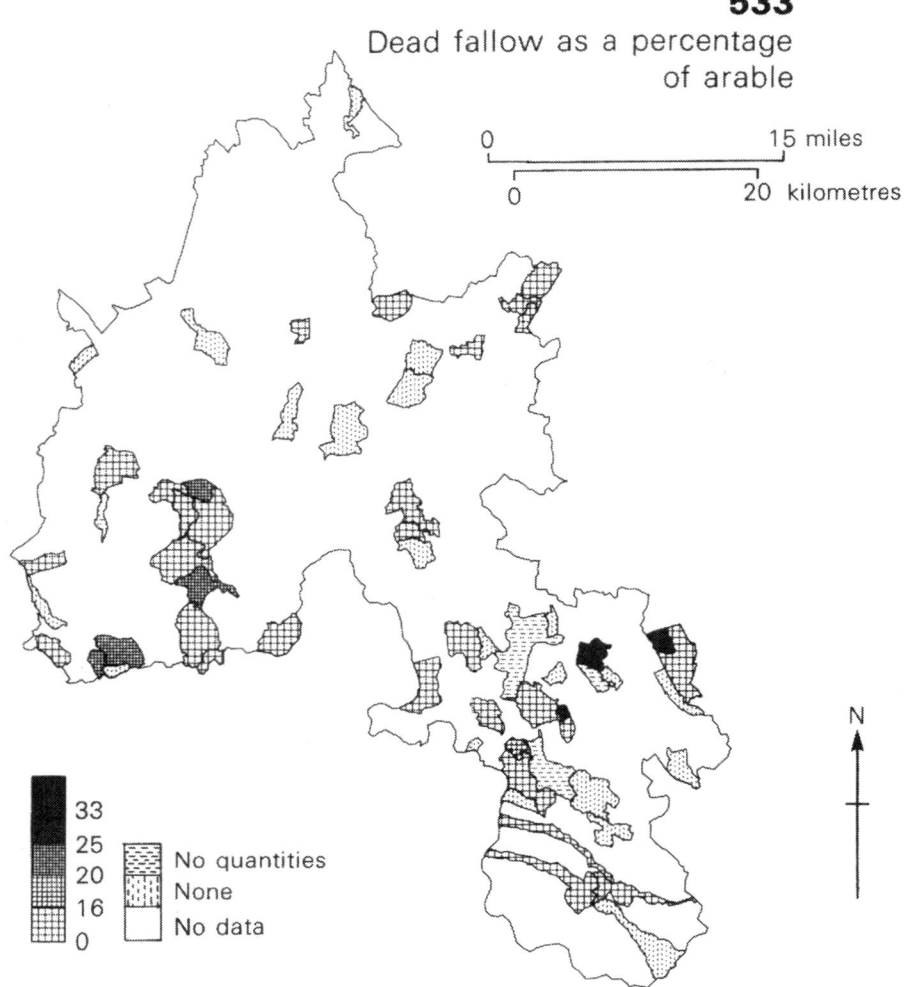

533 Dead fallow as a percentage of arable

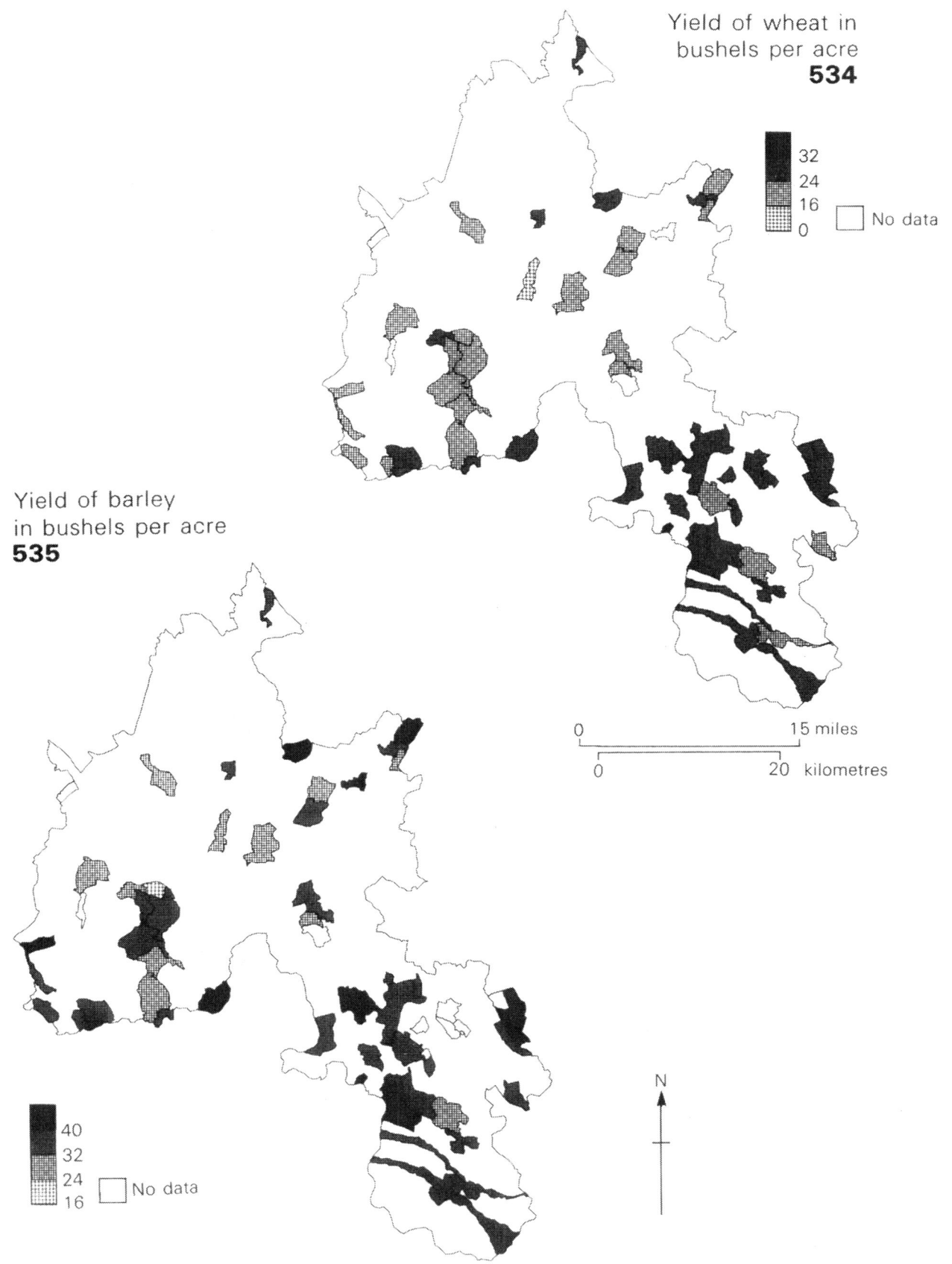

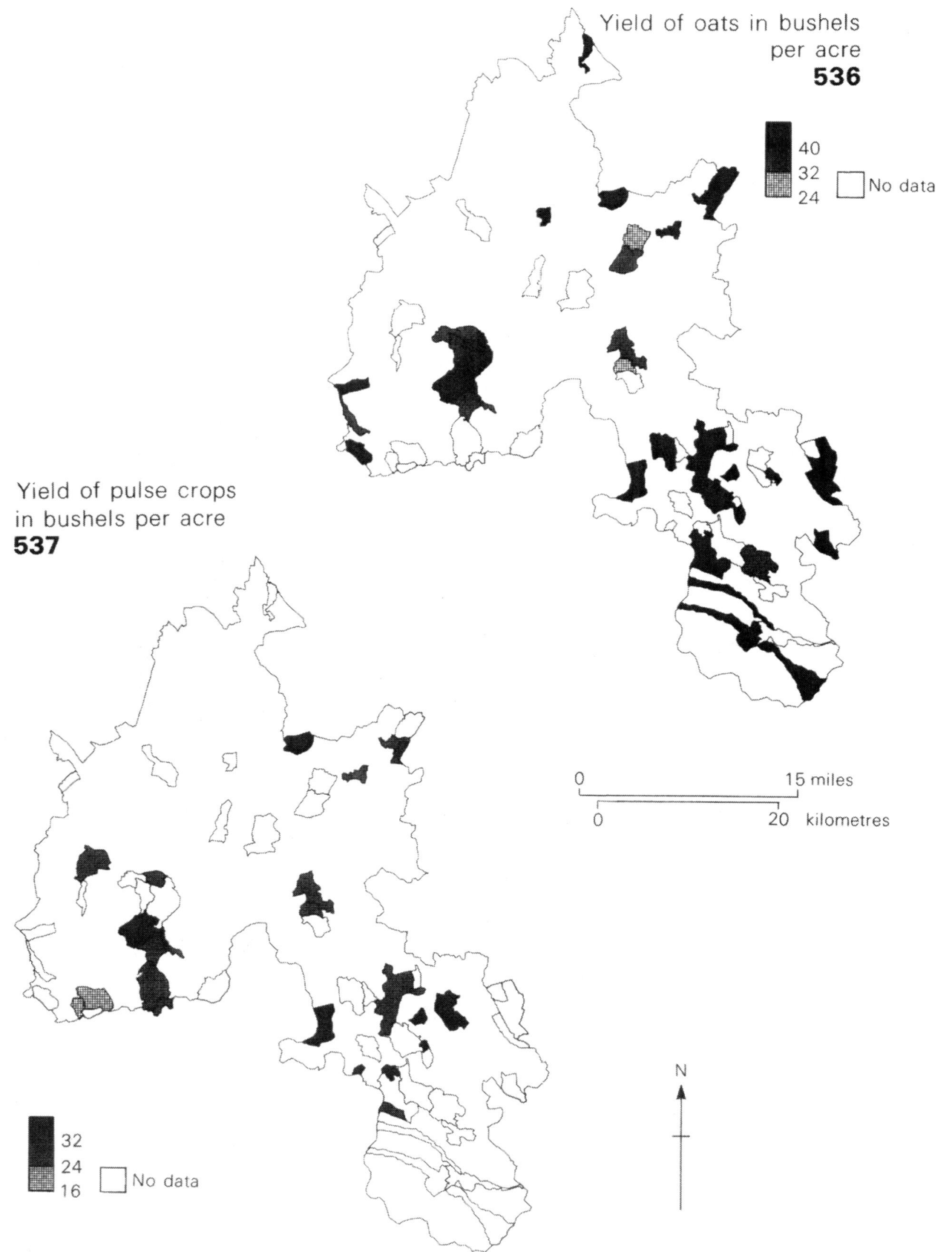

Oxfordshire

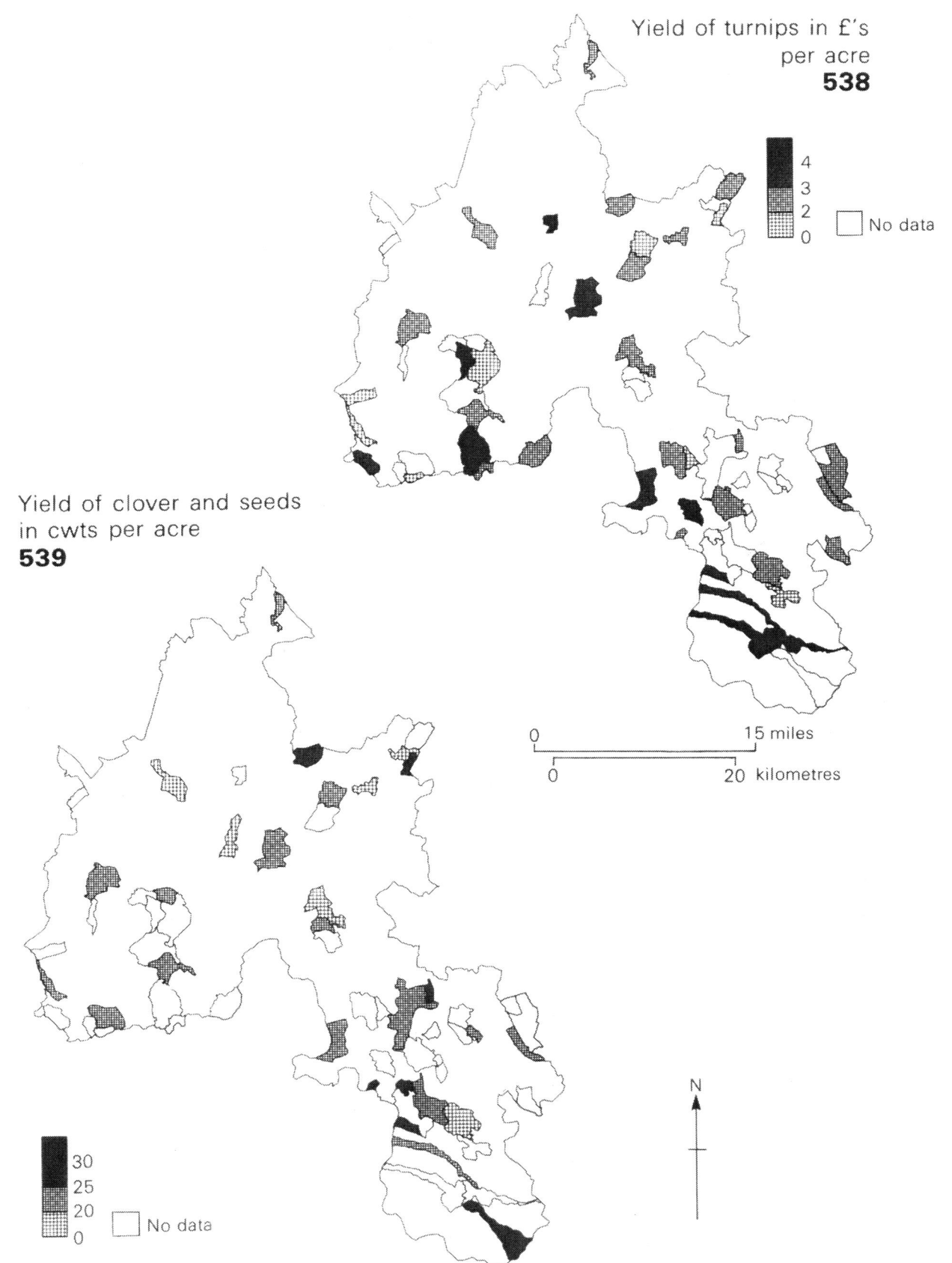

Yield of turnips in £'s per acre
538

Yield of clover and seeds in cwts per acre
539

Midland counties

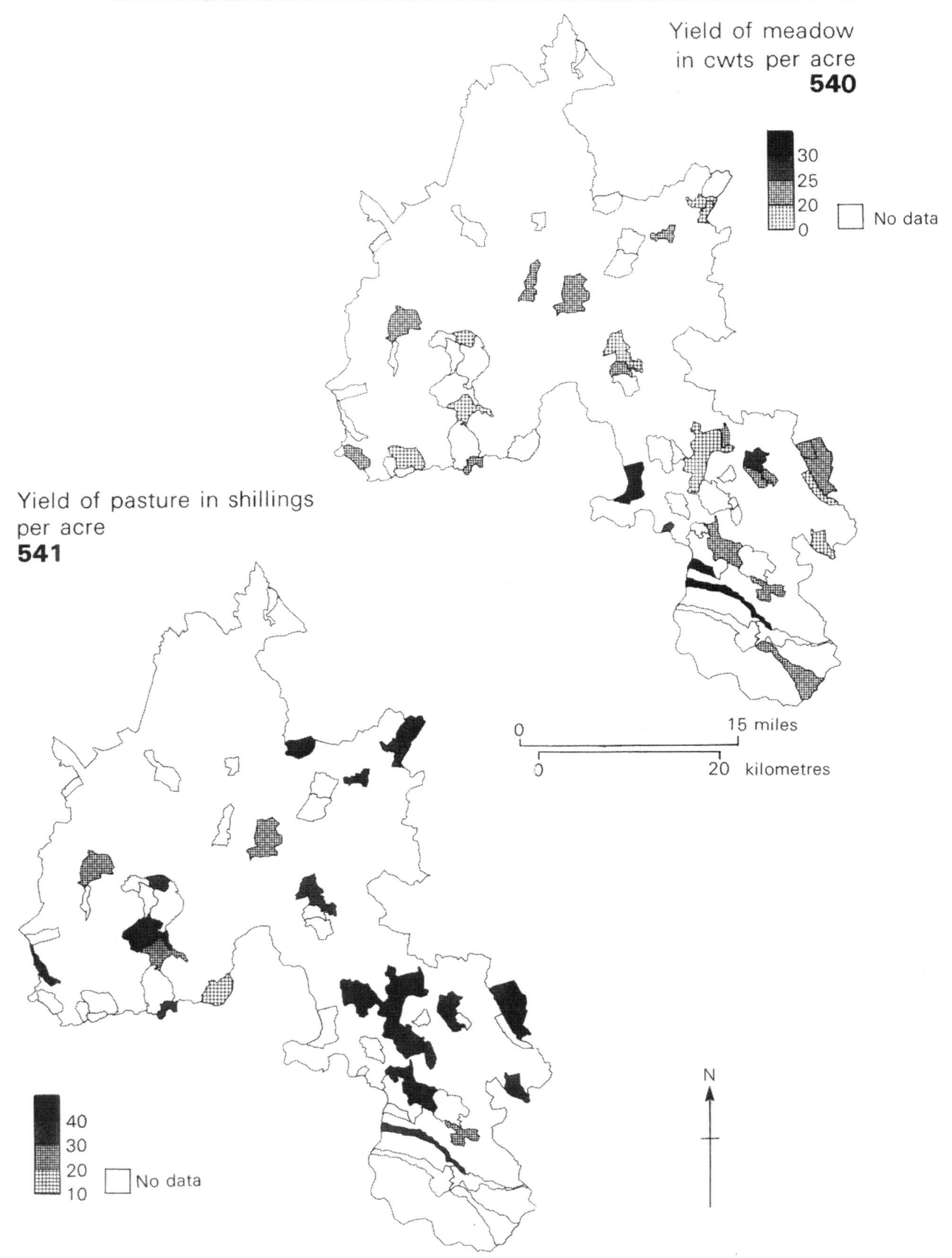

540 Yield of meadow in cwts per acre

541 Yield of pasture in shillings per acre

Buckinghamshire

214 tithe districts
59 reports on tithe agreements

F. D. Hartley (1953) has used tithe apportionments and maps to reconstruct the pattern of land use *c.* 1840 in Chiltern Buckinghamshire.

Buckinghamshire is the county with the smallest proportion (18 per cent) of tithe districts with complete data mapped in this study. Data coverage in the Vale of Aylesbury and north Buckinghamshire is particularly sparse (Map 542) as a result of parliamentary enclosure of many parishes; indeed at Quainton and a few other places enclosure was in progress at the time of tithe commutation. Chiltern beech woodlands were exempt from tithe by prescription. Nine assistant commissioners and local agents wrote reports on Buckinghamshire agreements (Table 75) and as a result these vary considerably in comprehensiveness and detail. The fullest accounts of farm management are to be found in Thomas Smith Woolley's reports, John West's are the briefest and least informative. At Astwood, near Newport Pagnell, 'a storm of snow prevented any great inspection of the land' by Horace William Meteyard on his visit in 1839, 'but this was quite unnecessary as I am well acquainted with the county and had most intelligent men to discuss the qualities of the soil with'.

Table 76 presents data on land use aggregated for the county as a whole and Maps 544–7 indicate the distribution of arable, grass, wood and common respectively. In Chiltern parishes the arable acreage was generally greater than that of grass; in the Vale of Aylesbury the reverse obtained. Assistant commissioners described Vale pastures as among the richest in England, though sometimes requiring drainage for their most effective exploitation. Dairying was of especial importance in this region; Thomas Smith Woolley reported that 'most of the land in the hamlets of Denham, Shipton and Doddershall is pasture for dairying – the dairying in this district "the Vale of Aylesbury" is confined to *butter*'. Skim milk was used for fattening pigs. In the Chilterns, the only good meadows noticed in tithe file reports were those along valley bottoms; meadow land in the Thames valley, both in the Chilterns and further north, received favourable comment.

The distributions of crops and their yields (Maps 548–60) and associated pattern of rotations accord closely with soil type. On still open fields in the Vale of Aylesbury, assistant commissioners and local tithe agents found the three-field system of wheat, beans and fallow still commonly practised, though in some parishes, Edlesborough for example, 'the general cultivation of the arable land is on a four-field turnip course. This prevails in the open, as well as in the inclosed ground, but in the former with much irregularity.' In north Buckinghamshire, four-course rotations were being adopted with much success; at Astwood, 'by feeding hoggetts through the winter on the land with turnips, selling them at Lady Day and then feeding the green crops with wethers through the summer, in short following the "Holkham farming" together with subsoil ploughing etc. double crops of at least five coombes of wheat have been got'. The lighter soils of the Chilterns were ideal for barley, rotations were very variable but usually, as at Great Hampden, on a five-course with one year in seeds. Over-cropping of the arable was a tendency often recorded. Some Chiltern parishes had very poor soils: at Fingest, Horace William Meteyard was of the opinion that 'the land would be most productive as beechwood'. The clay lands were too wet for barley; wheat was the chief corn crop grown in the Vale of Aylesbury. In these dairying districts straw was so valuable that as at Shenley, for instance, Thomas Smith Woolley remarked 'the great object appears to be to grow straw for bedding the cattle in winter'.

High farming is not mentioned in the agreement reports but low farming was noticed in this county (see Subject Index). At Marsh Gibbon in the clay vale: 'the pasture is a fine staple of land, and a similar soil is some of the richest and most productive pastures in England. But here there is no drainage, no top dressing, or any attention to the husbandry – the grass is coarse and sour and covered with ant hills.' At Aston Sandford, south-west of Aylesbury, F. Browne Browne declared 'the land is stiff and clayey, and a considerable part of it very wet. The soil is said to retain the wet so near a drain, that draining would not answer, but this appears to be excuse only for slovenly farming.'

Table 75 *Reports on agreements for commutation of tithes in Buckinghamshire*

Assistant commissioner/ local tithe agent	1837	1838	1839	1840	1841	1842	1843	1844	Totals
F. Browne Browne			12	7					19
Joseph Townsend	5	7		1					13
Thomas Smith Woolley	1		2	1		4		1	9
John West	1	1	3						5
Horace William Meteyard			4						4
John Mee Mathew		1	2						3
John Pickering		1	1			1			3
Henry Jemmett			2						2
Roger Kynaston		1							1
Totals	7	11	26	9		5		1	59

Table 76 *Land use, crops and yields in Buckinghamshire c. 1836*

A	Land use	Percentage of total land area enumerated in reports on tithe agreements	Estimated acreage in whole county
	Arable	55.8	260,405
	Grass	30.1	140,408
	Wood	9.2	42,879
	Common	3.9	18,309

B	Crop	Mean percentage of arable	Mean yield per acre	Estimated acreage in whole county
	Wheat	23.3	21.0 bushels	60,609
	Barley	14.8	28.4 bushels	38,414
	Oats	10.0	34.7 bushels	26,050
	Pulses	7.2	25.5 bushels	18,655
	Turnips	13.8	£3.56	35,871
	Seeds	20.5	19.1 cwts	53,399
	Fallows	6.9	—	18,077

414　Midland counties

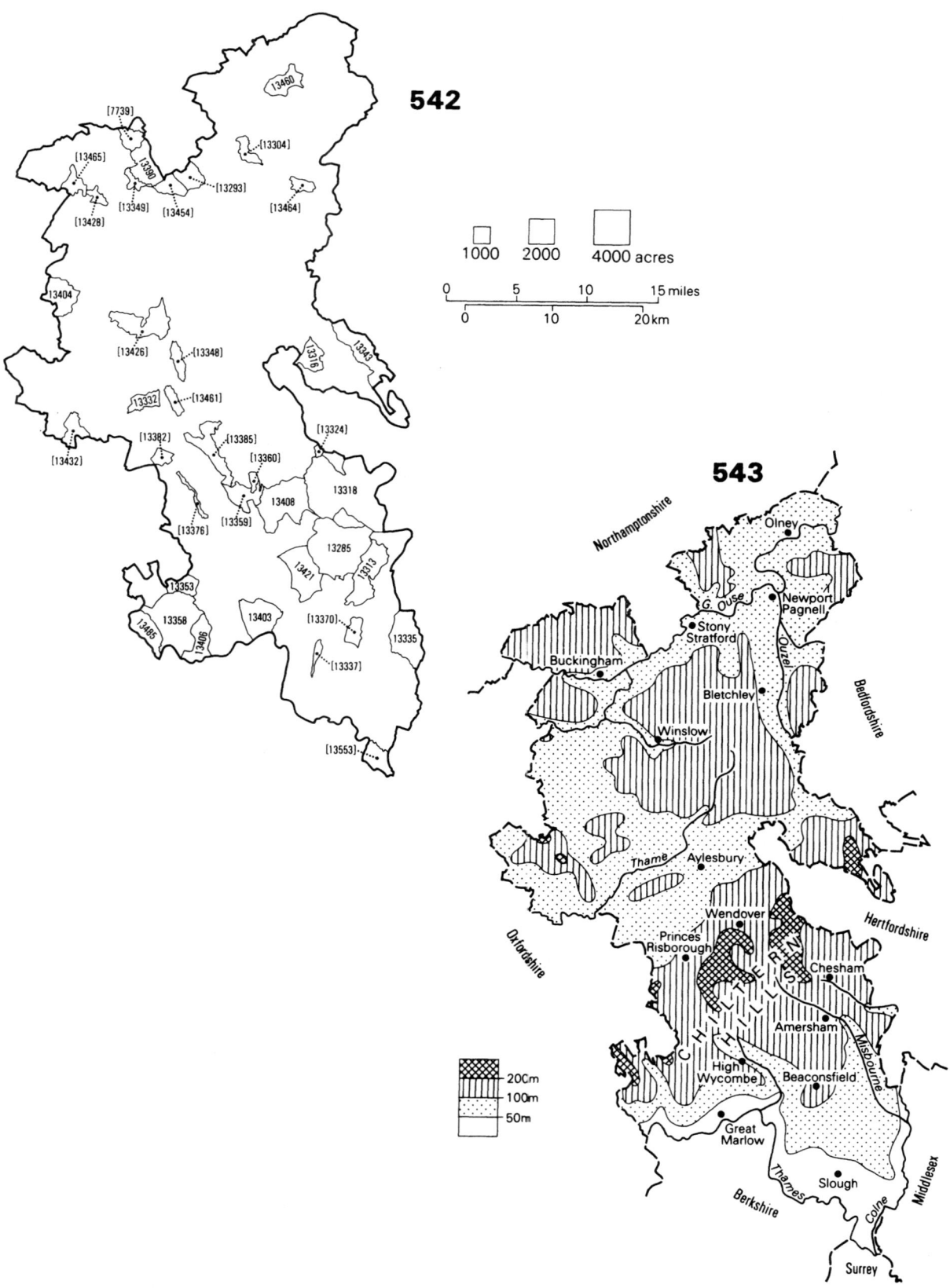

Buckinghamshire

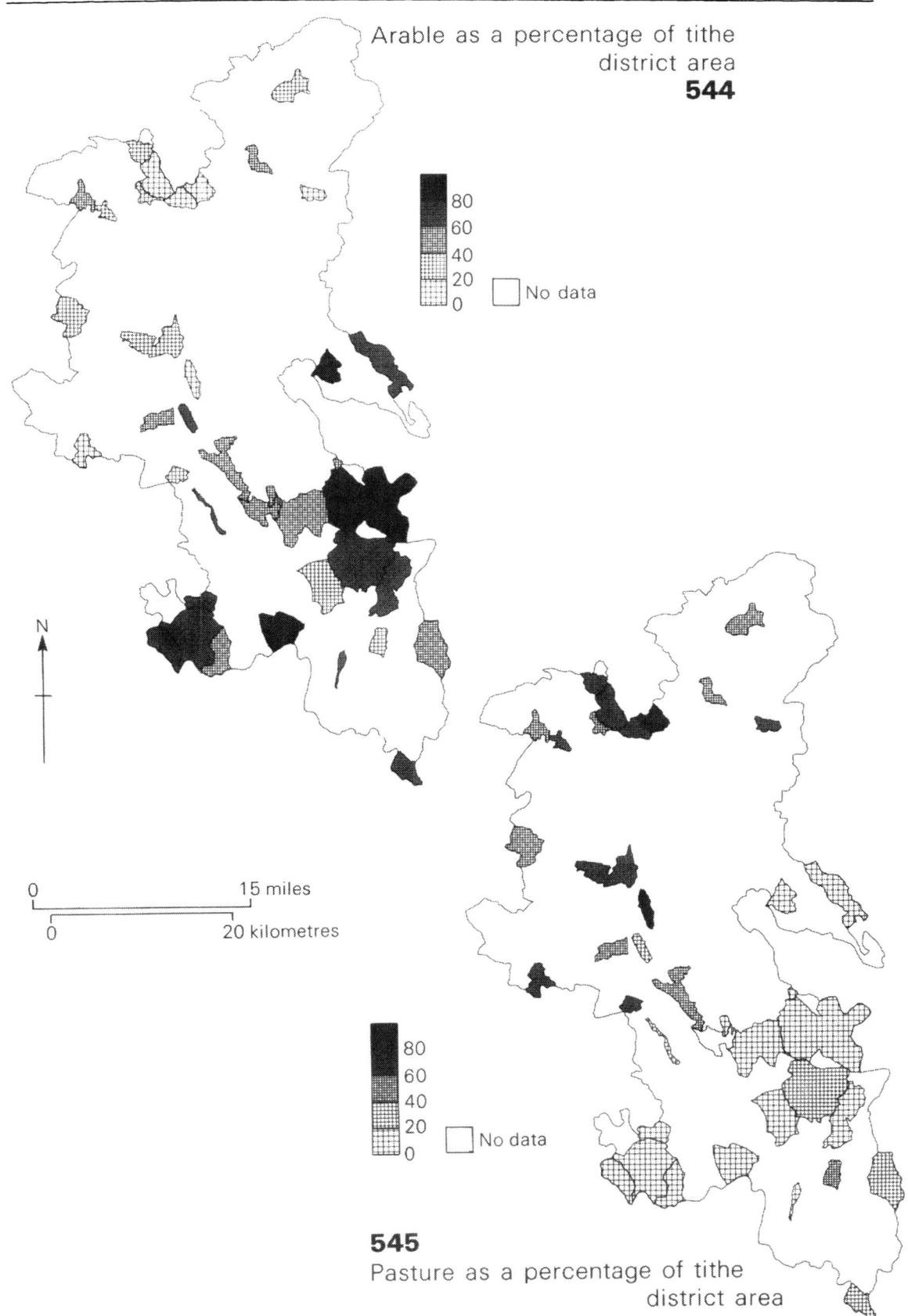

544 Arable as a percentage of tithe district area

545 Pasture as a percentage of tithe district area

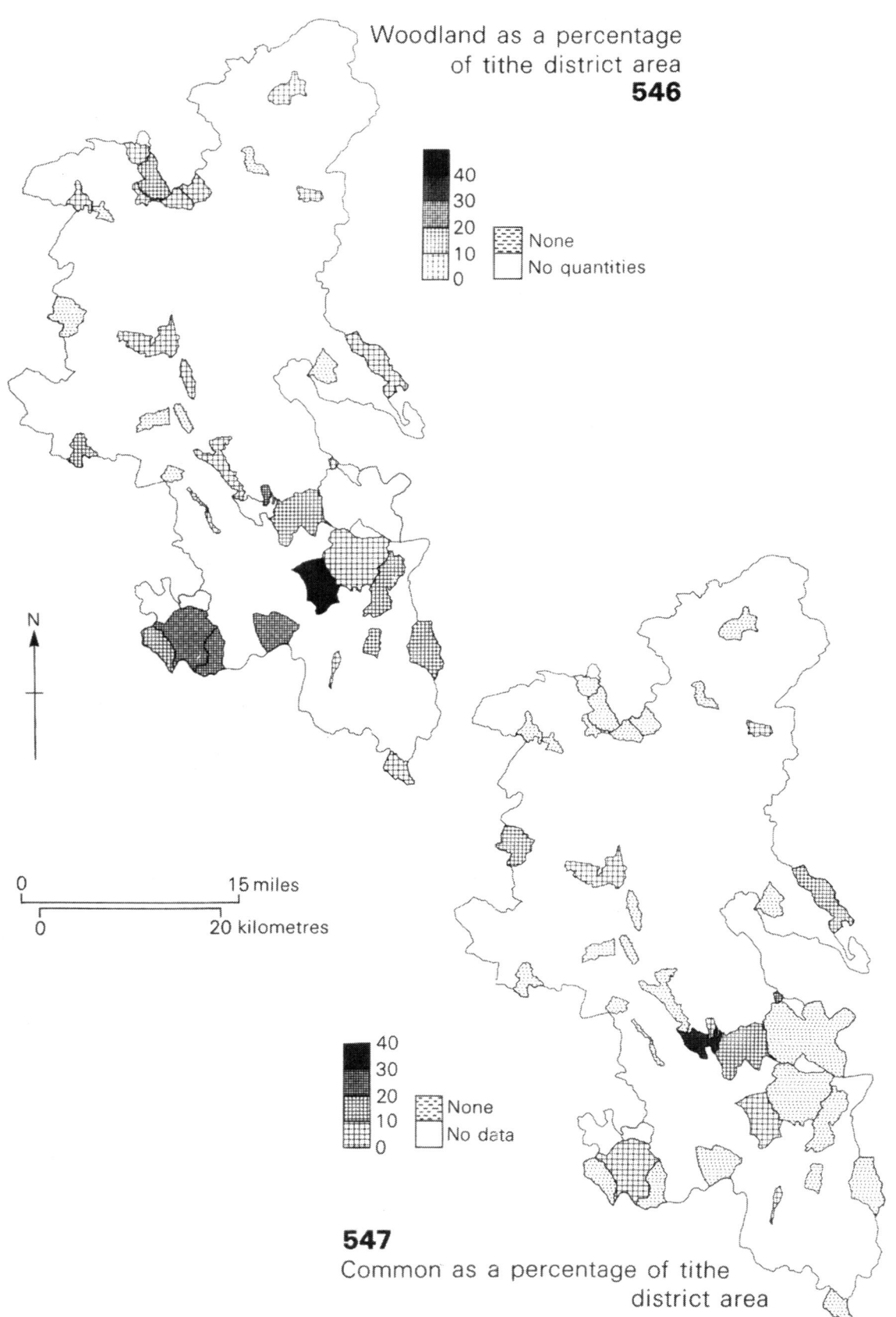

546 Woodland as a percentage of tithe district area

547 Common as a percentage of tithe district area

Buckinghamshire

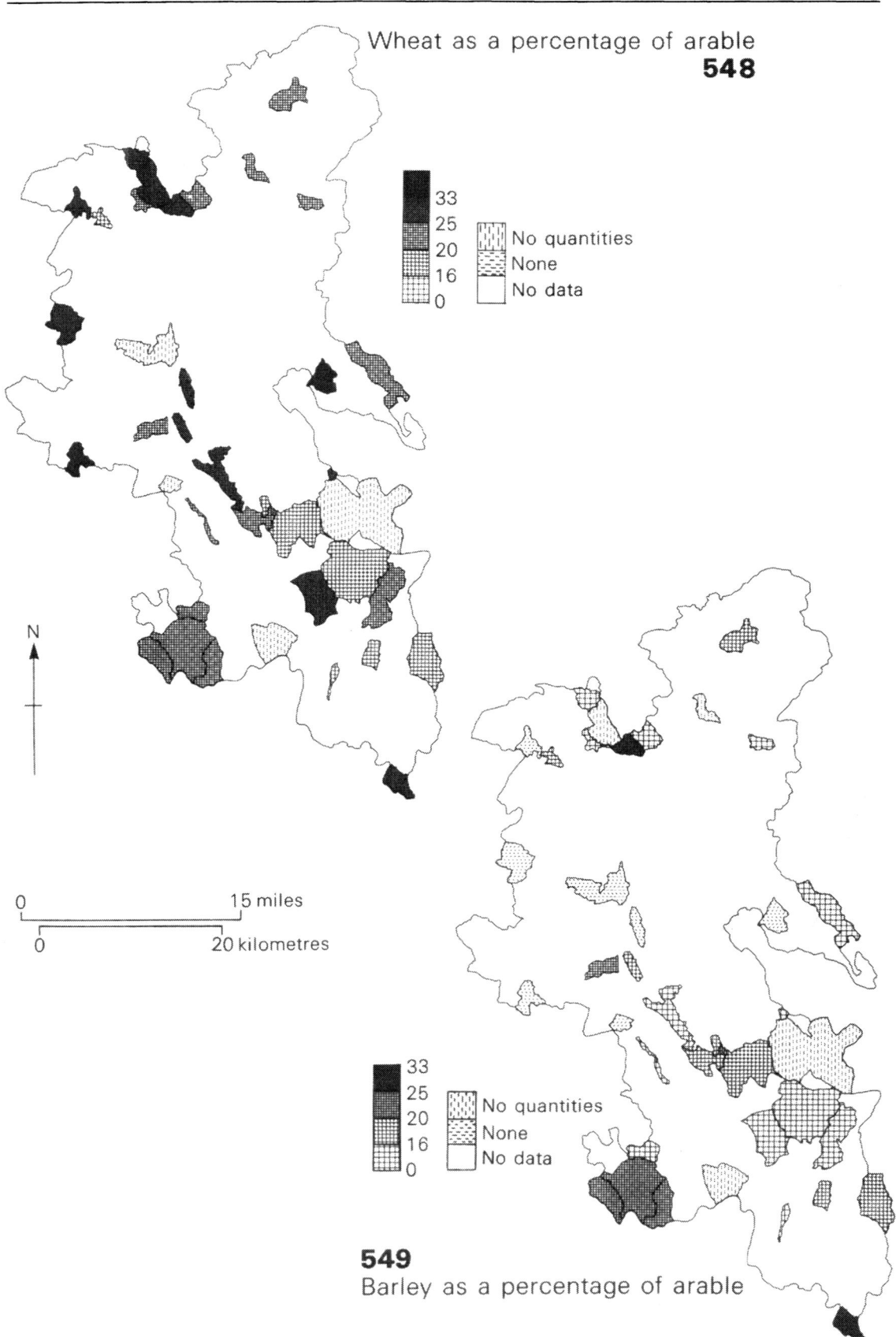

548 Wheat as a percentage of arable

549 Barley as a percentage of arable

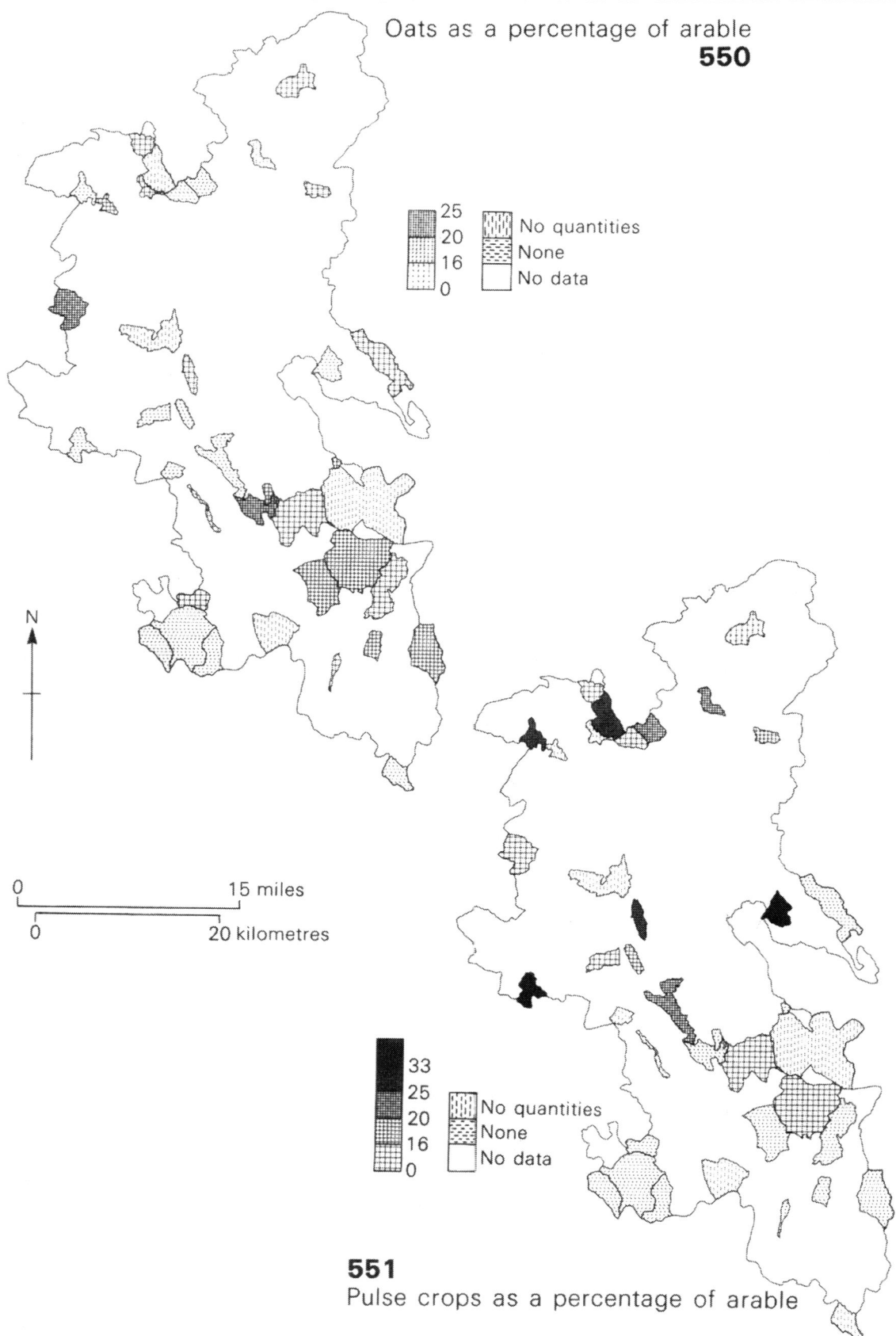

550 Oats as a percentage of arable

551 Pulse crops as a percentage of arable

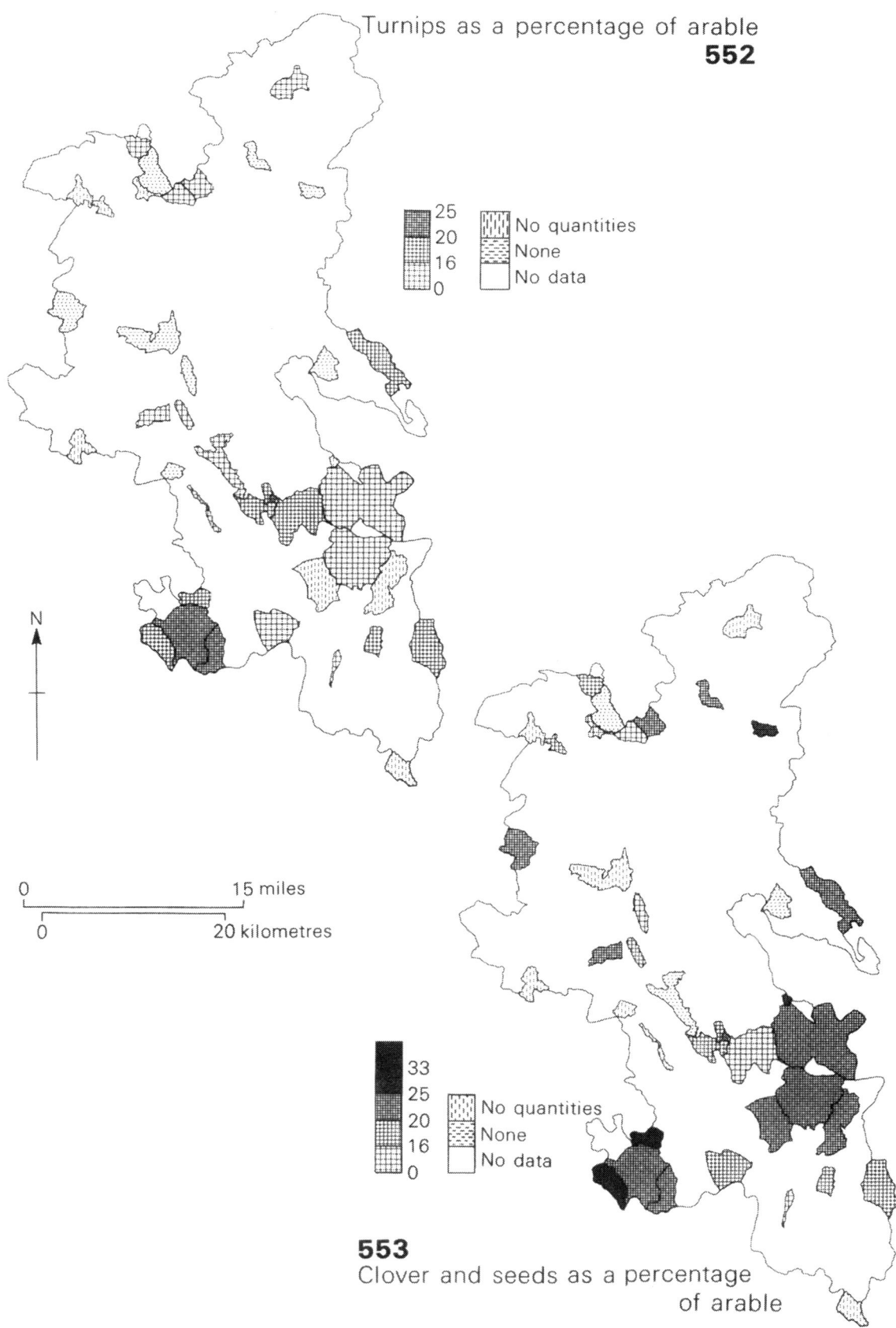

552 Turnips as a percentage of arable

553 Clover and seeds as a percentage of arable

Midland counties

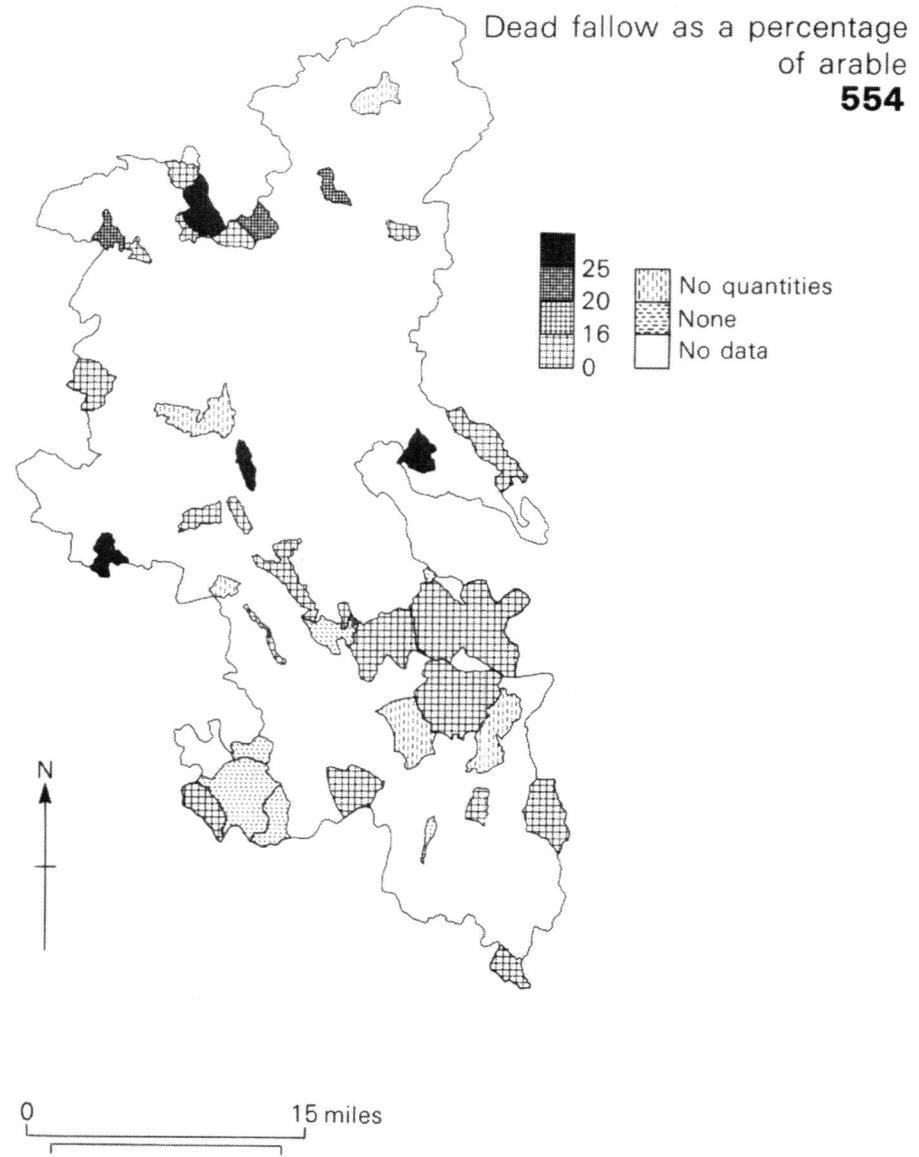

Dead fallow as a percentage of arable
554

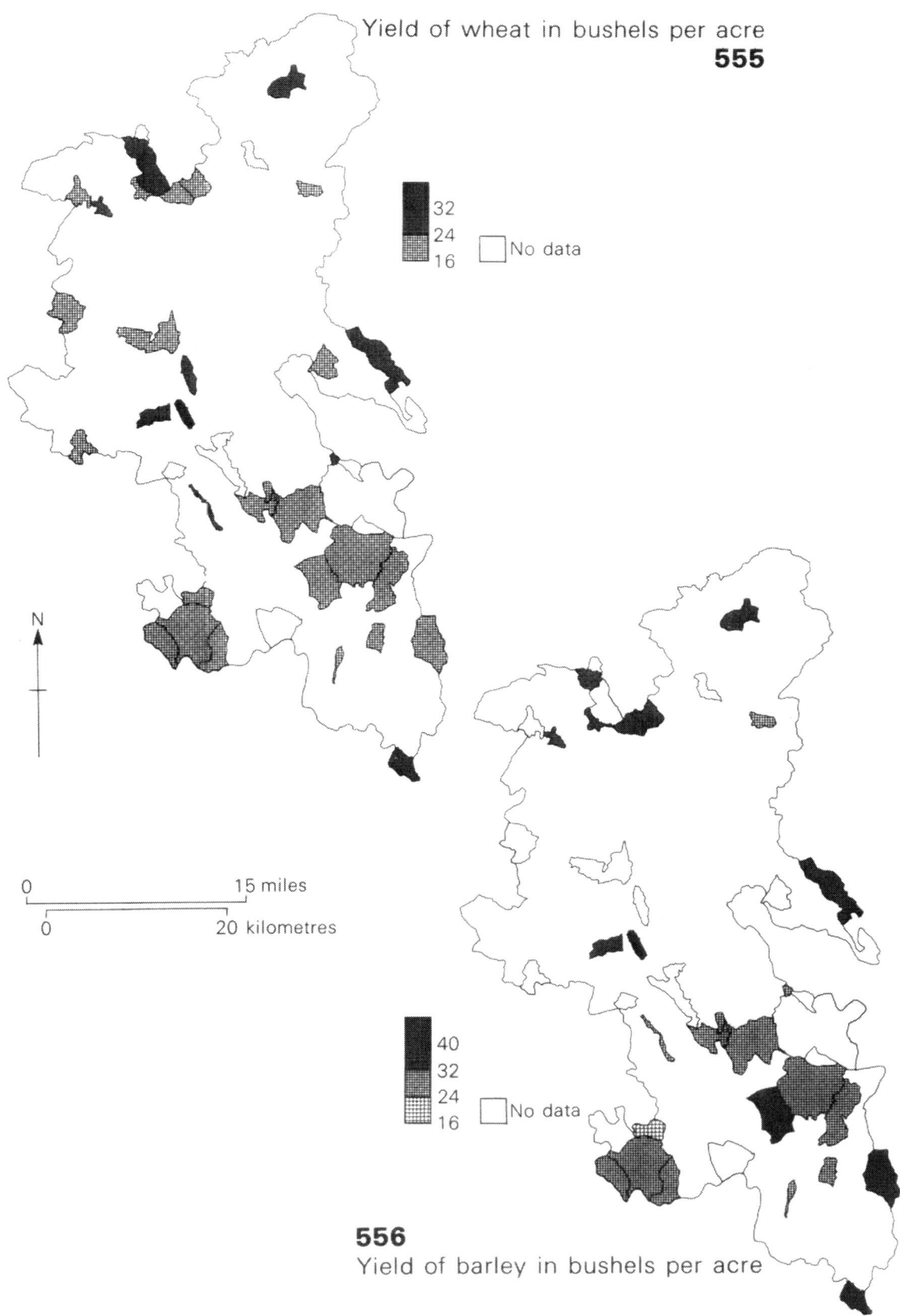

555 Yield of wheat in bushels per acre

556 Yield of barley in bushels per acre

422   Midland counties

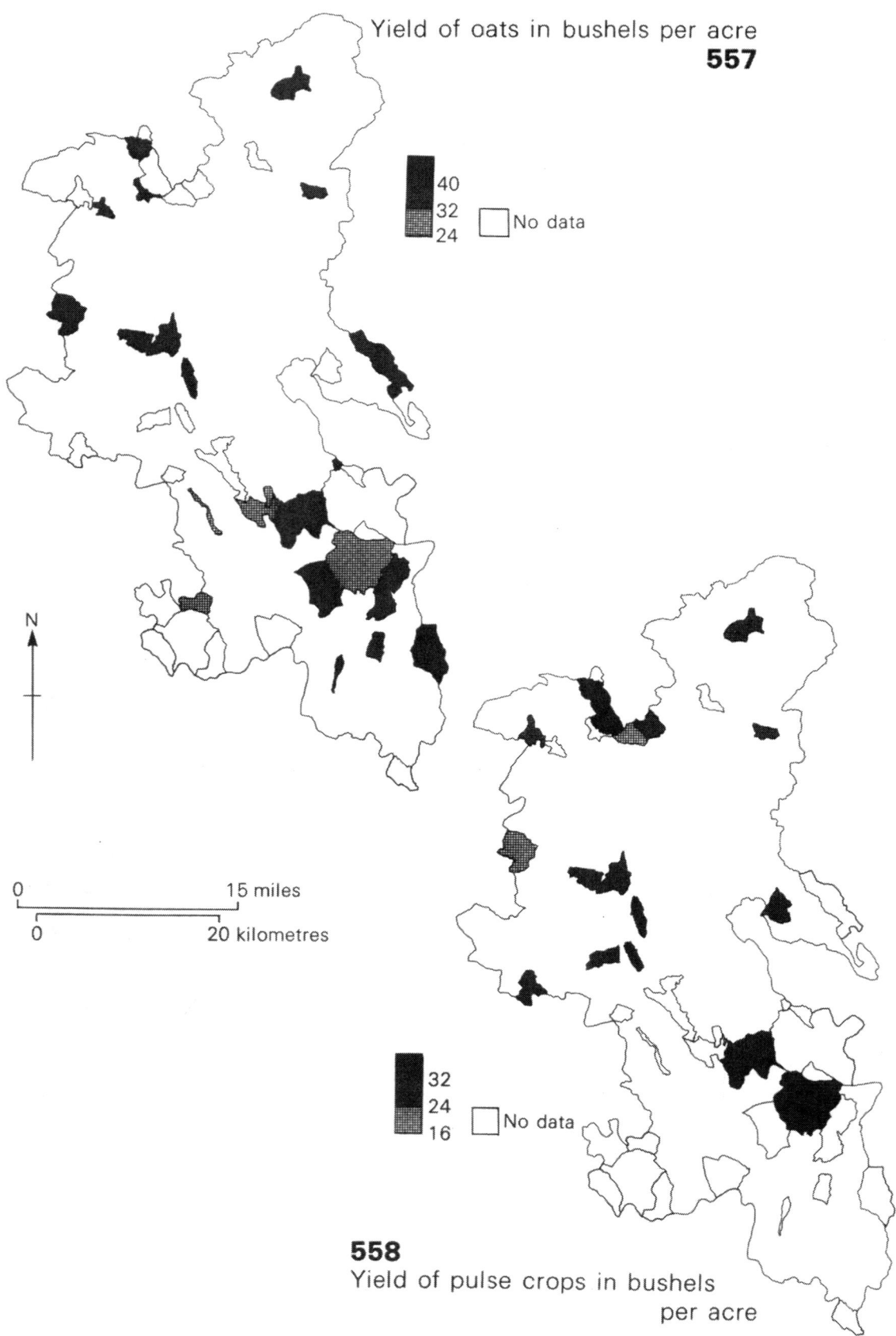

Yield of oats in bushels per acre
557

558
Yield of pulse crops in bushels per acre

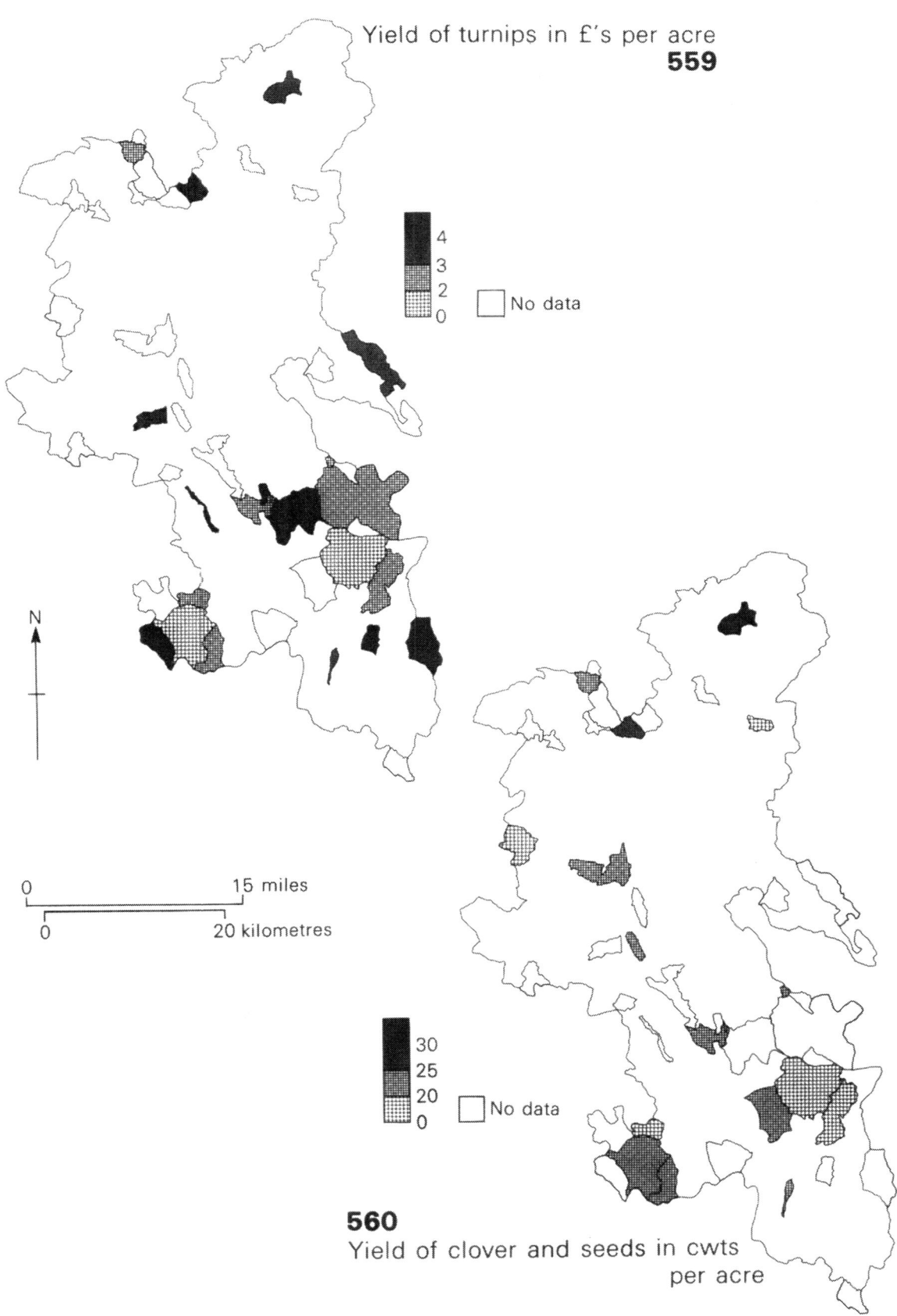

559 Yield of turnips in £'s per acre

560 Yield of clover and seeds in cwts per acre

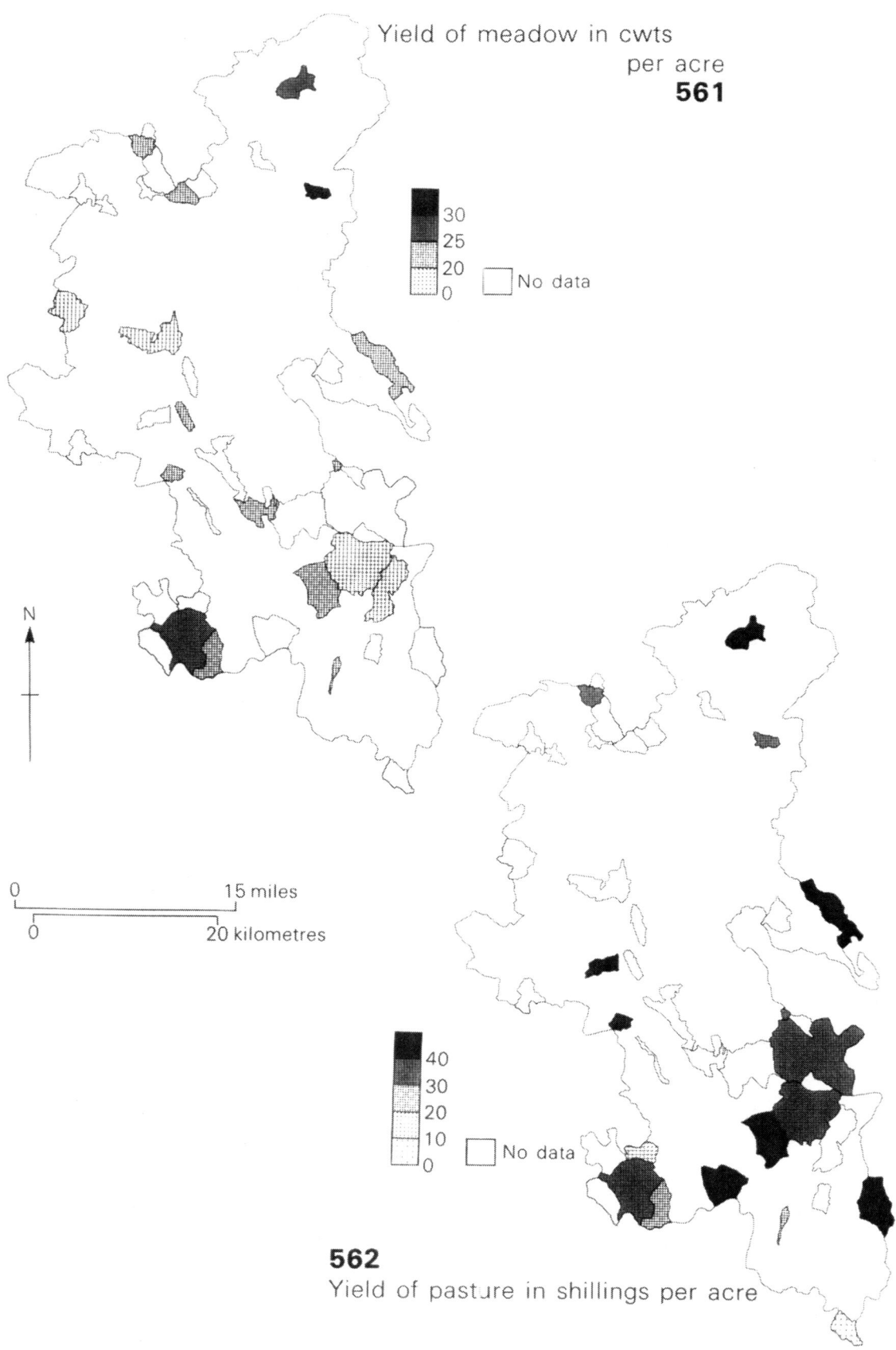

Bedfordshire

128 tithe districts
23 reports on tithe agreements

More than half the parishes in Bedfordshire were entirely tithe free by 1836 as a result of parliamentary enclosure and in a few others tithes had been replaced by a corn-rent. Of the twenty-three tithe districts with reports on agreements, sixteen possess land use and crop data for more than 90 per cent of their total area and these data have been aggregated in Table 78. This 13 per cent sample is biased, of course, in that it contains only early enclosed or still open parishes and is not representative of those enclosed in the eighteenth and nineteenth centuries. Assistant commissioners and local tithe agents were not much impressed with the quality of agriculture in open field parishes. Quite typical is the opinion that Thomas Smith Woolley voiced at Westoning where 'like open lands in general the farming is usually of the worst description – many of the crops being very light and full of weeds'. Improvements were, however, taking place with, wherever possible, fallows planted with some potatoes, tares on clay soils, and turnips on light soils (see Subject Index). Three-course rotations were disappearing; on the chalk/clay soils of Totternhoe in 1840, for example, 'the course of husbandry is irregular, the old system was three crops to a fallow, but at present land is not allowed to remain a whole year absolutely unproductive. The prevalent system may be taken as a five course of barley or oats, clover, wheat, beans and turnips.' There are a number of references (see Subject Index) to the advance of draining on clay soils, although at Edworth, Edward Greathed speaks disparagingly of the way farmers filled their drains with 'rotten bushes' with the result that after seven years they were filled in and quite useless.

None of grassland and livestock husbandry, woodland, or common occasioned much comment in the tithe files of this county where the ratio of arable to grass was 2 to 1 and where Tithe Commission reporters were most concerned to discuss the arable sector when assessing the fairness of an agreement or when framing an award.

Table 77 *Reports on agreements for commutation of tithes in Bedfordshire*

Assistant commissioner/ local tithe agent	1837	1838	1839	1840	1841	1842	1843	Totals
John Pickering		1	3		1			5
Thomas Smith Woolley	2		2		1			5
F. Browne Browne		1		3				4
John West	1	2						3
William Heard			1				1	2
Joseph Townsend		2						2
Edward Greathed		1						1
Roger Kynaston			1					1
Totals	3	7	7	3	2		1	23

Table 78 *Land use, crops and yields in Bedfordshire c. 1836*

	Land use	Percentage of total land area enumerated in reports on tithe agreements		Estimated acreage in whole county
A	Arable	60.1		177,557
	Grass	31.2		92,254
	Wood	5.6		16,545
	Crop	Mean percentage of arable	Mean yield per acre	Estimated acreage in whole county
B	Wheat	22.8	22.7 bushels	40,397
	Barley	13.2	31.4 bushels	23,366
	Oats	7.4	36.9 bushels	13,155
	Pulses	13.6	21.8 bushels	24,194
	Turnips	11.4	£3.50	20,196
	Seeds	16.5	21.0 cwts	29,317
	Fallows	16.0	—	28,412

Leicestershire

353 tithe districts
43 reports on tithe agreements

Leicestershire has one of the highest proportions (37 per cent) of completely tithe free districts of any county and, conversely, the smallest proportion of reports on tithe agreements, just 12 per cent, a figure which reduces further to 8 per cent when those covering less than 90 per cent of a tithe district are excluded. In consequence, data for the very small sample of twenty-eight places with representative coverage are not aggregated to form a table of county estimates. Tithe awards are mostly quite late in date (1845–50) and, as with agreements, few refer to substantial parts of a township but usually just that small part enclosed in the pre-parliamentary period. Nevertheless, minutes and papers in these files do contain useful accounts of landscape and farming (see Subject Index). The Index reveals that enclosure and its agrarian consequences were topics much written about; a preponderance of entries relates to grassland and livestock farming and its produce, rather than to the arable sector. Files listed against the heading 'exemptions from tithe' provide a wealth of information on the very complex pattern of tithing that arose where part only of a township was enclosed. At Snarestone, Richard Burton Phillipson wrote, doubtless in exasperation, that 'having the titheable and modus lands so much intermixed as to chequer the map renders it difficult to find them out in a survey'.

Table 79 *Reports on agreements for commutation of tithes in Leicestershire*

Assistant commissioner/ local tithe agent	1838	1839	1840	1841	1842	1843	1844	1848	Totals
John Pickering		11	4	2					17
Thomas Smith Woolley	6	5			1		1		13
Edward Greathed	5								5
Richard Burton Phillipson				1	1		1		3
Henry Pilkington						2			2
Horace William Meteyard			1						1
John Job Rawlinson			1						1
Joseph Townsend								1	1
Totals	11	16	6	3	2	2	2	1	43

Northamptonshire

340 tithe districts
40 reports on tithe agreements

No fewer than 160 Northamptonshire tithe districts were exempt from tithe by 1836; in 78 per cent of districts where some tithe remained, commutation was effected by compulsory award. The result is that just 12 per cent of Northamptonshire districts have reports on tithe agreements, a fact which places this county alongside Leicestershire at the foot of a national league of coverage. This figure reduces still further to 7 per cent of all districts when agreements covering restricted parts of a district are excluded. As in Leicestershire, parliamentary enclosure is again the key to explaining these low figures. Extant data are insufficient either for mapping statistics of land use, crops and yields, district-by-district, or for producing reliable county aggregates.

As a body, Northamptonshire files are not as rich a source on agricultural practices as those of Leicestershire – even enclosure does not get the weight of attention that might be expected. Exceptions to this are places such as Stoke Bruern where Thomas Smith Woolley remarked that the

> hamlet has only recently been inclosed in the course of the last year. All the arable land during the years of the average was open and very ill farmed in the common open field course of two crops and a dead fallow. The arable land is of a character which the system it has hitherto been farmed upon is very ill adapted for and I think it will be benefited beyond measure by the inclosure.

On the other hand, Northamptonshire files, particularly those for places where awards were imposed, contain a wealth of information on the Church, its incomes, tithing practices and exemptions (see Subject Index headings 1–8). All of this material was collected by assistant tithe commissioners during the process of framing an award.

Table 80 *Reports on agreements for commutation of tithes in Northamptonshire*

Assistant commissioner/ local tithe agent	1838	1839	1840	1841	1842	1843	Totals
John West	7	9					16
Thomas Smith Woolley	3	2		2	2		9
F. Browne Browne		4	3				7
John Pickering	1		2			1	4
Henry Pilkington		3					3
Joseph Townsend	1						1
Totals	12	18	5	2	2	1	40

WALES

Anglesey
Brecon*
Caernarvonshire*
Cardiganshire*
Carmarthenshire*
Denbighshire
Flintshire
Glamorgan*
Merionethshire
Montgomeryshire
Pembrokeshire*
Radnorshire*

The 'pastoral' type of printed form used for reporting on tithe agreements in Welsh counties requires estimates of land uses, the course of crops and the number of stock and asks assistant tithe commissioners and local tithe agents for their 'remarks, stating the peculiar circumstances of the parish which may affect the value of the tithe'.

* For these counties crop acreages are insufficient for compiling county figures.

Anglesey

76 tithe districts
55 reports on tithe agreements

The usual system of tithing in Anglesey was by annual auction – 'a great deal of unpleasant competition is resorted to, and which is now happily on the point of being abolished'. Included in the total of fifty-five reports are eleven valuations made by assistant tithe commissioner Aneurin Owen in the course of drafting compulsory awards. As their form and content are identical with John Fenton's reports on agreements, they have been added to the Anglesey data base. Statistical data in Anglesey files are a good deal richer than for most Welsh counties, but neither Fenton nor Owen provide any yield data. Fenton's landscape descriptions are particularly full and vivid with comments on the large tracts of waste and bog and the rarity of hedgerows and trees. Mining and quarrying in the mountainous part of the county are described; Amlwch parish contained the 'celebrated copper mines which are still worked but not to the extent they were some years ago. Owing to the quantity of mineral raised and smelted here the general aspect of the district is barren and the proportion of the naked rock (at least 400 acres) is immense.'

Soils are not discussed in much detail but the general picture that comes across from the files is one of poor, unproductive soils, very light on the limestone plateau and needing much manure to produce good crops, or else heavy and in need of draining. Fenton found, however, very great differences in the quality of farming from parish to parish on these poor lands. At Llanddeusant, he considered that there was 'very little improvable land in this parish. The system of farming is slovenly and under a better course, the crops might be much increased in value.' By contrast, at Llanfaethlu, 'the system of farming is good, and the crops in general are abundant; but the land is brought to its highest state of cultivation and no great future improvement can be contemplated'. Rotations are not stated with much precision in the parish descriptions and were often irregular. A six- or seven-course of seeds for three years; broken up for oats; potatoes or turnips; barley or wheat is that most often recorded. Potatoes were a vitally important element of the farming system, especially for feeding to pigs, and a common practice was for farmers to allow the parish poor to grow potatoes on their fallow fields – a practice described by Aneurin Owen at Aberffraw.

> This parish [he said] is distinguished by the large quantity of potatoes grown. The population is considerable and they busily collect sea tang, at all convenient opportunities, for manure and are allowed by the farmers such ground for potatoes as may be required on

condition of manuring it. Thus about half the quantity grown is the result of this extraneous manure, and the corn crops owing to it are largely extended.

Three other topics receive frequent comment in Anglesey files. The need of plantations to act as wind breaks is the first. At Llangaffo, 'planting belts of timber across exposed situations is much needed to break the force of the prevailing winds. The trees at Dinan thrive well and are the only ones in the parish, although planted in a high locality prove what may be done.' A second topic concerns manuring the arable. Lime was easily obtained in Anglesey and there was a regular export trade to the mainland through Red Wharf Bay. Sea sand and shells are also noted. Finally, the marketing of produce much concerned both Fenton and Owen as they had to make some allowance for costs when commuting tithes. At Trefdraeth, 'the distance from markets and the extreme badness of the road to Carnarvon (the principal market) and the ferry at Talyfoel, put the inhabitants to considerable inconvenience and expense in the transportation of their produce'.

Table 81 *Reports on agreements for commutation of tithes in Anglesey*

Assistant commissioner/ local tithe agent	1839	1840	1841	1842	1843	1844	1845	1846	1847	1848	Totals
John Fenton	5	12	14	6	5						42
Aneurin Owen					9		1	1		2	13
Totals	5	12	14	6	14		1	1		2	55

Table 82 *Land use and crops in Anglesey c. 1836*

	A	Land use	Percentage of total land area enumerated in reports on tithe agreements	Estimated acreage in whole county
		Arable	34.6	66,978
		Grass	56.4	109,064
		Common	2.7	5,128
	B	Crop	Mean percentage of arable	Estimated acreage in whole county
		Wheat	9.4	6,303
		Barley	19.7	13,221
		Oats	43.8	29,324

Brecon

84 tithe districts
60 reports on tithe agreements

Only three Brecon parishes were tithe free and, as in Wales generally, a high proportion (71 per cent) of voluntary commutations were achieved. Unfortunately, the information on rural landscapes and farming contained in Brecon files is not as rich as this high coverage might suggest. Rarely do either Thomas Hoskins, who wrote 87 per cent of the reports, or John Johnes, who completed the remainder (Table 83), provide crop acreages. They never record crop yields or write parish descriptions. Information entered on the printed questionnaire is minimal and stated quantities are, as the two assistant commissioners acknowledged, very rough and ready. In particular, both men found gross inaccuracies in acreages of commons. At Modrydd, Johnes reported in 1838 that 'some say 1000, others 2000 acres, the acreage of the common lands is not well ascertained – from my own view I should consider it more than 1000 acres and I did not see the whole of it'. There is, however, much more detailed information in that much smaller number of files (twenty-one) relating to parishes where compulsory awards were framed. That for Llanganten, for example, contains a valuation of crops received by assistant commissioner Aneurin Owen and a further series of counter valuations as opposing parties presented their various cases. These can be exceptionally detailed – for Llanfillo and Llangattock parishes, for instance, there are valuations of the crops and animals on each field of each farm.

Aggregated data on land use in Brecon are presented in Table 84 which, in view of the cautions on accuracy made above, should be viewed as a guide to proportions of arable, grass, wood and common, rather than as a statement of precise acreages. There is very little supplementary information in the files on arable farming practices in this county. The most that is available for anything like a representative sample of places is a view of the usual arable rotation. The kinds of variations noted can be gauged from the following examples:

'fallow, wheat, barley, clover 2–3 years, fallow for turnips';
'fallow, wheat, barley, clover 4–5 years, oats, barley';
'fallow, wheat, barley, clover, wheat, barley';
'fallow, wheat, barley, oats, clover 2–4 years – sometimes oats, or fallow';
'fallow, wheat, barley, clover, wheat, oats, grass 4–5 years';
'fallow, wheat, barley, clover, wheat, oats'.

In short the basic system was to fallow land for wheat and then to sow barley. After this there would be a clover ley of from two to five years and then oats. The four-course wheat, turnips, barley, clover system was general in only a small minority of Brecon parishes (see Subject Index) but in others a small quantity of land might be farmed in this way, whilst the rest was tilled according to more traditional rotations. It is reported that potatoes occasionally formed part of the field crop rotation but that pulses were uncommon. On really poor soils, leys might be as long as seven or eight years and oats the main crop. On the whole, though, long leys and successive crops of oats were not as common in Brecon as in parts of central and North Wales.

The Subject Index indicates the near silence of Brecon tithe files on grassland farming and livestock husbandry.

Table 83 *Reports on agreements for commutation of tithes in Brecon*

Assistant commissioner/ local tithe agent	1838	1839	1840	1841	1842	1843	Totals
Thomas Hoskins		21	18	11		2	52
John Johnes	7	1					8
Totals	7	22	18	11		2	60

Table 84 *Land use in Brecon c. 1836*

Land use	Percentage of total land area enumerated in reports on tithe agreements	Estimated acreage in whole county
Arable	18.3	84,007
Grass	37.0	170,020
Wood	4.6	21,188
Common	40.9	188,339

Caernarvonshire

73 tithe districts
57 reports on tithe agreements

Caernarvonshire tithe file documents are very similar to those of other North Wales counties. A high proportion, 78 per cent, contain reports on the voluntary agreements by which tithe commutation was achieved. John Fenton, who reported on 88 per cent of these (Table 85), provides no estimates of crop yields and his crop acreages are not consistently recorded. His colleague, Aneurin Owen, states crop yields for just two parishes where late agreements were assessed in 1845. As a record of land use and cropping patterns, Caernarvonshire tithe files are thus flawed in much the same way as those for other Welsh counties. Therefore, the aggregate figures in Table 86 should be read with circumspection.

A complicated series of exemptions and moduses in lieu of tithes operated in this county. Moduses for hay and meadows affected management practices in some tithe districts. For example, John Fenton wrote in 1841 that 'there is a large proportion of grassland in this parish (Trefriw) and its neighbour (Llanrhychwyn) owing to the exemption from hay tithe under a modus of two pence from each farm'. Tithe of livestock was very commonly paid as a modus; potatoes, much grown especially in mining and quarrying districts, were often not tithed at all; nor sometimes were turnips. Woodland was generally tithe free as elsewhere in North Wales. In short, there was no one system of tithing which applied throughout this county (see Subject Index).

Arable rotations varied according to altitude and soil quality. In some upland districts, oats were the only corn grown and the rotation consisted of breaking up a ley for potatoes, then growing a couple of crops of oats, before laying the land down again. In bad seasons even oats were an uncertain crop in these areas. Elsewhere, assistant commissioners considered that rotations were characterised by their irregularity with numerous variations in each of the succession of corn crops grown, the fallow and root crops, and the numbers of years of ley. Some examples of actual rotations cited in the files are:

> 'seeds 2 yrs, oats, potatoes, barley, seeds, fallow for a little wheat';
> 'ley (sometimes turnips), oats, potatoes, wheat, barley, ley';
> 'seeds and natural mountain grass, potatoes, barley, oats, oats';
> '3 yrs ley, oats, barley (seldom any wheat sown)';
> '2 yrs ley, oats, barley, potatoes, barley, seeds (sometimes fallow for wheat)'.

Many parishes had extensive areas of poor upland pastures often interspersed with bog and rocks. At Dolwyddelan,

> the upper land which is the largest portion, is very poor grazing ground, quite in a state of nature and not admitting of cultivation with a view to profit. It is thickly interspersed with loose rocks of enormous size, lofty precipices and interminable bogs, swamps and lakes, so that at a rough calculation there may be upwards of two thousand acres of waste contained in it.

Livestock husbandry, though, is poorly detailed in Caernarvonshire tithe files. Cattle breeding and feeding, dairying in mining and quarrying districts, sheep, pigs and mountain ponies are noted but receive scant discussion (see Subject Index).

Apart from arable farming, there are only two recurrent topics with detailed comment. The first concerns the management of plantations of coniferous and deciduous woodland made on estates of large landowners in parishes such as Beddgelert, Llandor, Bodean and Bettws-y-Coed. This last was

> a part of the domain of Lord Willoughby de Eresby, is very extensively planted and kept in its natural state . . . it forms one of the most interesting portions of mountain scenery in north Wales and it is not likely so long as it may remain in the possession of the House of Gulir ever to alter its character for the sake of any agricultural improvement.

The second topic concerns the agrarian consequences and, therefore, effects on value of tithes of an increasing mining and quarrying population. 'The parish of Bettws Garmon lies high among the range of the Snowdonian Hills . . . The produce is consumed on the spot where the vicinity of the mines and slate quarries cause a great consumption of provisions of every kind.' In nearby Llanddeiniolen parish, 'dairy produce is the principal desideratum, the quarrymen generally feeding on bread, butter, ptoatoes, and milk, seldom using flesh. What corn is sown is tolerably productive and any surplus commands a high price.'

Caernarvonshire

Table 85 *Reports on agreements for commutation of tithes in Caernarvonshire*

Assistant commissioner/ local tithe agent	1839	1840	1841	1842	1843	1844	1845	Totals
John Fenton	14	21	9	6				50
Aneurin Owen	2					1	4	7
Totals	16	21	9	6		1	4	57

Table 86 *Land use in Caernarvonshire c. 1836*

Land use	Percentage of total land area enumerated in reports on tithe agreements	Estimated acreage in whole county
Arable	14.0	51,724
Grass	71.3	264,082
Wood	3.3	12,206
Common	10.2	38,323

Cardiganshire

74 tithe districts
54 reports on tithe agreements

Very nearly the whole of this county was titheable in 1836 and in a high proportion (68 per cent) of tithe districts, commutation was effected voluntarily. It was usual in this part of Wales for woodland to be tithe free but there were some exceptional instances of tithed woods in this county. At Llanfihangel Geneu'r Glynn acreages of coppice, plantation and timber woodland were distinguished in a valuation prior to award so that the valuable tithe of coppice could be accurately assessed. At Llanfihangel y Creuddyn, a proposed agreement foundered over the level of woodland tithe and a separate valuation of each piece of woodland was called prior to the imposition of a compulsory award. Both Thomas Hoskins (78 per cent of reports) and John Johnes (20 per cent of reports) (Table 87), are concerned about inaccuracies in acreages in schedules of proposed agreements. It is evident that neither suspected any intention to deceive but errors resulted from the combined effects of using old, out-of-date surveys, the sheer difficulty of estimating acreages accurately in mountainous terrain and also some confusion over the definition of arable land – whether this should or should not exclude seeds. Only Aneurin Owen in his one report for Cardiganshire provides crop acreages; there are no yield figures in any of this county's printed reports. Thus Table 88 contains only land use figures and no maps are produced for Cardiganshire.

The skeletal nature of responses to questions on the printed forms means that these provide few details other than a classification of soil type and a listing of crop rotations. It is as if the grassland and livestock sector was non-existent. More detail on farming practices emerges from evidence presented at award meetings, but, nevertheless, the Subject Index for Cardiganshire is one of few entries.

In essence, a typical rotation at this time would begin with breaking up some ley grass, then growing a number of corn crops with perhaps a dead fallow or a crop of potatoes in the sequence, before laying the land down again for at least three to four years, but up to as many as seven to eight years either by sowing clover or, quite commonly, by allowing grasses to regenerate naturally. In detail, the files record almost as many variations on this theme of white crops followed by several years of leys as there were parishes. Furthermore, different rotations are cited for different parts of the same parish where there are distinct areas of high and low land. At Llandewi Aberarth, for example, 'below the hill' it was 'wheat, barley, oats, barley, seed 2 years' but on the hillside 'barley, oats 3 or 4 years, then laid down to grass 7 years'. The one exception to these rotations involving leys of various lengths was at Llanrhystyd, where

> near the sea shore, facing St George's channel, there is some land of a very extraordinary nature, it is a fine rich loam, and extends to a considerable depth and very productive, – it is constantly manured with the seaweed which is driven in great abundance on the shore and one very large field which I saw, has produced a good crop of barley every year for 50 years *successively*, – the oldest man never remembers any other than barley growing in that field.

Table 87 *Reports on agreements for commutation of tithes in Cardiganshire*

Assistant commissioner/ local tithe agent	1837	1838	1839	1840	1841	1842	1843	1844	1845	Totals
Thomas Hoskins			27	3	5	2	5			42
John Johnes	4	7								11
Aneurin Owen									1	1
Totals	4	7	27	3	5	2	5		1	54

Table 88 *Land use in Cardiganshire c. 1836*

Land use	Percentage of total land area enumerated in reports on tithe agreements	Estimated acreage in whole county
Arable	28.6	126,772
Grass	52.5	232,653
Wood	2.1	9,176
Common	16.9	74,696

Carmarthenshire

83 tithe districts
56 reports on tithe agreements

All Carmarthenshire parishes were titheable in 1836 and in only one, Llanelly, had some tithe been commuted previously. Moduses for hay and agistment tithe prevailed in at least thirty-nine parishes but, nevertheless, tithe owners and payers in two-thirds of this county's tithe districts achieved agreements for commutation of tithes. Woodland was tithe free but its acreage was enumerated in reports by Thomas Hoskins but more rarely by John Johnes (Table 89). None of the reports provides crop acreage or yield data, though these topics are usually discussed and figures sometimes stated in evidence presented at award meetings (see Subject Index). Anything resembling a 'parish description' in the sense that this term can be applied to English tithe files is rare in Carmarthenshire reports on agreements so that entries in the Subject Index derive in the main from papers presented at award meetings. There is clearly room for bias in such a sample of documents, particularly in the picture of generally poor farming which comes across from farmers' evidence.

Arable rotations took from between seven and twelve years to complete and followed a system not unusual in Wales of a series of corn crops and then leys of three to eight years. In mountain parishes little or no wheat was cultivated, either oats and barley were sown together or, as at Eglwysfair a Churig, little but oats grown, a situation which elicited the following comment from Hoskins in 1843, that 'none but Welsh farmers who exist chiefly upon oaten bread could live there'. Morris Sayer, in the sole report on a tithe agreement which he wrote for the Tithe Commission, offers a striking comparison of Welsh mountain farming with England. At Cwmtwrch and Cwmcothi, he remarked that

> the method of husbandry in the mountainous districts of Wales differs widely from that in England; here they crop with oats for 4, 5 and even 6 consecutive years without any other manure than a sprinkling of lime and afterwards frequently allow it to remain to produce a natural herbage, and not an uncommon practice to pare and burn the sward (such as it is after such treatment) for wheat; clover is scantily used and a wonder to see an acre of turnips on a farm.

Yield figures noted in award minutes are very low. At Laugharne, for example, David Morris, a local farmer, records that in 1841 his wheat produced only 10 bushels an acre and barley and oats between 12 and 14 bushels. References to turnips are few and to potatoes fewer than in most Welsh counties (see Subject Index). Productive meadows along the

Towy, the poverty of upland pastures, dairying in the valleys and breeding sheep and bullocks are all recorded but there is little depth of detail on management practices in Carmarthenshire files.

Table 89 *Reports on agreements for commutation of tithes in Carmarthenshire*

Assistant commissioner/ local tithe agent	1837	1838	1839	1840	1841	1842	1843	Totals
Thomas Hoskins			12	7	7	1	2	29
John Johnes	7	16	3					26
Morris Sayer		1						1
Totals	7	17	15	7	7	1	2	56

Table 90 *Land use in Carmarthenshire c. 1836*

Land use	Percentage of total land area enumerated in reports on tithe agreements	Estimated acreage in whole county
Arable	26.0	157,725
Grass	60.8	368,716
Wood	4.9	29,775
Common	8.2	49,874

Denbighshire

107 tithe districts
94 reports on tithe agreements

J. B. Jarvis (1946) has used tithe maps and apportionments to reconstruct land use in southeast Denbighshire and J. W. Edwards (1963) consulted tithe files as well as apportionments and maps for his study of enclosure and agricultural improvement in the Vale of Clwyd.

More tithe (88 per cent of all tithe districts) was commuted by voluntary agreement in Denbighshire than in any other Welsh or English county. Both Aneurin Owen and John Fenton who together compiled all but four of the reports provide data on crop rotations and acreages. The Dean and Chapter of Winchester Cathedral owned the great tithes of many parishes and for some, including Erddig, Erbistock and Erlas, acreages of corn crops cited in reports are taken from surveys made on their behalf in 1839. Where acreages were obtained by the more usual method of estimation, both assistant commissioners expressed their usual reservations about accuracy, particularly in relation to that category of land which they called 'mountain land'. Not only did the nature of the terrain mean that this was difficult to estimate, but it is evident that this type of land is not consistently recorded in their reports – sometimes it is subsumed under the 'common', sometimes under the 'pasture' or sometimes included in 'total titheable acreage'. For example, '5000 acres of inferior mountain land' are included as 'pasture' at Llanrhaiadr in Cimmerch; '2008 acres mountain' are included in the total titheable acreage at Christionydd-Kenrich and '2000 acres mountain', '800 acres mountain' and '450 acres mountain' are entered under 'common' at Ruthin, Llangollen Fawr and Meivod respectively.

Owen and Fenton wrote lengthy parish descriptions. Owen's are especially informative with detailed commentaries on landscape and scenery. He contrasts carefully soil productivity in highland and vale areas, comments on roads, canals and markets and how these affected costs of tithe collection, and the ease or otherwise of procuring lime. Fenton's descriptions are perhaps not as informative on the local economy but he invariably comments on the Church and parochial matters such as the provision of schooling. He recounts tales of local folklore acquired on his travels, as, for instance, in the report for Llanelian yn Rhos, where

> a well existed bearing the saint's name which in the ages of superstition and even to a recent date, became the terror of the credulous, from its supposed property of inflicting divers disorders upon those whose names were inscribed on stones and thrown into it,

and which could not be removed but by a fee being given to the lady who kept the well, to reverse the malediction, and who did a thriving trade by her occupation.

Conventional three- or four-course rotations were not common in Denbighshire at this date (see Subject Index); leys of more than two years duration were normal and these when broken up were either limed for wheat or manured for potatoes. It is recorded that some inferior soils would produce only oats but in more fertile lowland areas, farmers concentrated on producing wheat or barley. References to turnips are numerous (seventy-seven places in the Subject Index) and most parishes (eighty-eight references in the Subject Index) grew some potatoes. For Holt on the river Dee, there is a quite detailed account of market gardening written by Aneurin Owen in 1843:

> The market gardeners [he said] have been accustomed to send their produce to Liverpool and Glasgow for sale; the competition is now so great and the facility afforded by steamers to convey produce from earlier but more distant parts so extensive, that the cultivation of garden crops is not remunerative. It is possible if a charge of 11s per acre tithe had been established that so considerable a check would have ensued as to have reduced the cultivation. Under the circumstances therefore I should consider an average arable charge upon such market gardens to be sufficient, as I have known to be accepted in many districts in England. The same remarks will apply to the lands under potatoes, an average arable charge might justly be extended to the lands upon which they are grown.

While the files of most Welsh counties are remarkable for their silence on livestock husbandry, particularly on the management of the ubiquitous sheep flock. John Fenton does remedy this for Denbighshire. He distinguishes, for example, between practices on newly enclosed and still open moorland. Of the former, he said at Llangadwaladr that 'the greater proportion of the side lands and hills is pasture – which feeds a good many cattle. The sheep are lessened in number since the mountain land has been enclosed and is improving; and the chief produce is derived from the dairies and sale of cattle.' By contrast, at Tir Ifan, 'this township is extensive and includes a large tract of mountain land fit only for the feeding of sheep of which a considerable number (principally wethers) are annually fattened for the markets of Llanrwst and other towns in the vicinity. There are few if any lambs bred upon the tract which is bleak and exposed.'

Table 91 *Reports on agreements for commutation of tithes in Denbighshire*

Assistant commissioner/ local tithe agent	1837	1838	1839	1840	1841	1842	1843	1844	1845	Totals
Aneurin Owen		11	8	2			13	11	2	47
John Fenton			7	11	12	10	3			43
John Johnes	3									3
Charles Pym	1									1
Totals	4	11	15	13	12	10	16	11	2	94

Table 92 *Land use, crops and yields in Denbighshire c. 1836*

A	Land use	Percentage of total land area enumerated in reports on tithe agreements	Estimated acreage in whole county
	Arable	23.9	92,167
	Grass	56.8	219,314
	Wood	5.1	19,683
	Common	14.2	55,134

B	Crop	Mean percentage of arable	Mean yield per acre	Estimated acreage in whole county
	Wheat	24.5	16.0 bushels	22,607
	Barley	24.9	20.0 bushels	22,991
	Oats	31.5	32.0 bushels	28,988
	Pulses	0.8	14.0 bushels	768

Flintshire

42 tithe districts
31 reports on tithe agreements

The documentary record in Flintshire files is in many respects similar to that of Denbighshire. The proportion of agreements is lower but, at 74 per cent of all tithe districts, is still high. Moduses were more common (twenty-seven places listed in the Subject Index) and covered milk, hay and potatoes. Woodland was tithe free. The main reason for the similarity of file contents of these two counties is that Aneurin Owen and John Fenton were the leading assistant tithe commissioners in both, responsible for 58 and 26 per cent respectively of Flintshire reports. Therefore, land use acreages (including that of tithe free woodland) crop rotations and parish descriptions are all extant. Yields of corn, roots and pulses are given for only that titheable part of one parish, Worthenbury, by assistant commissioner Charles Pym on one of his only two incursions into Wales to assess agreements.

Crop rotations (see Subject Index) recorded in the files are also similar to those of Denbighshire and follow with but slight variations that described by Owen at Northop: 'the system of cultivation is to sow wheat on a limed fallow, or clover ley, or after potatoes or turnips. Then oats, or where the soil is favourable, barley and seeds. Sometimes a pasture is broken up for oats, the stubble limed and sown with wheat. Very few peas or beans are grown.' After this succession, ley grasses would take over for a number of years.

A significant difference with Denbighshire is that Flintshire files contain little information on the livestock sector; in this respect they are more akin to those of other North Wales counties.

Table 93 *Reports on agreements for commutation of tithes in Flintshire*

Assistant commissioner/ local tithe agent	1837	1838	1839	1840	1841	1842	1843	1844	1845	Total
Aneurin Owen		5	11				1		1	18
John Fenton			2	4	1		1			8
John Johnes	4									4
Charles Pym	1									1
Totals	5	5	13	4	1		2		1	31

Table 94 *Land use and crops in Flintshire c. 1836*

A	Land use	Percentage of total land area enumerated in reports on tithe agreements	Estimated acreage in whole county
	Arable	30.6	56,550
	Grass	56.7	104,830
	Wood	5.2	9,648
	Common	7.4	13,647

B	Crop	Mean percentage of arable	Estimated acreage in whole county
	Wheat	32.0	18,095
	Barley	18.9	10,694
	Oats	28.2	15,958
	Pulses	1.3	761

Glamorgan

137 tithe districts
52 reports on tithe agreements

The contents of Glamorgan tithe files are very similar to those of other South Wales counties; Thomas Hoskins and John Johnes completed all the reports on agreements (Table 95) and neither man wrote a parish description, specified crop yields or presented crop acreages consistently. Johnes was also called on to draft compulsory awards in Glamorgan (awards were required at 60 per cent of titheable places) and these files contain much more information on agrarian practices and include, for example at Ystradowen, Llanharry and Llanwonno, detailed, field-by-field valuations of crops and stock. These apart, land use data were taken by estimation with acreages often rounded to the nearest 10 or 100. Thus figures in Table 96 are really only a guide to proportions of the various categories of land. Both commissioners did, though, record what they thought was the general arable rotation at each place they visited. Entries on rotations in the Subject Index, however, refer mostly to those award parishes where these were actually discussed. Four- and five-course turnip rotations were quite widespread at this date in Glamorgan, though there were still places, Michaelston-y-Vedw was one, where four-course shifts took the form of dead fallow, wheat, barley, clover. When such rotations were extended by allowing clover to lie from two to eight years, they were materially little different from typical Welsh long ley systems. Potatoes are rarely mentioned as an integral part of rotations but their cultivation is discussed in award evidence (see Subject Index).

Glamorgan files are near silent on grassland farming and livestock husbandry; the only topic regularly noted is the yield and quality of hay, as when covered by a modus payment (see Subject Index) the value of parochial tithes was depressed.

Table 95 *Reports on agreements for commutation of tithes in Glamorgan*

Assistant commissioner/ local tithe agent	1838	1839	1840	1841	1842	1843	1844	Totals
Thomas Hoskins	3	14	12	4		3	2	38
John Johnes	12	2						14
Totals	15	16	12	4		3	2	52

Table 96 *Land use in Glamorgan c. 1836*

Land use	Percentage of total land area enumerated in reports on tithe agreements	Estimated acreage in whole county
Arable	27.5	150,393
Grass	52.0	284,845
Wood	10.9	59,681
Common	8.7	47,678

Merionethshire

34 tithe districts
24 reports on tithe agreements

Merionethshire, with fewest tithe districts of any county unit used by the Tithe Commission, also has some of the largest. Of those tithe districts with reports on agreements (71 per cent of the total) ten extended over more than 10,000 acres and only two were of less than 5,000 acres. At ten places (see Subject Index) the difficulty and costs of collecting and marketing tithe from such large tithe districts with much mountainous terrain is remarked upon. Conversely the coastal parishes were in a very fortunate position in terms of accessibility to both markets and manures.

Tithe of meadow and hay was usually covered by moduses, woodland was tithe free and potatoes sometimes so. Merionethshire is the one county in England and Wales totally devoid of crop rotation data in reports on tithe agreements, but both Aneurin Owen and John Fenton, who completed all the reports (Table 97), did record the acreages of corn, root, pulse and fallow crops so that Table 98 includes aggregates for these as well as county land use statistics.

On the poorest soils in the more elevated parts of the county, successive crops of oats were taken and then the land returned to grass. 'The husbandry of these mountain districts', reported Owen at Mallwyd in 1838, 'seems well adapted to the locality, has been pursued in the same mode for ages and does not appear to be susceptible of much improvement. Turnip culture cannot be introduced on account of the sheep, which no fence scarcely could exclude.' Where the food demands of non-agrarian mountain populations were felt, as at Festiniog, 'a large district of land all more or less mountainous, traversed by torrents. The elevation and damp climate render it more eligible for pasturage than tillage although the dense population congregated to work the valuable slate quarries requires a considerable importation of corn.' On somewhat better soils more favourably situated, as at Penhal, 'Land is broked up for oats, sometimes denshired and burnt for barley, which crop is followed by potatoes. Wheat, or meslin, is generally sown on this ameliorated soil, and is considered to prosper better than after any other preparation. Barley and seeds follow.' Liming for corn and the introduction of potatoes into the rotation increased output.

> In this part of the country [Dolgelly] meslin and oats were formerly the grains mostly sown. Since the utility of lime has been acknowledged, and its use prevalent, meslin is not so much sown, wheat alone being considered more suitable. Potatoes are a great article

of growth and consumption and carefully cultivated; they are generally succeeded by wheat. Then barley follows with seeds.

Though actual acreages are not extant, it would seem from comments that very extensive spreads of potatoes were grown along the coast. At Llanenddwyn, for example, Owen reported that 'the principal peculiarity in the husbandry is the great breadth of potatoes planted; the manure for which is procured by carting the sea tang, mixing it with earth, and when decomposed using the compost. These potatoes, being watery and unpalatable from the nature of the manure, are used to feed hogs.'

The existence of large flocks of sheep, especially in those parishes with much common and mountain pasture, are noted and a seasonal transhumance was practised. Little else is noticed, however, about livestock farming methods other than a novel practice of animal feeding of supplementing scarce fodder by feeding horses on furze. In his report on the agreement at Trawsfynydd, Owen proclaimed that 'a small farmer in this vicinity deserves honourable notice from originating the use of brambles, cut in a straw cutter, for the provender of his horses. Upon this, I understand, they are solely fed.'

Table 97 *Reports on agreements for commutation of tithes in Merionethshire*

Assistant commissioner/ local tithe agent	1838	1839	1840	1841	1842	Totals
Aneurin Owen	10	5		1		16
John Fenton		1	1	3	3	8
Totals	10	6	1	4	3	24

Table 98 *Land use and crops in Merionethshire c. 1836*

A	Land use	Percentage of total land area enumerated in reports on tithe agreements	Estimated acreage in whole county
	Arable	6.6	24,832
	Grass	50.1	188,941
	Wood	3.6	13,557
	Common	39.7	149,349
B	Crop	Mean percentage of arable	Estimated acreage in whole county
	Wheat	13.9	3,940
	Barley	18.4	5,205
	Oats	47.0	13,277

Montgomeryshire

75 tithe districts
59 reports on tithe agreements

Parish summary land use acreages from tithe apportionments have been mapped for Montgomeryshire by J. M. Powell (1962, 1969) and fifty square miles of field-by-field land use mapping was conducted by L. S. Andrews and published by J. May and S. F. Wells (1942) in their Montgomeryshire report on the Land Utilisation Survey of Great Britain.

Montgomeryshire files are very similar in content to those of Merionethshire. Woodland was exempt from tithe and so not always enumerated; hay and potatoes were in many places tithe free or covered by a modus (see Subject Index). Rotation courses are not specified but all crop acreages except for seeds are given in a form which enables county figures to be aggregated (Table 100). Both John Fenton and Aneurin Owen, who together wrote all but two of this county's reports, provided quite full parish descriptions comprising statements of situation, quality of pasture and arable land, accessibility of markets and manures and the state of local roads.

Both men found that local farmers considered bare fallowing a necessary practice where the land was heavy. Liming was thought a vital prerequisite for good corn crops and there is some mention of it in almost every file. Assistant commissioners usually comment if it was expensive or difficult to obtain lime and sometimes say where it was obtained and by what means it was conveyed. For instance, at Machynlleth, lime and coal were imported by sea from Glamorgan and then burnt locally; at Mochdre, farmers bought lime from Newtown and it cost 14d per bushel and was used at a rate of 30 bushels an acre.

Crop rotations in Montgomeryshire did not much impress the assistant commissioners. As elsewhere in North Wales, the traditional system was to take four or five white crops and with the last of these clover or rye grass was sown and then the land returned to grass for several years. Variations on this general practice went some way towards what assistant commissioners considered 'improvement', as, for example, when a ley was ploughed and planted first with potatoes or, more occasionally, with turnips before being limed for wheat. The cultivation of both these root crops is much discussed in this county's files (fifty-six and fifty entries in the Subject Index respectively). In the very highest parts of Montgomeryshire, mountain 'friths' were broken up and sown with oats for several years in succession before land was laid again to pasture.

Near the river Severn there were some good meadows and pastures but in the higher parts of the county grass was judged poor and on assistant commissioners' valuations was worth little more than common land. Rentals of 3–4s an acre are recorded, while 10–12s would be an average encountered in the tithe files. In high parishes sheep were the main source of farmers' incomes; in lowland areas it is reported that sheep were brought in to eat any spare grass but few were kept permanently. At Mochdre in 1841, 'Nearly 2,700 sheep are summered in this parish, 2,000 of which are wintered in other parishes, about 1,800 is considered the number titheable to the impropriator.'

Table 99 *Reports on agreements for commutation of tithes in Montgomeryshire*

Assistant commissioner/ local tithe agent	1837	1838	1839	1840	1841	1842	1843	1844	Totals
John Fenton			11	22	4	3			40
Aneurin Owen		8	5		1			3	17
John Johnes	2								2
Totals	2	8	16	22	5	3		3	59

Table 100 *Land use and crops in Montgomeryshire c. 1836*

	A Land use	Percentage of total land area enumerated in reports on tithe agreements	Estimated acreage in whole county
	Arable	14.8	71,379
	Grass	47.0	227,192
	Wood	4.5	21,422
	Common	33.9	161,553
	B Crop	Mean percentage of arable	Estimated acreage in whole county
	Wheat	26.1	18,591
	Barley	20.9	14,933
	Oats	33.0	23,554
	Pulses	1.3	928

Pembrokeshire

147 tithe districts
94 reports on tithe agreements

T. R. B. Dicks (1964) has constructed maps of land use in Pembrokeshire from parish estimates in tithe apportionments. See *The tithe surveys of England and Wales* (pp. 193–6) for a discussion of land use data derived from tithe apportionments of western England and Wales.

Only five parishes were entirely tithe free in Pembrokeshire in 1836 and very many files (see Place Index) contain a copy of either a draft award or agreement. Files for parishes where commutation was compulsory generally contain a valuation of crops grown in the parish and their yields; those where John Johnes officiated at award meetings are especially detailed with even small acreages of turnips and potatoes, which are often omitted in agreement returns, carefully enumerated. The presence of these valuations in the files compensates to a considerable extent for the fact that all but two of the reports on tithe agreements were prepared by Thomas Hoskins and John Johnes who, as elsewhere in Wales, provide no 'parish descriptions', no crop acreages and no yields.

Long leys were a feature of the agriculture in most Pembrokeshire parishes and were the keystone of an agrarian system which received very negative comments from both Hoskins and Johnes. At St Nicholas, near Fishguard, for example, Johnes remarked that

> the land in this parish is generally of a fair arable quality, but there is but little pasture, the farmers depending mostly for the pasture in this as in the majority of parishes in the neighbourhood on the pasture arising from the land lying idle after tillage, and which in truth is allowed so to lie rather for the purpose of recovering from the usual severe course of cropping than for any other cause. If the land in this and other parishes were properly farmed, the produce would be larger and more free from weeds.

Hoskins, when reporting at St Ishmaels on Milford Haven, was even more severe with what he saw.

> There is some *very good* land in this parish, capable of *considerable produce*, if *well farmed*. The system throughout this part of the country is generally *bad*. I met with a Gentn here, who cultivates his own land, (from the Isle of Wight) and who has introduced the turnip and barley system and feeding off with sheep, to great advantage – but he says he 'can not make the Welshmen think so'. They *will follow* the system of their fore fathers.

This traditional system is described at many places (see Subject Index); Johnes put it neatly when assessing the rent-charge agreed for the poor soils of Penrydd parish (Newcastle Emlyn):

> the system of farming is bad, very little wheat is grown in the parish, the land is generally pared and burnt, a crop of oats is taken then barley or a mixture of barley and oats and then a crop of oats with rye grass. The land then lies idle for six or seven years until it begins to produce furze which it is prone to do.

Some examples of the various terms used by Thomas Hoskins to describe long leys in Pembrokeshire are listed in *The tithe surveys of England and Wales*, (p. 144).

As remarked above, many award valuations include small acreages of turnips and potatoes (twenty-three and thirty-nine places respectively). In a few parishes acreages were such as to elicit special comment from assistant commissioners at the end of their agreement reports. Of the 100 acres of potatoes at Begelly cum East Williamston, Johnes remarked that 'the quantity of potatoes appears excessive, but it was said that a large quantity is grown for the consumption of the colliers, this parish being above the coal measures', and at Prendergast, 'the potatoes are generally set by persons residing in the town (Haverfordwest), several persons having crops of potatoes in the same field, who it is probable would not raise them all at the same time'.

The poverty of data on livestock farming in this county's tithe files can be judged from the tiny number of just eighteen entries under grassland and livestock headings in the Subject Index.

Table 101 *Reports on agreements for commutation of tithes in Pembrokeshire*

Assistant commissioner/ local tithe agent	1837	1838	1839	1840	1841	1842	1843	1848	Totals
Thomas Hoskins			39	6	4	5	1		55
John Johnes	12	24	1						37
John Fenton						1			1
Aneurin Owen								1	1
Totals	12	24	40	6	4	6	1	1	94

Table 102 *Land use in Pembrokeshire c. 1836*

Land use	Percentage of total land area enumerated in reports on tithe agreements	Estimated acreage in whole county
Arable	25.2	101,170
Grass	69.5	279,121
Wood	2.7	10,888
Common	0.1	5,040

Radnorshire

53 tithe districts
31 reports on tithe agreements

All Radnorshire parishes were titheable in 1836, but with Thomas Hoskins and John Johnes responsible for all but one of the reports on agreements (Table 103) the contents of this county's tithe files are similar to those of Brecon, Cardiganshire, Carmarthenshire, Glamorgan and Pembrokeshire, i.e. there are no parish descriptions, no crop acreages and no yield data in the reports. The same caveats have to be applied as in those counties to the accuracy of land use estimates used to compile Table 104. To take just one instance, at Llangunllo, arable, pasture, wood and common acreages have been rounded to the nearest 100 and 1,000 acres in the tithe file.

As in Pembrokeshire, long rotations were the general rule in Radnorshire (see Subject Index) and these consisted of either successive white crops and then ley or, alternatively, some potatoes or turnips might be planted in the first year of ploughing. At Colva, 'on the higher lands, a crop of potatoes is taken, then wheat, barley or oats, and rye grass, sometimes two crops of oats – on the lower lands the system is much the same, substituting turnips, which are grazed off by the sheep, for potatoes'. At Llananno, Aneurin Owen had obtained 'a copy of a survey of the actual crops in 1801 which I judge would but little vary from present circumstances. The rye would be less the wheat more; but as the two crops are about the same intrinsic value in this country, it does not affect the comparative estimate.' At Pilleth, Johnes was astounded by a system of '2 crops of turnips in succession and then 2 crops of oats in succession and sometimes turnips – oats – turnips and oats again, a system I never heard of before'!

With just eight entries under grassland and livestock headings (see Subject Index), Radnorshire files rank as the least informative of any county on animal husbandry.

Table 103 *Reports on agreements for commutation of tithes in Radnorshire*

Assistant commissioner/ local tithe agent	1837	1838	1839	1840	1841	1842	1843	Totals
Thomas Hoskins		2	11	3	1	1	2	20
John Johnes	3	6	1					10
George Bolls			1					1
Totals	3	8	13	3	1	1	2	31

Table 104 *Land use in Radnorshire c. 1836*

Land use	Percentage of total land area enumerated in reports on tithe agreements	Estimated acreage in whole county
Arable	14.0	38,021
Grass	29.1	79,130
Wood	3.5	9,587
Common	53.3	144,644

ENGLAND AND WALES

A major lacuna in the foundations for an agrarian history of England and Wales is firm evidence on the gross output of the industry in the period before government becan collecting national statistics on an annual basis in 1866 (Kain, 1979b). For instance, Deane and Cole (1967, p. 62) state that 'for corn there are no production or quasi-production series which might be regarded as reliable guides, and we cannot place much faith in the pattern of change which might emerge from a comparison of the scattered accounts of contemporaries'. Instead, they estimate the output of British agriculture by reference to consumption data, an exercise which is fraught with many difficulties, not least the fact that consumers switched from one cereal to another in response to prices (Collins, 1975).

The calculation of gross agricultural output from estimates of crop acreages and yields was, however, a fundamental component of parish tithe commutation. One of the great strengths of the acreage and yield data now preserved in tithe files is that they can be aggregated to estimate not only county outputs (as presented in the county sections above), but also to compile regional and national output figures. Though these data are imperfect (see *The tithe surveys of England and Wales*, pp. 141–5), in both coverage of the country and in accuracy they are more reliable than any other similarly comprehensive source. For example, although evidence for Cumberland, Westmorland, Nottinghamshire, Leicestershire, Northamptonshire and Middlesex are too suspect and too sparse to be trustworthy, the tithe surveys provide data that are more representative of the country as a whole than the eleven county agricultural statistics of 1854 and information on a greater range of products than the 1801 Crop Return. Furthermore, there is no evidence of any consistent understatement of acreages as there is with the 1801 data (Turner, 1981). By contrast, tithe file evidence constitutes a fairly precise datum against which earlier and later information can be measured. This last is not undertaken in any detail in this book; tithe survey data generated by our project are being employed in a comparative sense by Mark Overton in a series of maps for a joint Economic History Society and Historical Geography Research Group *Atlas of the Industrial Revolution*, edited by John Langton and Robert Morris. Attention in this section of the *Atlas and Index* is focussed on first, the distribution of arable and pasture, secondly, on variations in crop relativities in England and Wales and thirdly, on national patterns of yields and gross outputs of grain crops in England *c*. 1836. As in the county sections, distribution patterns are not described at length but are communicated cartographically by a set of maps.

Arable and grass

The tithe files reveal that c. 1836 there were some 15.1 million acres of arable (excluding seed crops in western counties) and 16.4 million acres of grass (a figure which includes land classified as 'rough grazing' in later government statistics). Assuming the surface area of England and Wales at 37.3 million acres (that reported in the 1851 census of population and itself calculated from tithe maps), a figure of some 5.8 million acres of woodland, common and unfarmed land can be obtained. The ratio of arable:pasture at 0.9:1 c. 1836 contributes to the consistent trend of increasing arable relative to grass from a ratio of under 0.7:1 in the early part of the century, through parity in the 1840s, 1.2:1 in the 1850s to more than 1.5:1 by 1872 (Table 105). In *The tithe surveys of England and Wales* (pp. 173–6), Hugh Prince and I briefly discuss some evidence bearing on the timing of the maximum extension of arable farming in England and Wales. We conclude that within the span of time extending from the Napoleonic Wars to the onset of continuous decline in grain farming in the 1870s, the most likely period for the maximum is in the third quarter of the century. In national terms, therefore, the tithe surveys were completed some years before this maximum, though many of the studies reviewed in that book indicate that in highland Britain reclamation at the moorland edge had slowed down and in many districts had come to a halt before 1840 but that the process was still very active on lowland heaths.

Maps 563–5 reveal a marked distinction in amounts of arable and grass between the east and the west of the country. In all East Anglian counties arable exceeded 60 per cent of county area; in all western counties the figure was below 40 per cent and in some parts of central Wales, it was less than 20 per cent. In Midland counties, arable and grass were in approximate acreage balance at this date. Thus tithe file data provide some quantitative support for the line which divides England into corn and grazing districts on the frontispiece map of James Caird's *English agriculture in 1850–51* (Caird, 1852).

Crop relativities

Maps 566–72 indicate the distributions of wheat, barley, oats and pulse crops in English and Welsh counties, and of turnips, clover and seeds, and dead fallow for those English counties with 'arable' format reports on tithe agreements. Tables 106 and 107 present national acreages, percentages and mean yields of the same crops. Nationally, wheat was the leading grain crop and occupied almost as much of the arable as the two spring grains together. Regionally, it was especially significant in the crop mix of western and southwestern counties; in many parishes in the latter it was the only grain grown on land ploughed for a few seasons and then laid back to grass. However, although wheat was important relative to other grains in Cornwall, Devon, Somerset and Dorset, the acreages raised were small. Wheat was only displaced from its position as leading grain crop by oats in the northern counties of Northumberland, Lancashire, Cheshire and in those North Wales counties for which data are extant. In Derbyshire and Durham wheat and oats ranked about equal first. Thus the core area of oats dominance remained as in 1801 (Turner, 1981) though by c. 1836 it was more restricted in extent as by then wheat had supplanted oats as leading grain crop in Staffordshire, Lincolnshire and Cambridgeshire.

Table 105 *Area of arable, meadow and pasture in England and Wales 1801–72*

Date	Source	Arable land (acres)	Meadow and pasture (acres)	Cultivated area (acres)	Ratio of arable: grass
1801a	B. P. Capper	11,350,501	16,796,458	28,146,959	0.68
1801b	Crop return	7,860,000 (excluding fallow, etc.)	—	—	—
1808	W. T. Comber	11,575,000	17,495,000	29,070,000	0.66
1827	W. Couling	11,143,370	17,605,630	28,749,000	0.63
1836	Tithe files	15,092,555 (excluding seeds in western counties)	16,363,409 (includes some 'rough grazings')	31,455,964	0.92
1851	J. Caird	13,667,000	13,332,000	26,999,000	1.02
1854	Agricultural statistics	15,261,842 (including clover and seeds)	12,392,137	27,653,979	1.23
1872	Agricultural statistics	18,136,369	11,522,712	29,659,081	1.57

Sources:
1801a – B. P. Capper, *A statistical account of the population and cultivation, produce and consumption of England and Wales* (London, 1801).
1801b – M. Turner, 'Arable in England and Wales: estimates from the 1801 crop return', *Journal of Historical Geography*, 7 (1981), pp. 291–302.
1808 – W. T. Comber, *An inquiry into the state of national subsistence* (London, 1808); on Capper and Comber see also H. C. Prince, 'England c. 1800', in H. C. Darby (ed.), *A new historical geography of England* (Cambridge, 1973), p. 403.
1827 – W. Couling, 'Evidence to House of Commons Select Committee on emigration from the United Kingdom, 1827', cited in G. R. Porter, *The progress of the nation*, 2nd edition (London, 1847), pp. 155–8.
1836 – Estimates of land use in the tithe files. Only those data covering more than 90 per cent of a tithe district are included; county figures have been obtained by multiplying the sum of available tithe file acreages by weighting factors equivalent to total county area: area of county with tithe file data; county figures were then aggregated to produce national figures.
1851 – J. Caird, *English agriculture in 1850–51*, 2nd edition (London, 1852).
1854 – Agricultural statistics, 1854, British Parliamentary Papers, House of Commons, 1854–5, LIII, p. 495.
1872 – Agricultural statistics, published in L. D. Stamp, *The land of Britain, its use and misuse*, 3rd edition (London, 1962), appendix 8.

Table 106 *Grain and pulse crops in England c. 1836*

	Million acres	Percentage of arable	Mean yield in bushels per acre
Wheat	3.4	26.8	21.7
Barley	2.0	15.5	30.7
Oats	1.6	12.8	33.7
Pulses	0.6	5.0	24.0

Table 107 *Clover, seeds, roots and fallows in England c. 1836**

	Million acres	Percentage of arable	Mean yield per acre
Turnips	1.3	11.3	£2.80
Clover and seeds	2.6	22.4	22.6 cwts
Dead fallows	1.2	10.8	—

* Data relate to those English counties with 'arable' format reports on tithe agreements; these counties contained 90.3 per cent of the total English arable acreage *c.* 1836.

Table 108 *Gross per annum output of grain crops in England c. 1836*

Region* and size in million acres	Wheat	Barley	Oats	All grains
	(million bushels)			
South West	9.8	12.1	3.9	25.8
South	17.1	13.1	11.0	41.2
East	21.1	21.2	10.1	52.4
North East	9.9	5.9	13.2	29.0
West	11.7	5.6	9.4	26.7
England**	74.4	60.8	55.3	190.5

* Regions are as defined on Maps 579–82.
** Figures for England include extrapolated data for Cumberland, Westmorland, Nottinghamshire, Leicestershire and Northamptonshire and exclude Monmouthshire.

For the country as a whole, barley had replaced oats as the second grain by c. 1836. In eastern counties, notably Norfolk, Suffolk and Rutland, barley ran a close second to wheat c. 1836; in 1801 it had been the leading crop in Rutland and Norfolk. Clearly, therefore, there had been some considerable changes in the mix of cereals cultivated in England between 1801 and c. 1836. Nationally, pulse crops formed but a minor part of rotations in the 1830s, though on heavy soils in Bedfordshire, Kent, Essex, Huntingdonshire, Oxfordshire, Rutland, Suffolk, Herefordshire and Worcestershire they displaced one of the spring grains to attain third rank in county crop relativities.

For the 90 per cent of the tilled area for which data are available, clover and seed crops ran second to wheat in terms of overall acreage, while the total acreage of turnips in England c. 1836 just exceeded that of dead fallow. At a local level, assistant tithe commissioners considered that soil characteristics were important influences on particular crop relativities and rotations. When viewing the country as a whole, however, it is evident that a northern and a southern division of the country can be superimposed upon the east–west arable/pasture distinction, particularly in terms of percentages of arable devoted to each of wheat, barley and oats (Maps 566–8) and of turnips and dead fallows (Maps 570 and 572). It is important, though, to remember as noted earlier that these are maps of proportions and not quantities.

Crop yields and patterns of output

All grain and fallow crop yields were highest in eastern and south-eastern counties (Maps 573–8). For wheat and barley this mirrors the pattern of distribution, while for oats it is the reverse. Suffolk and Essex farmers with the smallest proportions of this spring grain obtained the highest yields; Cheshire with one of the highest proportions of oats to other grains exhibits one of the lower figures for overall yields.

The final four maps and the last table in this *Atlas and Index* summarise the gross output of the main grain crops in the mid-1830s. For these purposes the country is divided into five regions of approximately equal size (5.7–5.9 million acres) to permit legitimate comparison of absolute output figures. Gross wheat output in East Anglia was more than twice that in the South West but also twice that of the North East, which in turn was the source of little more than half the amount of wheat produced in the southern region. With barley, a north–south element in the distribution of output is even clearer; south-western farmers produced more than twice the amount of those in the North East or the West, but just about the same as farmers in the southern region. Oats on the other hand, had a primarily northern source – the two northern regions contributed almost as much as the total of the three southern and eastern groups of counties. When all grains are added together, the mirrored north–south elements in the distributions of individual crops are self-cancelling and reveal an East Anglian group of counties as clearly dominating the picture of total grain output. A third of all English grain was produced in these six counties, just about the same as the total of the two western regions added together. The southern group of counties generated a third as much grain again than the total of Yorkshire, Durham and Northumberland.

Arable as a percentage of total county area
563

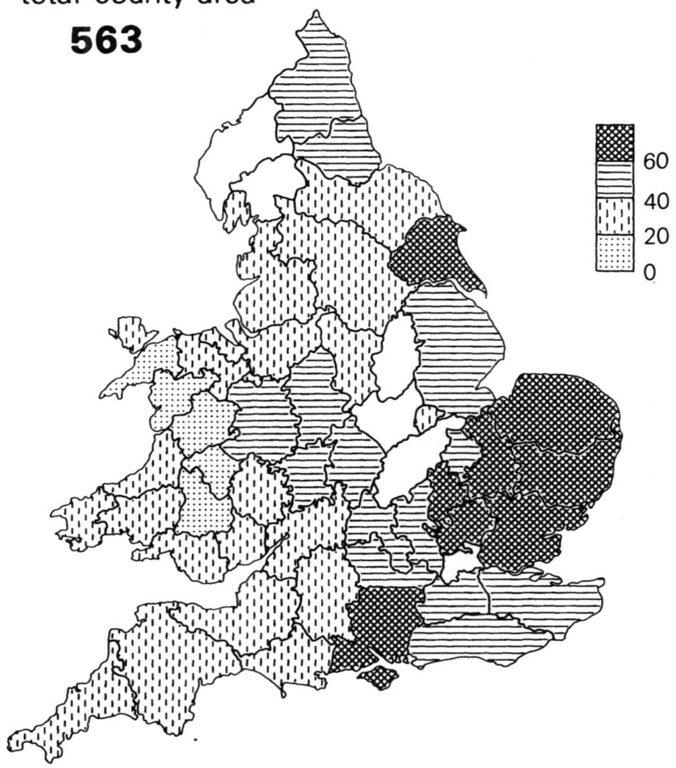

Pasture as a percentage of total county area
564

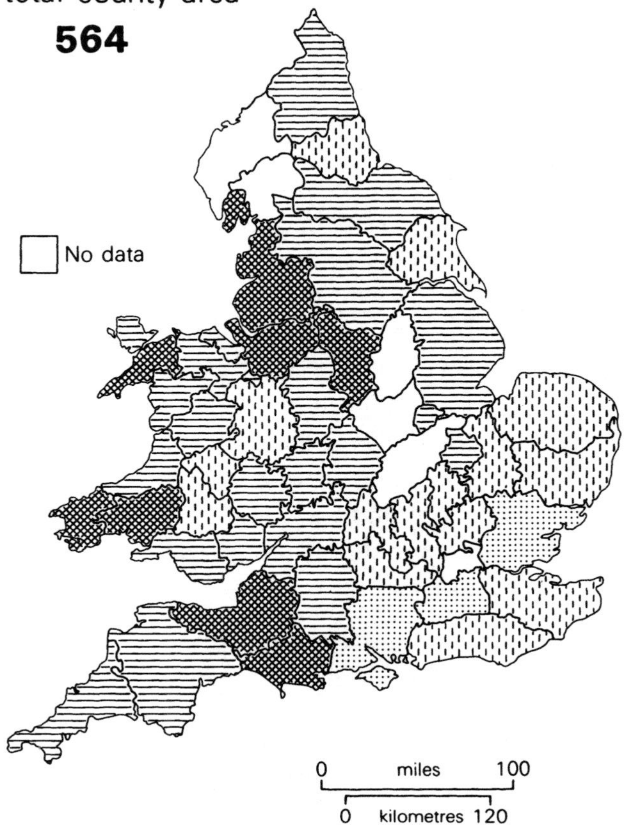

Ratio of arable to pasture
565

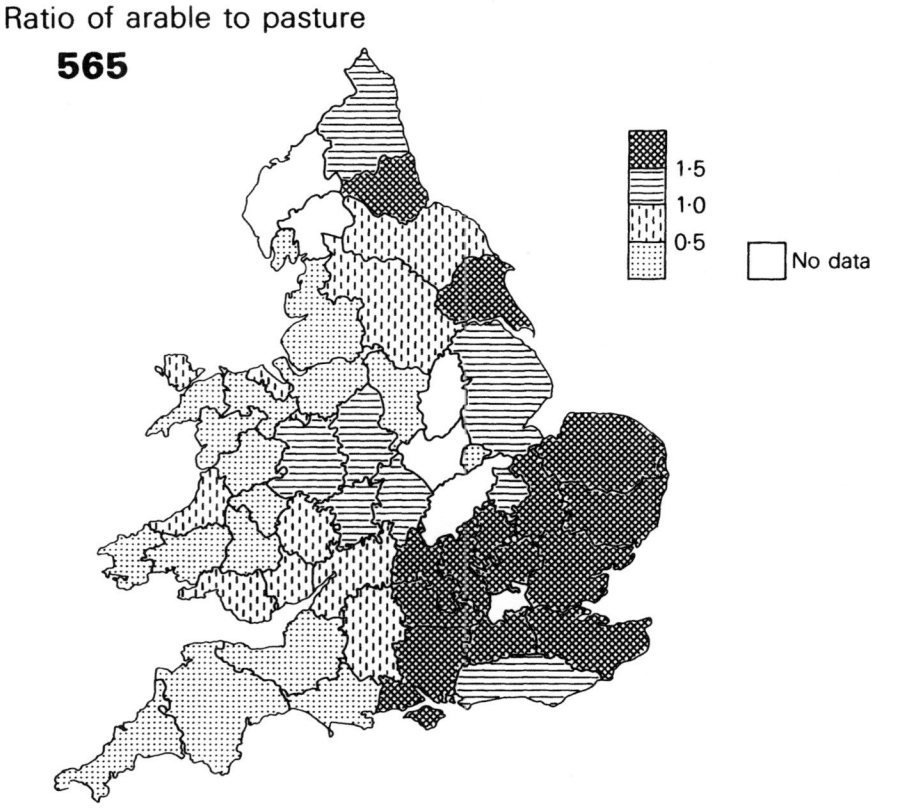

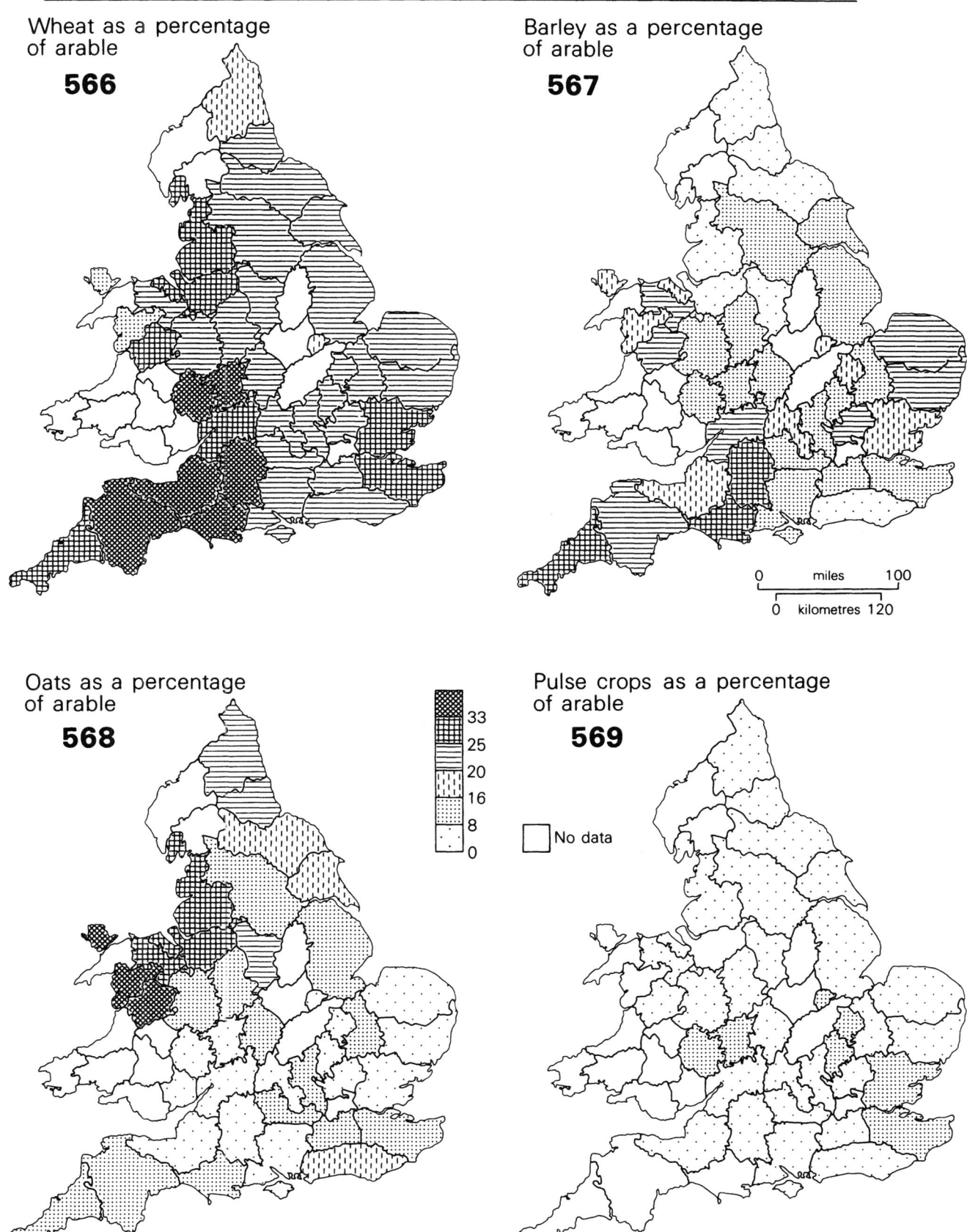

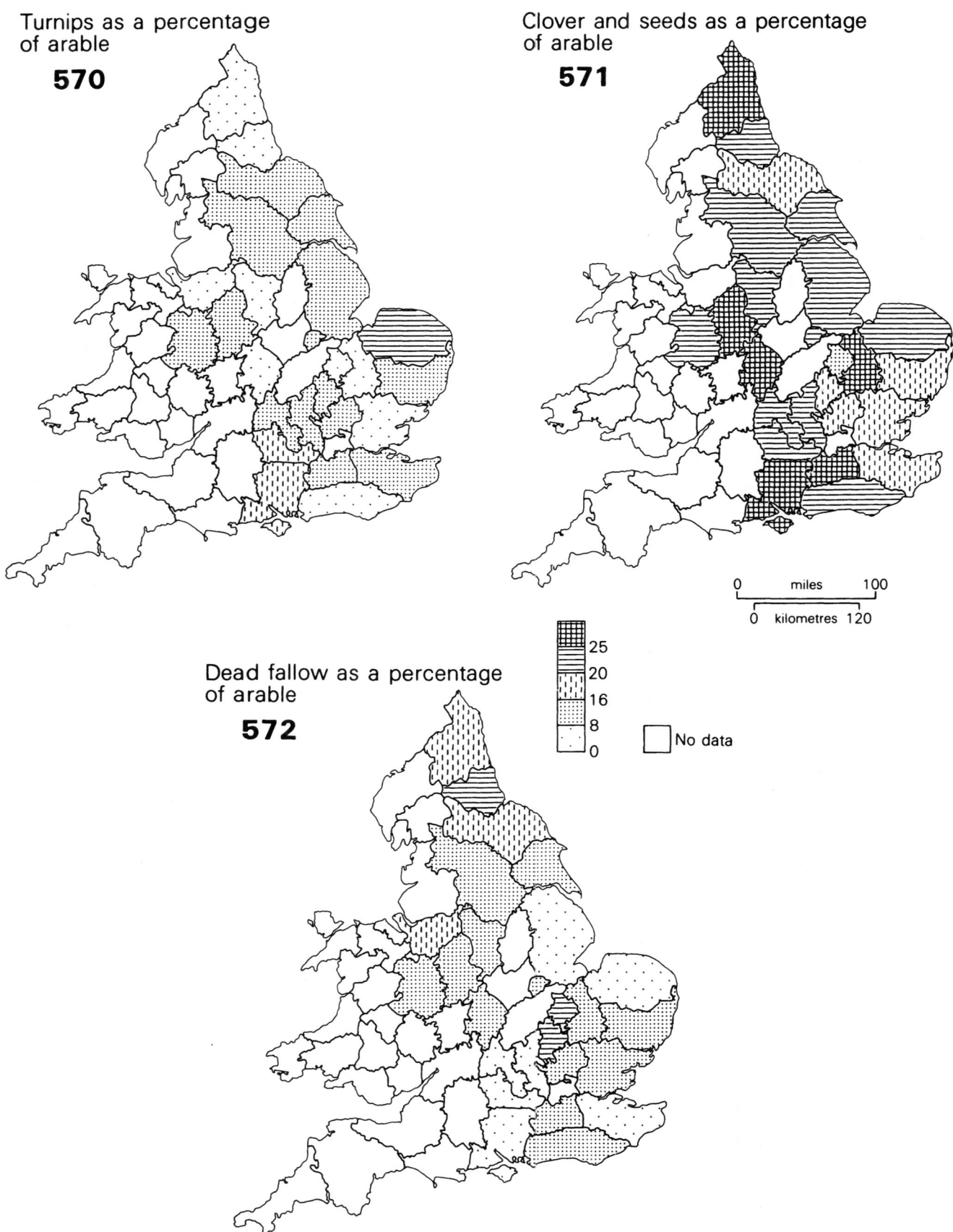

England and Wales

Yield of wheat in bushels per acre
573

Yield of barley in bushels per acre
574

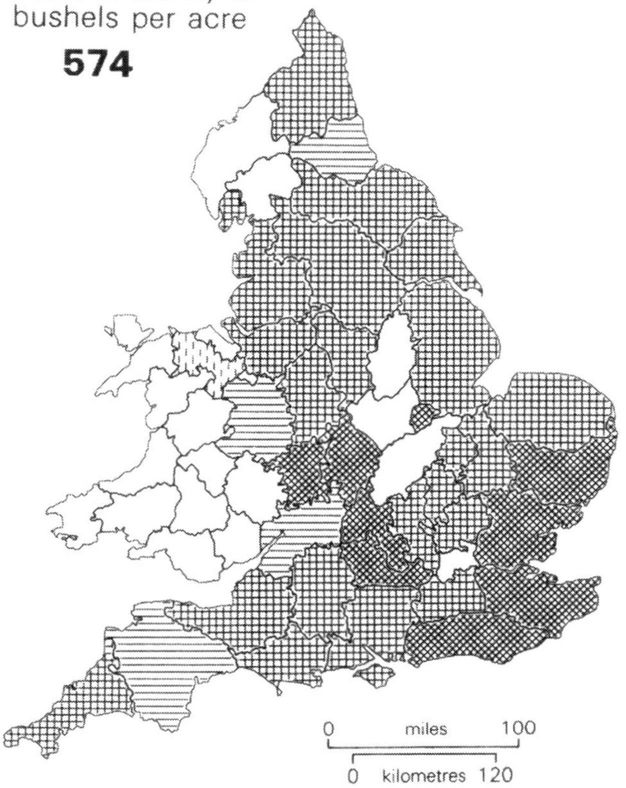

0 miles 100
0 kilometres 120

Yield of oats in bushels per acre
575

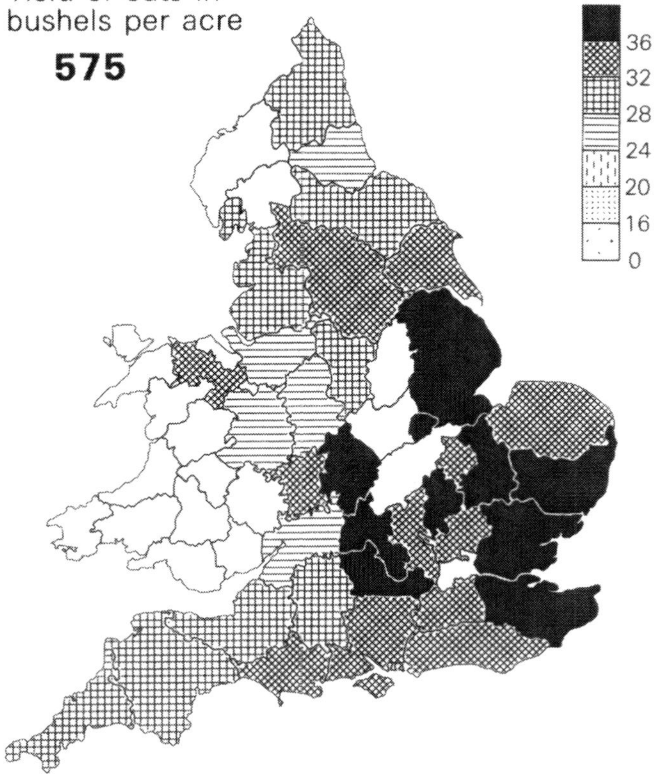

36
32
28
24
20
16
0

No data

Yield of pulse crops in bushels per acre
576

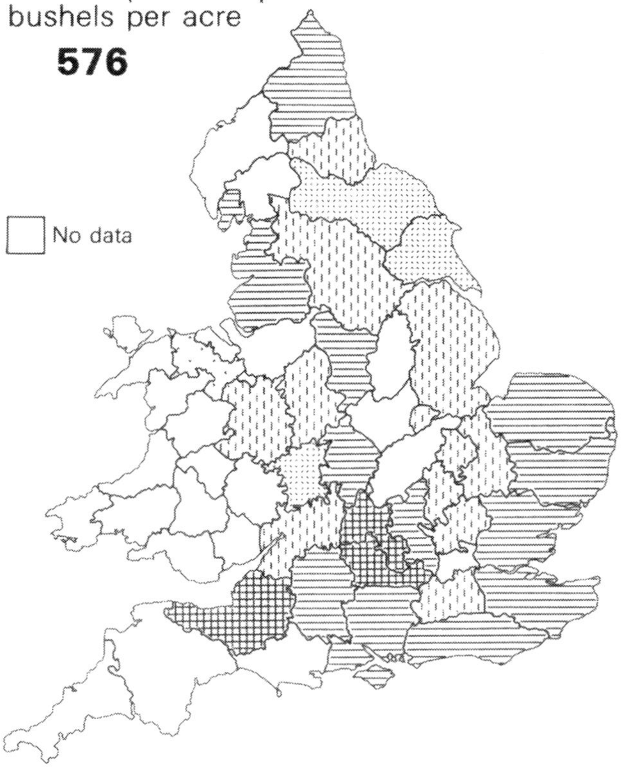

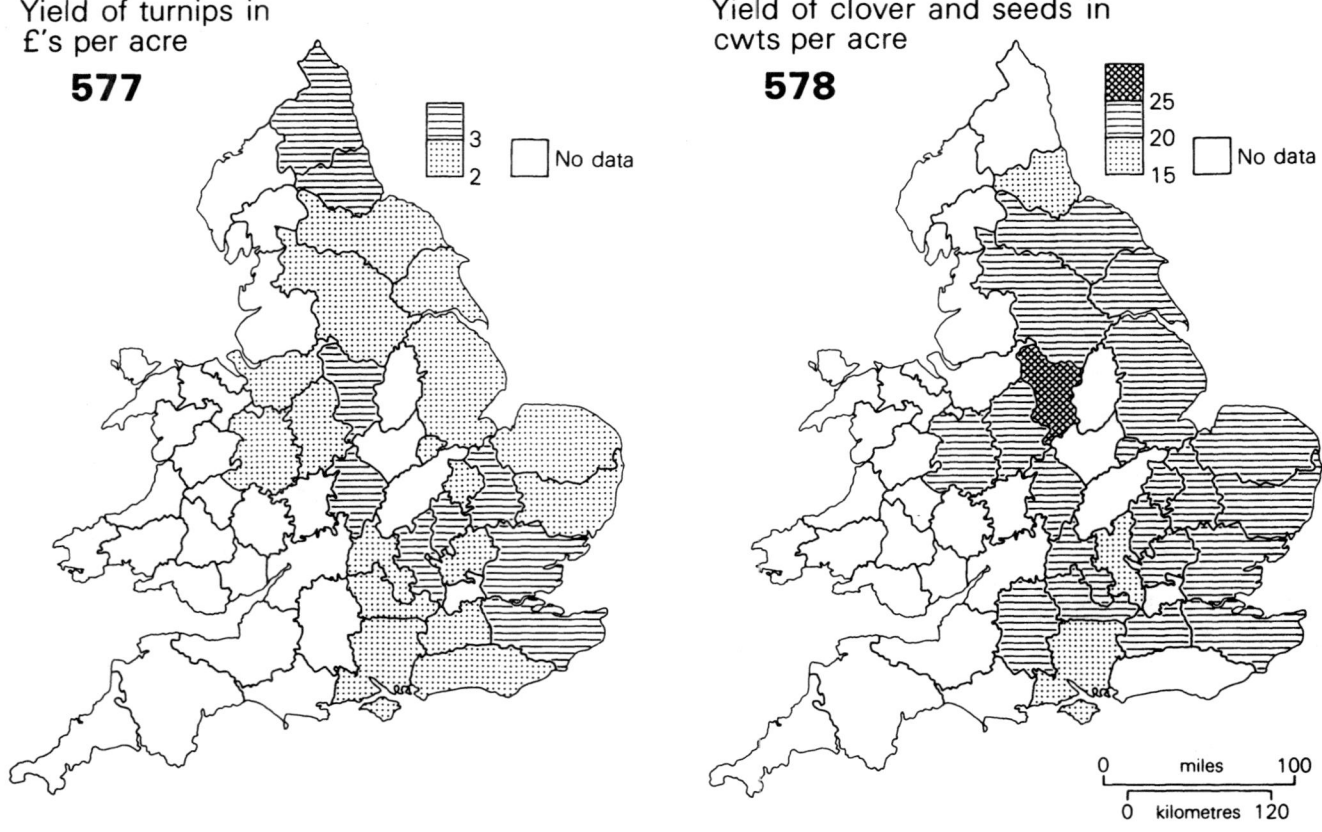

577 Yield of turnips in £'s per acre

578 Yield of clover and seeds in cwts per acre

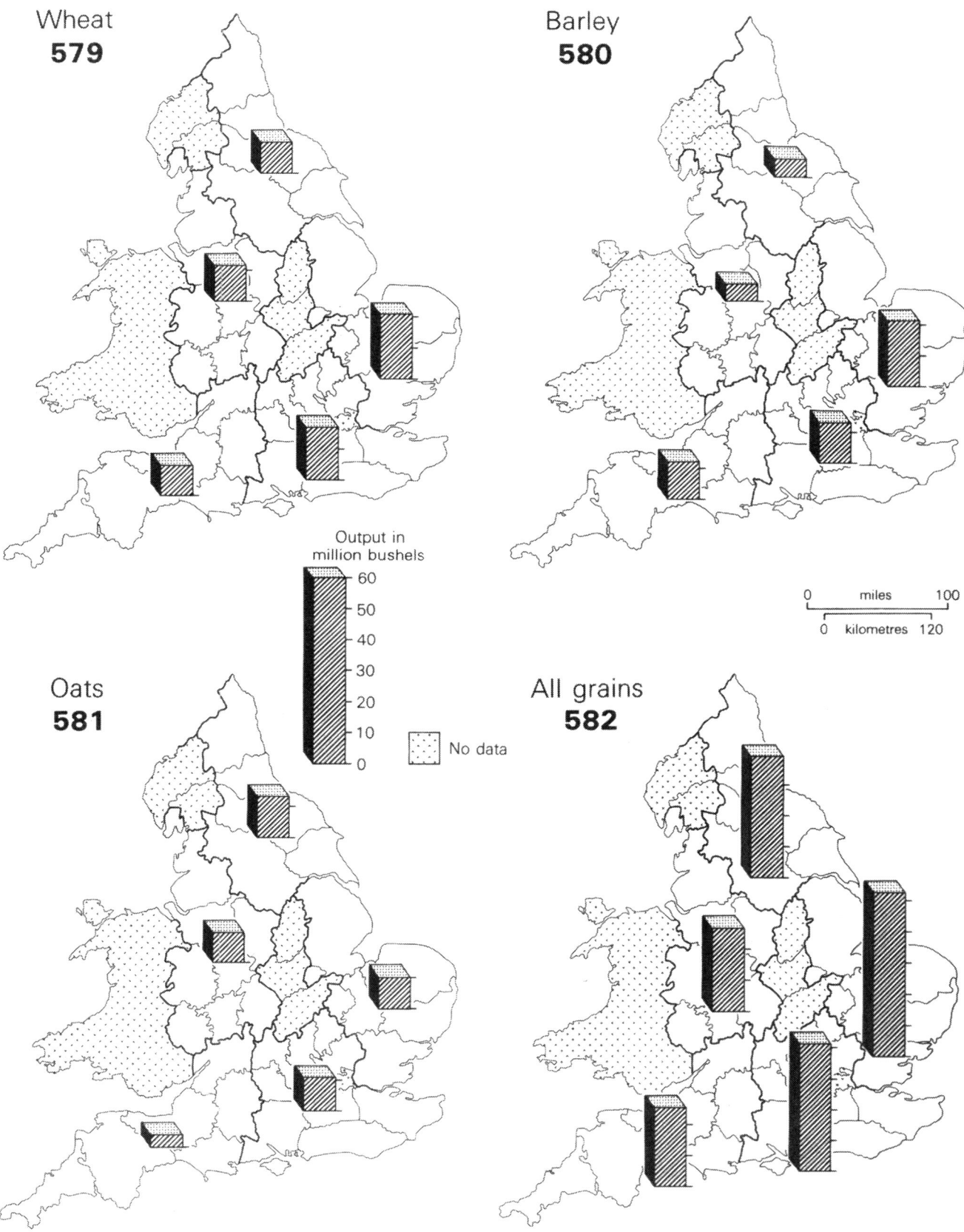

PLACE INDEX

The first of the two indexes lists all the tithe files and the main categories of papers they contain. It is arranged in alphabetical order of English and then Welsh counties; within counties, files are listed in numerical order of their unique Public Record Office press-marks. The following information is provided in the Place Index:

1. *Reference number*   This is the press-mark listed in the Public Record Office typescript catalogue of Class IR 18. These reference numbers are the same as those stamped on the outside cover of each file by the Tithe Redemption Commission.

2. *Tithe district name*   This is the name by which a district was known to the Tithe Commission at the time of commutation. We have retained the spelling as it appears in the file. For some places this is different from modern spelling and also from that used in other contemporary documents (e.g. the 1841 and 1851 censuses of population and Ordnance Survey maps).

3. *Category of tithe district*   Most tithe districts are coterminous with townships in northern England and parishes elsewhere. A minority are tithings, chapelries, manors, hamlets, extra-parochial places and such like; many of these enjoyed separate status solely for tithe commutation purposes. The following abbreviations are used in the Place Index:

B	Borough	BP	Borough and parish
C	Chapelry	EP	Extra-parochial place
D	District	ID	Tithe district
H	Hamlet	MH	Manor and hamlet
I	Tithing	MR	Manor and lordship
L	Liberty	PC	Parochial chapelry
M	Manor	PD	Parish and district
P	Parish	PH	Parish and hamlet
R	Lordship	PI	Parish and tithing
T	Township	PP	Part of a place
V	Village	TD	Township and district
		TH	Township and hamlet
		UP	United parishes

4. *Classes of document in the file*   The main types of document found in each file are listed following the code letters defining the category of tithe district. The following classification of papers is used:

> *N.t.p.* – (No tithes payable): These are files for places where either no tithe remained to be commuted in 1836 or where tithe liability had been, or was about to be, extinguished by a deed of merger in the land.
>
> *Agrmt.* – (*Agreement*): These files contain a copy or draft of a voluntary agreement for commutation of tithes.
>
> *Awd.* – (*Award*): A copy of a draft award imposed by an assistant tithe commissioner will be found in files where this entry appears in Place Index listings.
>
> *Min.* – (*Minutes*): All files where tithe was commuted by agreement or award and then apportioned by map and schedule of apportionment contain official notices, instructions and receipts from the Tithe Commission. Where a file contains a record of the process of commutation, problems encountered and solutions proposed, the entry 'Minutes' is used in the Place Index. If these papers contain more than an account of procedure, topics discussed in them will be found listed in the Subject Index.
>
> *Rep.* – (*Report and date of compilation*): One of the most valuable historical source documents in tithe files is the local tithe agent's or assistant commissioner's report on the fairness or otherwise of a voluntary agreement. As noted in the Introduction and at greater length in *The tithe surveys of England and Wales*, these 6,740 reports contain a massive amount of statistical data on local farming in the years around 1840, and also a wealth of descriptive material on local rural economy and society. The last is classified in the Subject Index below.

Bedfordshire

12965	Ampthill	P	N.t.p.,Min.
12966	Astwick	P	N.t.p.,Min.
12967	Apsley Guise	P	Awd.,Min.
12968	Barford Great	P	N.t.p.,Min.
12969	Barford Little	P	Min.,Rep. 1843
12970	Barton in the Clay	P	N.t.p.,Min.
12971	Battlesden	P	Awd.,Min.
12972	Bedford St Cuthbert	P	N.t.p.,Min.
12973	Bedford St John	P	N.t.p.,Min.
12974	Bedford St Peter	P	N.t.p.,Min.
12975	Bedford St Mary	P	N.t.p.,Min.
12976	Bedford St Paul	P	N.t.p.,Min.
12977	Biddenham	P	Awd.,Min.
12978	Blunham	P	N.t.p.,Min.
12979	Biggleswade	P	Agrmt.,Min.
12980	Billington	H	Min.
12981	Bletsoe	P	Agrmt.,Min.,Rep. 1839
12982	Bolnhurst	P	Awd.,Min.
12983	Bromham	P	Awd.,Min.
12984	Buckwood	D	Rep. 1841
12985	Campton	P	N.t.p.,Min.
12986	Cardington	P	Min.,Rep. 1840
12987	Carlton and Chellington	P	N.t.p.,Min.
12988	Chalgrave	P	N.t.p.,Min.
12989	Chicksands Priory	EP	N.t.p.
12990	Clapham	P	Awd.,Min.
12991	Clifton	P	N.t.p.,Min.
12992	Clophill	P	N.t.p.,Min.
12993	Cockayne Hatley	P	Rep. 1838
12994	Colmworth	P	N.t.p.,Min.
12995	Cople	P	Awd.,Min.
12996	Cranfield	P	N.t.p.,Min.
12997	Dean	P	N.t.p.,Min.
12998	Dunton	P	N.t.p.,Min.
12999	Dunstable	P	Min.,Rep. 1839
13000	Eaton Bray	P	Awd.,Min.
13001	Eaton Socon	P	N.t.p.,Min.
13002	Edworth	P	Agrmt.,Rep. 1838
13003	Eggington	H	Awd.,Min.
13004	Elstow	P	N.t.p.,Min.
13005	Eversholt	P	Agrmt.,Min.,Rep. 1837
13006	Everton	P	N.t.p.,Min.
13007	Eyeworth	P	Min.,Rep. 1838
13008	Farndish	P	N.t.p.,Min.
13009	Felmersham	P	N.t.p.,Min.
13010	Flitton	P	N.t.p.,Min.
13011	Flitwick	P	N.t.p.,Min.
13012	Goldington	P	Awd.,Min.
13013	Gravenhurst Upper	P	N.t.p.,Min.
13014	Gravenhurst Lower	P	N.t.p.
13015	Harold	P	N.t.p.,Min.
13016	Hawnes	P	Min.,Rep. 1840
13017	Harlington	P	N.t.p.,Min.
13018	Heath and Reach	C	Awd.,Min.
13019	Henlow	P	Awd.,Min.
13020	Higham Gobion	P	Min.,Rep. 1837
13021	Hockliffe	P	Awd.,Min.
13022	Holcut	P	Awd.,Min.
13023	Holwell	P	N.t.p.
13024	Houghton Conquest	P	Awd.,Min.
13025	Salford	P	N.t.p.,Min.
13026	Houghton Regis	P	N.t.p.,Min.
13027	Husborn Crawley	P	N.t.p.,Min.
13028	Kempston	P	Awd.,Min.
13029	Keysoe	P	Min.
13030	Knotting	P	Min.,Rep. 1839
13031	Langford	P	N.t.p.,Min.
13032	Lidlington	P	Awd.,Min.
13033	Leighton Buzzard	T	Awd.,Min.
13034	Luton	P	Awd.,Min.
13035	Maulden	P	N.t.p.,Min.
13036	Melchbourn	P	Agrmt.,Awd.,Min.,Rep. 1838
13037	Meppershall	P	Awd.,Min.
13038	Marston Moretaine	P	N.t.p.,Min.
13039	Milbrooke	P	N.t.p.,Min.
13040	Milton Bryant	P	N.t.p.,Min.
13041	Milton Ernest	P	N.t.p.,Min.
13042	Northill	P	N.t.p.,Min.
13043	Oakley	P	Awd.,Min.
13044	Odell	P	Awd.,Min.
13045	Pavenham	P	N.t.p.,Min.
13046	Pertenhall	P	Agrmt.,Rep. 1838
13047	Potsgrove	P	Awd.,Min.
13048	Potton	P	N.t.p.,Min.
13049	Puddington	P	N.t.p.,Min.
13050	Pulloxhill	P	N.t.p.,Min.
13051	Ravensden	P	N.t.p.,Min.
13052	Renhold	P	Agrmt.,Min.,Rep. 1838
13053	Ridgmont with Sedgenhoe	P	Awd.,Min.
13054	Riseley	P	Awd.,Min.
13055	Roxton	P	N.t.p.,Min.
13056	Sandy	P	N.t.p.,Min.
13057	Sharnbrook	P	N.t.p.,Min.
13058	Shefford Hardwicks	EP	N.t.p.
13059	Shelton	P	N.t.p.,Min.
13060	Shitlington	P	N.t.p.,Min.
13061	Stepingley	P	N.t.p.,Min.
13062	Streatley	P	Awd.,Min.
13063	Studham	P	Awd.,Min.
13064	Sundon	P	N.t.p.,Min.
13065	Souldrope	P	Rep. 1841
13066	Southill	P	N.t.p.,Min.
13067	Stagsden	P	Rep. 1839
13068	Stanbridge	T	Awd.,Min.
13069	Staughton Little	P	N.t.p.,Min.
13070	Steventon	P	N.t.p.,Min.
13071	Stondon Upper	P	N.t.p.
13072	Stotfold	P	Awd.,Min.
13073	Tempsford	P	N.t.p.,Min.
13074	Thurleigh	P	N.t.p.,Min.
13075	Tilsworth	P	N.t.p.,Min.
13076	Tingrith	P	Agrmt.,Min.,Rep. 1838
13077	Toddington	P	N.t.p.,Min.
13078	Totternhoe	P	Min.,Rep. 1840
13079	Turvey	P	Agrmt.,Min.,Rep. 1837
13080	Old Warden	P	Awd.,Min.
13081	Westoning	P	Rep. 1839
13082	Whipsnade	P	Awd.,Min.
13083	Wilden	P	N.t.p.,Min.
13084	Willington	P	Min.,Rep. 1839
13085	Wilshamstead	P	N.t.p.,Min.
13086	Woburn	P	Awd.,Min.
13087	Wootton	P	Awd.,Min.
13088	Wrestlingworth	P	N.t.p.,Min.
13089	Wymington	P	Awd.,Min.
13090	Yeldon	P	Min.
13091	Tilbrook	P	N.t.p.,Min.
14825	Sutton	P	Rep. 1839

Berkshire

13092	Ashbury	P	N.t.p.,Min.
13093	Aston Tirrold	P	Agrmt.,Min.,Rep. 1838
13094	Avington	P	Agrmt.,Rep. 1838
13095	Arborfield	P	Min.,Rep. 1841
13096	Ardington	P	Awd.,Min.
13097	Ashampstead	P	Min.
13098	Abingdon St Helen	P	Awd.,Min.
13099	Abingdon St Nicholas	P	Awd.,Min.
13100	Aldermaston	P	Agrmt.,Min.,Rep. 1838
13101	Aldworth	P	Min.,Rep. 1840
13102	Appleford	H	Agrmt.,Min.,Rep. 1839
13103	Appleton	P	Min.,Rep. 1839
13104	Bourton and Watchfield	I	N.t.p.,Min.
13105	Boxford	P	Agrmt.,Min.,Rep. 1837
13106	Bradfield	P	Awd.,Min.
13107	Blewberry	P	Agrmt.,Min.,Rep. 1838
13108	Bagley Wood	EP	N.t.p.,Min.
13109	Bagnor	I	Awd.,Min.
13110	Barkham	P	Min.,Rep. 1839
13111	Basildon	P	Agrmt.,Min.,Rep. 1838
13112	Baulking	H	Agrmt.,Min.,Rep. 1837
13113	Beadon	P	Min.,Rep. 1841
13114	Beckett	I	N.t.p.,Min.
13115	Beenham Vallence	P	N.t.p.,Min.
13116	Besselsleigh	P	Min.,Rep. 1841
13117	Bisham	P	Awd.,Min.
13118	Binfield	P	Agrmt.,Min.,Rep. 1837
13119	Bray	P	Min.,Rep. 1842
13120	Brightwaltham	P	Agrmt.,Min.,Rep. 1838
13121	Brightwell	P	Min.,Rep. 1840
13122	Brimpton	P	Min.,Rep. 1839
13123	Bryants Fee	I	Awd.,Min.
13124	Buckland	P	Min.,Rep. 1839
13125	Bucklebury	I	Min.,Rep. 1840
13126	Burghfield	P	Awd.,Min.
13127	Buscot	P	Min.,Rep. 1839
13128	Catmore	P	Awd.,Min.
13129	Chaddleworth	P	Min.,Rep. 1840
13130	West Challow	H	N.t.p.,Min.
13131	Chandlings	EP	N.t.p.,Min.
13132	East Challow	H	Awd.,Min.
13133	Childrey	P	N.t.p.,Min.
13134	Chieveley	H	Awd.,Min.
13135	Chilton	P	Awd.,Min.
13136	Cholsey	P	Awd.,Min.
13137	Clewer	P	Min.,Rep. 1839
13138	Coleshill	P	Min.,Rep. 1840
13139	Compton	P	Agrmt.,Awd.,Min.,Rep. 1839
13140	Compton Beauchamp	P	Agrmt.,Rep. 1838
13141	Cookham	P	Rep. 1843
13142	Courage	I	Min.,Rep. 1839
13143	Great Coxwell	P	Rep. 1842
13144	Cumner	P	N.t.p.,Min.
13145	Dedworth	H	Awd.,Min.
13146	Denchworth	P	N.t.p.,Min.
13147	Didcot	P	Min.,Rep. 1839
13148	Draycott Moor	T	Awd.,Min.
13149	Drayton	P	N.t.p.,Min.
13150	Earley	L	Min.,Rep. 1840
13151	East Hampstead	P	Min.,Rep. 1841

Berkshire contd.

13152	Eaton Hastings	P	Awd.,Min.
13153	Enbourne	P	Min.,Rep. 1840
13154	Englefield	P	Min.,Rep. 1843
13155	Faringdon	P	Awd.,Min.
13156	Farnborough	P	Agrmt.,Rep. 1838
13157	Farringdon Little	T	Rep. 1840
13158	Fernham	H	Min.,Rep. 1841
13159	Fawley North	P	N.t.p.
13160	Finchampstead	P	Awd.,Min.
13161	Frilford	H	Min.
13162	Frilsham	P	Agrmt.,Min.,Rep. 1839
13163	Fyfield	P	N.t.p.,Min.
13164	Garford	H	Awd.,Min.
13165	Garston East	P	Agrmt.,Min.,Rep. 1841
13166	Goosey	T	Awd.,Min.
13167	Graseley	I	Awd.,Min.
13168	Greenham	C	Min.,Rep. 1840
13169	Hanney East	T	Min.
13170	Hagbourne	P	Min.,Rep. 1841
13171	Hampstead Norris	P	Agrmt.,Min.,Rep. 1838
13172	Hampstead Marshall	P	Min.,Rep. 1840
13173	Hanney West	P	Min.,Rep. 1841
13174	Hardwell	D	Awd.,Min.
13175	Harwell	P	Min.,Rep. 1840
13176	Hatford	P	Agrmt.,Rep. 1839
13177	Hendred East	P	Min.,Rep. 1839
13178	Hendred West	P	Awd.,Min.
13179	Hinton Waldridge	P	N.t.p.,Min.
13180	Hinksey South	P	N.t.p.,Min.
13181	Hinksey North	P	N.t.p.,Min.
13182	Hungerford	P	Awd.,Min.
13183	Hurley	P	Min.,Rep. 1842
13184	Hurst	P	Agrmt.,Min.,Rep. 1840
13185	Ilsley East	P	Agrmt.,Min.,Rep. 1839
13186	Ilsley West	P	N.t.p.,Min.
13187	Inkpen	P	Min.,Rep. 1840
13188	Kingston Bagpuize	P	Awd.,Min.
13189	Kingston Lisle	H	Min.,Rep. 1840
13190	Kintbury	P	Min.,Rep. 1841
13191	Lambourne	P	Awd.,Min.
13192	Langford	T	N.t.p.,Min.
13193	Leckhampstead	C	Min.,Rep. 1841
13194	Letcombe Bassett	P	Awd.,Min.
13195	Letcombe Regis	P	Awd.,Min.
13196	Lockinge East	P	Min.,Rep. 1840
13197	Longcott	C	N.t.p.,Min.
13198	Longworth	P	Awd.,Min.
13199	Lyford	H	N.t.p.,Min.
13200	Marcham	P	N.t.p.,Min.
13201	Midgham	C	Min.,Rep. 1841
13202	Milton	P	Awd.,Min.
13203	Marlston	I	Min.,Rep. 1839
13204	Moreton South	P	Awd.,Min.
13205	Moreton North	P	Awd.,Min.
13206	Mortimer	P	Min.,Rep. 1838
13207	Moulsford	P	Min.,Rep. 1840
13208	Newbury	P	Min.,Rep. 1839
13209	Oare	C	Agrmt.,Min.,Rep. 1839
13210	Padworth	P	Agrmt.,Min.,Rep. 1838
13211	Pangbourn	P	Agrmt.,Min.,Rep. 1838
13212	Peasemore	P	Agrmt.,Min.,Rep. 1838
13213	Pewsey	P	N.t.p.,Min.
13214	Radley	P	Awd.,Min.
13215	Reading,St Giles	P	Agrmt.,Min.,Rep. 1838
13216	Reading,St Laurence	P	Min.
13217	Reading,St Mary	P	Min.,Rep. 1838
13218	Remenham	P	Min.,Rep. 1840
13219	Ruscombe	P	Min.,Rep. 1840
13220	Sandhurst	P	Agrmt.,Min.,Rep. 1841
13221	Seacourt	EP	N.t.p.,Min.
13222	Shaw cum Donnington	P	Agrmt.,Min.,Rep. 1838
13223	Shefford East	P	Agrmt.,Min.,Rep. 1843
13224	Sonning Town	L	Awd.,Min.
13225	Sotwell	H	Agrmt.,Min.,Rep. 1838
13226	Speen	P	N.t.p.,Min.
13227	Sutton Courtney	P	Awd.,Min.
13228	Sutton Wick	T	N.t.p.,Min.
13229	Swallowfield	P	Awd.,Min.
13230	Shilton	P	Agrmt.,Min.,Rep. 1839
13231	Shinfield	P	Agrmt.,Min.,Rep. 1839
13232	Shottesbrook	P	Min.,Rep. 1843
13233	Shrivenham	P	Min.,Rep. 1840
13234	Snelsmore	I	Min.,Rep. 1839
13235	Sparsholt	P	Agrmt.,Min.,Rep. 1838
13236	Stanford Dingley	P	Agrmt.,Min.,Rep. 1838
13237	Stanford in the Vale	P	Awd.,Min.
13238	Steventon	P	Min.
13239	Streatly	P	Min.,Rep. 1840
13240	Sulham	P	Rep. 1840
13241	Sulhampstead Abbotts	UP	Awd.,Min.
13242	Sunninghill	P	Agrmt.,Awd.,Min.,Rep. 1839
13243	Sunningwell	P	Min.,Rep. 1840
13245	Shefford Great	P	Agrmt.,Min.,Rep. 1838
13246	Shillingford	P	Awd.,Min.
13247	Tilehurst	P	Awd.,Min.
13248	Tidmarsh	P	Agrmt.,Min.,Rep. 1839
13249	Thatcham	P	Min.,Rep. 1841
13250	Tubney	P	Min.,Rep. 1840
13251	Uffington	P	N.t.p.,Min.
13252	Ufton Nervet	P	Awd.,Min.
13253	Wallingford,All Hallows	P	Min.,Rep. 1839
13254	Wallingford Castle	EP	N.t.p.,Min.
13255	Wallingford St Leonard	P	Awd.,Min.
13256	Wallingford St Mary	P	Min.
13257	Wallingford St Peter	P	Awd.,Min.
13258	Waltham,St Lawrence	P	Min.,Rep. 1839
13259	White Waltham	P	Min.,Rep. 1843
13260	Wantage	P	Awd.,Min.
13261	Warfield	P	Min.,Rep. 1841
13262	Wargrave	P	Min.,Rep. 1839
13263	Wasing	P	Awd.,Min.
13264	Welford	P	Min.,Rep. 1837
13265	Whitchurch	P	Agrmt.,Min.,Rep. 1838
13266	Windsor New	P	Awd.,Min.
13267	Windsor Old	P	Min.
13268	Windsor Castle	D	N.t.p.
13269	Winkfield North	P	Agrmt.,Min.,Rep. 1839
13270	Winkfield South	D	Awd.,Min.
13271	Winterbourne	I	Min.,Rep. 1839
13272	Witham	P	N.t.p.,Min.
13273	Wittenham Long	P	N.t.p.,Min.
13274	Wittenham Little	P	Awd.,Min.
13275	Wokingham	P	Awd.,Min.
13276	Woodhay West	P	Min.,Rep. 1837
13277	Woodley Sandford	L	Min.,Rep. 1840
13278	Woolhampton	P	Min.,Rep. 1839
13279	Wootton	P	Awd.,Min.
13280	Yattenden	P	Min.,Rep. 1843
14803	Purley	P	Min.,Rep. 1839

Buckinghamshire

7730	Kingsey	P	Awd.,Min.
13244	Shalston	P	Awd.,Min.
13281	Abbey Bradwell	EP	N.t.p.
13282	Addington	P	Awd.,Min.
13283	Adstock	P	N.t.p.
13284	Akeley cum Stockholt	P	Awd.,Min.
13285	Amersham	P	Agrmt.,Rep. 1837
13286	Ashenden	P	Awd.,Min.
13287	Astwood	P	Agrmt.,Min.,Rep. 1839
13288	Aston Abbotts	P	Awd.,Min.
13289	Aston Clinton	P	Awd.,Min.
13290	Aston Sandford	P	Agrmt.,Min.,Rep. 1839
13291	Aylesbury	P	Awd.,Min.
13292	Barton Hartshorne	P	Min.
13293	Beachampton	P	Agrmt.,Rep. 1839
13294	Beaconsfield	P	Awd.,Min.
13295	Biddlesden	P	N.t.p.
13296	Bierton with Broughton	P	Awd.,Min.
13297	Bledlow	P	Min.
13298	Bletchley	P	N.t.p.
13299	Boarstall	P	Awd.,Min.
13300	Bourton	H	Awd.,Min.
13301	Boveney Lower	H	Awd.,Min.,Rep. 1839
13302	Brayfield Cold	P	N.t.p.
13303	Bradenham	P	Awd.,Min.
13304	Bradwell	P	Agrmt.,Rep. 1839
13305	Brickhill Great	P	Agrmt.,Min.,Rep. 1839
13306	Brickhill Little	P	N.t.p.
13307	Brill	P	Awd.,Min.
13308	Buckingham	P	Awd.,Min.
13309	Buckland	P	Awd.,Min.
13310	Burnham	P	Agrmt.,Min.,Rep. 1838
13311	Calverton	P	N.t.p.
13312	Castle Thorpe	P	N.t.p.
13313	Chalfont St Giles	P	Agrmt.,Min.,Rep. 1838
13314	Chalfont St Peter	P	Awd.,Min.
13315	Chearsley	P	N.t.p.
13316	Cheddington	P	Agrmt.,Rep. 1839
13317	Chenies	P	Agrmt.,Min.,Rep. 1837
13318	Chesham	P	Agrmt.,Min.,Rep. 1842
13319	Chesham Bois	P	Agrmt.,Min.,Rep. 1838
13320	Crendon Long	P	N.t.p.
13321	Creslow	P	N.t.p.
13322	Chicheley	P	Awd.,Min.
13323	Chetwode	P	N.t.p.
13324	Cholesbury	P	Agrmt.,Rep. 1837
13325	Chilton	P	N.t.p.
13326	Claydon Middle	P	Awd.,Min.
13327	Claydon East	P	Awd.,Min.
13328	Clifton Reynes	P	Min.
13329	Cowley	H	Agrmt.,Rep. 1839
13330	Crawley North	P	Awd.,Min.
13331	Cublington	P	N.t.p.
13332	Cuddington	P	Agrmt.,Min.,Rep. 1840
13333	Datchet	P	N.t.p.
13334	The Den or Old Wick	EP	N.t.p.
13335	Denham	P	Agrmt.,Rep. 1840
13336	Dinton or Donnington	P	N.t.p.
13337	Dorney	P	Agrmt.,Min.,Rep. 1839

Buckinghamshire contd.

13338	Dorton	P	Awd.,Min.
13339	Drayton Beauchamp	P	Agrmt.,Rep. 1837
13340	Drayton Parslow	P	N.t.p.
13341	Dunton	P	N.t.p.,Min.
13342	Edgecott	P	N.t.p.,Min.
13343	Edlesborough	P	Agrmt.,Min.,Rep. 1839
13344	Ellesborough	P	Awd.,Min.
13345	Emberton	P	N.t.p.
13346	Eton	P	Agrmt.,Rep. 1839
13347	Farnham Royal	P	Agrmt.,Min.,Rep. 1839
13348	Fleet Marston	P	Agrmt.,Min.,Rep. 1840
13349	Foscott	P	Agrmt.,Rep. 1839
13350	Fulmer	P	Agrmt.,Awd.,Min.
13351	Gayhurst	P	Awd.,Min.
13352	Fenny Stratford	P	Min.
13353	Fingest	P	Agrmt.,Rep. 1839
13354	Grandborough	P	N.t.p.
13355	Grendon Underwood	P	Awd.,Min.
13356	Grove	P	Awd.,Min.
13357	Haddenham	P	N.t.p.
13358	Hambleden	P	Agrmt.,Min.,Rep. 1837
13359	Hampden Great	P	N.t.p.,Rep. 1839
13360	Hampden Little	P	Agrmt.,Rep. 1839
13361	Hanslope	P	N.t.p.,Min.
13362	Horwood Little	P	Awd.,Min.
13363	Hardmead	P	Agrmt.,Rep. 1838
13364	Hardwick with Weedon	PH	N.t.p.
13365	Hartwell with Sedrup	PH	N.t.p.
13367	Halton	P	Awd.,Min.
13368	Haversham	P	N.t.p.
13369	Hawridge	P	Min.,Rep. 1838
13370	Hedgerley	P	Agrmt.,Rep. 1840
13371	Hedsor	P	Agrmt.,Rep. 1838
13372	Hillesden	P	Awd.,Min.
13374	Hoggeston	P	Awd.,Min.
13375	Hogshaw cum Fulbrook	PH	Awd.,Min.
13376	Horsenden	P	Agrmt.,Rep. 1839
13377	Horton	P	Min.
13378	Horwood Great	P	Awd.,Min.
13379	Hughendon	P	Agrmt.,Min.,Rep. 1842
13380	Hulcot	P	Awd.,Min.
13381	Ickford	P	Awd.,Min.
13382	Illmire	P	Agrmt.,Rep. 1839
13383	Iver	P	Awd.,Min.
13384	Ivinghoe	P	Agrmt.,Rep. 1839
13385	Kimble Great	P	Agrmt.,Min.,Rep. 1839
13386	Kimble Little	P	N.t.p.
13387	Langley Marish	P	Awd.,Min.
13388	Lathbury	P	Awd.,Min.
13389	Lavendon	P	N.t.p.
13390	Leckhampstead	P	Agrmt.,Rep. 1839
13391	Lee	P	N.t.p.
13392	Lenborough	H	Awd.,Min.
13393	Lillingstone Dayrell	P	Agrmt.,Min.,Rep. 1837
13394	Linford Great	P	Awd.,Min.
13395	Linford Little	P	N.t.p.
13396	Linslade	P	N.t.p.
13397	Longmarston and Ashthorpe	EP	N.t.p.
13398	Loughton	P	N.t.p.
13399	Ludgershall	P	N.t.p.
13400	Luffield Abbey	EP	N.t.p.
13401	Maids Moreton	P	N.t.p.
13402	Marlow Great	P	Awd.,Min.
13403	Marlow Little	P	Agrmt.,Rep. 1844
13404	Marsh Gibbon	P	Agrmt.,Rep. 1839
13405	Marston North	P	N.t.p.
13406	Medmenham	P	Agrmt.,Rep. 1838
13407	Mentmore	P	Min.
13408	Missenden Great	P	Min.,Rep. 1840
13409	Missenden Little	P	Awd.,Min.
13410	Monks Risborough	P	N.t.p.
13411	Moulsoe	P	N.t.p.
13412	Mursley and Salden	PH	Awd.,Min.
13413	Newport Pagnel	P	Awd.,Min.
13414	Newton Blossomville	P	N.t.p.
13415	Newton Longville	P	Awd.,Min.
13416	Oakley	P	N.t.p.
13417	Olney	P	N.t.p.
13418	Oving	P	Awd.,Min.
13419	Padbury	P	Awd.,Min.
13420	Middleton (Milton Keynes)	P	Agrmt.,Rep. 1837
13421	Penn	P	Agrmt.,Rep. 1838
13422	Pightlesthorne (Pitstone)	P	Min.,Rep. 1838
13423	Pitchcott	P	Awd.,Min.
13424	Preston Bissett	P	N.t.p.
13425	Princes Risborough	P	N.t.p.
13426	Quainton	P	Agrmt.,Min.,Rep. 1842
13427	Quarrendon	H	Awd.,Min.
13428	Radclive	P	Agrmt.,Rep. 1840
13429	Radnage	P	Awd.,Min.
13430	Ravenstone	P	Awd.,Min.
13431	Saunderton	P	Awd.,Min.
13432	Shabbington	P	Agrmt.,Rep. 1839
13433	Sherrington	P	N.t.p.
13434	Stoke Hammond	P	N.t.p.
13435	Shenley	P	Agrmt.,Min.,Rep. 1840
13436	Simpson	P	N.t.p.
13437	Singleborough	H	N.t.p.
13438	Slapton	P	N.t.p.
13439	Soulbury	P	Awd.,Min.
13440	Stanton Bury	P	N.t.p.
13441	Stewkley	P	N.t.p.
13442	Steeple Claydon	P	Awd.,Min.
13443	Stoke Goldington	P	Awd.,Min.
13444	Stoke Mandeville	P	N.t.p.
13445	Stoke Poges	P	Agrmt.,Min.,Rep. 1842
13446	Stone	P	Awd.,Min.
13447	Stony Stratford	UP	N.t.p.
13448	Stowe	P	Awd.,Min.
13449	Studley	H	N.t.p.
13450	Swanbourne	P	Awd.,Min.
13451	Taplow	P	N.t.p.
13452	Tattenhoe	P	Awd.,Min.
13453	Thornborough	P	Awd.,Min.
13454	Thornton	P	Agrmt.,Rep. 1838
13455	Tingewick	P	Awd.,Min.
13456	Towersey	P	N.t.p.
13457	Turweston	P	N.t.p.
13458	Turville	P	Agrmt.,Min.
13459	Twyford	P	N.t.p.
13460	Tyringham with Filgrave	P	Agrmt.,Rep. 1838
13461	Upton	H	Agrmt.,Rep. 1840
13462	Upton cum Chalvey	P	Awd.,Min.
13463	Waddesdon	P	Awd.,Min.
13464	Walton	P	Agrmt.,Rep. 1839
13465	Water Stratford	P	Agrmt.,Min.,Rep. 1839
13466	Wavenden	P	Awd.,Min.
13467	Wendover	P	Agrmt.,Min.,Rep. 1842
13468	Westbury	P	Min.
13469	Weston Turville	P	Awd.,Min.
13470	Weston Underwood	P	Awd.,Min.
13471	Wexham	P	Awd.,Min.
13472	Whaddon	P	N.t.p.
13473	Whitchurch	P	N.t.p.
13474	Willen	P	Awd.,Min.
13475	Winchendon Upper	P	Awd.,Min.
13476	Winchendon Nether	P	N.t.p.
13477	Wing	P	Awd.,Min.
13478	Wingrave with Rowsham	P	N.t.p.
13479	Winslow	P	N.t.p.
13480	Wolverton	P	Awd.,Min.
13481	Wooburn	P	Awd.,Min.
13482	Woolstone Great	P	N.t.p.
13485	Fawley	P	Agrmt.,Min.,Rep. 1840
13546	Woolstone Little	P	Min.
13547	Wootton under Wood	P	Min.
13548	Worminghall	P	Awd.,Min.
13549	Woughton on the Green	P	N.t.p.
13550	Wycombe West	P	Awd.,Min.
13551	Wycombe Borough of	B	Awd.,Min.
13552	Wycombe High or Chipping	P	Awd.,Min.
13553	Wyrardisbury	P	Agrmt.,Rep. 1839
14804	Broughton	P	N.t.p.
14805	Marsworth	P	N.t.p.
14829	Brickhill Bow	P	N.t.p.

Cambridgeshire

9842	Kennett	P	Min.
13483	Bywall Fen	D	Agrmt.,Min.,Rep. 1839
13484	Carlton cum Willingham	P	N.t.p.
13486	Castle Camps	P	Agrmt.,Min.,Rep. 1840
13487	Chatteris Adventurers Hall	PD	N.t.p.
13488	Chesterton	P	Agrmt.,Min.,Rep. 1839
13489	Comberton	P	Min.,Rep. 1839
13490	Cherry Hinton	P	N.t.p.
13491	Cheveley	P	Rep. 1838
13492	Childerley	P	Awd.,Min.
13493	Chippenham	P	Min.,Rep. 1839
13494	Connington	P	N.t.p.
13495	Coton	P	N.t.p.
13496	Cottenham	P	Min.,Rep. 1838
13497	Coveney	P	Rep. 1841
13498	Croxton	P	N.t.p.
13499	Croydon cum Clapton	P	Agrmt.,Min.,Rep. 1839
13500	Doddington	T	Min.,Rep. 1839
13501	Downham	P	Rep. 1838
13502	Dry Drayton	P	N.t.p.
13503	Dullingham	P	N.t.p.
13504	Duxford St Peter,St John	P	Agrmt.,Rep. 1839
13505	Elm and part of Outwell	P	Min.,Rep. 1839
13506	Elsworth	P	N.t.p.
13507	Eltisley	P	Rep. 1841
13508	Eversden Great	P	N.t.p.
13509	Ely Holy Trinity,St Mary	P	Min.
13510	Abington Great	P	N.t.p.
13511	Abington Little	P	N.t.p.
13512	Abington Pigotts	P	Agrmt.,Rep. 1838
13513	Arrington	P	Agrmt.,Min.
13514	Ashley cum Silverley	P	N.t.p.
13515	Babraham	P	Rep. 1845

Cambridgeshire contd.

13516	Balsham	P	N.t.p.
13517	Barrington	P	N.t.p.,Min.
13518	Bartlow	P	Awd.,Min.
13519	Barton	P	Min.,Rep. 1840
13520	Bassingbourne	P	N.t.p.
13521	Bourn	P	Min.,Rep. 1840
13522	Bottisham	P	N.t.p.
13523	Boxworth	P	Agrmt.,Min.,Rep. 1838
13524	Brinkley	P	N.t.p.
13525	Burrough Green	P	Agrmt.,Min.,Rep. 1837
13526	Burwell	P	Awd.,Min.
13527	Benwick (Doddington P.)	H	Rep. 1839
13528	Caldecote	P	Min.
13529	Cambridge St Andrew Less	P	Awd.,Min.
13530	Caxton	P	N.t.p.
13531	Cambridge All Saints	P	N.t.p.
13532	Cambridge St Andrew the Gt	P	N.t.p.
13533	Cambridge St Benedict	P	N.t.p.
13534	Cambridge St Botolph	P	N.t.p.
13535	Cambridge St Clement	P	N.t.p.
13536	Cambridge St Edward	P	N.t.p.
13537	Cambridge St Giles	P	N.t.p.
13538	Cambridge St Michael	P	N.t.p.
13539	Cambridge St Mary the Less	P	Min.
13540	Cambridge St Mary the Gt	P	N.t.p.
13541	Cambridge St Peter	P	N.t.p.
13542	Cambridge St Sepulchre	P	N.t.p.
13543	Cambridge St Thomas	P	N.t.p.
13544	Cambridge Holy Trinity	P	N.t.p.
13545	Cambridge University	P	N.t.p.
13567	Eversden Little	P	N.t.p.
13568	Fen Ditton	P	N.t.p.
13569	Fen Drayton	P	Rep. 1840
13570	Fordham	P	N.t.p.
13571	Foulmire	P	Awd.,Min.
13572	Foxton	P	Agrmt.,Min.
13573	Fulbourn	P	N.t.p.
13574	Gamlingay	P	Awd.,Min.
13575	Girton	P	Awd.,Min.,Rep. 1841
13576	Gransden Little	P	N.t.p.
13577	Granchester	P	N.t.p.
13578	Graveley	P	N.t.p.
13579	Grunty Fen	EP	Awd.,Min.
13580	Haddenham	P	Rep. 1843
13581	Hardwick	P	Min.
13582	Harlton	P	N.t.p.
13583	Harston	P	N.t.p.
13584	Haslingfield	P	Min.,Rep. 1841
13585	Hatley East	P	Rep. 1842
13586	Hatley St George	P	Agrmt.,Min.,Rep. 1838
13587	Hauxton cum Newton	P	N.t.p.
13588	Hildersham	P	Agrmt.,Min.,Rep. 1837
13589	Hinxton	P	N.t.p.
13590	Histon	P	N.t.p.
13591	Horningsea	P	N.t.p.
13592	Horseheath	P	Rep. 1839
13593	Ickleton	P	N.t.p.,Min.
13594	Impington	P	N.t.p.
13595	Isleham	P	Min.
13596	Kingston	P	N.t.p.
13597	Kirtling	P	N.t.p.
13598	Knapwell	P	N.t.p.
13599	Kneesworth	H	Rep. 1839
13600	Landbeach	P	N.t.p.
13601	Landwade	P	N.t.p.
13602	Leverington	P	Awd.,Min.
13603	Linton	P	Min.,Rep. 1839
13604	Litlington	P	Min.,Rep. 1841
13605	Littleport	P	Agrmt.,Min.,Rep. 1839
13606	Lolworth	P	Rep. 1840
13607	Madingley	P	Rep. 1841
13608	March	T	Min.,Rep. 1839
13609	Melbourn	P	Agrmt.,Min.,Rep. 1839
13610	Meldreth	P	N.t.p.
13611	Mepal	P	Agrmt.,Min.,Rep. 1838
13612	Milton	P	N.t.p.
13613	Newmarket All Saints	P	N.t.p.
13614	Newmarket St Mary	P	N.t.p.
13615	Newton (Thriplow Hundred)	P	Min.,Rep. 1841
13616	Newton (Isle of Ely)	P	Min.,Rep. 1841
13617	Oakington	P	N.t.p.
13618	Orwell	P	N.t.p.
13619	Outwell	PP	Min.,Rep. 1839
13620	Over	P	N.t.p.
13621	Pampisford	P	N.t.p.
13622	Papworth St Agnes	P	Agrmt.,Min.,Rep. 1838
13623	Papworth St Everard	P	Min.,Rep. 1840
13624	Rampton	P	Min.,Rep. 1842
13625	Sawston	P	N.t.p.
13626	Shelford Great	P	N.t.p.
13627	Shelford Little	P	N.t.p.
13628	Shepreth	P	Min.,Rep. 1839
13629	Shingay	P	N.t.p.
13630	Shudy Camps	P	Min.,Rep. 1840
13631	Snailwell	P	Rep. 1839
13632	Soham	P	Agrmt.,Min.,Rep. 1837
13633	Stanton Long All Saints	P	N.t.p.
13634	Stanton Long St Michael	P	Awd.,Min.
13635	Stapleford	P	N.t.p.
13636	Steeple Morden	P	Agrmt.,Min.,Rep. 1838
13637	Stetchworth	P	N.t.p.
13638	Stow Long	P	N.t.p.
13639	Stow cum Quy	P	Min.,Rep. 1837
13640	Stretham	P	N.t.p.,Agrmt.,Min.
13641	Stuntney	H	Agrmt.,Min.,Rep. 1838
13642	Sutton	P	Agrmt.,Min.,Rep. 1837
13643	Swaffham Bulbeck	P	N.t.p.
13644	Swavesey	P	Min.,Rep. 1838
13645	Tadlow	P	Min.,Rep. 1842
13646	Teversham	P	N.t.p.
13647	Thetford	H	Agrmt.,Rep. 1838
13648	Thorney	P	N.t.p.
13649	Toft	P	Awd.,Min.
13650	Trumpington	P	N.t.p.
13651	Tyd St Giles	P	Awd.,Min.
13652	Thriplow	P	Rep. 1840
13653	Upwell cum Welney	P	Min.
13654	Guilden Morden	P	N.t.p.
13655	Manea	P	Min.
13656	Wentworth	P	Awd.,Min.
13657	Waterbeach	P	Agrmt.,Rep. 1838
13658	Wendye	P	Awd.,Min.
13659	Westley Waterless	P	Min.,Rep. 1838
13660	Weston Colville	P	N.t.p.
13661	Westwick	H	Rep. 1838
13662	Whaddon	P	Min.,Rep. 1838
13663	Whittlesey St Andrew	UP	Awd.,Min.
13664	Whittlesford	P	N.t.p.
13665	Wicken	P	Agrmt.,Awd.,Min.
13666	Wickham West	P	N.t.p.,Awd.
13667	Wilbraham Great	P	N.t.p.
13668	Wilbraham Little	P	N.t.p.
13669	Wilburton	P	Agrmt.,Rep. 1838
13670	Willingham	P	Agrmt.,Awd.,Min.,Rep. 1837
13671	Wimblington	H	Min.,Rep. 1839
13672	Wimpole	P	Agrmt.,Rep. 1837
13673	Wisbech St Mary	P	Min.,Rep. 1838
13674	Wisbech St Peter	P	Min.,Rep. 1840
13675	Witcham	P	Awd.,Min.
13676	Witchford	P	Min.,Rep. 1839
13677	Wolvey Hills and Hole	EP	N.t.p.
13678	Wood Ditton	P	N.t.p.
13679	Wratting West	P	Awd.,Min.
14830	Swaffham Prior	P	N.t.p.

Cheshire

1	Daresbury	T	Awd.,Min.
2	Darnhall	T	Awd.,Min.
3	Davenham	T	Agrmt.,Min.,Rep. 1838
4	Davenport	T	Agrmt.,Rep. 1838
5	Delamere	T	N.t.p.,Min.
6	Disley	T	Agrmt.,Awd.,Min.,Rep. 1840
7	Doddington	T	Awd.,Min.
8	Dodcott cum Wilksley	T	Agrmt.,Min.,Rep. 1839
9	Dodleston	P	Agrmt.,Min.
10	Duckinfield	T	Awd.,Min.
11	Duckington	T	Agrmt.,Min.,Rep. 1838
12	Duddon	T	Agrmt.,Min.,Rep. 1838
13	Dunham	T	Agrmt.,Rep. 1838
14	Dunham Massey	T	Min.,Rep. 1838
15	Dutton	T	Agrmt.,Rep. 1840
16	Earnshaw Hall Farm	D	Agrmt.,Rep. 1841
17	Eastham	T	Agrmt.,Min.,Rep. 1839
18	Eaton	T	Rep. 1839
19	Eaton (Davenham Parish)	T	Agrmt.,Rep. 1838
20	Eaton	T	Agrmt.,Min.,Rep. 1838
21	Ecclestone	P	Agrmt.,Min.
22	Edge	T	Agrmt.,Min.,Rep. 1838
23	Edlestone	T	Agrmt.,Rep. 1839
24	Egerton	T	Agrmt.,Rep. 1838
25	Elton	T	Agrmt.,Min.,Rep. 1838
26	Elton	T	Rep. 1838
27	Etchells	T	Agrmt.,Rep. 1840
28	Etchells	T	Agrmt.,Rep. 1839
29	Faddiley	T	Agrmt.,Rep. 1839
30	Fallybroome	T	Awd.,Min.
31	Farndon	T	Agrmt.,Min.,Rep. 1839
32	Foulk Stapleford	T	Agrmt.,Min.,Rep. 1838
33	Frankby	T	Awd.,Min.
34	Frodsham Lordship	T	Agrmt.,Awd.,Min.,Rep. 1840
35	Frodsham	T	Agrmt.,Awd.,Min.,Rep. 1840
36	Fulshaw	T	Agrmt.,Rep. 1839
37	Gawsworth	P	Awd.,Min.
38	Grafton	P	Awd.,Min.
39	Grange	T	Awd.,Min.
40	Grappenhall	T	Min.
41	Greasby	T	Awd.,Min.
42	Godley	T	Awd.,Min.
43	Golborne David	T	Awd.,Min.
44	Goostrey cum Barnshaw	T	Agrmt.,Awd.,Min.,Rep. 1838

Cheshire contd.

45	Guilden Sutton	P	Awd.,Min.
46	Hale	T	Rep. 1838
47	Halton	T	Awd.,Min.
48	Hampton	T	Agrmt.,Min.,Rep. 1837
49	Handforth cum Bosden	T	Awd.,Min.
50	Handley	T	Agrmt.,Min.,Rep. 1838
51	Lyme Handley	T	Awd.,Min.
52	Hankelow	T	Agrmt.,Rep. 1838
53	Hapsford	T	Agrmt.,Min.,Rep. 1838
54	Haslington	T	Agrmt.,Min.,Rep. 1840
55	Hartford	T	Awd.,Min.
56	Harthill	P	Agrmt.,Rep. 1838
57	Hassall	T	Agrmt.,Min.,Rep. 1840
58	Hatherton	T	Awd.,Min.
59	Hatton	T	Awd.,Min.
60	Hatton	T	Agrmt.,Min.,Rep. 1838
61	Haughton	T	Agrmt.,Min.,Rep. 1839
62	Henbury cum Pexall	T	Awd.,Min.
63	Henhull	T	Agrmt.,Min.,Rep. 1839
64	Heswall	P	Awd.,Min.
65	Hilbre Island	EP	N.t.p.,Min.
66	Hilsby	T	Agrmt.,Awd.,Min.,Rep. 1840
67	Hockenhull	T	Agrmt.,Rep. 1838
68	Hollingworth	T	Awd.,Min.
69	Hoole	T	Agrmt.,Rep. 1838
70	Hoose	T	Awd.,Min.
71	Hooton	T	Agrmt.,Min.,Rep. 1839
72	Horton	T	Agrmt.,Min.,Rep. 1838
73	Horton cum Peele	T	Awd.,Min.
74	Hough	T	Agrmt.,Min.,Rep. 1838
75	Hulmewalfield	T	Min.,Rep. 1840
76	Hulse	T	Awd.,Min.
77	Hunsterson	T	Awd.,Min.
78	Huntingdon	T	Awd.,Min.
79	Hurdsfield	T	Awd.,Min.
80	Hurleston	T	Agrmt.,Min.,Rep. 1839
81	Huxley	T	Agrmt.,Min.,Rep. 1838
82	Hyde	T	Agrmt.,Min.,Rep. 1839
83	Iddinshall	T	N.t.p.,Min.
84	Ince	P	N.t.p.,Min.
85	Irby	T	Min.
86	Irby	T	Awd.,Min.
87	St John the Baptist	P	Awd.,Min.
88	Keckwick	T	Awd.,Min.,Rep. 1844
89	Kelsall	T	Agrmt.,Min.,Rep. 1838
90	Kermincham	T	Agrmt.,Min.,Rep. 1839
91	Kettleshulme	T	Awd.,Min.
92	Kinderton cum Hulme	T	Agrmt.,Min.,Rep. 1842
93	Kingsley	T	Agrmt.,Awd.,Min.,Rep. 1840
94	Kingsmarsh	EP	Awd.,Min.
95	Kirby West	T	Awd.,Min.
96	Kingswood	T	N.t.p.
97	Knutsford Nether	T	Awd.,Min.,Rep. 1841
98	Knutsford Over	T	Awd.,Min.
99	Lache Dennis	T	Awd.,Min.
100	Landican	T	Awd.,Min.
101	Latchford	T	N.t.p.
102	Lea	T	Agrmt.,Min.,Rep. 1839
103	Lea	T	Agrmt.,Rep. 1838
104	Lea Newbold	T	Agrmt.,Rep. 1839
105	Lees	T	Agrmt.,Awd.,Min.,Rep. 1841
106	Ledsham	T	Agrmt.,Min.,Rep. 1839
107	Leftwich	T	Awd.,Min.
108	Leighton	T	Awd.,Min.
109	High Leigh	T	Awd.,Min.
110	Little Leigh	T	Agrmt.,Min.,Rep. 1839
111	Leighton	T	Awd.,Min.
112	Liscard	T	Agrmt.,Min.,Rep. 1839
113	Littleton	T	Awd.,Min.
114	Lostock Gralam	T	Awd.,Min.
115	Lymm	P	Agrmt.,Min.,Rep. 1837
116	Macclesfield	T	Awd.,Min.
117	Macclesfield Forest	T	Awd.,Min.
118	Macefen	T	Agrmt.,Rep. 1837
119	Malpas	T	Agrmt.,Min.,Rep. 1839
120	Manley	T	Agrmt.,Awd.,Min.,Rep. 1840
121	Marbury	T	Agrmt.,Awd.,Min.,Rep. 1843
122	Marbury cum Quoisley	T	Agrmt.,Min.,Rep. 1837
123	Marlston cum Lache	T	Agrmt.,Min.,Rep. 1842
124	Marple	T	Awd.,Min.
125	Marston	T	Awd.,Min.
126	Marthall cum Warford	T	Agrmt.,Min.,Rep. 1841
127	Marton	T	Awd.,Min.
128	Marton	T	Agrmt.,Min.,Rep. 1845
129	Marton	T	Awd.,Min.
130	St Mary on the Hill	P	Agrmt.,Min.,Rep. 1839
131	Matley	T	Agrmt.,Min.,Rep. 1839
132	Meolse Great	T	Awd.,Min.
133	Meolse Little	T	Awd.,Min.
134	Mere	T	Awd.,Min.
135	Mickle Trafford	T	Agrmt.,Min.,Rep. 1838
136	Middlewich and Newton	T	Awd.,Min.
137	Millington	T	Agrmt.,Min.,Rep. 1841
138	Minshull Vernon	T	Awd.,Min.
139	Mobberley	P	Agrmt.,Awd.,Min.,Rep. 1843
140	Mollington Little	T	Agrmt.,Min.,Rep. 1838
141	Mollington Great	T	Agrmt.,Min.,Rep. 1838
142	Moorsbarrow with Parm	T	Awd.,Min.
143	Monks Coppenhall	T	Min.,Rep. 1840
144	Moor	T	Awd.,Min.
145	Middleton Grange	PC	Min.
146	Moreton cum Alcumlow	T	Agrmt.,Rep. 1838
147	Moston	T	Agrmt.,Min.,Rep. 1838
148	Moston	T	Agrmt.,Min.,Rep. 1838
149	Mottram St Andrew	T	Awd.,Min.
150	Mottram in Longdendale	T	Awd.,Min.
151	Mouldsworth	T	Agrmt.,Rep. 1838
152	Moulton	T	Awd.,Min.
153	Nantwich	T	Awd.,Min.
154	Ness	T	Agrmt.,Min.,Rep. 1839
155	Neston Great	T	Awd.,Min.
156	Newall	T	Agrmt.,Min.,Rep. 1838
157	Newbold Astbury	T	Agrmt.,Min.,Rep. 1838
158	Newhall	T	Agrmt.,Min.,Rep. 1839
159	Newton	T	Agrmt.,Awd.,Min.,Rep. 1840
160	Neston Little	T	Awd.,Min.
161	Newton	T	Awd.,Min.
162	Newton by Daresbury	T	Awd.,Min.
163	Newton	T	Agrmt.,Min.,Rep. 1839
164	Newton	T	Awd.,Min.
165	Newton	T	Awd.,Min.
166	Newton	T	Agrmt.,Rep. 1838
167	Noctorum	T	Awd.,Min.
168	Norbury	T	Agrmt.,Min.,Rep. 1837
169	Norbury	T	Agrmt.,Awd.,Min.,Rep. 1840
170	Norley	T	Agrmt.,Awd.,Min.,Rep. 1840
171	Norton	T	Min.
172	Northen	T	Agrmt.,Min.,Rep. 1840
173	Northwich	T	Awd.,Min.
174	Occlestone	T	Awd.,Min.
175	Odd Rode	T	Agrmt.,Min.,Rep. 1838
176	Offerton	T	Awd.,Min.
177	Oldcastle	T	Agrmt.,Min.,Rep. 1837
178	Ollerton	T	Agrmt.,Awd.,Min.,Rep. 1841
179	St Oswald	P	Awd.,Min.
180	Oulton Low	T	Agrmt.,Min.,Rep. 1839
181	Over	T	Agrmt.,Min.,Rep. 1845
182	Over	T	Agrmt.,Min.,Rep. 1846
183	Overchurch	P	Agrmt.,Rep. 1837
184	Overton	T	Agrmt.,Min.,Rep. 1838
185	Oxton	T	Awd.,Min.
186	Partington	T	Min.,Rep. 1838
187	Pensley	T	Awd.,Min.
188	Peckforton	T	Agrmt.,Min.,Rep. 1846
189	Peover Inferior	T	Agrmt.,Awd.,Min.,Rep. 1842
190	Peover Nether	T	Agrmt.,Awd.,Min.,Rep. 1842
191	Peover Over	T	Agrmt.,Awd.,Min.,Rep. 1841
192	Pickmere	T	Agrmt.,Awd.,Min.,Rep. 1842
193	Picton	T	Agrmt.,Min.,Rep. 1838
194	Plumley	T	Agrmt.,Min.,Rep. 1842
195	Poole	T	Agrmt.,Min.,Rep. 1839
196	Poolton cum Seacombe	T	Agrmt.,Min.,Rep. 1839
197	Poolton cum Spittle	T	Agrmt.,Min.,Rep. 1842
198	Pott Shrigley	T	Awd.,Min.
199	Pownall Fee	T	Agrmt.,Min.,Rep. 1839
200	Poynton	T	Awd.,Min.
201	Prenton	T	Agrmt.,Rep. 1845
202	Prestbury	T	Awd.,Min.
203	Preston on the Hill	T	Awd.,Min.
204	Puddington	T	Agrmt.,Rep. 1839
205	Pulford	P	Agrmt.,Min.
206	Raby	T	Awd.,Min.
207	Radnorshire	T	Agrmt.,Rep. 1842
208	Rainow	T	Awd.,Min.
209	Ravenscroft	T	Awd.,Min.
210	Ridley	T	Agrmt.,Min.,Rep. 1840
211	North Rode	T	Awd.,Min.
212	Romiley	T	Agrmt.,Awd.,Min.,Rep. 1839
213	Rope	T	Agrmt.,Rep. 1838
214	Rostherne	T	Agrmt.,Min.,Rep. 1841
215	Rowton	T	Awd.,Min.
216	Rudheath	R	Awd.,Min.
217	Rudheath	T	Awd.,Min.
218	Runcorn	T	Awd.,Min.
219	Saighton	T	Agrmt.,Min.,Rep. 1839
220	Sale	T	Awd.,Min.
221	Church Hulme	T	Agrmt.,Min.,Rep. 1840
222	Sandbach	T	Min.,Rep. 1840
223	Saughall Great	T	Agrmt.,Awd.
224	Saughall Little	T	Agrmt.,Min.,Rep. 1842
225	Seven Oaks	T	Agrmt.,Awd.,Min.,Rep. 1843
226	Stockton	T	Agrmt.,Rep. 1837
227	Shavington cum Gresty	T	Agrmt.,Min.,Rep. 1838
228	Shipbrooke	T	Agrmt.,Min.,Rep. 1838
229	Shocklach	P	Agrmt.,Min.,Rep. 1838
230	Shotwick Park	EP	Min.
231	Shurlach	T	Awd.,Min.
232	Shotwick	T	Awd.,Min.
233	Siddington	T	Awd.,Min.
234	Smallwood	T	Agrmt.,Min.,Rep. 1838
235	Snelson	T	Agrmt.,Awd.,Min.,Rep. 1841
236	Somerford Booths	T	Agrmt.,Min.,Rep. 1838

Cheshire contd.

237	Somerford Radnor	T	Agrmt.,Rep. 1842
238	Sound	T	Agrmt.,Min.,Rep. 1839
239	Sproston	T	Agrmt.,Min.,Rep. 1839
240	Spurstow	T	Agrmt.,Min.,Rep. 1839
241	Stanlow	EP	Min.
242	Stanney Great	EP	Awd.,Min.
243	Stanney Little	T	Awd.,Min.
244	Stanthorne	T	Awd.,Min.
245	Stapeley	T	Agrmt.,Min.,Rep. 1838
246	Stayley	T	Agrmt.,Min.,Rep. 1839
247	Stockham	T	Awd.,Min.
248	Stockton Heath	D	Min.
249	Stoke	T	Agrmt.,Min.,Rep. 1839
250	Stoke	T	Awd.,Min.
251	Storeton	T	Agrmt.,Rep. 1839
252	Stublach	T	Awd.,Min.
253	Sutton	T	N.t.p.,Awd.,Min.
254	Sutton	T	Awd.,Min.
255	Sutton	T	Awd.,Min.
256	Sutton Great	T	Awd.,Min.
257	Sutton Little	T	Awd.,Min.
258	Stretton	T	Awd.,Min.
259	Stretton	T	Agrmt.,Min.,Rep. 1840
260	Swettenham	T	Agrmt.,Min.,Rep. 1839
261	Tabley Nether	T	Awd.,Min.
262	Tabley Over	T	Awd.,Min.
263	Tattenhall	P	Min.,Rep. 1838
264	Tarporley	T	Agrmt.,Min.,Rep. 1838
265	Tarvin	T	Agrmt.,Min.,Rep. 1838
266	Tatton	T	Agrmt.,Awd.,Min.,Rep. 1841
267	Taxal	T	Awd.,Min.
268	Tetton	T	Agrmt.,Min.,Rep. 1838
269	Thelwall	T	Awd.,Min.
270	Thingwell	T	Awd.,Min.
271	Thornton	T	Agrmt.,Min.,Rep. 1838
272	Thornton Hough	T	Awd.,Min.
273	Thurstaston and Irby	P	Awd.,Min.
274	Threapwood	EP	N.t.p.,Min.
275	Tilson	T	Agrmt.,Min.,Rep. 1840
276	Tilstone	T	Agrmt.,Rep. 1839
277	Timperley	T	Min.,Rep. 1838
278	Tintwistle	T	Awd.,Min.
279	Titherington	T	Awd.,Min.
280	Tittenley	T	Awd.,Min.
281	Tiverton	T	Agrmt.,Min.,Rep. 1839
282	Toft	T	Agrmt.,Awd.,Min.,Rep. 1842
283	Torkington	T	Agrmt.,Awd.,Min.,Rep. 1840
284	Tranmore	T	Awd.,Min.
285	Tushingham cum Grindley	T	Agrmt.,Rep. 1838
286	Twemlow	T	Agrmt.,Min.,Rep. 1839
287	Upton	T	Agrmt.,Rep. 1839
288	Upton	T	Awd.,Min.
289	Walgherton	T	Awd.,Min.
290	Walton Higher	T	Awd.,Min.
291	Walton Lower	T	Awd.,Min.
292	Wallasey	T	Agrmt.,Min.,Rep. 1840
293	Warburton	P	Agrmt.,Min.,Rep. 1837
294	Wardle	T	Agrmt.,Min.,Rep. 1839
295	Warmingham	T	Agrmt.,Min.,Rep. 1838
296	Waverham	T	Awd.,Min.
297	Waverton	T	Agrmt.,Min.
298	Weaverham	P	Agrmt.,Min.,Rep. 1839
299	Wharton	T	Agrmt.,Min.,Rep. 1838
300	Werneth	T	Agrmt.,Min.,Rep. 1839
301	Wervin	T	Agrmt.,Awd.,Min.,Rep. 1839
302	Weston	T	Awd.,Min.
303	Weston	T	Agrmt.,Awd.,Min.,Rep. 1842
304	Wetenhall	T	Agrmt.,Min.,Rep. 1841
305	Whalley cum Yerdsley	T	Awd.,Min.
306	Whatcroft	T	Agrmt.,Rep. 1838
307	Wheelock	T	Agrmt.,Min.,Rep. 1839
308	Whitby,Overpool	T	Agrmt.,Min.
309	Whitley Higher	T	Awd.,Min.,Rep. 1842
310	Whitley Lower	T	Awd.,Min.
311	Wigland	T	Agrmt.,Min.,Rep. 1838
312	Wildboar Clough	T	Awd.,Min.
313	Willaston	T	Agrmt.,Awd.,Min.,Rep. 1844
314	Willaston	T	Awd.,Min.
315	Willaston	T	Agrmt.,Awd.,Min.,Rep. 1839
316	Willington	EP	Awd.,Min.
317	Wimboldsley	T	N.t.p.,Min.
318	Wimbolds Trafford	T	Agrmt.,Min.,Rep. 1838
319	Wincham	T	Agrmt.,Awd.,Min.,Rep. 1842
320	Wincle	T	Awd.,Min.
321	Winnington	T	Agrmt.,Awd.,Min.,Rep. 1843
322	Wirswall	T	Agrmt.,Min.,Rep. 1837
323	Wistaston	P	Agrmt.,Rep. 1839
324	Withington Lower	T	Awd.,Min.
325	Withington Old	T	Awd.,Min.
326	Witton cum Twambrook	T	Agrmt.,Min.,Rep. 1839
327	Woodbank	T	Awd.,Min.
328	Woodchurch	T	Awd.,Min.
329	Woodcote	T	Agrmt.,Rep. 1838
330	Woodford	T	Awd.,Min.
331	Woolstanwood	T	Agrmt.,Min.,Rep. 1839
332	Worleston	T	Agrmt.,Min.,Rep. 1842
333	Worth	T	Awd.,Min.
334	Wrenbury	T	Agrmt.,Rep. 1838
335	Wybunbury	T	Agrmt.,Awd.,Min.,Rep. 1839
336	Wychough	T	Agrmt.,Rep. 1839
13366	Hattersley	T	Min.,Rep. 1839
13680	Acton	T	Agrmt.,Min.,Rep. 1839
13681	Acton Grange	T	Awd.,Min.
13682	Adlington	T	Awd.,Min.
13683	Agden	T	Rep. 1839
13684	Agden	T	Agrmt.,Min.,Rep. 1838
13685	Agden	T	Awd.,Min.
13686	Alderley	T	Awd.,Min.
13687	Aldford	P	Agrmt.,Min.
13688	Allostock	T	Awd.,Min.
13689	Alpraham	T	Agrmt.,Min.,Rep. 1839
13690	Alsager	T	Agrmt.,Min.,Rep. 1838
13691	Altrincham	T	Min.,Rep. 1838
13692	Alvanley	T	Agrmt.,Awd.,Min.,Rep. 1840
13693	Alvaston	T	Agrmt.,Min.,Rep. 1840
13694	Austerson	T	Agrmt.,Rep. 1838
13695	Audlem	T	Agrmt.,Min.,Rep. 1839
13696	Ashton	T	Agrmt.,Min.,Rep. 1838
13697	Ashton by Sutton	T	Awd.,Min.
13698	Aston Grange	T	Awd.,Min.
13699	Astbury	P	Min.
13700	Aston	T	Agrmt.,Min.,Rep. 1839
13701	Aston	T	Agrmt.,Awd.,Min.,Rep. 1842
13702	Ashton upon Mersey	P	Agrmt.,Min.,Rep. 1842
13703	Ashton upon Mersey	T	Min.,Rep. 1838
13704	Arrow	T	Awd.,Min.
13705	Ashley	T	Min.,Rep. 1838
13706	Arclid	T	Agrmt.,Rep. 1839
13707	Appleton	T	Agrmt.,Awd.,Min.,Rep. 1842
13708	Anderton	T	Agrmt.,Awd.,Min.,Rep. 1843
13709	Antrobus	T	Agrmt.,Awd.,Min.,Rep. 1842
13710	Bache	T	Awd.,Min.
13711	Backford	T	Agrmt.,Min.,Rep. 1839
13712	Baddiley	P	Agrmt.,Min.,Rep. 1839
13713	Baddington	T	Agrmt.,Min.,Rep. 1838
13714	Barrow	P	Agrmt.,Min.,Rep. 1838
13715	Baguley	T	Agrmt.,Min.,Rep. 1840
13716	Barton	T	Agrmt.,Min.,Rep. 1840
13717	Barnton	T	Agrmt.,Awd.,Min.,Rep. 1843
13718	Barnston	T	Awd.,Min.
13719	Bartherton	T	Agrmt.,Min.,Rep. 1838
13720	Barthomley	T	Agrmt.,Rep. 1838
13721	Bartington	T	Agrmt.,Rep. 1840
13722	Basford	T	Agrmt.,Min.,Rep. 1838
13723	Bebbington Higher	T	Awd.,Min.
13724	Bebbington Lower	T	Awd.,Min.
13725	Beeston	T	Min.,Rep. 1846
13726	Betchton	T	Awd.,Min.,Rep. 1840
13727	Bexton	T	Agrmt.,Awd.,Min.,Rep. 1841
13728	Bickerton	T	Agrmt.,Min.,Rep. 1838
13729	Bidstone	P	Min.,Rep. 1838
13730	Biley cum Yatehouses	T	Agrmt.,Rep. 1842
13731	Birches	T	Awd.,Min.
13732	Birkenhead	PC	N.t.p.,Min.
13733	Bollington	T	Awd.,Min.
13734	Bollington	T	Awd.,Min.
13735	Bollington	D	Min.,Rep. 1839
13736	Birtles	T	Awd.,Min.
13737	Blackden	T	Min.,Rep. 1840
13738	Bosley	T	Awd.,Min.
13739	Bostock	T	Agrmt.,Rep. 1838
13740	Bradley	T	Agrmt.,Min.,Rep. 1839
13741	Bradwall	T	Agrmt.,Rep. 1839
13742	Bredbury	T	Agrmt.,Min.,Rep. 1839
13743	Brereton cum Smethwick	P	Awd.,Min.
13744	Bridgmere	T	Awd.,Min.
13745	Bridge Trafford	T	Agrmt.,Rep. 1838
13746	St Bridget	P	Awd.,Min.
13747	Brindley	T	Agrmt.,Min.,Rep. 1839
13748	Brinnington	T	Agrmt.,Min.,Rep. 1839
13749	Brimstage	T	Agrmt.,Rep. 1840
13750	Bowdon	T	Agrmt.,Min.,Rep. 1838
13751	Boughton Great	T	Awd.,Min.
13752	Bollin Fee	T	Agrmt.,Min.,Rep. 1839
13753	Blakenhall	T	Awd.,Min.
13754	Blacon with Crabhall	T	Awd.,Min.
13755	Blakeley Brow	D	Awd.,Min.
13756	Bromborow	T	Agrmt.,Min.,Rep. 1839
13757	Broomhall	T	Agrmt.,Rep. 1838
13758	Broxton	T	Agrmt.,Min.,Rep. 1838
13759	Bruen Stapleford	T	Agrmt.,Rep. 1838
13760	Budworth Little	P	Min.,Rep. 1839
13761	Budworth Great	T	Agrmt.,Awd.,Min.,Rep. 1842
13762	Buerton	T	Awd.,Min.
13763	Buglawton	T	Agrmt.,Min.,Rep. 1840
13764	Bunbury	T	Agrmt.,Min.,Rep. 1839
13765	Burland	T	Agrmt.,Min.,Rep. 1839
13766	Burton	T	Awd.,Min.
13767	Burton	T	Agrmt.,Rep. 1838
13768	Burwardsley	T	Agrmt.,Min.,Rep. 1840
13769	Butley	T	Awd.,Min.
13770	Caldy	T	Awd.,Min.

Cheshire contd.

13771	Calveley	T	Min.
13772	Capenhurst	T	Agrmt.,Min.,Rep. 1839
13773	Capesthorne	T	Awd.,Min.
13774	Carden	T	Agrmt.,Min.,Rep. 1840
13775	Carrington	T	Min.,Rep. 1838
13776	Caughall	T	Agrmt.,Rep. 1838
13777	Cheadle Bulkeley	T	Awd.,Min.
13778	Checkley cum Wrinehill	T	Awd.,Min.
13779	Chelford	T	Awd.,Min.
13780	Chester, Holy Trinity	P	Agrmt.,Rep. 1838
13781	Chidlow	T	Agrmt.,Rep. 1839
13782	Childer Thornton	T	Agrmt.,Min.,Rep. 1839
13783	Cholmondeley	T	Agrmt.,Min.,Rep. 1838
13784	Cholmondeston	T	Awd.,Min.
13785	Cheadle Moseley	T	Awd.,Min.
13786	Chorley	T	Agrmt.,Min.,Rep. 1839
13787	Chorley	T	Agrmt.,Min.,Rep. 1839
13788	Chorlton	T	Awd.,Min.
13789	Chorlton	T	Agrmt.,Min.,Rep. 1837
13790	Chorlton	T	Awd.,Min.
13791	Christleton	T	Awd.,Min.
13792	Church Coppenhall	T	Agrmt.,Min.,Rep. 1841
13793	Church Lawton	P	Agrmt.,Min.,Rep. 1838
13794	Church Minshull	P	Agrmt.,Min.,Rep. 1838
13795	Churton Heath	T	Agrmt.,Rep. 1839
13796	Churton by Farndon	T	Agrmt.,Min.,Rep. 1839
13797	Claughton cum Grange	T	Awd.,Min.
13798	Claverton	T	Agrmt.,Min.,Rep. 1838
13799	Clifton cum Rock Savage	T	Min.,Rep. 1844
13800	Clive	T	Min.,Rep. 1840
13801	Clotton Hoolfield	T	Agrmt.,Min.,Rep. 1838
13802	Clutton	T	Agrmt.,Min.,Rep. 1840
13803	Coddington	P	Agrmt.,Min.,Rep. 1838
13804	Cogshall	T	Awd.,Min.
13805	Congleton	T	Min.,Rep. 1843
13806	Coole Pilate	T	Agrmt.,Rep. 1839
13807	Cotton Abbott	T	Awd.,Min.
13808	Cotton Edmunds	T	Awd.,Min.
13809	Cotton	T	Agrmt.,Rep. 1839
13810	Cranage	T	Min.,Rep. 1843
13811	Crewe	T	Agrmt.,Min.,Rep. 1838
13812	Crewe	T	Awd.,Min.
13813	Croughton	T	Agrmt.,Awd.,Min.,Rep. 1839
13814	Crowley	T	Agrmt.,Awd.,Min.,Rep. 1842
13815	Croxton	T	N.t.p.,Awd.,Min.
13816	Cuddington	T	Agrmt.,Min.,Rep. 1838
14823	Stockport	T	Awd.,Min.
14824	Bramall	T	Agrmt.,Awd.,Min.,Rep. 1839
14835	Comberbach	T	Awd.,Min.

Cornwall

337	Advent	P	Min.
338	St Agnes	P	Agrmt.,Min.,Rep. 1841
339	St Allen	P	Rep. 1840
340	Alternun	P	Awd.,Min.
341	Anthony in the East	P	Agrmt.,Rep. 1841
342	St Anthony in Meneage	P	Rep. 1840
343	St Anthony in Roseland	P	Rep. 1839
344	St Austell	P	Awd.,Min.
345	St Blazey	P	Rep. 1839
346	Blisland	P	Awd.,Min.
347	Boconnoc	P	Agrmt.,Rep. 1837
348	Bodmin	BP	Awd.,Min.
349	Botus Fleming	P	Awd.,Min.
350	Boyton	P	Min.
351	Braddock	P	Agrmt.,Rep. 1837
352	Bradridge	D	Min.
353	Breage	P	Rep. 1842
354	St Breock	P	Awd.,Min.
355	St Breward	P	Rep. 1843
356	Bridgerule West	P	Awd.,Min.
357	Budock	P	Agrmt.,Rep. 1843
358	St. Buryan	P	Rep. 1838
359	Callington	P	Min.
360	Calstock	P	Min.
361	Camborne	P	Min.,Rep. 1840
362	Cardynham	P	Agrmt.,Rep. 1839
363	St Cleather	P	Min.
364	St Cleer	P	Agrmt.,Awd.,Rep. 1839
365	St Clements	P	Agrmt.,Min.
366	Colan	P	Awd.,Min.
367	St Columb Major	P	Rep. 1840
368	Cornelly	P	Rep. 1844
369	St Columb Minor	P	Rep. 1840
370	Constantine	P	Agrmt.,Rep. 1842
371	Crantock	P	Min.,Rep. 1840
372	Creed	P	Min.
373	Crowan	P	Agrmt.,Rep. 1841
374	Cubert	P	Min.
375	Cuby	P	Awd.,Min.
376	Cury	P	Rep. 1839
377	Davidstone	P	Rep. 1838
378	St Dennis	P	Min.
379	St Dominick	P	Awd.,Min.
380	Duloe	P	Rep. 1841
381	Egloshayle	P	Rep. 1840
382	Egloskerry	P	Min.,Rep. 1838
383	Endellion	P	Awd.,Rep. 1838
384	St Enoder	P	Awd.,Min.
385	St Erme	P	Rep. 1840
386	St Erth	P	Rep. 1842
387	St Ervan	P	Agrmt.,Min.
388	St Eval	P	Awd.,Min.
389	St Ewe	P	Agrmt.,Rep. 1839
390	Falmouth	P	Min.
391	Feock	P	Awd.,Min.
392	Filley	P	Awd.,Min.
393	Forrabury	P	Agrmt.,Min.,Rep. 1839
394	Fowey	P	Min.
395	St Gennys	P	Agrmt.,Min.,Rep. 1839
396	St Germans	P	Awd.,Min.
397	Germoe	P	Agrmt.,Rep. 1840
398	Gerrans	P	Min.
399	St Gluvias	P	Awd.,Rep. 1844
400	Golant	P	Rep. 1839
401	St Gorran	P	Awd.,Min.
402	Grade	P	Min.
403	Gulval	P	Rep. 1842
404	Gunwalloe	P	Awd.,Min.
405	Gwennap	P	Rep. 1838
406	Gwinear	P	Rep. 1841
407	Gwithian	P	Min.,Rep. 1838
408	Helland	P	Min.
409	Helston	B	Rep. 1838
410	St Hilary	P	Min.
411	Illogan	P	Agrmt.,Min.,Rep. 1840
412	St Issey	P	Min.
413	St Ive	P	Rep. 1840
414	St Ives	P	Min.
415	Jacobstow	P	Awd.,Min.
416	St Johns	P	Rep. 1840
417	St Juliot	P	Min.
418	St Just in Penwith	P	Rep. 1842
419	St Just in Roseland	P	Rep. 1840
420	Kea	P	Rep. 1842
421	St Keverne	P	Awd.,Min.
422	St Kew	P	Min.
423	St Keyne	P	Rep. 1839
424	Kilkhampton	P	Min.
425	Ladock	P	Awd.,Min.
426	Lamorran	P	Agrmt.,Rep. 1840
427	Laneast	P	Rep. 1840
428	Landewednack	P	Rep. 1841
429	Landrake with St Erney	P	Awd.,Min.
430	Landulph	P	Rep. 1840
431	Lanhydrock	P	Rep. 1840
432	Lanivet	P	Awd.,Min.
433	Lanlivery	P	Rep. 1840
434	Lanreath	P	Agrmt.,Rep. 1842
435	Lansallos	P	Min.
436	Lanteglos by Camelford	P	Min.
437	Lanteglos by Fowey	P	Rep. 1839
438	Launcells	P	Rep. 1840
439	Lawhitton	P	Rep. 1840
440	Lesnewth	P	Awd.,Min.
441	St Levan	P	Rep. 1838
442	Lewannick	P	Rep. 1841
443	Lezant	P	Awd.,Min.
444	Linkinhorne	P	Agrmt.,Min.,Rep. 1839
445	Liskeard	P	Min.
446	Lostwithiel	P	Rep. 1839
447	Ludgvan	P	Rep. 1839
448	Luxulian	P	Agrmt.,Rep. 1839
449	Mabe	P	Min.
450	St Mabyn	P	Awd.,Min.
451	Madron	P	Rep. 1840
452	Manaccan	P	Rep. 1840
453	Marazion	P	Awd.,Min.
454	Marham Church	P	Agrmt.,Min.,Rep. 1839
455	St Martin or St Keyne	P	Agrmt.,Rep. 1839
456	St Martin in Meneage	P	Agrmt.,Rep. 1841
457	St Mary Magdalene	P	Agrmt.,Rep. 1841
458	St Mary Scilly Isles	D	Awd.,Min.
459	St Mary Truro	P	Min.
460	Mawgan in Meneage	P	Rep. 1841
461	Mawgan in Pyder	P	Agrmt.,Rep. 1840
462	Mawnan	P	Rep. 1839
463	St Mellion	P	Rep. 1840
464	Menheniot	P	Awd.,Min.
465	St Mewan	P	Rep. 1838
466	Moorwinstow	P	Agrmt.,Rep. 1840
467	Morvah	P	Awd.,Min.
468	Morval	P	Min.,Rep. 1845
469	Mullion	P	Min.
470	Mylor	P	Awd.,Min.
471	St Merryn	P	Min.
472	Merther	P	Rep. 1843
473	Mevagissey	P	Min.
474	St Michael Carhayes	P	Min.
475	St Michael Penkivel	P	Agrmt.,Rep. 1840

Cornwall contd.

476	Kenwyn	P	Rep. 1840
477	Michaelstow	P	Awd.,Min.
478	Minster	P	Agrmt.,Rep. 1839
479	St Minver	P	Rep. 1838
480	St Neot	P	Awd.,Min.
481	Newlyn	P	Rep. 1840
482	North Hill	P	Awd.,Min.
483	Otterham	P	Min.
484	Padstow	P	Min.
485	Paul	P	Min.
486	Pelynt	P	Rep. 1840
487	Penryn	B	Agrmt.,Rep. 1844
488	Penzance	P	Min.
489	Perranarworthal	P	Agrmt.,Rep. 1842
490	Perranuthnoe	P	Rep. 1840
491	Perranzabucoe	P	Rep. 1841
492	Petherwin South	P	Agrmt.,Min.
493	Petherick Little	P	Min.
494	Phillack	P	Rep. 1840
495	Pillaton	P	Awd.,Min.
496	Pinnock St	P	Min.
497	Poughill	P	Min.
498	Poundstock	P	Min.,Rep. 1840
499	Probus	P	Rep. 1843
500	Quethiock	P	Min.,Rep. 1841
501	Rame	P	Min.
502	Redruth	P	Rep. 1841
503	Roche	P	Min.,Rep. 1838
504	Ruan Lanihorne	P	Min.
505	Ruan Major	P	Rep. 1838
506	Ruan Minor	P	Min.
507	Sancreed	P	Min.
508	Scilly Isles		Awd.,Min.
509	Sennen	P	Min.,Rep. 1838
510	Sheviock	P	Agrmt.,Rep. 1841
511	Sithney	P	Rep. 1842
512	South Hill	P	Min.
513	St Stephens in Branwell	P	Rep. 1838
514	St Stephens in Launceston	P	Rep. 1840
515	St Stephens by Saltash	P	Agrmt.,Rep. 1841
516	Stithians	P	Min.
517	Stoke Climsland	P	Min.
518	Stratton	P	Agrmt.,Rep. 1838
519	Talland	P	Min.
520	Tamerton North	P	Min.
521	St Teath	P	Min.
522	Temple	P	Min.
523	St Thomas the Apostle	P	Min.
524	Tintagel	P	Min.
525	Towednack	P	Rep. 1841
526	Tregavethan	D	Rep. 1841
527	Tregony Borough	B	Min.
528	Tregony St James	P	Awd.,Min.
529	Treneglos	P	Agrmt.,Min.,Rep. 1839
530	Tremayne	P	Rep. 1838
531	Tresmeer	P	Agrmt.,Rep. 1839
532	Trevalga	P	Awd.,Min.
533	Trewarlet	H	Min.
534	Trewenn	P	Min.,Rep. 1843
535	St Tudy	P	Awd.,Min.
536	Tywardreth	P	Rep. 1839
537	Uny Lelant	P	Rep. 1839
538	Veep St	P	Rep. 1839
539	Veryan	P	Min.
540	Warbstow	P	Min.
541	Warleggan	P	Agrmt.,Rep. 1839
542	Week St Mary	P	Agrmt.,Rep. 1840
543	Wendron	P	Min.,Rep. 1841
544	Wenn St	P	Min.
545	Winnow St	P	Rep. 1839
546	Whitstone	P	Rep. 1840
547	Withiel	P	Agrmt.,Rep. 1841
548	Zennor	P	Min.

Cumberland

549	Allhallows	P	N.t.p.,Min.
550	Allonby	T	Awd.,Min.
551	Alston	P	Agrmt.,Min.,Rep. 1841
552	Armathwaite,Nunclose	T	Awd.,Min.
553	Ainstable	P	Awd.,Min.
554	Allerby	P	Awd.,Min.
555	Aikton	P	Min.
556	Aglionby	T	Awd.,Min.
557	Arthuret	P	Awd.,Min.
558	Bampton Little	T	Agrmt.,Min.,Rep. 1839
559	Bassenthwaite	P	N.t.p.,Min.
560	St Bees	T	Agrmt.,Min.,Rep. 1838
561	Berrier and Murrah	T	Awd.,Min.
562	Bewcastle	P	Agrmt.,Min.,Rep. 1839
563	Birkby	T	Awd.,Min.
564	Birker and Austhwaite	T	Min.
565	Blackhall High Quarter	T	Awd.,Min.
566	Blackhall Low Quarter	T	Awd.,Min.
567	Blencogo	T	Awd.,Min.
568	Blencow Great	T	N.t.p.
569	Blencow Little	T	Awd.,Min.
570	Blindbothal	T	N.t.p.,Min.
571	Bolton Highside Quarter	T	Awd.,Min.
572	Bootle	P	Agrmt.,Min.,Rep. 1838
573	Botchardgate	T	Awd.,Min.
574	Botcherby	T	Awd.,Min.
575	Bowness	P	Min.,Rep. 1839
576	Bowscale and Mossdale	T	Awd.,Min.
577	Brackenthwaite	T	Awd.,Min.
578	Brampton	P	Awd.,Min.
579	Bridekirk	T	Agrmt.,Awd.,Min.
580	St Bridget Beckermont	P	Awd.,Min.
581	Brigham	T	N.t.p.,Min.
582	Brisco	T	Awd.,Min.
583	Brisco	D	Min.,Rep. 1840
584	Breconhill Quarter	T	Awd.,Min.
585	Broadfield	D	Awd.,Min.
586	Bromfield	T	N.t.p.,Min.
587	Broughton Great	T	N.t.p.
588	Broughton Little	T	N.t.p.
589	Burtholme	T	N.t.p.
590	Burgh on Sands	P	Awd.,Min.
591	Buttermere	T	Awd.,Min.
592	Bolton Low Quarter	T	Awd.,Min.
593	Caldbeck	P	Awd.,Min.
594	Caldewgate	T	Awd.,Min.
595	Calthwaite	H	Awd.,Min.
596	Camerton	T	Min.,Rep. 1840
597	Cargo	T	Awd.,Min.
598	Carlatton	EP	Min.
599	Carleton	T	Awd.,Min.
600	Castle Carrock	P	N.t.p.,Min.
601	Castle Sowerby	P	Awd.,Min.
602	Chapel Sucken	T	Awd.,Min.
603	Cleator	P	Agrmt.,Awd.,Min.,Rep. 1839
604	Clifton Great	T	N.t.p.,Min.
605	Cloffock	EP	N.t.p.,Min.
606	Clifton Little	T	N.t.p.,Min.
607	Cockermouth	T	Agrmt.,Min.,Rep. 1840
608	Corby Little	T	Min.,Rep. 1839
609	Corby and Warwick Bridge	T	Awd.,Min.
610	Corney	P	Awd.,Min.
611	Cross Cannonby	T	Awd.,Min.
612	Crofton Quarter	T	Awd.,Min.
613	Croglin	P	N.t.p.,Min.
614	Crosby upon Eden	P	Awd.,Min.
615	Crosby	T	Awd.,Min.
616	Crosthwaite	P	Agrmt.,Awd.,Min.
617	Culgaith	T	Awd.,Min.
618	Cummersdale	T	Awd.,Min.
619	Cumrew	P	Agrmt.,Min.,Rep. 1837
620	Cumwhinton and Coathill	T	Awd.,Min.
621	Cumwhitton	P	Min.,Rep. 1838
622	St Cuthbert	P	N.t.p.
623	Dacre and Soulby	T	Awd.,Min.
624	Dalston	P	Awd.,Min.
625	Dean	P	Awd.,Min.
626	Dearham	T	Agrmt.,Min.,Rep. 1839
627	Denton Nether	P	N.t.p.,Min.
628	Denton Upper	P	N.t.p.,Min.
629	Distington	P	N.t.p.,Min.
630	Dovenby	D	Rep. 1838
631	Drigg	T	N.t.p.,Min.
632	Dundraw	T	N.t.p.,Min.
633	Easby	T	N.t.p.
634	Edenhall	P	Awd.,Min.
635	Egremont	P	Awd.,Min.
636	Ellenborough and Unerigg	T	Awd.,Min.
637	Embleton	T	Agrmt.,Min.,Rep. 1839
638	English Street	T	N.t.p.
639	Ennerdale	T	Awd.,Min.
640	Etterby	T	Awd.,Min.
641	Farlam West	T	N.t.p.,Min.
642	Flimby	P	Awd.,Min.
643	Frizington	T	Awd.,Min.,Rep. 1839
644	Gamblesby	T	Agrmt.,Min.,Rep. 1839
645	Gilcrux	P	Awd.,Min.
646	Glassonby	T	Awd.,Min.
647	Gosforth	P	N.t.p.,Min.
648	Grey Southen	T	N.t.p.,Min.
649	Greystoke	T	Awd.
650	Grinsdale	P	N.t.p.,Min.
651	Hameshill	H	Min.,Rep. 1838
652	Hail and Wilton	T	N.t.p.,Min.
653	Harraby	T	Awd.,Min.
654	Harrington	P	Awd.,Min.
655	Hayton and Melay	T	Awd.,Min.
656	Hayton,Fenton,Faugh	D	Awd.,Min.,Rep. 1839
657	Hensingham	T	N.t.p.,Min.
658	Hesket Nether	T	Min.,Rep. 1842
659	Hesket Upper	T	Awd.,Min.
660	Holm Cultram	P	Awd.,Min.
661	Houghton	T	Awd.,Min.
662	Hutton Soil	T	Awd.,Min.
663	Hutton	P	Min.,Rep. 1839

Cumberland contd.

664	Hutton John	T	Min.,Rep. 1838
665	Hutton Roof	T	Awd.,Min.
666	Irton	P	Awd.,Min.
667	Ireby Low	T	Awd.,Min.
668	Ireby High	T	Awd.,Min.
669	Irthington	T	Awd.,Min.
670	Isell	P	Awd.,Min.
671	Itonfield	T	Awd.,Min.
672	St John Beckermont	P	Awd.,Min.
673	Johnby	T	Awd.,Min.
674	Kelton and Arcledon		N.t.p.
675	Kingmoor	EP	Awd.,Min.
676	Kingwater	T	N.t.p.
677	Kinnyside	T	Awd.,Min.
678	Kirkandrews upon Eden	P	N.t.p.,Min.
679	Kirkandrews upon Esk	P	Min.
680	Kirkbampton	T	Min.,Rep. 1839
681	Kirkbride	P	Awd.,Min.
682	Kirkland	T	Awd.,Min.
683	Kirklinton	P	Agrmt.,Rep. 1839
684	Kirkoswald High Quarter	T	Awd.,Min.
685	Kirkoswald Low Quarter	T	Awd.,Min.
686	Lamplugh	P	Agrmt.,Min.,Rep. 1837
687	Lanercost	P	Awd.,Min.
688	Laversdale	T	Awd.,Min.
689	Lazonby	T	Awd.,Min.
690	Linstock	T	Awd.,Min.
691	Longtown Quarter	T	Awd.
692	Longwathby	P	Awd.,Min.
693	Lorton	T	Agrmt.,Min.,Rep. 1840
694	Loweswater	T	Awd.,Min.
695	Lowside Quarter	T	Agrmt.,Min.,Rep. 1838
696	Low Quarter	T	Awd.
697	Lyneside Quarter	T	Awd.,Min.
698	St Mary,Carlisle	P	N.t.p.
699	Matterdale	T	Awd.,Min.
700	Melmerby	P	Agrmt.,Min.,Rep. 1839
701	Middle Quarter	T	Awd.
702	Middlesceugh	H	Awd.,Min.
703	Midge Holme	EP	N.t.p.
704	Millom Lower	T	Awd.,Min.
705	Millom Upper	T	Awd.,Min.
706	Moat Quarter	T	Awd.
707	Moresby	P	Agrmt.,Min.,Rep. 1838
708	Mosser	T	Awd.,Min.
709	Motherby and Gill	T	Awd.,Min.
710	Muncaster	P	Awd.,Min.
711	Mungrisdale	T	Awd.,Min.
712	Naworth	T	N.t.p.
713	Nealhouse	T	Awd.,Min.
714	Netherhall	T	Awd.,Min.
715	Netherby Quarter	T	Awd.
716	Nether Wasdale	T	Agrmt.,Min.,Rep. 1839
717	Newbiggin	T	N.t.p.
718	Newby	T	Awd.,Min.
719	Newton	P	Min.,Rep. 1838
720	West Newton	T	Min.
721	Newtown	T	Awd.,Min.
722	Nichol Forest	T	Awd.,Min.
723	Orton	P	Awd.,Min.
724	Oughterby	T	Min.,Rep. 1839
725	Oughterside	T	Awd.,Min.
726	Oulton	T	Awd.,Min.
727	Ousby	P	Awd.,Min.
728	Papcastle	T	Min.,Rep. 1838
729	Parton	T	N.t.p.,Min.
730	Parton and Micklethwaite	T	Awd.,Min.
731	Penrith	P	Awd.,Min.
732	Petteril Crooks	T	Awd.,Min.
733	Petteril Crooks	T	Min.,Rep. 1839
734	Plumbland	P	Awd.,Min.
735	Plumpton Street	T	Awd.,Min.
736	Plumpton Wall	T	Awd.,Min.
737	Ponsonby	T	Awd.,Min.
738	Preston Quarter	T	Awd.,Min.
739	Priestgate	D	Awd.,Min.
740	Redmain	T	Rep. 1837
741	Renwick	P	Awd.,Min.
742	Ribton	T	Agrmt.,Rep. 1840
743	Rickerby	T	Awd.,Min.
744	Rickergate	T	Awd.,Min.
745	Rockcliff	P	Awd.,Min.
746	Rottington	T	Awd.,Min.
747	Salkeld Great	P	Awd.,Min.
748	Salkeld Little	T	N.t.p.,Min.
749	Salter and Esket	EP	N.t.p.,Min.
750	Scotby	T	Awd.,Min.
751	Sandwith	T	Awd.,Min.,Rep. 1838
752	Scaleby	P	Agrmt.,Min.,Rep. 1839
753	Seaton	T	Min.,Rep. 1840
754	Stainton	T	Awd.,Min.
755	Setmurthy	T	Agrmt.,Min.,Rep. 1840
756	Sebergham	P	Awd.,Min.
757	Skelton	P	Min.,Rep. 1841
758	Soulby	T	N.t.p.
759	Soulfitts	D	Agrmt.,Awd.,Min.
760	Staffield	T	Awd.,Min.
761	Stainton,Great and Little	T	Awd.,Min.
762	Stanwix	T	Awd.,Min.
763	Stapleton	P	Awd.,Min.
764	Stoneraise	T	N.t.p.
765	Talkin	T	Agrmt.,Min.,Rep. 1839
766	Tallentire	T	Min.,Rep. 1838
767	Tarraby	T	Awd.,Min.
768	Threlkeld	T	Awd.,Min.
769	Thursby	T	Min.,Rep. 1840
770	Thwaites	T	Awd.,Min.
771	Torpenhow	P	Min.
772	Uldale	P	Min.,Rep. 1840
773	Ulpha	T	Awd.,Min.
774	Upperby	T	Awd.,Min.
775	Waberthwaite	P	Awd.,Min.
776	Walton	P	Awd.,Min.
777	Warwick	P	Awd.,Min.
778	Water Head	T	N.t.p.
779	Watermillock	T	Awd.,Min.
780	Waverton	T	N.t.p.
781	Westward	P	N.t.p.,Min.
782	Wetheral	P	Awd.,Min.
783	Wheddicar	T	Awd.,Min.
784	Whinfell	T	Agrmt.,Min.,Rep. 1840
785	Whicham	P	Agrmt.,Min.,Rep. 1838
786	Whillimoor	T	N.t.p.,Min.
787	Whitbeck	P	Agrmt.,Rep. 1838
788	Whitehaven	T	Awd.,Min.
789	Wigton,Woodside,Waverton	T	N.t.p.,Min.
790	Winscales	T	N.t.p.,Min.
791	Woodside Quarter	T	N.t.p.
792	Workington	T	N.t.p.,Min.
793	Wreay	T	Min.,Rep. 1839
794	Wreay Hall	D	Min.,Rep. 1842
795	Wythop	T	Awd.,Min.

Derbyshire

796	Abney and Abney Grange	T	Awd.,Min.
797	Alderwasley	T	Awd.,Min.
798	Aldwark	T	Awd.,Min.
799	Alfreton	P	Awd.,Min.
800	Alkmonton	T	Agrmt.,Rep. 1838
801	St Alkmund	T	Awd.,Min.
802	Allestree	P	Awd.,Min.
803	Alsop le Dale	T	Awd.,Min.
804	Alveston	C	N.t.p.
805	Appleby	P	N.t.p.,Min.
806	Arleston	T	Awd.,Min.
807	Ash	T	Agrmt.,Rep. 1838
808	Ashbourne	T	Awd.,Min.
809	Ashford	T	Agrmt.,Awd.,Min.,Rep. 1841
810	Ashleyhay	T	Awd.,Min.
811	Ashover	T	Awd.,Min.
812	Aston upon Trent	T	N.t.p.,Min.
813	Aston (Hope)	T	Awd.,Min.
814	Atlow	C	Agrmt.,Rep. 1838
815	Ault Hucknall	P	Agrmt.,Rep. 1838
816	Bakewell	T	N.t.p.,Min.
817	Ballidon	T	Awd.,Min.
818	Bamford	T	Agrmt.,Min.,Rep. 1840
819	Barlborough	P	Agrmt.,Min.,Rep. 1839
820	Barlow Little	H	N.t.p.
821	Barrow on Trent	P	N.t.p.
822	Baslow	T	Awd.,Min.
823	Barton Blount	P	Awd.,Min.
824	Bearward Cote	T	Awd.,Min.
825	Beauchief Abbey	EP	N.t.p.
826	Beard,Ollersett,Whittle,	T	Agrmt.,Rep. 1840
827	Beeley	T	N.t.p.
828	Beighton	P	N.t.p.
829	Belper	T	Awd.,Min.
830	Bentley	T	Rep. 1839
831	Biggin	T	Awd.,Min.
832	Blackwell (Bakewell)	T	Agrmt.,Awd.,Min.,Rep. 1841
833	Blackwell (Scarsdale)	P	Agrmt.,Rep. 1838
834	Bolsover	T	Awd.,Min.
835	Bonsall	P	Awd.,Min.
836	Boulton	C	N.t.p.,Min.
837	Boundary (Derby/Leicester)	D	N.t.p.
838	Boylston	P	Awd.,Min.
839	Brackenfield and Woolley	T	Agrmt.,Rep. 1839
840	Bradborne	T	Rep. 1840
841	Bradley	P	Agrmt.,Rep. 1838
842	Bradwell	T	Agrmt.,Rep. 1843
843	Brailsford	P	Agrmt.,Min.
844	Brampton	P	Agrmt.,Rep. 1838
845	Brassington	C	N.t.p.
846	Breadsall	P	N.t.p.,Min.
847	Breaston	T	Agrmt.,Rep. 1839
848	Brough and Shatton	T	Agrmt.,Rep. 1843
849	Broughton West	T	Awd.,Min.
850	Brushfield	T	Agrmt.,Awd.,Min.,Rep. 1840
851	Bubnell	T	Agrmt.,Rep. 1839

Derbyshire contd.

No.	Place	Type	Details
852	Burnaston	T	Awd.,Min.
853	Buxton	T	Awd.,Min.,Rep. 1841
854	Calke	P	Awd.,Min.
855	Calow (Chesterfield)	T	Awd.,Min.
856	Callow (Wirksworth)	T	Awd.,Min.
857	Calver	T	Awd.,Min.
858	Carsington	P	Agrmt.,Rep. 1838
859	Castle Gresley	H	Awd.,Min.
860	Castleton	P	Agrmt.,Rep. 1839
861	Cauldwell	T	Agrmt.,Rep. 1839
862	Chaddesden	P	N.t.p.
863	Chapel en le Frith	P	Agrmt.,Awd.,Min.,Rep. 1844
864	Charlesworth	D	Awd.,Min.
865	Chatsworth	T	Awd.,Min.
866	Chellaston	P	Awd.,Min.
867	Chelmorton and Flagg	T	N.t.p.,Min.
868	Chester Little	T	Awd.,Min.
869	Chesterfield	P	Awd.,Min.
870	Chinley,Bugsworth,Brownsid	T	Agrmt.,Min.,Rep. 1840
871	Chilcote	T	Awd.,Min.
872	Church Gresley	T	Awd.,Min.
873	Claylane	T	Awd.,Min.
874	Church Broughton	P	Awd.,Min.
875	Clifton	T	Awd.,Min.
876	Clown	P	Agrmt.,Rep. 1838
877	Coal Aston	T	Awd.,Min.
878	Codnor Park	EP	Awd.,Min.
879	Coton in the Elms	T	Agrmt.,Rep. 1840
880	Cotton	T	Rep. 1839
881	Crich	T	Awd.,Min.
882	Cromford	T	Agrmt.,Rep. 1839
883	Croxall	T	Agrmt.,Rep. 1839
884	Cubley	P	Agrmt.,Rep. 1839
885	Curbar	T	Awd.,Min.
886	Dalbury and Lees	P	Agrmt.,Rep. 1838
887	Dale Abbey	EP	N.t.p.
888	Darley and Little Rowsley	T	Agrmt.,Rep. 1839
889	Darley Abbey	T	N.t.p.,Awd.,Min.
890	Denby	P	Agrmt.,Rep. 1843
891	Derby All Saints	P	N.t.p.
892	Derby Hills	EP	Awd.,Min.
893	Derwent	C	N.t.p.,Min.
894	Dethick,Lea,Holloway	H	Awd.,Min.
895	Donisthorpe	T	Agrmt.,Rep. 1843
896	Dore	C	N.t.p.
897	Doveridge	T	Awd.,Min.
898	Drakelow	T	Awd.,Min.
899	Dronfield	T	Awd.,Min.
900	Duffield	T	Agrmt.,Rep. 1838
901	Eaton and Sedsall	T	Awd.,Min.
902	Eaton Little	T	Awd.,Min.
903	Eaton Long	T	N.t.p.,Min.
904	Eckington	P	N.t.p.,Min.
905	Edale	T	Agrmt.,Rep. 1839
906	Edensor	T	Agrmt.,Rep. 1840
907	Fenny Bentley	P	Min.,Rep. 1840
908	Fernilee	T	Agrmt.,Awd.,Min.,Rep. 1844
909	Edlaston	P	Awd.,Min.
910	Egginton	P	Awd.,Min.
911	Elmton	P	Awd.,Min.
912	Elton and Winster	T	N.t.p.
913	Elvaston	P	Awd.,Min.
914	Etwall	T	Awd.,Min.
915	Eyam	T	Agrmt.,Rep. 1839
916	Eyam Woodland	T	Agrmt.,Rep. 1839
917	Fairfield	T	Agrmt.,Rep. 1841
918	Findern	T	N.t.p.
919	Foolow	T	Agrmt.,Rep. 1839
920	Foremark and Ingleby	P	N.t.p.,Min.
921	Froggatt	T	Awd.,Min.
922	Glapwell	H	Awd.,Min.
923	Glossop	P	Min.
924	Gratton	T	N.t.p.
925	Griff Grange	EP	N.t.p.
926	Grindlow	T	Awd.,Min.
927	Haddon Nether	T	Awd.,Min.
928	Hadfield	T	Awd.,Min.
929	Hallam West	P	Agrmt.,Rep. 1837
930	Harthill	T	Awd.,Min.
931	Hartington	P	N.t.p.
932	Hartshorn	P	N.t.p.
933	Hassop	T	Awd.,Min.
934	Hathersage	T	N.t.p.,Min.
935	Hatton	T	N.t.p.,Min.
936	Hayfield	T	Awd.,Min.
937	Hazelbache	T	Agrmt.,Awd.,Min.,Rep. 1839
938	Hazelwood	T	Awd.,Min.
939	Heage	T	Awd.,Min.
940	Heanor	T	Awd.,Min.
941	Heath	P	Agrmt.,Rep. 1838
942	Codnor and Loscoe	T	Awd.,Min.
943	Highlow	T	Awd.,Min.
944	Hilton	T	Agrmt.,Min.,Rep. 1842
945	Hognaston	T	Agrmt.,Min.,Rep. 1842
946	Holbrook	T	Agrmt.,Rep. 1839
947	Hollington	T	N.t.p.
948	Holmesfield	C	N.t.p.
949	Hoon	T	Awd.,Min.
950	Hopton	T	Awd.,Min.
951	Hopwell	H	Awd.,Min.
952	Horsley	T	Awd.,Min.
953	Hope	T	Awd.,Min.
954	Horsley Woodhouse	T	Awd.,Min.
955	Hucklow Little	T	Awd.,Min.
956	Hucklow Great	T	Awd.,Min.
957	Hulland	T	Awd.,Min.
958	Hulland Ward Intake	T	Awd.,Min.
959	Ible	T	Awd.,Min.
960	Ilkestone	P	Awd.,Min.
961	Ironbrook Grange	T	Awd.,Min.
962	Kedleston	P	Min.
963	Kilbourne	T	Awd.,Min.
964	Killamarsh	P	Agrmt.,Awd.,Min.
965	Kirkhallam	P	Agrmt.,Rep. 1846
966	Mapperley	T	Min.,Rep. 1842
967	Kirk Ireton	P	Awd.,Min.
968	Kirk Langley	P	Awd.,Min.,Rep. 1843
969	Kniveton	P	Awd.,Min.
970	Langwith Upper	P	Agrmt.,Rep. 1838
971	Lea Hall	H	Awd.,Min.
972	Linton	T	Awd.,Min.
973	Litton	T	Awd.,Min.
974	Littleover	T	Awd.,Min.
975	Lullington	T	Awd.,Min.
976	Longford	T	Agrmt.,Rep. 1838
977	Longstone Great	T	Agrmt.,Awd.,Min.,Rep. 1841
978	Longstone Little	T	Awd.,Min.
979	Mackworth	P	Awd.,Min.
980	Mappleton	P	Agrmt.,Rep. 1839
981	Marston on Dove	T	Agrmt.,Rep. 1839
982	Marston Montgomery	P	Agrmt.,Rep. 1839
983	Matlock	P	Awd.,Min.
984	Measham	T	Awd.,Min.
985	Melbourn	P	Awd.,Min.
986	Mellor	P	Awd.,Min.
987	Mercaston	T	Awd.,Min.
988	St.Michael's	P	N.t.p.
989	Mickleover	T	Agrmt.,Rep. 1839
990	Middleton by Wirksworth	T	Awd.,Min.
991	Monyash	T	Awd.,Min.
992	Morley	P	Agrmt.,Rep. 1843
993	Morton	P	Awd.,Min.
994	Mugginton	T	Awd.,Min.
995	Newton Grange	T	Awd.,Min.
996	Newton Solney	P	Awd.,Min.
997	Norbury and Roston	P	Awd.,Min.
998	Normanton	T	Awd.,Min.
999	Normanton South	P	Agrmt.,Min.,Rep. 1838
1000	Norton	P	Agrmt.,Rep. 1842
1001	Oakthorpe	T	Agrmt.,Min.,Rep. 1843
1002	Ockbrook	P	N.t.p.
1003	Oslaston and Thurwaston	T	N.t.p.
1004	Osmaston next Ashbourne	P	Agrmt.,Min.
1005	Osmaston next Derby	P	Awd.,Min.
1006	Osmaston Moor Meadow	D	N.t.p.
1007	Padley Nether	T	Agrmt.,Rep. 1841
1008	Parwich	T	Awd.,Min.
1009	Peak High (or Peak Forest)	EP	Awd.,Min.
1010	Pentrich	T	Awd.,Min.
1011	Peter's St and Litchurch	C	Awd.,Min.
1012	Pilsley	T	Awd.,Min.
1013	Pinxton	P	Agrmt.,Rep. 1838
1014	Quorndon	PC	Awd.,Min.
1015	Radbourne	P	Awd.,Min.
1016	Ravensdale Park	T	Awd.,Min.
1017	Ripley	T	Agrmt.,Min.,Rep. 1838
1018	Rodsley	T	Agrmt.,Rep. 1838
1019	Rostliston	P	Agrmt.,Rep. 1839
1020	Rowland	T	Awd.,Min.
1021	Sandiacre	P	Awd.,Min.
1022	Sawley	T	Awd.,Min.
1023	Snelston	P	N.t.p.
1024	Scropton	P	Awd.,Min.
1025	Scarcliff	P	Awd.,Min.
1026	Offerton	T	Awd.,Min.
1027	Offcote Underwood	T	Awd.,Min.
1028	Shardlow	T	Awd.,Min.
1029	Sheldon	T	Agrmt.,Awd.,Min.,Rep. 1841
1030	Shipley	T	N.t.p.
1031	Shirland	P	Agrmt.,Min.,Rep. 1839
1032	Shirley	T	Agrmt.,Min.
1033	Shottle and Postern	T	Awd.,Min.
1034	Sinfin Moor	D	Awd.,Min.
1035	Packington	P	N.t.p.
1036	Padfield	D	Min.
1037	Smalley	T	Agrmt.,Min.,Rep. 1838
1038	Smisby	P	N.t.p.
1039	Smerrill	T	Agrmt.,Rep. 1839
1040	Somershall Herbert	P	Awd.,Min.
1041	Spondon	T	Awd.,Min.
1042	Stanton and Birchover	T	N.t.p.
1043	Stanton by Bridge	P	Agrmt.,Awd.,Min.

Derbyshire contd.

1044	Stanton juxta Dale Abbey	P	Awd.,Min.
1045	Simmondby	D	Min.
1046	Rowsley Great	T	Agrmt.,Awd.,Min.,Rep. 1839
1047	Repton and Bretby	T	Awd.,Min.
1048	Pleasley	P	Agrmt.,Min.,Rep. 1842
1049	Pilsley	T	Agrmt.,Rep. 1840
1050	Stanton and New Hall	T	Awd.,Min.
1051	Stapenhill	T	Awd.,Min.
1052	Stanley	T	Awd.,Min.
1053	Staunton (Stanton)	T	N.t.p.
1054	Staveley	P	Agrmt.,Rep. 1838
1055	Stoke	T	Awd.,Min.
1056	Stoney Middleton	T	Agrmt.,Min.,Rep. 1840
1057	Stretton en le Field	P	Rep. 1844
1058	Stretton	T	Awd.,Min.
1059	Sutton cum Duckmanton	P	Agrmt.
1060	Swadlincote	T	Awd.,Min.
1061	Swarkeston	P	Awd.,Min.
1062	Taddington and Priestcliff	T	Agrmt.,Awd.,Min.,Rep. 1842
1063	Tadswell Fee	EP	N.t.p.
1064	Tansley	T	Awd.,Min.
1065	Thornhill	T	Awd.,Min.
1066	Thorpe	P	Awd.,Min.
1067	Thurvaston, Oslaston,	T	Agrmt.,Rep. 1840
1068	Tibshelf	P	Awd.,Min.
1069	Ticknall	P	Awd.,Min.
1070	Tideswell	T	Rep. 1840
1071	Tissington	P	Agrmt.,Rep. 1840
1072	Totley	T	Agrmt.,Rep. 1838
1073	Trusley	P	Agrmt.,Rep. 1838
1074	Tupton	T	Awd.,Min.
1075	Turnditch	T	Awd.,Min.
1076	Twyford	T	Awd.,Min.
1077	Unstone	T	Awd.,Min.
1078	Walton upon Trent	P	Agrmt.,Rep. 1839
1079	Wardlow	T	Awd.,Min.
1080	Wensley and Snitterton	T	Awd.,Min.
1081	Werburgh St.	P	Agrmt.,Min.,Rep. 1843
1082	Wessington	T	Awd.,Min.
1083	Weston upon Trent	P	N.t.p.
1084	Weston Underwood	T	Awd.,Min.
1085	Whetstone	T	Agrmt.,Rep. 1840
1086	Whitfield	T	Awd.,Min.
1087	Whittington	P	N.t.p.,Min.
1088	Whitwell	P	Agrmt.,Rep. 1838
1089	Willesley	P	N.t.p.
1090	Willington	P	N.t.p.
1091	Wilne Church and Draycott	L	Awd.,Min.
1092	Risley	T	Agrmt.,Min.,Rep. 1839
1093	Wilsthorpe	H	Awd.,Min.
1094	Windley	T	Rep. 1840
1095	Wingerworth	P	Rep. 1842
1096	Wingfield North	T	Awd.,Min.
1097	Idridgehay and Alton	T	Awd.,Min.
1098	Wingfield South	P	Min.
1099	Winshill	T	Awd.,Min.
1100	Winster	T	Awd.,Min.
1101	Wirksworth	T	Awd.,Min.
1102	Woodlands	T	Awd.,Min.
1103	Woodthorpe	T	Awd.,Min.
1104	Wormhill	T	Awd.,Min.
1105	Yeaveley	T	Agrmt.,Rep. 1839
1106	Yieldersley	T	Min.
1109	Youlgreave	P	N.t.p.
1110	Sutton on the Hill	T	Agrmt.,Rep. 1838
1111	Sudbury	P	Awd.,Min.,Rep. 1842
1112	Sturstow	T	Awd.,Min.
1113	Stydd	EP	N.t.p.

Devon

350	Boyton	P	Min.
1107	Bratton Fleming	P	Min.
1108	Braunton	P	Min.
1114	Bratton Clovelly	P	Awd.,Min.
1115	Branscombe	P	Rep. 1841
1116	Brampford Speke	P	Min.
1117	Bradworthy	P	Agrmt.,Awd.,Min.
1118	Bradstone	P	Rep. 1839
1119	Bradninch	P	Min.,Rep. 1838
1120	Bradford	P	Agrmt.,Rep. 1840
1121	Bow or Nymet Tracy	P	Awd.,Min.,Rep. 1840
1122	Bovey Tracey	P	Awd.,Min.
1123	Bampton	P	Agrmt.,Rep. 1843
1124	Barnstaple	P	Awd.,Min.
1125	Beaworthy	P	Min.
1126	Beaford	P	Min.,Rep. 1839
1127	Beerferris	P	Awd.,Min.
1128	Belstone	P	Min.
1129	Berry Pomeroy	P	Rep. 1841
1130	Bickleigh	P	Rep. 1839
1131	Berrynarbor	P	Agrmt.,Min.
1132	Bickington	P	Rep. 1839
1133	Bickleigh	P	Awd.,Min.
1134	Bicton	P	Rep. 1839
1135	Bideford	P	N.t.p.
1136	Bigbury	P	Awd.,Min.
1137	Bickington High	P	Rep. 1840
1138	Bishops Nympton	P	Awd.,Rep. 1841
1139	Bishops Tawton	P	Agrmt.,Awd.,Min.,Rep. 1839
1140	Bishopsteignton	P	Agrmt.
1141	Bittadon	P	Rep. 1838
1142	Blackawton	P	Awd.,Min.
1143	Blackborough	P	Awd.,Rep. 1844
1144	Bondleigh	P	Min.
1145	Bovey North	P	Rep. 1839
1146	Brendon	P	Min.
1147	Brent South	P	Min.
1148	Brent Tor	P	Agrmt.,Awd.,Min.
1149	Bridestow	P	Awd.,Min.
1150	Bridford	P	Rep. 1840
1151	Brixham	P	Min.
1152	Brixton	P	Agrmt.,Min.,Rep. 1840
1153	Broadhembury	P	Awd.,Min.
1154	Broadhempston	P	Awd.,Min.
1155	Broadnymet	P	Rep. 1841
1156	Broadwood Kelly	P	Awd.,Min.
1157	Bridgerule East	P	Min.
1158	Broadwoodwidger	P	Awd.,Min.
1159	Brushford	P	Awd.,Min.
1160	Buckfastleigh	P	Awd.,Min.
1161	Buckerell	P	Awd.,Min.
1162	Buckland Brewer	P	Agrmt.,Min.
1163	Buckland East	P	Agrmt.,Min.
1164	Buckland Filleigh	P	Awd.,Min.
1165	Buckland Monachorum	P	Rep. 1842
1166	Buckland in the Moor	P	Rep. 1840
1167	Buckland Tout Saints	P	Agrmt.
1168	Buckland West	P	Rep. 1839
1169	Budeaux St	P	Awd.,Min.
1170	Budleigh East	P	Awd.,Min.
1171	Bulkworthy	P	Awd.,Min.
1172	Bulworthy	P	Min.
1173	Burlescombe	P	Agrmt.,Min.
1174	Burrington	P	Rep. 1838
1175	Butterleigh	P	Agrmt.
1176	Bystock	D	Awd.,Min.
1177	Abbots Bickington	P	Rep. 1839
1178	Abbotsham	P	Rep. 1840
1179	Abbotskerswell	P	Rep. 1838
1180	All Fours (Tiverton)	D	Min.
1181	Allington East	P	Agrmt.,Min.,Rep. 1839
1182	Alphington	P	Awd.,Min.
1183	Alverdiscott	P	Rep. 1840
1184	Alvington West	P	Min.
1185	Alvington	P	Agrmt.,Min.
1186	Anstey East	P	Min.
1187	Anstey West	P	Min.
1188	Arlington	P	Awd.,Min.
1189	Ashburton	P	Min.,Rep. 1840
1190	Ashbury	P	Awd.,Min.
1191	Ashcombe	P	Rep. 1840
1192	Ashford	P	Awd.,Min.,Rep. 1842
1193	Ashprington	P	Awd.,Min.
1194	Ashreigney	P	Min.
1195	Ashton	P	Min.,Rep. 1839
1196	Ashwater	P	Awd.,Min.
1197	Atherington	P	Min.
1198	Aveton Gifford	P	Min.
1199	Awliscombe	P	Awd.,Rep. 1840
1200	Axminster	P	Min.
1201	Axmouth	P	Awd.,Min.
1202	Cadbury	P	Min.
1203	Cadeleigh	P	Rep. 1840
1204	Calverleigh	P	Rep. 1838
1205	Chagford	P	Awd.,Min.
1206	Challacombe	P	Agrmt.,Rep. 1838
1207	Charles the Martyr	P	Awd.
1208	Charleton	P	Agrmt.,Rep. 1839
1209	Chawley	P	Awd.,Min.
1210	Cheldon	P	Agrmt.
1211	Cheriton Bishop	P	Rep. 1838
1212	Cheriton Fitzpaine	P	Rep. 1838
1213	Chittlehampton	P	Awd.,Min.
1214	Chilston	D	Awd.,Min.
1215	Chilverstone	P	Awd.,Min.
1216	Christow	P	Rep. 1841
1217	Chudleigh	P	Rep. 1838
1218	Chulmleigh	P	Awd.,Min.
1219	Church Stanton	P	N.t.p.
1220	Churchstow	P	Rep. 1839
1221	Churton Ferrers	P	Agrmt.,Rep. 1840
1222	Clannaborough	P	Rep. 1838
1223	Clare	D	Awd.,Min.
1224	Clawton	P	Agrmt.,Awd.,Min.
1225	Clayhanger	P	Min.
1226	Clayhidon	P	Min.,Rep. 1837
1227	Clist Broad	P	Awd.,Min.
1228	Clist St. George	P	Awd.,Min.
1229	Clist Honiton	P	Agrmt.,Rep. 1839
1230	Clist Hydon	P	Rep. 1841

480

Devon contd.

No.	Place	Type	Details
1231	Clist St. Lawrence	P	Awd.,Min.
1232	Clist St. Mary	P	Rep. 1838
1233	Aylesbeare	P	N.t.p.
1234	Clovelly	P	Agrmt.,Min.,Rep. 1838
1235	Cockington	P	Min.
1236	Coffinswell	P	Rep. 1842
1237	Colaton Raleigh	P	Awd.,Min.
1238	Coldridge	P	Awd.,Min.
1239	Colebrook	P	Awd.,Min.
1240	Colyton	P	Min.,Rep. 1841
1241	Combeinteignhead	P	Agrmt.,Min.,Rep. 1837
1242	Combmartin	P	Awd.,Min.
1243	Combpyne	P	Agrmt.,Rep. 1844
1244	Compton Gifford	T	Rep. 1840
1245	Coombe Raleigh	P	Rep. 1840
1246	Cookbury	P	Awd.,Min.
1247	Cornwood	P	Awd.,Min.
1248	Cornworthy	P	Awd.,Min.
1249	Coryton	P	Awd.,Min.
1250	Cotleigh	P	Agrmt.,Rep. 1840
1251	Countisbury	P	Rep. 1838
1252	Cowley	H	Min.
1253	Creacombe	P	Awd.,Min.
1254	Crediton	P	Awd.,Min.,Rep. 1839
1255	Cruwys Morchard	P	Awd.,Min.,Rep. 1838
1256	Cullompton	P	Awd.,Min.
1257	Culmstock	P	Rep. 1841
1258	Dalwood	P	Agrmt.,Min.,Rep. 1844
1259	Dartington	P	Rep. 1839
1260	Lydford & Dartmoor Forest	PD	Agrmt.,Rep. 1839
1261	Dartmouth St Petrox	P	N.t.p.
1262	Dartmouth St Saviours	P	N.t.p.
1263	Dawlish	P	Awd.,Min.
1264	Dean Prior	P	Awd.,Min.
1265	Denbury	P	Agrmt.,Rep. 1839
1266	Diptford	P	Min.,Rep. 1838
1267	Dittisham	P	Min.,Rep. 1839
1268	Dodbrooke	P	Awd.,Min.
1269	Doddiscombsleigh	P	Rep. 1838
1270	Dolton	P	Awd.,Min.
1271	Dotton	EP	Min.
1272	Dowland	P	Rep. 1838
1273	Down St. Mary	P	Min.
1274	Down East	P	Awd.
1275	Down West	P	Awd.,Min.
1276	Drewsteignton	P	Agrmt.
1277	Dunchideock	P	Awd.,Min.
1278	Dunkeswell	P	Agrmt.,Rep. 1844
1279	Dunsford	P	Agrmt.
1280	Dunterton	P	Min.
1281	Eggbuckland	P	Agrmt.,Rep. 1838
1282	Eggesford & Barton	PD	Awd.,Min.
1283	Ermington	P	Min.
1284	Exbourne	P	Awd.,Min.
1285	Exeter Holy Trinity	P	Awd.,Min.
1286	Exeter St. David	P	Min.
1287	Exeter St. Edmund	P	Awd.,Min.
1288	Exeter St. Mary Steps	P	Awd.,Min.
1289	Exeter St. Olave	P	N.t.p.
1290	Exeter St. Stephen	P	N.t.p.
1291	Exminster	P	Rep. 1839
1292	Exmoor Forest (part of)	EP	N.t.p.
1293	Farringdon	P	Rep. 1838
1294	Farway	P	Min.
1295	Feniton	P	Rep. 1838
1296	Filleigh	P	Agrmt.,Min.
1297	Fremington	P	Min.,Rep. 1838
1298	Frithelstock	P	Rep. 1838
1299	Georgeham	P	Awd.,Min.
1300	Georgenympton	P	Min.
1301	Germansweek	P	Min.
1302	St. Giles on the Heath	P	Rep. 1840
1303	St. Giles in the Wood	P	Min.
1304	Gidley	P	Awd.,Min.
1305	Gittisham	P	Rep. 1838
1306	Goodleigh	P	Agrmt.,Min.,Rep. 1839
1307	Haccombe	P	Min.
1308	Halberton	P	Agrmt.,Rep. 1840
1309	Halwell	P	Rep. 1839
1310	Halwell (Black Torrington)	P	Min.
1311	Harberton	P	Min.
1312	Harford	P	Rep. 1838
1313	Harpford	P	Awd.,Min.,Rep. 1839
1314	Hartland	P	Awd.,Min.
1315	Hatherleigh	P	Min.,Rep. 1841
1316	Heanton Punchardon	P	Rep. 1838
1317	Heavitree	P	Min.
1318	Hempston Little	P	Rep. 1838
1319	Hemyock	P	Awd.,Min.
1320	Hennock	P	Rep. 1838
1321	Holsworthy	P	Min.
1322	Hollacombe	P	Awd.,Min.
1323	Holne	P	Agrmt.,Rep. 1838
1324	Honeychurch	P	Rep. 1838
1325	Highampton	P	Min.
1326	Highbray	P	Rep. 1838
1327	Highley St Mary	EP	N.t.p.
1328	Highweek	P	Agrmt.,Rep. 1840
1329	Hittisleigh	P	Rep. 1841
1330	Hockworthy	P	Awd.,Min.
1331	Holberton	P	Rep. 1839
1332	Holcombe Burnell	P	Agrmt.,Min.
1333	Holcombe Rogus	P	Agrmt.,Rep. 1840
1334	Honiton	P	Awd.,Min.
1335	Horwood	P	Awd.,Min.
1336	Huish	P	Agrmt.,Awd.,Min.
1337	Huish North	P	Min.,Rep. 1840
1338	Huish South	P	Min.
1339	Huntsham	P	Agrmt.,Awd.,Min.,Rep. 1840
1340	Huntshaw	P	Rep. 1841
1341	Huxham	P	Agrmt.,Min.
1342	Hurley's District Uffculme	D	Min.
1343	Iddesleigh	P	Awd.,Min.
1344	Ide	P	Min.
1345	Ideford	P	Agrmt.,Rep. 1839
1346	Ilfracombe	P	Awd.,Min.
1347	Ilsington	P	Rep. 1838
1348	Instow	P	Awd.,Min.
1349	Inwardleigh	P	Awd.,Min.
1350	Ipplepen	P	Awd.,Min.,Rep. 1839
1351	Jacobstow	P	Awd.,Rep. 1838
1352	Kelly	P	Rep. 1838
1353	Kenn	P	Rep. 1841
1354	Kennerleigh	P	Rep. 1839
1355	Kentisbeare	P	Min.,Rep. 1841
1356	Kentisbury	P	Min.,Rep. 1839
1357	Kenton	P	Awd.,Min.
1358	Kilmington	P	Rep. 1838
1359	Kingsnympton	P	Min.
1360	Kingsbridge	P	N.t.p.
1361	Kingskerswell	P	Agrmt.,Rep. 1840
1362	Kingsteignton	P	Rep. 1840
1363	Kingston	P	Min.
1364	Kingswear	P	Agrmt.,Rep. 1840
1365	Knowstone	P	Min.
1366	Lamerton	P	Awd.,Min.
1367	Landcross	P	Rep. 1838
1368	Landkey	P	Awd.,Min.
1369	Langtree	P	Awd.,Min.,Rep. 1838
1370	Lapford	P	Min.
1371	St. Leonards	P	Rep. 1839
1372	Lewtrenchard	P	Rep. 1839
1373	Lifton	P	Min.
1374	Littleham	P	Awd.,Rep. 1839
1375	Littleham and Exmouth	P	Min.
1376	Loddeswell	P	Min.,Rep. 1838
1377	Loxbear	P	Rep. 1842
1378	Loxhore	P	Min.
1379	Luffincott	P	Agrmt.,Awd.
1380	Old Lydford	D	Min.,Rep. 1844
1381	Luppitt	P	Awd.,Min.
1382	Lustleigh	P	Agrmt.
1383	Lympston	P	Agrmt.,Rep. 1839
1384	Lynton	P	Min.,Rep. 1839
1385	Maker	P	Min.
1386	Malborough	P	Awd.,Min.
1387	Mamhead	P	Rep. 1838
1388	Manaton	P	Min.
1389	Marldon	P	Agrmt.,Rep. 1839
1390	Martinhoe	P	Awd.,Min.
1391	Marwood	P	Awd.,Min.
1392	Maryansleigh	P	Rep. 1839
1393	St Mary Church	P	Rep. 1840
1394	Marystow	P	Min.
1395	Mary Tavy	P	Agrmt.,Rep. 1843
1396	Meavy	P	Rep. 1839
1397	Meeth	P	Min.,Rep. 1839
1398	Membury	P	Min.,Rep. 1840
1399	Merton	P	Rep. 1841
1400	Meshaw	P	Rep. 1838
1401	Milton South	P	Min.
1402	Milton Abbott	P	Awd.,Min.,Rep. 1839
1403	Milton Damerel	P	Rep. 1840
1404	Modbury	P	Awd.,Min.
1405	Molland	P	Min.
1406	Molton North	P	Rep. 1840
1407	Molton South	P	Awd.,Min.,Rep. 1839
1408	Monk Okehampton	P	Awd.,Min.
1409	Monkton	P	Agrmt.,Rep. 1842
1410	Morchard Bishop	P	Min.,Rep. 1838
1411	Moreton Hampstead	P	Min.
1412	Morebath	P	Min.,Rep. 1837
1413	Morley	P	Min.
1414	Morthoe	P	Agrmt.,Min.
1415	Musbury	P	Rep. 1839
1416	Monkleigh	P	Awd.,Min.
1417	Netherexe	P	N.t.p.
1418	Newton Ferrers	P	Agrmt.,Min.,Rep. 1839
1419	Newton St Cyres	P	Min.
1420	Newton St Petrock	P	Min.,Rep. 1840
1421	Newton Tracey	P	Awd.,Min.
1422	St. Nicholas	P	Min.

Devon contd.

1423	Northam	P	Rep. 1838
1424	Northcot	H	Awd.,Min.
1425	Northleigh	P	Min.,Rep. 1839
1426	Northlew	P	Min.
1427	Nymet Rowland	P	Min.
1428	Oakford	P	Min.,Rep. 1840
1429	Offwell	P	Awd.,Min.
1430	Ogwell East	P	Agrmt.,Rep. 1841
1431	Ogwell West	P	Awd.,Rep. 1838
1432	Okehampton	P	Awd.,Min.
1433	Otterton	P	Awd.,Min.
1434	Ottery St. Mary	P	Awd.,Min.
1435	Poltimore	P	Agrmt.
1436	Powderham	P	Rep. 1838
1437	Paignton	P	Min.,Rep. 1840
1438	Pancrasweek	P	Awd.,Min.
1439	Parkham	P	Awd.,Min.
1440	Parracombe	P	Rep. 1838
1441	Payhembury	P	Rep. 1839
1442	Peters Marland	P	Rep. 1839
1443	Petherwin North	P	Awd.,Min.
1444	Petertavy	P	Min.,Rep. 1839
1445	Petrockstow	P	Agrmt.
1446	Pilton	P	Min.
1447	Pinhoe	P	Agrmt.,Rep. 1838
1448	Pitt (Tiverton)	D	Min.
1449	Plymouth St Andrew	P	Awd.,Min.
1450	Plympton St. Mary	P	Min.,Rep. 1840
1451	Plympton St. Maurice	P	Min.
1452	Plymstock	P	Min.
1453	Plymtree	P	Min.
1454	Pool South	P	Agrmt.,Awd.,Min.,Rep. 1840
1455	Portlemouth East	P	Min.
1456	Poughill	P	Awd.,Min.
1457	Priors (Tiverton)	D	Awd.,Min.
1458	Puddington	P	Agrmt.,Min.,Rep. 1838
1459	Putford East	P	Awd.,Min.
1460	Putford West	P	Rep. 1838
1461	Pyworthy	P	Min.,Rep. 1838
1462	Rackenford	P	Min.
1463	Rattery	P	Awd.,Min.
1464	Revelstoke	P	Agrmt.,Min.,Rep. 1840
1465	Rew	P	Agrmt.,Awd.,Min.,Rep. 1837
1466	Ringmore	P	Min.
1467	Roborough	P	Awd.,Min.
1468	Rockbeare	P	Awd.,Min.
1469	Romansleigh	P	Min.,Rep. 1839
1470	Rose Ash	P	Awd.,Min.
1471	Rousdon St. Pancras	P	Min.,Rep. 1843
1472	Salcombe Regis	P	Agrmt.,Rep. 1839
1473	Sampford Courtenay	P	Min.
1474	Sampford Peverell	P	Awd.,Min.
1475	Sampford Spiney	P	Awd.,Min.
1476	Shaugh	P	Awd.,Min.
1477	Shebbear	P	Awd.,Min.
1478	Sheepstor	P	Agrmt.,Rep. 1842
1479	Sheepwash	P	Rep. 1839
1480	Sheldon	P	Min.,Rep. 1838
1481	Sherford	P	Awd.,Min.
1482	Sherwill	P	Rep. 1838
1483	Shillingford	P	Agrmt.,Rep. 1838
1484	Shobrooke	P	Awd.,Min.
1485	Shute	P	Rep. 1842
1486	Sidbury	P	Rep. 1840
1487	Sidmouth	P	Rep. 1840
1488	St. Sidwell	P	Min.
1489	Silverton	P	Agrmt.,Min.,Rep. 1842
1490	Slapton	P	Awd.,Min.
1491	Sourton	P	Min.
1492	Southleigh	P	Rep. 1838
1493	Sowton	P	Agrmt.,Rep. 1837
1494	Spreyton	P	Min.
1495	Staverton	P	Min.
1496	Stockleigh English	P	Min.
1497	Stockleigh Pomeroy	P	Awd.,Min.
1498	Stoke Canon	P	Agrmt.,Rep. 1840
1499	Stoke Damerel	P	Rep. 1840
1500	Stokefleming	P	Min.
1501	Stoke Gabriel	P	Awd.,Min.
1502	Stokeinteignhead	P	Awd.,Min.
1503	Stokenham	P	Min.,Rep. 1842
1504	Stoke Rivers	P	Rep. 1842
1505	Stonehouse East	P	N.t.p.
1506	Stoodleigh	P	Agrmt.,Min.,Rep. 1841
1507	Stowford	P	Rep. 1838
1508	Sutcombe	P	Rep. 1842
1509	Swimbridge	P	Awd.,Min.
1510	Sydenham South	P	Rep. 1840
1511	Talaton	P	Rep. 1839
1512	Tamerton Folliott	P	Rep. 1839
1513	Tavistock	P	Min.,Rep. 1843
1514	Tawstock	P	Rep. 1842
1515	Tawton North	P	Min.
1516	Tawton South	P	Awd.,Min.
1517	Tedburn St Mary	P	Agrmt.,Min.
1518	Teignmouth West	P	Rep. 1839
1519	Teingrace	P	Rep. 1838
1520	Templeton	P	Min.
1521	Tetcott	P	Agrmt.,Rep. 1837
1522	Thelbridge	P	Awd.,Min.
1523	St. Thomas the Apostle	P	Agrmt.,Rep. 1838
1524	Thornbury	P	Rep. 1839
1525	Thorncombe	P	Rep. 1841
1526	Thorverton	P	Min.
1527	Throwley	P	Agrmt.,Rep. 1840
1528	Tidcombe (Tiverton)	D	Rep. 1841
1529	Thurleston	P	Min.
1530	Thrushelton	P	Rep. 1839
1531	Tiverton All Fours	D	Min.
1532	Topsham	P	Awd.,Min.
1533	Torbrian	P	Agrmt.,Min.,Rep. 1839
1534	Tormoham	P	Awd.,Min.
1535	Torrington Black	P	Agrmt.,Min.
1536	Torrington Great	P	Min.
1537	Torrington Little	P	Rep. 1838
1538	Totnes	P	Min.
1539	Teignmouth East	P	Rep. 1840
1540	Townstall	P	Awd.,Min.
1541	Sandford	P	Rep. 1838
1542	Seaton and Beer	Pl	Rep. 1839
1543	Satterleigh	P	Rep. 1839
1544	Trentishoe	P	Min.
1545	Trusham	P	Agrmt.,Rep. 1838
1546	Twitchen	P	Rep. 1840
1547	Uffculme	P	Agrmt.,Awd.,Min.
1548	Ugborough	P	Min.
1549	Uplowman	P	Awd.
1550	Uplyme	P	Rep. 1838
1551	Upottery	P	Rep. 1840
1552	Upton Hellions	P	Rep. 1840
1553	Upton Pyne	P	Rep. 1837
1554	Upton Weaver (Cullompton)	D	Awd.,Min.
1555	Ven Ottery	P	Agrmt.,Rep. 1839
1556	Virginstow	P	Rep. 1839
1557	Walkhampton	P	Rep. 1839
1558	Warkleigh	P	Rep. 1841
1559	Washfield	P	Rep. 1838
1560	Washford Pyne	P	Rep. 1839
1561	Wear Gifford	P	Agrmt.,Min.
1562	Welcomb	P	Awd.,Min.
1563	Wembury	P	Rep. 1838
1564	Wemworthy	P	Agrmt.,Rep. 1837
1565	Weston Peverel	I	Rep. 1840
1566	Whimple	P	N.t.p.
1567	Whitchurch	P	Awd.,Min.
1568	Werrington	P	Rep. 1839
1569	Westleigh	P	Min.
1570	Whitestone	P	Awd.,Min.
1571	Widdecombe in the Moor	P	Awd.,Min.
1572	Widworthy	P	Rep. 1838
1573	Willand	P	Min.
1574	Winkleigh	P	Awd.,Min.
1575	Witheridge	P	Agrmt.,Rep. 1837
1576	Withycombe Rawleigh	P	Min.,Rep. 1838
1577	Wolborough	P	Awd.,Min.
1578	Woodbury	P	Min.
1579	Woodland	P	Rep. 1838
1580	Woodleigh	P	Min.
1581	Woolfardisworthy	P	Min.
1582	Woolfardisworthy Hartland	P	Min.
1583	Worlington East	P	Min.
1584	Worlington West	P	Min.
1585	Yarcombe	P	Awd.,Min.
1586	Yarnscombe	P	Rep. 1840
1587	Yealmpton	P	Awd.,Min.
1588	Zeal Monachorum	P	Agrmt.,Min.,Rep. 1840

Dorset

1589	Abbotsbury	P	Rep. 1841
1590	Affpuddle	P	Rep. 1838
1591	Allington	P	Rep. 1839
1592	Almer & Mapperton	P	Rep. 1843
1593	Alderholt	I	Awd.,Min.
1594	Alton Pancras	P	Awd.,Min.
1595	Anderson	P	Agrmt.,Rep. 1837
1596	Arne	C	Awd.,Min.
1597	Askerswell	P	Awd.,Min.
1598	Athelhampton	P	Awd.,Min.
1599	Ashmore	P	Awd.,Min.
1600	Batcombe	P	Agrmt.,Rep. 1838
1601	Beaminster	P	Min.,Rep. 1841
1602	Beerhackett	P	Rep. 1839
1603	Belchalwell	P	Rep. 1840
1604	Bere Regis	P	Agrmt.,Rep. 1842
1605	Bettiscombe	P	Agrmt.,Rep. 1839
1606	Bincombe	P	Agrmt.,Rep. 1838
1607	Bishops Caundle	P	Awd.,Min.
1608	Blagdon and Boveridge	I	N.t.p.,Min.
1609	Blandford Forum	P	Agrmt.,Rep. 1837
1610	Blandford	P	Agrmt.,Rep. 1837

Dorset contd.

1611	Bloxworth	P	Agrmt.,Rep. 1844
1612	Bothenhampton	P	Awd.,Min.
1613	Bradford Abbas	P	Agrmt.,Min.,Rep. 1838
1614	Bradford Peverell	P	N.t.p.,Min.
1615	Bradpole	P	Awd.,Min.
1616	Bredy Little	P	Awd.,Min.
1617	Bridport	P	Awd.,Min.
1618	Broad Maine	P	N.t.p.,Min.
1619	Broadway	P	Agrmt.,Min.,Rep. 1837
1620	Broad Windsor	P	Rep. 1838
1621	Bryanston	P	Agrmt.
1622	Buckhorn Weston	P	Rep. 1838
1623	Buckland Newton	P	Agrmt.,Min.,Rep. 1838
1624	Buckland Ripers	P	Agrmt.,Min.,Rep. 1837
1625	Burlestone	P	Rep. 1843
1626	Burstock	P	Rep. 1840
1627	Burton Bradstock	P	Rep. 1840
1628	Canford Great(Middle Div)	D	Rep. 1841
1629	Canford Great(Western Div)	D	Rep. 1841
1630	Castleton	P	Awd.,Min.
1631	Catherston Leweston	P	Awd.,Min.
1632	Caundle Marsh	P	Agrmt.,Rep. 1837
1633	Cattistock	P	Agrmt.,Rep. 1839
1634	Cerne Abbas	P	Agrmt.,Min.
1635	Cerne Nether	P	Awd.,Min.
1636	Chalbury	P	Min.,Rep. 1840
1637	Charborough	P	Agrmt.,Awd.,Min.
1638	Chardstock	P	Min.,Rep. 1839
1639	Charlton Marshall	PC	N.t.p.,Min.
1640	Charminster	P	Agrmt.,Rep. 1837
1641	Charmouth	P	Awd.,Min.
1642	Cheddington	P	Agrmt.,Rep. 1838
1643	W. Chelborough	P	Agrmt.,Rep. 1839
1644	E. Chelborough	P	Agrmt.,Rep. 1839
1645	Cheselbourne	P	Awd.,Min.
1646	Chetnole	C	Awd.,Min.
1647	Chettle	P	Awd.,Min.
1648	Chickerell	P	Agrmt.,Rep. 1838
1649	Chideock	P	Awd.,Min.
1650	Chilcomb	P	Agrmt.,Rep. 1840
1651	Child Okeford	P	Agrmt.,Rep. 1839
1652	Chilfrome	P	Awd.,Min.
1653	Church Knowle	P	Awd.,Min.
1654	Clifton Maybank	P	Agrmt.,Rep. 1838
1655	Compton Abbas(Dorchester)	P	Awd.,Min.
1656	Compton Abbas(Shaftsbury)	P	Awd.,Min.
1657	Compton Nether	P	Agrmt.,Rep. 1838
1658	Compton Over	P	Agrmt.,Rep. 1838
1659	Compton Valance	P	Rep. 1839
1660	Coombe Keynes cum Wool	P	Agrmt.,Rep. 1839
1661	Corfe Castle	P	Awd.,Min.
1662	Corscombe	P	Agrmt.,Min.,Rep. 1838
1663	Corfe Mullen	P	Agrmt.,Rep. 1837
1664	Cranborne	P	Min.
1665	Cranborne and Holwell	I	Awd.,Min.
1666	Critchell Long	P	Awd.,Min.
1667	Dewlish	P	Min.
1668	Dorchester All Saints	P	N.t.p.
1669	Dorchester Holy Trinity	P	Min.
1670	Dorchester St Peter	P	N.t.p.,Min.
1671	Durweston	P	Agrmt.,Min.
1672	Edmondsham	P	Agrmt.,Rep. 1838
1673	Evershot	UP	Agrmt.,Rep. 1838
1674	Fairwood	I	Awd.,Min.
1675	Farnham	P	Agrmt.,Awd.,Min.,Rep. 1839
1676	Fifehead Magdalen	P	Agrmt.,Rep. 1839
1677	Fifehead Neville	P	Agrmt.,Rep. 1839
1678	Fleet	P	Agrmt.,Rep. 1838
1679	Folke	P	Agrmt.,Rep. 1839
1680	Fontmell Magna	P	Agrmt.,Rep. 1837
1681	Fordington	P	Awd.,Min.
1682	Frampton	P	Agrmt.,Rep. 1839
1683	Frome Vauchurch	P	Agrmt.,Rep. 1838
1684	Gillingham	P	Awd.,Min.
1685	Glanville Wootton	P	Agrmt.,Rep. 1838
1686	Godmanstone	P	Agrmt.,Rep. 1838
1687	Gussage	P	Min.,Rep. 1839
1688	Gussage St Michael	P	Awd.,Min.
1689	Halstock	P	Agrmt.,Rep. 1842
1690	Hammoon	P	Rep. 1838
1691	Hampreston	P	Min.,Rep. 1837
1692	Hamworthy	P	Agrmt.,Rep. 1838
1693	Hanford	EP	N.t.p.
1694	Hawkchurch	P	Awd.,Min.
1695	Haydon	P	Agrmt.,Min.,Rep. 1839
1696	Hazelbury	P	Agrmt.,Rep. 1838
1697	Hermitage	P	Rep. 1840
1698	Hillfield	P	Awd.,Min.
1699	Hilton	P	Awd.,Min.
1700	Hinton Martel	P	Agrmt.,Rep. 1838
1701	Hinton Parva	P	Rep. 1841
1702	Hinton St Mary	P	Awd.,Min.
1703	Holme East	P	Rep. 1841
1704	Holnest	P	Min.,Rep. 1843
1705	Hook	P	Agrmt.,Min.,Rep. 1839
1706	Horton	P	Min.,Rep. 1840
1707	Ibberton	P	Agrmt.,Rep. 1838
1708	Iwerne Courtney	P	Agrmt.,Min.,Rep. 1838
1709	Iwerne Minster	P	Awd.,Min.
1710	Kimmeridge Great	P	N.t.p.
1711	Kingston Russell	P	Rep. 1838
1712	Kingston Magna	P	Awd.,Min.
1713	Kinson	C	Agrmt.,Min.,Rep. 1838
1714	W. Knighton	P	Min.,Rep. 1843
1715	Langton Herring	P	Awd.,Min.
1716	Langton	P	Agrmt.,Min.,Rep. 1839
1717	Langton Matravers	P	Agrmt.,Min.,Rep. 1839
1718	Leigh	C	Awd.,Min.
1719	Leweston	EP	N.t.p.,Min.
1720	Lillington,Inner,Outer	D	Min.
1721	Litton Cheney	P	Agrmt.,Min.,Rep. 1839
1722	Loders	P	Awd.,Min.
1723	Longbredy	P	Agrmt.,Min.,Rep. 1839
1724	Longburton	P	Awd.,Min.
1725	Longfleet	I	Awd.,Min.
1726	E. Lulworth	P	Rep. 1839
1727	Lydlinch	P	Agrmt.,Min.,Rep. 1840
1728	Lyme Regis	P	Rep. 1842
1729	Lytchett Matravers	P	Rep. 1837
1730	Lytchett Minster	P	Agrmt.,Min.,Rep. 1838
1731	Maiden Newton	P	Min.,Rep. 1837
1732	Manston	P	Awd.,Min.
1733	Mapperton	P	Agrmt.,Rep. 1837
1734	Mappowder	P	Agrmt.,Min.,Rep. 1841
1735	Margaret Marsh	P	Awd.,Min.
1738	Marnhull	P	Min.,Rep. 1837
1739	Marshwood	P	Awd.,Min.
1740	Melbury Abbas	P	Agrmt.,Rep. 1838
1741	Melbury Bubb	P	Agrmt.,Rep. 1838
1742	Melbury Osmond	P	Agrmt.,Rep. 1838
1743	Melbury Sampford	P	Agrmt.,Rep. 1838
1744	Melcomb Horsey	P	Min.,Rep. 1840
1745	Milborne	P	Agrmt.,Rep. 1839
1746	Milton Abbas	P	N.t.p.
1747	Mintern Magna	P	Awd.,Min.
1748	Moreton	P	Rep. 1838
1749	Monckton up Wimborne	I	N.t.p.,Min.
1750	Moore Critchell	P	Awd.,Min.
1751	Morden	P	Min.,Rep. 1845
1752	Mosterton	P	Agrmt.,Rep. 1838
1753	Motcomb	P	Agrmt.,Rep. 1838
1754	Netherbury	P	Agrmt.,Rep. 1839
1755	Nutford	I	Awd.,Min.
1756	Oborne	P	Agrmt.,Rep. 1838
1757	Okeford Fitzpaine	P	Agrmt.,Min.,Rep. 1838
1758	Orchard East or Hartgrove	P	Awd.,Min.
1759	Orchard West	P	Awd.,Min.
1760	Osmington	P	Agrmt.,Rep. 1837
1761	Ower Moigne	P	Min.,Rep. 1840
1762	Parkstone	I	Awd.,Min.
1763	W. Parley	P	Min.,Rep. 1839
1764	Pentridge	P	Agrmt.,Rep. 1838
1765	Perrot South	P	Agrmt.,Rep. 1838
1766	Piddlehinton	P	Rep. 1838
1767	Piddletown	P	Min.,Rep. 1839
1768	Piddletrenthide	P	Agrmt.,Rep. 1838
1769	Pilsdon	P	Agrmt.,Rep. 1841
1770	Pimperne	P	N.t.p.,Min.
1771	Poole St James	P	N.t.p.,Min.
1772	Powerstock	P	Agrmt.,Min.,Rep. 1839
1773	N. Poorton	P	Agrmt.,Rep. 1837
1774	Portisham	P	Agrmt.,Awd.,Min.
1775	Portland	P	Agrmt.,Min.,Rep. 1839
1776	Poxwell	P	Agrmt.,Rep. 1840
1777	Preston & Sutton Pointz	P	Agrmt.,Min.,Rep. 1838
1778	Pulham	P	Min.,Rep. 1838
1779	Puncknoll	P	Awd.,Min.
1780	Purse Caundle	P	Agrmt.,Rep. 1838
1781	Radipole	P	Agrmt.,Min.,Rep. 1837
1782	Rampisham	P	Min.,Rep. 1839
1783	Ryme Intrinsica	P	Min.,Rep. 1839
1784	Shapwick	P	Awd.,Min.
1785	Shaftesbury Holy Trinity	P	Rep. 1840
1786	Shaftesbury St James	P	Min.,Rep. 1840
1787	Shaftesbury St Rumbold	P	Min.,Rep. 1840
1788	Stratton	P	Min.,Rep. 1838
1789	Sherborne	P	Awd.,Min.
1790	Shillingstone	P	Min.,Rep. 1838
1791	Silton	P	Agrmt.,Rep. 1837
1792	Sixpenny Handley	P	Min.,Rep. 1841
1793	Spetisbury	P	Min.,Rep. 1838
1794	W. Stafford	P	Agrmt.,Rep. 1838
1795	Stalbridge	P	Agrmt.,Rep. 1839
1796	Stanton St Gabriel	P	Awd.,Min.
1797	Steeple	P	Awd.,Min.
1798	Stoke Abbott	P	Min.,Rep. 1839
1799	Steepleton Preston	P	Agrmt.,Rep. 1839
1800	Stintsford	P	Agrmt.,Rep. 1837
1801	Stoke Gaylard	P	Agrmt.,Min.,Rep. 1841
1802	Stockland	P	Agrmt.,Min.,Rep. 1844
1803	Stockwood	P	Agrmt.,Min.,Rep. 1839
1804	Stoke East	P	Awd.,Min.

Dorset contd.

1805	Stoke Wake	P	Min.,Rep. 1839
1806	Stourpain	P	Min.,Rep. 1840
1807	Stourton Caundle	P	Min.,Rep. 1839
1808	Stower Provost	P	Awd.,Min.
1809	E. Stower	P	Agrmt.,Min.,Rep. 1842
1810	W. Stower	P	Min.,Rep. 1842
1811	Sturminster Marshall	P	Agrmt.,Min.,Rep. 1838
1812	Swyer	P	Agrmt.,Min.,Rep. 1838
1813	Studland	P	Min.,Rep. 1839
1814	Sturminster Newton	P	Min.,Rep. 1839
1815	Sutton Waldron	P	Min.
1816	Swanage	P	Agrmt.,Min.,Rep. 1839
1817	Sydling	P	Agrmt.,Min.,Rep. 1839
1818	Symondsbury	P	Min.,Rep. 1839
1819	Tarent Crawford	P	Awd.,Min.
1820	Tarent Hinton	P	Min.
1821	Tarent Rushton	P	Awd.,Min.
1822	Tarrant Gunville	P	Awd.,Min.
1823	Tarrant Keinston	P	Agrmt.,Min.,Rep. 1838
1824	Tarrant Monkton and Laun	P	Rep. 1839
1825	Tarrant Rawston	P	Agrmt.,Min.,Rep. 1838
1826	Thornford	P	Awd.,Min.
1827	Tincleton	P	Awd.,Min.
1828	Todber	P	Min.,Rep. 1840
1829	Toller Fratrum	P	Awd.,Min.
1830	Toller Porcorum	P	Rep. 1843
1831	Tolpuddle	P	Min.,Rep. 1841
1832	Tomson	P	Agrmt.,Rep. 1838
1833	Toners Puddle	P	Rep. 1838
1834	Turnworth	P	Agrmt.,Min.,Rep. 1840
1835	Tyneham	P	Agrmt.,Rep. 1840
1836	Upcerne	P	Agrmt.,Rep. 1839
1837	Upwey	P	Agrmt.,Rep. 1838
1838	Walditch	P	Agrmt.,Min.,Rep. 1838
1839	Wareham Holy Trinity	P	Awd.,Min.
1840	Wareham St Martin	P	Awd.,Min.
1841	Wareham,Lady Saint Mary	P	Awd.,Min.
1842	Warmbrook	P	Awd.,Min.
1843	Warmwell	P	Rep. 1841
1844	West End(Loders)	H	Awd.,Min.
1845	Watercombe	EP	N.t.p.
1846	Weymouth	P	Agrmt.,Min.
1847	Whitchurch Canonicorum	P	Awd.,Min.
1848	Whitcombe	P	N.t.p.
1849	Wimborne Minster	P	Awd.,Min.
1850	Wimborne	P	Agrmt.,Rep. 1838
1851	Winfrith Newburgh	P	Min.
1852	Winterborne Abbas	P	Agrmt.,Rep. 1839
1853	Winterborne Game	P	Awd.,Min.
1854	Winterborne Clenstone	P	Agrmt.,Rep. 1839
1855	Winterborne Kingston	P	Agrmt.,Rep. 1842
1856	Winterborne Martin	P	Awd.,Min.
1857	Winterborne Monkton	P	Min.
1858	Winterborne Houghton	P	Agrmt.,Rep. 1838
1859	Winterborne Steepleton	P	Awd.,Min.
1860	Winterborne Strickland	P	N.t.p.,Min.
1861	Winterborne Whitechurch	P	Agrmt.,Min.
1862	Winterborne Zelstone	P	Min.,Rep. 1839
1863	Witchampton	P	Rep. 1838
1864	Witherstone	P	Agrmt.,Rep. 1839
1865	Woodsford	P	Min.,Rep. 1840
1866	Woodyate West	EP	Awd.,Min.
1867	Woolland	P	Min.,Rep. 1839
1868	Wootton Fitzpaine	P	Rep. 1841
1869	Wootton North	P	Awd.,Min.
1870	Worth Matravers	P	Agrmt.,Min.,Rep. 1839
1871	Wraxall	P	Rep. 1839
1872	Wyke Regis	P	Agrmt.,Min.,Rep. 1839
1873	Wynford Eagle	P	Agrmt.,Rep. 1838
1874	Yetminster	P	Awd.,Min.

Durham

1736	Byers Green	T	Min.,Rep. 1842
1737	Butterwick and Old Acres	T	Min.,Rep. 1838
1875	Ancroft	T	Awd.,Min.
1876	Archdeacon Newton	T	Awd.,Min.
1877	Auckland St Andrew	T	Awd.,Min.
1878	Auckland St Helen	T	Agrmt.,Min.,Rep. 1839
1879	Auckland West	T	Awd.,Min.
1880	Aycliffe Great	T	Min.,Rep. 1838
1881	Barmpton	T	Min.,Rep. 1842
1882	Barmston	T	Agrmt.,Rep. 1840
1883	Barnard Castle	T	Agrmt.,Min.,Rep. 1840
1884	Barns High and Low	D	Awd.,Min.
1885	Bedburn North	T	Awd.,Min.
1886	Bedburn South	T	Awd.,Min.
1887	Bedlington	T	Min.,Rep. 1838
1888	Bishopwearmouth Pans	T	N.t.p.,Min.
1889	Benfieldside	T	Awd.,Min.
1890	Berrington Law	H	Rep. 1839
1891	Biddick South	T	Awd.,Min.
1892	Billingham	T	Min.,Rep. 1838
1893	Billingside	T	Awd.,Min.
1894	Binchester	T	N.t.p.,Min.
1895	Birtley	T	Awd.,Min.
1896	Bishop Auckland	T	Awd.,Min.
1897	Bishop Middleham	T	Agrmt.,Rep. 1839
1898	Bishopton	T	Min.,Rep. 1839
1899	Bishop Wearmouth	T	Min.,Rep. 1843
1900	Blackwell	T	Awd.,Min.
1901	Blakiston	R	Awd.,Min.
1902	Bolam	T	Agrmt.,Min.,Rep. 1840
1903	Boldon	P	Agrmt.,Rep. 1838
1904	Bourn Moor	T	Awd.,Min.
1905	Bradbury	T	Agrmt.,Rep. 1838
1906	Brancepeth	T	Agrmt.,Min.,Rep. 1838
1907	Brandon and Byshottles	T	Agrmt.,Min.,Rep. 1838
1908	Brearton	T	Awd.,Min.
1909	Broom	T	Min.,Rep. 1838
1910	Burdon	T	Agrmt.,Rep. 1839
1911	Burdon	T	Rep. 1838
1912	Burnhope and Hamsteels	T	Agrmt.,Rep. 1839
1913	Butsfield East and West	D	Min.,Rep. 1840
1914	Carlton	T	Agrmt.,Min.,Rep. 1839
1915	Cassop	T	Agrmt.,Min.,Rep. 1840
1916	Castle Eden	P	Agrmt.,Rep. 1838
1917	Castle Precincts	EP	N.t.p.,Min.
1918	Chester le Street	T	Awd.,Min.,Rep. 1840
1919	Cheswick	T	Agrmt.,Min.,Rep. 1841
1920	Chilton	T	Agrmt.,Min.,Rep. 1838
1921	Choppington	T	Awd.,Min.
1922	Chopwell	T	Awd.,Min.
1923	Claxton	T	Min.,Rep. 1842
1924	Cleatlam	T	Agrmt.,Min.,Rep. 1841
1925	Coatham Mandeville	T	Min.,Rep. 1838
1926	Coats A Moor	T	Awd.,Min.
1927	Cocken	T	Awd.,Min.
1928	Cockerton	D	Awd.,Min.
1929	Cockfield	P	Agrmt.,Min.,Rep. 1838
1930	Cold Pig Hill	D	Agrmt.,Min.,Rep. 1838
1931	Cold Rowley	T	Agrmt.,Min.,Rep. 1840
1932	College the	EP	N.t.p.,Min.
1933	Collierley and Pontop	T	Awd.,Min.
1934	Coniscliffe	P	Agrmt.,Min.,Rep. 1840
1935	Conside and Knitsley	T	Awd.,Min.
1936	Brafferton	T	Min.,Rep. 1839
1937	Cornforth	T	Agrmt.,Min.,Rep. 1839
1938	Cornhill	T	Agrmt.,Awd.,Min.
1939	Cornsay	T	Agrmt.,Rep. 1839
1940	Coundon	T	Awd.,Min.
1941	Coundon Grange	T	Agrmt.,Rep. 1839
1942	Cowpen Bewley	T	Agrmt.,Min.,Rep. 1838
1943	Coxhoe	T	Min.,Rep. 1841
1944	Craike	P	Min.,Rep. 1839
1945	Crawcrook	T	Agrmt.,Rep. 1839
1946	Crook and Billy Row	T	Agrmt.,Min.,Rep. 1838
1947	Crossgate	T	Min.,Rep. 1838
1948	Dalton le Dale	T	Min.,Rep. 1839
1949	Dalton Piercy	T	Agrmt.,Min.,Rep. 1839
1950	Darlington	D	Awd.,Min.
1951	Darlington and Cockerton	D	Agrmt.,Min.,Rep. 1838
1952	Dawdon	T	Awd.,Min.
1953	Denton	T	Agrmt.,Min.,Rep. 1838
1954	Dinsdale	P	Agrmt.,Min.,Rep. 1839
1955	Duddo	T	Awd.,Min.
1956	Durham,St Mary le Bow	P	N.t.p.,Min.
1957	Durham,St Mary the Less	P	N.t.p.,Min.
1958	Durham,St Nicholas	P	Awd.,Min.
1959	Easington	P	Agrmt.,Min.,Rep. 1838
1960	Ebchester	C	N.t.p.,Min.
1961	Edmondbyers	P	Agrmt.,Min.,Rep. 1839
1962	Elwick	T	Agrmt.,Min.,Rep. 1839
1963	Elwick Hall	P	Agrmt.,Min.,Rep. 1839
1964	Emelden	T	Min.,Rep. 1838
1965	Eppleton	T	Min.,Rep. 1838
1966	Eppleton Little	T	Agrmt.,Rep. 1839
1967	Escomb	T	Awd.,Min.
1968	Eshe	T	Agrmt.,Min.,Rep. 1839
1969	Evenwood	T	Awd.,Min.
1970	Edmondsley	T	Awd.,Min.
1971	Egglescliffe	P	Agrmt.,Min.,Rep. 1838
1972	Eggleston	T	Awd.,Min.
1973	Eldon	T	N.t.p.,Min.
1974	Elstob	T	Agrmt.,Rep. 1838
1975	Elton	P	Agrmt.,Rep. 1838
1976	Elvet	T	Min.,Rep. 1838
1977	Felkington	T	Awd.,Min.
1978	Felling	D	Awd.,Min.
1979	Fenham	T	Awd.,Min.
1980	Fern Islands	EP	N.t.p.
1981	Ferryhill	T	Agrmt.,Rep. 1838
1982	Fishburn	T	Agrmt.,Rep. 1838
1983	Ford	T	Awd.,Min.
1984	Forest and Frith	T	Awd.,Min.
1985	Forest Quarter	T	Awd.,Min.
1986	Foxton cum Shotton	T	Agrmt.,Rep. 1838
1987	Framwellgate	T	Agrmt.,Min.,Rep. 1838
1988	Fulwell	T	Awd.,Min.
1989	Gainford	T	Min.,Rep. 1841
1990	Garmondsway Moor	EP	Awd.,Min.

Durham contd.

No.	Place	Type	Details
1991	Gateshead	P	Min.,Rep. 1838
1992	Gateshead Fell	P	Agrmt.,Rep. 1840
1993	St Giles, Durham	P	Awd.,Min.
1994	Greatham	T	Agrmt.,Min.,Rep. 1839
1995	Greencroft	T	Agrmt.,Min.,Rep. 1839
1996	Grindon	P	Min.
1997	Grindon	T	Awd.,Min.
1998	Hamsterley	T	Awd.,Min.
1999	Hall Garth	D	Awd.,Min.
2000	Heighington	T	Min.,Rep. 1838
2001	Helmington Row	T	Agrmt.,Rep. 1838
2002	Harraton	T	Awd.,Min.
2003	Hart	T	Agrmt.,Rep. 1839
2004	Hartburn	T	Agrmt.,Min.,Rep. 1839
2005	Hartlepool	T	Agrmt.,Awd.,Min.,Rep. 1840
2006	Harton	T	Agrmt.,Rep. 1838
2007	Headlam	T	Agrmt.,Min.,Rep. 1840
2008	Healey Field	T	Min.,Rep. 1842
2009	Heaton	T	Awd.,Min.
2010	Hedley Hope	T	Agrmt.,Min.,Rep. 1839
2011	Hedworth	T	Awd.,Min.
2012	Henknowle and Coppycrooks	D	Agrmt.,Rep. 1839
2013	Herrington, East and Middle	T	Awd.,Min.
2014	Herrington West	T	Awd.,Min.
2015	Heseldon	T	Agrmt.,Min.,Rep. 1838
2016	Hett	T	Agrmt.,Min.,Rep. 1838
2017	Hetton le Hole	T	Rep. 1838
2018	Heworth	D	Min.
2019	Hilton	T	Agrmt.,Min.,Rep. 1838
2020	Holmside	D	Awd.,Min.,Rep. 1842
2021	Holmside	T	Awd.,Min.
2022	Holy Island	P	Awd.,Min.
2023	Horden	M	N.t.p.,Min.
2024	Horncliffe	T	Agrmt.,Min.,Rep. 1840
2025	Horncliff Loanend	T	Agrmt.,Min.,Rep. 1839
2026	Houghton le Side	T	Agrmt.,Min.,Rep. 1840
2027	Houghton le Skerne	T	Min.,Rep. 1838
2028	Houghton le Spring	T	Min.,Rep. 1841
2029	Hunstonworth	T	N.t.p.,Min.
2030	Hunwick and Helmington	T	Awd.,Min.
2031	Hurworth	T	Agrmt.,Min.,Rep. 1838
2032	Hutton Henry	T	Agrmt.,Min.,Rep. 1837
2033	Hylton	T	Awd.,Min.
2034	Ingleton	T	Agrmt.,Min.,Rep. 1838
2035	Iveston	T	Agrmt.,Awd.,Min.,Rep. 1840
2036	Jarrow	T	Awd.,Min.
2037	Kelloe	T	Agrmt.,Rep. 1839
2038	Killerby	T	Agrmt.,Min.,Rep. 1838
2039	Kimblesworth	EP	Awd.,Min.
2040	Kyloe	T	Agrmt.,Min.,Rep. 1843
2041	Kyo	T	Awd.,Min.
2042	Lambton	T	Awd.,Min.
2043	Lamesley	C	Awd.,Min.
2044	Lanchester	T	Awd.,Min.
2045	Langley	T	Awd.,Min.
2046	Langleydale and Shotton	T	Agrmt.,Min.,Rep. 1839
2047	Langton	T	Agrmt.,Min.,Rep. 1838
2048	Lumley Great and Little	T	Agrmt.,Rep. 1840
2049	Morden	T	Agrmt.,Min.,Rep. 1838
2050	Longridge	T	Agrmt.,Rep. 1841
2051	Lynesack and Softley	T	Awd.,Min.
2052	Magdalen Close	EP	Awd.,Min.
2053	Mainsforth	T	Min.,Rep. 1844
2054	Marwood	T	Min.,Rep. 1841
2055	Merrington	T	Agrmt.,Min.,Rep. 1839
2056	Middlestone	T	Awd.,Min.
2057	Middleton in Teesdale	T	Awd.,Min.
2058	Middleton St George	P	Agrmt.,Min.,Rep. 1838
2059	Medomsley	T	Min.,Rep. 1841
2060	Netherton	T	Rep. 1838
2061	Midridge	T	Awd.,Min.
2062	Midridge Grange	T	Awd.,Min.
2063	Monk Heseldon	T	Agrmt.,Min.,Rep. 1837
2064	Monkhouse	EP	N.t.p.,Min.
2065	Monkton	T	Agrmt.,Min.,Rep. 1838
2066	Monk Wearmouth	T	Min.,Rep. 1839
2067	Monk Wearmouth Shore	T	Awd.,Min.
2068	Moorhouse	T	Awd.,Min.
2069	Moorsley	T	Min.,Rep. 1838
2070	Morton	T	Rep. 1840
2071	Morton Grange	T	Awd.,Min.
2072	Morton Palmes	T	Rep. 1838
2073	Muggleswick	PC	Awd.,Min.
2074	Murton	T	Agrmt.,Min.,Rep. 1839
2075	Nesbit	T	Agrmt.,Min.,Rep. 1839
2076	Nesham	T	Agrmt.,Min.,Rep. 1838
2077	Newbiggin	T	Min.,Rep. 1839
2078	Newbiggin	T	Awd.,Min.
2079	Newbottle	T	Min.,Rep. 1838
2080	Newfield	T	Agrmt.,Min.,Rep. 1839
2081	Newlandside Quarter	T	Awd.,Min.
2082	Newton Long	P	Agrmt.,Min.,Rep. 1837
2083	Newton Bewley	T	Agrmt.,Min.,Rep. 1838
2084	Newton Cap	T	Awd.,Min.
2085	Norham	T	Agrmt.,Min.,Rep. 1839
2086	Norham Mains	T	Min.,Rep. 1839
2087	Norton	P	Agrmt.,Awd.,Min.,Rep. 1841
2088	Offerton	T	Awd.,Min.
2089	Ord	T	Agrmt.,Awd.,Min.,Rep. 1843
2090	Ouston	T	Awd.,Min.
2091	Old Park	T	Awd.,Min.
2092	Painshaw	T	Awd.,Min.
2093	Park Quarter	T	Awd.,Min.
2094	Pelton	T	Awd.,Min.
2095	Piersbridge	T	Agrmt.,Rep. 1838
2096	Pittington	D	Min.,Rep. 1840
2097	Plawsworth	T	Awd.,Min.
2098	Pollards Lands	T	Min.,Rep. 1838
2099	Preston	T	Min.,Rep. 1838
2100	Preston le Skerne	T	Agrmt.,Min.,Rep. 1839
2101	Quarrington	T	Agrmt.,Rep. 1838
2102	Raby and Keverstone	T	Agrmt.,Min.,Rep. 1838
2103	Rainton East	T	Min.,Rep. 1838
2104	Rainton West	T	Agrmt.,Min.,Rep. 1839
2105	Redmarshall	T	Min.,Rep. 1838
2106	Redworth	T	Awd.,Min.
2107	Ross	T	Min.,Rep. 1840
2108	Ryhope	T	Agrmt.,Min.,Rep. 1839
2109	Ryton	T	Agrmt.,Min.,Rep. 1839
2110	Ryton Woodside	T	Rep. 1838
2111	Sadberge	H	Awd.,Min.
2112	Satley	T	Agrmt.,Rep. 1838
2113	School Aycliffe	T	Agrmt.,Rep. 1838
2114	Scremerston	P	Agrmt.,Min.,Rep. 1840
2115	Seaham	T	Agrmt.,Min.,Rep. 1839
2116	Seaton Carew	T	Agrmt.,Rep. 1838
2117	Sedgefield	T	Agrmt.,Min.,Rep. 1838
2118	Shadforth	T	Agrmt.,Min.,Rep. 1838
2119	Sheraton and Hulam	EP	Awd.,Min.
2120	Sherburn House	T	Min.,Rep. 1838
2121	Sherburn	T	N.t.p.,Min.
2122	Shields South	T	Agrmt.,Rep. 1840
2123	Shildon	T	Agrmt.,Min.,Rep. 1838
2124	Shincliffe	T	Min.,Rep. 1841
2125	Shoreswood	T	Min.,Rep. 1838
2126	Silksworth	T	Rep. 1838
2127	Sleekburn East	T	Rep. 1838
2128	Sleekburn West	T	Agrmt.,Rep. 1838
2129	Snotterton	T	Agrmt.,Rep. 1839
2130	Sockburn	T	Min.,Rep. 1839
2131	Southwick	T	Agrmt.,Min.,Rep. 1843
2132	Spittle	T	Agrmt.,Min.,Rep. 1838
2133	Staindrop	T	Agrmt.,Min.,Rep. 1841
2134	Stainton and Streatlam	T	Agrmt.,Min.,Rep. 1838
2135	Stainton le Street	T	Min.,Rep. 1839
2136	Stainton Little	T	Awd.,Min.
2137	Stanhope Quarter	T	Min.,Rep. 1838
2138	Stella	T	Agrmt.,Min.,Rep. 1839
2139	Stillington	T	Awd.,Min.
2140	Stockton	T	Agrmt.,Min.,Rep. 1838
2141	Stranton	T	Agrmt.,Min.,Rep. 1838
2142	Stockley	T	Agrmt.,Min.,Rep. 1838
2143	Summerhouse	P	N.t.p.,Min.
2144	Sunderland	T	Agrmt.,Rep. 1839
2145	Sunderland Bridge	T	N.t.p.,Min.
2146	Thickley East	D	Awd.,Min.
2147	Tanfield	T	Agrmt.,Rep. 1839
2148	Thrislington	T	Min.,Rep. 1843
2149	Thornley	T	Min.,Rep. 1840
2150	Thorp	T	Agrmt.,Min.,Rep. 1837
2151	Thorpe Bulmer	T	Agrmt.,Rep. 1839
2152	Throston	T	Agrmt.,Min.,Rep. 1839
2153	Tilmouth	P	Agrmt.,Min.,Rep. 1839
2154	Trimdon	T	Agrmt.,Min.,Rep. 1838
2155	Tudhoe	T	Min.,Rep. 1838
2156	Tunstall	T	Awd.,Min.
2157	Tweedmouth	T	Agrmt.,Min.,Rep. 1839
2158	Twisel	H	Agrmt.,Min.,Rep. 1839
2159	Unthank	T	Agrmt.,Awd.,Min.,Rep. 1839
2160	Urpeth	T	Awd.,Min.
2161	Usworth Great	T	Agrmt.,Min.,Rep. 1838
2162	Wackerfield	T	Agrmt.,Min.,Rep. 1840
2163	Waldridge	T	Agrmt.,Min.,Rep. 1838
2164	Walworth	T	Awd.,Min.
2165	Warden Law	T	Agrmt.,Min.,Rep. 1843
2166	Washington	T	Agrmt.,Min.,Rep. 1839
2167	Westerton	T	Min.,Rep. 1838
2168	Westoe	T	Agrmt.,Awd.,Min.,Rep. 1842
2169	Westwick	T	Min.,Rep. 1838
2170	Whessoe	P	Min.,Rep. 1839
2171	Whitburn	P	Min.,Rep. 1838
2172	Whickham	T	Agrmt.,Min.,Rep. 1839
2173	Whitton	EP	Awd.,Min.
2174	Whitwell House	T	Awd.,Min.,Rep. 1843
2175	Whitworth	T	Agrmt.,Awd.,Min.,Rep. 1840
2176	Whorlton	T	Min.,Rep. 1838
2177	Willington	T	N.t.p.,Min.
2178	Windlestone	T	Agrmt.,Min.,Rep. 1839
2179	Wingate	T	Agrmt.,Min.,Rep. 1837
2180	Winlaton	T	Agrmt.,Min.,Rep. 1840
2181	Winstone	T	Agrmt.,Min.,Rep. 1838
2182	Witton Gilbert	T	Agrmt.,Min.,Rep. 1838

Durham contd.

2183	Witton le Wear	T	Awd.,Min.
2184	Wolsingham	P	Agrmt.,Min.,Rep. 1838
2185	Wolviston	T	Agrmt.,Min.,Rep. 1838
2186	Woodham	T	Min.,Rep. 1838

Essex

2187	Abberton	P	Min.,Rep. 1838
2188	Abbotts Roothing	P	Awd.,Min.
2189	Aldham	P	Awd.,Min.
2190	Alphamstone	P	Min.,Rep. 1839
2191	Alresford	P	Min.,Rep. 1842
2192	Althorne	P	Min.,Rep. 1838
2193	Ardleigh	P	Awd.,Min.
2194	Arkesden	P	N.t.p.,Min.
2195	Ashdon	P	Awd.,Min.
2196	Asheldham	P	Min.,Rep. 1838
2197	Ashen	P	Min.,Rep. 1838
2198	Ashingdon	P	Min.,Rep. 1838
2199	Aveley	P	Min.,Rep. 1838
2200	Aythorpe Roding	P	Awd.,Min.
2201	Bardfield Great	P	Min.,Rep. 1841
2202	Baddow Great	P	Agrmt.,Min.,Rep. 1838
2203	Ballingdon	H	Awd.,Min.
2204	Barking	P	Awd.,Min.
2205	Barling	P	Min.,Rep. 1838
2206	Basildon	P	Agrmt.,Min.,Rep. 1837
2207	Baddow Little	P	Min.,Rep. 1839
2208	Barnston	P	Min.,Rep. 1838
2209	Beauchamp Roothing	P	Min.,Rep. 1840
2210	Beaumont	P	Min.,Rep. 1838
2211	Belchamp North End	EP	N.t.p.
2212	Belchamp Otten	P	Agrmt.,Min.,Rep. 1839
2213	Bardfield Little	P	Min.,Rep. 1839
2214	Bardfield Saling	P	Awd.,Min.
2215	Belchamp St Paul	P	Min.,Rep. 1840
2216	Belchamp Walter	P	Awd.,Min.
2217	Bemfleet North	P	Awd.,Min.
2218	Bemfleet South	P	Awd.,Min.
2219	Bentley Great	P	Min.,Rep. 1840
2220	Bentley Little	P	Min.,Rep. 1839
2221	Berden	P	Rep. 1838
2222	Berechurch	P	Min.
2223	Bergholt West	P	Agrmt.,Min.,Rep. 1842
2224	Berners Roothing	P	Min.,Rep. 1839
2225	Birch Great and Little	P	Min.,Rep. 1841
2226	Birchanger	P	Min.,Rep. 1839
2227	Birdbrook	P	Min.,Rep. 1839
2228	Blackmore	P	Awd.,Min.
2229	Bocking	P	Min.,Rep. 1838
2230	Bobbingworth	P	Agrmt.,Min.,Rep. 1837
2231	Boreham	P	Min.,Rep. 1838
2232	Borley	P	Min.,Rep. 1838
2233	Bowers Gifford	P	Awd.,Min.
2234	Boxtead	P	Min.,Rep. 1838
2235	Bradfield	P	Agrmt.,Min.,Rep. 1839
2236	Bradwell next Coggeshall	P	Min.,Rep. 1840
2237	Bradwell by the Sea	P	Min.,Rep. 1836
2238	Braintree	P	Awd.,Min.
2239	Braxted Great	P	Min.,Rep. 1838
2240	Braxted Little	P	Rep. 1840
2241	Brightlingsea	P	Min.,Rep. 1838
2242	Bromley Great	P	Awd.,Min.
2243	Broomfield	P	Awd.,Min.
2244	Broxtead	P	Awd.,Min.,Rep. 1839
2245	Bromley Little	P	Min.,Rep. 1839
2246	Bulmer	P	Awd.,Min.
2247	Bulphan	P	Agrmt.,Min.,Rep. 1837
2248	Bumpstead Helion	P	Agrmt.,Min.,Rep. 1839
2249	Bures Hamlet	P	Agrmt.,Min.,Rep. 1838
2250	Bures Mount	P	Min.,Rep. 1838
2251	Burnham	P	Awd.,Min.
2252	Burstead Great	P	Min.,Rep. 1839
2253	Burstead Little	P	Min.,Rep. 1837
2254	Buttsbury	P	Min.,Rep. 1838
2255	Canvey Island	P	Min.,Rep. 1839
2256	Canewdon	P	Awd.,Min.
2257	Canfield Great	P	Awd.,Min.
2258	Canfield Little	P	Min.,Rep. 1842
2259	Chadwell	P	Min.,Rep. 1839
2260	Chapel	P	Min.,Rep. 1841
2261	Chelmsford	P	Min.,Rep. 1840
2262	Chesterford Great	P	N.t.p.,Min.
2263	Chesterford Little	P	N.t.p.,Min.
2264	Chich St Osyth	P	Min.,Rep. 1838
2265	Chickney	P	Min.,Rep. 1838
2266	Chignal Great	P	Awd.,Min.
2267	Chignal Little	P	Awd.,Min.
2268	Chigwell	P	Min.,Rep. 1838
2269	Childerditch	P	Min.,Rep. 1839
2270	Chingford	P	Min.,Rep. 1838
2271	Chrishall Great	P	N.t.p.,Min.
2272	Chrishall Little	P	N.t.p.,Min.
2273	Chrishall	P	N.t.p.,Min.
2274	Clacton Little	P	Min.,Rep. 1840
2275	Clacton Great	P	Min.,Rep. 1841
2276	Clavering	P	Min.,Rep. 1839
2277	Coggeshall Little	P	Awd.,Min.
2278	Colchester All Saints	P	Min.,Rep. 1838
2279	Colchester St Botolph	P	Min.,Rep. 1838
2280	Colchester St Giles	P	Min.,Rep. 1838
2281	Colchester St Leonard	P	Awd.,Min.
2282	Colchester St James	P	Awd.,Min.
2283	Colchester St Mary	P	N.t.p.,Min.
2284	Colchester St Mary	P	Min.,Rep. 1845
2285	Colchester St Michael	P	Min.,Rep. 1842
2286	Colchester St Nicholas	P	Awd.,Min.
2287	Colchester St Peter	P	Awd.,Min.
2288	Colchester St Runwald	P	N.t.p.,Min.
2289	Colchester Holy Trinity	P	Min.,Rep. 1845
2290	Colne Earls	P	Min.,Rep. 1838
2291	Coggeshall Great	P	Awd.,Min.
2292	Colne Engaine	P	Min.,Rep. 1838
2293	Colne Wakes	P	Min.,Rep. 1839
2294	Colne White	P	Min.,Rep. 1838
2295	Copford	P	Min.,Rep. 1839
2296	Corringham	P	Min.,Rep. 1839
2297	Cranham	P	Min.,Rep. 1839
2298	Creeksea	P	Min.,Rep. 1844
2299	Cressing	P	Min.,Rep. 1838
2300	Dagenham	P	Min.,Rep. 1841
2301	Danbury	P	Min.,Rep. 1839
2302	Debden	P	Agrmt.,Awd.,Min.,Rep. 1838
2303	Dedham	P	Min.
2304	Dengie	P	Min.,Rep. 1838
2305	Doddinghurst	P	Awd.,Min.
2306	Donyland East	P	Min.,Rep. 1840
2307	Dovercourt	P	Awd.,Min.
2308	Downham	P	Agrmt.,Awd.,Min.,Rep. 1839
2309	Dunmow Great	P	Min.,Rep. 1836
2310	Dunmow Little	P	Min.,Rep. 1839
2311	Colchester St Martin	P	Awd.,Min.
2312	Easter Good	P	Agrmt.,Min.,Rep. 1839
2313	Easter High	P	Awd.,Min.
2314	Easthorpe	P	Min.,Rep. 1840
2315	Easton Great	P	Min.,Rep. 1839
2316	Easton Little	P	Agrmt.,Min.,Rep. 1838
2317	Eastwood	P	Awd.,Min.
2318	Elmdon	P	N.t.p.,Min.
2319	Elmstead	P	Awd.,Min.
2320	Elsenham	P	Min.,Rep. 1839
2321	Epping	P	Min.,Rep. 1838
2322	Farnham	P	Min.,Rep. 1839
2323	Faulkbourn	P	Min.,Rep. 1838
2324	Feering	P	Min.,Rep. 1840
2325	Felstead	P	Awd.,Min.
2326	Finchingfield	P	Agrmt.,Min.,Rep. 1838
2327	Dunton	P	Min.,Rep. 1837
2328	Fingeringhoe	P	Awd.,Min.
2329	Fobbing	P	Awd.,Min.
2330	Fordham	P	Rep. 1837
2331	Foxearth	P	Min.,Rep. 1839
2332	Foulness Island	D	Awd.,Min.
2333	Frating	P	Min.,Rep. 1841
2334	Fairsted	P	Min.,Rep. 1837
2335	Fambridge South	P	Agrmt.,Min.,Rep. 1837
2336	Fambridge North	P	Min.,Rep. 1840
2337	Frinton	P	Min.,Rep. 1839
2338	Fryerning	P	Min.,Rep. 1842
2339	Fyfield	P	Min.,Rep. 1840
2340	Gestingthorpe	P	Min.,Rep. 1838
2341	Goldhanger	P	Min.,Rep. 1839
2342	Gosfield	P	Rep. 1841
2343	Greenstead	P	Min.,Rep. 1839
2344	Grinstead	P	Agrmt.,Min.,Rep. 1838
2345	Hadleigh	P	Awd.,Min.
2346	Hadstock	P	N.t.p.,Min.
2347	Hainault Forest	D	Awd.,Min.
2348	Halstead	P	Min.,Rep. 1838
2349	Hallingbury Great	P	Rep. 1838
2350	Hallingbury Little	P	Min.,Rep. 1838
2351	Ham West	P	Awd.,Min.
2352	Ham East	P	Min.,Rep. 1838
2353	Ham West	P	Min.
2354	Hanningfield East	P	Min.,Rep. 1840
2355	Hanningfield South	P	Agrmt.,Min.,Rep. 1837
2356	Hanningfield West	P	Awd.,Min.
2357	Harlow	P	Awd.,Min.
2358	Harwich St Nicholas	P	Min.,Rep. 1842
2359	Hatfield Broad Oak	P	Min.,Rep. 1838
2360	Hatfield Peverel	P	Min.,Rep. 1839
2361	Havengore Island	D	N.t.p.,Min.
2362	Havering	P	Awd.,Min.
2363	Hawkwell	P	Agrmt.,Min.,Rep. 1838
2364	Hazeleigh	P	Awd.,Min.
2365	Hedingham Castle	P	Awd.,Min.
2366	Hedingham Sible	P	Min.,Rep. 1839
2367	Hempstead	P	Min.,Rep. 1842
2368	Henny Great	P	Min.,Rep. 1840
2369	Henny Little	P	Min.,Rep. 1839
2370	Heybridge	P	Awd.,Min.

Essex contd.

2371	Henham	P	Min.,Rep. 1839
2372	Heydon	P	Min.,Rep. 1838
2373	Hockley	P	Awd.,Min.
2374	Holland Great	P	Rep. 1838
2375	Holland Little	P	Min.,Rep. 1839
2376	Holyfield Upshire	H	Min.,Rep. 1840
2377	Horkesley Great	P	Min.,Rep. 1839
2378	Horkesley Little	P	Awd.,Min.
2379	Hornchurch	P	Awd.,Min.
2380	Horndon East	P	Awd.,Min.
2381	Horndon West	P	N.t.p.,Min.
2382	Horndon on the Hill	P	Min.,Rep. 1840
2383	Hutton	P	Min.,Rep. 1838
2384	Ilford Little	P	Min.,Rep. 1838
2385	Ingatestone	P	Min.,Rep. 1837
2386	Ingrave	P	Min.,Rep. 1839
2387	Inworth	P	Min.,Rep. 1838
2388	Kelvedon	P	Agrmt.,Min.,Rep. 1837
2389	Kelvedon Hatch	P	Agrmt.,Min.
2390	Kirby le Soken	P	Awd.,Min.
2391	Laindon	P	Agrmt.,Min.,Rep. 1837
2392	Laindon Hills	P	Awd.,Min.
2393	Langford	P	Min.,Rep. 1837
2394	Langham	P	Min.,Rep. 1838
2395	Langley	P	Rep. 1838
2396	Lamarsh	P	Min.,Rep. 1839
2397	Lambourne	P	Min.,Rep. 1841
2398	Langenhoe	P	Min.,Rep. 1838
2399	Latchingdon	P	Min.,Rep. 1839
2400	Latton	P	Min.,Rep. 1838
2401	Laver High	P	Awd.,Min.
2402	Laver Little	P	Awd.,Min.
2403	Laver Magdalen	P	Awd.,Min.
2404	Lawford	P	Min.,Rep. 1839
2405	Layer Breton	P	Awd.,Min.
2406	Layer de la Hay	P	Min.,Rep. 1838
2407	Layer Marney	P	Min.,Rep. 1838
2408	Lee Chapel	EP	Awd.,Min.
2409	Great Leigh	P	Min.,Rep. 1838
2410	Leigh	P	Awd.,Min.
2411	Little Leighs	P	Min.,Rep. 1838
2412	Lexden	P	Min.,Rep. 1838
2413	Leyton	P	Agrmt.,Min.,Rep. 1839
2414	Lindsell	P	Awd.,Min.
2415	Liston	P	Agrmt.,Min.,Rep. 1839
2416	Littlebury	P	N.t.p.,Min.
2417	Loughton	P	Awd.,Min.
2418	Maldon All Saints	P	Awd.,Min.
2419	Maldon St Mary	P	Awd.,Min.
2420	Maldon St Peter	P	Min.,Rep. 1839
2421	Manningtree	P	N.t.p.,Min.
2422	Manuden	P	Min.,Rep. 1838
2423	Maplestead Great	P	Min.,Rep. 1840
2424	Mayland	P	Agrmt.,Min.,Rep. 1837
2425	Matching	P	Min.,Rep. 1840
2426	Maplestead Little	P	Min.,Rep. 1839
2427	Margaretting	P	Agrmt.,Min.,Rep. 1837
2428	Marks Hall	P	Min.,Rep. 1839
2429	Mashbury	P	Awd.,Min.
2430	Mersea West	P	Min.,Rep. 1839
2431	Messing	P	Min.,Rep. 1839
2432	Mersea East	P	Agrmt.,Min.,Rep. 1837
2433	Middleton	P	Min.
2434	Mistley	P	Min.,Rep. 1841
2435	Moreton	P	Min.,Rep. 1838
2436	Mountnessing	P	Min.,Rep. 1838
2437	Mucking	P	Awd.,Min.
2438	Munden	P	Awd.,Min.
2439	Navestock	P	Min.,Rep. 1838
2440	Nazeing	P	Awd.,Min.
2441	Netteswell	P	Agrmt.,Min.,Rep. 1837
2442	Nevenden	P	Min.,Rep. 1839
2443	Newland St Lawrence	P	Agrmt.,Min.,Rep. 1837
2444	Newport	P	Min.,Rep. 1839
2445	Norton Cold	P	Min.,Rep. 1839
2446	Norton Mandeville	P	Min.,Rep. 1847
2447	Northweald Bassett	P	Min.,Rep. 1838
2448	Notley Black	P	Agrmt.,Min.,Rep. 1837
2449	Notley White	P	Min.,Rep. 1839
2450	Oakley Great	P	Min.,Rep. 1841
2451	Oakley Little	P	Awd.,Min.
2452	Ockendon North	P	Agrmt.,Min.,Rep. 1838
2453	Ockendon South	P	Awd.,Min.
2454	Ongar Chipping	P	Min.,Rep. 1838
2455	Ongar High	P	Awd.,Min.
2456	Orsett	P	Min.,Rep. 1839
2457	Orsett	H	Awd.,Min.
2458	Ovington	P	Min.,Rep. 1838
2459	Paglesham	P	Min.,Rep. 1838
2460	Panfield	P	Rep. 1838
2461	Parndon Great	P	Awd.,Min.
2462	Parndon Little	P	Awd.,Min.
2463	Pattiswick	P	Min.,Rep. 1841
2464	Pebmarsh	P	Min.,Rep. 1838
2465	Peldon	P	Min.,Rep. 1839
2466	Pentlow	P	Rep. 1838
2467	Pitsea	P	Awd.,Min.
2468	Pleshy	P	Awd.,Min.
2469	Prittlewell	P	Awd.,Min.
2470	Purleigh	P	Awd.,Min.
2471	Quendon	P	Min.,Rep. 1838
2472	Radwinter	P	Min.,Rep. 1838
2473	Rainham	P	Min.,Rep. 1838
2474	Ramsden Crays	P	Min.,Rep. 1845
2475	Ramsden Bellhouse	P	Min.,Rep. 1839
2476	Ramsey	P	Awd.,Min.
2477	Rawreth	P	Min.,Rep. 1838
2478	Rayleigh	P	Awd.,Min.
2479	Rayne	P	Agrmt.,Min.,Rep. 1837
2480	Rettendon	P	Min.,Rep. 1838
2481	Rickling	P	Min.,Rep. 1838
2482	Ridgewell	P	Min.,Rep. 1839
2483	Rivenhall	P	Rep. 1838
2484	Rochford	P	Min.,Rep. 1838
2485	Romford	P	Min.
2486	Roothing High	P	Min.,Rep. 1838
2487	Roothing Leaden	P	Awd.,Min.
2488	Roothing Margaret	P	Min.,Rep. 1844
2489	Roothing White and Morrell	P	Min.,Rep. 1838
2490	Roxwell	P	Min.,Rep. 1839
2491	Roydon	P	Min.,Rep. 1841
2492	Runwell	P	Min.,Rep. 1845
2493	Saffron Walden	P	Min.,Rep. 1841
2494	Saling Great	P	Agrmt.,Min.,Rep. 1839
2495	Salcott	P	Rep. 1840
2496	Sampford Great	P	Min.,Rep. 1842
2497	Sampford New	P	Min.,Rep. 1839
2498	Sandon	P	Min.,Rep. 1839
2499	Sewardstone	H	Awd.,Min.
2500	Shalford	P	Awd.,Min.
2501	Sheering	P	Min.,Rep. 1840
2502	Shelley	P	Agrmt.,Min.,Rep. 1837
2503	Shellow Bowells	P	Min.,Rep. 1837
2504	Shenfield	P	Min.,Rep. 1838
2505	Shoebury North	P	Min.,Rep. 1838
2506	Shoebury South	P	Min.,Rep. 1838
2507	Southchurch	P	Min.,Rep. 1838
2508	Southminster	P	Min.,Rep. 1842
2509	Springfield	P	Rep. 1839
2510	Stambourne	P	Min.,Rep. 1842
2511	Stambridge Great	P	Min.,Rep. 1840
2512	Stambridge Little	P	Agrmt.,Min.,Rep. 1837
2513	Stanford le Hope	P	Awd.,Min.
2514	Shopland	P	Rep. 1839
2515	Snoreham	P	Min.,Rep. 1840
2516	Stanford Rivers	P	Min.,Rep. 1837
2517	Stapleford Abbotts	P	Awd.,Min.
2518	Stanstead Mount Fitchett	P	Min.,Rep. 1842
2519	Stanway	P	Min.,Rep. 1839
2520	Stapleford Tawney	P	Agrmt.,Min.,Rep. 1837
2521	Stebbing	P	Min.,Rep. 1838
2522	Steeple	P	Awd.,Min.
2523	Steeple Bumpstead	P	Awd.,Min.
2524	Stifford	P	Min.,Rep. 1837
2525	Stisted	P	Rep. 1839
2526	Stock	P	Min.,Rep. 1841
2527	Stondon Massey	P	Awd.,Min.
2528	Stowe Maries	P	Min.,Rep. 1839
2529	Streethall	P	Awd.,Min.
2530	Sturmer	P	Min.,Rep. 1839
2531	Sutton	P	Min.,Rep. 1838
2532	Takeley	P	Min.,Rep. 1839
2533	Tendring	P	Awd.,Min.,Rep. 1840
2534	Terling	P	Min.,Rep. 1841
2535	Tey Great	P	Min.,Rep. 1838
2536	Tey Little	P	Min.,Rep. 1840
2537	Tey Marks	P	Min.,Rep. 1841
2538	Thaxted	P	Awd.,Min.
2539	Theydon Mount	P	Agrmt.,Min.,Rep. 1837
2540	Thorington	P	Awd.,Min.
2541	Thorpe le Soken	P	Awd.,Min.
2542	Thoydon Bois	P	Awd.,Min.
2543	Theydon Gernon	P	Rep. 1837
2544	Thundersley	P	Min.,Rep. 1838
2545	Thurrock Grays	P	Min.,Rep. 1841
2546	Thurrock Little	P	Awd.,Min.
2547	Thurrock West	P	Min.,Rep. 1837
2548	Tilbury juxta Clare	P	Awd.,Min.,Rep. 1838
2549	Tilbury East	P	Min.,Rep. 1838
2550	Tilbury West	P	Min.,Rep. 1838
2551	Tillingham	P	Min.,Rep. 1837
2552	Tilty	P	N.t.p.,Min.
2553	Tolleshunt Darcy	P	Min.,Rep. 1839
2554	Tolleshunt Major	P	Awd.,Min.
2555	Tolleshunt Knights	P	Min.,Rep. 1838
2556	Toppesfield	P	Min.,Rep. 1839
2557	Totham Great	P	Min.,Rep. 1842
2558	Totham Little	P	Min.,Rep. 1839
2559	Tollesbury	P	Awd.,Min.
2560	Twinstead	P	Awd.,Min.
2561	Ugley	P	Agrmt.,Min.,Rep. 1838
2562	Ulting	P	Awd.,Min.,Rep. 1837

Essex contd.

2563	Upminster	P	Min.,Rep. 1842
2564	Vange	P	Min.,Rep. 1839
2565	Virley	P	Min.,Rep. 1839
2566	Wakering Great	P	Min.,Rep. 1838
2567	Wakering Little	P	Min.,Rep. 1841
2568	Waltham Great	P	Agrmt.,Min.,Rep. 1839
2569	Waltham Little	P	Agrmt.,Min.,Rep. 1837
2570	Walthamstow	P	Awd.,Min.,Rep. 1841
2571	Walton le Soken	P	Min.,Rep. 1839
2572	Warley Great	P	Agrmt.,Min.,Rep. 1837
2573	Wanstead	P	Min.,Rep. 1840
2574	Warley Little	P	Min.,Rep. 1837
2575	Weald South	D	Min.,Rep. 1839
2576	Weald South	P	Min.,Rep. 1837
2577	Weeley	P	Min.,Rep. 1840
2578	Wendens Ambo	P	N.t.p.,Min.
2579	Wenden Lofts	P	N.t.p.,Min.
2580	Wennington	P	Agrmt.,Min.,Rep. 1839
2581	Wethersfield	P	Awd.,Min.,Rep. 1842
2582	Wickham Bishops	P	Min.,Rep. 1840
2583	Wicken Bonant	P	Awd.,Min.
2584	Wimbish cum Thunderley	P	Min.,Rep. 1839
2585	Wickham St Pauls	P	Min.,Rep. 1837
2586	Wickford	P	Min.,Rep. 1839
2587	Widdington	P	Min.,Rep. 1838
2588	Widford	P	Min.,Rep. 1838
2589	Wigborough Great	P	Agrmt.,Awd.,Min.,Rep. 1842
2590	Wigborough Little	P	Min.,Rep. 1838
2591	Willingale Doe	P	Min.,Rep. 1837
2592	Willingale Spain	P	Agrmt.,Min.,Rep. 1837
2593	Witham	P	Agrmt.,Min.,Rep. 1839
2594	Wivenhoe	P	Min.,Rep. 1838
2595	Wix	P	Min.,Rep. 1843
2596	Woodford	P	Min.,Rep. 1838
2597	Woodham Ferris	P	Min.,Rep. 1839
2598	Woodham Mortimer	P	Min.,Rep. 1838
2599	Woodham Walter	P	Awd.,Min.
2600	Wormingford	P	Min.,Rep. 1838
2601	Wrabness	P	Min.,Rep. 1840
2602	Writtle	P	Min.,Rep. 1839
2603	Yeldham Great	P	Min.,Rep. 1840
2604	Yeldham Little	P	Min.,Rep. 1840

Gloucestershire

2605	Abinghall	P	Rep. 1838
2606	Ablington	I	Rep. 1840
2607	Acton Turville	P	Rep. 1839
2608	Adlestrop	P	N.t.p.
2609	Alderley	P	Min.,Rep. 1838
2610	Alderton	P	N.t.p.
2611	Aldsworth	P	N.t.p.
2612	Alveston	P	Awd.,Min.
2613	Alvington	P	N.t.p.,Min.
2614	Ampney St Peter	P	Awd.,Min.
2615	Arle,Arlestone	I	N.t.p.,Min.
2616	Arlingham	P	N.t.p.,Min.
2617	Arlington,Winson	H	Awd.,Min.
2618	Ashchurch	P	Awd.,Min.
2619	Ashelworth	P	N.t.p.,Min.
2620	Ashton Cold	P	Awd.,Min.
2621	Ashton Cold	P	N.t.p.
2622	Aston Subedge	P	N.t.p.
2623	Aston Underhill	H	Awd.,Min.
2624	Awre	P	Agrmt.,Min.,Rep. 1840
2625	Avening	P	Rep. 1838
2626	Almondsbury	P	Min.,Rep. 1838
2627	Badgeworth,Shurdington	P	Rep. 1838
2628	Badminton Great	P	N.t.p.
2629	Bagendon	P	Min.,Rep. 1838
2630	Banks Fee	H	Min.,Rep. 1842
2631	Barnsley	P	Rep. 1841
2632	Barnwood	P	Rep. 1838
2633	Barrington Great	P	Rep. 1841
2634	Barrington Little	P	N.t.p.,Min.
2635	Batsford	P	Agrmt.,Rep. 1839
2636	Baunton	P	Awd.,Min.
2637	Beckford	P	N.t.p.
2638	Berkeley	P	Min.,Rep. 1838
2639	Beverstone	P	N.t.p.
2640	Bibury	P	N.t.p.
2641	Bishops Cleeve	P	Min.
2642	Bisley	P	Min.,Rep. 1841
2643	Bitton	H	Min.
2644	Blaisdon	P	Min.
2645	Bleddington	P	N.t.p.
2646	Bourton on the Water	P	Min.
2647	Boxwell	P	Rep. 1838
2648	Briavels Common	EP	Awd.,Min.
2649	Briavels St	P	Rep. 1839
2650	Brimpsfield	P	Rep. 1837
2651	Bristol (15 Parishes)	P	N.t.p.,Min.
2652	Bristol Castle	EP	N.t.p.
2653	Bristol Christchurch	P	N.t.p.
2654	Bourton on Hill,Moreton	P	N.t.p.
2655	Broadwell	P	N.t.p.
2656	Brockworth	P	Awd.,Min.
2657	Brockthorp	P	Awd.,Min.
2658	Bromsberrow	P	Agrmt.,Rep. 1837
2659	Buckland	P	N.t.p.
2660	Bulley	P	Rep. 1838
2661	Cam	P	Min.,Rep. 1839
2662	Campden	P	Awd.,Min.
2663	Castlett	H	Awd.,Min.
2664	Cerney North	P	Min.
2665	Cerney South	P	N.t.p.,Min.
2666	Charfield	P	Min.,Rep. 1839
2667	Charingworth	H	Awd.,Min.
2668	Charlton	D	Rep. 1840
2669	Charlton Abbotts	P	Min.
2670	Charlton Kings	P	Awd.,Min.
2671	Cherington	P	N.t.p.,Min.
2672	Childwickham	P	N.t.p.
2673	Chipping Sodbury	P	Awd.,Min.
2674	Churcham	P	N.t.p.
2675	Churchdown	P	Agrmt.,Min.
2676	Cirencester	P	Rep. 1838
2677	Clifford Chambers	P	Awd.,Min.
2678	Clifton	P	Awd.,Min.
2679	Coaley	P	Agrmt.,Min.
2680	Coates	P	N.t.p.,Min.
2681	Colesbourne	P	Min.,Rep. 1839
2682	Compton Little	P	N.t.p.,Min.
2683	Coln St Denis	P	N.t.p.,Min.
2684	Condicote	P	Awd.,Min.
2685	Compton Abdale	P	Awd.,Min.
2686	Compton Greenfield	P	Rep. 1840
2687	Coln St Aldwin's	MR	N.t.p.,Min.
2688	Coln Rogers	P	Agrmt.,Rep. 1839
2689	Corse	P	N.t.p.,Min.
2690	Cowhoneyborn	MH	N.t.p.
2691	Cowley	P	Rep. 1838
2692	Cranham	P	Rep. 1838
2693	Cromhall	P	Rep. 1839
2694	Cubberley	P	Rep. 1838
2695	Daglinworth	P	Agrmt.,Rep. 1837
2696	Dean Forest	D	N.t.p.
2697	Deerhurst	P	N.t.p.,Min.
2698	Didbrooke	P	Awd.,Min.
2699	Didcote	H	Awd.,Min.
2700	Didmarton	P	Rep. 1838
2701	Dixton	H	Agrmt.,Rep. 1838
2702	Dodington	P	Rep. 1838
2703	Donnington	H	N.t.p.
2704	Dowdeswell	P	Min.,Rep. 1839
2705	Down Ampney	P	Awd.,Min.
2706	Downhatherley	P	Awd.,Min.
2707	Doynton	P	N.t.p.
2708	Driffield,Kempsford	P	N.t.p.
2709	Dumbleton	P	Agrmt.,Min.,Rep. 1843
2710	Duntisborne Abbot's	P	N.t.p.
2711	Duntisborne Rouse	P	N.t.p.
2712	Dursley	P	Awd.,Min.
2713	Dyrham cum Hinton	P	Awd.,Min.
2714	Dymock	P	Awd.,Min.
2715	Eastington	P	Min.,Rep. 1839
2716	Eastleech Martin	P	N.t.p.,Min.
2717	Eastington	I	N.t.p.,Min.
2718	Eastleech Turville	P	N.t.p.,Min.
2719	Ebrington,Hilcoat	TH	N.t.p.
2720	Edgeworth	P	Rep. 1839
2721	Elberton	P	Awd.,Min.
2722	Elkstone	P	Rep. 1841
2723	Elmore	P	Awd.,Min.
2724	Elmstone Hardwicke	P	Rep. 1838
2725	English Bicknor	P	Rep. 1838
2726	Eyford	P	N.t.p.
2727	Fairford	P	Awd.,Min.
2728	Farmcote	H	Awd.,Min.
2729	Filton	P	Rep. 1838
2730	Flaxley	P	N.t.p.,Min.
2731	Forthampton	P	N.t.p.,Min.
2732	Frampton on Severn	P	N.t.p.
2733	French Hay	P	Awd.,Min.
2734	Fretherne	P	Min.,Rep. 1838
2735	Frocester	P	Awd.,Min.
2736	St George	P	Awd.,Min.
2737	Gloucester	P	Awd.,Min.
2738	Gloucester St Mary	P	Min.
2739	Gotherington	H	N.t.p.
2740	Greet	H	N.t.p.,Min.
2741	Gretton	H	N.t.p.
2742	Guiting Power	P	N.t.p.,Min.
2743	Guiting Grange	H	Awd.,Min.
2744	Hailes	P	Min.
2745	Hampnett	P	Awd.,Min.
2746	Hardwick	P	Awd.,Min.
2747	Hanham	H	Min.
2748	Harescombe	P	Rep. 1839
2749	Haresfield	P	N.t.p.,Min.
2750	Harnhill	P	Rep. 1838

Gloucestershire contd.

2751	Hartpury	P	Awd.,Min.
2752	Haselton	P	N.t.p.
2753	Hasfield	P	N.t.p.
2754	Hatherop	P	N.t.p.
2755	Hawkesbury	P	Agrmt.,Awd.,Min.,Rep. 1840
2756	Hawling	P	Awd.,Min.
2757	Hempstead	P	Awd.,Min.
2758	Henbury	P	Min.
2759	Hewelsfield	P	Rep. 1839
2760	Highnam Over Linton	H	Awd.,Min.
2761	Hill	P	Rep. 1841
2762	Hinton on the Green	P	Awd.,Min.
2763	Holyrood Ampney	P	N.t.p.,Min.
2764	Horsley	P	Min.,Rep. 1840
2765	Horton	P	Rep. 1838
2766	Huntley	P	Rep. 1838
2767	Icomb	P	Awd.,Min.
2768	Ilmington	P	Awd.,Min.
2769	Iron Acton	P	Min.,Rep. 1838
2770	Kemmerton	P	N.t.p.,Min.
2771	Kempley	P	Min.,Rep. 1840
2772	Kingscote	P	Rep. 1838
2773	King Stanley	P	Min.,Rep. 1839
2774	Lancaut	P	Min.,Rep. 1839
2775	Lasborough	P	Awd.,Min.
2776	Lassington	P	Rep. 1839
2777	Lea	P	Awd.,Min.
2778	Leckhampton	P	N.t.p.,Min.
2779	Lechlade	P	Agrmt.,Rep. 1838
2780	Littleton upon Severn	P	Awd.,Min.
2781	Littleton West	P	Min.,Rep. 1840
2782	Littleworth	EP	N.t.p.
2783	Longborough	P	N.t.p.,Min.
2784	Longmarston	P	N.t.p.,Min.
2785	Longney	P	N.t.p.,Min.
2786	Lydney	P	Agrmt.,Min.,Rep. 1840
2787	Lye	P	N.t.p.,Min.
2788	Longhope	P	Min.,Rep. 1838
2789	Frampton Cotterell	P	Min.,Rep. 1840
2790	Horfield	P	Awd.,Min.
2791	Littleden	P	Agrmt.,Min.,Rep. 1839
2792	Lemington Lower	P	N.t.p.,Min.
2793	Dorsington	P	N.t.p.,Min.
2794	Maisemore	P	N.t.p.,Min.
2795	Mangersbury	H	N.t.p.,Min.
2796	Mangotsfield	P	Awd.,Min.
2797	Marshfield	P	Agrmt.,Min.
2798	Meysey Hampton	P	N.t.p.,Min.
2799	St Michael,Gloucester	P	Awd.,Min.
2800	Mickleton	P	Agrmt.,Min.
2801	Minety	P	Min.,Rep. 1838
2802	Minsterworth	P	Rep. 1839
2803	Minchinhampton,Rod	P	Min.,Rep. 1839
2804	Miserdine	P	Min.,Rep. 1838
2805	Mitcheldean	P	Min.
2806	Moreton Valence	P	Rep. 1840
2807	Moreton in the Marsh	P	N.t.p.,Min.
2808	Naunton	P	Agrmt.,Rep. 1840
2809	Newent	P	Min.,Rep. 1838
2810	Newington Bagpath	P	Min.,Rep. 1839
2811	Newland	P	Awd.,Min.
2812	Newnham	P	Min.,Rep. 1839
2813	Nibley North	P	Awd.,Min.
2814	North Hamlet	EP	N.t.p.
2815	Northleach	P	Awd.,Min.
2816	Northway,Newton	I	Awd.,Min.
2817	Norton	P	Rep. 1840
2818	Notgrove	P	N.t.p.,Min.
2819	Nympsfield	P	Min.,Rep. 1838
2820	Oddington	P	N.t.p.,Min.
2821	Oldbury on the Hill	P	Rep. 1838
2822	Oldland	H	Min.
2823	Olveston	P	Awd.,Min.
2824	Owlpen	P	Min.,Rep. 1838
2825	Oxenhall	P	Agrmt.,Min.,Rep. 1841
2826	Oxenton	P	N.t.p.,Min.
2827	Ozleworth	P	Min.,Rep. 1838
2828	Painswick	P	Min.
2829	Pebworth	P	N.t.p.,Min.
2830	Pauntley	P	Min.,Rep. 1839
2831	St Philip,Jacob	P	Awd.,Min.
2832	Pinnock,Hyde	P	Awd.,Min.
2833	Pitchcombe	P	Min.,Rep. 1838
2834	Prescott	EP	N.t.p.
2835	Prestbury	P	Min.,Rep. 1838
2836	Preston	P	Awd.,Min.
2837	Preston,Stratton	P	N.t.p.,Min.
2838	Preston upon Stour	P	Min.
2839	Prinknash Park	EP	N.t.p.
2840	Pucklechurch	P	Awd.,Min.
2841	Quedgley	P	Agrmt.,Min.,Rep. 1839
2842	Quenington	P	N.t.p.,Min.
2843	Quinton	P	Min.,Rep. 1839
2844	Randwick	P	Awd.,Min.
2845	Rangeworthy	C	Awd.,Min.
2846	Rendcomb	P	Agrmt.,Rep. 1837
2847	Rissington Little	P	Min.
2848	Rissington Great	P	N.t.p.,Min.
2849	Rissington Wick	P	Min.
2850	Rockhampton	P	Agrmt.,Min.,Rep. 1837
2851	Rodmarton,Coates	P	Awd.,Min.
2852	Rowell	EP	Awd.,Min.
2853	Ruardean	P	Awd.,Min.
2854	Rudford	P	Min.,Rep. 1837
2855	Saintbury	P	Awd.,Min.
2856	Salperton	P	N.t.p.,Min.
2857	Sandhurst	P	Agrmt.,Min.,Rep. 1838
2858	Saperton	P	Awd.,Min.
2859	Saul	P	Min.,Rep. 1838
2860	Sevenhampton	P	N.t.p.,Min.
2861	Sezincote	P	Awd.,Min.
2862	Shinnington	P	N.t.p.,Min.
2863	Shipton Moyne	P	Min.,Rep. 1838
2864	Shipton Sollars	P	N.t.p.,Min.
2865	Shireborne,Windrush	P	N.t.p.,Min.
2866	Chedworth	P	Rep. 1842
2867	Shirehampton	I	Min.,Rep. 1840
2868	Siddington	P	N.t.p.,Min.
2869	Siston	P	Rep. 1839
2870	Slaughter,Lower and Upper	P	N.t.p.,Min.
2871	Snowshill	P	Min.
2872	Snowshill(Staunton)	M	N.t.p.,Min.
2873	Sodbury Little	P	Min.,Rep. 1838
2874	Sodbury Old	P	Agrmt.,Min.,Rep. 1838
2875	Somerville Aston	P	Agrmt.,Rep. 1837
2876	South Hamlet	EP	N.t.p.
2877	Southrop	P	Awd.,Min.
2878	Standish	P	Awd.,Min.
2879	Stanley Pontlarge	P	N.t.p.,Min.
2880	Stanway	P	N.t.p.,Min.
2881	Stapleton	P	Agrmt.,Min.,Rep. 1842
2882	Staunton	P	Awd.,Min.
2883	Staunton	P	N.t.p.,Min.
2884	Stinchcombe	P	Agrmt.,Min.,Rep. 1839
2885	Stoke Orchard	H	Agrmt.,Min.,Rep. 1837
2886	Staverton	P	N.t.p.,Min.
2887	Stowell	P	N.t.p.,Min.
2888	Stoke Gifford	P	Awd.,Min.
2889	Stonehouse	P	Min.
2890	Stow on the Wold	P	N.t.p.,Min.
2891	Sudeley	P	Awd.,Min.
2892	Sutton	P	N.t.p.,Min.
2893	Swell Lower	P	N.t.p.,Min.
2894	Swell Over	P	N.t.p.,Min.
2895	Swindon	P	Min.,Rep. 1839
2896	Syde	P	Rep. 1838
2897	Taynton	P	Awd.,Min.
2898	Temple Guiting	P	N.t.p.,Min.
2899	Tetbury	P	Min.
2900	Tewkesbury	P	Awd.,Min.
2901	Thomarton	P	N.t.p.,Min.
2902	Thornbury	P	Min.,Rep. 1839
2903	Tibberton	P	Min.,Rep. 1838
2904	Tidenham	P	Awd.,Min.
2905	Toddington	P	Awd.,Min.
2906	Todenham	P	Agrmt.,Rep. 1840
2907	Tormarton	P	Min.,Rep. 1839
2908	Tortworth	P	Awd.,Min.
2909	Tredington	P	N.t.p.,Min.
2910	Twyning	P	Awd.,Min.
2911	Trinley	P	N.t.p.,Min.
2912	Tuffley	H	Min.,Rep. 1840
2913	Turkdean	P	N.t.p.,Min.
2914	Tytherington	P	Rep. 1838
2915	Uley	P	Min.,Rep. 1838
2916	Up Hatherley	EP	N.t.p.,Min.
2917	Tresham	M	N.t.p.,Min.
2918	Upleadon	P	Awd.,Min.
2919	Uchington	H	Awd.,Min.
2920	Upton St Leonards	P	Awd.,Min.
2921	Wapley	P	Agrmt.,Min.,Rep. 1839
2922	Westall Naunton	H	Awd.,Min.
2923	Woodchester	P	Min.,Rep. 1838
2924	Witcombe Great	P	Agrmt.,Rep. 1837
2925	Walton Cardiff	P	Awd.,Min.
2926	Washbourne Great	P	N.t.p.,Min.
2927	Welford	P	N.t.p.,Min.
2928	Westbury upon Severn	P	Agrmt.,Min.,Rep. 1839
2929	Westbury	T	Awd.,Min.
2930	Westerleigh	P	Awd.,Min.
2931	Weston Birt	P	Min.,Rep. 1839
2932	Weston on Avon	P	N.t.p.,Min.
2933	Weston sub Edge	P	Awd.,Min.
2934	Westcote	P	Awd.,Min.
2935	Whaddon	P	Min.
2936	Wheatenhurst	P	Agrmt.,Rep. 1837
2937	Whittington	P	Min.,Rep. 1838
2938	Wick,Abson	P	Awd.,Min.
2939	Wickwar	P	Min.
2940	Widford	P	Agrmt.,Rep. 1838
2941	Willersley	P	N.t.p.,Min.
2942	Winchcombe	P	N.t.p.,Min.

Gloucestershire contd.

2943	Windrush	P	N.t.p.,Min.
2944	Winstone	P	Rep. 1842
2945	Winterbourne	P	Awd.,Min.
2946	Withington	P	N.t.p.,Min.
2947	Woolastone	P	Min.,Rep. 1838
2948	Woolstone	P	Min.,Rep. 1838
2949	Wormington	P	N.t.p.,Min.
2950	Yanworth	P	Rep. 1838
2951	Wootton under Edge	P	Awd.,Min.
2952	Yate	P	Min.,Rep. 1838
2969	Bicknor Welsh	P	N.t.p.

Hampshire

8716	Petersfield	P	Agrmt.,Rep. 1841
8873	Abbotts Ann	P	Agrmt.,Rep. 1839
8874	Aldershott	P	Awd.,Min.
8875	Alresford New	P	Awd.,Min.
8876	Alresford Old	P	Awd.,Min.
8877	Alton	P	Agrmt.,Rep. 1839
8878	Alverstoke	P	Agrmt.,Rep. 1840
8879	Amport	P	Agrmt.,Rep. 1838
8880	Andover cum Foxcott	P	Awd.,Min.
8881	Andwell	EP	N.t.p.
8882	Appleshaw	P	Agrmt.,Rep. 1839
8884	Arreton	P	Awd.,Min.
8885	Ashe	P	Awd.,Min.
8886	Ashley	P	Agrmt.,Rep. 1840
8887	Ashmansworth	P	Awd.,Min.
8888	Avington	P	Agrmt.,Rep. 1838
8889	Baddesley North	P	N.t.p.
8890	Barton Stacey	P	Agrmt.,Rep. 1839
8891	Basing	P	Agrmt.,Rep. 1841
8892	Basingstoke	P	Agrmt.,Rep. 1840
8893	Baughurst	P	Agrmt.,Rep. 1838
8894	Beaulieu	P	N.t.p.
8895	Beaworth	P	Agrmt.,Rep. 1837
8896	Bedhampton	P	Rep. 1841
8897	Bentley	P	Min.
8898	Bentworth	P	Agrmt.,Rep. 1840
8899	Bighton	P	Agrmt.,Rep. 1838
8900	Binstead	P	Min.
8901	Binsted near Alton	P	Awd.,Min.
8902	Bishopstoke	P	Agrmt.,Rep. 1839
8903	Bishops Sutton	P	Awd.,Min.
8904	Bishops Waltham	P	Agrmt.,Rep. 1840
8905	Blendworth	P	Agrmt.,Rep. 1840
8906	Boldre	P	Awd.,Min.
8907	Bonchurch (Isle of Wight)	P	Agrmt.,Rep. 1842
8908	Botley	P	Agrmt.,Rep. 1838
8909	Bossington	P	Agrmt.,Rep. 1837
8910	Brading	P	Agrmt.,Rep. 1842
8911	Bradley	P	Rep. 1839
8912	Bramdean	P	Agrmt.,Rep. 1839
8913	Bramley	P	Agrmt.,Rep. 1838
8914	Bramshaw	P	Agrmt.,Rep. 1839
8915	Bramshott	P	Awd.,Min.
8916	Breamore	P	Awd.,Min.
8917	Brighstone (Isle of Wight)	P	Rep. 1838
8918	Brockenhurst	P	Awd.,Min.
8919	Brooke	P	Awd.,Min.
8920	Broughton	P	Agrmt.,Rep. 1837
8921	Brown Candover	P	Agrmt.,Rep. 1841
8922	Boarhunt	P	Agrmt.,Rep. 1840
8923	Buckholt	P	Rep. 1839
8924	Bullington	P	Agrmt.,Rep. 1840
8925	Bursledon	P	Agrmt.,Rep. 1839
8926	Burghclere	P	Agrmt.,Rep. 1837
8927	Buriton	P	Agrmt.,Rep. 1841
8928	Burley Lodge	EP	N.t.p.
8929	Burley Ville	EP	N.t.p.
8930	Calbourne	P	Agrmt.,Rep. 1838
8931	Calshot Castle	EP	N.t.p.
8932	Carisbrooke	P	Awd.,Min.
8933	Catherington	P	Agrmt.,Rep. 1841
8934	Chale	P	Min.
8935	Charlton	P	Agrmt.,Rep. 1840
8936	Chawton	P	Agrmt.,Rep. 1839
8937	Cheriton	P	Min.,Rep. 1837
8938	Chilbolton	P	Agrmt.,Rep. 1838
8939	Chilcomb	P	Agrmt.,Rep. 1838
8940	Chilton Candover	P	Agrmt.,Min.,Rep. 1841
8941	Chilworth	P	N.t.p.
8942	Charford North	P	N.t.p.,Min.
8943	Charford South	T	Awd.,Min.
8944	Christchurch	P	Agrmt.,Min.,Rep. 1838
8945	Church Oakley	P	Awd.,Min.
8946	Clanfield	P	Agrmt.,Rep. 1840
8947	Clatford Upper	P	Awd.,Min.
8948	Clatford Lower	P	N.t.p.
8949	Cliddesden	P	Agrmt.,Rep. 1842
8950	Colemore and Priorsdean	P	Awd.,Min.
8951	Colrey	EP	N.t.p.
8952	Combe	P	Awd.,Min.
8953	Compton	P	Awd.,Min.
8954	Corhampton	P	N.t.p.
8955	Crawley	P	Agrmt.,Min.
8956	Crondall	P	Awd.,Min.
8957	Crown Farm	EP	N.t.p.
8958	Crux Easton	P	Awd.,Min.
8959	Culverley	EP	N.t.p.
8960	Deane	P	Agrmt.,Rep. 1839
8961	Deane East	P	Agrmt.,Rep. 1839
8962	Dibden	P	Agrmt.,Rep. 1842
8963	Dockenfield	I	Min.
8964	Dogmersfield	P	Agrmt.,Rep. 1837
8965	Droxford	P	Agrmt.,Rep. 1840
8966	Dummer	P	Agrmt.,Rep. 1837
8967	Dunwood	EP	N.t.p.
8968	Durley	P	Agrmt.,Rep. 1839
8969	Eastmeon	P	Awd.,Min.
8970	Easton	P	Agrmt.,Rep. 1839
8971	Eastrop	P	Agrmt.,Rep. 1838
8972	Ecchinswell	P	Awd.,Min.
8973	Eldon Upper	P	Min.
8974	Eling	P	Awd.,Min.
8975	Ellingham	P	Awd.,Min.
8976	Elvetham	P	Agrmt.,Rep. 1839
8977	Empshott	P	Agrmt.,Rep. 1842
8978	Eversley	P	Agrmt.,Min.
8979	Ewhurst	P	Agrmt.,Rep. 1843
8980	Exbury	P	Agrmt.,Min.,Rep. 1838
8981	Exton	P	Agrmt.,Rep. 1839
8982	Faccombe	P	Awd.,Min.
8983	Fareham	P	Awd.,Min.
8984	Farleigh Wallop	P	Agrmt.,Rep. 1842
8985	Farley Chamberlayne	P	Agrmt.,Rep. 1838
8986	Farlington	P	Rep. 1839
8987	Farnborough	P	Agrmt.,Rep. 1839
8988	Farringdon	P	Agrmt.,Rep. 1839
8989	Fawley	P	Rep. 1838
8991	Fordingbridge	P	Agrmt.,Rep. 1839
8992	Freefolk	P	Min.
8993	Freshwater (Isle of Wight)	P	Agrmt.,Rep. 1837
8994	Froyle	P	Agrmt.,Rep. 1845
8995	Froxfield	P	Awd.,Min.
8996	Fyfield	P	Agrmt.,Rep. 1839
8997	Gatcombe	P	Awd.,Min.
8998	Godsfield	EP	N.t.p.
8999	Godshill	P	Awd.,Min.
9000	Godshill Wood	EP	N.t.p.
9001	Goodworth Clatford	P	Agrmt.,Rep. 1837
9002	Grateley	P	Agrmt.,Rep. 1837
9003	Greatham	P	Agrmt.,Rep. 1842
9004	Grewell	P	Awd.,Min.
9005	Hale	P	Agrmt.,Rep. 1840
9006	Hamble	P	Agrmt.,Rep. 1838
9007	Hambledon	P	Awd.,Min.
9008	Hannington	P	Agrmt.,Rep. 1839
9009	Harbridge	P	Agrmt.,Rep. 1840
9010	Hartley Mauditt	P	Rep. 1839
9011	Hartley Westpall	P	Rep. 1838
9012	Hartley Wintney	P	Awd.,Min.
9013	Havant	P	Agrmt.,Rep. 1838
9014	Hawkley	P	Awd.,Min.
9015	Hayling North	P	Awd.,Min.
9016	Hayling South	P	Min.
9017	Headbourne Worthy	P	Agrmt.,Min.
9018	Headley	P	Min.
9019	Heckfield	P	Agrmt.,Rep. 1839
9020	Helens St.(Isle of Wight)	P	Agrmt.,Rep. 1840
9021	Herriard	P	Rep. 1839
9022	Highclere	P	Agrmt.,Min.,Rep. 1837
9023	Hinton Ampner	P	Agrmt.,Rep. 1838
9024	Holybourne	P	Agrmt.,Rep. 1842
9025	Hordle	P	Agrmt.,Rep. 1843
9026	Houghton	P	Agrmt.,Rep. 1842
9027	Hound	P	Rep. 1838
9028	Hunton	P	Agrmt.,Rep. 1838
9029	Hursley	P	Agrmt.,Rep. 1839
9030	Hurstbourne Priors	P	Awd.,Min.
9031	Hurstbourne Tarrant	P	Rep. 1839
9032	Ibsley	P	Agrmt.,Rep. 1840
9033	Idsworth	P	Agrmt.,Rep. 1840
9034	Illsfield	P	Min.
9035	Ipersbridge	EP	N.t.p.
9036	Itchen Abbas	P	Agrmt.,Rep. 1838
9037	Itchen Stoke	P	Rep. 1838
9038	Kilmiston	P	Agrmt.,Rep. 1837
9039	Kimpton	P	Agrmt.,Rep. 1837
9040	Kingsclere	P	Agrmt.,Rep. 1841
9041	Kingsley	P	Awd.,Min.
9042	Kings Somborne	P	Agrmt.,Awd.,Min.
9043	Kingstone	P	Agrmt.,Min.,Rep. 1838
9044	Kingsworthy	P	Agrmt.,Rep. 1838
9045	Knights Enham	P	Agrmt.,Min.,Rep. 1838
9046	Lainstone	P	Min.
9047	Lasham	P	Agrmt.,Rep. 1838
9048	Lawrence St.	P	Min.
9049	Linford	EP	N.t.p.
9050	Laverstoke	P	Awd.,Min.

Hampshire contd.

9051	Leckford	P	Agrmt.,Rep. 1842
9052	Linwood	EP	N.t.p.
9053	Liss	P	Agrmt.,Rep. 1841
9054	Litchfield	P	Agrmt.,Rep. 1839
9055	Linkenholt	P	Agrmt.,Rep. 1838
9056	Littleton	P	Agrmt.,Rep. 1839
9057	Lockerley	P	Agrmt.,Rep. 1840
9058	Longparish	P	Awd.,Min.
9059	Longstock	P	Agrmt.,Rep. 1840
9060	Lymington	P	Awd.,Min.
9061	Lyndhurst	P	Agrmt.,Rep. 1838
9062	Mapplederwell	P	Agrmt.,Rep. 1839
9063	Martyr Worthy	P	Agrmt.,Rep. 1839
9064	Mary St. Bourne	P	Awd.,Min.
9065	Medstead	P	Awd.,Min.
9066	Meonstoke	P	Agrmt.,Rep. 1840
9067	Milbrook	P	Agrmt.,Rep. 1843
9068	Milford	P	Agrmt.,Rep. 1839
9069	Milland (Ville)	EP	Min.
9070	Milton	P	Awd.,Min.
9071	Minesteed	P	Agrmt.
9072	Mitchelmersh	P	Agrmt.,Rep. 1839
9073	Monk Sherborne	P	Rep. 1839
9074	Monxton	P	Agrmt.,Min.,Rep. 1838
9075	Morestead	P	Agrmt.,Rep. 1841
9076	Mottisfont	P	Agrmt.,Rep. 1839
9077	Mottistone (Isle of Wight)	P	Agrmt.,Rep. 1839
9078	Nateley Scures	P	Agrmt.,Rep. 1839
9079	Neatham	EP	N.t.p.
9080	Newchurch (Isle of Wight)	P	Awd.,Min.
9081	New Forest	EP	Min.
9082	Newnham	P	Agrmt.,Rep. 1840
9083	Newport (Isle of Wight)	P	N.t.p.
9084	Newton Valence	P	Agrmt.,Rep. 1843
9085	Newtown	P	Agrmt.,Rep. 1837
9086	Nicholas St	P	N.t.p.
9087	Niton	P	Agrmt.,Rep. 1838
9088	Northington	P	Agrmt.,Awd.,Min.,Rep. 1840
9089	Northwood	P	Awd.,Min.
9090	Nursling	P	Min.
9091	Nutley	P	Agrmt.,Rep. 1838
9092	Odiham	P	Awd.,Min.
9093	Ogdens	EP	N.t.p.
9094	Otterbourne	P	Agrmt.,Rep. 1840
9095	Overton	P	Awd.,Min.
9096	Ovington	P	Min.
9097	Owslebury	P	Awd.,Min.
9098	Pamber	P	Rep. 1838
9099	Park House	EP	N.t.p.
9100	Parkhurst Forest	D	N.t.p.
9101	Penton Mewsey	P	Agrmt.,Rep. 1837
9102	Picket Post,Picket Gate	EP	N.t.p.
9103	Popham	H	Awd.,Min.
9104	Portchester	P	Agrmt.,Rep. 1839
9105	Portsea	P	Agrmt.,Awd.,Min.,Rep. 1838
9106	Portsmouth	P	N.t.p.
9107	Preston Candover	P	Agrmt.,Rep. 1838
9108	Privett	P	Awd.,Min.
9109	Quarley	P	Awd.,Min.
9110	Ringwood	P	Awd.,Min.
9111	Ropley	P	Awd.,Min.
9112	Rockbourne	P	Agrmt.,Rep. 1839
9113	Romsey	P	Awd.,Min.
9114	Rotherwick	P	Agrmt.,Rep. 1841
9115	Rowner	P	Agrmt.,Rep. 1839
9116	Salterns Great	EP	N.t.p.
9117	Selborne	P	Awd.,Min.
9118	Shalden	P	Agrmt.,Rep. 1840
9119	Shanklin	P	Awd.,Min.
9120	Shalfleet	P	Awd.,Min.
9121	Sheet	I	Agrmt.,Rep. 1841
9122	Sherborne St John	P	Agrmt.,Rep. 1840
9123	Sherfield English	P	Rep. 1840
9124	Sherfield upon Loddon	P	Agrmt.,Rep. 1840
9125	Shipton Bellinger	P	Agrmt.,Min.,Rep. 1840
9126	Shobley	EP	N.t.p.
9127	Shorwell (Isle of Wight)	P	Agrmt.,Rep. 1843
9128	Sidmonton	P	Awd.,Min.
9129	Silchester	P	Agrmt.,Rep. 1839
9130	Soberton	P	Agrmt.,Rep. 1840
9131	Sopley	P	Agrmt.,Rep. 1839
9132	South (East Bere)	D	N.t.p.
9133	Southampton All Saints	P	Awd.,Min.
9134	Southampton Holy Rood	P	N.t.p.,Min.
9135	Southampton Holy Trinity	P	Min.
9136	Southampton St John	P	N.t.p.
9137	Southampton St Mary	P	Min.
9138	Southampton St Michael	P	N.t.p.,Min.
9139	Southampton St Paul	P	N.t.p.
9140	Southwick	P	Agrmt.,Rep. 1840
9141	Sparsholt	P	Agrmt.,Min.,Rep. 1842
9142	Steep	P	Rep. 1841
9143	Steventon	P	Agrmt.,Rep. 1839
9144	Stockbridge	P	Awd.,Min.
9145	Stoke Charity	P	Rep. 1837
9147	Stoneham North	P	Awd.,Min.
9148	Stoneham South	P	Awd.,Min.
9149	Stratfield Saye	P	Agrmt.,Min.,Rep. 1839
9150	Stratfield Turgis	P	Agrmt.,Rep. 1839
9151	Stratton East	P	N.t.p.
9152	Stratton West	P	N.t.p.
9153	Sutton Long	P	Awd.,Min.
9154	Swarraton	P	Agrmt.,Rep. 1839
9155	Tadley	P	Agrmt.,Rep. 1838
9156	Tangley	P	Agrmt.,Rep. 1837
9157	Tedworth South	P	Agrmt.,Rep. 1840
9158	Thorley (Isle of Wight)	P	Agrmt.,Awd.,Rep. 1843
9159	Thruxton	P	Agrmt.,Rep. 1839
9160	Tichborne	P	Agrmt.,Rep. 1839
9161	Timsbury	P	Min.
9162	Twyford	P	Awd.,Min.
9163	Tisted East	P	Agrmt.,Min.,Rep. 1840
9164	Tisted West	P	Agrmt.,Rep. 1844
9168	Titchfield	P	Agrmt.,Min.,Rep. 1837
9169	Titherley East	P	Awd.,Min.
9170	Tufton	P	Awd.,Min.
9171	Tunworth	P	Agrmt.,Rep. 1838
9172	Tytherly West	P	Agrmt.,Rep. 1837
9173	Up Eldon	P	Awd.,Min.
9174	Upham	P	Agrmt.,Min.,Rep. 1839
9175	Up Nately	P	Agrmt.,Rep. 1841
9176	Upton Gray	P	Agrmt.,Min.,Rep. 1839
9177	Ventnor	P	N.t.p.
9178	Vernham Dean	C	N.t.p.
9179	Wallop Over	P	Awd.,Min.
9180	Waltham North	P	Rep. 1839
9181	Wallop Nether	P	Min.
9182	Warblington	P	Agrmt.,Min.,Rep. 1838
9183	Warnborough South	P	Agrmt.,Rep. 1839
9184	Warnford	P	Agrmt.,Rep. 1839
9185	Waterloo Ville	EP	N.t.p.
9186	Week	P	Awd.,Min.
9187	Wellow East	P	Agrmt.,Rep. 1837
9188	Westmeon	P	Min.,Rep. 1839
9189	Weston Corbet	EP	N.t.p.
9190	Weston Patrick	P	Agrmt.,Rep. 1841
9191	Weyhill	P	Agrmt.,Rep. 1838
9192	Wherwell	P	Agrmt.,Rep. 1840
9193	Whippingham, Isle of Wight	P	Awd.,Min.
9194	Walkhampton	P	N.t.p.
9195	Whitechurch	P	Awd.,Min.
9196	Whitsbury	P	Awd.,Min.
9197	Whitwell	P	Awd.,Min.
9198	Wickham	P	Awd.,Min.
9199	Wickham Forest	EP	Min.
9200	Widley	P	Awd.,Min.
9201	Wield	P	Agrmt.,Rep. 1844
9202	Winchester St Bartholomew	P	Awd.,Min.
9203	Winchester St Clement	P	Min.
9204	Winchester St Faiths	P	Awd.,Min.
9205	Winchester St John Baptist	C	N.t.p.
9206	Winchester St Laurence	P	N.t.p.
9207	Winchester St Maurice	P	N.t.p.,Min.
9208	Winchester St Michael	P	N.t.p.
9209	Winchester St Peter	P	N.t.p.,Min.
9210	Winchester St Swithin	P	N.t.p.
9211	Winchfield	P	Awd.,Min.
9212	Winnall	P	Agrmt.,Min.
9213	Winslade and Kempshott	P	Agrmt.,Min.,Rep. 1838
9214	Wonston	P	Agrmt.,Rep. 1838
9215	Woodcote	P	N.t.p.,Min.
9216	Woodgreen	EP	N.t.p.
9217	Woodhay East	P	Min.,Rep. 1837
9218	Woodmancott	P	Agrmt.,Rep. 1839
9219	Woolverton	P	Agrmt.,Rep. 1839
9220	Wootton (Isle of Wight)	P	Awd.,Min.
9221	Wootton St. Lawrence	P	Min.
9222	Worldham East	P	Agrmt.,Rep. 1840
9223	Worldham West	P	Awd.,Min.
9224	Worting	P	Agrmt.,Min.,Rep. 1838
9225	Wymering	P	Min.,Rep. 1839
9226	Yarmouth (Isle of Wight)	P	Awd.,Min.
9227	Yateley	P	Awd.,Min.
9228	Yaverland (Isle of Wight)	P	Agrmt.,Rep. 1838
9714	Mitcheldever	P	Awd.,Min.
14807	Southampton St Lawrence	P	N.t.p.
14808	Winchester St John	P	N.t.p.

Herefordshire

2953	Abbey Dore	P	Agrmt.,Rep. 1839
2954	Aconbury	P	Awd.,Min.
2955	Allensmore	P	Agrmt.,Min.,Rep. 1840
2956	All Saints	P	Agrmt.,Min.,Rep. 1841
2957	Almeley	P	Agrmt.,Rep. 1839
2958	Amberley	T	Awd.,Min.
2959	Ashperton	P	Agrmt.,Min.,Rep. 1838
2960	Aston	P	Awd.,Min.
2961	Aston Ingham	P	Agrmt.,Rep. 1838
2962	Bosbury	P	Min.,Rep. 1839
2963	Aymestrey	P	Awd.,Min.

Herefordshire contd.

No.	Place		Details
2964	Avenbury	P	Agrmt.,Min.,Rep. 1840
2965	Aylton	P	Awd.,Min.
2966	Bacton	P	Agrmt.,Min.,Rep. 1839
2967	Ballingham	P	Agrmt.,Min.,Rep. 1842
2968	Bartestree	C	Agrmt.,Min.,Rep. 1839
2970	Blakemere	P	Awd.,Min.
2971	Little Birch	P	Awd.,Min.
2972	Much Birch	P	Awd.,Min.
2973	Birley	P	Awd.,Min.,Rep. 1837
2974	Bishops Frome	P	Awd.,Min.
2975	Bishopstone	P	Awd.,Min.
2976	Bodenham	P	N.t.p.,Min.
2977	Bolston	P	Agrmt.,Rep. 1840
2978	Brampton Abbotts	P	Rep. 1838
2979	Brampton Brian	P	Agrmt.,Min.,Rep. 1839
2980	Bredwardine	P	Agrmt.,Rep. 1841
2981	Breinton	P	Agrmt.,Rep. 1840
2982	Brilley	P	Min.,Rep. 1840
2983	Bridenbury	P	Agrmt.,Rep. 1839
2984	Bridge Sollers	P	Rep. 1842
2985	Bridstow	P	Rep. 1839
2986	Brinsop	P	Awd.,Min.
2987	Brobury	P	Awd.,Min.
2988	Brockhampton	P	Agrmt.,Rep. 1840
2989	Brockhampton	C	N.t.p.
2990	Bromyard Town	D	Awd.,Min.
2991	Bullingham Lower	T	N.t.p.
2992	Bullingham Upper	P	Awd.,Min.
2993	Burghill	P	Min.
2994	Burrington	P	Awd.
2995	Bwlch Trewyn	H	Min.,Rep. 1839
2996	Byford	P	Agrmt.,Rep. 1842
2997	Byton	P	Awd.,Min.
2998	Callow	P	Agrmt.,Rep. 1840
2999	Canon Frome	P	Min.,Rep. 1838
3000	Canon Pion	P	Agrmt.,Min.,Rep. 1841
3001	Castle Frome	P	Agrmt.,Rep. 1840
3002	Clehonger	P	Agrmt.,Min.,Rep. 1840
3003	Craswell	T	Awd.,Min.,Rep. 1841
3004	Credenhill	P	Agrmt.,Min.,Rep. 1842
3005	Croft	T	Agrmt.,Min.,Rep. 1842
3006	Cusop	P	Agrmt.,Rep. 1839
3007	Clifford	P	Min.,Rep. 1845
3008	Coddington	P	Agrmt.,Rep. 1838
3009	Collington	P	Agrmt.,Rep. 1838
3010	Colwall	P	Awd.,Min.
3011	Brimfield	P	Agrmt.,Min.,Rep. 1840
3012	Little Cowarne	P	Agrmt.,Rep. 1839
3013	Much Cowarne	P	Awd.,Min.
3014	Cradley	P	Agrmt.,Min.,Rep. 1838
3015	St Devereux	P	Agrmt.,Rep. 1838
3016	Little Dewchurch	P	Agrmt.,Rep. 1840
3017	Dewsall	P	Agrmt.,Rep. 1840
3018	Dilwyn	P	Min.,Rep. 1837
3019	Dinedor	P	N.t.p.
3020	Docklow	P	Agrmt.,Rep. 1840
3021	Donnington	P	Agrmt.,Rep. 1837
3022	Dormington	P	Agrmt.,Min.,Rep. 1842
3023	Dorstone	P	Agrmt.,Min.,Rep. 1840
3024	Downton	P	Min.
3025	Dulas	P	Rep. 1845
3026	Dunmore	EP	Min.
3027	Eardisland	P	Min.,Rep. 1842
3028	Eardisley	P	Agrmt.,Min.
3029	Eaton Bishop	P	Awd.,Min.
3030	Eastmor	P	Agrmt.,Rep. 1838
3031	Edwin Ralph	P	Awd.,Min.
3032	Elton	P	Awd.,Min.
3033	Evesbatch	P	Awd.,Min.
3034	Ewias Harold	P	Awd.,Min.
3035	Eye Morton,Ashton	T	Awd.,Min.
3036	Eyton	P	Agrmt.,Awd.,Min.,Rep. 1838
3037	Farlow	C	Agrmt.,Awd.,Rep. 1844
3038	Felton	P	Awd.,Min.
3039	Fordisbridge	D	Awd.,Min.
3040	Fownhope	P	Awd.,Min.
3041	Foy	P	Rep. 1838
3042	Fwddog	T	Agrmt.,Awd.,Min.,Rep. 1840
3043	Ganerew	P	Rep. 1842
3044	Garway	P	Min.,Rep. 1840
3045	Gooderich	P	Min.,Rep. 1837
3046	Grafton	T	Agrmt.,Awd.,Min.
3047	Grendon Bishop	P	Agrmt.,Rep. 1840
3048	Grendon Warren	EP	N.t.p.,Min.
3049	Hampton Bishop	T	Awd.,Min.
3050	Hampton New,Wafer	EP	N.t.p.
3051	Harewood	P	N.t.p.
3052	Hatfield	P	Awd.,Min.
3053	Haywood Forest	EP	N.t.p.
3054	Hentland	P	Agrmt.,Rep. 1840
3055	Hereford St John	P	Agrmt.,Rep. 1840
3056	Hereford Little	P	Awd.,Min.
3057	Hereford St Martin	P	Awd.,Min.
3058	Hereford St Nicholas	P	Min.,Rep. 1842
3059	Hereford St Owen	P	Agrmt.,Rep. 1845
3060	Hereford St Peter	P	Agrmt.,Min.
3061	Holme Lacy	P	Agrmt.,Min.,Rep. 1840
3062	Holmer	P	Agrmt.,Min.,Rep. 1840
3063	Hope under Dinmore	P	Awd.,Min.
3064	Hope Mansel	P	Agrmt.,Rep. 1839
3065	How Caple	P	Rep. 1839
3066	Humber	P	Awd.,Min.
3067	Huntington	P	Awd.,Min.
3068	Huntington(Holmer)	T	Agrmt.,Rep. 1840
3069	Kenderchurch	P	Awd.,Min.
3070	Kentchester	P	Awd.,Min.
3071	Kentchurch	P	Agrmt.,Min.,Rep. 1839
3072	Kilpeck	P	Min.
3073	Kimbolton	P	Min.,Rep. 1840
3074	Kings Caple	P	Agrmt.,Min.,Rep. 1838
3075	Kingsland	P	Agrmt.,Min.
3076	Kings Pyon	P	Agrmt.,Min.,Rep. 1838
3077	Kingstone	P	Agrmt.,Min.,Rep. 1840
3078	Kington	P	Awd.,Min.
3079	Kinnersley	P	Agrmt.,Min.,Rep. 1840
3080	Kinsham Upper	P	Awd.,Min.
3081	Knill	P	Awd.,Min.
3082	Laysters	P	Awd.,Min.
3083	Ledbury	P	Agrmt.,Min.,Rep. 1839
3084	Leinthall Starks	P	Awd.,Min.
3085	Leintwardine	P	Agrmt.,Min.
3086	Leominster	P	Awd.,Min.
3087	Upper Hide	T	Awd.,Min.
3088	Letton	P	Agrmt.,Min.,Rep. 1840
3089	Lingen	P	Awd.,Min.
3090	Linton	P	Agrmt.,Min.,Rep. 1839
3091	Linton(Bromyard)	T	Agrmt.,Rep. 1841
3092	Llancillow	P	Rep. 1841
3093	Llandinabo	P	Rep. 1842
3094	Llangarren	P	Agrmt.,Min.,Rep. 1840
3095	Llanrothal	P	Agrmt.,Min.,Rep. 1840
3096	Llanveynoe	T	Min.,Rep. 1841
3097	Llanwarne	P	Rep. 1841
3098	Longtown	T	Min.,Rep. 1841
3099	Lucton	P	Agrmt.,Min.,Rep. 1842
3100	Ludford	P	Awd.,Min.
3101	Lugwardine	P	Awd.,Min.
3102	Luston	T	Min.,Rep. 1841
3103	Lyonshall	P	Agrmt.,Min.,Rep. 1839
3104	Madley	P	Min.,Rep. 1842
3105	Mansel Gamage	P	Agrmt.,Min.,Rep. 1842
3106	Mansel Lacy	P	Min.,Rep. 1839
3107	Marcle Little	P	Min.,Rep. 1838
3108	Marden	P	Agrmt.,Min.,Rep. 1842
3109	Marcle Much	P	Min.,Rep. 1839
3110	Margarets St.	P	Awd.,Min.
3111	Marston	P	Agrmt.,Min.,Rep. 1839
3112	Michaelchurch Exley	P	Awd.,Min.
3113	Middleton on the Hill	P	Min.,Rep. 1840
3114	Moccas	P	Agrmt.,Min.,Rep. 1837
3115	Monkland	P	Agrmt.,Rep. 1840
3116	Monnington on Wye	P	Agrmt.,Min.,Rep. 1837
3117	Mordiford	P	Agrmt.,Min.,Rep. 1840
3118	Moreton upon Lugg	P	Awd.,Min.
3119	Morton Jeffries	P	Awd.,Min.
3120	Much Dewchurch	P	Awd.,Min.
3121	Munsley	P	Agrmt.,Rep. 1837
3122	Newton	T	Min.,Rep. 1841
3123	Welsh Newton	P	Awd.,Min.
3124	Newton	T	Agrmt.,Min.,Rep. 1838
3125	Norton	T	Agrmt.,Rep. 1838
3126	Norton Canon	P	Agrmt.,Rep. 1840
3127	Ocle Pitchard	P	Awd.,Min.
3129	Orleton	P	Agrmt.,Min.
3130	Orcop	P	Min.,Rep. 1842
3131	Parkhold	T	N.t.p.,Min.
3132	Pembridge	P	Awd.,Min.
3133	Pencombe	P	Agrmt.,Rep. 1837
3134	Pencoyd	P	Awd.,Min.
3135	Peterchurch	P	Min.
3136	Peterstow	P	Min.,Rep. 1840
3137	Pipe,Lyde	P	Agrmt.,Min.,Rep. 1838
3138	Pixley	P	Rep. 1838
3139	Preston on Wye	P	Awd.,Min.
3140	Preston Wynn	P	Agrmt.,Rep. 1839
3141	Pudleston	P	Awd.,Min.
3142	Putley	P	Min.,Rep. 1839
3143	Richards Castle	P	Rep. 1839
3144	Rochford	P	Awd.,Min.
3145	Ross	P	Min.,Rep. 1843
3146	Rowlstone	P	Awd.,Min.,Rep. 1841
3147	Sapey Upper	P	Agrmt.,Min.,Rep. 1838
3148	Saltmarsh	EP	N.t.p.
3149	Sarnesfield	P	Awd.,Min.
3150	Sellack	P	Agrmt.,Min.,Rep. 1840
3151	Shobdon	P	N.t.p.,Min.
3152	Sollars Hope	P	Agrmt.,Min.,Rep. 1839
3153	Stanage	R	Agrmt.,Awd.,Min.,Rep. 1839
3154	Stanford Bishop	P	Agrmt.,Rep. 1838
3155	Stanton upon Arrow	P	Min.,Rep. 1839
3156	Staunton on Wye	P	N.t.p.
3157	Stoke Bliss	P	Agrmt.,Min.,Rep. 1839

Herefordshire contd.

3158	Stoke Prior	P	Agrmt.,Min.,Rep. 1840
3159	Stretford	P	Agrmt.,Rep. 1838
3160	Stretton Grandsome	P	N.t.p.,Min.
3161	Stretton Sugwas	P	Agrmt.,Min.,Rep. 1839
3162	Sutton St Michael	P	Awd.,Min.
3163	Sutton St Nicholas	P	Awd.,Min.
3164	Tarrington	P	Agrmt.,Min.,Rep. 1839
3165	Tedstone Delamere	P	Agrmt.,Rep. 1841
3166	Tedstone Wafer	P	Agrmt.,Min.,Rep. 1837
3167	Stoke Edith	P	Agrmt.,Min.,Rep. 1839
3168	Stoke Lacy	P	Awd.,Min.
3169	Thornbury	P	Awd.,Min.
3170	Thruxton	P	Agrmt.,Min.,Rep. 1839
3171	Tibberton	P	Agrmt.,Min.,Rep. 1842
3172	Titley	P	Agrmt.,Min.,Rep. 1842
3173	Tretire,Michaelchurch	P	Agrmt.,Min.,Rep. 1839
3174	Treville	EP	Awd.
3175	Tupsley	T	Awd.,Min.
3176	Turnastone	P	Agrmt.,Min.,Rep. 1838
3177	Upton Bishop	P	Agrmt.,Min.,Rep. 1840
3178	Ullingswick	P	Agrmt.,Min.,Rep. 1838
3179	Vowchurch	P	Awd.,Min.
3180	Fenn,Fern	I	Agrmt.,Min.,Rep. 1840
3181	Wacton	P	Agrmt.,Min.
3182	Walford	P	Awd.,Min.
3183	Walterstone	P	Awd.,Min.
3184	Wellington	P	Min.,Rep. 1841
3185	Weobley	P	Min.,Rep. 1838
3186	Weonards St	P	Agrmt.,Rep. 1839
3187	Westhide	P	Agrmt.,Rep. 1839
3188	Weston Beggard	P	Agrmt.,Min.,Rep. 1839
3189	Weston upon Penyard	P	Agrmt.,Rep. 1838
3190	Whitbourn	P	Min.,Rep. 1839
3191	Whitchurch	P	Awd.,Min.
3192	Whitney	P	Agrmt.,Rep. 1839
3193	Wigmore	P	Min.,Rep. 1840
3194	Willersley	P	Agrmt.,Rep. 1840
3196	Winforton	P	Agrmt.,Min.,Rep. 1839
3197	Winslow	T	Agrmt.,Min.,Rep. 1838
3198	Wisterstone	C	N.t.p.
3199	Withington	P	Awd.,Min.
3200	Wolferlow	P	Agrmt.,Min.,Rep. 1839
3201	Woolhope	P	Awd.,Min.
3202	Wormbridge	P	Rep. 1839
3203	Wormesley	P	Awd.,Min.
3204	Yarkhill	P	Agrmt.,Min.,Rep. 1844
3205	Yarpole	P	Agrmt.,Min.,Rep. 1841
3206	Yatton	T	Agrmt.,Min.,Rep. 1839
3207	Yazor	P	Awd.,Min.

Hertfordshire

3195	Willian	P	Agrmt.,Min.,Rep. 1837
3208	Abbots Langley	P	Min.,Rep. 1840
3209	Albury	P	Awd.,Min.
3210	Albans Saint	P	Min.
3211	Aldbury	P	Awd.,Min.
3212	Anstey	P	N.t.p.,Min.
3213	Aldenham	P	Min.,Rep. 1840
3214	All Saints and St John	P	Awd.,Min.
3215	Amwell Great	P	Rep. 1839
3216	Andrew Saint	P	Agrmt.,Rep. 1838
3217	Ashwell	P	Awd.,Min.
3218	Aspeden	P	Agrmt.,Min.,Rep. 1840
3219	Aston	P	Agrmt.,Min.,Rep. 1839
3220	Ayott St Lawrence	P	Min.
3221	Ayott St Peter	P	Agrmt.,Rep. 1838
3222	Baldock	P	Awd.,Min.
3223	Barkway	P	Awd.,Min.
3224	Barnet East and High	P	Min.,Rep. 1839
3225	Barley	P	Rep. 1839
3226	Bayford	P	Agrmt.,Rep. 1837
3227	Bengeo	P	Agrmt.,Rep. 1841
3228	Bennington	P	Agrmt.,Min.,Rep. 1838
3229	Berkhamstead Little	P	Agrmt.,Min.,Rep. 1838
3230	Berkhamstead St Peter's	P	Agrmt.,Min.,Rep. 1839
3231	Bishops Stortford	P	Rep. 1839
3232	Bovingdon	P	Agrmt.,Rep. 1838
3233	Bramfield	P	Agrmt.,Rep. 1838
3234	Braughing	P	N.t.p.
3235	Brent Pelham	P	Agrmt.,Min.,Rep. 1837
3236	Bushey	P	Rep. 1839
3237	Broadfield	P	N.t.p.,Min.
3238	Broxbourne	P	Min.,Rep. 1839
3239	Buckland	P	Min.,Rep. 1838
3240	Bygrave	P	Min.
3241	Caddington	P	N.t.p.,Min.
3242	Caldecott	P	Agrmt.,Rep. 1838
3243	Cheshunt	P	Awd.,Min.
3244	Clothall	P	Agrmt.,Rep. 1839
3245	Codicote	P	Rep. 1841
3246	Coleshill	H	Min.
3247	Cottered	P	N.t.p.,Min.
3248	Datchworth	P	Agrmt.,Min.,Rep. 1838
3249	Digswell	P	Awd.,Min.
3250	Eastwick	P	Min.
3251	Elstree	P	N.t.p.,Min.
3252	Essendon	P	Agrmt.,Rep. 1837
3253	Flansted	P	Min.
3254	Flaunden	H	Agrmt.,Rep. 1838
3255	Furneux Pelham	P	Agrmt.,Min.,Rep. 1837
3256	Gaddesden Great	P	Agrmt.,Min.,Rep. 1838
3257	Gaddesden Little	P	Agrmt.,Rep. 1839
3258	Gilston	P	Min.
3259	Gravely cum Chisfield	P	Agrmt.,Min.,Rep. 1838
3260	Hadham Little	P	Awd.,Min.
3261	Hadham Much	P	Rep. 1838
3262	Harpenden	P	Min.,Rep. 1837
3263	Hatfield Bishops	P	Agrmt.,Min.,Rep. 1838
3264	Hemel Hempstead	P	Agrmt.,Min.,Rep. 1842
3265	Hertingfordbury	P	Agrmt.,Min.,Rep. 1838
3266	Hexton	P	Rep. 1837
3267	Hinxworth	P	N.t.p.,Min.
3268	Hitchin	P	Awd.,Min.
3269	Hoddesdon	H	Min.,Rep. 1840
3270	Hormead Little	P	Min.,Rep. 1838
3271	Hormead Great	P	N.t.p.,Min.
3272	Hunsdon	P	Rep. 1837
3273	Ickleford	P	Awd.,Min.
3274	Ippolitts	P	N.t.p.,Min.
3275	Kelshall	P	N.t.p.
3276	Kensworth	P	N.t.p.,Min.
3277	Kimpton	P	Agrmt.,Rep. 1837
3278	King's Langley	P	Agrmt.,Min.,Rep. 1837
3279	King's Walden	P	N.t.p.,Min.
3280	Knebworth	P	Agrmt.,Rep. 1845
3281	Layston	P	Awd.,Min.
3282	Letchworth	P	Rep. 1838
3283	Lilley	P	Min.
3284	London Colney	H	Min.
3285	Margaret's Saint	P	Agrmt.,Min.
3286	Measden	P	Rep. 1838
3287	Michael Saint(St Albans)	P	Awd.,Min.
3288	Mimms North	P	Min.
3289	Munden Great	P	Agrmt.,Min.,Rep. 1841
3290	Munden Little	P	Agrmt.,Min.,Rep. 1840
3291	Newnham	P	Min.,Rep. 1842
3292	Northaw	P	Awd.,Min.
3293	Northchurch	P	Agrmt.,Min.,Rep. 1838
3294	Norton	P	N.t.p.,Min.
3295	Offley	P	Min.
3296	Paul's St. Walden	P	Awd.,Min.
3297	Peter St.(St Albans)	P	Agrmt.,Awd.,Min.
3298	Pirton	P	N.t.p.
3299	Puttenham	P	N.t.p.,Min.
3300	Radwell	P	Agrmt.,Min.
3301	Redbourn	P	Awd.,Min.
3302	Reed	P	N.t.p.,Min.
3303	Ridge	P	Agrmt.,Rep. 1839
3304	Royston	P	Awd.,Min.
3304	Royston	P	Awd.,Min.
3305	Rushden	P	Awd.,Min.
3306	Rickmansworth	P	Agrmt.,Min.,Rep. 1838
3307	Sacomb	P	Agrmt.,Rep. 1837
3308	Sandon	P	Awd.,Min.
3309	Sandridge	P	Awd.,Min.
3310	Sarratt	P	Rep. 1840
3311	Sawbridgeworth	P	Min.,Rep. 1838
3312	Sheephall	P	Awd.,Min.
3313	Stephen's St.(St Albans)	P	Min.
3314	Stevenage	P	Agrmt.,Rep. 1837
3315	Stocking Pelham	P	Agrmt.,Rep. 1837
3316	Shenley	P	Awd.,Min.
3317	Standon	P	Rep. 1838
3318	Stanstead Abbott	P	Min.,Rep. 1839
3319	Stapleford	P	Agrmt.,Rep. 1837
3320	Studham	P	Min.,Rep. 1839
3321	Tewin	P	Agrmt.,Rep. 1838
3322	Therfield	P	Min.,Rep. 1840
3323	Tring	P	N.t.p.,Min.
3324	Thorley	P	Rep. 1845
3325	Throcking	P	Agrmt.,Rep. 1841
3326	Thundridge	P	Min.,Rep. 1845
3327	Totteridge	P	Agrmt.,Rep. 1840
3328	Wakeley	P	N.t.p.
3329	Walkern	P	Agrmt.,Rep. 1838
3330	Wallington	P	Agrmt.,Min.,Rep. 1839
3331	Watford	P	Awd.,Min.
3332	Watton	P	Agrmt.,Min.,Rep. 1837
3333	Ware	P	Min.,Rep. 1845
3334	Welwyn	P	Agrmt.,Rep. 1837
3335	Westmill	P	Agrmt.,Min.,Rep. 1838
3336	Wormley	P	Rep. 1838
3337	Wigginton	P	Agrmt.,Rep. 1842
3338	Widford	P	Min.,Rep. 1838
3339	Widdial	P	Min.,Rep. 1841
3340	Whethampstead	P	Agrmt.,Min.,Rep. 1839
3341	Weston	P	Awd.,Min.
3342	Wymondley Great	P	N.t.p.,Min.
3343	Yardley	P	Min.,Rep. 1839

Huntingdonshire

3128	Old Hurst	P	N.t.p.,Min.
3344	Abbotsley	P	N.t.p.,Min.
3345	Abbots Ripton	P	Awd.,Min.,Rep. 1840
3346	Alconbury	P	Awd.,Min.
3347	Alwalton	P	N.t.p.
3348	Barham	P	Min.
3349	Bedford Level	D	Min.
3350	Bevill's Wood	EP	Awd.,Min.
3351	Bluntisham cum Earith	P	Awd.,Min.
3352	Brampton	P	Agrmt.,Min.,Rep. 1839
3353	Brington	P	N.t.p.,Min.
3354	Broughton	P	N.t.p.,Min.
3355	Buckden	P	N.t.p.,Min.
3356	Buckworth	P	Agrmt.,Rep. 1838
3357	Bury	P	Min.
3358	Bythorn	P	Rep. 1839
3359	Caldecot	P	Awd.,Min.
3360	Caldecote(Eynesbury)	H	Agrmt.,Rep. 1838
3361	Catworth Great	P	N.t.p.,Min.
3362	Catworth Little	P	Min.
3363	Chesterton	P	Agrmt.,Rep. 1837
3364	Colne	P	Agrmt.,Rep. 1838
3365	Connington	P	Agrmt.,Rep. 1838
3366	Coppingford	P	Awd.,Min.
3367	Covington	P	Awd.,Min.
3368	Denton	P	N.t.p.,Min.
3369	Diddington	P	N.t.p.,Min.
3370	Drewell's	D	Awd.,Min.
3371	Easton	P	Rep. 1842
3372	Ellington	P	N.t.p.,Min.
3373	Elton	P	N.t.p.,Min.
3374	Eynesbury	P	N.t.p.,Min.
3375	Farcett	P	Awd.,Min.
3376	Fen Stanton	P	N.t.p.,Min.
3377	Fletton	P	Awd.,Min.
3378	Folksworth	P	Min.
3379	Gidding Great	P	Min.,Rep. 1842
3380	Gidding Little	P	Awd.,Min.
3381	Godmanchester	P	N.t.p.,Min.
3382	Graffham	P	N.t.p.,Min.
3383	Gransden Great	P	Awd.,Min.
3384	Haddon	P	Agrmt.,Rep. 1837
3385	Hail Weston	P	Agrmt.,Min.,Rep. 1837
3386	Hamerton	P	Agrmt.,Rep. 1838
3409	Glatton	P	N.t.p.,Min.
3410	Hartford	P	N.t.p.,Min.
3411	Hemingford Abbotts	P	N.t.p.,Min.
3412	Hemingford Grey	P	N.t.p.,Min.
3413	Hilton	P	Agrmt.,Rep. 1839
3414	Hinchinbrook	EP	N.t.p.,Min.
3415	Houghton cum Witton	P	N.t.p.,Min.
3416	Holme	P	Awd.,Min.
3417	Holywell cum Needingworth	P	Awd.,Min.
3418	Huntingdon All Saints	P	Awd.,Min.
3419	Huntingdon St Benedict	P	Awd.,Min.
3420	Huntingdon St John	P	Awd.,Min.
3421	Huntingdon St Mary	P	Awd.,Min.
3422	Ives St.	P	N.t.p.,Min.
3423	Keyston	P	Agrmt.,Min.,Rep. 1838
3424	Kimbolton	P	Awd.,Min.
3425	Kings Delph,Eight Roods	D	Agrmt.,Awd.,Min.
3426	Kings Ripton	P	Awd.,Min.
3427	Lancelynsbury	H	Rep. 1841
3428	Leighton Bromswold	P	Awd.,Min.
3431	Lutton	P	Min.,Rep. 1839
3432	Midloe	EP	N.t.p.,Min.
3433	Molesworth	P	Agrmt.,Rep. 1838
3434	Morborne	P	Agrmt.,Rep. 1838
3435	Neots Saint	P	N.t.p.,Min.
3436	Offord Cluny	P	N.t.p.,Min.
3437	Offord Darcey	P	Rep. 1840
3438	Orton Cherry	P	N.t.p.
3439	Overton Longville	P	N.t.p.
3440	Paxton Great	P	N.t.p.,Min.
3441	Paxton Little	P	Awd.,Min.
3442	Pidley cum Fenton	P	Min.,Rep. 1839
3443	Ramsey	P	Agrmt.,Min.,Rep. 1838
3444	Raveley Great	P	N.t.p.,Min.
3445	Raveley Little	P	Awd.,Min.
3446	Washingley	P	Awd.,Min.
3447	Water Newton	P	Agrmt.,Rep. 1837
3448	Sapley	R	N.t.p.,Min.
3449	Sawtrey All Saints	P	N.t.p.
3450	Sawtrey St Andrew	P	N.t.p.,Min.
3451	Sawtrey St Judith	EP	N.t.p.,Min.
3452	Somersham	P	Agrmt.,Rep. 1838
3453	Southoe	P	N.t.p.,Min.
3454	Spaldwick	P	N.t.p.,Min.
3455	Stanground	P	N.t.p.,Min.
3456	Staughton Great	P	N.t.p.,Min.
3457	Steeple Gidding	P	Rep. 1838
3458	Stibbington	P	N.t.p.,Min.
3459	Stilton	P	N.t.p.,Min.
3460	Stow	P	Rep. 1839
3461	Swineshead	P	N.t.p.,Min.
3462	Stukeley Little	P	N.t.p.,Min.
3463	Stukeley Great	P	N.t.p.,Min.
3464	Tetworth	P	Rep. 1839
3465	Upwood	P	Agrmt.,Awd.,Min.
3466	Upton	P	N.t.p.,Min.
3467	Warboys	P	Agrmt.,Rep. 1838
3468	Waresley	P	Rep. 1841
3469	Weald	H	Agrmt.,Rep. 1838
3470	Weston Old	P	Awd.,Min.
3471	Winwick	P	N.t.p.,Min.
3472	Wistow	P	N.t.p.,Min.
3473	Woodhurst	P	N.t.p.,Min.
3474	Woodstone	P	N.t.p.,Min.
3475	Woolley	P	Awd.,Min.
3476	Woodwalton	P	Min.,Rep. 1839
3477	Yaxley	P	Awd.,Min.
3478	Yelling	P	N.t.p.,Min.

Kent

3387	Cray North	P	Rep. 1837
3388	St Pauls Cray	P	Rep. 1839
3389	Crundale	P	Rep. 1838
3390	Cudham	P	Min.
3391	Coxtone	P	Rep. 1842
3392	Darenth	P	Awd.,Min.
3393	Dartford	P	Rep. 1840
3394	Davington	P	N.t.p.
3395	Deal	P	Awd.,Min.
3396	Debtling	P	Rep. 1838
3397	Denton near Dover	P	Awd.,Min.
3398	Denton near Gravesend	P	Awd.,Min.
3399	Deptford	P	Awd.,Min.
3400	Ditton	P	Min.
3401	Doddington	P	Awd.,Min.
3402	Dover Castle Etc	EP	N.t.p.
3403	Dover St James	P	Awd.,Min.
3404	Down	P	Min.
3405	Dunkirk	EP	N.t.p.
3406	Dymchurch	P	Rep. 1841
3407	Eastbridge	P	Awd.,Min.
3408	Eastchurch	P	Min.
3479	Acol	P	Min.
3480	Acrise	P	Rep. 1839
3481	Addington	P	Min.
3482	Adisham	P	Rep. 1840
3483	Aldington	P	Min.
3484	Alkham	P	Rep. 1840
3485	Allhallows	P	Rep. 1840
3486	Allington	P	Min.
3487	Appledore	P	Min.
3488	Ash	P	Rep. 1839
3489	Ash next Wingham	P	Agrmt.
3490	Ashford	P	Agrmt.
3491	Ashurst	P	Rep. 1843
3492	Aylesford	P	Min.
3493	Badlesmere and Leveland	P	Rep. 1839
3494	Bapchild	P	Rep. 18 0
3494	Bapchild	P	Rep. 1839
3495	Barfreston	P	Min.
3496	Barham	P	Min.
3497	Barming East	P	Rep. 1839
3498	Barming West	EP	Min.
3499	Beakesbourne	P	Min.
3500	Bearsted	P	Min.
3501	Beckenham	P	Rep. 1838
3502	Benenden	P	Rep. 1839
3503	Bethersden	P	Rep. 1838
3504	Betshanger	P	Min.
3505	Bexley	P	Min.
3506	Bicknor	P	Min.
3507	Bidborough	P	Rep. 1838
3508	Biddenden	P	Min.
3509	Bilsington	P	Rep. 1840
3510	Birchington	P	Min.
3511	Bircholt	P	Min.
3512	Birling	P	N.t.p.
3513	Bishopsbourn	P	Rep. 1839
3514	Boughton Aluph	P	Rep. 1839
3515	Blackmanstone	P	Min.
3516	Bobbing	P	Rep. 1839
3517	Bonnington	P	Rep. 1840
3518	Borden	P	Rep. 1839
3519	Boughton under Blean	P	Min.
3520	Boughton Malherbe	P	Rep. 1838
3521	Boughton Monchelsea	P	Min.
3522	Brenzett	P	Min.
3523	Boxley	P	Min.
3524	Brabourne	P	Rep. 1839
3525	Brasted	P	Min.
3526	Bredhurst	P	Rep. 1838
3527	Bredgar	P	Rep. 1839
3528	Brenchley	P	Awd.,Min.
3529	Broomhill	P	Min.

Kent contd.

3530	Bridge and Patrixbourne	P	Rep. 1838
3531	Bromley	P	Rep. 1840
3532	Brooke	P	Rep. 1837
3533	Brookland	P	Min.
3534	Broomfield	P	Min.
3535	Buckland next Dover	P	Min.
3536	Buckland near Faversham	P	Min.
3537	Burmarsh	P	Min.
3538	Burham	P	Min.
3539	Canterbury All Saints Etc	P	N.t.p.
3540	Canterbury City Parishes	P	N.t.p.
3541	Canterbury Holy Cross	P	Min.
3542	Canterbury St Dunstan	P	Min.
3543	Canterbury St Mary Bredin	P	Min.
3544	Canterbury St Martin	P	Rep. 1839
3545	Canterbury St Mary N Gate	P	Min.
3547	Canterbury St Mildred	P	Min.
3548	Canterbury St Paul	P	Rep. 1843
3549	Canterbury St Peter	P	Awd.,Min.
3550	Capel	P	Min.
3551	Capel le Ferne	P	Rep. 1842
3552	Chalk	P	Rep. 1840
3553	Challock	P	Rep. 1841
3554	Charing	P	Rep. 1840
3555	Charlton next Dover	P	Min.
3556	Charlton	P	Rep. 1838
3557	Chart Great	P	Rep. 1839
3558	Chart Little	P	Awd.
3559	Chart Sutton	P	Min.
3560	Chartham	P	Rep. 1842
3561	Chatham	P	Min.
3562	Chelsfield	P	Rep. 1838
3563	Cheriton	P	Rep. 1839
3564	Chevening	P	N.t.p.
3565	Chiddingstone	P	Rep. 1838
3566	Chilham	P	Rep. 1840
3567	Chillenden	P	Awd.,Min.
3568	Cobham	P	Awd.,Min.
3569	Coldred	P	Awd.,Min.
3570	Cosmos St	P	Rep. 1839
3571	Cooling or Cowling	P	Rep. 1839
3572	Footscray	P	Rep. 1838
3573	Crayford	P	Rep. 1839
3574	St Mary Cray	P	Rep. 1843
3575	Chislehurst	P	Awd.,Min.
3576	Chislet	P	Min.
3577	Cliffe at Hoo	P	Min.
3578	Cliffe West	P	Rep. 1840
3579	Cowden	P	Rep. 1842
3580	Cranbrook	P	Rep. 1839
3581	Eastling	P	Rep. 1842
3582	Eastry	P	Rep. 1839
3583	Eastwell	P	Rep. 1838
3584	Eboney	P	Min.
3585	Edenbridge	P	Min.
3586	Egerton	P	Min.
3587	Elham	P	Min.
3588	Elmley	P	Rep. 1843
3589	Elmstead	P	Rep. 1841
3590	Elmstone	P	Rep. 1841
3591	Eltham	P	Rep. 1841
3592	Erith	P	Min.
3593	Ewell	P	Awd.,Min.
3594	Eynesford	P	Min.
3595	Eythorne	P	Min.
3596	Fairfield	P	Awd.,Min.
3597	Farleigh East	P	Min.
3598	Farleigh West	P	Awd.,Min.
3599	Farnborough	P	Rep. 1840
3600	Farningham	P	Awd.,Min.
3601	Faversham	P	Min.
3602	Fawkham	P	Rep. 1838
3604	Folkestone	L	Awd.,Min.
3605	Fordwich	P	Awd.,Min.
3606	Frindsbury	P	Rep. 1840
3607	Frinstead	P	Rep. 1840
3608	Frittenden	P	Min.
3609	Gillingham	P	Rep. 1840
3610	Godmersham	P	Rep. 1839
3611	Goodneston	P	Rep. 1837
3612	Goodnestone near Wingham	P	Min.
3613	Goudhurst	P	Min.
3614	Graveney	P	Awd.,Min.
3615	Gravesend	P	Rep. 1839
3616	Greenwich	P	Awd.,Min.
3618	Guston	P	Awd.,Min.
3619	Hackington	P	Rep. 1839
3620	Hadlow	P	Min.
3621	High Halden	P	N.t.p.
3622	Halling	P	Rep. 1839
3623	Halstead	P	Awd.,Min.
3624	Halstow High	P	Rep. 1839
3625	Lower Halstow	P	Awd.,Min.
3626	Ham	P	Awd.,Min.
3628	Harbledown St Michael	P	Agrmt.,Min.
3628	Harbledown	P	Agrmt.,Min.
3629	Hardres Great	P	Rep. 1839
3630	Hardres Lower	P	Rep. 1838
3631	Harrietsham	P	Rep. 1839
3632	Hartley	P	Awd.,Min.
3633	Hartlip	P	Min.
3634	Hastingleigh	P	Rep. 1840
3635	Hawkhurst	P	Min.
3636	Hawkinge	P	Min.
3637	Hayes	P	Rep. 1838
3638	Headcorn	P	Min.
3639	Herne	P	Rep. 1839
3640	Hernhill	P	Rep. 1839
3641	Hever	P	Rep. 1840
3642	Higham	P	Awd.,Min.
3643	Hinxhill	P	Rep. 1839
3644	Hoath	P	Rep. 1839
3645	Hollingbourne	P	Rep. 1840
3646	Hope All Saints	P	Awd.,Min.
3647	Horsmonden	P	Rep. 1839
3648	Horton Kirby	P	Min.
3649	Hothfield	P	Awd.,Min.
3650	Hougham	P	Rep. 1842
3651	Hucking	P	Rep. 1841
3652	Hunton	P	Rep. 1838
?653	Hythe St Leonard	P	Awd.,Min.
?654	Hythe West	P	Min.
3655	Ickham and Well	P	Rep. 1841
3656	Ifield	P	Rep. 1839
3657	Ightham	P	Rep. 1839
3658	Ivychurch	P	Min.
3659	Iwade	P	Rep. 1840
3660	Isle of Grain	P	Awd.,Min.
3661	Margate St John Baptist	P	Awd.,Min.
3662	Kemsing	P	Rep. 1840
3663	Kennardington	P	Rep. 1839
3664	Kennington	P	Rep. 1840
3665	Keston	P	Rep. 1838
3666	Kidbrook	L	Rep. 1844
3667	Kingsdown Nr Farningham	P	Awd.,Min.
3668	Kingsdown	P	Rep. 1839
3669	Kingsnorth	P	Rep. 1839
3670	Kingstone	P	Awd.,Min.
3671	Knockholt	P	Rep. 1843
3672	Knowlton	P	Rep. 1842
3673	Lamberhurst	P	Rep. 1841
3674	Langdon East	P	Awd.,Min.
3675	Langdon West	P	Rep. 1840
3676	Langley	P	Awd.,Min.
3677	Hurst	P	Awd.,Min.
3678	St Lawrence Thanet	P	Min.
3679	Lee	P	Min.,Rep. 1839
3680	Leeds	P	Awd.,Min.
3681	Leigh	P	Rep. 1839
3682	Lenham	P	Rep. 1839
3683	Lewisham	P	Awd.
3684	Leybourne	P	Rep. 1842
3685	Leysdown	P	Rep. 1840
3686	Lidsing	V	Rep. 1841
3687	Linstead	P	Min.
3688	Linton	P	Rep. 1840
3689	Littlebourn	P	Min.
3690	Longfield	P	Min.
3691	Loose	P	Min.
3692	Luddenham	P	Rep. 1840
3693	Lullingstone	P	Awd.,Min.
3694	Lydd	P	N.t.p.
3695	Luddesdown	P	Rep. 1840
3696	Lydden	P	Awd.,Min.
3697	Lympne	P	Rep. 1840
3698	Lyminge	P	Awd.,Min.
3699	Maidstone	P	Min.
3700	Malling East	P	Rep. 1838
3701	Malling West	P	Awd.,Min.
3702	Marden	P	Min.
3703	Cliffe	P	Rep. 1840
3704	Hoo	P	Rep. 1840
3704	St Mary Romney Marsh	P	Min.
3706	Meopham	P	Min.
3707	Mereworth	P	Rep. 1840
3708	Mersham	P	Rep. 1841
3709	Merston	P	Awd.,Min.
3710	Midley	P	Awd.,Min.
3711	Milstead	P	Awd.,Min.
3712	Milton near Canterbury	P	Awd.,Min.
3713	Milton near Gravesend	P	Awd.,Min.
3714	Milton	P	Rep. 1839
3715	Minster	P	Rep. 1841
3716	Minster Thanet	P	Rep. 1841
3717	Molash	P	Rep. 1841
3718	Mongeham Great	P	Rep. 1839
3719	Mongeham Little	P	Awd.,Min.
3720	Monks Horton	P	Rep. 1839
3721	Monkton	P	Rep. 1839
3722	Mottingham	EP	Awd.,Min.
3723	Murston	P	Rep. 1839
3724	Nackington	P	Min.

Kent contd.

3725	Nettlestead	P	Awd.,Min.
3726	Newchurch	P	Rep. 1841
3727	Newenden	P	Rep. 1839
3728	Newington	P	Rep. 1840
3729	Newington (Sittingbourne)	P	Awd.,Min.
3730	Newnham	P	Awd.,Min.
3731	Nicholas St at Wade	P	Rep. 1839
3732	Nonington and Womenswould	P	Rep. 1838
3733	Northbourne	P	Awd.,Min.
3734	Norton	P	Rep. 1839
3735	Northfleet	P	Rep. 1838
3736	Nursted	P	Rep. 1838
3737	Oare	P	Rep. 1839
3738	Offham	P	Awd.,Min.
3738	Poulton	P	N.t.p.
3739	Orgarswick	P	Rep. 1841
3740	Orlestone	P	Rep. 1838
3741	Ospringe	P	Rep. 1840
3742	Orpington	P	Rep. 1843
3743	Otford	P	Min.
3744	Otham	P	Rep. 1838
3745	Otterden	P	Rep. 1839
3746	Oxney	P	Rep. 1839
3747	Paddlesworth (Rochester)	P	Agrmt.,Min.
3748	Paddlesworth	P	Rep. 1838
3749	Peckham East	P	Min.
3750	Peckham West	P	Awd.,Min.
3751	Pembury	P	Awd.,Min.
3752	Penshurst	P	Rep. 1838
3753	Thanet St Peter	P	Rep. 1839
3754	Petham	P	Agrmt.,Rep. 1837
3755	Pluckley	P	Rep. 1837
3756	Plumstead	P	Min.
3757	Postling	P	Awd.,Min.
3759	Preston next Faversham	P	Awd.,Min.
3760	Preston next Wingham	P	Awd.,Min.
3761	Queenborough	P	N.t.p.
3762	Rainham	P	Rep. 1838
3763	Ramsgate St George	P	Awd.,Min.
3764	Reculver	P	Rep. 1839
3765	Ridley	P	Rep. 1839
3766	Ringwould	P	Rep. 1839
3767	Ripple	P	Awd.
3768	River	P	Min.
3769	Rochester Cathedral	P	N.t.p.
3770	Rochester St Margaret	P	Awd.,Min.
3771	Rochester St Nicholas Etc	P	N.t.p.
3772	Rodmersham	P	Rep. 1839
3773	Rolvenden	P	Rep. 1838
3775	Romney Old	P	Awd.,Min.
3776	New Romney	P	Rep. 1842
3777	Ruckinge	P	Rep. 1839
3778	Ryarsh	P	Min.
3779	Saltwood	P	Awd.,Min.
3780	Sandhurst	P	Rep. 1837
3781	Sandwich St Clement	P	Awd.,Min.
3782	Sandwich St Mary	P	Awd.,Min.
3783	Sandwich St Peter	P	Min.
3784	Sarre	P	Rep. 1841
3785	Seal	P	Rep. 1841
3786	Seasalter	P	Rep. 1840
3787	Selling	P	Rep. 1839
3788	Sellinge	P	Rep. 1840
3789	Sevenoaks	P	Rep. 1838
3790	Sevington	P	Rep. 1838
3791	Shadoxhurst	P	Rep. 1841
3793	Sholden	P	Awd.,Min.
3794	Shoreham	P	Rep. 1840
3794	Romney Marsh	PP	Min.
3795	Shorne	P	Awd.,Min.
3796	Sibertswould	P	Awd.,Min.
3797	Sittingbourne	P	Rep. 1840
3798	Smarden	P	Min.
3799	Smeeth	P	Min.
3800	Snargate	P	Awd.,Min.
3801	Snave	P	Awd.,Min.
3802	Snodland	P	Min.
3803	Southfleet	P	Rep. 1839
3804	Speldhurst	P	Rep. 1839
3805	Standford	P	Rep. 1838
3806	Stansted	P	Awd.,Min.
3807	Stalisfield	P	Rep. 1839
3808	Staple	P	Rep. 1840
3809	Staplehurst	P	Rep. 1838
3810	Stelling	P	Min.
3811	Stelling Minnis	EP	N.t.p.
3813	Stodmarsh	P	Awd.,Min.
3814	Stoke	P	Awd.,Min.
3815	Stone near Dartford	P	Agrmt.,Min.
3816	Stone	P	Rep. 1839
3817	Stone next Faversham	P	Awd.,Min.
3818	Stourmouth	P	Min.
3819	Stonar	P	N.t.p.
3820	Stowting	P	Awd.,Min.
3821	Strood	P	Awd.,Min.
3822	Sturry	P	Rep. 1840
3823	Sundridge	P	Agrmt.
3824	Sutton near Dover	P	Awd.,Min.
3825	Sutton East	P	Awd.
3826	Sutton at Hone	P	Min.
3827	Swingfield	P	Awd.,Min.
3828	Sutton Valence	P	Awd.,Min.
3829	Swalecliffe	P	Min.
3830	Swanscombe	P	Rep. 1843
3831	St Thomas Isle of Harty	P	N.t.p.
3832	Tenterden	P	Min.
3833	Teston	P	Awd.
3834	Teynham	P	Min.
3835	Thanington	P	Rep. 1838
3836	Tilmanstone	P	Rep. 1840
3837	Thornham	P	Awd.,Min.
3838	Throwley	P	Rep. 1840
3839	Tonbridge	P	Rep. 1840
3840	Tonge	P	Agrmt.,Min.
3841	Trotterscliffe	P	Awd.,Min.
3842	Tudeley	P	Awd.,Min.
3843	Tunstall	P	Rep. 1839
3844	Ulcomb	P	Rep. 1838
3845	Upchurch	P	Awd.,Min.
3846	Waltham	P	Rep. 1840
3847	Waldershare	P	Awd.,Min.
3848	Walmer	P	Awd.,Min.
3849	Warden	P	Rep. 1841
3850	Warehorne	P	Awd.,Min.
3851	Wateringbury	P	Rep. 1840
3852	Hoo St Werburgh	P	Min.
3853	Westbere	P	Rep. 1837
3854	Westerham	P	Awd.,Min.
3855	Westwell	P	Rep. 1841
3856	Whitfield	P	Awd.,Min.
3857	Whitstable	P	Rep. 1840
3858	Wickham East	P	Awd.,Min.
3859	Wickham West	P	Rep. 1838
3860	Wickhambreux	P	Agrmt.,Min.
3861	Wittersham	P	Rep. 1838
3862	Willesborough	P	Awd.,Min.
3863	Wilmington	P	Awd.,Min.
3864	Wingham	P	Rep. 1840
3865	Witchling	P	Awd.,Min.
3867	Woodchurch	P	Rep. 1838
3868	Woodnesborough	P	Awd.,Min.
3869	Wormshill	P	Rep. 1839
3870	Wouldham	P	Awd.,Min.,Rep. 1841
3871	Woolwich	P	Min.
3872	Wootton	P	Rep. 1840
3873	Worth	P	Min.
3874	Wrotham	P	Min.
3875	Wye	P	Rep. 1841
3876	Yalding	P	Min.
10432	Penshurst	P	Agrmt.,Min.,Rep. 1839
14826	Sheldwich	P	Rep. 1841

Lancashire

3878	Abram	T	Agrmt.,Rep. 1839
3879	Accrington New	T	Awd.
3880	Accrington Old	T	Awd.,Min.
3881	Adlington	T	Agrmt.,Rep. 1842
3882	Aighton Bailey Chaigley	T	Awd.,Min.
3883	Ainsworth	T	Agrmt.,Rep. 1839
3884	Aintree	T	Agrmt.,Min.,Rep. 1843
3885	Aldcliffe	T	Awd.,Min.
3886	Aldingham	P	Awd.,Min.
3887	Alkrington	T	Agrmt.,Rep. 1838
3888	Allerton	T	Agrmt.,Min.,Rep. 1839
3889	Allithwaite Lower	T	N.t.p.
3890	Allithwaite Upper	T	N.t.p.
3891	Alston	T	Agrmt.,Min.
3892	Altcar	P	Awd.,Min.
3893	Altham	T	Awd.,Min.
3894	Anderton	T	Awd.,Rep. 1842
3895	Angerton	EP	Agrmt.,Min.,Rep. 1839
3896	Anglezark	T	Awd.,Min.
3897	Ardwick	T	Awd.,Min.
3898	Arkholme with Cawood	T	Awd.,Min.
3899	Ashton under Lyne	T	Awd.,Min.
3900	Ashton within Mackerfield	T	Agrmt.,Min.,Rep. 1838
3901	Ashton with Stodday	T	Min.,Rep. 1840
3902	Ashworth	T	Agrmt.,Rep. 1839
3903	Aspull	T	Agrmt.,Rep. 1839
3904	Astley	T	Awd.,Min.
3905	Atherton	T	Agrmt.,Rep. 1838
3906	Aughton	P	Agrmt.,Rep. 1843
3907	Balderstone	T	Awd.,Min.
3908	Barley with Wheatley Booth	T	Awd.,Min.
3909	Barnacre with Bonds	H	Agrmt.,Rep. 1839
3910	Barrowford Booth	T	Awd.,Min.
3911	Barton	T	Awd.,Min.
3912	Barton upon Irwell	T	Awd.,Min.
3913	Bedford	T	Awd.,Min.
3914	Birtle cum Bamford	T	Awd.,Min.

Lancashire contd.

3915	Bickerstaffe	T	Agrmt.,Rep. 1839
3916	Billinge Chapel End	T	Agrmt.,Rep. 1838
3917	Billinge Higher End	T	Agrmt.,Rep. 1838
3918	Billington	T	Awd.,Min.
3919	Bilsborough	T	Agrmt.,Rep. 1839
3920	Birkdale	T	Awd.,Min.
3921	Bispham with Norbreck	T	Awd.,Min.
3922	Bispham	T	Agrmt.,Rep. 1840
3923	Blackburn	P	Awd.,Min.
3924	Blackrod	T	Rep. 1839
3925	Bleasdale	T	Awd.,Min.
3926	Blackley	T	Awd.,Min.
3927	Blatchinworth, Calderbrook	T	Awd.
3928	Blawith	T	Awd.,Min.
3929	Bonds	H	Awd.,Min.
3930	Bolton Little	D	Awd.,Min.
3931	Booths Higher	T	Awd.,Min.
3932	Booths Lower	T	Awd.,Min.
3933	Bootle cum Linacre	T	Agrmt.,Rep. 1839
3934	Borwick	T	Awd.,Min.
3935	Bowland with Leagrim	T	Awd.,Min.
3936	Bold	T	Agrmt.,Rep. 1839
3937	Bolton Great	T	Awd.,Min.
3938	Bolton le Sands	T	Awd.,Min.
3939	Bradford	T	Awd.,Min.
3940	Bradshaw	T	Awd.,Min.
3941	Bretherton	T	Agrmt.,Rep. 1838
3942	Briercliffe with Extwistle	T	Min.
3943	Breightmet	T	Awd.,Min.
3944	Brindle	P	Agrmt.,Rep. 1838
3945	Broughton in Furness	T	Awd.,Min.
3946	Broughton (Manchester)	T	Awd.,Min.
3947	Broughton (Preston)	T	Agrmt.,Rep. 1839
3948	Broughton West	T	N.t.p.
3949	Bryning with Kellamergh	T	Agrmt.,Min.,Rep. 1838
3950	Bulk	T	Awd.,Min.
3951	Burnage	T	Awd.,Min.
3952	Burrow with Burrow	T	Awd.,Min.
3953	Burscough	T	Awd.,Min.
3954	Burtonwood	T	Agrmt.,Min.,Rep. 1837
3955	Bury	T	Agrmt.,Min.
3956	Butterworth	T	Awd.,Min.
3957	Cabus and Nether Wyersdale	TD	Awd.,Min.
3958	Cantsfield	T	Agrmt.,Rep. 1845
3959	Carleton	T	Agrmt.,Rep. 1839
3960	Carnforth	T	Awd.,Min.
3961	Cartmel	P	Awd.,Min.
3962	Cartmel Fell	T	N.t.p.
3963	Castleton	T	Awd.,Min.
3964	Caton	T	Awd.,Min.
3965	Catteral	T	Awd.,Min.
3966	Chadderton	T	Agrmt.,Rep. 1839
3967	Charnock Richard	T	Agrmt.,Rep. 1842
3968	Chatburn	T	Awd.,Min.
3969	Cheetham	T	Awd.,Min.
3970	Childwall	T	Awd.,Min.
3971	Chipping	P	Agrmt.,Rep. 1839
3972	Chorley	T	Agrmt.,Rep. 1843
3973	Chorlton cum Hardy	T	Awd.,Min.
3974	Chorlton on Medlock	T	Awd.,Min.
3975	Church	T	Awd.,Min.
3976	Church Conistone	T	Awd.,Min.
3977	Claife	T	Awd.,Min.
3978	Claughton (Garstang)	T	Agrmt.,Rep. 1838
3979	Claughton	P	Min.
3980	Clayton le Dale	T	Awd.,Min.
3981	Clayton le Moors	T	N.t.p.
3982	Clayton le Woods	T	Agrmt.,Rep. 1838
3983	Cleveley	T	Awd.,Min.
3984	Clifton	T	Awd.,Min.
3985	Clifton with Salwick	T	Agrmt.,Rep. 1838
3986	Clitheroe	T	Awd.,Min.
3987	Cliviger	T	Awd.,Min.
3988	Cockerham	T	Awd.,Min.
3989	Colne	T	Awd.,Min.
3990	Colton	P	Awd.,Min.
3991	Coppul	T	Agrmt.,Rep. 1842
3992	Cowpe Lenches, New Hall	T	Agrmt.,Rep. 1838
3993	Crompton	T	Agrmt.,Awd.,Min.,Rep. 1845
3994	Cronton	T	Awd.,Rep. 1838
3995	Crosby Little	T	Agrmt.,Rep. 1843
3996	Croston	T	Agrmt.,Min.,Rep. 1838
3997	Crosby Great	T	Agrmt.,Min.,Rep. 1843
3998	Croxteth Park	EP	Agrmt.,Rep. 1838
3999	Cuerdale	T	N.t.p.
4000	Cuerden	T	Agrmt.,Rep. 1838
4001	Cuerdley	T	Agrmt.,Rep. 1839
4002	Dalton	P	Agrmt.,Rep. 1839
4003	Culcheth	T	Rep. 1838
4004	Dalton (Burton)	T	Agrmt.,Rep. 1837
4005	Dalton (Wigan)	T	Agrmt.,Min.,Rep. 1839
4006	Darwen Over or Upper	T	Awd.,Min.
4007	Darcy Lever	T	Awd.,Min.
4008	Darwen Lower	T	Awd.,Min.
4009	Deane	P	Min.
4010	Denton	T	Awd.,Min.
4011	Derby West	T	Agrmt.,Min.,Rep. 1839
4012	Didsbury	T	Awd.,Min.
4013	Dilworth	T	Agrmt.,Rep. 1838
4014	Dinkley	T	Awd.,Min.
4015	Ditton	T	Awd.,Min.
4016	Dolphinholme House	D	Agrmt.,Rep. 1838
4017	Downholland	T	Awd.,Min.
4018	Downham	T	Awd.,Min.
4019	Droylsden	T	Awd.,Min.
4020	Dunnerdale	T	Agrmt.,Awd.,Min.
4021	Dunnockshaw	T	Awd.,Min.
4022	Dutton	T	Agrmt.,Min.,Rep. 1838
4023	Duxbury	T	Agrmt.,Rep. 1842
4024	Eccles	P	Min.
4025	Eccleshill	T	Rep. 1843
4026	Eccleston	T	Agrmt.,Min.,Rep. 1841
4027	Eccleston Great	T	Agrmt.,Min.,Rep. 1838
4028	Eccleston Little	T	Agrmt.,Min.,Rep. 1838
4029	Eccleston (Prescot)	T	Agrmt.,Rep. 1839
4030	Edgeworth	T	Awd.,Min.
4031	Egton with Newland	T	Awd.,Min.
4032	Ellel	T	Awd.,Min.
4033	Elston	T	Agrmt.,Rep. 1837
4034	Elswick	T	Agrmt.,Rep. 1839
4035	Elton	T	Agrmt.,Rep. 1838
4036	Entwisle	T	Awd.,Min.
4037	Euxton	T	Awd.,Min.
4038	Everton	C	Awd.,Min.
4039	Failsworth	T	Awd.,Min.
4040	Farington	T	Agrmt.,Rep. 1842
4041	Farleton	T	Awd.,Min.
4042	Farnworth	T	Awd.,Min.
4043	Fazakerly	T	Awd.,Min.
4044	Fishwick	T	Rep. 1843
4045	Fleetwood on Wyre	D	N.t.p.
4046	Flixton	T	Awd.,Min.
4047	Flookburgh	T	N.t.p.
4048	Formby	T	Awd.,Min.
4049	Forton	T	N.t.p.
4050	Forton (Garstang)	D	Agrmt.,Awd.,Min.
4051	Foulridge	T	Agrmt.,Rep. 1838
4052	Freckleton	T	Agrmt.,Min.,Rep. 1838
4053	Fulwood	T	Awd.,Min.
4054	Garstang	T	Awd.,Min.
4055	Garston	T	Agrmt.,Rep. 1840
4056	Golborne	T	Agrmt.,Min.,Rep. 1838
4057	Goldshaw Booth	T	Awd.,Min.
4058	Goosnargh with Newsham	T	Awd.,Min.
4059	Gorton	T	Awd.,Min.
4060	Greenalgh	H	Agrmt.,Min.,Rep. 1838
4061	Gressingham	T	Awd.,Min.
4062	Grimsargh with Brockholes	T	Min.,Rep. 1841
4063	Habergham Eaves	T	Awd.,Min.
4064	Halsall	T	Awd.,Min.
4065	Haigh	T	Agrmt.,Rep. 1838
4066	Haighton	T	Agrmt.,Rep. 1839
4067	Hale	T	Agrmt.,Rep. 1841
4068	Halewood	T	Agrmt.,Rep. 1839
4069	Halliwell and Horwich	T	Awd.,Min.
4070	Halton	P	Agrmt.,Rep. 1838
4071	Hambleton	T	Agrmt.,Rep. 1839
4072	Hapton	T	Awd.,Min.
4073	Hardhorn with Newton	T	Agrmt.,Rep. 1839
4074	Harwood	T	Awd.,Min.
4075	Harwood Little	T	Awd.,Min.
4076	Harpurhey	T	Awd.,Min.
4077	Haslingden	T	Awd.,Min.
4078	Haughton	T	Awd.,Min.
4079	Harwood Great	T	Awd.,Min.
4080	Haydock	T	Agrmt.,Rep. 1838
4081	Hawkshead	T	Awd.,Min.
4082	Heap	T	Agrmt.,Rep. 1838
4083	Heapey	T	Awd.,Min.
4084	Heath Charnock	T	Agrmt.,Rep. 1842
4085	Heaton (Deane)	T	Awd.,Min.
4086	Heaton Great (Prestwich)	T	Agrmt.,Rep. 1839
4087	Heaton Little (Prestwich)	T	Awd.,Min.
4088	Heaton Norris	T	Awd.,Min.
4089	Heaton with Oxcliffe	T	Agrmt.,Rep. 1838
4090	Henhead	T	Awd.,Min.
4091	Hesketh with Becconsall	P	Agrmt.,Rep. 1839
4092	Heskin	T	Agrmt.,Rep. 1841
4093	Heyhouses	EP	Awd.,Min.
4094	Heysham	P	Agrmt.,Rep. 1838
4095	Higham	T	Awd.,Min.
4096	Hindley (Wigan)	T	Agrmt.,Rep. 1839
4097	Houghton (Leyland)	T	Awd.,Min.
4098	Holker Lower	T	N.t.p.
4099	Holker Upper	T	N.t.p.
4100	Holleth	T	Agrmt.,Rep. 1839
4101	Hoole	P	Agrmt.,Rep. 1839
4102	Hopwood (Middleton)	T	Agrmt.,Rep. 1839
4103	Hornby	T	Awd.,Min.
4104	Hothersall	T	Agrmt.,Rep. 1838
4105	Houghton with Middleton	T	Agrmt.,Rep. 1838
4106	Houghton West	T	Awd.,Min.

Lancashire contd.

No.	Place	Type	Details
4107	Howick	T	Agrmt.,Rep. 1839
4108	Hulme	T	Awd.,Min.
4109	Hulton Little or Peel	T	Awd.,Min.
4110	Hulton Middle	T	Awd.,Min.
4111	Huncoat	T	Awd.,Min.
4112	Hundersfield	T	Min.
4113	Hutton	T	Awd.,Min.
4114	Hutton Priest	T	Awd.,Min.
4115	Hulton Over	T	N.t.p.
4116	Huyton	T	Agrmt.,Awd.,Min.,Rep. 1840
4117	Ightonhill Park	T	Agrmt.,Rep. 1838
4118	Ince Blundell	T	Agrmt.,Rep. 1843
4119	Ince within Mackerfield	T	Agrmt.,Rep. 1839
4120	Inskip with Sowerby	T	Agrmt.,Rep. 1839
4121	Kellet Over	PC	Agrmt.,Awd.,Min.
4122	Kenyon	T	Agrmt.,Rep. 1838
4123	Kersley	T	Awd.,Min.
4124	Kirkby	T	Agrmt.,Rep. 1839
4125	Low Quarter Middle Quarter	T	Awd.,Min.,Rep. 1842
4126	Kirkdale	T	Rep. 1839
4127	Kirkham	T	Agrmt.,Rep. 1838
4128	Kirkland	T	Awd.,Min.
4129	Knowsley	T	Agrmt.,Awd.,Min.,Rep. 1839
4130	Lancaster	T	Awd.,Min.
4131	Lancaster Castle	EP	N.t.p.
4132	Langho	T	Min.
4133	Lathom	T	Agrmt.,Rep. 1838
4134	Laund Booth Old	T	Awd.,Min.
4135	Layton with Warbreck	T	Agrmt.,Rep. 1839
4136	Lea,Ashton,Ingol,Cottam	T	Agrmt.,Min.,Rep. 1838
4137	Leck	T	Agrmt.,Rep. 1845
4138	Leigh West	T	Agrmt.,Awd.,Min.
4139	Levenshulme	T	Awd.,Min.
4140	Lever Great	T	Agrmt.,Rep. 1838
4141	Lever Little	T	Awd.,Min.
4142	Leyland	T	Agrmt.,Rep. 1838
4143	Lindale	C	N.t.p.
4144	Litherland	T	Agrmt.,Rep. 1843
4145	Liverpool	P	N.t.p.,Min.
4146	Livesey	T	Awd.,Min.
4147	Longton	T	Agrmt.,Rep. 1838
4148	Longworth	T	Awd.,Min.
4149	Lostock	T	Rep. 1839
4150	Lowick	T	Awd.,Min.
4151	Lowton	T	Agrmt.,Rep. 1838
4152	Lunt	T	Agrmt.,Rep. 1843
4153	Lydiate	T	Awd.,Min.
4154	Lytham	T	Agrmt.,Rep. 1839
4155	Maghull	T	Agrmt.,Rep. 1839
4156	Manchester	T	Awd.,Min.
4157	Mansriggs	T	Min.
4158	Marsden,Great and Little	T	Min.
4159	Melling cum Wrayton	T	Awd.,Min.
4160	Melling cum Cunscough	T	Agrmt.,Rep. 1839
4161	Mary St,Manchester	T	N.t.p.
4162	Mawdesley	T	Agrmt.,Rep. 1839
4163	Marton	T	Agrmt.,Rep. 1839
4164	Mearley	T	Awd.,Min.
4165	Medlar with Wesham	T	Agrmt.,Min.,Rep. 1839
4166	Crumpsall	T	Awd.,Min.
4167	Mellor	T	Awd.,Min.
4168	Meols North	T	Agrmt.,Rep. 1839
4169	St Michael upon Wyre	P	N.t.p.
4170	Middleton (Lancaster)	T	Agrmt.,Awd.,Min.
4171	Middleton	T	Agrmt.,Rep. 1839
4172	Mitton Little	T	N.t.p.
4173	Mitton Henthorne Coldcoats	T	Awd.,Min.
4174	Monk Coniston and Skelwith	T	Awd.,Min.
4175	Mosshouses, Waitham Hill	T	Min.
4176	Mosside	T	Awd.,Min.
4177	Moston	T	Awd.,Min.
4178	Musbury,Mugden Head	T	Awd.,Min.
4179	Myerscough	T	Awd.,Min.
4180	Netherton	T	Agrmt.,Rep. 1843
4181	Nateby	T	Awd.,Min.
4182	Nether Kellet	T	Agrmt.,Rep. 1839
4183	Newburgh	H	Awd.,Min.
4184	New Church in Rossendale	T	Awd.,Min.
4185	Newchurch in Pendle	C	Min.
4186	Newton	T	Awd.,Min.
4187	Newton within Mackerfield	T	Agrmt.,Min.,Rep. 1838
4188	Newton with Scales	T	Agrmt.,Rep. 1838
4189	Oldham	T	Awd.,Min.,Rep. 1845
4190	Openshaw	T	Awd.,Min.
4191	Ormskirk	T	Awd.,Min.
4192	Orrell	T	Agrmt.,Rep. 1838
4193	Orrell and Ford	T	Agrmt.,Rep. 1843
4194	Osbaldestone	T	Awd.,Min.
4195	Osbaldwisle	T	Awd.,Min.
4196	Overton	T	Awd.,Min.
4197	Out Rawcliffe	T	Min.
4198	Osmotherley	T	Awd.,Min.
4199	Padiham	T	Agrmt.,Rep. 1838
4200	Parbold	T	Agrmt.,Rep. 1841
4201	Parr	T	Agrmt.,Rep. 1839
4202	Pemberton	T	Agrmt.,Min.,Rep. 1844
4203	Pendlebury	T	Awd.,Min.
4204	Pendleton (Eccles)	T	Awd.,Min.
4205	Pendleton (Whally)	TH	Awd.,Min.
4206	Pennington	T	Awd.,Min.
4207	Pennington	P	Agrmt.,Rep. 1839
4208	Penketh	T	Rep. 1839
4209	Penwortham	T	Agrmt.,Rep. 1838
4210	Pilkington	T	Min.,Rep. 1840
4211	Pilling	T	Awd.,Min.
4212	Pilling Lane	H	Awd.,Min.
4213	Pilsworth	T	Agrmt.,Rep. 1839
4214	Pleasington	T	Awd.,Min.
4215	Poulton	T	Agrmt.,Rep. 1839
4216	Poulton,Bare,Torrisholme	T	Agrmt.,Min.,Rep. 1838
4217	Poulton with Fearnhead	T	Awd.,Min.
4218	Preesall with Hackensall	T	Agrmt.,Rep. 1840
4219	Prescot	T	Min.,Rep. 1840
4220	Preston	T	Agrmt.,Rep. 1839
4221	Prestwich	T	Agrmt.,Rep. 1839
4222	Quarlton	T	Awd.,Min.
4223	Quernmore	T	Awd.,Min.
4224	Quick Mere	T	N.t.p.
4225	Radcliffe	P	Agrmt.,Rep. 1839
4226	Rainford	T	Agrmt.,Awd.,Min.,Rep. 1839
4227	Rainhill	T	Awd.,Min.,Rep. 1840
4228	Ramsgreave	T	Awd.,Min.
4229	Rawcliffe Upper	T	Awd.,Min.
4230	Read	T	Awd.,Min.
4231	Reddish	T	Awd.,Min.
4232	Rawcliffe Upper	D	Agrmt.,Rep. 1840
4233	Reedley Hollows	T	Awd.,Min.
4234	Ribby with Wrea	T	Agrmt.,Rep. 1838
4235	Ribbleton	T	Agrmt.,Rep. 1843
4236	Ribchester	T	Rep. 1838
4237	Rishton	T	Awd.,Min.
4238	Rivington	T	Awd.,Min.
4239	Rixton with Glazebrook	T	Min.
4240	Rochdale	P	N.t.p.
4241	Roeburndale	T	Awd.,Min.
4242	Rough Lee Booth	T	Awd.,Min.
4243	Royton	T	Agrmt.,Awd.,Min.,Rep. 1845
4244	Roby	T	Agrmt.,Rep. 1840
4245	Rufford	P	Agrmt.,Rep. 1839
4246	Rumworth	T	Awd.,Min.
4247	Rusholme	T	Awd.,Min.
4248	Salford	T	Awd.,Min.
4249	Salisbury	T	Awd.,Min.
4250	Samlesbury	T	Awd.,Min.
4251	Sankey Great	T	Agrmt.,Rep. 1839
4252	Satterthwaite	C	Awd.,Min.
4253	Scarisbrick	T	Agrmt.,Rep. 1839
4254	Scotforth	T	Awd.,Min.
4255	Seathwaite	T	Agrmt.,Rep. 1839
4256	Sefton	T	Agrmt.,Min.,Rep. 1843
4257	Sharples	D	Awd.,Min.
4258	Shevington	T	Agrmt.,Awd.,Rep. 1842
4259	Simonswood	EP	Agrmt.,Rep. 1839
4260	Simonstone	T	Awd.,Min.
4261	Singleton Great and Little	T	Agrmt.,Rep. 1838
4262	Silverdale	T	Awd.,Min.
4263	Skelmersdale	T	Agrmt.,Rep. 1838
4264	Skerton	T	Agrmt.,Awd.,Min.,Rep. 1838
4265	Slyne with Hest	T	Awd.,Min.
4266	Southworth with Croft	T	Agrmt.,Min.,Rep. 1838
4267	Speke	T	Agrmt.,Rep. 1841
4268	Spotland	T	Awd.,Min.
4269	Stalmine with Staynall	T	Agrmt.,Rep. 1840
4270	Standish with Langtree	T	Agrmt.,Awd.,Min.,Rep. 1842
4271	Stavely	C	N.t.p.
4272	Stretford	T	Agrmt.,Min.,Rep. 1839
4273	Subberthwaite	T	Awd.,Min.
4274	Sutton	T	Agrmt.,Rep. 1839
4275	Tarbock	T	Awd.,Min.
4276	Tarleton	P	Agrmt.,Rep. 1839
4277	Tatham	P	Awd.,Min.
4278	Thistleton	H	Agrmt.,Min.,Rep. 1838
4279	Thornham	T	Agrmt.,Rep. 1839
4280	Thornton	T	Agrmt.,Rep. 1843
4281	Thornton (Poulton)	T	Agrmt.,Rep. 1839
4283	Thurnham	T	Agrmt.,Rep. 1841
4284	Tottington Higher End	T	Agrmt.,Rep. 1838
4285	Tockholes	T	Min.
4286	Todmorden and Walsden	T	Awd.,Min.
4287	Tonge	T	Agrmt.,Rep. 1838
4288	Tonge with Haulgh	T	Awd.,Min.
4289	Torver	T	Awd.,Min.
4290	Tottington Lower End	T	Agrmt.,Rep. 1838
4291	Toxteth Park	EP	Awd.,Min.
4292	Trawden	T	Min.
4293	Treales,Roseacre,Wharles	T	Agrmt.,Rep. 1839
4294	Tunstal	T	Agrmt.,Rep. 1845
4295	Turton	C	Awd.,Min.
4296	Twiston	T	Awd.,Min.
4297	Tyldesley with Shakerley	T	Awd.,Min.
4298	Ulneswalton	T	Agrmt.,Rep. 1838
4299	Ulverston	T	Awd.,Min.

Lancashire contd.

4300	Upholland	T	Agrmt.,Awd.,Min.,Rep. 1844
4301	Urswick	P	Awd.,Min.
4302	Urmston	T	Awd.,Min.
4303	Walmersley	T	Agrmt.,Rep. 1838
4304	Walton le Dale	T	Agrmt.,Rep. 1838
4305	Walton on the Hill	T	Awd.,Min.
4306	Wardleworth	T	Awd.,Min.
4307	Warrington	T	Agrmt.,Rep. 1838
4308	Warton	T	Min.
4309	Warton with Lindeth	T	Awd.,Min.
4310	Wavertree	T	Awd.,Min.
4311	Weeton with Preese	T	Agrmt.,Min.,Rep. 1838
4312	Welch Whittle	T	Agrmt.,Rep. 1842
4313	Whalley	T	Awd.,Min.
4314	Wennington	T	Awd.,Min.
4315	Westby with Plumpton	T	Agrmt.,Rep. 1838
4316	Wheatley Carr	T	Awd.,Min.
4317	Wheelton	T	Awd.,Min.
4318	Whiston	T	Min.,Rep. 1840
4319	Whittingham	T	Awd.,Min.
4320	Whittington	P	Awd.,Min.
4321	Whittle le Woods	T	Awd.,Min.
4322	Widnes	T	Min.,Rep. 1839
4323	Wigan	T	Agrmt.,Rep. 1839
4324	Wilpshire	T	Awd.,Min.
4325	Winmarleigh	T	Agrmt.,Rep. 1838
4326	Windle	T	Agrmt.,Rep. 1839
4327	Winstanley	T	Agrmt.,Rep. 1837
4328	Winwick with Hulme	T	Agrmt.,Rep. 1838
4329	Wiswell	T	Awd.,Min.
4330	Withington	T	Awd.,Min.
4331	Withnell	T	Awd.,Min.
4332	Witton	T	Awd.,Min.
4333	Woodplumpton	T	Agrmt.,Min.,Rep. 1839
4334	Woolton Little	T	Awd.,Min.
4335	Woolton Great	T	Agrmt.,Rep. 1842
4336	Woolston with Martinscroft	T	Awd.,Min.
4337	Worsley	T	Awd.,Min.
4338	Worsthorn and Hurstwood	T	N.t.p.,Min.
4339	Worston	T	Awd.,Min.
4340	Worthington	T	Agrmt.,Rep. 1842
4341	Wray with Bottom	T	Awd.,Min.
4342	Wrightinton	T	Agrmt.,Rep. 1841
4343	Wuerdle and Wardle	T	Awd.,Min.
4344	Wyersdale Over	T	Awd.,Min.
4345	Yate and Pickup Bank	T	Awd.,Min.
4346	Yealand Conyers	T	Awd.,Min.
4347	Yealand Redmayne	T	Awd.,Min.

Leicestershire

4282	Thrussington	P	Awd.,Min.
4348	Alexton	P	Agrmt.,Min.,Rep. 1840
4349	All Saints (Leicester)	P	Awd.,Min.
4350	Arnesby	P	N.t.p.
4351	Anstey	D	Awd.,Min.
4352	Anstey Pastures	EP	N.t.p.
4353	Ashfordby	P	Awd.,Min.
4354	Ashby de la Zouch	T	Awd.,Min.
4355	Ashby Folville and Barsby	T	Awd.,Min.
4356	Ashby Parva	T	Awd.,Min.
4357	Abkettleby	T	Awd.,Min.
4358	Ashby Magna	T	Awd.,Min.
4359	Aston Flamville	P	Agrmt.,Awd.,Min.,Rep. 1839
4360	Atterton	T	Awd.,Min.
4361	Ayleston	T	N.t.p.
4362	Baggrave	H	N.t.p.
4363	Bardon Park	EP	Awd.,Min.
4364	Barkby	P	Awd.,Min.
4365	Barrons Park	T	Awd.
4366	Barron on Soar	L	N.t.p.,Min.
4367	Barsby	T	Awd.,Min.
4368	Barton in the Beans	T	Awd.,Min.
4369	Barton in the Beans	T	N.t.p.
4370	Barton in the Beans	H	Awd.,Min.
4371	Barwell	P	Agrmt.,Rep. 1838
4372	Bassett House,Knoll House	EP	Min.
4373	Beaumont Leys	EP	N.t.p.,Min.
4374	Barkestone	P	N.t.p.
4375	Blackfordby and Boothorpe	T	Awd.,Min.
4376	Beeby	P	Agrmt.,Min.,Rep. 1839
4377	Belgrave	P	Awd.,Min.
4378	Belton	P	Awd.,Min.
4379	Belvoir	EP	N.t.p.,Min.
4380	Bescaby	EP	N.t.p.
4381	Billesdon	T	Awd.,Min.
4382	Bilstone	T	Awd.,Min.
4383	Birstall	C	Awd.,Min.
4384	Bittesby	H	Awd.,Min.
4385	Bitteswell	P	Awd.,Min.
4386	Blaby cum Countessthorp	P	Min.
4387	Black Friars	EP	N.t.p.
4388	Blaston St Michael	P	Agrmt.,Rep. 1842
4389	Bottesford	T	Awd.,Min.
4390	Bowden Great	T	Awd.,Min.
4391	Branstone	P	N.t.p.
4392	Breedon,Tonge,Wilson	T	N.t.p.
4393	Bringhurst	P	N.t.p.,Min.
4394	Broadgate	EP	N.t.p.
4395	Brookesby	P	Awd.,Min.
4396	Broughton Astley	D	Awd.,Min.
4397	Broughton Nether	P	Awd.,Min.
4398	Bruntingthorpe	P	N.t.p.
4399	Buckminster	P	Agrmt.,Rep. 1839
4400	Burbage	P	Agrmt.,Min.,Rep. 1839
4401	Burrow or Burrough	P	Agrmt.,Rep. 1843
4405	Burton Lazaars	P	Awd.,Min.
4406	Burton on the Wolds	T	Awd.,Min.
4407	Burton Overy	P	N.t.p.
4408	Bushby	H	Awd.,Min.
4409	Cadeby	P	Agrmt.,Rep. 1839
4410	Carlton	T	Awd.,Min.
4411	Carlton Curlieu	T	Awd.,Min.
4412	Castle Donington	T	Awd.,Min.
4413	Castle View	EP	N.t.p.
4414	Catthorpe	P	Awd.,Min.
4415	Charley	EP	N.t.p.
4416	Charnwood Forest	EP	N.t.p.,Min.
4417	Church Langton	P	N.t.p.
4418	Clawton or Long Clawson	P	Awd.,Min.
4419	Claybrooke Little	T	N.t.p.,Min.
4420	Claybrooke Great	T	Awd.,Min.
4421	Coates	T	N.t.p.
4422	Cold Overton	P	Agrmt.,Rep. 1838
4423	Cole Orton	P	Awd.,Min.
4424	Congerston	P	N.t.p.,Min.
4425	Coton	T	Min.
4426	Cosby	P	Awd.,Min.
4427	Cossington	P	Awd.,Min.
4428	Coston	P	Agrmt.,Rep. 1844
4429	Cottesbach	P	Awd.,Min.
4430	Cranoe	P	N.t.p.
4431	Croxton South	P	Awd.,Min.
4432	Croft	P	N.t.p.,Min.
4433	Cropston	T	N.t.p.,Min.
4434	Croxton Keyrial	P	N.t.p.
4435	Dadlington	C	Awd.,Min.
4436	Dalby Great	P	Agrmt.,Min.,Rep. 1840
4437	Dalby Little	P	Awd.,Min.
4438	Dalby Old	EP	Awd.,Min.
4439	Desford	T	Awd.,Min.
4440	Diseworth	P	N.t.p.
4441	Dishley	C	Min.
4442	Drayton	T	Min.
4443	Dunton Bassett	P	N.t.p.,Min.
4444	Earl Shilton	T	Awd.,Min.
4445	Easthope	H	N.t.p.
4446	Easton Magna	C	N.t.p.
4447	Eastwell	P	Awd.,Min.
4448	Eaton	P	Min.
4449	Edmondthorpe	P	Awd.,Min.
4450	Elmsthorpe	P	Awd.,Min.
4451	Emmanuel	P	Awd.,Min.
4452	Enderby	P	Min.,Rep. 1848
4453	Evington	P	Awd.,Min.
4454	Eye Kettleby	T	Awd.,Min.
4455	Fenny Drayton	P	Awd.,Min.
4456	Fleckney	P	N.t.p.,Min.
4457	Foston	P	Awd.,Min.
4458	Foxton	P	N.t.p.,Min.
4459	Freeby	D	Awd.,Min.
4460	Frisby	C	Awd.,Min.
4461	Frisby on the Wreak	P	N.t.p.
4462	Frolesworth	P	Agrmt.,Rep. 1838
4463	Galby	T	Awd.,Min.
4464	Garendon	EP	Awd.,Min.
4465	Glenn Little	H	Agrmt.,Rep. 1839
4466	Gaddesby	PC	Awd.,Min.
4467	Garthorpe	P	Agrmt.,Rep. 1839
4468	Giles St. in Blaston	P	Agrmt.,Rep. 1839
4469	Gilmorton	P	N.t.p.
4470	Gilroe or Gilroes	EP	N.t.p.
4471	Glenfield	P	Awd.,Min.
4472	Glenfield Frith	EP	N.t.p.,Min.
4473	Glen Magna	P	N.t.p.
4474	Glooston	P	N.t.p.
4475	Goadby	T	Awd.,Min.
4476	Goadby Marwood	P	Agrmt.,Rep. 1839
4477	Gopsall Hall	EP	Awd.,Min.
4478	Gores Land	D	Awd.,Min.
4479	Grimstone	P	Awd.,Min.
4480	Groby	H	N.t.p.,Min.
4481	Gumley	P	Awd.,Min.
4482	Hallick or Holy Oaks	H	N.t.p.
4483	Hallaton	P	Awd.,Min.
4484	Halstead	T	Agrmt.,Awd.,Min.
4485	Hamilton or Hambleton	H	N.t.p.
4486	Harborough (Market)	T	Awd.,Min.
4487	Harby	P	N.t.p.
4488	Harston	P	Agrmt.,Rep. 1839
4489	Hathern	P	N.t.p.

Leicestershire contd.

No.	Place	Type	Details
4490	Heather	P	Awd.,Min.
4491	Hemington	T	N.t.p.
4492	Higham on the Hill	P	N.t.p.
4493	Hinckley	T	Awd.,Min.
4494	Hoby	P	Awd.,Min.
4495	Holt with Bradley	P	Awd.,Min.
4496	Holwell	T	Awd.,Min.
4497	Hose	P	N.t.p.,Min.
4498	Horninghold	P	Awd.,Min.
4499	Hoton	T	N.t.p.
4500	Houghton on the Hill	P	N.t.p.
4501	Hugglescote and Donington	T	Agrmt.,Min.,Rep. 1838
4502	Humberston	P	N.t.p.
4503	Huncote	T	Agrmt.,Rep. 1840
4504	Hungerton	P	N.t.p.,Min.
4505	Husbands Bosworth	P	N.t.p.,Min.
4506	Ibstock	T	Agrmt.,Rep. 1838
4507	Illston	T	Awd.,Min.
4508	Ingarsby	H	N.t.p.
4509	Isley Walton	T	Agrmt.,Rep. 1840
4510	Kegworth	P	N.t.p.
4511	Keyham	C	N.t.p.
4512	Kibworth Beauchamp	L	N.t.p.
4513	Kibworth Harcourt	L	N.t.p.
4514	Kilworth South	P	N.t.p.
4515	Kimcote	P	N.t.p.
4516	Kilby	P	N.t.p.
4517	Kilworth North	P	N.t.p.
4518	Kings Norton	P	Awd.,Min.
4519	Kirby Frith	EP	N.t.p.,Min.
4520	Kirby Bellars	P	Awd.,Min.
4521	Kirby Mallory	T	Awd.,Min.
4522	Knaptoft	P	Awd.,Min.
4523	Knighton	C	Awd.,Min.
4524	Knipton	P	N.t.p.
4525	Knight Thorpe	T	N.t.p.
4526	Knossington or Knawston	P	Awd.,Min.
4527	Langley Priory	EP	N.t.p.,Min.
4528	Tur Langton	T	N.t.p.
4529	Langton East	T	N.t.p.
4530	Langton West	T	N.t.p.
4531	Laund	EP	N.t.p.,Min.
4532	Laughton	P	Agrmt.,Rep. 1838
4533	Leicester Abbey	EP	N.t.p.,Min.
4534	Leicester Forest East	EP	N.t.p.
4535	Leire	P	N.t.p.,Min.
4536	Leonard St with Abbeygate	P	Awd.,Min.
4537	Lockington	P	Awd.,Min.
4538	Lindley and Rowden	T	N.t.p.
4539	Loughborough	P	Awd.,Min.
4540	Loddington	P	Awd.,Min.
4541	Lowesby and Cold Newton	P	Awd.,Min.
4542	Lubbenham	T	Awd.,Min.
4543	Lubbesthorpe	T	Awd.,Min.
4544	Lutterworth	P	Awd.,Min.
4545	Marefield	T	Awd.,Min.
4546	Market Bosworth	T	Awd.,Min.
4547	Markfield	P	Awd.,Min.
4548	Margaret St	P	Awd.,Min.
4549	Martins St	P	N.t.p.
4550	Mary St,Bromkinsthorpe	P	Awd.,Min.
4551	Medbourn	P	Awd.,Min.
4552	Melstone	P	Min.
4553	Merevale	P	N.t.p.,Min.
4554	Melton Mowbray	T	Min.
4555	Misterton and Poultney	H	Agrmt.,Rep. 1838
4556	Mountsorrel	T	N.t.p.,Min.
4557	Mowsley,Shearsby	H	N.t.p.
4558	Muston	P	Awd.,Min.
4559	Mythe the	EP	Min.
4560	Naneley	T	Min.
4561	Nailstone	P	Agrmt.,Rep. 1840
4562	Narborough	T	Agrmt.,Awd.,Min.,Rep. 1841
4563	Newbold de Verdon	P	N.t.p.
4564	Newparks	T	N.t.p.
4565	Newton Harcourt	C	N.t.p.
4566	Newtown	T	Awd.,Min.
4567	Newton Linford	P	Min.
4568	Nicholas St	P	Awd.,Min.
4569	Newarks	L	N.t.p.,Min.
4570	Normanton	H	N.t.p.
4571	Normanton Turville	T	Awd.,Min.
4572	Norton	T	Min.
4573	Norton East	P	Agrmt.,Rep. 1838
4574	Norton juxta Twycross	P	Awd.,Min.
4575	Noseley	P	Awd.,Min.
4576	Oadby	P	N.t.p.,Min.
4577	Odestone	T	Awd.,Min.
4578	Orton on the Hill	P	N.t.p.,Min.
4579	Osbaston	T	Awd.,Min.
4580	Osgathorpe	P	N.t.p.
4581	Owston and Newbold	P	N.t.p.
4582	Packington with Snibstone	P	Awd.,Min.
4583	Peatling Magna	P	Awd.,Min.
4584	Peatling Parva	P	Awd.,Min.
4585	Peckleton	P	Min.,Rep. 1844
4586	Pickwell with Leesthorpe	P	Awd.,Min.
4587	Plungar	P	N.t.p.
4588	Potters Marston	T	Awd.,Min.
4589	Prestwold	T	Awd.,Min.
4590	Quenby	H	N.t.p.
4591	Queeniborough	P	N.t.p.
4592	Quorndon	L	N.t.p.,Min.
4593	Ragdale or Wreakdale	P	N.t.p.,Min.
4594	Ratby	T	Awd.,Min.
4595	Ratcliffe Culey	R	N.t.p.
4596	Ratcliffe on the Wreak	P	N.t.p.,Min.
4597	Ravenstone	P	N.t.p.
4598	Rearsby	P	Awd.,Min.
4599	Redmile	P	N.t.p.
4600	Rolleston	T	Awd.,Min.
4601	Rotherby	P	Awd.,Min.
4602	Rothley	P	Awd.,Min.
4603	Rothley Temple	EP	N.t.p.
4604	Saddington	P	N.t.p.,Min.
4605	Saltby	P	Min.
4606	Sapcote	P	Awd.,Min.
4607	Saxelby	P	Awd.,Min.
4608	Scalford	P	Awd.,Min.
4609	Scraptoft	P	Awd.,Min.
4610	Seagrave	P	N.t.p.
4611	Sewsterne	C	Agrmt.,Rep. 1839
4612	Shackerstone	T	Awd.,Min.
4613	Shangton or Shankton	P	Agrmt.,Rep. 1842
4614	Sharnford	P	Awd.,Min.
4615	Shawell	P	Agrmt.,Rep. 1839
4616	Shearsby	L	N.t.p.
4617	Sheepshead	P	Awd.,Min.
4618	Sheepy Magna	T	Awd.,Min.
4619	Sheepy Parva	T	Awd.,Min.
4620	Shenton	T	Awd.,Min.
4621	Shoby or Shouldby	EP	N.t.p.
4622	Shermans	EP	N.t.p.
4623	Sibson	T	Awd.,Min.
4624	Sileby	P	N.t.p.
4625	Slawston	P	N.t.p.
4626	Smeaton Westerby	H	N.t.p.
4627	Snareston	P	Agrmt.,Rep. 1841
4628	Somerby	P	Awd.,Min.
4629	Seal	P	Awd.,Min.
4630	Saxby	P	Awd.,Min.
4631	Stapleford	P	N.t.p.,Min.
4632	Sproxton	P	Awd.,Min.
4633	Stanton under Bardon	T	N.t.p.,Min.
4634	Stapleton	P	Agrmt.,Rep. 1838
4635	Stapleton	H	N.t.p.
4636	Statherne	P	N.t.p.
4637	Staunton Harold	T	N.t.p.
4638	Stoughton	T	Awd.,Min.
4639	Stockerstone	P	Rep. 1839
4640	Stoke Golding	T	Awd.,Min.
4641	Stonesby	P	N.t.p.,Min.
4642	Stonton Wyville	P	Min.
4643	Stoney Stanton	P	N.t.p.,Min.
4644	Stretton Great	T	Agrmt.,Awd.,Rep. 1841
4645	Stretton Parva	C	N.t.p.,Min.
4646	Sutton Cheney	T	N.t.p.
4647	Swannington	T	Awd.,Min.
4648	Swepstone	P	Agrmt.,Rep. 1839
4649	Swinford	P	N.t.p.
4650	Swithland	P	Awd.,Min.
4651	Sysonby	H	Agrmt.,Rep. 1843
4652	Syston	P	Awd.,Min.
4653	Temple Hall	H	N.t.p.
4654	Theddingworth	T	Awd.,Min.
4655	Thornton	T	N.t.p.
4656	Thorpe Arnold	P	Awd.,Min.
4657	Thorpe Langton	T	N.t.p.
4658	Thorpe Satchville	T	Awd.,Min.
4659	Thringstone	T	N.t.p.
4660	Thurcaston	T	N.t.p.
4661	Thurlaston	P	Awd.,Min.
4662	Thurmaston South	C	Awd.,Min.
4663	Thurnby	T	Awd.,Min.
4664	Tilton on the Hill	P	Agrmt.,Rep. 1839
4665	Tooley	T	Awd.,Min.
4666	Tugby	P	Awd.,Min.
4667	Twycross	P	Awd.,Min.
4668	Twyford	T	Awd.,Min.
4669	Ullesthorpe	H	Awd.,Min.
4670	Ulverscroft	EP	N.t.p.
4671	Upton	T	Awd.,Min.
4672	Waltham	P	N.t.p.
4673	Walton on the Wolds	P	N.t.p.
4674	Walcote and Poulteney	H	Awd.,Min.
4675	Wanlip	P	Agrmt.,Rep. 1838
4676	Wartnaby	P	Awd.,Min.
4677	Welby	H	Agrmt.,Rep. 1838
4678	Welham	P	Awd.,Min.
4679	Westrill with Starmore	EP	N.t.p.
4680	Whatborough	T	Awd.,Min.
4681	Whatton Long	P	N.t.p.,Min.

Leicestershire contd.

4682	Whetstone	P	Awd.,Min.
4683	White or Augustine Friars	EP	N.t.p.
4684	Whitwick	T	N.t.p.
4685	Wigston Great	P	N.t.p.
4686	Wigston Parva	H	Awd.,Min.
4687	Willoughby Waterless	P	Awd.,Min.
4688	Wimeswold	P	Awd.,Min.
4689	Wistow	T	N.t.p.
4690	Withcote	P	Awd.,Min.
4691	Witherley	T	Awd.,Min.
4692	Worthington with Newbold	C	N.t.p.,Min.
4693	Woodhouse	T	Agrmt.,Rep. 1840
4694	Woodthorpe	H	Awd.,Min.
4695	Wyford cum Brentingby	T	Awd.,Min.
4696	Wycombe with Chadwell	H	N.t.p.,Min.
4697	Wykeham and Caldwell	L	N.t.p.
4698	Wykin	H	Awd.,Min.
4699	Wymondham	P	Agrmt.,Rep. 1839
4736	Barlestone	T	Awd.,Min.
5453	Skeffington	P	Awd.,Min.
14833	Bagworth	C	N.t.p.,Min.

Lincolnshire

4402	Addlethorpe	P	Agrmt.,Min.,Rep. 1842
4403	Ailsby	P	Agrmt.,Min.,Rep. 1840
4404	Aisby	T	N.t.p.,Min.
4700	Aisthorpe	P	Awd.,Min.
4701	Alford with Tothby,Rigsby	P	Min.,Rep. 1838
4702	Alkborough	P	Agrmt.,Min.,Rep. 1841
4703	Allington East	P	N.t.p.,Min.
4704	Althorpe	T	Awd.,Min.
4705	Alvingham	P	N.t.p.,Min.
4706	Amcotts	T	Agrmt.,Rep. 1838
4707	Ancaster	P	Awd.,Min.
4708	Anderby	P	Awd.,Min.
4709	Anwick	P	N.t.p.,Min.
4710	Apley	P	Awd.,Min.
4711	Appleby	P	Awd.,Min.
4712	Asgarby	P	Awd.,Min.
4713	Asgarby(Spalding)	P	Awd.,Min.
4714	Ashby	T	N.t.p.
4715	Ashby by Partney	P	N.t.p.,Min.
4716	Ashby cum Fenby	P	Agrmt.,Awd.,Min.
4717	Ashby Puerorum	P	Awd.,Min.
4718	Ashby de la Laund	P	N.t.p.,Min.
4719	Ashby West	P	Awd.,Min.
4720	Aslackby	P	Awd.,Min.
4721	Asterby	P	Min.
4722	Aswarby	P	Agrmt.,Rep. 1837
4723	Aswardby	P	Agrmt.,Awd.,Min.,Rep. 1842
4724	Atterby	T	N.t.p.,Min.
4725	Aubourn	P	Awd.,Min.
4726	Aunby	H	N.t.p.,Min.
4727	Aunsby	P	Agrmt.,Rep. 1838
4728	Authorpe	P	Agrmt.,Min.,Rep. 1838
4729	Bag Enderby	P	Agrmt.,Rep. 1838
4730	Bardney	P	Awd.,Min.
4731	Barholme cum Stowe	P	Agrmt.,Min.,Rep. 1838
4732	Barkston	P	Agrmt.,Rep. 1838
4733	Barkwith East	P	N.t.p.,Min.
4734	Barkwith West	P	Awd.,Min.
4735	Barlings	P	N.t.p.,Min.
4737	Barnetby le Wold	P	N.t.p.,Min.
4738	Barnoldby le Beek	P	N.t.p.,Min.
4739	Barrow upon Humber	P	N.t.p.,Min.
4740	Barrowby	P	Awd.,Min.
4741	Barton upon Humber	P	N.t.p.,Min.
4742	Basingthorpe with Westby	P	Agrmt.,Rep. 1839
4743	Bassingham	P	Awd.,Min.
4744	Baston	P	N.t.p.,Min.
4745	Baumber	P	N.t.p.,Min.
4746	Beckingham	P	N.t.p.,Min.
4747	Beelsby	P	Awd.,Min.
4748	Beesby	P	Agrmt.,Min.,Rep. 1839
4749	Belchford	P	Awd.,Min.
4750	Belleau cum Aby	P	Awd.,Min.
4751	Belton	P	N.t.p.,Min.,Rep. 1837
4752	Belton in Axholme	P	Awd.,Min.
4753	St Benedict	P	Min.
4754	Benington	P	N.t.p.,Min.
4755	Bennington Grange	EP	N.t.p.
4756	Bennington Long	P	N.t.p.,Min.
4757	Benniworth	P	Awd.,Min.
4758	Bicker	P	N.t.p.,Min.
4759	Bigby	P	Agrmt.,Rep. 1839
4760	Billingborough	P	N.t.p.,Min.
4761	Billinghay	P	N.t.p.,Min.
4762	Bilsby	P	Awd.,Min.
4763	Binbrook St Gabriel	P	Min.
4764	Binbrook St Mary	P	Min.
4765	Birthorpe	T	N.t.p.,Min.
4766	Biscathorpe	P	N.t.p.,Min.
4767	Bishops Norton	P	N.t.p.,Min.
4768	Bitchfield	P	Awd.,Min.
4769	Bloxholm	P	Agrmt.,Min.,Rep. 1837
4770	Blyborough	P	Agrmt.,Rep. 1837
4771	Blyton	P	N.t.p.,Min.
4772	Bolingbroke	P	Awd.,Min.
4773	Bonby	P	Awd.,Min.
4774	Boothby Graffoe	P	N.t.p.,Min.
4775	Blankney	P	N.t.p.,Min.
4776	Boston East	P	Awd.,Min.
4777	St Botolph	P	Awd.,Min.
4778	Bottesford	T	N.t.p.,Min.
4779	Boultham	P	Awd.,Min.
4780	Boothby Pagnell	P	Agrmt.,Min.,Rep. 1838
4781	Bourne	P	Awd.,Min.
4782	Boston West	P	Awd.,Min.
4783	Braceborough	P	N.t.p.,Min.
4784	Bracebridge	P	Awd.,Min.
4785	Brackenborough	P	Awd.,Min.
4786	Braceby	P	Agrmt.,Min.,Rep. 1838
4787	Bradley	P	Agrmt.,Rep. 1839
4788	Brauncewell	P	Awd.,Min.
4789	Brattleby	P	Min.
4790	Brant Broughton	P	Agrmt.,Min.,Rep. 1838
4791	Branston	P	Awd.,Min.
4792	Brampton	T	N.t.p.,Min.
4793	Brigsley	P	Awd.,Min.
4794	Bromby	T	Awd.,Min.
4795	Brinkhill	P	N.t.p.,Min.
4796	Brocklesby	P	Min.
4797	Brothertoft	C	N.t.p.,Min.
4798	Broughton	P	Awd.,Min.
4799	Broxholme	P	Agrmt.,Rep. 1840
4800	Buckland and Farforth	P	Awd.,Min.
4801	Bucknall	P	Rep. 1839
4802	Bullington	T	Awd.,Min.
4803	Burgh le Marsh	P	Awd.,Min.
4804	Burgh upon Bane cum Girsby	P	Agrmt.,Min.,Rep. 1842
4805	Burringham	T	Awd.,Min.
4806	Burton by Lincoln	P	Awd.,Min.
4807	Burton Pedwardine	P	Awd.,Min.
4808	Burton Coggles	P	Agrmt.,Min.,Rep. 1838
4809	Burton upon Stather	P	N.t.p.,Min.
4810	Buslingthorpe	P	Agrmt.,Rep. 1838
4811	Butterwick East	T	Awd.,Min.
4812	Butterwick West,Kelfield	T	Awd.,Min.
4813	Bytham Little	P	N.t.p.,Min.
4814	Cabourn	P	N.t.p.,Min.
4815	Castle Bytham	P	N.t.p.,Min.
4816	Cadney cum Housham	P	Awd.,Min.
4817	Caenby	P	Awd.,Min.
4818	Caistor	P	Awd.,Min.
4819	Calcethorpe	P	Awd.,Min.
4820	Cammeringham	P	Awd.,Min.
4821	Candlesby	P	N.t.p.,Min.
4822	Canwick	P	N.t.p.,Min.
4823	Careby	P	Agrmt.,Rep. 1838
4824	Carlby	P	N.t.p.,Min.
4825	Carlton Castle	P	N.t.p.,Min.
4826	Carlton Great	P	Agrmt.,Min.,Rep. 1838
4827	Carlton Little	P	Agrmt.,Min.,Rep. 1840
4828	Carlton le Moorland	P	Awd.,Min.
4829	Carlton North	P	Awd.,Min.
4830	Carlton Scroop	P	Agrmt.,Rep. 1837
4831	Carlton South	P	Awd.,Min.
4832	Carrington	PC	N.t.p.,Min.
4833	Castle Dykings	EP	N.t.p.,Min.
4834	Cawkwell	P	N.t.p.,Min.
4835	Cawthorpe Little	P	Rep. 1838
4836	Caythorpe with Friston	P	Awd.,Min.
4837	Cherry Willingham	P	Awd.,Min.
4838	Claxby Pluckacre	P	Agrmt.,Rep. 1839
4839	Claypole	P	N.t.p.,Min.
4840	Claythorpe	H	Agrmt.,Rep. 1839
4841	Cleatham	T	Agrmt.,Rep. 1844
4842	Clee	P	Awd.,Min.
4843	Clixby	P	Agrmt.,Awd.,Min.,Rep. 1839
4844	Coates	P	Awd.,Min.
4845	Coates Great	P	Agrmt.,Rep. 1839
4846	Coates Little	P	Agrmt.,Rep. 1844
4847	Coats North	P	Awd.,Min.
4848	Cockerington North	P	Agrmt.,Rep. 1840
4849	Cockerington South	P	Agrmt.,Awd.,Min.,Rep. 1840
4850	Coleby	P	N.t.p.,Min.
4851	Corringham Great	H	Agrmt.,Rep. 1838
4852	Corringham Little	H	Agrmt.,Min.,Rep. 1838
4853	Coningsby	P	Awd.,Min.
4854	Conisholme	P	Agrmt.,Min.,Rep. 1839
4855	Claxby by Normanby	P	Awd.,Min.
4856	Colsterworth	P	Min.
4857	Copping Syke	EP	Min.
4858	Corby	P	Agrmt.,Min.,Rep. 1841
4859	Covenham,St Bartholomew	P	Awd.,Min.
4860	Covenham,St Mary	P	N.t.p.,Min.
4861	Cowbit	P	N.t.p.,Min.
4862	Cranwell	P	Awd.,Min.
4863	Creeton	P	Agrmt.,Min.,Rep. 1840
4864	Croft	P	Awd.,Min.

Lincolnshire contd.

4865	Crofton	H	N.t.p.
4866	Crosby	T	N.t.p.,Min.
4867	Crowland	P	N.t.p.,Min.
4868	Crowle	P	N.t.p.,Min.
4869	Croxby	P	Agrmt.,Rep. 1837
4870	Croxton	P	N.t.p.,Min.
4871	Cumberworth	P	N.t.p.,Min.
4872	Cuxwold	P	Agrmt.,Rep. 1838
4873	Dalby	P	Awd.,Min.
4874	The Decreed Lands	D	N.t.p.
4875	Deeping Fen	EP	N.t.p.,Min.
4876	Deeping Market	P	N.t.p.,Min.
4877	Deeping St James	P	N.t.p.,Min.
4878	Deeping West	P	N.t.p.,Min.
4879	Dembleby	P	Agrmt.,Rep. 1837
4880	Denton	P	Agrmt.,Rep. 1839
4881	Digby's Wash	EP	N.t.p.,Min.
4882	Digby	P	Agrmt.,Rep. 1839
4883	Doddington	P	Agrmt.,Awd.,Min.,Rep. 1839
4884	Dogdyke	T	N.t.p.
4885	Donington	P	N.t.p.,Min.
4886	Donington upon Bain	P	N.t.p.,Min.
4887	Dorrington	P	Awd.,Min.
4888	Dowsby	P	Agrmt.,Min.,Rep. 1837
4889	Drainage Marsh	EP	N.t.p.,Min.
4890	Dry Doddington	T	N.t.p.
4891	Dunholme	P	Min.
4892	Dunsby	P	Agrmt.,Rep. 1838
4893	Dunstall and Bonsdale	H	Agrmt.,Rep. 1838
4894	Dunston	P	N.t.p.,Min.
4895	Dyke	D	Min.
4896	Eagle	P	Awd.,Min.
4897	Eagle Woodhouse	EP	N.t.p.,Min.
4898	Eagle Hall	EP	N.t.p.,Min.
4899	Edenham	P	Awd.,Min.
4900	Edlington	P	Awd.,Min.
4901	Elkington North	P	Agrmt.,Rep. 1838
4902	Elkington South	P	Agrmt.,Rep. 1839
4903	Elsham	P	Min.
4904	Epworth	P	Awd.,Min.
4905	Evedon	P	Agrmt.,Awd.,Min.,Rep. 1838
4906	Ewerby	P	Awd.,Min.
4907	Falkingham and Laughton	P	Agrmt.,Rep. 1838
4908	Farforth cum Maidenwell	P	Awd.,Min.
4909	Fens East and West	D	Min.
4910	Fenton	P	Awd.,Min.
4911	Ferriby South	P	N.t.p.,Min.
4912	Ferry Corner	EP	N.t.p.,Min.
4913	Ferry East	T	N.t.p.
4914	Fillingham	P	N.t.p.,Min.
4915	Firsby (Candleshoe)	P	Agrmt.,Rep. 1839
4916	Firsby East	H	Agrmt.,Min.,Rep. 1839
4917	Firsby West	P	Agrmt.,Rep. 1840
4918	Fiskerton	P	N.t.p.,Min.
4919	Fishtoft	P	N.t.p.,Min.
4920	Fleet	P	Agrmt.,Rep. 1838
4921	Flixborough with Normanby	T	Agrmt.,Rep. 1839
4922	Forty Foot Bank North	EP	Min.
4923	Forty Foot Bridge	EP	Min.
4924	Faldingworth	P	N.t.p.,Min.
4925	Foston	P	N.t.p.,Min.
4926	Fotherby	P	N.t.p.,Min.
4927	Frampton	P	N.t.p.,Min.
4928	Frieston and Butterwick	P	N.t.p.,Min.
4929	Friskney	P	Agrmt.,Min.,Rep. 1839
4930	Fristhorpe	P	Agrmt.,Awd.,Rep. 1844
4931	Frodingham	T	N.t.p.,Min.
4932	Fulbeck	P	Min.
4933	Fulletby	P	N.t.p.,Min.
4934	Fulstow	P	N.t.p.,Min.
4935	Gainsborough	T	Awd.,Min.
4936	Garwick	H	N.t.p.,Min.
4937	Gate Burton	P	Awd.,Min.
4938	Gautby	P	Agrmt.,Min.,Rep. 1838
4939	Gayton le Marsh	P	Agrmt.,Rep. 1839
4940	Gayton le Wold	P	Agrmt.,Min.,Rep. 1839
4941	Gedney	P	Agrmt.,Min.,Rep. 1839
4942	Gibbet Hills	EP	N.t.p.,Min.
4943	Glanford Brigg	C	N.t.p.,Min.
4944	Glentham	P	N.t.p.,Min.
4945	Glentworth	P	Agrmt.,Min.,Rep. 1839
4946	Gonerby Great	P	N.t.p.,Min.
4947	Goltho	T	Awd.,Min.
4948	Goulsby	P	N.t.p.,Min.
4949	Gosberton	P	N.t.p.,Min.
4950	Goxhill	P	Awd.,Min.
4951	Graby and Millthorpe	H	Min.
4952	Grainsby	P	Agrmt.,Rep. 1839
4953	Grantham	P	Awd.,Min.
4954	Grasby	P	N.t.p.,Min.
4955	Grimsby Little	P	Awd.,Min.
4956	Grimsby Great	P	Awd.,Min.
4957	Grainthorpe	P	Awd.,Min.
4958	Greenhill	EP	N.t.p.
4959	Grayingham	P	Agrmt.,Awd.,Min.
4960	Greatford	P	N.t.p.,Min.
4961	Greetham	P	N.t.p.,Min.
4962	Greetwell	P	Awd.,Min.
4963	Grimblethorpe	EP	N.t.p.,Min.
4964	Grimoldby	P	Awd.,Min.
4965	Grimsthorpe	T	N.t.p.
4966	Gunby	P	Rep. 1838
4967	Gunby St Nicholas	P	N.t.p.,Min.
4968	Gunhouse	T	Agrmt.,Min.,Rep. 1838
4969	Haddington	T	Min.
4970	Hagnaby	P	Awd.,Min.
4971	Hagworthingham	P	N.t.p.,Min.
4972	Hainton	P	Awd.,Min.
4973	Hale Little	T	Min.
4974	Hale Great	P	Awd.,Min.
4975	Hallington	P	Awd.,Min.
4976	Halton Holegate	P	Awd.,Min.
4977	Harrington	P	Agrmt.
4978	Harts Grounds	EP	N.t.p.,Min.
4979	Hatcliffe	P	Agrmt.,Rep. 1838
4980	Hatton	P	Awd.,Min.
4981	Haugh	EP	Awd.,Min.
4982	Haugham	P	Agrmt.,Rep. 1839
4983	Havenbank	EP	Min.
4984	Haverholme Priory	EP	N.t.p.,Min.
4985	Hawerby cum Beesby	P	Agrmt.,Rep. 1838
4986	Haxey	P	Awd.,Min.
4987	Haydor	P	N.t.p.,Min.
4988	Haltham upon Bain	P	Awd.,Min.
4989	Halton East	P	N.t.p.,Min.
4990	Halton West	T	Agrmt.,Rep. 1838
4991	Hammeringham	P	N.t.p.,Min.
4992	Hanbeck	H	Agrmt.,Rep. 1839
4993	Hanby	H	Awd.,Min.
4994	Hannah	P	N.t.p.,Min.
4995	Hanworth Cold	P	Awd.,Min.,Rep. 1839
4996	Hareby	P	Awd.,Min.
4997	Hardwick	T	Awd.,Min.
4998	Harlaxton	P	N.t.p.,Min.
4999	Harmston	P	N.t.p.,Min.
5000	Harrowby	T	Agrmt.,Rep. 1839
5001	Harpswell	P	Awd.,Min.
5002	Habrough	P	N.t.p.,Min.
5003	Hacconby	P	Awd.,Min.
5004	Haceby	P	Agrmt.,Rep. 1837
5005	Hackthorn	P	N.t.p.,Min.
5006	Healing	P	Agrmt.,Rep. 1839
5007	Heapham	P	N.t.p.,Min.
5008	Heckington	P	N.t.p.,Min.
5009	Heighington	T	N.t.p.
5010	Helpringham	P	N.t.p.,Min.
5011	Hemingby	P	Awd.,Min.
5012	Hemswell	P	N.t.p.,Min.
5013	Hibaldstowe	P	N.t.p.,Min.
5014	Hogsthorpe	P	N.t.p.,Min.
5015	Holbeach	P	Agrmt.,Min.
5016	Horbling	P	N.t.p.,Min.
5017	Howell	P	Awd.,Min.
5018	Holbeck	EP	Min.
5019	Holdingham	H	N.t.p.
5020	Holne	T	Awd.,Min.
5021	Holton cum Beckering	P	Awd.,Min.
5022	Holton le Clay	P	Agrmt.,Min.,Rep. 1839
5023	Holton le Moor	P	Rep. 1838
5024	Honington	P	Agrmt.,Rep. 1839
5025	Horkstowe	P	Agrmt.,Min.,Rep. 1840
5026	Horsington	P	N.t.p.,Min.
5027	Hough on the Hill	P	Awd.,Min.
5028	Horncastle	P	N.t.p.,Min.
5029	Hougham and Marston	P	Awd.,Min.
5030	Huckerby	H	Agrmt.,Rep. 1838
5031	Humberstone	P	Awd.,Min.
5032	Hundleby	P	Awd.,Min.
5033	Huttoft	P	Awd.,Min.
5034	Hykeham North	P	Min.
5035	Hykeham North	P	N.t.p.
5036	Hykeham South	P	Awd.,Min.
5037	Immingham	P	Awd.,Min.
5038	Ingham	P	Awd.,Min.
5039	Ingoldmells	P	Agrmt.,Min.,Rep. 1843
5040	Ingoldsby	P	Awd.,Min.
5041	Irby upon Humber	P	Agrmt.,Rep. 1837
5042	Irby in the Marsh	P	Min.,Rep. 1841
5043	Irnham	P	Agrmt.,Min.,Rep. 1839
5044	John Saint	P	Awd.,Min.
5045	Keadby	T	Awd.,Min.
5046	Keal East	P	Awd.,Min.
5047	Keal West	P	Awd.,Min.
5048	Keddington	P	N.t.p.,Min.
5049	Keelby	P	Agrmt.,Min.,Rep. 1844
5050	Kirmington	P	Awd.,Min.
5051	Keisby	H	Awd.,Min.
5052	Kelby	T	Awd.,Min.
5053	Kelsey North	P	N.t.p.,Min.
5054	Kelsey South	P	Awd.,Min.
5055	Kelstern	H	Awd.,Min.
5056	Kettlethorpe	P	Awd.,Min.

Lincolnshire contd.

No.	Place	Type	Details
5057	Killingholme	P	Awd.,Min.
5058	Kingerby	P	Awd.,Min.
5059	Kirkby East	P	Awd.,Min.
5060	Kirby Green	P	Agrmt.,Rep. 1839
5061	Kirkby upon Bane	P	Awd.,Min.
5062	Kirkby cum Osgodby	P	N.t.p.,Min.
5063	Kirkby Laythorpe	P	Awd.,Min.
5064	Kirkby Underwood	P	N.t.p.,Min.
5065	Kirmond le Mire	P	Agrmt.,Rep. 1838
5066	Kirkstead	P	N.t.p.,Min.
5067	Kirton (Boston)	P	N.t.p.,Min.
5068	Kirton in Lindsey	P	N.t.p.,Min.
5069	Knaith	P	Awd.,Min.
5070	Kyme North	T	Awd.,Min.
5071	Kyme South	P	Awd.,Min.
5072	Laceby	P	Agrmt.,Min.,Rep. 1840
5073	Lambcroft	D	Min.
5074	Llangrick Ferry	EP	N.t.p.,Min.
5075	Llangriville	T	N.t.p.,Min.
5076	Langtoft	P	N.t.p.,Min.
5077	Langton (Spilsby)	P	Agrmt.,Rep. 1838
5078	Langton (Wragby)	P	Rep. 1843
5079	Langton Woodhouse	EP	Awd.,Min.
5080	Langton (Horncastle)	P	N.t.p.,Min.
5081	Langworth	T	Min.
5082	Laughton	P	Agrmt.,Awd.,Min.,Rep. 1843
5083	Lavington or Lenton	T	Agrmt.,Awd.,Min.,Rep. 1839
5084	Lavington or Lenton	H	Awd.,Min.
5085	Lea	P	Agrmt.,Rep. 1837
5086	Leadenham	P	N.t.p.,Min.
5087	Leake	P	N.t.p.,Min.
5088	Leasingham	P	Agrmt.,Min.,Rep. 1839
5089	Legbourne	P	N.t.p.,Min.
5090	Legsby	P	Awd.,Min.
5091	Leverton	P	N.t.p.,Min.
5092	Limber Magna	P	Awd.,Min.
5093	Limber Parva	H	Awd.,Min.
5094	Linwood	H	Awd.,Min.
5095	Linwood	P	Agrmt.,Rep. 1839
5096	Lissington	P	Agrmt.,Rep. 1839
5097	Londonthorpe	P	N.t.p.,Min.
5098	Louth	P	Awd.,Min.
5099	Ludford Magna	P	Awd.,Min.
5100	Ludborough	P	Awd.,Min.
5101	Luddington	P	N.t.p.,Min.
5102	Ludford Parva	P	N.t.p.,Min.
5103	Lusby	P	Awd.,Min.
5104	Mablethorpe St Mary	P	Awd.,Min.
5105	Mablethorpe St Peter	P	N.t.p.
5106	Maidenhouse	EP	N.t.p.
5107	Maidenwell	P	Min.
5108	Maltby	D	Min.
5109	Maltby le Marsh	P	Agrmt.,Rep. 1838
5110	Manby	P	N.t.p.,Min.
5111	Manthorpe cum Little Goner	T	N.t.p.,Min.
5112	Manton	P	N.t.p.,Min.
5113	Mareham le Fen	P	Awd.,Min.
5114	Mareham on the Hill	P	N.t.p.,Min.
5115	St Margaret	P	Awd.,Min.
5116	Markby	P	Agrmt.,Rep. 1839
5117	Market Deeping	P	N.t.p.,Min.
5118	Market Rasen	P	Awd.,Min.
5119	Market Stainton	P	Awd.,Min.
5120	St Mark	P	Awd.,Min.
5121	Marsh Chapel	P	Awd.,Min.
5122	Mavis Enderby	P	Awd.,Min.
5123	Marston	P	Awd.,Min.
5124	Martin	P	Agrmt.,Min.,Rep. 1839
5125	Martin Dales	D	Awd.,Min.
5126	St Martin	P	Awd.,Min.
5127	Martin(Timberland)	H	N.t.p.,Min.
5128	Marton	P	N.t.p.,Min.
5129	St Mary le Wigford	P	Awd.,Min.
5130	St Mary Magdalene	P	Awd.,Min.
5131	Mere Hall	P	Awd.,Min.
5132	Melton Ross	P	Awd.,Min.
5133	Messingham	P	N.t.p.,Min..
5134	Metheringham	P	Awd.,Min.
5135	St Michael on the Mount	P	N.t.p.
5136	Midville	T	N.t.p.,Min.
5137	Millthorpe	H	N.t.p.
5138	Minting	P	Agrmt.,Min.,Rep. 1842
5139	Miningsby	P	Awd.,Min.
5140	Monks Liberty	EP	N.t.p.,Min.
5141	Moorby	P	Awd.,Min.
5142	Morton	P	Awd.,Min.
5143	Morton	T	N.t.p.,Min.
5144	Morton by Swinderby	EP	N.t.p.,Min.
5145	Moulton	P	Awd.,Min.
5146	Muckton	P	Agrmt.,Awd.,Min.,Rep. 1838
5147	Mumby cum Chapel	P	Awd.,Min.
5148	Navenby	P	N.t.p.,Min.
5149	Nettleham	P	N.t.p.,Min.
5150	Nettleton	P	N.t.p.,Min.
5151	Newsham	EP	N.t.p.,Min.
5152	Newton	P	N.t.p.,Min.
5153	Newton next Toft	P	Awd.,Min.
5154	Newton upon Trent	P	N.t.p.,Min.
5155	St Nicholas	P	Awd.,Min.
5156	Nocton	P	Awd.,Min.
5157	Normanby next Spittal	P	N.t.p.,Min.
5158	Northolme	P	Awd.,Min.
5159	Normanby on the Wolds	P	Awd.
5160	Normanton	P	N.t.p.,Min.
5161	Northorpe	P	Rep. 1838
5162	Norton Disney	P	Agrmt.,Rep. 1839
5163	Nuncotham	EP	N.t.p.,Min.
5164	Orby	P	Awd.,Min.
5165	Orford	D	Awd.,Min.
5166	Ormsby North	P	Awd.,Min.
5167	Ormsby South cum Ketsby	P	Agrmt.,Rep. 1839
5168	Osbournby	P	N.t.p.,Min.
5169	Oseby	T	N.t.p.
5170	Osgodby	T	Agrmt.,Rep. 1839
5171	Owersby	P	Agrmt.,Min.,Rep. 1838
5172	Owmby	P	N.t.p.,Min.
5173	Owston and West Butterwick	P	Awd.,Min.
5174	Oxcombe	P	Agrmt.,Rep. 1840
5175	The Paddock	EP	N.t.p.,Min.
5176	Panton	P	Agrmt.,Rep. 1838
5177	Louth Park	T	N.t.p.,Min.
5178	Partney	P	Agrmt.,Rep. 1838
5179	St Paul	P	N.t.p.
5180	Pelhams Lands	EP	N.t.p.,Min.
5181	Pepper Gowt Plot	EP	N.t.p.
5182	St Peter at Arches	P	Awd.,Min.
5183	St Peter at Gowts	P	Awd.,Min.
5184	St Peter in Eastgate	P	Awd.,Min.
5185	Pickworth	P	Awd.,Min.
5186	Pilham	P	Awd.,Min.
5187	Pinchbeck	P	N.t.p.,Min.
5188	Pointon	T	Awd.,Min.
5189	Ponton Great	P	N.t.p.,Min.
5190	Ponton Little	P	N.t.p.,Min.
5191	Potter Hanworth	P	Awd.,Min.
5192	Quadring	P	N.t.p.,Min.
5193	Quarrington	P	N.t.p.,Min.
5194	Raithby	P	Awd.,Min.
5195	Raithby with Maltby	P	Agrmt.,Min.,Rep. 1839
5196	Rakes Farm	EP	N.t.p.,Min.
5197	Ranby	P	Awd.,Min.
5198	Rauceby,North and South	P	N.t.p.,Min.
5199	Rand with Futtleby	P	Awd.,Min.
5200	Middle Rasen	T	Awd.,Min.
5201	West Rasen	P	N.t.p.,Min.
5202	Ravendale East	P	Agrmt.,Awd.,Min.,Rep. 1839
5203	Ravendale West	P	N.t.p.,Min.
5204	Redbourne	P	Agrmt.,Rep. 1841
5205	Repham	P	Agrmt.,Rep. 1841
5206	Reston North	P	Agrmt.,Rep. 1839
5207	Reston South	P	Awd.,Min.
5208	Revesby	P	N.t.p.,Min.
5209	Riby	P	Agrmt.,Rep. 1838
5210	Rippingale	P	N.t.p.,Min.
5211	Risby	T	Awd.,Min.
5212	Riseholme	P	N.t.p.,Min.
5213	Ropsley and Little Humby	P	Awd.,Min.
5214	Rothwell	P	N.t.p.,Min.
5215	Roughton	P	Awd.,Min.
5216	Rowlands Marsh	EP	N.t.p.
5217	Roulston	P	Agrmt.,Min.,Rep. 1843
5218	Roxby cum Risby	P	Agrmt.,Rep. 1840
5219	Roxholme	T	Awd.,Min.
5220	Royalty	EP	N.t.p.,Min.
5221	Ruskington	P	Awd.,Min.
5222	Saleby	P	N.t.p.,Min.
5223	Salmonby	P	Awd.,Min.
5224	Saltfleetby All Saints	P	Agrmt.,Rep. 1838
5225	Saltfleetby St Clements	P	Agrmt.,Min.,Rep. 1838
5226	Saltfleetby St Peters	P	Agrmt.,Min.,Rep. 1839
5227	Santon East	H	N.t.p.
5228	Sapperton	P	Awd.,Min.
5229	Sausthorpe	P	Agrmt.,Rep. 1839
5230	Saxby	P	Agrmt.,Min.,Rep. 1837
5231	Saxby in Aslacoe	P	Awd.,Min.
5232	Saxelby with Ingleby	P	N.t.p.,Min.
5233	Scamblesby	P	N.t.p.,Min.
5234	Scampton	P	Awd.,Min.
5235	Scarle North	P	Agrmt.,Rep. 1839
5236	Scate Intack,Wroot Acres	D	Awd.,Min.
5237	Scartho	P	N.t.p.,Min.
5238	Scawby	P	N.t.p.,Min.
5239	Scopwick	P	N.t.p.,Min.
5240	Sothern	P	Awd.,Min.
5241	Scotter	P	N.t.p.,Min.
5242	Scottlethorpe	H	N.t.p.
5243	Scotton	P	Agrmt.,Rep. 1838
5244	Scot Willoughby	P	Rep. 1837
5245	Scrafield	P	Agrmt.,Rep. 1840
5246	Scredington	P	N.t.p.,Min.
5247	Scremby	P	N.t.p.,Min.
5248	Scrivelsby	P	Awd.,Min.

Lincolnshire contd.

5249	Sedgebrook	P	Agrmt.,Awd.,Min.,Rep. 1845
5250	Searby cum Owmby	P	N.t.p.,Min.
5251	Silk Willoughby	P	Agrmt.,Rep. 1839
5252	Silt Pits	EP	N.t.p.,Min.
5253	Sixhills	P	Awd.,Min.
5254	Skegness	P	Agrmt.,Awd.,Min.,Rep. 1842
5255	Skendleby	P	Agrmt.,Min.,Rep. 1846
5256	Skidbrook cum Saltfleet	P	Agrmt.,Rep. 1837
5257	Semperingham	T	N.t.p.,Min.
5258	Sibsey	P	N.t.p.,Min.
5259	Skellingthorpe	P	N.t.p.,Min.
5260	Skillington	P	N.t.p.,Min.
5261	Skinnand	P	Awd.,Min.
5262	Skirbeck	P	N.t.p.,Min.
5263	Skirbeck Quarter	D	N.t.p.,Min.
5264	Sleaford New	P	N.t.p.,Min.
5265	Sleaford Old	P	N.t.p.,Min.
5266	Snarford	P	Awd.,Min.
5267	Snelland	P	Agrmt.,Min.,Rep. 1839
5268	Snitterby	T	N.t.p.,Min.
5269	Somerby	P	Awd.,Min.
5270	Somerby(Corringham)	T	Agrmt.,Rep. 1838
5271	Somerby	P	N.t.p.,Min.
5272	Somercotes North	P	Awd.,Min.
5273	Somercotes South	P	Agrmt.,Min.,Rep. 1839
5274	Somersby	P	Agrmt.,Rep. 1838
5275	Somerton Castle	M	Agrmt.,Rep. 1842
5276	Sotby	P	N.t.p.,Min.
5277	Southorpe	EP	Min.
5278	Southrey	T	Min.
5279	Spalding	P	N.t.p.,Min.
5280	Spanby	P	Awd.,Min.
5281	Spilsby with Eresby	PH	N.t.p.,Min.
5282	Spittlegate Houghton	T	N.t.p.,Min.
5283	Spridlington	P	N.t.p.,Min.
5284	Springthorpe	P	Agrmt.,Min.,Rep. 1838
5285	Stainby	P	N.t.p.,Min.
5286	Stainfield	P	Awd.,Min.
5287	Stainsby	T	Min.
5288	Stainton le Vale	P	N.t.p.,Min.
5289	Stallingborough	P	Agrmt.,Rep. 1842
5290	Stamford All Saints	P	Awd.,Min.
5291	Stamford St George	P	Agrmt.,Min.,Rep. 1841
5292	Stamford St John	P	Awd.,Min.
5293	Stamford St Mary	P	N.t.p.,Min.
5294	Stamford St Michael	P	Awd.,Min.
5295	Stane	H	Awd.,Min.
5296	Stainton by Langworth	P	Agrmt.,Min.,Rep. 1838
5297	Stapleford	P	Awd.,Min.
5298	Steeping Great	P	Agrmt.,Rep. 1841
5299	Steeping Little	P	Awd.,Min.
5300	Stenigot	P	Agrmt.,Rep. 1839
5301	Stewton	P	Agrmt.,Rep. 1837
5302	Stockwith East	T	N.t.p.,Min.
5303	Stoke North and South	P	N.t.p.,Min.
5304	Stowe (Well Wapentake)	P	Agrmt.,Awd.,Min.,Rep. 1839
5305	Stragglethorpe	P	N.t.p.,Min.
5306	Stroxton	P	Awd.,Min.
5307	Stickford	P	Awd.,Min.
5308	Stickney	P	Awd.,Min.
5309	Stixwould	P	Awd.,Min.
5310	Strubby	P	N.t.p.,Min.
5311	Stubton	P	Agrmt.,Min.,Rep. 1837
5312	Sturton Great	P	N.t.p.,Min.
5313	Sudbrooke	P	Agrmt.,Rep. 1838
5314	Surfleet	P	Awd.,Min.
5315	Sutterby	P	Agrmt.,Min.,Rep. 1838
5316	Sutterton	EP	N.t.p.,Min.
5317	Sutton St Edmunds	C	Awd.,Min.
5318	Sutton St James	H	Agrmt.,Min.,Rep. 1839
5319	Sutton in the Marsh	P	Agrmt.,Rep. 1839
5320	Sutton St Mary	P	Agrmt.,Min.,Rep. 1841
5321	Sutton St Nicholas	H	Agrmt.,Min.,Rep. 1841
5322	Swaby	P	N.t.p.,Min.
5323	Swallow	P	N.t.p.,Min.
5324	Swarby	P	N.t.p.,Min.
5325	Swaton	P	N.t.p.,Min.
5326	Swayfield	P	N.t.p.,Min.
5327	Swinderby	P	Awd.,Min.
5328	Swineshead	P	N.t.p.,Min.
5329	Swinethorpe	EP	N.t.p.,Min.
5330	Swinhop	P	Agrmt.,Min.,Rep. 1838
5331	Swinstead	P	N.t.p.,Min.
5332	St Swithin	P	Awd.,Min.
5333	Syston	P	N.t.p.,Min.
5334	Tallington	P	Agrmt.,Rep. 1839
5335	Farlesthorpe	P	Agrmt.,Rep. 1839
5336	Tathwell	P	Awd.,Min.
5337	Tattershall	P	Awd.,Min.
5338	Tealby	P	Awd.,Min.
5339	Temple Bruer	EP	N.t.p.,Min.
5340	Tetford	P	N.t.p.,Min.
5341	Tetney	P	Min.
5342	Theddlethorpe All Saints	P	Agrmt.,Min.,Rep. 1838
5343	Theddlethorpe St Helens	P	Agrmt.,Min.,Rep. 1838
5344	Thimbleby	P	Awd.,Min.
5345	Thoresby North	P	Awd.,Min.
5346	Thoresby South	P	Agrmt.,Awd.,Min.,Rep. 1842
5347	Thoresway	P	N.t.p.,Min.
5348	Thorganby	P	Agrmt.,Min.,Rep. 1841
5349	Thornton	P	Agrmt.,Rep. 1839
5350	Thornton le Moor	P	Awd.,Min.
5351	Thornton Curtin	P	Awd.,Min.
5352	Thorpe Acre	P	N.t.p.,Min.
5353	Thorpe in the Fallows	P	Awd.,Min.
5354	Thorpe Latimer	H	N.t.p.
5355	Thorpe Hall	I	Min.
5356	Thorpe on the Hill	P	Awd.,Min.
5357	Thorpe St Peter	P	Awd.,Min.
5358	Thorpe Tilney	T	Agrmt.,Rep. 1839
5359	Threckingham with Stow	P	Awd.,Min.
5360	Thurlby	P	N.t.p.,Min.
5361	Thurlby (Boothby Graffo)	P	Agrmt.,Min.,Rep. 1838
5362	Tiley	P	Min.
5363	Timberland	P	N.t.p.,Min.
5364	Toft	P	Awd.,Min.
5365	Torrington East	P	Awd.,Min.
5366	Torksey	T	N.t.p.,Min.
5367	Torrington West	P	Agrmt.,Awd.,Min.,Rep. 1838
5368	Tothill	P	Awd.,Min.
5369	Toynton All Saints	P	Awd.,Min.
5370	Toynton High	P	Awd.,Min.
5371	Toynton Low	P	Awd.,Min.
5372	Toynton St Peters	P	N.t.p.
5373	Trusthorpe	P	N.t.p.,Min.
5374	Tupholme	P	Awd.,Min.
5375	Twigmoor	T	Awd.,Min.
5376	Tyd St Mary	P	Agrmt.,Min.,Rep. 1838
5377	Uffington	P	Agrmt.,Rep. 1838
5378	Ulceby	P	N.t.p.,Min.
5379	Ulceby	P	N.t.p.,Min.
5380	Upton	P	N.t.p.,Min.
5381	Usselby	P	Awd.,Min.
5382	Utterby	P	Agrmt.,Min.
5383	Ville East	T	N.t.p.,Min.
5384	Ville West	T	N.t.p.,Min.
5385	Waddingham	P	Agrmt.,Min.,Rep. 1837
5386	Waddington	P	N.t.p.,Min.
5387	Waddingworth	P	Agrmt.,Rep. 1837
5388	Wainfleet All Saints	P	Agrmt.,Min.,Rep. 1838
5389	Walkerith	T	N.t.p.,Min.
5390	Walmsgate	P	Awd.,Min.
5391	Waltham	P	N.t.p.,Min.
5392	Walesby	T	Agrmt.,Awd.,Min.,Rep. 1838
5393	Washingborough	P	Awd.,Min.
5394	Welby	P	N.t.p.,Min.
5395	Wellingore	P	N.t.p.,Min.
5396	Welton in the Marsh	P	N.t.p.,Min.
5397	Wainfleet St Mary	P	Agrmt.,Min.,Rep. 1839
5398	Waith	P	N.t.p.,Min.
5399	Walcot	P	Agrmt.,Min.,Rep. 1840
5400	Well with Dexthorpe	P	Agrmt.,Min.,Rep. 1839
5401	Whaplode	P	Agrmt.,Min.,Rep. 1839
5402	Welbourne cum Sapperton	P	N.t.p.,Min.
5403	Whisby	T	Agrmt.,Rep. 1838
5404	Welton (near Louth)	P	N.t.p.,Min.
5405	Welton (near Lincoln)	P	N.t.p.,Min.
5406	Welton le Wold	P	Awd.,Min.
5407	Westborough	P	N.t.p.,Min.
5408	Weston	P	Agrmt.,Min.
5409	Whitton	P	N.t.p.,Min.
5410	Wickenby cum Westaby	P	Agrmt.,Awd.,Min.
5411	Wigtoft	P	N.t.p.,Min.
5412	Wildsworth	P	Min.
5413	Wilksby	P	Awd.,Min.
5414	Willingham	P	N.t.p.,Min.
5415	Willingham North	P	N.t.p.,Min.
5416	Willingham South	P	N.t.p.,Min.
5417	Wildmore Fen,East and West	D	N.t.p.
5418	Winteringham	P	Awd.,Min.
5419	Witham on the Hill	P	N.t.p.,Min.
5420	Witham North	P	Awd.,Min.
5421	Witham South	P	N.t.p.,Min.
5422	Willoughby with Sloothby	P	Agrmt.,Rep. 1838
5423	Willoughton	P	N.t.p.,Min.
5424	Wilsford	P	Min.
5425	Wilsthorpe	C	N.t.p.,Min.
5426	Winceby	P	Agrmt.,Min.,Rep. 1838
5427	Woolsthorpe	P	Awd.,Min.
5428	Wingland(New Saltmarsh)	EP	Awd.,Min.
5429	Winterton	P	Agrmt.,Min.,Rep. 1839
5430	Winthorpe	P	Awd.,Min.
5431	Wispington	P	Agrmt.,Rep. 1838
5432	Withcall	P	N.t.p.,Min.
5433	Withern	P	Agrmt.,Min.,Rep. 1838
5434	Wrangle	P	Awd.,Min.
5435	Wold Newton	P	Awd.,Min.
5436	Wood Enderby	P	Awd.,Min.
5437	Woodhall	P	N.t.p.,Awd.,Min.
5438	Woodhouse Farm	T	Agrmt.,Rep. 1838
5439	Worlaby	P	Awd.,Min.
5440	Worlaby	P	Awd.,Min.

Lincolnshire contd.

5441	Wootton	P	N.t.p.,Min.
5442	Wragby	P	Awd.,Min.
5443	Wrawby	P	N.t.p.,Min.
5444	Wroot	P	N.t.p.
5445	Wroot	P	Awd.,Min.
5446	Wyberton	P	Agrmt.,Rep. 1840
5447	Wyham with Cadeby	P	Awd.,Min.
5448	Wykeham East	P	Awd.,Min.
5449	Wyvill with Hungerton	P	Awd.,Min.
5450	Yaddlethorpe	T	N.t.p.
5451	Yarborough	P	N.t.p.,Min.
5452	Yawthorpe	T	Agrmt.,Rep. 1838
5607	Burwell	P	Awd.,Min.
7475	Misson	P	Awd.,Min.

Middlesex

5454	Acton	P	Awd.,Min.
5455	Allhallows the Less	P	N.t.p.
5456	Andrew St. Holborn	P	N.t.p.
5457	Ashford	P	Min.,Rep. 1839
5458	Barking Allhallows	P	N.t.p.
5459	Bedfont	P	Awd.,Min.
5460	Bethnal Green,St. Matthew	P	Min.
5461	Botolph St. Aldersgate	P	N.t.p.
5462	Botolph St. Aldgate	P	N.t.p.
5463	Brentford New	P	Min.,Rep. 1838
5464	Bromley St Leonard	P	Awd.,Min.
5465	Chelsea	P	Min.
5466	Chelsea	P	Awd.,Min.
5467	Chiswick	P	Awd.,Min.
5468	Christchurch,Spitalfields	P	N.t.p.
5469	Clement St. Danes	P	Min.
5470	Clerkenwell,St. James	P	N.t.p.
5471	Cowley	P	Awd.,Min.
5472	Cranford	P	Min.,Rep. 1838
5473	Drayton West	P	N.t.p.,Min.
5474	Ealing	P	Min.,Rep. 1840
5475	Edgeware	P	Awd.,Min.
5476	Edmonton	P	N.t.p.,Min.
5477	Enfield	P	Awd.,Min.
5478	Feltham	P	N.t.p.,Min.
5479	Finchley	P	Min.,Rep. 1839
5480	Finsbury Park	D	Min.
5481	Friern Barnet	P	Awd.,Min.
5482	Fulham	P	Awd.,Min.
5483	George St. Bloomsbury	P	N.t.p.
5484	George St. in the East	P	N.t.p.
5485	George St. Hanover Square	P	N.t.p.
5486	Giles St. in the Fields	P	N.t.p.
5487	Greenford Great	P	Min.,Rep. 1839
5488	Hackney St. John	P	Awd.,Min.
5489	Hackney South	P	Awd.,Min.
5490	Hackney West	P	Min.
5491	Hadley	P	Awd.,Min.
5492	Hammersmith	P	Awd.,Min.
5493	Hampstead,St. John	P	Min.,Rep. 1839
5494	Hampton	P	Awd.,Min.
5495	Hanwell	P	Min.
5496	Hanworth	P	N.t.p.,Min.
5497	Harefield	P	Awd.,Min.
5498	Harlington	P	Min.,Rep. 1839
5499	Harmondsworth	P	N.t.p.,Min.
5500	Harrow on the Hill	P	N.t.p.
5501	Hayes	P	N.t.p.,Min.
5502	Hendon	P	Awd.,Min.,Rep. 1842
5503	Heston	P	Min.
5504	Hillingdon	P	N.t.p.,Min.
5505	Hornsey	P	Min.
5506	Ickenham	P	Min.,Rep. 1839
5507	Isleworth	P	Min.,Rep. 1839
5508	Islington St Mary	P	Awd.,Min.
5509	James St. Westminster	P	N.t.p.
5510	John St. the Evangelist	P	N.t.p.
5511	Kensington	P	Min.
5512	Kingsbury	P	Min.,Rep. 1838
5513	Laleham	P	Agrmt.,Awd.,Min.
5514	Leonard St. Foster Lane	P	N.t.p.
5515	Limehouse,St. Anne	P	N.t.p.
5516	Littleton	P	Awd.,Min.
5517	Luke St. City Road	L	N.t.p.
5518	St. Margaret,Westminster	P	Awd.
5519	St. Margaret,Westminster	P	Awd.,Min.
5520	Martin St. in the Fields	P	Awd.,Min.
5521	Margaret St. Westminster	P	Awd.,Min.
5522	Mary St. le Strand	P	N.t.p.
5523	Marylebone St.	P	Awd.,Min.
5524	Mimms South	P	Awd.,Min.
5525	Northolt	P	Agrmt.,Min.,Rep. 1836
5526	Norwood Precinct	C	N.t.p.
5527	Paddington	P	Awd.,Min.
5528	Pancras St.	P	Awd.,Min.
5529	Paul St. Covent Garden	P	N.t.p.,Min.
5530	Perivale	P	Awd.,Min.
5531	Peter St. Ad Vincula	P	N.t.p.
5532	Pinner	P	N.t.p.,Min.
5533	Poplar	P	Awd.,Min.
5534	Ruislip	P	N.t.p.,Min.
5535	Saffron Hill,Hatton Garden	L	N.t.p.
5536	Sepulchre St.	P	Min.
5537	Shadwell,St. Paul	P	N.t.p.
5538	Shepperton	P	Awd.,Min.
5539	Shoreditch,St. Leonard	P	N.t.p.
5540	Stanmore Great	P	Min.,Rep. 1838
5541	Stanmore Little	P	Rep. 1838
5542	Stanwell	P	Min.,Rep. 1843
5543	Staines	P	Awd.,Min.,Rep. 1840
5544	Stoke Newington	P	Awd.,Min.
5545	Stratford le Bow,St. Mary	P	Awd.,Min.
5546	Stepney	P	Awd.,Min.
5547	Sunbury	P	N.t.p.,Min.
5548	Teddington	P	N.t.p.,Min.
5549	Tottenham	P	Awd.,Min.
5550	Twickenham	P	Awd.,Min.
5551	Twyford West	P	Awd.,Min.
5552	Wapping,St. John	P	N.t.p.
5553	Whitechapel,St. Mary	P	Min.
5554	Willesden	P	N.t.p.,Min.
6657	St. Anne, Soho	P	N.t.p.

Monmouthshire

5555	Monmouth Co. Union Rep.s	D	Min.
5556	Abergavenny	P	Awd.,Min.
5557	Aberystruth	P	Min.,Rep. 1840
5558	Arvans St	P	Awd.,Min.
5559	Bassalleg	P	Min.,Rep. 1840
5560	Bedwas	P	Min.,Rep. 1840
5561	Bedwelty	P	Awd.,Min.
5562	Bettws	P	Min.,Rep. 1841
5563	Bettws Newydd	P	Awd.,Min.
5564	Bicknor Welsh	P	Agrmt.,Rep. 1838
5565	Bishton	P	Awd.,Min.
5566	Brides St	P	Min.,Rep. 1840
5567	Brides St Netherwent	P	Min.,Rep. 1839
5568	Bryngwyn	P	Min.,Rep. 1839
5569	Caerwent and Crick	P	Min.,Rep. 1843
5570	Caldicott	P	Awd.,Min.
5571	Old Castle	P	Agrmt.,Rep. 1839
5572	Chapel Hill	P	N.t.p.
5573	Chepstow	P	Awd.,Min.
5574	Christchurch	P	Agrmt.,Min.,Rep. 1839
5575	Clytha	H	Awd.,Min.
5576	Coedkernew	P	Min.,Rep. 1842
5577	Cwmcarvon	P	Agrmt.,Min.
5578	Cwmyoy	P	Awd.,Min.
5579	Dinham	H	Rep. 1839
5580	Dingestow	P	Min.
5581	Dixton	P	Awd.,Min.
5582	Glascoed	H	Agrmt.,Min.,Rep. 1840
5583	Goldcliff	P	Rep. 1840
5584	Goytrey	P	Agrmt.,Min.,Rep. 1838
5585	Gracedieu Park	P	N.t.p.
5586	Grosmont	P	Min.,Rep. 1840
5587	Gwehellog	H	Awd.,Min.
5588	Gwernesney	P	Awd.,Min.
5589	Henllis	P	Min.,Rep. 1842
5590	Howick	P	Awd.,Min.
5591	Ifton	P	N.t.p.,Min.
5592	Itton	P	Awd.,Min.
5593	Kemeys Commander	P	Agrmt.,Rep. 1838
5594	Kemeys Inferior	P	Agrmt.,Min.
5595	Cilgwrrwg	P	Awd.,Min.
5596	Langstone	P	Awd.,Min.
5597	Langua	P	Agrmt.,Min.,Rep. 1837
5598	Llanishen	P	Agrmt.,Min.,Rep. 1840
5599	Llanmartin	P	Min.,Rep. 1839
5600	Llanarth	P	Awd.,Min.
5601	Llanbaddock	P	Awd.,Min.
5602	Llanbedr	H	Awd.,Min.
5603	Llandevaud	H	Awd.,Min.
5604	Llandenny	P	Agrmt.,Min.,Rep. 1840
5605	Llandevenny	H	N.t.p.
5606	Llandogo	P	Awd.,Min.
5608	Llanvrechva	P	Min.,Rep. 1840
5609	Llandegfydd	P	Agrmt.,Rep. 1838
5610	Llanellan	P	Awd.,Min.
5611	Llanfoist	P	Awd.,Min.
5612	Llangattock juxta Caerleon	P	Awd.,Min.
5613	Llangattock Lingoed	P	Awd.,Min.
5614	Llangattock Vibon Avel	P	Agrmt.,Min.,Rep. 1838
5615	Llangeview	P	Awd.,Min.
5616	Llangoven	P	Agrmt.,Min.,Rep. 1841
5617	Llangunnock	P	Awd.,Min.
5618	Llanhillith	P	Min.,Rep. 1839
5619	Llangattock juxta Usk	P	Min.,Rep. 1840
5620	Llangibby	P	Agrmt.,Min.,Rep. 1838
5621	Llangwm Issaf and Uchaf	P	Awd.,Min.
5622	Llanhenoch	P	Min.,Rep. 1838
5623	Llanllowel	P	Agrmt.,Min.,Rep. 1837

Monmouthshire contd.

5624	Llantrissent	P	Agrmt.,Min.,Rep. 1839
5625	Llanthewy Rytherch	P	Min.,Rep. 1840
5626	Llanvaches	P	Min.,Rep. 1840
5627	Llansoy	P	Awd.,Min.
5628	Llanvapley	P	Agrmt.,Min.,Rep. 1838
5629	Llantillio Crosseny	P	Awd.,Min.
5630	Llanfihangel Crucorney	P	Awd.,Min.
5631	Llanthewy Skirrid	P	Min.,Rep. 1839
5632	Llantillio Portholey	P	Min.,Rep. 1839
5633	Llanover	P	Agrmt.,Min.,Rep. 1843
5634	Llanvair Discoed	P	Agrmt.,Min.
5635	Llanthewy Vach	P	Min.,Rep. 1842
5636	Llanvetherine	P	Min.,Rep. 1839
5637	Llansaintfraed	P	Awd.,Min.
5638	Llanvihangel juxta Roggett	P	Min.,Rep. 1839
5639	Llanvihangel juxta Usk	P	Awd.,Min.
5640	Llanvihangel Ystern	P	Min.,Rep. 1839
5641	Llanwenarth	P	Min.,Rep. 1842
5642	Llanwern	P	Agrmt.,Rep. 1838
5643	Llanvair Kilgeddin	P	Min.,Rep. 1840
5644	Llanvihangel Llantarnam	P	Agrmt.,Min.
5645	Llanvihangel Pontymoil	P	Rep. 1839
5646	Llanvihangel Tor Y Mynydd	P	Agrmt.,Min.,Rep. 1838
5647	Machen	P	Agrmt.,Min.,Rep. 1838
5648	Magor	P	Awd.,Min.
5649	Malpas	P	Rep. 1839
5650	Mamhilad	P	Awd.,Min.
5651	Marshfield	P	Min.,Rep. 1840
5652	Matherne and Runston	P	Awd.,Min.
5653	Maughans St	P	Awd.,Min.
5654	Mellons St	P	Awd.,Min.
5655	Mitchel Troy	P	Agrmt.,Min.,Rep. 1841
5656	Monkswood	P	N.t.p.
5657	Monmouth	P	Awd.,Min.
5658	Mounton	P	Awd.,Min.
5659	Nash	P	Min.,Rep. 1840
5660	Newchurch East and West	P	Agrmt.,Min.,Rep. 1839
5661	Newport	P	N.t.p.
5662	Panteague	P	Rep. 1837
5663	Penallt	P	Awd.,Min.
5664	Penbiddle	H	N.t.p.
5665	Penhow	P	Agrmt.,Min.,Rep. 1842
5666	Portskewett and Southbrook	P	Agrmt.,Min.,Rep. 1838
5667	Penrose	P	Awd.,Min.
5668	Penterry	P	Awd.,Min.
5669	Peny Clawdd	P	Min.,Rep. 1841
5670	Peterstone	P	Min.,Rep. 1840
5671	Pierre St	P	Rep. 1838
5672	Ragland	P	Min.
5673	Redwick	P	Awd.,Min.
5674	Risca	P	Min.,Rep. 1842
5675	Rockfield	P	Awd.,Min.
5676	Rogerstone	H	N.t.p.
5677	Pierre St and Runstone	P	N.t.p.
5678	Pontypool	P	Min.
5679	Roggett	P	Rep. 1839
5680	Rumney	P	Agrmt.,Min.,Rep. 1840
5681	Runstone	P	Min.
5682	Shirenewton	P	Agrmt.,Awd.,Min.,Rep. 1838
5683	Skenfrith	P	Awd.,Min.
5684	Tregare	P	Awd.,Min.
5685	Trelleck Grange	C	Min.
5686	Trevethin	P	Awd.,Min.
5687	Tintern Parva	P	Awd.,Min.
5688	Tredunnock	P	Agrmt.,Min.,Rep. 1838
5689	Trelleck	P	Awd.,Min.
5690	Treworgan	EP	N.t.p.,Min.
5691	Trostrey	P	Min.,Rep. 1839
5692	Undy	P	Min.,Rep. 1839
5693	Usk	P	Awd.,Min.
5694	Whitson	P	Awd.,Min.
5695	Wilcrick	P	Agrmt.,Min.,Rep. 1838
5696	Wolves Newton	P	Agrmt.,Min.,Rep. 1838
5697	Wonastow	P	Awd.,Min.
5698	Saint Woollos	P	Min.,Rep. 1841
14586	Mynyddysllwyn	P	Awd.,Min.,Rep. 1839

Norfolk

5699	Ashby	P	Rep. 1839
5700	Ashwelthorpe	P	Awd.,Min.
5701	Ashwicken	P	Rep. 1842
5702	Aslacton	P	Agrmt.,Rep. 1839
5703	Attlebridge	P	N.t.p.
5704	Attleburgh	P	Rep. 1838
5705	Aylmerton	P	Rep. 1842
5707	Aylsham	P	Rep. 1838
5708	Babingley	P	Rep. 1838
5709	Baconsthorpe	P	Min.
5710	Bale	P	Rep. 1838
5711	Banham	P	Awd.,Min.
5712	Bacton	P	Awd.,Min.
5713	Bagthorp	P	Rep. 1838
5714	Banningham	P	Rep. 1842
5715	Barford	P	Rep. 1838
5716	Barmer	P	Min.
5717	Acle	P	Rep. 1838
5718	Alborough	P	Rep. 1839
5719	Alburgh	P	Agrmt.,Rep. 1838
5720	Alby	P	Rep. 1838
5721	Aldeby	P	Awd.,Min.
5722	Alderford	P	Rep. 1840
5723	Alethorpe	P	Awd.,Min.
5724	Yelverton cum Alpington	P	Rep. 1838
5725	Anmer	P	Rep. 1838
5726	Antingham St Mary	P	Rep. 1838
5727	Appleton	P	Rep. 1839
5728	Arminghall	P	Rep. 1839
5729	Ashby,Oby and Thirne	P	Awd.,Min.
5730	Ashill	P	Rep. 1838
5731	Ashmanhaugh	P	Rep. 1840
5732	Barney	P	Rep. 1838
5733	Barnham Broom	ID	Rep. 1846
5734	Barningham Norwood	P	Awd.,Min.
5735	Barningham Parva	P	Rep. 1838
5736	Barningham Winter	P	Agrmt.,Min.,Rep. 1839
5737	Barrett Ringstead	P	Rep. 1843
5738	Barsham East	P	Rep. 1838
5739	Barsham North	P	Rep. 1839
5740	Barsham West	P	Awd.,Min.
5741	Barton Bendish	P	N.t.p.
5742	Barton Turf	P	Min.,Rep. 1838
5743	Barwick	P	Awd.,Min.
5744	Bawburgh	P	Rep. 1839
5745	Bawsey	P	Min.
5746	Bawdeswell	P	Awd.,Min.
5747	Bayfield	P	Rep. 1839
5748	Beachamwell St Mary	UP	Awd.,Min.
5749	Beachamwell All Saints	P	Awd.,Min.
5750	Beckham East	P	Awd.,Min.
5751	Beckham West	P	Rep. 1843
5752	Bedingham	P	Rep. 1839
5753	Beeston next Mileham	P	Min.,Rep. 1838
5754	Beeston St Andrew	P	Awd.,Min.
5755	Beeston St Lawrence	P	Min.,Rep. 1838
5756	Beeston Regis	P	Rep. 1838
5757	Beetley	P	Awd.,Min.
5758	Beighton	P	Min.,Rep. 1839
5759	Belaugh	P	Rep. 1839
5760	Bergh Apton and Holveston	P	Rep. 1839
5761	Bessingham	ID	Min.,Rep. 1839
5762	Besthorpe	P	Awd.,Min.
5763	Buckenham Old	P	Rep. 1841
5764	Bexwell	P	Rep. 1838
5765	Billingford	P	Agrmt.,Min.,Rep. 1837
5766	Billingford	P	Rep. 1839
5767	Billockby	P	Rep. 1838
5768	Bilney East	P	Rep. 1838
5769	Bilney West	P	N.t.p.
5770	Binham	P	Rep. 1838
5771	Bintry	P	Awd.,Min.
5772	Bircham Great	P	Rep. 1838
5773	Bircham Newton	P	Rep. 1838
5774	Bircham Tofts	P	Rep. 1838
5775	Bittering Little	P	Rep. 1838
5776	Bixley cum Framingham Earl	P	N.t.p.
5777	Blakeney	P	N.t.p.
5778	Blickling	P	Rep. 1839
5779	Blofield	P	Awd.,Min.
5780	Blo Norton	P	Rep. 1838
5781	Bodham	P	Min.,Rep. 1839
5782	Bodney	P	Rep. 1839
5783	Booton	P	Rep. 1839
5784	Boughton	P	Rep. 1842
5785	Bowthorpe	P	N.t.p.
5786	Bracon Ash	P	Awd.,Min.
5787	Bradeston	P	Awd.,Min.
5788	Bradenham West	P	Rep. 1838
5789	Bradenham East	P	Rep. 1838
5790	Bradfield	P	Rep. 1839
5791	Bramerton	P	Rep. 1838
5792	Brampton	P	Agrmt.,Min.,Rep. 1839
5793	Bressingham	D	Awd.,Min.
5794	Brettenham	P	Agrmt.,Rep. 1837
5795	Bridgham	P	Rep. 1837
5796	Briningham	P	Rep. 1838
5797	Brinton	P	Rep. 1838
5798	Briston	P	Awd.,Min.
5799	Brockdish	P	Rep. 1838
5800	Brooke	P	Rep. 1839
5801	Broome	P	Rep. 1839
5802	Bressingham	P	Rep. 1842
5803	Brandon Parva	P	Min.,Rep. 1838
5804	Breckles	P	Awd.,Min.
5805	Brandeston	P	Rep. 1841
5806	Brancaster	P	Awd.,Min.
5808	Brisley	P	Min.
5809	Brundall	P	Min.,Rep. 1838
5810	Brunstead	P	Rep. 1842
5811	Burgh	P	Agrmt.,Rep. 1837
5812	Burlingham St Edmund	P	Rep. 1839

Norfolk contd.

5813	Burlingham St Peter	P	Rep. 1839
5814	Burnham Deepdale	P	Awd.,Min.
5815	Burlingham St Andrew	P	Rep. 1839
5816	Buckenham	P	Rep. 1837
5817	Buckenham New	P	Awd.,Min.
5818	Buckenham near Toft	P	Min.
5819	Bunwell	P	Rep. 1838
5820	Burgh next Aylsham	P	Rep. 1838
5821	Burgh St Peter	P	Rep. 1838
5822	Burnham Norton	P	Min.,Rep. 1838
5823	Burnham Overy	P	Rep. 1838
5824	Burnham Sutton	P	Rep. 1838
5825	Burnham Thorpe	P	Rep. 1838
5826	Burnham Westgate	P	Agrmt.,Min.,Rep. 1837
5827	Burston	P	Rep. 1839
5828	Buxton	P	Rep. 1841
5829	Bylaugh	P	Rep. 1840
5830	Caister	P	Min.,Rep. 1841
5831	Caister St Edmunds	P	Rep. 1838
5832	Caldecot	P	Awd.,Min.
5833	Calthorpe	P	Rep. 1839
5834	Cantley	P	Agrmt.,Min.
5835	Carbrooke	P	Agrmt.,Min.,Rep. 1839
5836	Carleton	P	Rep. 1838
5837	Carlton East	P	Awd.,Min.
5838	Carleton Forehoe	P	N.t.p.
5839	Carleton Rode	P	Rep. 1838
5840	Carleton cum Ashby	P	Min.
5841	Castle Acre	P	Rep. 1838
5842	Castle Rising	P	Min.,Rep. 1837
5843	Caston	P	Min.
5844	Catfield	P	Min.,Rep. 1840
5845	Catton	P	Rep. 1843
5846	Cawston	P	Min.
5847	Chedgrave	P	Rep. 1838
5848	Choseley	EP	N.t.p.
5849	Claxton	P	Awd.,Min.
5850	Clenchwarton	P	Awd.,Min.
5851	Cley next the Sea	P	Rep. 1838
5852	Clippesby	P	Min.,Rep. 1839
5853	Cockley Cley All Saints	P	Awd.,Min.
5854	Cockthorpe	P	Rep. 1839
5855	Colby	P	Rep. 1839
5856	Colkirk	P	Min.,Rep. 1838
5857	Colney	P	Rep. 1839
5858	Coltishall	P	Agrmt.,Rep. 1837
5859	Colton	P	Awd.,Min.
5860	Colveston	P	Awd.,Min.
5861	Congham	P	Rep. 1837
5862	Corpusty	P	Rep. 1838
5863	Costessey	P	Min.,Rep. 1839
5864	Coston	P	Rep. 1842
5865	Cranwich	P	Min.,Rep. 1838
5866	Cranworth	P	Rep. 1838
5867	Creake North	P	Min.,Rep. 1839
5868	Creake South	P	Rep. 1838
5869	Cressingham Great	P	Rep. 1838
5870	Cressingham Little	P	Awd.,Min.
5871	Crimplesham	P	Rep. 1839
5872	Cringleford	P	Awd.,Min.
5873	Cromer	P	Awd.,Min.,Rep. 1838
5874	Crostwick	P	Agrmt.,Min.,Rep. 1838
5875	Crownthorpe	P	Rep. 1841
5876	Croxton	P	Min.
5877	Darsingham	P	Rep. 1840
5878	Denton	P	Rep. 1839
5879	Deopham	P	Awd.,Min.
5880	Dereham East	PH	Min.,Rep. 1838
5881	Denver	P	Rep. 1838
5882	Dereham West	P	Rep. 1845
5883	Dickleburgh	P	Awd.,Min.
5884	Didlington	P	Awd.,Min.
5885	Dilham	P	Rep. 1838
5886	Diss	P	Rep. 1837
5887	Ditchingham	P	Rep. 1839
5888	Docking	P	Awd.,Min.
5889	Doughton cum Dunton	P	N.t.p.
5890	Downham Market	P	Min.
5891	Drayton	P	Rep. 1839
5892	Dunham Great	P	Rep. 1838
5893	Dunham Little	P	Rep. 1838
5894	Dunston	P	Awd.,Min.
5895	Dunton	P	Rep. 1837
5896	Earsham	P	Rep. 1839
5897	Eccles	P	Agrmt.,Rep. 1838
5898	Eccles next the Sea	P	Rep. 1839
5899	Edgefield	P	Awd.,Min.
5900	Edingthorpe	P	Rep. 1839
5901	Egmere	P	Rep. 1838
5902	Ellingham	P	Rep. 1839
5903	Ellingham Great	P	Awd.,Min.
5904	Ellingham Little	P	Min.,Rep. 1839
5905	Elmham North	P	Min.,Rep. 1838
5906	Elsing	P	Min.,Rep. 1839
5907	Emneth	P	Awd.,Min.
5908	Erpingham	P	Rep. 1839
5909	Easton	P	Rep. 1843
5910	Eaton	P	Rep. 1838
5911	Fakenham	P	Awd.,Min.
5912	Felbrige	P	Rep. 1842
5913	Felmingham	P	Rep. 1839
5914	Felthorpe	P	Rep. 1840
5915	Feltwell St Mary	CP	Min.
5916	Fersfield	P	Rep. 1839
5917	Field Dalling	P	Rep. 1839
5918	Filby	P	Agrmt.,Min.,Rep. 1837
5919	Fincham St Michael	P	Min.,Rep. 1840
5920	Fishley	P	Agrmt.,Awd.,Min.,Rep. 1839
5921	Flitcham	P	Rep. 1838
5922	Flordon	P	Awd.,Min.
5923	Fordham	P	Rep. 1840
5924	Forncett St Mary	P	Awd.,Min.
5925	Forncett St Peter	P	Awd.,Min.
5926	Foulden	P	Min.,Rep. 1839
5927	Foulsham	P	Rep. 1838
5928	Foxley	P	Rep. 1839
5929	Framingham Pigot	P	Rep. 1840
5930	Fransham Great	P	Rep. 1838
5931	Fransham Little	P	Rep. 1838
5932	Freethorpe	P	Rep. 1840
5933	Frenze	P	Rep. 1839
5934	Frettenham	UP	Min.,Rep. 1840
5935	Fring	P	Rep. 1840
5936	Fritton	P	Rep. 1838
5937	Fulmodestone cum Croxton	P	Agrmt.,Rep. 1837
5938	Fundenhall	P	Min.
5939	Garboldisham	P	Rep. 1839
5940	Garvestone	P	Rep. 1839
5941	Gasthorpe	P	Rep. 1840
5942	Gateley	P	Min.
5943	Gatesend or Tattersett	P	Agrmt.,Min.,Rep. 1839
5944	Gayton	P	Rep. 1839
5945	Gayton Thorpe	P	Rep. 1841
5946	Gaywood	P	Rep. 1838
5947	Geldeston	P	Agrmt.,Rep. 1838
5948	Gillingham All Saints	P	Awd.,Min.,Rep. 1839
5949	Gimingham	P	Rep. 1839
5950	Gissing	P	Rep. 1839
5951	Glandford	P	Rep. 1839
5952	Gooderstone	P	Min.
5953	Gresham	P	Rep. 1842
5954	Gressenhall	P	Awd.,Min.
5955	Grimstone	P	N.t.p.
5956	Griston	P	Rep. 1839
5957	Guestwick	P	Awd.,Min.
5958	Guist	P	Awd.,Min.
5959	Gunthorpe	P	Rep. 1838
5960	Gunton	P	Rep. 1838
5961	Hackford	P	Rep. 1839
5962	Hackford next Reepham	P	Awd.,Min.
5963	Haddiscoe	P	Rep. 1840
5964	Hales	P	Rep. 1838
5965	Halvergate	P	Awd.,Min.
5966	Hanworth	P	Rep. 1838
5967	Happisburgh	P	Min.,Rep. 1840
5968	Hapton	P	Awd.,Min.
5969	Hardingham	P	Min.
5970	Hardley	P	Rep. 1839
5971	Hargham	P	Agrmt.,Rep. 1838
5972	Harling East	P	Awd.,Min.
5973	Harling West	P	N.t.p.
5974	Harpley	P	Min.,Rep. 1838
5975	Hassingham	P	N.t.p.
5976	Hautbois Magna	P	Min.,Rep. 1838
5977	Haveringland	P	Rep. 1840
5978	Haynford	P	Rep. 1837
5979	Heacham	P	Awd.,Min.
5980	Heckingham	P	Rep. 1838
5981	Hedenham	P	Rep. 1839
5982	Heigham	P	Min.
5983	Helhoughton	P	Rep. 1838
5984	Hellesdon	P	Rep. 1839
5985	Hemblington	P	Rep. 1840
5986	Hellington	P	Rep. 1838
5987	Hempnall	P	Rep. 1840
5988	Hempton	P	N.t.p.
5989	Hemsby	P	Rep. 1839
5990	Hempstead (near Holt)	P	Rep. 1839
5991	Hempstead	P	Rep. 1839
5992	Henstead cum Hulver St	P	Min.
5993	Hethel	P	Awd.,Min.
5994	Hethersett	P	Awd.,Min.
5995	Kempstone	P	Rep. 1838
5996	Hevingham	P	Min.,Rep. 1838
5997	Heydon	P	Rep. 1840
5998	Hickling	P	Awd.,Min.
5999	Hilborough	P	Awd.,Min.
6000	Hilgay	P	Rep. 1840
6001	Hillington near Lynn	P	Rep. 1838
6002	Hindolveston	P	Rep. 1839
6003	Hindringham	P	Rep. 1838
6004	Hingham	P	Awd.,Min.

Norfolk contd.

No.	Place	Type	Details
6005	Hockering	P	Agrmt.,Rep. 1838
6006	Hockham Great and Little	P	Agrmt.,Rep. 1837
6007	Hockwold cum Wilton (part)	P	Agrmt.,Min.
6008	Hockwold cum Wilton (part)	UP	Min.
6009	Holkham	P	Min.,Rep. 1837
6010	Runcton Holme	P	Rep. 1838
6011	Holme Hall	P	Rep. 1839
6012	Holme next the Sea	P	Rep. 1843
6013	Holt	P	Rep. 1839
6014	Honing	P	Awd.,Min.
6015	Honingham	P	Rep. 1840
6016	Hoo	P	Awd.,Min.
6017	Houghton	P	Rep. 1839
6018	Horning	P	Rep. 1839
6019	Horningtoft	P	Rep. 1844
6020	Horsey	P	Rep. 1838
6021	Horsford	P	Rep. 1841
6022	Horsham St Faiths	P	Rep. 1841
6023	Houghton next Walsingham	P	Rep. 1838
6024	Horstead	P	Min.
6025	Hoveton St John	P	Rep. 1841
6026	Hoveton St Peter	P	Rep. 1840
6027	Howe and West Poringland	P	Rep. 1838
6028	Hunstanton	P	Rep. 1843
6029	Hunworth	P	Min.,Rep. 1839
6030	Igborough and Langford	P	Rep. 1839
6031	Illington	P	Rep. 1842
6032	Ingham	P	Rep. 1841
6033	Intwood	P	Rep. 1839
6034	Irmingland	P	Rep. 1840
6035	Ingoldisthorpe	P	Rep. 1839
6036	Ingworth	P	Rep. 1839
6037	Irstead	P	Rep. 1838
6038	Itteringham	EP	Rep. 1838
6039	Kelling	P	Rep. 1838
6040	Kenninghall	P	Min.
6041	Keswick	P	Min.
6042	Ketteringham	P	Min.
6043	Kettlestone	P	Min.,Rep. 1839
6044	Kilverstone	P	Min.
6045	Kimberley	P	N.t.p.
6046	Kirby Bedon St Andrew	P	Rep. 1841
6047	Kirby Bedon St Mary	P	Awd.,Min.
6048	Kirby Cane	P	Rep. 1839
6049	Kirstead	P	Rep. 1842
6050	Knapton	P	Rep. 1839
6051	Lakenham	P	Awd.,Min.
6052	Lammas and Little Hautbois	P	Rep. 1839
6053	Langham	P	Min.
6054	Langley	P	Rep. 1838
6055	Larling	P	Rep. 1837
6056	Lessingham	P	Rep. 1840
6057	Letheringsett	P	Rep. 1838
6058	Letton	P	Rep. 1838
6059	Lexham East	P	Min.
6060	Lexham West	P	Min.
6061	Leziate	P	Min.
6062	Limpenhoe	P	Awd.,Min.
6064	Lingwood	P	Min.,Rep. 1839
6065	Litcham	P	Awd.,Min.
6066	Loddon	P	Rep. 1838
6067	Longham	P	Rep. 1838
6068	Lopham South	P	Awd.,Min.
6069	Lopham North	P	Rep. 1845
6070	Ludham	P	Rep. 1841
6071	Lyndford	P	N.t.p.
6072	Lyng	P	Min.,Rep. 1839
6073	Lynn North	P	Rep. 1838
6074	Lynn St Margarets	P	Awd.,Min.
6075	Lynn South	P	Agrmt.,Rep. 1840
6076	Lynn West St Peter	P	Awd.,Min.
6077	Marham	P	Awd.,Min.
6078	Marlingford	P	Rep. 1838
6079	Marsham	P	Rep. 1839
6080	Martham	P	Awd.,Min.
6081	Massingham Great	P	Rep. 1838
6082	Massingham Little	P	Rep. 1838
6083	Matlaske	P	Rep. 1839
6084	Mattishall	P	Rep. 1838
6085	Mattishall Burgh	P	Agrmt.,Min.
6086	Mautby	P	Rep. 1838
6087	Melton Constable	P	Rep. 1838
6088	Melton Great	P	Rep. 1839
6089	Melton Little	P	Awd.,Min.
6090	Merton	P	Agrmt.,Min.
6091	Metton	P	Rep. 1842
6092	Middleton	P	Min.
6093	Mileham	P	Rep. 1840
6094	Mintlyn	P	Awd.,Min.
6095	Morley	P	Rep. 1839
6096	Morston	P	Rep. 1838
6097	Morton	P	Rep. 1841
6098	Moulton	P	Awd.,Min.
6099	Methwold	P	Rep. 1840
6100	Moulton St Michael	P	Agrmt.,Min.,Rep. 1837
6101	Mourning Thorpe	P	Rep. 1838
6102	Mulbarton	P	Awd.,Min.
6103	Mundesley	P	Rep. 1838
6104	Mundford	P	Rep. 1842
6105	Mundham	P	Rep. 1838
6106	Narborough	P	Rep. 1838
6107	Narford	P	Rep. 1839
6108	Neatishead	P	Rep. 1840
6109	Necton	P	Rep. 1840
6110	Needham	P	Rep. 1841
6111	Newton by Castle Acre	P	Awd.,Min.
6112	Newton Flotman	P	Awd.,Min.,Rep. 1837
6113	Newton West	P	Rep. 1838
6114	Northwold	D	Min.
6115	Norton Subcourse	P	Rep. 1838
6116	Norwich All Saints	P	Awd.,Min.
6117	Norwich St Andrew	P	N.t.p.
6118	Norwich St Augustine	P	N.t.p.
6119	Norwich St Benedict	P	N.t.p.
6120	Norwich St Clement	P	Awd.,Min.
6121	Norwich County Gaol	EP	N.t.p.
6122	Norwich Earlham St Mary	P	Awd.,Min.
6123	Norwich St Edmund	P	N.t.p.
6124	Norwich St Ethelred	P	Awd.,Min.
6125	Norwich St George Colegate	P	N.t.p.
6126	Norwich St George Tombland	P	N.t.p.
6127	Norwich St Giles	P	N.t.p.
6128	Norwich St Gregory	P	N.t.p.
6129	Norwich St Helen	P	N.t.p.
6130	Norwich St James	PH	N.t.p.
6131	Norwich St John Baptist	P	Awd.,Min.
6132	Norwich St John Maddermark	P	N.t.p.
6133	Norwich St John Sepulchre	P	Awd.,Min.
6134	Norwich St Julian	P	Awd.,Min.
6135	Norwich St Lawrence	P	N.t.p.
6136	Norwich St Margaret	P	N.t.p.
6137	Norwich St Martin at Oak	P	N.t.p.
6138	Norwich St Martin	P	N.t.p.
6139	Norwich St Mary Coslany	P	N.t.p.
6140	Norwich St Mary	P	N.t.p.
6141	Norwich St Michael	P	N.t.p.
6142	Norwich St Michael	P	Awd.,Min.
6143	Norwich St Paul	P	N.t.p.
6144	Norwich St Peter Mancroft	P	N.t.p.
6145	Norwich St Peter Hungate	P	N.t.p.
6146	Norwich St Peter Per Mount	P	Awd.,Min.
6147	Norwich St Peter Southgate	P	Awd.,Min.
6148	Norwich St Saviour	P	N.t.p.
6149	Norwich St Simon,St Jude	P	N.t.p.
6150	Norwich St Stephen	P	N.t.p.
6151	Norwich St Swithin	P	N.t.p.
6152	Norwich	EP	N.t.p.
6153	Ormesby St Margaret	P	Min.,Rep. 1838
6154	Osmondeston or Scole	P	Rep. 1839
6155	Oulton	P	Rep. 1839
6156	Outwell	P	Rep. 1839
6157	Overstrand	P	Rep. 1838
6158	Ovington	P	Awd.,Min.
6159	Oxborough	P	Awd.,Min.
6160	Oxmead	P	Rep. 1839
6161	Oxwick	P	Min.,Rep. 1840
6162	Palgrave Parva	P	Rep. 1838
6163	Palling	P	Rep. 1838
6164	Panxworth	P	Rep. 1839
6165	Paston	P	Awd.,Min.
6166	Pattisley	P	Awd.,Min.
6167	Pensthorpe	P	Rep. 1838
6168	Pentney	P	Awd.,Min.
6169	Pickenham North	P	Agrmt.,Rep. 1839
6170	Pickenham South	P	Rep. 1841
6171	Plumstead	P	Min.,Rep. 1839
6172	Plumstead Great	P	Rep. 1838
6173	Plumstead Little	P	Rep. 1838
6174	Poringland East	P	N.t.p.
6175	Poringland Great or East	P	Awd.,Min.
6176	Postwick	P	Min.,Rep. 1838
6177	Potter Heigham	P	Rep. 1838
6178	Pudding Norton	P	Awd.,Min.
6179	Pulham St Mary the Virgin	P	Agrmt.,Rep. 1837
6180	Quarles	EP	N.t.p.
6181	Rackheath	P	Rep. 1837
6182	Raveningham	P	Rep. 1838
6183	Quidenham	P	Rep. 1842
6184	Raynham East	P	Rep. 1839
6185	Raynham South	P	Rep. 1839
6186	Raynham West	P	Rep. 1838
6187	Ranworth	P	Rep. 1839
6188	Redenhall with Harlestone	P	Rep. 1838
6189	Reedham	P	Rep. 1840
6190	Reifham St Mary	P	Min.,Rep. 1844
6191	Repps North	P	Rep. 1838
6192	Repps South	P	Rep. 1839
6193	Repps with Bastwick	P	Min.,Rep. 1838
6194	Reymerston	P	Rep. 1838
6195	Ridlington	P	Awd.,Min.
6196	Riddlesworth	P	Rep. 1840
6197	Ringland	P	Awd.,Min.

Norfolk contd.

6198	Ringstead Barrett	P	N.t.p.
6199	Ringstead Great	P	Rep. 1841
6200	Rockland All Saints	UP	Min.
6201	Rockland St Mary	P	Awd.,Min.
6202	Rockland St Peter	P	Rep. 1838
6203	Rollesby	P	Rep. 1839
6204	Roudham	P	Rep. 1842
6205	Rougham	P	Rep. 1842
6206	Roughton	P	Rep. 1838
6207	Roydon (Castle Rising)	P	Rep. 1837
6208	Roydon (Diss Hundred)	P	Min.,Rep. 1839
6209	Rudham East	P	Rep. 1838
6210	Rudham West	P	Awd.,Min.
6211	Runcton North	P	Rep. 1840
6212	Runcton South	P	Rep. 1838
6213	Runhall	P	Rep. 1844
6214	Runham	P	Min.
6215	Runton	P	Rep. 1838
6216	Rushall	P	Rep. 1842
6217	Rushford	P	N.t.p.
6218	Ruston East	P	Rep. 1840
6219	Ryburgh Great	P	N.t.p.
6220	Ryburgh Little	P	N.t.p.
6221	Ryston and Roxham	P	Rep. 1840
6222	Saham Toney	P	Awd.,Min.
6223	Salhouse	P	Rep. 1842
6224	Sall	P	Rep. 1838
6225	Salthouse	P	Rep. 1838
6226	Saltmarsh New	EP	Min.
6227	Sandringham	P	Rep. 1838
6228	Santon	P	Awd.,Min.
6229	Saxlingham	P	Awd.,Min.
6230	Saxthorpe	P	Min.,Rep. 1841
6231	Scarning	P	Min.
6232	Saxlingham Thorpe	P	Awd.,Min.
6233	Shelfanger	P	Min.
6234	Shimpling	P	Awd.,Min.
6235	Shingham	P	Rep. 1839
6236	Shipdam	P	Min.
6237	Sco Ruston	P	Awd.,Min.
6238	Scottowe	P	Rep. 1839
6239	Scoulton	P	Rep. 1838
6240	Sculthorpe	P	Rep. 1838
6241	Sedgeford	P	Rep. 1840
6242	Seething	P	Rep. 1838
6243	Sharrington	P	Rep. 1840
6244	Shouldham Thorpe	P	Awd.,Min.
6245	Shropham	P	Rep. 1838
6246	Sidestrand	P	Rep. 1838
6247	Sisland	P	Rep. 1838
6248	Skeyton	P	Min.,Rep. 1840
6249	Sloley	P	Rep. 1837
6250	Smallburgh	P	Rep. 1838
6251	Snare Hill	EP	N.t.p.
6252	Snetterton	P	Min.,Rep. 1843
6253	Snettisham	P	N.t.p.
6254	Snoring Great	P	Rep. 1840
6255	Snoring Little	P	Rep. 1838
6256	Somorfield or Southmere	P	Awd.,Min.
6257	Somerton East	P	Rep. 1840
6258	Shotesham All Saints	P	Rep. 1840
6259	Shouldham	P	Rep. 1843
6260	Shelton and Hardwick	P	Agrmt.,Rep. 1837
6261	Shereford	P	Rep. 1839
6262	Sheringham	P	Rep. 1839
6263	Shernborne	P	N.t.p.
6264	Somerton West	P	Rep. 1840
6265	Southacre	P	Agrmt.,Rep. 1837
6266	Southbergh	P	Rep. 1837
6267	Southery	P	Rep. 1838
6268	Southwood	P	Awd.,Min.
6269	Sparham	P	Rep. 1842
6270	Spixworth	P	Agrmt.,Rep. 1837
6271	Sporle	P	Agrmt.,Rep. 1838
6272	Sprowston	P	Min.
6273	Stalham	P	Rep. 1843
6274	Stanfield	P	Min.,Rep. 1838
6275	Stanford	P	Rep. 1839
6276	Stanhoe	P	Min.,Rep. 1838
6277	Starston	P	Agrmt.,Min.,Rep. 1837
6278	Stibbard	P	Min.
6279	Stiffkey	P	Min.
6280	Stockton	P	Awd.,Min.
6281	Stody	P	Rep. 1839
6282	Stoke Ferry	P	Awd.,Min.
6283	Stokesby cum Herringby	P	Agrmt.,Rep. 1838
6284	Stoke Holy Cross	P	Agrmt.,Awd.,Min.
6285	Stow Bardolph	P	Awd.,Min.
6286	Stow Bedon	P	Awd.,Min.
6287	Stradsett	P	Rep. 1839
6288	Stratton St Mary	P	Rep. 1839
6289	Stratton St Michael	P	Rep. 1839
6290	Stratton Strawless	P	Rep. 1838
6291	Strumpshaw	P	Awd.,Min.
6292	Sturston	P	N.t.p.
6293	Suffield	P	Rep. 1838
6294	Surlingham St Mary	P	Min.
6295	Sustead	P	Awd.,Min.
6296	Sutton	P	Min.,Rep. 1839
6297	Swaffham	P	Rep. 1839
6298	Swafield	P	Rep. 1839
6299	Swainsthorpe	P	Min.,Rep. 1837
6300	Swanington	P	Awd.,Min.
6301	Swanton Abbott	P	Rep. 1838
6302	Swanton Morley	P	Awd.,Min.
6303	Swanton Novers	P	Rep. 1838
6304	Swardeston	P	Awd.,Min.
6305	Syderstone	P	Awd.,Min.
6306	Tacolnestone	P	Awd.,Min.
6307	Tasburgh	P	Rep. 1840
6308	Tatterford	P	Rep. 1839
6309	Taverham	P	Awd.,Min.
6310	Terrington St Clements	P	Rep. 1839
6311	Testerton	P	Min.
6312	Tharston	P	Rep. 1838
6313	Thelveton	P	Rep. 1838
6314	Themelthorpe	P	Rep. 1838
6315	Thetford St Cuthbert	P	Awd.,Min.
6316	Thetford St Mary	P	Awd.,Min.
6317	Thetford St Peter	P	Awd.,Min.
6318	Thirning	P	Rep. 1837
6319	Thompson	P	Awd.,Min.
6320	Thornage	P	Rep. 1838
6321	Thornham	P	Rep. 1840
6322	Thorpe Abbotts	P	Min.
6323	Thorpe next Norwich	P	Awd.,Min.
6324	Thorpe Parva	P	Rep. 1840
6325	Thorpe Market	P	Rep. 1838
6326	Thorpe next Haddiscoe	P	Rep. 1838
6327	Thursford	P	Awd.,Min.
6328	Thurton	P	Rep. 1838
6329	Threxton	P	Rep. 1837
6330	Thrigby	P	Rep. 1837
6331	Thurgarton	P	Rep. 1837
6332	Thurlton	P.	Rep. 1838
6333	Tofts West	P	Min.
6334	Topcroft	P	Rep. 1839
6335	Tottenhill	P	N.t.p.
6336	Tottington	P	Awd.,Min.
6337	Trimingham	P	Rep. 1838
6338	Troughton	P	N.t.p.
6339	Trowse Newton	P	Awd.,Min.
6340	Trunch	P	Rep. 1839
6341	Tuddenham East	P	Rep. 1839
6342	Tuddenham North	P	Rep. 1839
6343	Tunstall	P	Awd.,Min.
6344	Tunstead	P	Awd.,Min.
6345	Tuttington	P	Rep. 1839
6346	Twyford	P	Rep. 1838
6347	Thuxton	P	Awd.,Min.
6348	Thwaite All Saints	P	Rep. 1841
6349	Thwaite St Mary	P	Min.,Rep. 1840
6350	Tibenham	P	Rep. 1839
6351	Tilney St Lawrence	P	Agrmt.,Awd.,Min.
6352	Titchwell	P	Rep. 1838
6353	Tittleshall cum Godwick	P	Agrmt.,Min.,Rep. 1837
6354	Tivetshall St Margaret	P	Agrmt.,Rep. 1838
6355	Tivetshall St Mary	P	Agrmt.,Rep. 1838
6356	Toft Trees	P	Min.,Rep. 1839
6357	Toft Monks	P	Rep. 1840
6358	Upton	P	Rep. 1839
6359	Waborne or Waybourne	P	Rep. 1839
6360	Wacton Magna	P	Rep. 1839
6361	Walsingham Great or Old	P	N.t.p.,Min.
6362	Walcote	P	Rep. 1839
6363	Wallington	P	Rep. 1839
6364	Walpole St Andrew	P	Rep. 1839
6365	Walpole St Peter	P	Rep. 1839
6366	Walsingham Little or New	P	N.t.p.
6367	Walsham North	P	Awd.,Min.
6368	Walsham South St Lawrence	P	Rep. 1839
6369	Walsoken	P	Min.
6370	Walton East	P	Awd.,Rep. 1841
6371	Walton West	P	Rep. 1839
6372	Warham All Saints	P	Rep. 1838
6373	Warham St Mary the Virgin	P	Rep. 1837
6374	Waterden	P	Rep. 1837
6375	Watlington	P	Rep. 1838
6376	Wereham	P	Awd.,Min.
6377	Watton	P	Rep. 1840
6378	Waxham	P	Rep. 1838
6379	Weasenham All Saints	P	Rep. 1839
6380	Weasenham St Peter	P	Rep. 1839
6381	Weeting	P	Awd.,Min.
6382	Welborne	P	Min.,Rep. 1838
6383	Wellingham	P	Agrmt.,Rep. 1837
6384	Wells next the Sea	P	Rep. 1842
6385	Wendling	P	Min.
6386	Westacre	P	N.t.p.
6387	Westfield	P	Rep. 1838
6388	Weston Longville	P	Rep. 1840
6389	Westwick	P	Min.,Rep. 1837

Norfolk contd.

6390	Wheatacre All Saints	P	Rep. 1840
6391	Whinbergh	P	Min.,Rep. 1839
6392	Whissonsett	P	Awd.,Min.
6393	Whitwell	P	Awd.,Min.
6394	Wickhampton	P	Rep. 1842
6395	Wicklewood	P	Rep. 1843
6396	Witchingham Great	P	Rep. 1841
6397	Winterton	P	Awd.,Min.
6398	Wiggenhall St Mary	P	Min.
6399	Wiggenhall	P	Min.,Rep. 1838
6400	Wiggenhall St Peter	P	Rep. 1838
6401	Wighton	P	Rep. 1839
6402	Wilby	P	Min.,Rep. 1838
6403	Wimbotsham	P	Rep. 1842
6404	Winch East	P	Rep. 1838
6405	Winch West	P	Rep. 1838
6406	Winfarthing	P	Awd.,Min.
6407	Witchingham Little	P	Awd.,Min.
6408	Witlingham	P	Rep. 1840
6409	Witton (Blofield Hundred)	P	Rep. 1838
6410	Witton (Tunstead Hundred)	P	Rep. 1838
6411	Wiveton	P	Rep. 1842
6412	Woodbastwick	P	Rep. 1838
6413	Wooddalling	P	Min.,Rep. 1839
6414	Wood Norton	P	Rep. 1842
6415	Woodrising	P	Rep. 1837
6416	Woodton	P	Rep. 1840
6417	Woolferton	P	Rep. 1838
6418	Wolterton cum Wickmere	P	Rep. 1839
6419	Wootton North	P	Rep. 1837
6420	Wootton South	P	Min.
6421	Wormegay	P	Rep. 1838
6422	Wiggenhall St Germans	P	Rep. 1838
6423	Worstead	P	Awd.,Min.
6424	Wramplingham	P	Rep. 1838
6425	Wreningham	P	Rep. 1839
6426	Wretham East and West	P	Awd.,Rep. 1839
6427	Wretton	P	Rep. 1839
6428	Wroxham	P	Rep. 1839
6429	Wymondham	P	Rep. 1839
6430	Yarmouth Great	P	Awd.,Min.
6431	Yaxham	P	Min.,Rep. 1838
7473	Norwich St Michael	P	N.t.p.

Northamptonshire

3431	Lutton	P	Awd.,Min.,Rep. 1839
6432	Abingdon	P	Agrmt.,Rep. 1840
6433	Abthorpe	P	Rep. 1838
6434	Addington Great	P	N.t.p.
6435	Addington Little	P	N.t.p.
6436	Alderton	P	N.t.p.
6437	Aldwinckle All Saints	P	N.t.p.
6438	Aldwinckle St Peter's	P	Awd.
6439	Althorpe	EP	N.t.p.
6440	Andrew St. Priory or Town	EP	N.t.p.
6441	Apethorpe	P	N.t.p.
6442	Arthingworth	P	Awd.,Min.
6443	Ashby Mears	P	N.t.p.
6444	Ashby St. Ledgers	P	Awd.,Min.
6445	Ashley	P	N.t.p.
6446	Ashby Cold	P	N.t.p.
6447	Ashton	P	N.t.p.
6448	Aston le Walls		Min.
6448	Aston le Walls	P	Awd.,Min.
6449	Astwell and Fawcott	H	Min.
6450	Aynhoe	P	Min.
6451	Aynhoe	D	Min.
6452	Badby	P	N.t.p.
6453	Bainton	P	N.t.p.
6454	Barby	P	Min.
6455	Barford	EP	N.t.p.
6456	Barnwell All Saints	EP	Awd.
6457	Barnack	P	N.t.p.
6458	Barnwell St. Andrew	UP	N.t.p.
6459	Barton Seagrave	P	Awd.,Min.
6460	Benefield Upper and Lower	P	Awd.,Min.
6461	Billing Great	P	N.t.p.
6462	Billing Little	P	Rep. 1840
6463	Blakesley	P	Agrmt.,Rep. 1840
6464	Blatherwycke	P	Awd.,Min.
6465	Blisworth	P	Awd.,Min.
6466	Boddington	P	N.t.p.
6467	Borough Fen	EP	N.t.p.
6468	Boughton	P	N.t.p.
6469	Bowden Little	P	Min.
6470	Bozeat	P	N.t.p.
6471	Brackley St. James	P	N.t.p.
6472	Braybrook	P	Awd.
6473	Brackley St. Peter	P	Agrmt.,Rep. 1839
6474	Bradden	P	N.t.p.
6475	Brafield on the Green	P	N.t.p.
6476	Brampton	P	Awd.
6476	Brampton Ash	P	N.t.p.
6477	Braunston	P	Min.
6478	Brigstock	P	Awd.,Min.
6479	Brington	P	Rep. 1839
6480	Brixworth	P	N.t.p.
6481	Brockhall	P	Rep. 1838
6482	Broughton	P	N.t.p.
6483	Buckby Long	P	Awd.
6484	Bugbrook	P	Awd.
6485	Bulwick	EP	Awd.,Min.
6486	Bulwick Short Leys	EP	N.t.p.
6487	Burton Latimer	P	N.t.p.
6488	Byfield	P	N.t.p.
6489	Canons Ashby		N.t.p.
6490	Carlton East	P	Awd.,Min.
6491	Castle Ashby	P	Agrmt.,Rep. 1840
6492	Castor	P	Awd.,Min.
6493	Catesby with Newbold	PH	N.t.p.
6494	Chacombe	P	Agrmt.,Rep. 1839
6495	Charwelton	P	Rep. 1839
6496	Cranford St. Andrew	P	Awd.,Min.
6497	Cranford St. John	P	N.t.p.
6498	Chelveston	P	N.t.p.
6499	Chipping Warden	P	Agrmt.,Rep. 1838
6500	Church Brampton	P	Awd.
6501	Cogenhoe or Cooknoe	P	Min.
6502	Cold Higham	P	N.t.p.
6503	Collingtree	P	N.t.p.
6504	Colly Weston	P	Agrmt.,Rep. 1839
6505	Clapton	P	Agrmt.,Rep. 1839
6506	Claycoton	P	Agrmt.,Rep. 1839
6507	Clipston	P	Min.
6508	Corby	P	Awd.,Min.
6509	Cosgrove	P	Min.
6510	Cotterstock	P	N.t.p.
6511	Cottesbrooke	P	Awd.,Min.
6512	Cottingham cum Middleton	P	Min.
6513	Courteenhall	P	Rep. 1838
6514	Cransley	P	Awd.,Min.
6515	Creaton Great	P	N.t.p.
6516	Crick	P	N.t.p.
6517	Croughton	P	N.t.p.
6518	Culworth	P	Agrmt.,Rep. 1839
6519	Dallington	P	Min.
6520	Daventry	P	N.t.p.
6521	Deene with Deenthorpe	PH	Awd.,Min.
6522	Denford	P	N.t.p.
6523	Denton	P	N.t.p.
6524	Desborough	P	N.t.p.
6525	Dingley	P	Agrmt.
6526	Doddington Great	P	N.t.p.
6527	Dodford	P	Awd.,Min.
6528	Draughton	P	Agrmt.
6529	Drayton	T	N.t.p.
6530	Duddington	P	N.t.p.
6531	Duston	P	N.t.p.
6532	Easton on the Hill	P	N.t.p.
6533	Earls Barton	P	Awd.,Min.
6534	Easton Maudit	P	Rep. 1838
6535	Easton Neston with Hulcote	P	Awd.,Min.
6536	Ecton	P	N.t.p.
6537	Edgcott	P	Awd.
6538	Elkington	P	N.t.p.
6539	Elmington	H	Agrmt.
6540	Etton	P	N.t.p.
6541	Evenley	P	Rep. 1839
6542	Everdon	P	N.t.p.
6543	Eydon	P	Min.
6544	Eye	P	N.t.p.
6545	Farndon East	P	Agrmt.
6546	Farthinghoe	P	Agrmt.,Awd.,Min.
6547	Faxton cum Mawsley	P	Agrmt.,Rep. 1839
6548	Farthingston	P	Awd.,Min.
6549	Fawsley	P	Awd.,Min.
6550	Faxton	P	Min.
6551	Finedon	P	N.t.p.
6552	Fineshade	EP	N.t.p.
6553	Flore	T	Awd.,Min.
6554	Fotheringhay	P	Min.
6555	Furtho	P	Awd.,Min.
6556	Gayton	P	Awd.,Min.
6557	Geddington	P	N.t.p.,Awd.
6558	Clapthorn	P	N.t.p.
6559	Glasthorpe	H	Awd.,Min.
6560	Glendon	P	N.t.p.
6561	Glinton	P	N.t.p.
6562	Grafton Regis	P	Awd.,Min.
6563	Grafton Underwood	P	N.t.p.
6564	Greatworth	P	Awd.,Min.
6565	Greens Norton	P	Min.
6566	Grendon	P	N.t.p.
6567	Gretton	P	N.t.p.
6568	Guilsborough	P	N.t.p.
6569	Haddon East	P	Awd.,Min.
6570	Haddon West	P	N.t.p.
6571	Handley	T	Awd.,Min.
6572	Hannington	P	N.t.p.
6573	Hardingstone	P	N.t.p.

Northamptonshire contd.

6574	Hardwick	P	Rep. 1839
6575	Hargrave	P	N.t.p.
6576	Harlestone	P	Awd.
6577	Harpole	P	N.t.p.
6578	Harrington	P	Agrmt., Rep. 1839
6579	Harringworth	P	N.t.p.
6580	Harrowden Magna and Parva	PH	Awd., Min.
6581	Hartwell	P	Agrmt., Awd.
6582	Hartwell Lodge	EP	N.t.p.
6583	Hellidon	P	N.t.p.
6584	Helmdon	P	Min.
6585	Helpstone	P	N.t.p.
6586	Hemington	P	Min.
6587	Heyford Nether	H	Awd., Min.
6588	Heyford Upper (part of)	H	Awd., Min.
6589	Heyford Upper (part of)	H	Awd.
6590	Heyford Upper (part of)	H	Awd.
6591	Higham Ferrers	P	N.t.p.
6592	Higham Park	EP	Agrmt., Rep. 1838
6593	Hinton in the Hedges	P	N.t.p.
6594	Holcot	P	N.t.p.
6595	Holdenby	P	Awd., Min.
6596	Horton	P	N.t.p.
6597	Hollowell	T	Awd., Min.
6598	Hothorpe	T	N.t.p.
6599	Houghton Little	P	N.t.p.
6600	Houghton Great	P	Rep. 1838
6601	Irchester	P	Awd., Min.
6602	Irthlingborough	P	N.t.p.
6603	Isham	P	N.t.p.
6604	Islip	P	N.t.p.
6605	Kelmarsh	P	Agrmt.
6606	Kettering	P	N.t.p.
6607	Kilsby	P	Awd., Min.
6608	Kings Cliffe	P	N.t.p.
6609	Kings Sutton	P	Awd., Min.
6610	Kingsthorpe	P	N.t.p.
6611	Kislingbury	P	N.t.p.
6612	Lamport & Hanging Houghton	PH	N.t.p.
6613	Laxton	P	N.t.p.
6614	Lilbourne	P	N.t.p.
6615	Lilford with Wigsthorpe	PH	N.t.p.
6616	Litchborough	P	Awd., Min.
6617	Loddington	P	Awd., Min.
6618	Longthorpe	H	N.t.p.
6619	Lowick	P	N.t.p.
6620	Luddington in the Brook	P	N.t.p.
6621	Maidford	P	Awd., Min.
6622	Maidwell	P	N.t.p.
6623	Marholm	P	Awd., Min.
6624	Marston St. Lawrence	P	N.t.p.
6625	Marston Trussell	P	N.t.p.
6626	Maxey	P	N.t.p.
6627	Middleton Cheney	P	N.t.p.
6628	Milton or Middleton Malzor	P	N.t.p.
6629	Moreton Pinckney	P	Min.
6630	Moulton	P	Awd.
6631	Moulton Park	EP	N.t.p.
6632	Naseby	P	N.t.p.
6633	Nassington	P	N.t.p.
6634	Newbottle	P	Awd.
6635	Newborough	P	N.t.p.
6636	Newnham	P	Awd., Min.
6637	Newton	P	N.t.p.
6638	Newton Bromshold	P	N.t.p.
6639	Northampton All Saints	P	N.t.p.
6640	Northampton St. Andrew	EP	N.t.p.
6641	Northampton St. Edmund	P	N.t.p.
6642	Northampton St. Giles	P	N.t.p.
6643	Northampton St. Katharine	P	N.t.p.
6644	Northampton Minster Close	EP	N.t.p.
6645	Northampton St. Peter	P	N.t.p.
6646	Northampton St. Sepulchre	P	Agrmt., Rep. 1843
6647	Northborough	P	N.t.p.
6648	Nortoft	T	Awd., Min.
6649	Norton	P	Awd., Min.
6650	Oakley Great	P	Awd., Min.
6651	Oakley Little	P	N.t.p.
6652	Old or Wold	P	N.t.p.
6653	Orlingbury	P	Awd., Min.
6654	Oundle	P	Awd.
6655	Oxenden Magna	P	N.t.p.
6656	Overstone	P	N.t.p.
6658	Peterborough St. John	P	N.t.p.
6659	Passenham	P	Awd.
6660	Paston	P	Agrmt., Rep. 1838
6661	Pattishall	P	N.t.p.
6662	Paulerspury	P	Awd., Min.
6663	Peakirk	P	N.t.p.
6664	Peterborough Minster	P	N.t.p.
6665	Piddington and Cackleton	PH	Awd., Min.
6666	Pilton	P	Agrmt.
6667	Pisford or Pitsford	P	N.t.p.
6668	Plumpton	P	Awd., Min.
6669	Polebrook	P	Awd., Min.
6670	Potterspury	P	Awd., Min.
6671	Preston Capes	P	Awd., Min.
6672	Preston Deanery	P	Rep. 1839
6673	Preston Little	H	Agrmt., Min.
6674	Pytchley	P	Awd., Min.
6675	Quinton	P	Awd.
6676	Radstone or Roddestone	P	N.t.p.
6677	Raunds	P	N.t.p.
6678	Ravensthorpe	P	N.t.p.
6679	Ringstead	P	Rep. 1838
6680	Roade	P	N.t.p.
6681	Rockingham	P	Agrmt., Rep. 1840
6682	Rothersthorpe	P	N.t.p.
6683	Rothwell and Orton	P	Awd.
6684	Rushden	P	N.t.p.
6685	Rushton	P	Agrmt., Rep. 1841
6686	Salcey Lodge	EP	N.t.p.
6687	Salcey Forest	EP	N.t.p.
6688	Scaldwell	P	Awd.
6689	Shutlanger	H	Rep. 1842
6690	Sibbertoft	P	Agrmt., Rep. 1838
6691	Silverston	H	Awd., Min.
6692	Slapton	P	Awd.
6693	Slipton	P	Awd., Min.
6694	Snorscombe	H	Agrmt., Rep. 1839
6695	Southorpe with Walcot	T	Agrmt., Rep. 1838
6696	Southwick	P	Awd., Min.
6697	Spratton	P	N.t.p.
6698	Stanwick	P	N.t.p.
6699	Stanford	P	N.t.p.
6700	Stanford Baron St. Martin	P	N.t.p.
6701	Stanion	P	N.t.p.
6702	Staverton	P	N.t.p.
6703	Stean or Stene	P	Awd., Min.
6704	Stoke Albany	P	Agrmt., Rep. 1841
6705	Stoke Bruern	P	Agrmt., Rep. 1842
6706	Stoke Doyle	P	Awd., Min.
6707	Stowe Nine Churches	P	Rep. 1839
6708	Strixton	P	Awd., Min.
6709	Stuchbury	P	Awd., Min.
6710	Sudborough	P	Agrmt., Min.
6711	Sulby	EP	N.t.p.
6712	Sulgrave	P	N.t.p.
6713	Sutton Bassett	P	N.t.p.
6714	Sutton	T	Min.
6715	Syresham	P	N.t.p.
6716	Sywell	P	Awd., Min.
6717	Tansor	P	N.t.p.
6718	Teeton	H	Awd., Min.
6719	Thenford	P	Awd.
6720	Thornby	P	Awd., Min.
6721	Thornhaugh & Wansford	P	Agrmt., Rep. 1838
6722	Thorpe Achurch	P	N.t.p.
6723	Thorpe Lubbenham	EP	N.t.p.
6724	Thorpe Malsor	P	Awd., Min.
6725	Thorpe Mandeville	P	N.t.p.
6726	Thrapston	P	N.t.p.
6727	Thurning	P	Agrmt.
6728	Tiffield	P	N.t.p.
6729	Titchmarsh	P	Awd., Min.
6730	Towcester	P	Awd., Min.
6731	Twywell	P	N.t.p.
6732	Ufford	P	N.t.p.
6733	Upton Nr. Northampton	P	N.t.p.
6734	Upton (Castor)	T	Min.
6735	Wadenhoe	P	N.t.p.
6736	Wakerley	P	N.t.p.
6737	Waldgrave	P	N.t.p.
6738	Warkton	P	N.t.p.
6739	Warkworth	P	N.t.p.
6740	Warmington	P	Min.
6741	Watford	P	Awd., Min.
6742	Weedon Beck	P	Min.
6743	Weedon Loys & Milthorpe	P	N.t.p.
6744	Weekley	P	N.t.p.
6745	Weldon Great & Little	P	N.t.p.
6746	Welford	P	Awd., Min.
6747	Welton	P	N.t.p.
6748	Wellingborough	P	Awd., Min.
6749	Weston by Welland	P	N.t.p.
6750	Weston Favell	P	Awd., Min.
6751	Whilton	P	N.t.p.
6752	Whiston	P	Rep. 1839
6753	Whittlebury	T	Awd., Min.
6754	Whitfield	P	Min.
6755	Whittering	P	N.t.p.
6756	Wicken	P	Agrmt.
6757	Wilbarston	PH	Min.
6758	Wilby	P	N.t.p.
6759	Winwick	P	Agrmt.
6760	Wollaston & Lodge Farm	P	Awd., Min.
6761	Woodend	H	N.t.p.
6762	Woodford	P	N.t.p.
6763	Woodford cum Membris	P	Agrmt., Rep. 1839
6764	Wood Newton	P	N.t.p.
6766	Yardley Hastings	P	N.t.p.
6767	Yarwell	P	N.t.p.

Northamptonshire contd.

6768	Yelvertoft	P	Awd.
8020	Hazelbeech	P	Awd.,Min.
14831	Wootton	P	Awd.,Min.

Northumberland

5706	Earl or Yearle	T	Awd.,Min.
5807	Eachwick	T	Awd.,Min.
6769	Abberwick	T	Rep. 1844
6770	Abbey Lands	T	N.t.p.
6771	Acklington	T	Agrmt.,Rep. 1838
6772	Acklington Park	T	Agrmt.,Rep. 1838
6773	Acomb	T	Agrmt.,Rep. 1838
6774	Acton, Old Felton	T	Rep. 1841
6775	Adderstone	T	Awd.,Min.
6776	Akeld	T	Agrmt.,Rep. 1839
6777	Allendale	P	Awd.,Min.
6778	Allenton	T	Awd.,Min.
6779	All Saints (Newcastle)	T	Awd.,Min.
6780	Alnham	T	Awd.,Min.
6781	Alnwick South Side	T	Agrmt.,Rep. 1839
6782	Alnwick	T	Min.
6783	Alnmouth	T	Agrmt.,Rep. 1841
6784	Amble	T	Min.,Rep. 1840
6785	Angerton High	T	Awd.,Min.
6786	Angerton Low	T	Awd.,Min.
6787	Andrew St (Newcastle)	PC	Awd.,Min.
6788	Anick	T	Agrmt.,Rep. 1838
6789	Anick Grange	T	Awd.,Min.
6790	Aydon	T	Awd.,Min.
6791	Aydon Castle	T	Awd.,Min.
6792	Bavington Little	T	Min.
6793	Backworth	T	Min.
6794	Backworth (Earsdon)	T	Min.,Rep. 1843
6795	Bamburgh	T	Awd.,Min.
6796	Bamburgh Castle	T	N.t.p.,Awd.
6797	Barmoor	T	Agrmt.,Rep. 1839
6798	Barrasford	T	Agrmt.,Rep. 1839
6799	Barrow	T	N.t.p.
6800	Bassington	T	Rep. 1839
6801	Bavington Great	T	Rep. 1839
6802	Beadnell	T	Rep. 1841
6803	Beal, Lowlin	T	Awd.,Min.
6804	Beanley	T	Agrmt.,Rep. 1839
6805	Bebside	PC	Awd.,Min.
6806	Bellasis	T	Rep. 1839
6807	Belford	T	Awd.,Min.
6808	Bellingham	P	Awd.,Min.
6809	Bellister	T	Awd.,Min.
6810	Belsay	T	Rep. 1839
6811	Benridge	T	Rep. 1838
6812	Benton Little	T	Agrmt.,Rep. 1839
6813	Benton Long	T	Agrmt.,Rep. 1839
6814	Benwell	T	Rep. 1840
6815	Berrington	T	Awd.,Min.
6816	Berwick upon Tweed	P	Awd.,Min.
6817	Berwick Hill	T	Agrmt.,Rep. 1840
6818	Berwick New	T	Rep. 1839
6819	Berwick Old	T	Agrmt.,Rep. 1839
6820	Bickerton	T	Rep. 1842
6821	Biddleston	T	Awd.,Min.
6822	Bigges Quarter	T	Awd.,Min.,Rep. 1841
6823	Bilton	T	Agrmt.,Rep. 1839
6824	Bingfield	C	Agrmt.,Rep. 1839
6825	Birling	T	Agrmt.,Rep. 1838
6826	Birtley High Division	C	Awd.,Min.,Rep. 1845
6827	Birtley Low Division	C	Min.,Rep. 1845
6828	Bitchfield	T	Agrmt.,Rep. 1839
6829	Black Carts, Ryehill	EP	Min.
6830	Blagdon	T	Awd.,Min.
6831	Blanchland High	C	N.t.p.,Min.
6832	Blenkinsopp	T	Awd.,Min.
6833	Bockenfield	T	Awd.,Min.
6834	Bolam	T	Agrmt.,Rep. 1839
6835	Bolam Vicarage	T	Rep. 1839
6836	Bolton	T	Rep. 1845
6837	Borowden	T	N.t.p.
6838	Borrowden	T	Awd.,Min.
6839	Bothal	P	Min.
6840	Boulmer, Seaton House	T	Agrmt.,Rep. 1839
6841	Bowsden	T	Min.,Rep. 1846
6842	Bradford	T	Rep. 1841
6843	Bradford (Bolam)	T	Agrmt.,Rep. 1839
6844	Brainshaugh	PC	Agrmt.,Min.
6845	Brandon	T	Min.,Rep. 1842
6846	Branton	T	Agrmt.,Rep. 1839
6847	Branxton	P	Agrmt.,Awd.,Min.,Rep. 1839
6848	Brenkley	T	Agrmt.,Rep. 1840
6849	Brinkburn Low Ward	T	Awd.,Min.
6850	Brinkburn High Ward	T	Awd.,Min.
6851	Brinkburn South Side	T	Awd.,Min.
6852	Broome Park	T	Min.,Rep. 1844
6853	Brotherwick	T	Agrmt.,Rep. 1838
6854	Broxfield	T	Awd.
6855	Brunton	T	Awd.,Min.
6856	Brunton East	T	Rep. 1839
6857	Brunton West	T	Rep. 1839
6858	Buckton	T	N.t.p.
6859	Budle	T	Min.,Rep. 1842
6860	Buller's Green	T	N.t.p.,Min.
6861	Bullocks Hall	T	Agrmt.,Rep. 1839
6862	Burradon	T	Agrmt.,Rep. 1839
6863	Burton	T	Awd.
6864	Buston High	T	Agrmt.,Rep. 1838
6865	Buston Low	T	Agrmt.,Rep. 1839
6866	Butterlaw	T	Awd.,Min.
6867	Byker	T	Agrmt.,Min.,Rep. 1843
6868	Bywell St Andrew	P	Agrmt.,Min.,Rep. 1840
6869	Bywell St Peter	P	Agrmt.,Rep. 1838
6870	Cacherside	T	Agrmt.,Rep. 1839
6871	Caistron	T	Awd.,Min.
6872	Callaby, Yettington	T	Awd.,Min.
6873	Callerton Black	T	Awd.,Min.
6874	Callerton High	T	Agrmt.,Awd.,Min.,Rep. 1840
6875	Callerton Little	T	Agrmt.,Rep. 1840
6876	Cambo	T	Awd.,Min.
6877	Camboise	T	Awd.,Min.
6878	Canongate	T	N.t.p.
6879	Capheaton	T	Rep. 1839
6880	Carham	T	Rep. 1843
6881	Carrow	T	Awd.,Min.
6882	Cartington	T	Rep. 1839
6883	Carry Coats	T	Awd.,Min.
6884	Chathill	T	Awd.,Min.
6885	Chatton	T	Awd.,Min.
6886	Cheeseburn Grange	T	Agrmt.,Rep. 1839
6887	Chevington East	T	Agrmt.,Rep. 1840
6888	Chevington West	T	Agrmt.,Rep. 1840
6889	Chipchase	T	Awd.,Min.
6890	Chollerton	T	Agrmt.,Rep. 1840
6891	Colwell, Great Swinburne	T	Rep. 1843
6892	Coquet Island	T	N.t.p.
6893	Corridge	T	Awd.,Min.
6894	Corsenside	P	Agrmt.,Rep. 1838
6895	Couldsmouth, Thompson's	T	Min.,Rep. 1842
6896	Coupland	T	Min.,Rep. 1839
6897	Cowpen	T	Agrmt.,Rep. 1840
6898	Coxlodge	T	Rep. 1839
6899	Cramlington	PC	Agrmt.,Rep. 1839
6900	Craster	T	Rep. 1841
6901	Crawley	T	Rep. 1839
6902	Coanwood	T	Awd.,Min.
6903	Coat Yards	T	Awd.,Min.
6904	Cocklaw	T	Agrmt.,Rep. 1838
6905	Coldcoats	T	Agrmt.,Rep. 1840
6906	Coldmartin	T	Rep. 1841
6907	Corbridge and Thornborough	T	Agrmt.,Rep. 1839
6908	Chillingham	P	Min.
6909	Chirdon	T	N.t.p.
6910	Chirton	T	Rep. 1840
6911	Coldwell	T	Rep. 1839
6912	Clarewood	T	Awd.,Min.
6913	Clennell	T	N.t.p.
6914	Clinch	H	Agrmt.,Rep. 1839
6915	Catchburn	T	Awd.,Min.,Rep. 1842
6916	Charlton East	Q	N.t.p.
6917	Charlton North	T	Awd.,Min.
6918	Charlton South	T	Awd.,Min.
6919	Charlton West	Q	N.t.p.
6920	Chartington	T	N.t.p.
6921	Cresswell	T	Awd.,Min.
6922	Crookdean	T	Awd.,Min.
6923	Crookham	T	Awd.,Min.
6924	Crookhouse	T	Agrmt.,Min.,Rep. 1839
6925	Cullercoates	T	N.t.p.
6926	Dalton	T	Agrmt.,Rep. 1839
6927	Darras Hall	T	Agrmt.,Rep. 1840
6928	Deanham	T	Awd.,Min.
6929	Debdon	T	Awd.,Min.
6930	Denton East	T	Awd.,Min.
6931	Denton West	T	Awd.,Min.
6932	Denwick	T	Agrmt.,Rep. 1839
6933	Detchant	T	N.t.p.
6934	Dilston	T	Awd.,Min.
6935	Dinnington	T	Agrmt.,Rep. 1840
6936	Dissington North	T	Agrmt.,Rep. 1839
6937	Dissington South	T	Agrmt.,Rep. 1839
6938	Ditchburn	T	Agrmt.,Rep. 1839
6939	Doddington	T	Awd.,Min.
6940	Downham	T	Agrmt.,Rep. 1839
6941	Doxford	T	Awd.,Min.
6942	Duddo	T	Awd.
6943	Dueshill	T	Awd.,Min.
6944	Dukeshagg	T	N.t.p.
6945	Dunston	T	Awd.,Min.
6946	Earsdon	T	Agrmt.,Rep. 1839
6947	Easington	T	Awd.,Min.
6948	Easington Grange	T	Awd.,Min.
6949	Edington	T	Rep. 1838
6950	Edlingham	T	Awd.,Min.
6951	Eglingham	T	Rep. 1841

Northumberland contd.

6952	Elford	T	Awd.,Min.
6953	Ellingham	T	Awd.,Min.
6954	Ellington	T	Agrmt.,Rep. 1839
6955	Elsdon	P	Agrmt.,Min.,Rep. 1838
6956	Elswick,Westgate	T	Awd.,Min.
6957	Eltringham	T	Agrmt.,Rep. 1839
6958	Elwick	T	Agrmt.,Rep. 1838
6959	Elyhaugh	T	N.t.p.
6960	Embleton	T	Awd.,Min.
6961	Eshot	T	Rep. 1841
6962	Eslington	D	N.t.p.
6963	Etal	T	Awd.,Min.
6964	Ewart	T	Awd.,Min.
6965	Ewesley	T	Awd.,Min.
6966	Ewesley	T	Min.,Rep. 1841
6967	Fairhaugh	T	Awd.,Min.
6968	Fairnley	T	Awd.,Min.
6969	Falloden	T	Awd.,Min.
6970	Fallowfield	T	N.t.p.,Min.
6971	Fallowlees	T	Rep. 1841
6972	Falstone	P	Awd.,Min.
6973	Farnham	T	N.t.p.
6974	Fawns	T	Rep. 1839
6975	Featherstone	T	Awd.,Min.
6976	Felton	T	Awd.,Min.
6977	Fenham	T	Rep. 1840
6978	Fenton	T	Awd.,Min.
6979	Fenwick	T	N.t.p.,Min.
6980	Fenwick(Stamfordham)	T	Agrmt.,Rep. 1839
6981	Fawdon(Ingram)	T	Rep. 1839
6982	Fawdon(St Nicholas)	T	Agrmt.,Rep. 1839
6983	Fleetham	T	Awd.,Min.
6984	Flotterton	T	Agrmt.,Rep. 1839
6985	Ford	T	Awd.,Min.
6986	Fowberry	T	Agrmt.,Rep. 1839
6987	Framlington	T	N.t.p.
6988	Freeholders Quarter	T	Agrmt.,Rep. 1840
6989	Gallow	T	Agrmt.,Rep. 1839
6990	Glanton	T	Awd.,Min.,Rep. 1841
6991	Glosterhill	T	N.t.p.
6992	Gosforth North	T	Rep. 1839
6993	Gosforth South	T	Rep. 1839
6994	Goswick	T	Awd.,Min.
6995	Greenleighton	T	Awd.,Min.
6996	Greens,Glantlees	T	Rep. 1839
6997	Grey's Forest	T	Awd.,Min.
6998	Greystead	P	Rep. 1843
6999	Gunnerton	T	Rep. 1841
7000	Guyson	T	N.t.p.
7001	Hadston	T	Agrmt.,Rep. 1838
7002	Haggerston	T	N.t.p.,Min.
7003	Hallington	T	Awd.,Min.
7004	Halliwell	T	Agrmt.,Rep. 1839
7005	Halton	T	Awd.,Min.
7006	Halton Shields	T	Awd.,Min.
7007	Haltwhistle	T	Awd.,Min.
7008	Halystone	P	Awd.,Min.
7009	Harbottle	T	Agrmt.,Rep. 1839
7010	Harle Little	T	Agrmt.,Rep. 1839
7011	Harle West	T	Agrmt.,Rep. 1839
7012	Harlow Hill	T	Rep. 1839
7013	Harnham	T	Agrmt.,Rep. 1839
7014	Hareup	T	Rep. 1839
7015	Hartburn	T	N.t.p.
7016	Hartburn Grange	T	Rep. 1838
7017	Hartford East	T	Agrmt.,Rep. 1839
7018	Hartford West	T	Agrmt.,Rep. 1838
7019	Hartington	T	Awd.,Min.
7020	Hartington Hall	T	Awd.,Min.
7021	Hartleyburn	T	Awd.,Min.
7022	Hartside	T	Rep. 1842
7023	Harwood	T	Awd.,Min.
7024	Hauxley	T	Min.,Rep. 1840
7025	Hawick	T	Awd.,Min.
7026	Hawkhill	T	Agrmt.,Rep. 1839
7027	Hawkwell	T	Agrmt.,Rep. 1839
7028	Haydon	C	Agrmt.,Min.,Rep. 1838
7029	Hazleridge	T	Rep. 1842
7030	Hazon,Hartlaw	T	Agrmt.,Rep. 1838
7031	Healey,Combhill	T	Awd.,Min.
7032	Heatherslaw,Flodden	T	Awd.,Min.
7033	Heathpool	T	Awd.,Min.
7034	Heaton	T	Rep. 1841
7035	Hebburn	T	N.t.p.
7036	Heddon Black	T	Awd.,Min.,Rep. 1839
7037	Heddon East	T	Agrmt.,Rep. 1843
7038	Heddon West	T	Rep. 1839
7039	Heddon on the Wall	T	Agrmt.,Min.,Rep. 1843
7040	Hedgeley	T	Agrmt.,Rep. 1839
7041	Hedley	T	Agrmt.,Rep. 1843
7042	Hedley Woodside	T	Agrmt.,Awd.,Rep. 1843
7043	Henshaw	T	Awd.,Min.
7044	Hepple	T	Rep. 1843
7045	Hepple Demesne	T	Rep. 1843
7046	Hepscott	T	Awd.,Min.,Rep. 1842
7047	Hesleyhurst	T	Awd.,Min.
7048	Hetton	T	Agrmt.,Rep. 1839
7049	Hetton House	T	Min.
7050	Heugh	T	Agrmt.,Rep. 1839
7051	Hexham West Quarter	T	Agrmt.,Rep. 1839
7052	Hexham	T	Agrmt.,Rep. 1839
7053	Hexham Low Quarter	T	Agrmt.,Rep. 1839
7054	Hexham High Quarter	T	Agrmt.,Rep. 1839
7055	Hexham Middle Quarter	T	Agrmt.,Rep. 1839
7056	Highley,High,Low	T	Agrmt.,Rep. 1838
7057	Higham Dykes	T	Agrmt.,Rep. 1840
7058	High Laws	T	Awd.,Min.
7059	Hilliwell	D	N.t.p.
7060	Hirst	T	Agrmt.,Awd.,Min.
7061	Holburn	T	Min.
7062	Hollinghill	T	Awd.,Min.
7063	Houghton,Close House	T	Agrmt.,Rep. 1843
7064	Holywell	T	N.t.p.
7065	Horsley	T	Agrmt.,Rep. 1839
7066	Horton	T	Awd.,Min.
7067	Horton(Chatton)	T	Rep. 1841
7068	Horton Grange	T	Agrmt.,Rep. 1840
7069	Houghton Little	T	Awd.,Min.
7070	Howden Pans	T	Awd.,Min.
7071	Howick	P	Agrmt.
7072	Howtell	T	Awd.,Min.
7073	Huln Parks	T	N.t.p.
7074	Humbleton	T	Awd.,Min.
7075	Ilderton	T	Awd.,Min.
7076	Inghoe	T	Rep. 1840
7077	Ingram Linhope	T	Agrmt.,Rep. 1842
7078	Jesmond	T	Rep. 1839
7079	John St.	T	N.t.p.,Min.
7080	Kearsley	T	Agrmt.,Rep. 1839
7081	Kenton	T	Rep. 1839
7082	Kidlands	EP	N.t.p.,Min.
7083	Kilham	T	Awd.,Min.
7084	Killingworth	T	Agrmt.,Min.,Rep. 1839
7085	Kirkharle	T	N.t.p.,Min.
7086	Kirkhaugh	P	Awd.,Min.
7087	Kirkheaton	EP	N.t.p.,Min.
7088	Kirkley	T	Agrmt.,Rep. 1840
7089	Kirknewton	T	Min.,Rep. 1843
7090	Kirkwhelpington	T	Awd.,Min.,Rep. 1839
7091	Kimmerston,Broomridge	T	Awd.,Min.
7092	Knaresdale	P	Min.
7093	Lambley	P	Agrmt.,Rep. 1838
7094	Lanton	T	Awd.,Min.
7095	Lowick	T	Awd.,Min.
7096	Learchild	T	Awd.,Min.
7097	Learmouth	T	Rep. 1843
7098	Leemailing	T	N.t.p.
7099	Lee Ward	T	Awd.,Min.
7100	Lemington	T	Awd.,Min.
7101	Lesbury	T	Agrmt.,Rep. 1841
7102	Lilburn East	T	Agrmt.,Rep. 1839
7103	Lilburn West	T	Agrmt.,Rep. 1839
7104	Linbriggs(Linbridge)	T	Awd.,Min.
7105	Linemouth	T	Awd.,Min.
7106	Linsheeles	T	Awd.,Min.
7107	Long Framlington	C	Agrmt.,Rep. 1839
7108	Long Horsley	P	N.t.p.
7109	Longhoughton	T	Awd.,Min.
7110	Longridge	T	N.t.p.
7111	Longshaws	T	Awd.,Min.
7112	Longwitton	T	Awd.,Min.
7113	Lorbottle	T	Awd.,Min.
7114	Lucker	T	Awd.,Min.
7115	Lyham	T	Agrmt.,Rep. 1839
7116	Manorial Allotment	D	Awd.,Min.
7117	Mason	T	Agrmt.,Rep. 1840
7118	Masters Close	EP	N.t.p.,Min.
7119	Matfen East	T	Agrmt.,Rep. 1839
7120	Matfen West	T	Rep. 1839
7121	Middleton South	T	Awd.,Min.
7122	Middleton South(Hartburn)	T	Awd.,Min.
7123	Middleton	T	N.t.p.
7124	Middleton Hall	T	Awd.,Min.
7125	Middleton North,Todridge	T	Awd.,Min.
7126	Meldon	T	Awd.,Min.
7127	Melkridge	T	Awd.,Min.
7128	Merryshields	D	Agrmt.,Rep. 1839
7129	Mickley	T	Agrmt.,Rep. 1839
7130	Middleton North	T	Awd.,Min.
7131	Milburn	T	Rep. 1841
7132	Milburn Grange	T	Agrmt.,Rep. 1840
7133	Milfield	T	Agrmt.,Min.,Rep. 1839
7134	Mindrum	T	Agrmt.,Rep. 1839
7135	Mitford,Molesdon	T	Awd.,Min.
7136	Moneylaws	T	Min.,Rep. 1845
7137	Monkseaton	T	Min.,Rep. 1844
7138	Morpeth	BP	Awd.,Min.
7139	Morrick	T	Agrmt.,Rep. 1838
7140	Mount Healey	T	Awd.,Min.
7141	Mousen	T	Awd.
7142	Murton	T	Agrmt.,Rep. 1840
7143	Nafferton	T	Agrmt.,Rep. 1839

Northumberland contd.

7144	Nesbit	T	Awd.,Min.
7145	Nesbitt(Stamfordham)	T	Agrmt.,Rep. 1839
7146	Netherton North Side	T	Min.
7147	Netherton South Side	T	Min.
7148	Netherwitton	T	Awd.,Min.
7149	Newbiggin	T	Awd.,Min.
7150	Newbiggin(Shotley)	T	Agrmt.,Rep. 1844
7151	Newbiggin(Woodhorn)	T	Awd.,Min.
7152	Newburn	T	Awd.,Min.
7153	Newburn Hall	T	Awd.,Min.
7154	Newtown	T	Awd.,Min.
7155	Newham	T	Awd.
7156	Newham(Whalton)	T	Agrmt.,Rep. 1839
7157	Newminster Abbey	T	Awd.,Min.
7158	Newsham,South Blyth	T	Agrmt.,Rep. 1839
7159	Newstead	T	Awd.
7160	Newton on the Moor	T	Agrmt.,Rep. 1841
7161	Newton by the Sea	T	Awd.,Min.
7162	Newton Park	T	Agrmt.,Rep. 1839
7163	Newton Underwood	T	Agrmt.,Rep. 1839
7164	Newton West	T	Awd.,Min.
7165	Nicholas St.	P	Min.
7166	Nunnykirk	T	Awd.,Min.
7167	Nunriding	T	Awd.
7168	Ogle	T	Awd.,Min.
7169	Outchester	T	Agrmt.,Rep. 1839
7170	Ovingham	T	Agrmt.,Rep. 1839
7171	Ovington	T	Agrmt.,Rep. 1839
7172	Owston	T	Agrmt.,Rep. 1839
7173	Paston	T	Agrmt.,Awd.,Min.,Rep. 1839
7174	Pauperhaugh	T	Awd.,Min.
7175	Peels	T	N.t.p.
7176	Pigdon	T	Agrmt.,Rep. 1839
7177	Plainmellor	T	Awd.,Min.
7178	Plashetts	T	Agrmt.,Rep. 1840
7179	Plessey,Shotton	T	Agrmt.,Rep. 1840
7180	Ponteland	T	Rep. 1841
7181	Portgate	T	Agrmt.,Rep. 1838
7182	Prendwick	T	Awd.,Min.
7183	Presson	T	Rep. 1843
7184	Preston	T	Rep. 1841
7185	Preston(Tynemouth)	D	Min.,Rep. 1840
7186	Prestwick	T	Rep. 1841
7187	Prudhoe	T	Agrmt.,Min.,Rep. 1843
7188	Prudhoe Castle	T	Agrmt.,Rep. 1839
7189	Ramshope	EP	N.t.p.,Min.
7190	Ratchwood	T	Awd.,Min.
7191	Raw	T	Awd.,Min.
7192	Rennington	T	Awd.,Min.
7193	Riddell's Quarter	T	Awd.,Min.
7194	Ridley	T	Awd.,Min.
7195	Riplington	T	Agrmt.,Rep. 1839
7196	Ritton Colt Park	T	Awd.,Min.
7197	Ritton White House	T	Awd.,Min.
7198	River Green	EP	N.t.p.,Min.
7199	Rock	T	Awd.
7200	Roddam	T	Awd.,Min.
7201	Rosedon	T	Awd.,Min.
7202	Rothbury	T	Awd.,Min.
7203	Rothley	T	Awd.,Min.
7204	Rudchester	T	Agrmt.,Rep. 1839
7205	Ryal	T	Agrmt.,Awd.,Min.,Rep. 1839
7206	Ryle Great	T	Awd.,Min.
7207	Ryle Little	T	Awd.,Min.
7208	Saltwick	T	Rep. 1839
7209	Sandoe	T	Agrmt.,Rep. 1838
7210	Screnwood	T	Awd.,Min.
7211	Seaton Delaval,Hartley	T	Agrmt.,Rep. 1840
7212	Seaton North	T	Awd.,Min.
7213	Selby's Forest	T	Awd.,Min.
7214	Seghill	T	Agrmt.,Rep. 1839
7215	Shaftoe East	T	Awd.,Min.
7216	Shaftoe West	T	Awd.,Min.
7217	Sharperton	T	Awd.,Min.
7218	Shawdon	T	Rep. 1841
7219	Shields North,Culler	T	N.t.p.,Min.
7220	Shilbottle	T	Agrmt.,Rep. 1839
7221	Shilvington	T	Awd.,Min.
7222	Shipley	T	Rep. 1841
7223	Shire Moor	D	Rep. 1844
7224	Shoeston	T	Awd.,Min.
7225	Snitter	T	Agrmt.,Rep. 1841
7226	Spittle Hill	T	Agrmt.,Rep. 1838
7227	Spittle	T	Agrmt.,Rep. 1839
7228	Stamford	T	Awd.,Min.
7229	Shortflatt	T	Agrmt.,Rep. 1839
7230	Shotley Lower Quarter	T	Awd.,Min.
7231	Simonburn	P	Agrmt.,Rep. 1840
7232	Slaley	P	Awd.,Min.
7233	Stannington	T	Agrmt.,Rep. 1840
7234	Stanton	T	Awd.,Min.
7235	Sturton Grange	T	Agrmt.,Rep. 1839
7236	Sunderland North	T	Awd.,Min.
7237	Swarland	T	N.t.p.
7238	Sweethope	T	Awd.,Min.
7239	Swinburne Little	T	Rep. 1843
7240	Swinhoe	T	Agrmt.,Rep. 1838
7241	Tarset	T	Agrmt.,Rep. 1838
7242	Thirlwall	T	Awd.,Min.
7243	Thirston East,West	T	Agrmt.,Rep. 1841
7244	Thockrington	T	Awd.,Min.
7245	Thorneyburn	T	Agrmt.,Rep. 1839
7246	Thorn Grafton	T	Awd.,Min.
7247	Thornton(Norham)	T	Awd.,Min.,Rep. 1841
7248	Thornton East	T	Awd.,Min.
7249	Thornton West	T	Awd.,Min.
7250	Throckley	T	Awd.,Min.
7251	Throckley Fell	D	Awd.,Min.
7252	Thropple	T	Agrmt.,Rep. 1839
7253	Thropton	T	Agrmt.,Rep. 1840
7254	Titlington	T	Rep. 1841
7255	Todburn	T	Awd.,Min.
7256	Todridge	T	N.t.p.,Min.
7257	Togston	T	Agrmt.,Rep. 1839
7258	Tone	T	Awd.
7259	Tosson Great,Ryehill	T	Agrmt.,Rep. 1839
7260	Tosson Little	T	Rep. 1840
7261	Tranwell,High Church	T	Awd.,Min.
7262	Trewick	T	Agrmt.,Rep. 1839
7263	Tughall	T	Awd.,Min.
7264	Twizell	T	Awd.,Min.
7265	Tynemouth	T	Min.,Rep. 1844
7266	Ulgham	C	Min.
7267	Unthank	T	Awd.,Min.
7268	Walbottle	T	Awd.,Min.
7269	Walker	T	Agrmt.,Rep. 1839
7270	Walkmill	T	Awd.,Min.
7271	Wall	T	Rep. 1838
7272	Wallridge	T	Agrmt.,Rep. 1839
7273	Walls' End	T	Rep. 1838
7274	Wallington	T	Awd.,Min.
7275	Wall Town	T	Awd.,Min.
7276	Warden	D	Min.,Rep. 1840
7277	Warenford	T	Awd.,Min.
7278	Warenton	T	Awd.,Min.
7279	Wark	P	Agrmt.,Rep. 1838
7280	Wark,Sunnilaws	T	Rep. 1843
7281	Warkworth	T	Agrmt.,Rep. 1838
7282	Warton	T	Agrmt.,Rep. 1839
7283	Weetsleet	T	Agrmt.,Rep. 1839
7284	Weetwood	T	Awd.,Min.
7285	Welton	T	Agrmt.,Rep. 1839
7286	Whalton	T	Agrmt.,Rep. 1840
7287	Whelpington West	T	Agrmt.,Awd.,Min.,Rep. 1839
7288	Whitchester	T	Agrmt.,Rep. 1839
7289	Whiteside Law	T	Rep. 1843
7290	Whitley	T	Rep. 1839
7291	Whitfield	P	Agrmt.,Min.
7292	Whitridge	T	Awd.,Min.
7293	Whittingham	P	Awd.,Min.
7294	Whittington Little	T	Rep. 1838
7295	Whittle	T	Agrmt.,Rep. 1839
7296	Whittle(Shilbottle)	T	Rep. 1839
7297	Whitton	T	Awd.,Min.
7298	Whorlton	T	Awd.,Min.
7299	Widdrington	T	Awd.,Min.
7300	Willington	T	Rep. 1838
7301	Wingates	T	Awd.,Min.
7302	Witton Shields	T	Agrmt.,Rep. 1838
7303	Wooden	T	Agrmt.,Rep. 1839
7304	Woodhorn	T	Awd.,Min.
7305	Woodhouse	T	Agrmt.,Rep. 1838
7306	Woodhorn Demesne	T	Agrmt.,Rep. 1839
7307	Wooler	T	Rep. 1841
7308	Woolsington	T	Awd.,Min.
7309	Wooperton	T	Agrmt.,Rep. 1839
7310	Wreigh Hill	T	Awd.,Min.
7311	Wylam	T	Agrmt.,Rep. 1843
7312	Yeavering	T	Agrmt.,Awd.,Min.,Rep. 1839
8019	Clifton,Coldwell	T	Awd.,Min.
8067	Trewhitt,High,Low	T	Agrmt.,Rep. 1841

Nottinghamshire

7313	Alverton	T	N.t.p.,Min.
7314	Annesley	P	N.t.p.,Awd.,Min.
7315	Applesthorpe	P	N.t.p.,Min.
7316	Arnold	P	Awd.,Min.
7317	Askham	P	Awd.,Min.
7318	Awsworth	H	Awd.,Min.
7319	Aslockton	T	N.t.p.,Min.
7320	Averham	P	Rep. 1838
7321	Babworth	P	Agrmt.,Rep. 1838
7322	Balderton	P	Awd.,Min.
7323	Barnby in the Willows	P	Agrmt.,Min.,Rep. 1841
7324	Barnby Moor	T	Awd.,Min.
7325	Barnstone	T	Awd.,Min.
7326	Barton	P	N.t.p.,Min.
7327	Basford	P	N.t.p.,Min.
7328	Beauvale Brooks	D	Min.
7329	Beckingham	P	N.t.p.,Min.

Nottinghamshire contd.

7330	Beeston	P	N.t.p.,Min.
7331	Bevercoates	T	Awd.,Min.
7332	Besthorpe	T	Min.,Rep. 1838
7333	Bilbrough	P	N.t.p.,Min.
7334	Bilby	H	Rep. 1841
7335	Bilsthorpe	P	Agrmt.,Rep. 1838
7336	Bingham	P	Agrmt.,Min.,Rep. 1838
7337	Bleasby	P	N.t.p.,Min.
7338	Blidworth	P	N.t.p.,Min.
7339	Blyth	T	Awd.,Min.,Rep. 1841
7340	Bole	P	Awd.,Min.
7341	Bothamsall	P	Awd.,Min.
7342	Bottoms	H	N.t.p.,Min.
7343	Boughton	P	Awd.,Min.
7344	Bramcote	P	Awd.,Min.
7345	Brewhouse Yard	EP	Awd.,Min.
7346	Bridgford East	P	N.t.p.,Min.
7347	Bridgford West	P	Rep. 1838
7348	Brinsley	H	Awd.,Min.
7349	Broughton Sulney	P	N.t.p.,Min.
7350	Budby	T	Awd.
7351	Bulcote	T	Awd.,Min.
7352	Bulwell	P	Agrmt.,Min.
7353	Bunny with Bradmore	P	N.t.p.,Min.
7354	Burton Joyce	P	N.t.p.,Min.
7355	Burton West	P	N.t.p.,Min.
7356	Calverton	P	N.t.p.,Min.
7357	Carburton	T	Awd.,Min.
7358	Carcolston	P	N.t.p.,Min.
7359	Carlton	T	N.t.p.,Min.
7360	Carlton in Lindrick	P	N.t.p.,Min.
7361	Carlton upon Trent	T	N.t.p.,Min.
7362	Caunton	P	N.t.p.,Min.
7363	Chilwell	T	Awd.,Min.
7364	Clareborough	P	Awd.,Min.
7365	Clayworth	T	Agrmt.,Min.
7366	Clifton cum Glapton	P	Awd.,Min.
7367	Clifton North	T	Awd.,Min.
7368	Clifton South	T	Awd.,Min.
7369	Clipstone	T	Awd.,Min.
7370	Coddington	P	N.t.p.,Min.
7371	Collingham North	P	N.t.p.,Min.
7372	Collingham South	P	Awd.,Min.
7373	Colston Basset	P	Awd.,Min.
7374	Colwick	P	Awd.,Min.
7375	Costock	P	N.t.p.,Min.
7376	Cotgrave	P	N.t.p.,Min.
7377	Cotham	P	N.t.p.,Min.
7378	Cromwell	P	N.t.p.,Min.
7379	Cropwell Bishop	P	N.t.p.,Min.
7380	Cropwell Butler	T	N.t.p.,Min.
7381	Cuckney	P	Rep. 1839
7382	Darlton	P	Awd.,Min.
7383	Drayton East	P	Awd.,Min.
7384	Drayton West	P	Awd.,Min.
7385	Dunham and Ragnall	P	Awd.,Min.
7386	Eakring	P	Min.,Rep. 1838
7387	Eastwood	P	N.t.p.,Min.
7388	Eaton	P	N.t.p.,Min.
7389	Edingley	P	N.t.p.,Min.
7390	Edwalton	P	Awd.,Min.
7391	Edwinstowe	T	Awd.,Min.
7392	Egmanton	P	N.t.p.,Min.
7393	Elksley	P	N.t.p.,Min.
7394	Elston	P	N.t.p.,Min.
7395	Elton	P	N.t.p.,Min.
7396	Epperstone	P	Rep. 1838
7397	Everton	T	Awd.,Min.
7398	Farndon	P	N.t.p.,Min.
7399	Farnsfield	P	N.t.p.,Min.
7400	Felley	EP	N.t.p.
7401	Fishpool	H	N.t.p.,Min.
7402	Fiskerton	T	Awd.,Min.
7403	Finningley	P	Rep. 1838
7404	Flawborough	PC	Awd.,Min.
7405	Fledborough	P	Min.,Rep. 1838
7406	Flintham	P	N.t.p.,Min.
7407	Fullwood	EP	N.t.p.,Min.
7408	Gamston	P	N.t.p.,Min.
7409	Gateford	T	Awd.,Min.
7410	Gedling	P	N.t.p.,Min.
7411	Greasley	T	Min.
7412	Girton	P	Min.,Rep. 1838
7413	Gonalston	P	Awd.,Min.
7414	Gotham	P	N.t.p.,Min.
7415	Granby cum Sutton	P	N.t.p.,Min.
7416	Grange Leys and Highfields	D	Agrmt.,Rep. 1842
7417	Gringley Little	H	Min.,Rep. 1838
7418	Gringley on the Hill	P	N.t.p.,Min.
7419	Grove	P	Awd.,Min.,Rep. 1838
7420	Halam	P	N.t.p.,Min.
7421	Halloughton	P	Awd.,Min.
7422	Harby	T	N.t.p.,Min.
7423	Harworth	P	N.t.p.,Min.
7424	Hawksworth	P	N.t.p.,Min.
7425	Hawton	P	Awd.,Min.
7426	Hayton and Tiln	H	Agrmt.,Min.,Rep. 1839
7427	Haywood Oaks	EP	N.t.p.,Min.
7428	Headon cum Upton	P	N.t.p.,Min.
7429	Hickling	P	N.t.p.,Min.
7430	Hockerton	P	Awd.,Min.
7431	Hodsock	T	Awd.,Min.
7432	Holme	P	N.t.p.,Min.
7433	Holme Pierrepont	P	Rep. 1838
7434	Houghton	P	Awd.,Min.
7435	Hoveringham	P	Awd.,Min.
7436	Hucknall under Huthwaite	T	N.t.p.,Min.
7437	Hucknall Torkard	P	N.t.p.,Min.
7438	Kelham	P	Awd.,Min.
7439	Kersall	T	N.t.p.,Min.
7440	Keyworth	P	N.t.p.,Min.
7441	Kilvington	P	N.t.p.,Min.
7442	Kimberley	T	Awd.,Min.
7443	Kingston upon Soar	P	Awd.,Min.
7444	Kinoulton	P	Awd.,Min.
7445	Kirkby in Ashfield	P	N.t.p.,Min.
7446	Kirklington	P	Awd.,Min.
7447	Kirton	P	N.t.p.,Min.
7448	Kneesall and Ompton	P	Agrmt.,Min.,Rep. 1839
7449	Kneeton	P	Awd.,Min.
7450	Lambley	P	Awd.,Min.
7451	Laneham	P	Min.,Rep. 1839
7452	Langar	T	Awd.,Min.
7453	Langford	P	Awd.,Min.
7454	Leake East	P	N.t.p.,Min.
7455	Leake West	P	N.t.p.,Min.
7456	Lenton	P	Awd.,Min.
7457	Leverton North	P	N.t.p.,Min.
7458	Leverton South	P	N.t.p.,Min.
7459	Lexington	P	Min.,Rep. 1839
7460	Lindhurst	EP	Awd.,Min.
7461	Littleborough	P	N.t.p.,Min.
7462	Lodge on the Wolds	EP	N.t.p.,Awd.,Min.
7463	Lound	T	N.t.p.
7464	Lowdham	P	Min.,Rep. 1838
7465	Lyndby	P	Awd.,Min.,Rep. 1841
7466	Mansfield	P	Awd.,Min.
7467	Mansfield Woodhouse	P	Awd.,Min.
7468	Maplebeck	P	Awd.,Min.
7469	Markham East	P	N.t.p.,Min.
7470	Markham West	P	N.t.p.,Min.
7471	Marnham	P	Agrmt.,Rep. 1843
7472	Mattersey	P	N.t.p.,Awd.,Min.
7474	Mering	EP	Awd.,Min.
7475	Misson	P	Awd.,Min.
7476	Misterton	P	N.t.p.,Min.
7477	Moorgate and Bollam	H	Agrmt.,Min.,Rep. 1839
7478	Moor Green	T	Awd.,Min.
7479	Morton	P	N.t.p.,Min.
7480	Muskham North	P	N.t.p.,Min.
7481	Muskham South	P	Min.
7482	Newark	P	Awd.,Min.
7483	Newstead	EP	N.t.p.,Min.
7484	Newthorpe	T	N.t.p.,Min.
7485	Newton	T	N.t.p.,Min.
7486	Normanton upon Trent	P	N.t.p.,Min.
7487	Normanton on the Wolds	H	Min.,Rep. 1839
7488	Norwell	P	N.t.p.,Min.
7489	Nottingham St Mary	P	Awd.,Min.
7490	Nottingham St Nicholas	P	N.t.p.,Min.
7491	Nuthall	T	Awd.,Min.
7492	Oldcoates	T	Agrmt.,Awd.,Min.,Rep. 1840
7493	Ollerton	T	Awd.
7494	Ordsall	P	Min.,Rep. 1838
7495	Orston	P	N.t.p.,Min.
7496	Osberton	T	Rep. 1845
7497	Ossington	P	Awd.,Min.
7498	Owthorpe	P	Awd.,Min.
7499	Oxton	P	Awd.,Min.
7500	Papplewick	P	Awd.,Min.
7501	Perlethorpe	T	Awd.
7502	Plumtree	P	N.t.p.,Min.
7503	Radcliffe on Trent	P	N.t.p.,Min.
7504	Radford	P	N.t.p.,Min.
7505	Ragnall	T	N.t.p.,Min.
7506	Rainworth	H	N.t.p.
7507	Rampton	P	Min.,Rep. 1839
7508	Ranskill	T	Min.,Rep. 1839
7509	Ratcliffe on Soar	P	N.t.p.,Min.
7510	Rempstone	P	N.t.p.,Min.
7511	Retford East	P	Awd.,Min.
7512	Retford West	P	N.t.p.,Min.
7513	Rolleston	T	N.t.p.,Min.
7514	Ruddington	P	N.t.p.,Min.
7515	Rufford	EP	Awd.,Min.
7516	Saundby	P	Rep. 1838
7517	Saxondale	T	N.t.p.,Min.
7518	Scaftworth	T	Awd.,Min.
7519	Scarle South	T	Min.,Rep. 1838
7520	Scarrington	P	N.t.p.,Min.
7521	Screveton	P	N.t.p.,Min.
7522	Scrooby	P	Awd.,Min.

Nottinghamshire contd.

7523	Selston	P	Awd.,Min.
7524	Shelford	P	N.t.p.,Min.
7525	Shelton	P	Awd.,Min.
7527	Shireoaks and Haggonfield	T	Min.,Rep. 1845
7528	Sibthorpe	P	N.t.p.,Min.
7529	Skegby	T	Awd.,Min.
7530	Skegby	P	Awd.,Min.
7531	Snenton	P	N.t.p.,Min.
7532	Southwell	P	Awd.,Min.
7533	Spalford	H	N.t.p.,Min.
7534	Standard Hill	EP	N.t.p.,Min.
7535	Stanford	P	Rep. 1838
7536	Stanton on the Wolds	P	Awd.,Min.
7537	Stapleford	P	Awd.,Min.
7538	Staunton	P	Awd.,Min.
7539	Staythorpe	T	Rep. 1838
7540	Stoke Bardolph	P	N.t.p.,Min.
7541	Stoke East	P	Awd.,Min.
7542	Stokeham	P	Agrmt.,Rep. 1839
7543	Strelley	P	N.t.p.,Min.
7544	Sturton	P	N.t.p.,Min.
7545	Styrrup	T	Awd.,Min.,Rep. 1841
7546	Sutton in Ashfield	P	N.t.p.,Min.
7547	Sutton Bonnington St Anne	P	N.t.p.,Min.
7548	Sutton Bonnington	P	Awd.,Min.
7549	Sutton cum Lound	P	Awd.,Min.
7550	Sutton upon Trent	P	Awd.,Min.
7551	Syerston	P	N.t.p.
7552	Teversal	P	Rep. 1840
7553	Thorney	P	Rep. 1839
7554	Thorpe	P	Min.,Rep. 1838
7555	Thorpe Bochart	P	Awd.,Min.
7556	Thrumpton	P	Awd.,Min.
7557	Thurgarton	P	N.t.p.,Min.
7558	Tollerton	P	N.t.p.,Min.
7559	Torworth	T	Agrmt.,Rep. 1839
7560	Toton	H	Awd.,Min.
7561	Treswell	P	Awd.,Min.
7562	Trowell	P	N.t.p.,Min.
7563	Tuxford	P	N.t.p.,Min.
7564	Tythby	T	Awd.,Min.
7565	Upton	P	N.t.p.,Min.
7566	Walesby	P	N.t.p.
7567	Walkeringham	P	N.t.p.,Min.
7568	Wallingwells	EP	Awd.,Min.
7569	Warsop	P	N.t.p.,Min.
7570	Watnall Cantelupe	T	Agrmt.,Rep. 1841
7571	Watnall Chaworth	T	Agrmt.,Rep. 1842
7572	Welbeck	EP	Awd.,Min.
7573	Welham	H	Awd.,Min.
7574	Wellow	P	Awd.,Min.
7575	Weston	P	N.t.p.,Min.
7576	Whatton	P	N.t.p.,Min.
7577	Wheatley North	P	Rep. 1838
7578	Wheatley South	P	Agrmt.,Rep. 1839
7579	Widmerpool	P	N.t.p.,Min.
7580	Wigsley	T	Awd.,Min.
7581	Wilford	P	Awd.,Min.
7582	Willoughby on the Wolds	P	N.t.p.,Min.
7583	Winkbourn	P	Awd.,Min.
7584	Winthorpe	P	Awd.,Min.
7585	Wiseton	T	Min.,Rep. 1837
7586	Wiverton	EP	Awd.,Min.
7587	Woodborough	P	N.t.p.,Min.
7588	Woodhouse Hall	EP	N.t.p.
7589	Wollaton cum Cossall	P	Awd.,Min.,Rep. 1838
7590	Worksop and Radford	T	Min.
7591	Wysall	P	N.t.p.,Min.
8883	Normanton upon Soar	P	N.t.p.,Min.

Oxfordshire

7592	Adderbury	P	N.t.p.
7593	Adwell	P	Rep. 1839
7594	Albury	P	Awd.,Min.
7595	Alkerton	P	N.t.p.
7596	Alvercot	P	N.t.p.,Min.
7597	Ambrosden	P	Awd.,Min.
7598	Ardley	P	Agrmt.,Rep. 1839
7599	Arncott	C	N.t.p.,Min.
7600	Ascot under Wychwood	P	Awd.,Min.
7601	Asthall	P	N.t.p.,Min.
7602	Aston and Coate	H	Agrmt.,Min.,Rep. 1839
7603	Aston Middle	H	N.t.p.,Min.
7604	Aston North	P	Awd.,Min.
7605	Aston Rowant	P	Agrmt.,Min.,Rep. 1839
7606	Attington	EP	Awd.,Min.
7607	Bampton	P	Awd.,Min.
7608	Barford St John St Michael	C	N.t.p.,Min.
7609	Barton Westcott	P	N.t.p.,Min.
7610	Banbury	P	Awd.,Min.
7611	Blackbourton	P	N.t.p.
7612	Baynton	H	Rep. 1843
7613	Beckley	P	N.t.p.,Min.
7614	Begbroke	P	Min.,Rep. 1840
7615	Bensington	P	Min.,Rep. 1840
7616	Berrick Salome	P	Agrmt.,Min.,Rep. 1838
7617	Bicester King's End	T	N.t.p.,Min.
7618	Bicester Market End	T	N.t.p.,Min.
7619	Binsey	P	N.t.p.
7620	Bix	P	Min.,Rep. 1840
7621	Baldon Marsh, Baldon Foot	P	N.t.p.,Min.
7622	Blackthorn	C	N.t.p.,Min.
7623	Bladon cum Woodstock	P	Awd.,Min.
7624	Blenheim Park	EP	N.t.p.,Min.
7625	Bletchington	P	Min.,Rep. 1839
7626	Bloxham	P	N.t.p.,Min.
7627	Bowld	H	Min.
7628	Brighthampton	H	Awd.,Min.
7629	Brightwell Baldwin	P	N.t.p.,Min.
7630	Britwell Prior	P	Awd.,Min.
7631	Britwell Salome	P	Min.
7632	Broadwell	P	N.t.p.,Min.
7633	Broughton	P	Awd.,Min.
7634	Broughton Poggs	P	Min.,Rep. 1839
7635	Bruerne	EP	N.t.p.
7636	Bucknell	P	Awd.,Min.
7637	Burford	P	N.t.p.,Min.
7638	Burroway Meadow, Charney	D	Awd.,Min.
7639	Cassington	P	Awd.,Min.
7640	Caversfield	P	Awd.,Min.
7641	Caversham	P	Awd.,Min.
7642	Chalgrove	P	Min.,Rep. 1840
7643	Charlbury	P	Awd.,Min.
7644	Charlton on Otmoor	P	Awd.,Min.
7645	Chastleton	P	Awd.,Min.
7646	Checkendon	P	Agrmt.,Min.,Rep. 1838
7647	Chesterton	P	N.t.p.,Min.
7648	Chimney	H	Min.,Rep. 1846
7649	Chinnor	P	Min.,Rep. 1840
7650	Chislehampton	P	N.t.p.,Min.
7651	Chippenhurst	H	Awd.,Min.
7652	Chipping Norton	P	Awd.,Min.
7653	Churchill	P	N.t.p.,Min.
7654	Clanfield	P	Agrmt.,Min.,Rep. 1838
7655	Clattercote	EP	N.t.p.
7656	Clifton	T	N.t.p.
7657	Clifton Hampden	P	N.t.p.,Min.
7658	Coggs	P	N.t.p.,Min.
7659	Combe Long	P	N.t.p.,Min.
7660	Cornbury Park	EP	Awd.,Min.
7661	Cornwell	P	N.t.p.,Min.
7662	Cottesford	P	Awd.,Min.
7663	Cowley	P	Min.
7664	Crawley	H	Min.,Rep. 1839
7665	Cropredy	P	Min.,Rep. 1842
7666	Crowell	P	Rep. 1839
7667	Crowmarsh Gifford	P	Min.,Rep. 1845
7668	Cuddesden	P	Min.,Rep. 1840
7669	Culham	P	Awd.,Min.
7670	Curbridge	H	Min.,Rep. 1840
7671	Cuxham	P	Min.,Rep. 1840
7672	Dean	H	Awd.,Min.
7673	Deddington	P	N.t.p.,Min.
7674	Denton	C	Min.,Rep. 1841
7675	Ditchley	T	N.t.p.,Min.
7676	Dorchester	P	Awd.,Min.
7677	Drayton Rectory	P	N.t.p.,Min.
7678	Drayton	P	Min.,Rep. 1839
7679	Ducklington	P	Agrmt.,Min.,Rep. 1838
7680	Dunstew	P	N.t.p.,Min.
7681	Easington	P	Agrmt.,Min.,Rep. 1839
7682	Elsfield	P	Rep. 1840
7683	Emmington	P	Rep. 1840
7684	Ensham	P	N.t.p.,Min.
7685	Enstone	P	Awd.,Min.
7686	Epwell	T	N.t.p.,Min.
7687	Ewelme	P	Min.,Rep. 1839
7688	Eye and Dunsden	D	Min.,Rep. 1839
7689	Fifield	P	Awd.,Min.
7690	Forest Hill	P	N.t.p.,Min.
7691	Fringford	P	Awd.,Min.
7692	Finmere	P	Min.,Rep. 1840
7693	Fritwell	P	N.t.p.,Min.
7694	Fulbrook	P	Awd.,Min.
7695	Garsington	P	Min.,Rep. 1841
7696	Glympton	P	Agrmt.,Rep. 1837
7697	Goring	P	Awd.,Min.
7698	Grafton	T	Min.,Rep. 1839
7699	Saint Giles (Oxford)	P	Awd.,Min.
7700	Goddington	P	N.t.p.,Min.
7701	Hailey	H	Min.,Rep. 1840
7702	Hampton Gay	P	N.t.p.,Min.
7703	Hampton Poyle	P	N.t.p.,Min.
7704	Handborough	P	N.t.p.,Min.
7705	Hanwell	P	N.t.p.,Min.
7706	Hardwick	P	Awd.,Min.
7707	Hardwick	C	Awd.,Min.
7708	Hardwick Heath	D	Awd.,Min.
7709	Harpsden cum Bolney	P	Min.,Rep. 1841
7710	Haseley Great	P	Agrmt.,Min.,Rep. 1838

Oxfordshire contd.

7711	Headington	P	N.t.p.,Min.
7712	Henley on Thames	P	Min.,Rep. 1842
7713	Hempton	T	N.t.p.
7714	Heyford Lower	P	N.t.p.,Min.
7715	Heyford Upper	P	N.t.p.,Min.
7716	Heythrop	P	Agrmt.,Rep. 1838
7717	Holton	P	Awd.,Min.
7718	Holwell	H	Rep. 1840
7719	Hook Norton	P	N.t.p.,Min.
7720	Horsepath	P	Awd.,Min.
7721	Ibstone	P	Rep. 1841
7722	Idbury	P	Awd.,Min.
7723	Iffley	P	Awd.,Min.
7724	Islip	P	Rep. 1842
7725	Kelmscot	H	N.t.p.,Min.
7726	Kencott	P	Min.
7727	Kiddington	P	Awd.,Min.
7728	Kidlington cum Gosford	P	Awd.,Min.
7729	Kingham	P	Awd.,Min.
7730	Kingsey	P	Awd.,Min.
7731	Kirtlington	P	N.t.p.,Min.
7732	Langley	H	Agrmt.,Rep. 1838
7733	Launton	P	Awd.,Min.
7734	Leafield	D	Agrmt.,Min.,Rep. 1838
7735	Leigh North	P	N.t.p.,Min.
7736	Leigh South	P	Awd.,Min.
7737	Lewknor	P	Min.
7738	Lewknor Uphill	P	Min.,Rep. 1840
7739	Lillingstone Lovell	P	Agrmt.,Rep. 1838
7740	Littlemore	D	N.t.p.,Min.
7741	Lyneham	H	N.t.p.
7742	Mapledurham	P	Min.,Rep. 1840
7743	Marston	P	Awd.,Min.
7744	Merton	P	N.t.p.,Min.
7745	Middleton Stoney	P	Rep. 1840
7746	Milcombe	C	N.t.p.,Min.
7747	Milton	H	Awd.,Min.
7748	Milton Great	P	Agrmt.,Min.,Rep. 1838
7749	Milton Little	H	N.t.p.
7750	Minster Lovell	P	Agrmt.,Min.,Rep. 1838
7751	Mixbury	P	Awd.,Min.
7752	Mongewell	P	Rep. 1840
7753	Nettlebed	P	Rep. 1842
7754	Newington	P	Agrmt.,Min.,Rep. 1839
7755	Newington North	T	Awd.,Min.
7756	Newington South	P	N.t.p.,Min.
7757	Newnham Courtnay	P	Agrmt.,Min.,Rep. 1838
7758	Newnham Murren	P	Min.
7759	Newton Purcell	P	Rep. 1843
7760	Noke	P	Agrmt.,Awd.,Min.,Rep. 1841
7761	Northmoor	P	Min.,Rep. 1840
7762	Norton Brize	P	N.t.p.,Min.
7763	Nuffield	P	Agrmt.,Min.,Rep. 1837
7764	Oddington	P	Awd.,Min.
7765	Overy	H	Min.,Rep. 1839
7766	St Aldate	P	Awd.,Min.
7767	Oxford City,All Saints	P	Awd.,Min.
7768	Oxford St Clement	P	Awd.,Min.
7769	Oxford St Peter	P	Awd.,Min.
7770	Oxford St Thomas	P	Awd.,Min.
7771	Oxford University	EP	N.t.p.,Min.
7772	Piddington	P	Awd.,Min.
7773	Pishill	P	Min.,Rep. 1848
7774	Pyrton	P	Awd.,Min.
7775	Radcot	H	N.t.p.,Rep. 1840
7776	Ramsden	H	Agrmt.,Min.,Rep. 1838
7777	Rollright Great	P	N.t.p.,Min.
7778	Rollright Little	P	Awd.,Min.
7779	Rotherfield Greys	P	Awd.,Min.
7780	Rotherfield Peppard	P	Min.,Rep. 1839
7781	Rousham	P	N.t.p.,Min.
7782	Salford	P	N.t.p.,Min.
7783	Sandford	P	Awd.,Min.
7784	Sandford (Bullingdon)	P	N.t.p.,Min.
7785	Shelswell	P	Rep. 1843
7786	Sarsden	P	N.t.p.,Min.
7787	Shifford	H	Awd.,Min.
7788	Shipton under Wychwood	T	Agrmt.,Min.,Rep. 1839
7789	Shiplake	P	Awd.,Min.
7790	Shipton upon Charwell	P	N.t.p.,Min.
7791	Shirburn	P	Min.,Rep. 1840
7792	Shotover	EP	N.t.p.,Min.
7793	Showel	C	Awd.,Min.
7794	Shutford	H	N.t.p.,Min.
7795	Shutford East	C	N.t.p.,Min.
7796	Broad Sibford	T	N.t.p.,Min.
7797	Sibford Ferris	T	N.t.p.,Min.
7798	Somerton	P	N.t.p.,Min.
7799	Souldern	P	Agrmt.,Min.,Rep. 1839
7800	Spelsbury	P	N.t.p.,Min.
7801	Stadhampton	P	Awd.,Min.
7802	Standhill	H	Rep. 1839
7803	Standlake	P	Awd.,Min.
7804	Stanton Harcourt	P	N.t.p.,Min.
7805	Stanton St John	P	N.t.p.,Min.
7806	Steeple Aston	P	N.t.p.,Min.
7807	Steeple Barton	P	Awd.,Min.
7808	North Stoke cum Ipsden	P	Awd.,Min.
7809	Stokenchurch	P	Awd.,Min.,Rep. 1842
7810	South Stoke cum Woodcote	P	Awd.,Min.
7811	Stoke Lyne and Fewcott	L	N.t.p.,Min.
7812	Stoke Talmage	P	Min.,Rep. 1839
7813	Stonelands	EP	N.t.p.,Min.
7814	Stonesfield	P	N.t.p.,Min.
7815	Stowood	P	N.t.p.,Min.
7816	Stratton Audley	P	N.t.p.,Min.
7817	Swalecliffe	P	Awd.,Min.
7818	Swinbrooke	P	N.t.p.,Min.
7819	Swyncombe	P	Rep. 1839
7820	Sydenham	P	N.t.p.,Min.
7821	Tackley	P	Agrmt.,Rep. 1839
7822	Tadmarton,Upper and Lower	P	N.t.p.,Min.
7823	Taynton	P	N.t.p.,Min.
7824	Tetsworth	P	Agrmt.,Min.,Rep. 1839
7825	Tew Great	P	N.t.p.,Min.
7826	Tew Little	H	N.t.p.,Min.
7827	Thame	P	Awd.,Min.
7828	Tiddington	T	Min.,Rep. 1838
7829	Tusmore	P	Awd.,Min.
7830	Upton	H	Min.
7831	Warborough	P	N.t.p.,Min.
7832	Warpsgrove	P	Awd.,Min.
7833	Over Warton	P	Rep. 1839
7834	Waterperry	P	Awd.,Min.
7835	Waterstock	P	Awd.,Min.
7836	Watlington	P	Min.
7837	Wendlebury	P	N.t.p.,Min.
7838	Weston South	P	Awd.,Min.
7839	Westwell	P	N.t.p.,Min.
7840	Wheatfield	P	Agrmt.,Min.,Rep. 1838
7841	Wheatley	H	N.t.p.,Min.
7842	Wigginton	P	N.t.p.,Min.
7843	Whitchurch	P	N.t.p.,Min.
7844	Whitchurch Common	D	N.t.p.,Min.
7845	Wickham	T	Awd.,Min.
7846	Wilcote	P	Awd.,Min.
7847	Witney	P	Min.,Rep. 1840
7848	Woodeaton	P	Agrmt.,Rep. 1837
7849	Woolvercott	P	Awd.,Min.
7850	Wooton	P	Rep. 1841
7851	Worton Nether	P	N.t.p.,Min.
7852	Wroxton and Balscot	P	N.t.p.,Min.
7853	Wychwood Forest	D	Min.
7854	Yarnton	P	Min.
7855	Yelford	P	Awd.,Min.
9165	Weston on the Green	P	Awd.,Min.
9166	Horley with Hornton	P	Min.
9167	Heath	P	N.t.p.,Min.

Rutland

7856	Ashwell	P	Agrmt.,Rep. 1838
7857	Ayston	P	Awd.,Min.
7858	Barleythorpe	H	N.t.p.
7859	Barrowden	P	Agrmt.,Min.,Rep. 1842
7860	Beaumont Chase	EP	Awd.,Min.
7861	Belton	P	N.t.p.
7862	Bisbrooke	P	Awd.,Min.
7863	Braunston	P	N.t.p.
7864	Brooke	T	Awd.,Min.
7865	Burley	P	Min.
7866	Caldecott	P	Awd.,Min.
7867	Casterton Great	P	N.t.p.
7868	Casterton Little	P	N.t.p.
7869	Clipsham	P	Agrmt.,Rep. 1838
7870	Cottesmore with Barrow	P	N.t.p.
7871	Edithweston	P	Awd.,Min.
7872	Egleton	P	N.t.p.,Min.
7873	Empingham	P	N.t.p.
7874	Essendine	P	Awd.,Min.
7875	Exton	P	N.t.p.
7876	Flitteris Park	D	Awd.,Min.
7877	Glaston	P	Rep. 1840
7878	Greetham	P	Agrmt.,Rep. 1838
7879	Gunthorpe	T	Awd.,Min.
7880	Hambleton	P	Awd.,Min.
7881	Hambleton Little	H	N.t.p.
7882	Ketton	P	N.t.p.,Awd.,Min.
7883	Horn	P	Rep. 1838
7884	Langham	T	Awd.,Min.
7885	Leighfield Forest	EP	Awd.,Min.
7886	Luffenham North	P	Awd.,Min.
7887	Luffenham South	P	Awd.,Min.
7888	Lyddington	P	Awd.,Min.
7889	Lyndon	P	Rep. 1839
7890	Manton	P	N.t.p.,Min.
7891	Market Overton	P	N.t.p.
7892	Martinsthorpe	P	Agrmt.,Rep. 1844
7893	Morcott	P	Agrmt.,Rep. 1839
7894	Normanton	P	N.t.p.
7895	Oakham	P	N.t.p.

Rutland contd.

7896	Pickworth	P	N.t.p.
7897	Pilton	P	Agrmt.,Rep. 1838
7898	Preston	P	N.t.p.
7899	Ryhall with Belminsthorpe	P	N.t.p.
7900	Ridlington	P	Agrmt.,Rep. 1839
7901	Seaton	P	Awd.,Min.
7902	Stoke Dry	P	Agrmt.,Rep. 1841
7903	Stretton	P	Agrmt.,Rep. 1837
7904	Teigh	P	Awd.,Min.
7905	Thistleton	P	N.t.p.
7906	Thorpe by Water	D	Awd.,Min.
7907	Tickencote	P	Agrmt.,Rep. 1837
7908	Tinwell	P	Awd.,Min.
7909	Tixover	P	Awd.,Min.
7910	Uppingham	P	Awd.,Min.
7911	Wardley	P	Awd.,Min.
7912	Whissendine	P	N.t.p.
7913	Whitwell	P	Agrmt.,Rep. 1838
7914	Wing	P	N.t.p.

Shropshire

7526	Shelvoke and Wikey	T	Agrmt.,Min.,Rep. 1838
7915	Abcott	D	N.t.p.
7916	Abdon	P	Awd.,Min.
7917	Abertanat	T	Awd.,Min.,Rep. 1838
7918	Acton	D	N.t.p.
7919	Acton Burnell	P	Agrmt.,Awd.,Min.
7920	Acton Round	P	Agrmt.,Rep. 1838
7921	Acton Scott	P	Agrmt.,Min.,Rep. 1838
7922	Adderley	P	Agrmt.,Rep. 1837
7923	Adney	D	N.t.p.
7924	Adston	T	Awd.,Min.
7925	Alberbury Quarter	D	Min.,Rep. 1843
7926	Albrightlee	T	Awd.,Min.
7927	Albrighton	P	Awd.,Min.
7928	Albrighton	P	Awd.,Min.
7929	Alderton	T	Awd.,Min.
7930	Aldon	T	Agrmt.,Min.,Rep. 1844
7931	Alkmere	T	Awd.,Min.
7932	Alkmond St.	P	Awd.,Min.
7933	All Stretton	D	N.t.p.
7934	Alkmond Park	D	Awd.,Min.
7935	Alveley	P	Awd.,Min.
7936	Arscott	T	Agrmt.,Min.
7937	Arlestone	D	N.t.p.
7938	Ashford Bowdler	P	Awd.,Min.
7939	Ashford Carbonell	P	Awd.,Min.
7940	Astley	T	Agrmt.,Min.,Rep. 1837
7941	Asterton	D	N.t.p.
7942	Astley Abbotts	P	Agrmt.,Awd.,Min.,Rep. 1840
7943	Aston,Hisland and Wootton	T	Agrmt.,Min.,Rep. 1837
7944	Aston Manor	D	N.t.p.
7945	Aston	D	N.t.p.
7946	Aston Botterell	P	Min.,Rep. 1838
7947	Aston Eyre	T	Agrmt.,Rep. 1839
7948	Atcham	P	Awd.,Min.
7949	Atterley	T	Awd.,Min.
7950	Badger	P	Agrmt.,Min.,Rep. 1837
7951	Bardley and Harcourt	T	Agrmt.,Min.,Rep. 1840
7952	Barrow	P	Agrmt.,Rep. 1838
7953	Baschurch	P	Awd.,Min.
7954	Battlefield	P	N.t.p.,Min.
7955	Beckbury	P	Agrmt.,Min.,Rep. 1838
7956	Beckjay	D	N.t.p.
7957	Bedstone	P	Min.,Rep. 1843
7958	Bennetts End	T	Min.
7959	Benthall	P	Agrmt.,Awd.,Min.,Rep. 1839
7960	Berghill	T	Agrmt.,Rep. 1837
7961	Berrington	P	Agrmt.,Min.,Rep. 1843
7962	Betton	T	Min.,Rep. 1841
7963	Bettus	D	N.t.p.
7964	Bicton and Calcott	T	Agrmt.,Awd.,Min.,Rep. 1842
7965	Billingsley	P	Rep. 1839
7966	Bin Weston	D	Awd.,Min.
7967	Bishops Castle	T	Min.,Rep. 1842
7968	Bitterley	P	Agrmt.,Min.,Rep. 1838
7969	Blodwel	T	Min.,Rep. 1839
7970	Bolas Magna	P	Agrmt.,Rep. 1837
7971	Bonninghall	P	Agrmt.,Min.,Rep. 1837
7972	Boraston and Whatmore	T	Agrmt.,Min.,Rep. 1839
7973	Boscobel	EP	Awd.,Min.
7974	Bourton and Callaughton	T	Agrmt.,Awd.,Min.
7975	Brace Meole	P	Agrmt.,Min.,Rep. 1843
7976	Broadward	D	N.t.p.
7977	Brockton	P	Min.,Rep. 1840
7978	Lee Brockhurst	P	Awd.,Min.
7979	Bromfield	P	Agrmt.,Min.,Rep. 1842
7980	Bromlow	D	Awd.,Min.
7981	Broncroft	T	Agrmt.,Rep. 1841
7982	Broom and Rowton	D	N.t.p.
7983	Broome	T	Awd.,Min.
7984	Broseley	P	Agrmt.,Min.,Rep. 1838
7985	Broughton	P	Awd.,Min.
7986	Broughton	P	N.t.p.
7987	Bryn	T	Rep. 1839
7988	Bucknell	P	Agrmt.,Min.,Rep. 1840
7989	Buildwas	P	Awd.,Min.
7990	Bulthey	T	Agrmt.,Rep. 1839
7991	Burford	T	Agrmt.,Awd.,Min.,Rep. 1839
7992	Burlton	T	Agrmt.,Min.,Rep. 1837
7993	Burwarton	P	Agrmt.,Rep. 1838
7994	Cainham	P	Awd.,Min.
7995	Cakemore	T	Agrmt.,Min.,Rep. 1841
7996	Cardington	T	Agrmt.,Awd.,Min.,Rep. 1843
7997	Cardiston	P	Awd.,Min.
7998	Castle Ward within	T	Awd.,Min.
7999	Cause,Wallop and Forest	T	Agrmt.,Rep. 1839
8000	St Chad	P	Min.
8001	Charlton	T	Agrmt.,Rep. 1837
8002	Chatwall	T	Agrmt.,Min.,Rep. 1838
8003	Chelmarsh	P	Agrmt.,Min.
8004	Cheswardine	P	Agrmt.,Min.,Rep. 1841
8005	Chetton	P	Agrmt.,Min.,Rep. 1838
8006	Chetwynd	P	Agrmt.,Min.,Rep. 1838
8007	Chetwynd Aston	T	Awd.,Min.
8008	Childs Ercall	P	Agrmt.,Min.,Rep. 1839
8009	Chirbury	P	Min.,Rep. 1842
8010	Chorley and Northwood	T	Agrmt.,Min.,Rep. 1841
8011	Church Aston	T	Awd.,Min.
8012	Church Harwood	D	N.t.p.
8013	Church Preen	P	Awd.,Min.
8014	Church Pulverbatch	T	Agrmt.,Min.,Rep. 1839
8015	Church Stretton	P	Agrmt.,Min.,Rep. 1838
8016	Claverley	P	Min.,Rep. 1839
8017	Clee St. Margaret	P	Awd.,Min.
8018	Clee Stanton	T	Agrmt.,Min.,Rep. 1841
8021	Cleobury Mortimer	D	Agrmt.,Awd.,Min.,Rep. 1844
8022	Cleobury North	P	Awd.,Min.
8023	Clive and Sansaw	T	Awd.,Min.
8024	Clun	P	Awd.,Min.
8025	Clunbury	T	Awd.,Min.
8026	Clungunford	P	Agrmt.,Awd.,Min.
8027	Clunton	T	Min.,Rep. 1843
8028	Colbatch	T	Agrmt.,Min.,Rep. 1840
8029	Cold Weston	P	Awd.,Min.
8030	Coleham	T	Awd.,Min.
8031	Condover	P	Agrmt.,Min.,Rep. 1839
8032	Conley and Boteville	D	N.t.p.
8033	Coreley	P	Agrmt.,Min.,Rep. 1840
8034	Corfton	T	Awd.,Min.
8035	Coston	D	N.t.p.
8036	Coton	T	Awd.,Min.
8037	Cotton	T	Awd.,Min.
8038	Cound	P	Min.,Rep. 1841
8039	Cressage	T	Awd.,Min.
8040	Crickheath	T	Agrmt.,Min.,Rep. 1837
8041	Crieve	D	N.t.p.
8042	Crow Meole	T	Awd.,Min.
8043	Culmington	P	Awd.,Min.
8044	Dawley Great	P	Awd.,Min.
8045	Dawley Little	T	Agrmt.,Rep. 1839
8046	Deuxhill	P	Agrmt.,Rep. 1838
8047	Diddlebury	P	Awd.,Min.
8048	Dinmore	EP	N.t.p.
8049	Dinthill	T	Awd.,Min.
8050	Ditton Priors	P	N.t.p.,Min.
8051	Doddington	T	Agrmt.,Min.,Rep. 1839
8052	Donnington	P	Agrmt.,Rep. 1838
8053	Dowles	P	Agrmt.,Rep. 1840
8054	Down Rossall	D	N.t.p.
8055	Down Lower	D	N.t.p.
8056	Downton and Hopton	T	Awd.,Min.
8057	Drayton in Hales	P	Agrmt.,Min.,Rep. 1837
8058	Eaton Constantine	P	Min.,Rep. 1837
8059	Eardington	T	Agrmt.,Min.,Rep. 1842
8060	Eardiston	T	Awd.,Min.
8061	Earnestrey Park	T	Agrmt.,Min.,Rep. 1841
8062	Easthorpe	P	Awd.,Min.
8063	Eaton	P	Agrmt.,Min.,Rep. 1841
8064	Edeclift	D	N.t.p.
8065	Edenhope	T	Agrmt.,Min.,Rep. 1840
8066	Edgmond	P	Awd.,Min.
8068	Edgton	P	Agrmt.,Min.,Rep. 1839
8069	Ellesmere	P	Min.,Rep. 1839
8070	Ellerdine	T	Agrmt.,Min.,Rep. 1839
8071	Emstrey	T	Agrmt.,Rep. 1839
8072	Enchmarsh	D	N.t.p.
8073	Ercall	T	Agrmt.,Min.,Rep. 1839
8074	Eyton	T	Agrmt.,Min.,Rep. 1837
8075	Farley Wyke and Bradley	T	Awd.,Min.
8076	Felton Butler	T	Rep. 1843
8077	Felton West	P	Agrmt.
8078	Fennemere	T	Agrmt.,Min.,Rep. 1842
8079	Fitz	P	Min.,Rep. 1837
8080	Ford	T	Awd.,Min.
8081	Frankwell	T	Awd.,Min.
8082	Frodesley	P	Awd.,Min.
8083	Glazeley	P	Agrmt.,Rep. 1838
8084	Greete	P	Awd.,Min.
8085	Greete	T	Awd.,Min.

Shropshire contd.

8086	Gretton	T	Awd.,Min.
8087	Grinshill	P	Agrmt.,Rep. 1838
8088	Habberley	P	Agrmt.,Rep. 1838
8089	Halesowen	T	Awd.,Min.
8090	Halford	C	N.t.p.
8091	Halston	M	N.t.p.
8092	Hamlets East	T	Awd.,Min.
8093	Hamlets West	T	Awd.,Min.
8094	Hanwood	P	Awd.,Min.
8095	Harcourt	T	Agrmt.,Rep. 1839
8096	Harlescott	T	Awd.,Min.
8097	Harley	P	Agrmt.,Min.,Rep. 1837
8098	Harley Wigwig and Homer	T	Awd.,Min.
8099	Hasbury	T	Awd.,Min.
8100	Hatton High and Booley	T	Agrmt.,Rep. 1839
8101	Haughmond	EP	N.t.p.
8102	Haughton and Poynton	T	Agrmt.,Min.,Rep. 1839
8103	Hawn	P	Awd.,Min.
8104	Hayton Lower	T	Awd.,Min.
8105	Hayton Upper	T	Awd.,Min.
8106	Heath	C	Awd.,Min.
8107	Heath	D	Awd.,Min.
8108	Hencott	D	Awd.,Min.
8109	Highley	P	Agrmt.,Min.,Rep. 1839
8110	Hill the	T	Awd.,Min.
8111	Hinstock	P	Agrmt.,Min.,Rep. 1837
8112	Hobendrid	D	N.t.p.
8113	Hodnet	P	Min.,Rep. 1840
8114	Holy Cross and St Giles	P	Min.,Rep. 1840
8115	Holgate	P	Agrmt.,Min.,Rep. 1842
8116	Holt Preen	T	Awd.,Min.
8117	Home	T	Awd.,Min.
8118	Hope Baggott	P	Awd.,Min.
8119	Hope Bowdler	P	Awd.,Min.
8120	Hopesay	P	Agrmt.,Rep. 1840
8121	Hopton Castle	P	Agrmt.,Rep. 1839
8122	Hopton Congeford	P	Awd.,Min.
8123	Hopton Wafers	P	Agrmt.,Rep. 1839
8124	Horderley Hall	EP	N.t.p.
8125	Hordley	P	Awd.,Min.
8126	Hortons Wood	T	Min.,Rep. 1842
8127	Hughley	P	Agrmt.,Rep. 1838
8128	Hunnington	T	Awd.,Min.
8129	Ightfield	P	Awd.,Min.,Rep. 1845
8130	Illey	T	Awd.,Min.
8131	Ingardine and the Lowe	T	Agrmt.,Rep. 1840
8132	Isombridge	T	Min.,Rep. 1843
8133	St Julian	P	Min.
8134	Kemberton	P	Agrmt.,Min.,Rep. 1839
8135	Kempton	T	N.t.p.
8136	Kenley	P	Agrmt.,Awd.,Min.,Rep. 1837
8137	Ketley	D	N.t.p.
8138	Kevencalonog	T	Agrmt.,Min.,Rep. 1839
8139	Kingswood	T	Awd.,Min.
8140	Kinlet	P	Agrmt.,Rep. 1840
8141	Kinnersley	P	Agrmt.,Rep. 1839
8142	Kinnerley	P	Awd.,Min.
8143	Kinnerton and Ritton	T	Awd.,Min.
8144	Kinton	T	Awd.,Min.
8145	Knockin	P	Min.,Rep. 1838
8146	Knuck	D	N.t.p.
8147	Kynaston	T	Awd.,Min.
8148	Langley and Ruckley	PC	Awd.,Min.
8149	Lappall	T	Awd.,Min.
8150	Lawrence St	P	Awd.,Min.
8151	Lawton	T	Awd.,Min.
8152	Lea and Oakley	T	Awd.,Min.
8153	Leaton	T	Min.,Rep. 1841
8154	Wrockwardine	P	Agrmt.,Min.,Rep. 1838
8155	Lee Botwood	P	Agrmt.,Rep. 1839
8156	Leigh and Hope	D	N.t.p.
8157	Leighton	P	Awd.,Min.
8158	Leonard St Bridgenorth	P	Agrmt.,Min.,Rep. 1839
8159	Lilleshall	P	Awd.,Min.
8160	Llwyntidmon and Treprenal	T	Min.,Rep. 1837
8161	Linley	P	Awd.,Min.
8162	Llanforda	T	Min.,Rep. 1839
8163	Llanvair Waterdine	P	Agrmt.,Awd.,Min.,Rep. 1839
8164	Llanyblodwell	P	N.t.p.
8165	Llanymynech	P	N.t.p.
8166	Llynelys	T	Awd.,Min.
8167	Longden	T	Agrmt.,Min.,Rep. 1839
8168	Longden upon Tern	P	Agrmt.,Rep. 1839
8169	Longford	T	Agrmt.,Rep. 1838
8170	Longner	T	N.t.p.
8171	Longnor	P	N.t.p.
8172	Loppington	P	Agrmt.,Min.,Rep. 1838
8173	Loughton	C	Rep. 1838
8174	Ludford	P	N.t.p.
8175	Lydbury North	P	Awd.,Min.
8176	Lydham	T	Awd.,Min.
8177	Lydley Hays	D	N.t.p.
8178	Maesbrook Issa	T	Awd.,Min.
8179	Mainstone	P	Agrmt.,Awd.,Min.,Rep. 1840
8180	Malinslee	T	Awd.,Min.
8181	Martin St	P	Min.,Rep. 1837
8182	Middleton Scriven	P	Agrmt.,Min.,Rep. 1839
8183	Middle	P	Agrmt.,Min.,Rep. 1837
8184	Middlehope	T	Agrmt.,Rep. 1842
8185	Middleton	T	Min.,Rep. 1838
8186	Madeley	P	Awd.,Min.
8187	Milson	P	Awd.,Min.
8188	Mindtown	P	Awd.,Min.
8189	Moreton Say	P	Min.,Rep. 1837
8190	Monk Hopton	P	Awd.,Min.
8191	Montford	P	Rep. 1843
8192	More the	P	Agrmt.,Min.,Rep. 1839
8193	St Mary	P	Min.
8194	St Mary Magdalen	P	Agrmt.,Min.,Rep. 1840
8195	Medlicott	D	N.t.p.
8196	Meerhouse	D	N.t.p.
8197	Melverley	P	Agrmt.,Min.,Rep. 1840
8198	Minsterley	T	Agrmt.,Rep. 1837
8199	Moreton Corbet	P	Agrmt.,Rep. 1838
8200	Morton	T	Min.,Rep. 1838
8201	Morville	T	Agrmt.,Awd.,Min.,Rep. 1839
8202	Mucklewick	T	N.t.p.
8203	Munslow	P	Awd.,Min.
8204	Muxton	D	N.t.p.
8205	Nash and Tilsop	T	Awd.,Min.
8206	Neen Savage	P	Agrmt.,Rep. 1838
8207	Neen Sollars	P	Agrmt.,Rep. 1839
8208	Neenton	P	Awd.,Min.
8209	Ness Great and Hopton	P	Awd.,Min.
8210	Ness Little	C	Awd.,Min.
8211	Netley	T	Rep. 1842
8212	Newcastle	D	N.t.p.
8213	Newport	P	Rep. 1839
8214	Newton	T	Awd.,Min.
8215	Newton and Wettleton	D	N.t.p.
8216	Noneley	T	Agrmt.,Min.,Rep. 1837
8217	Norbury	T	Awd.,Min.
8218	Nordley Regis	D	N.t.p.
8219	Norton in Hales	P	N.t.p.
8220	Obley	T	Agrmt.,Min.,Rep. 1842
8221	Oldbury and Langley	T	Min.,Rep. 1839
8222	Oldbury	P	Agrmt.,Min.,Rep. 1838
8223	Onibury	P	Agrmt.,Rep. 1839
8224	Onslow	T	N.t.p.
8225	Oreton	H	Awd.,Min.
8226	Osbaston	T	Agrmt.,Awd.,Min.,Rep. 1843
8227	Oswestry	T	Min.,Rep. 1838
8228	Overton	D	N.t.p.
8229	Park Lower	D	N.t.p.
8230	Patten	T	Awd.,Min.
8231	Peaton	P	Agrmt.,Rep. 1841
8232	Petton	P	Agrmt.,Rep. 1842
8233	Pickthorn	H	Awd.,Min.
8234	Pitchford	P	Awd.,Min.
8235	Plaish	T	Agrmt.,Rep. 1838
8236	Pontesbury	P	Min.
8237	Posenhall	EP	N.t.p.
8238	Poston Great	D	Rep. 1842
8239	Prees	P	Agrmt.,Rep. 1839
8240	Presthope	T	Awd.,Min.
8241	Preston	T	Min.,Rep. 1840
8242	Preston Gubbals	P	Agrmt.,Rep. 1837
8243	Preston Montford	T	Awd.,Min.
8244	Preston upon the Wild Moor	P	N.t.p.
8245	Pulley	T	Awd.,Min.
8246	Purslow	D	N.t.p.
8247	Quatford	T	Awd.,Min.
8248	Quatt	P	Awd.,Min.
8249	Quinton	D	N.t.p.
8250	Rattlinghope	T	Awd.,Min.
8251	Reilth	T	Agrmt.,Awd.,Min.,Rep. 1840
8252	Rhugantin	T	Agrmt.,Rep. 1839
8253	Ridgeacre	T	Agrmt.,Awd.,Min.,Rep. 1842
8254	Rock and Henley	T	Awd.,Min.
8255	Roden	T	Awd.,Min.
8256	Rodington	P	Awd.,Min.
8257	Romsley	T	Agrmt.,Rep. 1840
8258	Rossall	T	Awd.,Min.
8259	Rowton and Amaston	T	Agrmt.,Min.,Rep. 1843
8260	Rudge	T	Agrmt.,Rep. 1839
8261	Rushbury	P	Agrmt.,Min.,Rep. 1839
8262	Ruyton	T	Agrmt.,Rep. 1839
8263	Ryton	P	Agrmt.,Rep. 1839
8264	Scefton	D	N.t.p.
8265	Shawbury	P	Agrmt.,Rep. 1838
8266	Selley	D	N.t.p.
8267	Sheinton	P	Agrmt.,Rep. 1840
8268	Shelderton	D	N.t.p.
8269	Shelton	T	Awd.,Min.
8270	Shelton and Oxon	T	Awd.,Min.,Rep. 1842
8271	Shelve	P	Agrmt.,Rep. 1839
8272	Sheriff Hales	P	Awd.,Min.
8273	Shiffnal	P	Agrmt.,Rep. 1839
8274	Shipton	P	Awd.,Min.
8275	Shottaton	T	Agrmt.,Rep. 1838
8276	Sibdon	P	Awd.,Min.
8277	Sidbury	P	Awd.,Min.

Shropshire contd.

8278	Silvington	P	Awd.,Min.
8279	Skirmage	EP	N.t.p.
8280	Smethcott	P	Awd.,Min.
8281	Shrawardine	P	Agrmt.,Awd.,Min.,Rep. 1843
8282	Stanton and Brockton	P	Awd.,Min.
8283	Stanton and Moston	T	Rep. 1839
8284	Stanton Long and Holdgate	P	Min.
8285	Stanton Lacy	T	Awd.,Min.
8286	Stapleton	T	Agrmt.,Min.,Rep. 1838
8287	Stirchley	P	Rep. 1839
8288	Stitt and Gatten	T	Awd.,Min.
8289	Stockton	P	Agrmt.,Rep. 1838
8290	Stockton	P	Awd.,Min.
8291	Stoke	T	Awd.,Min.
8292	Stoke St Milborough	C	Min.
8293	Stoke upon Tearn	P	Agrmt.,Rep. 1837
8294	Stokesay,Newton,Wettleton	T	Agrmt.,Min.,Rep. 1839
8295	Stoneward	D	Awd.,Min.
8296	Stoneward	D	N.t.p.
8297	Stottesdon	P	Awd.,Min.
8298	Stowe	P	Agrmt.,Awd.,Min.,Rep. 1839
8299	Stretton Little	D	N.t.p.
8300	Sutton	D	N.t.p.
8301	Sutton Great	P	Awd.,Min.
8302	Sutton Little	T	Awd.,Min.
8303	Sutton Maddock	P	Agrmt.,Min.,Rep. 1839
8304	Sydney Moor	D	N.t.p.
8305	Sylattyn	P	Min.,Rep. 1838
8306	Sweeney,Weston,Cotton	T	Agrmt.,Min.
8307	Tasley	T	Agrmt.,Rep. 1838
8308	Tearn Cold Hatton	T	Rep. 1839
8309	Tibberton and Cherrington	T	Agrmt.,Rep. 1839
8310	Ticklerton	D	N.t.p.
8311	Tir Y Coed	T	Awd.,Min.
8312	Tong	P	Agrmt.,Min.,Rep. 1838
8313	Trebrodier	T	Agrmt.,Min.,Rep. 1839
8314	Trefnant	T	Agrmt.,Min.,Rep. 1842
8315	Trefonnen	T	Awd.,Min.
8316	Tugford	P	Agrmt.,Min.,Rep. 1839
8317	Uffington	P	Awd.,Min.
8318	Uppington	P	Agrmt.,Min.,Rep. 1839
8319	Upton Cressett	P	Agrmt.,Rep. 1841
8320	Upton Magna	P	Awd.,Min.
8321	Waters Upton	P	Agrmt.,Min.,Rep. 1837
8322	Walton Prescott	T	Awd.,Min.
8323	Warley Salop	T	Min.,Rep. 1840
8324	Welchampton	P	Agrmt.,Min.,Rep. 1842
8325	Welsh Ward	D	Awd.,Min.
8326	Wellington	P	Awd.,Min.
8327	Wem	P	Agrmt.,Min.,Rep. 1839
8328	Wenlock Much	P	Awd.,Min.
8329	Wenlock Little	P	Agrmt.
8330	Westbury	T	Agrmt.,Min.,Rep. 1839
8331	Westbury	P	Min.
8332	Westhope	T	Awd.,Min.
8333	Westley	T	Agrmt.,Min.,Rep. 1840
8334	Weston	D	N.t.p.
8335	Weston	T	Awd.,Min.
8336	Weston under Red Castle	D	N.t.p.
8337	Wheathill	P	Agrmt.,Min.,Rep. 1838
8338	Whitchurch	P	Agrmt.,Rep. 1837
8339	Whittington	P	Agrmt.,Min.,Rep. 1837
8340	Whitton	T	Agrmt.,Min.,Rep. 1840
8341	Whitcott and Hardwick	D	N.t.p.
8342	Whitley and Welbatch	T	Agrmt.,Rep. 1841
8343	Whitton	T	Awd.,Min.
8344	Whixall	T	Min.,Rep. 1842
8345	Wilcott and Nescliff	T	Awd.,Min.
8346	Wilderley and Cothercott	T	Agrmt.,Min.,Rep. 1838
8347	Willey	P	Agrmt.,Min.,Rep. 1838
8348	Withington	P	Awd.,Min.
8349	Wilstone	D	N.t.p.
8350	Winnington	T	Agrmt.,Min.,Rep. 1842
8351	Wistanstow	P	Awd.,Min.
8352	Wollascot Great and Little	T	Awd.,Min.
8353	Wollaston	T	Agrmt.,Awd.,Min.
8354	Wolstaston	P	Agrmt.,Min.,Rep. 1840
8355	Wombridge	P	Awd.,Min.
8356	Woodbatch	T	Rep. 1839
8357	Woodcot and Horton	T	Min.,Rep. 1841
8358	Woodcote	C	Awd.,Min.
8359	Wooton	T	Awd.,Min.
8360	Worfield	P	Agrmt.,Min.,Rep. 1837
8361	Worthen	D	Awd.,Min.
8362	Wrickton	T	Awd.,Min.
8363	Wrockwardine Wood	P	Awd.,Min.
8364	Wroxeter	P	Agrmt.,Min.,Rep. 1839
8365	Wykey	D	N.t.p.
8366	The Yelds	D	Awd.,Min.
8367	Yockleton	T	Agrmt.,Rep. 1839
8368	Yoreton	T	Agrmt.,Rep. 1838
8369	Yorton	TH	N.t.p.
9484	Stony Stretton	T	Awd.,Min.

Somerset

8370	Somerset Union Rep.s	D	Min.
8371	Abbas and Temple Combe	P	Rep. 1839
8372	Abbotts Leigh	P	Rep. 1838
8373	Alford	P	Rep. 1839
8374	Aller	P	Rep. 1838
8375	Almsford	P	Rep. 1838
8376	Alston Sutton	C	Rep. 1838
8377	Angersleigh	P	Rep. 1840
8378	Ansford	P	N.t.p.
8379	Ashbrittle	P	Rep. 1839
8380	Ashill	P	Rep. 1837
8381	Ashington	P	Rep. 1838
8382	Ashcott	P	Agrmt.,Rep. 1839
8383	Asholt	P	Awd.,Min.
8384	Ash Priors	P	Agrmt.,Rep. 1837
8385	Ashton Long	P	Awd.,Min.
8386	Ashwick	P	Agrmt.,Rep. 1840
8387	Axbridge	P	Rep. 1839
8388	Babcary	P	Rep. 1839
8389	Babington	P	Rep. 1838
8390	Backwell	P	Awd.,Min.
8391	Badgeworth	P	Rep. 1839
8392	Bagborough West	P	Min.
8393	Baltonsborough	P	Awd.,Min.
8394	Banwell	P	Agrmt.,Rep. 1837
8395	Barrington	P	Min.,Rep. 1839
8396	Barrow	P	Rep. 1838
8397	Bathford	P	Agrmt.,Rep. 1839
8398	Barrow North	P	Rep. 1838
8399	Barrow South	P	Awd.,Min.
8400	Barton St Davids	P	Rep. 1840
8401	Barwick	P	Rep. 1838
8402	Batcombe	P	Awd.,Min.
8403	Bathampton	P	Agrmt.,Rep. 1844
8404	Bathealton	P	Rep. 1840
8405	Batheaston	P	Rep. 1841
8406	Bath St James	P	N.t.p.
8407	Bath St Michael	P	N.t.p.
8408	Bath St Peter,St Paul	P	N.t.p.
8409	Bathwick	P	Rep. 1838
8410	Bawdrip	P	Min.
8411	Beckington	P	Agrmt.,Min.
8412	Bedminster	P	Agrmt.,Rep. 1840
8413	Beercrocombe	P	Min.,Rep. 1837
8414	Beere and Idstock	EP	Awd.,Min.
8415	Berkley	P	Rep. 1839
8416	Berrow	P	Rep. 1838
8417	Bickenhall	P	Rep. 1837
8418	Bicknoller	P	Rep. 1838
8419	Biddisham	P	Rep. 1838
8420	Binegar	P	Agrmt.,Rep. 1840
8421	Bishops Hull	P	Awd.,Min.
8422	Bishops Lydeard	P	Rep. 1837
8423	Blackford(Wedmore)	D	Min.,Rep. 1838
8424	Blackford	P	Rep. 1838
8425	Blagdon	P	Min.
8426	Bleadon	P	Awd.,Min.
8427	Brislington	P	Awd.,Min.
8428	Bradford	P	Awd.,Min.
8429	Bradley West	P	Rep. 1842
8430	Bradon South	P	Awd.,Min.
8432	Bratton St Maur	P	Rep. 1839
8433	Brean	P	Rep. 1838
8434	Brent East	P	Rep. 1840
8435	Brent South	P	Rep. 1841
8436	Brewham North	P	Agrmt.,Rep. 1840
8437	Bridgwater	P	Awd.,Min.
8438	Broadway New Enclosures	D	Min.
8439	Broadway Old Enclosures	D	Min.
8440	Brockley	P	Awd.
8441	Brompton Ralph	P	Agrmt.,Rep. 1840
8442	Broomfield	P	Rep. 1838
8443	Bruham South	P	Min.
8444	Brushford	P	Agrmt.,Rep. 1839
8445	Brimpton	P	Rep. 1838
8446	Bruton	P	Rep. 1841
8447	Buckland Dinham	P	Rep. 1840
8448	Buckland St Mary	P	Rep. 1839
8449	Buckerell	D	N.t.p.
8450	Buckland West	P	Awd.,Min.
8451	Burnett	P	Rep. 1838
8452	Burnham	P	Rep. 1838
8453	Burrington	P	Rep. 1838
8454	Butcombe	P	Agrmt.,Rep. 1838
8455	Butleigh	P	Awd.,Min.
8456	Cadbury North	P	Rep. 1837
8457	Cadbury South	P	Agrmt.,Rep. 1842
8458	Catcott	H	Awd.,Min.
8459	Castle Cary	P	Rep. 1839
8460	Camely	P	Rep. 1838
8461	Camel West	P	Agrmt.,Rep. 1839
8462	Camerton	P	Rep. 1844
8463	Cannington	P	Min.,Rep. 1839
8464	Capland Old Enclosures	D	Awd.,Min.
8465	Carhampton	P	Agrmt.,Rep. 1839

Somerset contd.

8466	Catherine St	H	Rep. 1841
8467	Chaffcombe	P	Min.,Rep. 1839
8468	Chard	P	Rep. 1842
8469	Charlcombe	P	Rep. 1839
8470	Charlinch	P	Min.,Rep. 1837
8471	Charlton Adam	P	Awd.,Min.
8472	Charlton Horethorne	P	Awd.,Min.
8473	Charlton Mackrell	P	N.t.p.
8474	Charlton Musgrave	P	Rep. 1838
8475	Chapel Allerton	P	Min.
8476	Charterhouse	EP	N.t.p.
8477	Cheddon Fitzpain	P	Agrmt.,Min.,Rep. 1837
8478	Chedzoy	P	Agrmt.,Rep. 1840
8479	Chelvey	P	Agrmt.,Rep. 1837
8480	Chelwood	P	Agrmt.,Min.,Rep. 1837
8481	Cheriton North	P	Rep. 1838
8482	Chew Magna	P	Awd.,Min.
8483	Chewton Mendip	P	Min.
8484	Chew Stoke	P	Min.
8485	Chilcompton	P	Awd.,Min.
8486	Chillington	P	Min.,Rep. 1839
8487	Chilton Cantilo	P	Awd.,Min.
8488	Chilton super Polden	H	Rep. 1839
8489	Chilton Trinity	P	Agrmt.,Min.,Rep. 1839
8490	Chinnock East	P	Awd.,Min.
8491	Chipstable	P	Awd.,Min.
8492	Churchill	P	Awd.,Min.
8493	Cheddar	P	Agrmt.,Min.,Rep. 1837
8494	Chinnock Middle	P	Rep. 1839
8495	Chinnock West	P	Rep. 1839
8496	Chiselborough	P	Min.,Rep. 1839
8497	Chilthorne Dorner	P	Awd.,Min.
8498	Christon	P	Agrmt.,Min.,Rep. 1839
8499	Clapton	P	Agrmt.,Rep. 1837
8500	Clatworthy	P	Rep. 1837
8501	Claverton	P	Rep. 1839
8502	Cleeve Old	P	Rep. 1838
8503	Clevedon	P	Min.,Rep. 1838
8504	Cloford	P	Rep. 1838
8505	Closworth	P	Agrmt.,Rep. 1836
8506	Clutton	P	Rep. 1837
8507	Coker East	P	Rep. 1840
8508	Coker West	P	Rep. 1838
8509	Combeflorey	P	Rep. 1838
8510	Combe Hay	P	Rep. 1839
8511	Compton Bishop	P	Rep. 1838
8512	Compton Dando	P	Awd.,Min.
8513	Compton Martin	P	Awd.,Min.
8514	Compton Pauncefoot	P	Rep. 1838
8515	Congresbury	P	Agrmt.,Rep. 1839
8516	Combe St Nicholas	P	Rep. 1839
8517	Compton Dundon	P	Awd.,Min.
8518	Corfe	P	Rep. 1838
8519	Corston	P	Awd.,Min.
8520	Corton Denham	P	Agrmt.,Rep. 1836
8521	Cossington	P	Min.,Rep. 1839
8522	Cothelstone	P	Rep. 1838
8523	Cranmore East	P	Min.,Rep. 1838
8524	Cranmore West	P	Rep. 1840
8525	Creech St Michael	P	Awd.,Min.
8526	Crewkerne	P	Awd.,Min.
8527	Cricket Malherbie	P	Awd.,Min.
8528	Cricket St. Thomas	P	Rep. 1838
8529	Croscombe	P	Rep. 1838
8530	Crowcombe	P	Awd.,Min.
8532	Cucklington,Stoke,Bayford	P	Rep. 1838
8533	Cudworth	P	Rep. 1841
8534	Culbone	P	Rep. 1838
8535	Curland	P	Rep. 1841
8536	Curry Mallett	P	Awd.,Min.
8537	Curry North	P	Awd.,Min.
8538	Curry Rivell	P	Awd.,Min.
8539	Cutcombe	P	Rep. 1840
8540	Cuthbert St.	EP	Min.,Rep. 1838
8541	Decumans St	P	Awd.,Min.
8542	Ditcheat	P	Rep. 1838
8543	Dinder	P	Rep. 1838
8544	Dinnington	P	Min.,Rep. 1839
8545	Dodington	P	Agrmt.,Rep. 1838
8546	Donyatt	P	Rep. 1838
8547	Doulting	P	Min.,Rep. 1838
8548	Dowlish Wake	P	Rep. 1838
8549	Downhead	P	Rep. 1838
8550	Drayton	P	Rep. 1839
8551	Dulverton	P	Agrmt.,Rep. 1839
8552	Dundry	P	Awd.,Min.
8553	Dunkerton	P	Awd.,Min.
8554	Dunster	P	Awd.,Min.
8555	Durleigh	P	Agrmt.,Rep. 1839
8556	Durston	P	Min.,Rep. 1838
8557	Earnshill	P	Rep. 1838
8558	Easthams	D	Agrmt.,Rep. 1840
8559	Eastrip	EP	N.t.p.,Min.
8560	Edington	P	Rep. 1838
8561	Elm	P	Rep. 1839
8562	Elworthy	P	Agrmt.,Rep. 1839
8563	Emberrow	P	Min.,Rep. 1839
8564	English Combe	P	Awd.,Min.
8565	Enmore	P	Min.,Rep. 1837
8566	Evercreech	P	Rep. 1838
8567	Exford	P	Agrmt.,Rep. 1839
8568	Exton	P	Rep. 1838
8569	Farmborough	P	Awd.,Min.
8570	Fiddington	P	Rep. 1837
8571	Fitzhead	P	Awd.,Min.
8572	Farrington Gurney	P	Rep. 1841
8573	Felton	P	Min.
8574	Fivehead	P	Min.,Rep. 1838
8575	Flax Bourton	P	Min.
8576	Foxcote	P	Rep. 1838
8577	Frampton Cotterill	D	N.t.p.
8578	Frome Selwood	P	Min.,Rep. 1840
8579	Easton in Gordano	P	Rep. 1839
8580	Glastonbury	P	Rep. 1840
8581	Goathill	P	Min.,Rep. 1839
8582	Goathurst	P	Agrmt.,Rep. 1845
8583	Grenton	P	Awd.,Min.,Rep. 1839
8584	Haburgin	D	Min.
8585	Halse	P	Agrmt.,Rep. 1839
8586	Ham High	P	Rep. 1838
8587	Hardington	P	Min.
8588	Hardington Mandeville	P	Awd.,Min.
8589	Harptree East	P	Min.,Rep. 1838
8590	Harptree West	P	Agrmt.,Min.,Rep. 1840
8591	Haselbury Plucknett	P	Awd.,Min.,Rep. 1837
8592	Hatch Beauchamp	P	Agrmt.,Min.,Rep. 1839
8593	Hatch West	P	Awd.,Min.
8594	Hawkridge	P	Rep. 1840
8595	Heathfield	P	Min.,Rep. 1838
8596	Hemington	P	Awd.,Min.
8597	Henstridge	P	Min.,Rep. 1838
8598	Hillfarrance	P	Min.
8599	Hinton Blewett	P	Min.,Rep. 1838
8600	Hinton Charterhouse	P	Awd.,Min.
8601	Hinton St. George	P	Min.,Rep. 1839
8602	Holcombe	P	Min.,Rep. 1839
8603	Holford	P	Agrmt.,Min.,Rep. 1840
8604	Holton	P	Min.,Rep. 1839
8605	Holwell	P	Agrmt.,Min.,Rep. 1839
8606	Hornblotton	P	Min.,Rep. 1838
8607	Horsington	P	Agrmt.,Min.,Rep. 1839
8608	Huish Champflower	P	Min.
8609	Huish Episcopi	P	Awd.,Min.,Rep. 1845
8610	Hungerford Farley	P	Min.,Rep. 1839
8611	Huntspill	P	Rep. 1838
8612	Hutton	P	Agrmt.,Min.,Rep. 1837
8613	Ilchester	P	Agrmt.,Min.,Rep. 1838
8614	Ilminster	P	Agrmt.,Min.,Rep. 1837
8615	Ilton	P	Rep. 1837
8616	Isle Abbotts	P	Min.
8617	Isle Brewers	P	Agrmt.,Min.,Rep. 1841
8618	Keinton Mandefield	P	Awd.,Min.
8619	Kelston	P	Rep. 1838
8620	Kenn	P	Awd.,Min.
8621	Kewstoke	P	Rep. 1838
8622	Keynsham	P	Agrmt.,Min.,Rep. 1840
8623	Kilmersdon	P	Min.,Rep. 1838
8624	Kilmington	P	Min.,Rep. 1839
8625	Kilton	P	Awd.,Min.
8626	Brompton Regis	P	Agrmt.,Min.,Rep. 1840
8627	Klive cum Stringston	P	Awd.,Min.
8628	Kingsbury Episcopi	P	Awd.,Min.
8629	Kingsdon	P	Min.,Rep. 1839
8630	Kingston	P	Min.
8631	Kingstone	P	Min.
8632	Kingston Seymour	P	Awd.,Min.
8633	Kingweston	P	Agrmt.,Rep. 1839
8634	Kittisford	P	Min.,Rep. 1842
8635	Knowle St Giles	P	Min.,Rep. 1838
8636	Lackington White	P	Min.
8637	Lamyat	P	Awd.,Min.
8638	Langford Budville	P	Min.,Rep. 1840
8639	Langport Eastover	P	Min.,Rep. 1838
8640	Langridge	P	Min.
8641	Laverton	P	Min.
8642	Leigh	C	Awd.,Min.
8643	Lilstock	P	Min.,Rep. 1838
8644	Limington	P	Min.,Rep. 1839
8645	Littleton High	P	Min.,Rep. 1839
8646	Litton	P	Min.,Rep. 1838
8647	Locking	P	Min.,Rep. 1838
8648	Lopen	P	Min.,Rep. 1839
8649	Lovington	P	Min.,Rep. 1839
8650	Loxton	P	Rep. 1840
8651	Luckham	P	Agrmt.,Min.,Rep. 1840
8652	Lufton	P	Min.,Rep. 1838
8653	Lullington	P	Awd.,Min.
8654	Luxborough	P	Awd.,Min.
8655	Lydiard St Lawrence	P	Agrmt.,Min.,Rep. 1839
8656	Lydford East	P	Min.,Rep. 1838
8657	Lydford West	P	N.t.p.,Min.
8658	Lympsham	P	Min.,Rep. 1838

Somerset contd.

No.	Place		Details
8659	Lyncombe and Widcombe	P	Agrmt.,Min.,Rep. 1839
8660	Lyng	P	Min.,Rep. 1838
8661	Mark	P	Agrmt.,Min.
8662	Maperton	P	Min.,Rep. 1839
8663	Marksbury	P	Awd.,Min.
8664	Marston Bigot	P	Min.,Rep. 1839
8665	Marston Magna	P	Min.,Rep. 1839
8666	Martock	P	Min.,Rep. 1841
8667	Meare	P	Awd.,Min.
8668	Mells	P	Min.
8669	Merriott	P	Awd.,Min.
8670	Michael Church	P	Rep. 1839
8671	Middlezoy	P	Awd.,Min.
8672	Midsomer Norton	P	Min.,Rep. 1839
8673	Milborne Port	P	Min.,Rep. 1839
8674	Milton Clevedon	P	Rep. 1842
8675	Milverton	P	Awd.,Min.
8676	Minehead	P	Min.
8677	Misterton	P	Rep. 1840
8678	Monksilver	P	Min.,Rep. 1841
8679	Monkton Combe	P	Awd.,Min.
8680	Monkton West	P	Rep. 1840
8681	Montacute	P	Min.,Rep. 1838
8682	Moorlinch	P	Agrmt.,Awd.,Min.,Rep. 1837
8683	Muchelney	P	Min.,Rep. 1841
8684	Mudford	P	Min.,Rep. 1839
8685	Nailsea	P	Agrmt.,Min.,Rep. 1840
8686	Nempnett	P	Awd.,Min.
8687	Nettlecombe	P	Rep. 1837
8688	Newton St Loe	P	Min.,Rep. 1839
8689	Niden	EP	N.t.p.
8690	Northover	P	Min.,Rep. 1838
8691	Norton Fitzwarren	P	Awd.,Min.,Rep. 1839
8692	Norton Hawkfield	D	Awd.,Min.
8693	Norton Malreward	P	Min.,Rep. 1838
8694	Norton St Philip	P	Min.,Rep. 1838
8695	Norton sub Hambdon	P	Rep. 1837
8696	Nunney	P	Min.,Rep. 1840
8697	Nylands with Badcombe	P	N.t.p.
8698	Nynehead	P	Agrmt.,Min.,Rep. 1837
8699	Oake	P	Min.,Rep. 1839
8700	Oare	P	Rep. 1840
8701	Odcombe	P	Min.,Rep. 1839
8702	Orchardleigh	P	Awd.,Min.
8703	Orchard Portman	P	Rep. 1837
8704	Othery	P	Awd.,Min.
8705	Otterford	P	Awd.,Min.
8706	Otterhampton	P	Min.,Rep. 1838
8707	Overstowey	P	Min.,Rep. 1838
8708	Paulton	P	Min.,Rep. 1839
8709	Pawlet	P	Min.,Rep. 1838
8710	Pen	D	N.t.p.
8711	Pendomer	P	Min.,Rep. 1840
8712	Pennard East	P	Awd.,Min.
8713	Pennard West	P	Min.,Rep. 1840
8714	Penselwood	P	Rep. 1838
8715	Perrott North	P	Min.,Rep. 1838
8717	Petherton South	P	Min.,Rep. 1839
8718	Petherton North	P	Awd.,Min.,Rep. 1838
8719	Pitcombe	P	Awd.
8720	Pitminster	P	Rep. 1838
8721	Pitney	P	Min.
8722	Pilton	P	Rep. 1838
8723	Pitney Lortie	P	N.t.p.,Min.
8724	Pointington	P	Min.
8725	Porlock	P	Awd.,Min.
8726	Portbury	P	Awd.,Min.
8727	Portishead	P	Awd.,Min.
8728	Preston Plucknett	P	Awd.,Min.
8729	Priddy	P	Min.,Rep. 1839
8730	Priston	P	Min.
8731	Publow	P	Min.
8732	Puckington	P	Min.
8733	Puddimore	P	Min.,Rep. 1838
8734	Puriton	P	Awd.,Min.
8735	Puxton	P	Min.,Rep. 1839
8736	Pylle	P	Agrmt.,Min.
8737	Quantoxhead East	P	Rep. 1839
8738	Quantoxhead West	P	Min.,Rep. 1840
8739	Queen Camel	P	Min.
8740	Queen Charlton	P	Awd.,Min.
8741	Radstock	P	Min.,Rep. 1838
8742	Raddington	P	Min.
8743	Regilbury	D	Awd.,Min.
8744	Rimpton	P	Min.,Rep. 1840
8745	Road and Wolverton	P	Agrmt.,Min.,Rep. 1839
8746	Rodden	P	Awd.,Min.
8747	Rodney Stoke	P	Min.,Rep. 1839
8748	Rowberrow	P	Awd.,Min.
8749	Rowington	P	Agrmt.,Rep. 1837
8750	Ruishton	P	Awd.,Min.
8751	Saltford	P	Agrmt.,Min.,Rep. 1837
8752	Sampford Arundel	P	Min.,Rep. 1839
8753	Sampford Brett	P	Min.,Rep. 1840
8754	Sandford Orcas	P	Min.,Rep. 1838
8755	Seaborough	P	Rep. 1839
8756	Selworthy	P	Agrmt.,Min.,Rep. 1840
8757	Sevington St Mary	P	Min.,Rep. 1840
8758	Sevington St Michael	P	Min.,Rep. 1839
8759	Shapwick	P	Awd.,Min.
8760	Shepton Beauchamp	P	Min.,Rep. 1839
8761	Shepton Mallett	P	Awd.,Min.
8762	Shepton Montague	P	Min.,Rep. 1839
8763	Shipham	P	Min.
8764	Skilgate	P	Agrmt.,Min.
8765	Sock Dennis	D	Rep. 1839
8766	Somerton	P	Min.,Rep. 1841
8767	Sparkford	P	Min.,Rep. 1838
8768	Spaxton	P	Min.,Rep. 1838
8769	Standerwick	P	Rep. 1839
8770	Stanton Drew	P	Awd.,Min.
8771	Stanton Prior	P	Min.,Rep. 1839
8772	Staple Fitzpaine	P	Min.
8773	Staplegrove	P	Agrmt.,Min.,Rep. 1837
8774	Stawell	H	Min.,Rep. 1839
8775	Stawley	P	Awd.,Min.
8776	Stockland Gaunts	P	Min.,Rep. 1837
8777	Stocklinch Magdalen	P	Awd.,Min.
8778	Stocklinch Ottersey	P	Min.,Rep. 1838
8779	Stogumber	P	Awd.,Min.
8780	Stogursey	P	Agrmt.,Min.,Rep. 1840
8781	Stowell	P	Rep. 1838
8782	North Stoke	P	Min.,Rep. 1838
8783	Stoke Pero	P	Agrmt.,Min.,Rep. 1839
8784	Stoke St Gregory	P	Min.,Rep. 1838
8785	Stoke St Mary	P	Agrmt.,Rep. 1837
8786	Stoke St Michael	P	Min.,Rep. 1839
8787	South Stoke	P	Min.,Rep. 1841
8788	Stoke under Hamden	P	Awd.,Min.
8789	Stone Easton	P	Min.,Rep. 1839
8790	Stowey	P	Min.
8791	Nether Stowey	P	Agrmt.,Min.,Rep. 1839
8792	Street	P	Awd.,Min.
8793	Stratton on the Foss	P	Min.,Rep. 1840
8794	Stringston	P	Min.
8795	Sutton Bingham	P	Rep. 1840
8796	Sutton Long	P	Agrmt.,Min.,Rep. 1842
8797	Sutton Mallet	H	Agrmt.,Min.,Rep. 1837
8798	Sutton Montis	P	Min.,Rep. 1838
8799	Swainswick	P	Min.,Rep. 1838
8800	Swell	P	Rep. 1838
8801	Taunton St George	D	N.t.p.
8802	Taunton St James	P	Min.,Rep. 1839
8803	Taunton St Mary	P	Min.,Rep. 1839
8804	Tellisford	P	Min.,Rep. 1838
8805	Thorn Coffin	P	Awd.,Min.
8806	Thorn Falcon	P	Min.,Rep. 1837
8807	Thorne St Margaret	P	Agrmt.,Min.,Rep. 1840
8808	Thurlbeer	P	Min.
8809	Thurloxton	P	Min.,Rep. 1837
8810	Tickenham	P	Awd.,Min.
8811	Timberscombe	P	Awd.,Min.
8812	Timsbury	P	Min.,Rep. 1838
8813	Tintinhull	P	Rep. 1838
8814	Tolland	P	Min.,Rep. 1838
8815	Treborough	P	Awd.,Min.
8816	Trent	P	Min.,Rep. 1839
8817	Trull	P	Awd.,Min.
8818	Twiverton	P	Agrmt.,Min.,Rep. 1840
8819	Ubley	P	Min.,Rep. 1838
8820	Uphill	P	Awd.,Min.
8821	Upton	P	Min.,Rep. 1838
8822	Upton Noble	P	Awd.,Min.
8823	Vagg Farm	D	N.t.p.
8824	Walcot	P	Awd.,Min.
8825	Walton	P	Awd.,Min.,Rep. 1842
8826	Walton in Gordano	P	Agrmt.,Min.,Rep. 1837
8827	Wanstrow	P	Min.,Rep. 1838
8828	Wayford	P	Awd.,Min.
8829	Weare	P	Min.,Rep. 1839
8830	Wedmore and Northload	P	Rep. 1838
8831	Week St Lawrence	P	Min.,Rep. 1838
8832	Wellington	P	Awd.,Min.
8833	Wellow	P	Rep. 1840
8834	Wells St Andrew	EP	N.t.p.
8835	Wembdon	P	Awd.,Min.
8836	Werberg St	P	N.t.p.
8837	Westbury	P	Min.,Rep. 1838
8838	Weston Zoyland	P	Min.,Rep. 1840
8839	West Moor	EP	N.t.p.
8840	Weston	P	Min.
8841	Weston Bampfylde	P	Rep. 1838
8842	Weston in Gordano	P	Agrmt.,Min.,Rep. 1837
8843	Weston super Mare	P	Agrmt.,Min.,Rep. 1837
8844	Whatley	P	Min.,Rep. 1838
8845	Wheathill	P	Rep. 1838
8846	White Stanton	P	Min.,Rep. 1838
8847	Widcombe	I	Min.,Rep. 1839
8848	Wilton	P	Min.
8849	Wincanton	P	Min.,Rep. 1839
8850	Winford	P	Min.,Rep. 1838
8851	Winnall	D	N.t.p.

Somerset contd.

8852	Winscombe	P	Min.,Rep. 1838
8853	Winsford	P	Agrmt.,Min.,Rep. 1838
8854	Winsham	P	Min.,Rep. 1839
8855	Witham Friary	P	N.t.p.
8856	Withiel Florey	P	Min.,Rep. 1839
8857	Withycombe	P	Min.,Rep. 1839
8858	Wiveliscombe	P	Awd.,Min.
8859	Wookey	P	Agrmt.,Min.
8860	Woolavington	P	Awd.,Min.
8861	Woolley	P	Rep. 1838
8862	Wootton Courtnay	P	Agrmt.,Rep. 1842
8863	Wootton North	P	Agrmt.,Min.,Rep. 1840
8864	Worle	P	Agrmt.,Min.,Rep. 1838
8865	Wraxall	P	Agrmt.,Min.,Rep. 1837
8866	Wrington	P	Min.,Rep. 1838
8867	Writhlington	P	Min.,Rep. 1840
8868	Withypoole	P	Min.,Rep. 1838
8869	Yarlington	P	Min.,Rep. 1838
8870	Yatton	P	Min.,Rep. 1841
8871	Yeovil	P	Awd.,Min.
8872	Yeovilton	P	Min.,Rep. 1838
9652	Freshford	P	Min.,Rep. 1837

Staffordshire

8531	Croxton	T	Agrmt.,Min.,Rep. 1841
9229	Acton Trussell	T	Awd.,Min.
9230	Adbaston	T	Min.,Rep. 1840
9231	Admaston	D	N.t.p.
9232	Abbotts Bromley	P	Agrmt.,Min.,Rep. 1844
9233	Aldridge	P	Agrmt.,Min.,Rep. 1839
9234	Alrewas Hays	EP	N.t.p.
9235	Alrewas	P	Agrmt.,Min.,Rep. 1840
9236	Alstonefield	P	N.t.p.,Min.
9237	Alton	P	Awd.,Min.
9238	Amblecoat	H	Agrmt.,Min.,Rep. 1838
9239	Amerton and Stowe	T	Min.
9240	Anslow	T	Awd.,Min.
9241	Armitage	P	Min.,Rep. 1840
9242	Ashley	P	Agrmt.,Min.,Rep. 1837
9243	Arley	P	Agrmt.,Min.,Rep. 1839
9244	Aspley	P	Agrmt.,Min.,Rep. 1838
9245	Aston,Burston,Stoke	T	Min.,Rep. 1843
9246	Audley	P	Agrmt.,Min.,Rep. 1837
9247	Bagnall	T	Min.
9248	Balterley	T	Agrmt.,Min.,Rep. 1838
9249	Barlaston	P	Awd.,Min.
9250	Barton under Needwood	T	Agrmt.,Min.,Rep. 1837
9251	Basford	T	Awd.,Min.
9252	Beech	T	Awd.,Min.
9253	Bemersley	T	N.t.p.
9254	Bentley	T	Awd.,Min.
9255	Berkswick	T	Awd.,Min.
9256	Betley	P	Agrmt.,Awd.,Min.,Rep. 1843
9257	Biddulph	P	Agrmt.,Min.,Rep. 1839
9258	Bilbrooke	P	Agrmt.,Min.,Rep. 1840
9259	Bilston	T	Awd.,Min.
9260	Bishops Offley	P	Agrmt.,Min.,Rep. 1840
9261	Blackwood and Crowborough	T	Awd.,Min.
9262	Blithfield	P	Awd.,Min.
9263	Blore with Swainscoe	T	Awd.,Min.
9264	Bloxwich	D	N.t.p.
9265	Broughton	T	Awd.,Min.
9266	Blurton	T	Awd.,Min.
9267	Blymhill	P	Agrmt.,Min.,Rep. 1839
9268	Bobbington	P	Agrmt.,Min.,Rep. 1839
9269	Bonehill	L	N.t.p.
9270	Botteslow	T	Awd.,Min.
9271	Bradley	P	Awd.,Min.
9272	Bradley in the Moors	P	Awd.,Min.
9273	Bradnop	T	Awd.,Min.
9274	Bromwich West	P	Agrmt.,Min.,Rep. 1839
9275	Bramshall	P	Awd.,Min.
9276	Branston	T	Awd.,Min.
9277	Brewood	P	Min.,Rep. 1838
9278	Bridgeford Great	H	Min.
9279	Bridgeford Little	H	Min.
9280	Brocton	T	Awd.,Min.
9281	Bromley	T	Agrmt.,Rep. 1838
9282	Bromley Bagots	T	Awd.,Min.
9283	Bromley Hurst	T	N.t.p.
9284	Broom	P	Agrmt.,Rep. 1838
9285	Bucknall	T	Awd.,Min.
9286	Burntwood	T	Awd.,Min.,Rep. 1839
9287	Burslem	P	Awd.,Min.
9288	Burton upon Trent	T	Awd.,Min.
9289	Burton Extra	T	Awd.,Min.
9290	Bushbury	T	Awd.,Min.,Rep. 1846
9291	Butterton	T	Awd.,Min.
9292	Butterton	T	Awd.,Min.
9293	Calton	T	N.t.p.
9294	Calton	T	Awd.,Min.
9295	Calton	T	Awd.,Min.
9296	Calton	T	Awd.,Min.
9297	Calwich	T	Awd.,Min.
9298	Cannock	P	Min.,Rep. 1840
9299	Canwell	EP	N.t.p.,Min.
9300	Castle Church	P	Awd.,Min.
9301	Cauldon	P	Awd.,Min.
9302	Caverswall	P	Awd.,Min.,Rep. 1840
9303	St Chad	P	Awd.,Min.
9304	St Chad	P	N.t.p.,Min.
9305	Charnes	T	Agrmt.,Awd.,Min.,Rep. 1843
9306	Chapel Chorlton	T	Rep. 1838
9307	Chartley Holme	EP	N.t.p.,Min.
9308	Chatcull	T	Agrmt.,Awd.,Min.,Rep. 1843
9309	Cheadle	P	Awd.,Min.
9310	Chebsey	P	Min.,Rep. 1843
9311	Checkley	P	Awd.,Min.
9312	Cheddleton cum Rownall	T	Awd.,Min.
9313	Cheslyn Hay	EP	Awd.,Min.
9314	Church Eaton	P	Agrmt.,Min.,Rep. 1838
9315	Church Stoke	D	N.t.p.
9316	Clayton and Seabridge	T	Awd.,Min.
9317	Clayton Griffith	T	Awd.,Min.
9318	Clent	P	Agrmt.,Min.,Rep. 1838
9319	Clifton and Haunton	T	Agrmt.,Rep. 1838
9320	Codsall	P	Awd.,Min.
9321	Cold Meece	T	Awd.,Min.
9322	Colton	P	Awd.,Min.
9323	Colton	P	Agrmt.,Awd.,Min.
9324	Colwich	P	Awd.,Min.,Rep. 1840
9325	Cotes	T	Awd.,Min.
9326	Coppenhall	T	Awd.,Min.
9327	Coton	T	Awd.,Min.
9328	Coven	D	N.t.p.
9329	Cresswell	EP	Awd.,Min.
9330	Croxden	P	N.t.p.,Min.
9331	Cunsall	T	Awd.,Min.
9332	Darlaston	T	Awd.,Min.
9333	Darlaston	P	Min.,Rep. 1840
9334	Denstone	T	N.t.p.
9335	Dilhorn	P	Agrmt.,Min.,Rep. 1838
9336	Draycott in the Moors	P	Agrmt.,Min.,Rep. 1837
9337	Draycott	T	Min.,Rep. 1838
9338	Drayton Bassett	P	Agrmt.,Rep. 1837
9339	Drayton in Hales	P	Agrmt.,Rep. 1838
9340	Drointon	T	Min.
9341	Dunstall	T	Agrmt.,Min.,Rep. 1837
9342	Dunston	C	Min.,Rep. 1840
9343	Eaves	T	Min.
9344	Eccleshall	T	Agrmt.,Rep. 1838
9345	Edengale	P	N.t.p.,Min.
9346	Elford	P	Agrmt.,Min.,Rep. 1839
9347	Elkstone Lower	C	N.t.p.,Min.
9348	Elkstone Upper	T	Awd.,Min.
9349	Ellaston	T	Awd.,Min.
9350	Ellenhall	P	Awd.,Min.
9351	Endon	C	Awd.,Min.
9352	Enville	P	Agrmt.,Awd.,Min.,Rep. 1838
9353	Essington	T	Agrmt.,Min.,Rep. 1839
9354	Fairfield Head	T	N.t.p.,Min.
9355	Farewell	P	Agrmt.,Min.,Rep. 1839
9356	Fazeley	T	Awd.,Min.
9357	Fauld	T	Awd.,Min.,Rep. 1838
9358	Featherstone	T	Agrmt.,Min.,Rep. 1840
9359	Fenton Calvert	T	Min.
9360	Fenton Vivian	T	Min.
9361	Field	D	N.t.p.
9362	Fisherwick	T	Rep. 1842
9363	Flashbrook	T	Min.,Rep. 1840
9364	Forton	P	Agrmt.,Min.,Rep. 1838
9365	Fradswell	C	Min.,Rep. 1840
9366	Freeford	T	Awd.,Min.
9367	Fulfin	EP	Min.,Rep. 1838
9368	Fulford	L	Awd.,Min.
9369	Gayton	P	Awd.,Min.
9370	Gnosall	P	Min.,Rep. 1837
9371	Gratwich	P	Agrmt.,Min.,Rep. 1837
9372	Greenhill	T	Min.
9373	Grindley	T	Min.
9374	Grindon	P	Agrmt.,Min.,Rep. 1839
9375	Hamstall Ridware	P	Agrmt.,Min.,Rep. 1838
9376	Hammerwick	T	Awd.,Min.
9377	Hanbury	P	Min.,Rep. 1838
9378	Hanchurch	T	Awd.,Min.
9379	Handsworth	P	Agrmt.,Min.,Rep. 1838
9380	Hanford	T	Awd.,Min.
9381	Harbourne	P	Agrmt.,Min.,Rep. 1838
9382	Harlaston	T	Awd.,Min.
9383	Hatherton	T	Min.,Rep. 1840
9384	Hanley and Shelton	T	Awd.,Min.
9385	Haslour	EP	Awd.,Min.,Rep. 1841
9386	Haughton	P	Agrmt.,Min.
9387	Haunton	T	Min.
9388	Haywood Great	T	Min.
9389	Haywood Little	T	Min.
9390	Heathy Lee	T	N.t.p.,Min.
9391	Heaton	T	Awd.,Min.
9392	Herberton	T	Awd.,Min.
9393	Highlands Park	D	Agrmt.,Rep. 1837

Staffordshire contd.

9394	Hilderstone	T	Agrmt.,Min.,Rep. 1841
9395	Hilton	T	Min.,Rep. 1842
9396	Himley	P	Agrmt.,Min.,Rep. 1839
9397	Hints	P	Awd.,Min.
9398	Hixon	T	Min.
9399	Hollinsclough	T	N.t.p.,Min.
9400	Hopton	T	Agrmt.,Rep. 1838
9401	Hopwas Hayes	EP	N.t.p.,Min.
9402	Horninglow	T	Awd.,Min.
9403	Horseley	T	Agrmt.,Min.,Rep. 1838
9404	Horton and Horton Hay	T	Awd.,Min.
9405	Ilam	P	Agrmt.,Min.,Rep. 1838
9406	Ingestre	P	Agrmt.,Rep. 1838
9407	Ipstones	D	N.t.p.
9408	Keel	P	Awd.,Min.
9409	Kibblestone	M	Min.
9410	Kings Bromley	P	Awd.,Min.,Rep. 1842
9411	Kingsley	P	Agrmt.,Min.,Rep. 1839
9412	Kingstone	P	Agrmt.,Min.,Rep. 1838
9413	Kingswinford	P	Agrmt.,Min.,Rep. 1839
9414	Kingswood	T	Agrmt.,Min.,Rep. 1840
9415	Kinvaston	T	Awd.,Min.
9416	Kinver	P	Awd.,Min.
9417	Lapley	P	Agrmt.,Awd.,Min.,Rep. 1838
9418	Leek and Lowe	T	Awd.,Min.
9419	Leek	P	Min.
9420	Leek Frith	T	Awd.,Min.
9421	Leigh	P	Agrmt.,Min.,Rep. 1840
9422	St Michael,Lichfield	T	Awd.,Min.
9423	St Mary,Lichfield	P	Awd.,Min.
9424	Longdon	P	Min.,Rep. 1841
9425	Longnor	C	Awd.,Min.
9426	Longsdon	T	Awd.,Min.
9427	Longton and Lane End	T	Awd.,Min.
9428	Madeley	P	Agrmt.,Min.,Rep. 1839
9429	Maer	P	Agrmt.,Min.,Rep. 1838
9430	Marchington	T	Agrmt.,Min.,Rep. 1842
9431	Marchington Woodlands	T	Agrmt.,Min.,Rep. 1842
9432	Marston	T	Agrmt.,Min.,Rep. 1838
9433	Mavesyn Ridware	P	Agrmt.,Rep. 1838
9434	Meaford and Oulton	T	Min.,Rep. 1842
9435	Mayfield	T	Awd.,Min.
9436	Mill Meece	T	Agrmt.,Min.,Rep. 1839
9437	Milwich	P	Agrmt.,Min.,Rep. 1838
9438	Moddershall	T	Awd.,Min.
9439	Morridge	T	N.t.p.
9440	Moseley and Coven	T	Awd.,Min.
9441	Mucclestone	P	Agrmt.,Min.,Rep. 1837
9442	Musden Grange	EP	Awd.,Min.
9443	Needwood Forest	D	N.t.p.
9444	Newborough	T	Min.,Rep. 1838
9445	Newcastle under Lyme	P	Min.,Rep. 1841
9446	Newton	L	N.t.p.
9447	Norbury	P	Agrmt.,Min.,Rep. 1838
9448	Normicott	T	Awd.,Min.
9449	Norton	T	N.t.p.
9450	Norton Caynes	P	Agrmt.,Min.,Rep. 1837
9451	Norton on the Moors	P	Min.,Rep. 1842
9452	Oaken	T	Agrmt.,Min.,Rep. 1838
9453	Oakley	T	Agrmt.,Min.,Rep. 1839
9454	Oakover	P	N.t.p.,Min.
9455	Offley High	P	Agrmt.,Min.,Rep. 1838
9456	Ogley Hay	EP	N.t.p.
9457	Onecote	T	Awd.,Min.
9458	Orton	D	Min.,Rep. 1840
9459	Packington	T	Agrmt.,Awd.,Min.,Rep. 1842
9460	Patshull	P	Awd.,Min.
9461	Pattingham	P	Rep. 1840
9462	Pelsall	T	Awd.,Min.
9463	Penkhull and Boothen	T	Awd.,Min.
9464	Penkridge	P	Min.,Rep. 1840
9465	Penn	P	Min.,Rep. 1842
9466	Pershall	T	Agrmt.,Rep. 1839
9467	Pipe Hill	T	Min.
9468	Pipe Ridware	P	Agrmt.,Min.,Rep. 1840
9469	Podmore	T	Agrmt.,Rep. 1838
9470	Prestwood	T	Awd.,Min.
9471	Quarnford	C	N.t.p.,Min.
9472	Ramshorn	T	Awd.,Min.
9473	Ranton	T	Awd.,Min.
9474	Rocester	P	Awd.,Min.
9475	Rolleston	T	Agrmt.,Min.,Rep. 1837
9476	Ronton Abbey	EP	Awd.,Min.
9477	Rowley Regis	P	N.t.p.,Min.
9478	Rownall	T	N.t.p.
9479	Rudyard	T	Awd.,Min.
9480	Rugeley	P	Agrmt.,Min.,Rep. 1840
9481	Rushall	P	Agrmt.,Min.
9482	Rushton James	T	Awd.,Min.
9483	Rushton Spencer	T	Awd.,Min.
9485	Salt and Enson	T	Agrmt.,Min.,Rep. 1838
9486	Sandon	P	Agrmt.,Min.,Rep. 1838
9487	Seabridge	T	Min.
9488	Sedgley	P	Awd.,Min.
9489	Seighford	P	Agrmt.,Min.,Rep. 1842
9490	Seisdon	D	N.t.p.
9491	Shareshill	P	Min.,Rep. 1840
9492	Sheen	P	Awd.,Min.
9493	Shelton	T	Min.
9494	Slindon	T	Agrmt.,Min.,Rep. 1839
9495	Stafford St Mary	P	N.t.p.
9496	Stallington	L	Awd.,Min.
9497	Standon	P	Agrmt.,Min.,Rep. 1837
9498	Shenstone	P	Agrmt.,Min.,Rep. 1838
9499	Stanley	T	Awd.,Min.
9500	Stanton	T	Awd.,Min.
9501	Statfold	P	Awd.,Min.
9502	Stone	T	Awd.,Min.
9503	Streethay	T	Awd.,Min.
9504	Stoke upon Trent	P	Min.
9505	Stowe	P	Awd.,Min.
9506	Stretton	T	Awd.,Min.
9507	Stretton	T	Awd.,Min.
9508	Sugnall Magna	T	Agrmt.,Awd.,Min.,Rep. 1842
9509	Sugnall Parva	T	Min.,Rep. 1842
9510	Swinfen	T	Awd.,Min.
9511	Swynnerton	P	Awd.,Min.
9512	Swindon	T	N.t.p.,Min.
9513	Tamhorn	R	Min.
9514	Teddesley Hay	EP	Min.
9515	Tatenhill	T	Agrmt.,Min.,Rep. 1837
9516	Tettenhall	P	Awd.,Min.
9517	Thorpe Constantine	P	Agrmt.,Rep. 1839
9518	Three Farms	T	Min.,Rep. 1840
9519	Tillington	T	Min.,Rep. 1840
9520	Tipton	P	Awd.,Min.
9521	Tittensor	T	Awd.,Min.
9522	Tittisworth	T	Awd.,Min.
9523	Tixall	P	Awd.,Min.
9524	Trentham	T	Awd.,Min.
9525	Trysull and Seisdon	P	Awd.,Min.
9526	Tunstall	T	Agrmt.,Min.,Rep. 1840
9527	Tutbury	P	Min.
9528	Uttoxeter	P	Min.,Rep. 1839
9529	Wall	T	Min.
9530	Walsall	P	Min.,Rep. 1843
9531	Walton	T	Agrmt.,Min.,Rep. 1838
9532	Walton	P	Min.,Rep. 1843
9533	Warslow	C	N.t.p.,Min.
9534	Water Eaton	T	Awd.,Min.
9535	Waterfall	T	Awd.,Min.
9536	Wednesbury	P	Awd.,Min.
9537	Wednesfield	T	Awd.,Min.
9538	Weeford	P	Awd.,Min.
9539	Weston under Lizard	P	Min.,Rep. 1838
9540	Weston upon Trent	P	Min.,Rep. 1842
9541	Wetton	P	Awd.,Min.
9542	Whiston	T	N.t.p.
9543	Whitgrave	T	Awd.,Min.
9544	Whitmore	P	Agrmt.,Rep. 1839
9545	Whittington	P	Agrmt.,Min.,Rep. 1837
9546	Wichnor	C	Awd.,Min.
9547	Wightwick	T	Agrmt.,Min.,Rep. 1840
9548	Willenhall	T	Awd.,Min.
9549	Wolstanton	P	Agrmt.,Min.,Rep. 1838
9550	Wolverhampton	T	Awd.,Min.
9551	Wombourn	D	Awd.,Min.,Rep. 1840
9552	Woodford Grange	EP	N.t.p.
9553	Woodhouses	T	Awd.,Min.
9554	Wootton	T	Agrmt.,Min.,Rep. 1838
9555	Wootton	T	Awd.,Min.
9556	Wigginton	T	Awd.,Min.
9557	Worston	L	Agrmt.,Awd.,Min.,Rep. 1838
9558	Wyrley Great	T	N.t.p.
9559	Yarlet	L	Awd.,Min.
9560	Yoxall	P	Agrmt.,Min.,Rep. 1839

Suffolk

6217	Rushford	P	N.t.p.
9561	Bacton	P	Rep. 1839
9562	Badingham	P	Rep. 1838
9563	Badley	P	N.t.p.
9564	Badwell Ash	P	Agrmt.,Rep. 1839
9565	Baylham	P	Min.,Rep. 1840
9566	Bardwell	P	Agrmt.,Min.,Rep. 1838
9567	Barham	P	Awd.,Min.
9568	Barningham & Coney Weston	P	Awd.,Min.
9569	Barking cum Needham	PH	Rep. 1841
9570	Barnby	P	Rep. 1839
9571	Barnardiston	P	Awd.,Min.
9572	Barnham	P	Rep. 1837
9573	Barrow	P	Agrmt.,Rep. 1839
9574	Barsham	P	Rep. 1839
9575	Barton Great	P	Min.
9576	Barton Mills	P	N.t.p.,Min.
9577	Battisford	P	Rep. 1841
9578	Bawdsey	P	Rep. 1842
9579	Bealings Great	P	Min.,Rep. 1839
9580	Bealings Little	P	Awd.,Min.
9581	Beccles	P	Rep. 1840

Suffolk contd.

9582	Bedfield	P	Rep. 1840
9583	Bedingfield	P	Rep. 1839
9584	Belstead	P	Rep. 1840
9585	Belton	P	Min.
9586	Benacre	P	Rep. 1839
9587	Benhall	P	Awd.,Min.
9588	Bentley	P	Awd.,Min.
9589	Bergholt East	P	Agrmt.,Rep. 1837
9590	Beyton	P	Agrmt.,Rep. 1837
9591	Bildeston	P	Agrmt.,Rep. 1838
9592	Blakenham Magna	P	Rep. 1838
9593	Blakenham Little	P	Rep. 1839
9594	Blaxhall	P	Agrmt.
9595	Blundeston and Flixton	P	Agrmt.,Rep. 1837
9596	Blyford	P	Rep. 1842
9597	Blythburgh	P	Agrmt.,Rep. 1840
9598	Boulge	P	Rep. 1838
9599	Boxford	P	Rep. 1841
9600	Boxted	P	Rep. 1839
9601	Boyton	P	Rep. 1843
9602	Bradfield Combust	P	Rep. 1838
9603	Bradfield St Clare	P	Rep. 1840
9604	Bradfield St George	P	Rep. 1839
9605	Bradley Great	P	Awd.,Min.
9606	Bradley Little	P	Min.,Rep. 1839
9607	Bradwell	P	Rep. 1839
9608	Braiseworth	P	Rep. 1839
9609	Acton	P	Agrmt.,Rep. 1839
9610	Akenham	P	Agrmt.,Rep. 1837
9611	Aldborough	P	Awd.,Min.
9612	Alderton	P	Min.,Rep. 1840
9613	Aldham	P	Awd.,Min.
9614	Aldringham with Thorpe	P	Rep. 1840
9615	Alpheton	P	Agrmt.,Rep. 1838
9616	Ampton	P	Agrmt.,Rep. 1839
9617	Ash Bocking	P	Rep. 1837
9618	Ashby	P	Rep. 1838
9619	Ashfield Great	P	Awd.,Min.
9620	Ashfield with Thorpe	P	Agrmt.,Min.
9621	Aspall	P	Awd.,Min.
9622	Assington	P	Agrmt.,Min.,Rep. 1837
9623	Athelington	P	Rep. 1837
9624	Brandeston	P	Awd.,Min.
9625	Brantham	P	Rep. 1837
9626	Brandon	P	Agrmt.,Min.,Rep. 1838
9627	Bramfield	P	Awd.,Min.
9628	Bramford	P	Awd.,Min.
9629	Brampton	P	Awd.,Min.,Rep. 1838
9630	Bredfield	P	Agrmt.,Min.,Rep. 1837
9631	Brent Eleigh	P	Rep. 1838
9632	Brettenham	P	Awd.,Min.
9633	Bricett Great	P	Awd.,Min.
9634	Brightwell	P	Awd.,Min.
9635	Brockley	P	Awd.,Min.
9636	Brome	P	Rep. 1839
9637	Bromeswell	P	Rep. 1843
9638	Bruisyard	P	Rep. 1840
9639	Brundish	P	Rep. 1840
9640	Bucklesham	P	Awd.,Min.,Rep. 1839
9641	Bulchamp	P	Awd.,Min.
9642	Bungay St Mary	P	Awd.,Min.
9643	Bungay Holy Trinity	P	Awd.,Min.
9644	Bures St Mary	P	Agrmt.,Min.,Rep. 1838
9645	Burgate	P	Rep. 1838
9646	Burgh	P	Rep. 1838
9647	Burgh Castle	P	Min.,Rep. 1838
9648	Burstall	P	Awd.,Min.
9649	Bury St Edmunds	P	Awd.,Min.
9650	Butley	P	Awd.,Min.
9651	Buxhall	P	Agrmt.
9652	Campsey Ash	P	Rep. 1838
9653	Capel St Andrew	P	Awd.,Min.
9654	Carlton	P	Rep. 1842
9655	Carlton	P	Rep. 1842
9656	Capel St Mary	P	Rep. 1840
9657	Carlton Colville	D	Agrmt.,Rep. 1837
9658	Carlton Colville	D	Awd.,Min.
9659	Cavendish	P	Awd.,Min.
9660	Cavenham	P	N.t.p.
9661	Charsfield	P	Rep. 1839
9662	Chattisham	P	Rep. 1839
9663	Chedburg	P	Agrmt.,Rep. 1837
9664	Chediston	P	Rep. 1839
9665	Clements St (Ipswich)	P	N.t.p.
9666	Chellesworth	P	Agrmt.,Min.,Rep. 1838
9667	Chelmondiston	P	Rep. 1838
9668	Chevington	P	Agrmt.,Rep. 1837
9669	Chillesford	P	Agrmt.,Min.,Rep. 1839
9670	Chilton	P	Rep. 1839
9671	Chimney Mills	EP	Min.
9672	Clare	P	Min.
9673	Claydon	P	Agrmt.
9674	Clopton	P	Awd.,Min.
9675	Cockfield	P	Awd.,Min.
9676	Coddenham	P	Min.,Rep. 1837
9677	Cookley	P	Min.
9678	Combs	P	Awd.,Min.
9679	Cornard Great	P	Agrmt.,Rep. 1839
9680	Cornard Little	P	Rep. 1842
9681	Corton	P	Rep. 1839
9682	Cotton	P	Rep. 1839
9683	Cove Hithe or North Hales	P	Rep. 1840
9684	Cove North	P	Rep. 1839
9685	Cove South	P	Rep. 1838
9686	Cowlinge	P	Awd.,Min.
9687	Cransford	P	Rep. 1839
9688	Cratfield	P	Rep. 1840
9689	Creeting St Mary	UP	Rep. 1838
9690	Creeting St Peter	P	Rep. 1838
9691	Cretingham	P	Awd.,Min.
9692	Copdock	P	Rep. 1838
9693	Crowfield	PC	Awd.,Min.
9694	Culford	P	Agrmt.,Rep. 1837
9695	Culpho	P	Min.
9696	Dalham	P	N.t.p.
9697	Dallinghoo	P	Min.
9698	Darsham	P	Rep. 1842
9699	Debach	P	Rep. 1839
9700	Debenham	P	Agrmt.
9701	Denardiston	P	Awd.,Min.
9702	Dennington	P	Rep. 1838
9703	Denham near Newmarket	P	Awd.,Min.
9704	Denham	P	Rep. 1840
9705	Depden	P	Rep. 1837
9706	Drinkstone	P	Agrmt.,Rep. 1838
9707	Downham Santon	P	N.t.p.,Min.
9708	Dunwich	BP	Rep. 1838
9709	Earl Soham	P	Rep. 1840
9710	Earl Stonham	P	Min.,Rep. 1838
9711	Easton	P	Rep. 1838
9712	Easton Bavents	P	Rep. 1839
9713	Edwardston	P	Agrmt.,Min.,Rep. 1837
9715	Ellough	P	Awd.,Min.
9716	Elmham South	P	Rep. 1839
9717	Elmham South St Cross	P	Min.,Rep. 1839
9718	Elmham South St James	P	Rep. 1839
9719	Elmham South St Margaret	P	Rep. 1840
9720	Elmham South St Michael	P	Rep. 1845
9721	Elmham South St Peter	P	Min.,Rep. 1839
9722	Elmsett	P	Min.,Rep. 1841
9723	Elmswell	P	Rep. 1840
9724	Elvedon	P	Rep. 1840
9725	Eriswell	P	Rep. 1839
9726	Erwarten	P	Rep. 1838
9727	Euston	P	Rep. 1837
9728	Exning	P	N.t.p.
9729	Eye	P	Rep. 1840
9730	Fakenham Great	P	Agrmt.,Awd.
9731	Falkenham	P	Rep. 1838
9732	Farnham	P	Rep. 1838
9733	Felixstow	P	Min.
9734	Felsham St Peter	P	Agrmt.,Rep. 1837
9735	Flempton	P	Agrmt.,Rep. 1838
9736	Flixton	P	Rep. 1843
9737	Flowton	P	Agrmt.,Min.
9738	Finborough Great	P	Awd.,Min.
9739	Finborough Little	P	Rep. 1838
9740	Finningham	P	Rep. 1839
9741	Fordley	P	Rep. 1838
9742	Fornham St Martin	P	N.t.p.
9743	Fornham St Genieveve	P	N.t.p.
9744	Fornham All Saints	P	Rep. 1837
9745	Foxhall	P	Awd.,Min.
9746	Framlingham	P	Rep. 1842
9747	Framsden	P	Rep. 1839
9748	Freckenham	P	N.t.p.
9749	Fressingfield	P	Min.,Rep. 1841
9750	Freston	P	Rep. 1839
9751	Friston	P	Awd.,Min.
9752	Fritton	P	Rep. 1837
9753	Frostenden	P	Rep. 1838
9754	Gazeley	P	Rep. 1840
9755	Gedding	P	Rep. 1841
9756	Gipping	P	Awd.,Min.
9757	Gisleham	P	Rep. 1841
9758	Gislingham	P	Rep. 1839
9759	Glemham Great	P	Rep. 1840
9760	Glemham Little	P	Min.,Rep. 1838
9761	Glemsford	P	Min.,Rep. 1840
9762	Gorleston	P	Rep. 1840
9763	Gorleston with South Town	P	N.t.p.
9764	Gosbeck	P	Awd.,Min.
9765	Groton	P	Agrmt.,Min.,Rep. 1838
9766	Grundisburgh	P	Rep. 1841
9767	Gunton	P	Rep. 1838
9768	Hacheston	P	Rep. 1839
9769	Hadleigh	P	Min.,Rep. 1838
9770	Halesworth	P	Min.,Rep. 1840
9771	Hardwick	EP	N.t.p.
9772	Hargrave	P	Rep. 1838
9773	Harkstead	P	Rep. 1838
9774	Harleston	P	Awd.,Min.
9775	Hartest	P	Min.,Rep. 1839

Suffolk contd.

9776	Hasketon	P	Min.,Rep. 1840
9777	Gassocks First and Second	D	Awd.,Min.
9778	Haughley	P	Min.
9779	Havergate Island	P	N.t.p.
9780	Haverhill	P	Min.,Rep. 1839
9781	Hawkedon	P	Rep. 1839
9782	Hawstead	P	Rep. 1842
9783	Hazlewood	P	Awd.,Min.
9784	Helmingham	P	Rep. 1839
9785	Hemingstone	P	Agrmt.
9786	Hemingstone	D	Awd.
9787	Hemley	P	Rep. 1840
9788	Hintlesham	P	Agrmt.,Rep. 1837
9789	Hengrave	P	Agrmt.,Rep. 1838
9790	Henham	P	N.t.p.
9791	Henstead cum Hulver Street	P	Rep. 1838
9792	Henley	P	Rep. 1837
9793	Hepworth	P	Awd.,Min.
9794	Herringfleet	P	Awd.,Min.
9795	Herringswell	P	N.t.p.
9796	Hessett	P	Agrmt.,Rep. 1837
9797	Heveningham	P	Rep. 1840
9798	Higham	P	Rep. 1838
9799	Hinderclay	P	Rep. 1843
9800	Hitcham	P	Agrmt.,Rep. 1839
9801	Holbrook	P	Rep. 1838
9802	Hollesley	P	Awd.,Min.
9803	Holton St Mary	P	Rep. 1838
9804	Holton St Peter	P	Rep. 1840
9805	Honington	P	Rep. 1838
9806	Homersfield	P	Rep. 1839
9807	Hoo	P	Min.
9808	Hopton	P	Min.
9809	Hopton by Lowestoft	P	Rep. 1843
9810	Horham	P	Rep. 1838
9811	Horningsheath	P	Agrmt.,Rep. 1837
9812	Hoxne	P	Rep. 1842
9813	Hundon	P	Awd.,Min.
9814	Hunston	P	Awd.,Min.
9815	Huntingfield	P	Awd.,Min.
9816	Icklingham	P	N.t.p.
9817	Icklingham All Saints	P	Agrmt.,Rep. 1839
9818	Icklingham St James	P	Agrmt.,Rep. 1839
9819	Ickworth	P	Rep. 1837
9820	Iken	P	Min.,Rep. 1839
9821	Ilketshall St Andrew	P	Min.
9822	Ilketshall St John	P	Rep. 1838
9823	Ilketshall St Lawrence	P	Awd.,Min.
9824	Ilketshall St Margaret	P	Rep. 1839
9825	Ingham	P	Agrmt.,Rep. 1837
9826	Ipswich Holy Trinity	P	N.t.p.
9827	Ipswich St Clement	P	Rep. 1841
9828	Ipswich St Helen	P	Rep. 1841
9829	Ipswich St Lawrence	P	N.t.p.
9830	Ipswich St Margaret	P	Awd.,Min.
9831	Ipswich St Mary at the Elm	P	N.t.p.
9832	Ipswich St Mary (Quay)	P	N.t.p.
9833	Ipswich St Mary (Town)	P	N.t.p.
9834	Ipswich St Mary Stoke	P	Rep. 1839
9835	Ipswich St Matthew	P	Awd.,Min.
9836	Ipswich St Nicholas	P	N.t.p.
9837	Ipswich St Peter	P	Awd.,Min.
9838	Ipswich St Stephen	EP	Awd.,Min.
9839	Ixworth	P	Awd.,Min.
9840	Kedington	P	Awd.,Min.
9841	Kelsale	P	Rep. 1842
9842	Kennett	P	Min.
9843	Kentford	P	Rep. 1840
9844	Kenton	P	Rep. 1839
9845	Kersey	P	Rep. 1839
9846	Kesgrave	P	Awd.,Min.
9847	Kessingland	P	Rep. 1838
9848	Kettlebastone	P	Rep. 1842
9849	Kettleburgh	P	Rep. 1839
9850	Kirkley	P	Rep. 1838
9851	Kirton	P	Rep. 1838
9852	Knettishall	P	Rep. 1840
9853	Knodishall	P	Awd.,Min.
9854	Lackford	P	Rep. 1843
9855	Lakenheath Fen	D	Awd.,Min.
9856	Lakenheath	P	Awd.,Min.
9857	Langham	P	Rep. 1838
9858	Lavenham	P	Rep. 1842
9859	Lawshall	P	Rep. 1839
9860	Laxfield	P	Rep. 1840
9861	Layham	P	Agrmt.,Min.
9862	Leiston	P	Min.,Rep. 1838
9863	Letheringham	P	Rep. 1842
9864	Lidgate	P	Awd.,Min.
9865	Lindsey	P	Rep. 1838
9866	Linstead Magna	P	Rep. 1840
9867	Linstead Parva	P	Rep. 1840
9868	Livermere Great	P	Agrmt.,Awd.,Min.,Rep. 1840
9869	Livermere Little	P	Awd.,Min.,Rep. 1840
9870	Lound	P	Rep. 1838
9871	Lowestoft	P	Rep. 1837
9872	Marlesford	P	Rep. 1841
9873	Martlesham	P	Agrmt.,Rep. 1837
9874	Mellis	P	Rep. 1839
9875	Metfield	P	Rep. 1841
9876	Melford Long	P	Awd.,Min.
9877	Melton	P	Agrmt.,Rep. 1837
9878	Mendlesham	P	Rep. 1839
9879	Mendham	P	Rep. 1840
9880	Mettingham	P	Awd.,Min.
9881	Mickfield	P	Agrmt.,Rep. 1838
9882	Middleton	P	Min.,Rep. 1838
9883	Milden	P	Rep. 1838
9884	Mildenhall	P	Awd.,Min.
9885	Monewden	P	Rep. 1838
9886	Monk Soham	P	Rep. 1840
9887	Monks Eleigh	P	Min.,Rep. 1840
9888	Monks Risbridge	L	N.t.p.
9889	Moulton	P	Min.,Rep. 1838
9890	Mutford	P	Rep. 1844
9891	Naughton	P	Awd.,Min.
9892	Nacton and Levington	P	Rep. 1837
9893	Nedging	P	Agrmt.,Rep. 1838
9894	Nettlestead	P	Rep. 1839
9895	Newbourn	P	Awd.,Min.
9896	Newton	P	Awd.,Min.
9897	Newton Old	P	Min.
9898	Norton	P	Rep. 1839
9899	Nowton	P	Rep. 1839
9900	Occold	P	Rep. 1838
9901	Oakley	P	Rep. 1839
9902	Offton and Little Bricett	P	Rep. 1839
9903	Onehouse	P	Awd.,Min.
9904	Orford	P	Agrmt.,Rep. 1838
9905	Ottley	P	Agrmt.,Rep. 1839
9906	Ousden	P	Agrmt.,Rep. 1838
9907	Pakefield	P	Rep. 1842
9908	Nayland	P	Rep. 1838
9909	Oulton	P	Rep. 1837
9910	Pakenham	P	Awd.,Min.
9911	Palgrave	P	Rep. 1837
9912	Parham	P	Agrmt.,Rep. 1839
9913	Playford	P	Awd.,Min.
9914	Peasenhall	P	Rep. 1840
9915	Pettaugh	P	Rep. 1839
9916	Pettistree	P	Rep. 1839
9917	Polstead	P	Agrmt.,Rep. 1839
9918	Poslingford	P	Agrmt.,Rep. 1840
9919	Preston	P	Agrmt.,Rep. 1838
9920	Ramsholt	P	Rep. 1840
9921	Rattlesden	P	Rep. 1838
9922	Raydon	P	Rep. 1838
9923	Rede	P	Agrmt.,Rep. 1837
9924	Redgrave	P	Awd.,Min.
9925	Redisham Great	P	Rep. 1842
9926	Redlingfield	P	Rep. 1839
9927	Rendham	P	Rep. 1840
9928	Rendlesham	P	Rep. 1839
9929	Reydon	P	Rep. 1841
9930	Rickinghall	D	Rep. 1840
9931	Ringsfield	P	Awd.,Min.
9932	Ringshall	P	Agrmt.,Rep. 1838
9933	Risby	P	Rep. 1839
9934	Rishangles	P	Awd.,Min.
9935	Rougham	P	Min.
9936	Rumburgh	P	Rep. 1843
9937	Rushbrooke	P	Rep. 1839
9938	Rushmere St Andrew	P	Awd.,Min.
9939	Rushmere	P	Rep. 1837
9940	Sapiston	P	N.t.p.
9941	Saxham Little	P	Awd.,Min.
9942	Saxham Great	P	Agrmt.,Rep. 1839
9943	Saxmundham	P	Min.,Rep. 1840
9944	Saxted	P	Rep. 1838
9945	Seamer	P	Min.,Rep. 1838
9946	Shaddingfield	P	Rep. 1840
9947	Shelland	P	Rep. 1839
9948	Shelley	P	Rep. 1841
9949	Shimpling Thorne	P	Rep. 1838
9950	Sibton	P	Rep. 1842
9951	Somerton	P	Rep. 1839
9952	Shipmeadow	P	Rep. 1839
9953	Shotley	P	Rep. 1838
9954	Shottisham	P	Rep. 1839
9955	Snape	P	Rep. 1846
9956	Somerleyton	P	Rep. 1837
9957	Somersham	P	Rep. 1839
9958	Sotherton	P	Rep. 1838
9959	Sotterley	P	Rep. 1840
9960	Southolt	P	Rep. 1838
9961	South Town	P	Rep. 1839
9962	Southwell Park	EP	Min.
9963	Southwold	P	Awd.,Min.
9964	Spexhall	P	Agrmt.,Min.,Rep. 1837
9965	Sproughton	P	Min.,Rep. 1837
9966	Stanningfield	P	Rep. 1838
9967	Stowupland	P	Rep. 1840

Suffolk contd.

9968	Sudborne	P	Agrmt.,Rep. 1838
9969	Sudbury	P	Awd.,Min.
9970	Sudbury St Bartholomew	EP	N.t.p.
9971	Stansfield	P	Agrmt.,Rep. 1837
9972	Stanstead	P	Agrmt.,Rep. 1838
9973	Stanton	P	Agrmt.,Rep. 1839
9974	Sternfield	P	Awd.,Min.
9975	Stoke Ash	P	Rep. 1840
9976	Stoke juxta Clare	P	Rep. 1839
9977	Stoke by Nayland	P	Agrmt.,Rep. 1837
9978	Stonham Little	P	Rep. 1839
9979	Stonham Aspall	P	Agrmt.,Min.,Rep. 1838
9980	Stoven	P	Rep. 1838
9981	Stowmarket St Mary	P	N.t.p.
9982	Stowmarket	P	Min.,Rep. 1840
9983	Stow West	P	N.t.p.
9984	Stowlangtoft	P	Awd.,Min.
9985	Stradbrooke	P	Min.
9986	Stradishall	P	Agrmt.,Rep. 1838
9987	Stratford St Andrew	P	Agrmt.,Rep. 1846
9988	Stratford St Mary	P	Rep. 1838
9989	Stratton Hall	EP	N.t.p.
9990	Stuston	P	Agrmt.,Awd.,Rep. 1842
9991	Stutton	P	Awd.,Min.
9992	Sudbury St Gregory & Peter	P	Min.
9993	Sutton	P	Awd.,Min.
9994	Swefling	P	Rep. 1841
9995	Swilland	P	Rep. 1839
9996	Syleham	P	Agrmt.,Min.
9997	Tannington	P	Min.,Rep. 1840
9998	Tostock	P	Awd.,Min.
9999	Tattingstone	P	Min.
10000	Theberton	P	Min.,Rep. 1838
10001	Thelnetham	P	Awd.,Min.
10002	Thorington	P	Agrmt.,Min.,Rep. 1839
10003	Weston	P	Rep. 1839
10004	Thorndon	P	Rep. 1839
10005	Thornham Great & Little	P	Awd.,Min.
10006	Thorpe Morieux	P	Rep. 1843
10007	Thorpe by Ixworth	P	N.t.p.
10008	Thrandeston	P	Awd.,Min.
10009	Thurlow Little	P	Awd.,Min.
10010	Thurlow Great	P	Rep. 1839
10011	Thurston	P	Agrmt.,Rep. 1839
10012	Thwaite	P	Rep. 1839
10013	Timworth	P	Agrmt.,Min.,Rep. 1837
10014	Trimley St Mary	P	Rep. 1838
10015	Trimley St Martin	P	Rep. 1838
10016	Troston	P	Rep. 1841
10017	Tunstall	P	Awd.,Min.
10018	Tuddenham St Martin	P	Rep. 1838
10019	Tuddenham St Mary	P	Agrmt.
10020	Ubbeston	P	Rep. 1838
10021	Ufford	P	Min.,Rep. 1843
10022	Uggeshall	P	Rep. 1838
10023	Waldingfield Great	P	Agrmt.,Rep. 1838
10024	Waldingfield Little	P	Rep. 1839
10025	Waldringfield	P	Min.,Rep. 1839
10026	Walpole	P	Awd.,Min.
10027	Walberswick	P	Rep. 1840
10028	Walsham le Willows	P	Awd.,Min.
10029	Walton	P	Min.
10030	Wangford	P	Rep. 1839
10031	Wangford by Brandon	P	Rep. 1842
10032	Wantisden	P	Awd.,Min.
10033	Washbrook	P	Rep. 1838
10034	Wattisfield	P	Awd.,Min.
10035	Wattisham	P	Awd.,Rep. 1837
10036	Weltenham	P	Agrmt.,Rep. 1838
10037	Wenham Great	P	Rep. 1843
10038	Wenham Little	P	Rep. 1843
10039	Wenhaston & Mells	PH	Rep. 1839
10040	Westerfield	P	Agrmt.,Rep. 1839
10041	Westhall	P	Rep. 1840
10042	Westhorpe	P	Rep. 1839
10043	Westleton	P	Rep. 1840
10044	Westley	P	Agrmt.,Min.
10045	Weston Market	P	Rep. 1841
10046	Wetherden	P	Awd.,Min.
10047	Wetheringsett	P	Awd.,Min.
10048	Weybread	P	Rep. 1839
10049	Whatfield	P	Awd.,Min.
10050	Whelnetham	P	Awd.,Min.
10051	Whelnetham Great	P	Awd.,Min.
10052	Whepstead	P	Awd.,Min.
10053	Wherstead	P	Rep. 1839
10054	Whitton	P	Rep. 1838
10055	Wickhambrook	P	Rep. 1839
10056	Wickham Market	P	Awd.,Min.
10057	Wickham Skeith	P	Rep. 1839
10058	Wilby	P	Rep. 1838
10059	Willingham	P	Rep. 1839
10060	Willisham	P	Rep. 1839
10061	Wingfield	P	Rep. 1840
10062	Winston	P	Awd.,Min.
10063	Wissett	P	Rep. 1840
10064	Wiston	P	Agrmt.,Rep. 1839
10065	Withersdale	P	Rep. 1839
10066	Withersfield	P	Awd.,Min.
10067	Witnesham	P	Agrmt.,Min.,Rep. 1842
10068	Wixoe	P	Agrmt.,Rep. 1838
10069	Woodbridge	P	Rep. 1840
10070	Woolpit	P	Awd.,Min.
10071	Woolverstone	P	Rep. 1838
10072	Wordwell	P	Agrmt.,Min.,Rep. 1837
10073	Worlingham	P	Rep. 1840
10074	Worlington	P	N.t.p.
10075	Worlingworth	P	Agrmt.,Min.,Rep. 1837
10076	Wortham	P	Min.,Rep. 1840
10077	Wratting Great	P	Awd.,Min.
10078	Wratting Little	P	Min.
10079	Wrentham	P	Rep. 1839
10080	Wyverstone	P	Rep. 1838
10081	Yaxley	P	Rep. 1842
10082	Yoxford	P	Rep. 1839
14827	Eyke	P	Rep. 1845

Surrey

10083	Abinger	P	Agrmt.,Min.,Rep. 1838
10084	Addington	P	Min.,Rep. 1837
10085	Aldbury	P	Min.,Rep. 1838
10086	Alfold	P	Agrmt.,Min.,Rep. 1839
10087	Ashe	P	Awd.,Min.
10088	Ashtead	P	Agrmt.,Min.
10089	Banstead	P	Agrmt.,Min.,Rep. 1840
10090	Barnes	P	Agrmt.,Min.,Rep. 1837
10091	Battersea	P	Agrmt.,Min.,Rep. 1839
10092	Beddington	P	Agrmt.,Min.,Rep. 1839
10093	Betchworth	P	Awd.,Min.,Rep. 1840
10094	Bermondsey St Mary	P	N.t.p.
10095	Bisley	P	Awd.,Min.
10096	Bletchingley	P	Agrmt.,Min.,Rep. 1840
10097	Bookham Great	P	Awd.,Min.
10098	Bookham Little	P	Agrmt.,Min.,Rep. 1839
10099	Bramley	P	Agrmt.,Min.,Rep. 1841
10100	Burstow	P	Min.,Rep. 1839
10101	Byfleet	P	Agrmt.,Awd.,Min.
10102	Capel	P	Agrmt.,Min.,Rep. 1838
10103	Carshalton	P	Awd.,Min.
10104	Caterham	P	Agrmt.,Min.,Rep. 1839
10105	Chaldon	P	Agrmt.,Min.,Rep. 1837
10106	Charlwood	P	Min.,Rep. 1839
10107	Cheam	P	Min.,Rep. 1840
10108	Chertsey	P	Awd.,Min.
10109	Chessington	P	Agrmt.,Min.,Rep. 1838
10110	Chiddingfold	P	Agrmt.,Min.,Rep. 1841
10111	Chilworth	P	Awd.,Min.
10112	Chipstead	P	Agrmt.,Min.,Rep. 1844
10113	Chobham	P	Awd.,Min.
10114	Churt	I	Min.
10115	Clandon East	P	Awd.,Min.
10116	Clandon West	P	Agrmt.,Min.,Rep. 1838
10117	Cobham	P	Agrmt.,Min.,Rep. 1848
10118	Compton	P	Agrmt.,Min.,Rep. 1840
10119	Coulsdon	P	Agrmt.,Min.,Rep. 1837
10120	Cranley	P	Agrmt.,Awd.,Min.,Rep. 1840
10121	Crowhurst	P	Agrmt.,Min.,Rep. 1841
10122	Croydon	P	Awd.,Min.
10123	Cuddington	P	Min.,Rep. 1839
10124	Dorking	P	Awd.,Min.
10125	Dunsfold	P	Awd.,Min.
10126	Effingham	P	Agrmt.,Awd.,Min.,Rep. 1838
10127	Egham	P	Agrmt.,Min.,Rep. 1840
10128	Elstead	P	Agrmt.,Min.,Rep. 1840
10129	Epsom	P	Awd.,Min.
10130	Esher	P	Awd.,Min.
10131	Ewell	P	N.t.p.,Min.
10132	Ewhurst	P	Agrmt.,Min.,Rep. 1840
10133	Farleigh	P	Agrmt.,Min.,Rep. 1839
10134	Farnham	P	Awd.,Min.
10135	Fetcham	P	Min.
10136	Frensham	P	Agrmt.,Min.,Rep. 1839
10137	Frimley	C	Awd.,Min.
10138	Gatton	P	Agrmt.,Rep. 1838
10139	Godalming	P	Agrmt.,Min.,Rep. 1842
10140	Godstone	P	Agrmt.,Min.,Rep. 1842
10141	Guildford St Nicholas	P	Agrmt.,Min.,Rep. 1841
10142	Guildford Holy Trinity	P	Agrmt.,Min.,Rep. 1843
10143	Ham	P	Agrmt.,Min.,Rep. 1840
10144	Hambledon	P	Awd.,Min.
10145	Hascomb	P	Agrmt.,Min.,Rep. 1841
10146	Haslemere	P	Agrmt.,Min.,Rep. 1841
10147	Headley	P	Agrmt.,Min.,Rep. 1839
10148	Horley	P	Awd.,Min.
10149	Horne	P	Agrmt.,Min.,Rep. 1842
10150	Horsell	P	Awd.,Min.
10151	Horsley East	P	Awd.,Min.
10152	Horsley West	P	Agrmt.,Min.,Rep. 1838
10153	Kew	P	Awd.,Min.
10154	Kingston on Thames	P	Min.,Rep. 1839

Surrey contd.

10155	Kingswood	L	Awd.,Min.
10156	Leatherhead	P	Awd.,Min.
10157	Leigh	P	Awd.,Min.
10158	Limpsfield	P	Awd.,Min.
10159	Lingfield	P	Agrmt.,Awd.,Min.
10160	Long Ditton	P	Awd.,Min.
10161	Malden	P	Agrmt.,Min.,Rep. 1839
10162	Merrow	P	Agrmt.,Min.,Rep. 1838
10163	Merstham	P	Rep. 1840
10164	Merton	P	Awd.,Min.
10165	Mickleham	P	Agrmt.,Min.,Rep. 1838
10166	Mordon	P	Agrmt.,Awd.,Min.,Rep. 1837
10167	Mortlake	P	Min.,Rep. 1839
10168	Moulsey East	P	N.t.p.,Min.
10169	Moulsey West	P	N.t.p.,Min.
10170	Newdigate	P	Agrmt.,Min.,Rep. 1840
10171	Norwood St Luke	D	Awd.,Min.
10172	Nutfield	P	Awd.,Min.
10173	Ockley	P	Agrmt.,Min.,Rep. 1840
10174	Oxted	P	Agrmt.,Min.,Rep. 1839
10175	Peper Harrow	P	Agrmt.,Min.,Rep. 1841
10176	Petersham	P	Awd.,Min.
10177	Pirbright	P	Agrmt.,Min.,Rep. 1841
10178	Putney	P	Awd.,Min.
10179	Puttenham	P	Awd.,Min.
10180	Pyrford	P	Awd.,Min.
10181	Richmond	P	Awd.,Min.
10182	Richmond Park	D	Awd.,Min.
10183	Reigate	P	Awd.,Min.
10184	Sanderstead	P	Agrmt.,Min.,Rep. 1843
10185	Seale	P	Agrmt.,Min.,Rep. 1839
10186	Send and Ripley	P	Awd.,Min.
10187	Shalford	P	Awd.,Min.
10188	Shere	P	Awd.,Min.
10189	Stoke next Guildford	P	Agrmt.,Min.,Rep. 1841
10190	Stoke D'Abernon	P	Awd.,Min.
10191	Sutton next Woking	I	Awd.,Min.
10192	Sutton	P	Agrmt.,Min.,Rep. 1839
10193	Tandridge	P	Agrmt.,Min.,Rep. 1844
10194	Tatsfield	P	Awd.,Min.
10195	Thames Ditton	P	Agrmt.,Min.,Rep. 1843
10196	Thorpe	P	Min.,Rep. 1840
10197	Thursley	P	Awd.,Min.
10198	Titsey	P	Awd.,Min.
10199	Walton on the Hill	P	Agrmt.,Min.,Rep. 1839
10200	Walton on Thames	P	Agrmt.,Min.,Rep. 1842
10201	Wanborough	P	N.t.p.,Min.
10202	Wandsworth	P	Awd.,Min.
10203	Warlingham cum Chelsham	P	Awd.,Min.
10204	Waterloo St John	D	Awd.,Min.
10205	Waverley Ville	EP	N.t.p.
10206	Weybridge	P	Awd.,Min.
10207	Wimbledon	P	Awd.,Min.
10208	Windlesham	P	Agrmt.,Awd.,Min.
10209	Wisley	P	Awd.,Min.
10210	Witley	P	Agrmt.,Min.,Rep. 1843
10211	Woking	P	Awd.,Min.
10212	Woldingham	P	Awd.,Min.
10213	Wonersh	P	Agrmt.,Awd.,Min.
10214	Woodmansterne	P	Awd.,Min.
10215	Worplesdon	P	Agrmt.,Min.,Rep. 1838
10216	Wotton	P	Agrmt.,Min.,Rep. 1839
10217	Buckland	P	Awd.,Min.
10218	Ockham	P	Agrmt.,Min.,Rep. 1838
13554	Clapham	P	Agrmt.,Rep. 1837
13555	Kennington	P	Awd.,Min.
13556	Lambeth Church	P	Awd.,Min.
13557	Mitcham	P	Awd.,Min.
13558	Newington St Peter	C	N.t.p.
13559	Newington St Mary	P	Awd.,Min.
13560	Streatham	P	Agrmt.,Rep. 1839
13561	Tooting Graveney	P	Awd.,Min.
13566	Brixton	P	Min.
14809	Camberwell	P	Agrmt.,Min.
14810	Rotherhithe	P	Agrmt.,Awd.,Min.
14811	Southwark,Christchurch	P	N.t.p.,Min.
14812	Southwark,St George	P	N.t.p.,Min.
14828	St John,Horsleydown	P	N.t.p.

Sussex

10219	Albourne	P	Agrmt.,Rep. 1839
10220	Alciston	P	Min.
10221	Aldingbourne	P	Awd.,Min.
10222	Aldrington	P	Awd.,Min.
10223	Alfriston	P	Awd.,Min.
10224	Amberley	P	Awd.,Min.
10225	Ambersham North	I	Awd.,Min.
10226	Ambersham South	I	Awd.,Min.
10227	Angmering	P	Agrmt.,Min.,Rep. 1839
10228	Appledram	P	Awd.,Min.
10229	Ardingley	P	Awd.,Min.
10230	Arlington	P	Awd.,Min.
10231	Arundel	P	Awd.,Min.
10232	Ashburnham	P	Agrmt.,Min.,Rep. 1839
10233	Ashington	P	Awd.,Min.
10234	Ashurst	P	Awd.,Min.
10235	Balcombe	P	Agrmt.,Min.,Rep. 1839
10236	Barcombe	P	Awd.,Min.
10237	Barlton	P	Agrmt.,Min.,Rep. 1839
10238	Barnham	P	Awd.,Min.
10239	Baybush	D	Agrmt.,Min.,Rep. 1839
10240	Beckley	P	Agrmt.,Min.,Rep. 1839
10241	Beddingham	P	Awd.,Min.
10242	Bepton	P	Min.,Rep. 1838
10243	Bersted South	P	Agrmt.,Min.,Rep. 1841
10244	Beeding	I	Agrmt.,Min.,Rep. 1842
10245	Berwick	P	Min.,Rep. 1838
10246	Bexhill	P	Min.,Rep. 1840
10247	Bignor	P	Awd.,Min.
10248	Billingshurst	P	Agrmt.,Min.,Rep. 1840
10249	Binderton	P	Awd.,Min.
10250	Binstead	P	Agrmt.,Min.,Rep. 1840
10251	Birdham	P	Awd.,Min.
10252	Bishopstone	P	Awd.,Min.
10253	Blatchington East	P	Awd.,Min.
10254	Blatchington West	P	Agrmt.,Min.,Rep. 1839
10255	Botolphs	P	Awd.,Min.
10256	Bodecton	P	Agrmt.,Min.,Rep. 1843
10257	Bodiam	P	Agrmt.,Min.,Rep. 1839
10258	Bolney	P	Awd.,Min.
10259	Bosham	P	Agrmt.,Min.,Rep. 1841
10260	Boxgrove	P	Min.,Rep. 1838
10261	Bramber	P	Agrmt.,Min.,Rep. 1839
10262	Brede	P	Min.
10263	Brightling	P	Agrmt.,Min.,Rep. 1839
10264	Brighton	P	Awd.,Min.
10265	Broadwater	P	Awd.,Min.
10266	Buddington	I	Agrmt.,Min.,Rep. 1840
10267	Burwash	P	Agrmt.,Min.,Rep. 1839
10268	Burpham	P	Agrmt.,Min.,Rep. 1840
10269	Bury	P	Agrmt.,Min.,Rep. 1839
10270	Buxted	P	Min.,Rep. 1841
10271	Catsfield	P	Agrmt.,Min.,Rep. 1839
10272	Chailey	P	Agrmt.,Rep. 1838
10273	Chalvington	P	Agrmt.,Min.,Rep. 1838
10274	North Chapel	P	Agrmt.,Min.,Rep. 1837
10275	Chichester City Parishes	P	Min.
10276	Chichester All Saints	P	Awd.,Min.
10277	Chichester All Saints	P	Min.
10278	Chichester St Bartholomew	P	Awd.,Min.
10279	Chichester St Paul	P	Min.
10280	Chichester Cathedral Close	EP	N.t.p.
10281	Chichester St James	EP	N.t.p.
10282	Chichester Newtown	EP	N.t.p.,Min.
10283	Chichester St Olave	P	Min.
10284	Chichester St Peter	P	N.t.p.,Min.
10285	Chiddingly	P	Agrmt.,Min.,Rep. 1839
10286	Chidham	P	Awd.,Min.
10287	Chiltington	P	Rep. 1837
10288	Chiltington West	P	Agrmt.,Min.,Rep. 1839
10289	Chithurst	P	Agrmt.,Min.,Rep. 1840
10290	Clapham	P	Awd.,Min.
10291	Clayton	P	Agrmt.,Min.,Rep. 1838
10292	Climping	P	Agrmt.,Rep. 1843
10293	Coates	P	Agrmt.,Min.,Rep. 1840
10294	Cocking	P	Min.
10295	Coldwaltham	P	Agrmt.,Min.,Rep. 1840
10296	Compton	P	Agrmt.,Min.,Rep. 1841
10297	Coombes	P	Agrmt.,Rep. 1841
10298	Cowfold	P	Agrmt.,Min.,Rep. 1839
10299	Crawley	P	Agrmt.,Min.,Rep. 1839
10300	Crowhurst	P	Agrmt.,Min.,Rep. 1840
10301	Cuckfield	P	Awd.,Min.
10302	Dallington	P	Awd.,Min.
10303	East Dean	P	Awd.,Min.
10304	East Dean	P	Awd.,Min.
10305	Westdean	P	Min.,Rep. 1841
10306	West Dean	P	Awd.,Min.
10307	Denton	P	Agrmt.,Rep. 1839
10308	Didling	P	Awd.,Min.
10309	Ditcheling	P	Agrmt.,Min.,Rep. 1839
10310	Donnington	P	Agrmt.,Min.,Rep. 1842
10311	Duncton	P	Agrmt.,Rep. 1837
10312	Durrington	P	Agrmt.,Min.,Rep. 1839
10313	Earnley	P	Agrmt.,Rep. 1845
10314	Eartham	P	Agrmt.,Min.,Rep. 1839
10315	Easebourne	P	Awd.,Min.
10316	Eastbourne	P	Agrmt.,Min.,Rep. 1841
10317	Eastergate	P	Awd.,Min.
10318	Eckington	P	Agrmt.,Min.,Rep. 1837
10319	Edburton	P	Awd.,Min.
10320	Egdean	P	Agrmt.,Rep. 1837
10321	Elsted	P	Awd.,Min.
10322	Etchingham	P	Agrmt.,Min.
10323	Ewhurst	P	Awd.,Min.
10324	Fairlight	P	Agrmt.,Min.,Rep. 1839
10325	Flitchling	D	Awd.,Min.
10326	Falmer	P	Agrmt.,Rep. 1838
10327	Farnhurst	D	Awd.,Min.
10328	Felpham	P	Agrmt.,Rep. 1844

Sussex contd.

10329	Ferring	P	Agrmt.,Min.,Rep. 1840
10330	Finden	P	Agrmt.,Rep. 1838
10331	Firle West	P	Awd.,Min.
10332	Fittleworth	P	Agrmt.,Rep. 1839
10333	Folkington	P	Agrmt.,Min.,Rep. 1838
10334	Ford	P	Agrmt.,Rep. 1839
10335	Framfield	P	Min.,Rep. 1839
10336	Frant	P	Awd.,Min.
10337	Friston	P	Min.
10338	Funtington	P	Agrmt.,Rep. 1838
10339	Glynde	P	Rep. 1839
10340	Goring	P	Agrmt.,Min.,Rep. 1843
10341	Graffham	P	Agrmt.,Rep. 1841
10342	Greatham	P	Agrmt.,Rep. 1837
10343	East Grinstead	P	Agrmt.,Rep. 1842
10344	West Grinstead	P	Agrmt.,Min.,Rep. 1836
10345	Guestling	P	Agrmt.,Min.,Rep. 1840
10346	East Guldeford	P	Agrmt.,Rep. 1842
10347	Hailsham	P	Agrmt.,Rep. 1841
10348	Ham and Bircham	D	Awd.,Min.
10349	Hamsey	P	Agrmt.,Min.,Rep. 1838
10350	Hangleton	P	Awd.,Min.
10351	Hardham	P	Awd.,Min.
10352	Hartfield	P	Agrmt.,Min.,Rep. 1842
10353	Harting	P	Agrmt.,Rep. 1841
10354	Hastings All Saints	P	Agrmt.,Min.,Rep. 1838
10355	Hastings St Clement	P	Agrmt.,Min.,Rep. 1838
10356	Hastings St Mary	P	N.t.p.
10357	Haysholt	P	Agrmt.,Rep. 1839
10358	Heathfield	P	Agrmt.,Min.,Rep. 1841
10359	Heene	P	Agrmt.,Rep. 1839
10360	Heighton South	P	Agrmt.,Min.,Rep. 1841
10361	Hellingby	P	Agrmt.,Rep. 1839
10362	Henfield	P	Awd.,Min.
10363	Hollington	P	Awd.,Min.
10364	Hooe	P	Agrmt.,Rep. 1839
10365	Horsham	P	Awd.,Min.
10366	Horsted Keynes	P	Agrmt.,Min.,Rep. 1839
10367	Horsted Little	P	Agrmt.,Min.,Rep. 1839
10368	East Hoathly	P	Agrmt.,Rep. 1839
10369	Houghton	P	Awd.,Min.
10370	Hove	P	Agrmt.,Min.,Rep. 1840
10371	Hunston	P	Awd.,Min.
10372	Hurstmonceaux	P	Agrmt.,Rep. 1839
10373	Hurst Pierpoint	P	Agrmt.,Min.,Rep. 1842
10374	Itchenor West	P	Agrmt.,Min.,Rep. 1838
10375	Icklesham	P	Min.
10376	Iden	P	Agrmt.,Min.,Rep. 1843
10377	Ifield	P	Agrmt.,Rep. 1841
10378	Iford	P	Awd.,Min.
10379	Iping	P	Agrmt.,Rep. 1841
10380	Isfield	P	Agrmt.,Min.,Rep. 1840
10381	Itchingfield	P	Agrmt.,Rep. 1840
10382	Jevington	P	Agrmt.,Rep. 1838
10383	Keymer	P	Awd.,Min.
10384	Kings Barns	I	Agrmt.,Min.,Rep. 1840
10385	Kingston	P	Agrmt.,Min.,Rep. 1841
10386	Kingstone	P	Awd.,Min.
10387	Kingston on Sea	P	Awd.,Min.
10388	Kirdford	P	Min.
10389	Lancing	P	Agrmt.,Rep. 1838
10390	Laughton	P	Agrmt.,Min.,Rep. 1838
10391	Mid Lavant	P	Awd.,Min.
10392	East Lavant	P	Rep. 1839
10393	Leominster	P	Agrmt.,Rep. 1838
10394	Lewes Castle Precincts	EP	N.t.p.,Min.
10395	Lewes St Thomas at Cliffe	P	Awd.,Min.
10396	Lewes St Michael	P	Awd.,Min.
10397	Lewes St Peter	P	Agrmt.,Min.,Rep. 1842
10398	Linchmere	P	Awd.,Min.
10399	Linch	P	Awd.,Min.
10400	Lindfield	P	Awd.,Min.
10401	Littlehampton	P	Agrmt.,Rep. 1841
10402	Littlington	P	Awd.,Min.
10403	Lodsworth	P	Agrmt.,Min.,Rep. 1841
10404	Lullington	P	Awd.,Min.
10405	Lurgashall	P	Agrmt.,Rep. 1840
10406	Madehurst	P	Agrmt.,Min.,Rep. 1840
10407	Malling South	P	Min.
10408	Marden East	P	Awd.,Min.
10409	Marden North	P	Agrmt.,Rep. 1840
10410	Maresfield	P	Awd.,Min.
10411	Mayfield	P	Min.
10412	Merston	P	Agrmt.,Rep. 1841
10413	Middleton	P	Awd.,Min.
10414	Midhurst	P	Awd.,Min.
10415	Mountfield	P	Agrmt.,Min.,Rep. 1839
10416	Mundham North	P	Awd.,Min.
10417	Newick	P	Agrmt.,Rep. 1839
10418	Newhaven	P	Agrmt.,Rep. 1841
10419	Newtimber	P	Agrmt.,Min.,Rep. 1839
10420	Ninfield	P	Agrmt.,Rep. 1841
10421	Newfishborne	P	Agrmt.,Min.,Rep. 1840
10422	Northiam	P	Min.
10423	Nuthurst	P	Awd.,Min.
10424	Ore	P	Min.
10425	Oving	P	Agrmt.,Rep. 1839
10426	Ovingdean	P	Agrmt.,Rep. 1839
10427	Parham	P	Agrmt.,Min.,Rep. 1839
10428	Pagham	P	Awd.,Min.
10429	Patcham	P	Awd.,Min.
10430	Patching	P	Awd.,Min.
10431	Peasmarsh	P	Agrmt.,Rep. 1839
10433	Pett	P	Awd.,Min.
10434	Petworth	P	Agrmt.,Rep. 1837
10435	Pevensey	P	Agrmt.,Min.,Rep. 1839
10436	Piddinghoe	P	Awd.,Min.
10437	Portslade	P	Agrmt.,Min.,Rep. 1841
10438	Playden	P	Agrmt.,Min.,Rep. 1843
10439	Plompton	P	Agrmt.,Rep. 1839
10440	Poling	P	Agrmt.,Min.,Rep. 1838
10441	Poynings	P	Agrmt.,Min.,Rep. 1842
10442	Preston	P	Agrmt.,Min.,Rep. 1840
10443	Preston East	P	Agrmt.,Min.,Rep. 1841
10444	Pyecombe	P	Agrmt.,Min.,Rep. 1839
10445	Pulborough	P	Agrmt.,Rep. 1839
10446	Racton	P	Agrmt.,Min.,Rep. 1840
10447	Ringmer	P	Awd.,Min.
10448	Rodmell	P	Agrmt.,Rep. 1838
10449	Rogate	P	Awd.,Min.
10450	Rotherfield	P	Agrmt.,Rep. 1838
10451	Rottingdean	P	Agrmt.,Rep. 1838
10452	Rudgwick	P	Agrmt.,Rep. 1840
10453	Rumboldswyke	P	Awd.,Min.
10454	Rusper	P	Agrmt.,Rep. 1842
10455	Rustington	P	Agrmt.,Min.,Rep. 1839
10456	Rye	P	Agrmt.,Rep. 1841
10457	Salehurst	P	Awd.,Min.
10458	Sedlescomb	P	Agrmt.,Rep. 1842
10459	Selham	P	Awd.,Min.
10460	Selmeston	P	Agrmt.,Rep. 1841
10461	Selsey	P	Agrmt.,Rep. 1841
10462	Shermanbury	P	Agrmt.,Min.,Rep. 1837
10463	Shipley	P	Awd.,Min.
10464	Shoreham Old	P	Awd.,Min.
10465	Shoreham New	P	Awd.,Min.
10466	Sidlesham	P	Awd.,Min.
10467	Singleton	P	Awd.,Min.
10468	Slaugham	P	Awd.,Min.
10469	Slindon	P	Agrmt.,Min.,Rep. 1839
10470	Slinfold	P	Awd.,Min.
10471	Sompting	P	Awd.,Min.
10472	Southease	P	Agrmt.,Min.,Rep. 1841
10473	Southover	P	Awd.,Min.
10474	Southwick	P	Awd.,Min.
10475	Stanmer	P	Rep. 1838
10476	Stedham	P	Awd.,Min.
10477	Steyning	P	Agrmt.,Min.,Rep. 1840
10478	Stoke North	P	N.t.p.,Min.
10479	Stoke South	P	Awd.,Min.
10480	Stoke West	P	Awd.,Min.
10481	Stopham	P	Agrmt.,Min.,Rep. 1838
10482	Storrington	P	Agrmt.,Min.,Rep. 1839
10483	Stoughton	P	Agrmt.,Min.,Rep. 1840
10484	Street	P	Agrmt.,Min.,Rep. 1838
10485	Sutton	P	Agrmt.,Rep. 1837
10486	Sutton cum Seaford	P	Agrmt.,Min.,Rep. 1839
10487	Tangmere	P	Min.,Rep. 1838
10488	Tarring Neville	P	Agrmt.,Rep. 1841
10489	Tarring West	P	Agrmt.,Min.,Rep. 1839
10490	Telscombe	P	Awd.,Min.
10491	Terwick	P	Agrmt.,Min.,Rep. 1839
10492	Thakeham	P	Agrmt.,Min.,Rep. 1840
10493	Thorney West	P	N.t.p.,Min.
10494	Ticehurst	P	Awd.,Min.
10495	Tillington	P	Agrmt.,Min.,Rep. 1837
10496	Tortington	P	Agrmt.,Min.,Rep. 1840
10497	Treyford	P	Awd.,Min.
10498	Trotton cum Tuxlith	P	Agrmt.,Min.,Rep. 1839
10499	Sullington	P	Agrmt.,Min.,Rep. 1840
10500	Twineham	P	Agrmt.,Min.
10501	Uckfield	P	Min.,Rep. 1841
10502	Udimore	P	Agrmt.,Min.,Rep. 1838
10503	Upmarden	P	Agrmt.,Min.,Rep. 1842
10504	Upwaltham	P	Agrmt.,Rep. 1837
10505	Wadhurst	P	Agrmt.,Min.,Rep. 1839
10506	Walberton	P	Awd.,Min.
10507	Waldron	P	Agrmt.,Min.,Rep. 1842
10508	Warbleton	P	Agrmt.,Min.,Rep. 1837
10509	Warminghurst	P	Awd.,Min.
10510	Warnham	P	Awd.,Min.
10511	Warning Camp	P	Min.,Rep. 1838
10512	Wartling	P	Agrmt.,Min.,Rep. 1839
10513	Washington	P	Agrmt.,Min.,Rep. 1840
10514	Westbourn	P	Awd.,Min.
10515	Westfield	P	Awd.,Min.
10516	Westmeston cum Chitlington	P	Agrmt.,Min.,Rep. 1838
10517	Westham	P	Agrmt.,Min.,Rep. 1838
10518	Westhampnett	P	Agrmt.,Min.,Rep. 1838
10519	Whatlington	P	Agrmt.,Min.,Rep. 1839
10520	Wiggonholt	P	Agrmt.,Min.,Rep. 1837
10521	Willingdon	P	Awd.,Min.

Sussex contd.

10522	Wilmington	P	Agrmt.,Min.,Rep. 1838
10523	Wisboroughgreen	P	Agrmt.,Min.,Rep. 1842
10524	Withyham	P	Agrmt.,Min.,Rep. 1843
10525	Wiston	P	Agrmt.,Min.,Rep. 1839
10526	Wittering East	P	Awd.,Min.
10527	Wittering West	P	Awd.,Min.
10528	Wivelsfield	P	Agrmt.,Min.,Rep. 1838
10529	Woodmancote	P	Agrmt.,Min.,Rep. 1839
10530	Woolavington	P	Agrmt.,Min.,Rep. 1841
10531	Woolbeding	P	Agrmt.,Min.,Rep. 1839
10532	Worth	P	Agrmt.,Min.,Rep. 1842
10533	Yapton	P	Agrmt.,Min.,Rep. 1841
13562	St Peter the Great	P	Min.
14802	Hoathly West	P	Awd.,Min.
14813	Battle	P	Awd.,Min.
14814	Chichester St Andrew	P	Min.
14815	Chichester St Martin	P	Min.
14816	Chichester St Pancras	P	Awd.,Min.
14817	Lewes St John	P	Agrmt.,Min.,Rep. 1842
14818	Lewes All Saints	P	Awd.,Min.
14819	Winchelsea	P	Awd.,Min.

Warwickshire

10534	Alcester	P	Awd.,Min.
10535	Allesley	P	Rep. 1839
10536	Alne Great	P	Rep. 1838
10537	Alveston	P	Min.
10538	Ansley	P	Agrmt.,Awd.,Min.,Rep. 1839
10539	Ansty	P	Awd.,Min.
10540	Arley	P	Min.,Rep. 1839
10541	Armington	T	Awd.,Min.
10542	Arrow	P	Awd.,Min.
10543	Ashow	P	Agrmt.,Rep. 1838
10544	Astley	P	N.t.p.,Awd.,Min.
10545	Aston Cantlow	P	N.t.p.
10546	Austrey	P	Awd.,Min.
10547	Aston juxta Birmingham	P	Awd.,Min.
10548	Avon Dassett	P	Min.
10549	Baddesley Clinton	P	Awd.,Min.
10550	Baddesley Ensor	P	Awd.,Min.
10551	Baginton	P	Rep. 1840
10552	Barcheston	P	Awd.,Min.
10553	Barford	P	Awd.,Min.
10554	Barton on the Heath	P	Awd.,Min.
10555	Baxterly	P	Awd.,Min.
10556	Bearley	P	N.t.p.,Min.
10557	Beaudesert	P	Rep. 1839
10558	Bedworth	P	Rep. 1839
10559	Berkswell	P	Awd.,Min.
10560	Bickenhill	P	Agrmt.,Rep. 1837
10561	Bidford	P	Awd.,Min.
10562	Billesley	P	Awd.,Min.
10563	Bilton	P	Rep. 1839
10564	Binley	P	N.t.p.
10565	Binton and Drayton	P	Awd.,Min.
10566	Birbury and Marton	P	N.t.p.
10567	Birmingham St George	P	Min.
10568	Birmingham St Martin	P	Min.
10569	Bourton on Dunsmore	P	Awd.,Min.
10570	Brailes	P	Awd.,Min.
10571	Bramcote	P	Min.
10572	Bolehall and Glascote	T	Awd.,Min.
10573	Brandon and Bretford	T	Agrmt.,Min.,Rep. 1840
10574	Brinklow	P	N.t.p.
10575	Brownsover	T	Awd.,Min.
10576	Bubbenhall	P	N.t.p.
10577	Budbrook	P	Awd.,Min.
10578	Bulkington	P	Min.,Rep. 1840
10579	Burmington	P	Awd.,Min.
10580	Burton Dassett	P	Min.
10581	Burton Hastings	P	Min.
10582	Bushwood Old Stratford	H	Awd.,Min.
10583	Butlers Marston	P	N.t.p.,Min.
10584	Caldecote	P	Rep. 1839
10585	Cesters Over	H	Awd.,Min.
10586	Chadshunt	P	Agrmt.,Rep. 1837
10587	Chapel Ascote	EP	N.t.p.
10588	Charlcote	P	Awd.,Min.
10589	Cherrington	P	N.t.p.
10590	Chesterton	T	Awd.,Min.
10591	Chilvers Coton	P	N.t.p.
10592	Church Lawford	P	Awd.,Min.
10593	Churchover	P	N.t.p.,Min.
10594	Claverdon and Norton	P	Rep. 1837
10595	Clifton	T	Awd.,Min.
10596	Compton Fenny	P	N.t.p.
10597	Compton Long	P	Awd.,Min.
10598	Compton Verney	EP	N.t.p.
10599	Compton Wyniates	P	Awd.,Min.
10600	Coombe Fields	EP	N.t.p.
10601	Copston Magna	T	Awd.,Min.
10602	Corley	P	Awd.,Min.
10603	Cosford	T	Rep. 1839
10604	Coton	T	N.t.p.
10605	Coughton	T	Rep. 1838
10606	Coundon	H	Rep. 1840
10607	Coventry Holy Trinity	P	Awd.,Min.
10608	Coventry St Michael	P	Awd.,Min.
10609	Cubbington	P	N.t.p.
10610	Curdworth	P	Min.
10611	Dordon	T	Awd.,Min.
10612	Dosthill	D	Rep. 1839
10613	Dunchurch	P	Rep. 1838
10614	Hall End and Freazley	H	Awd.,Min.
10615	Hampton in Arden	H	Awd.,Min.
10616	Harborough Magna	P	Awd.,Min.
10617	Haselor	P	N.t.p.
10618	Haseley	P	Rep. 1840
10619	Hatton	P	Awd.,Min.
10620	Harbury	P	Awd.,Min.
10621	Hampton Lucy	P	Awd.,Min.
10622	Hillmorton	P	Awd.,Min.
10623	Honily	P	Awd.,Min.
10624	Honington	P	Min.,Rep. 1843
10625	Easenhall	T	Rep. 1839
10626	Eatington Upper and Lower	P	N.t.p.,Min.
10627	Edgbaston	P	Awd.,Min.
10628	Elmdon	P	Rep. 1839
10629	Exhall	P	Awd.,Min.
10630	Exhall cum Wixford	P	N.t.p.
10631	Fillongley	P	Awd.,Min.
10632	Foleshill	P	Rep. 1840
10633	Frankton	P	Min.
10634	Gaydon	P	N.t.p.
10635	Grafton(Temple and Arden)	P	Awd.,Min.
10636	Grandborough	P	Awd.,Min.
10637	Grendon	P	Awd.,Min.
10638	Halford	P	N.t.p.
10639	Hunningham	P	Awd.,Min.
10640	Idlicote	P	Min.
10641	Ipsley	P	Rep. 1841
10642	Itchington Bishops	P	Min.,Rep. 1837
10643	Itchington Long	P	N.t.p.,Min.
10644	Kenilworth	P	Awd.,Min.
10645	Keresley	H	Min.
10646	Atherstone on Stour	P	Rep. 1844
10647	Barston	P	Rep. 1840
10648	Farnborough	P	Rep. 1840
10649	Kingsbury	P	Awd.,Min.
10650	Kingston or Chesterton	T	Awd.,Min.
10651	Knowle	H	Rep. 1839
10652	Lambcote	H	Awd.,Min.
10653	Lapworth	P	Min.,Rep. 1838
10654	Ladbrooke	P	Rep. 1837
10655	Lawford Little	T	Awd.,Min.
10656	Kineton	P	Awd.,Min.
10657	Leamington Priors	P	Awd.,Min.
10658	Leamington Hastings	P	Awd.,Min.,Rep. 1838
10659	Lawford Long	H	Awd.,Rep. 1839
10660	Lea Marston	P	N.t.p.,Min.
10661	Leek Wootton	P	Awd.,Min.
10662	Lighthorne	P	Rep. 1838
10663	Lillington	P	Rep. 1838
10664	Loxley	P	Awd.,Min.
10665	Luddington and Dodwell	H	N.t.p.,Min.
10666	Mancetter	P	N.t.p.,Min.
10667	Marton	P	N.t.p.
10668	Maxstoke	P	Awd.,Min.
10669	Merevale	P	N.t.p.,Min.
10670	Meriden	P	N.t.p.,Min.
10671	Middleton	P	N.t.p.
10672	Milverton	P	Awd.,Min.
10673	Monks Kirby Etc.	T	Agrmt.,Rep. 1839
10674	Morton Bagott	P	N.t.p.
10675	Morton Morrell	P	Awd.,Min.
10676	Napton on the Hill	P	Min.
10677	Newbold	T	Awd.,Min.
10678	Newbold Pacey	P	Awd.,Min.
10679	Newnham Regis	P	Awd.,Min.
10680	Newton and Biggin	T	Awd.,Min.
10681	Newton Regis	P	N.t.p.
10682	Nuneaton	P	Rep. 1841
10683	Newbold Revel	T	Agrmt.,Rep. 1839
10684	Nuthurst	P	Rep. 1839
10685	Offchurch	P	Awd.,Min.
10686	Oversley	H	Awd.,Min.
10687	Oxhill	P	N.t.p.,Min.
10688	Packington Little	P	N.t.p.
10689	Packington Great	P	Rep. 1840
10690	Packwood	P	Rep. 1838
10691	Pailton	H	Rep. 1840
10692	Perry Crofts	D	Min.
10693	Pillerton Mersey	P	N.t.p.,Min.
10694	Pinley	EP	N.t.p.,Min.
10695	Pooley	H	Awd.,Min.
10696	Preston Bagott	P	Rep. 1838
10697	Princethorpe	T	Awd.,Min.
10698	Hardwick Priors	P	Min.
10699	Priors Marston	P	Awd.,Min.
10700	Polesworth	H	Awd.,Min.

Warwickshire contd.

10701	Radbourne	P	Awd.,Min.
10702	Radford Semele	P	Awd.,Rep. 1841
10703	Radway	P	Min.
10704	Ratley	T	Awd.,Min.
10705	Rowington	P	Awd.,Min.
10706	Rugby	P	N.t.p.,Min.
10707	Ryton upon Dunsmoor	P	N.t.p.
10708	Salford Priors	P	Awd.,Min.
10709	Seckington	P	Rep. 1842
10710	Salford Abbots	T	Awd.,Min.
10711	Southam	P	N.t.p.,Min.
10712	Stockton	P	N.t.p.
10713	Sheldon	P	Rep. 1838
10714	Sherbourne	P	N.t.p.
10715	Shilton	P	Min.,Rep. 1840
10716	Shotteswell	P	N.t.p.,Min.
10717	Shuckborough Lower,Upper	P	N.t.p.,Min.
10718	Shustoke	P	Rep. 1838
10719	Shuttington	P	N.t.p.
10720	Snitterfield	P	Rep. 1839
10721	Solihull	P	Agrmt.,Rep. 1837
10722	Sow	P	Rep. 1842
10723	Spernall	P	Agrmt.,Rep. 1838
10724	Strivichall	H	N.t.p.
10725	Stoke City of Coventry	P	Rep. 1840
10726	Stoneleigh	P	Rep. 1843
10727	Stratford Old	BP	Awd.,Min.
10728	Stretton Baskerville	P	Awd.,Min.
10729	Stretton upon Dunsmore	P	Awd.,Min.
10730	Stretton on the Fosse	P	Agrmt.,Min.
10731	Studley	P	Awd.,Min.
10732	Syerscote	T	N.t.p.,Min.
10733	Sutton Coldfield	P	Awd.,Min.
10734	Bishops Tachbrooke	P	Awd.,Min.
10735	Tamworth	B	Min.
10736	Tamworth Castle	L	Awd.,Min.
10737	Tanworth	P	Rep. 1838
10738	Thornton	H	Awd.,Min.
10739	Tysoe	P	Awd.,Min.
10740	Ufton	P	Rep. 1840
10741	Upton	T	Awd.,Min.
10742	Walton D'Eville and Maudit	T	Agrmt.,Rep. 1839
10743	Warmington	P	Rep. 1840
10744	Warton	T	Awd.,Min.
10745	Warwick St Mary	P	Awd.,Min.
10746	Warwick St Nicholas	P	Awd.,Min.
10747	Wasperton	P	Rep. 1840
10748	Watergall	EP	N.t.p.
10749	Weddington	P	Rep. 1839
10750	Weethley	T	Rep. 1839
10751	Welford	P	Rep. 1839
10752	Wellesbourne Hastings	H	N.t.p.,Min.
10753	Weston under Weatherley	P	N.t.p.,Min.
10754	Wellesbourne Mountford	T	Awd.,Min.
10755	Whatcott	P	N.t.p.
10756	Whateley	D	Agrmt.
10757	Whateley	D	Awd.,Min.
10758	Whichford	P	N.t.p.
10759	Whitacre Nether	P	N.t.p.
10760	Whitacre Over	P	Min.
10761	Whitchurch	P	Agrmt.,Rep. 1842
10762	Whitnash	P	Agrmt.,Rep. 1837
10763	Wibtoft	H	Awd.,Min.
10764	Willenhall	T	N.t.p.
10765	Willey	P	N.t.p.,Min.
10766	Willington	H	Rep. 1839
10767	Wishaw	P	Min.
10768	Withybrook	P	Awd.,Min.
10769	Wolfhamcote	P	Awd.,Min.
10770	Wolford Great	P	Rep. 1845
10771	Wolford Little	H	Rep. 1839
10772	Wolford Little	H	Awd.
10773	Wolston and Marston	T	Awd.,Min.
10774	Wolverton	P	Awd.,Min.
10775	Wormleighton	P	N.t.p.
10776	Wilmcote	H	N.t.p.,Min.
10777	Wolvey	P	Awd.,Min.
10778	Wootton Waiven	P	Min.,Rep. 1838
10779	Wroxhall	P	N.t.p.,Min.
10780	Wyken	P	Awd.,Min.
12924	Wappenbury	P	Awd.,Min.

Westmorland

10781	Ambleside Above Stock	T	Agrmt.,Min.,Rep. 1838
10782	Ambleside Below Stock	T	Agrmt.,Rep. 1838
10783	Appleby	T	Awd.,Min.
10784	Applethwaite	T	Agrmt.,Min.,Rep. 1838
10785	Asby	P	Awd.,Min.
10786	Askham	P	Rep. 1838
10787	Bampton	P	Min.,Rep. 1838
10788	Barbon	T	Agrmt.,Min.,Rep. 1840
10789	Barton High	T	Min.,Rep. 1839
10790	Beetham	T	Awd.,Min.,Rep. 1839
10791	Birkbeck Fells	T	Agrmt.,Min.,Rep. 1839
10792	Bleatarn	T	Awd.,Min.
10793	Bolton	T	N.t.p.,Min.
10794	Bondgate	T	Awd.,Min.
10795	Brampton	P	Min.,Rep. 1841
10796	Bretherdale	T	Agrmt.,Min.,Rep. 1839
10797	Brough	T	Awd.,Min.
10798	Brough Sowerby	T	Awd.,Min.
10799	Brougham	P	Rep. 1839
10800	Burralls	T	Awd.,Min.
10801	Burton	T	Awd.,Min.
10802	Burton in Kendal	T	Awd.,Min.
10803	Casterton	T	Agrmt.,Rep. 1843
10804	Cliburn	P	Awd.,Min.
10805	Clifton	P	N.t.p.,Min.
10806	Colby	T	Awd.,Min.
10807	Crackenthorpe	T	Awd.,Min.
10808	Crosby Garrett	T	Awd.,Min.
10809	Crosby Ravensworth	P	Agrmt.,Awd.,Min.
10810	Drybeck	T	Awd.,Min.
10811	Dufton	P	Awd.,Min.
10812	Farleton	T	Min.,Rep. 1839
10813	Firbank	T	Min.,Rep. 1841
10814	Grasmere	T	Agrmt.,Min.,Rep. 1838
10815	Hartley	T	Awd.,Min.
10816	Hartsop and Patterdale	T	Rep. 1839
10817	Haverbrack	T	Agrmt.,Rep. 1838
10818	Hardendale	T	Rep. 1838
10819	Heversham	P	Awd.,Min.
10820	Hilbeck	T	Awd.,Min.
10821	Hilton	T	Min.,Rep. 1839
10822	Hoffe	T	N.t.p.,Min.
10823	Holme	T	Awd.,Min.
10824	Holmescales	H	Awd.,Min.
10825	Hutton Roof	T	Awd.,Min.
10826	Kaber	T	Agrmt.,Awd.,Min.
10827	Kendal	P	Awd.,Min.
10828	Killington	T	Min.,Rep. 1841
10829	Kings Meaburn	T	Awd.,Min.
10830	Kirby Thore	T	N.t.p.,Min.
10831	Kirkby Longsdale	T	Awd.,Min.
10832	Kirkby Stephen	T	Agrmt.,Awd.,Min.
10833	Knock	T	N.t.p.,Min.
10834	Langdale	T	Rep. 1838
10835	Langdale	T	Awd.,Min.
10836	Lowther	P	Rep. 1837
10837	Lupton	T	Awd.,Min.
10838	Mallerstang	T	Agrmt.,Awd.,Min.
10839	Mansergh	T	Awd.,Min.
10840	Martindale	T	Min.,Rep. 1838
10841	Marton Long	T	Agrmt.,Rep. 1838
10842	Meathop and Ulpha	T	Awd.,Min.
10843	Middleton	T	Agrmt.,Rep. 1842
10844	Milburne	T	Min.,Rep. 1839
10845	Morland	T	N.t.p.
10846	Murton	T	Min.,Rep. 1839
10847	Musgrave Great	P	Awd.,Min.
10848	Musgrave Little	T	Awd.,Min.
10849	Nateby	T	Agrmt.,Awd.,Min.
10850	Newbiggin	P	Awd.,Min.
10851	Newby	T	Min.,Rep. 1839
10852	Ormside Great	T	Awd.,Min.
10853	Orton and Raisebeck	T	Min.,Rep. 1840
10854	Preston Patrick	T	Awd.,Min.
10855	Ravenstonedale	P	N.t.p.,Min.
10856	Rosegill	T	Agrmt.,Min.,Rep. 1838
10857	Rydal and Loughrigg	T	Agrmt.,Min.,Rep. 1838
10858	Sandford	T	Awd.,Min.
10859	Scattergate	T	Awd.,Min.
10860	Sleagill	T	N.t.p.,Min.
10861	Smardale	T	Agrmt.,Min.,Rep. 1839
10862	Sockbridge	T	Rep. 1839
10863	Soulby	T	Agrmt.,Awd.
10864	Stainmoor	T	Awd.,Min.
10865	Strickland Great	T	Rep. 1838
10866	Strickland Little	T	Awd.,Min.
10867	Tebay	T	Agrmt.,Rep. 1839
10868	Temple Sowerby	T	Agrmt.,Min.,Rep. 1838
10869	Thrimby	T	Rep. 1839
10870	Troutbeck	T	Agrmt.,Min.,Rep. 1839
10871	Undermilbeck	T	Agrmt.,Min.,Rep. 1838
10872	Waitby	T	Agrmt.,Awd.,Min.
10873	Warcop	T	N.t.p.,Awd.,Min.
10874	Wharton	T	Agrmt.,Awd.,Min.
10875	Witherslack	T	Awd.,Min.
10876	Winder Low	T	Min.,Rep. 1839
10877	Winton	T	Agrmt.,Awd.,Min.,Rep. 1839
10878	Yanwath	T	Awd.,Min.

Wiltshire

10879	Aldbourn	P	Agrmt.,Min.,Rep. 1837
10880	Alderbury	P	Awd.,Min.
10881	Alderton	P	Agrmt.,Min.,Rep. 1839
10882	Allcannings	P	Min.
10883	Allenford Farm	EP	N.t.p.

Wiltshire contd.

10884	Allington	I	Min.,Rep. 1839
10885	Allington	P	Awd.,Min.
10886	Alton Barnes	P	Agrmt.,Min.,Rep. 1839
10887	Alton Priors	P	Awd.,Min.
10888	Alvediston	P	Awd.,Min.
10889	Amesbury	P	Awd.,Min.
10890	Anstey	P	N.t.p.,Min.
10891	Berwick St James	P	Min.,Rep. 1843
10892	Ashley	P	Min.,Rep. 1838
10893	Ashton Keynes	P	N.t.p.,Min.
10894	Ashton West	P	Agrmt.,Min.,Rep. 1838
10895	Avebury	P	Awd.,Min.
10896	Baverstock	P	Agrmt.,Rep. 1839
10897	Barford St Martin	P	Min.,Rep. 1840
10898	Baydon	P	Awd.,Min.
10899	Bedwin Great	P	Awd.,Min.,Rep. 1848
10900	Bedwin Little	P	Agrmt.,Min.,Rep. 1841
10901	Beechingstoke	P	Agrmt.,Min.,Rep. 1838
10902	Berwick Basset	P	Awd.,Min.
10903	Berwick St John	P	Min.,Rep. 1840
10904	Berwick St Leonard	P	N.t.p.,Min.
10905	Biddestone St Nicholas	P	Min.,Rep. 1839
10906	Biddestone St Peter	P	Min.,Rep. 1839
10907	Bishops Cannings	P	Awd.,Min.
10908	Bishops Cannings St James	PC	Awd.,Min.
10909	Bishopstrow	P	Rep. 1839
10910	Bishopstone	P	Agrmt.,Min.,Rep. 1838
10911	Blackland	P	Awd.,Min.
10912	Blagden	EP	Awd.,Min.
10913	Blunsden St Andrew	P	Agrmt.,Rep. 1837
10914	Boscombe	P	Awd.,Min.
10915	Bower Chalke	P	Awd.,Min.
10916	Bowood	L	Awd.,Min.
10917	Box	P	Min.,Rep. 1838
10918	Boyton	P	Awd.,Min.
10919	Bradford	P	Min.,Rep. 1840
10920	Bradley North	P	Awd.,Min.
10921	Bradon	T	Rep. 1838
10922	Bremhill	P	Awd.,Min.
10923	Bremilham	P	Rep. 1838
10924	Brinkworth	P	Agrmt.,Awd.,Min.
10925	Britford	P	Agrmt.,Min.,Rep. 1838
10926	Brixton Deverell	P	Agrmt.,Rep. 1838
10927	Broad Chalke	P	Awd.,Min.
10928	Broad Hinton	P	Awd.,Min.
10929	Bromham	P	Min.,Rep. 1843
10930	Broughton Gifford	P	Min.,Rep. 1840
10931	Bulford	P	Agrmt.,Min.,Rep. 1838
10932	Bulkington	I	Min.,Rep. 1839
10933	Burbage	P	Awd.,Min.
10934	Burcombe South	P	Min.
10935	Buttermere	P	Min.,Rep. 1839
10936	Calne	P	Awd.,Min.
10937	Calstone Wellington	P	Awd.,Min.
10938	Castle Combe	P	Awd.,Min.
10939	Castle Eaton	P	Min.,Rep. 1839
10940	Chalfield Great	P	Agrmt.,Min.,Rep. 1837
10941	Chalfield Little	EP	N.t.p.
10942	Charlton	P	Awd.,Min.
10943	Charlton Brokenborough	P	Agrmt.,Min.
10944	Cherhill	P	Awd.,Min.
10945	Cheriton with	P	Awd.,Min.
10946	Cheverell Great and Little	P	N.t.p.,Min.
10947	Chicklade	P	Min.,Rep. 1838
10948	Chilmark	P	Min.,Rep. 1839
10949	Chilton Folliott	P	N.t.p.,Min.
10950	Chippenham	P	Awd.,Min.
10951	Chiseldon	P	Awd.,Min.
10952	Chisenbury de la Folly	I	N.t.p.,Min.
10953	Chisenbury East	I	Awd.,Min.
10954	Chitterne All Saints	P	Min.,Rep. 1840
10955	Chitterne St Mary	P	Agrmt.,Min.,Rep. 1841
10956	Chittoe	T	Awd.,Min.
10957	Cholderton	P	Awd.,Min.
10958	Christian Malford	P	Agrmt.,Min.,Rep. 1838
10959	Chute	P	Awd.,Min.
10960	Chute Forest, East and West	EP	Agrmt.,Min.,Rep. 1839
10961	Clarendon	EP	Awd.,Min.
10962	Clatford	I	Awd.,Rep. 1840
10963	Cliffe Pypard	P	Min.
10964	Coate	I	Awd.,Min.
10965	Codford St Mary	P	Awd.,Min.
10966	Codford St Peter	P	Awd.,Min.
10967	Colerne	P	N.t.p.,Min.
10968	Collingbourne Ducis	P	Min.,Rep. 1845
10969	Collingbourne Kingston	P	Awd.,Min.
10970	Compton	I	N.t.p.,Min.
10971	Compton Bassett	P	Agrmt.,Min.,Rep. 1838
10972	Compton Chamberlain	P	Awd.,Min.
10973	Coombe	I	Awd.,Min.
10974	Coombe Bissett	P	Min.,Rep. 1839
10975	Corsley	P	Awd.,Min.
10976	Corsham	P	Agrmt.,Min.,Rep. 1836
10977	Coulston	P	Agrmt.,Min.,Rep. 1839
10978	Cricklade St Sampson	P	Awd.,Min.
10979	Cricklade St Mary	P	Awd.,Min.
10980	Crudwell	P	Awd.,Min.,Rep. 1838
10981	Damerham South	P	Min.,Rep. 1845
10982	Dauntsey	P	Min.,Rep. 1839
10983	Dean West	P	Awd.,Min.
10984	Devizes St John	P	Agrmt.,Min.,Rep. 1839
10985	Dinton	P	Awd.,Min.,Rep. 1840
10986	Ditteridge	P	Agrmt.,Min.,Rep. 1838
10987	Donhead St Andrew	P	Awd.,Min.
10988	Donhead St Mary	P	Awd.,Min.
10989	Downton	P	Agrmt.,Min.,Rep. 1838
10990	Draycot Cerne	P	Min.,Rep. 1839
10991	Draycott Foliatt	P	Agrmt.,Rep. 1839
10992	Durnford	P	Min.,Rep. 1840
10993	Durrington	P	Min.,Rep. 1839
10994	Earldoms	EP	N.t.p.
10995	Easterton	I	Min.,Rep. 1839
10996	Earl Stoke	P	N.t.p.,Min.
10997	Easton Grey	P	Rep. 1838
10998	Ebbesborne Wake	P	Min.,Rep. 1843
10999	Edington	P	Awd.,Min.
11000	Eisey	P	Awd.,Min.
11001	Enford	I	Awd.,Min.
11002	Everleigh	P	Rep. 1841
11003	Fifield Brabant	P	Awd.,Min.
11004	Figheldean	P	Min.,Rep. 1839
11005	Fisherton	P	Awd.,Min.
11006	Fisherton de la Mere	P	Agrmt.,Rep. 1838
11007	Fittleton	P	Agrmt.,Min.,Rep. 1838
11008	Fonthill Bishop	P	Agrmt.,Min.,Rep. 1837
11009	Fonthill Gifford	P	Min.,Rep. 1840
11010	Fovant	P	Agrmt.,Min.,Rep. 1839
11011	Foxley	P	Agrmt.,Rep. 1841
11012	Froxfield	P	Awd.,Min.
11013	Frugglestone St Peter	P	Min.,Rep. 1840
11014	Garsdon	P	Min.,Rep. 1839
11015	Grinstead East	P	Awd.,Min.
11016	Grinstead West	P	Agrmt.,Min.,Rep. 1837
11017	Grittleton	P	Min.,Rep. 1838
11018	Ham	P	Rep. 1838
11019	Hankerton	P	Min.,Rep. 1841
11020	Hannington	P	Agrmt.,Rep. 1839
11021	Hardenhuish	P	Agrmt.,Min.,Rep. 1838
11022	Harnham West	P	Awd.,Min.
11023	Heddington	P	Agrmt.,Min.,Rep. 1841
11024	Heytesbury	P	N.t.p.,Min.
11025	Highway	P	Rep. 1839
11026	Highworth	P	Min.,Rep. 1838
11027	Hilperton	P	Agrmt.,Min.,Rep. 1837
11028	Hill Deverill	P	Awd.,Min.
11029	Hillmarton	P	Rep. 1842
11030	Hinton Parva	P	Min.,Rep. 1840
11031	Hinton	I	Min.,Rep. 1841
11032	Hindon	P	Awd.,Min.
11033	Hipperscomb	EP	Awd.,Min.
11034	Holdfast	H	N.t.p.,Min.
11035	Homington	P	Awd.,Min.
11036	Horningsham	P	Awd.,Min.
11037	Hullavington	P	Min.,Rep. 1841
11038	Idmiston	P	Awd.,Min.
11039	Imber	P	Min.,Rep. 1838
11040	Inglesham	P	Awd.,Min.
11041	Keevil	M	N.t.p.,Min.
11042	Kelloways	P	Agrmt.,Rep. 1839
11043	Kemble	P	N.t.p.,Min.
11044	Kennett East	P	Rep. 1838
11045	Kingswood	P	N.t.p.,Min.
11046	Kington Deverill	P	N.t.p.,Min.
11047	Kington St Michael	P	Awd.,Min.
11048	Kington West	P	Awd.,Min.
11049	Knook	P	N.t.p.,Min.
11050	Knoyle East	P	Rep. 1838
11051	Knoyle West	P	Min.,Rep. 1839
11052	Lacock	P	Agrmt.,Min.,Rep. 1837
11053	Lake	I	Awd.,Min.
11054	Landford	P	Agrmt.,Min.,Rep. 1839
11055	Langdon Wyke	I	Awd.,Min.
11056	Langford Little	P	Agrmt.,Rep. 1838
11057	Langley Burrell	P	Awd.,Min.
11058	Avon	P	Awd.,Min.
11059	Huish	P	Rep. 1839
11060	Ashton Steeple	I	Min.,Rep. 1841
11061	Lavington East	I	Awd.,Min.
11062	Lavington West	P	Min.,Rep. 1838
11063	Latton	P	N.t.p.,Min.
11064	Laverstock	P	Agrmt.,Min.,Rep. 1841
11065	Lea and Cleverton	P	Min.,Rep. 1840
11066	Leigh	H	Min.,Rep. 1840
11067	Leigh de la Mere	P	Awd.,Min.
11068	Liddington	P	Min.,Rep. 1840
11069	Littlecot	I	Rep. 1840
11070	Littleton Drew	P	Agrmt.,Min.,Rep. 1838
11071	Longbridge Deverill	P	Agrmt.,Min.,Rep. 1838
11072	Longstreet	I	Awd.,Min.
11073	Luckington	P	Min.,Rep. 1839
11074	Ludgershall	P	Min.
11075	Lydiard Millicent	P	Min.,Rep. 1839

Wiltshire contd.

11076	Lydiard Tregoze	P	Agrmt.,Min.,Rep. 1839
11077	Lyneham	P	Awd.,Min.
11078	Maddington	P	Awd.,Min.
11079	Maiden Bradley	P	Awd.,Min.
11080	Malmsbury	P	Min.,Rep. 1840
11081	Manningford Abbots	P	Awd.,Min.
11082	Manningford Bohun	P	Min.,Rep. 1839
11083	Manningford Bruce	P	Agrmt.,Rep. 1838
11084	Manton and Elcot	D	Awd.,Min.
11085	Marden	P	Agrmt.,Rep. 1839
11086	Marlborough St Mary	P	Awd.,Min.
11087	Marlborough St Peter	P	Awd.,Min.
11088	Marston Maisey	P	Min.,Rep. 1839
11089	Martin	P	Min.,Rep. 1845
11090	Melksham	P	Min.,Rep. 1836
11091	Mere	P	Awd.,Min.
11092	Milford	D	Awd.,Min.
11093	Milston cum Brigmerston	P	Min.,Rep. 1840
11094	Milton Lilbourne	P	Awd.,Min.
11095	Mildenhall	P	Agrmt.,Min.,Rep. 1838
11096	Monkton Farleigh	P	Agrmt.,Rep. 1842
11097	Monkton Deverill	P	Agrmt.,Rep. 1838
11098	Netheravon	P	N.t.p.,Min.
11099	Netherhampton	P	Agrmt.,Min.,Rep. 1844
11100	Nettleton	P	Min.,Rep. 1838
11101	Newnton Long	P	Min.,Rep. 1838
11102	Newnton North and Hilcott	P	Min.,Rep. 1839
11103	Newton South	P	Awd.,Min.
11104	Newton Toney	P	Agrmt.,Rep. 1839
11105	No Man's Land	EP	N.t.p.
11106	Norton Bavant	P	Awd.,Min.
11107	Norton Coleparle	P	Rep. 1840
11108	Nunton and Bodenham	P	N.t.p.
11109	Oaksey	P	Awd.,Min.
11110	Odstock	P	N.t.p.,Min.
11111	Ogbourn St Andrew	P	Min.,Rep. 1839
11112	Ogbourn St George	P	Awd.,Min.
11113	Orcheston St Mary	P	Agrmt.,Rep. 1838
11114	Overton	P	N.t.p.,Min.
11115	Patney	P	N.t.p.,Min.
11116	Pertwood	P	Agrmt.,Rep. 1838
11117	Pewsey	P	Agrmt.,Min.,Rep. 1838
11118	Pewsham	H	Min.
11119	Pitton and Farley	P	Min.,Rep. 1839
11120	Plaitford	P	Min.,Rep. 1843
11121	Polshot	P	Agrmt.,Min.,Rep. 1837
11122	Poole Keynes	P	N.t.p.,Min.
11123	Potterne	P	Agrmt.,Min.,Rep. 1839
11124	Poulton	P	N.t.p.,Min.
11125	Purton	P	Agrmt.,Min.,Rep. 1838
11126	Ramsbury	P	Agrmt.,Min.,Rep. 1841
11127	Rodborne Cheney	P	Awd.,Min.
11128	Rollestone	P	Rep. 1839
11129	Rowde	P	Min.,Rep. 1840
11130	Rushall	P	Awd.,Min.
11131	St Thomas (Salisbury)	P	N.t.p.,Min.
11132	St Edmund (Salisbury)	P	N.t.p.,Min.
11133	St Martin (Salisbury)	P	Awd.,Min.
11134	Savernake	L	
11135	Seagry	P	Min.,Rep. 1840
11136	Sedghill	P	Agrmt.,Rep. 1837
11137	Semington	C	Agrmt.,Min.,Rep. 1838
11138	Semley	P	Min.,Rep. 1838
11139	Shalbourn	P	Agrmt.,Awd.,Min.,Rep. 1840
11140	Shaw	I	Min.,Rep. 1841
11141	Sherrington	P	Min.
11142	Sherston Magna	P	Min.,Rep. 1839
11143	Sherston Parva	P	Agrmt.,Min.,Rep. 1842
11144	Shorncote	P	Agrmt.,Rep. 1840
11145	Shrewton	P	Agrmt.,Min.,Rep. 1838
11146	Somerford Great	P	N.t.p.,Min.
11147	Somerford Keynes	P	N.t.p.,Min.
11148	Somerford Little	P	Awd.,Min.
11149	Sopworth	P	Rep. 1838
11150	Standlinch	P	Min.,Rep. 1840
11151	Stanley and Nethermore	I	Awd.,Min.
11152	Stanton St Quintin	P	N.t.p.,Min.
11153	Stapleford	P	Awd.,Min.
11154	Staunton St Bernard	P	Min.,Rep. 1845
11155	Steeple Langford	P	Agrmt.,Min.,Rep. 1838
11156	Stert	I	Awd.,Min.
11157	Stratton St Margaret	P	N.t.p.,Min.
11158	Stockton	P	N.t.p.,Min.
11159	Stourton	P	Agrmt.,Min.,Rep. 1839
11160	Stanton Fitzwarren	P	Awd.,Min.
11161	Stratford Tony	P	Agrmt.,Rep. 1838
11162	Stratford	P	Agrmt.,Min.,Rep. 1839
11163	Sutton Benger	P	Min.,Rep. 1839
11164	Sutton Mandeville	P	Agrmt.,Rep. 1838
11165	Sutton Veny	P	N.t.p.,Min.
11166	Swallowclift	P	Awd.,Min.
11167	Swallowfield	P	Min.,Rep. 1841
11168	Swindon	P	Awd.,Min.
11169	Tedworth North	P	Rep. 1839
11170	Teffont Evias	P	Awd.,Min.
11171	Tidcombe	P	Rep. 1839
11172	Tilshead	P	Awd.,Min.
11173	Tisbury	P	Agrmt.,Min.,Rep. 1838
11174	Tockenham	P	Agrmt.,Rep. 1838
11175	Tollard Royal	P	Agrmt.,Min.,Rep. 1838
11176	Trowbridge	P	Agrmt.,Min.,Rep. 1837
11177	Tytherton Lucas	I	Min.,Rep. 1838
11178	Whiteparish	P	Min.,Rep. 1840
11179	Uffcott	I	N.t.p.,Min.
11180	Uphaven	P	Agrmt.,Rep. 1839
11181	Upton Lovell	P	Agrmt.,Rep. 1838
11182	Uptonscudamore	P	Min.,Rep. 1838
11183	Urchfont	P	Agrmt.,Min.,Rep. 1841
11184	Wanborough	P	Awd.,Min.
11185	Warminster	P	Awd.,Min.
11186	Wellow West	P	Agrmt.,Min.,Rep. 1837
11187	Westbury	P	Agrmt.,Min.,Rep. 1840
11188	Westwood	P	Awd.,Min.
11189	Whaddon	P	Agrmt.,Rep. 1839
11190	Wick	I	Min.
11191	Widhill	I	Agrmt.,Rep. 1838
11192	Wilcot	P	Agrmt.,Min.,Rep. 1838
11193	Wilsford	P	Awd.,Min.
11194	Wilsford	P	Awd.,Min.
11195	Wilton	P	Agrmt.,Min.,Rep. 1844
11196	Wily	P	Min.,Rep. 1838
11197	Wingfield	P	Agrmt.,Min.,Rep. 1839
11198	Winterbourne Basset	P	Rep. 1840
11199	Winterbourne Dauntsey	P	Awd.,Min.
11200	Winterbourne Earls	P	Agrmt.,Min.,Rep. 1839
11201	Winterbourne Gunner	P	Min.,Rep. 1840
11202	Winterbourne Monckton	P	N.t.p.,Min.
11203	Winterbourne Stoke	P	Min.,Rep. 1839
11204	Winterslow	P	Agrmt.,Awd.,Min.
11205	Wishford Magna	P	Agrmt.,Min.,Rep. 1838
11206	Woodborough	P	Agrmt.,Min.,Rep. 1838
11207	Woodford	P	Awd.,Min.
11208	Wooton Bassett	P	Agrmt.,Min.,Rep. 1840
11209	Wootton Rivers	P	Min.,Rep. 1838
11210	Wraxall North	P	Agrmt.,Min.,Rep. 1837
11211	Wroughton	P	Awd.,Min.
11212	Yatesbury	P	Min.,Rep. 1840
11213	Yatton Keynell	P	Awd.,Min.
11353	Orcheston St George	P	Agrmt.,Min.,Rep. 1838

Worcestershire

11214	Abberley	P	Min.,Rep. 1842
11215	Abberton	P	Rep. 1844
11216	Abbots Lench	H	Awd.,Min.
11217	Abbots Morton	P	N.t.p.
11218	Acton Beauchamp	P	Min.,Rep. 1840
11219	Alderminster	P	Min.
11220	Alfrick	H	Min.,Rep. 1838
11221	Alvechurch	P	Awd.,Min.
11222	Areley Kings	P	Awd.,Min.
11223	Astley	P	Min.,Rep. 1839
11224	Aston	H	Min.,Rep. 1840
11225	Atch Lench	H	Awd.,Min.
11226	Badsey	P	N.t.p.,Min.
11227	Bayton	P	N.t.p.,Min.
11228	Bedwardine St John	P	Awd.,Min.
11229	Bedwardine St Michael	P	Awd.,Min.
11230	Bellbroughton	P	Awd.,Min.
11231	Bengeworth	P	N.t.p.,Min.
11232	Beoley	P	Min.,Rep. 1841
11233	Berrington	T	Awd.,Min.
11234	Berrow	P	Awd.,Min.
11235	Besford	P	Min.
11236	Bewdley	H	Awd.,Min.
11237	Birtsmorton	P	Min.,Rep. 1839
11238	Bishampton	P	Awd.,Min.
11239	The Blockhouse	EP	N.t.p.
11240	Blockley	P	Awd.,Min.
11241	Bockleton	P	Awd.,Min.
11242	Bredicot	P	Awd.,Min.
11243	Bromsgrove	P	Min.,Rep. 1839
11244	Birlingham	H	Awd.,Min.
11245	Bredon	P	N.t.p.,Min.
11246	Bretforton	P	Min.
11247	Brickhampton	P	N.t.p.,Min.
11248	Broadwas	P	Min.,Rep. 1839
11249	Broadway	P	N.t.p.,Min.
11250	Broughton Hackett	P	N.t.p.,Min.
11251	Chaceley	P	Rep. 1840
11252	Chaddesley Corbett	P	Min.,Rep. 1839
11253	Church Honeybourne	P	Awd.,Min.
11254	Churchill	P	Min.,Rep. 1839
11255	Cleeve Prior	P	N.t.p.,Min.
11256	Claines	P	Awd.,Min.
11257	Clifton upon Teme	P	Rep. 1844
11258	Cofton Hackett	P	Min.,Rep. 1838
11259	Comberton Great,Little	P	N.t.p.,Min.
11260	Cotheridge	P	Awd.,Min.
11261	Cutsden	H	Awd.,Min.
11262	Cradley	T	Awd.,Min.

Worcestershire contd.

11263	Crome D'Abitot	P	Awd.,Min.
11264	Crome Earls	P	Rep. 1838
11265	Croome Hill	P	Min.,Rep. 1839
11266	Cropthorne	P	Awd.,Min.
11267	Crowle	P	N.t.p.,Min.
11268	Daylesford	P	Agrmt.,Min.,Rep. 1841
11269	Defford	C	Awd.,Min.
11270	Ditchford	H	Awd.,Min.
11271	Dodenham	P	Agrmt.,Awd.,Min.,Rep. 1839
11272	Dodderhill	P	Awd.,Min.
11273	Dormstone	P	N.t.p.,Min.
11274	Dorn	H	Awd.,Min.
11275	Doverdale	P	Min.,Rep. 1838
11276	Droitwich St Andrew	P	Min.,Rep. 1838
11277	Droitwich St Nicholas	P	Min.,Rep. 1838
11278	Droitwich St Peter	P	Min.,Rep. 1840
11279	Dudley	P	N.t.p.,Min.
11280	Eastham	P	Awd.,Min.
11281	Eckington	P	N.t.p.,Min.
11282	Edwin Loach	P	Awd.,Min.
11283	Eldersfield	P	Min.,Rep. 1841
11284	Elmbridge	C	Awd.,Min.
11285	Elmley Castle	P	Awd.,Min.
11286	Elmley Lovett	P	Awd.,Min.
11287	Evenlode	P	Agrmt.,Rep. 1839
11288	Evesham All Saints	P	N.t.p.,Min.
11289	Evesham St Lawrence	P	N.t.p.,Min.
11290	Feckenham	P	Min.,Rep. 1839
11291	Fladbury	H	N.t.p.,Min.
11292	Flyford Flavell	P	N.t.p.,Min.
11293	Frankley	P	Min.,Rep. 1840
11294	Grafton Flyford	P	N.t.p.,Min.
11295	Grimley	P	Min.,Rep. 1838
11296	Hadsor	P	N.t.p.,Min.
11297	Hagley	P	Agrmt.,Min.,Rep. 1837
11298	Hallow	P	Awd.,Min.
11299	Hampton Great and Little	P	N.t.p.,Min.
11300	Hampton Lovett	P	Min.,Rep. 1838
11301	Hanbury	P	Min.,Rep. 1838
11302	Hanley Castle	P	N.t.p.,Min.
11303	Hanley Child	H	Agrmt.,Min.,Rep. 1840
11304	Hanley William	P	Agrmt.,Min.,Rep. 1839
11305	Hartlebury	P	Min.,Rep. 1838
11306	Harvington	P	N.t.p.,Min.
11307	Hill and Moor	H	N.t.p.,Min.
11308	Hillhampton	H	Rep. 1840
11309	Himbleton	P	N.t.p.,Min.
11310	Hindlip	P	Rep. 1838
11311	Holt with Little Witley	P	Min.,Rep. 1838
11312	Huddington	P	N.t.p.
11313	Hurcott and Comberton	H	Agrmt.,Min.,Rep. 1841
11314	Iccomb	P	N.t.p.,Min.
11315	Inkberrow	P	Min.,Rep. 1839
11316	Kempsey	P	Min.,Rep. 1839
11317	Kenswick	D	N.t.p.,Min.
11318	Kidderminster	B	Min.,Rep. 1842
11319	Kidderminster	D	Awd.,Min.
11320	Knightwick	P	Awd.,Min.,Rep. 1839
11321	Kington	P	Rep. 1839
11322	Kyre or Kyre Wyard	P	Agrmt.,Rep. 1839
11323	Leigh	P	Min.,Rep. 1838
11324	Church Lench	T	Rep. 1839
11325	Lindridge	P	Agrmt.,Min.,Rep. 1839
11326	Littleton South	P	Agrmt.,Awd.,Min.,Rep. 1839
11327	Longdon	P	Awd.,Min.
11328	Luttley	T	Awd.,Min.
11329	Lulsley	H	Min.,Rep. 1838
11330	Madresfield	P	Agrmt.,Min.,Rep. 1840
11331	Malvern Little and Welland	D	Awd.,Min.
11332	Malvern Little	P	Awd.,Min.
11333	Malvern Great	P	Awd.,Min.
11334	Mamble	P	Agrmt.,Rep. 1838
11335	Martin Hussingtree	P	Min.,Rep. 1840
11336	Castle Morton	P	Min.,Rep. 1838
11337	Martley	P	Min.,Rep. 1843
11338	Mathon	P	Min.,Rep. 1840
11339	Lower Mitton	H	Awd.,Min.
11340	Naunton Beauchamp	P	N.t.p.,Min.
11341	Newbold upon Stour	P	Agrmt.,Min.,Rep. 1840
11342	Newland	H	Min.,Rep. 1842
11343	Northfield	P	Min.,Rep. 1839
11344	Northwick	H	Awd.,Min.
11345	Norton by Bredon	H	N.t.p.,Min.
11346	Norton juxta Kempsey	P	Min.,Rep. 1841
11347	King's Norton	P	Min.,Rep. 1838
11348	Norton and Lenchwick	P	Awd.,Min.
11349	Oddingley	P	Min.,Rep. 1838
11350	Offenham	P	Awd.,Min.
11351	Oldberrow	P	Rep. 1837
11352	Ombersley	P	Min.,Rep. 1839
11354	Orleton	H	Agrmt.,Min.,Rep. 1839
11355	Overbury	P	N.t.p.,Min.
11356	Paxford	H	N.t.p.,Min.
11357	Pedmore	P	Awd.,Min.
11358	Pendock	P	Awd.,Min.
11359	Peopleton	P	Awd.,Min.
11360	Pershore St Andrew	C	Awd.,Min.
11361	Pensham	H	N.t.p.,Min.
11362	Queenhill	H	N.t.p.,Min.
11363	Pershore, Holy Cross	P	Awd.,Min.
11364	Piddle North	P	N.t.p.,Min.
11365	Piddle Wyre	H	Awd.,Min.
11366	Pinvin	C	N.t.p.,Min.
11367	Pirton	P	Awd.,Min.
11368	Powick	P	Awd.,Min.
11369	Redmarley D'Abitot	P	Awd.,Min.,Rep. 1838
11370	Ribbesford	R	Agrmt.,Rep. 1839
11371	Ripple	P	N.t.p.,Min.
11372	Rock	P	Awd.,Min.
11373	Rous Lench and Radford	M	N.t.p.,Min.
11374	Rushock	P	Awd.,Min.
11375	Salwarp	P	N.t.p.,Min.
11376	Sapey Lower or Pitchard	P	Min.,Rep. 1841
11377	Sedgberrow	P	N.t.p.,Min.
11378	Shell	EP	N.t.p.,Min.
11379	Shelsey Beauchamp	P	Awd.,Min.
11380	Shelsey Walsh	P	Awd.,Min.
11381	Shipston on Stour	P	Awd.,Min.
11382	Shrawley	P	Rep. 1838
11383	Spetchley	P	Min.,Rep. 1840
11384	Stanford	P	Agrmt.,Rep. 1839
11385	Staunton	P	Min.,Rep. 1842
11386	Stock and Bradley	C	Awd.,Min.
11387	Stockton	P	Agrmt.,Min.,Rep. 1841
11388	Stoulton	P	Rep. 1838
11389	Stoke Prior	P	Awd.,Min.
11390	Severn Stoke	P	Awd.,Min.
11391	Stone	P	Awd.,Min.
11392	Sheriffs Lench	H	Awd.,Min.
11393	Strensham	P	N.t.p.,Min.
11394	Suckley	P	Min.,Rep. 1838
11395	Sutton	H	Awd.,Min.
11396	Swinford Old	P	N.t.p.,Min.
11397	Tardebigg	P	Min.,Rep. 1839
11398	Tenbury	T	Awd.,Min.
11399	The Foreign of Tenbury	T	Awd.,Min.
11400	Throckmorton	H	Awd.,Min.
11401	Tibberton	P	N.t.p.,Min.
11402	Tidmington	P	Awd.,Min.
11403	Tredington	P	Agrmt.,Min.,Rep. 1840
11404	Upton on Severn	P	Awd.,Min.
11405	Upton Snodsbury	P	Agrmt.,Min.,Rep. 1839
11406	Upton Warren	P	Min.,Rep. 1838
11407	Warley Wigorn	T	Min.,Rep. 1840
11408	Warndon	P	Awd.,Min.
11409	Welland	P	Awd.,Min.
11410	White Ladies Aston	P	Min.,Rep. 1838
11411	Whittington	C	Awd.,Min.
11412	Wichenford	P	Min.,Rep. 1838
11413	Wick juxta Pershore	H	N.t.p.,Min.
11414	Wickhamford	P	Agrmt.,Rep. 1842
11415	Witley Great	P	Min.,Rep. 1839
11416	Wolverley	P	Agrmt.,Min.,Rep. 1839
11417	Worcester St Andrew	P	N.t.p.,Min.
11418	Worcester St Martin	P	Awd.,Min.
11419	Worcester St Peter	P	Awd.,Min.
11420	Worcester St Albans	P	N.t.p.,Min.
11421	Worcester St Clements	P	Awd.,Min.
11422	Yardley	P	Min.

York City and Ainsty

11423	York City & Ainsty	P	Min.
11424	Acaster Malbis	P	Awd.,Min.
11425	Acaster Sailby	T	Rep. 1838
11426	Acomb	T	N.t.p.,Min.
11427	Appleton Roebuck	T	N.t.p.,Min.
11428	Askham Bryan	P	N.t.p.,Min.
11429	Askham Richard	P	N.t.p.,Min.
11430	Bickerton	T	Awd.,Min.
11431	Bilton	T	Min.
11432	Bilbrough	P	Min.,Rep. 1838
11433	Bishopthorpe	P	Awd.,Min.
11434	Bolton Percy	T	Awd.,Min.
11435	Clifton	T	Awd.,Min.
11436	Colton	T	Awd.,Min.
11437	Copmanthorpe	T	Min.,Rep. 1837
11438	Cuthbert St	P	Min.,Rep. 1845
11439	Dennis St in Walmgate	P	Awd.,Min.
11440	Dringhouses	T	Agrmt.,Min.,Rep. 1839
11441	Healaugh	P	Awd.,Min.
11442	St Helen on the Walls	P	Awd.,Min.
11443	Hessay	T	N.t.p.,Min.
11444	St Lawrence	P	Awd.,Min.
11445	St Mary, Bishophill	T	Awd.,Min.
11446	St Mary, Bishophill	T	Awd.,Min.
11447	St Maurice in the Suburbs	P	Awd.,Min.
11448	Knapton	T	N.t.p.,Awd.,Min.
11450	Mary St Bishophill	T	Awd.,Min.
11451	Middlethorpe	T	Min.,Rep. 1838
11452	Rawcliffe	T	Awd.,Min.

York City and Ainsty contd.

11453	Rufforth	P	Awd.,Min.
11454	Saviour St	P	Awd.,Min.
11455	Steeton	T	Awd.,Min.
11456	Thorp Arch	P	Awd.,Min.
11457	Walton	P	Awd.,Min.
11458	Wighill	P	Awd.,Min.
11807	Wilstrop	T	Agrmt.,Rep. 1839

Yorkshire, East Riding

11459	Acklam	T	Awd.,Min.
11460	Aike	T	N.t.p.,Min.
11461	Aldborough	T	Awd.,Min.
11462	Allerthorpe	T	Min.,Rep. 1839
11463	Anlaby	T	Min.
11465	Argam	P	Awd.,Min.
11466	Arnold	T	N.t.p.,Min.
11467	Arras	H	Awd.,Min.
11468	Asselby	T	Awd.,Min.
11469	Atwick	P	Min.,Rep. 1839
11470	Aughton	P	Awd.,Min.
11471	Bainton and Neswick	T	N.t.p.,Min.
11472	Balkholme	T	Awd.,Min.
11473	Barlby	T	Awd.,Min.
11474	Barmby on the Marsh	T	Awd.,Min.
11475	Barmby on the Moor	T	N.t.p.,Min.
11476	Barmston	P	N.t.p.,Min.
11477	Barthorpe	T	Awd.,Min.
11478	Beeford	T	Awd.,Min.
11479	Belby	T	Awd.,Min.
11480	Bellasize	T	Awd.,Min.
11481	Belthorpe	T	Awd.,Min.
11482	Bempton	P	N.t.p.,Min.
11483	Benningholme	T	N.t.p.,Min.
11484	Bentley	T	Min.,Rep. 1838
11485	Bessingby	P	Awd.,Min.
11486	Beswick	T	Awd.,Min.
11487	Beverley St Martin	P	Min.
11488	Beverley St Mary	P	Awd.,Min.
11489	Beverley St Nicholas	P	Awd.,Min.
11490	Bewick	T	Min.
11491	Bielby	C	N.t.p.,Min.
11492	Bilton	T	Awd.,Min.
11493	Binnington	T	N.t.p.,Min.
11494	Birdsall	P	Rep. 1838
11495	Bishop Burton	P	N.t.p.,Min.
11496	Bishop Wilton	T	N.t.p.,Min.
11497	Blacktoft	P	Agrmt.,Min.,Rep. 1837
11498	Bolton	T	Agrmt.,Min.,Rep. 1840
11499	Bonwick	T	Min.,Rep. 1839
11500	Boreas Hill	H	Awd.,Min.
11501	Boynton	P	Awd.,Min.
11502	Bracken	T	Awd.,Min.
11503	Brackenholme cum Woodhall	T	Awd.,Min.
11504	Brands Burton	T	Awd.,Min.
11505	Brantingham	P	Agrmt.,Min.,Rep. 1844
11506	Breighton	T	Awd.,Min.
11507	Bridlington	T	N.t.p.,Min.
11508	Brigham	T	N.t.p.,Min.
11509	Bubwith	T	Min.
11510	Buckton	T	Awd.,Min.
11511	Bugthorpe	P	Awd.,Min.
11512	Burnby	P	Awd.,Min.
11513	Burton Agnes	D	Agrmt.,Min.,Rep. 1839
11514	Burton North	P	Min.,Rep. 1839
11515	Burton Constable	T	N.t.p.,Min.
11516	Burton North	P	N.t.p.,Min.
11517	Burton Pidsea	P	N.t.p.,Min.
11518	Carlton	T	Min.
11519	Burythorpe	P	Min.,Rep. 1838
11520	Carnaby	P	Awd.,Min.
11521	Catfoss	T	Min.,Rep. 1838
11522	Catton High	T	Awd.,Min.
11523	Catton Low	T	Awd.,Min.
11524	Catwick	P	Awd.,Min.
11525	Cave North	P	Agrmt.,Min.,Rep. 1839
11526	Cave South	T	Agrmt.,Min.,Rep. 1839
11527	Cavil with Portington	T	Agrmt.,Min.,Rep. 1840
11528	Cheapsides	EP	N.t.p.,Min.
11529	Cliffe North	T	Awd.,Min.
11530	Cliffe South	T	Agrmt.,Rep. 1837
11531	Cliffe cum Lund	T	Awd.,Min.
11532	Cowlam	P	Awd.,Min.
11533	Cotness	T	N.t.p.,Min.
11534	Cottam	T	Awd.,Min.
11535	Cottingham	P	Awd.,Min.,Rep. 1838
11536	Cottingwith East	T	N.t.p.,Min.
11537	Cowden Great	T	N.t.p.,Min.
11538	Cowden Little	H	Awd.,Min.
11539	Dalton North	P	N.t.p.,Min.
11540	Dalton South	P	N.t.p.,Min.
11541	Danthorpe	T	Awd.,Min.
11542	Deighton	P	Awd.,Min.
11543	Driffield Great and Little	T	Agrmt.,Min.,Rep. 1844
11544	Drypool	P	Awd.,Min.
11545	Dringhoe	T	N.t.p.,Min.
11546	Duffield North	T	N.t.p.,Min.
11547	Duffield South	T	N.t.p.,Min.
11548	Duggleby	T	Awd.,Min.
11549	Dunnington	P	Awd.,Min.
11550	Dunnington	P	Min.,Rep. 1838
11551	Easington	T	N.t.p.,Min.
11552	Eastburn	T	Awd.,Min.
11553	Easton	T	N.t.p.,Min.
11554	Eastrington	T	Awd.,Min.
11555	Ellerby	T	Awd.,Min.
11556	Elloughton	P	N.t.p.,Min.
11557	Elmswell	T	Agrmt.,Awd.,Min.,Rep. 1842
11558	Elstronwick	T	N.t.p.,Min.
11559	Elvington	T	Agrmt.,Min.,Rep. 1844
11560	Emmotland	T	Rep. 1840
11561	Escrick	T	N.t.p.,Min.
11562	Eske	T	N.t.p.,Min.
11563	Etton	P	Awd.,Min.
11564	Everingham	T	N.t.p.,Min.
11565	Fangfoss cum Spittle	P	Awd.,Min.
11566	Faxfleet	T	Agrmt.,Min.,Rep. 1844
11567	Ferriby North	P	Awd.,Min.
11568	Filey	T	N.t.p.,Min.
11569	Fitling	T	Awd.,Min.
11570	Flinton	T	Awd.,Min.
11571	Flotmanby East	T	Min.
11572	Foggathorpe	T	Awd.,Min.
11573	Folkton	P	Awd.,Min.
11574	Fordon	T	N.t.p.,Min.
11575	Fosham	T	Awd.,Min.
11576	Foston on the Wolds	P	N.t.p.,Min.
11577	Foxholes	P	Min.,Rep. 1838
11578	Fraisthorpe with Auburn	P	Awd.,Min.
11579	Fridaythorpe	P	N.t.p.,Min.
11580	Frodingham South	T	Awd.,Min.
11581	Frodingham North	P	Awd.,Min.
11582	Fulford Gate	T	N.t.p.,Min.
11583	Fulford Water	P	N.t.p.,Min.
11584	Full Sutton	P	N.t.p.,Min.
11585	Ganton	P	Min.
11586	Ganstead	T	Awd.,Min.
11587	Garrison Side	EP	Awd.,Min.
11588	Garton cum Grimston	T	Awd.,Min.
11589	Garton on the Wolds	P	Awd.,Min.
11590	Gembling	T	Awd.,Min.
11591	Gilberdyke	T	Awd.,Min.
11592	Givendale Great	T	Rep. 1839
11593	Goodmanham	P	N.t.p.,Min.
11594	Goxhill	P	Min.,Rep. 1839
11595	Gransmoor	T	Min.,Rep. 1838
11596	Gribthorpe	T	Agrmt.,Rep. 1841
11597	Grimston North	P	N.t.p.,Min.
11598	Grimthorpe	T	Awd.,Min.
11599	Grindale	T	Awd.,Min.
11600	Halsham	P	Awd.,Min.
11601	Harpham	T	N.t.p.,Min.
11602	Harsewell	P	Agrmt.,Rep. 1840
11603	Hatfield Great	T	Rep. 1839
11604	Hatfield Little	T	Rep. 1839
11605	Hayton	P	Rep. 1838
11606	Hedon	P	Awd.,Min.
11607	Helperthorpe	P	N.t.p.,Min.
11608	Hemingbrough	T	Awd.,Min.
11609	Hempsholme	T	Awd.,Min.
11610	Heslerton East	T	N.t.p.,Min.
11611	Heslington St Lawrence	T	Min.,Rep. 1839
11612	Heslington St Paul	T	Agrmt.,Min.,Rep. 1839
11613	Hessle	P	N.t.p.,Min.
11614	Hilderthorpe	T	Awd.,Min.
11615	Hilston	P	Awd.,Min.
11616	Holme on Spalding Moor	P	Awd.,Min.
11617	Hornsea Burton	T	Awd.,Min.
11618	Hotham	P	Rep. 1839
11619	Howden	T	Awd.,Min.
11620	Howden	T	Awd.,Min.
11621	Howsham	T	Rep. 1839
11622	Huggate	P	Awd.,Min.
11623	Humbleton	T	Awd.,Min.
11624	Hunmanby	T	N.t.p.,Min.
11625	Hunsley	H	Rep. 1838
11626	Hutton Cranswick	T	Awd.,Min.
11627	Holme on the Wolds	P	N.t.p.,Min.
11628	Houghton	T	N.t.p.
11629	Holmpton	P	N.t.p.,Min.
11630	Kelfield	T	Min.,Rep. 1838
11631	Kelk Great	T	Min.,Rep. 1840
11632	Kelk Little	EP	Awd.,Min.
11633	Kennythorpe	T	Agrmt.,Rep. 1839
11634	Kexby	T	Awd.
11635	Keyingham	P	Awd.,Min.
11636	Kilham	P	Awd.,Min.
11637	Kilnsea	P	Awd.,Min.
11638	Kilnwick	T	N.t.p.,Awd.,Min.
11639	Kilnwick Percy	P	Min.,Rep. 1837
11640	Kilpin	T	Awd.,Min.

Yorkshire, East Riding contd.

11641	Kingston upon Hull	P	Awd.,Min.
11642	Kingston upon Hull	P	N.t.p.,Min.
11643	Kirby under Dale	P	Rep. 1838
11644	Kirkbrn	T	Awd.,Min.
11645	Kirkby Grindalyth	T	Awd.,Min.
11646	Kirk Ella	T	N.t.p.,Min.
11647	Kirkham	EP	N.t.p.
11648	Knapton	T	Awd.,Min.
11649	Knedlington	T	Awd.,Min.
11650	Laxton	T	Awd.,Min.
11651	Langtoft	T	N.t.p.,Min.
11652	Langton	T	Awd.,Min.
11653	Langwith	T	Rep. 1839
11654	Laytham	T	Min.
11655	Lelley	T	N.t.p.,Min.
11656	Leckonfield	P	N.t.p.,Awd.,Min.
11657	Leven	T	Agrmt.,Awd.,Min.,Rep. 1839
11658	Leppington	T	Awd.,Min.
11659	Lissett	T	N.t.p.,Min.
11660	Lockington	T	Awd.,Min.
11661	Londesborough	P	N.t.p.,Min.
11662	Lowthorpe	P	N.t.p.,Min.
11663	Lund	P	N.t.p.,Min.
11664	Lutton East and West	T	N.t.p.,Min.
11665	Mappleton	P	Min.,Rep. 1838
11666	Marfleet	P	Awd.,Min.
11667	Marton	T	Awd.,Min.
11668	Melton	T	N.t.p.,Min.
11669	Menthorpe	T	Min.,Rep. 1839
11670	Metham	T	N.t.p.,Min.
11671	Middleton	T	N.t.p.,Min.
11672	Millington	T	Awd.,Min.,Rep. 1841
11673	Molescroft	T	Awd.,Min.
11674	Moor Town	T	Awd.,Min.
11675	Moreby		Rep. 1842
11676	Muston	T	Agrmt.,Awd.,Min.,Rep. 1837
11677	Naburn	T	Awd.,Min.
11678	Nafferton	P	N.t.p.,Min.
11679	Newbald North and South	P	N.t.p.,Min.
11680	Newton West	T	Awd.,Min.
11681	Newton East	T	Awd.,Min.
11682	Newport Wallingfen	T	N.t.p.,Min.
11683	Newsome Field	D	Min.,Rep. 1840
11684	New Village	EP	Awd.,Min.
11685	Norton	P	Awd.,Min.
11686	Nunburnholme	T	Awd.,Min.
11687	Nunkeeling cum Bewholme	P	Awd.,Min.
11688	Octon Grange	H	Rep. 1838
11689	Osgodby	T	Awd.,Min.
11690	Owstwick	T	Awd.,Min.
11691	Outnewton	T	Rep. 1839
11692	Owborough	H	Agrmt.,Rep. 1839
11693	Otteringham	P	N.t.p.,Min.
11694	Owthorne	T	Awd.,Min.
11695	Owsthorpe	T	Awd.,Min.
11696	Patrington	P	Awd.,Min.
11697	Paull	T	Awd.,Min.
11698	Preston	T	Awd.,Min.
11699	Pocklington	P	N.t.p.,Min.
11700	Raisthorpe	T	N.t.p.,Min.
11701	Riccall	P	Awd.,Min.
11702	Righton	P	Awd.,Min.
11703	Rillington	T	N.t.p.,Min.
11704	Rimswell	T	Awd.,Min.
11705	Risby	T	Agrmt.,Rep. 1839
11706	Rise	P	Rep. 1838
11707	Riston Long	P	N.t.p.,Min.
11708	Roos	T	N.t.p.,Min.
11709	Rotsea	T	Awd.,Min.
11710	Routh	P	Awd.,Min.
11711	Rowley	P	Min.
11712	Rudstone	T	N.t.p.,Min.
11713	Ruston Parva	P	N.t.p.,Min.
11714	Ryhill and Camerton	T	N.t.p.,Min.
11715	Saltmarshe	T	Awd.,Min.
11716	Sancton	T	Min.,Rep. 1841
11717	Sewerby and Marton	T	N.t.p.,Min.
11718	Settrington	T	N.t.p.,Min.
11719	Seaton Ross	P	Awd.,Min.
11720	Seaton	T	Min.,Rep. 1839
11721	Sculcoates	P	N.t.p.,Min.
11722	Scrayingham	T	N.t.p.,Min.
11723	Scorborough	P	Min.,Rep. 1839
11724	Scampston	T	Agrmt.,Awd.,Min.,Rep. 1843
11725	Sigglesthorne	T	N.t.p.,Min.
11726	Sherburn	P	Awd.,Min.
11727	Skipwith	T	Min.,Rep. 1839
11728	Skipsea	T	N.t.p.,Min.
11729	Skidby	P	N.t.p.,Min.
11730	Skelton	T	Awd.,Min.
11731	Skerne	P	Awd.,Min.
11732	Skeckling with Burstwick	P	Awd.,Min.
11733	Skirlaugh North	H	Awd.,Min.
11734	Skirlaugh South	T	Awd.,Min.
11735	Skirlaugh South	D	Agrmt.,Rep. 1839
11736	Skirpenbeck	P	Awd.,Min.
11737	Sledmere with Croom	P	N.t.p.,Min.
11738	Southcoates	T	Awd.,Min.
11739	South Burn	P	Awd.,Min.
11740	Spaldington	T	Awd.,Min.
11741	Speeton	T	N.t.p.,Min.
11742	Sproatley	R	N.t.p.,Min.
11743	Stamford Bridge East	T	Awd.
11744	Stamford Bridge West	T	Agrmt.,Min.,Rep. 1841
11745	Staxton	T	N.t.p.,Min.
11746	Stillingfleet	P	N.t.p.,Min.
11747	Storkhill with Sandholme	T	Awd.,Min.
11748	Sunderlandwick	P	Awd.,Min.
11749	Sunk Island	P	N.t.p.,Min.
11750	Sutton and Stoneferry	T	Awd.,Min.
11751	Sutton on Derwent	P	Awd.,Min.,Rep. 1838
11752	Swanland	T	Min.,Rep. 1839
11753	Swine	T	Awd.,Min.
11754	Thearne	T	Awd.,Min.
11755	Thirtleby	T	Agrmt.,Min.,Rep. 1842
11756	Thirkleby	T	Agrmt.,Rep. 1842
11757	Thixondale	T	Awd.,Min.
11758	Thorganby cum Cottingwith	P	Awd.,Min.
11759	Thorngumbald	T	Awd.,Min.
11760	Thornton	T	Awd.,Min.
11761	Thorpe	T	Awd.,Min.
11762	Thorpe Bassett	P	Awd.,Min.
11763	Thorpe le Street	T	Agrmt.,Rep. 1837
11764	Thurnholme	T	Min.,Rep. 1840
11765	Thwing	P	N.t.p.,Min.
11766	Tibthorpe	T	N.t.p.,Min.
11767	Tickton with Hull Bridge	T	Awd.,Min.
11768	Tunstall	P	Awd.,Min.
11769	Ulrome	C	Awd.,Min.
11770	Walkington	P	N.t.p.,Min.
11771	Waghen	T	Awd.,Min.
11772	Waplington	T	Agrmt.,Rep. 1839
11773	Warter	P	Awd.,Min.
11774	Wassand	D	Rep. 1839
11775	Watton	P	Awd.,Min.
11776	Waxholme	T	Awd.,Min.
11777	Weaverthorpe	P	Awd.,Min.
11778	Weel	T	Awd.,Min.
11779	Weeton Little	T	N.t.p.,Min.
11780	Welton	T	N.t.p.,Min.
11781	Welwick	P	Awd.,Min.
11782	Wold Newton	T	N.t.p.,Min.
11783	West Ella	T	N.t.p.,Min.
11784	Westow	P	Min.,Rep. 1839
11785	Wetwang and Fimber	T	N.t.p.,Min.
11786	Wharram Percy	T	Awd.,Min.
11787	Wharram le Street	P	Min.,Rep. 1838
11788	Wheldrake	T	Awd.,Min.
11789	Wilberfoss	P	N.t.p.,Min.
11790	Willerby	T	N.t.p.,Min.
11791	Willerby	T	N.t.p.,Min.
11792	Willitoft	T	Awd.,Min.
11793	Winestead	P	Awd.,Min.
11794	Winton cum Barmston	T	N.t.p.
11795	Winteringham	T	Awd.,Min.
11796	Withernwick	P	Awd.,Min.
11797	Woodmansey	T	Awd.,Min.
11798	Wressle	P	Min.,Rep. 1839
11799	Wyton	T	Agrmt.,Rep. 1842
11800	Yapham cum Meltonby	T	Awd.,Min.
11801	Yeddingham	P	N.t.p.,Min.
11802	Yokefleet	T	Awd.,Min.
11803	Youlthorpe with Gowthorpe	T	N.t.p.,Min.
11804	Bowthorpe	T	N.t.p.,Min.
11805	Meaux	T	N.t.p.,Min.
11806	Towthorpe	T	N.t.p.,Min.
11822	Market Weighton	P	Agrmt.,Awd.,Min.
11911	Coniston		
12518	Ellerton Priory	P	Awd.,Min.
12612	Hollym cum Withernsea	T	N.t.p.,Min.
13563	Skeffling	P	N.t.p.

Yorkshire, North Riding

1944	Craike	P	Rep. 1839
11808	Abbotside High	T	Rep. 1840
11809	Abbotside Low	T	Rep. 1840
11810	Acklam in Cleveland	P	Awd.,Min.
11811	Agglethorpe	H	N.t.p.
11812	Ainderby Quernhow	T	Rep. 1840
11813	Ainderby Steeple	T	Awd.,Min.
11814	Aislaby (Middleton)	T	Awd.,Min.
11815	Aislaby (Whitby)	T	Awd.,Min.
11816	Akebor	T	N.t.p.,Min.
11817	Aldborough	T	Awd.,Min.
11818	Aldwark	T	Agrmt.,Rep. 1841
11819	Allerston	P	Awd.,Min.
11820	Alne	T	Awd.,Min.
11821	Alverton	T	Awd.,Min.
11823	Amotherby	T	Awd.,Min.
11824	Ampleforth	T	N.t.p.,Min.

Yorkshire, North Riding contd.

11825	Angram Grange	T	Agrmt.,Rep. 1839
11826	Appleton	T	Awd.,Min.
11827	Appleton le Moors	T	Awd.,Min.,Rep. 1842
11828	Appleton le Street	T	Awd.,Min.
11829	Appleton upon Wiske	P	Agrmt.,Awd.,Min.
11830	Arden,Ardenside	T	Awd.,Min.
11831	Arkendale	P	Agrmt.,Rep. 1838
11832	Arkleside	H	Awd.,Min.
11833	Arundel Grange	H	Awd.,Min.
11834	Aryholme	T	N.t.p.,Min.
11835	Asenby	T	Rep. 1838
11836	Aske	T	Awd.,Min.
11837	Askrigg	T	Rep. 1839
11838	Aysgarth	T	Awd.,Min.
11839	Ayton Great	T	Awd.,Min.
11840	Ayton East	T	N.t.p.,Min.
11841	Ayton Little	T	Awd.,Min.
11842	Ayton West	T	N.t.p.
11843	Bagby	C	Awd.,Min.
11844	Bainbridge	T	Awd.,Min.
11845	Baldersby	T	Rep. 1838
11846	Barforth	T	Awd.,Min.
11847	Barnby	T	Awd.,Min.
11848	Barton	T	Agrmt.,Min.,Rep. 1841
11849	Barugh,Great,Little	T	Awd.,Min.
11850	Barton le Street	T	Awd.,Min.
11851	Bedale	P	Agrmt.,Rep. 1838
11852	Bellerby	T	N.t.p.
11853	Bilsdale West Side	T	Awd.,Min.
11854	Birdforth	T	Agrmt.,Rep. 1839
11855	Birkby	P	Rep. 1839
11856	Bishopdale	T	Rep. 1839
11857	Boldron	T	Agrmt.,Rep. 1842
11858	Boltby	T	Awd.,Min.
11859	Bolton Castle	C	Min.
11860	Bolton on Swale	T	Rep. 1839
11861	Borrowby(Leake)	T	Awd.,Min.
11862	Borrowby(Lythe)	T	Awd.,Min.
11863	Bossall,Barnby	H	Awd.,Min.
11864	Bowes	T	Agrmt.,Min.,Rep. 1839
11865	Brafferton	T	Awd.,Min.
11866	Brampton	H	Agrmt.,Awd.,Rep. 1843
11867	Brandsby	P	Rep. 1839
11868	Bransdale West Side	T	Awd.,Min.
11869	Brawby	T	Rep. 1840
11870	Brignall	P	Agrmt.,Rep. 1838
11871	Brompton(Northallerton)	T	Min.,Rep. 1839
11872	Brompton on Swale	T	Awd.,Min.
11873	Brompton	T	Awd.,Min.
11874	Brotton	T	Agrmt.,Rep. 1845
11875	Brough	T	Awd.,Min.
11876	Broughton	T	Awd.,Min.
11877	Bulmer	P	N.t.p.,Min.
11878	Burneston	T	Agrmt.,Rep. 1838
11879	Burton upon Yore	T	Rep. 1838
11880	Burton, Walden	T	Awd.,Min.
11881	Busby Great	T	Agrmt.,Rep. 1837
11882	Busby Little	T	Agrmt.
11883	Buttercrambe,Aldby	P	Awd.,Min.
11884	Butterwick	T	Rep. 1838
11885	Byland Abbey	T	Awd.,Min.
11886	Byland Old	P	Awd.,Min.
11887	Caldbergh	T	Min.,Rep. 1843
11888	Caldwell	T	Awd.,Min.
11889	Carkin	T	Awd.,Min.
11890	Carlton	T	N.t.p.,Min.
11891	Carlton Husthwaite	T	Agrmt.,Rep. 1839
11892	Carlton Highdale	T	Min.
11893	Carthorpe	T	Agrmt.,Rep. 1838
11894	Carperby,Thoresby	T	Rep. 1839
11895	Catterick	T	Awd.,Min.
11896	Catton	T	Agrmt.,Rep. 1838
11897	Carlton Miniott	T	Agrmt.,Awd.,Min.
11898	Carlton Town	T	Awd.,Min.
11899	Carleton	P	Awd.,Min.
11901	Castle Leavington	T	Rep. 1839
11902	Cawthorn	T	N.t.p.
11903	Cawton	T	Rep. 1838
11904	Cayton	T	Awd.,Min.
11905	Claxton	T	Awd.,Min.
11906	Cleasby	P	Awd.,Min.
11907	Colburn	T	Awd.,Min.
11908	Coulton	T	Awd.,Min.
11909	Commondale	T	Awd.,Min.
11910	Coneysthorpe	T	Awd.,Min.
11912	Constable Burton	T	Agrmt.,Awd.,Rep. 1838
11913	Cornborough	T	Awd.,Min.
11914	Cotherston	T	Agrmt.,Rep. 1839
11915	Coverham	T	Rep. 1840
11916	Cowesby	P	Rep. 1837
11917	Cowton East	P	Rep. 1838
11918	Cowton North	T	Agrmt.,Rep. 1838
11919	Cowton South	T	Awd.,Min.,Rep. 1842
11920	Coxwold	T	Agrmt.,Rep. 1839
11921	Crambe,Barton	T	Agrmt.,Rep. 18 4
11922	Crathorne	P	Awd.,Min.
11923	Croft	T	Awd.,Min.
11924	Cropton	T	Awd.,Min.
11925	Crosby	T	Awd.,Min.
11926	Crosby Cote	D	Awd.,Min.
11927	Cundall	T	Awd.,Min.
11928	Dale Town,Murton	T	Awd.,Min.
11929	Dalton	T	Awd.,Min.
11930	Dalton(Topcliffe)	T	Min.,Rep. 1840
11931	Dalton on Tees	T	Awd.,Min.
11932	Danby	P	Awd.,Min.
11933	Danby Wiske	T	Agrmt.,Rep. 1839
11934	Deighton	T	Rep. 1841
11935	Dishforth	T	Agrmt.,Rep. 1840
11936	Downholme	T	Awd.,Min.
11937	Earswick	T	N.t.p.,Min.
11938	Easby	T	Awd.,Min.
11939	Easby	T	Rep. 1838
11940	Easington	T	Agrmt.,Rep. 1837
11941	Easingwold	T	Awd.,Min.
11942	Ebberston	P	Awd.,Min.
11943	Edston Great	T	Min.
11944	Egglestone Abbey	T	N.t.p.
11945	Egton	T	Agrmt.,Rep. 1841
11946	Ellerbeck	T	N.t.p.
11947	Ellerburn Parish	P	N.t.p.
11948	Ellerby	T	Rep. 1840
11949	Ellerton Abbey	T	Awd.,Min.
11950	Ellerton upon Swale	T	Rep. 1839
11951	Ellingstring	T	Rep. 1838
11952	Ellington	T	Rep. 1838
11953	Elmire	T	Rep. 1840
11954	Eppleby	T	Awd.,Min.,Rep. 1843
11955	Eryholme	PC	Rep. 1839
11956	Eskdaleside	T	Awd.,Min.
11957	Eston	T	Rep. 1838
11958	Exelby Leeming	T	Agrmt.,Rep. 1838
11959	Faceby	T	Awd.,Min.
11960	Fadmoor	T	Awd.,Min.
11961	Farlington	T	Rep. 1840
11962	Farmanby	T	N.t.p.
11963	Farndale High Quarter	T	Awd.,Min.
11964	Farndale East Side	T	Rep. 1838
11965	Farndale Low Quarter	T	Awd.,Min.
11966	Fawdington	T	Awd.,Min.
11967	Fearby	T	Rep. 1838
11968	Felixkirk	P	Awd.,Min.
11969	Fingall	T	Rep. 1838
11970	Flawith	T	N.t.p.
11971	Flaxton	T	Awd.,Min.
11972	Forcett	T	Awd.,Min.
11973	Foston	T	N.t.p.
11974	Foxton	H	Awd.,Min.
11975	Fryton	T	N.t.p.
11976	Fylingdales	T	Awd.,Min.
11977	Ganthorpe	H	N.t.p.
11978	Garriston	T	Awd.,Min.
11979	Gate Helmsley	T	N.t.p.
11980	Gatenby	T	Rep. 1839
11981	Gayles	T	Awd.,Min.
11982	Gillamoor	T	Awd.,Min.
11983	Gilmonby	T	Agrmt.,Rep. 1847
11984	Girsby and Over Dinsdale	T	Awd.,Min.
11985	Gisborough	T	Awd.,Min.
11986	Glaisdale	T	Awd.,Min.
11987	Goathland	T	Awd.,Min.
11988	Grimstone	T	Rep. 1838
11989	Grinton	T	Rep. 1841
11990	Gristhorpe	T	Awd.,Min.
11991	Gueldable	T	Awd.,Min.
11992	Habton Great	T	Awd.,Min.
11993	Habton Little	T	Agrmt.,Rep. 1841
11994	Hackness	T	Agrmt.,Rep. 1846
11995	Harlsey East	P	Awd.,Min.
11996	Harlsey West	T	Awd.,Min.
11997	Harmby	T	Agrmt.,Awd.,Min.
11998	Hartoft	T	Awd.,Min.
11999	Harton	T	Rep. 1840
12000	Harwood Dale	T	N.t.p.
12001	Bilsdale	T	Agrmt.,Rep. 1841
12002	Falsgrave	T	Awd.,Min.
12003	Hawes	T	Min.,Rep. 1839
12004	Hawkeswell	T	Awd.,Min.
12004	Seamer(Scarborough)	T	Awd.,Min.
12005	Hawnby	T	Agrmt.,Awd.,Min.,Rep. 1844
12006	Hawsker,Stainsacre	T	Awd.,Min.
12007	Haxby	P	N.t.p.
12008	Healey with Sutton	T	Rep. 1838
12009	Helmsley	T	Agrmt.,Awd.,Min.,Rep. 1844
12010	Helmsley Over	P	N.t.p.
12011	Helperby	T	N.t.p.,Min.
12012	Hemlington	T	Awd.,Min.
12013	Heworth(part)	T	N.t.p.,Min.
12014	Heworth(part)	T	N.t.p.,Min.
12015	Hilton	P	Min.,Rep. 1839
12016	Hinderskelf	P	Awd.,Min.
12017	Hinderwell	P	Rep. 1838

Yorkshire, North Riding contd.

No.	Place		Details
12018	Hildenley	T	Awd.,Min.
12019	Hipswell, St Martin	TH	Awd.,Min.
12020	Holme	T	Rep. 1839
12021	Holme cum Howgrave	T	Agrmt.,Rep. 1838
12022	Holme South	T	Rep. 1839
12023	Holwick	T	N.t.p.,Min.
12024	Hood Grange	H	Awd.,Min.
12025	Hornby	P	Rep. 1839
12026	Hovingham	T	Awd.,Min.
12027	Howe	T	Awd.,Min.
12028	Hudswell	T	Awd.,Min.
12029	Hunderthwaite	T	Agrmt.,Min.,Rep. 1839
12030	Huntington	T	Awd.,Min.
12031	Hunton	T	Awd.,Min.
12032	Husthwaite	T	Agrmt.,Min.,Rep. 1839
12033	Huttons Ambo	P	N.t.p.,Min.
12034	Hutton Bushel	T	N.t.p.
12035	Hutton Conyers	T	Awd.,Min.
12036	Hutton le Hole	T	Rep. 1839
12037	Hutton Long Villiers	T	Agrmt.,Rep. 1838
12038	Hutton Lowcross	T	Awd.,Min.
12039	Hutton Mulgrave	T	Awd.,Min.
12040	Hutton	T	Min.,Rep. 1838
12041	Ilton cum Pott	T	Rep. 1838
12042	Ingleby Arncliffe	P	Awd.,Min.
12043	Ingleby Barwick	T	Awd.,Min.
12044	Ingleby Greenhow	P	Rep. 1839
12045	Irton	T	N.t.p.,Min.
12046	Kepwick	T	Awd.,Min.
12047	Kilburn	T	Min.,Rep. 1839
12048	Kildale	P	Awd.,Min.
12049	Killerby	T	Awd.,Min.
12050	Kilton	T	Rep. 1845
12051	Kilvington North	T	Agrmt.,Awd.,Min.
12052	Kilvington South	T	Awd.,Min.
12053	Kingthorpe	T	N.t.p.,Min.
12054	Kiplin	T	Rep. 1839
12055	Kirby in Cleveland	P	Min.,Rep. 1842
12056	Kirby Cold	P	Awd.,Min.
12057	Kirby Knowle	T	Rep. 1839
12058	Kirby Misperton	T	Awd.,Min.
12059	Kirby Moorside	T	Awd.,Min.
12060	Kirby Wiske	T	Min.
12061	Kirby Fleetham	P	Agrmt.,Rep. 1838
12062	Kirkby Ravensworth	T	Awd.,Min.
12063	Kirkby Sigston	T	Awd.,Min.
12064	Kirkdale	P	N.t.p.,Min.
12065	Kirkleatham	T	Agrmt.,Rep. 1839
12066	Kirkleavington	T	Rep. 1839
12067	Kirklington	T	Agrmt.,Rep. 1838
12068	Knayton with Brawith	T	Awd.,Min.
12069	Landmouth with Catto	T	Awd.,Min.
12070	Langton upon Swale	T	Agrmt.
12071	Lartington	T	Agrmt.,Rep. 1839
12072	Lastingham	T	Awd.,Min.
12073	Laysthorpe	T	Awd.,Min.
12074	Layton East	T	Awd.,Min.
12075	Layton West	T	Agrmt.,Awd.,Min.,Rep. 1838
12076	Leake	T	Awd.,Min.
12077	Levisham	P	Awd.,Min.
12078	Leyburn	T	Min.,Rep. 1839
12079	Libberston	T	Awd.,Min.
12080	Lilling East, West	T	Awd.,Min.
12081	Linthorpe	T	N.t.p.
12082	Linton upon Ouse	T	N.t.p.
12083	Liverton	T	Agrmt.
12084	Lockton	T	N.t.p.,Min.
12085	Lofthouse	P	Agrmt.,Min.
12086	Lunedale	T	N.t.p.,Min.
12087	Lythe	T	Awd.,Min.
12088	Maltby	T	Awd.,Min.
12089	Malton St Leonard	P	N.t.p.,Min.
12090	Malton Old	P	Awd.,Min.
12091	Manfield	P	Rep. 1840
12092	Marishes	T	Agrmt.,Awd.,Min.,Rep. 1839
12093	Marton in Cleveland	P	Rep. 1839
12094	Marton le Moor	T	Rep. 1838
12095	Marton in the Forest	P	Awd.,Min.
12096	Marrick	P	Awd.,Min.
12097	Marsk in Cleveland	P	Awd.,Min.
12098	Marske	P	Agrmt.,Awd.,Min.,Rep. 1840
12099	Masham	T	Rep. 1838
12100	Maunby	T	Min.
12101	Melbecks	T	Awd.,Min.
12102	Melmerby	T	Awd.,Min.
12103	Melmerby	T	Agrmt.,Rep. 1838
12104	Melsonby	T	Rep. 1840
12105	Mickleby	T	Awd.,Min.
12106	Mickleton	T	N.t.p.,Min.
12107	Middleham	P	Min.,Rep. 1839
12108	Middlesborough	P	Awd.,Min.
12109	Middleton on Leven	T	Min.,Rep. 1839
12110	Middleton Tyas	T	Agrmt.,Rep. 1840
12111	Middleton Quernhow	T	Agrmt.,Rep. 1838
12112	Middleton	T	Awd.,Min.
12113	Milby	T	Awd.,Min.,Rep. 1842
12114	Monk End	D	Agrmt.,Rep. 1843
12115	Moorsome, Great, Little	T	Agrmt.,Rep. 1839
12116	Morton	T	Agrmt.,Rep. 1838
12117	Morton upon Swale	T	Rep. 1840
12118	Moulton	T	Agrmt.,Rep. 1840
12119	Moxby	P	N.t.p.
12120	Muker	T	Awd.,Min.
12121	Murton	T	Agrmt.,Rep. 1841
12122	Muscoates	T	Awd.,Min.
12123	Myton on Swale	P	Awd.,Min.
12124	Nawton	T	Awd.,Min.
12125	Ness East	T	N.t.p.,Min.
12126	Ness West	T	N.t.p.,Min.
12127	Newbiggin	T	Rep. 1839
12128	Newbrough	T	Awd.,Min.
12129	Newby Wiske	T	Min.
12130	New Forest	T	Rep. 1838
12131	Newholme cum Dunsley	T	Awd.,Min.
12132	Newsham Manor	T	Rep. 1838
12133	Newsham	T	Agrmt.,Rep. 1840
12134	Newsham	T	Min.
12135	Newton	P	Agrmt.,Min.
12136	Newton East	R	Agrmt.,Rep. 1839
12137	Newton Morrell	T	Rep. 1839
12138	Newton Mulgrave	T	Awd.,Min.
12139	Newby	T	Min.,Rep. 1838
12140	Newby	T	N.t.p.
12141	Newton upon Ouse	T	N.t.p.,Min.
12142	Newton upon Rawcliffe	T	Awd.,Min.
12143	Newton le Willows	T	Rep. 1838
12144	Northallerton	T	Agrmt.,Rep. 1842
12145	Normanby(Ormseby)	T	Rep. 1838
12146	Normanby(Normanby)	T	Rep. 1838
12147	Northolme	T	Awd.,Min.
12148	Norton le Clay	T	Awd.,Min.
12149	Nunnington	P	N.t.p.,Min.
12150	Nunwick cum Howgrave	T	Agrmt.,Rep. 1838
12151	Nunthorpe	T	Awd.,Min.
12152	Osbaldwick	P	Awd.,Min.
12153	Oldstead	T	Agrmt.,Awd.,Min.,Rep. 1842
12154	Ormesby	T	Agrmt.,Rep. 1838
12155	Osgodby	T	Awd.,Min.
12156	Osmotherley	P	Awd.,Min.
12157	Oswaldkirk	P	Rep. 1838
12158	Otterington North	T	Awd.,Min.
12159	Otterington South	P	Awd.,Min.
12160	Oulston	T	Agrmt.,Rep. 1839
12161	Overton	P	Awd.,Min.
12162	Ovington	T	Rep. 1838
12163	Patrick Brompton	T	Min.,Rep. 1838
12164	Pickering(District)	T	Awd.,Min.
12165	Pickering	T	Awd.,Min.,Rep. 1838
12166	Pickhill with Roxby	T	Agrmt.,Rep. 1838
12167	Picton	T	Awd.,Min.
12168	Pinchinthorpe	T	Agrmt.
12169	Pool	T	Awd.,Min.
12170	Potto	T	Rep. 1840
12171	Preston	T	Rep. 1839
12172	Rainton with Newby	T	Agrmt.,Rep. 1838
12173	Raskelf	C	Awd.,Min.
12174	Ravensworth	T	Awd.,Min.
12175	Redmire	T	Rep. 1842
12176	Reeth	T	Awd.
12177	Richmond	P	Min.,Rep. 1839
12178	Rokeby	P	Agrmt.,Rep. 1838
12179	Romaldkirk	T	N.t.p.,Min.
12180	Romanby	T	Rep. 1839
12181	Rosedale East Side	T	Awd.,Min.
12182	Rosedale West Side	T	Rep. 1838
12183	Rounton East	T	Awd.,Min.
12184	Rounton West	P	Rep. 1838
12185	Rudby in Cleveland	P	Awd.,Min.
12186	Ruswarp, Whitby	T	Awd.,Min.
12187	Ryton	T	Awd.,Min.
12188	Salton	T	Awd.,Min.
12189	Sandhutton	T	Awd.,Min.
12190	Sandhutton(Thirsk)	T	Agrmt.,Min.,Rep. 1841
12191	Sawden	T	N.t.p.
12192	Scackleton	T	Awd.,Min.
12193	Scalby	P	N.t.p.,Min.
12194	Scarborough	T	Awd.,Min.
12195	Scawton	P	Rep. 1839
12196	Skinningrove	T	Agrmt.,Rep. 1845
12197	Scorton	T	Rep. 1839
12198	Scotton(Catterick)	T	Awd.,Min.
12199	Scotton	T	Awd.,Min.
12200	Sneaton	P	N.t.p.,Min.
12201	Scrafton West	T	Awd.,Min.
12202	Scruton	P	Rep. 1839
12203	Seamer(in Cleveland)	T	Min.,Rep. 1838
12205	Sessay cum Hutton	P	Rep. 1841
12206	Sexhow	T	Rep. 1838
12207	Sheriff Hutton	T	Awd.,Min.
12208	Silton Nether	T	Awd.,Min.
12209	Silton Over	T	Agrmt.,Rep. 1839
12210	Sinderby	T	Agrmt.,Rep. 1838

Yorkshire, North Riding contd.

12211	Sinnington with Marton	P	N.t.p.
12212	Skeeby	T	Awd.,Min.
12213	Skelton	T	N.t.p.,Min.
12214	Skelton	T	Agrmt.,Rep. 1845
12215	Skiplam	T	Awd.,Min.
12216	Skipton upon Swale	T	Rep. 1840
12217	Skutterskelfe	T	Rep. 1839
12218	Slingsby	P	Awd.,Min.
12219	Smeaton Great	P	Awd.,Min.
12220	Snainton	C	Awd.,Min.
12221	Snape	T	N.t.p.
12222	Smilesworth	T	Awd.,Min.
12223	Sowerby	T	Awd.,Min.
12224	Sowerby under Cotcliffe	T	Awd.,Min.
12225	Spaunton	T	Awd.,Min.
12226	Spennithorne	T	Awd.,Min.
12227	Stainton Dale	T	N.t.p.
12228	Stapleton	T	Min.,Rep. 1841
12229	Startforth	T	Agrmt.,Rep. 1839
12230	Stillington	P	Agrmt.,Rep. 1839
12231	Stittenham	T	Awd.,Min.
12232	Stockton on the Forest	P	Awd.,Min.
12233	Stokesley	T	Agrmt.,Min.
12234	Stonegrave	T	Min.
12235	Strensall	T	Awd.,Min.
12236	Sutton under White	T	Awd.,Min.
12237	Sutton on the Forest	T	Awd.,Min.
12238	Sutton cum Howgrave	T	Agrmt.,Rep. 1838
12239	Swainby cum Allerthorpe	T	Agrmt.,Rep. 1839
12240	Swinton	T	Awd.,Min.
12241	Swinton	T	Rep. 1838
12242	Tanfield East	T	Agrmt.,Rep. 1838
12243	Tanfield West	P	Agrmt.,Min.
12244	Terrington	P	N.t.p.
12245	Theakstone	T	Agrmt.,Min.,Rep. 1838
12246	Thimbleby	T	Awd.,Min.
12247	Thirkleby	P	Awd.,Min.
12248	Thirlby	T	Awd.,Min.
12249	Thirsk	T	Awd.,Min.
12250	Thoralby	T	Min.,Rep. 1839
12251	Thornaby	T	Awd.,Min.
12252	Thornbrough	T	Awd.,Min.,Rep. 1840
12253	Thornton	P	N.t.p.,Min.
12254	Thornton cum Baxby	T	Agrmt.,Rep. 1839
12255	Thornton le Beans	T	Awd.,Min.
12256	Thornton Briggs	T	Awd.,Min.
12257	Thornton le Clay	T	Awd.,Min.
12258	Thornton Dale	P	Awd.,Min.
12259	Thornton le Moor	T	Awd.,Min.
12260	Thornton Riseborough	T	Agrmt.,Min.
12261	Thornton Rust	T	Rep. 1839
12262	Thornton le Street	T	Awd.,Min.
12263	Thornton Steward	P	Rep. 1839
12264	Thornton Watlass	P	Agrmt.,Min.
12265	Thormanby	P	Rep. 1841
12266	Thorpe le Willows	T	Agrmt.,Rep. 1839
12267	Thorpfield	H	Rep. 1839
12268	Thrintoft	T	Rep. 1840
12269	Throxenby	T	N.t.p.
12270	Tocketts	T	Rep. 1841
12271	Tollerton	T	Awd.,Min.
12272	Tolthorpe, Flawith	T	N.t.p.
12273	Topcliffe	T	Rep. 1838
12274	Towthorpe	T	Awd.,Min.
12275	Troutsdale	T	Awd.,Min.
12276	Tunstall	T	Awd.,Min.
12277	Uckerby	T	Agrmt.,Rep. 1841
12278	Ugglebarnby	T	Awd.,Min.
12279	Ugthorpe	T	Awd.,Min.
12280	Upleatham	P	Rep. 1841
12281	Upsall	T	Awd.,Min.
12282	Upsil	T	Agrmt.,Rep. 1838
12283	Walburn	P	N.t.p.
12284	Warlaby	T	Awd.,Min.
12285	Warthill	P	N.t.p.,Min.
12286	Wass	T	Awd.,Min.
12287	Wath	T	Agrmt.,Rep. 1838
12288	Wath	T	N.t.p.
12289	Welburn	T	N.t.p.,Min.
12290	Welburn (Kirkdale)	T	Awd.,Min.
12291	Welbury	P	Agrmt.,Rep. 1841
12292	Well	P	Awd.,Min.
12293	Wensley	T	Rep. 1840
12294	Westerdale	T	Rep. 1838
12295	Whashton	T	Awd.,Min.
12296	Whenby	P	Rep. 1838
12297	Whitby	T	Awd.,Min.
12298	Whitwell	T	Awd.,Min.
12299	Whitwell on the Hill	T	N.t.p.
12300	Trenholme	H	Awd.,Min.
12301	Wigginton	P	Awd.,Min.
12302	Wildon Grange	T	Rep. 1839
12303	Wilton	P	Awd.,Min.
12304	Wilton	C	N.t.p.,Min.
12305	Winton	T	Awd.,Min.
12306	Witton East	P	Awd.,Min.
12307	Witton West	T	Min.,Rep. 1839
12308	Wombleton	T	N.t.p.
12309	Worsall High	T	Awd.,Min.
12310	Worsall Low	T	Awd.,Min.
12311	Wrelton	T	Awd.,Min.
12312	Wycliffe	P	Rep. 1840
12313	Wykeham	P	Awd.,Min.
12314	Yafforth	T	Rep. 1842
12315	Yarm	P	Agrmt.,Min.
12316	Youlton	T	Awd.,Min.
12317	Yearsley	T	Agrmt.,Rep. 1839
12318	Holtby	P	Min.,Rep. 1838
12319	Swainby	H	Rep. 1839
12367	Barningham	P	Agrmt.,Rep. 1840
12627	Huby	T	Rep. 1838
12648	Kirby Hill	T	Min.,Rep. 1840
12666	Langthorpe	T	Rep. 1841
12738	Norton Conyers	T	Agrmt.,Rep. 1839
12749	Stainton	T	Awd.,Min.
12850	Stainton	T	Awd.,Min.
12854	Stanwick St John	T	Awd.,Min.
13565	Gilling	T	Awd.,Min.
14822	Dalby	P	Rep. 1838

Yorkshire, West Riding

8431	Brampton en le Morthen	T	N.t.p.
11449	Ouseburn Little	T	N.t.p.,Min.
11464	Ardsley East	P	N.t.p.,Min.
11900	Castleford	P	Awd.,Min.
12169	Pool	T	Awd.,Min.
12263	Knottingley	T	Awd.,Min.
12320	Aberford	T	Awd.,Min.
12321	Ackton	T	Awd.,Min.
12322	Ackworth	P	N.t.p.,Min.
12323	Addingham	T	Agrmt.,Min.,Rep. 1843
12324	Addle cum Eccup	T	Awd.,Min.
12325	Adlingfleet	T	Awd.,Min.
12326	Admergill	T	Awd.,Min.
12327	Adwick le Street	T	Awd.,Min.
12328	Airton	T	Awd.,Min.
12329	Aismunderby with Bondgate	T	Agrmt.,Rep. 1839
12330	Aldfield	T	Rep. 1840
12331	Alwoodley	T	Awd.,Min.
12332	Appletreewick	T	N.t.p.,Min.
12333	Allerton	T	Awd.,Min.
12334	Allerton Bywater	T	N.t.p.,Min.
12335	Allerton Mauleverer	P	Awd.,Min.
12336	Almondbury	T	Awd.,Min.
12337	Altofts	T	Min.,Rep. 1838
12338	Alverthorpe	D	Awd.,Min.
12339	Anston North	P	Awd.,Min.
12340	Ardsley	T	Rep. 1838
12341	Ardsley West	P	N.t.p.
12342	Arkendale	T	N.t.p.,Min.
12343	Armin	C	N.t.p.,Min.
12344	Armley	T	Agrmt.,Rep. 1845
12345	Armthorpe	P	N.t.p.
12346	Arncliffe	T	Awd.,Min.
12347	Askern	T	N.t.p.,Min.
12348	Asquith	T	N.t.p.,Min.
12349	Attercliffe cum Darnall	T	Awd.,Min.
12350	Aston cum Aughton	P	Rep. 1838
12351	Austerfield	T	Rep. 1839
12352	Austhorpe	T	Rep. 1839
12353	Austonley	T	Awd.,Min.
12354	Austwick and Lawkland	T	Awd.,Min.,Rep. 1843
12355	Azerley	T	Agrmt.,Min.,Rep. 1838
12356	Baildon	T	Awd.,Min.
12357	Balne	T	N.t.p.,Min.
12358	Badsworth	P	Rep. 1839
12359	Barden	T	Awd.,Min.,Rep. 1843
12360	Bardsey cum Rigton	T	Agrmt.,Awd.,Min.,Rep. 1840
12361	Barkstone	T	N.t.p.
12362	Barlow	T	Awd.,Min.
12363	Barkisland	T	N.t.p.
12364	Barnbrough	P	Rep. 1838
12365	Barnby upon Don	T	N.t.p.,Min.
12366	Barnesley	T	N.t.p.,Min.
12367	Barrowby	T	Rep. 1840
12368	Barugh	T	Min.
12370	Barwick in Elmett	T	N.t.p.,Min.
12371	Bashall Eaves	T	Awd.,Min.
12372	Batley	T	Min.
12373	Bawtry	T	Min.,Rep. 1839
12374	Beal and Kellingley	T	Agrmt.,Awd.,Min.,Rep. 1839
12375	Bentham	T	Min.,Rep. 1839
12376	Bentley and Arksey	T	N.t.p.,Min.
12377	Bewerley	T	Agrmt.,Min.,Rep. 1838
12378	Beeston	T	Awd.,Min.
12379	Beamsley	T	Agrmt.,Min.,Rep. 1842
12380	Beamsley near Skipton	T	Agrmt.,Rep. 1839
12381	Bierley North	T	Awd.,Min.
12382	Biggin and Little Fenton	T	N.t.p.,Min.
12383	Bilham	T	Awd.,Min.

Yorkshire, West Riding contd.

No.	Place	Type	Details
12384	Billingley	T	Rep. 1839
12385	Bilton with Harrogate	T	Awd.,Min.
12386	Bilton Park	D	Agrmt.,Rep. 1839
12387	Bingley	P	Min.,Rep. 1844
12388	Bishopside High and Low	T	Min.,Rep. 1838
12389	Birstwith	T	Awd.,Min.
12390	Birkin	T	Awd.,Min.
12391	Bishop Monkton	T	Agrmt.,Rep. 1839
12392	Bishop Thornton	T	Min.,Rep. 1839
12393	Bishopton	T	Agrmt.,Min.,Rep. 1838
12394	Blubberhouses	T	Awd.,Min.
12395	Bolton Abbey	T	N.t.p.,Min.
12396	Bolton by Bolland	P	Agrmt.,Rep. 1839
12397	Bolton	T	Awd.,Min.
12398	Bolton upon Dearne	P	Agrmt.,Min.
12399	Bordley	T	Awd.,Min.
12400	Boroughbridge	T	Awd.,Min.
12401	Bowland Higher Division	T	Agrmt.,Min.,Rep. 1843
12402	Bowland Lower Division	T	N.t.p.,Min.
12403	Bowling	T	Awd.,Min.
12404	Bracewell	P	Awd.,Min.
12405	Barnoldswick	T	Awd.,Min.
12406	Bradford West	T	Awd.,Min.
12407	Bradfield	C	Awd.,Min.
12408	Bradford	T	Awd.,Min.
12409	Bradleys Both	T	Rep. 1840
12410	Braithwell	T	Rep. 1838
12411	Bramham	T	Awd.,Min.
12412	Bramhope	T	Min.
12413	Bramley in Braithwell	T	Rep. 1839
12414	Bramley	T	Min.,Rep. 1845
12415	Brampton en le Morthen	T	Awd.,Min.
12416	Bramwith Sand	T	Rep. 1840
12417	Brayton	P	Min.
12418	Brearton	T	Agrmt.,Rep. 1839
12419	Bretton West	T	Awd.,Min.
12420	Bretton West	T	N.t.p.,Min.
12421	Bridge Hewick	T	Awd.,Min.
12422	Brierley	T	Min.,Rep. 1839
12423	Brightside	T	N.t.p.
12424	Brinsworth	T	Awd.,Min.
12425	Brodsworth	P	Agrmt.,Rep. 1845
12426	Brogden	T	N.t.p.,Min.
12427	Brotherton	T	Awd.,Min.
12428	Broughton	T	Agrmt.,Awd.,Min.,Rep. 1841
12429	Buckden	T	Agrmt.,Min.,Rep. 1840
12430	Burghwallis	T	Awd.,Min.
12431	Burley	T	Agrmt.,Min.,Rep. 1844
12432	Burn	T	Awd.,Min.
12433	Burnsal with Thorpe	T	Awd.,Min.
12434	Burton in Lonsdale	P	N.t.p.
12435	Burton Leonard	P	Awd.,Min.
12436	Burton Salmon	T	Awd.,Min.
12437	Bryam cum Poole	T	Awd.,Min.
12438	Calton	T	N.t.p.,Awd.,Min.
12439	Castley	T	Awd.,Min.
12440	Carlton	P	Agrmt.,Min.,Rep. 1839
12441	Carleton	T	N.t.p.,Min.
12442	Carlton	T	Awd.,Min.
12443	Carlton	T	N.t.p.,Min.
12444	Carlton	H	Min.,Rep. 1838
12445	Calverley	T	Awd.,Min.
12446	Campsall	T	N.t.p.,Min.
12447	Cantley	P	Awd.,Min.
12448	Cartworth	T	Awd.,Min.
12449	Cattal	T	Min.
12450	Catterton	T	Awd.,Min.
12451	Cawthorne	P	Awd.,Min.
12452	Cawood	P	N.t.p.,Min.
12453	Chapel Allerton	T	Min.,Rep. 1844
12454	Chapel Haddlesey	T	Rep. 1838
12455	Chevet	T	Awd.,Min.
12456	Churwell	T	Awd.,Min.
12457	Clapham with Newby	T	Awd.,Min.
12458	Clareton	T	N.t.p.,Min.
12459	Clayton with Frickley	P	Awd.,Min.
12460	Clayton West	T	Awd.,Min.
12461	Clayton	T	Awd.,Min.
12462	Cleckheaton	T	Awd.,Min.
12463	Clifford	T	Awd.,Min.
12464	Clifton	T	Awd.,Min.
12465	Clifton Crookhill	D	Rep. 1839
12466	Clifton with Norwood	T	Awd.,Min.
12467	Clotherholme	T	Agrmt.,Rep. 1838
12468	Coates	T	Awd.,Min.
12469	Coldcotes	H	Min.,Rep. 1844
12470	Cold Hiendley	T	Rep. 1840
12471	Collingham	P	Awd.,Min.
12472	Coneythorpe	T	N.t.p.,Min.
12473	Conisbrough	T	Min.,Rep. 1839
12474	Conisbrough Parks	D	Awd.,Min.
12475	Coniston	H	Awd.,Min.
12476	Cononley	T	Min.,Rep. 1839
12477	Crigglestone	T	Awd.,Min.
12478	Copgrove	P	Rep. 1840
12479	Copt Hewick	T	Agrmt.,Min.,Rep. 1841
12480	Cowling	T	Awd.,Min.,Rep. 1844
12481	Cowthorpe	P	Awd.,Min.
12482	Cracoe	T	Agrmt.,Min.,Rep. 1839
12483	Cridling Stubbs	T	Awd.,Min.
12484	Crofton	P	Awd.,Min.
12485	Crossland South	T	Awd.,Min.,Rep. 1840
12486	Crowle	P	Min.
12487	Cudworth	T	Awd.,Min.
12488	Cumberworth	T	N.t.p.,Min.
12489	Dacre	T	Awd.,Min.
12490	Dalton	T	N.t.p.,Awd.,Min.
12491	Darfield	T	Rep. 1839
12492	Darton	P	Awd.,Min.
12493	Denby	T	N.t.p.,Min.
12494	Dent	T	Awd.,Min.
12495	Deighton North	T	Awd.,Min.
12496	Dennaby	T	Rep. 1839
12497	Denton	T	Awd.,Min.
12498	Dewsbury	T	Awd.,Min.
12499	Dinnington	P	N.t.p.,Min.
12500	Doncaster	P	Agrmt.,Min.,Rep. 1838
12501	Draughton	T	Awd.,Min.,Rep. 1844
12502	Drax	P	Min.,Rep. 1838
12503	Drighlington	T	Awd.,Min.
12504	Dodworth	T	Awd.,Min.
12505	Dunkeswick and Weston	T	N.t.p.,Min.
12506	Dunsforth Lower	T	N.t.p.,Min.
12507	Darrington	P	Rep. 1838
12508	Dunsforth Upper, Branton	T	N.t.p.,Min.
12509	Easington	T	Min.,Rep. 1840
12510	Eastoft	T	Min.,Rep. 1838
12511	Eavestone	T	Awd.,Min.
12512	Ecclesall	T	N.t.p.,Min.
12513	Ecclesfield	T	N.t.p.,Min.
12514	Eccleshill	T	Awd.,Min.
12515	Edlington	P	Rep. 1839
12516	Egborough	T	Min.,Rep. 1838
12517	Ellenthorpe	T	Awd.,Min.
12519	Elmley	T	Awd.,Min.
12520	Elmsall North	T	Agrmt.,Min.,Rep. 1841
12521	Elslack	T	Min.,Rep. 1839
12522	Elmsall South	T	Awd.,Min.
12523	Embsay	T	Awd.,Min.
12524	Esholt	T	Awd.,Min.
12525	Fairburn	T	Agrmt.,Rep. 1839
12526	Farnham	P	Awd.,Min.
12527	Farnhill	T	Awd.,Min.
12528	Farnley Tyas	T	Agrmt.,Awd.,Min.,Rep. 1839
12529	Farnley	T	Min.,Rep. 1844
12530	Farnley	T	Awd.,Min.
12531	Fockerby	T	Awd.,Min.
12532	Fountain's Earth	T	Agrmt.,Min.,Rep. 1838
12533	Felliscliffe	T	Awd.,Min.
12534	Fenwick	T	Awd.,Min.
12535	Ferensby	T	Awd.,Min.
12536	Ferrinsby	T	Agrmt.,Min.,Rep. 1839
12537	Ferry Fryston	P	Awd.,Min.,Rep. 1838
12538	Fewston	T	Awd.,Min.
12539	Firbeck	P	Min.,Rep. 1840
12540	Fishlake	P	N.t.p.,Min.
12541	Flaxby	T	N.t.p.,Min.
12542	Flockton	T	Awd.,Min.
12543	Follifoot	T	Awd.,Min.
12544	Friar Mere	D	Awd.,Min.
12545	Fulstone	T	Awd.,Min.
12546	Garforth	T	Agrmt.,Min.,Rep. 1841
12547	Gargrave	P	Awd.,Min.
12548	Gawthorpe	T	Awd.,Min.
12549	Garsdale	T	Min.,Rep. 1840
12550	Giggleswick	P	Awd.,Min.
12551	Gildersome	T	Awd.,Min.
12552	Gildingwells	T	Min.,Rep. 1840
12553	Gisburn	T	Awd.,Min.
12554	Gisburn Forest	T	Awd.,Min.
12555	Givendale	T	Rep. 1840
12556	Glusburn	T	Awd.,Min.,Rep. 1844
12557	Golcar	T	Agrmt.,Awd.,Min.
12558	Goldsbrough	T	Awd.,Min.
12559	Gomersal	T	Awd.,Min.
12560	Goole	T	Awd.,Min.
12561	Gowdall	T	N.t.p.,Min.
12562	Grantley	T	Awd.,Min.
12563	Grassington	T	Awd.,Min.
12564	Greasborough	T	Awd.,Min.
12565	Grewelthorpe	T	Agrmt.,Min.,Rep. 1839
12566	Grindleton	T	Awd.,Min.
12567	Guiseley	T	Min.,Rep. 1839
12568	Gunthwaite	T	Awd.,Min.
12569	Haddlesey West	T	N.t.p.,Min.
12570	Haldenby	T	Agrmt.,Min.,Rep. 1840
12571	Halifax	P	N.t.p.,Min.
12572	Hallam, Upper and Nether	T	N.t.p.,Min.
12573	Halton West	T	Rep. 1839
12574	Halton East	T	Agrmt.,Min.,Rep. 1841
12575	Halton Gill	T	Agrmt.,Min.,Rep. 1840
12576	Hammerton Green	T	N.t.p.,Min.

Yorkshire, West Riding contd.

No.	Place		Details
12577	Hampsthwaite	T	Awd.,Min.
12578	Handsworth	P	Awd.,Min.
12579	Hanlith	T	Awd.,Min.
12580	Hardwick East	T	Awd.,Min.
12581	Hardwick West	T	Awd.,Min.
12582	Harewood	T	Awd.,Min.
12583	Harthill	P	Min.,Rep. 1840
12584	Hartlington	T	Awd.,Min.
12585	Hartshead	T	Awd.,Min.
12586	Hartwith Winsley	T	Awd.,Min.
12587	Hatfield	P	Min.,Rep. 1840
12588	Havercroft	T	Agrmt.,Min.,Rep. 1839
12589	Hawkswick	T	Agrmt.,Min.,Rep. 1840
12590	Hawksworth	T	Awd.,Min.
12591	Haworth	T	Awd.,Min.
12592	Hazlewood	T	Awd.,Min.,Rep. 1843
12593	Hazlewood	T	Awd.,Min.
12594	Headingley cum Burley	T	Agrmt.,Rep. 1844
12595	Heaton	T	Awd.,Min.
12596	Hebden	T	Awd.,Min.
12597	Heck	T	N.t.p.,Min.
12598	Heckmondwike	T	Agrmt.,Awd.,Min.,Rep. 1842
12599	Hellifield	T	Min.,Rep. 1839
12600	Hemsworth	P	N.t.p.,Min.
12601	Hensal	T	N.t.p.,Min.
12602	Hepworth	T	Awd.,Min.
12603	Hessle	T	Awd.,Min.
12604	Hetton	T	Agrmt.,Min.,Rep. 1839
12605	Hickleton	P	Awd.,Min.
12606	Hiendley South	T	Min.
12607	Hillam	T	N.t.p.,Min.
12608	Hill Top	T	Awd.,Min.
12609	Hirst Courtney	T	Min.,Rep. 1838
12610	Hirst Temple	T	N.t.p.,Min.
12611	Holbeck	T	Awd.,Min.
12612	Holme	T	Awd.,Min.
12613	Honley	T	N.t.p.,Min.
12614	Hook	T	Awd.,Min.
12615	Hooton Pagnell	P	Awd.,Min.
12616	Hooton Roberts	P	Rep. 1839
12617	Horbury	T	Awd.,Min.
12618	Horton	T	Awd.,Min.
12619	Horton	T	Awd.,Min.
12620	Horton in Ribblesdale	P	Awd.,Min.
12621	Horsforth	T	Min.,Rep. 1839
12622	Houghton Great	T	Rep. 1840
12623	Houghton Little	T	Rep. 1839
12624	Hoyland High	T	Agrmt.,Awd.,Min.
12625	Hoyland Swaine	T	Awd.,Min.
12626	Huddersfield	T	Awd.,Min.
12628	Hunshelff	T	N.t.p.,Min.
12629	Hunsingore	T	Awd.,Min.
12630	Hunslet	T	Min.,Rep. 1844
12631	Hunsworth	T	Awd.,Min.
12632	Humberton	T	Awd.,Min.
12633	Idle	T	Awd.,Min.
12634	Ilkley	T	Awd.,Min.
12635	Ingburchworth	T	N.t.p.,Min.
12636	Ingerthorpe	T	Awd.,Min.
12637	Ingleton	T	Min.,Rep. 1839
12638	Keighley	P	Min.,Rep. 1840
12639	Kellington	T	Min.,Rep. 1839
12640	Keswick East	T	N.t.p.,Min.
12641	Kettlewell	T	Awd.,Min.
12642	Kexborough	T	Awd.,Min.
12643	Kildwick	T	Awd.,Min.,Rep. 1844
12644	Kilnsay	T	Awd.,Min.
12645	Kimberworth	T	Awd.,Min.
12646	Kippax	T	N.t.p.,Min.
12647	Kirkby Hall	T	Awd.,Min.
12649	Kirk Deighton	T	Agrmt.,Min.,Rep. 1846
12650	Kirk Hammerton	P	Awd.,Min.
12651	Kirkheaton	P	Awd.,Min.
12652	Kirk Bramwith	P	Awd.,Min.
12653	Kirkburton	T	Awd.,Min.
12654	Kirkby Malzeard	T	Agrmt.,Min.,Rep. 1838
12655	Kirkby Overblow	T	Agrmt.,Rep. 1838
12656	Kirkby Wharfe	T	Awd.,Min.
12657	Kirkby in Malham Dale	T	Awd.,Min.
12658	Kirk Sandall	T	Awd.,Min.
12659	Kirkby South	T	Min.
12660	Kirksmeaton	P	N.t.p.,Min.
12661	Knaresborough	P	Awd.,Min.
12662	Langold and Letwell	T	Rep. 1840
12664	Langset	T	N.t.p.
12665	Laverton	T	Agrmt.,Min.,Rep. 1838
12667	Laughton en le Morthen	P	Agrmt.,Rep. 1839
12668	Lead Hall	T	Awd.,Min.
12669	Leathley	T	Awd.,Min.
12670	Ledsham	T	Agrmt.,Rep. 1840
12671	Ledstone	T	Rep. 1840
12672	Leeds	T	Awd.,Min.
12673	Lindley cum Quarmby	C	Min.
12674	Lindley	T	Awd.,Min.
12675	Lindrick	T	Agrmt.,Rep. 1838
12677	Lingards	T	Agrmt.,Awd.,Min.,Rep. 1839
12678	Linthwaite	T	Awd.,Min.
12679	Linton	T	Awd.,Min.
12680	Featherstone	T	Awd.,Min.
12681	Hamphall Stubbs	T	Min.,Rep. 1838
12682	Linton	T	Min.,Rep. 1838
12683	Litton	T	Agrmt.,Min.,Rep. 1840
12684	Liversedge	T	Awd.,Min.
12685	Lockwood	T	Awd.,Min.,Rep. 1840
12686	Lofthouse	T	Min.,Rep. 1838
12687	Longwood	C	N.t.p.,Min.
12688	Lords Mere	D	Awd.,Min.
12689	Lotherton	T	Agrmt.,Rep. 1839
12690	Malham	T	Awd.,Min.
12691	Malham Moor	T	Awd.,Min.
12692	Maltby	P	Min.,Rep. 1838
12693	Manningham	T	Awd.,Min.
12694	Markenfield	T	Awd.,Min.
12695	Markington with Waller	T	Awd.,Min.
12696	Marr	P	Awd.,Min.
12697	Marsden	T	Awd.,Min.
12698	Marsden	T	Awd.,Min.
12699	Marston Long	P	Min.,Rep. 1839
12700	Marton cum Grafton	P	Awd.,Min.,Rep. 1841
12701	Martons Both	P	Min.,Rep. 1843
12702	Meltham	T	Awd.,Min.
12703	Melton on the Hill	P	Awd.,Min.
12704	Menstone	T	Awd.,Min.
12705	Menwith with Darley	T	Awd.,Min.
12706	Methley	P	N.t.p.,Min.
12707	Mexbrough	P	Agrmt.,Rep. 1838
12708	Micklefield	T	Min.,Rep. 1839
12709	Middleton	T	Awd.,Min.
12710	Middleton	T	Agrmt.,Min.,Rep. 1839
12711	Middop (or Midhope)	T	Awd.,Min.
12712	Midhope	D	Awd.,Min.
12713	Milford South and Lumby	T	N.t.p.,Min.
12714	Minskip	T	Agrmt.,Min.,Rep. 1840
12715	Mirfield	P	Awd.,Min.
12716	Mitton with Crook	T	Awd.,Min.
12717	Monk Bretton	T	N.t.p.,Min.
12718	Monk Fryston	T	Awd.,Min.
12719	Monkhill	T	N.t.p.,Min.
12720	Morley	T	Awd.,Min.
12721	Morton East and West	T	Awd.,Min.
12722	Morton cum Fareholm	D	N.t.p.
12723	Moss	T	Awd.,Min.
12724	Nappa	T	Awd.,Min.
12725	Nesfield with Langbar	T	Awd.,Min.
12726	Newall with Clifton	T	Awd.,Min.
12727	Newby with Mulwith	T	Awd.,Min.
12728	Newhay	P	Min.
12729	Newpark	D	Min.
12730	Newsholme	T	Awd.,Min.
12731	Newthorpe and Huddleston	T	Agrmt.,Min.,Rep. 1839
12732	Newton	T	Min.,Rep. 1840
12733	Newton Kyme with Towlston	P	Awd.,Min.
12734	Nidd	P	Awd.,Min.,Rep. 1841
12735	Norland	T	N.t.p.
12736	Normanton	T	Min.,Rep. 1839
12737	Norton	T	N.t.p.,Min.
12739	Nostel cum Hurstwick	T	Awd.,Min.
12740	Notton	T	Rep. 1839
12741	Nun Monkton	P	Agrmt.,Rep. 1839
12742	Nunwicke	T	Rep. 1838
12743	Oldcoats	T	Min.
12744	Orgreave	T	Awd.,Min.
12745	Osmondthorpe	D	Min.,Rep. 1844
12746	Ossett	T	Awd.,Min.
12747	Otley	T	Awd.,Min.
12748	Otterburn	T	Awd.,Min.
12749	Oulton with Woodlesford	T	Min.,Rep. 1839
12750	Ouseburn Great	P	N.t.p.,Min.
12751	Ousefleet	T	Min.
12752	Ovenden	T	Min.
12753	Owram South	T	N.t.p.
12754	Owram North	T	N.t.p.
12755	Owston	T	Awd.,Min.
12756	Oxspring	T	Awd.,Min.
12757	Oxton	T	Awd.,Min.
12758	Parlington	T	Awd.,Min.
12759	Paythorne	T	Awd.,Min.
12760	Peniston	T	N.t.p.,Min.
12761	Pigburn	D	N.t.p.
12762	Plumpton	T	Awd.,Min.
12763	Pollington	T	N.t.p.,Min.
12764	Pontefract	T	Awd.,Min.
12765	Pontefract Park	EP	N.t.p.,Min.
12766	Potter Newton	T	Min.,Rep. 1844
12767	Preston Great and Little	T	Agrmt.,Awd.,Min.,Rep. 1842
12768	Preston Long	T	Min.,Rep. 1839
12769	Pudsey	T	Awd.,Min.
12770	Purston Jaglin	T	Awd.,Min.
12771	Quick Mere	D	Awd.,Min.
12772	Catcliffe	T	Awd.,Min.
12773	Ravenfield	P	Awd.,Min.
12774	Rawcliffe	T	Awd.,Min.

Yorkshire, West Riding contd.

No.	Place	Type	Details
12775	Rawden	T	Min.,Rep. 1837
12776	Rawmarsh	P	Agrmt.,Awd.,Min.,Rep. 1844
12777	Reedness	T	Awd.,Min.
12778	Ribston Great	T	Awd.,Min.
12779	Ribston Little	T	Awd.,Min.
12780	Rigton	T	Min.
12781	Rilston	T	Min.,Rep. 1839
12782	Rimington	T	Awd.,Min.
12783	Ripon	T	Agrmt.,Min.,Rep. 1838
12784	Ripley	P	Agrmt.,Rep. 1839
12785	Rishworth	T	N.t.p.
12786	Roecliffe	T	Awd.,Min.
12787	Rossington	P	Rep. 1838
12788	Rotherham	T	Awd.,Min.
12789	Rothwell Haigh	T	Agrmt.,Min.,Rep. 1838
12790	Rothwell cum Royds	T	Agrmt.,Rep. 1844
12791	Roundhay	T	N.t.p.,Min.
12792	Royston	P	Awd.,Min.
12793	Ryhill	T	Awd.,Min.
12794	Ryther cum Ossendike	T	Min.,Rep. 1838
12795	Saddleworth with Quick	T	Min.
12796	Salterforth	T	Awd.,Min.
12797	Sandal Great	T	Awd.,Min.
12798	Sawley	T	Min.,Rep. 1841
12799	Sawley with Tosside	EP	N.t.p.
12800	Scammonden	T	Awd.,Min.
12801	Seacroft	T	Min.,Rep. 1839
12802	Sedbergh	T	Agrmt.,Min.,Rep. 1839
12803	Selby	P	N.t.p.,Min.
12804	Shadwell	T	N.t.p.,Min.
12805	Sharleston	T	Agrmt.,Rep. 1841
12806	Shaw Mere	D	Awd.,Min.
12807	Sharow	T	Agrmt.,Min.,Rep. 1841
12808	Saxton with Scarthingwell	T	Awd.,Min.
12809	Scarcroft	T	N.t.p.,Min.
12810	Scausby	D	N.t.p.
12811	Scholes	H	Awd.,Min.
12812	Scosthrop	T	Awd.,Min.
12813	Scotton	T	N.t.p.,Min.
12814	Scriven with Tentergate	T	Agrmt.,Min.,Rep. 1839
12815	Shittlington	T	Awd.,Min.
12816	Sicklinghall cum Woodhall	T	Agrmt.,Rep. 1838
12817	Silkstone	T	Awd.,Min.,Rep. 1839
12818	Silsden	T	Awd.,Min.
12819	Skelbrooke	T	Awd.,Min.
12820	Sheffield	T	Awd.,Min.
12821	Shelf	T	N.t.p.
12822	Shelley	T	Awd.,Min.
12823	Shepley	T	Awd.,Min.
12824	Sherburn	T	N.t.p.,Min.
12825	Shipley	T	Awd.,Min.
12826	Skelding	T	Awd.,Min.
12827	Skellow	T	Agrmt.,Rep. 1838
12828	Skelmanthorpe	T	Awd.,Min.
12829	Skelton	T	Rep. 1842
12830	Skipton	T	Agrmt.,Min.,Rep. 1839
12831	Skircoat	T	N.t.p.
12832	Slaidburn	T	Min.,Rep. 1840
12833	Slaithwaite	T	Awd.,Min.
12834	Smeaton Little	T	N.t.p.,Min.
12835	Snaith and Cowick	T	Min.,Rep. 1839
12836	Snydale	T	Agrmt.,Min.,Rep. 1839
12837	Soothill Upper	T	Awd.,Min.
12838	Soothill Nether	T	Awd.,Min.
12839	Sowerby	T	N.t.p.
12840	Soyland	T	Min.
12841	Spofforth	T	Awd.,Min.
12842	Sprotbrough	P	Agrmt.,Min.,Rep. 1846
12843	Stainborough	T	Awd.,Min.
12844	Stainburn	T	N.t.p.,Min.
12846	Stainland with Old Lindley	T	N.t.p.
12847	Stainley North	T	Min.,Rep. 1840
12848	Stainley South	P	Min.
12851	Stainton cum Hellaby	P	Agrmt.,Min.,Rep. 1838
12852	Stannington Storrs	D	Awd.,Min.
12853	Stansfield	T	N.t.p.
12855	Staveley	P	Awd.,Min.
12856	Stirton with Thorlby	T	Rep. 1839
12857	Stockheld	T	N.t.p.
12858	Stonebeck Down	T	Agrmt.,Min.,Rep. 1838
12859	Stonebeck UP	T	Agrmt.,Min.,Rep. 1838
12860	Steeton with Eastburn	T	Agrmt.,Awd.,Min.,Rep. 1844
12861	Stotfold	EP	Awd.,Min.
12862	Studley Magna	T	Agrmt.,Rep. 1838
12863	Studley Parva	T	Rep. 1840
12864	Sturton	T	Awd.,Min.
12865	Stutton	T	Agrmt.,Min.,Rep. 1843
12866	Sutton Grange	T	N.t.p.,Min.
12867	Sutton	T	Awd.,Min.
12868	Sutton	T	Min.,Rep. 1838
12869	Sutton	T	Min.,Rep. 1839
12870	Swinden	T	Awd.,Min.
12871	Swinefleet	T	Awd.,Min.
12872	Swillington and Astley	P	N.t.p.,Min.
12873	Stanley with Wrenthorpe	T	Awd.,Min.
12874	Starbotton	T	Awd.,Min.
12875	Tadcaster East	T	Agrmt.,Awd.,Min.,Rep. 1843
12876	Tadcaster West	T	Awd.,Min.
12877	Tankersley	P	Min.,Rep. 1839
12878	Tanshelf	T	N.t.p.,Min.
12879	Temple Newsam	T	Awd.,Min.
12880	Thong Upper	T	Awd.,Min.
12881	Thong Nether	T	Agrmt.,Awd.,Min.
12882	Thorne	P	Min.,Rep. 1840
12883	Thorner	T	N.t.p.,Min.
12884	Thornes	T	Awd.,Min.
12885	Thornhill	T	Awd.,Min.
12886	Thornthwaite with Padside	T	Awd.,Min.
12887	Thornton	T	Awd.,Min.
12888	Thornton	P	N.t.p.
12889	Thornville	T	Min.
12890	Thorpe	T	N.t.p.
12891	Thorpe	T	Rep. 1839
12892	Thorpe in Balne	T	Agrmt.,Awd.,Min.,Rep. 1844
12893	Thorpe Salvin	P	Awd.,Min.
12894	Thorpe Willoughby	T	N.t.p.
12895	Thorpe Underwood	T	Awd.,Min.
12896	Thorpe Stapleton	T	Awd.,Min.
12897	Thornton in Craven	P	N.t.p.,Min.
12898	Thornton in Lonsdale	P	Min.,Rep. 1840
12899	Threshfield	T	Awd.,Min.
12900	Throapham and Thwaites	D	Min.,Rep. 1840
12901	Todwick	P	Awd.,Min.
12902	Thrybergh	P	Rep. 1839
12903	Thurcross	T	Awd.,Min.
12904	Thurgoland	T	Awd.,Min.
12905	Thurlstone	T	N.t.p.,Min.
12906	Thurnscoe	P	Min.,Rep. 1839
12907	Thurstonland	T	Awd.,Min.
12908	Tickhill	P	Awd.,Min.
12909	Timble Great	T	Awd.,Min.
12910	Timble Little	T	Awd.,Min.
12911	Tinsley	T	Awd.,Min.
12912	Tong	T	Awd.,Min.
12913	Towton	T	Awd.,Min.
12914	Treeton and Manor of Wales	T	Agrmt.,Min.,Rep. 1838
12915	Trumfleet	T	Agrmt.,Rep. 1840
12916	Ulley	T	N.t.p.,Min.
12917	Ulleskelf	T	Agrmt.,Awd.,Min.,Rep. 1841
12918	Totley	T	N.t.p.
12919	Waddington	T	Awd.,Min.
12920	Wadsworth (and Haworth)	P	Min.
12921	Wadworth	P	Min.
12922	Wakefield	T	Awd.,Min.
12923	Wales Manor	P	Min.
12925	Walkingham Hill	T	Agrmt.,Rep. 1839
12926	Walton	T	Awd.,Min.
12927	Warmfield cum Heath	T	Min.,Rep. 1839
12928	Warmsworth	P	Agrmt.,Min.,Rep. 1838
12929	Warsill	T	N.t.p.,Min.
12930	Wath upon Dearne	P	Min.,Rep. 1840
12931	Weardley	T	N.t.p.,Min.
12932	Weston	T	Awd.,Min.
12933	Westwick	T	Awd.,Min.
12934	Wetherby	T	Min.,Rep. 1838
12935	Whiston	T	Min.
12936	Whiston	T	Awd.,Min.
12937	Whitcliffe with Thorpe	T	Min.,Rep. 1839
12938	Whitgift	T	Awd.,Min.
12939	Whitley	T	N.t.p.,Min.
12940	Whitley Lower	T	Awd.,Min.
12941	Whitwood	T	Awd.,Min.
12942	Whixley	P	Awd.,Min.
12943	Wickersley	T	N.t.p.,Min.
12944	Widdington	T	Awd.,Min.
12945	Wigglesworth	T	Min.,Rep. 1839
12946	Wigton	T	N.t.p.
12947	Wike	T	Awd.,Min.
12948	Wike	T	Rep. 1839
12949	Wilsden	T	Awd.,Min.
12950	Winksley	T	Awd.,Min.
12951	Wintersett	T	Awd.,Min.
12952	Wistow	P	N.t.p.,Min.
12953	Wombwell	T	Min.,Rep. 1838
12954	Womersley	T	N.t.p.,Min.
12955	Woodsetts	T	Awd.,Min.
12956	Wooldale	T	Awd.,Min.
12957	Woolley	T	Rep. 1839
12958	Wortley	T	Awd.,Min.
12959	Worsbrough	T	Min.,Rep. 1838
12960	Wothersome	T	Agrmt.,Min.,Rep. 1840
12961	Wragby	P	Min.
12962	Yeadon	T	Min.,Rep. 1837
12963	Weeton	T	N.t.p.
12964	Warley	T	N.t.p.
13564	Aldborough	P	N.t.p.
14820	Pannal	P	N.t.p.,Min.
14832	Carleton	T	N.t.p.,Min.
14834	Arthington	T	Awd.,Min.

Anglesey

13817	Aberfraw	P	Awd.,Min.
13818	Amlwch	P	Rep. 1841
13819	Beaumaris	P	Awd.,Min.
13820	Bodedern	P	Rep. 1840
13821	Bodewryd	P	N.t.p.
13822	Bodwrog	P	Rep. 1843
13823	Cerrigceinwen	P	Rep. 1841
13824	Ceirchiog	P	Awd.,Min.
13825	Coedana	P	Rep. 1840
13826	Gwaredog	C	Rep. 1842
13827	Heneglwys	P	Rep. 1841
13828	Holyhead	P	Rep. 1840
13829	Llanallgo	P	Awd.,Min.
13830	Llanbabo	P	Rep. 1841
13831	Llanbadrig	P	Min.,Rep. 1843
13832	Llanbedrgoch	P	Rep. 1841
13833	Llanbeulan	P	Awd.,Min.
13834	Llanddaniel	P	Awd.
13835	Llanddausaint	P	Rep. 1841
13836	Llanddona	P	Awd.,Min.
13837	Llanddyfnan	P	Min.,Rep. 1841
13838	Llandegvan	P	Awd.,Min.
13839	Llandisilio	P	Rep. 1842
13840	Llandrigarn	P	Rep. 1840
13841	Llanerchymedd	EP	N.t.p.
13842	Llaneilian	P	Awd.,Min.,Rep. 1843
13843	Llanengrad	P	Awd.,Min.
13844	Llanedwen	P	Awd.,Min.
13845	Llanfaethly	P	Rep. 1840
13846	Llanfair Mathafarn Eithaf	P	Rep. 1841
13847	Llanfairpwllgwyngyll	P	Rep. 1842
13848	Llanfairyneubwll	P	Agrmt.,Rep. 1840
13849	Llanfairynghornwy	P	Rep. 1841
13850	Llanfihangel Din Sylwy	P	Awd.,Min.
13851	Llanfihangel Trerbeirdd	P	Rep. 1840
13852	Llanfihangelynhowyn	P	Agrmt.,Rep. 1840
13853	Llanfihangel Esgeifiog	P	Rep. 1843
13854	Llanflewyn	P	Rep. 1841
13855	Llanfechell	P	Min.,Rep. 1842
13856	Llanfwrog	P	Rep. 1840
13857	Llangadwaladr	P	Rep. 1843
13858	Llangaffo	P	Agrmt.,Rep. 1839
13859	Llangainwen	P	Agrmt.,Rep. 1839
13860	Llangefni	P	Rep. 1842
13861	Llangwyllog	P	Awd.,Min.
13862	Llangwyfan	P	Rep. 1839
13863	Llangoed	P	Awd.,Min.
13864	Llangristiolus	P	Rep. 1841
13865	Llanidan	P	Awd.,Min.
13866	Llaniestin	P	Awd.,Min.
13867	Llanllibio	P	Awd.,Min.
13869	Llanrhwydrys	P	Agrmt.,Rep. 1840
13871	Llanrhyddlad	P	Rep. 1843
13873	Llasadwrn	P	Rep. 1839
13875	Llantrisaint	P	Awd.,Min.
13876	Llanvaelog	P	Awd.,Min.
13877	Llanvachraith	P	Awd.,Min.
13878	Llanvaes	P	Awd.,Min.
13879	Llanvair Yn Y Cymwd	P	Awd.,Min.
13880	Llanvigael	P	Awd.,Min.
13881	Llangwenllwyfo	P	Min.,Rep. 1842
13882	Llanynghenedl	P	Awd.,Min.
13883	Llechcynvarwy	P	Awd.,Min.
13884	Llechylched	P	Awd.,Min.
13885	Newborough	P	Awd.,Min.
13886	Pentraeth	P	Rep. 1841
13887	Penrhos Llugwy	P	Awd.,Min.
13888	Penmynydd	P	Min.,Rep. 1843
13889	Penmon	P	Awd.,Min.
13890	Rhodygeidio	P	Awd.,Min.
13891	Rhosbeirio	P	Rep. 1841
13892	Rhoscolyn	P	Agrmt.,Rep. 1840
13893	Rhos Y Myneich	D	Awd.,Min.
13894	Trefdraeth	P	Rep. 1841
13895	Tregayan	P	Agrmt.,Rep. 1839
13896	Trewalchmai	P	Agrmt.,Rep. 1840

Brecon

13874	Llanspyddyd	P	Min.,Rep. 1838
13897	Aberllunvey	P	Awd.,Min.
13898	Aberyscir	P	Agrmt.
13899	Alltmawr	P	Rep. 1840
13900	Battle	P	Min.
13901	Bronllys	P	Rep. 1839
13902	Builth	P	Agrmt.,Rep. 1840
13903	Cantriff	P	Rep. 1838
13904	Castle Inn	EP	N.t.p.
13905	Christ's College	EP	N.t.p.
13906	Cray	H	Min.,Rep. 1840
13907	Crickadarn	P	Rep. 1841
13908	Crickhowell	P	Rep. 1839
13909	St Michael Cwmdu	P	Awd.,Min.
13910	St Davids	P	Agrmt.,Min.,Rep. 1841
13911	Great Forest of Brecon	D	Min.
13912	Garthbrengy	P	Rep. 1839
13913	Glasbury	P	Agrmt.,Min.,Rep. 1841
13914	Glyn	H	Rep. 1840
13915	Glyntawe	T	Rep. 1840
13916	Grwynefaur	T	Min.,Rep. 1839
13917	Gwenddwr and Troscoed	P	Rep. 1840
13918	Hay	P	Awd.,Min.
13919	St John the Evangelist	P	Min.,Rep. 1839
13920	Llanavanfawr	P	Rep. 1840
13921	Llanvanfechan	P	Rep. 1840
13922	Llanbeder	P	Min.,Rep. 1840
13923	Llandewi Abergwessin	P	Awd.,Min.
13924	Llandewi Cwm	P	Rep. 1839
13925	Llandefalley	P	Min.,Rep. 1841
13926	Llandevailogfach	P	Rep. 1839
13927	Llandilofane	P	Agrmt.,Min.,Rep. 1839
13928	Llandulas	P	Awd.,Min.
13929	Llanelly	P	Min.,Rep. 1839
13930	Llanelieu	P	Agrmt.,Min.,Rep. 1839
13931	Llanfihangel Aberwissin	P	Rep. 1840
13932	Llanfihangel Brynfrabean	P	Min.,Rep. 1840
13933	Llanfihangel Nantbraen	P	Agrmt.,Min.,Rep. 1839
13934	Llanfihangel Talyllyn	P	Agrmt.,Min.
13935	Llanfrynach	P	Rep. 1840
13936	Llanganten	P	Awd.,Min.
13937	Llangastytallyllyn	P	Rep. 1841
13938	Llangattock	P	Awd.,Min.
13939	Llangenny	P	Rep. 1839
13940	Llangorse	P	Rep. 1841
13941	Llangunnider	P	Agrmt.,Awd.,Min.,Rep. 1840
13942	Llangynog	P	Min.
13943	Llanhamlach	P	Rep. 1838
13944	Llanigan	P	Awd.,Min.
13945	Llanlleonfel	P	Agrmt.,Awd.,Min.
13946	Llansaintfraed	P	Min.
13947	Llanthetty	P	Rep. 1839
13948	Llanthew	P	Agrmt.,Min.,Rep. 1841
13949	Llanvigan	P	Rep. 1840
13950	Llanvillo	P	Awd.,Min.
13951	Llanwrthol	P	Awd.,Min.
13952	Llanwrtyd	P	Awd.,Min.
13953	Llanynis	P	Min.,Rep. 1839
13954	Llanywern	P	Awd.,Min.
13955	Llysdinam	P	Agrmt.,Rep. 1840
13956	Llyswen	P	Min.,Rep. 1839
13957	Maescar	H	Rep. 1838
13958	Maesmynis	P	Min.,Rep. 1841
13959	Mary St	C	Rep. 1838
13960	Merthyr Cynog	P	Rep. 1839
13961	Modridd	H	Rep. 1838
13962	Patrishow	P	Rep. 1841
13963	Penbuallt	H	Agrmt.,Min.,Rep. 1843
13964	Penderyn	P	Rep. 1839
13965	Penpont	H	Min.,Rep. 1838
13966	Rhosferrig	H	Min.,Rep. 1840
13967	Senny	P	Rep. 1840
13968	Talachddu	P	Awd.,Min.
13969	Talgarth	P	Min.,Rep. 1839
13970	Trayanglaes	H	Rep. 1839
13971	Trayenmawr	H	Min.,Rep. 1839
13972	Trefilis	H	Rep. 1843
13973	Trelong	P	Awd.,Min.
13974	Tyrabbott	D	N.t.p.
13975	Vaynor	P	Rep. 1840
13976	Ysclydach	H	Rep. 1841
13977	Ystradfellty	P	Rep. 1841
13978	Ystradgunlais	P	Min.,Rep. 1839
13979	Cathedine	P	Rep. 1839

Caernarvonshire

13870	Llanrhychwyn	P	Min.,Rep. 1841
14088	Aber	P	Awd.,Min.
14089	The Abbey	EP	N.t.p.
14090	Aberconwy	P	Awd.,Min.
14091	Aberdaron	P	Rep. 1840
14092	Abererch	P	Rep. 1844
14093	Bangor	P	Rep. 1840
14094	Bardsey Isle	EP	N.t.p.
14095	Beddgelert	P	Agrmt.,Rep. 1839
14096	Bettws Garmon	P	Agrmt.,Min.,Rep. 1839
14097	Bettws Y Coed	P	Rep. 1841
14098	Bodean	P	Agrmt.,Awd.,Min.,Rep. 1840
14099	Bodferin	P	Min.,Rep. 1840
14100	Bottwnog	P	Min.,Rep. 1840
14101	Bryncroes	P	Rep. 1840
14102	Caerhun	P	Awd.,Min.
14103	Carngwych	P	Rep. 1840
14104	Ceidio	P	Min.
14105	Clynog	P	Agrmt.,Awd.,Min.,Rep. 1840
14107	Crickieth	P	Agrmt.,Rep. 1839
14108	Gyfin	P	Awd.,Min.
14109	Deneio	P	Awd.,Min.

Caernarvonshire contd.

14110	Dolbenmaen	P	Agrmt.,Rep. 1839
14111	Dolgarog and Ardda	T	Awd.,Min.
14112	Dolwyddelen	P	Min.,Rep. 1841
14113	Dwygyfylchi	P	Rep. 1842
14114	Edeyrn	P	Agrmt.,Min.,Rep. 1840
14115	Eglws Rhos	P	Rep. 1845
14116	Eidda	T	Min.
14117	Gwydir	T	Min.,Rep. 1842
14118	Llanaelhaiarn	P	Rep. 1840
14119	Llanarmon	P	Awd.,Min.,Rep. 1841
14120	Llambeblig	P	Agrmt.,Rep. 1839
14121	Llanbedr and Tal Y Cavn	T	Awd.,Min.
14122	Llanbedrog,Llangian	P	Rep. 1839
14123	Llanberris	P	Agrmt.,Min.,Rep. 1839
14124	Llanddeiniolen	P	Agrmt.,Min.
14125	Llandegai	P	Agrmt.,Min.,Rep. 1840
14126	Llandegwning	P	Awd.,Min.,Rep. 1842
14127	Llandudno	P	Min.,Rep. 1845
14128	Llandudwen	P	Awd.,Min.
14129	Llandwrog	P	Agrmt.,Awd.,Min.,Rep. 1840
14130	Llanengan	P	Rep. 1840
14131	Llanfaelrhys	P	Agrmt.,Awd.,Min.,Rep. 1841
14132	Llanfaglan	P	Agrmt.,Awd.,Min.,Rep. 1839
14133	Llanfairisgaer	P	Agrmt.,Rep. 1839
14135	Llangelynin	P	Rep. 1845
14136	Llangwnodle	P	Min.,Rep. 1841
14137	Llangwstenin	P	Min.,Rep. 1845
14138	Llangybi	P	Rep. 1841
14139	Llanieston	P	Agrmt.,Rep. 1840
14140	Llanllechid	P	Agrmt.,Min.,Rep. 1839
14141	Llanllyfni	P	Rep. 1839
14142	Llannor	P	Agrmt.,Awd.,Min.,Rep. 1840
14143	Llanrug	P	Rep. 1839
14144	Llanvairvechan	P	Awd.,Min.
14145	Llanwnda	P	Agrmt.,Min.,Rep. 1839
14146	Llanystymdwy	P	Rep. 1841
14147	Llysfaen	P	Rep. 1842
14148	Maenan	D	Awd.,Min.
14149	Mellteyrn	P	Min.,Rep. 1840
14150	Nefyn	P	Agrmt.,Rep. 1840
14151	Penllech	P	Min.,Rep. 1840
14152	Penmachno	P	Rep. 1842
14153	Penmorfa	P	Agrmt.,Awd.,Min.,Rep. 1839
14154	Penrhos	P	Agrmt.,Rep. 1840
14155	Pistyll	C	Min.,Rep. 1840
14156	Rhiw	P	Min.
14157	Treflys	P	Agrmt.,Rep. 1839
14158	Trefrhiw	P	Min.,Rep. 1841
14159	Tydweilog	P	Agrmt.,Rep. 1840
14160	Ynscynhairn	P	Rep. 1842
14270	Llanfihangel Y Pennant	P	Agrmt.,Min.,Rep. 1839

Cardiganshire

13868	Llanllwchairn	P	Awd.,Min.
13872	Llanrhystid	P	Min.,Rep. 1839
13980	Aberporth	P	Agrmt.,Rep. 1838
13981	Bangor	P	Agrmt.,Rep. 1837
13982	Bettws Bledrws	P	Rep. 1839
13983	Bettws Evan	P	Rep. 1839
13984	Bettws Leiki	T	Awd.,Min.
13985	Blaenpennal	T	Rep. 1842
13986	Blaenporth	P	Agrmt.,Min.,Rep. 1837
13987	Brongwynn	P	Awd.,Min.
13988	Cardigan St Mary	P	Agrmt.,Rep. 1839
13989	Caron	P	Min.,Rep. 1839
13990	Cellan	P	Agrmt.,Awd.,Min.
13991	Cilcennin	P	Rep. 1840
13992	Cilieayron	P	Min.,Rep. 1839
13993	Cydplwf	H	Awd.,Min.
13994	Dihewid	P	Awd.,Min.
13995	Doithie Pysgottwr	T	Min.,Rep. 1839
13996	Doithie Camddwr	T	Rep. 1839
13997	Garth and Ystrad	T	Rep. 1841
13998	Gartheli	H	Awd.,Min.
13999	Gogoyan	T	Awd.,Min.
14000	Gorwith	T	Min.,Rep. 1839
14001	Gwynfil	T	Rep. 1841
14002	Gwnnws	P	Awd.,Min.
14003	Henllan	P	Rep. 1839
14004	Henvynyw	P	Rep. 1845
14005	Lampeter Pont Stephen	P	Rep. 1839
14006	Llanarth	P	Agrmt.,Min.,Rep. 1837
14007	Llanavan	P	Rep. 1843
14008	Llanbadarnfawr	P	Awd.,Min.
14009	Llanbadarntrefeglwys	P	Agrmt.,Min.,Rep. 1837
14010	Llanbadarn Odyn	P	Awd.,Min.
14011	Llanddinol	P	Rep. 1839
14012	Llandewy Aberath	P	Rep. 1839
14013	Llandissiliogogo	P	Rep. 1841
14014	Llandugroydd	P	Rep. 1839
14015	Llandyfriog	P	Min.,Rep. 1839
14016	Llandyssil	P	Min.
14017	Llanerchayron	P	Rep. 1839
14018	Llancynfelyn	P	Awd.,Min.
14019	Llanfair Clydogan	P	Rep. 1839
14020	Llanfair Orllwyn	P	Min.,Rep. 1839
14021	Llanfair Trefligen	P	Rep. 1840
14022	Llanfihangel Geneu Glyn	P	Awd.,Min.
14023	Llanfihangelycroyddyn	P	Awd.,Min.
14024	Llanfihangel Ystrad	P	Min.,Rep. 1838
14025	Llangeitho	P	Min.,Rep. 1839
14026	Llangrannog	P	Rep. 1840
14027	Llangrwyddon	P	Rep. 1843
14028	Llangoedmore	P	Min.,Rep. 1838
14029	Llanguby	P	Rep. 1839
14030	Llangunllo	P	Rep. 1839
14031	Llanilar	P	Min.,Rep. 1843
14032	Llanina	P	Min.
14033	Llanio	T	Min.,Rep. 1841
14034	Llansaintfraed	P	Min.
14035	Llanwenog	P	Min.,Rep. 1842
14036	Llanwnen	P	Awd.,Min.
14037	Llanychaiarn	P	Rep. 1843
14038	Llechryd	C	Rep. 1839
14039	Lledrod	P	Min.,Rep. 1843
14040	Mount	P	N.t.p.
14041	Nantcwnlle	P	Min.,Rep. 1839
14042	Pembryn	P	Agrmt.,Rep. 1838
14043	Prisk and Carvan	T	Min.,Rep. 1839
14044	Rhosdie	P	Rep. 1839
14045	Silian	P	Awd.,Min.
14046	Sputty Ystradmeurig	P	Min.,Rep. 1839
14047	Sputty Ystwyth	P	Awd.,Min.,Rep. 1841
14048	Trefilan	P	Rep. 1838
14049	Tremain	P	Min.,Rep. 1838
14050	Troedyraur	P	Rep. 1837
14051	Verwig	P	Agrmt.,Rep. 1838

Carmarthenshire

14052	Llangain	P	Min.,Rep. 1841
14053	Llangadock	P	Agrmt.,Rep. 1837
14054	Llangathen	P	Rep. 1838
14055	Llangeller	P	Rep. 1839
14056	Llangennech	P	Awd.,Min.
14057	Llanginning	P	Min.,Rep. 1838
14058	Llanglydwen	P	Awd.,Min.
14059	Llangunnog	P	Agrmt.,Min.,Rep. 1839
14060	Llangunnor	P	Min.
14061	Llangyndeyrn	P	Awd.,Min.
14062	Llanllawddog	P	Awd.,Min.,Rep. 1838
14063	Llanllwny	P	Agrmt.,Min.,Rep. 1841
14064	Llanon	P	Rep. 1841
14065	Llanpimpsaint	P	Rep. 1838
14066	Llansadurnen	P	Rep. 1841
14067	Llansadwrn	P	Min.,Rep. 1838
14068	Llansawel	P	Min.,Rep. 1838
14069	Llanstephan	P	Rep. 1840
14070	Llanddoysaint	P	Rep. 1837
14071	Llanvallteg	P	Rep. 1843
14072	Llanfihangel Abercowin	P	Rep. 1841
14073	Llanwinnio	P	Min.
14074	Llanwrda	P	Agrmt.,Min.,Rep. 1837
14075	Llanybyther	P	Rep. 1840
14076	Llanycrwys	P	Rep. 1839
14077	Marros	P	Rep. 1839
14078	Merthyr	P	Rep. 1838
14079	Mothfey	P	Min.,Rep. 1838
14080	Mydrim	P	Agrmt.,Rep. 1841
14081	Newchurch	P	Awd.,Min.,Rep. 1839
14082	Pemboyr	P	Rep. 1838
14083	Pembrey	P	Awd.,Min.,Rep. 1839
14084	Pencarreg	P	Agrmt.,Min.,Rep. 1841
14085	Pendine	P	Min.,Rep. 1839
14086	Treleach Ar Bettws	P	Agrmt.,Min.
14087	Wen	H	Agrmt.,Rep. 1837
14161	Talley	P	Agrmt.,Min.,Rep. 1838
14162	Abergwilli	P	Rep. 1838
14163	Abernant	P	Agrmt.,Rep. 1840
14164	Bettws	P	Min.
14165	Brechfa	P	Awd.,Min.
14166	Carmarthen,St. Peter	P	Agrmt.,Min.,Rep. 1837
14167	Castelldwyron and Grondu	H	Awd.,Min.
14168	Castle Green	EP	Min.
14169	Cilycwm	P	Awd.,Min.
14170	Cilymaenllwyd	P	Agrmt.,Min.,Rep. 1837
14171	St. Clears	P	Agrmt.,Min.,Rep. 1838
14172	Conwillgaio	P	Min.,Rep. 1839
14173	Conwill in Elvet	P	Awd.,Min.
14174	Cwmtwrch and Cwmcothy	H	Agrmt.,Min.,Rep. 1838
14175	Eglwyscummin	P	Agrmt.,Min.,Rep. 1842
14176	Eglwysfairacherig	C	Agrmt.,Min.,Rep. 1843
14177	Egremont	P	Awd.,Min.
14178	Henllan Amgoed	P	Awd.,Min.
14179	St. Ishmael	P	Awd.,Min.
14180	Kennarth	P	Min.,Rep. 1838
14181	Kidwelly	P	Awd.,Min.
14182	Kiffig	P	Min.,Rep. 1839
14183	Kilrhedyn	P	Awd.,Min.

Carmarthenshire contd.

14184	Langan	P	Min.
14185	Laugharne	P	Awd.,Min.
14186	Laugharne	T	Awd.,Min.
14187	Llanarthney	P	Awd.,Min.
14188	Llanboidy	P	Agrmt.,Min.,Rep. 1837
14189	Llandawke	P	Rep. 1839
14190	Llandibie	P	Agrmt.,Min.,Rep. 1840
14191	Llanddarog	P	Min.,Rep. 1839
14192	Llandefailog	P	Awd.,Min.
14193	Llandefeysant	P	Rep. 1838
14194	Llandilo Abercowin	P	Rep. 1840
14195	Llandilofawr	P	Min.
14196	Llandingat	P	Rep. 1838
14197	Llandisilio	P	Min.,Rep. 1839
14198	Llandowror	P	Min.
14199	Llanegwadd	P	Min.
14200	Llanedy	P	Awd.,Min.
14201	Llanfairarybrin	P	Min.,Rep. 1838
14202	Llanfihangel Aberbythych	P	Rep. 1839
14203	Llanfihangel Ar Arth	P	Min.,Rep. 1840
14204	Llanfyhangel Cilyfargen	P	Min.,Rep. 1839
14205	Llanfihangel Rhos Y Corn	P	Awd.,Min.
14206	Llanfynydd	P	Min.,Rep. 1839
14821	Llanelly	P	Min.,Rep. 1840

Denbighshire

14106	Coedrwg	T	Min.,Rep. 1841
14134	Llanganhaval	P	Agrmt.,Min.,Rep. 1839
14207	Abenbury Vechan	T	Min.,Rep. 1842
14208	Abergele	P	Rep. 1840
14209	Aberwhiler	T	Rep. 1842
14210	Acton	T	Min.,Rep. 1839
14211	Allington	T	Min.,Rep. 1843
14212	Bannister Issa	T	Agrmt.,Min.,Rep. 1842
14213	Bannister Ucha	T	Agrmt.,Min.,Rep. 1842
14214	Bersham	T	Min.,Rep. 1840
14215	Bettws Yn Rhos	P	Agrmt.,Rep. 1840
14216	Bieston and Gourton	T	Min.,Rep. 1842
14217	Boddyn Wyddog,Bryntangor	T	Min.,Rep. 1841
14218	Bodigre Yr Abbott	T	Awd.,Min.
14219	Broughton	T	Agrmt.,Min.,Rep. 1844
14220	Burras Hovah	T	Min.,Rep. 1839
14221	Bwraes Rifri	T	Min.,Rep. 1843
14222	Burton	T	Awd.,Min.,Rep. 1843
14223	Cacca Dutton	T	Agrmt.,Min.,Rep. 1843
14224	Carreghofa	T	Agrmt.,Rep. 1837
14225	Cerrig Y Druidion	P	Awd.,Min.
14226	Christionydd Kenrick	T	Min.,Rep. 1844
14227	Chirk	R	Agrmt.,Rep. 1837
14228	Clocaenog	P	Agrmt.,Min.,Rep. 1839
14229	Creigiog Is Glan	T	Awd.,Min.
14230	Crogen Iddon	T	Min.,Rep. 1839
14231	Cyfnant	T	Agrmt.,Min.,Rep. 1842
14232	Cyffylliog	P	Agrmt.,Awd.,Min.,Rep. 1841
14233	Denbigh	P	Agrmt.,Min.,Rep. 1840
14234	Derwenynial	P	Min.,Rep. 1842
14235	Dinbryn	T	Agrmt.,Min.,Rep. 1844
14236	Dutton Y Crain	T	Agrmt.,Min.,Rep. 1843
14237	Dutton Difaeth	T	Agrmt.,Min.,Rep. 1843
14238	Efenechtyd	P	Rep. 1841
14239	Erbistock	P	Agrmt.,Min.,Rep. 1844
14240	Eglwys Vach	P	Awd.,Min.
14241	Eglwys Hegl	T	Min.,Rep. 1844
14242	Erddig	T	Min.,Rep. 1843
14243	Erlas	T	Min.,Rep. 1843
14244	Esclusham Above	T	Agrmt.,Min.,Rep. 1845
14245	Esclusham Below	T	Min.,Rep. 1844
14246	Garthewin	T	Agrmt.,Min.,Rep. 1844
14247	Gellygynnon	T	Agrmt.,Awd.,Min.,Rep. 1843
14248	St George	T	Rep. 1840
14249	Gresford	T	Min.,Rep. 1843
14250	Gwerni Hywel	D	Awd.,Min.
14251	Gwersyllt	T	Agrmt.,Min.,Rep. 1843
14252	Gwytherin	P	Min.,Rep. 1840
14253	Gwythrania	T	Min.,Rep. 1841
14254	Havodgynvawr	T	Min.,Rep. 1838
14255	Holt	T	Awd.,Min.,Rep. 1839
14256	Holt Parks	D	Awd.,Min.
14257	Llai	T	Agrmt.,Min.,Rep. 1843
14258	Llanarmon Dyfryn Ceiriog	P	Min.,Rep. 1838
14259	Llanarmon Mynydd Mawr	P	Min.,Rep. 1839
14260	Llanbedr Dyffryn Clwyd	P	Agrmt.,Min.,Rep. 1837
14261	Llandulas	P	Agrmt.,Min.,Rep. 1842
14262	Llandegla	P	Awd.,Min.
14263	Llandoget	P	Agrmt.,Rep. 1837
14264	Llandrillo Yn Rhos	P	Awd.,Min.
14265	Llandyrnog	P	Min.,Rep. 1839
14266	Llanelian Yn Rhos	P	Agrmt.,Min.,Rep. 1841
14267	Llanelidan	P	Agrmt.,Awd.,Min.,Rep. 1839
14268	Llanfair Dyffryn Clwyd	P	Agrmt.,Min.,Rep. 1838
14269	Llanfihangel Glyn Myfyr	P	Min.,Rep. 1839
14270	Llangadwaladr	P	Agrmt.,Min.,Rep. 1839
14271	Llangedwin	P	Min.,Rep. 1839
14272	Llangernyw	P	Min.,Rep. 1838
14273	Llangollen Fawr	T	Min.,Rep. 1839
14274	Llanferres	P	Agrmt.,Min.,Rep. 1838
14275	Llanfwrog	P	Agrmt.,Min.,Rep. 1841
14276	Llangollen Vechan	T	Min.,Rep. 1838
14277	Llangwm	P	Min.,Rep. 1840
14278	Llangwyfan	P	Min.,Rep. 1840
14279	Llannevydd	P	Awd.,Min.
14280	Llanrhaiadr in Cinmerch	P	Agrmt.,Min.,Rep. 1840
14281	Llanrwst	P	Min.,Rep. 1841
14282	Llansanan	P	Min.
14283	Llansantffraid	P	Min.,Rep. 1838
14284	Llansantffraid Glan Conwy	P	Min.,Rep. 1842
14285	Llanychan	P	Agrmt.,Min.,Rep. 1838
14286	Llanynys	P	Awd.,Min.,Rep. 1841
14287	Lledrod and Estynallan	T	Min.,Rep. 1838
14288	Lleweni Isav	T	Agrmt.,Awd.,Min.,Rep. 1841
14289	Maesyr Uchain	T	Rep. 1841
14290	Marchweil	P	Agrmt.,Min.,Rep. 1840
14291	Meifod	T	Rep. 1840
14292	Meiriadog	T	Awd.,Min.
14293	Meivod	T	Min.,Rep. 1839
14294	Minera	T	Agrmt.,Min.,Rep. 1845
14295	Moelvre	T	Min.,Rep. 1844
14296	Nantglyn	P	Agrmt.,Min.,Rep. 1840
14297	Pengwern	T	Rep. 1839
14298	Pryssyllygoed	T	Min.,Rep. 1842
14299	Ridley	T	Rep. 1843
14300	Ruabon	P	Agrmt.,Min.,Rep. 1844
14301	Ruthin and Llanryhdd	P	Agrmt.,Min.,Rep. 1841
14302	Stansty	T	Agrmt.,Min.,Rep. 1844
14303	Sutton	T	Min.,Rep. 1843
14304	Sycharth,Priddbwlch	T	Min.,Rep. 1840
14305	Tir Evan	T	Min.,Rep. 1843
14306	Trebrys	T	Min.,Rep. 1843
14307	Trevor Isav	T	Min.,Rep. 1838
14308	Trevor Uchav	T	Min.,Rep. 1838
14309	Tyr Yr Abbot Isav	D	Awd.,Min.
14310	Wrexham Regis and Wrexham	T	Awd.,Min.
14311	Brymbo	T	Agrmt.,Min.,Rep. 1844

Flintshire

14313	Bangor	P	Agrmt.,Min.
14314	Bettisfield	T	Agrmt.,Min.,Rep. 1839
14315	Boddlewyddan	T	Min.,Rep. 1840
14316	Bodfary	D	Awd.,Min.
14317	Bodidris	T	Awd.,Min.
14318	Bronnington	T	Agrmt.,Rep. 1839
14319	Caerwys	P	Awd.,Min.
14320	Cilcen	P	Min.,Rep. 1839
14321	Cil Owain	T	Awd.,Min.
14322	Cwm	P	Min.,Rep. 1843
14323	Cyrchynan	T	Awd.,Min.
14324	Dymerchion	P	Agrmt.,Awd.,Min.,Rep. 1840
14325	Dyserth	P	N.t.p.,Min.,Rep. 1839
14326	Faenol	T	Rep. 1840
14327	Flint	P	Agrmt.,Min.,Rep. 1837
14328	Gwaenysgor	P	Awd.,Min.
14329	Halghton	T	Agrmt.,Min.,Rep. 1839
14330	Halkin	P	Min.,Rep. 1839
14331	Hanmer	T	Agrmt.,Min.,Rep. 1839
14332	Hawarden	P	Rep. 1839
14333	Holywell	P	Agrmt.,Min.,Rep. 1841
14334	Hope	P	Awd.,Min.
14335	Iscoyd	T	Agrmt.,Min.,Rep. 1838
14336	Llanasa	P	Min.,Rep. 1839
14337	Marford and Hosely	T	Rep. 1843
14338	Meliden	P	Min.,Rep. 1839
14339	Mold	P	Agrmt.,Min.,Rep. 1837
14340	Nannerch	T	Min.,Rep. 1838
14341	Nercwys	T	Rep. 1838
14342	Newmarket	P	Min.,Rep. 1845
14343	Northop	P	Min.,Rep. 1838
14344	Overton	P	Agrmt.,Min.,Rep. 1837
14345	Pengwern	T	Min.,Rep. 1840
14346	Penley	T	Agrmt.,Min.,Rep. 1837
14347	Rhuddlan	P	Min.,Rep. 1839
14348	Talar,Brynpolyn	T	Awd.,Min.
14349	Treuddyn	T	Rep. 1838
14350	Tybroughton	T	Agrmt.,Rep. 1839
14351	Whitford	P	Awd.,Min.
14352	Willington	T	Agrmt.,Min.,Rep. 1839
14353	Worthenbury	P	Agrmt.,Min.,Rep. 1837
14354	Ysgeiviog	D	Awd.,Min.

Glamorgan

14355	Baglan	P	Awd.,Min.
14356	Aberdare	P	Awd.,Min.
14357	Aberavon	P	Min.
14358	St. Andrew	P	Rep. 1840
14359	Andrew St Minor	P	N.t.p.
14360	St. Athan	P	Agrmt.,Rep. 1839
14361	Barry	P	Rep. 1839

Glamorgan contd.

14362	Bettws	P	Rep. 1843
14363	Bishopstone	P	Awd.,Min.
14364	Blaengwrach	H	Awd.,Min.
14365	Bonvilstone	P	Rep. 1839
14366	St Bride Minor	H	Awd.,Min.
14367	St Bride Major with Wick	P	Awd.,Min.
14368	St Bride super Ely	P	Min.
14369	Britonferry	P	N.t.p.,Min.
14370	Cadoxton juxta Barry	P	Rep. 1843
14371	Cadoxton juxta Neath	P	Awd.,Min.
14372	Cardiff St John	P	Awd.,Min.
14373	Cardiff St Mary	P	Awd.,Min.
14374	Cayra	P	Agrmt.,Rep. 1839
14375	Cheriton	P	Awd.,Min.
14376	Clyne	H	Awd.,Min.
14377	Coity Higher	H	Agrmt.,Rep. 1839
14378	Coity Lower	H	Agrmt.,Min.
14379	Colwinstone	P	Agrmt.,Min.,Rep. 1838
14380	Cowbridge	P	Agrmt.,Rep. 1840
14381	Coychurch Higher	H	Rep. 1839
14382	Coychurch Lower	H	Rep. 1841
14383	St Donatts	P	Awd.,Min.
14384	Eglwysbrewis	P	Rep. 1839
14385	Eglwyslian	P	Awd.,Min.
14386	Ewenny	P	Awd.,Min.
14387	St Fagan's	P	Awd.,Min.
14388	Flemingstone	P	Awd.,Min.
14389	St George	P	Awd.,Min.
14390	Gileston	P	Awd.,Min.
14391	Gellygaer	P	Awd.,Min.
14392	Glyncorrwg	H	Awd.,Min.
14393	Highlight	EP	N.t.p.
14394	Hilary St	P	Rep. 1838
14395	Ilston	P	Awd.,Min.
14396	St John	P	Awd.,Min.
14397	Kilybebyll	P	Agrmt.,Min.,Rep. 1838
14398	Knelston	P	Awd.,Min.
14399	Laleston	P	Awd.,Min.
14400	Landow	P	Rep. 1841
14401	Langan	P	Rep. 1840
14402	Lantwit Major	P	Min.,Rep. 1840
14403	Lavernock	P	Awd.,Min.
14404	Lisfane	P	Awd.,Min.
14405	Lisworney	P	Agrmt.,Rep. 1838
14406	Llanblethian	P	Min.,Rep. 1840
14407	Llancarvon	P	Rep. 1840
14408	Llandaff	P	Awd.,Min.
14409	Llandefodog	P	Awd.,Min.
14410	Llandewi	P	Awd.,Min.
14411	Llandilio Tal Y Bont	P	Awd.,Min.
14412	Llandough	P	Awd.,Min.
14413	Llandough,Cogan,Leckwith	P	Rep. 1841
14414	Llanedarne	P	Awd.,Min.
14415	Llangeinor	P	Awd.,Min.
14416	Llangennith	P	Awd.,Min.
14417	Llangevelach	P	Min.,Rep. 1838
14418	Llangonoyd	P	Awd.,Min.
14419	Llanguicke	P	Rep. 1838
14420	Llanharron	P	Rep. 1838
14421	Llanharry	P	Min.
14422	Llanishen	P	Awd.,Min.
14423	Llanilid	P	Awd.,Min.
14424	Llanmadock	P	Min.
14425	Llanmaes	P	Awd.,Min.
14426	Llanmihangel	P	Awd.,Min.
14427	Llanrhidian Lower	P	Awd.,Min.
14428	Llanrhidian Upper	D	Awd.,Min.
14429	Llansamlet	P	Awd.,Min.
14430	Llansannor	P	Awd.,Min.
14431	Llantrisant	P	Awd.,Min.
14432	Llantrythid	P	Rep. 1839
14433	Llantwit Lower	H	Awd.,Min.
14434	Llantwit Vardre	P	Agrmt.,Rep. 1844
14435	Llanvabon	P	Awd.,Min.,Rep. 1840
14436	Llanwonno	P	Awd.,Min.
14437	Llanvithen	EP	Min.
14438	Loughor	P	Min.,Rep. 1839
14439	Lythans St	P	Agrmt.,Rep. 1838
14440	Marcross	P	Awd.,Min.
14441	Margam	P	N.t.p.
14442	St Marychurch	P	Awd.,Min.
14443	Merthyr Dovan	P	Min.,Rep. 1839
14444	Merthyrmawr	P	Awd.,Min.
14445	Merthyr Tydfil	P	Awd.,Min.
14446	Michaelstone Higher	P	Rep. 1839
14447	Michaelstone Lower	H	Awd.,Min.
14448	Michaelstone le Pit	P	Min.,Rep. 1843
14449	Michaelstone super Ely	P	Agrmt.,Min.,Rep. 1839
14450	Michaelstone Y Vedw	P	Agrmt.,Min.,Rep. 1838
14451	Monknash	P	Awd.,Min.
14452	Nash	EP	N.t.p.
14453	Neath	P	Awd.,Min.
14454	Newton Nottage	P	Awd.,Min.
14455	Nicholas St	P	Agrmt.,Rep. 1838
14456	Nicholaston	P	Awd.,Min.
14457	Oxwich	P	Awd.,Min.
14458	Oystermouth	P	Agrmt.,Awd.,Min.,Rep. 1844
14459	Pencoed	H	Rep. 1839
14460	Pendoylan	P	Awd.,Min.
14461	Penlline	P	Agrmt.,Min.,Rep. 1838
14462	Penmaen	P	Awd.,Min.
14463	Penmark	P	Agrmt.,Rep. 1840
14464	Pennard	P	Awd.,Awd.,Min.
14465	Pennarth	P	Awd.,Min.
14466	Penrice	P	Awd.,Min.
14467	Pentyrch	P	Rep. 1839
14468	Peterstone super Ely	P	Awd.,Min.
14469	Peterstone super Montem	H	Agrmt.,Min.,Rep. 1841
14470	Porteynon	P	Awd.,Min.
14471	Porthkerry	P	Min.,Rep. 1838
14472	Pyle and Kenfig	P	Awd.,Min.
14473	Radyr	P	Rep. 1840
14474	Resolven	H	Min.,Rep. 1840
14475	Reynoldston	P	Min.,Rep. 1838
14476	Roath	P	Rep. 1839
14477	Rossilly	P	Awd.,Min.
14478	Ruddry	P	Min.,Rep. 1840
14479	Stembridge	EP	N.t.p.
14480	Sully	P	Awd.,Min.
14481	Swansea	P	Rep. 1838
14482	Tythegstone	P	Awd.,Min.
14483	Van	H	Awd.,Min.
14484	Welsh St Donats	P	Min.,Rep. 1840
14485	Wenvoe	P	Min.,Rep. 1839
14486	Whitchurch	P	Min.
14487	Ynysadwre	H	Awd.,Min.
14488	Ystradowen	P	Awd.,Min.
14489	Ystradyfodog	P	Awd.,Min.
14490	St Mary Hill	P	Min.
14491	Newcastle	P	Awd.,Min.

Merionethshire

14492	Dolgelly	P	Agrmt.,Rep. 1838
14493	Festiniog	P	Awd.,Min.,Rep. 1841
14494	Gwyddelwern	P	Min.,Rep. 1838
14495	Llanaber	P	Agrmt.,Awd.,Min.,Rep. 1839
14496	Llanbedr	P	Awd.,Min.
14497	Llandanwg	P	Awd.,Min.
14498	Llanddwywei	P	Awd.,Min.
14499	Llanddervel	P	Rep. 1838
14500	Llandecwyn	P	Rep. 1841
14501	Llandrillo	P	Rep. 1840
14502	Llanegryn	P	Awd.,Min.
14503	Llanelltyd	P	Awd.,Min.,Rep. 1842
14504	Llanenddwyn	P	Awd.,Min.
14505	Llanfair	P	Agrmt.,Min.,Rep. 1839
14506	Llanfihangel Y Pennant	P	Min.,Rep. 1838
14507	Llanfihangel Y Traethau	P	Min.,Rep. 1841
14508	Llangar	P	Rep. 1838
14509	Llangelynin	P	Agrmt.,Awd.,Min.,Rep. 1839
14510	Llangower	P	Agrmt.,Awd.,Min.,Rep. 1842
14511	Llansanfraid Glyn Dyvrdwy	P	Awd.,Min.
14512	Llanuwchlyn	P	Awd.,Min.
14513	Llanvachraith	P	Awd.,Min.
14514	Llanvor	P	Awd.,Min.
14515	Llanvrothen	P	Min.,Rep. 1839
14516	Llanycil	P	Rep. 1838
14517	Llanymowddwy	P	Min.,Rep. 1842
14518	Maentwrog	P	Awd.,Min.
14519	Mallwyd	P	Agrmt.,Min.,Rep. 1838
14520	Penhal	P	Awd.,Min.,Rep. 1838
14521	Tal Y Llyn	P	Min.,Rep. 1838
14522	Towyn	P	Agrmt.,Awd.,Min.,Rep. 1838
14523	Trawsfynydd	P	Agrmt.,Awd.,Min.,Rep. 1839
14524	Bettws Gwerfilgoch	P	Rep. 1841
14525	Corwen	P	Rep. 1839

Montgomeryshire

14526	Aberhafesp	T	Rep. 1839
14527	Aston	T	Awd.,Min.
14528	Batchddre and Hapton Issa	T	Agrmt.,Min.,Rep. 1839
14529	Bausley	T	Rep. 1840
14530	Bettws	P	Min.,Rep. 1840
14531	Berriew	P	Awd.,Min.,Rep. 1839
14532	Broniarth Upper and Lower	T	Min.,Rep. 1840
14533	Brompton,Riston	T	Agrmt.,Min.,Rep. 1840
14534	Carno	P	Awd.,Min.
14535	Castlecaereinion	P	Min.,Rep. 1839
14536	Castlewright	T	Agrmt.,Min.,Rep. 1840
14537	Cemaes	P	Min.,Rep. 1838
14538	Churchstoke and Hurdley	T	Agrmt.,Min.,Rep. 1840
14539	Coffronydd	T	Min.,Rep. 1840
14540	Criggion	T	Rep. 1839
14541	Darowen	P	Awd.,Min.
14542	Dolwar	T	N.t.p.,Min.,Rep. 1841
14543	Forden	P	Agrmt.,Min.,Rep. 1840
14544	Garthbeibio	P	Min.,Rep. 1838
14545	Garthbwlch	T	Agrmt.,Awd.,Min.,Rep. 1838

Montgomeryshire contd.

14546	Gungrogfechan	T	Awd.,Min.,Rep. 1840
14547	Hendrehen,Llan,Trawscoed	T	Min.,Rep. 1842
14548	Hengynwithfach	T	Agrmt.,Min.,Rep. 1840
14549	Hirnant	P	Agrmt.,Min.,Rep. 1839
14550	Hope and Cletterwood	T	Agrmt.,Min.,Rep. 1840
14551	Hopton Urcha	T	Agrmt.,Min.,Rep. 1840
14552	Hyssington	T	Min.,Rep. 1839
14553	Kerry	P	Awd.,Min.
14554	Llanbrinmair	P	Min.,Rep. 1839
14555	Llandinam	P	Awd.,Min.
14556	Llangynog	P	Min.,Rep. 1839
14557	Llanllugan	P	Awd.,Min.
14558	Llanllwchairn	P	Min.,Rep. 1841
14559	Llangyniw	P	Awd.,Min.
14560	Llandrino	P	Min.,Rep. 1840
14561	Llandysilio	P	Min.,Rep. 1839
14562	Llandyssil	P	Min.,Rep. 1840
14563	Llanercrochwell	T	Min.,Rep. 1840
14564	Llanervul	P	Awd.,Min.
14565	Llanfihangel	P	Agrmt.,Min.,Rep. 1844
14566	Llangadvan	P	Min.,Rep. 1838
14567	Llangirrig	P	Agrmt.,Min.,Rep. 1841
14568	Llanmerewig	P	Min.,Rep. 1840
14569	Llanrhaiadr Yn Mochnant	P	Min.,Rep. 1839
14570	Llanvechain	P	Min.,Rep. 1839
14571	Llanwddun	P	Awd.,Min.,Rep. 1840
14572	Llanwrin	P	Agrmt.,Min.,Rep. 1837
14573	Llanwyddelan	P	Awd.,Min.
14574	Llansanfraid Yn Mechain	P	Min.,Rep. 1838
14575	Llanvair Caer Einion	P	Min.,Rep. 1839
14576	Llanvyllin	P	Awd.,Min.
14577	Llanwnog	P	Awd.,Min.
14578	Manafon	P	Awd.,Min.
14579	Machynllaeth	P	Agrmt.,Min.,Rep. 1842
14580	Meifod	P	Awd.,Min.,Rep. 1839
14581	Mellington	T	Agrmt.,Min.,Rep. 1839
14582	Middletown	T	Agrmt.,Min.,Rep. 1838
14583	Montgomery	P	Agrmt.,Min.,Rep. 1838
14584	Morfodion	T	Awd.,Min.
14585	Mouchtre	P	Min.,Rep. 1841
14587	Penegoes	P	Agrmt.,Min.,Rep. 1837
14588	Newtown	P	Awd.,Min.
14589	Pennant	P	Min.,Rep. 1839
14590	Penstrowed	P	Agrmt.,Min.,Rep. 1840
14591	Pool (Lower Division)	D	Awd.,Min.,Rep. 1840
14592	Pool (Upper and Middle)	D	Awd.,Min.,Rep. 1840
14593	Snead	P	Awd.,Min.
14594	Tirymynach	T	Min.,Rep. 1840
14595	Tregynon	P	Min.,Rep. 1841
14596	Trelystan	T	Min.,Rep. 1844
14597	Trevedryd	T	Min.,Rep. 1838
14598	Treveglwys	P	Awd.,Min.
14599	Trewern	T	Agrmt.,Min.,Rep. 1840
14600	Uppington	T	Min.,Rep. 1844
14601	Varchoel	T	Min.,Rep. 1842

Pembrokeshire

14602	Ambleston	P	Awd.,Min.
14603	Amroth	P	Awd.,Min.
14604	Angle	P	Awd.,Min.
14605	Bayvil	P	Min.,Rep. 1843
14606	Begelly cum East William	PH	Awd.,Min.
14607	Bletherstone	P	Min.,Rep. 1839
14608	Boulston	P	Awd.,Min.
14609	Brawdy	P	Min.
14610	Bridell	P	Agrmt.,Rep. 1837
14611	Brides St	P	Rep. 1839
14612	Burton	P	Min.,Rep. 1838
14613	Caldy Island	EP	N.t.p.
14614	Camrose	P	Awd.,Min.
14615	Carew	P	Rep. 1838
14616	Castleblyth	P	Awd.,Min.
14617	Castlemartin	P	Agrmt.,Min.,Rep. 1837
14618	Capel Colman	C	Awd.,Min.
14619	Clarbeston	P	Rep. 1839
14620	Clydey	P	Agrmt.,Min.,Rep. 1839
14621	Coedcanlas	P	N.t.p.
14622	Cosheston	P	Awd.,Min.
14623	Crinow	P	Min.,Rep. 1840
14624	Crunwear	P	Min.,Rep. 1839
14625	Dale	P	Awd.,Min.
14626	David's St	P	Agrmt.,Min.,Rep. 1838
14627	Dinas	P	Min.,Rep. 1841
14628	Dogmells St	P	Agrmt.,Min.,Rep. 1838
14629	Dogwells St	P	Min.
14630	Edrens St	P	Awd.,Min.
14631	Eglwyswrw	P	Agrmt.,Min.,Rep. 1838
14632	Egremont	P	N.t.p.
14633	Elvis St	P	Agrmt.,Min.,Rep. 1837
14634	Florence St	P	Rep. 1839
14635	Freystrop	P	Agrmt.,Min.,Rep. 1837
14636	Fishguard	P	Min.,Rep. 1839
14637	Furzy Park and Portfield	EP	Min.
14638	Granston	P	Min.,Rep. 1838
14639	Gumfreston	P	Min.,Rep. 1839
14640	Haroldstone West	P	Min.,Rep. 1839
14641	Hasguard	P	Min.
14642	Haverfordwest St Martin	P	Awd.,Min.
14643	Haverfordwest St Mary	P	N.t.p.,Min.
14644	Haverfordwest St Thomas	P	Min.,Rep. 1839
14645	Hayscastle	P	Min.
14646	Henry's Moat	P	Min.,Rep. 1838
14647	Herbrainstone	P	Min.,Rep. 1838
14648	Hodgeston	P	Rep. 1839
14649	Hubberston	P	Rep. 1839
14650	Ishmaels St	P	Min.,Rep. 1839
14651	Issells St	P	Min.,Rep. 1839
14652	Jefferston	P	Awd.,Min.
14653	Johnstone	P	Min.,Rep. 1842
14654	Jordanstone	P	Agrmt.,Min.,Rep. 1842
14655	Kilgerran	P	Min.,Rep. 1838
14656	Lambston	P	Min.,Rep. 1839
14657	Lampeter Velfrey	P	Min.,Rep. 1842
14658	Lamphey	P	Agrmt.,Min.,Rep. 1839
14659	Lawrence St	P	Min.,Rep. 1838
14660	Lawrenny	P	Min.,Rep. 1841
14661	Letterston	P	Agrmt.,Min.,Rep. 1838
14662	Llandeloy	P	Min.
14663	Llandewi Velfry	P	Min.
14664	Llandilo	P	Min.,Rep. 1839
14665	Llanfairnant Gwynne	P	Agrmt.,Min.,Rep. 1837
14666	Llanfair Nant Y Goff	P	Min.,Rep. 1838
14667	Llanfihangel Penbedw	P	Agrmt.,Min.,Rep. 1837
14668	Llanfirnach	P	Agrmt.,Min.,Rep. 1838
14669	Llangolman	P	Min.,Rep. 1839
14670	Llangwm	P	Min.,Rep. 1840
14671	Llanhowell	P	Min.
14672	Llanllawer	P	Awd.,Min.
14673	Llanrian	P	Awd.,Min.
14674	Llanrithan	P	Agrmt.,Min.,Rep. 1838
14675	Llanstadwell	P	Agrmt.,Rep. 1837
14676	Llanstadwell	D	Agrmt.,Min.,Rep. 1848
14677	Llanstinnan	P	Awd.,Min.
14678	Llantood	P	Min.,Rep. 1838
14679	Llanwnda	P	Awd.,Min.
14680	Llanycefn	P	Awd.,Min.
14681	Llanychare	P	Min.,Rep. 1841
14682	Llanychlwydog	P	Min.,Rep. 1842
14683	Llawhaden	P	Min.,Rep. 1839
14684	Llysyfrane	P	Min.,Rep. 1839
14685	Loveston	P	Min.,Rep. 1840
14686	Ludchurch	P	Min.,Rep. 1839
14687	Maenclochog	P	Min.,Rep. 1839
14688	Manerdify	P	Agrmt.,Min.,Rep. 1838
14689	Manorbeer	P	Awd.,Min.
14690	Manorowen	P	Agrmt.,Min.,Rep. 1837
14691	Marloes	P	Awd.,Min.
14692	Martletwy	P	Min.,Rep. 1840
14693	Mathry	P	Min.,Rep. 1838
14694	Meline	P	Agrmt.,Rep. 1838
14695	Minwere	P	Awd.,Min.
14696	Moilgrove	P	Awd.,Min.
14697	Monachlogddu	P	Min.,Rep. 1839
14698	Monington	P	Agrmt.,Min.,Rep. 1837
14699	Monkton	P	Min.,Rep. 1839
14700	Morville	P	Agrmt.,Min.,Rep. 1839
14701	Mounton	C	Awd.,Min.
14702	Narberth	P	Min.,Rep. 1840
14703	Nash	P	Min.,Rep. 1839
14704	Nevern	P	Awd.,Min.
14705	Newcastle Little	P	Awd.,Min.
14706	New Moat	P	Min.,Rep. 1839
14707	Newport	P	Awd.,Min.
14708	Nicholas Saint	P	Min.,Rep. 1838
14709	Nolton	P	Agrmt.,Rep. 1838
14710	Pembroke St Mary	P	Min.,Rep. 1839
14711	Pembroke St Michael	P	Min.,Rep. 1839
14712	Penally	P	Awd.,Min.
14713	Penrith	P	Agrmt.,Rep. 1837
14714	Petrox Saint	P	Rep. 1839
14715	Pontfaen	P	Awd.,Min.
14716	Prendergast	P	Awd.,Min.
14717	Puncheston	P	Min.,Rep. 1841
14718	Pwllcrochon	P	Min.,Rep. 1839
14719	Redburth	P	Awd.,Min.
14720	Reynoldstone	P	Min.,Rep. 1842
14721	Rhoscrowther	P	Min.,Rep. 1839
14722	Roch	P	Agrmt.,Rep. 1837
14723	Tenby St Mary	P	Min.,Rep. 1839
14724	Trefgarn Great	P	Awd.,Min.
14774	Robeston Wathen	C	Awd.,Min.
14775	Rosemarket	P	Awd.,Min.
14776	Rudbaxton	P	Awd.,Min.
14777	Spittal	P	Rep. 1838
14778	Stackpole Bosher	P	Rep. 1837
14779	Stackpole Elidor	P	Rep. 1839
14780	Stainton	P	Rep. 1839
14781	Slebeck	P	Awd.,Min.
14782	Stainton Impropriators Div	P	Min.
14783	Stainton Vicars Division	P	Awd.,Min.

Pembrokeshire contd.

14784	Stokam Island	EP	N.t.p.
14785	Talbenny	P	Rep. 1839
14787	Twinnells Saint	P	Rep. 1838
14788	Uzmaston	P	Rep. 1839
14789	Walton East	P	Rep. 1839
14790	Walwyns Castle	P	Awd.,Min.
14791	Walton West	P	Agrmt.,Rep. 1840
14792	Warren	P	Rep. 1839
14793	Wiston	P	Rep. 1838
14794	Whitechurch in Dewsland	P	Rep. 1838
14796	Whitechurch in Kemes	P	Rep. 1839
14797	Yerbestone	P	Awd.,Min.
14798	Robertson West	P	Rep. 1842
14801	Harroldstone St Issello	P	N.t.p.

Radnorshire

14725	Aberedw	P	Min.,Rep. 1843
14726	Beguildy	P	Min.
14727	Bettws Disserth	P	Rep. 1838
14728	Bleddfa	P	Min.,Rep. 1838
14729	Boughrood	P	Agrmt.,Min.,Rep. 1839
14730	Bryngwyn	P	Awd.,Min.
14731	Clirow	P	Agrmt.,Min.,Rep. 1839
14732	Cefnllys	P	Agrmt.,Min.,Rep. 1838
14733	Cregrina	P	Min.,Rep. 1838
14734	Colva	P	Min.,Rep. 1837
14735	Church	T	Min.
14736	Disserth	P	Agrmt.,Min.,Rep. 1838
14737	Cascob	P	Min.,Rep. 1839
14738	Gladestry	P	Min.,Rep. 1839
14739	Glascombe	P	Min.,Rep. 1837
14740	Golon and Cefn Pawl	T	Min.,Rep. 1839
14741	Harmon Saint	P	Min.,Rep. 1839
14742	Heyop	P	Min.,Rep. 1841
14743	Knighton	P	Agrmt.,Min.,Rep. 1839
14744	Llanbadarn Fawr	P	Min.,Rep. 1838
14745	Llanbadarn Y Garreg	P	Min.,Rep. 1838
14746	Llanbadarn Vynydd	P	Awd.,Min.
14747	Llanno	P	Awd.,Min.
14748	Llanbedr Painscastle	P	Min.
14749	Llanbister	P	Awd.
14750	Llandegley	P	Agrmt.,Min.,Rep. 1840
14751	Llandewifach	P	Awd.,Min.
14752	Llandewy Ystradenny	P	Min.,Rep. 1839
14753	Llandilo Graban	P	Agrmt.,Min.,Rep. 1839
14754	Llandrindod	P	Min.,Rep. 1840
14755	Llanelwedd	P	Min.
14756	Llanfihangel Helygen	C	Min.
14757	Llangunllo	P	Min.,Rep. 1839
14758	Llansaintfraed in Elvel	P	Agrmt.,Min.,Rep. 1837
14759	Llanstephan	P	Min.,Rep. 1840
14760	Llanvihangel Nantmellan	P	Agrmt.,Min.,Rep. 1842
14761	Llanvihangel Rhydithon	P	Min.,Rep. 1839
14762	Llanyre	C	Awd.,Min.
14763	Llowes	P	Awd.,Min.
14764	Michaelchurch on Arrow	P	Awd.,Min.
14765	Nantmel	P	Awd.,Min.
14766	Newchurch	P	Awd.,Min.
14767	Norton	P	Awd.,Min.
14768	Pilleth	P	Awd.,Min.
14769	Presteign	P	Min.
14770	Radnor New	P	Awd.,Min.
14771	Radnor Old	P	Agrmt.,Rep. 1839
14772	Rhyadr Ar Gwy	C	Awd.,Min.
14773	Rhulan	P	Min.
14786	Trewern and Gwaithla	T	Min.,Rep. 1839
14795	Whitton	P	Agrmt.,Min.
14799	Llansaintfraed Cwmtoyddwr	P	Min.,Rep. 1838
14800	Llanfaredd	P	Min.,Rep. 1843

SUBJECT INDEX

Each county is indexed separately and counties appear in the same order as in the Place Index. Against each of 182 subject headings, the P.R.O. reference numbers of those files with material on that topic are listed in numerical order. Thus a researcher interested in ascertaining what might be found in the file of a particular place would turn first to the Place Index of the relevant county and identify the reference number of that place. The Subject Index for the county is then scanned for headings against which that number is listed. As all the reference numbers listed against each heading are arranged in numerical order, this is not a difficult task. The following example illustrates the procedure. To obtain a résumé of the contents of the tithe file of Chalfont St Giles in Buckinghamshire the Place Index for Buckinghamshire is first consulted which provides the reference number (13313) and reveals that Chalfont St Giles is a parish where tithes were commuted by agreement, that the file contains minutes of meetings and a record of papers and evidence produced during commutation, and that a report on the tithe agreement was written by a local agent of the Tithe Commission in 1838. The reference number 13313 is then referred to the Buckinghamshire Subject Index which reveals that the papers in the tithe file contain information on reasons for some land being exempt from tithe, a description of local topography, that a variety of soils including chalk and sand occur there, that general comments on rotations are made and that a four-course rotation was generally adopted with turnip cultivation particularly noted; sheep fattening and deer are also remarked upon.

Researchers concerned with particular topics simply note the reference numbers printed against relevant headings in the same way as the subject index of a book is used. The tithe districts to which these reference numbers refer can be identified by scanning the appropriate county section of the Place Index. The subject material included under each index heading in the Subject Index is defined below.

Tithe and local tithe customs

The first eight headings are concerned with material in tithe files relating to local tithe systems; see Chapter 1 of *The tithe surveys of England and Wales* for definitions of tithing terms.

1. Tithe free district
   No tithe payable in 1836; papers in file provide reasons.
2. History of tithe payment
   This entry identifies those files in which especially detailed information is provided

on the amounts of tithe paid and the nature of titheable produce in the past (often back to the seventeenth century).

3. Tithe practices and agriculture

   Past customs of tithe payment and how these affected local agricultural practices; indications of ways in which the 1836 commutation might affect farming in a locality.

4. Exemptions from tithe

   The reasons for part of a district or some products being exempt from tithe are discussed.

5. Tithe in kind

   This heading identifies those districts in which it was stated that tithe was still collected in kind.

6. Compositions

   The collection of some, or all, tithe as a money payment prior to 1836.

7. Moduses

   Districts where it was noted that moduses (customary, usually small, money payments in lieu of tithe) were in force over some lands or for some products.

8. Glebe

   Discussion of the extent or value of glebe lands.

Rural landscapes

General topographic descriptions

9. Local topography described

   In these files will be found descriptions of local scenery, landform and the appearance of the countryside.

10. Regional topography described

    Similar information as the above but dealing with an area wider than a single tithe district.

Settlements

These are matters of infrequent note in the files.

11. Village morphology

    The form and layout of rural settlements in a district.

12. Church

    Architectural descriptions of church buildings.

13. Country houses and ornamental gardens

    Descriptions of principal residences and their grounds.

14. Farm houses and buildings

    These are usually comments on the suitability of farm buildings for the type of agriculture practised and their state of repair.

15. Cottages and cottage gardens
    Labourers dwellings, often with notes on the amount and quality of garden produce.

Fields

16. Field boundaries
    Usually the type of boundary is described in these files.
17. Open fields
    The extent/location of any open fields.
18. Small, irregular closes
    Field size and shape were factors which local agents thought would affect the ease of tithe collection; they sometimes noted where exceptionally small or irregularly shaped fields would increase costs of tithe collection by comparison with neighbouring districts.
19. Large, regular fields
    These were noted for reasons opposite to the previous category.

Woodland

20. Hedgerow timber
    Hedgerows often provided a timber resource as well as field boundaries: in 'pastoral' format reports, the species of trees are usually identified.
21. Coppice
    Coppicing of woodland noted.
22. Plantations
    References to woodland plantations.
23. Woodland management
    Usually with comments on frequency of cutting of coppice, etc.
24. Productive woodland
    As with most categories of land, local tithe agents often provide a value judgement of quality of titheable woodland; (in many places only underwood, not timber, was tithed, and so comments under 24 and 25 may relate only to this); this heading includes those places which they considered above average quality.
25. Poor woodland
    Woodlands of below average productivity; as with the previous category, such judgements were usually made only where woodland was titheable.

Unfarmed land

26. Commons
    Under this heading will be found comments on both the extent and vegetation of commons, though often only where this was titheable.
27. Furze, gorse and heathlands
    Comments on such unreclaimed lands.

28. Moorland
    Comments on such unreclaimed lands.
29. Mosses
    Comments on such unreclaimed lands.
30. Fens
    Comments on undrained fenland.
31. Wasteland
    Land which local agents considered would be forever unproductive of tithe, such as sea cliffs and beaches.

Agriculture

Environmental factors

In the middle years of the nineteenth century, environmental factors such as natural soil fertility, drainage and land altitude were judged potent influences on agricultural output and, therefore, on the value of tithes. Local agents looked particularly closely at the nature of soils.

32. Climatic hazards
    Entries under this head relate mostly to places where exposure to high winds was thought to reduce the value of arable and pasture.
33. Excessively steep land
    Places where local agents considered some land too steeply sloping to be ploughed.
34. Land requires drainage
    Land which for want of drainage would not yield a full tithe.
35. Land liable to flood
    Land which in some seasons or years would be inundated by river or sea with a consequent reduction of its produce.
36. Productive soil
    As well as commenting on the nature of soil (see 38–44 below) local agents often made a judgement based on their experience and perception as to whether local soils were naturally more productive than average;
37. Poor soil
    or whether soils were less fertile than average and so might yield a reduced titheable product.
38. Heavy (clay) soil
    Soils which local agents classified as heavy included not only those developed on a clay subsoil but others which in their view were likely to produce depressed yields in wet seasons unless underdrained. A commonly used yardstick was whether or not soils were suited to turnips.
39. Loamy (turnip) soil
    Loams, or 'turnip soils' as they are frequently described, were those considered best adapted to high-output, convertible husbandry at this time.

40. Light soils

This category includes land on which pasture was likely to 'burn' in dry summers and on which wheat did not yield well.

41. Peat

Where soil was developed on a peat subsoil.

42. Chalk

Where soil was developed on chalk strata.

43. Sand or gravel

Soils developed on these parent materials.

44. Several varieties of soil

Soil type varies from one part of a tithe district to another and even, as in parts of Kent, for example, from one part of a field to another. Where local agents' descriptions suggest that soil variations were particularly marked, this heading is employed.

Transport and marketing of produce

Transport and marketing factors are commented on in tithe files because of the influence they had on the ease or otherwise with which tithe could be collected in kind and then sold. Assistant commissioners and local tithe agents deducted a sum, perhaps as much as 30 per cent, from the gross value of a rent-charge as an allowance for the fact that money payments would not incur any costs of collections.

45. Fields remote from farms

If landholdings were scattered over a wide area of a district then the cost of collecting tithe would be especially high.

46. Good local roads

The nature of local roads also had a bearing on the costs of tithe collection and so local agents often commented where these were good;

47. Poor local roads

and also where they were in a bad condition, perhaps impassable for a part of the year.

48. Turnpike and main roads

Similar comments were made about roads leading out of a district to the main produce markets.

49. Roads recently improved

Assistant commissioners were careful to note any improvements which might affect the local tithe situation in the five years prior to 1836; improvement of roads was one such matter.

50. Water carriage

Water carriage, if available, usually receives some comment, both for its use for marketing produce and also for importing manures.

51. Canals

Occasionally these are separately distinguished in the files.

52. Railways

Comments on these again relate mainly to the effect of rail transport on the marketing of agricultural produce.

53. Markets accessible

Distance from market was also a factor taken into account by local agents when calculating costs of collecting tithe; this heading indicates those places where local agents were prompted to comment that a district was favourably located in this respect;

54. Markets inaccessible

and this heading where in their opinion distance incurred an above average cost of tithe collection.

55. Provincial markets

In a few files markets themselves are discussed, particularly whether they specialised in grain or livestock.

56. London market

Places located with access to the London market and where this facility was judged to affect prices obtained for titheable produce.

57. Fairs

Rarely described.

58. Market prices

Notional prices for titheable products used for calculating gross rent-charges are to be found in many thousands of files, especially those with reports on tithe agreements. They are 'notional' in that they do not always display that regional variation which is known to have existed. This index heading identifies those files in which market prices are discussed or actual prices listed.

Land management

This sub-section contains a wide range of topics, all broadly related to land management.

59. Landowners and their estates

In all files with a report on a tithe agreement there is a statement of the number of landowners in the district. Acreages are rarely stated (the tithe apportionment is the best source for these), but matters relating to the structure of landownership are discussed in a few files identified by this heading.

60. Land occupiers

Again a tithe apportionment is the best source for a list of names; this heading identifies files where some characteristics of land occupation are noted.

61. Farm size

Always consult the tithe apportionment and map to reconstruct sizes and boundaries of farms; these files contain comments on farm size, often in relation to its effect on agricultural production.

62. Leases

These are not often discussed but are mentioned in some files, again perhaps where they have some particular bearing on output or are not in line with those of neighbouring districts.

63. Farm implements

As noted in the Introduction, implements and machinery are rarely objects of mention in tithe file papers.

64. Common grazing

Many commons were either tithe free or generated very little titheable produce and so their use occasioned little comment in tithe files.

65. Lammas and other common rights

Where these existed and had a bearing on titheable produce they might be discussed.

66. Rents

All 'pastoral' format reports on agreements and many of 'arable' type contain statistics on the rental of land; in files identified by this heading, the general question of land rents is discussed.

67. Urban influences on value of land

Competing demands close to large urban areas and their effect on land prices occasioned comment in these files.

68. Rates

In a few files the question of rates and their relationship to tithe and poor relief is discussed.

69. Farm labour and wages

One of the weaknesses of tithe surveys as a source for studying nineteenth-century rural economy and society is their silence on those who peopled the landscape, not least on agricultural labourers; there are very few files listed under this heading.

Agricultural change

When assessing a fair rent-charge, assistant commissioners and local tithe agents were required to note any recent changes which might increase or depress the gross value of tithes. 'Recent' usually related to the years of average (1829–35), though some files contain information on, for example, improvements initiated in the early 1820s and many on what was likely to happen in the near future as a direct result of tithe commutation. Great caution should be used if inferring absence of an improving practice at a particular place from data in this sub-section of the index; the only systematic basis for local agents commenting on these matters was if they considered that they had materially affected, or would materially affect, the gross value of titheable produce either upwards or downwards.

70. Enclosure or improvement of waste

The bringing of previously unproductive land into cultivation had clear consequences for tithe, even though such land might be tithe free for a number of years after initial reclamation.

71. Enclosure of commons

Comments as the previous heading.

72. Enclosure of open fields
    There were still quite a number of parishes with open fields as late as *c.* 1836; recent or expected enclosure is usually commented on in tithe files.
73. Enlargement of fields
    Few instances of field enlargement receive comment in tithe files.
74. Occasional ploughing of grassland
    Under this head will be found comments on infield–outfield systems (see also 108 and 109 below).
75. Conversion of grass to arable
    The ploughing up of pasture had an immediate effect on the value of tithes; there is much speculation in the files about whether the Tithe Commutation Act might itself be an important influence on this.
76. Conversion of arable to pasture
    The laying down of arable to permanent grass, as when emparking, would depress the value of tithe and so occasioned comment.

77–86: Under these heads are listed those places where use of these particular methods of land improvement is commented on.
77. Paring and burning
78. Warping
79. Subsoil ploughing
80. Reclaiming and embanking
81. Marsh drainage
82. Drainage channels and ditches
83. Steam pumps
84. Ridge-and-furrow
85. Underdrainage
86. Tile drains

87–100: Under these heads comments on use of specific marls, manures and fertilisers are made; absence of an entry for a place does not imply that the practice was not employed.
87. Marl
88. Chalk
89. Lime
90. Seasand
91. Soot
92. Dung
93. Seaweed
94. Fish
95. Bones
96. Copralite
97. Guano
98. Rape cake

Subject Index

99. Chemical fertiliser
100. Oil dust, unspecified fertiliser or manure

Arable farming

101–9: Rotations. The usual way in which local tithe agents and assistant commissioners calculated the gross output of agricultural produce in a district was by establishing the crop rotation or rotations normally followed in the parish. This was a fundamental step in their calculation and so it is not surprising that rotations elicit considerable comment in tithe files. They are listed in this index according to the number of courses followed. Although the nature of farming systems under three-, four- or five-course systems varies from one part of the country to another, they provide some guide to the proportions of wheat grown. Longer rotations are very much more varied; there is a world of difference, for example, between a six- or seven-course in Devon with three or four years in seeds and the same in east Kent with perhaps three crops of wheat and no bare fallows.

101. General comments on rotations
    This heading indicates those files in which there is some discussion of crop rotations, often at length.
102. Irregular rotations
    This heading identifies parishes in which local tithe agents considered that no one rotation was adopted generally.
103. Three-course rotation
104. Four-course rotation
105. Five-course rotation
106. Six-course rotation
107. Seven-course rotation
108. Eight–ten-course rotation
109. More than ten-course rotation
    Headings 108 and 109 mainly identify those districts where the plough was taken around the farm at intervals of as long as ten years.

110–14: Corn crops. In almost all files where the Place Index indicates that there is a report on a tithe agreement, estimated acreages and yields of corn crops grown in a district will be found. The cultivation of grains for bread and animal feed was a normal practice in most tithe districts *c.* 1836 and so the simple presence of these crops occasioned little comment in any written descriptions made by local tithe agents or in papers of evidence. These index headings do not, therefore, give any indication of what was grown where or in what quantity; the likelihood of this information being in a file can be ascertained by checking whether the Place Index indicates that it contains a report on a tithe agreement. Headings 110–14 of this Subject Index identify only those places at which cultivation of grain crops is discussed at some length.

110. Wheat
111. Barley

112. Oats
113. Rye or meslin
114. Corn yields

115–33: Pulse, seed, forage and root crops, and fallows. Exactly the same caveats apply to these headings as to those of corn crops. These crops, however, elicited much more comment from local agents; some were interchangeable, and so there may be comments on which ones were grown, for example. Others were adapted to particular soil characteristics – peas were favoured on lighter soils, beans on heavier land. The turnip was used by many commentators as an indicator of convertible husbandry and of the elimination of what they saw as wasteful bare fallowing (see also 136 below).

115. Beans
116. Peas
117. Rape
118. Coleseed
119. Mustard
120. Caraway
121. Canary
122. Unspecified grass seed
123. Clover
124. Sainfoin
125. Trefoil
126. Tares and vetches
127. Lucerne
128. Kale
129. Turnips
130. Mangolds
131. Swedes
132. Potatoes
133. Bare fallows

134–8: The quality of arable farming. Value judgements on the general quality of local farming are often recorded by Tithe Commission agents in justification of the level of rent-charge assessed.

134. High farming

On 'arable' format report forms, local agents were asked specifically to note any instances of abnormally high or low farming which might have influenced the amount of tithe actually paid during the years of average. High farming was not defined according to any clearly stated criteria, indeed some local agents often used the term as a synonym for exceptionally good husbandry.

135. Low farming

Term used to denote under-capitalised or just bad, slovenly arable husbandry.

136. Remarks on the absence of turnips

The cultivation of turnips and elimination of dead fallows were often taken by local agents as indicators of a reasonable farming system. By contrast, absence of turnips at places where environmental factors were considered suitable for their cultivation signified poor farming practices.

137. Remarks on pests and diseases

These are not noted in any systematic way but are remarked upon in those places where one crop or another was particularly susceptible to disease problems or where these had depressed the yield of tithe during the years of average.

138. Recent increase or decrease in productivity

Assistant commissioners and local agents were asked to note particularly any recent changes affecting productivity which might affect the representativeness of the years of average as a basis on which to assess rent-charge.

Livestock farming

In very many tithe districts, animal products and the produce of grassland generally were liable to small or vicarial tithes, the great or rectorial tithes being those emanating from the arable. Hay was usually a great tithe but sometimes a small tithe. Vicarial tithes were worth much less than rectorial tithes and were those most likely to be covered by small customary payments or moduses in lieu of their full value. On an average, tithe files contain much less descriptive information about the livestock sector than about the arable. 'Pastoral' format reports usually contain estimates of livestock numbers but these are of questionable accuracy (see *The tithe surveys of England and Wales*, Chapter 4).

139–45: Grassland

139. Good quality pastures

As with other categories of land, a value judgement of the quality of grassland was often given. Comments which suggest an above average appraisal are indexed with this heading;

140. Poor quality pastures

while this heading indicates places where pastures were considered of below average quality.

141. Meadows

Produce of these could be very valuable so where they were extensive, comment would be elicited in justification of the amount of tithe they generated.

142. Irrigation and water meadows

This heading indicates comment on these practices.

143. Marsh grassland

144. Parks

Ornamental parks used for grazing would generate titheable produce and so might be described; emparking, especially if from arable, would reduce tithe liability and almost certainly elicited comment.

145. Accommodation land

Accommodation land on the edge of urban areas could command very high rents but often it was covered by a modus and so received little comment.

146–8: Livestock. These index headings identify comments on particular management practices and on particular types of animals and animal feedstuffs and products.
146. Cattle breeding
147. Cattle fattening
148. Dairying
149. Cow keeping
150. Sheep breeding
151. Sheep fattening
152. Droving
    Used to indicate those files in which there is comment on movement of animals from one part of the country to another; not, though, a topic of frequent comment.
153. Horses
154. Pigs
155. Oxen
    Very few comments on these animals.
156. Poultry
    Very few comments, probably due to lapse of tithe collection.
157. Rabbits
    Also includes those files where warrens are discussed.
158. Deer
159. Animal diseases
    As with crop pests and diseases, animal diseases are remarked upon where particular troubles were endemic or where incidence of disease affected titheable produce during the years of average.
160. Straw
161. Hay
162. Manufactured feedstuffs (cake, etc.)
163. Stall or yard feeding
164. Milk
165. Butter
166. Cheese
167. Wool
168. Eggs

Fruit, vegetables and industrial crops

Orchards and fruit, hops and some market gardens by virtue of the very high value of output per acre were liable in some parts of the country to an additional payment in lieu of tithes known as an extraordinary tithe rent-charge. Other crops noted in this final section of the Subject Index were either cultivated mainly in gardens and so contributed only a notional amount to the rent-charge if any at all, or else were 'recent' introductions and not, therefore, crops customarily tithed. Both these facts help explain why there are so few entries under these headings.

Subject Index 561

169. Good orchards

   An assessment of the quality of these might be made in the course of determining gross rent-charge.

170. Poor orchards

   Those assessed at below average productivity.

171. Fruit

   Rarely are individual varieties of fruit crops discussed.

172. Market gardens

   Absence of this code does not mean that market gardens were not worked in a tithe district (this can be ascertained by referring to the schedule of apportionment); files are entered under this heading only if local market gardens elicited some specific comment.

173. Allotments

   A rarely used heading.

174. Cabbages
175. Carrots
176. Onions
177. Other vegetables
178. Hops
179. Flax and hemp
180. Dyestuffs
181. Reeds and oziers
182. Teasels

Bedfordshire

1. Tithe-free district 12965 12966 12968 12970 12972 12973 12974 12975 12976 12978 12985 12987 12988 12989 12991 12992 12994 12996 12997 12998 13001 13004 13006 13008 13009 13010 13011 13013 13014 13015 13017 13023 13025 13026 13027 13031 13035 13039 13040 13041 13042 13043 13045 13048 13049 13050 13051 13055 13056 13057 13058 13059 13060 13061 13064 13066 13069 13070 13071 13073 13074 13075 13077 13083 13085 13088 13091
2. History of tithe payment 13036 13079
4. Exemptions from tithe 12969 12977 12981 12982 12983 12990 12999 13012 13016 13028 13032 13034 13044 13046 13053 13054 13062 13063 13072 13078 14825
5. Tithe in kind 13012 13018 13033 13068 13076
6. Compositions 12979 12980 12982 12983 12990 12995 13000 13003 13005 13012 13018 13021 13024 13029 13033 13037 13038 13047 13062 13063 13068 13072 13082
7. Moduses 12981 13000 13003 13016 13018 13032 13033 13034 13036 13038 13053 13065 13078 13086 13089 13090
8. Glebe 12984 13021 13033 13038 13090
9. Local topographic descriptions 13005
10. Regional topographic descriptions 12969 13020 13052 13078
11. Village morphology 12969 13036
12. Church 12986 13016 13036 13052 13078
13. Country houses and ornamental gardens 13036 13076 13076 13079
14. Farm houses and buildings 13020
15. Cottages and cottage gardens 12969 13067 13079 13081
16. Field boundaries 12983
17. Open fields 12986 13000 13003 13016 13052 13078 13081 13090
21. Coppice 13002 13046 13079
22. Plantations 12969 12984 13036 13067 13076 13079
24. Productive woodland 12981 13067 13079
25. Poor woodland 13002 13081
28. Moorland 13076
32. Climatic hazards 13067
34. Land requires drainage 13081
36. Productive soil 12981 13030 13079
37. Poor soil 12969 12981 13002 13030 13046 13052 13065 13067 13079
38. Heavy (clay) soil 12969 12981 12983 12986 12993 13002 13007 13016 13036 13065 13067 13078 13079 13081 13084
39. Loamy (turnip) soil 12981 12983 12986 13076 13079 13081 13084
40. Light soil 13005
41. Several varieties of soil 13081
42. Chalk 12999 13078
43. Sand or gravel 12969 12984 13005 13007 13016
44. Peat 12969
45. Fields remote from farms 13020 13036
46. Good local roads 12981 12984 12986 13030 13036 13052
47. Poor local roads 12969
48. Turnpike and main roads 12969 12981 12999
53. Markets accessible 12999
55. Provincial markets 12981
58. Market prices 12999
60. Land occupiers 13020
61. Farm size 12986 13016 13052 13078
62. Leases 13030 13052
64. Common grazing 13078
65. Lammas and other common rights 12980 13000 13076 13078 13078 13090
66. Rents 13052
72. Enclosure of open fields 12968 12970 12977 12980 12987 12991 12994 12996 13017 13018 13028 13031 13033 13043 13048 13054 13057 13060 13061 13083 13085
76. Conversion of arable to pasture 12969
85. Underdrainage 12981 12993 13002 13016 13030 13067
101. General comments on crop rotations 13002 13078
102. Irregular rotations 13036 13067 13078
103. 3-course rotation 12981 12986 13000 13003 13016 13046 13052 13068 13081
104. 4-course rotation 12969 12981 12983 12986 12993 13005 13007 13016 13030 13068 13078 13084
105. 5-course rotation 12984 13078
106. 6-course rotation 12969
110. Wheat 12999
114. Corn yields 12969 12983 12995 13000 13003 13012 13021 13047 13081
115. Beans 12969 12983 12986 12993 12995 13002 13003 13007 13012 13016 13030 13036 13078 13081 13084
116. Peas 12969 13002 13012 13081
122. Unspecified grass seeds 12984 13020
123. Clover 12969 12993 13007 13016 13030 13036 13052 13078 13084
126. Tares and vetches 12969 12993 12995 13002 13012 13036 13052 13067
129. Turnips 12969 12983 12984 12995 12999 13002 13005 13007 13016 13030 13052 13067 13078 13081 13084
130. Mangolds 12969
132. Potatoes 13081
133. Bare fallows 12969 12981 12986 12993 12995 13002 13003 13007 13016 13036 13046 13052 13078 13081 13084
135. Low farming 13002 13081
137. Remarks on pests and crop diseases 13046
138. Recent increase in productivity 13002 13067
139. Good quality pastures 12969 12981 13076 13081 13081
140. Poor quality pastures 12981 13002 13007 13036 13067 13076 13079 13081
141. Meadows 13052 13067 13079 13081
144. Parks 13005 13036
146. Cattle breeding 12981 13030 13036
147. Cattle fattening 12981 13030 13036
148. Dairying 12981 13005 13020
150. Sheep breeding 12969 13030 13036
151. Sheep fattening 13036
155. Oxen 13036
160. Straw 12999
161. Hay 12969 12983 13012 13036 13079
164. Milk 12999
169. Good orchards 13079
172. Market gardens 12979 13033

Berkshire

1. Tithe-free district 13092 13104 13108 13114 13115 13130 13131 13133 13134 13144 13146 13149 13159 13163 13179 13180 13181 13186 13192 13197 13199 13200 13213 13221 13226 13228 13251 13254 13268 13272 13273

Berkshire contd.

3	Tithe practices and agriculture	13140 13183
4	Exemptions from tithe	13093 13098 13100 13101 13111 13119 13120 13121 13122 13124 13125 13129 13136 13139 13143 13151 13165 13169 13170 13177 13183 13187 13190 13193 13196 13201 13203 13207 13209 13215 13216 13218 13225 13229 13230 13232 13235 13239 13243 13249 13253 13259 13261 13269 13275 13277
5	Tithe in kind	13098 13102 13140 13141 13148 13175 13198 13220 13225 13239 13259 13269
6	Compositions	13097 13098 13126 13135 13152 13167 13227 13229 13246 13252 13275
7	Moduses	13125 13151 13160 13172 13173 13177 13183 13184 13196 13208 13220 13235 13243 13249 13259
9	Local topographic descriptions	13140 13171 13211 14803
10	Regional topographic descriptions	13093 13113 13156 13162
11	Village morphology	13122 13223 13253 13261 13271 13280
12	Church	13103 13124 13127 13177 13203 13209 13212 13217 13231 13269 13271 14803
13	Country houses and ornamental gardens	13141 13211 13218 13218 13242 13242 13265 13265 13276 13278
15	Cottages and cottage gardens	13141 13143 13223 13232 13276
16	Field boundaries	13122 13258
17	Open fields	13105 13126 13141 13147 13177 13189 13196 13212 13225 13231
18	Small, irregular closes	13258 13261
19	Large, regular fields	13105
20	Hedgerow timber	13258 13261 13269
21	Coppice	13105 13118 13122 13124 13127 13154 13177 13218 13219 13223 13269 13276 14803
22	Plantations	13102 13105 13137 13142 13153 13172 13218 13219 13220 13242 13264 13276
23	Woodland management	13223
24	Productive woodland	13110 13280
25	Poor woodland	13162 13183
26	Commons	13125 13141 13141 13196 13207 13219 13249 13276
27	Furze, gorse and heathlands	13105 13110 13118 13120 13142 13151 13220 13250 13264 13276
31	Wasteland	13118 13151 13220 13249 13250
32	Climatic hazards	13103 13110 13177 13185 13215 13258 13261
34	Land requires drainage	13100 13126 13127 13143 13183 13201 13208 13209 13223 13258 13261 13269 13276 13280
35	Land liable to flood	13100 13124 13126 13183 13201 13215 13230 13261 13262
36	Productive soil	13093 13095 13102 13105 13112 13119 13120 13122 13127 13137 13140 13141 13147 13154 13158 13170 13173 13175 13176 13177 13183 13184 13185 13193 13196 13211 13212 13217 13218 13231 13232 13235 13240 13243 13245 13253 13259 13262 13271 13276 13280 14803
37	Poor soil	13093 13105 13125 13126 13137 13140 13141 13142 13143 13183 13183 13185 13189 13203 13206 13208 13209 13218 13220 13223 13232 13242 13245 13250 13259 13261 13262 13276
38	Heavy (clay) soil	13094 13095 13100 13101 13102 13103 13110 13111 13112 13118 13119 13120 13121 13124 13125 13126 13127 13129 13137 13138 13140 13141 13143 13147 13151 13153 13156 13157 13162 13171 13172 13177 13183 13184 13185 13201 13203 13209 13215 13222 13223 13231 13232 13235 13240 13243 13258 13259 13269 13278
39	Loamy (turnip) soil	13095 13100 13102 13105 13111 13113 13116 13119 13120 13143 13175 13207 13209 13211 13212 13217 13223 13231 13232 13243 13276 13277 13280 14803
40	Light soil	13093 13100 13105 13113 13118 13124 13129 13140 13142 13154 13162 13165 13176 13177 13183 13185 13196 13207 13210 13212 13239 13248 13258 13277
41	Several varieties of soil	13093 13094 13103 13107 13111 13119 13120 13137 13142 13190 13206 13209 13215 13218 13223 13235 13245 13262 13276
42	Chalk	13094 13101 13105 13111 13129 13139 13140 13141 13147 13154 13156 13165 13172 13177 13183 13185 13189 13193 13196 13203 13218 13223 13225 13234 13235 13236 13239 13240 13248 13262 13264 13265 13280 14803
43	Sand or gravel	13094 13095 13100 13103 13107 13110 13111 13112 13119 13120 13122 13124 13125 13126 13137 13142 13143 13153 13154 13157 13158 13162 13170 13172 13173 13176 13184 13187 13190 13203 13206 13207 13208 13209 13210 13215 13218 13219 13220 13222 13230 13234 13235 13236 13242 13248 13249 13250 13253 13259 13261 13264 13265 13269 13276 13278 14803
44	Peat	13122 13142 13190 13208 13222 13242 13264 13278
46	Good local roads	13105 13142 13208 13261 13278
48	Turnpike and main roads	13094 13100 13154 13156 13183 13210 13218 13245 13258
50	Water carriage	13102
51	Canals	13100 13173 13187 13249
52	Railways	13111 13119 13143 13147 13154 14803
53	Markets accessible	13102 13137 13142 13153 13173 13196 13249 13253
54	Markets inaccessible	13100
55	Provincial markets	13137 13208
56	London market	13118 13187 13249
58	Market prices	13242
59	Landowners and their estates	13122 13124 13218 13245 13278
60	Land occupiers	13094 13111 13154 13171 13171 13225 13232 13245 14803
61	Farm size	13094 13095 13103 13122 13124 13127 13158 13177 13203 13209 13269 13271
65	Lammas and other common rights	13126 13141
68	Rates	13103 13122 13124 13127 13177 13203 13209 13269 13271 14803
70	Enclosure or improvement of waste	13105 13110 13119 13119 13120
71	Enclosure of commons	13266
72	Enclosure of open fields	13163 13164 13186 13200 13204 13225 13226 13239 13241 13261 13273
76	Conversion of arable to pasture	13183 13265
85	Underdrainage	13102
95	Bones	13207
98	Rape cake	13100
100	Oil dust, unspecified fertilisers or manures	13102 13207
101	General comments on crop rotations	13107 13129 13141 13215 13220
102	Irregular rotations	13177 13201 13208 13242 13261
103	3-course rotation	13118
104	4-course rotation	13093 13094 13095 13100 13101 13103 13105 13107 13110 13111 13113 13116 13118 13119 13120 13121 13122 13125 13127 13137 13138 13139 13141 13142 13143 13147 13153 13154 13156 13157 13158 13165 13170 13173 13175 13177 13184 13185 13187 13189 13190 13193 13196 13201 13203 13209 13210 13211 13212 13215 13217 13218 13219 13222 13225 13231 13232 13235 13236 13239 13240 13242 13243 13245 13248 13249 13253 13258 13261 13264 13265 13269 13271 13277 13278 13280 14803
105	5-course rotation	13093 13100 13105 13107 13110 13124 13129 13151 13183 13210 13234 13258 13261
106	6-course rotation	13123
108	8-10-course rotation	13207
110	Wheat	13177
113	Rye or meslin	13139 13208 13242 13276
114	Corn yields	13106 13118 13123 13125 13126 13142 13148 13160 13188 13217 13231 13267
115	Beans	13093 13095 13100 13102 13103 13107 13110 13112 13118 13119 13120 13121 13124 13126 13127 13138 13143 13147 13151 13157 13158 13162 13170 13171 13173 13175 13177 13184 13185 13190 13196 13201 13206 13207 13215 13217 13223 13225 13231 13234 13235 13240 13243 13258 13262 13269
116	Peas	13100 13119 13120 13137 13143 13196 13223 13225 13236
123	Clover	13095 13102 13103 13105 13110 13113 13118 13119 13120 13121 13122 13124 13125 13129 13137 13138 13142 13143 13151 13154 13157 13158 13165 13171 13173 13175 13176 13177 13183 13184 13185 13187 13189 13190 13193 13196 13203 13206 13207 13208 13209 13211 13212 13219 13222 13223 13232 13235 13240 13261 13262 13269 13271 13276 13277 13278 13280 14803
124	Sainfoin	13094 13129 13139 13140 13165 13177 13189 13196 13203 13209 13223 13235 13245 13264 13280 14803
125	Trefoil	13209 13211
126	Tares and vetches	13100 13102 13112 13118 13119 13120 13147 13153 13175 13185 13208 13223 13235 13240 13262

Berkshire contd.

129	Turnips	13093 13094 13095 13100 13101 13102 13103 13105 13107 13112 13113 13116 13119 13120 13121 13122 13124 13125 13126 13129 13137 13139 13140 13141 13142 13143 13147 13151 13153 13154 13156 13157 13158 13162 13170 13175 13176 13177 13184 13185 13187 13189 13190 13193 13196 13203 13206 13207 13208 13209 13210 13211 13212 13217 13218 13219 13222 13223 13225 13231 13232 13234 13235 13236 13242 13243 13245 13248 13253 13258 13261 13262 13264 13265 13271 13276 13277 13278 13280 14803
131	Swedes	13110
132	Potatoes	13102 13110 13125 13137 13193 13201 13208 13249
133	Bare fallows	13093 13095 13101 13103 13110 13118 13119 13120 13121 13124 13126 13127 13138 13143 13151 13157 13170 13177 13184 13187 13189 13196 13201 13206 13207 13209 13215 13217 13219 13223 13225 13231 13232 13235 13240 13242 13243 13258 13269 13271 13276 13278 13280 14803
134	High farming	13111 13121 13140 13154 13176 13212 13217 13231
135	Low farming	13183 13225 13245
139	Good quality pastures	13100 13105 13110 13112 13119 13120 13127 13137 13140 13143 13173 13183 13185 13189 13196 13210 13215 13223 13231 13232 13262 13276 13280
140	Poor quality pastures	13119 13120 13126 13129 13140 13143 13147 13187 13208 13209 13219 13248 13250 13258 13261 13276
141	Meadows	13111 13120 13127 13137 13141 13142 13147 13157 13183 13196 13207 13210 13211 13215 13218 13222 13223 13230 13232 13242 13248 13253 13261 13262 13276 13278 13280
142	Irrigation and water meadows	13094 13100 13105 13187 13217 13223 13236 13245 13264 13278 13280
143	Marsh grassland	13219
144	Parks	13111 13124 13129 13137 13183 13218 13232 13242 13276 13280
147	Cattle fattening	13118 13127 13278
148	Dairying	13112 13127 13170 13173 13190
150	Sheep breeding	13094 13105 13113 13116 13119 13120 13139 13142 13151 13158 13165 13170 13173 13177 13183 13185 13190 13193 13201 13212 13220 13231 13232 13245 13249 13265
154	Pigs	13105 13141 13183 13223 13232 13280
156	Poultry	13141 13280
160	Straw	13137
161	Hay	13119 13120 13141 13142 13154 13211 13223 13230 13232 13242 13245 13276 13278
169	Good orchards	13173
170	Poor orchards	13141
172	Market gardens	13137 13217
173	Allotments	13127 13142 13261
174	Cabbages	13110 13137 13208
181	Reeds and oziers	13100 13122 13141 13183 13217 13232 13262

Buckinghamshire

1	Tithe-free district	13281 13283 13295 13298 13302 13306 13311 13312 13315 13320 13321 13323 13325 13331 13333 13334 13336 13340 13341 13342 13345 13354 13357 13359 13361 13364 13365 13368 13386 13389 13391 13395 13396 13397 13398 13399 13400 13401 13405 13410 13411 13414 13416 13417 13424 13425 13433 13434 13436 13437 13438 13440 13441 13444 13447 13449 13451 13456 13457 13459 13472 13473 13476 13478 13479 13482 13549 14804 14805 14829
2	History of tithe payment	13337 13375 13383 13402 13552
4	Exemptions from tithe	13290 13301 13303 13313 13316 13317 13318 13319 13324 13332 13339 13347 13349 13353 13358 13359 13360 13369 13371 13394 13403 13422 13429 13432 13467 13485 13550
5	Tithe in kind	13329 13379 13402
6	Compositions	13285 13374 13378 13383 13387 13388 13394 13402 13429 13548 13550
7	Moduses	13337 13388 13412 13420 13426 13435 13469
9	Local topographic descriptions	13285 13301 13313 13316 13318 13319 13332 13335 13343 13346 13347 13358 13360 13370 13376 13379 13384 13385 13403 13406 13432 13485
10	Regional topographic descriptions	13379
11	Village morphology	13370 13379 13382
12	Church	13290 13293 13316 13332 13335 13343 13348 13349 13360 13370 13371 13376 13384 13408 13428 13432 13465 13485 13553
13	Country houses and ornamental gardens	13337 13454 13460
15	Cottages and cottage gardens	13318
16	Field boundaries	13316 13363
17	Open fields	13316 13343 13404 13415 13422
20	Hedgerow timber	13432
21	Coppice	13421
22	Plantations	13435 13466
23	Woodland management	13293 13318 13370 13485
24	Productive woodland	13285 13335
26	Commons	13301 13301 13358 13359 13379
27	Furze, gorse and heathlands	13285 13305 13445
32	Climatic hazards	13305 13318 13319 13346 13421
34	Land requires drainage	13290 13293 13316 13348 13349 13384 13403 13404 13426 13432 13465
35	Land liable to flood	13301 13337 13358 13406
36	Productive soil	13310 13335 13346 13382 13426
37	Poor soil	13287 13329 13353 13360 13363 13370 13371 13379 13461 13467 13485
38	Heavy (clay) soil	13290 13293 13304 13310 13316 13318 13332 13335 13339 13348 13349 13358 13360 13363 13369 13376 13382 13390 13393 13403 13422 13426 13428 13432 13435 13454 13460 13461 13464 13465 13467
39	Loamy (turnip) soil	13301 13305 13310 13324 13337 13343 13347 13369 13376 13385 13420 13426 13445 13460 13461 13553
40	Light soil	13319 13332
41	Several varieties of soil	13310 13313 13316 13317 13319 13324 13339 13343 13358 13359 13360 13370 13371 13403 13406 13408 13421 13422 13428 13454 13464
42	Chalk	13285 13313 13318 13339 13358 13359 13360 13371 13376 13379 13385 13403 13406 13408 13421 13422 13467 13485
43	Sand or gravel	13285 13305 13310 13313 13317 13335 13337 13346 13347 13349 13360 13370 13406 13421 13422 13428 13445 13485
44	Peat	13317 13428
46	Good local roads	13358
47	Poor local roads	13316
48	Turnpike and main roads	13317 13385
52	Railways	13304 13316 13422
55	Provincial markets	13346 13445
56	London market	13382
58	Market prices	13287 13464
59	Landowners and their estates	13285 13287 13318 13337 13371 13408 13553
60	Land occupiers	13287 13346 13359 13460
61	Farm size	13290 13316 13332 13335 13346 13348 13349 13359 13360 13370 13376 13408 13428 13432 13454 13465 13485 13553
62	Leases	13427
64	Common grazing	13343 13346 13359
65	Lammas and other common rights	13343 13346
68	Rates	13316 13485
71	Enclosure of commons	13285
72	Enclosure of open fields	13285 13347 13384 13426
76	Conversion of arable to pasture	13349
79	Subsoil ploughing	13287 13404 13464

Buckinghamshire contd.

85	Underdrainage	13464
88	Chalk	13353
92	Dung	13335
101	General comments on crop rotations	13313 13346 13387 13402 13403
102	Irregular rotations	13343 13435 13454
103	3-course rotation	13290 13293 13316 13329 13348 13376 13384 13385 13426 13432 13461 13465 13553
104	4-course rotation	13293 13301 13304 13310 13313 13332 13343 13347 13349 13358 13363 13371 13382 13385 13390 13406 13408 13421 13445 13454 13460 13461 13465 13467 13485
105	5-course rotation	13304 13310 13318 13335 13337 13353 13359 13360 13370 13376 13379 13408 13428
106	6-course rotation	13445
110	Wheat	13415
111	Barley	13285 13310 13432
114	Corn yields	13387 13388 13402
115	Beans	13332 13408 13415 13428
116	Peas	13403 13408
123	Clover	13301 13318 13335 13346 13358 13403 13408
124	Sainfoin	13317 13358 13376 13403 13485
125	Trefoil	13310
126	Tares and vetches	13290 13304 13310 13382 13403 13461
129	Turnips	13287 13310 13313 13319 13332 13403 13421 13464
133	Bare fallows	13421 13465
135	Low farming	13290 13353 13359 13384 13404
136	Remarks on the absence of turnips	13346 13379
139	Good quality pastures	13310 13376 13382 13404 13406 13426 13464 13553
140	Poor quality pastures	13317 13329 13379 13467
141	Meadows	13318 13319 13347 13403 13406 13426 13460 13467
142	Irrigation and water meadows	13317 13318 13332 13358
144	Parks	13318 13359 13379 13403 13422
145	Accommodation land	13318
146	Cattle breeding	13382 13408 13467 13548
147	Cattle fattening	13304 13348 13363 13432 13435 13548
148	Dairying	13293 13304 13305 13318 13329 13348 13349 13382 13390 13393 13407 13426 13432 13435 13454 13460 13548
150	Sheep breeding	13378 13548
151	Sheep fattening	13287 13293 13305 13313 13318 13454 13464 13548
153	Horses	13548
154	Pigs	13287 13379 13382 13426 13454 13548
157	Rabbits	13385
158	Deer	13313
159	Animal diseases	13290 13293
160	Straw	13435
161	Hay	13285 13318 13347 13359
162	Manufactured feedstuffs (cake etc.)	13382 13454
165	Butter	13382 13426 13435 13454
167	Wool	13313 13318 13343 13407 13548
169	Good orchards	13318 13358 13382 13403
170	Poor orchards	13379
171	Fruits	13343
172	Market gardens	13318
173	Allotments	13324
181	Reeds and oziers	13553

Cambridgeshire

1	Tithe-free district	13484 13487 13490 13494 13495 13498 13502 13503 13506 13508 13510 13511 13514 13516 13517 13520 13522 13524 13530 13531 13532 13533 13534 13535 13536 13537 13538 13540 13541 13542 13543 13544 13545 13567 13568 13570 13573 13576 13577 13578 13582 13583 13587 13589 13590 13591 13593 13594 13596 13597 13598 13600 13601 13610 13612 13613 13614 13617 13618 13620 13621 13625 13626 13627 13629 13633 13635 13637 13638 13640 13643 13646 13648 13650 13654 13660 13664 13666 13667 13668 13677 13678 14830
2	History of tithe payment	13529
4	Exemptions from tithe	13488 13491 13493 13496 13497 13500 13539 13579 13580 13584 13599 13603 13624 13631 13645 13647 13657 13665 13670
5	Tithe in kind	13525 13624
6	Compositions	13513 13525 13526 13571 13574 13581 13595 13602 13649 13651 13665
7	Moduses	13497 13574 13640 13665 13676
8	Glebe	13525 13580 13641
9	Local topographic descriptions	13483 13491 13513 13521 13523 13525 13569 13584 13592 13603 13605 13606 13607 13608 13622 13623 13630 13631 13632 13652 13674
10	Regional topographic descriptions	13500 13504 13521 13585 13661 13671
11	Village morphology	13584 13669
12	Church	13505 13584 13592 13606 13607 13623 13652 13674
13	Country houses and ornamental gardens	13491 13588 13672
14	Farm houses and buildings	13661
15	Cottages and cottage gardens	13661 13669
16	Field boundaries	13499 13512 13645
17	Open fields	13488 13489 13501 13507 13519 13523 13571 13580 13588 13592 13599 13606 13607 13609 13615 13624 13630 13632 13639 13642 13644 13647 13652 13661 13669 13670 13676
18	Small, irregular closes	13523 13581 13592 13603 13642 13644
19	Large, regular fields	13504
21	Coppice	13525
22	Plantations	9842 13493 13515 13628 13672
23	Woodland management	13515 13523 13584 13592 13606 13607 13623 13630 13641 13652 13659
25	Poor woodland	13585
26	Commons	13507 13507 13523 13616 13632 13647 13669
27	Furze, gorse and heathlands	9842 13491 13588 13603 13609 13631
28	Moorland	13605
30	Fens	13483 13493 13497 13500 13501 13504 13527 13580 13605 13608 13611 13616 13631 13632 13641 13657 13669 13671 13673 13674 13676
31	Wasteland	13647
32	Climatic hazards	13486 13489 13493 13505 13512 13523 13527 13609 13622 13632 13671
34	Land requires drainage	13486 13488 13489 13499 13504 13507 13575 13581 13585 13585 13603 13609 13624 13645 13676
35	Land liable to flood	13501 13644
36	Productive soil	13491 13505 13512 13569 13599 13619 13632 13657
37	Poor soil	13489 13581 13606 13607 13609 13623 13632 13652 13662
38	Heavy (clay) soil	13486 13489 13491 13496 13497 13499 13501 13507 13512 13513 13519 13521 13523 13525 13575 13580 13585 13586

Cambridgeshire contd.

		13588 13592 13606 13607 13611 13622 13623 13624 13630 13641 13642 13644 13647 13659 13661 13662 13672 13676
39	Loamy (turnip) soil	13501 13525 13580 13604 13628 13645 13659 13661 13669 13674
40	Light soil	13493 13504 13525 13575 13588 13603 13604 13607 13609 13615
41	Several varieties of soil	13504 13603 13631 13632 13636 13652 13669 13670 13672
42	Chalk	13513 13515 13584 13592 13599 13630 13636
43	Sand or gravel	13491 13496 13515 13569 13584 13622 13631 13642 13652 13670
44	Peat	13501 13527 13642 13647
45	Fields remote from farms	13632
46	Good local roads	13491 13525 13670
47	Poor local roads	13632
48	Turnpike and main roads	13488 13523
50	Water carriage	13488 13491 13500 13671
53	Markets accessible	13489 13505 13603 13608 13609 13622 13647
54	Markets inaccessible	13500 13630
55	Provincial markets	13504 13641 13676
56	London market	13491
58	Market prices	13605 13628
59	Landowners and their estates	13488 13493 13505 13512 13515 13575 13607 13623 13623 13631 13655 13662 13672
60	Land occupiers	13499 13500 13505 13515 13652 13671
61	Farm size	13512 13569 13584 13592 13606 13607 13628 13630 13631
64	Common grazing	13500 13615 13624 13632 13639 13644 13647 13665
65	Lammas and other common rights	13488 13493 13496 13500 13599 13602 13603 13608 13608 13608 13609 13615 13624 13632 13639 13639 13644 13647 13665 13670 13671
69	Farm labour and wages	13630 13657 13657
70	Enclosure or improvement of waste	13632
71	Enclosure of commons	13581
72	Enclosure of open fields	13488 13489 13519 13521 13569 13575 13580 13588 13599 13603 13604 13609 13624 13644 13652
75	Conversion of grass to arable	13644
77	Paring and burning	13483 13505 13608 13609 13632 13671 13676
80	Reclaiming and embanking	13670
81	Marsh drainage	13497 13500 13527 13580 13605 13608 13611 13632 13669 13671 13673
82	Drainage channels and ditches	13483 13507 13608 13616 13619 13673
83	Steam pumps	13505 13605 13608 13632 13669
84	Ridge-and-furrow	13488 13507
85	Underdrainage	13504 13512 13622 13636 13661
86	Tile drains	13488
87	Marl	13497 13501 13527 13605 13608 13611 13642 13671
92	Dung	13488 13493 13505 13662
95	Bones	13504 13505 13609
100	Oil dust, unspecified fertilisers or manures	13603
101	General comments on crop rotations	13497 13499 13527 13592 13608 13616 13622 13624 13632 13636 13652 13669 13670 13671 13673
102	Irregular rotations	13505 13521 13603 13608 13636 13674
103	3-course rotation	13507 13519 13521 13523 13586 13606 13615 13616 13630 13641 13644 13647 13652 13670
104	4-course rotation	13486 13488 13489 13491 13493 13497 13499 13504 13512 13515 13521 13523 13525 13569 13575 13580 13584 13585 13592 13603 13604 13605 13616 13624 13628 13631 13642 13645 13657 13659 13662 13669 13676
105	5-course rotation	13496 13505 13527 13580 13605 13607 13609 13623 13641 13642 13647 13673
106	6-course rotation	13497
107	7-course rotation	13483
110	Wheat	13486 13488 13491 13513 13527 13657
111	Barley	13488 13489 13491 13504 13505 13521
112	Oats	13486 13489 13605
113	Rye or meslin	13493 13504 13599 13609
115	Beans	13489 13491 13603 13608
116	Peas	13493 13599 13603 13609 13616 13652
117	Rape	13580 13657 13673
118	Coleseed	13497 13504 13505 13527 13605 13608 13616 13619 13628 13641 13647 13669 13671 13673 13674 13674 13676
123	Clover	13486 13488 13489 13499 13504 13512 13588 13599 13628 13676
124	Sainfoin	13504 13599 13603
125	Trefoil	13486 13488 13504 13609
126	Tares and vetches	13486 13489 13493 13499 13512 13584 13603 13607 13608 13619 13631 13632 13652 13676
129	Turnips	13486 13488 13504 13505 13512 13515 13521 13569 13588 13608 13645 13674
130	Mangolds	13486 13489 13500 13580 13608 13657 13671
131	Swedes	13676
132	Potatoes	13499 13500 13505 13527 13608 13616 13619 13670 13671
133	Bare fallows	13486 13489 13491 13584 13586 13624
134	High farming	13504 13505 13512 13515 13575 13584 13592 13599 13604 13607 13616 13619 13631
135	Low farming	13488 13507 13580 13624 13669
136	Remarks on the absence of turnips	13489 13615 13623 13644 13676
137	Remarks on pests and crop diseases	13641 13671
138	Recent increase in productivity	13505
139	Good quality pastures	13486 13505 13521 13580 13611 13616 13616
140	Poor quality pastures	13489 13507 13513 13585 13641 13645
141	Meadows	13504 13586 13588 13603 13605 13609
142	Irrigation and water meadows	13515
144	Parks	13491 13493 13607 13672
147	Cattle fattening	13604 13608 13644 13659 13673
148	Dairying	13505 13604 13608 13622
150	Sheep breeding	13588
151	Sheep fattening	13486 13489 13493 13504 13515 13588 13603 13608 13622 13628 13630 13641 13644 13659 13669 13673
153	Horses	13644 13657
154	Pigs	13501 13661
156	Poultry	13661
159	Animal diseases	13622
161	Hay	13486 13504 13575 13603 13608 13615 13632 13644 13659 13671
162	Manufactured feedstuffs (cake etc.)	13505 13505
167	Wool	13493 13504 13630 13644
169	Good orchards	13632 13669
170	Poor orchards	13628
171	Fruits	13661
177	Other vegetables	13674
179	Flax and hemp	13619 13619

Cheshire

#	Topic	Page references
1	Tithe-free district	5 65 83 84 101 253 274 317 13732 13815
2	History of tithe payment	162 171 218 241
3	Tithe practices and agriculture	7 201
4	Exemptions from tithe	8 12 14 27 34 91 92 99 104 105 127 139 142 174 175 196 214 219 221 239 241 242 252 261 271 283 332 13696 13701 13706 13716 13726 13741 13761 13783 13798 13809 13810
5	Tithe in kind	8 15 17 22 27 34 56 58 66 67 88 90 92 93 97 102 104 105 106 110 112 119 120 121 123 125 126 128 130 137 139 140 141 146 148 154 158 159 163 166 169 170 172 175 178 180 181 184 189 190 191 192 194 195 196 197 201 204 207 210 214 219 221 222 225 226 229 234 235 236 237 239 240 259 260 266 268 275 282 285 286 287 289 292 295 298 301 303 304 307 311 315 323 327 329 331 334 335 336 13684 13692 13694 13695 13706 13711 13713 13716 13721 13727 13728 13730 13737 13740 13741 13749 13756 13757 13758 13760 13763 13768 13772 13774 13781 13782 13783 13790 13792 13795 13796 13800 13802 13806 13813 13816
6	Compositions	7 37 39 51 58 59 73 79 94 98 109 128 131 164 167 181 215 216 243 267 284 289 291 314 13743 13744 13746 13762 13777 13790
7	Moduses	1 2 4 6 8 14 15 17 19 22 27 31 34 37 38 43 50 54 55 58 59 60 61 66 67 68 69 72 73 76 88 93 95 102 104 106 110 112 119 120 121 123 129 130 135 139 142 143 144 148 150 151 152 159 162 163 170 171 177 180 181 182 186 189 190 192 194 196 206 210 216 218 219 226 231 236 239 243 244 249 252 254 255 258 259 260 261 263 263 265 267 268 269 272 275 276 277 280 282 283 286 287 292 293 294 295 296 298 299 300 304 306 307 311 315 323 327 328 329 332 334 335 336 13366 13680 13683 13684 13689 13690 13692 13694 13695 13696 13697 13698 13700 13701 13706 13707 13709 13713 13714 13715 13716 13720 13721 13728 13735 13739 13740 13741 13745 13747 13749 13750 13752 13755 13756 13757 13758 13760 13761 13763 13764 13765 13767 13768 13774 13775 13781 13783 13786 13787 13792 13795 13796 13798 13799 13800 13801 13802 13806 13809 13813 13814 13816 14823 14835
9	Local topographic descriptions	122
10	Regional topographic descriptions	61 102 118 122 154 157 164 168 175 268 276 311 13689 13690 13713 13729 13752 13758 13764 13803 13811
11	Village morphology	95 112 246 13798
12	Church	13712 13764
13	Country houses and ornamental gardens	69 147 13712 13811
16	Field boundaries	48
18	Small, irregular closes	89 13748
19	Large, regular fields	48 177
22	Plantations	34 122 188 13798
26	Commons	95 122 132
27	Furze, gorse and heathlands	54 90 95 188 188 13810 13810
29	Mosses	54 120 122 13702 13703 14824
31	Wasteland	188 13728 13783
32	Climatic hazards	44 70 132 133 300 321 13696 13763
33	Excessively steep land	212
34	Land requires drainage	20 25 32 41 50 81 106 122 123 132 140 141 146 148 151 168 188 189 204 210 213 227 234 245 263 268 271 277 292 295 318 322 332 13366 13705 13713 13715 13719 13720 13722 13725 13730 13749 13750 13756 13786 13792 13794 13800 13801 13811 14824
35	Land liable to flood	32 135 186 13714 13798
36	Productive soil	3 11 12 14 25 29 48 56 57 66 67 69 75 82 89 104 115 135 139 151 157 159 169 184 186 195 214 226 227 234 240 245 249 259 263 265 271 289 293 307 313 315 318 319 321 335 13683 13689 13691 13696 13703 13709 13714 13715 13722 13726 13728 13744 13745 13747 13750 13752 13756 13758 13759 13761 13764 13767 13770 13774 13775 13793 13794
37	Poor soil	4 8 11 12 14 15 32 33 46 53 54 63 72 77 81 82 89 90 92 115 119 120 131 133 139 147 151 186 197 199 201 204 212 214 219 235 238 240 263 265 271 289 299 306 331 335 13684 13690 13694 13696 13705 13715 13719 13722 13737 13740 13742 13748 13749 13750 13756 13759 13761 13767 13772 13775 13786 13792 13794 13801 13806 13814 13816
38	Heavy (clay) soil	3 4 6 8 11 12 15 17 18 19 20 22 23 24 25 26 27 28 29 31 32 33 34 35 36 41 44 46 48 50 52 53 54 57 58 60 61 63 71 72 77 81 82 88 89 90 92 93 97 102 103 104 105 106 110 115 118 119 120 121 123 126 128 130 131 135 137 139 140 141 143 146 147 148 154 156 157 158 163 164 166 168 169 172 175 177 178 180 181 182 183 184 189 190 191 192 193 194 195 196 197 199 201 204 210 212 213 214 219 221 222 224 225 227 229 234 235 238 239 240 245 246 249 251 259 263 264 265 266 268 271 275 276 277 281 282 283 285 286 287 289 292 293 294 295 298 299 300 301 303 304 306 307 309 311 322 323 327 329 331 334 335 336 13366 13680 13684 13689 13690 13692 13693 13694 13695 13700 13701 13705 13706 13707 13708 13709 13711 13712 13713 13714 13715 13716 13717 13719 13720 13721 13722 13725 13726 13727 13729 13730 13735 13737 13739 13740 13741 13742 13744 13745 13747 13748 13749 13750 13752 13758 13759 13760 13761 13763 13768 13770 13772 13776 13781 13782 13783 13786 13787 13789 13790 13792 13793 13794 13795 13796 13798 13799 13800 13801 13802 13803 13805 13806 13809 13810 13811 13813 13814 13816 14824
39	Loamy (turnip) soil	11 16 18 22 25 29 36 56 57 60 67 88 95 105 115 126 130 151 154 159 163 169 172 175 199 219 221 227 245 263 268 271 275 282 287 300 307 318 329 334 336 13692 13693 13708 13714 13715 13722 13737 13741 13752 13768 13770 13783 13787 13793 13796 13816
40	Light soil	14 20 54 58 77 80 90 115 159 172 188 236 277 281 286 289 293 303 13690 13702 13703 13715 13725 13740 13767 13770 13780 13793 13805
41	Several varieties of soil	151 222 260 286 309 13366 13693 13712 13765 13799 13801 13803 13805
43	Sand or gravel	3 8 12 14 15 17 18 20 24 26 31 34 35 44 46 50 52 54 57 66 70 71 74 75 81 90 92 93 95 97 102 103 110 112 118 119 120 121 122 128 131 132 133 137 139 143 147 151 157 158 159 166 168 169 170 172 175 177 178 181 182 184 188 189 190 191 195 197 199 207 210 214 225 235 236 238 239 240 246 249 251 259 260 264 266 268 276 281 282 285 286 289 292 296 298 301 306 307 309 311 313 315 319 321 322 323 335 336 13680 13684 13689 13692 13695 13700 13701 13702 13703 13706 13708 13711 13712 13717 13720 13721 13722 13725 13726 13727 13728 13729 13730 13735 13737 13740 13742 13744 13747 13749 13750 13756 13757 13758 13759 13760 13761 13764 13765 13768 13774 13775 13781 13782 13783 13786 13787 13789 13790 13793 13800 13802 13805 13809 13810 13811 13816
44	Peat	14 56 74 147 148 169 178 192 235 285 295 13684 13702 13727 13740 13768 13783 13802 13805 13810
46	Good local roads	11 48 89 118 177 322 13696 13702 13789
47	Poor local roads	32 44 235 13767
48	Turnpike and main roads	11 12 13759 13767 13801
50	Water carriage	197
51	Canals	148 212 281 294 301 13683 13712 13726 13735 13813
52	Railways	143
53	Markets accessible	6 14 27 130 140 151 163 172 196 222 236 246 265 283 287 289 300 301 319 321 332 13696 13720 13729 13748 13780 13798 13813
54	Markets inaccessible	32 44 13705
55	Provincial markets	18 25 27 28 89 95 112 123 130 131 132 172 181 186 192 194 201 225 263 277 281 13366 13683 13691 13696 13703 13715 13720 13735 13750 13759 13761 13767
58	Market prices	61 13680 13761
59	Landowners and their estates	37 61 71 121 122 249 13680 13693 13763 13770 13707 13713 13757 13787 13795
60	Land occupiers	61 77 133 197 204 224 259 296 303 321 329 13693 13707 13713 13757 13787 13795

Cheshire contd.

#	Topic	References
61	Farm size	61 82 89 95 204 259 13693 13739 14824
62	Leases	39 41 195 249 294 13680 13693 13713 13757
66	Rents	23 29 63 75 80 128 139 143 181 182 188 195 197 201 204 224 225 226 238 293 309 313 13680 13693 13700 13701 13707 13708 13709 13717 13725 13726 13747 13761 13765 13770 13786 13799 13810 13814
67	Urban influences on value of land	63 319 321 13729 13780 13798
70	Enclosure or improvement of waste	13765 13765
71	Enclosure of commons	131 13792
72	Enclosure of open fields	304
75	Conversion of grass to arable	13803
76	Conversion of arable to pasture	17 71 82 131 183 225 235 238 13713 13729 13739 13756 13772
80	Reclaiming and embanking	13702 14824
85	Underdrainage	157 175 178 190 210 225 304 306 332 13712 13741 13748 13763 13770 14824
86	Tile drains	13803 13806
87	Marl	121 264 13775
92	Dung	14 18 27 28 44 69 112 163 172 196 197 222 224 225 277 283 287 289 13683 13691 13702 13703 13715 13750 13775
95	Bones	8 61 131 175 178 190 225 238 281 286 304 306 329 331 13680 13694 13712 13806
101	General comments on crop rotations	6 13 17 18 22 28 31 33 39 41 54 72 92 93 95 97 102 106 110 139 143 148 156 164 169 170 188 191 192 199 201 210 212 214 219 221 222 226 229 235 249 268 286 294 295 298 299 301 315 323 331 334 335 336 13680 13683 13690 13694 13695 13706 13708 13711 13716 13721 13725 13727 13730 13737 13739 13747 13749 13756 13760 13761 13763 13774 13781 13782 13783 13787 13789 13792 13793 13795 13796 13800 13802 13806 13809 13811 13813
102	Irregular rotations	22 75 118 128 166 181 226 229 322 13684 13725 13726 13740 13761 13816
103	3-course rotation	4 8 23 24 29 31 34 50 54 57 58 77 92 93 102 104 119 123 143 146 180 234 289 332 13744 13790
104	4-course rotation	4 16 24 26 54 58 67 77 121 157 158 172 184 224 225 289 303 309 311 319 334 13701 13707 13709 13717 13744 13761 13770 13783 13790 13814
105	5-course rotation	118 122 168 322 13717 13728
106	6-course rotation	48 132 133
107	7-course rotation	70 132
108	8-10-course rotation	128
109	More than 10-course rotation	3 181 228
111	Barley	263 13712
114	Corn yields	6 15 17 22 63 75 80 90 118 123 143 154 159 163 181 197 210 226 287 292 300 335 13711 13727 13740 13747 13752 13765 13766 13786 13793 13812
115	Beans	102 135 201 287 332 13750 13770
116	Peas	102 13750
123	Clover	6 8 17 25 27 53 54 57 58 60 72 74 75 81 88 97 103 104 106 110 139 148 151 158 166 169 172 189 191 196 201 204 212 214 221 224 227 229 235 239 251 259 263 265 268 275 282 283 286 287 300 307 315 334 335 336 13683 13691 13709 13719 13722 13726 13728 13735 13739 13742 13759 13760 13763 13767 13768 13774 13782 13789 13792 13795 13798 13801 13802 13805 13809 13816 14824
126	Tares and vetches	27 75 172 201 13702
129	Turnips	8 17 18 20 24 31 48 54 56 57 58 61 67 70 71 77 80 92 97 112 119 126 131 135 137 139 143 147 154 158 163 164 166 168 169 172 177 178 184 190 191 196 197 201 204 214 219 221 222 224 226 235 236 239 246 251 259 264 266 276 281 286 287 289 292 296 298 303 311 313 314 315 323 334 335 336 13683 13684 13689 13695 13706 13712 13727 13728 13730 13735 13740 13741 13744 13745 13748 13749 13756 13760 13761 13765 13768 13770 13774 13780 13781 13782 13783 13789 13790 13793 13796 13798 13809 13816 14824
131	Swedes	27 239 286 307 332
132	Potatoes	3 6 8 12 14 15 17 18 20 22 24 25 27 29 31 34 53 54 56 57 58 60 61 63 66 67 69 70 71 72 74 75 77 80 81 82 88 89 90 92 93 95 97 102 103 105 106 110 112 119 120 121 123 126 128 130 132 133 135 137 139 140 141 143 147 151 154 158 159 163 164 166 169 170 172 178 181 182 184 186 188 189 190 191 192 193 194 195 196 197 199 201 204 210 212 214 219 221 222 224 225 227 229 234 235 236 238 239 240 245 249 251 259 260 263 264 265 266 268 271 275 276 281 282 283 286 287 289 292 294 295 296 298 300 301 303 307 309 311 313 314 315 319 321 323 327 331 332 334 335 336 13366 13680 13683 13684 13689 13690 13691 13692 13693 13695 13700 13702 13705 13706 13707 13708 13709 13711 13712 13713 13715 13716 13717 13719 13720 13721 13722 13725 13726 13727 13728 13730 13735 13737 13740 13741 13742 13744 13745 13747 13749 13750 13752 13756 13757 13759 13760 13761 13763 13764 13765 13768 13770 13774 13781 13782 13783 13786 13787 13790 13795 13796 13798 13799 13800 13801 13802 13805 13806 13809 13813 13814 13816 14824
133	Bare fallows	3 6 8 15 17 18 20 22 25 27 31 48 50 54 56 57 58 60 63 71 72 74 75 77 80 81 88 90 92 93 97 102 103 104 105 106 110 119 120 123 126 130 135 137 139 140 141 146 147 148 157 158 164 166 168 175 177 178 180 182 184 188 189 190 191 192 193 195 196 199 201 210 212 214 219 222 224 225 227 228 229 234 238 239 240 249 251 259 263 264 265 268 271 275 276 282 283 286 287 289 292 295 298 299 300 301 303 304 319 321 323 327 329 331 332 334 335 336 13680 13690 13692 13694 13695 13700 13705 13706 13707 13708 13709 13711 13713 13716 13717 13719 13720 13721 13722 13725 13726 13727 13730 13737 13739 13740 13741 13742 13745 13747 13749 13750 13752 13756 13757 13758 13760 13763 13764 13765 13770 13772 13774 13781 13782 13783 13786 13787 13789 13790 13792 13793 13794 13795 13796 13799 13800 13801 13802 13806 13809 13811 13813 13814
134	High farming	57 61 66 137 159 169 172 184 190 214 222 296 306 13689 13737 13809
135	Low farming	3 17 19 22 57 106 140 166 197 226 228 236 251 268 295 301 13711 13740 13749 13756 13772 13782 13813 14824
136	Remarks on the absence of turnips	44 13749 13757
138	Recent increase in productivity	8 27 34 54 66 67 92 93 97 102 110 112 119 137 158 169 178 184 190 191 192 194 214 221 222 239 259 260 282 298 307 311 315 329 334 336 13683 13692 13695 13706 13721 13728 13735 13737 13741 13756 13758 13774 13781 13795 13796 13802 13809
139	Good quality pastures	11 25 26 41 81 95 135 146 148 186 193 226 229 234 245 268 318 332 13702 13714 13745 13775 13789 13793
140	Poor quality pastures	4 13 32 95 146 285 13780
141	Meadows	25 32 53 81 122 135 186 193 293 294 318 332 13714 13745 13759 13775
142	Irrigation and water meadows	27 183 263 13702 13803
143	Marsh grassland	34 35 66 13799
144	Parks	7 71 121 266 13744 13774 13811
145	Accommodation land	63 69 224 332 13691 13798
146	Cattle breeding	13796
147	Cattle fattening	54 95 112 126 132 133 196 286 300 323 13759 13774
148	Dairying	3 6 8 12 13 15 16 17 18 19 22 23 24 25 26 27 28 29 31 34 35 36 41 44 50 54 56 57 58 60 61 63 67 74 75 77 80 82 88 89 90 95 102 103 104 110 112 118 119 121 126 130 132 135 139 140 141 143 151 154 156 158 164 166 169 175 177 182 184 188 191 195 196 199 201 204 210 213 219 221 225 226 229 234 235 236 237 238 239 240 245 246 251 259 260 265 266 268 271 275 285 286 287 292 294 295 298 299 300 301 303 307 309 309 311 313 315 318 319 321 323 327 329 331 334 335 336 13680 13684 13690 13693 13694 13695 13700 13701 13706 13707 13708 13709 13711 13713 13714 13716 13717 13719 13720 13721 13722 13725 13726 13728 13737 13739 13741 13744 13745 13747 13748 13749 13756 13757 13758 13759 13760 13761

Cheshire contd.

		13763	13765	13767	13768	13772	13774	13776	13782	13783	13786	13787	13789	13790	13792	13794	13795	13796	13801	13802	13806	13809
		13811	13813	13814	13816	14824
149	Cow keeping	224	13748
150	Sheep breeding		17	54	88	266		303	13689	13707	13763	13770
151	Sheep fattening	224	286
153	Horses	266	13805
154	Pigs	313
157	Rabbits	132
158	Deer	266	13744
160	Straw	22	166	226	251	306	13684
161	Hay	25	69	112	132	135	163	172	193	292	13691	13702	13714	13739	13745	13775	13805	13816
162	Manufactured feedstuffs (cake etc.)			131	166	226	246	13760
164	Milk	6	27	69	112	123	130	131	163	169	172	192	194	212	246	283	292	300	319	13366	13683
	13735	13748	13749
165	Butter	131	246	13366	13683
166	Cheese	6	16	22	24	26	34	35	36	57	66	92	93	95	97	105	106	118	120	123	128
		137	148	159	163	170	178	180	189	190	192	194	199	210	222	226	227	235	268	282	283	295
		304	319	322	13680	13683	13692	13719	13727	13730	13735	13752	13757	13764	13792	13800	13816
172	Market gardens		14	130	13702	13703	13715	13750
174	Cabbages	13702
175	Carrots	186	277	13691	13750
176	Onions	13702	13750

Cornwall

2	History of tithe payment		378	458	492	517
4	Exemptions from tithe		352	362	396	401	427	433	470	523
5	Tithe in kind	341	351	355	371	395	400	437	448	450	462	474	479	513	538	540
6	Compositions	337	348	349	354	359	372	375	378	379	384	387	388	390	391	392	394	396	398	401
		402	408	412	415	417	421	422	424	425	435	440	443	445	449	464	467	469	470	471	473	474
		477	482	484	485	488	492	493	495	496	497	501	504	507	512	516	519	520	521	522	524	527
		528	532	533	535	539	540	544	548
7	Moduses	337	347	350	356	366	379	387	396	402	408	422	441	471	477	493	495	509	517	520
		521	524
8	Glebe	340	347	354	359	360	363	365	372	375	384	387	391	392	396	398	401	402	404	408	410
		415	417	422	425	429	432	436	443	445	450	464	468	470	473	480	483	493	495	496	497	504
		506	507	512	516	519	522	524	527	528	532	535	539	544	548
9	Local topographic descriptions		364	389	400	448	466	541
10	Regional topographic descriptions	347	377	389	395	400	455	505
11	Village morphology	351	447	536
14	Farm houses and buildings	468	468
17	Open fields	448	462	537
20	Hedgerow timber	339	341	342	345	355	357	358	361	362	364	367	368	369	370	373	376	377	380
		381	382	383	385	389	395	399	400	405	406	407	409	411	413	416	420	423	426	430	431	433
		434	437	438	439	442	444	446	448	452	454	455	456	457	460	461	462	463	465	466	468	472
		475	476	481	487	489	491	494	498	499	500	502	505	510	511	513	514	515	525	526	531	536
		538	541	542	543	545	546	547
21	Coppice	351	362	368	370	380	399	413	419	422	423	430	431	444	463	468	476	478	486	489
		492	499	500	510	515	547
22	Plantations	347	351	361	370	385	407	411	423	427	437	448	451
23	Woodland management	347
25	Poor woodland		472	478	489	498	511	526
26	Commons	378	405
27	Furze, gorse and heathlands		358	479
28	Moorland	355
32	Climatic hazards	395	461	466	478	529
34	Land requires drainage		373	389	416	542
36	Productive soil	345	367	371	376	381	403	515	538
37	Poor soil	343	367	381	395	478	491	505
38	Heavy (clay) soil	338	339	341	342	357	361	364	368	369	373	376	380	385	389	395	397	399	406
		411	413	416	419	420	427	428	430	434	438	439	442	452	456	457	460	463	465	468	472	476
		479	481	486	490	491	498	500	502	505	510	513	514	515	518	525	526	530	541	545
39	Loamy (turnip) soil	361	362	371	382	389	405	416	431	442	446	461	466	510	513	514	545
40	Light soil	347	371	376	393	395	399	400	406	407	423	426	428	433	437	444	448	451	455	456
		457	460	461	472	475	478	531	536	538	541
41	Several varieties of soil	362	364	368	369	373	545
43	Sand or gravel	341	405	494	515	518
44	Peat	355	405	411	431	442	502	503	513	525	546
46	Good local roads	407	448	462
47	Poor local roads	351	364	377	383	389	395	400	423	437	531	537	542
48	Turnpike and main roads	377	537	545
50	Water carriage	343	364	426	475	515	545
51	Canals	448
52	Railways	448	541	545
53	Markets accessible	403	447	515
54	Markets inaccessible	351	395	400	466	531
55	Provincial markets	347	488	537
56	London market	403
59	Landowners and their estates	357	362	441	461
61	Farm size	347	468	513	537
62	Leases	373	380	411	451
64	Common grazing	505
65	Lammas and other common rights	503	513
66	Rents	403	419	451
89	Lime	364	367	381	455	461	475	513	531	542	545
90	Seasand	364	367	381	385	455	461	475	513	531	541	542	545
93	Seaweed	455
101	General comments on crop rotations		343	371	376	381	382	383	385	400	405	407	409	426	437	441	444
		447	448	454	455	461	462	465	466	475	478	492	505	509	513	529	531	536	538	541	542	545
102	Irregular rotations	446
103	3-course rotation	358	364	367	518	534
104	4-course rotation	377	389	393	395	403	457	472	518	530
105	5-course rotation	338	341	342	347	351	353	357	361	368	369	370	373	380	386	397	399	406	411
		416	418	419	420	423	428	430	433	438	439	451	452	456	460	468	476	479	481	486	489	490

Cornwall contd.

		491	492	494	498	499	500	503	510	511	514	515	525	526	543	547				
106	6-course rotation				338	339	362	413	416	427	431	433	434	463	487	498	502			
107	7-course rotation				442	453	537													
109	More than 10-course rotation						546													
114	Corn yields	389																		
123	Clover	351	361	367	479															
129	Turnips	455	461	492																
132	Potatoes	341	345	364	376	381	383	385	393	395	400	401	403	405	409	416	423	426	433	437
		438	444	446	447	448	451	454	455	461	462	465	466	478	486	488	492	505	513	515	531	536
		537	538	541	542	545														
134	High farming	451	476																	
135	Low farming	416																		
139	Good quality pastures				409															
142	Irrigation and water meadows					377	444													
143	Marsh grassland	363																		
146	Cattle breeding	541																		
147	Cattle fattening	441																		
148	Dairying	441																		
150	Sheep breeding	347	448	541																
153	Horses	378																		
154	Pigs	389	395	405	407	448	462													
156	Poultry	389	395	405	407	462														
161	Hay	358	389																	
165	Butter	492																		
171	Fruits	360	360																	
174	Cabbages	409	488																	
176	Onions	488																		
181	Reeds and oziers	421																		

Cumberland

1	Tithe-free district	549	559	568	570	581	586	587	588	600	604	605	606	613	622	627	628	629	631
		632	633	638	641	647	648	650	652	657	678	698	703	712	717	729	748	749	758	764	778	780
		781	786	789	790	791	792												
2	History of tithe payment				593		660	792											
3	Tithe practices and agriculture			557	560	637	716	719	757										
4	Exemptions from tithe			578	580	590	593	599	601	614	616	623	624	625	626	630	634	639	646	651
		669	670	679	685	686	688	695	702	705	716	721	723	726	727	728	733	734	738	742	756	757
		761	763	766	771	772	776	782	783	785	787	793							
5	Tithe in kind	553	555	563	567	569	572	574	593	597	603	607	610	621	630	649	658	661	664	666
		688	689	693	709	710	719	728	734	741	751	766	769	776	777	795			
6	Compositions	555	556	557	566	571	594	595	597	614	618	620	624	635	653	661	666	681	689	692
		694	708	709	723	727	732	736	767	775	776	777	779	782					
7	Moduses	550	552	553	554	560	561	563	565	566	569	571	573	574	575	575	576	577	578	579
		580	582	583	585	590	591	593	595	599	601	602	608	609	610	611	612	614	615	616	617	618
		624	635	636	637	639	640	642	643	643	644	649	653	655	656	659	662	663	665	666	668	671
		672	673	679	680	682	684	687	689	690	693	695	699	702	704	707	708	710	713	716	719	722
		725	731	732	733	734	735	736	738	739	740	744	745	747	749	754	755	756	757	760	761	763
		768	770	772	773	775	776	779	782	783	785	793	795						
8	Glebe	557	610	616	624	634	649	679	689	751	792								
9	Local topographic descriptions				603														
10	Regional topographic descriptions			596	607	679	787												
11	Village morphology	651	740																
14	Farm houses and buildings			557															
15	Cottages and cottage gardens			557															
16	Field boundaries	572																	
18	Small, irregular closes		558	608	621	644	663	700	724	752	765								
22	Plantations	662	679	740															
24	Productive woodland			663															
26	Commons	572	572	596	644	765	772	773											
27	Furze, gorse and heathlands		551	572	572														
28	Moorland	551	680																
29	Mosses	575	621																
32	Climatic hazards	551	560	626	643	643	644	658	693	700	751	765	772	787	794				
34	Land requires drainage	572	643	651	663	707	719	724	733	793	794								
35	Land liable to flood	794																	
36	Productive soil	572	575	644	686	693	700	707	719	755	757	784	785	787					
37	Poor soil	551	558	560	572	575	583	603	621	626	643	656	663	693	707	719	728	733	740	752
		753	755	766	769	784	785	787											
38	Heavy (clay) soil	551	558	583	596	608	626	630	643	656	663	680	719	724	733	742	752	753	766
		769	785	787	794														
39	Loamy (turnip) soil	658	663	664	686	700	724	785											
40	Light soil	558	560	608	621	679	680	695	751	765	772	794							
41	Several varieties of soil		558	656	733	752	769												
43	Sand or gravel	551	558	583	596	621	644	656	658	680	695	724	742	752	753	765	769	772	
44	Peat	558	575	621	643	656	679	752	765										
46	Good local roads		608	693	700	752	784												
47	Poor local roads		765	766	784	785													
48	Turnpike and main roads		658																
51	Canals	575																	
53	Markets accessible	551	607	695	751														
54	Markets inaccessible	572	785	787															
55	Provincial markets	663																	
58	Market prices	571	603	692															
59	Landowners and their estates		621	621	707														
60	Land occupiers	603																	
61	Farm size	621	707	742															
62	Leases	751																	
64	Common grazing	644	716																
66	Rents	619	728																
70	Enclosure or improvement of waste		553	557	571	607	643	753	784										
71	Enclosure of commons	553	571	607	663	733	742	753	757	784									
76	Conversion of arable to pasture	603																	
80	Reclaiming and embanking	557																	

Cumberland contd.

92	Dung	607	695														
101	General comments on crop rotations				557	572	607	621	626	630	637	733					
102	Irregular rotations	656	658	663	724												
103	3-course rotation	752															
104	4-course rotation	637	656	695	707	751	752										
105	5-course rotation	619	637	643	656	658	664	680	695	707	719	751	769	785			
106	6-course rotation	558	607	608	619	644	656	663	664	680	686	700	707	719	724	728	751	765	794
107	7-course rotation	572	607														
108	8-10-course rotation	572	607	621													
110	Wheat 644 765																
111	Barley 630																
112	Oats 772																
113	Rye or meslin 621																
114	Corn yields	560	571	607	634	733	765										
123	Clover 583	651	686	751	769	785											
129	Turnips	558	572	583	596	603	608	621	630	637	643	644	656	658	663	664	680	686	695	700
	707	719	724	728	733	735	742	751	753	765	769	772	785	794			
132	Potatoes	572	583	596	603	630	637	651	663	680	686	695	707	719	724	728	735	742	751	753
	765	769	772	785	794												
133	Bare fallows	558	572	583	596	603	626	637	651	656	663	664	680	695	719	724	728	733	752	753
	765	769	785	794													
134	High farming 769																
135	Low farming	560	695	751	753	769											
136	Remarks on the absence of turnips			766													
138	Recent increase in productivity	557															
139	Good quality pastures	551	757														
140	Poor quality pastures	551															
143	Marsh grassland	575	679														
146	Cattle breeding	651	757	772													
147	Cattle fattening	695	740														
148	Dairying	607	728	751													
150	Sheep breeding	560	621	644	693	716	757	772	779								
151	Sheep fattening	621															
153	Horses 707																
154	Pigs 793																
156	Poultry 793																
157	Rabbits 572																
160	Straw	583	692	772													
161	Hay	607	621	651	707												
164	Milk	603	707	728	751												

Derbyshire

1	Tithe-free district	804	805	812	816	820	821	825	827	828	836	845	846	862	867	887	889	891	893
	896	903	904	912	918	920	924	925	931	932	934	935	947	948	988	1002	1003	1023	1030	1038	1042
	1053	1063	1083	1087	1089	1090	1109	1113										
2	History of tithe payment	811	823	850	865	869	872	894	911	913	914	954	993	1069	1098	1111	1111	
4	Exemptions from tithe	798	801	811	822	833	851	866	868	874	881	899	902	910	914	921	922	958
	959	960	962	964	971	977	978	980	984	985	989	991	992	997	1021	1026	1028	1047	1050	1051	1052
	1079	1091															
5	Tithe in kind	798	799	810	839	852	907	909	913	961	993	997	1025	1105				
6	Compositions	796	799	803	808	810	813	822	823	829	831	834	849	852	855	856	857	869	871	897
	901	909	910	913	914	921	933	936	943	950	953	955	956	957	958	959	963	964	967	968	971
	973	974	977	978	983	986	987	990	993	994	1008	1010	1015	1016	1026	1028	1033	1040	1044	1055	1061
	1065	1080	1084	1091	1097	1101	1106										
7	Moduses	798	799	806	811	817	823	824	831	835	838	846	849	852	855	859	864	865	866	869
	871	875	881	894	899	901	909	911	913	914	923	926	927	928	930	936	944	949	951	953	956
	957	960	961	962	963	964	967	973	977	983	985	990	994	997	1011	1015	1016	1024	1028	1033	1036
	1041	1045	1050	1058	1064	1066	1080	1086	1091	1104	1112						
8	Glebe	860	875	909	962	967	975	987	1015	1040	1084							
9	Local topographic descriptions	839	840	848	860	863	882	886	888	905	907	908	915	916	937	968	976
	980	982	1017	1039	1046	1049	1056	1057	1110	1111							
10	Regional topographic descriptions	800	807	815	850	870	976	992	999	1001	1017	1018	1049	1105			
11	Village morphology	819	851	879	888	929											
12	Church 819																
13	Country houses and ornamental gardens	819	976														
14	Farm houses and buildings	1046															
15	Cottages and cottage gardens	819	882	1046	1073												
16	Field boundaries	1057															
17	Open fields 968																
18	Small, irregular closes	982	1017	1031	1054												
20	Hedgerow timber 976																
21	Coppice 811																
22	Plantations	819	832	880	882	886	888	929	1048	1073							
23	Woodland management	815	1111														
24	Productive woodland	815															
25	Poor woodland	819	886	888													
26	Commons	848	886														
27	Furze, gorse and heathlands	818															
28	Moorland	888	905	990													
29	Mosses 917																
32	Climatic hazards	826	839	842	858	860	870	906	907	945	982	1007	1048	1056	1057	1085	1111
34	Land requires drainage	839	884	966	982	989	999	1017	1031	1046							
35	Land liable to flood	847	981	1092	1111												
36	Productive soil	818	843	847	851	858	886	895	907	968	970	1019	1031	1054	1071	1073	1085	1092	1094
37	Poor soil	814	818	826	839	841	843	851	870	882	886	890	946	966	981	982	989	1000	1007	1013
	1037	1056	1070	1085	1088	1105											
38	Heavy (clay) soil	807	814	819	830	833	839	840	841	842	843	848	858	861	870	876	879	880	883
	884	886	890	900	907	929	941	945	965	968	980	982	989	999	1007	1017	1031	1054	1057	1067	1071
	1073	1088	1092	1105	1110	1111											
39	Loamy (turnip) soil	807	809	818	819	830	847	850	858	860	861	888	917	945	968	970	977	1007	1019
	1031	1048	1054	1057	1067	1078	1088										
40	Light soil	832	833	842	876	884	929	1048	1070	1071							
41	Several varieties of soil	840	844	905	1095	1111											

Derbyshire contd.

43	Sand or gravel		839	841	843	847	861	870	900	980	1031	1092	1105	1111	
44	Peat	844	853	917	981	1019									
45	Fields remote from farms			863											
46	Good local roads		879	900											
47	Poor local roads		839	1017	1054										
48	Turnpike and main roads		839	844	1017	1046									
49	Roads recently improved		886	929											
51	Canals	965	1001												
52	Railways		900	1054											
53	Markets accessible		879	968	992	1000	1001								
54	Markets inaccessible		1073												
55	Provincial markets		839	880	1078	1092									
58	Market prices		1048												
59	Landowners and their estates		839	851	882	888	919	929	929	981	1000	1031	1039	1039	
60	Land occupiers		818	819	861	884	888	1017	1057						
61	Farm size	839	844	882	888	906	915	916	937	982	989	999	1017	1031	
64	Common grazing		886												
65	Lammas and other common rights				819										
66	Rents	841	861	907	915	916	968	976	982	1057	1062	1071			
68	Rates	968	982	1001	1017										
69	Farm labour and wages		1017												
70	Enclosure or improvement of waste			802	1005										
71	Enclosure of commons		905	981	982	1028									
72	Enclosure of open fields		802	874	913	968	985								
80	Reclaiming and embanking		844												
85	Underdrainage		907	929	982										
89	Lime	815	982												
92	Dung	807	888	929	968										
95	Bones	1048													
101	General comments on crop rotations			1054											
102	Irregular rotations	809	814	826	832	847	853	888	919	941	977	980	1029	1031	1054
103	3-course rotation	818	833	860	883	890	907	968	980	989	1037	1062	1072	1094	1095
104	4-course rotation	800	807	815	818	839	844	848	851	884	907	941	965	966	968	1031	1048	1056	1067	1088	1105	1111
105	5-course rotation	807	814	830	861	876	945	965	976	982	999	1001	1013	1017	1018	1019	1048	1110
106	6-course rotation	847	876	879	900	1057									
107	7-course rotation	879	880	1092											
108	8-10-course rotation	1039	1073	1078											
110	Wheat	842	879	929											
111	Barley	992													
112	Oats	826	858	888	906	908	1049	1056	1062						
114	Corn yields	883	929	945	989	1048	1054	1110							
115	Beans	965	992												
123	Clover	814	1048												
126	Tares and vetches	814	1031	1057											
129	Turnips	807	809	818	832	841	852	853	929	977	1017	1039	1062	1067	1088	1092	1094	1095	1104	1111
130	Mangolds	839													
132	Potatoes	809	832	850	853	861	882	890	907	917	945	966	968	1000	1017	1029	1056	1062	1094	1095	1104	1111
133	Bare fallows	851	907	946	992	1105									
134	High farming	847	848	1048											
135	Low farming	819	826	850	851	870	886	906	966	989	999	1017	1070	1085	
136	Remarks on the absence of turnips		819	861	1105										
139	Good quality pastures	807	833	847	858	863	888	900	968	976	981	1046	1054	1067	1073	1078	1081	1110
140	Poor quality pastures	819	882	1017	1031	1037	1056								
141	Meadows	847	853	880	882	883	888	900	929	980	981	1048	1056	1062	1078	1092	1111
144	Parks	830	976	1111											
145	Accommodation land		860	1081											
146	Cattle breeding	839	841	860	890	905	907	919	965	966	968	980	1057	1062	1111	
147	Cattle fattening	809	832	853	860	870	880	888	905	917	919	937	977	1019	1029	1039	1062
148	Dairying	809	818	830	839	840	841	858	860	880	882	884	886	888	890	905	907	908	915	916	917	919	929	937	945	965	966	968	980	982	1004	1007	1017	1019	1029	1048	1057	1073	1094	1110
150	Sheep breeding	840	888	890	905	907	968	1039	1057	1104					
151	Sheep fattening	809	818	832	840	848	853	860	870	908	915	916	917	937	945	965	1007	1019	1029	1048	1062
153	Horses	908	915	916	919	945	1039	1081							
154	Pigs	882	1062	1073	1111										
156	Poultry	1111													
158	Deer	1111													
160	Straw	915	916												
161	Hay	809	819	888	915	916	945	1062							
164	Milk	860	863	937											
165	Butter	842	848	863	1062										
166	Cheese	842	847	848	879	880	890	929	1062	1067	1071	1092	1111		
171	Fruits	941													
173	Allotments	929													
174	Cabbages	929	1062												
181	Reeds and oziers		880	981											

Devon

1	Tithe-free district	1219	1261	1262	1289	1290	1292	1327	1360	1417	1505										
2	History of tithe payment	1107	1108	1115	1116	1117	1119	1120	1122	1123	1124	1125	1126	1127	1128	1129	1132	1133
	1134	1135	1136	1137	1138	1140	1141	1142	1144	1146	1150	1151	1152	1154	1156	1157	1158	1161	1162	1189	1191
	1192	1195	1203	1204	1205	1206	1207	1208	1211	1212	1215	1217	1220	1221	1222	1228	1229	1230	1232	1233	1234
	1236	1237	1238	1240	1241	1243	1246	1247	1249	1251	1252	1254	1256	1257	1259	1260	1263	1265	1266	1267	1269
	1270	1272	1273	1275	1276	1278	1281	1283	1285	1286	1288	1291	1293	1294	1295	1296	1297	1298	1299	1300	1301
	1302	1303	1304	1305	1308	1309	1310	1313	1316	1317	1318	1319	1320	1321	1322	1324	1325	1326	1328	1330	1332
	1333	1334	1335	1338	1339	1340	1341	1343	1344	1345	1345	1346	1347	1348	1349	1350	1352	1353	1354	1356	1357
	1358	1359	1361	1363	1365	1366	1367	1369	1370	1371	1372	1373	1374	1376	1378	1380	1381	1382	1383	1384	1385
	1387	1388	1389	1390	1391	1392	1393	1394	1395	1396	1397	1400	1401	1403	1404	1405	1407	1408	1409	1410	1411
	1412	1413	1414	1416	1418	1419	1421	1422	1423	1425	1426	1427	1428	1429	1432	1433	1434	1435	1436	1437	1438
	1439	1440	1441	1442	1443	1444	1446	1447	1448	1451	1452	1453	1454	1455	1456	1457	1458	1458	1459	1460	1461
	1462	1463	1464	1465	1466	1467	1470	1473	1474	1475	1476	1477	1478	1479	1480	1482	1483	1484	1485	1486	1487

Devon contd.

```
        1488  1489  1492  1493  1494  1495  1496  1497  1498  1500  1501  1502  1504  1506  1507  1508  1511  1512  1513  1517  1518
        1520  1521  1522  1523  1525  1526  1527  1529  1532  1533  1535  1537  1539  1541  1542  1543  1544  1545  1546  1547  1549
        1550  1551  1552  1555  1556  1557  1558  1560  1562  1563  1564  1565  1566  1567  1568  1569  1571  1572  1573  1575  1577
        1578  1579  1580  1581  1583  1584  1586  1587  1588
 3  Tithe practices and agriculture    1214  1258  1298  1313  1501
 4  Exemptions from tithe        1124  1130  1131  1140  1147  1151  1152  1153  1160  1161  1195  1208  1226  1234  1240  1248  1255
        1264  1271  1272  1274  1282  1283  1298  1314  1315  1319  1333  1347  1353  1376  1381  1382  1387  1404  1414  1418  1419
        1423  1436  1446  1450  1468  1478  1478  1487  1492  1499  1503  1506  1512  1513  1523  1525  1536  1538  1548  1554  1563
        1568
 5  Tithe in kind   1129  1131  1151  1168  1189  1222  1223  1225  1226  1228  1229  1231  1239  1245  1251  1260  1268  1269  1270
        1284  1312  1331  1342  1354  1384  1399  1406  1428  1433  1439  1440  1441  1442  1448  1474  1486  1521  1546  1574
 6  Compositions    350   1107  1108  1114  1115  1117  1118  1119  1120  1121  1122  1123  1124  1125  1126  1127  1128  1129  1130
        1131  1132  1134  1135  1136  1137  1138  1139  1140  1141  1142  1143  1144  1145  1147  1148  1149  1150  1151  1152  1153
        1154  1155  1156  1157  1158  1159  1160  1161  1163  1168  1177  1178  1181  1183  1185  1186  1188  1189  1191  1192  1195
        1202  1203  1204  1205  1206  1207  1208  1209  1210  1211  1212  1213  1214  1215  1216  1217  1218  1220  1222  1223  1224
        1225  1226  1227  1228  1229  1230  1231  1232  1234  1236  1236  1238  1239  1241  1242  1243  1245  1252  1253  1254  1255
        1256  1257  1258  1259  1260  1263  1265  1266  1268  1269  1270  1272  1274  1277  1278  1279  1280  1281  1282  1283
        1284  1285  1291  1293  1295  1297  1298  1299  1300  1302  1304  1305  1306  1308  1309  1310  1312  1313  1314  1315  1316
        1317  1318  1319  1320  1322  1323  1324  1325  1326  1328  1329  1331  1333  1334  1335  1336  1337  1338  1341  1342  1343
        1344  1345  1346  1347  1348  1349  1350  1351  1352  1353  1354  1355  1356  1357  1358  1361  1362  1363  1365  1366  1367
        1368  1369  1371  1372  1373  1374  1375  1376  1377  1378  1379  1380  1382  1383  1384  1385  1386  1387  1388  1389  1390
        1391  1392  1393  1394  1395  1397  1398  1399  1400  1401  1403  1405  1406  1407  1408  1409  1410  1412  1413  1414  1415
        1416  1418  1419  1420  1423  1424  1425  1426  1427  1428  1429  1430  1431  1432  1433  1434  1435  1436  1437  1438  1439
        1440  1441  1442  1443  1444  1445  1446  1447  1448  1449  1450  1451  1452  1453  1454  1455  1456  1457  1458  1459  1460
        1461  1462  1463  1464  1466  1467  1468  1469  1470  1472  1473  1475  1476  1477  1478  1479  1480  1482  1483  1484  1485
        1486  1487  1488  1489  1491  1492  1493  1494  1495  1496  1497  1498  1499  1500  1501  1502  1503  1504  1506  1507  1508
        1509  1510  1511  1512  1513  1514  1515  1516  1517  1518  1519  1520  1521  1522  1523  1524  1525  1526  1527  1529  1530
        1532  1533  1535  1536  1537  1538  1539  1540  1542  1543  1544  1545  1547  1548  1549  1550  1551  1552  1553  1555  1556
        1557  1558  1559  1560  1561  1562  1563  1564  1565  1566  1567  1568  1569  1570  1572  1573  1574  1575  1576  1577  1578
        1579  1580  1581  1582  1583  1584  1585  1586  1587  1588
 7  Moduses         350   1119  1123  1134  1141  1149  1153  1161  1173  1180  1202  1203  1205  1209  1227  1233  1240  1256  1260
        1276  1295  1296  1314  1315  1346  1350  1355  1357  1368  1373  1375  1381  1382  1393  1410  1418  1434  1435  1441
        1445  1448  1453  1467  1471  1472  1485  1495  1497  1509  1542  1547  1561  1566  1568  1573  1579  1587
 8  Glebe           1107  1114  1119  1121  1123  1126  1127  1128  1133  1134  1136  1137  1138  1140  1141  1142  1145  1147  1149  1150
        1151  1153  1154  1161  1191  1203  1204  1205  1206  1210  1211  1212  1213  1217  1218  1220  1247  1248  1251  1257  1263
        1265  1266  1269  1274  1276  1279  1280  1281  1284  1293  1295  1297  1304  1305  1307  1310  1312  1316  1317  1318  1320
        1323  1324  1325  1326  1329  1330  1332  1333  1343  1345  1347  1348  1350  1351  1353  1355  1356  1361  1366  1367
        1369  1372  1374  1375  1376  1380  1381  1383  1384  1385  1387  1392  1393  1395  1397  1399  1400  1401  1404  1407  1408
        1410  1419  1420  1421  1423  1425  1431  1433  1436  1440  1444  1445  1447  1451  1453  1455  1456  1458  1460  1461  1462
        1463  1465  1466  1468  1470  1473  1483  1484  1487  1493  1495  1496  1497  1500  1502  1503  1504  1506  1507
        1508  1512  1514  1517  1519  1524  1525  1529  1537  1543  1544  1545  1550  1551  1552  1553  1555  1556  1558  1559  1560
        1561  1564  1566  1567  1569  1570  1571  1572  1573  1575  1576  1580  1584  1585  1587  1588
 9  Local topographic descriptions      1128  1141  1145  1151  1163  1168  1173  1206  1251  1266  1285  1297  1312  1320  1323  1324
        1326  1331  1340  1354  1356  1363  1371  1406  1415  1423  1431  1440  1460  1472  1541
10  Regional topographic descriptions   1173  1205  1391  1433  1482  1493  1499  1541
11  Village morphology      1260
12  Church          1155
16  Field boundaries        1128  1141  1206  1351
18  Small, irregular closes       1173
19  Large, regular fields   1469
20  Hedgerow timber 1115  1118  1119  1120  1121  1123  1126  1129  1130  1132  1134  1137  1138  1139  1143  1145  1150  1152
        1155  1165  1166  1168  1174  1177  1178  1179  1183  1189  1191  1192  1195  1199  1203  1204  1208  1211  1212  1216  1217
        1220  1221  1222  1226  1229  1230  1232  1236  1240  1241  1243  1244  1245  1250  1251  1254  1255  1257  1258  1259  1260
        1265  1266  1267  1274  1278  1281  1291  1293  1295  1297  1298  1302  1305  1306  1308  1309  1312  1313  1315  1316
        1318  1320  1323  1324  1326  1328  1329  1331  1333  1337  1339  1340  1345  1347  1350  1351  1352  1353  1354  1355  1356
        1358  1361  1362  1364  1367  1369  1371  1372  1374  1376  1377  1380  1383  1384  1387  1389  1392  1393  1395  1396  1397
        1398  1399  1400  1402  1403  1406  1407  1409  1410  1412  1415  1418  1420  1423  1425  1428  1430  1431  1436  1437  1440
        1441  1442  1444  1447  1450  1458  1460  1461  1464  1465  1469  1469  1471  1472  1478  1479  1480  1482  1483  1485  1486
        1487  1489  1492  1498  1499  1503  1504  1506  1507  1508  1510  1511  1512  1513  1514  1518  1519  1523  1524  1525  1527
        1528  1530  1533  1537  1539  1542  1543  1545  1546  1550  1551  1552  1553  1555  1556  1557  1558  1559  1560  1563  1564
        1565  1568  1572  1575  1576  1579  1586  1588
21  Coppice         1123  1126  1130  1137  1138  1141  1150  1166  1173  1195  1217  1243  1266  1269  1270  1280  1281  1297  1298
        1302  1305  1306  1318  1323  1326  1336  1340  1347  1351  1354  1356  1359  1367  1369  1372  1374  1384  1392  1397
        1418  1433  1435  1443  1444  1445  1450  1461  1479  1482  1492  1506  1512  1537  1543  1555  1556  1559  1560  1563  1564
        1568  1579
22  Plantations     1134  1173  1179  1185  1191  1195  1232  1241  1260  1272  1291  1296  1328  1336  1351  1383  1387  1409  1423
        1433  1436  1437  1445  1454  1482  1487  1493  1551  1555  1559  1564
23  Woodland management     1145  1163  1222  1251  1269  1279  1296  1313  1316  1352  1435  1482  1507  1512  1563
24  Productive woodland     1482  1541
25  Poor woodland   1217  1251
26  Commons         1128  1211  1251  1257  1265  1323  1323  1347  1440  1472  1519  1550
27  Furze, gorse and heathlands   1138  1168  1203  1251  1276  1276  1281  1332  1415  1440  1472  1519  1521
28  Moorland        1222  1395  1400  1445  1458  1469  1560  1575
31  Wasteland       1297  1299  1460  1519  1521
32  Climatic hazards      1472  1563  1571
34  Land requires drainage        1150  1155  1177  1222  1232  1392  1511  1543  1558  1560
35  Land liable to flood   1229  1465
36  Productive soil       1129  1259  1291  1295  1316  1351  1352  1389  1423  1437  1461  1465  1565
37  Poor soil       1166  1168  1203  1211  1251  1298  1302  1312  1323  1324  1326  1340  1347  1351  1369  1384  1428  1431  1458
        1460  1469  1521  1530  1546  1557  1561  1563  1586
38  Heavy (clay) soil     1119  1121  1123  1126  1129  1137  1138  1139  1143  1150  1155  1163  1165  1166  1168  1173  1174  1177
        1178  1183  1185  1189  1192  1195  1199  1203  1206  1208  1210  1211  1212  1216  1217  1221  1222  1226  1229  1230  1232
        1234  1236  1240  1243  1244  1251  1255  1257  1259  1265  1266  1267  1269  1272  1278  1279  1281  1291  1293
        1295  1296  1297  1298  1302  1305  1309  1315  1316  1318  1320  1323  1324  1328  1329  1336  1339  1340  1345  1347  1350
        1351  1352  1354  1356  1358  1361  1362  1367  1369  1372  1374  1376  1377  1380  1383  1389  1392  1393  1397  1399
        1400  1403  1407  1409  1411  1412  1415  1420  1425  1428  1431  1435  1436  1440  1441  1442  1444  1445  1447  1450
        1458  1460  1461  1465  1469  1479  1480  1483  1489  1492  1498  1506  1507  1508  1511  1512  1514  1518  1519  1521  1524
        1525  1530  1533  1537  1539  1541  1543  1545  1550  1551  1552  1553  1555  1556  1558  1559  1560  1561  1564  1568  1575
        1576  1579  1586  1588
39  Loamy (turnip) soil   1121  1123  1152  1155  1204  1212  1216  1221  1226  1230  1232  1234  1254  1265  1306  1309  1316  1328
        1333  1352  1353  1355  1358  1361  1371  1374  1393  1402  1423  1430  1454  1482  1493  1498  1518  1523  1528  1541  1542
        1552
40  Light soil      1129  1130  1163  1173  1177  1181  1185  1195  1208  1250  1328  1336  1369  1382  1403  1418  1464  1472  1487
        1499  1504  1525  1563
41  Several varieties of soil     1126  1132  1137  1138  1165  1179  1183  1189  1205  1254  1259  1266  1267  1272  1281  1293  1296
```

Devon contd.

```
              1306 1308 1318 1331 1333 1337 1347 1350 1354 1356 1358 1362 1372 1377 1380 1398 1399 1420 1430 1431 1437
              1460 1479 1485 1507 1508 1512 1519 1524 1533 1537 1542 1545 1551 1579
 42  Chalk    1243 1471
 43  Sand or gravel      1115 1119 1134 1139 1143 1145 1150 1166 1189 1191 1192 1206 1220 1222 1226 1229 1236 1240
     1241 1251 1257 1258 1260 1278 1291 1295 1316 1320 1323 1345 1350 1351 1353 1355 1377 1383 1384 1387 1389
     1396 1409 1435 1436 1437 1441 1447 1465 1472 1480 1483 1485 1486 1487 1489 1511 1523 1527 1528 1539 1543
     1550 1553 1555 1559 1564 1572 1575 1588
 44  Peat    1120 1206 1260 1312 1355 1389 1400 1440 1482 1489 1558 1572
 45  Fields remote from farms  1260
 46  Good local roads   1163 1259 1296 1493
 47  Poor local roads   1168 1173 1177 1250 1331 1406 1460 1486 1506 1530 1545 1546 1557 1586
 49  Roads recently improved  1458
 50  Water carriage     1316
 51  Canals  1333
 53  Markets accessible  1128 1138 1139 1259 1297 1316 1318 1345 1358 1367 1374 1383 1431 1441 1444 1447 1469 1482
     1523 1552 1565
 54  Markets inaccessible 1145 1173 1174 1177 1191 1206 1242 1250 1251 1251 1270 1272 1324 1326 1351 1354 1356 1384
     1397 1399 1440 1460 1486 1506 1543 1556
 55  Provincial markets  1205 1245 1345 1352 1472 1493 1499
 57  Fairs   1205 1259 1499
 58  Market prices      1326 1354 1358 1391 1399 1415 1482
 59  Landowners and their estates  1117 1129 1131 1135 1142 1143 1145 1150 1157 1158 1163 1168 1177 1191 1191 1203
     1204 1208 1210 1211 1212 1222 1271 1282 1296 1313 1348 1351 1353 1354 1373 1377 1387 1394 1399 1400 1410 1411
     1418 1419 1421 1426 1428 1428 1438 1440 1443 1453 1458 1472 1473 1483 1506 1513 1519 1563 1564
 60  Land occupiers     1168 1212 1232 1254 1291 1367 1441 1441 1558
 61  Farm size  1163 1205 1471 1483 1521 1557
 62  Leases  1377 1399 1506
 63  Farm implements    1173
 64  Common grazing     1276 1323 1347 1440 1472
 65  Lammas and other common rights  1134 1218 1251 1383 1444 1472 1478 1550
 66  Rents   1168 1232 1326 1467 1518
 68  Rates   1284 1367 1387 1399
 69  Farm labour and wages  1173 1269 1351 1387 1399
 70  Enclosure or improvement of waste  1191 1214 1326 1400 1511 1521 1524
 71  Enclosure of commons  1323 1353
 74  Occasional ploughing of grassland  1251 1524
 75  Conversion of grass to arable  1251
 76  Conversion of arable to pasture  1387
 77  Paring and burning  1120 1177 1276 1403 1442 1558
 85  Underdrainage      1222 1458
 89  Lime  1128 1163 1217 1265 1282 1312 1326 1351 1352 1367 1431 1460 1558
 92  Dung  1174 1523
100  Oil dust, unspecified fertilisers or manures  1151 1173 1297 1316 1358 1374 1383 1423 1428 1447
101  General comments on crop rotations  1114 1119 1120 1134 1136 1138 1141 1141 1143 1151 1168 1174 1191 1205 1212
     1214 1234 1241 1251 1272 1297 1312 1326 1376 1387 1415 1433 1458 1461 1472 1478 1519 1550 1575 1576
102  Irregular rotations  1557
103  3-course rotation   1258 1336 1396 1465
104  4-course rotation   1119 1163 1199 1204 1217 1226 1240 1254 1258 1293 1336 1355 1440 1450 1485 1487 1518 1528
     1539 1550 1555 1572
105  5-course rotation   1119 1121 1123 1130 1137 1145 1150 1165 1166 1168 1174 1179 1181 1183 1185 1189 1191 1192
     1195 1203 1208 1210 1217 1221 1229 1232 1236 1243 1245 1251 1254 1255 1257 1258 1266 1278 1281 1291 1295
     1296 1297 1305 1309 1313 1315 1316 1318 1320 1323 1324 1328 1329 1333 1340 1347 1350 1351 1353 1354 1356
     1358 1361 1362 1367 1374 1380 1382 1383 1389 1392 1393 1395 1398 1399 1407 1409 1410 1412 1415 1420 1423
     1425 1430 1431 1433 1436 1437 1441 1445 1447 1466 1471 1479 1483 1486 1489 1492 1493 1498 1503 1504 1506
     1507 1508 1510 1511 1513 1521 1523 1524 1525 1527 1537 1542 1543 1545 1551 1552 1555 1556 1558 1559 1563
     1564 1565 1588
106  6-course rotation   1126 1129 1137 1138 1139 1150 1152 1155 1178 1211 1220 1222 1230 1234 1244 1250 1259 1265
     1267 1269 1272 1298 1302 1308 1345 1352 1354 1369 1372 1376 1377 1397 1400 1418 1441 1442 1444 1454 1461
     1464 1469 1482 1512 1553 1559 1560 1568 1579
107  7-course rotation   1115 1118 1132 1216 1306 1337 1339 1354 1364 1384 1387 1460 1480 1514
108  8-10-course rotation  1326 1331 1354 1402 1403 1406 1428 1530 1546 1586
109  More than 10-course rotation  1120 1260
110  Wheat  1145 1309 1326 1391
111  Barley 1141 1168 1177 1309 1391
112  Oats   1128 1260 1309 1391 1489
117  Rape   1132
123  Clover 1415 1521
126  Tares and vetches   1363 1511 1542
129  Turnips     1173 1177 1245 1270 1312 1472
130  Mangolds    1362
132  Potatoes    1118 1119 1121 1130 1134 1140 1141 1145 1152 1163 1166 1178 1179 1189 1191 1192 1195 1197 1206
     1217 1218 1221 1232 1244 1251 1265 1267 1270 1272 1281 1295 1296 1306 1313 1316 1324 1326 1331 1337 1340
     1342 1345 1351 1352 1356 1358 1362 1363 1367 1377 1382 1387 1391 1397 1399 1400 1410 1412 1423 1425 1433
     1440 1444 1447 1454 1458 1460 1482 1483 1498 1504 1506 1507 1511 1512 1523 1527 1542 1543 1545 1556 1557
     1575 1579
133  Bare fallows  1177
134  High farming  1119 1151 1173 1174 1212 1222 1265 1272 1293 1297 1316 1318 1358 1367 1374 1383 1389 1431 1437
     1444 1523 1542 1545 1555
135  Low farming   1177 1376
136  Remarks on the absence of turnips  1168
139  Good quality pastures      1118 1558
140  Poor quality pastures      1173 1177 1205 1372 1469 1471
141  Meadows     1132 1155 1163 1173 1177 1382 1400 1435 1469 1558
142  Irrigation and water meadows  1163 1173 1181 1241
144  Parks  1387 1435 1485
145  Accommodation land         1487
146  Cattle breeding            1407
147  Cattle fattening           1118 1141 1173 1244 1251 1371 1382 1402 1445 1499 1565
148  Dairying    1205 1284 1499
150  Sheep breeding             1163 1205 1296 1445
151  Sheep fattening            1118 1178 1244 1284 1382 1402
154  Pigs   1168 1218 1340 1382 1399 1441 1469 1493 1521
156  Poultry     1382 1493 1521
157  Rabbits     1145
158  Deer   1435
```

Devon contd.

159	Animal diseases	1576	
161	Hay	1174	
171	Fruits	1445	
174	Cabbages	1565	
178	Hops	1416	
181	Reeds and oziers	1286	1529

Dorset

#	Topic	Years
1	Tithe-free district	1608 1614 1618 1639 1668 1670 1693 1710 1719 1746 1749 1770 1771 1845 1848 1860
2	History of tithe payment	1594 1665 1674 1722 1745 1745 1775 1789 1856
3	Tithe practices and agriculture	1616 1648
4	Exemptions from tithe	1591 1592 1597 1604 1611 1632 1637 1657 1660 1662 1681 1682 1698 1702 1703 1708 1709 1713 1714 1724 1756 1769 1774 1775 1784 1786 1789 1800 1804 1826 1834 1839 1841 1849 1851 1873
5	Tithe in kind	1615 1675 1685 1691 1712 1721 1793 1806 1808 1819 1851
6	Compositions	1593 1597 1599 1607 1615 1616 1617 1630 1634 1637 1641 1645 1652 1656 1661 1665 1666 1669 1674 1677 1684 1688 1694 1698 1699 1702 1709 1712 1715 1720 1721 1729 1732 1735 1739 1747 1750 1759 1762 1779 1784 1796 1797 1804 1808 1815 1819 1820 1821 1822 1826 1827 1829 1839 1840 1842 1844 1847 1853 1856 1857 1869 1874
7	Moduses	1597 1601 1612 1615 1627 1629 1632 1633 1645 1647 1649 1651 1652 1661 1662 1684 1698 1699 1713 1714 1721 1722 1726 1731 1751 1758 1761 1765 1766 1773 1774 1775 1782 1788 1789 1796 1797 1798 1804 1811 1817 1818 1821 1829 1837 1843 1851 1853 1874
8	Glebe	1631 1666 1671 1709 1712 1724 1797 1815 1820 1821 1822 1826 1836
9	Local topographic descriptions	1805 1817
10	Regional topographic descriptions	1814 1849 1868
13	Country houses and ornamental gardens	1616 1750
16	Field boundaries	1616
17	Open fields	1597 1680 1775 1788 1836
20	Hedgerow timber	1590 1591 1592 1600 1601 1602 1603 1604 1605 1610 1611 1613 1620 1622 1623 1625 1626 1627 1628 1629 1633 1636 1638 1642 1643 1644 1648 1650 1651 1654 1657 1658 1659 1660 1662 1663 1672 1673 1675 1676 1679 1682 1683 1685 1687 1689 1690 1692 1695 1696 1697 1700 1701 1703 1704 1705 1706 1707 1708 1713 1716 1717 1721 1723 1726 1727 1730 1734 1738 1740 1741 1742 1744 1745 1751 1752 1753 1754 1756 1757 1763 1765 1767 1769 1772 1773 1778 1782 1783 1785 1786 1787 1788 1790 1791 1793 1795 1798 1799 1800 1801 1802 1803 1805 1807 1809 1810 1811 1812 1813 1814 1816 1818 1824 1825 1828 1830 1832 1833 1836 1837 1843 1850 1852 1854 1855 1858 1862 1863 1864 1868 1870 1871 1872 1873
21	Coppice	1592 1602 1603 1604 1619 1626 1627 1628 1632 1633 1671 1687 1689 1694 1703 1706 1707 1709 1713 1714 1728 1742 1743 1745 1753 1761 1764 1767 1769 1776 1777 1782 1787 1790 1792 1795 1800 1801 1806 1807 1809 1814 1816 1817 1818 1820 1823 1824 1828 1830 1831 1832 1833 1834 1835 1836 1838 1850 1854 1864 1868 1870 1871 1873
22	Plantations	1592 1610 1613 1663 1671 1687 1689 1694 1708 1714 1724 1743 1747 1763 1776 1781 1789 1793 1797 1800 1804 1814 1852 1872
27	Furze, gorse and heathlands	1604 1653 1661 1661 1663 1683 1686 1692 1714 1715 1725 1729 1729 1730 1747 1751 1761 1763 1797 1797 1804 1813 1813 1827 1831 1843 1865
32	Climatic hazards	1773 1805
33	Excessively steep land	1756 1805
34	Land requires drainage	1685 1704 1727 1765 1850 1863
36	Productive soil	1619 1686 1691 1721 1765 1795 1800
37	Poor soil	1662 1673 1683 1692 1703 1715 1729 1741 1748 1752 1765 1805 1813 1817 1830
38	Heavy (clay) soil	1589 1602 1603 1605 1611 1619 1623 1624 1627 1629 1636 1638 1643 1644 1648 1650 1654 1659 1667 1672 1676 1679 1683 1685 1689 1690 1695 1696 1697 1701 1704 1708 1715 1717 1721 1726 1727 1728 1730 1734 1738 1740 1742 1743 1744 1753 1757 1760 1761 1763 1765 1769 1772 1773 1774 1776 1777 1778 1780 1781 1782 1783 1785 1786 1790 1791 1795 1801 1803 1805 1807 1809 1810 1811 1812 1814 1816 1817 1828 1830 1835 1836 1837 1843 1864 1865 1868 1870 1871 1872 1873
39	Loamy (turnip) soil	1650 1654 1675 1676 1679 1690 1691 1705 1706 1716 1723 1778 1802 1806 1814 1854 1862
40	Light soil	1592 1605 1613 1620 1622 1625 1642 1678 1679 1685 1711 1714 1715 1731 1734 1738 1741 1756 1765 1768 1772 1774 1780 1791 1794 1795 1799 1809 1810 1812 1828 1837 1838 1864
41	Several varieties of soil	1667 1685 1721 1729 1738 1765 1830
42	Chalk	1600 1603 1604 1606 1609 1610 1623 1625 1633 1636 1638 1640 1644 1651 1660 1667 1672 1675 1682 1683 1686 1687 1700 1706 1707 1714 1716 1721 1723 1726 1744 1751 1757 1761 1764 1767 1774 1776 1777 1788 1790 1792 1793 1799 1806 1811 1823 1824 1825 1830 1831 1832 1837 1843 1850 1852 1855 1858 1863 1873
43	Sand or gravel	1589 1590 1591 1601 1604 1609 1611 1620 1623 1626 1628 1629 1640 1642 1644 1651 1657 1658 1660 1663 1673 1682 1689 1692 1695 1696 1703 1708 1713 1714 1721 1726 1729 1730 1733 1738 1740 1744 1745 1748 1751 1754 1757 1763 1765 1766 1767 1769 1772 1776 1778 1785 1786 1787 1788 1790 1794 1798 1799 1800 1802 1805 1807 1813 1817 1818 1823 1825 1831 1832 1833 1838 1843 1855 1858 1863 1865 1868 1873
44	Peat	1700 1714 1730 1751 1830 1833 1850 1865
46	Good local roads	1592 1680 1729 1873
47	Poor local roads	1605 1644 1773 1774 1799 1805
48	Turnpike and main roads	1675 1721
53	Markets accessible	1592 1679 1795 1800 1838
54	Markets inaccessible	1605 1644 1799 1803 1805
55	Provincial markets	1795
58	Market prices	1744
59	Landowners and their estates	1683 1756 1775 1789 1799
60	Land occupiers	1644 1681 1728 1799 1827
61	Farm size	1691
62	Leases	1683 1756 1799
64	Common grazing	1613 1836
65	Lammas and other common rights	1613 1686 1752 1775 1836
66	Rents	1775
71	Enclosure of commons	1660
72	Enclosure of open fields	1817
74	Occasional ploughing of grassland	1652 1663
76	Conversion of arable to pasture	1616
92	Dung	1795 1800
100	Oil dust, unspecified fertilisers or manures	1611
101	General comments on crop rotations	1627 1727 1742 1744 1765 1773 1775 1795 1827
102	Irregular rotations	1657 1683
103	3-course rotation	1591 1602 1651 1676 1680 1685 1696 1704 1740 1778 1782 1783 1788 1837 1838 1855 1872
104	4-course rotation	1589 1590 1592 1600 1603 1604 1606 1610 1613 1620 1622 1623 1624 1626 1628 1629 1633 1638 1640 1642 1648 1650 1654 1658 1659 1663 1663 1672 1673 1678 1680 1683 1685 1691 1695 1697 1700 1701 1705 1706 1708 1711 1713 1714 1717 1721 1723 1729 1730 1731 1733 1734 1738 1741 1744 1745 1751 1752 1753 1754 1756 1757 1760 1761 1763 1766 1767 1769 1777 1781 1785 1788 1790 1791 1793 1794 1795 1798 1801 1805 1806 1807 1809 1810 1811 1812 1813 1816 1817 1818 1823 1825 1828 1830 1833 1835 1836 1852 1855 1858 1863 1864 1868 1870 1871 1871

Dorset contd.

105	5-course rotation		1592	1595	1601	1605	1609	1611	1619	1625	1636	1643	1644	1647	1660	1662	1673	1675	1679	1682
	1686	1687	1703	1716	1726	1728	1742	1744	1748	1751	1754	1768	1772	1774	1776	1780	1786	1792	1795	1799	1800
	1803	1814	1817	1820	1824	1832	1836	1850	1854	1862	1865	1873									
106	6-course rotation		1707	1729	1817	1832	1843														
108	8-10-course rotation	1802																			
110	Wheat 1744 1820																				
111	Barley 1625 1820																				
112	Oats 1820																				
113	Rye or meslin		1787	1813																	
114	Corn yields 1597		1599	1615	1637	1677	1680	1681	1739												
115	Beans 1631 1704		1712	1779	1795	1814	1838														
116	Peas 1631 1838																				
123	Clover 1600 1605		1615	1619	1620	1622	1624	1636	1642	1644	1649	1654	1662	1673	1677	1678	1682	1683	1691	1711
	1712	1724	1741	1742	1744	1748	1752	1760	1766	1768	1772	1775	1779	1780	1781	1794	1799	1813	1817	1827	1847
124	Sainfoin 1820																				
126	Tares and vetches		1615	1619	1631	1649	1772	1795	1847	1868											
129	Turnips 1592		1595	1600	1605	1609	1615	1619	1620	1625	1637	1642	1644	1654	1660	1662	1673	1675	1678	1679
	1680	1682	1683	1686	1691	1711	1714	1726	1730	1741	1742	1744	1748	1752	1766	1768	1772	1773	1778	1779	1780
	1794	1795	1799	1800	1802	1803	1813	1817	1820	1827	1873										
132	Potatoes 1605		1615	1631	1648	1649	1660	1675	1677	1682	1686	1712	1724	1726	1742	1772	1779	1795	1799	1800
	1802	1803	1813	1814	1817	1838	1847	1861	1873												
133	Bare fallows 1624		1677	1704	1712	1760	1779	1781	1813	1817											
134	High farming 1644		1800																		
135	Low farming 1765																				
139	Good quality pastures			1609	1619	1683	1685														
140	Poor quality pastures			1686	1813																
141	Meadows 1609		1685	1714	1752	1850															
142	Irrigation and water meadows			1597	1667	1750	1794	1827	1831												
144	Parks 1616 1637		1743																		
146	Cattle breeding		1830																		
147	Cattle fattening		1632	1774																	
148	Dairying 1632		1680	1683	1704	1774	1805	1830													
149	Cow keeping 1795																				
150	Sheep breeding		1601	1620	1623	1647	1659	1662	1667	1687	1744	1751	1754	1766	1767	1768	1776	1792	1794	1818
	1823	1824	1831	1835	1852	1855	1865	1871													
151	Sheep fattening		1628	1629	1663	1692	1713	1728	1734												
158	Deer 1637																				
161	Hay 1619																				
165	Butter 1632																				
166	Cheese 1632																				
169	Good orchards		1680	1772																	
172	Market gardens		1768	1795																	
178	Hops 1745																				
179	Flax and hemp		1591	1615	1620	1649	1847														
181	Reeds and oziers		1591	1781																	

Durham

1	Tithe-free district		1888	1894	1917	1932	1956	1957	1960	1973	1980	2023	2029	2064	2122	2144	2146	2178			
2	History of tithe payment		2070	2112	2181																
3	Tithe practices and agriculture		1903	1910	1920	2003	2031	2050	2075	2151											
4	Exemptions from tithe			1736	1878	1883	1884	1897	1910	1912	1916	1931	1937	1942	1953	1962	1985	1989	2008	2010
	2012	2020	2022	2030	2035	2037	2051	2078	2083	2087	2097	2098	2104	2108	2114	2116	2123	2133	2141	2148	2150
	2158	2163	2169	2171	2182																
5	Tithe in kind		1914	1946	1974	2011	2053	2056	2096	2105	2139	2173	2179	2182							
6	Compositions		1875	1885	1964	1977	1984	1997	2009	2011	2013	2014	2022	2057	2093	2112	2120	2137	2157		
7	Moduses		1737	1876	1881	1883	1884	1886	1896	1899	1900	1901	1906	1907	1910	1918	1920	1921	1922	1923	1924
	1925	1934	1937	1938	1943	1945	1946	1949	1950	1952	1955	1959	1963	1964	1965	1971	1972	1977	1978	1981	1983
	1984	1985	1987	1989	1991	1992	1994	1997	2001	2002	2006	2007	2010	2014	2015	2016	2020	2025	2026	2037	2038
	2042	2047	2054	2057	2058	2059	2060	2063	2065	2072	2073	2074	2075	2076	2078	2079	2080	2081	2083	2085	2086
	2093	2096	2099	2100	2103	2104	2106	2110	2111	2118	2124	2126	2127	2131	2134	2136	2137	2142	2143	2145	2148
	2149	2150	2153	2154	2155	2158	2163	2164	2167	2168	2169	2170	2171	2175	2176	2177	2179	2181	2182	2186	
8	Glebe 1959 2154																				
9	Local topographic descriptions		2151	2176	2179																
10	Regional topographic descriptions		1887	1903	1912	1944	1946	2019	2047	2065	2077	2083	2102	2106	2113	2128	2136	2142			
	2143	2152	2155	2186																	
11	Village morphology		1737	1931	1941	1943	2005	2074	2096	2123	2138	2149	2168	2180	2184						
14	Farm houses and buildings		1915	1930	2072																
15	Cottages and cottage gardens		1737																		
16	Field boundaries		2024	2138	2158																
18	Small, irregular closes		1890	1899	1909	1923	1961	1976	1992	1995	2000	2016	2027	2047	2072	2106	2118	2145	2164		
	2169	2176																			
19	Large, regular fields		1887	1920	1953	1976	2025	2060	2085	2089	2095	2109	2110	2111	2118	2125	2127	2128	2129	2133
	2153	2158																			
22	Plantations 2106																				
25	Poor woodland		1974																		
26	Commons 1939																				
27	Furze, gorse and heathlands		1883	1939	1959	2040	2184														
28	Moorland 1913		1961																		
32	Climatic hazards		1887	1902	1906	1907	1911	1912	1914	1915	1916	1929	1930	1931	1939	1946	1961	1964	1968	1974
	1981	1992	1995	2001	2010	2017	2025	2035	2046	2054	2069	2103	2109	2111	2124	2126	2135	2138	2166		
33	Excessively steep land		1961	1992	2131	2138	2148	2182													
34	Land requires drainage		1878	1880	1881	1902	1909	1910	1925	1947	1974	1976	1995	2040	2054	2104	2115	2124	2142
	2163	2170	2171	2175	2181	2182															
35	Land liable to flood		1905	1906	1994	2048	2186														
36	Productive soil		1878	1883	1887	1892	1899	1906	1911	1919	1920	1934	1936	1942	1951	1953	1954	1976	1981	1987
	1989	1991	2000	2005	2006	2012	2017	2024	2025	2027	2037	2048	2054	2055	2079	2080	2085	2086	2087	2095	2096
	2104	2111	2118	2129	2130	2133	2139	2145	2158	2160	2166	2167	2169	2170	2171	2182	2184				
37	Poor soil		1737	1878	1880	1882	1883	1897	1902	1903	1907	1909	1913	1914	1915	1918	1925	1929	1934	1936	1943
	1946	1947	1948	1949	1954	1959	1964	1966	1968	1974	1986	1987	1995	2001	2004	2006	2012	2016	2017	2026	2035
	2037	2050	2054	2055	2069	2074	2076	2080	2082	2100	2101	2104	2105	2115	2116	2117	2118	2119	2124	2125	2135
	2136	2138	2139	2141	2142	2145	2148	2150	2151	2155	2159	2163	2167	2169	2170	2171	2173	2177	2179	2180	2182
	2184	2185	2186																		
38	Heavy (clay) soil		1736	1737	1878	1880	1881	1882	1883	1887	1890	1897	1898	1899	1902	1903	1905	1906	1907	1909

Durham contd.

		1910	1911	1912	1913	1914	1916	1918	1919	1920	1923	1924	1925	1929	1930	1931	1934	1937	1939	1942	1943	1944
		1946	1948	1949	1951	1954	1959	1962	1963	1964	1965	1966	1968	1974	1975	1976	1981	1982	1986	1989	1994	1995
		2000	2001	2003	2004	2006	2007	2010	2012	2015	2016	2017	2019	2025	2026	2027	2028	2031	2034	2035	2037	2038
		2040	2047	2048	2050	2053	2054	2058	2059	2060	2063	2065	2066	2069	2070	2072	2075	2076	2077	2079	2080	2082
		2086	2087	2089	2095	2096	2099	2100	2103	2104	2105	2108	2111	2115	2116	2117	2119	2121	2123	2124	2125	2126
		2127	2128	2130	2131	2134	2135	2136	2139	2141	2145	2149	2151	2152	2153	2154	2155	2156	2158	2162	2163	2164
		2166	2168	2169	2170	2171	2175	2176	2177	2181	2182	2186										
39	Loamy (turnip) soil		1736	1890	1892	1897	1899	1930	1945	1953	1965	1989	2024	2025	2028	2040	2048	2060	2080	2083
		2085	2086	2087	2095	2115	2121	2125	2129	2133	2139	2158	2162	2166	2169	2171	2175	2181
40	Light soil		1902	1920	1941	1947	1954	1976	1981	1992	1995	2007	2025	2027	2031	2034	2050	2055	2066	2086	2099
		2110	2130	2132	2138	2141	2150	2160	2164	2167	2171	2182
41	Several varieties of soil			1878	1929	1937	1941	1943	1953	1965	2007	2016	2017	2028	2032	2037	2048	2054	2059	2079
		2089	2100	2125	2131	2135	2163	2169
43	Sand or gravel		1736	1737	1878	1902	1906	1907	1911	1913	1918	1919	1920	1923	1925	1934	1939	1942	1945	1946
		1954	1961	1962	1965	1974	1976	1987	1995	2000	2001	2007	2031	2035	2038	2053	2066	2070	2080	2085	2095	2096
		2105	2108	2109	2110	2119	2124	2130	2145	2153	2154	2158	2160	2169	2170	2173	2175	2177	2182
44	Peat		1918	1946	1995	2010	2015	2035	2054	2100	2119	2125
46	Good local roads		1899	1951	1976	1987	1992	2024	2025	2027	2079	2095	2099	2104	2111	2129	2133	2156	2164	2182
47	Poor local roads		1736	1737	1890	1906	1907	1911	1914	1915	1916	1923	1925	1930	1936	1945	1946	1961	1964	1965
		1966	1968	1974	1981	1995	2001	2016	2025	2028	2065	2072	2082	2100	2105	2106	2110	2115	2124	2126	2128	2135
		2142	2153	2155	2158	2164	2166	2175	2177	2179
48	Turnpike and main roads		1878	1911	1945	1947	1951	1963	1976	2085	2095	2110	2119	2153	2158
50	Water carriage		1903	2180
52	Railways		1878	1903	1916	1936	1945	1951	2005	2010	2074	2080	2096	2099	2109	2126	2138	2139	2179	2180
53	Markets accessible		1878	1881	1892	1899	1903	1909	1911	1924	1945	1947	1951	1953	1976	1992	2004	2024	2027	2031
		2035	2038	2054	2066	2089	2099	2103	2105	2108	2109	2115	2124	2126	2133	2145	2156	2166	2169	2172
54	Markets inaccessible		1961	1995	2040	2162
55	Provincial markets		1899	1924	2006	2024	2038	2066	2106	2108	2133	2156	2176
58	Market prices		1948	2028	2096
59	Landowners and their estates			1887	1919	1920	1966	2012	2114	2121	2150	2151	2151
60	Land occupiers		1880	1897	1911	1912	1954	1965	2026	2050	2086	2114	2119	2121	2175
61	Farm size		1912	1954	2046	2154
62	Leases	2156	2168
63	Farm implements		2069
64	Common grazing		2116
65	Lammas and other common rights			2005
66	Rents	1878	1882	1883	1892	1897	1902	1903	1905	1913	1919	1929	1931	1934	1936	1954	1965	1982	1986	1989	1991
		2007	2026	2032	2034	2046	2049	2050	2054	2055	2058	2063	2080	2082	2117	2130	2139	2149	2150	2151	2154	2160
		2167	2168	2171	2172	2173	2176	2179	2181	2184	2185
67	Urban influences on value of land		1899	1951	1992	2005	2066	2096	2123
70	Enclosure or improvement of waste		1883	1913	2054	2172
71	Enclosure of commons		1960	2022	2147
79	Subsoil ploughing		1887
80	Reclaiming and embanking	2050
82	Drainage channels and ditches		1909
86	Tile drains	1919
89	Lime	1878	1936	1948	2006	2028	2096	2100	2131	2139	2156	2167	2179
92	Dung	1878	1899	1945	1951	1992	2006	2017	2040	2065	2066	2089	2108	2109	2126	2131	2135	2163	2171	2172	2180
93	Seaweed	2066	2171
94	Fish	2141
95	Bones	2028	2069
101	General comments on crop rotations		1878	1890	1897	1899	1911	1959	2065	2139	2171
102	Irregular rotations	1915	1918	1923	1930	1968	1981	1992	1995	2028	2040	2053	2054	2069	2104	2105	2108	2111	2119
		2121	2139	2145	2169
103	3-course rotation		1736	1737	1881	1882	1883	1897	1898	1910	1916	1918	1923	1929	1931	1934	1936	1937	1944	1949
		1954	1963	1965	1966	1975	1976	1981	1994	2003	2004	2007	2015	2028	2034	2035	2037	2048	2053	2055	2058	2063
		2075	2077	2079	2089	2096	2101	2103	2104	2105	2116	2118	2126	2130	2135	2136	2141	2142	2145	2150	2151	2152
		2156	2163	2168	2170	2171	2176	2182
104	4-course rotation		1736	1881	1882	1883	1887	1890	1897	1902	1903	1912	1913	1916	1918	1919	1930	1931	1934	1939
		1945	1953	1962	1989	1992	2006	2007	2012	2024	2025	2028	2032	2035	2040	2046	2048	2053	2054	2060	2070	2079
		2080	2082	2087	2089	2095	2096	2099	2103	2104	2109	2110	2111	2117	2119	2123	2125	2127	2129	2130	2132	2133
		2134	2139	2148	2163	2166	2168	2169	2172	2175	2176	2181
105	5-course rotation		1882	1890	1897	1914	1918	1930	1953	1954	1968	1995	2006	2025	2032	2034	2040	2048	2050	2059
		2085	2086	2105	2125	2149	2153	2158	2175	2184
106	6-course rotation		2025	2164
110	Wheat	1948	1981	2027	2046	2111	2115
111	Barley	2038	2166
112	Oats	1981	2156
113	Rye or meslin		1918	2053
114	Corn yields		1878	1882	1897	1907	1913	1924	1931	1945	1954	1959	1963	1964	2001	2015	2016	2026	2028	2046	2050
		2055	2070	2072	2074	2083	2115	2123	2124	2130	2134	2148	2149	2152	2163	2177	2180	2181
115	Beans	1890	1892	1898	1911	1914	1919	1925	1937	1942	1944	1949	1976	1991	1994	2004	2007	2025	2027	2031	2032
		2038	2050	2058	2060	2063	2070	2072	2077	2082	2083	2099	2103	2111	2123	2127	2132	2136	2141	2172	2176
116	Peas	1919	1925	1942	2083	2172
123	Clover	1737	1878	1880	1882	1883	1887	1897	1898	1899	1910	1911	1913	1915	1916	1923	1925	1930	1931	1936	1942
		1944	1945	1947	1948	1949	1959	1962	1963	1964	1965	1966	1975	1976	1981	1991	1992	2012	2015	2016	2024	2025
		2027	2028	2031	2032	2037	2046	2048	2050	2054	2055	2055	2058	2060	2063	2065	2069	2070	2072	2074	2075
		2076	2079	2082	2083	2089	2095	2099	2100	2101	2102	2103	2104	2109	2111	2113	2116	2117	2118	2121	2123	2124
		2125	2126	2127	2128	2129	2130	2131	2132	2133	2135	2139	2141	2143	2145	2148	2151	2152	2154	2155	2156	2160
		2162	2163	2164	2166	2167	2163	2170	2171	2172	2173	2175	2180	2181
125	Trefoil	1915
126	Tares and vetches		2024	2115	2172
129	Turnips		1736	1881	1883	1887	1890	1897	1898	1899	1902	1903	1911	1919	1923	1929	1930	1934	1936	1945	1947
		1948	1954	1965	1966	1968	1976	1981	1989	1992	2003	2007	2012	2015	2016	2024	2025	2026	2027	2028	2031	2032
		2034	2035	2038	2047	2048	2050	2054	2055	2060	2066	2069	2070	2072	2076	2083	2085	2086	2087	2089	2095	2096
		2101	2103	2105	2106	2108	2109	2110	2115	2116	2117	2118	2121	2123	2125	2126	2128	2129	2131	2132	2134	2138
		2139	2143	2145	2148	2149	2150	2153	2156	2158	2160	2162	2163	2164	2166	2169	2171	2175	2176	2179	2181	2182
		2184
131	Swedes		1945	2038	2079	2095
132	Potatoes		1736	1883	1887	1899	1903	1923	1936	1945	1947	1948	1962	1965	1976	1981	1989	1991	2003	2005	2016
		2026	2028	2031	2047	2055	2066	2070	2076	2087	2089	2096	2108	2109	2110	2121	2126	2128	2131	2132	2139	2150
		2156	2160	2162	2166	2171	2176	2179	2182	2184
133	Bare fallows		1737	1878	1880	1881	1881	1882	1883	1887	1890	1897	1898	1899	1910	1912	1913	1914	1915	1916	1923
		1925	1929	1930	1936	1937	1939	1944	1945	1947	1948	1949	1959	1962	1963	1964	1966	1968	1975	1976	1981
		1989	1994	1995	2004	2007	2012	2015	2016	2025	2027	2028	2031	2032	2034	2035	2037	2046	2048	2053	2054	2055

Durham contd.

2058 2059 2060 2063 2069 2070 2072 2074 2075 2076 2077 2079 2082 2083 2086 2087 2089 2095 2096 2099 2100 2101 2102 2103 2104 2105 2106 2113 2116 2117 2118 2121 2123 2124 2125 2126 2127 2128 2129 2130 2131 2132 2133 2134 2135 2136 2138 2139 2141 2143 2145 2148 2149 2150 2151 2152 2153 2154 2155 2156 2158 2160 2162 2163 2164 2166 2167 2168 2169 2171 2173 2175 2176 2179 2180 2181 2182 2184

134 High farming 2012 2085 2086 2095 2102 2114 2125 2133 2158

135 Low farming 1880 1881 1898 1903 1907 1909 1914 1925 1936 1942 1943 1947 1949 1965 1968 1974 1976 1995 2000 2003 2028 2037 2046 2053 2054 2055 2069 2079 2115 2121 2124 2142 2151 2159 2173 2177 2186

136 Remarks on the absence of turnips 1914 1916 1937 1944 1953 1959 1962 1987 2053 2111 2121 2167

137 Remarks on pests and crop diseases 1981 2006

138 Recent increase in productivity 2166 2176

139 Good quality pastures 1903 1911 1953 2040 2047 2059 2095 2123 2133 2152 2168

140 Poor quality pastures 1905 1944 1949 1959 2136

141 Meadows 2059

143 Marsh grassland 1905 2049

144 Parks 2150

145 Accommodation land 1883 2133

146 Cattle breeding 1897 1902 1919 1924 1934 1954 1989 2007 2024 2046 2066 2085 2086 2096 2115 2130 2134 2150 2176 2181

147 Cattle fattening 1934 1953 1989 2024 2152

148 Dairying 1913 1934 1954 1989 2005 2007 2026 2046 2066 2096 2123 2130 2132 2156 2168 2171 2176 2181

149 Cow keeping 2066

150 Sheep breeding 1897 1902 1915 1919 1924 1934 1954 1989 2007 2024 2026 2050 2085 2086 2087 2134 2150 2176 2181

151 Sheep fattening 2024

153 Horses 1966 2005 2066 2156

160 Straw 1919 2006 2156 2171

161 Hay 1915 1951 2005 2006 2046 2096 2103 2115 2126 2156 2172

162 Manufactured feedstuffs (cake etc.) 1919 1934 2171

164 Milk 2096 2132 2156 2168

165 Butter 1902 1924 1934 1989 2134 2150 2176

172 Market gardens 1991 2027 2031 2172

Essex

1 Tithe-free district 2194 2262 2263 2271 2272 2273 2283 2288 2318 2346 2361 2381 2416 2421 2552 2578 2579

2 History of tithe payment 2332 2436

3 Tithe practices and agriculture 2431 2456 2505 2593

4 Exemptions from tithe 2204 2215 2228 2241 2252 2254 2258 2261 2269 2279 2280 2282 2284 2285 2286 2289 2290 2299 2301 2306 2307 2312 2316 2321 2326 2341 2342 2343 2344 2351 2359 2371 2376 2379 2397 2398 2401 2402 2409 2412 2413 2417 2420 2430 2431 2436 2463 2467 2475 2485 2490 2490 2493 2493 2494 2502 2514 2517 2518 2525 2534 2537 2543 2545 2547 2553 2557 2568 2570 2571 2573 2575 2580 2595 2597

5 Tithe in kind 2220 2270 2275 2297 2300 2304 2309 2320 2337 2386 2422 2430 2444 2456 2460 2461 2465 2471 2489 2505 2510 2511 2514 2521 2523 2531 2532 2534 2563 2571 2575 2584

6 Compositions 2188 2189 2193 2195 2200 2203 2214 2216 2228 2233 2238 2242 2243 2246 2251 2256 2266 2281 2303 2305 2307 2308 2317 2325 2328 2337 2345 2351 2356 2357 2362 2365 2370 2380 2390 2392 2401 2402 2403 2405 2419 2429 2433 2437 2438 2440 2453 2455 2461 2462 2469 2470 2476 2487 2500 2513 2523 2527 2529 2538 2540 2541 2547 2554 2559 2593

7 Moduses 2201 2239 2244 2254 2256 2257 2261 2276 2277 2291 2303 2313 2331 2362 2371 2379 2382 2394 2420 2423 2432 2440 2441 2449 2456 2475 2485 2488 2491 2493 2509 2512 2519 2544 2568 2573 2584 2599

8 Glebe 2188 2370 2396 2479

9 Local topographic descriptions 2187 2232 2253 2268 2386 2420 2426 2466 2516 2543 2587

10 Regional topographic descriptions 2197 2206 2241 2244 2250 2293 2297 2306 2308 2324 2355 2359 2396 2445 2452 2524 2534 2558 2577 2584

11 Village morphology 2223 2229 2260 2265 2268 2284 2290 2348 2388 2398 2411 2449 2452 2454 2479 2512 2521 2571

12 Church 2192 2196 2210 2232 2239 2241 2268 2276 2292 2302 2320 2344 2359 2363 2388 2400 2409 2426 2449 2454 2483 2484 2515 2516 2543 2561 2567 2571 2576 2586 2598 2602

13 Country houses and ornamental gardens 2196 2202 2202 2268 2269 2316 2409 2434 2434 2471 2479 2509 2543 2543 2596

15 Cottages and cottage gardens 2427 2479 2510

16 Field boundaries 2496

17 Open fields 2202 2221 2231 2284 2320 2395 2444 2481 2566 2580 2587

18 Small, irregular closes 2223

19 Large, regular fields 2496 2600

21 Coppice 2223 2241 2260 2292 2308 2315 2316 2320 2330 2331 2355 2363 2367 2383 2404 2415 2441 2460 2471 2479 2496 2497 2510 2530 2539 2557 2563 2580 2581 2587 2589 2595 2597 2602

22 Plantations 2191 2444 2474 2492 2508 2530 2543 2544 2573 2600

24 Productive woodland 2268 2323 2330 2367 2436 2471 2483 2508 2561 2584 2587

25 Poor woodland 2223 2245 2338 2427 2448 2463 2484 2492 2510 2516 2557 2582

26 Commons 2223 2247 2268 2301 2427 2475 2549 2558 2562 2563

27 Furze, gorse and heathlands 2223 2259 2259 2359 2456

30 Fens 2456

31 Wasteland 2223 2398 2475 2558 2596

32 Climatic hazards 2247 2275 2279 2301 2306 2323 2335 2384 2391 2393 2445 2448 2506 2528 2589 2604

33 Excessively steep land 2259 2260

34 Land requires drainage 2196 2202 2212 2224 2235 2249 2254 2258 2265 2269 2301 2312 2321 2323 2337 2338 2386 2394 2396 2409 2411 2426 2439 2448 2474 2482 2491 2508 2510 2512 2516 2528 2530 2563 2564 2581 2584 2585 2597

35 Land liable to flood 2206 2207 2223 2231 2234 2236 2247 2260 2270 2343 2391 2404 2430 2459 2491 2496 2497 2501 2564 2567 2571 2582

36 Productive soil 2199 2201 2202 2205 2207 2209 2227 2229 2232 2235 2239 2247 2249 2250 2260 2264 2268 2269 2270 2275 2284 2289 2290 2294 2297 2304 2322 2324 2326 2330 2331 2336 2337 2339 2341 2344 2348 2352 2358 2360 2363 2366 2368 2372 2377 2382 2383 2384 2387 2388 2394 2396 2400 2409 2415 2420 2422 2426 2427 2430 2436 2443 2445 2449 2450 2454 2479 2481 2483 2484 2490 2492 2505 2506 2507 2512 2519 2524 2526 2528 2530 2533 2535 2545 2551 2567 2571 2580 2581 2582 2588 2589 2600 2601 2602

37 Poor soil 2191 2192 2199 2201 2206 2207 2215 2219 2225 2235 2249 2259 2260 2264 2265 2270 2274 2279 2280 2284 2285 2297 2298 2306 2309 2310 2337 2342 2348 2363 2391 2394 2396 2397 2423 2427 2431 2435 2479 2482 2484 2490 2493 2510 2519 2520 2521 2525 2526 2544 2545 2548 2550 2568 2574 2575 2580 2582 2585 2589 2593 2597

38 Heavy (clay) soil 2190 2192 2196 2197 2198 2201 2202 2206 2208 2209 2210 2212 2213 2215 2220 2221 2223 2224 2225 2226 2227 2230 2231 2235 2236 2240 2241 2244 2247 2248 2250 2252 2253 2258 2260 2265 2268 2269 2270 2274 2275 2276 2278 2279 2285 2290 2292 2293 2295 2296 2298 2299 2301 2302 2304 2308 2309 2312 2314 2315 2316 2320 2321 2322 2324 2326 2327 2330 2331 2335 2336 2337 2338 2340 2341 2342 2348 2349 2350 2354 2355 2359 2360 2363 2366 2367 2368 2369 2371 2372 2374 2375 2376 2382 2383 2385 2386 2387 2388 2391 2394 2395 2396 2397 2398 2399 2400 2404 2406 2407 2411 2412 2413 2420 2422 2425 2426 2428 2431 2432 2435 2441 2442 2443 2445 2446 2447 2448 2449 2456 2458 2459 2460 2463 2464 2465 2466 2472 2474 2475 2477 2480 2481 2482

Essex contd.

2484 2486 2488 2489 2490 2491 2492 2493 2494 2495 2496 2497 2498 2501 2504 2508 2509 2511 2512 2514 2515
2516 2518 2521 2524 2526 2528 2530 2534 2535 2536 2537 2539 2543 2548 2551 2553 2555 2556 2557 2558 2561
2563 2564 2565 2566 2567 2568 2571 2572 2574 2576 2577 2580 2581 2582 2584 2585 2586 2587 2589 2592 2593
2595 2596 2597 2598 2602 2603 2604
39 Loamy (turnip) soil 2191 2199 2201 2202 2207 2213 2215 2219 2221 2223 2226 2229 2231 2232 2235 2239 2245 2249
2250 2253 2255 2265 2274 2275 2278 2289 2290 2292 2295 2296 2297 2309 2315 2322 2326 2330 2331 2336 2337
2339 2341 2342 2344 2348 2349 2352 2354 2358 2360 2369 2375 2377 2387 2391 2393 2396 2406 2411 2412 2420
2422 2423 2430 2430 2431 2432 2434 2436 2450 2452 2454 2456 2463 2466 2475 2480 2483 2491 2498 2501 2505
2506 2507 2508 2509 2511 2514 2518 2519 2525 2530 2531 2533 2549 2550 2551 2553 2561 2562 2563 2567 2573
2576 2577 2580 2581 2582 2587 2588 2593 2595 2600 2601 2603
40 Light soil 2187 2190 2199 2206 2226 2229 2234 2239 2252 2261 2264 2268 2280 2290 2294 2296 2300 2316 2322
2339 2343 2393 2394 2406 2420 2422 2423 2426 2434 2452 2475 2484 2506 2507 2512 2516 2518 2519 2524 2526
2531 2543 2549 2550 2557 2562 2569 2572 2574 2576 2580 2593 2594 2598
41 Several varieties of soil 2190 2202 2206 2223 2229 2230 2253 2268 2269 2279 2293 2312 2316 2340 2348 2363 2368
2371 2374 2387 2394 2409 2426 2427 2431 2432 2442 2449 2452 2456 2479 2501 2518 2520 2545 2551 2553 2557
2561 2569 2574 2576 2577 2582 2598
42 Chalk 2276 2372 2471 2493
43 Sand or gravel 2187 2190 2191 2199 2205 2207 2219 2220 2221 2223 2225 2234 2239 2240 2241 2250 2259 2260
2261 2268 2276 2278 2279 2284 2285 2290 2293 2294 2300 2301 2308 2322 2324 2326 2327 2333 2340 2343 2348
2350 2352 2355 2366 2368 2371 2372 2382 2384 2385 2387 2388 2394 2397 2404 2409 2413 2431 2441 2444 2448
2452 2459 2471 2472 2473 2481 2493 2498 2504 2507 2516 2519 2524 2530 2531 2533 2534 2543 2544 2545 2549
2551 2557 2569 2572 2574 2577 2582 2598 2600
44 Peat 2524 2544
46 Good local roads 2190 2227 2231 2260 2304 2308 2323 2327 2355 2359 2366 2377 2439 2443 2449 2452 2464 2493
2505 2509 2510 2535 2562 2596
47 Poor local roads 2265 2312 2335 2589
48 Turnpike and main roads 2221 2226 2227 2236 2289 2293 2301 2314 2324 2338 2340 2360 2371 2384 2397 2427 2471
2481 2486 2520 2532 2536 2537 2555 2556 2568 2577 2588 2593 2601 2603
50 Water carriage 2235 2275 2279 2298 2308 2355 2420 2434 2443 2473 2491 2495 2524 2528 2545 2565
53 Markets accessible 2190 2202 2227 2231 2250 2280 2338 2343 2352 2360 2384 2404 2413 2420 2448 2464 2471 2473
2481 2493 2509 2519 2573 2588 2596
54 Markets inaccessible 2548
55 Provincial markets 2250 2348 2355 2420 2443 2493
56 London market 2199 2270 2275 2300 2308 2321 2352 2355 2384 2400 2413 2441 2443 2473 2573 2596
58 Market prices 2276 2304 2359 2521 2577
59 Landowners and their estates 2192 2192 2253 2264 2264 2471 2486 2589 2593 2602
60 Land occupiers 2235 2335 2369 2441 2448 2452 2475 2486 2521 2550 2588 2598
61 Farm size 2187 2210 2241 2253 2260 2276 2296 2304 2320 2359 2398 2400 2449 2479 2486 2515 2567 2600 2602
62 Leases 2294 2359
64 Common grazing 2247 2268 2441 2562
65 Lammas and other common rights 2247 2502 2562
66 Rents 2199 2241 2253 2265 2343 2355 2359 2363 2394 2454 2459 2471 2520 2521 2539 2550 2576 2596
68 Rates 2210 2229 2232 2265 2276 2320 2443 2449 2482 2521 2567 2580 2586 2602
70 Enclosure or improvement of waste 2191 2191 2235 2285 2398 2465 2506
71 Enclosure of commons 2463
72 Enclosure of open fields 2194 2481
80 Reclaiming and embanking 2241
82 Drainage channels and ditches 2247 2375 2439
85 Underdrainage 2197 2265 2316 2458 2604
87 Marl 2208 2290 2299 2411
88 Chalk 2252 2298 2304 2341 2508 2511 2558 2586 2588 2597 2602
89 Lime 2254 2386 2439 2564 2586 2598 2602
92 Dung 2275 2280 2352 2384 2448 2472 2473 2539 2573 2588 2598
94 Fish 2279 2348 2507
100 Oil dust, unspecified fertilisers or manures 2276
101 General comments on crop rotations 2224 2244 2248 2250 2310 2326 2352 2384 2435 2473 2486 2488 2489 2507 2510
2521 2532 2548 2556 2568 2592 2594 2596
102 Irregular rotations 2248 2265 2296 2413 2596
103 3-course rotation 2196 2248 2258 2359 2363 2400 2439 2441 2444 2446 2481 2486 2521 2530 2587 2592
104 4-course rotation 2187 2190 2191 2196 2197 2198 2199 2201 2202 2205 2206 2206 2208 2210 2213 2215 2219 2220
2223 2225 2226 2227 2229 2232 2234 2235 2240 2244 2247 2248 2249 2250 2252 2254 2258 2259 2260 2261 2265
2265 2268 2269 2274 2275 2276 2278 2279 2284 2285 2289 2290 2292 2293 2294 2299 2306 2308 2309 2310 2314
2315 2316 2320 2321 2322 2323 2324 2330 2331 2333 2336 2337 2338 2339 2340 2342 2343 2344 2350 2354 2358
2360 2366 2368 2369 2375 2376 2377 2383 2385 2386 2391 2393 2396 2397 2400 2404 2406 2407 2409 2420 2422
2423 2425 2426 2427 2430 2431 2434 2435 2436 2441 2442 2444 2445 2446 2448 2449 2450 2454 2460 2463 2464
2465 2466 2471 2472 2473 2475 2480 2481 2482 2484 2488 2490 2493 2494 2495 2496 2497 2498 2501 2507 2508
2509 2515 2516 2518 2519 2525 2526 2528 2530 2532 2533 2534 2535 2536 2539 2548 2549 2553 2555 2556 2557
2561 2562 2563 2564 2565 2567 2568 2571 2575 2576 2577 2581 2582 2584 2585 2587 2588 2590 2594 2595 2600
2601 2602 2603 2604
105 5-course rotation 2239 2245 2249 2269 2279 2295 2335 2355 2382 2411 2459 2483 2505 2580 2586
106 6-course rotation 2192 2199 2207 2241 2255 2298 2304 2308 2341 2398 2399 2407 2422 2432 2443 2448 2450 2459
2474 2484 2492 2508 2511 2514 2528 2531 2558 2566 2567 2589 2590 2597
107 7-course rotation 2199 2491
110 Wheat 2221 2224 2232 2276 2302 2308 2335 2359 2382 2443 2521
111 Barley 2247 2330 2400 2521
113 Rye or meslin 2270 2413 2456 2475 2480
114 Corn yields 2206 2220 2234 2239 2247 2253 2254 2265 2268 2302 2307 2312 2330 2336 2339 2363 2383 2391 2398
2420 2432 2444 2448 2454 2465 2472 2481 2483 2484 2491 2519 2535 2539 2543 2562 2565 2576 2598
115 Beans 2187 2190 2192 2196 2197 2198 2201 2202 2205 2206 2207 2208 2209 2210 2212 2213 2215 2220 2223 2225
2227 2229 2232 2236 2239 2241 2244 2247 2248 2249 2250 2252 2253 2255 2258 2259 2260 2265 2270 2274 2275
2279 2280 2292 2293 2295 2296 2297 2298 2299 2302 2304 2308 2309 2310 2314 2315 2316 2320 2321 2322 2323
2324 2326 2330 2331 2335 2336 2337 2338 2340 2341 2342 2343 2349 2354 2355 2359 2360 2363 2366 2367 2368
2371 2372 2375 2376 2382 2383 2388 2391 2393 2395 2396 2397 2398 2399 2400 2406 2407 2411 2412 2415 2422
2423 2425 2430 2431 2432 2435 2436 2442 2443 2445 2446 2447 2448 2449 2450 2452 2454 2456 2458 2459 2460
2463 2464 2465 2466 2471 2472 2474 2475 2477 2480 2482 2483 2484 2488 2492 2494 2495 2496 2497 2498 2501
2505 2506 2507 2509 2511 2514 2516 2518 2521 2525 2526 2528 2530 2531 2535 2536 2537 2543 2544 2548 2551
2553 2555 2556 2558 2562 2563 2564 2565 2566 2567 2568 2571 2575 2576 2581 2584 2585 2586 2589 2590 2592
2593 2595 2597 2601 2602 2603 2604
116 Peas 2191 2202 2207 2208 2210 2213 2220 2225 2232 2241 2248 2249 2259 2270 2280 2285 2296 2297 2299 2302
2304 2315 2316 2323 2326 2330 2331 2339 2349 2359 2367 2375 2394 2398 2400 2406 2411 2413 2432 2436 2445
2449 2452 2456 2460 2471 2473 2480 2481 2482 2483 2494 2496 2497 2501 2504 2511 2518 2521 2524 2528 2531
2551 2557 2562 2563 2565 2567 2584 2585 2586 2592 2593 2602
117 Rape 2505
118 Coleseed 2205 2225 2255 2394 2444 2505 2505 2506 2507 2508 2512 2514 2566
119 Mustard 2205 2505 2528 2551 2566

Essex contd.

120	Caraway		2505	2528	2551															
123	Clover	2187	2190	2191	2192	2196	2197	2198	2201	2202	2205	2206	2207	2208	2210	2212	2213	2220	2223	2227	2229
		2232	2239	2241	2244	2245	2247	2249	2250	2252	2254	2255	2258	2259	2260	2265	2270	2276	2280	2284	2285
		2289	2292	2294	2295	2296	2297	2298	2299	2300	2302	2304	2308	2310	2312	2315	2316	2320	2323	2326	2330	2331
		2335	2336	2337	2338	2339	2341	2344	2349	2355	2358	2359	2363	2366	2367	2375	2377	2383	2385	2386	2386	2388
		2391	2393	2394	2395	2396	2398	2399	2404	2406	2407	2409	2411	2413	2415	2420	2422	2432	2434	2435	2436	2441
		2442	2443	2444	2445	2446	2448	2449	2450	2452	2456	2459	2460	2463	2464	2465	2466	2471	2474	2475	2477	2480
		2482	2483	2484	2488	2489	2491	2492	2493	2494	2496	2497	2501	2504	2505	2506	2509	2511	2511	2512	2514	2516
		2518	2519	2524	2528	2530	2531	2535	2539	2543	2544	2548	2550	2551	2557	2558	2562	2563	2564	2565	2566
		2567	2571	2575	2580	2581	2584	2585	2586	2587	2588	2589	2592	2593	2595	2596	2597	2598	2602
124	Sainfoin		2227	2372																	
125	Trefoil	2197	2250	2330	2435	2480	2519	2535	2548												
126	Tares and vetches		2187	2197	2202	2205	2208	2210	2212	2213	2221	2223	2231	2248	2250	2259	2265	2270	2280	2296
		2297	2299	2301	2302	2304	2308	2310	2316	2321	2326	2330	2359	2398	2400	2411	2413	2422	2427	2435	2439	2449
		2456	2466	2472	2481	2482	2486	2496	2504	2506	2510	2521	2524	2525	2531	2535	2544	2563	2563	2565	2567	2575
		2576	2586	2593	2602																
129	Turnips		2191	2199	2201	2202	2205	2207	2208	2210	2213	2215	2219	2221	2223	2225	2226	2229	2231	2232	2234
		2239	2240	2241	2244	2245	2247	2249	2250	2252	2259	2260	2261	2270	2274	2275	2276	2278	2279	2280	2284	2285	2289
		2292	2294	2295	2300	2301	2302	2304	2306	2308	2309	2310	2312	2314	2315	2316	2323	2324	2326	2330	2331	2333
		2336	2337	2339	2340	2341	2342	2343	2344	2350	2358	2360	2366	2367	2368	2369	2371	2372	2375	2377	2382	2388
		2393	2394	2396	2398	2400	2404	2406	2407	2409	2412	2413	2415	2422	2423	2426	2427	2432	2434	2435	2436	2439	2441
		2442	2444	2448	2449	2450	2452	2454	2456	2459	2463	2466	2471	2473	2475	2480	2481	2483	2484	2489	2491	2493
		2498	2501	2504	2505	2506	2507	2508	2509	2511	2512	2514	2518	2519	2521	2521	2524	2525	2530	2531	2533	2534
		2545	2549	2550	2551	2557	2561	2562	2563	2567	2575	2576	2577	2580	2582	2586	2587	2588	2593	2594	2595	2598
		2600	2601	2602																	
130	Mangolds		2197	2208	2229	2254	2270	2308	2330	2338	2341	2428	2448	2452	2466	2480	2508	2531	2535	2551	2568
		2589	2595																		
131	Swedes		2270	2330	2338	2428															
132	Potatoes	2199	2205	2229	2270	2300	2384	2413	2422	2448	2473	2524	2531	2539	2545	2551	2573	2576	2596		
133	Bare fallows	2187	2190	2191	2192	2197	2198	2201	2202	2205	2206	2208	2209	2212	2213	2215	2221	2223	2224	2227
		2231	2236	2239	2244	2245	2247	2248	2249	2250	2252	2254	2255	2258	2259	2260	2265	2269	2274	2275	2276	2279
		2293	2294	2295	2296	2297	2298	2299	2302	2308	2309	2310	2314	2315	2316	2320	2321	2322	2323	2324	2326	2330
		2331	2335	2337	2338	2340	2340	2341	2342	2349	2350	2354	2355	2359	2360	2363	2363	2366	2367	2371	2372	2375
		2376	2382	2383	2385	2386	2388	2391	2393	2395	2396	2397	2398	2399	2404	2406	2407	2409	2412	2415	2422	2423
		2425	2431	2432	2435	2436	2439	2441	2442	2443	2445	2446	2447	2448	2449	2450	2452	2454	2456	2458	2459
		2463	2464	2465	2466	2472	2474	2477	2480	2481	2482	2483	2486	2488	2489	2490	2491	2492	2494	2495	2496	2497
		2501	2504	2505	2506	2509	2510	2511	2514	2514	2515	2516	2518	2521	2524	2525	2526	2528	2530	2531	2532	2535	2536
		2537	2543	2544	2548	2551	2553	2555	2556	2557	2558	2562	2563	2564	2565	2567	2568	2575	2576	2577	2580	2581
		2584	2585	2586	2587	2589	2590	2592	2593	2595	2596	2597	2602	2603	2604							
134	High farming	2192	2199	2201	2212	2220	2229	2235	2268	2275	2300	2322	2343	2348	2352	2369	2374	2384	2397	2428
		2430	2452	2452	2458	2473	2484	2486	2490	2498	2508	2509	2566	2573	2582	2589	2593	2598	2600			
135	Low farming	2225	2265	2274	2297	2333	2366	2471	2493	2495	2534	2544	2565	2589							
136	Remarks on the absence of turnips			2210	2253	2302	2320	2335	2359	2558	2568	2585									
137	Remarks on pests and crop diseases			2567																
138	Recent increase in productivity		2208	2293	2348	2411	2422	2431	2436	2466	2472	2482	2489	2593	2598	2604					
139	Good quality pastures		2191	2198	2199	2202	2207	2223	2226	2236	2239	2247	2248	2253	2254	2260	2261	2268	2274
		2285	2293	2297	2309	2315	2316	2321	2322	2323	2324	2331	2338	2354	2358	2363	2371	2376	2382	2388	2422	2427
		2436	2448	2454	2466	2474	2479	2483	2484	2491	2497	2498	2508	2518	2576	2581	2587	2596	2600			
140	Poor quality pastures		2201	2212	2215	2219	2224	2234	2244	2258	2269	2275	2296	2297	2298	2301	2302	2304	2306
		2309	2315	2338	2341	2342	2374	2375	2376	2383	2386	2397	2399	2423	2427	2430	2432	2448	2452	2458	2463	2464
		2474	2479	2488	2489	2490	2491	2492	2493	2495	2497	2510	2511	2518	2525	2530	2544	2545	2549	2550	2553	2566
		2589	2590	2597	2603	2604															
141	Meadows	2187	2191	2201	2202	2207	2223	2225	2231	2234	2236	2241	2261	2285	2293	2300	2301	2324	2330	2343
		2359	2360	2394	2404	2423	2427	2444	2466	2471	2491	2497	2501	2524	2525	2530	2533	2539	2562	2568	2582	2588
		2596	2600	2603																	
142	Irrigation and water meadows			2596	2602															
143	Marsh grassland	2199	2205	2210	2241	2255	2259	2275	2296	2298	2300	2304	2327	2335	2336	2337	2341	2352	2358
		2384	2398	2413	2420	2430	2459	2465	2473	2505	2508	2511	2545	2549	2550	2557	2564	2567	2571	2589	2590
144	Parks	2301	2316	2323	2386	2413	2428	2434	2452	2471	2534	2545	2596								
145	Accommodation land		2493																	
146	Cattle breeding	2508	2511	2531																	
147	Cattle fattening	2265	2308	2323	2355	2397	2400	2441	2443	2534											
148	Dairying	2248	2268	2413	2427	2516	2539	2543													
150	Sheep breeding	2197	2265	2290	2304	2326	2366	2415	2427	2441	2443	2458	2510	2531							
151	Sheep fattening	2308	2323	2355	2397	2441	2456	2458	2511	2534											
154	Pigs	2308	2355	2427	2443	2479															
156	Poultry	2308	2355	2427	2443																
158	Deer	2323																			
160	Straw	2302	2471																		
161	Hay	2192	2198	2206	2207	2208	2223	2224	2234	2239	2244	2245	2253	2254	2258	2260	2270	2295	2306	2363	2376
		2383	2386	2393	2397	2404	2413	2415	2422	2454	2471	2483	2484	2492	2494	2496	2516	2539	2543	2544	2562	2576
		2581	2596	2598																	
162	Manufactured feedstuffs (cake etc.)			2229	2456	2472	2511													
165	Butter	2516	2543																		
169	Good orchards		2279																		
170	Poor orchards		2371																		
171	Fruits	2279	2279	2279																	
172	Market gardens		2190	2229	2261	2268	2270	2279	2280	2289	2300	2348	2366	2384	2413	2420	2423	2454	2524	2535
		2573	2581																		
173	Allotments	2330																			
174	Cabbages	2199	2308	2452	2480																
175	Carrots	2581																			
176	Onions	2366	2535	2581																	
178	Hops	2190	2229	2292	2326	2348	2366	2423	2460	2490	2494	2581									
181	Reeds and oziers	2508	2550																		

Gloucestershire

1	Tithe-free district	2608	2610	2611	2613	2615	2616	2619	2621	2622	2628	2634	2637	2639	2640	2645	2651	2652	2653
		2654	2655	2659	2665	2671	2672	2674	2680	2682	2683	2687	2689	2690	2696	2697	2703	2708	2710	2711	2716	2717
		2718	2719	2726	2730	2731	2732	2739	2740	2741	2742	2749	2752	2753	2754	2763	2770	2778	2782	2783	2784	2785
		2787	2792	2793	2794	2795	2798	2807	2814	2818	2820	2826	2829	2834	2837	2839	2842	2848	2856	2860	2862	2864
		2865	2868	2870	2872	2876	2879	2880	2883	2886	2890	2892	2893	2894	2898	2901	2909	2911	2913	2916	2917	2926
		2927	2932	2941	2942	2943	2946	2949														

Gloucestershire contd.

2	History of tithe payment		2636	2757	2760	2764														
3	Tithe practices and agriculture		2642																	
4	Exemptions from tithe		2618	2627	2631	2638	2641	2643	2644	2646	2656	2662	2664	2667	2670	2677	2681	2684	2685
	2704	2705	2713	2714	2723	2727	2747	2751	2755	2757	2760	2768	2771	2775	2786	2810	2811	2812	2813	2816	2819
	2822	2824	2828	2838	2840	2841	2844	2847	2849	2858	2877	2878	2891	2902	2904	2906	2910	2920	2923	2924	2931
	2939																				
5	Tithe in kind		2699	2724	2775	2874	2900	2933													
6	Compositions		2617	2643	2644	2646	2657	2663	2664	2668	2675	2678	2685	2698	2699	2707	2712	2713	2727	2733	2735
	2736	2745	2746	2757	2758	2775	2777	2797	2800	2805	2811	2813	2815	2822	2823	2828	2836	2840	2844	2845	2850
	2853	2871	2887	2888	2889	2891	2897	2899	2904	2908	2910	2918	2925	2930	2933	2933	2934	2945	2951		
7	Moduses		2614	2626	2627	2638	2650	2660	2661	2667	2673	2677	2678	2684	2698	2705	2707	2712	2727	2735	2755
	2764	2767	2769	2772	2779	2780	2790	2797	2813	2835	2836	2838	2845	2850	2851	2858	2861	2891	2895	2902	2915
	2928	2938																			
8	Glebe		2657	2689	2709	2758	2762	2877	2888	2919											
9	Local topographic descriptions			2692	2803	2915															
11	Village morphology		2815	2822																	
17	Open fields		2919	2933																	
18	Small, irregular closes		2624																		
20	Hedgerow timber		2605	2606	2607	2609	2624	2625	2626	2627	2629	2630	2631	2632	2633	2635	2638	2642	2647	2649
	2650	2658	2660	2661	2666	2668	2676	2681	2686	2688	2692	2693	2694	2700	2701	2702	2715	2720	2722	2724
	2725	2729	2734	2748	2750	2755	2759	2761	2764	2765	2766	2769	2771	2772	2773	2774	2776	2779	2781	2786	2788
	2789	2791	2801	2802	2803	2804	2806	2808	2809	2810	2812	2817	2819	2821	2824	2825	2827	2830	2833	2835	2841
	2843	2857	2859	2863	2866	2867	2874	2881	2884	2895	2896	2902	2903	2906	2907	2912	2914	2921	2923
	2928	2931	2936	2937	2940	2944	2947	2948	2950	2952											
21	Coppice		2607	2624	2629	2633	2644	2722	2788	2802	2805	2812	2830	2843	2846	2854	2904				
22	Plantations		2644	2658	2661	2776	2803	2846	2867	2875	2881										
24	Productive woodland			2638	2750	2761															
25	Poor woodland		2607	2801																	
26	Commons		2627	2642	2661	2781	2869	2910	2921	2934											
27	Furze, gorse and heathlands		2658	2661	2904																
32	Climatic hazards		2771	2776	2813																
33	Excessively steep land		2788	2803	2810																
34	Land requires drainage		2624	2630	2771	2869	2875	2885	2907	2921	2924										
35	Land liable to flood		2624	2776	2830	2854	2904														
36	Productive soil		2638	2661	2709	2769	2801	2867	2867	2895											
37	Poor soil		2630	2681	2801	2852	2866	2904	2944												
38	Heavy (clay) soil		2607	2624	2626	2627	2630	2631	2632	2635	2638	2643	2649	2658	2661	2668	2686	2701	2702	2704
	2715	2724	2729	2734	2747	2748	2755	2759	2761	2764	2766	2771	2776	2776	2779	2781	2786	2788	2789	2791	2801
	2802	2806	2808	2809	2812	2817	2824	2825	2830	2835	2841	2843	2850	2857	2859	2863	2866	2866	2869	2873	2875
	2881	2885	2895	2903	2906	2907	2912	2921	2928	2931	2936	2940	2948	2952							
39	Loamy (turnip) soil		2607	2638	2695	2750	2773	2869	2884	2928											
40	Light soil		2606	2625	2626	2629	2630	2631	2633	2638	2642	2650	2661	2666	2676	2681	2688	2692	2693	2694	2695
	2700	2702	2704	2720	2722	2725	2734	2755	2759	2764	2755	2766	2772	2781	2803	2804	2808	2810	2819	2821	2824	2825
	2827	2833	2846	2863	2866	2866	2873	2874	2896	2907	2914	2921	2923	2924	2937	2944	2950				
41	Several varieties of soil		2624	2638	2642	2764	2776	2803	2869	2873	2881	2903									
43	Sand or gravel		2605	2609	2627	2632	2635	2643	2647	2658	2661	2702	2747	2755	2766	2771	2774	2776	2779	2786
	2789	2809	2810	2817	2824	2825	2830	2835	2850	2854	2857	2859	2867	2881	2895	2902	2906	2915	2931	2940	2944
	2947																				
44	Peat		2801																		
46	Good local roads		2661	2695	2699	2704	2781	2806	2866	2869	2907										
47	Poor local roads		2810	2921																	
48	Turnpike and main roads		2632	2919	2921																
53	Markets accessible		2632	2661	2704	2729	2776	2806	2866	2867	2869	2881	2907	2919	2921						
58	Market prices		2813	2820																	
59	Landowners and their estates		2658	2764																	
60	Land occupiers		2875	2895	2896																
61	Farm size		2624	2642	2764	2773	2803	2869													
63	Farm implements		2630	2933																	
64	Common grazing		2673	2781	2803	2859															
65	Lammas and other common rights			2673	2734	2779															
66	Rents	2643	2867	2895	2896																
68	Rates		2775																		
69	Farm labour and wages		2933																		
70	Enclosure or improvement of waste			2712																	
71	Enclosure of commons		2677																		
72	Enclosure of open fields		2756	2768	2806	2847															
75	Conversion of grass to arable			2712																	
77	Paring and burning		2630																		
85	Underdrainage		2607																		
89	Lime	2830																			
92	Dung	2895																			
95	Bones	2630																			
101	General comments on crop rotations			2686	2722	2747	2759	2789	2801	2850	2859	2903	2936								
102	Irregular rotations		2624	2643	2747	2773	2867	2895	2921												
103	3-course rotation		2605	2607	2609	2638	2660	2715	2734	2761	2771	2802	2806	2809	2812	2817	2825	2841	2857	2859
	2881	2884	2903	2912	2915	2928	2948	2952													
104	4-course rotation		2606	2625	2626	2627	2631	2632	2638	2661	2666	2668	2676	2692	2693	2701	2702	2709	2724	2725
	2729	2748	2750	2755	2766	2769	2774	2776	2779	2786	2808	2809	2810	2817	2825	2830	2854	2863	2874	2875	2885
	2906	2907	2915	2944	2947	2950															
105	5-course rotation		2630	2631	2633	2635	2649	2650	2658	2688	2694	2695	2720	2755	2764	2765	2779	2781
	2803	2804	2819	2824	2833	2835	2866	2873	2874	2904	2914	2923	2924	2931	2940	2950					
106	6-course rotation		2631	2635	2642	2647	2658	2681	2691	2700	2704	2720	2772	2821	2827	2835	2841	2846	2873	2874
	2896	2937	2940	2944																	
108	8-10-course rotation		2695	2808																	
114	Corn yields		2617	2666	2695	2700	2712	2713	2773	2775	2812	2813	2832	2833	2914	2919	2920	2924	2928	2931	2933
	2934	2937	2947	2948																	
115	Beans	2626	2627	2658	2748	2779	2786	2825	2835	2875	2906	2948									
116	Peas	2902	2906																		
122	Unspecified grass seeds		2764																		
123	Clover	2626	2635	2748	2772	2779	2786	2789	2808	2824	2827	2835	2846	2875	2896	2902	2924	2952			
124	Sainfoin		2630	2681	2722	2808	2896	2950													
126	Tares and vetches		2607	2643	2695	2747	2748	2779	2878												
129	Turnips		2606	2607	2630	2635	2642	2649	2649	2658	2695	2704	2720	2722	2759	2764	2769	2772	2779	2781	2786
	2789	2803	2808	2810	2824	2825	2827	2835	2846	2878	2896	2902	2904	2907	2923	2924	2940	2950			
132	Potatoes		2626	2643	2668	2686	2707	2712	2747	2789	2791	2801	2902	2921	2952						

Gloucestershire contd.

133	Bare fallows	2606	2607	2626	2627	2635	2649	2649	2658	2701	2748	2759	2769	2779	2786	2788	2791	2824	2825	2835
	2843	2854	2875	2903	2906	2921	2940												
135	Low farming	2921																	
136	Remarks on the absence of turnips			2761	2789														
139	Good quality pastures		2624	2642	2776	2801	2803	2806	2830	2881									
140	Poor quality pastures		2624	2630	2642	2781	2801	2869	2907	2924									
141	Meadows	2642	2764	2776	2781	2803	2830	2866	2867	2895									
143	Marsh grassland		2624																
144	Parks	2704	2713	2846	2924														
145	Accommodation land			2695															
146	Cattle breeding		2607	2642	2764	2771	2803	2907	2921	2944									
148	Dairying	2607	2624	2630	2642	2661	2764	2771	2776	2806	2866	2881	2895	2904	2907	2921			
150	Sheep breeding		2609	2642	2695	2722	2724	2764	2781	2803	2866	2907	2944						
151	Sheep fattening		2661	2702	2803	2924													
153	Horses	2638																	
155	Oxen	2803	2810	2830	2871														
158	Deer	2704																	
161	Hay	2624	2869																
166	Cheese	2904																	
169	Good orchards			2903	2904														
170	Poor orchards		2850																
171	Fruits	2928																	
172	Market gardens		2707																
173	Allotments		2689	2859															

Hampshire

1	Tithe-free district	8881	8889	8894	8929	8931	8941	8942	8951	8954	8957	8959	8967	8998	9000	9035	9049	9052	9083
	9086	9093	9099	9102	9106	9116	9127	9135	9139	9185	9189	9205	9207	9208	9209	9210	9215	9216	14807 14808
2	History of tithe payment		8932																
3	Tithe practices and agriculture			8961	9112														
4	Exemptions from tithe		8920	8939	8944	8950	8974	8983	9029	9042	9063	9064	9072	9095	9103	9107	9113	9119	9120
	9123	9131	9144	9145	9181	9193	9197	9206											
5	Tithe in kind	8897	8932	8965	8986	8991	9054	9074	9117	9179									
6	Compositions	8897	8906	8915	8918	8952	8953	8956	8974	8983	9001	9004	9007	9012	9014	9015	9016	9030	9034	9041
	9042	9058	9060	9064	9065	9070	9080	9089	9092	9095	9097	9108	9109	9110	9111	9113	9117	9119	9120	9129	9138
	9147	9148	9153	9161	9162	9170	9179	9181	9186	9193	9195	9196	9197	9198	9200	9203	9204	9220	
7	Moduses	8920	8939	8943	8991	9016	9042	9080	9119	9120	9147	9161	9172	9173	9181	9193	9203	9206	9220	9227
8	Glebe	8915	8918	8974	8983	9012	9015	9016	9034	9060	9070	9080	9095	9097	9109	9111	9117	9119	9120	9147
	9153	9162	9170	9186	9195	9200	9211	9220	9221	9223	9226	9227	9714						
9	Local topographic descriptions		8878	8892	8898	8907	8985	8987	9013	9031	9040	9115	9143						
10	Regional topographic descriptions		8897	8899	8911	8935	8940	8984	8988	9021	9036								
11	Village morphology		9008	9038	9067	9130	9172	9218											
12	Church	8716	8891	8892	8896	8933	8940	8944	8961	9040	9053	9075	9104	9125	9126	9143	9159	9175	9190
13	Country houses and ornamental gardens			8891	8907	8964	8964	8987	8989	9037	9087	9088	9163						
15	Cottages and cottage gardens			8964	9008	9187													
16	Field boundaries		9053	9091	9159														
17	Open fields	8877	9126																
18	Small, irregular closes		8908	8968	9008	9053	9150	9155											
19	Large, regular fields	8890	8960	8981	9008	9023	9047	9183											
20	Hedgerow timber	8893	8913	9150	9217														
21	Coppice	8897	8937	8964	8994	9019	9031	9038	9045	9064	9071	9174	9187						
22	Plantations	8949	8976	8987	8996	9005	9009	9022	9038	9067	9154	9156	9164	9174					
23	Woodland management		8933	8940	9121	9125	9183												
24	Productive woodland		8886	8960	8977	9003	9039	9073	9098	9101	9156	9183	9217						
25	Poor woodland	8873	8905	8917	8923	8930	8937	8944	8962	8994	9008	9013	9025	9027	9033	9038	9044	9057	9084
	9158	9164	9168	9187	9201	9214													
26	Commons	8925	8927	8937	8937	8944	9009	9013	9019	9027	9027	9032	9053	9061	9078	9085	9115	9123	9145	9155
	9168																		
27	Furze, gorse and heathlands		8917	8926	8989	9005	9009	9019	9027	9032	9078	9078	9084	9091	9115	9187	9187		
31	Wasteland	8976																	
32	Climatic hazards	8886	8912	8923	9005	9009	9010	9027	9028	9031	9044	9045	9053	9054	9077	9118	9128	9146	9176
	9201	9222																	
33	Excessively steep land		8925	8994															
34	Land requires drainage		8914	8968	8977	8979	8980	8986	9011	9077	9114	9124	9141	9143	9149	9150	9155	9158	9182
	9217																		
36	Productive soil	8892	8895	8896	8902	8908	8913	8920	8960	8964	8991	9002	9013	9027	9031	9038	9066	9105	9115
	9128	9160	9168	9182	9184	9218													
37	Poor soil	8882	8888	8895	8896	8899	8904	8905	8923	8930	8933	8935	8937	8940	8946	8961	8964	8968	8970	8976
	8985	9002	9005	9009	9013	9022	9027	9036	9038	9053	9055	9059	9061	9066	9075	9091	9098	9118
	9126	9130	9132	9142	9149	9154	9156	9159	9160	9171	9175	9176	9180	9182	9187	9213	9218	9225
38	Heavy (clay) soil	8879	8891	8893	8896	8898	8902	8908	8909	8910	8913	8914	8917	8922	8924	8925	8927	8930	8936
	8937	8949	8961	8964	8965	8966	8976	8993	8994	8996	9002	9003	9008	9010	9011	9019	9020	9021	9029
	9031	9036	9038	9040	9047	9053	9057	9061	9062	9068	9072	9073	9074	9076	9078	9082	9091	9094	9098	9105	9107
	9114	9115	9118	9123	9124	9125	9130	9141	9143	9149	9150	9155	9157	9158	9164	9172	9174	9175	9176	9187	9188
	9191	9192	9218	9219	9222	9228													
39	Loamy (turnip) soil	8892	8895	8908	8917	8920	8926	8937	8949	8964	8965	8966	8968	8971	8986	8991	9008	9024	9038
	9039	9043	9053	9067	9071	9076	9087	9168	9182	9224	9228								
40	Light soil	8879	8895	8905	8936	8937	8965	8985	8987	9023	9025	9028	9044	9054	9063	9084	9091	9101	9104
	9123	9128	9130	9146	9158	9180	9192	9201	9213	9218	9224								
41	Several varieties of soil	8877	8878	8888	8896	8899	8902	8910	8911	8926	8930	8933	8936	8937	8964	8965	8968	8986
	8993	9002	9019	9021	9022	9029	9053	9057	9072	9076	9077	9094	9112	9124	9158	9174	9187	9225
42	Chalk	8873	8879	8882	8886	8890	8891	8896	8898	8899	8905	8910	8912	8917	8921	8922	8923	8924	8926	8927	8933
	8935	8936	8938	8939	8940	8946	8960	8961	8965	8966	8979	8981	8986	8996	9008	9024	9026	9028	9031	9036	9038
	9040	9045	9051	9053	9055	9059	9066	9073	9074	9077	9087	9107	9112	9118	9142	9143	9154	9157	9159	9163	9164
	9171	9172	9174	9176	9180	9183	9188	9190	9191	9192	9201	9213	9214	9217	9219	9225	9228		
43	Sand or gravel	8716	8882	8896	8902	8904	8908	8912	8913	8914	8917	8925	8926	8944	8946	8964	8965	8968	8976
	8979	8980	8989	8993	8994	9003	9005	9006	9009	9022	9025	9027	9028	9029	9031	9032	9040	9043	9045	9053	9061
	9067	9068	9072	9073	9076	9077	9078	9085	9088	9105	9121	9124	9131	9141	9143	9144	9146	9150	9155	9164	9168
	9171	9172	9187	9188	9192	9201	9225												
44	Peat	8914	8968	9022	9026	9059	9076	9146	9187	9214									
45	Fields remote from farms		8970	9074	9160														
46	Good local roads	8882	8960	9024	9027	9168	9225												
47	Poor local roads	8968	9008	9053	9055	9222													

Hampshire contd.

#	Topic	References
48	Turnpike and main roads	8877 8893 9021 9037 9062 9078 9085 9121 9124 9144 9149 9163 9182 9213 9218 9224
50	Water carriage	8925 9027 9168
51	Canals	9072
52	Railways	8987
53	Markets accessible	8877 8882 8886 8925 8936 8938 8949 8960 8971 8981 8991 8996 9003 9024 9027 9045 9082 9112 9168 9176 9183 9225
54	Markets inaccessible	8921 8935 8940 9055 9172 9222
55	Provincial markets	8892
57	Fairs	8882 9191
58	Market prices	8716 8961
59	Landowners and their estates	8886 8914 8927 8949 8979 8988 9005 9011 9029 9037 9056 9067 9088 9112 9115 9149 9150 9154 9187 9218 9219
60	Land occupiers	8884 8884 8890 8994 8996 9021 9029 9054 9055 9077 9105 9115 9217 9218
61	Farm size	8891 8893 8896 8917 8933 8961 8986 8988 8993 8996 9032 9040 9053 9074 9075 9076 9114 9121 9126 9143 9146 9155 9159 9163 9175 9190
62	Leases	8906 9112 9159 9218
63	Farm implements	9029
64	Common grazing	9187
65	Lammas and other common rights	8937 8938 9013 9057 9174
66	Rents	8716 8907 8935 9013 9075
69	Farm labour and wages	9011
70	Enclosure or improvement of waste	9191
71	Enclosure of commons	8882 9028 9100 9133
72	Enclosure of open fields	8938 9107
73	Enlargement of fields	8897
75	Conversion of grass to arable	8890 8897 8985
76	Conversion of arable to pasture	9154
81	Marsh drainage	8989
85	Underdrainage	8925 9028 9044 9098 9115 9132 9150
86	Tile drains	9150
88	Chalk	8893 8989 9072 9073 9082 9091
92	Dung	8904 8925 9105
95	Bones	9063 9201 9218
97	Guano	9201
101	General comments on crop rotations	9011 9036 9067 9068 9074 9218
102	Irregular rotations	8893 8910 8911 8914 8923 8930 8965 8968 8991 9011 9074 9076 9105 9112 9125 9157 9160 9190 9218 9222
103	3-course rotation	8891 8910 8944 8977 8994 9019 9175
104	4-course rotation	8716 8877 8878 8879 8882 8891 8892 8893 8896 8898 8908 8910 8922 8925 8930 8933 8936 8944 8949 8960 8961 8968 8971 8976 8977 8979 8986 8988 8991 8993 8994 9005 9006 9008 9009 9010 9013 9019 9021 9024 9025 9027 9037 9038 9040 9043 9047 9051 9053 9057 9067 9071 9073 9078 9082 9084 9085 9087 9094 9101 9104 9114 9115 9121 9123 9126 9128 9130 9141 9142 9143 9149 9158 9159 9163 9168 9175 9213 9217 9222 9225 9228
105	5-course rotation	8873 8879 8886 8888 8893 8898 8904 8905 8908 8909 8912 8913 8917 8921 8924 8925 8927 8935 8936 8940 8946 8965 8970 8980 8981 8985 8988 8994 9020 9023 9027 9028 9029 9031 9033 9036 9043 9045 9047 9051 9054 9055 9056 9072 9073 9075 9077 9088 9098 9123 9124 9125 9130 9131 9132 9144 9150 9154 9156 9164 9172 9174 9176 9180 9183 9184 9188 9191 9192 9201 9218 9219
106	6-course rotation	8899 8907 8927 8935 8946 9002 9039 9074 9107 9118 9132 9142 9146 9157 9160 9214
107	7-course rotation	9063 9160
110	Wheat	8902 8913 8964 9160
111	Barley	8902
112	Oats	9187
113	Rye or meslin	8882 9053 9187
114	Corn yields	8904 8945 9028 9038 9044 9073 9082 9089 9131
115	Beans	8913 9029 9073 9077 9098 9114 9123 9125 9158 9183 9222
116	Peas	8977 9025 9063 9084 9112 9222
117	Rape	9087 9142 9146
123	Clover	8896 8904 8907 8925 8933 8935 8946 8965 9025 9028 9044 9045 9063 9067 9071 9072 9073 9084 9098 9101 9114 9115 9121 9125 9143 9158 9171 9180 9187 9190 9201 9222
124	Sainfoin	8873 8886 8890 8899 8912 8924 8933 8937 8961 8965 8981 9002 9008 9022 9023 9024 9033 9038 9039 9047 9055 9056 9062 9063 9072 9073 9075 9088 9091 9101 9107 9118 9131 9142 9146 9154 9156 9157 9159 9160 9163 9171 9172 9174 9176 9184 9188 9190 9192 9214 9217 9218
125	Trefoil	9045 9176
126	Tares and vetches	8882 8917 8949 8977 9028 9029 9044 9054 9063 9067 9112 9149 9163 9180 9190
127	Lucerne	9131
129	Turnips	8716 8878 8896 8902 8907 8908 8909 8917 8946 8949 8977 8993 8994 9008 9010 9025 9028 9029 9029 9037 9038 9039 9040 9054 9056 9063 9067 9071 9073 9075 9076 9084 9088 9091 9094 9101 9107 9112 9115 9118 9121 9123 9126 9128 9131 9142 9143 9146 9150 9154 9156 9158 9158 9159 9164 9168 9171 9172 9175 9180 9187 9190 9192 9201 9214 9217 9222
132	Potatoes	8907
133	Bare fallows	8878 8893 8908 8911 8925 8949 8977 9021 9040 9073 9076 9077 9078 9094 9112 9114 9115 9123 9125 9158 9164 9175 9192
134	High farming	8892 8927 8986 9038 9104 9225
135	Low farming	8910 8930 8933 8935 8946 8981 8984 8986 9029 9054 9061 9098 9144
136	Remarks on the absence of turnips	9149
137	Remarks on pests and crop diseases	8921
139	Good quality pastures	8873 8877 8879 8895 8902 8910 8920 8927 8981 8991 8994 9013 9038 9053 9059 9073 9104 9105 9164 9168 9183 9217 9228
140	Poor quality pastures	8873 8895 8910 8912 8917 8930 8933 8937 8968 8976 8979 8980 8996 9002 9010 9027 9033 9038 9039 9043 9045 9051 9053 9059 9063 9076 9078 9084 9094 9098 9101 9104 9107 9124 9149 9156 9157 9172 9187 9214
141	Meadows	8716 8944 8964 9010 9019 9033 9053 9057 9067 9076 9123 9132 9146
142	Irrigation and water meadows	8873 8888 8890 8895 8902 8904 8909 8913 8920 8921 8921 8924 8937 8940 8940 8965 8970 9005 9009 9019 9026 9031 9032 9036 9037 9038 9057 9059 9063 9066 9076 9094 9131 9146 9160 9192 9214
143	Marsh grassland	8910 8927 8939 8971 8981 8989 9006
144	Parks	8888 8964 8989 9005 9009 9019 9022 9033 9037 9088 9150 9157 9163 9187 9213
145	Accommodation land	8716 8927
146	Cattle breeding	8914 8962 9071
147	Cattle fattening	9002 9067 9078 9217
148	Dairying	8907 8913 8927 8991
149	Cow keeping	9105
150	Sheep breeding	8882 8910 8949 8962 8977 9003 9005 9024 9026 9037 9051 9054 9055 9059 9061 9115 9128 9157 9159 9188 9190 9191 9192 9201 9213
151	Sheep fattening	8902 8977 9009 9024 9071 9164 9217
153	Horses	9029 9071

Hampshire contd.

154	Pigs	8976	9071	9082												
156	Poultry		9053													
157	Rabbits		9010	9075												
158	Deer	9005	9009	9037												
159	Animal diseases			8902												
160	Straw	8949														
161	Hay	8716	8891	8909	8914	8944	8970	8994	9008	9013	9025	9044	9061	9063	9067	9072
163	Stall or yard feeding		9071													
170	Poor orchards		9187													
171	Fruits	9187														
172	Market gardens		9105													
173	Allotments	9067														
178	Hops	8897	8901	8964	8977	8994	9117	9143	9153	9163	9183					

Herefordshire

1	Tithe-free district	2976	2989	3048	3053	3131	3148	3151	3156	3160	3198								
4	Exemptions from tithe		2971	2998	3010	3020	3023	3025	3039	3044	3057	3060	3063	3073	3075	3076	3087	3089	3102
	3106	3108	3109	3113	3123	3135	3140	3146	3158	3168	3193	3200							
5	Tithe in kind	2970	2975	2987	3129	3139	3144	3145	3201	3207									
6	Compositions	2963	2971	2972	2974	2975	2986	2997	3010	3013	3028	3029	3031	3032	3033	3034	3038	3046	3049	3066
	3067	3070	3072	3078	3081	3082	3084	3085	3089	3100	3101	3106	3110	3112	3120	3123	3127	3132	3134	3144	3149
	3162	3168	3169	3175	3179	3180	3181	3182	3183	3199	3207								
7	Moduses	2962	2995	3003	3011	3023	3039	3047	3056	3062	3063	3075	3083	3087	3092	3096	3098	3102	3106	3112
	3113	3122	3129	3132	3135	3144	3146	3158	3193	3199	3205	3207							
8	Glebe	2958	2960	2965	2971	3066	3081	3143	3168	3182									
9	Local topographic descriptions			3003	3147	3165													
10	Regional topographic descriptions			3107	3147	3166													
15	Cottages and cottage gardens			3024															
17	Open fields	3029																	
20	Hedgerow timber		2953	2955	2956	2957	2959	2961	2962	2964	2966	2967	2968	2973	2977	2978	2979	2981	2982	2983
	2984	2985	2988	2995	2996	2998	2999	3000	3001	3002	3003	3004	3005	3006	3007	3008	3009	3011	3012	3014	3015
	3016	3017	3020	3022	3023	3025	3027	3030	3036	3037	3041	3042	3043	3044	3045	3054	3055	3058	3059	3061	3062
	3064	3065	3068	3071	3074	3076	3077	3079	3083	3088	3090	3091	3092	3093	3094	3095	3096	3097	3098	3099
	3102	3103	3104	3105	3107	3108	3109	3111	3113	3115	3117	3122	3124	3125	3126	3130	3133	3136	3137	3138	3140
	3142	3143	3145	3146	3147	3150	3152	3153	3154	3155	3157	3158	3159	3161	3164	3165	3167	3168	3170	3171	3172
	3173	3176	3177	3178	3180	3184	3185	3186	3187	3188	3189	3190	3192	3193	3196	3197	3200	3202	3204	3205	3206
21	Coppice	2982	3008	3016	3018	3030	3036	3097	3103	3116	3130	3137	3149	3164	3171	3172	3177	3178	3180	3189
	3197	3203																	
22	Plantations	2980	3024	3109	3119	3171													
23	Woodland management			3021															
24	Productive woodland		2978	3014	3088	3108	3109	3142	3167	3171	3172	3173	3187	3188						
25	Poor woodland		3020																
32	Climatic hazards		3097																
34	Land requires drainage		3024	3083	3088	3094	3165												
35	Land liable to flood		3145																
36	Productive soil	2978	3012	3041	3054	3166													
37	Poor soil	2967	3094	3158	3165	3167	3186												
38	Heavy (clay) soil		2953	2956	2959	2961	2962	2964	2966	2967	2968	2973	2977	2980	2981	2982	2983	2986	2995	2998
	2999	3000	3001	3002	3003	3004	3005	3006	3007	3008	3009	3010	3011	3012	3014	3015	3016	3017	3018	3021	3022
	3023	3027	3036	3047	3055	3061	3062	3071	3073	3076	3079	3083	3088	3090	3091	3092	3095	3096	3098	3099	3101
	3102	3103	3104	3105	3107	3108	3109	3113	3114	3115	3116	3117	3122	3124	3125	3126	3130	3133	3137	3138	3140
	3142	3143	3146	3147	3152	3153	3154	3157	3158	3164	3165	3166	3167	3168	3170	3172	3176	3177	3178	3180	3185
	3187	3188	3190	3193	3197	3200	3202	3204	3205	3206									
39	Loamy (turnip) soil	2956	2964	2978	2982	3005	3007	3014	3024	3027	3104	3109	3130	3145	3153	3166	3171	3173	3176
	3184	3187	3196	3206															
40	Light soil	2961	2967	2986	2995	2999	3008	3014	3020	3022	3030	3037	3042	3058	3091	3092	3097	3099	3101	3116
	3146	3155	3167	3170	3192	3193													
41	Several varieties of soil	2967	2980	3137															
43	Sand or gravel		2955	2957	2967	2973	2978	2979	2980	2981	2984	2985	2988	2996	3002	3004	3006	3007	3009	3011
	3016	3023	3025	3027	3037	3041	3042	3043	3044	3045	3054	3055	3058	3059	3061	3062	3064	3065	3068	3073	3074
	3076	3077	3083	3090	3093	3094	3095	3097	3103	3104	3105	3108	3111	3114	3115	3117	3126	3136	3137	3143	3145
	3150	3152	3158	3159	3161	3170	3171	3172	3173	3177	3180	3185	3186	3189	3192	3193	3194			
46	Good local roads	2980																	
47	Poor local roads	3003	3037	3107	3165														
48	Turnpike and main roads		3121																
53	Markets accessible	2980	3019	3047	3059														
54	Markets inaccessible	3003	3037																
56	London market	2980	3079																
58	Market prices	2970	3024																
59	Landowners and their estates			3061															
61	Farm size	3037	3079	3165															
62	Leases	3044																	
66	Rents	3059	3075	3168															
67	Urban influences on value of land			2956															
70	Enclosure or improvement of waste			3141															
101	General comments on crop rotations			3010	3013	3115	3143	3157	3172	3187									
102	Irregular rotations	2956	2957	3010	3027														
103	3-course rotation	2953	2958	2959	2962	2964	2966	2968	2977	2983	2986	2995	2998	2999	3000	3001	3002	3003	3006
	3009	3011	3012	3014	3016	3017	3020	3021	3022	3062	3071	3073	3075	3076	3077	3079	3082	3089	3091	3096	3098
	3101	3102	3108	3109	3113	3121	3122	3124	3137	3138	3140	3142	3158	3159	3164	3165	3166	3167	3168	3170	3178
	3184	3188	3193	3196	3200	3204	3206												
104	4-course rotation	2955	2957	2961	2967	2978	2979	2980	2981	2984	2985	2986	2987	2988	2995	2996	2998	3000	3004
	3005	3007	3008	3011	3014	3015	3017	3019	3023	3024	3037	3041	3043	3044	3045	3054	3055	3058	3061	3062	3064
	3065	3068	3073	3074	3075	3077	3088	3090	3091	3093	3094	3095	3097	3099	3101	3103	3104	3105	2107	3108	3109
	3111	3114	3116	3117	3125	3130	3136	3143	3145	3146	3147	3150	3152	3153	3154	3155	3170	3171	3173	3182	3184
	3185	3186	3188	3189	3190	3193	3194	3197	3202	3206									
105	5-course rotation	2957	2994	3002	3007	3025	3030	3059	3092	3094	3103	3108	3133	3143	3166	3171	3187	3192	3204
	3205																		
106	6-course rotation	2982	3018	3055	3094	3126	3161	3176	3205										
107	7-course rotation	2982	3094	3117	3144														
108	8-10-course rotation	2973	3036	3042															
110	Wheat	3097																	
111	Barley	3097																	

Herefordshire contd.

114	Corn yields	2958	2963	2965	2971	2972	2974	2986	2987	2991	2992	2994	2997	3010	3013	3019	3024	3029	3031	3032
		3033	3034	3035	3036	3038	3040	3046	3057	3066	3067	3070	3075	3078	3082	3087	3089	3100	3101	3110	3116	3119
		3120	3127	3132	3135	3144	3163	3168	3169	3175	3179	3182	3183	3191	3199	3201	3207
115	Beans	2953	2962	2964	2968	2977	2983	2991	2992	2998	2999	3000	3001	3002	3008	3010	3011	3012	3019	3021	3029
		3030	3035	3036	3038	3047	3057	3058	3059	3061	3062	3066	3076	3079	3082	3087	3090	3091	3101	3103	3107	3108
		3110	3113	3115	3117	3119	3120	3121	3126	3127	3133	3140	3141	3142	3144	3152	3154	3157	3163	3164	3165	3166
		3167	3168	3169	3170	3175	3178	3179	3184	3185	3187	3188	3190	3193	3197	3199	3200	3201	3204	3205	3206
116	Peas	2953	2962	2964	2968	2973	2977	2982	2986	2991	2992	2994	2997	2998	3000	3001	3002	3006	3010	3011	3012
		3015	3019	3020	3021	3029	3035	3038	3041	3057	3062	3066	3070	3073	3076	3077	3078	3082	3087	3088	3089
		3091	3092	3100	3101	3103	3108	3110	3113	3119	3120	3121	3125	3126	3130	3132	3141	3142	3146	3149	3152	3158
		3161	3163	3164	3169	3170	3172	3176	3178	3179	3183	3185	3188	3193	3199	3200	3201	3205	3206	3207
123	Clover	2955	2957	2958	2963	2964	2967	2968	2981	2982	2983	2984	2986	2987	2988	2991	2992	2994	2995	2996	2997	2998
		3001	3002	3004	3006	3007	3010	3011	3012	3015	3018	3019	3023	3029	3030	3036	3037	3038	3042	3043	3044	3045
		3054	3057	3058	3061	3062	3064	3068	3070	3073	3082	3088	3089	3090	3092	3093	3094	3095	3099	3103	3104	3105
		3106	3108	3114	3115	3116	3117	3119	3120	3127	3130	3132	3133	3135	3136	3140	3141	3144	3145	3146
		3149	3150	3155	3157	3161	3163	3167	3168	3169	3172	3175	3176	3179	3182	3183	3184	3185	3186	3189	3191	3193
		3194	3197	3199	3202	3204	3205	3207
126	Tares and vetches		2962	2982	3001	3002	3010	3022	3030	3041	3058	3059	3070	3082	3089	3090	3103	3126	3149	3161
		3163	3190	3193	3201	3204
129	Turnips	2955	2957	2967	2973	2978	2980	2981	2982	2984	2985	2986	2987	2988	2991	2992	2994	2995	2996	2997
		3000	3002	3004	3006	3007	3010	3011	3022	3023	3024	3025	3035	3037	3038	3040	3041	3043	3044	3045	3054	3057
		3058	3059	3061	3062	3064	3066	3068	3070	3077	3078	3079	3089	3090	3093	3094	3095	3097	3099	3100	3103	3104
		3105	3108	3109	3110	3114	3115	3116	3117	3119	3120	3127	3132	3135	3136	3139	3140	3141	3143	3145	3149	3150
		3155	3161	3163	3167	3168	3169	3170	3172	3173	3175	3176	3179	3182	3184	3185	3186	3187	3188	3189	3192	3193
		3194	3199	3201	3206	3207
131	Swedes	3024
132	Potatoes	2958	2992	2994	3024	3035	3040	3057	3058	3059	3066	3070	3078	3100	3110	3119	3120	3135	3139	3149
		3163	3168	3169	3179	3183	3201
133	Bare fallows	2953	2958	2962	2964	2968	2973	2977	2982	2983	2986	2987	2995	2998	2999	3000	3001	3002	3006	3007
		3008	3011	3015	3020	3021	3022	3023	3030	3036	3061	3073	3075	3076	3077	3079	3082	3088	3091	3092	3095	3096
		3098	3101	3107	3113	3115	3116	3117	3121	3122	3125	3126	3130	3133	3140	3142	3143	3144	3146	3152	3154	3157
		3158	3164	3165	3166	3167	3168	3170	3178	3184	3185	3187	3188	3190	3193	3200	3202	3204	3205	3206
139	Good quality pastures		2956	3024
140	Poor quality pastures		2980	3010	3024	3165
141	Meadows	2980
142	Irrigation and water meadows		2980
145	Accommodation land		3059
146	Cattle breeding		2980	3018	3024	3047	3075	3114	3165
147	Cattle fattening		2991	3018	3019	3075	3079	3114	3116
148	Dairying	3047	3097	3165
149	Cow keeping	2956	3059
150	Sheep breeding		2959	2967	3018	3020	3021	3078	3097	3114	3116	3145
151	Sheep fattening		2959	3021	3114	3116	3145
154	Pigs	2994	3018	3110
155	Oxen	2980	2991	3079	3097
156	Poultry	3018
157	Rabbits	3155
159	Animal diseases	3079
160	Straw	2997
161	Hay	2994	3078	3182	3201
167	Wool	3078
169	Good orchards		2962	2991	2992	2994	2997
170	Poor orchards		2975	3024	3087
171	Fruits	3024
172	Market gardens		3078	3125	3190
178	Hops	2957	2959	2962	2964	2968	2977	2991	2992	2998	3000	3001	3005	3008	3009	3010	3014	3017	3019	3022	3027
		3031	3035	3036	3038	3047	3061	3062	3066	3073	3076	3091	3101	3102	3105	3107	3108	3109	3113	3115	3119	3121
		3125	3126	3129	3132	3133	3137	3140	3141	3142	3147	3149	3155	3157	3158	3159	3164	3167	3168	3187	3188	3190
		3197	3199	3200	3205

Hertfordshire

1	Tithe-free district	3212	3234	3237	3241	3247	3251	3267	3271	3274	3275	3276	3279	3294	3298	3299	3302	3323	3328
		3342
3	Tithe practices and agriculture		3300	3322
4	Exemptions from tithe		3195	3208	3210	3211	3213	3214	3217	3225	3225	3227	3229	3230	3236	3238	3243	3245	3254
		3258	3266	3268	3269	3273	3277	3283	3287	3289	3290	3292	3296	3300	3303	3310	3313	3316	3317	3318	3327	3331
		3336	3337
5	Tithe in kind	3209	3217	3235	3243	3248	3281
6	Compositions	3209	3211	3214	3217	3235	3240	3243	3249	3250	3255	3256	3260	3264	3268	3281	3287	3288	3292	3296
		3313	3331
7	Moduses	3211	3223	3229	3252	3281	3296	3316	3317
8	Glebe	3209	3240	3242	3248	3260	3283	3312
9	Local topographic descriptions		3213	3229	3230	3254	3256	3266	3310	3322
10	Regional topographic descriptions		3229	3233	3262	3293	3326
11	Village morphology	3257	3303
12	Church	3221	3224	3231	3236	3244	3254	3259	3261	3303	3318	3338	3340
13	Country houses and ornamental gardens		3224	3238	3263	3266	3300	3300	3327	3332	3332	3333	3334	3339
14	Farm houses and buildings	3303
15	Cottages and cottage gardens		3238	3262	3266	3278	3307
16	Field boundaries	3228	3262	3289	3307	3319
17	Open fields	3215	3218	3235	3244	3255	3259	3262	3289	3290	3293	3300	3308	3315	3322	3329	3336	3338	3339
18	Small, irregular closes		3216	3254	3289
19	Large, regular fields	3289	3300
20	Hedgerow timber	3224	3230	3289	3319
21	Coppice	3262	3277	3278	3285	3289	3319	3324
22	Plantations	3195	3266	3291	3307	3332
24	Productive woodland		3213	3238	3254	3256	3261	3277	3285	3286	3319	3322	3333
25	Poor woodland	3216	3219	3221	3229	3231	3232	3264	3265	3270	3280	3289	3320	3337
26	Commons	3232	3256	3266	3278	3337
27	Furze, gorse and heathlands		3278
31	Wasteland	3262
32	Climatic hazards	3227	3232	3256	3265	3338
33	Excessively steep land		3266	3307	3319

Hertfordshire contd.

34	Land requires drainage	3236	3259	3263	3278	3280	3316	3322	3324	3325	3326	3338					
35	Land liable to flood	3289															
36	Productive soil	3195	3215	3238	3255	3266	3277	3278	3285	3293	3311	3319	3326	3333	3334	3337	3340
37	Poor soil 3208	3216	3227	3238	3244	3262	3263	3266	3277	3278	3282	3285	3286	3293	3307	3310	3311	3319	3322
	3330 3333 3334																
38	Heavy (clay) soil	3213	3218	3219	3224	3225	3227	3231	3232	3233	3235	3236	3239	3245	3248	3252	3255	3257	3259
	3261 3262 3263 3264 3266 3270 3272 3280 3282 3285 3286 3289 3290 3291 3293 3303 3307 3311 3315 3316 3317																
	3318 3319 3320 3322 3324 3325 3326 3327 3329 3330 3333 3334 3335 3336 3337 3338 3339 3343																
39	Loamy (turnip) soil	3195	3213	3218	3219	3230	3238	3257	3259	3266	3272	3278	3285	3290	3300	3311	3314	3316	3317
	3321 3324 3334 3336 3338																
40	Light soil 3221	3225	3231	3232	3233	3252	3262	3263	3264	3265	3269	3270	3280	3289	3300	3310	3316	3318	3320
	3329 3330 3332 3338																
41	Several varieties of soil	3215	3233	3242	3245	3255	3256	3257	3259	3266	3272	3289	3338	3339				
42	Chalk 3195	3232	3244	3245	3254	3255	3256	3259	3264	3266	3278	3291	3329	3330	3343			
43	Sand or gravel	3195	3208	3213	3216	3219	3221	3224	3225	3227	3231	3232	3242	3245	3248	3254	3255	3256	3259
	3262 3263 3264 3277 3278 3280 3282 3293 3314 3319 3320 3321 3326 3327 3329 3334 3339 3340 3343																
44	Peat 3254 3332																
46	Good local roads	3226	3228	3252	3262	3278	3332	3339	3340								
47	Poor local roads	3214	3244	3286	3289												
48	Turnpike and main roads	3195	3218	3219	3224	3225	3238	3242	3244	3245	3248	3255	3259	3262	3269	3270	3272	3300
	3311 3314 3318 3319 3322 3324 3325 3332 3333 3334 3335 3336																
50	Water carriage 3324																
52	Railways 3208	3230	3232	3238	3324	3337											
53	Markets accessible	3195	3226	3228	3252	3334											
54	Markets inaccessible	3244	3286	3315													
56	London market	3213	3226	3230	3316	3318	3327	3333	3343								
59	Landowners and their estates	3213	3257	3263	3286	3293	3300	3300	3336								
60	Land occupiers	3225	3226	3270	3282	3291	3317										
61	Farm size 3224	3236	3244	3252	3270	3278	3303										
62	Leases 3208 3213 3321 3339																
64	Common grazing	3232	3266	3290	3310	3322	3337										
65	Lammas and other common rights	3217	3266	3269	3269	3290	3293	3321									
66	Rents 3252 3286																
68	Rates 3270																
71	Enclosure of commons	3236															
72	Enclosure of open fields	3213	3225	3255	3266	3317	3322										
76	Conversion of arable to pasture	3282	3300	3339													
85	Underdrainage 3307	3318	3343														
88	Chalk 3232																
91	Soot 3330																
92	Dung 3293 3327 3336																
98	Rape cake 3330																
100	Oil dust, unspecified fertilisers or manures	3291															
101	General comments on crop rotations	3215	3221	3224	3282	3286	3289	3293	3311	3321							
103	3-course rotation	3218	3232	3236	3239	3244	3286	3311	3315	3317	3322	3336	3339				
104	4-course rotation	3195	3208	3213	3215	3216	3218	3224	3225	3226	3227	3228	3229	3230	3231	3233	3235	3236	3238
	3239 3244 3252 3257 3259 3261 3263 3264 3265 3269 3270 3278 3280 3289 3290 3291 3293 3300 3303 3314 3315																
	3317 3318 3320 3322 3324 3325 3326 3329 3330 3333 3335 3336 3337 3338 3339 3343																
105	5-course rotation	3213	3221	3245	3262	3289	3289	3293	3310	3316	3321	3337					
106	6-course rotation	3256															
110	Wheat 3325 3336																
114	Corn yields 3308	3313	3316	3331													
115	Beans 3195 3213	3218	3219	3231	3236	3238	3239	3259	3263	3264	3280	3289	3290	3303	3311	3317	3318	3320	3324
	3329 3335 3338 3343																
116	Peas 3195 3218	3219	3221	3231	3238	3245	3259	3263	3264	3280	3289	3290	3291	3293	3310	3311	3317	3320	3322
	3324 3329 3335 3337 3338 3339																
123	Clover 3195 3208	3213	3216	3218	3219	3221	3225	3227	3230	3231	3232	3235	3236	3238	3242	3244	3245	3257	3259
	3261 3263 3264 3269 3270 3280 3289 3290 3291 3293 3303 3310 3311 3315 3317 3318 3320 3321 3322 3324 3325																
	3326 3329 3330 3335 3337 3338 3340 3343																
124	Sainfoin 3230 3242 3259																
126	Tares and vetches	3213	3233	3239	3242	3245	3256	3259	3265	3270	3286	3289	3293	3310	3325	3326	3335	3339
129	Turnips 3195 3208	3213	3216	3218	3219	3221	3225	3227	3228	3229	3230	3231	3232	3233	3236	3238	3239
	3239 3242 3244 3245 3252 3256 3257 3259 3262 3263 3264 3269 3270 3280 3289 3290 3291 3293 3303 3307 3310																
	3311 3317 3318 3320 3321 3322 3324 3325 3326 3329 3330 3335 3337 3338 3339 3340 3343																
130	Mangolds 3326																
132	Potatoes 3224 3326 3327 3336																
133	Bare fallows 3195	3218	3221	3225	3227	3230	3231	3232	3233	3235	3236	3238	3239	3242	3244	3245	3257	3259	3263
	3264 3270 3280 3289 3290 3291 3307 3311 3315 3317 3318 3320 3322 3324 3325 3326 3329 3330 3335 3336 3337																
	3338 3343																
134	High farming 3263	3300	3316	3330													
135	Low farming 3214	3221	3235	3282	3316	3339											
136	Remarks on the absence of turnips	3218															
137	Remarks on pests and crop diseases	3233	3335														
138	Recent increase in productivity	3225	3317	3339													
139	Good quality pastures	3216	3218	3227	3230	3231	3232	3236	3245	3255	3259	3261	3264	3270	3278	3326	3332	3333
	3334 3343																
140	Poor quality pastures	3208	3216	3219	3225	3231	3242	3245	3259	3277	3278	3280	3285	3289	3290	3300	3307	3310
	3321 3322 3325 3329 3330 3334 3337 3338 3339																
141	Meadows 3218	3227	3231	3236	3254	3255	3262	3278	3285	3289	3311	3316	3318	3319	3324	3326	3333	3334	3336
	3340 3343																
143	Marsh grassland 3269																
144	Parks 3238 3257	3258	3263	3266	3277	3307	3316	3327	3332	3333							
145	Accommodation land	3216															
146	Cattle breeding	3333	3343														
147	Cattle fattening	3227															
148	Dairying 3227	3289	3333	3339													
150	Sheep breeding	3208	3225	3227	3256	3291	3306	3333	3337	3339							
151	Sheep fattening	3226	3227	3245	3252	3310											
153	Horses 3289 3291																
154	Pigs 3289 3343																
156	Poultry 3343																
158	Deer 3257 3332																
160	Straw 3333																
161	Hay 3213 3218	3219	3225	3230	3245	3269	3289	3307	3310	3318	3327	3343					
162	Manufactured feedstuffs (cake etc.)	3252	3333														

Hertfordshire contd.

163	Stall or yard feeding	3227	
165	Butter	3343	
169	Good orchards	3254	3278
170	Poor orchards	3266	

Huntingdonshire

1	Tithe-free district	3128 3344 3347 3353 3354 3355 3361 3368 3369 3372 3373 3374 3376 3381 3382 3409 3410 3411 3412 3414 3415 3422 3432 3435 3436 3438 3439 3440 3444 3448 3449 3450 3451 3453 3454 3455 3456 3458 3459 3461 3462 3463 3466 3471 3472 3473 3474 3478
2	History of tithe payment	3346 3424
3	Tithe practices and agriculture	3413
4	Exemptions from tithe	3345 3348 3352 3356 3358 3362 3367 3371 3377 3378 3416 3417 3419 3421 3426 3428 3433 3437 3441 3442 3452 3464 3467 3475 3477
5	Tithe in kind	3366 3383
6	Compositions	3345 3351 3359 3375 3380 3416 3419 3420 3421 3424 3470
7	Moduses	3345 3346 3383 3418 3419 3431 3433 3442 3452
8	Glebe	3351 3383
10	Regional topographic descriptions	3360 3468 3469
12	Church	3431
15	Cottages and cottage gardens	3385
16	Field boundaries	3371
17	Open fields	3379 3384 3385 3413 3423 3431
18	Small, irregular closes	3385
19	Large, regular fields	3384
21	Coppice	3384 3385
22	Plantations	3363
24	Productive woodland	3464 3468
25	Poor woodland	3358 3363 3427 3468
26	Commons	3379 3421 3431
27	Furze, gorse and heathlands	3358 3363
30	Fens	3364 3365 3416 3442 3443 3452 3467 3476 3477
31	Wasteland	3442
32	Climatic hazards	3356 3457
34	Land requires drainage	3363 3385 3413 3431 3460
36	Productive soil	3356 3363 3364 3365 3384 3443 3468
37	Poor soil	3352 3356 3358 3360 3363 3365 3384 3427 3437 3460 3464 3467 3468 3469 3476
38	Heavy (clay) soil	3345 3358 3360 3364 3365 3371 3379 3384 3385 3386 3413 3427 3431 3433 3434 3437 3442 3447 3452 3457 3460 3464 3468 3469
39	Loamy (turnip) soil	3363 3385 3443 3447 3452 3468
40	Light soil	3442 3452
41	Several varieties of soil	3447 3452
43	Sand or gravel	3364 3447
44	Peat	3365 3442
45	Fields remote from farms	3467
46	Good local roads	3469
47	Poor local roads	3360 3365 3434 3442 3467 3468
48	Turnpike and main roads	3363 3365 3384 3385 3434 3447
53	Markets accessible	3469
54	Markets inaccessible	3468
55	Provincial markets	3365
58	Market prices	3474
59	Landowners and their estates	3379 3385 3423 3443 3443 3468
60	Land occupiers	3384 3457 3469
61	Farm size	3360
62	Leases	3460
65	Lammas and other common rights	3379 3379 3413 3420 3423
66	Rents	3352 3423 3469
68	Rates	3359
71	Enclosure of commons	3356 3413
72	Enclosure of open fields	3352 3358 3385 3409 3413 3440 3458 3460 3467 3472 3474
75	Conversion of grass to arable	3358 3431 3457
76	Conversion of arable to pasture	3468
81	Marsh drainage	3443 3467
82	Drainage channels and ditches	3413
84	Ridge-and-furrow	3379 3413 3469
85	Underdrainage	3413 3464
86	Tile drains	3413
87	Marl	3443 3452
101	General comments on crop rotations	3464
103	3-course rotation	3352 3360 3365 3371 3379 3431 3434 3460 3469
104	4-course rotation	3363 3365 3371 3384 3385 3386 3413 3423 3427 3431 3433 3437 3442 3447 3464 3468 3476
105	5-course rotation	3442
106	6-course rotation	3467
110	Wheat	3356 3379
111	Barley	3457
112	Oats	3467
114	Corn yields	3351 3383 3467
115	Beans	3351 3356 3363 3364 3371 3379 3384 3385 3386 3413 3423 3427 3431 3433 3437 3442 3460 3469
116	Peas	3351 3363 3364 3371
118	Coleseed	3351 3364 3365 3442 3452 3467 3476
123	Clover	3356 3360 3363 3371 3384 3385 3386 3413 3427 3431 3447 3464 3467
125	Trefoil	3413 3464
126	Tares and vetches	3351 3385 3386 3413 3423 3460
129	Turnips	3351 3363 3364 3371 3413 3447 3452
130	Mangolds	3469
133	Bare fallows	3351 3352 3356 3360 3363 3364 3371 3379 3385 3386 3413 3423 3427 3431 3433 3434 3437 3452 3460 3469 3476
134	High farming	3356 3384 3468
135	Low farming	3384 3385 3413
136	Remarks on the absence of turnips	3434 3460
137	Remarks on pests and crop diseases	3452
138	Recent increase in productivity	3452
139	Good quality pastures	3345 3363 3371 3379 3384 3385 3413 3468

Huntingdonshire contd.

140	Poor quality pastures		3345	3358	3363	3384	3423	3427	3442	3457	3460
141	Meadows	3352	3363	3371	3379	3447					
144	Parks	3421	3468								
146	Cattle breeding		3457								
147	Cattle fattening		3379								
148	Dairying	3379	3464	3468							
150	Sheep breeding		3379	3457	3464	3468					
151	Sheep fattening		3423								
152	Droving	3464									
161	Hay	3384									
166	Cheese	3431									
169	Good orchards		3385								

Kent

1	Tithe-free district		3402	3405	3539	3540	3738	3761	3769	3771	3811	3819	3831				
2	History of tithe payment			3407	3700	3702	3776	3783									
3	Tithe practices and agriculture			3406	3408	3487	3533	3654	3694	3704	3829	3857					
4	Exemptions from tithe		3403	3407	3541	3545	3568	3666	3701	3725	3747	3785					
5	Tithe in kind	3648	3855														
7	Moduses		3406	3487	3515	3533	3726	3728	3739	3777							
9	Local topographic descriptions				3388	3389	3391	3484	3501	3520	3527	3544	3559	3578	3584	3641	3643	3650	3657	3663
	3664	3665	3669	3682	3697	3704	3715	3728	3731	3736	3748	3762	3789	3794	3804	3809	3822	3844	3846	3855	3861
	3864	3872															
10	Regional topographic descriptions			3390	3487	3591											
11	Village morphology		3557														
12	Church	3655	3728														
13	Country houses and ornamental gardens			3387	3531	3556	3666	3679	3859								
14	Farm houses and buildings		3867														
15	Cottages and cottage gardens			3650	3671	3875											
16	Field boundaries	3404	3508	3520	3579	3681	3717	3717	3746	3755	3785	3791	3828	3869			
17	Open fields	3578	3721	3746	3766	3836											
18	Small, irregular closes		3404	3508	3520	3579	3586	3621	3755	3785	3791						
19	Large, regular fields	3544	3721	3745	3755												
21	Coppice	3390															
22	Plantations	3387	3736	3746													
23	Woodland management		3602	3741													
24	Productive woodland		3387	3388	3513	3518	3556	3560	3574	3582	3631	3634	3668	3669	3671	3682	3695	3714	3724
	3734	3736	3745	3788	3789	3807	3808	3830	3840	3843	3864	3869	3872			
25	Poor woodland	3391	3482	3506	3512	3531	3532	3534	3544	3554	3562	3599	3611	3628	3651	3682	3715	3724	3744
	3754	3820	3844	3855	14826											
26	Commons	3400	3525	3553	3575	3589	3673	3673	3694	3785	3802	3802	3839	3855			
27	Furze, gorse and heathlands			3657													
31	Wasteland	3551	3694	3735													
32	Climatic hazards		3531	3532	3544	3548	3551	3554	3566	3581	3602	3631	3634	3650	3662	3684	3715	3717	3742	3744
	3748	3762	3777	3802	3809	3828	3855	3857	14826							
34	Land requires drainage		3387	3508	3517	3520	3526	3532	3557	3565	3572	3579	3677	3717	3777	3780	3786	3802	3809
	3839	3844	3861													
35	Land liable to flood		3610	3659	3832	3851											
36	Productive soil	3389	3406	3482	3485	3494	3497	3512	3513	3514	3518	3548	3560	3581	3582	3609	3611	3615	3619
	3622	3639	3643	3644	3647	3650	3652	3655	3656	3657	3662	3664	3668	3672	3673	3685	3692	3694	3708	3714	3718
	3721	3723	3726	3734	3739	3741	3742	3753	3755	3762	3764	3765	3776	3784	3788	3797	3803	3808	3814	3829	3835
	3836	3840	3843	3851	3853	3864	3875									
37	Poor soil	3480	3502	3503	3506	3507	3508	3511	3516	3520	3527	3551	3553	3560	3565	3572	3573	3574	3579	3580
	3581	3589	3599	3602	3606	3607	3609	3622	3634	3637	3639	3645	3647	3650	3651	3655	3665	3673	3679	3682	3686
	3703	3708	3710	3720	3727	3740	3742	3745	3746	3748	3755	3775	3777	3778	3785	3789	3791	3806	3807	3829	3838
	3846	3855	3872	3875												
38	Heavy (clay) soil	3387	3388	3408	3484	3485	3493	3503	3507	3508	3509	3512	3514	3520	3548	3551	3554	3557	3563
	3564	3565	3566	3570	3579	3580	3583	3591	3606	3607	3621	3630	3639	3640	3641	3645	3650	3659	3662	3663	3666
	3668	3671	3673	3677	3681	3684	3685	3686	3688	3704	3707	3708	3715	3717	3720	3723	3727	3740	3745	3748	3752
	3754	3755	3773	3777	3780	3786	3789	3791	3794	3805	3809	3828	3839	3849	3855	3857	3861	3867	3869	10432	14826
39	Loamy (turnip) soil	3389	3406	3484	3485	3488	3491	3509	3512	3514	3518	3526	3530	3531	3554	3557	3560	3562	3564
	3566	3571	3574	3580	3581	3582	3610	3615	3619	3640	3644	3655	3657	3662	3664	3669	3672	3673	3685	3692	3694
	3695	3697	3700	3708	3714	3716	3721	3731	3737	3739	3744	3753	3754	3755	3762	3764	3765	3776	3794	3803	3808
	3816	3828	3835	3839	3840	3843	3859	3864	3875							
40	Light soil	3491	3502	3526	3530	3544	3562	3602	3606	3610	3630	3631	3643	3655	3657	3675	3695	3703	3732	3790
	3804	3807	3830	3836	3855	3859	10432	14826								
41	Several varieties of soil			3387	3388	3391	3393	3394	3396	3484	3493	3497	3513	3517	3520	3524	3526	3554	3556	3557
	3559	3560	3562	3563	3564	3566	3574	3580	3606	3609	3622	3628	3631	3639	3647	3652	3655	3657	3673	3682	3708
	3723	3735	3741	3772	3773	3787	3788	3797	3804	3820	3828	3830	3853	3870	14826	
42	Chalk	3387	3388	3391	3396	3482	3484	3513	3518	3527	3544	3551	3552	3554	3560	3563	3564	3566	3573	3574	3578
	3581	3582	3589	3599	3606	3610	3615	3622	3629	3630	3634	3645	3650	3651	3662	3675	3695	3703	3716	3723	3732
	3734	3735	3736	3741	3742	3745	3746	3754	3762	3766	3787	3794	3807	3830	3838	3843	3864	3872	3875	
43	Sand or gravel	3514	3516	3518	3527	3531	3554	3563	3564	3572	3574	3583	3591	3599	3628	3637	3663	3664	3665
	3668	3669	3673	3679	3707	3723	3732	3734	3742	3744	3748	3773	3785	3789	3804	3816	3830	3855			
45	Fields remote from farms			3655	3710	3865											
46	Good local roads		3610	3648	3664	3718	3735	3736	14826								
47	Poor local roads	3532	3557	3586	3621	3650	3651	3695	3748	3785	3789	3791	3844	3846	3867	3869	3875
48	Turnpike and main roads		3611	3621	3797	3867											
50	Water carriage	3393	3493	3512	3611	3615	3622	3642	3656	3685	3795	3797	3857				
53	Markets accessible	3530	3544	3610	3615	3619	3630	3651	3656	3664	3695	3700	3718	3735	3736	3753	3763	3853	3873
54	Markets inaccessible	3389	3488	3493	3508	3511	3527	3532	3624	3641	3651	3744	3745	3748	3775	3791	3829	3869	3875
55	Provincial markets	3483	3505	3548	3598	3601	3648	3744	3839								
56	London market	3387	3390	3393	3493	3512	3531	3536	3574	3577	3591	3601	3615	3642	3736	3795	3830	3839	3857
	3859	3870														
57	Fairs	3556															
59	Landowners and their estates			3577	3585	3610	3638	3658	3671	3728	3754	3859	3869				
60	Land occupiers		3585	3585	3805												
61	Farm size	3388	3491	3501	3641	3650	3659	3671	3681	3688	3695	3704	3707	3723	3745	3754	3804	3810	3867
62	Leases	3487	3514	3521	3585	3803	3805										
63	Farm implements		3526	3637	3723												
66	Rents	3493	3501	3507	3514	3557	3563	3564	3615	3619	3706	3731	3806	3868			
67	Urban influences on value of land				3556	3615	3666										
68	Rates	3868															

Kent contd.

71	Enclosure of commons	3531	3620	3688												
73	Enlargement of fields	3820														
75	Conversion of grass to arable	3406	3408	3483	3487	3509	3533	3654	3694	3726	3740	3800	3801			
76	Conversion of arable to pasture	3408	3487	3650	3704	3726	3740	3800	3829	14826						
79	Subsoil ploughing	3816														
85	Underdrainage	3508	3514	3640	3669	3673	3708	3780	3786	3805	3816	3820	3857	3867		
86	Tile drains	3805														
87	Marl	3669	3816	3867												
88	Chalk	3408	3816													
89	Lime	3408	3727	3789	3867											
92	Dung	3505	3512	3530	3531	3577	3615	3622	3630	3642	3656	3700	3718	3735	3736	3744	3795	3858
94	Fish	3577	3607	3736	3805											
95	Bones	3736														
100	Oil dust, unspecified fertilisers or manures			3493	3640	3692	3700	3753								
101	General comments on crop rotations		3590	3624	3721	3731	3735	3828								
102	Irregular rotations	3393	3517	3524	3531	3548	3564	3566	3591	3610	3639	3641	3659	3671	3704	3715	3745	3746	3794
	3809	3828	3869	3870												
103	3-course rotation	3394	3503	3530	3639	3641	3652	3861								
104	4-course rotation	3388	3389	3393	3396	3488	3491	3501	3502	3514	3516	3517	3524	3526	3530	3552	3554	3556	3562
	3565	3573	3580	3583	3599	3606	3622	3637	3641	3644	3647	3652	3669	3679	3686	3720	3732	3752	3762	3773	3788
	3789	3790	3803	3804	3805	3820	3836	3851	3861	10432						
105	5-course rotation	3394	3509	3514	3526	3544	3602	3610	3637	3643	3688	3707	3741	3803	3809	3816
106	6-course rotation	3408	3482	3485	3491	3502	3513	3518	3524	3566	3570	3582	3631	3634	3663	3664	3682	3684	3685	3695	3697
	3703	3714	3718	3734	3737	3748	3772	3784	3786	3807	3808	3820	3822	3843	3849	3872
107	7-course rotation	3494	3551	3566	3607	3650	3692	3734	3736	3741	3786	3787	3843			
110	Wheat	3867														
112	Oats	3610														
114	Corn yields	3586	3595	3599	3621	3745	3749	3754	3814	3828	3868					
116	Peas	3390	3556	3573	3574	3742	3830									
118	Coleseed	3576														
119	Mustard	3829														
120	Caraway	3576	3639	3786												
123	Clover	3830	3839													
124	Sainfoin	3553	3589	3855	3875	14826										
126	Tares and vetches	3666														
129	Turnips	3396	3573	3637												
130	Mangolds	3591														
131	Swedes	3867														
132	Potatoes	3387	3387	3395	3548	3556	3574	3576	3589	3591	3666	3753	3786	3858	3873	
133	Bare fallows	3491	3508	3513	3651	3671	3753	3777	3867							
134	High farming	3393	3408	3493	3496	3544	3591	3640	3644	3650	3656	3669	3673	3692	3700	3721	3728	3731	3736	3744
	3753	3754	3762	3784	3786	3789	3795	3797	3803	3830	3835	3836	3840	3849	3851	3858	3859
135	Low farming	3551	3565	3513	3581	3629	3650	3697	3740	3745	3754	3777	3786	3789	3791	3809	3837	3846	3855	3869
136	Remarks on the absence of turnips		3613	3621	3681	3745	3753									
138	Recent increase in productivity	3591	3669	3717	3778	3828	3857	3870								
139	Good quality pastures	3391	3396	3485	3491	3502	3503	3507	3509	3511	3513	3524	3530	3544	3548	3563	3566	3572	3574	3588	3591
	3610	3622	3631	3643	3647	3664	3669	3672	3673	3681	3697	3700	3714	3721	3726	3734	3736	3737	3762	3776	3786
	3788	3797	3816	3830	3835	3839	3843	3849	3851	3875					
140	Poor quality pastures	3393	3396	3485	3491	3502	3503	3507	3509	3511	3512	3513	3524	3531	3554	3557	3560	3580
	3581	3591	3607	3610	3611	3621	3622	3631	3634	3639	3641	3645	3647	3650	3651	3655	3665	3669	3672	3682	3686
	3703	3708	3715	3720	3735	3740	3745	3748	3784	3785	3786	3787	3794	3807	3822	3830	3835	3836	3840	3844	3846
	3855	3861	3869	3872	3875										
141	Meadows	3491	3560	3659												
142	Irrigation and water meadows		3560	3700												
143	Marsh grassland	3391	3606	3624	3660	3704	3716	3721	3731	3764	3816	3830	3832	3853		
144	Parks	3480	3556	3560	3589	3637	3655	3672	3684	3688	3708	3720	3785	3789	3838	3839	14826
145	Accommodation land	3637														
146	Cattle breeding	3574	3742													
147	Cattle fattening	3573	3585													
148	Dairying	3839														
150	Sheep breeding	3694	3839													
151	Sheep fattening	3588														
158	Deer	3400														
159	Animal diseases	3532														
160	Straw	3505	3548	3601	3638	3648	3763	3793								
161	Hay	3531	3577	3591	3638	3648	3702	3875								
162	Manufactured feedstuffs (cake etc.)		3577	3637												
163	Stall or yard feeding	3867														
169	Good orchards	3387	3391	3497	3560	3562	3566	3573	3581	3590	3594	3598	3609	3688	3700	3714	3716	3736	3762
	3797	3830	3840	3851												
170	Poor orchards	3554	3579	3599	3715	3735	3838	3840								
171	Fruits	3387	3387	3390	3556	3591	3687	3687	3687	3687	3840	3840				
172	Market gardens	3390	3548	3556	3591	3666	3718									
174	Cabbages	3591	3679													
175	Carrots	3591														
176	Onions	3556	3591													
177	Other vegetables	3591														
178	Hops	3391	3491	3514	3521	3530	3548	3553	3554	3559	3562	3564	3566	3577	3579	3581	3585	3586	3590	3598	3600
	3602	3609	3620	3629	3630	3635	3644	3651	3657	3662	3668	3673	3681	3684	3688	3689	3690	3691	3695	3696	3699
	3700	3717	3724	3729	3735	3741	3749	3780	3785	3787	3789	3798	3799	3803	3807	3820	3835	3839	3840	3845
	3851	3855	3867	3874												
181	Reeds and oziers	3704														

Lancashire

1	Tithe-free district	3889	3890	3962	3981	3999	4045	4047	4049	4098	4099	4115	4131	4143	4145	4161	4169	4271
2	History of tithe payment	4145	4178	4217	4239	4256	4268									
3	Tithe practices and agriculture	4065	4163													
4	Exemptions from tithe	3959	4002	4004	4011	4121	4125	4170	4204	4232	4300					
5	Tithe in kind	4013	4016	4080	4188	4223										
6	Compositions	3886	3926	4194	4256	4302	4309	4314	4317							
7	Moduses	3895	3898	3938	3951	3964	3965	4002	4068	4125	4149	4150	4159	4163	4189	4198	4202	4217	4256	4288
	4302	4309	4314	4317												
8	Glebe	4307														

Lancashire contd.

9	Local topographic descriptions		3900	3933	3971	4013	4070	4082	4084	4094	4101	4107	4117	4122	4125	4137	4187	4215
	4216	4255	4294															
10	Regional topographic descriptions		3902	3915	3958	3959	3985	4027	4028	4029	4034	4052	4055	4060	4062	4066	4067	4073
	4080	4091	4092	4102	4105	4113	4119	4124	4155	4187	4188	4208	4226	4258	4261	4263	4269	4276	4278	4279	4290
11	Village morphology	3997	4126															
15	Cottages and cottage gardens		3933															
17	Open fields	4234																
18	Small, irregular closes		3900	3982	4003	4035	4056	4082	4122	4199	4207	4264	4266	4303				
19	Large, regular fields	3978	4094															
20	Hedgerow timber	4028																
21	Coppice	4016																
22	Plantations	4016	4065	4280														
26	Commons	3895	3966	4259														
28	Moorland	4101	4125	4137	4182	4241	4307											
29	Mosses	3903	3909	3947	3954	3988	3996	3998	4003	4029	4034	4040	4071	4084	4089	4094	4133	4142	4144	4147
	4154	4162	4168	4180	4193	4226	4253	4259	4263	4283	4298	4315						
31	Wasteland	3988	3993	4027														
32	Climatic hazards	3944	3952	3996	4013	4026	4027	4080	4092	4104	4135	4187	4236	4261	4284	4315		
34	Land requires drainage		3900	4016	4025	4026	4027	4033	4052	4060	4080	4092	4136	4187	4188	4253	4274	4303
35	Land liable to flood	3941	3996	4000	4120	4163	4168	4192	4232	4236	4293	4307						
36	Productive soil	3884	3933	3944	3952	3967	3982	3985	3992	4001	4004	4023	4034	4070	4071	4100	4107	4116	4119
	4125	4129	4133	4135	4144	4188	4216	4219	4227	4245	4272	4276	4300					
37	Poor soil	3883	3887	3895	3900	3903	3909	3936	3952	3971	3998	4003	4016	4022	4025	4028	4033	4055	4080	4082
	4091	4122	4182	4189	4200	4201	4225	4263	4274	4284	4290	4304						
38	Heavy (clay) soil	3878	3881	3883	3884	3887	3888	3894	3900	3901	3902	3909	3915	3916	3919	3922	3924	3933	3941
	3947	3967	3971	3972	3978	3982	3991	3994	3996	3998	4000	4002	4011	4013	4022	4025	4026	4027	4028	4033
	4034	4035	4040	4044	4055	4056	4060	4062	4066	4067	4068	4071	4080	4082	4084	4086	4091	4094	4096	4100	4104
	4107	4117	4119	4120	4122	4133	4135	4136	4137	4142	4144	4149	4151	4154	4155	4160	4162	4165	4168	4171	4180
	4189	4193	4199	4200	4202	4208	4209	4210	4213	4215	4219	4220	4221	4225	4226	4227	4232	4234	4235	4236	4244
	4245	4251	4253	4258	4259	4263	4270	4272	4274	4278	4279	4281	4283	4284	4287	4290	4293	4294	4300	4303	4304
	4307	4311	4312	4318														
39	Loamy (turnip) soil	3881	3894	3916	3944	3949	3954	3967	3982	3985	3991	3995	3996	4000	4001	4002	4013	4023	4029
	4044	4056	4065	4068	4070	4104	4105	4107	4118	4122	4127	4147	4152	4165	4187	4192	4199	4207	4209	4216	4232
	4236	4251	4256	4266	4270	4280	4294	4298	4303	4315								
40	Light soil	4035	4080	4264														
41	Several varieties of soil		3895	3902	3906	3909	3922	3972	3978	3982	3994	4000	4003	4022	4029	4055	4082	4094	4129
	4142	4147	4155	4220														
43	Sand or gravel		3884	3887	3888	3900	3901	3902	3906	3915	3933	3944	3947	3958	3972	3978	3992	3994	3995	3997
	3998	4002	4011	4025	4040	4044	4055	4056	4067	4071	4082	4086	4091	4096	4100	4102	4120	4122	4124	4133	4144
	4147	4149	4151	4154	4155	4160	4162	4168	4171	4180	4193	4208	4209	4210	4218	4219	4221	4225	4226	4227
	4235	4243	4244	4253	4255	4263	4264	4267	4269	4272	4274	4284	4287	4290	4300	4304	4318		
44	Peat	3881	3884	3894	3895	3915	3944	3947	3949	3954	3991	4027	4084	4086	4094	4102	4118	4120	4124	4142	4144
	4162	4163	4165	4209	4216	4221	4226	4232	4243	4253	4259	4272	4274	4278	4281	4293	4300	4307		
46	Good local roads	4105	4142	4187	4264													
47	Poor local roads	3900	3971	3996	4003	4035	4080	4082	4104	4122	4216	4236	4303					
48	Turnpike and main roads		4137	4187	4216													
50	Water carriage	4267																
51	Canals	3884	4005	4065	4133	4144	4155	4160	4180	4187	4193	4245	4253	4276				
52	Railways	4003	4056	4080	4105	4151	4187											
53	Markets accessible	3888	3902	4056	4066	4105	4127	4144	4151	4187	4202	4216	4220	4251	4272	4300		
54	Markets inaccessible	3971																
55	Provincial markets	3883	4267															
57	Fairs	3952																
58	Market prices	4003	4187	4234														
59	Landowners and their estates		3915	3978	4065	4067	4067	4068	4105	4107	4151	4154	4234	4245	4275	4287	4293	4311
60	Land occupiers	3967	4023	4062	4073	4225	4258	4267	4270	4304	4318							
61	Farm size	3902	3905	3915	3924	4003	4011	4056	4086	4102	4105	4124	4125	4127	4142	4151	4155	4160	4171	4187
	4189	4207	4221	4225	4279	4304	4318											
62	Leases	3955	4275	4293	4311	4318												
64	Common grazing	4016																
66	Rents	3922	4033	4062	4136	4137	4220	4264	4294	4300								
67	Urban influences on value of land	4243																
68	Rates	4278																
69	Farm labour and wages		4052															
70	Enclosure or improvement of waste			4031	4040	4254												
71	Enclosure of commons	3887	4207	4220	4254													
72	Enclosure of open fields	3952																
73	Enlargement of fields	3978																
75	Conversion of grass to arable	4220																
76	Conversion of arable to pasture	3881	3938	3971														
77	Paring and burning	4163	4283															
80	Reclaiming and embanking	3985	3988	4089	4154	4272	4276	4283										
81	Marsh drainage	4154	4272	4283														
82	Drainage channels and ditches		4060	4293														
85	Underdrainage	3998	4086	4100	4107	4133	4221	4234	4251	4279								
87	Marl	3959	3996	4071	4135	4142	4154	4163	4215	4234	4269	4283	4311	4312	4315			
89	Lime	3883	3909	4005														
92	Dung	3883	3884	3888	3906	3933	3994	3995	3998	4005	4029	4033	4035	4066	4068	4080	4082	4086	4089	4102	4105
	4118	4133	4136	4144	4152	4155	4160	4180	4187	4193	4199	4201	4202	4209	4216	4221	4226	4245	4264	4267	4272
	4274	4280	4300	4307														
93	Seaweed	4216																
95	Bones	4119																
101	General comments on crop rotations		3903	3917	3919	3954	3966	4029	4033	4060	4151	4215	4218	4245	4251	4266		
102	Irregular rotations	3944	3949	3955	3996	4003	4094	4105	4122	4142	4147	4163	4187	4199	4209	4216	4234	4298
103	3-course rotation	3883	3936	3949	3958	3959	3978	3985	4013	4016	4027	4028	4034	4035	4056	4060	4082	4102	4116
	4120	4137	4188	4213	4215	4227	4234	4236	4243	4253	4259	4267	4278	4279	4293	4294	4303	4311	4318
104	4-course rotation	3878	3901	3903	3916	3917	3941	3978	4001	4022	4044	4065	4068	4086	4096	4192	4221	4234	4264
	4274	4276	4280	4287	4298	4304												
105	5-course rotation	3881	3894	3915	3967	3991	3992	3998	4071	4182	4251	4256	4269	4270	4283			
106	6-course rotation	3997	4070	4094	4133	4147	4209	4234										
107	7-course rotation	4089																
108	8-10-course rotation	4163																
110	Wheat	3992	4026	4092	4105	4188	4259											
111	Barley	3906	3966	4003	4082	4266												
112	Oats	4025	4040	4117	4259													

Lancashire contd.

114	Corn yields	3985	4016	4026	4033	4034	4068	4089	4091	4092	4135	4144	4162	4180	4193	4200	4276	4312	
115	Beans	3906	4003	4060	4066	4135													
116	Peas	4060																	
123	Clover	3924	3959	4027	4029	4051	4065	4073	4094	4107	4116	4142	4182	4192	4201	4226	4234	4251	4263	4281	4283
		4298	4307	4318															
126	Tares and vetches			4060	4067														
129	Turnips			4073	4281														
132	Potatoes	3878	3881	3883	3884	3887	3888	3894	3900	3903	3905	3906	3909	3915	3916	3917	3922	3924	3933	3936
		3941	3944	3947	3949	3959	3966	3967	3982	3985	3991	3992	3993	3994	3995	3997	3998	4000	4003	4005	4011	4013
		4016	4022	4023	4026	4029	4034	4035	4040	4044	4052	4055	4056	4060	4062	4065	4067	4068	4071	4073	4080	4082
		4084	4086	4091	4092	4094	4096	4100	4102	4104	4107	4116	4118	4119	4120	4122	4124	4126	4127	4129	4133	4135
		4137	4142	4144	4147	4151	4152	4155	4160	4162	4163	4165	4168	4171	4180	4182	4187	4188	4189	4192	4193	4199
		4200	4201	4202	4208	4209	4210	4213	4218	4219	4220	4220	4221	4225	4226	4227	4235	4236	4243	4244	4245	4251
		4253	4256	4258	4259	4263	4264	4266	4267	4269	4270	4272	4274	4278	4279	4280	4281	4284	4287	4290	4293	4298
		4300	4303	4304	4307	4311	4312	4315	4318											
133	Bare fallows	3978	3991	4135	4165														
134	High farming	3884	3978	4067	4086	4116	4133	4154	4155	4227	4272	4276	4318							
135	Low farming	3887	3919	3922	3944	3992	4001	4003	4011	4022	4025	4096	4107	4136	4165	4187	4269	4281	4284	4287
		4304																	
136	Remarks on the absence of turnips			3978	3982	4016	4070	4082	4105	4119	4187	4266							
139	Good quality pastures	3958	4001	4011	4220	4304													
140	Poor quality pastures		4028	4040	4060														
143	Marsh grassland	3901	3985	4052	4188	4264	4281												
144	Parks	3952	3995	4023	4065	4080													
145	Accommodation land			4011															
146	Cattle breeding		4068	4137	4234	4258													
147	Cattle fattening	3958	3978	4023	4052	4068	4201	4226	4294										
148	Dairying	3881	3883	3884	3888	3894	3902	3933	3947	3958	3966	3967	3972	3991	3993	3995	3997	4013	4016	4052
		4062	4073	4082	4086	4113	4118	4125	4126	4137	4187	4188	4189	4210	4219	4221	4225	4232	4234	4243	4251	4256
		4270	4272	4280	4294															
150	Sheep breeding		3924	3958	4037	4311													
151	Sheep fattening		3958	4137	4294														
153	Horses	3884	3995	3997	4052	4065	4073	4118	4256	4280	4294								
154	Pigs	3881	3884	3958	4037														
156	Poultry	3884																	
157	Rabbits	3995	4005	4118															
158	Deer	3915	3936	3952	4208	4226													
160	Straw	3886	3902	3985	4068	4234													
161	Hay	4065	4068	4127	4137	4144	4188	4234	4251	4267									
162	Manufactured feedstuffs (cake etc.)			3924															
164	Milk	3894	3902	3933	3972	3991	3997	4011	4013	4044	4126	4219	4235	4251						
165	Butter	3883	3902	4011	4044	4137	4251	4294											
166	Cheese	3894	3905	4016	4137	4232	4234	4294											
167	Wool	4016	4207																
169	Good orchards			4266															
172	Market gardens		4126	4307															
174	Cabbages	4094	4307																
175	Carrots	4094	4147	4276															
181	Reeds and oziers	4307																	

Leicestershire

1	Tithe-free district	4350	4352	4361	4362	4366	4373	4374	4379	4380	4387	4391	4392	4393	4394	4398	4407	4413	4415
		4416	4417	4419	4421	4424	4430	4432	4433	4434	4440	4443	4445	4446	4456	4458	4461	4469	4470	4472	4473	4474
		4480	4482	4487	4489	4491	4492	4497	4499	4500	4502	4504	4505	4508	4510	4511	4512	4513	4514	4515	4516	4517
		4519	4524	4525	4527	4528	4529	4530	4531	4533	4534	4538	4549	4553	4556	4557	4563	4565	4569	4570	4574	4576
		4578	4580	4581	4587	4590	4591	4592	4593	4595	4596	4597	4599	4603	4604	4610	4616	4621	4622	4624	4625	4626
		4631	4633	4635	4636	4637	4641	4643	4645	4646	4649	4657	4659	4660	4662	4670	4672	4673	4674	4679	4681	4683
		4684	4685	4689	4692	4696	4697	14833												
2	History of tithe payment		4356	4358	4396	4405	4428	4450	4455	4460	4583								
3	Tithe practices and agriculture		4399	4611															
4	Exemptions from tithe		4282	4353	4375	4378	4381	4383	4385	4386	4389	4390	4405	4410	4426	4431	4439	4441	4448
		4455	4479	4481	4501	4506	4518	4521	4522	4523	4526	4539	4542	4543	4544	4547	4548	4550	4554	4567	4574	4585
		4588	4598	4602	4605	4606	4607	4612	4614	4618	4619	4623	4628	4629	4630	4632	4642	4650	4652	4654	4655	4661
		4663	4666	4667	4669	4676	4682	4688												
5	Tithe in kind	4401	4678																
6	Compositions	4356	4360	4370	4375	4378	4383	4384	4385	4395	4396	4411	4414	4423	4426	4427	4431	4435	4447	4449
		4451	4459	4495	4496	4523	4550	4566	4586	4598	4600	4601	4609	4620	4628	4629	4640	4647	4656	4667	4669	4671
		4682	4686	4687	4691	4694	4698	5453												
7	Moduses	4282	4348	4355	4358	4363	4364	4368	4382	4405	4406	4412	4423	4431	4450	4452	4454	4467	4475	4485
		4494	4542	4544	4546	4547	4566	4571	4577	4579	4582	4585	4594	4605	4609	4620	4623	4627	4629	4652	4658	4661
		4663	4665	4671	4678	4687	4690	4691	4736											
8	Glebe	4356	4396	4437	4447	4455	4457	4460	4463	4506	4526	4584	4607	4617	4618	4620	4623	4629	4642	4643	4654
		4667	4678	4698	4736															
9	Local topographic descriptions		4401	4585	4607	4627													
10	Regional topographic descriptions		4503	4509	4562	4585	4648												
11	Village morphology	4376	4400	4409	4462	4468	4506	4573											
12	Church	4422	4441	4468	4531														
13	Country houses and ornamental gardens		4476	4639	4675														
14	Farm houses and buildings		4460	4607	4613														
15	Cottages and cottage gardens		4376	4409	4462	4468	4477	4501	4506	4555	4573	4613	4639	4675					
16	Field boundaries	4400	4428	4488	4488														
17	Open fields	4388																	
18	Small, irregular closes	4400	4462																
19	Large, regular fields	4639																	
20	Hedgerow timber	4488																	
22	Plantations	4376	4477	4555	4573	4639	4675												
23	Woodland management	4639																	
25	Poor woodland	4409	4429	4555															
26	Commons	4551																	
27	Furze, gorse and heathlands	4585																	
34	Land requires drainage	4428	4436	4506	4551	4677	4693												
36	Productive soil	4371	4395	4400	4409	4476	4503	4506	4532	4555	4585	4627	4648	4677					
37	Poor soil	4400	4428	4465	4467	4501	4506	4555	4585	4611									

Leicestershire contd.

38	Heavy (clay) soil	4348	4376	4399	4400	4401	4422	4428	4429	4436	4462	4465	4467	4476	4477	4488	4501	4503	4506
	4509	4555	4561	4562	4585	4607	4611	4613	4615	4627	4634	4644	4648	4651	4664	4675	4699		
39	Loamy (turnip) soil		4359	4452	4462	4488	4501	4506	4555	4627	4675	4699							
40	Light soil	4409																	
41	Several varieties of soil			4468	4488	4506	4585												
43	Sand or gravel		4399	4400	4476	4488	4503	4506	4561	4562	4585	4611	4615	4634	4648	4664			
44	Peat	4585	4693																
45	Fields remote from farms			4428	4501														
46	Good local roads		4400	4462	4476	4501	4615	4648	4675										
47	Poor local roads		4401	4422	4532	4634													
48	Turnpike and main roads		4429	4465	4555	4562	4573	4615	4651										
51	Canals	4465	4627																
52	Railways	4506																	
53	Markets accessible		4400	4465	4501	4555	4651	4675											
55	Provincial markets		4399	4488	4611	4664	4677												
56	London market	4664																	
59	Landowners and their estates			4359	4406	4428	4468	4476	4639										
60	Land occupiers		4428	4503	4506	4573	4627	4634											
61	Farm size	4409	4585	4639															
62	Leases	4638																	
64	Common grazing	4388	4468																
66	Rents	4348	4388	4422	4428	4436	4503	4585	4651	4664									
71	Enclosure of commons	4693																	
72	Enclosure of open fields	4381	4386	4444	4475	4501	4520	4521	4539	4546	4551	4554	4600	4608	4614				
75	Conversion of grass to arable		4429	4467	4611														
82	Drainage channels and ditches		4634																
85	Underdrainage		4460	4555	4613	4634													
89	Lime	4648																	
101	General comments on crop rotations			4503	4648														
102	Irregular rotations	4376	4422	4428	4436	4468	4532	4562	4693										
103	3-course rotation	4532	4551	4644	4690	4699													
104	4-course rotation	4399	4401	4462	4467	4476	4488	4561	4573	4611	4613	4615	4627	4648	4651	4664	4675	4677	4699
105	5-course rotation	4395	4648	4651	4693														
106	6-course rotation	4371	4400	4409	4428	4465	4501	4503	4506	4509	4585	4634	4675						
107	7-course rotation	4585																	
108	8-10-course rotation	4562																	
109	More than 10-course rotation		4648																
110	Wheat	4677																	
113	Rye or meslin	4648																	
114	Corn yields	4396	4532	4607	4677	4690	4693												
115	Beans	4428	4467	4509	4551	4573	4644	4651	4664										
118	Coleseed	4677																	
123	Clover	4551																	
126	Tares and vetches	4644																	
129	Turnips	4399	4400	4409	4428	4462	4465	4476	4488	4501	4503	4509	4555	4561	4562	4613	4615	4627	4634	4648
	4675	4677	4693																
133	Bare fallows	4400	4401	4428	4467	4501	4509	4551	4555	4562	4573	4585	4613	4627	4634	4644	4664	4675	4677	4690
	4693																		
134	High farming	4376	4477	4488	4555	4573													
135	Low farming	4376	4428	4436	4615	4677													
136	Remarks on the absence of turnips		4460	4573	4607	4611													
139	Good quality pastures	4348	4359	4376	4388	4409	4422	4428	4429	4501	4506	4532	4555	4573	4613	4639	4651	4675	
	4699																		
140	Poor quality pastures	4359	4428	4429	4460	4467	4468	4477	4501	4506	4555	4573	4585	4607	4613	4639	4675	4699	
141	Meadows	4371	4422	4428	4429	4457	4551	4675											
142	Irrigation and water meadows		4501	4506															
144	Parks	4409	4477																
145	Accommodation land		4555	4651															
146	Cattle breeding	4348	4428	4465	4468	4488	4613	4627	4639	4648									
147	Cattle fattening	4348	4388	4399	4422	4428	4462	4476	4483	4561	4585	4611	4613	4615	4648	4664	4699		
148	Dairying	4376	4388	4409	4422	4428	4429	4465	4476	4501	4506	4561	4585	4627	4634	4648			
150	Sheep breeding	4348	4401	4428	4465	4468	4476	4488	4503	4506	4613	4615	4627	4639	4648	4699			
151	Sheep fattening	4348	4388	4400	4462	4476	4488	4503	4585	4611	4613	4615	4639	4648	4699				
153	Horses	4651																	
154	Pigs	4462	4468	4573															
155	Oxen	4699																	
156	Poultry		4462	4468	4573														
159	Animal diseases	4467																	
160	Straw	4422	4465	4607	4615														
161	Hay	4388	4462	4465	4573	4634	4651	4677	4690	4699									
166	Cheese	4388	4400	4436	4503	4615													
169	Good orchards		4409	4462	4501	4506	4555												
170	Poor orchards		4468																

Lincolnshire

1	Tithe-free district	4404	4703	4705	4709	4714	4715	4718	4724	4726	4733	4735	4737	4738	4739	4741	4744	4745	4746
	4754	4755	4756	4758	4761	4765	4766	4767	4771	4774	4775	4778	4783	4792	4795	4797	4809	4813	4814	4815	4821
	4822	4824	4825	4832	4833	4834	4839	4850	4860	4861	4865	4866	4867	4868	4870	4871	4875	4876	4877	4878	4881
	4884	4885	4886	4889	4890	4894	4897	4898	4911	4912	4914	4918	4919	4924	4925	4926	4927	4928	4931	4933	4934
	4936	4942	4943	4944	4946	4948	4949	4954	4958	4960	4961	4963	4967	4971	4978	4984	4987	4989	4991	4994	4998
	4999	5002	5005	5007	5008	5010	5012	5013	5014	5016	5019	5026	5028	5048	5052	5053	5062	5064	5066	5067	5068
	5074	5075	5076	5080	5086	5087	5089	5091	5093	5097	5101	5102	5106	5110	5111	5112	5114	5117	5127	5128	5133
	5135	5136	5140	5143	5144	5148	5149	5150	5151	5152	5154	5157	5160	5163	5168	5169	5172	5175	5177	5179	5180
	5181	5186	5187	5189	5190	5192	5193	5196	5198	5201	5203	5208	5210	5212	5214	5216	5220	5221	5222	5227	5232
	5233	5237	5238	5239	5241	5246	5247	5250	5252	5257	5258	5259	5260	5262	5263	5264	5265	5268	5271	5276	5279
	5281	5282	5283	5285	5288	5293	5302	5305	5312	5316	5322	5324	5325	5326	5328	5329	5331	5334	5339
	5340	5347	5352	5354	5360	5363	5366	5373	5378	5379	5380	5383	5384	5386	5389	5391	5394	5395	5396	5398	5402
	5404	5405	5407	5409	5411	5414	5415	5416	5419	5421	5423	5425	5432	5437	5441	5443	5451				
2	History of tithe payment		4734	4743	4753	4828	4837	4844	4945	4957	4974	4986	5001	5017	5025	5070	5073	5125	5131
	5197	5234	5309	5318	5320	5375	5418	5447													
3	Tithe practices and agriculture		4716	4835	5146	5243	5254	5256	5284	5313									
4	Exemptions from tithe		4702	4704	4706	4707	4708	4711	4713	4719	4720	4721	4730	4731	4734	4743	4749	4750	4752
	4757	4760	4763	4764	4768	4776	4777	4779	4781	4782	4789	4791	4798	4806	4812	4817	4826	4828	4829	4843	4848

Lincolnshire contd.

```
       4849 4852 4853 4856 4857 4858 4859 4888 4892 4899 4904 4909 4910 4922 4923 4935 4950 4955 4956 4964 4976
       4986 4988 4990 4996 5003 5021 5022 5033 5034 5038 5044 5045 5046 5047 5049 5050 5054 5056 5057 5085 5092
       5094 5098 5099 5100 5103 5118 5129 5131 5132 5134 5141 5142 5145 5147 5156 5166 5173 5191 5194 5197 5200
       5205 5213 5215 5240 5248 5253 5261 5269 5289 5291 5292 5294 5299 5307 5308 5313 5314 5327 5337 5338 5341
       5344 5353 5356 5357 5359 5369 5370 5371 5377 5393 5399 5406 5413 5418 5420 5424 5427 5428 5429 5436 5445
       5446
 5  Tithe in kind       4700 4803 4843 4848 4849 4851 4863 4915 4974 5043 5058 5121 5138 5199 5200 5202 5266 5284 5298
       5304 5317 5359 5408 5438 5452
 6  Compositions        4700 4704 4711 4712 4717 4719 4720 4743 4747 4752 4762 4768 4784 4788 4798 4805 4806 4807 4816
       4818 4820 4829 4831 4836 4847 4862 4864 4873 4891 4900 4903 4906 4908 4937 4951 4953 4956 4959 4964 4980
       4986 4993 4997 5017 5020 5021 5027 5040 5051 5055 5058 5071 5082 5083 5084 5090 5108 5113 5118 5120 5125
       5153 5164 5183 5185 5188 5199 5202 5223 5234 5236 5266 5272 5280 5295 5306 5309 5310 5314 5317 5345 5350
       5353 5359 5364 5365 5368 5410 5420 5435 5439 5445 5449
 7  Moduses             4402 4716 4725 4740 4752 4762 4793 4803 4807 4812 4817 4818 4819 4820 4827 4844 4854 4856 4887
       4893 4896 4906 4915 4916 4938 4956 4957 4969 4981 4986 5017 5027 5037 5042 5043 5045 5061 5063 5082
       5104 5125 5153 5164 5173 5182 5211 5231 5254 5270 5272 5278 5298 5310 5317 5318 5320 5332 5345 5351 5365
       5375 5392 5400 5418 5430 5433 5438 5448
 8  Glebe       4712 4796 4800 4816 4817 4818 4836 4957 4966 5017 5029 5112 5123 5139 5164
 9  Local topographic descriptions      4402 4701 4941 5039 5041 5096 5161 5256 5315 5358 5426
10  Regional topographic descriptions   4729 4801 4854 4858 4891 4901 4920 4966 5065 5072 5096 5108 5109 5124 5176 5202
       5205 5273 5274 5296 5300 5315 5318 5320 5321 5330 5348 5358 5452
11  Village morphology  4742 4790 4810 4858 4872 4905 4907 5024 5065 5218 5254 5298 5313 5315 5330 5346 5348 5426
12  Church      4748 4838 4966 5180 5304 5400
13  Country houses and ornamental gardens  4751 4751 4804 4880 4883 4905 4966 5043 5077 5209 5229 5270 5311 5313 5330
       5400
14  Farm houses and buildings   4748 4810 4872 4907 5024 5065 5301 5315
15  Cottages and cottage gardens        4701 4702 4728 4728 4742 4790 4810 4851 4852 4872 4880 4893 4902 4905 4907 4907
       4979 5024 5043 5065 5065 5085 5146 5171 5209 5229 5270 5284 5311 5330 5342 5361 5392 5426 5433 5452
16  Field boundaries    5039 5161 5273
17  Open fields 4701 4851 4852 5006 5109 5116 5202 5243 5278 5284 5291 5345 5422 5433
19  Large, regular fields       4917 5025 5251
20  Hedgerow timber     4769 5138
21  Coppice     4701 4892 4982 5243 5311 5349 5367 5400
22  Plantations 4701 4747 4751 4790 4843 4869 4872 4880 4882 4883 4902 4966 4979 4980 5000 5023 5024 5065 5077
       5085 5162 5174 5209 5229 5270 5313 5330 5346 5367 5400 5426
23  Woodland management 4982 5095
24  Productive woodland 4804 4982 5077 5124 5349 5433
25  Poor woodland       4701 4787 4810 4843 4851 4902 4905 5043 5095 5146 5162 5270 5361 5377 5403 5452
26  Commons     4851 4851 4852 4930 4930 4952 5024 5096 5243 5284
27  Furze, gorse and heathlands 4732 4851 4852 4902 4921 4938 4952 5023 5095 5124 5171 5205 5349 5392 5403 5452
28  Moorland    5023 5300 5349 5361 5392
30  Fens        4713 4799 4826 4854 4857 4882 4892 4915 4920 4929 4941 5109 5217 5224 5225 5230 5318 5320 5321 5335
       5358 5376 5397 5401
31  Wasteland   4852 4864
32  Climatic hazards    4938 4939 4940 5109 5161 5218 5346 5348 5361 5387
33  Excessively steep land      4872 5392
34  Land requires drainage      4701 4722 4723 4728 4748 4786 4801 4810 4838 4851 4852 4854 4858 4882 4888 4915 4930
       4939 4968 5023 5024 5043 5077 5078 5082 5088 5124 5146 5167 5171 5205 5243 5244 5278 5284 5335 5358 5359
       5361 5387 5426
35  Land liable to flood        4799 4891 4905 4930 4937 5042 5085 5161 5235 5273 5275 5298 5377 5433
36  Productive soil     4402 4702 4724 4732 4751 4770 4780 4830 4845 4848 4851 4864 4869 4872 4892 4901 4902
       4940 4941 4945 4968 4985 4990 5017 5039 5072 5077 5082 5205 5218 5230 5243 5254 5255 5256 5274 5284 5291
       5318 5330 5342 5343 5346 5388 5399 5401 5403 5422
37  Poor soil   4403 4728 4731 4751 4804 4838 4841 4854 4858 4863 4869 4872 4879 4883 4888 4893 4916 4917 4938
       4945 4966 4968 4995 5000 5023 5024 5030 5042 5043 5082 5085 5088 5096 5146 5170 5204 5218 5235 5243 5245
       5251 5254 5267 5270 5278 5318 5346 5348 5349 5358 5361 5367 5387 5403 5431 5438 5452
38  Heavy (clay) soil   4403 4711 4722 4723 4742 4751 4759 4760 4780 4786 4790 4799 4808 4820 4823 4826 4827
       4835 4838 4840 4841 4845 4846 4848 4849 4852 4854 4858 4863 4879 4880 4891 4892 4893 4902 4905 4907 4915 4916
       4917 4930 4937 4938 4939 4940 4945 4952 4966 4968 4982 4985 4992 4995 5000 5006 5022 5023 5025 5030 5039
       5041 5042 5060 5072 5078 5082 5083 5088 5090 5095 5096 5109 5116 5124 5138 5146 5161 5162 5170 5171 5176
       5178 5195 5204 5205 5206 5217 5235 5243 5244 5249 5251 5254 5255 5256 5267 5270 5275 5289 5291 5298 5301
       5304 5311 5313 5319 5335 5343 5346 5349 5361 5376 5385 5387 5388 5399 5400 5431 5433 5438 5452
39  Loamy (turnip) soil 4403 4711 4722 4723 4728 4751 4770 4799 4804 4808 4820 4823 4843 4852 4879 4880 4892 4905 4907
       4921 4941 4945 4990 5023 5024 5043 5060 5077 5096 5171 5202 5206 5209 5217 5243 5249 5275 5296 5311 5346
       5348 5361 5385 5400 5401 5403 5426 5429
40  Light soil  4723 4729 4751 4770 4840 4841 4864 4869 4891 4979 5082 5116 5176 5204 5218 5230 5245 5251 5255
       5274 5291 5399 5433
41  Several varieties of soil   4787 4841 4854 4863 4879 4891 4905 4907 4929 5043 5078 5085 5088 5161 5171 5205 5243
       5244 5311 5313 5359 5392 5399
42  Chalk       4759 4835 4902 4940 4982 4985 5065 5072 5077 5146 5167 5174 5195 5300 5315
43  Sand or gravel      4723 4731 4759 4787 4790 4840 4838 4840 4841 4845 4845 4879 4882 4891 4905 4917 4921 4937 4941
       4992 5000 5025 5072 5082 5088 5090 5095 5096 5124 5162 5167 5170 5171 5178 5204 5205 5209 5218 5229 5235
       5243 5245 5251 5254 5255 5291 5300 5311 5318 5346 5349 5358 5361 5387 5392
44  Peat        4706 4759 4883 5082 5204 5217 5229 5300 5385 5433
45  Fields remote from farms    4845 4920 5433
46  Good local roads    4751 4790 4801 4840 4845 4854 4880 4945 4952 4966 4982 5039 5077 5116 5124 5161 5178 5195
       5209 5224 5235 5251 5267 5347 5357
47  Poor local roads    4727 4742 4799 4810 4838 4845 4854 4893 4917 4920 4940 4941 5030 5096 5146 5205 5225 5243
       5251 5304 5315 5385
48  Turnpike and main roads     4722 4907 4920 4952 4982 5022 5024 5095 5205 5251 5376
50  Water carriage      4845 5349 5358
51  Canals      5397
53  Markets accessible  4751 4790 4921 4952 4966 5039 5230 5311 5358
54  Markets inaccessible        4742
55  Provincial markets  4702 4845 4880 5024 5251 5349
57  Fairs       4804
58  Market prices       4794 5346 5439
59  Landowners and their estates        4748 4787 4799 4804 4846 4847 4869 4879 4880 4902 4907 4917 4938 4982 4982 5023
       5023 5025 5085 5095 5095 5146 5209 5209 5275 5311 5313 5315 5330 5348 5392 5400 5400 5426
60  Land occupiers      4403 4810 4838 4841 4848 4869 4872 4891 4893 4902 4982 5077 5095 5109 5146 5422 5426
61  Farm size   4863 4872 4907 4917 5025 5146 5161 5235 5251 5348 5359
62  Leases      4846 4848 5315
63  Farm implements     4938 4941 5025
64  Common grazing      4930 5243 5284 5291
65  Lammas and other common rights      4851 4852 5284 5291 5403
```

Lincolnshire contd.

66	Rents	4403	4723	4731	4759	4769	4770	4826	4827	4830	4835	4841	4863	4869	4879	4891	4892	4920	4930	4938	4941
		4968	4990	5049	5078	5090	5138	5146	5178	5217	5230	5249	5291	5301	5319	5335	5359	5385	5387	5399	5446
67	Urban influences on value of land				4701																
68	Rates 5350 5364																				
69	Farm labour and wages 4872																				
70	Enclosure or improvement of waste				4732	4869	4883	4902	4904	5109	5113	5139	5145	5171	5300	5325	5335	5361	5392		
	5397 5403																				
71	Enclosure of commons			4887	4904	4937	5023	5042	5094	5129	5221	5318	5325	5434							
72	Enclosure of open fields		4701	4728	4751	4763	4781	4783	4835	4848	4853	4858	4954	5002	5036	5053	5073	5087	5091		
	5098	5109	5110	5122	5160	5173	5226	5227	5237	5241	5273	5289	5298	5369	5370	5371	5379	5418	5419	5420	
75	Conversion of grass to arable		4700	4810	4816	4823	4891	4907	4915	4930	4940	5030	5042	5090	5096	5109	5161	5205			
	5254 5349 5452																				
76	Conversion of arable to pasture		4880	5330																	
78	Warping 5243 5397																				
80	Reclaiming and embanking	4706	4759	4799	4845	4846	4929	4941	5039	5145	5180	5318	5320	5335	5397	5401					
81	Marsh drainage	4706	4711	4713	4799	4854	4915	4929	5060	5109	5204	5217	5229	5342	5358	5376	5392	5428	5446		
82	Drainage channels and ditches	4402	4706	4787	4799	4845	4345	4854	5025	5060	5171	5446									
85	Underdrainage	4700	4787	4801	4810	4820	4838	4847	4891	4937	4938	4939	4966	5006	5023	5030	5090	5095	5096		
	5109	5116	5146	5161	5176	5251	5275	5298	5313	5335	5359	5367	5399	5426	5431	5452					
87	Marl	4706	4804	5023	5025	5095	5204	5229	5367	5392											
88	Chalk	4835	4901	4902	5025																
89	Lime	4810	5023																		
92	Dung	4917																			
95	Bones	4700	4701	4788	4804	4810	4835	4872	4902	4940	5023	5025	5065	5077	5209	5330	5348	5367	5426		
100	Oil dust, unspecified fertilisers or manures				4751	4869	4891														
101	General comments on crop rotations		4706	4769	4799	4845	4848	4891	4920	5041	5072	5082	5109	5167	5226	5298	5301				
	5304	5318	5330	5385	5387	5422	5431														
102	Irregular rotations	4879	5082	5095	5235	5256															
103	3-course rotation	4402	4403	4701	4748	4780	4786	4801	4826	4827	4835	4849	4851	4854	4888	4892	4915	4920	4921		
	4938	4939	4945	5025	5041	5109	5116	5176	5224	5225	5273	5289	5291	5296	5298	5301	5319	5343	5349	5358	5376
	5387	5388	5399	5431																	
104	4-course rotation	4402	4403	4701	4722	4723	4728	4731	4732	4742	4748	4751	4759	4770	4786	4787	4799	4801	4808		
	4826	4835	4838	4840	4841	4843	4845	4846	4848	4849	4852	4854	4863	4872	4880	4882	4892	4893	4905	4907	4915
	4920	4939	4940	4941	4945	4952	4966	4968	4982	4995	5006	5024	5025	5030	5041	5060	5065	5077	5078	5082	5083
	5088	5090	5095	5096	5109	5116	5138	5146	5161	5162	5167	5170	5176	5178	5195	5206	5209	5217	5218	5229	5235
	5249	5251	5267	5275	5284	5296	5300	5304	5315	5318	5330	5335	5345	5346	5349	5358	5367	5376	5388	5392	5397
	5399	5400	5426	5433																	
105	5-course rotation	4723	4727	4804	4830	4841	4863	4869	4882	4901	4929	4990	4992	5000	5024	5041	5088	5124	5174		
	5209	5217	5229	5230	5245	5330	5335	5348	5358	5403											
106	6-course rotation	4921																			
110	Wheat 5330 5349																				
111	Barley 5095 5209 5349																				
112	Oats 5387																				
113	Rye or meslin		4801	4843	4921	5085	5095	5171	5235	5243	5349	5361	5403								
114	Corn yields	4403	4768	4790	4803	4938	4986	5040	5041	5055	5090	5230	5284	5298	5387	5399	5401				
115	Beans	4403	4722	4768	4770	4780	4804	4823	4845	4848	4849	4851	4852	4854	4863	4891	4907	4915	4920		
	4937	4938	4939	4966	4968	4992	5006	5025	5030	5041	5042	5082	5083	5088	5109	5116	5138	5146	5161	5205	5217
	5243	5249	5254	5273	5275	5291	5296	5298	5301	5311	5320	5321	5343	5346	5358	5359	5376	5385	5399	5401	5422
	5452																				
116	Peas	4731	4863	4937	4990	4992	5116	5284	5346	5359											
117	Rape	4826	4920	5109	5318	5319	5376	5385													
118	Coleseed	4845	4854	4864	4882	4888	4892	4905	4915	4920	4941	4941	5171	5224	5225	5226	5318	5320	5320	5321	
	5321	5358	5376	5397	5401	5401															
122	Unspecified grass seeds		4830	5006	5161	5346															
123	Clover	4403	4722	4786	4804	4808	4830	4849	4852	4863	4864	4907	4915	4941	4990	5006	5041	5060	5077	5083	5096
	5138	5161	5162	5178	5202	5205	5206	5217	5243	5284	5298	5311	5318	5320	5321	5346	5359	5399	5426		
126	Tares and vetches		4722	4830	4864	4941	4990	5096	5359	5385											
129	Turnips	4402	4403	4727	4728	4729	4731	4742	4751	4770	4786	4787	4790	4799	4804	4820	4823	4830	4835	4838	
	4840	4845	4848	4849	4854	4863	4864	4869	4879	4882	4891	4892	4901	4902	4905	4907	4915	4920	4921	4929	4937
	4940	4941	4945	4952	4966	4968	4982	4985	4990	4992	5000	5023	5024	5025	5041	5042	5060	5065	5072	5077	5078
	5082	5083	5085	5088	5090	5095	5096	5109	5116	5124	5138	5146	5161	5162	5167	5170	5171	5174	5176	5178	5195
	5205	5206	5217	5224	5225	5229	5230	5235	5243	5245	5249	5251	5254	5270	5273	5274	5275	5289	5300	5304	5311
	5318	5319	5320	5321	5330	5335	5346	5348	5349	5358	5359	5367	5385	5387	5392	5397	5399	5401	5403	5422	5426
	5433																				
130	Mangolds	4941																			
131	Swedes	5320	5321																		
132	Potatoes	4702	4706	4851	4852	4864	4891	4920	4941	4968	5030	5039	5042	5082	5095	5138	5243	5298	5318	5320	
	5321	5359	5452																		
133	Bare fallows	4402	4403	4722	4728	4751	4768	4786	4801	4808	4820	4823	4827	4835	4845	4848	4851	4852	4863	4888	
	4891	4892	4907	4915	4945	4952	4966	4968	4995	5006	5023	5025	5030	5039	5041	5042	5060	5085	5088	5090	5096
	5109	5116	5138	5146	5161	5162	5167	5170	5178	5202	5205	5217	5235	5249	5251	5267	5273	5275	5284	5291	5296	5298
	5301	5304	5311	5335	5342	5343	5349	5358	5367	5376	5387	5388	5399	5422	5431	5438	5452				
134	High farming	4701	4723	4820	4830	4880	4901	4902	4917	4979	5017	5055	5065	5077	5095	5161	5209	5218	5313	5330	
	5348	5392	5399	5400																	
135	Low farming	4731	4801	4843	4852	4939	4940	5082	5124	5146	5244	5301	5315	5359	5388	5438					
136	Remarks on the absence of turnips				5202	5291															
137	Remarks on pests and crop diseases			4787	4838	5349	5433														
138	Recent increase in productivity		5204	5330	5335	5426	5433														
139	Good quality pastures		4402	4701	4706	4732	4742	4751	4770	4780	4790	4804	4810	4823	4830	4840	4846	4854	4880		
	4891	4892	4905	4907	4920	4921	4929	4941	5000	5039	5041	5065	5072	5077	5083	5085	5116	5161	5170	5206	5209
	5217	5218	5224	5225	5244	5289	5319	5335	5342	5343	5361	5392	5397	5422	5426	5433	5446				
140	Poor quality pastures		4701	4728	4732	4742	4751	4810	4823	4851	4852	4858	4893	4902	4905	4907	4917	4920	4921		
	4930	4938	4940	4945	4952	5023	5024	5030	5065	5085	5109	5146	5161	5162	5170	5205	5209	5229	5243	5244	5270
	5284	5289	5298	5311	5315	5330	5348	5361	5367	5426	5429	5433	5438	5452							
141	Meadows	4701	4732	4751	4790	4810	4840	4851	4880	4891	4893	4905	4930	5085	5162	5167	5205	5226	5230	5275	
	5284	5298	5342	5346	5348	5361	5367	5377	5422	5429	5433										
142	Irrigation and water meadows			5330																	
143	Marsh grassland		4708	4849	4854	4864	4915	4929	4937	4939	4941	5006	5039	5226	5254	5273	5289	5319	5320	5342	
	5397	5446																			
144	Parks	4751	4880	4905	4966	5043	5204	5209	5313	5400											
145	Accommodation land		4846	5000																	
146	Cattle breeding		4759	4801	4838	4840	4845	4863	4882	4891	4917	4930	4945	4952	4966	4982	4995	5006	5022	5060	
	5078	5083	5088	5090	5095	5096	5109	5124	5170	5178	5226	5249	5251	5267	5289	5304	5315	5318	5348	5349	5358
	5359	5401																			
147	Cattle fattening		4706	4723	4729	4748	4826	4840	4845	4854	4864	4917	4929	4941	4945	5083	5124	5178	5226	5251	

Lincolnshire contd.

```
         5275  5318  5359  5399  5401  5422
148  Dairying          4723  4748  4801  4827  4841  4863  4891  4930  4966  5000  5022  5078  5090  5109  5162  5235  5249  5349
150  Sheep breeding          4723  4727  4729  4748  4759  4801  4804  4808  4827  4838  4840  4841  4845  4863  4869  4882  4891  4917
     4930  4945  4952  4966  4982  4995  5006  5025  5060  5072  5078  5083  5088  5090  5095  5096  5109  5124  5162  5170  5174
     5195  5202  5204  5206  5217  5226  5243  5249  5251  5267  5274  5275  5289  5296  5304  5346  5348  5358  5387  5388  5399
     5401
151  Sheep fattening          4706  4840  4845  4854  4864  4929  4941  4945  5025  5162  5225  5226  5318  5422
153  Horses  4748  4827  4852  4917  4995  5078  5348
154  Pigs    4852  4979
155  Oxen    4748  5320  5321  5349
156  Poultry       4702  4851  4852  4979  5243
157  Rabbits       5023  5171  5218  5243
158  Deer    4732
159  Animal diseases       4786  4787  4838  4930  4938  4995  5006  5162  5170  5278  5304  5387
160  Straw   4941
161  Hay     4732  4790  4845  4851  4939  5000  5042  5116  5146  5230  5298  5311  5346  5348  5367  5377  5387  5426  5433
162  Manufactured feedstuffs (cake etc.)    4872  4917
165  Butter  5162  5315
167  Wool    5256  5388
169  Good orchards       4701  4790  4851  5243  5311  5392  5433
170  Poor orchards       4742
172  Market gardens      4907  5429
174  Cabbages      4941
175  Carrots       4864
176  Onions        4702
179  Flax and hemp       4941
```

Middlesex

```
1    Tithe-free district       5470  5473  5476  5477  5478  5496  5499  5501  5504  5515  5529  5532  5534  5547  5548  5554
4    Exemptions from tithe     5471  5475  5481  5482  5491  5493  5494  5503  5505  5506  5508  5513  5524  5536  5538  5542  5543
5    Tithe in kind  5454  5487  5502  5549
6    Compositions   5454  5459  5460  5466  5467  5475  5481  5482  5488  5489  5490  5497  5524  5527  5530  5538  5544  5545  5546
     5549  5550
7    Moduses        5479  5505  5508  5513  5528  5533  5544  5546
8    Glebe    5459  5481  5516
9    Local topographic descriptions       5493
10   Regional topographic descriptions    5474  5512  5541
11   Village morphology     5493
12   Church         5472  5506  5507  5541  5543
13   Country houses and ornamental gardens   5472  5472  5474  5493
17   Open fields    5543
19   Large, regular fields    5542
20   Hedgerow timber          5498
21   Coppice        5507
22   Plantations    5472  5542
25   Poor woodland  5540
27   Furze, gorse and heathlands   5493
32   Climatic hazards         5457  5474  5479  5512
36   Productive soil          5472  5498  5507
37   Poor soil      5457  5540
38   Heavy (clay) soil        5474  5479  5487  5502  5506  5525  5540  5541
39   Loamy (turnip) soil      5498  5512
40   Light soil     5457  5472  5512  5542
43   Sand or gravel           5474  5479  5493  5512  5525  5543
46   Good local roads         5506  5540
47   Poor local roads         5525
51   Canals  5472  5525
52   Railways       5498
53   Markets accessible       5454  5457  5474  5512
56   London market            5479  5502  5506  5512  5540
58   Market prices            5474  5541  5542
59   Landowners and their estates   5472  5506
60   Land occupiers           5506
61   Farm size      5506  5507  5543
63   Farm implements          5525
67   Urban influences on value of land   5512
68   Rates   5506  5507  5543
70   Enclosure or improvement of waste   5525
71   Enclosure of commons     5493
72   Enclosure of open fields 5459  5494  5496  5503  5525  5554
76   Conversion of arable to pasture    5525
82   Drainage channels and ditches      5525
92   Dung    5457  5472  5474  5479  5506  5512  5525  5525  5540  5541
101  General comments on crop rotations  5457  5463  5479  5512  5541
102  Irregular rotations      5457  5474
103  3-course rotation        5472  5525
104  4-course rotation        5487  5507  5543
110  Wheat   5472
113  Rye or meslin   5512  5541
114  Corn yields    5516
115  Beans   5472  5487  5502  5512  5525  5540  5541  5543
116  Peas    5457  5472  5474  5542  5543
123  Clover  5463  5472  5474  5487  5498  5502  5507  5516  5525  5542  5543
126  Tares and vetches  5474  5479  5487  5502  5512  5525  5540  5541
129  Turnips        5457  5474  5479  5507  5512  5542  5543
131  Swedes         5512
132  Potatoes       5472  5474  5512  5541
133  Bare fallows   5512  5525  5540  5541  5543
134  High farming   5472
139  Good quality pastures    5463  5487  5498  5507  5512  5525  5540  5541
140  Poor quality pastures    5472
141  Meadows        5472  5487  5493  5498  5507  5516  5525
144  Parks   5472  5474  5540
```

Middlesex contd.

145	Accommodation land		5463										
151	Sheep fattening		5525										
153	Horses	5512											
158	Deer	5472											
161	Hay	5454	5457	5472	5474	5487	5493	5502	5506	5512	5525	5540	5541	5542
162	Manufactured feedstuffs (cake etc.)					5512	5541						
169	Good orchards		5498	5542									
172	Market gardens		5454	5463	5464	5474	5487	5507	5543				
174	Cabbages		5512										
181	Reeds and oziers		5463	5474	5543								

Monmouthshire

1	Tithe-free district	5572	5585	5591	5656	5690															
2	History of tithe payment		5578																		
4	Exemptions from tithe		5555	5556	5558	5559	5571	5574	5580	5614	5626	5643	5644	5645	5657	5659	5665	5667	5683		
	5685	5687	5689	5692																	
5	Tithe in kind	5565	5570	5581	5612	5654	5694														
6	Compositions	5555	5563	5573	5575	5577	5583	5586	5587	5588	5590	5595	5601	5606	5610	5615	5617	5626	5627	5629	
	5630	5648	5650	5654	5657	5663	5667	5668	5682	5684	5686	5687	5689	5693	5694						
7	Moduses	5555	5558	5563	5565	5566	5568	5569	5574	5575	5583	5586	5600	5614	5619	5624	5625	5629	5632	5635	
	5650	5651	5652	5653	5659	5667	5670	5673	5675	5680	5683	5697									
8	Glebe	5563	5565	5611	5617	5629	5654	5667	5682												
10	Regional topographic descriptions				5642																
12	Church	5617																			
20	Hedgerow timber	5557	5559	5560	5562	5564	5566	5567	5568	5569	5571	5574	5576	5579	5582	5583	5584	5586	5589		
	5593	5598	5599	5604	5608	5609	5614	5616	5618	5619	5620	5622	5623	5624	5625	5626	5628	5631	5632	5633	5635
	5636	5638	5640	5641	5642	5643	5645	5646	5647	5649	5651	5655	5659	5660	5662	5665	5666	5669	5670	5671	5674
	5679	5680	5682	5688	5691	5692	5695	5696	5698	14586											
21	Coppice	5569	5577	5586	5594	5596	5610	5611	5626	5627	5630	5642	5644	5653	5663						
24	Productive woodland		5624	5666	5671																
25	Poor woodland	5569	5622	5651																	
26	Commons	5618	5682																		
31	Wasteland	5608																			
32	Climatic hazards	5569																			
34	Land requires drainage	5568	5569	5622	5642	5682	5688	5696													
36	Productive soil	5586	5628	5631	5679	5680	5688	5691	5692												
37	Poor soil	5557	5568	5569	5584	5586	5618	5666	5671	5696											
38	Heavy (clay) soil	5557	5559	5562	5564	5566	5567	5568	5569	5571	5574	5576	5582	5583	5584	5586	5588	5589	5598		
	5604	5608	5614	5616	5619	5622	5624	5625	5628	5631	5632	5635	5636	5640	5642	5643	5645	5646	5649		
	5651	5655	5659	5666	5669	5670	5680	5682	5688	5692	5695	5696	5698	14586							
39	Loamy (turnip) soil	5562	5586	5620	5631	5635	5636	5638	5641	5655	5666	5671	5679	5680	5691	5692					
40	Light soil	5564	5569	5574	5576	5584	5593	5603	5609	5618	5620	5622	5623	5628	5638	5642	5646	5649	5660	5662	
	5665	5679	5682																		
41	Several varieties of soil		5586	5646	5688	14586															
43	Sand or gravel	5559	5560	5564	5567	5569	5574	5576	5579	5586	5589	5593	5599	5618	5619	5622	5624	5625	5628		
	5632	5633	5636	5638	5641	5643	5647	5651	5660	5666	5674	5679	5688	5698							
44	Peat	5560																			
47	Poor local roads	5564																			
48	Turnpike and main roads	5570																			
53	Markets accessible	5611	5620																		
58	Market prices	5564	5601	5612																	
59	Landowners and their estates		5579																		
60	Land occupiers	5579																			
61	Farm size	5584	5646	5649																	
66	Rents	5569	5597	5642																	
67	Urban influences on value of land	5642																			
68	Rates	5564																			
70	Enclosure or improvement of waste	5603																			
71	Enclosure of commons	5682																			
100	Oil dust, unspecified fertilisers or manures		5658																		
101	General comments on crop rotations	5557	5562	5564	5566	5568	5571	5583	5593	5598	5599	5604	5608	5609	5614	5616					
	5618	5619	5620	5622	5623	5624	5628	5636	5641	5647	5651	5655	5659	5660	5662	5670	5672	5682	5692	5698	
103	3-course rotation	5597	5640	5649	5669																
104	4-course rotation	5569	5603	5625	5629	5630	5632	5633	5636	5638	5643	5645	5665	5666	5671	5675	5679	5688	5691		
	5695	5696																			
105	5-course rotation	5567	5569	5576	5631	5646	5649	5665	5666	5671	5680										
106	6-course rotation	5559	5567	5574	5579	5586	5630	5646	5663	5665	5680	5689									
107	7-course rotation	5559	5579	5626	5646	5674	5689														
108	8-10-course rotation	5560	5589	5635	5674	14586															
109	More than 10-course rotation		5560																		
114	Corn yields	5563	5565	5570	5573	5575	5577	5580	5586	5587	5588	5592	5594	5595	5596	5600	5606	5610	5611	5612	
	5613	5615	5621	5627	5629	5630	5634	5637	5639	5644	5648	5650	5653	5654	5657	5658	5663	5667	5668	5672	5675
	5682	5684	5686	5687	5689																
115	Beans	5569	5613	5657	5680	5692															
116	Peas	5569	5586	5587	5609	5610	5611	5613	5615	5627	5636	5657	5667	5680							
123	Clover	5559	5560	5562	5564	5566	5567	5569	5571	5576	5579	5580	5582	5586	5587	5588	5589	5592	5593	5594	5595
	5596	5599	5600	5601	5603	5604	5606	5608	5609	5610	5611	5613	5614	5615	5616	5619	5620	5621	5622	5623	5625
	5626	5627	5628	5629	5630	5631	5632	5633	5634	5635	5636	5637	5639	5641	5643	5644	5645	5646	5647	5651	5653
	5657	5662	5663	5665	5666	5668	5669	5670	5671	5672	5674	5675	5680	5682	5684	5688	5689	5691	5692	5695	5696
	5698	14586																			
126	Tares and vetches	5603																			
129	Turnips	5558	5559	5563	5564	5567	5569	5571	5573	5574	5575	5576	5579	5580	5587	5592	5594	5596	5599	5600	
	5601	5603	5606	5610	5611	5613	5620	5621	5622	5625	5626	5628	5629	5630	5631	5632	5633	5634	5636	5637	5638
	5639	5641	5643	5644	5647	5648	5649	5651	5654	5655	5660	5663	5665	5666	5668	5671	5672	5675	5679	5682	5684
	5687	5688	5689	5691	5698																
132	Potatoes	5558	5563	5573	5575	5577	5580	5583	5587	5588	5592	5594	5595	5596	5600	5601	5603	5606	5610	5611	
	5613	5615	5621	5623	5626	5627	5629	5630	5634	5637	5639	5644	5647	5648	5653	5654	5655	5657	5659	5663	5668
	5672	5682	5684	5687	5689																
133	Bare fallows	5567	5568	5571	5574	5579	5582	5584	5586	5589	5597	5598	5604	5608	5609	5614	5616	5618	5619	5622	
	5623	5624	5625	5628	5630	5631	5635	5636	5640	5643	5646	5647	5649	5655	5660	5663	5666	5669	5671	5674	5675
	5680	5682	5688	5692	5695	5696	14586														
135	Low farming	5584																			
137	Remarks on pests and crop diseases		5614																		

Monmouthshire contd.

139	Good quality pastures	5583	5597	5646	
140	Poor quality pastures			5646	
141	Meadows	5569	5629		
143	Marsh grassland			5670	
147	Cattle fattening			5642	5659
153	Horses	5662			
160	Straw	5612			
161	Hay	5629	5662		
164	Milk	5601			

Norfolk

1	Tithe-free district	5741	5769	5776	5777	5785	5838	5848	5955	5988	6045	6071	6117	6118	6119	6121	6123	6125	6126
		6127	6128	6129	6130	6132	6135	6136	6137	6138	6139	6140	6141	6143	6144	6145	6148	6149	6150	6151	6152	6180
		6217	6219	6220	6251	6253	6263	6292	6335	6338	6361	6366	6386	7473					
2	History of tithe payment		5727	6228	6231	6232												
3	Tithe practices and agriculture		5813	6099	6169	6173	6183											
4	Exemptions from tithe		5770	5823	5845	5867	5880	5885	6008	6051	6278	6316	6376					
5	Tithe in kind	5802	5806	5830	6040	6111												
6	Compositions	5711	5712	5721	5734	5743	5746	5749	5750	5754	5762	5771	5779	5786	5787	5798	5806	5808	5814	5830
		5837	5843	5846	5849	5853	5859	5860	5872	5876	5879	5888	5890	5894	5899	5903	5907	5924	5938	5942	5954	5957
		5958	5962	5965	5968	5969	5972	5979	5994	5998	5999	6004	6007	6013	6016	6051	6068	6076	6077	6080	6089	6090
		6092	6102	6106	6111	6120	6122	6133	6134	6158	6159	6165	6195	6197	6200	6201	6210	6214	6222	6229	6231	6232
		6234	6237	6256	6268	6278	6279	6280	6282	6284	6291	6294	6295	6300	6302	6304	6305	6306	6309	6319	6327	6336
		6347	6351	6367	6376	6392	6393	6397	6398	6399	6406	6407	6420	6423					
7	Moduses		5736	5779	5793	5817	5835	5837	5841	5876	5905	5957	6008	6016	6053	6055	6156	6158	6168	6197	6209
		6227	6231	6232	6233	6236	6241	6278	6311	6316	6324	6369	6391	6393	6406				
8	Glebe	5712	5749	5762	5779	5786	5790	5793	5798	5808	5814	5853	5866	5884	5952	5962	6007	6089	6106	6114	6158
		6222	6260	6291	6294	6299	6352	6368	6398	6406									
9	Local topographic descriptions		5703	5710	5713	5715	5720	5724	5728	5730	5739	5742	5744	5747	5752	5756	5760	5770
		5780	5812	5815	5819	5823	5861	5862	5863	5867	5868	5869	5873	5898	5909	5910	5919	5921	5926	5935	5936	5943
		5947	5949	5951	5980	5989	6001	6003	6015	6019	6020	6027	6028	6033	6035	6039	6050	6072	6075	6078	6082	6087
		6099	6154	6156	6157	6163	6172	6184	6185	6188	6215	6225	6242	6245	6262	6274	6281	6310	6359	6363	6365	6371
		6372	6387	6389	6413														
10	Regional topographic descriptions		5714	5737	5810	5812	5825	5831	5892	5901	5906	5931	5935	5941	5949	5961	5975	6086
		6172	6185	6211	6266	6287	6364	6370	6413	6418									
11	Village morphology		5701	5704	5732	5747	5770	5778	5802	5816	5829	5831	5854	5866	5873	5880	5886	5898	5910	5966
		5976	5977	6043	6103	6157	6163	6167	6188	6194	6204	6216	6262	6287	6359	6377	6378	6396	
12	Church	5701	5704	5715	5720	5727	5733	5736	5747	5750	5761	5770	5781	5823	5831	5866	5898	5934
		5951	5967	5977	5996	6052	6066	6081	6084	6087	6157	6163	6179	6188	6191	6204	6212	6242	6257	6258	6266	6274
		6310	6359	6371	6378	6399	6408	6424											
13	Country houses and ornamental gardens				5736	5747	5778	5829	5845	5863	5912	5971	6009	6017	6262	6287	6301	6313	6378
		6389	6418																
14	Farm houses and buildings	5831	5841	5841	5864	5864	5895	5948	6034	6342	6379	6414						
15	Cottages and cottage gardens		5707	5736	5761	5847	5858	5861	5868	5908	5929	5948	5959	5960	6009	6017	6183	6211
		6223	6250	6250	6313	6321	6375	6419											
16	Field boundaries		5755	5791	5831	5895	5897	5908	5913	5926	6096	6100	6184	6206	6211	6215	6242	6247	6249	6314
		6329	6342	6356	6374	6379	6380	6401											
17	Open fields		5720	6153															
18	Small, irregular closes		5739	5761	5780	5802	5906	5929	5940	5967	6013	6067	6100	6101	6112	6157	6179	6277	6331
		6342																	
19	Large, regular fields	5699	5736	5756	5841	5847	5851	5895	5913	6039	6155	6176	6194	6247	6249	6265	6359	6365	6371
		6401																	
21	Coppice	5736	5755	5778	5781	5788	5816	5836	5856	5861	5867	5868	5901	5959	5966	5973	5995	6005	6037	6155
		6181	6182	6224	6250	6303	6313	6328	6331	6354	6355	6357	6412	6415	6418				
22	Plantations	5699	5704	5705	5725	5726	5738	5742	5745	5753	5756	5760	5764	5765	5775	5780	5783	5788	5790	5791
		5794	5795	5796	5797	5800	5803	5811	5820	5822	5823	5825	5829	5830	5836	5841	5842	5847	5852	5857	5858	5861
		5862	5867	5869	5878	5880	5887	5891	5893	5897	5901	5908	5912	5914	5921	5926	5927	5935	5939	5941	5943	5947
		5948	5949	5950	5954	5956	5960	5963	5966	5970	5971	5973	5974	5975	5976	5977	5978	5983	5985	5990	5995	5996	5997
		6001	6005	6006	6013	6015	6017	6023	6035	6036	6039	6043	6052	6058	6073	6079	6082	6083	6087	6101	6105	6112
		6113	6153	6160	6164	6171	6173	6181	6186	6187	6191	6192	6196	6199	6203	6205	6206	6215	6224	6238	6239	6240
		6241	6247	6248	6249	6257	6258	6262	6265	6271	6284	6293	6299	6301	6303	6308	6312	6320	6325	6329	6332
		6333	6340	6346	6359	6370	6372	6373	6375	6379	6384	6389	6401	6402	6404	6409	6410	6412	6413	6417	6418	6419
		6426	6428																
23	Woodland management		5738	6009	6046	6249	6262	6281	6360	6370									
24	Productive woodland		5778	5788	5800	5819	5928	5964	5981	6009	6019	6109	6188	6290	6377	6416	6425		
25	Poor woodland		5707	5708	5717	5718	5720	5728	5730	5736	5747	5753	5756	5764	5766	5767	5772	5774	5791	5799
		5816	5824	5825	5836	5847	5851	5855	5858	5861	5863	5867	5873	5878	5880	5897	5912	5913	5914	5921	5927	5932
		5947	5950	5953	5960	5966	5970	5974	5983	5997	6001	6006	6017	6023	6028	6032	6035	6038	6039	6043	6052	6054
		6106	6113	6155	6160	6173	6176	6227	6248	6255	6303	6328	6331	6332	6340	6346	6353	6355	6359	6373
		6375	6379	6388	6389	6390	6401	6408	6410	6417	6418	6428							
26	Commons	5718	5718	5720	5725	5735	5756	5790	5809	5816	5842	5842	5856	5858	5863	5868	5877	5906	5926	5936
		5939	5943	5950	5976	5983	6012	6021	6035	6096	6114	6153	6189	6206	6207	6208	6211	6218	6223
		6252	6258	6297	6297	6299	6308	6321	6333	6342	6348	6360	6404	6405	6419				
27	Furze, gorse and heathlands		5708	5720	5725	5735	5745	5756	5775	5775	5781	5782	5782	5791	5794	5795	5795	5801
		5821	5842	5851	5852	5861	5863	5865	5867	5874	5877	5897	5900	5904	5906	5912	5913	5914	5926
		5937	5939	5943	5944	5944	5945	5951	5966	5971	5974	5983	5996	6006	6011	6013	6030	6030	6035	6039	6039	6055
		6079	6096	6097	6104	6104	6106	6153	6171	6172	6181	6183	6186	6186	6191	6204	6206	6209	6215	6223	6225	6225
		6227	6252	6255	6252	6258	6281	6281	6290	6290	6297	6321	6333	6342	6348	6359	6359	6370	6370	6379	6380	6402
		6411	6417	6419	6421	6426													
28	Moorland	5701																	
30	Fens	5784	5881	5882	5923	5926	5946	6000	6099	6156	6221	6250	6267	6310	6403	6421	6427		
32	Climatic hazards		5701	5702	5703	5704	5705	5713	5756	5772	5784	5794	5801	5816	5828	5829	5830	5831	5833	5839
		5842	5847	5862	5863	5866	5874	5882	5898	5900	5902	5910	5921	5944	5945	5948	5967	5973	5989	6009	6025
		6029	6043	6052	6056	6072	6096	6103	6104	6154	6157	6163	6167	6181	6183	6191	6194	6199	6204	6215	6218	6223
		6225	6235	6242	6245	6262	6273	6281	6324	6337	6348	6365	6370	6371	6373	6374	6377	6378	6391	6396	6403	6411
		6419	6427																
34	Land requires drainage		5701	5702	5744	5753	5756	5760	5763	5784	5789	5795	5805	5816	5825	5892	5902	5909	5920
		5930	5936	5948	5970	5975	5991	6005	6019	6020	6022	6027	6032	6035	6037	6048	6054	6058	6067	6069	6101	6105
		6160	6163	6167	6186	6187	6193	6224	6326	6421									
35	Land liable to flood	5703	5728	5759	5766	5795	5801	5809	5816	5821	5831	5844	5847	5862	5863	5865	5896	5902	5946
		5947	5973	5976	6010	6055	6086	6110	6163	6177	6188	6225	6265	6266	6267	6299	6308	6318	6329	6373	6403
36	Productive soil		5714	5715	5717	5718	5724	5739	5760	5764	5767	5780	5791	5792	5796	5799	5800	5803	5809	5810
		5811	5812	5813	5815	5816	5819	5820	5821	5822	5823	5825	5827	5828	5833	5835	5839	5841	5847	5851	5852	5854

Norfolk contd.

```
        5855 5856 5858 5861 5868 5869 5871 5878 5881 5898 5913 5918 5923 5928 5929 5931 5932 5933 5937 5939 5940
        5956 5959 5964 5967 5974 5976 5980 5983 5985 5987 5989 5991 6003 6018 6020 6022 6026 6036 6037 6057 6069
        6070 6073 6079 6083 6088 6091 6100 6101 6108 6109 6153 6156 6176 6177 6185 6186 6189 6194 6218 6225 6248
        6249 6257 6261 6264 6273 6283 6289 6296 6297 6310 6312 6331 6332 6334 6342 6345 6350 6352 6353 6356 6357
        6358 6360 6362 6365 6368 6383 6387 6394 6395 6400 6421 6422 6424 6425 6428
37 Poor soil            5699 5701 5703 5726 5731 5736 5737 5745 5752 5756 5770 5772 5773 5781 5782 5783 5800 5805 5810
        5824 5825 5826 5830 5842 5847 5851 5861 5862 5864 5865 5868 5869 5873 5896 5906 5912 5914 5923 5939 5943
        5944 5945 5948 5950 5956 5964 5966 5973 5974 5984 5990 5997 6002 6009 6017 6027 6029 6030 6048 6056 6082
        6084 6088 6097 6103 6104 6108 6110 6135 6167 6170 6171 6172 6173 6181 6191 6196 6199 6202 6204 6205
        6206 6207 6221 6223 6227 6235 6248 6252 6262 6267 6281 6290 6296 6297 6303 6318 6325 6329 6333 6359 6363
        6365 6373 6389 6395 6408 6412 6414 6419 6424 6426 6427
38 Heavy (clay) soil   5702 5704 5713 5715 5719 5724 5745 5751 5752 5753 5761 5763 5764 5766 5775 5783 5784 5788
        5795 5799 5800 5802 5815 5819 5821 5835 5844 5847 5854 5856 5866 5875 5878 5880 5886 5887 5892 5893 5896
        5901 5902 5909 5916 5917 5921 5926 5927 5928 5930 5933 5940 5946 5948 5949 5950 5953 5959 5961 5964 5966
        5981 5995 6003 6005 6011 6015 6019 6048 6049 6050 6066 6067 6072 6073 6082 6087 6093 6101 6105 6109 6112
        6154 6157 6161 6162 6169 6179 6182 6188 6190 6216 6218 6224 6242 6258 6259 6260 6264 6266 6269 6271 6274
        6277 6283 6287 6288 6289 6297 6299 6308 6312 6313 6314 6318 6324 6334 6342 6349 6350 6353 6354 6355 6357
        6360 6365 6371 6372 6374 6379 6388 6390 6391 6396 6399 6400 6403 6411 6413 6414 6415 6416 6417 6422 6424
        6425 6431
39 Loamy (turnip) soil 5699 5702 5707 5714 5717 5718 5720 5728 5732 5733 5738 5739 5742 5747 5751 5753 5758 5764
        5778 5780 5783 5788 5791 5796 5801 5811 5819 5820 5822 5830 5844 5847 5852 5854 5855 5856 5861 5864 5866
        5868 5874 5875 5878 5880 5885 5886 5887 5892 5893 5895 5896 5902 5905 5908 5909 5913 5917 5918 5919 5920
        5923 5930 5935 5936 5937 5940 5943 5947 5949 5954 5961 5963 5970 5978 5981 5983 5985 5986 5987
        5991 5995 6000 6001 6002 6003 6005 6009 6010 6012 6013 6015 6018 6019 6020 6035 6036 6037 6038 6039 6043
        6046 6048 6049 6050 6052 6055 6056 6058 6064 6066 6067 6072 6081 6083 6084 6086 6095 6101 6103 6108 6109
        6112 6115 6153 6154 6160 6162 6163 6172 6176 6177 6181 6182 6184 6186 6188 6190 6193 6203 6208 6209
        6211 6224 6230 6238 6240 6242 6249 6250 6252 6254 6255 6258 6265 6267 6271 6274 6276 6277 6281 6283 6288
        6289 6293 6296 6301 6303 6312 6313 6320 6321 6326 6330 6331 6340 6341 6346 6348 6353 6357 6358 6359 6360
        6362 6363 6365 6374 6375 6377 6378 6379 6380 6382 6387 6388 6390 6394 6396 6403 6405 6409 6412 6413 6415
        6418 6427 6428 6429 6431
40 Light soil           5699 5705 5708 5710 5715 5726 5731 5735 5736 5737 5744 5747 5755 5756 5760 5763 5765 5770 5781
        5782 5783 5784 5790 5794 5795 5801 5809 5819 5820 5824 5828 5829 5830 5836 5863 5864 5867 5869 5875 5877
        5887 5896 5897 5906 5909 5910 5912 5913 5919 5921 5928 5934 5935 5943 5945 5946 5948 5953 5959 5963 5970
        5971 5990 5995 5996 6002 6003 6006 6011 6015 6025 6026 6028 6029 6030 6031 6038 6043 6048 6052 6054
        6056 6066 6072 6082 6093 6097 6101 6107 6108 6113 6155 6161 6162 6169 6171 6172 6182 6192 6204 6205 6206
        6211 6215 6223 6224 6230 6239 6241 6252 6261 6262 6264 6269 6271 6289 6297 6308 6312 6321 6324 6325 6328
        6337 6340 6341 6346 6402 6405 6417 6431
41 Several varieties of soil   5725 5730 5732 5744 5747 5753 5761 5763 5800 5801 5805 5826 5828 5831 5833 5835 5842
        5862 5864 5874 5875 5882 5887 5891 5893 5896 5904 5909 5926 5948 5961 5963 5966 5974 6011 6015 6031 6038
        6046 6050 6064 6066 6067 6072 6079 6099 6116 6169 6171 6182 6205 6208 6246 6252 6259 6265 6274 6296
        6299 6318 6371 6372 6388 6390 6396 6402 6403 6405 6410 6411 6414 6421 6431
42 Chalk    5824 5841 5921 6106 6109 6373 6429
43 Sand or gravel  5701 5703 5704 5707 5713 5715 5728 5732 5735 5745 5753 5759 5761 5764 5766 5768 5772 5773
        5774 5775 5778 5781 5788 5790 5800 5805 5821 5822 5823 5826 5830 5842 5845 5847 5851 5857 5861 5865 5866
        5868 5869 5873 5880 5891 5897 5901 5902 5905 5914 5926 5927 5936 5941 5943 5944 5947 5960 5961 5966 5973
        5974 5976 5977 5978 5980 5984 5989 5990 5996 5997 6001 6002 6009 6013 6017 6019 6022 6030 6034 6038 6039
        6050 6054 6055 6067 6078 6079 6081 6082 6084 6087 6088 6096 6101 6103 6105 6106 6154 6157 6164 6167 6170
        6171 6173 6176 6181 6183 6187 6188 6190 6191 6192 6196 6199 6205 6206 6207 6209 6212 6215 6223 6227 6235
        6238 6240 6243 6245 6247 6250 6255 6257 6259 6262 6265 6266 6270 6274 6275 6293 6298 6299 6303 6326 6328
        6329 6332 6333 6337 6342 6345 6352 6359 6363 6373 6374 6375 6377 6379 6380 6389 6395 6403 6404 6405 6408
        6410 6412 6414 6415 6419 6424 6425 6427 6428 6429
44 Peat      5745 5816 5865 5964 6043 6052 6208 6224 6242 6250 6267 6318 6395 6399
45 Fields remote from farms  5815 5984 6064 6176 6182
46 Good local roads      5731 5766 5830 5844 5855 5857 5865 5878 5887 5891 5895 5914 5928 5929 5932 5939 5946
        5948 5956 5977 5981 5987 5997 6010 6018 6030 6046 6088 6095 6097 6108 6167 6189 6199 6203 6223 6248 6258
        6332 6334 6345 6360 6400 6422 6425 6428
47 Poor local roads      6020 6160 6164 6187 6227 6235 6257 6267 6298 6350 6410 6416
48 Turnpike and main roads  5815 5852 5871 5880 5904 5910 5923 5928 5944 5963 5966 5971 6015 6022 6064 6079 6097
        6109 6172 6176 6191 6213 6287 6288 6307 6313 6341 6354 6355 6356 6358 6360 6363 6368 6371 6375 6396 6403
        6404 6405 6416 6429
49 Roads recently improved  6020
50 Water carriage   5719 5730 5731 5759 5784 5801 5810 5816 5823 5828 5833 5852 5855 5902 5932 5986 6010 6018
        6032 6046 6052 6070 6072 6104 6108 6110 6115 6169 6189 6218 6230 6252 6257 6264 6269 6273 6283 6297 6298
        6332 6352 6368 6377 6384 6390 6394 6403 6408 6427 6428
53 Markets accessible    5702 5705 5714 5718 5730 5731 5733 5739 5744 5747 5751 5752 5758 5759 5760 5763 5766 5778
        5781 5782 5784 5790 5800 5801 5802 5810 5812 5813 5815 5819 5828 5829 5830 5833 5835 5845 5851 5855 5857
        5863 5864 5869 5871 5875 5878 5887 5891 5896 5900 5902 5906 5909 5910 5914 5916 5919 5928 5933 5934 5944
        5945 5946 5948 5949 5951 5953 5956 5961 5963 5981 5984 5985 5986 6000 6011 6022 6025 6029 6030 6031 6039
        6043 6046 6049 6064 6069 6079 6088 6095 6104 6109 6110 6154 6156 6160 6167 6169 6172 6187 6191 6192 6208
        6211 6218 6221 6223 6230 6238 6252 6259 6261 6269 6270 6281 6297 6298 6310 6324 6334 6342 6345 6348 6349
        6356 6357 6363 6365 6368 6370 6377 6390 6400 6402 6403 6404 6405 6408 6416 6422
54 Markets inaccessible  5865 5866 5892 5930 5932 5939 5950 5980 6001 6019 6020 6032 6070 6235 6274 6350 6431
55 Provincial markets    5699 5702 5705 5722 5730 5737 5739 5744 5747 5751 5759 5763 5784 5805 5830 5874 5875 5882
        5910 5928 5945 5946 5953 5986 6011 6013 6015 6069 6072 6097 6110 6205 6264 6390 6394
56 London market         5739 6010 6081 6225 6384
57 Fairs    5718
58 Market prices  5829 5906 5945 6011 6102 6104 6188 6352 6403
59 Landowners and their estates  5701 5715 5725 5727 5737 5744 5755 5760 5760 5764 5770 5782 5783 5813 5816 5820
        5824 5829 5841 5847 5864 5868 5892 5895 5902 5912 5919 6033 6081 6081 6096 6104 6104 6157 6183 6184 6188
        6188 6261 6281 6324 6355 6356 6356 6363 6370 6370 6371 6374 6378 6402 6419
60 Land occupiers   5710 5715 5719 5764 5780 5813 5831 5839 5841 5866 5871 5905 5912 5916 5933 5945 5945 5986
        5986 6030 6069 6081 6084 6096 6106 6172 6208 6212 6250 6265 6283 6287 6297 6348 6354 6422 6424 6424 6426
        6427
61 Farm size         5727 5788 5791 5802 5830 5839 5854 5864 5895 5905 5934 5959 6034 6056 6058 6069 6100 6104 6157
        6176 6197 6209 6235 6239 6260 6329 6333 6340 6342 6354 6355 6389 6391
62 Leases   5813 5813 5815 5835 5910 5912 5945 6084 6163 6356
63 Farm implements  5805 5928 5944 5996 6245 6373
64 Common grazing   5791 5844 5858 5862 5915 5932 6211 6213 6297 6299
65 Lammas and other common rights  5765 5802 5816 5816 5833 5842 5877 5915 5926 5939 5975 5991 6025 6035 6039
        6055 6079 6099 6202 6207 6208 6211 6218 6250 6252 6297
66 Rents    5864 5866 5910 6009 6019 6086 6173 6235 6267 6283 6318 6365
68 Rates    5839 6029 6164 6221 6257 6267 6276
69 Farm labour and wages  6276
70 Enclosure or improvement of waste  5735 5801 5900 5905 5929 5945 5964 5978 5986 6019 6173 6177 6239 6241 6250
71 Enclosure of commons  5699 5714 5715 5732 5751 5761 5821 5833 5880 5917 5928 5930 5937 5959 5986 5991 6002
```

Norfolk contd.

6006 6026 6056 6172 6250 6273 6274 6301 6314 6395 6424
72 Enclosure of open fields 5841 5967 6107 6368 6393
74 Occasional ploughing of grassland 6358 6365
75 Conversion of grass to arable 5835 6075 6342 6411 6426
76 Conversion of arable to pasture 5869
77 Paring and burning 5882 6099 6213 6221 6267
80 Reclaiming and embanking 5821 5864 5885 5964 6020 6076 6226 6310 6352 6365 6417 6419
81 Marsh drainage 5717 5815 5830 5841 5864 5881 5898 5920 5923 5963 6000 6008 6037 6115 6156 6163 6172 6177
6188 6193 6221 6239 6264 6267 6310 6371 6390 6399 6403 6427
82 Drainage channels and ditches 5830 5916 5926 5948 6100 6156 6163 6184 6242 6329 6342 6365 6368 6371 6378 6399
83 Steam pumps 5830
85 Underdrainage 5702 5704 5719 5789 5800 5801 5869 5896 5901 5916 5928 5929 5953 6003 6010 6011 6015 6069
6072 6087 6100 6105 6110 6154 6169 6188 6202 6208 6212 6216 6218 6242 6269 6277 6288 6314 6324 6334 6342
6350 6355 6370 6377 6383 6388 6390 6391 6396 6416 6429
86 Tile drains 5719 5871 5875 6202 6208 6212 6342 6377 6390
87 Marl 5770 5810 5812 5813 5826 5831 5864 5869 5876 5928 5986 6000 6003 6010 6072 6160 6206 6212 6218 6221
6239 6248 6261 6262 6337 6345 6362 6368 6403 6424 6425 6427 6428
88 Chalk 5826 5935 6196
89 Lime 5715 5770 5831 5892 6424
91 Soot 6424
92 Dung 5744 5812 5813 5815 5821 5830 5833 5844 5896 5910 6003 6056 6064 6172 6188 6204 6218 6264 6270 6362
6368 6370 6373 6384 6391 6405 6429
93 Seaweed 6003 6199
94 Fish 5735 5770 5824 5900 6003 6029 6199 6283 6321 6352
95 Bones 5739 5770 5824 5826 5831 5900 6003 6169 6321 6352 6370 6424
97 Guano 6281
98 Rape cake 5770 5821 5823 5826 6003 6081 6188 6424 6431
99 Chemical fertilisers 5715 5735 5739 5763 5763 5770 5821 5821 5823 5831 5892 5930 6003 6027 6029 6072 6188 6281
6283 6283 6431
100 Oil dust, unspecified fertilisers or manures 5725 5739 5744 5760 5763 5782 5805 5810 5869 5909 5928 5944 5986 6011
6031 6033 6034 6072 6081 6104 6205 6245 6261 6269 6273 6342 6356 6370 6390 6394 6396 6402
101 General comments on crop rotations 5719 5725 5755 5763 5829 5830 5835 5882 5945 6091 6221 6274 6275 6310 6360
6371 6377 6403 6422
102 Irregular rotations 5710 5713 5715 5788 5794 6075 6097 6283 6384 6400
103 3-course rotation 5715 6221 6417
104 4-course rotation 5699 5701 5703 5704 5707 5708 5710 5714 5715 5717 5719 5722 5725 5726 5728 5730 5732 5733
5736 5737 5738 5739 5742 5744 5745 5747 5752 5753 5755 5758 5759 5760 5763 5764 5765 5766 5767 5768 5770
5772 5773 5774 5778 5780 5781 5782 5783 5784 5788 5789 5791 5792 5794 5795 5796 5797 5799 5800 5802 5803
5805 5809 5811 5812 5813 5815 5816 5820 5821 5826 5827 5828 5829 5831 5835 5836 5839 5841 5842 5844 5845
5847 5851 5852 5854 5856 5857 5858 5861 5862 5863 5864 5865 5866 5867 5868 5869 5871 5873 5874 5875 5878
5880 5881 5882 5885 5886 5887 5891 5892 5893 5895 5896 5897 5898 5901 5902 5904 5905 5906 5908 5909 5910
5913 5914 5916 5917 5918 5919 5920 5921 5926 5927 5928 5929 5930 5931 5932 5933 5934 5935 5936 5937 5939
5940 5941 5943 5944 5945 5946 5947 5948 5949 5950 5951 5956 5959 5961 5963 5964 5966 5966 5967 5970 5971
5974 5976 5977 5978 5980 5981 5983 5984 5985 5986 5987 5989 5990 5991 5995 5996 5997 6000 6001 6002 6003
6005 6006 6010 6011 6012 6013 6015 6018 6019 6020 6022 6023 6025 6026 6028 6031 6032 6033 6034 6035 6036
6037 6039 6046 6048 6049 6052 6054 6055 6056 6058 6064 6067 6067 6069 6070 6072 6073 6078 6079 6081 6084
6086 6087 6088 6093 6096 6099 6100 6101 6103 6105 6106 6107 6108 6109 6110 6112 6113 6115 6153 6154 6155
6157 6160 6161 6162 6163 6164 6167 6169 6170 6171 6172 6173 6176 6177 6179 6181 6182 6183 6184 6185 6186
6187 6188 6189 6190 6191 6192 6193 6194 6196 6199 6202 6203 6205 6206 6207 6208 6211 6212 6213 6215 6216
6218 6221 6223 6224 6225 6227 6230 6238 6239 6240 6241 6242 6243 6245 6246 6247 6248 6249 6250 6252 6254
6255 6257 6258 6259 6260 6261 6262 6264 6265 6266 6267 6269 6270 6271 6273 6274 6276 6277 6283 6287 6288
6289 6290 6293 6296 6297 6299 6301 6307 6308 6310 6312 6313 6314 6318 6320 6321 6324 6325 6326 6328 6329
6330 6331 6332 6334 6337 6340 6341 6342 6345 6346 6348 6349 6350 6352 6353 6354 6355 6356 6357 6358 6359
6360 6362 6363 6368 6370 6372 6373 6374 6375 6377 6379 6380 6382 6383 6384 6387 6388 6389 6390 6391 6394
6395 6396 6401 6402 6403 6404 6405 6408 6409 6410 6411 6412 6414 6415 6416 6417 6419 6421 6422 6424 6425
6426 6427 6428 6429 6431
105 5-course rotation 5713 5715 5735 5752 5810 5822 5824 5825 5826 5898 5918 5987 6000 6030 6031 6104 6156 6163
6199 6267 6274 6275 6348 6364 6365 6371 6378 6399 6426
106 6-course rotation 5705 5715 5718 5731 5735 5751 5833 5855 5900 5912 5923 5953 6003 6029 6091 6156 6199 6218
6267 6274 6281 6298
110 Wheat 5702 5735 5738 5801 5828 6273 6356 6403
111 Barley 5702 5714 5738 5744 5751 5823 5828 6039 6056 6082 6104 6356 6394
112 Oats 5737 5763 5782 5896 5916 6006 6030 6104 6156 6184 6223 6403 6426
113 Rye or meslin 5745 5765 5782 5794 5805 5829 5842 5861 5891 5909 5926 5941 5945 5971 5984 5996 6006 6030
6031 6033 6048 6104 6170 6196 6207 6223 6242 6275 6329 6370 6426
114 Corn yields 5705 5714 5717 5735 5752 5810 5812 5813 5815 5819 5829 5900 5909 5928 5945 6163 6235 6283 6362
6365 6378 6399 6426
115 Beans 5702 5704 5719 5763 5784 5827 5875 5882 5886 5896 5902 5916 5919 5933 5950 6020 6049 6064 6100 6154
6156 6163 6179 6190 6208 6212 6216 6277 6310 6313 6324 6334 6342 6350 6352 6362 6364 6365 6371 6375 6378
6399 6417
116 Peas 5714 5760 5763 5782 5803 5805 5828 5864 5875 5882 5906 5909 5945 6015 6056 6161 6163 6218 6269 6324
6342 6352 6356 6364 6371 6378 6426
118 Coleseed 5782 5829 5881 5882 6000 6156 6221 6241 6267 6310 6310 6364 6365 6365 6371 6375 6399 6400 6403
6422
122 Unspecified grass seeds 6012 6015 6091
123 Clover 5702 5704 5714 5719 5725 5737 5739 5751 5760 5782 5799 5801 5805 5812 5813 5815 5828 5833 5854 5864
5875 5882 5886 5896 5900 5902 5908 5909 5910 5913 5916 5928 5933 5949 5950 5953 5961 5967 5985 5986 5990
5991 5996 6003 6011 6015 6025 6028 6029 6034 6049 6056 6069 6072 6081 6081 6100 6104 6109 6110 6154 6161
6162 6163 6169 6171 6181 6182 6184 6185 6190 6193 6196 6205 6207 6208 6211 6213 6216 6218 6230 6241 6242
6243 6249 6252 6254 6259 6261 6264 6269 6283 6296 6297 6307 6313 6318 6321 6331 6334 6340 6342 6348 6352
6356 6362 6365 6370 6371 6377 6378 6384 6388 6389 6390 6391 6394 6396 6399 6418 6424 6427
124 Sainfoin 6027 6030 6426
125 Trefoil 5714 5725 5737 5739 5751 5760 5782 5805 5828 5833 5869 5875 5882 5896 5900 5902 5906 5909 5910 5916
5928 5933 5996 6003 6011 6025 6027 6029 6056 6069 6072 6081 6104 6110 6154 6169 6184 6205 6208 6218 6230
6252 6261 6264 6269 6297 6321 6342 6348 6352 6356 6370 6377 6384 6388 6390 6396 6427 6429
126 Tares and vetches 5702 5744 5760 5763 5784 5864 5906 5910 5916 5961 6110 6154 6170 6242 6297 6390 6391 6429
127 Lucerne 5910
128 Kale 6429
129 Turnips 5699 5701 5702 5704 5705 5707 5708 5710 5713 5714 5715 5717 5718 5720 5725 5726 5730 5731 5732
5733 5735 5736 5737 5738 5739 5742 5744 5747 5751 5753 5755 5756 5758 5759 5760 5761 5763 5764 5765 5766
5767 5768 5770 5772 5773 5774 5778 5780 5781 5782 5783 5784 5788 5789 5790 5791 5792 5794 5795 5796 5797
5799 5800 5801 5802 5803 5805 5809 5810 5811 5812 5813 5815 5816 5819 5820 5821 5822 5823 5824 5825 5826
5827 5828 5829 5830 5831 5833 5835 5836 5839 5841 5842 5844 5845 5847 5851 5852 5854 5855 5856 5857 5858
5861 5862 5863 5864 5865 5866 5867 5868 5868 5869 5871 5873 5874 5875 5878 5880 5881 5882 5885 5886 5887
5891 5892 5893 5895 5896 5897 5898 5900 5902 5904 5905 5906 5908 5909 5910 5912 5913 5914 5916 5917 5918

Norfolk contd.

```
      5919 5920 5921 5923 5926 5927 5928 5929 5930 5931 5932 5933 5934 5935 5936 5937 5939 5940 5941 5943 5944
      5945 5946 5947 5948 5949 5951 5953 5956 5959 5961 5963 5964 5966 5967 5970 5971 5974 5976 5977 5978 5980
      5981 5983 5984 5985 5986 5987 5989 5990 5991 5995 5996 5997 6000 6001 6003 6005 6006 6009 6010 6011 6012
      6013 6015 6018 6019 6020 6022 6023 6025 6026 6028 6029 6030 6034 6035 6036 6037 6038 6039 6048 6049 6052
      6054 6055 6056 6058 6064 6067 6069 6070 6072 6079 6081 6084 6086 6086 6091 6093 6095 6096 6100 6103 6104
      6106 6107 6108 6109 6110 6112 6113 6115 6153 6154 6155 6156 6157 6160 6161 6162 6163 6164 6167 6169 6170
      6171 6172 6173 6176 6177 6179 6181 6182 6183 6184 6185 6186 6187 6187 6188 6189 6190 6191 6192 6193 6194
      6196 6199 6202 6203 6205 6206 6207 6208 6209 6211 6212 6213 6215 6216 6218 6221 6223 6224 6225 6227 6230
      6235 6238 6239 6240 6241 6242 6243 6245 6246 6247 6248 6249 6250 6252 6254 6255 6257 6258 6259 6261 6262
      6264 6265 6266 6267 6269 6270 6271 6273 6274 6275 6276 6277 6281 6283 6287 6288 6289 6290 6293 6296 6297
      6298 6299 6301 6307 6308 6310 6312 6313 6314 6318 6320 6321 6324 6325 6326 6328 6330 6331 6332 6334 6337
      6340 6341 6342 6345 6346 6348 6349 6350 6352 6353 6354 6355 6356 6357 6358 6359 6360 6362 6363 6364 6365
      6368 6370 6371 6372 6373 6374 6375 6377 6378 6379 6380 6382 6383 6384 6387 6388 6389 6390 6391 6394 6396
      6400 6401 6402 6403 6408 6409 6410 6411 6412 6413 6414 6415 6416 6417 6418 6419 6421 6422 6424 6425 6426
      6427 6428 6429 6431
130   Mangolds      5715 5744 5751 5760 5763 5784 5788 5810 5813 5815 5830 5831 5882 5892 5896 5930 5953 5964 5986
      6005 6011 6049 6064 6069 6072 6110 6188 6190 6212 6218 6221 6264 6269 6273 6283 6297 6310 6312 6313 6321
      6365 6368 6377 6390
131   Swedes        5714 5831 6221 6261
132   Potatoes      5763 5830 5961 6156 6297 6310 6364 6365 6371
133   Bare fallows  5702 5733 5763 5784 5799 5801 5819 5823 5844 5875 5878 5892 5896 5902 5916 5923 5928 5930 5948
      5964 5981 5996 6011 6048 6049 6069 6081 6093 6110 6154 6156 6179 6188 6242 6258 6307 6313 6324 6334 6342
      6354 6355 6364 6373 6415 6427 6431
134   High farming  5707 5715 5726 5735 5739 5744 5760 5763 5770 5782 5783 5810 5812 5813 5815 5819 5824 5826 5827
      5829 5831 5836 5841 5861 5866 5867 5868 5871 5874 5895 5896 5900 5900 5901 5912 5919 5921 5934 5935 5945
      5951 5953 5977 5978 5983 5986 5995 5996 6003 6010 6015 6018 6027 6028 6031 6033 6054 6081 6169 6172 6183
      6184 6188 6205 6212 6224 6230 6249 6261 6264 6270 6281 6283 6287 6288 6329 6341 6342 6346 6348 6352 6354
      6356 6368 6373 6374 6381 6391 6394 6396 6401 6402 6409 6411 6418 6419 6424
135   Low farming   5926 5948 6019 6096 6224 6331 6337
136   Remarks on the absence of turnips  5719 5752 5799 5950 6399
137   Remarks on pests and crop diseases 5730 5896 5910 5964 6156 6194 6431
138   Recent increase in productivity    5728 6040 6169
139   Good quality pastures   5717 5718 5720 5755 5764 5766 5794 5796 5797 5799 5800 5815 5822 5824 5825 5831 5841
      5845 5856 5861 5871 5878 5881 5896 5901 5902 5904 5905 5912 5931 5936 5937 5939 5940 5946 5948 5956 5971
      5983 5985 5995 6010 6035 6036 6058 6072 6073 6075 6081 6082 6083 6101 6108 6109 6153 6157 6170 6184 6186
      6190 6230 6254 6257 6277 6288 6289 6307 6333 6346 6348 6350 6356 6358 6375 6384 6396 6400 6405 6418 6419
      6422
140   Poor quality pastures   5701 5705 5708 5726 5733 5742 5744 5747 5753 5759 5760 5761 5764 5767 5770 5775 5778
      5780 5781 5782 5783 5789 5790 5795 5802 5809 5819 5822 5831 5835 5836 5841 5844 5847 5856 5857 5858 5861
      5862 5864 5865 5873 5893 5897 5906 5908 5910 5914 5917 5926 5927 5928 5935 5941 5959 5971 5973 5980 5984
      5989 6003 6015 6017 6018 6020 6025 6037 6043 6050 6052 6056 6070 6078 6091 6093 6097 6112 6114 6155 6161
      6162 6163 6164 6167 6171 6176 6177 6179 6181 6183 6187 6204 6207 6213 6218 6221 6225 6238 6241 6245 6246
      6248 6250 6254 6257 6259 6260 6262 6264 6265 6275 6281 6290 6303 6310 6318 6325 6326 6337 6341 6353 6378
      6388 6389 6395 6402 6409 6412 6413 6414 6424 6426 6427
141   Meadows       5699 5702 5703 5707 5708 5715 5718 5720 5724 5725 5726 5732 5738 5742 5744 5745 5747 5753 5755
      5764 5766 5770 5778 5780 5781 5783 5788 5790 5791 5795 5799 5801 5803 5809 5820 5831 5833 5842 5857 5858
      5863 5868 5878 5880 5885 5895 5896 5904 5905 5906 5908 5910 5913 5916 5917 5921 5926 5928 5932 5933 5934
      5936 5940 5943 5949 5950 5951 5956 5959 5960 5970 5974 5975 5976 5984 5986 5990 5995 6001 6005 6011
      6013 6022 6037 6043 6048 6049 6055 6058 6064 6072 6096 6110 6112 6113 6153 6155 6160 6169 6191 6192 6202
      6206 6208 6224 6240 6242 6246 6247 6261 6266 6269 6289 6293 6297 6298 6299 6301 6312 6314 6318 6320 6328
      6329 6330 6331 6332 6340 6342 6345 6346 6354 6355 6371 6372 6373 6374 6377 6379 6380 6391 6395 6401 6408
      6409 6413 6414 6415 6417 6418 6422 6427 6428
142   Irrigation and water meadows       5841 6368 6401
143   Marsh grassland   5721 5728 5758 5759 5767 5811 5815 5816 5821 5823 5830 5836 5842 5847 5851 5852 5902 5920
      5932 5947 5948 5963 5964 5970 5980 5991 6020 6054 6064 6086 6096 6115 6163 6172 6176 6177 6182 6187 6188
      6189 6193 6203 6207 6211 6223 6225 6257 6264 6273 6283 6296 6310 6321 6326 6352 6358 6368 6370 6371 6372
      6373 6378 6384 6390 6394 6399 6405 6411 6412 6419
144   Parks        5720 5736 5747 5755 5778 5829 5836 5845 5847 5863 5867 5905 5909 5912 5916 5959 5960 5966 5996 6009
      6017 6054 6058 6087 6108 6181 6182 6183 6184 6186 6196 6221 6287 6325 6328 6331 6363 6384 6401 6418 6426
145   Accommodation land       5873 5910 6377
146   Cattle breeding    5715 5948 5996 6033 6034 6188 6242 6365 6390
147   Cattle fattening   5705 5708 5730 5736 5744 5751 5760 5784 5789 5801 5803 5810 5811 5812 5813 5815 5821 5828
      5830 5833 5869 5875 5896 5900 5902 5906 5928 5953 5981 5986 6011 6015 6029 6056 6058 6064 6069 6086 6154
      6179 6184 6204 6212 6218 6221 6230 6243 6252 6264 6269 6273 6283 6297 6307 6342 6348 6356 6368 6377 6384
      6388 6391 6396 6400 6422
148   Dairying      5701 5719 5730 5805 6029 6194 6264 6269 6273 6384
149   Cow keeping   6046
150   Sheep breeding    5715 5763 5782 5791 5805 5831 5868 5869 5871 5875 5904 5935 5944 5945 5996 6022 6030 6034
      6081 6104 6169 6183 6188 6194 6204 6223 6230 6242 6245 6252 6261 6269 6297 6324 6362 6365 6370 6384 6395
      6403 6404 6411 6426 6429
151   Sheep fattening   5702 5705 5725 5737 5739 5744 5751 5760 5763 5784 5801 5811 5812 5813 5815 5828 5829 5833
      5896 5902 5906 5953 5980 5981 5986 6003 6011 6025 6029 6033 6056 6058 6179 6184 6212 6218 6221 6235 6269
      6273 6342 6348 6356 6368 6377 6387 6390 6396
153   Horses        5714 5763 5805 5906 6022 6030 6086 6104 6252 6426 6429
154   Pigs          5948 6208
155   Oxen    6022  6349 6408
156   Poultry       5862 5868 5948 6035 6208 6252 6321
157   Rabbits       5782 5823 5833 6009 6104 6113 6169 6196 6227 6275 6333 6417
158   Deer    5703  5705 5829 5851 5869 6043 6072 6097 6104 6205 6249 6269 6275 6293 6325 6333 6373 6388 6401
159   Animal diseases   5801 5805 5902 6245 6329 6352
160   Straw         5704 5714 5813 5815 5900 5928 5984 6154 6204 6221 6281 6368 6403
161   Hay     5702  5705 5708 5714 5744 5759 5760 5763 5782 5788 5801 5810 5812 5813 5815 5828 5833 5842 5869 5871
      5875 5880 5882 5886 5887 5896 5900 5902 5906 5910 5916 5953 5960 5971 5981 5986 6011 6025 6029 6064 6072
      6095 6104 6109 6154 6208 6218 6230 6252 6259 6261 6264 6269 6310 6342 6348 6352 6356 6368 6371 6377 6384
      6388 6390 6391 6394 6396 6426 6427 6429
162   Manufactured feedstuffs (cake etc.)  5704 5715 5715 5719 5730 5735 5735 5739 5744 5751 5760 5763 5763 5801 5805
      5810 5812 5813 5815 5824 5829 5833 5875 5906 5909 5944 5945 5953 5985 6010 6011 6015 6029 6031 6031 6033
      6034 6064 6069 6081 6084 6154 6169 6183 6184 6188 6204 6205 6212 6218 6230 6243 6252 6261 6264 6269 6273
      6283 6297 6342 6348 6352 6356 6368 6373 6377 6384 6388 6390 6391 6394 6394 6396 6396 6426
163   Stall or yard feeding   5702 5714 5739 5751 5763 5801 5813 5821 5828 5831 5896 5898 5900 5916 6015 6037 6064 6110
      6184 6188 6208 6218 6230 6261 6264 6269 6310 6321 6342 6356 6377 6388 6391 6394 6396 6409 6429
164   Milk    5830
165   Butter  6029
169   Good orchards     5724 5791 5861 5940 5963 6223
172   Market gardens    5845 5918 6104 6192
```

Norfolk contd.

174	Cabbages	5882									
178	Hops	5722	6396								
181	Reeds and oziers			5781	5830	5855	5983	6241	6257	6271	6318	6331	6352

Northamptonshire

1	Tithe-free district	6434	6435	6436	6437	6439	6440	6441	6443	6445	6446	6447	6452	6453	6455	6457	6458	6461	6466
	6467	6468	6470	6471	6474	6475	6480	6482	6486	6487	6488	6489	6493	6497	6498	6502	6503	6510	6515	6516	6520
	6522	6523	6524	6526	6529	6530	6531	6532	6536	6538	6540	6542	6544	6551	6552	6557	6558	6560	6561	6563	6566
	6567	6568	6570	6572	6573	6575	6577	6579	6582	6583	6585	6591	6593	6594	6596	6598	6599	6602	6603	6604	6606
	6608	6610	6611	6612	6613	6614	6615	6618	6619	6620	6622	6626	6627	6628	6631	6632	6633	6635	6637	6638	6639
	6640	6641	6642	6643	6644	6645	6647	6651	6652	6655	6656	6658	6661	6663	6664	6667	6676	6677	6678	6680	6682
	6684	6686	6687	6697	6698	6699	6700	6701	6702	6711	6712	6713	6715	6717	6722	6723	6725	6726	6728	6731	6732
	6735	6736	6737	6738	6739	6743	6744	6745	6747	6749	6751	6755	6758	6761	6762	6764	6766	6767			
2	History of tithe payment		6442	6444	6449	6450	6451	6454	6460	6464	6465	6469	6472	6476	6476	6477	6478	6483	6484
	6485	6496	6507	6508	6509	6509	6512	6517	6519	6521	6533	6535	6543	6559	6565	6580	6584	6597	6601	6607	6609
	6621	6624	6625	6629	6636	6653	6665	6670	6683	6688	6691	6692	6693	6696	6724	6729	6730	6740	6741	6742	6746
	6748	6753	6754	6757	6760	6763	14831														
3	Tithe practices and agriculture		6689																
4	Exemptions from tithe		6442	6444	6449	6450	6451	6454	6460	6464	6465	6469	6472	6476	6477	6478	6483	6484	6485
	6496	6507	6512	6517	6519	6521	6533	6543	6559	6565	6571	6580	6584	6597	6601	6607	6609	6621	6634	6636	6649
	6650	6653	6654	6665	6668	6669	6670	6674	6675	6683	6688	6691	6692	6693	6696	6718	6720	6724	6729	6730	6740
	6741	6742	6746	6748	6753	6754	6757	6760	14831												
5	Tithe in kind	6505	6534	6548	6605	6616	6679	6685	6689	6721									
6	Compositions	6444	6448	6454	6459	6477	6483	6484	6485	6490	6492	6496	6509	6511	6512	6521	6525	6528	6543	6556
	6559	6564	6571	6580	6584	6595	6597	6601	6605	6609	6616	6617	6623	6648	6662	6666	6670	6673	6674	6683	6688
	6708	6714	6716	6718	6720	6724	6729	6733	6734	6741	6742	6748	6754	8020							
7	Moduses	6444	6454	6460	6463	6464	6469	6479	6483	6490	6492	6499	6509	6512	6521	6539	6545	6546	6562	6565
	6569	6578	6581	6621	6629	6653	6666	6669	6670	6679	6683	6685	6691	6696	6703	6705	6709	6718	6720	6730	6753
	6760	14831																			
8	Glebe	6554	6666	6671	6727														
9	Local topographic descriptions		3431	6462	6463	6481	6491	6504	6537	6547	6554	6578	6666	6681	6685	6694	6707	6752
10	Regional topographic descriptions		6660	6689	6690	6752												
11	Village morphology	6463	6660	6695	6727													
12	Church	3431	6462	6463	6473	6491	6547	6578	6660									
14	Farm houses and buildings		6504	6554														
15	Cottages and cottage gardens		6494	6537	6554	6600	6660	6695	6704	6721	6727							
17	Open fields	3431	6504	6679	6689	6695	6705	6721	6727									
18	Small, irregular closes		3431															
19	Large, regular fields	6505	6752															
20	Hedgerow timber	6537																
21	Coppice	6462	6671	6756														
22	Plantations	6494	6537	6605	6671	6721												
23	Woodland management		6462	6463	6473	6504	6547	6578	6660	6673	6685	6694	6704					
24	Productive woodland		6694	6704														
25	Poor woodland	6494	6499	6504	6695													
26	Commons	6660	6721	6727														
27	Furze, gorse and heathlands		6695															
34	Land requires drainage		3431	6547	6578	6685	6695	6704	6721									
35	Land liable to flood	6432	6504	6537	6554	6679	6689	6705										
36	Productive soil	6494	6554	6578	6660	6673	6679	6681										
37	Poor soil	6491	6495	6541	6592													
38	Heavy (clay) soil	3431	6433	6463	6491	6505	6534	6547	6574	6586	6592	6662	6666	6671	6673	6685	6763	
39	Loamy (turnip) soil	6462	6463	6481	6494	6537	6554	6578	6660	6681	6685	6690	6695	6704	6721	6727	6752	6763
40	Light soil	6504																
41	Several varieties of soil	6432	6463	6473	6504	6518	6537	6578	6605	6660	6672	6690	6707	6721	6752	6756		
45	Fields remote from farms	6600	6704															
46	Good local roads	6432	6660															
47	Poor local roads	6505	6506	6752														
48	Turnpike and main roads	6592	6721	6752	6756													
49	Roads recently improved	6671																
53	Markets accessible	6494	6504															
55	Provincial markets	6432	6592	6660	6752													
56	London market	6578	6600															
58	Market prices	6629																
59	Landowners and their estates		6513	6554	6605													
60	Land occupiers	6537																
61	Farm size	3431	6462	6463	6473	6547	6578											
62	Leases	6535	6571															
64	Common grazing	6646	6721	6727														
65	Lammas and other common rights		6660															
66	Rents	6514																
67	Urban influences on value of land		6646															
68	Rates	3431	6463	6473	6491	6547	6578	6609	6616	6617	6623	6662	6670	6673	6674	6727	6733	
71	Enclosure of commons	6695	6705															
72	Enclosure of open fields	6695	6705															
75	Conversion of grass to arable		6506	6592	6671													
76	Conversion of arable to pasture		3431															
82	Drainage channels and ditches		6660															
84	Ridge-and-furrow	6462																
85	Underdrainage	6513	6671	6681	6721													
100	Oil dust, unspecified fertilisers or manures			6504														
101	General comments on crop rotations		6463	6504	6554	6592	6671	6685	6705	6727								
102	Irregular rotations	6505	6646	6660														
103	3-course rotation	3431	6463	6547	6578	6679	6681	6727										
104	4-course rotation	3431	6432	6462	6463	6473	6481	6491	6505	6518	6554	6574	6578	6600	6671	6681	6690	6707	6721
	6752																				
105	5-course rotation	6432	6494	6505	6541	6574												
106	6-course rotation	6495	6763															
110	Wheat	6662	6727															
111	Barley	6504																
115	Beans	6662	6727															
126	Tares and vetches		6554															
129	Turnips	6554	6605	6660	6752													

Northamptonshire contd.

132	Potatoes	6646													
133	Bare fallows	6505	6752												
134	High farming	6495	6513	6534	6600	6662	6707								
135	Low farming	6629	6695												
136	Remarks on the absence of turnips			6505	6673	6705	6727								
139	Good quality pastures		6432	6463	6494	6547	6554	6578	6600	6605	6666	6704	6705	6721	6763
140	Poor quality pastures		6495	6586	6592	6671	6689	6695							
141	Meadows	6494	6537	6554	6600	6605	6666	6685	6705	6721	6763				
144	Parks	6491	6537	6685	6695	6705									
146	Cattle breeding		6537	6672											
147	Cattle fattening		6481	6554	6578	6600	6681	6690	6694	6704					
148	Dairying	6479	6494	6495	6537	6672	6673	6694	6721	6763					
150	Sheep breeding		6433	6537	6578	6592									
151	Sheep fattening		6704												
154	Pigs	6537	6705	6727											
155	Oxen	6600													
161	Hay	6537	6685	6705											
166	Cheese	3431													
169	Good orchards		6494	6554	6600	6660	6666	6704							
172	Market gardens		6646												
176	Onions		6463												
181	Reeds and oziers		6463												

Northumberland

1 Tithe-free district 6770 6796 6799 6831 6858 6860 6878 6913 6933 6944 6959 6970 6973 6979 7002 7015 7073 7079 7082 7085 7087 7118 7123 7175 7189 7198 7219 7237 7256
2 History of tithe payment 6795 6847 6850 6892 6994
3 Tithe practices and agriculture 6894 6897 7045 7113 7181 7209
4 Exemptions from tithe 6772 6773 6778 6780 6781 6782 6785 6795 6797 6803 6826 6846 6876 6886 6887 6893 6894 6901 6924 6934 6966 6999 7012 7066 7095 7122 7150 7173 7179 7181 7183 7203 7205 7235 7260 7265 7266 7283 7288 7289 7311
5 Tithe in kind 6769 6788 6802 6838 6840 6852 6885 6894 6906 7039 7124
6 Compositions 6782 6787 6790 6791 6792 6801 6805 6808 6815 6816 6826 6827 6830 6832 6838 6839 6847 6866 6872 6873 6876 6877 6884 6885 6893 6895 6902 6912 6915 6917 6924 6928 6930 6934 6939 6950 6963 6997 7003 7006 7043 7066 7072 7074 7075 7083 7105 7113 7125 7126 7127 7130 7136 7138 7144 7149 7152 7194 7212 7213 7215 7221 7232 7238 7242 7246 7249 7255 7261 7268 7275 7291 7292 7293 7298 7299 7301 7304
7 Moduses 5706 5807 6773 6777 6780 6782 6785 6786 6787 6788 6790 6791 6792 6795 6805 6809 6812 6813 6818 6819 6822 6826 6827 6846 6847 6851 6866 6868 6870 6871 6872 6877 6880 6882 6886 6893 6896 6902 6903 6915 6918 6921 6922 6924 6930 6931 6935 6939 6940 6949 6953 6955 6963 6964 6966 6980 6985 6986 6995 7005 7006 7007 7014 7020 7023 7031 7033 7037 7043 7044 7045 7047 7048 7051 7055 7058 7060 7062 7069 7072 7074 7075 7080 7083 7086 7094 7095 7099 7100 7102 7103 7105 7112 7113 7115 7121 7122 7124 7130 7132 7134 7138 7145 7149 7152 7153 7157 7160 7164 7166 7172 7173 7174 7177 7178 7182 7188 7191 7193 7195 7197 7200 7201 7202 7205 7206 7207 7209 7210 7212 7213 7215 7216 7221 7230 7232 7241 7245 7246 7248 7250 7255 7261 7264 7266 7268 7269 7270 7274 7275 7276 7279 7282 7285 7286 7288 7289 7291 7293 7297 7298 7301 7303 7304 7306 7308 7310
8 Glebe 6780 6835 6885 6915 6960 7266 7273 7293
9 Local topographic descriptions 6769 6773 6776 6783 6895 6911 6955 6971 6984 6998 6999 7063 7077 7133 7150 7178 7241 7259 7273
10 Regional topographic descriptions 6772 6788 6802 6817 6820 6826 6841 6869 6879 6888 6895 6981 7004 7051 7057 7067 7097 7139 7181 7226 7276 7279 7281
11 Village morphology 6824 6835 6938 6971 7272 7300
13 Country houses and ornamental gardens 7218
14 Farm houses and buildings 6824
15 Cottages and cottage gardens 6783
16 Field boundaries 6822 6887 6897 7139
18 Small, irregular closes 6794 6798 6806 6812 6813 6907 6936 6937 6988 7027 7040 7054 7056 7084 7129 7170 7179 7252 7253 7276 7283 7286
19 Large, regular fields 6776 6797 6804 6818 6819 6822 6823 6840 6847 6868 6880 6887 6891 6896 6914 6932 6940 6980 6981 6984 6986 7010 7011 7014 7024 7026 7036 7050 7065 7068 7080 7090 7102 7103 7117 7119 7120 7134 7142 7156 7176 7185 7188 7205 7208 7220 7239 7259 7276 7282 7285 7286 7290 7296 7309 7312
22 Plantations 6797 6804 6822 6823 6938 6955 6986 7136 7139 7235 7289
25 Poor woodland 7036
26 Commons 6783 6955 7009 7042 7107 7107
27 Furze, gorse and heathlands 6819 7051 7055 7189 7272
28 Moorland 6769 6804 6836 6870 6894 6904 6911 6955 6974 6977 6998 6999 7044 7045 7055 7090 7093 7178 7231 7241 7245 7279 7287 8067
32 Climatic hazards 6776 6781 6784 6794 6797 6801 6806 6812 6813 6818 6819 6823 6824 6826 6840 6846 6848 6852 6861 6870 6874 6887 6907 6911 6914 6936 6938 6955 6981 6988 6990 6999 7013 7014 7022 7024 7030 7039 7040 7041 7042 7044 7051 7053 7055 7056 7077 7080 7090 7093 7107 7115 7119 7120 7132 7134 7156 7171 7179 7205 7208 7220 7231 7253 7259 7260 7276 7282 7285 7287 7296 7309 7312
33 Excessively steep land 6776 6783 6895 6932 7050 7053 7055
34 Land requires drainage 6769 6771 6772 6781 6794 6798 6822 6825 6826 6827 6836 6841 6846 6852 6853 6886 6894 6897 6902 6905 6938 6951 6966 6980 7010 7011 7029 7036 7038 7040 7044 7076 7088 7119 7120 7129 7132 7139 7145 7150 7156 7160 7187 7193 7227 7252 7272 7283
35 Land liable to flood 6846 7040 7044 7307
36 Productive soil 6773 6783 6788 6794 6814 6819 6823 6825 6834 6842 6845 6846 6859 6864 6865 6868 6880 6890 6894 6896 6898 6907 6915 6924 6940 6946 6957 6958 6977 6982 6986 6989 6990 7001 7026 7027 7039 7040 7052 7078 7101 7102 7128 7133 7134 7136 7158 7166 7167 7169 7170 7171 7179 7183 7184 7185 7214 7218 7231 7235 7253 7259 7265 7266 7271 7273 7276 7279 7281 7300 7307 7311 7312
37 Poor soil 6781 6794 6798 6800 6810 6811 6848 6853 6870 6874 6875 6891 6894 6896 6899 6906 6911 6927 6938 6949 6951 6966 6996 7013 7016 7024 7036 7037 7040 7052 7053 7054 7055 7076 7088 7107 7115 7117 7129 7131 7145 7160 7218 7222 7227 7229 7231 7247 7252 7262 7266 7272 7283 7296 7300 7305 8067
38 Heavy (clay) soil 6781 6794 6798 6771 6772 6774 6781 6784 6788 6794 6797 6798 6802 6804 6806 6811 6812 6813 6817 6822 6823 6824 6826 6826 6827 6828 6836 6840 6841 6842 6846 6847 6848 6852 6856 6857 6861 6862 6867 6868 6874 6875 6886 6887 6890 6891 6897 6898 6900 6904 6905 6910 6915 6924 6926 6927 6935 6936 6937 6938 6946 6949 6951 6966 6977 6980 6982 6984 6986 6988 6992 6993 6999 7004 7010 7011 7014 7017 7018 7024 7027 7030 7034 7036 7037 7041 7042 7046 7050 7051 7052 7053 7054 7055 7056 7057 7065 7068 7076 7078 7080 7081 7084 7088 7090 7093 7107 7115 7117 7119 7120 7129 7131 7132 7137 7139 7142 7143 7145 7156 7158 7160 7162 7163 7170 7171 7172 7180 7184 7185 7186 7187 7188 7208 7209 7211 7214 7220 7222 7223 7225 7226 7227 7233 7235 7239 7240 7243 7245 7247 7252 7253 7254 7260 7266 7269 7272 7273 7276 7283 7285 7286 7288 7289 7290 7294 7295 7296 7300 7311 8067
39 Loamy (turnip) soil 6774 6776 6781 6783 6784 6788 6812 6814 6819 6836 6845 6847 6852 6868 6880 6890 6896 6900 6907 6907 6914 6915 6951 6957 6981 6984 6990 7011 7037 7038 7039 7041 7042 7046 7063 7101 7128 7133 7134

Northumberland contd.

		7183	7184	7187	7205	7208	7223	7225	7226	7231	7243	7252	7253	7254	7259	7265	7266	7276	7282	7307	7309
40	Light soil	6818	6907	6932	6998	7009	7054	7131	7205	7209	7289
41	Several varieties of soil			6869	6891	6898	6905	6907	6926	6977	6980	6992	7011	7024	7028	7034	7036	7050	7054	7065
	7067	7068	7076	7081	7132	7137	7150	7180	7188	7209	7211	7222	7223	7225	7231	7239	7247	7279
43	Sand or gravel		6773	6776	6798	6802	6804	6819	6823	6827	6840	6848	6874	6896	6907	6924	6927	6932	6937	6938
	6940	6957	6961	6986	6988	6998	7014	7018	7022	7024	7026	7027	7029	7038	7040	7044	7045	7051	7052	7053	7054
	7055	7065	7077	7078	7093	7102	7103	7115	7156	7162	7163	7170	7171	7178	7187	7188	7209	7218	7245	7252	7276
	7282	7296	7309	7311	7312
44	Peat	6788	6826	6827	6847	6894	7042	7120	7188	7247	7272
46	Good local roads		6784	6813	6819	6868	6896	6897	6932	7024	7046	7142	7143	7185	7253	7265	7266	7273
47	Poor local roads		6769	6794	6798	6806	6811	6818	6824	6826	6827	6828	6836	6848	6852	6874	6875	6905	6907	6914
	6935	6936	6937	6938	6981	6984	6988	7009	7010	7011	7014	7022	7030	7036	7041	7042	7051	7052	7053	7054	7055
	7057	7068	7076	7077	7088	7090	7093	7107	7115	7117	7132	7134	7145	7150	7162	7172	7176	7179	7187	7205	7226
	7231	7259	7260	7282	7285	7295
48	Turnpike and main roads		6774	6776	7056	7065	7088	7107	7129	7133	7179	7233	7285
50	Water carriage		6825	6859	6864	7257
52	Railways	6868	6869	6907	6957	7028	7039	7051	7052	7063	7128	7143	7170	7171	7273
53	Markets accessible		6773	6788	6794	6811	6813	6864	6867	6868	6869	6880	6897	6899	6907	6957	7026	7028	7046	7137
	7143	7171	7185	7209	7257	7266	7290
54	Markets inaccessible	6806	6820	6826	6827	6828	6848	6905	6914	6981	7009	7010	7013	7014	7022	7036	7041	7042	7044
	7076	7090	7145	7187	7245	7260	7282
55	Provincial markets	6899	7028	7046	7052
57	Fairs	6999	7241	7245
58	Market prices	6816	7016	7039	7046	7185	7265
59	Landowners and their estates		6771	6781	6800	6825	6859	6877	6887	6926	6926	7001	7016	7028	7044	7088	7113	7150
	7184	7257	7281	7306
60	Land occupiers		6769	6783	6820	6826	6836	6859	6862	6864	6906	6915	6927	6946	6958	6981	6992	7001	7026	7046
	7136	7180	7257	7294
61	Farm size	6826	6845	6875	6895	6906	6914	6915	6917	6971	7057	7132	7134	7170
62	Leases	6771	6880	6992	6993	7016
63	Farm implements	6840	7119
64	Common grazing	6783	6955
66	Rents	6774	6794	6802	6810	6814	6820	6823	6826	6836	6843	6869	6900	6906	6907	6910	6946	6951	6955	6971	6989
	6990	6996	7013	7016	7028	7034	7038	7044	7067	7101	7131	7160	7180	7184	7186	7195	7222	7225	7229	7231	7240
	7243	7247	7271	7273	7290	8067
70	Enclosure or improvement of waste		7202
71	Enclosure of commons	6894	6907	7202	7300
75	Conversion of grass to arable	6772	6810
76	Conversion of arable to pasture	6897
79	Subsoil ploughing	6794	7119
80	Reclaiming and embanking	6885	7218	7247
82	Drainage channels and ditches	6895
85	Underdrainage	6771
86	Tile drains	6859
92	Dung	6812	6813	6814	6856	6857	6867	6868	6898	6910	6977	6982	6992	6993	7034	7078	7081	7084	7137	7171	7180
	7223	7265	7266	7273	7283
93	Seaweed	6784	6840	7024	7211
95	Bones	6859
100	Oil dust, unspecified fertilisers or manures		6859
101	General comments on crop rotations		6932	6937	6938	6981	6998	7014	7016	7029	7041	7077	7088	7101	7150	7187	7265
	7281	7307
102	Irregular rotations	6769	6811	6822	6827	6836	6868	6915	6949	6966	7009	7014	7042	7054	7102	7137	7223	7253
103	3-course rotation	7222	7266	7300
104	4-course rotation	6771	6773	6776	6781	6788	6797	6798	6804	6806	6811	6812	6813	6814	6817	6823	6824	6825	6826
	6827	6828	6836	6840	6841	6846	6848	6852	6856	6857	6859	6862	6864	6867	6868	6869	6874	6875	6890	6891	6897
	6898	6899	6900	6904	6905	6907	6915	6926	6927	6935	6936	6937	6938	6940	6946	6949	6954	6957	6961	6966	6977
	6980	6982	6984	6990	6992	6993	7004	7010	7011	7012	7017	7018	7024	7026	7027	7030	7034	7036	7037	7038	7040
	7041	7042	7044	7045	7046	7050	7052	7053	7054	7055	7056	7057	7063	7065	7068	7076	7078	7080	7081	7084	7088
	7090	7102	7107	7117	7119	7129	7132	7137	7142	7143	7145	7156	7158	7160	7162	7163	7170	7171	7172	7176	7180
	7184	7185	7186	7188	7205	7208	7209	7211	7214	7218	7220	7222	7223	7225	7226	7227	7231	7233	7239	7240
	7252	7253	7254	7259	7260	7265	7266	7271	7273	7276	7281	7282	7283	7285	7286	7288	7289	7290	7295	7296	7300
	7311	8067
105	5-course rotation	6769	6776	6781	6797	6802	6818	6819	6822	6826	6842	6847	6859	6869	6880	6895	6906	6914	6924
	6938	6940	6958	6981	6986	6988	7001	7016	7022	7026	7029	7030	7052	7053	7054	7055	7067	7077	7089	7102	7103
	7133	7134	7136	7143	7162	7183	7188	7220	7247	7266	7271	7276	7312
106	6-course rotation	6781	6783	6845	6940	7093	7102	7243
107	7-course rotation	6783	7093	7162	7179
108	8-10-course rotation	7093
110	Wheat	6826	6840	6936	7120	7185	7309
111	Barley	6798	7028	7150	7185	7223	7309
112	Oats	6880	6911	7022	7026	7028	7296	7309
113	Rye or meslin	6896	6955	7055	7305
114	Corn yields	6812	6813	6814	6819	6820	6840	6865	6884	6885	6954	6981	7097	7183	7271	7291
115	Beans	6802	6836	6840	6842	6852	6897	6900	6993	7024	7039	7046	7101	7136	7142	7179	7184	7185	7225	7233	7247
	7273	7287	7290	7311	8067
116	Peas	6802	6842	6852	6900	7039	7041	7042	7044	7045	7052	7136	7162	7184	7187	7231	7247	7286	7311
123	Clover	6773	6813	6823	6828	6840	6845	6846	6852	6862	6868	6874	6875	6894	6899	6904	6907	6926	6927	6935	6936
	6937	6949	6955	6980	6984	6998	7010	7011	7012	7018	7024	7027	7036	7038	7039	7041	7042	7044	7045	7046	7050
	7056	7057	7063	7065	7067	7068	7076	7078	7080	7084	7090	7107	7117	7119	7129	7132	7136	7137	7142	7143	7145
	7156	7162	7163	7170	7171	7172	7176	7179	7183	7185	7187	7188	7205	7209	7222	7223	7226	7227	7231	7233	7245
	7247	7252	7253	7259	7260	7265	7273	7282	7283	7285	7286	7288	7290	7296	7311
129	Turnips	6769	6771	6773	6774	6781	6784	6788	6798	6802	6804	6806	6814	6817	6818	6819	6820	6823	6824	6825
	6826	6827	6836	6840	6842	6845	6846	6852	6856	6857	6864	6865	6867	6868	6874	6880	6890	6891	6894
	6894	6895	6896	6898	6905	6906	6907	6910	6914	6915	6917	6926	6932	6937	6938	6955	6957	6966	6977	6981	6984
	6986	6990	6992	6998	6999	7001	7010	7011	7016	7018	7022	7024	7026	7028	7029	7030	7034	7036	7037	7038
	7039	7040	7041	7042	7044	7045	7046	7050	7052	7056	7057	7063	7065	7067	7068	7076	7077	7078	7080	7081	7084
	7101	7102	7103	7107	7119	7120	7132	7133	7136	7137	7142	7143	7145	7156	7162	7163	7170	7171	7172	7176	7180
	7183	7184	7185	7186	7187	7188	7205	7208	7209	7211	7220	7222	7223	7225	7226	7233	7235	7239	7240	7243	7245	7247
	7252	7253	7259	7260	7265	7269	7282	7288	7289	7290	7294	7295	7296	7311	7312	8067
131	Swedes	6840
132	Potatoes	6794	6814	6817	6825	6827	6848	6856	6857	6867	6870	6874	6894	6898	6911	6915	6955	6992	6998	6999
	7011	7012	7028	7029	7034	7039	7052	7056	7068	7078	7081	7084	7132	7136	7180	7208	7223	7265	7269	7273	7287
	7288	7294	7300	7311
133	Bare fallows	6769	6771	6773	6784	6788	6794	6797	6798	6804	6811	6812	6813	6817	6819	6822	6823	6827	6828	6836
	6840	6846	6848	6852	6856	6857	6868	6874	6875	6880	6890	6891	6894	6897	6898	6899	6904	6907	6926	6927	6932	6935

Northumberland contd.

```
              6936  6937  6938  6949  6957  6966  6980  6981  6984  6986  6988  6998  7010  7011  7012  7018  7024  7026  7027  7029  7036
              7037  7039  7040  7041  7042  7044  7045  7050  7052  7054  7056  7057  7063  7065  7068  7076  7078  7080  7084  7090  7107
              7117  7119  7129  7132  7133  7137  7142  7143  7145  7156  7162  7163  7170  7171  7172  7176  7179  7188  7208  7211  7220
              7223  7226  7227  7231  7233  7245  7252  7253  7260  7265  7273  7282  7283  7285  7286  7289  7290  7295  7296  7311
134  High farming      6776  6845  6859  6880  6924  6940  6946  6958  7001  7034  7103  7131  7134  7312
135  Low farming       6769  6811  6824  6874  6905  6935  6954  7041  7265
136  Remarks on the absence of turnips    6911  7226
137  Remarks on pests and crop diseases   6917  7162
139  Good quality pastures      6773  6834  6847  6864  6895  6904  6907  7067  7218  7240  7312
140  Poor quality pastures      6801  6822  6827  6836  6840  6891  6894  6902  6904  6938  6974  6988  7024  7044  7131  7239  7276
142  Irrigation and water meadows    7307
144  Parks   6772  6986  7193
146  Cattle breeding   6769  6794  6801  6820  6841  6845  6862  6880  6897  6940  6946  6986  7004  7013  7026  7038  7097  7131
     7134  7158  7160  7183  7186  7214  7218  7222  7247  7272  7305  8067  7243  7294
147  Cattle fattening  6841  6842  6845  6887  6990  6999  7028  7101  7243  7294
148  Dairying   6773  6774  6783  6814  6818  6820  6856  6857  6862  6898  6900  6904  6910  6946  6951  6977  6982  6990  6992
     6993  7004  7034  7038  7078  7081  7101  7131  7158  7214  7218  7222  7225  7243  7247  7254  8067
149  Cow keeping  6814  6977
150  Sheep breeding    6769  6774  6802  6818  6820  6826  6827  6845  6880  6895  6900  6906  6914  6917  6940  6951  6955  6958
     6966  6971  6986  6990  7016  7026  7028  7067  7089  7097  7101  7113  7134  7136  7183  7218  7222  7240  7241  7243  7245
     7247  7254  7279  7291  7294  7309  8067
151  Sheep fattening   6801  6887  6894  6897  6904  7016  7294
152  Droving    7272
153  Horses   6774  6783  6794  6814  6856  6857  6898  6910  6946  6977  6982  6992  7004  7034  7038  7078  7081  7101  7158  7214
158  Deer     6769  6986  7044  7193
159  Animal diseases.  6794  7040  7240
160  Straw    6788  6802  6856  6857  6898  6982  6992  6993  7039  7081  7209
161  Hay      6776  6788  6856  6857  6895  6898  6905  6915  6955  6982  6992  6993  6999  7038  7039  7078  7081  7088  7180  7186
     7209  7288  7311
162  Manufactured feedstuffs (cake etc.)    7038
163  Stall or yard feeding   6802  6906  7029  7063
164  Milk     6773
167  Wool     6826
172  Market gardens    6907  6910  6915  7052  7078
174  Cabbages    7052
176  Onions      7052
```

Nottinghamshire

```
1   Tithe-free district    7313  7314  7315  7319  7326  7327  7329  7330  7333  7337  7338  7342  7346  7349  7353  7354  7355  7356
    7359  7360  7361  7362  7370  7371  7375  7376  7377  7378  7379  7380  7385  7387  7388  7389  7392  7393  7394  7395  7398
    7399  7401  7406  7407  7408  7410  7414  7415  7418  7420  7422  7423  7424  7427  7428  7429  7432  7436  7437  7439  7440
    7445  7447  7454  7455  7457  7458  7461  7462  7463  7469  7470  7472  7476  7480  7483  7484  7485  7486  7488  7490  7495
    7502  7503  7504  7505  7506  7510  7512  7514  7517  7520  7521  7524  7528  7531  7533  7534  7536  7540  7543  7544  7546
    7547  7551  7557  7558  7563  7565  7566  7567  7569  7575  7576  7579  7580  7582  7587  7591  8883
2   History of tithe payment     7340  7441  7443  7509
3   Tithe practices and agriculture   7417  7465  7536  7577
4   Exemptions from tithe    7316  7317  7322  7324  7325  7331  7335  7339  7340  7343  7344  7348  7351  7364  7366  7367  7368
    7373  7381  7382  7390  7396  7397  7409  7411  7412  7430  7431  7433  7435  7442  7446  7451  7453  7456  7464  7468  7475
    7477  7479  7482  7489  7492  7497  7500  7518  7522  7529  7532  7537  7538  7541  7548  7549  7550  7553  7554  7570  7571
    7573  7574  7577  7581  7584  7590
5   Tithe in kind   7323  7336  7339  7421  7426  7433  7450  7451  7464  7492  7499  7532  7577
6   Compositions    7316  7317  7322  7341  7343  7344  7358  7363  7366  7368  7373  7374  7382  7383  7384  7390  7391  7404  7421
    7431  7434  7438  7441  7442  7444  7446  7450  7466  7467  7468  7482  7489  7491  7492  7499  7518  7523  7525  7529  7530
    7536  7560  7573
7   Moduses   7316  7318  7321  7331  7332  7334  7344  7363  7372  7374  7382  7397  7403  7411  7421  7431  7434  7441  7456
    7465  7471  7474  7478  7492  7499  7522  7523  7525  7529  7532  7549  7550  7560  7561
8   Glebe   7366  7368  7373  7374  7438  7441  7450  7479
9   Local topographic descriptions    7381  7419
10  Regional topographic descriptions  7317  7334  7339  7402  7433  7451  7466  7545
11  Village morphology  7317  7321  7386  7419  7433  7539
12  Church   7321  7459
13  Country houses and ornamental gardens  7320  7339  7419  7496  7585
15  Cottages and cottage gardens   7317  7320  7332  7386  7412  7516  7535  7539  7554
17  Open fields  7386  7459  7507  7577
18  Small, irregular closes  7465
21  Coppice  7320  7386  7419
22  Plantations  7320  7321  7332  7487  7519  7535  7589
23  Woodland management  7351  7381  7419
24  Productive woodland  7464
25  Poor woodland   7396  7553  7589
26  Commons  7386  7465  7523
27  Furze, gorse and heathlands   7523
28  Moorland  7332
32  Climatic hazards   7335  7382  7508  7513  7559  7585
33  Excessively steep land  7467
34  Land requires drainage  7323  7416  7507  7516  7519  7523  7530  7539  7552
35  Land liable to flood  7321  7332  7402  7405  7412  7451  7492  7494  7513  7516  7535  7539  7585
36  Productive soil   7320  7323  7332  7336  7339  7347  7382  7386  7396  7405  7433  7451  7464  7471  7494  7507  7516  7519
    7535  7554  7577  7578  7585
37  Poor soil   7321  7323  7332  7381  7386  7402  7412  7416  7417  7419  7426  7465  7466  7467  7477  7508  7516  7519  7523
    7530  7553  7554  7559  7585  7589
38  Heavy (clay) soil   7320  7323  7332  7332  7335  7347  7382  7386  7396  7402  7405  7416  7417  7419  7426  7433  7438  7451
    7464  7465  7466  7467  7471  7487  7492  7494  7516  7519  7523  7530  7535  7552  7553  7577  7578  7585  7589
39  Loamy (turnip) soil   7320  7323  7332  7334  7347  7426  7433  7438  7471  7494  7519  7535  7539  7542  7554  7585
40  Light soil   7320  7323  7332  7405  7412  7448  7465  7466  7467  7471  7492  7496  7516  7530  7545  7571  7577
41  Several varieties of soil   7332  7335  7402  7403  7492
43  Sand or gravel   7321  7335  7347  7381  7402  7403  7405  7412  7426  7433  7448  7459  7464  7467  7477  7487  7496  7508
    7513  7542  7553  7559  7570  7571  7589
44  Peat   7459  7496  7542  7554  7585
45  Fields remote from farms  7438
46  Good local roads  7347  7464  7487  7535
47  Poor local roads  7335  7589
48  Turnpike and main roads   7320  7332  7336  7419  7464  7516
```

Nottinghamshire contd.

50	Water carriage	7320																
51	Canals 7589																	
53	Markets accessible	7320	7321	7336	7347	7464	7477	7535	7554	7589								
55	Provincial markets	7336	7347	7433	7589													
59	Landowners and their estates		7321	7321	7381	7467	7530	7530	7552	7585	7585							
60	Land occupiers	7321	7323	7336	7417	7438	7477	7577										
61	Farm size 7317	7417	7467	7471	7523													
62	Leases 7347 7453 7513																	
63	Farm implements 7381																	
65	Lammas and other common rights			7465	7466	7523												
66	Rents 7335 7347 7405 7416	7465	7487	7492	7496	7513	7523	7527	7530	7553								
67	Urban influences on value of land	7320	7477															
68	Rates 7465																	
70	Enclosure or improvement of waste		7553															
71	Enclosure of commons	7504	7533															
72	Enclosure of open fields	7338	7364	7402	7422	7428	7435	7469	7542	7544	7566	7569	7577	7578				
75	Conversion of grass to arable	7513	7585															
76	Conversion of arable to pasture	7426																
78	Warping 7585																	
82	Drainage channels and ditches	7492																
83	Steam pumps 7585																	
85	Underdrainage	7382	7467	7523	7530	7542	7553	7585										
86	Tile drains 7335 7419																	
87	Marl 7467																	
92	Dung 7335 7347 7451 7536																	
95	Bones 7335 7467																	
98	Rape cake 7467																	
100	Oil dust, unspecified fertilisers or manures		7334															
101	General comments on crop rotations	7459	7578															
102	Irregular rotations 7405																	
103	3-course rotation	7382	7386	7419	7451	7494	7507	7552	7577	7578								
104	4-course rotation	7320	7334	7335	7339	7381	7382	7396	7402	7416	7448	7451	7465	7467	7471	7487	7496	7527	7535
	7545 7553 7570 7585																	
105	5-course rotation	7321	7335	7347	7381	7402	7403	7433	7464	7465	7467	7494	7496	7508	7523	7527	7530	7559	7571
	7589																	
106	6-course rotation	7321	7335	7433	7530	7535												
110	Wheat 7403 7453																	
113	Rye or meslin	7323	7332	7403	7412	7496	7519	7553	7585									
114	Corn yields 7438 7467 7552 7554																	
115	Beans 7336 7347 7386 7396	7419	7426	7433	7451	7459	7494	7507	7516	7519	7530	7577	7578	7589				
116	Peas 7321 7402 7403 7438	7513	7530															
123	Clover 7335 7347 7381 7386	7402	7419	7433	7453	7471	7513	7516	7530	7535	7539	7542	7552	7578	7589			
126	Tares and vetches 7419 7530 7585																	
129	Turnips 7321 7332 7335 7336	7347	7381	7402	7403	7412	7433	7448	7459	7464	7465	7471	7477	7487	7494	7496		
	7508 7513 7519 7523 7527 7530 7535 7539 7542 7553 7554 7559 7570 7571 7585																	
132	Potatoes 7336 7438 7466 7519 7523 7530																	
133	Bare fallows 7332 7347 7416	7419	7433	7448	7464	7465	7471	7487	7494	7507	7523	7530	7535	7542	7552	7553	7554	
	7571 7577 7578 7589																	
134	High farming 7321 7467 7477 7508 7559 7585 7589																	
135	Low farming 7323 7552																	
136	Remarks on the absence of turnips	7417	7516															
138	Recent increase in productivity	7519	7536	7570	7585													
139	Good quality pastures	7320	7321	7323	7336	7347	7386	7405	7412	7417	7419	7426	7433	7466	7471	7477	7494	7513
	7516 7519 7535 7539 7554 7578																	
140	Poor quality pastures	7321	7323	7386	7405	7412	7507	7516	7554	7585	7589							
141	Meadows 7320 7321 7323 7336	7382	7386	7412	7426	7451	7466	7513	7516	7535	7539	7554						
142	Irrigation and water meadows	7405	7467	7467	7507													
143	Marsh grassland 7412																	
144	Parks 7320 7321 7339 7419 7535 7585 7589																	
145	Accommodation land 7320 7466 7477 7541																	
146	Cattle breeding 7396 7465 7471 7487 7492 7527 7553 7571 7589																	
147	Cattle fattening 7335 7405 7419 7433 7464 7471 7527 7570																	
148	Dairying 7396 7416 7419 7433 7466 7471 7523 7527 7570 7571																	
150	Sheep breeding 7321 7335 7396 7416 7433 7465 7466 7467 7487 7492 7496 7513 7527 7539 7553 7570 7571																	
151	Sheep fattening 7321 7323 7419 7508 7559																	
153	Horses 7466 7496																	
154	Pigs 7523																	
155	Oxen 7464																	
156	Poultry 7523																	
158	Deer 7589																	
159	Animal diseases 7419																	
160	Straw 7335 7405 7527																	
161	Hay 7320 7323 7347 7405 7513																	
162	Manufactured feedstuffs (cake etc.)	7467	7508	7559														
164	Milk 7347 7433 7466																	
165	Butter 7335 7487																	
166	Cheese 7335 7405 7419 7589																	
169	Good orchards 7336 7386 7426 7554																	
172	Market gardens 7336																	
178	Hops 7391 7419 7426 7573																	
181	Reeds and oziers 7513 7554																	

Oxfordshire

1	Tithe-free district	7592	7595	7596	7599	7601	7603	7608	7609	7611	7613	7617	7618	7619	7621	7622	7624	7626	7629
	7632	7637	7647	7650	7653	7655	7656	7657	7658	7659	7661	7673	7675	7677	7680	7684	7686	7690	7693	7700	7702
	7703	7704	7705	7711	7713	7714	7715	7719	7725	7731	7735	7740	7741	7744	7746	7756	7762	7767	7771	7777	7781
	7782	7784	7786	7790	7792	7794	7795	7796	7797	7798	7800	7804	7805	7806	7811	7813	7814	7815	7816	7818	7820
	7822	7823	7825	7826	7837	7839	7841	7842	7843	7844	7851	7852	9167						
2	History of tithe payment	7659	7768	7769	7801														
3	Tithe practices and agriculture	7646	7654																
4	Exemptions from tithe	7600	7614	7620	7623	7625	7633	7636	7639	7641	7643	7644	7646	7649	7652	7662	7663	7665
	7669	7670	7672	7676	7678	7687	7688	7691	7694	7697	7709	7710	7712	7720	7721	7722	7723	7726	7727	7728	7733
	7737	7738	7742	7743	7750	7752	7753	7754	7755	7758	7760	7763	7764	7765	7768	7770	7772	7773	7774	7780	7783

Oxfordshire contd.

```
              7791 7801 7803 7807 7808 7809 7810 7812 7817 7819 7830 7831 7835 7836 7846 7849 7850 9166
  5  Tithe in kind            7600 7604 7610 7638 7654 7676 7685 7726 7752 7765 7808 7809
  6  Compositions             7597 7604 7630 7631 7641 7644 7645 7662 7663 7669 7676 7685 7691 7706 7707 7717 7720 7726 7727
     7728 7729 7730 7733 7747 7749 7758 7766 7769 7770 7772 7774 7779 7783 7789 7793 7801 7803 7807 7808 7810
     7829 7831 7835 7838 7849 7854 7855
  7  Moduses          7610 7651 7654 7707 7729 7751 7760 7764 7785 7803 7807 7832 7854
  8  Glebe       7630 7643 7654 7685 7717 7720 7727 7730 7736 7774 7838
  9  Local topographic descriptions        7664 7666 7757 7776 7780 7812 7833
 10  Regional topographic descriptions     7615 7634 7732 7821
 11  Village morphology        7732 7739 7809 7847
 12  Church                    7602 7646 7664 7716 7734 7780 7785 7812
 13  Country houses and ornamental gardens 7593 7667 7710 7710 7716 7785
 16  Field boundaries          7664 7734
 17  Open fields               7602 7615 7642 7654 7666 7678 7698 7710 7729 7748 7775 7776
 21  Coppice                   7687 7694 7763 7776 7785
 22  Plantations               7848
 24  Productive woodland       7646 7664 7709
 25  Poor woodland             7710 7716 7759 7809
 26  Commons           7652 7652 7664 7698 7743 7748 7773 7809 7849
 31  Wasteland         7748 7759 7773 7776
 32  Climatic hazards  7712 7754 7780 7833
 33  Excessively steep land    7666 7773
 34  Land requires drainage    7612 7710 7754 7757 7759 7785 7802 7824
 35  Land liable to flood  7602 7648 7654 7667 7678 7688 7757 7761
 36  Productive soil           7615 7616 7649 7665 7667 7668 7678 7681 7688 7734 7739 7752 7765 7785 7799 7828 7833
 37  Poor soil         7598 7634 7666 7670 7679 7688 7701 7710 7716 7718 7721 7734 7738 7745 7773 7785 7791 7809
 38  Heavy (clay) soil         7593 7602 7605 7612 7616 7620 7625 7646 7648 7649 7654 7664 7667 7679 7681 7682 7683 7687
     7688 7692 7695 7698 7709 7710 7724 7732 7734 7738 7739 7748 7750 7752 7753 7754 7757 7759 7760 7761 7763
     7776 7785 7788 7812 7819 7824 7833 7840 7848
 39  Loamy (turnip) soil       7602 7625 7646 7668 7678 7724 7799
 40  Light soil        7614 7615 7654 7664 7667 7668 7670 7679 7696 7701 7716 7718 7732 7734 7745 7748 7750 7752 7757
     7763 7776 7788 7799 7821 7848 7850
 41  Several varieties of soil 7602 7620 7687 7752 7753 7776
 42  Chalk       7605 7620 7646 7666 7667 7687 7709 7721 7738 7742 7752 7763 7773 7780 7791 7809 7819
 43  Sand or gravel            7602 7614 7646 7671 7687 7688 7692 7698 7710 7712 7716 7748 7750 7752 7754 7763 7776 7780
     7785 7833
 45  Fields remote from farms  7598 7679
 46  Good local roads          7709 7712 7724 7850
 47  Poor local roads          7602 7646 7681 7802
 48  Turnpike and main roads   7748 7750 7754 7763 7765 7788 7809 7821 7824 7828
 50  Water carriage            7709
 53  Markets accessible        7674 7709 7712 7850
 55  Provincial markets        7674
 56  London market             7692 7759
 58  Market prices             7674 7732
 59  Landowners and their estates      7597 7667 7679 7716 7732 7739 7743 7745 7752 7802
 60  Land occupiers            7679 7681 7732 7739 7752 7757 7776
 61  Farm size                 7602 7642 7646 7664 7665 7678 7681 7709 7734 7750 7760 7780 7833
 62  Leases      7642
 64  Common grazing            7652 7732 7734 7776 7849
 65  Lammas and other common rights    7664 7743 7776 7788
 66  Rents       7716 7734 7739
 68  Rates       7644 7646 7664 7685 7734 7761 7780 7787 7808 7812 7833
 70  Enclosure or improvement of waste 7695 7697
 71  Enclosure of commons              7664 7697
 72  Enclosure of open fields          7599 7601 7613 7631 7641 7642 7654 7669 7679 7694 7695 7698 7723 7728 7731 7737 7748
     7760 7841 7852
 75  Conversion of grass to arable     7739
 82  Drainage channels and ditches     7824
 85  Underdrainage             7739 7754
 86  Tile drains       7754
 92  Dung        7709 7828
100  Oil dust, unspecified fertilisers or manures  7646
101  General comments on crop rotations    7612 7654 7681 7687 7718 7750 7776 7788 7802 7819
102  Irregular rotations       7598 7615 7721 7729 7750 7785
103  3-course rotation         7616 7681 7683 7692 7724 7812 7824 7840
104  4-course rotation         7593 7602 7605 7615 7620 7625 7642 7646 7648 7649 7654 7668 7670 7671 7674 7678 7681 7682
     7687 7688 7695 7698 7701 7710 7712 7721 7724 7734 7739 7742 7745 7748 7750 7752 7753 7754 7760 7761 7765
     7773 7776 7780 7788 7828 7848 7850
105  5-course rotation         7625 7634 7664 7666 7696 7709 7721 7734 7738 7759 7799 7819 7821 7828 7833
106  6-course rotation         7634 7718
107  7-course rotation         7716
110  Wheat       7678 7732
114  Corn yields       7641 7671 7676 7681 7724 7729 7732 7738 7745 7787 7829 7846
115  Beans       7602 7605 7615 7648 7649 7654 7667 7668 7678 7679 7681 7682 7683 7692 7698 7701 7718 7724 7739 7748
     7750 7757 7759 7761 7776 7788 7799 7802 7812 7824 7828 7840 7848
116  Peas        7667 7734 7748 7757
122  Unspecified grass seeds           7716
123  Clover      7602 7615 7646 7664 7668 7678 7682 7688 7692 7696 7701 7709 7712 7716 7718 7721 7734 7738 7742 7745
     7748 7753 7757 7760 7761 7773 7776 7780 7812 7828 7833 7840 7848
124  Sainfoin          7598 7634 7646 7667 7687 7716 7752 7763 7780 7850
126  Tares and vetches 7616 7681 7724 7734 7739 7750 7752 7763 7812 7840
129  Turnips     7602 7612 7615 7620 7634 7646 7648 7649 7654 7664 7665 7666 7667 7668 7678 7679 7682 7688 7692
     7696 7701 7709 7710 7712 7716 7718 7721 7724 7734 7738 7739 7742 7745 7748 7750 7752 7753 7754 7757 7759
     7760 7763 7773 7780 7788 7799 7819 7821 7828 7833 7840 7848 7850
130  Mangolds    7667
131  Swedes      7667
132  Potatoes    7615 7698 7718 7757
133  Bare fallows      7602 7605 7615 7616 7648 7649 7654 7678 7679 7683 7692 7698 7701 7718 7724 7739 7748 7750 7752
     7754 7757 7759 7761 7763 7799 7812 7824 7833 7840 7848
134  High farming      7625 7682 7752 7753
135  Low farming       7615 7642 7666 7679 7681 7698 7710 7757 7759 7785 7802
136  Remarks on the absence of turnips     7616 7809
139  Good quality pastures     7614 7665 7667 7668 7678 7682 7683 7698 7712 7724 7739 7748 7759 7765 7785 7799
140  Poor quality pastures     7612 7634 7679 7681 7695 7710 7712 7716 7745 7753 7754 7759 7761 7785 7802 7809 7819
```

Oxfordshire contd.

141	Meadows	7614	7620	7648	7654	7667	7668	7670	7679	7681	7688	7698	7701	7716	7724	7739	7757	7765	7775	7785
	7821	7847																	
143	Marsh grassland	7602																	
144	Parks	7696	7710	7716	7745	7785													
146	Cattle breeding	7615																	
147	Cattle fattening	7665	7692	7724	7775														
148	Dairying	7665	7674	7682	7695	7710	7739	7760	7840										
150	Sheep breeding	7687	7695	7696	7709	7721	7739	7753	7760	7791	7809	7848	7850						
151	Sheep fattening	7681	7696	7709	7739	7848													
153	Horses	7709	7760																
154	Pigs	7732	7809																
158	Deer	7716	7776																
161	Hay	7648	7667	7688	7716	7739	7754	7785	7828	7840									
162	Manufactured feedstuffs (cake etc.)			7802															
163	Stall or yard feeding	7739																	
165	Butter	7665	7739	7759	7828														
166	Cheese	7698	7739	7828															
169	Good orchards	7667																	
171	Fruits	7748																	
173	Allotments	7732																	
181	Reeds and oziers	7678																	

Rutland

1	Tithe-free district	7858	7861	7863	7867	7868	7870	7872	7873	7875	7882	7890	7891	7894	7895	7896	7898	7899	7905
	7912	7914																	
2	History of tithe payment	7879	7885																
4	Exemptions from tithe	7878	7900	7908	7910														
6	Compositions	7857	7862	7874	7876	7880	7886	7887	7901	7909	7911								
7	Moduses	7866	7879	7884	7888														
8	Glebe	7857	7901	7908	7911	7913													
10	Regional topographic descriptions	7856																	
14	Farm houses and buildings	7856																	
16	Field boundaries	7856																	
17	Open fields	7859	7888	7893	7897														
26	Commons	7859																	
32	Climatic hazards	7892																	
34	Land requires drainage	7897																	
35	Land liable to flood	7859																	
36	Productive soil	7856	7903																
37	Poor soil	7869	7883																
38	Heavy (clay) soil	7859	7869	7889	7892	7893	7903	7904	7913										
39	Loamy (turnip) soil	7877	7889	7893	7900	7903	7904	7907											
40	Light soil	7859	7869																
46	Good local roads	7856																	
47	Poor local roads	7869	7913																
48	Turnpike and main roads	7903	7907																
53	Markets accessible	7856	7913																
55	Provincial markets	7893																	
59	Landowners and their estates	7859																	
60	Land occupiers	7859	7893																
65	Lammas and other common rights	7859																	
66	Rents	7859	7902	7903															
68	Rates	7864																	
69	Farm labour and wages	7859																	
92	Dung	7893																	
101	General comments on crop rotations	7893																	
103	3-course rotation	7859	7889																
104	4-course rotation	7856	7869	7877	7897	7900	7913												
105	5-course rotation	7878	7900	7903	7904	7907													
106	6-course rotation	7859	7877	7883	7893	7904													
112	Oats	7907																	
115	Beans	7859	7889	7893	7904														
116	Peas	7859	7893																
118	Coleseed	7897																	
123	Clover	7900	7904	7907															
126	Tares and vetches	7907																	
129	Turnips	7856	7859	7869	7877	7878	7883	7893	7900	7903	7904	7907	7913						
133	Bare fallows	7856	7859	7869	7877	7878	7883												
134	High farming	7883	7903																
135	Low farming	7869																	
139	Good quality pastures	7856	7902																
141	Meadows	7859																	
144	Parks	7883																	
146	Cattle breeding	7877	7892																
147	Cattle fattening	7877	7889	7900	7902														
150	Sheep breeding	7892	7893	7900															
151	Sheep fattening	7889	7900																
153	Horses	7893																	
161	Hay	7859																	
181	Reeds and oziers	7907																	

Shropshire

1	Tithe-free district	7954	8048	8050	8090	8091	8101	8124	8135	8170	8171	8202	8219	8224	8237	8244	8279	8296	8369
2	History of tithe payment	7927	7938	7949	7953	8081	8129	8139	8161	8280	8351								
3	Tithe practices and agriculture	7925	8206	8323															
4	Exemptions from tithe	7526	7920	7925	7927	7938	7952	7959	7961	7965	7974	7975	7979	7988	7995	7996	7999	8000
	8002	8006	8010	8013	8021	8027	8043	8051	8057	8068	8074	8078	8087	8089	8095	8098	8099	8102	8109	8114
	8123	8125	8128	8134	8136	8140	8155	8162	8163	8166	8181	8183	8201	8250	8253	8254	8259	8267	8272	8288	8308
	8337	8347	8351	8364															
5	Tithe in kind	7526	7947	7977	7981	8006	8007	8043	8082	8083	8087	8106	8116	8119	8200	8267	8274	8275	8298	8321
6	Compositions	7916	7919	7924	7925	7928	7934	7972	7985	7989	7994	7997	8000	8007	8022	8023	8024	8026	8029	8037

Shropshire contd.

8043 8056 8060 8062 8075 8080 8082 8089 8094 8104 8108 8117 8119 8125 8133 8142 8151 8152 8157 8159 8175 8187 8193 8203 8208 8240 8247 8248 8254 8256 8267 8272 8274 8281 8285 8290 8291 8297 8315 8326 8328 8332 8335 8351 8352 8358 8359 8361 8363

7 Moduses 7917 7919 7921 7925 7927 7930 7938 7942 7948 7949 7951 7953 7959 7961 7966 7968 7970 7973 7978 7980 7981 7988 7990 7997 8004 8005 8006 8008 8009 8010 8017 8018 8022 8026 8031 8033 8034 8037 8038 8039 8043 8044 8047 8060 8061 8065 8071 8073 8078 8080 8082 8086 8089 8092 8093 8098 8102 8104 8105 8106 8107 8109 8115 8125 8127 8129 8132 8139 8140 8143 8145 8150 8151 8154 8155 8157 8160 8161 8167 8180 8183 8183 8184 8185 8186 8189 8191 8192 8194 8198 8203 8211 8231 8232 8235 8248 8251 8253 8254 8256 8259 8262 8275 8280 8281 8285 8286 8288 8290 8294 8297 8301 8302 8303 8306 8308 8309 8312 8313 8320 8322 8324 8325 8326 8327 8328 8333 8348 8350 8353 8361 8364

8 Glebe 7940 7969

9 Local topographic descriptions 7930 7965 7977 7981 8015 8028 8033 8063 8065 8131 8155 8163 8173 8179 8192 8239 8251 8253 8281 8298 8313 8314

10 Regional topographic descriptions 7946 7947 7970 7987 7992 8061 8076 8102 8231 8261 8303 8318 8333 8357 8364

11 Village morphology 8052 8088

12 Church 8088

14 Farm houses and buildings 8001 8038 8038

16 Field boundaries 7971 8323

18 Small, irregular closes 8001 8172 8257 8323

19 Large, regular fields 8327 8360

21 Coppice 7930 7950 7965 7972 8053 8267

22 Plantations 7925 7940 7965 7970 7971 8008 8057 8113 8172 8173 8181 8185 8216 8242 8293 8298 8306 8338 8360

23 Woodland management 8053 8153 8267

24 Productive woodland 8063 8111

25 Poor woodland 8120

26 Commons 7993 8015 8033 8061 8121 8163 8172 8173 8314

27 Furze, gorse and heathlands 7925 8065 8070 8283

28 Moorland 8216

31 Wasteland 7961 8163

32 Climatic hazards 7946 7990 7999 8015 8022 8038 8063 8065 8102 8163 8173 8194 8198 8220 8223 8238 8252 8261 8283 8314 8346 8350

33 Excessively steep land 7917 7961 7967 7968 7969 8015 8053 8062 8175 8194 8220 8238 8252 8257 8346

34 Land requires drainage 7940 7943 7946 7947 7961 7965 7970 7972 7984 7985 7990 8009 8010 8022 8033 8053 8058 8062 8063 8071 8079 8088 8115 8118 8132 8134 8136 8168 8175 8183 8185 8201 8232 8259 8286 8307 8319 8324

35 Land liable to flood 7925 7940 7977 7981 7985 8009 8038 8058 8063 8071 8079 8160 8178 8197 8198 8311 8321

36 Productive soil 7925 7950 7960 7965 7968 7971 7991 7996 8001 8006 8008 8016 8021 8038 8057 8069 8071 8073 8074 8079 8102 8111 8114 8121 8132 8158 8162 8169 8178 8179 8189 8194 8222 8223 8226 8239 8263 8273 8281 8283 8286 8293 8303 8305 8306 8309 8311 8316 8339 8342 8350 8360 8364 8368

37 Poor soil 7940 7947 7952 7960 7965 7967 7984 7985 7987 7990 7991 7995 7999 8001 8006 8009 8010 8015 8021 8022 8028 8053 8057 8061 8062 8068 8073 8079 8083 8100 8102 8111 8115 8121 8127 8155 8162 8163 8172 8179 8184 8191 8194 8197 8198 8201 8213 8221 8222 8238 8239 8241 8251 8252 8257 8271 8283 8286 8305 8313 8318 8319 8323 8342 8344 8346 8354

38 Heavy (clay) soil 7526 7917 7920 7921 7922 7925 7930 7936 7940 7942 7943 7946 7947 7951 7952 7959 7960 7961 7962 7964 7965 7968 7970 7971 7972 7975 7977 7979 7981 7984 7985 7987 7988 7990 7991 7993 7995 7999 8001 8004 8005 8009 8010 8014 8015 8016 8018 8021 8022 8031 8033 8038 8040 8045 8046 8051 8052 8053 8057 8058 8061 8062 8069 8070 8073 8078 8079 8087 8088 8097 8100 8109 8113 8123 8126 8129 8131 8134 8136 8140 8144 8145 8153 8154 8155 8158 8160 8167 8172 8173 8178 8181 8182 8183 8185 8189 8191 8197 8198 8199 8206 8207 8216 8221 8222 8226 8227 8231 8232 8235 8238 8239 8241 8242 8253 8257 8259 8261 8265 8270 8273 8281 8286 8287 8294 8303 8305 8306 8307 8311 8312 8314 8316 8318 8319 8321 8323 8324 8327 8330 8337 8338 8339 8340 8342 8344 8346 8347 8350 8357 8367

39 Loamy (turnip) soil 7917 7921 7925 7940 7947 7951 7959 7961 7965 7971 7975 7977 7979 7987 7991 7999 8001 8004 8006 8008 8009 8014 8015 8016 8021 8027 8031 8038 8045 8053 8057 8059 8062 8070 8071 8073 8074 8078 8087 8102 8111 8134 8153 8167 8168 8183 8185 8189 8201 8216 8223 8226 8232 8239 8241 8259 8261 8263 8265 8283 8286 8303 8305 8316 8327 8330 8356 8367

40 Light soil 7950 7955 7957 7969 7975 7977 8001 8002 8004 8008 8009 8031 8038 8057 8065 8070 8073 8088 8095 8097 8113 8120 8121 8126 8136 8138 8141 8175 8183 8191 8199 8211 8213 8220 8222 8223 8235 8239 8251 8252 8257 8259 8260 8262 8273 8283 8298 8309 8313 8314 8318 8321 8323 8327 8342 8350 8364 8368

41 Several varieties of soil 7930 7936 7962 7968 7977 7985 8004 8014 8051 8052 8057 8058 8071 8076 8087 8097 8113 8114 8129 8131 8132 8154 8155 8162 8168 8175 8181 8183 8189 8227 8239 8265 8273 8281 8283 8294 8298 8305 8306 8323 8324 8327 8338 8342

43 Sand or gravel 7526 7925 7930 7936 7940 7942 7943 7950 7955 7960 7962 7970 7971 7988 8001 8006 8008 8009 8016 8058 8070 8073 8076 8079 8095 8100 8113 8114 8121 8132 8144 8145 8169 8172 8179 8181 8189 8191 8192 8194 8198 8200 8201 8241 8242 8251 8265 8271 8275 8286 8289 8298 8306 8308 8309 8312 8321 8323 8324 8327 8338 8339 8347 8360 8364 8368

44 Peat 7940 7960 7970 8009 8070 8073 8074 8095 8102 8113 8169 8181 8183 8189 8200 8305 8321 8324 8327 8339

46 Good local roads 7943 7950 7969 7970 8022 8052 8070 8073 8074 8102 8181 8182 8183 8194 8201 8211 8239 8242 8251 8257 8263 8303 8318 8323 8327 8338 8360 8364

47 Poor local roads 7916 7940 7943 7946 7967 7990 8009 8058 8061 8063 8068 8088 8095 8131 8136 8138 8160 8172 8173 8175 8183 8184 8198 8201 8220 8242 8313 8338

48 Turnpike and main roads 7921 7930 7947 7962 7965 7979 7985 7987 8008 8010 8022 8031 8057 8088 8100 8109 8111 8115 8120 8123 8134 8140 8153 8154 8155 8167 8168 8199 8207 8260 8275 8294 8305 8342 8344 8357 8367

51 Canals 7943 8241

53 Markets accessible 7947 7964 7969 8016 8052 8071 8109 8123 8158 8181 8201 8239 8241 8253 8263 8270 8273 8303 8318 8323 8327 8339 8364

54 Markets inaccessible 7916 7990 8015 8061 8065 8068 8088 8095 8131 8136 8163 8175 8220 8261 8316

55 Provincial markets 8052 8073 8303 8323

57 Fairs 8022 8175

58 Market prices 7981

59 Landowners and their estates 7979 8001 8058 8069 8070 8097 8118 8136 8140 8153 8182 8192 8308 8312 8319 8354 8364

60 Land occupiers 7930 7940 7951 7985 8062 8076 8114 8121 8305 8305 8311 8312 8319 8337

61 Farm size 7995 8015 8178 8312

62 Leases 8175

63 Farm implements 8120 8136 8364

64 Common grazing 8033 8179

66 Rents 7930 7942 7950 7952 7961 7964 7970 7979 7985 7988 7996 8001 8004 8009 8021 8027 8057 8076 8111 8114 8126 8129 8132 8136 8138 8173 8178 8181 8191 8213 8220 8232 8238 8253 8270 8281 8318 8321 8324 8338

67 Urban influences on value of land 8158 8213 8257

68 Rates 7928 7943 7970 8291

70 Enclosure or improvement of waste 7999 8065 8136 8251 8344

71 Enclosure of commons 8057 8136 8314 8351

75 Conversion of grass to arable 8018 8082

76 Conversion of arable to pasture 8120 8123 8140

79 Subsoil ploughing 7979 8073 8153

80 Reclaiming and embanking 7960 8178 8241

Shropshire contd.

85	Underdrainage		7968	7979	7984	8009	8052	8070	8074	8140	8153	8199	8316	8339	8357				
86	Tile drains	8058	8070	8073	8201	8318	8327	8354	8364										
89	Lime	7922	7930	7984	8057	8063	8111	8118	8201										
92	Dung	7968	7970	8045	8073	8158	8227	8323											
95	Bones	8057																	
100	Oil dust, unspecified fertilisers or manures				7979	8199													
101	General comments on crop rotations			7921	7922	7946	7961	7979	8006	8040	8057	8058	8076	8100	8138	8140	8160	8169	
	8183	8191	8199	8216	8221	8231	8261	8289	8309	8311	8313	8323	8338						
102	Irregular rotations		7960	7969	8002	8040	8053	8172	8173	8175	8183	8241	8265	8306	8319	8323	8327	8350	
103	3-course rotation		7526	7942	7972	7981	7987	7995	8004	8016	8046	8051	8061	8062	8069	8083	8118	8184	8201	8261
	8286	8312	8346	8356															
104	4-course rotation		7917	7920	7921	7925	7929	7930	7940	7942	7943	7950	7951	7952	7957	7961	7962	7964	7964	7965
	7970	7971	7975	7977	7981	7985	7987	7988	7993	7996	8001	8004	8005	8006	8009	8010	8015	8016	8022	8027	8031
	8033	8038	8051	8052	8062	8070	8071	8074	8076	8078	8079	8095	8097	8102	8109	8111	8113	8114	8119	8126	8127
	8131	8132	8134	8136	8141	8144	8145	8154	8167	8168	8173	8181	8185	8191	8192	8194	8199	8200	8201	8206	8211
	8213	8220	8226	8232	8238	8241	8253	8259	8261	8262	8270	8271	8273	8281	8283	8286	8289	8294	8298	8303	8307
	8312	8314	8318	8324	8330	8333	8337	8347	8350	8360	8367	8368								
105	5-course rotation		7526	7921	7925	7929	7930	7940	7943	7946	7951	7952	7955	7962	7965	7967	7970	7977	7979	7981
	7988	7990	7999	8008	8015	8027	8028	8031	8038	8045	8053	8059	8061	8062	8068	8070	8076	8079	8097	8102	8111
	8113	8115	8119	8120	8121	8123	8126	8134	8136	8153	8154	8160	8163	8167	8172	8173	8175	8178	8179	8192	8198
	8207	8216	8221	8222	8223	8231	8232	8251	8252	8257	8260	8271	8275	8308	8309	8316	8324	8327	8330	8337	8338
	8340	8354	8357																	
106	6-course rotation		7922	8040	8070	8111	8129	8181	8185	8198	8227	8340								
108	8-10-course rotation		7991																	
110	Wheat	8002	8018	8144	8346															
111	Barley	7946	8173																	
112	Oats	7965	8065																	
113	Rye or meslin		7922	8063	8070	8100	8111													
114	Corn yields	8018	8058	8069	8083	8085	8120	8127	8134	8136	8141	8153	8155	8162	8181	8183	8192	8248	8263	8285
	8303	8327	8337	8361	8364															
115	Beans	7962	7968	7970	7972	7981	7991	7995	8018	8021	8033	8058	8061	8063	8071	8085	8111	8118	8140	8153	8207
	8231	8285	8294	8316	8342	8357														
116	Peas	7965	7972	8002	8022	8046	8085	8118	8285	8298	8303	8327								
123	Clover	7526	7917	7920	7921	7925	7928	7930	7940	7942	7943	7947	7951	7952	7955	7957	7962	7965	7967	7968	7970	7977	7979
	7981	7981	7984	7987	7990	7993	7999	8001	8002	8004	8005	8006	8008	8010	8014	8015	8021	8022	8028	8031	8033
	8038	8045	8046	8051	8052	8057	8058	8059	8061	8063	8065	8070	8071	8073	8074	8079	8083	8097	8100	8111	8115
	8119	8120	8121	8123	8127	8129	8134	8136	8138	8140	8141	8144	8145	8153	8154	8167	8168	8175	8181	8185	8191
	8197	8199	8200	8201	8206	8207	8222	8227	8232	8241	8248	8259	8261	8267	8275	8281	8294	8298	8303	8309	8312
	8313	8316	8318	8319	8323	8327	8330	8333	8337	8340	8342	8344	8347	8354	8356	8357	8360	8364	8367		
125	Trefoil	8045	8058																	
126	Tares and vetches		7930	8002	8014	8031	8085	8115	8123	8134	8154	8197	8207	8319	8323	8357	8367			
127	Lucerne	8360																		
129	Turnips	7526	7917	7921	7922	7925	7928	7930	7940	7942	7943	7950	7952	7955	7957	7959	7960	7961	7962	7964
	7967	7968	7969	7970	7971	7975	7977	7979	7981	7984	7985	7987	7988	7991	7996	7999	8001	8002	8004	8006	8008
	8009	8014	8015	8016	8021	8022	8028	8031	8038	8040	8053	8058	8059	8062	8065	8068	8069	8070	8071	8073
	8074	8076	8078	8079	8085	8087	8088	8095	8097	8100	8102	8109	8111	8113	8114	8114	8115	8119	8120	8121	8126
	8129	8131	8132	8134	8136	8140	8141	8144	8145	8153	8154	8159	8160	8162	8163	8167	8168	8172	8175	8179	8181
	8184	8185	8191	8194	8198	8199	8200	8201	8216	8220	8222	8226	8232	8241	8248	8251	8253	8259	8261	8267	8275
	8281	8285	8294	8298	8303	8305	8306	8309	8311	8312	8313	8314	8316	8318	8323	8324	8327	8330	8333	8338	8340
	8342	8347	8350	8360	8364	8367	8368													
131	Swedes	8061	8183	8231																
132	Potatoes	7526	7917	7969	7981	7985	7987	8021	8061	8062	8063	8065	8069	8085	8114	8118	8126	8129	8138	8145
	8154	8160	8172	8175	8200	8226	8231	8253	8257	8270	8275	8305	8311	8314	8323	8324	8327	8350			
133	Bare fallows	7526	7917	7920	7921	7922	7925	7928	7930	7940	7942	7943	7946	7952	7962	7964	7965	7968	7970	7972
	7975	7979	7981	7984	7985	7987	7990	7991	7993	7995	7999	8004	8005	8009	8010	8014	8015	8016	8021	8022	8027
	8031	8033	8038	8040	8046	8051	8052	8053	8058	8061	8062	8063	8070	8071	8076	8078	8079	8083	8085	8087	8088
	8097	8100	8102	8109	8111	8113	8114	8115	8118	8119	8123	8127	8129	8132	8138	8144	8145	8153	8154	8160	8162
	8167	8168	8172	8173	8175	8178	8179	8181	8182	8183	8184	8185	8191	8197	8198	8199	8201	8207	8222	8226	8227
	8232	8238	8241	8248	8251	8262	8281	8285	8294	8303	8305	8307	8311	8312	8314	8316	8318	8319			
	8324	8327	8330	8333	8337	8338	8340	8342	8344	8346	8347	8350	8354	8356	8357	8367					
134	High farming	8073	8111	8293	8309	8323	8357	8360												
135	Low farming	7947	7969	7971	7987	8002	8005	8033	8046	8058	8061	8068	8069	8113	8115	8127	8131	8132	8134	8138
	8145	8172	8198	8252	8263	8319	8327	8337	8340	8342	8344									
138	Recent increase in productivity		8073	8115	8185	8199	8260	8305	8312	8344	8357									
139	Good quality pastures		7922	7936	7940	7943	7959	7960	7967	7968	7981	7984	7991	7995	7999	8045	8052	8057	8063
	8065	8070	8071	8073	8121	8158	8162	8163	8179	8201	8222	8227	8239	8241	8251	8262	8281	8294	8305	8311	8338
	8339																			
140	Poor quality pastures		7943	7946	7962	7965	7981	7984	7991	7999	8009	8022	8051	8053	8061	8063	8065	8070	8071
	8088	8102	8115	8131	8138	8172	8179	8223	8239	8251	8287	8303	8307	8313	8316					
141	Meadows	7943	7950	7960	7968	7970	7972	7981	7985	7991	7999	8009	8022	8038	8052	8053	8057	8068	8095	8131
	8158	8162	8179	8251	8298	8303	8311	8354												
142	Irrigation and water meadows		7957	7970	8015	8057	8111	8175	8211	8216	8227	8293								
144	Parks	7922	8347																	
145	Accommodation land		8053	8194	8270															
146	Cattle breeding		7916	7930	7942	7975	7981	7988	8009	8022	8038	8058	8076	8118	8131	8136	8175	8178	8181	8184
	8191	8220	8251	8253	8259	8281	8311	8316												
147	Cattle fattening		7930	7961	7972	7975	8076	8114	8118	8178	8181	8197	8238	8241	8281					
148	Dairying	7526	7917	7930	7942	7964	7975	7985	7988	7996	7999	8004	8009	8021	8027	8058	8062	8065	8068	8076
	8078	8079	8100	8113	8114	8118	8126	8129	8132	8145	8178	8179	8184	8191	8197	8200	8220	8226	8232	8238
	8241	8253	8259	8262	8270	8281	8308	8311	8314	8324	8327	8338	8350							
149	Cow keeping	8114																		
150	Sheep breeding		7942	7950	7961	7970	7975	7988	7996	8004	8009	8015	8021	8022	8027	8028	8038	8062	8065	8068
	8073	8078	8088	8113	8114	8118	8121	8126	8132	8163	8175	8175	8179	8181	8184	8191	8220	8232	8241	8259	8270
	8281	8298	8314	8327	8350	8354														
151	Sheep fattening		7943	7950	8076															
153	Horses	7981	7995	8065	8073	8118	8136	8319												
154	Pigs	8324																		
156	Poultry		8324																	
158	Deer	7943	8175																	
160	Straw	8191	8201																	
161	Hay	7943	7950	7970	8009	8021	8058	8175	8197	8253	8257	8270	8298							
163	Stall or yard feeding		8113	8131																
165	Butter	7964	8184	8220	8311															
166	Cheese	8113	8129	8131	8311	8338														
167	Wool	8073	8175	8251																

Shropshire contd.

169　Good orchards　8053
178　Hops　7972　7991

Somerset

1	Tithe-free district		8406	8407	8408	8473	8476	8559	8657	8689	8697	8723	8855							
2	History of tithe payment			8390	8423	8437	8492	8587	8840											
3	Tithe practices and agriculture			8515	8572	8709	8718	8830	8831											
4	Exemptions from tithe		8371	8372	8375	8385	8393	8397	8399	8400	8401	8402	8409	8416	8420	8421	8423	8427	8429
	8440	8466	8477	8503	8503	8509	8512	8516	8518	8519	8540	8544	8546	8547	8550	8554	8556	8560	8573	8578	8580
	8583	8587	8588	8590	8594	8599	8609	8610	8611	8621	8622	8626	8640	8648	8650	8651	8653	8659	8660	8661	8664
	8665	8666	8671	8672	8673	8677	8680	8681	8682	8683	8684	8688	8694	8699	8706	8709	8718	8719	8720	8722	8728
	8733	8744	8752	8756	8757	8760	8762	8766	8777	8780	8784	8793	8800	8802	8812	8813	8819	8824	8827	8830	8833
	8846	8847	8849	8850	8852	8853	8854	8856	8864	8866	8872										
5	Tithe in kind		8401	8411	8463	8478	8493	8530	8542	8560	8565	8570	8596	8624	8628	8638	8669	8675	8732	8734	8780
	8784	8788	8796	8852	8860																
6	Compositions		8383	8393	8399	8402	8409	8411	8426	8427	8428	8430	8463	8491	8512	8526	8530	8536	8553	8554	8583
	8584	8588	8596	8598	8616	8625	8627	8628	8631	8638	8641	8653	8668	8675	8676	8682	8691	8692	8725	8726	8727
	8730	8732	8734	8739	8740	8742	8748	8750	8759	8763	8764	8770	8772	8775	8779	8788	8790	8810	8811	8815
	8820	8822	8824	8828	8835	8858	8860	8865													
7	Moduses		8372	8374	8379	8380	8381	8382	8384	8386	8393	8394	8395	8410	8423	8425	8427	8428	8429	8432	8435
	8437	8442	8452	8453	8456	8460	8463	8468	8478	8479	8483	8488	8489	8490	8494	8495	8503	8506	8511	8512	8513
	8515	8518	8521	8524	8528	8529	8530	8533	8538	8540	8542	8546	8552	8558	8560	8563	8566	8572	8573	8579	8580
	8582	8583	8586	8588	8590	8591	8592	8599	8602	8608	8609	8610	8611	8614	8615	8618	8620	8621	8622	8623	8626
	8628	8629	8632	8635	8638	8648	8649	8655	8656	8663	8666	8667	8669	8671	8672	8677	8679	8680	8682	8683	8690
	8691	8699	8708	8709	8715	8717	8722	8726	8728	8734	8739	8740	8750	8766	8770	8773	8776	8777	8780	8782	8784
	8785	8786	8789	8796	8798	8806	8809	8810	8825	8829	8830	8831	8833	8837	8847	8852	8860	8863	8865	8866	8870
	8871																				
8	Glebe	8371	8372	8373	8375	8379	8423	8475	8594	8795											
9	Local topographic descriptions		8372	8379	8382	8453	8489	8499	8500	8501	8511	8522	8528	8529	8576	8640	8651	8660
	8700	8737	8741	8783	8786	8821	8826	8838	8862	8866											
10	Regional topographic descriptions		8373	8374	8376	8394	8402	8415	8423	8440	8544	8589	8666	8804							
11	Village morphology	8557	8578	8594	8659	8685	8708	8765	8783	8799	8843										
12	Church	8423																			
13	Country houses and ornamental gardens		8799																		
17	Open fields	8778																			
18	Small, irregular closes		8516	8818																	
20	Hedgerow timber		8371	8372	8373	8374	8375	8376	8377	8379	8380	8381	8382	8386	8387	8389	8391	8395	8396	8397
	8398	8400	8401	8403	8404	8405	8409	8412	8415	8416	8417	8418	8419	8420	8422	8423	8424	8429	8432	8463	8467
	8480	8486	8489	8493	8496	8498	8503	8509	8516	8518	8521	8523	8528	8533	8535	8544	8546	8547	8555	8556	8560
	8563	8567	8574	8578	8581	8583	8585	8589	8590	8591	8592	8595	8597	8599	8601	8603	8604	8605	8606	8607	8610
	8611	8613	8614	8615	8617	8619	8621	8622	8623	8624	8629	8633	8634	8635	8636	8639	8640	8644	8645	8646	8647
	8649	8650	8651	8652	8655	8656	8658	8659	8660	8662	8664	8665	8666	8670	8672	8674	8677	8678	8680	8681	8682
	8683	8684	8685	8687	8688	8690	8691	8693	8694	8696	8699	8700	8701	8703	8706	8707	8708	8709	8713	8714
	8715	8717	8720	8722	8733	8735	8737	8738	8739	8741	8744	8747	8749	8752	8753	8754	8755	8756	8757	8758	8760
	8762	8765	8766	8767	8768	8769	8771	8774	8776	8778	8780	8781	8782	8783	8784	8786	8787	8789	8791	8793	8795
	8796	8797	8798	8799	8800	8802	8803	8804	8807	8809	8810	8813	8814	8816	8818	8819	8827	8829	8830	8831
	8833	8837	8838	8841	8844	8845	8846	8850	8852	8853	8854	8856	8857	8861	8862	8863	8864	8866	8867	8868	8869
	8870	8872																			
21	Coppice		8371	8386	8394	8396	8397	8440	8447	8448	8454	8466	8467	8469	8470	8486	8491	8493	8499	8500	8501
	8514	8515	8516	8529	8533	8534	8539	8540	8547	8549	8551	8561	8565	8579	8597	8602	8603	8607	8612	8626	8633
	8640	8651	8659	8664	8672	8695	8696	8698	8703	8714	8737	8747	8753	8762	8764	8767	8786	8787	8789	8819	8821
	8825	8826	8842	8844	8853	8868	9652														
22	Plantations		8372	8382	8386	8392	8420	8442	8462	8467	8468	8470	8480	8486	8491	8509	8514	8540	8547	8557	8563
	8565	8589	8601	8602	8613	8622	8624	8633	8649	8650	8651	8659	8664	8673	8680	8684	8695	8698	8699	8701	8706
	8715	8717	8733	8741	8747	8752	8768	8776	8782	8789	8791	8795	8797	8799	8804	8806	8819	8821	8826	8843	8846
	8853	8856	8865	8866	8869																
23	Woodland management		8392	8738																	
24	Productive woodland		8373	8442	8460	8614	8687	8688	8720	8789											
25	Poor woodland		8499	8500	8551	8607	8633	8696	8707	8738	8852										
26	Commons	8371	8375	8379	8396	8397	8426	8486	8498	8518	8534	8539	8551	8551	8568	8594	8594	8599	8603	8650
	8651	8672	8695	8700	8714	8720	8737	8738	8752	8756	8768	8771	8780	8821	8825	8826	8827	8847	8850	8853	8856
	8856	8857	8862	8862	8868																
27	Furze, gorse and heathlands			8442	8448	8493	8539	8551	8551	8567	8568	8568	8589	8594	8624	8624	8707	8714	8720
	8737	8737	8738	8752	8756	8764	8783	8816	8847	8850	8853	8853	8856	8857	8862						
28	Moorland		8382	8539	8594	8647	8660	8718	8783	8784	8796	8838									
31	Wasteland		8493	8621	8650	8659	8690	8781	8866												
32	Climatic hazards		8415	8444	8448	8502	8504	8534	8539	8540	8551	8624	8626	8633	8644	8700	8737	8764	8789	8821
	8825	8846	8850	8852	8853	8854	9652														
33	Excessively steep land			8448	8467	8539	8551	8562	8576	8678	8755	8782	8814	8862							
34	Land requires drainage		8371	8382	8388	8396	8398	8400	8405	8416	8419	8429	8445	8454	8459	8461	8463	8502	8504
	8507	8535	8540	8560	8574	8576	8578	8589	8595	8603	8605	8607	8617	8629	8646	8656	8660	8666	8694	8696
	8711	8722	8733	8735	8784	8819	8821	8825	8827	8830	8845	8847	8853	8866							
35	Land liable to flood		8374	8387	8478	8496	8498	8515	8550	8551	8574	8580	8597	8629	8647	8650	8660	8683	8688	8733
	8735	8780	8784	8813	8829	8838	8852														
36	Productive soil		8371	8374	8375	8387	8389	8397	8416	8419	8433	8434	8435	8445	8446	8451	8456	8457	8463	8477
	8478	8489	8494	8495	8496	8502	8503	8507	8508	8509	8514	8518	8522	8529	8540	8542	8548	8549	8557	8573	8579
	8580	8585	8588	8590	8610	8611	8613	8614	8619	8621	8636	8639	8640	8645	8648	8651	8658	8659	8662	8665	8670	8674
	8681	8695	8699	8701	8707	8713	8715	8718	8720	8747	8757	8758	8760	8762	8765	8768	8771	8773	8774	8778	8789
	8793	8802	8803	8812	8814	8831	8838	8841	8849	8861	8863										
37	Poor soil		8372	8374	8382	8388	8397	8418	8432	8436	8442	8444	8448	8454	8456	8466	8468	8489	8502	8503
	8504	8510	8516	8528	8529	8534	8540	8551	8557	8558	8560	8562	8562	8589	8590	8614	8626	8629	8633	8664	8693
	8696	8707	8708	8711	8718	8720	8729	8733	8768	8825	8829	8833	8842	8847	8852	8854	8856	8863	8866	8868	
38	Heavy (clay) soil		8371	8373	8374	8377	8379	8381	8382	8388	8391	8394	8395	8396	8397	8398	8400	8404	8412	8415
	8416	8417	8418	8419	8422	8423	8429	8432	8433	8434	8435	8436	8438	8446	8447	8448	8452	8454	8457	8459	8460
	8461	8463	8465	8468	8469	8470	8480	8481	8488	8488	8489	8493	8498	8500	8502	8503	8504	8506	8507
	8508	8516	8521	8523	8532	8533	8535	8539	8540	8542	8546	8550	8551	8555	8556	8557	8561	8566	8570	8572	8573
	8574	8576	8578	8580	8582	8583	8586	8590	8591	8592	8595	8597	8599	8602	8603	8604	8605	8606	8607	8610	8612
	8613	8614	8617	8621	8622	8624	8629	8633	8634	8635	8639	8640	8644	8645	8646	8647	8649	8650	8651	8652	8655
	8656	8658	8660	8661	8662	8664	8665	8666	8672	8673	8677	8678	8680	8681	8683	8685	8688	8690	8691	8693	8694	8696
	8699	8703	8706	8709	8711	8713	8714	8717	8722	8733	8735	8737	8738	8739	8744	8751	8752	8754	8755	8756	8762
	8765	8767	8768	8769	8774	8776	8780	8781	8786	8787	8791	8795	8796	8797	8799	8800	8803	8806	8807	8812	8813
	8816	8819	8825	8827	8829	8830	8831	8833	8838	8841	8844	8845	8847	8852	8854	8861	8862	8863	8864	8866	8867
	8870	8872	9652																		

Somerset contd.

#	Topic	Numbers
39	Loamy (turnip) soil	8375 8379 8386 8387 8389 8397 8409 8417 8420 8422 8441 8445 8456 8478 8496 8499 8501 8503 8524 8529 8532 8540 8545 8549 8585 8612 8615 8619 8623 8639 8640 8650 8651 8655 8665 8670 8674 8678 8680 8681 8684 8698 8715 8745 8747 8758 8771 8773 8784 8791 8802 8837 8841 8865
40	Light soil	8371 8372 8374 8376 8379 8381 8382 8389 8391 8397 8400 8401 8403 8404 8405 8415 8418 8420 8422 8432 8441 8442 8444 8446 8448 8451 8462 8463 8465 8466 8467 8468 8469 8479 8480 8481 8486 8489 8493 8494 8495 8498 8499 8501 8502 8504 8507 8508 8510 8516 8518 8522 8528 8529 8533 8534 8543 8545 8547 8548 8551 8555 8557 8558 8560 8562 8563 8566 8567 8568 8570 8574 8576 8578 8579 8581 8582 8591 8594 8595 8597 8599 8602 8603 8604 8607 8610 8612 8619 8622 8623 8629 8633 8640 8646 8647 8659 8661 8662 8664 8672 8673 8674 8677 8680 8682 8688 8693 8696 8699 8700 8708 8717 8718 8720 8722 8737 8738 8741 8745 8751 8752 8755 8756 8762 8764 8766 8767 8768 8769 8771 8778 8780 8782 8785 8786 8787 8789 8796 8798 8799 8800 8802 8804 8807 8809 8814 8818 8821 8825 8826 8827 8831 8833 8837 8842 8844 8846 8847 8849 8850 8852 8854 8856 8857 8861 8862 8865 8866 8867 8868 8869 8870 9652
41	Several varieties of soil	8377 8379 8380 8391 8396 8404 8405 8412 8415 8418 8432 8438 8446 8456 8460 8461 8463 8466 8503 8507 8511 8524 8532 8551 8591 8597 8610 8622 8624 8651 8662 8677 8680 8687 8688 8693 8694 8700 8707 8718 8720 8722 8762 8768 8780 8812 8819 8829 8849 8850 8854 8857 8863 8870
42	Chalk	8533
43	Sand or gravel	8375 8380 8384 8394 8395 8401 8404 8412 8415 8416 8417 8422 8424 8432 8433 8438 8441 8447 8448 8453 8456 8457 8459 8460 8463 8465 8479 8480 8481 8486 8494 8495 8496 8502 8506 8507 8508 8509 8509 8511 8514 8516 8522 8524 8543 8544 8545 8547 8548 8555 8556 8557 8561 8563 8570 8578 8579 8582 8585 8589 8590 8592 8601 8604 8606 8610 8614 8615 8621 8623 8624 8634 8635 8636 8645 8648 8649 8651 8652 8655 8659 8660 8670 8672 8673 8677 8681 8682 8684 8685 8687 8691 8694 8695 8701 8703 8708 8709 8711 8714 8715 8717 8733 8738 8739 8749 8752 8753 8754 8757 8758 8760 8768 8773 8774 8778 8781 8782 8783 8784 8791 8793 8795 8797 8807 8809 8814 8816 8819 8830 8833 8838 8843 8844 8849 8852 8854 8857 8863 8864 8866 8869 8872
44	Peat	8374 8382 8488 8540 8560 8682 8718 8766 8783 8784 8838
45	Fields remote from farms	8562
46	Good local roads	8371 8373 8381 8388 8389 8391 8394 8396 8400 8404 8419 8424 8434 8445 8447 8451 8453 8457 8459 8460 8462 8468 8470 8481 8486 8488 8494 8495 8496 8507 8508 8509 8511 8514 8522 8524 8533 8545 8547 8548 8549 8550 8560 8565 8572 8574 8580 8595 8597 8599 8601 8603 8604 8605 8610 8622 8624 8636 8644 8647 8648 8649 8658 8665 8673 8677 8694 8698 8699 8708 8713 8714 8733 8741 8744 8745 8752 8755 8778 8782 8784 8785 8793 8795 8804 8807 8813 8819 8826 8833 8841 8845 8846 8854 8857 8863 8864 8867 9652
47	Poor local roads	8379 8416 8448 8465 8467 8500 8502 8510 8516 8534 8539 8551 8551 8562 8567 8568 8576 8594 8606 8660 8678 8700 8735 8755 8783 8784 8814 8821 8853 8854 8856 8857 8861 8868
50	Water carriage	8463 8857
51	Canals	8698
52	Railways	8688 8698
53	Markets accessible	8371 8372 8373 8381 8388 8389 8391 8396 8397 8403 8405 8412 8434 8442 8445 8447 8451 8453 8457 8459 8460 8462 8463 8467 8468 8470 8481 8486 8488 8489 8493 8494 8495 8496 8507 8508 8522 8524 8545 8548 8549 8550 8563 8572 8579 8580 8581 8585 8595 8646 8659 8662 8695 8701 8714 8741 8762 8771 8799 8818 8837 8848 8861
54	Markets inaccessible	8465 8500 8534 8539 8551 8567 8594 8700 8735 8821 8831 8857 8868
55	Provincial markets	8381 8389 8391 8396 8397 8400 8404 8412 8424 8467 8480 8489 8493 8496 8509 8514 8533 8547 8551 8560 8574 8589 8597 8601 8603 8604 8605 8607 8622 8624 8636 8644 8646 8648 8649 8658 8662 8665 8673 8674 8677 8694 8699 8708 8713 8733 8744 8752 8778 8782 8791 8793 8795 8804 8807 8812 8813 8819 8833 8837 8845 8850 8854 8863 8867
56	London market	8463 8545 8550 8791 8872
58	Market prices	8402 8626 8629 8633 8669 8849
59	Landowners and their estates	8379 8379 8382 8382 8388 8442 8444 8460 8488 8493 8493 8504 8535 8540 8540 8551 8562 8578 8607 8636 8672 8681 8722 8738 8745 8780 8800 8845 8846 8853 8853 8861 8862 8863 8866 8868
60	Land occupiers	8387 8409 8412 8535 8605 8626 8670 8672 8696 8706 8802 8830 8847 8849 8868 8870
61	Farm size	8379 8381 8382 8405 8412 8415 8434 8435 8438 8444 8459 8488 8493 8494 8495 8507 8515 8551 8578 8626 8629 8666 8670 8673 8680 8695 8696 8703 8708 8713 8714 8752 8758 8780 8799 8847 8849 8854 8862
62	Leases	8440 8488 8504 8516 8544 8646 8799 8830
64	Common grazing	8371 8379 8397 8599 8672 8700 8783
65	Lammas and other common rights	8382 8486 8621 8640 8650 8700 8700 8720 8752 8783 8825 8827 8868
66	Rents	8415 8496 8698 8837 8866
67	Urban influences on value of land	8387 8409 8578 8639 8659 8799 8861
68	Rates	8387
70	Enclosure or improvement of waste	8529 8578 8718 8729
71	Enclosure of commons	8372 8395 8438 8468 8491 8562 8568 8590 8862
72	Enclosure of open fields	8493 8609 8656 8657 8838
75	Conversion of grass to arable	8525 8572 8830
76	Conversion of arable to pasture	8440 8444 8830
77	Paring and burning	8524 8540 8589 8700 8853
80	Reclaiming and embanking	8709 8830
81	Marsh drainage	8499 8515 8580 8718 8784 8830 8838
83	Steam pumps	8784
85	Underdrainage	8373 8415 8432 8445 8459 8467 8481 8488 8498 8499 8522 8574 8607 8629 8633 8636 8662 8680 8711 8722 8745 8755 8800 8845 8846 8861
87	Marl	8445
88	Chalk	8467
89	Lime	8444 8448 8504 8507 8539 8548 8549 8551 8563 8589 8708 8821 8853 8868
92	Dung	8528 8578 8758 8798 8866
95	Bones	8758 8760
101	General comments on crop rotations	8375 8376 8380 8382 8386 8387 8417 8420 8452 8454 8456 8463 8498 8540 8547 8597 8599 8655 8687 8688 8694 8695 8700 8707 8709 8720 8722 8744 8758 8763 8781 8782 8786 8787 8798 8799 8813 8821 8837 8856 8857 8861 8862 8866 8867 8868 8869
102	Irregular rotations	8371 8372 8386 8391 8394 8396 8405 8412 8420 8438 8446 8454 8456 8466 8563 8572 8578 8590 8640 8645 8658 8659 8672 8685 8699 8713 8714 8717 8771 8793 8803 8847 8849 8863 8870
103	3-course rotation	8373 8377 8381 8388 8391 8394 8398 8416 8417 8419 8420 8422 8429 8433 8434 8435 8436 8446 8452 8460 8461 8466 8469 8478 8503 8504 8518 8523 8524 8535 8539 8542 8543 8550 8555 8560 8570 8574 8583 8586 8595 8605 8606 8607 8611 8613 8617 8644 8647 8649 8656 8665 8666 8680 8683 8690 8693 8706 8713 8733 8735 8739 8744 8765 8774 8776 8780 8785 8796 8812 8825 8827 8829 8830 8831 8845 8870 8872
104	4-course rotation	8374 8379 8389 8395 8396 8403 8405 8412 8415 8418 8422 8424 8432 8441 8445 8447 8451 8453 8457 8461 8462 8465 8467 8468 8474 8477 8479 8486 8494 8495 8496 8499 8500 8506 8507 8508 8509 8510 8511 8514 8521 8522 8524 8532 8533 8534 8544 8545 8546 8548 8549 8555 8556 8558 8561 8562 8568 8572 8579 8581 8582 8585 8589 8591 8592 8597 8601 8603 8604 8612 8614 8615 8619 8622 8623 8624 8634 8635 8660 8662 8673 8677 8682 8684 8691 8696 8701 8738 8745 8751 8757 8762 8766 8773 8797 8806 8809 8818 8833 8865 9652
105	5-course rotation	8384 8404 8417 8442 8470 8524 8565 8566 8591 8651 8674 8678 8680 8698 8703 8717 8753 8754 8755 8756 8767 8769 8802 8816 8826 8843 8846 8867 9652
106	6-course rotation	8394 8842
108	8-10-course rotation	8372
110	Wheat	8396 8415 8649
111	Barley	8415
112	Oats	8563

Somerset contd.

```
114  Corn yields      8432  8491  8497  8516  8554  8560  8588  8624  8652  8666  8681  8722  8739  8760  8778  8813  8816  8844  8847
     8853  8868  8872
115  Beans     8373  8377  8382  8388  8395  8400  8416  8419  8422  8423  8429  8463  8477  8518  8521  8555  8560  8565  8574  8583
     8595  8605  8606  8607  8611  8612  8613  8614  8615  8617  8623  8629  8631  8636  8644  8649  8656  8665  8666  8680  8681
     8682  8683  8684  8690  8691  8693  8698  8699  8706  8709  8713  8717  8733  8735  8739  8744  8751  8754  8760  8765  8766
     8767  8773  8774  8776  8780  8784  8785  8795  8796  8797  8798  8800  8813  8813  8816  8825  8829  8830  8831  8841  8845
     8870  8872
116  Peas      8377  8493  8631  8691
122  Unspecified grass seeds        8372  8463
123  Clover    8394  8395  8401  8403  8428  8592  8717  8751  8754  8767  8784  8798  8816  8841  9652
126  Tares and vetches      8382  8394  8397  8417  8422  8428  8489  8493  8591  8646  8680  8706  8720  8747  8751  8752  8767  8773
     8785  8798  8800  8829  8831  8845  8854
129  Turnips   8377  8379  8384  8396  8397  8403  8405  8412  8415  8417  8418  8422  8424  8432  8463  8467  8470  8477  8500
     8509  8514  8528  8533  8544  8546  8547  8556  8565  8567  8585  8590  8591  8597  8601  8603  8604  8607  8614  8619  8623
     8624  8626  8629  8631  8636  8640  8645  8648  8651  8652  8655  8662  8670  8672  8673  8674  8677  8678  8680  8681  8687
     8691  8694  8695  8696  8698  8699  8700  8701  8707  8708  8715  8720  8737  8738  8741  8745  8749  8751  8752  8753  8755
     8756  8757  8758  8760  8768  8773  8778  8780  8782  8787  8787  8791  8793  8795  8802  8803  8807  8814  8816  8818  8821
     8833  8838  8841  8844  8846  8852  8853  8854  8856  8857  8861  8867  8868  8869  9652
130  Mangolds         8585  8681
131  Swedes           8698
132  Potatoes  8372  8375  8386  8387  8394  8396  8417  8419  8420  8428  8465  8488  8493  8535  8540  8567  8578  8579  8590
     8594  8599  8611  8612  8621  8639  8646  8650  8659  8682  8685  8691  8695  8700  8714  8714  8729  8747  8784  8812  8816
     8819  8820  8838  8843  8847  8850  8862  8863  8864
133  Bare fallows     8373  8377  8379  8382  8416  8422  8423  8429  8480  8489  8518  8521  8523  8555  8560  8574  8583  8595  8605
     8606  8607  8611  8612  8613  8617  8644  8665  8680  8682  8683  8690  8691  8693  8698  8703  8706  8709  8713  8722  8733
     8735  8739  8744  8749  8754  8765  8766  8767  8774  8776  8781  8784  8785  8795  8796  8798  8800  8813  8821  8825  8827
     8829  8830  8845  8865  8870  8872  9652
134  High farming     8403  8442  8459  8460  8510  8522  8548  8585  8633  8636  8681  8745  8758  8869
135  Low farming      8375  8376  8379  8396  8398  8416  8444  8452  8454  8488  8501  8504  8507  8510  8516  8535  8540  8551  8574
     8611  8626  8646  8659  8804  8827  8852
138  Recent increase in productivity      8459  8499  8510
139  Good quality pastures          8371  8372  8373  8375  8377  8381  8386  8391  8397  8403  8404  8405  8409  8412  8416  8420  8424
     8433  8435  8441  8444  8447  8448  8451  8452  8453  8456  8457  8459  8463  8465  8468  8481  8488  8495  8496  8499  8501
     8502  8503  8507  8508  8509  8511  8515  8516  8522  8524  8533  8540  8544  8548  8549  8550  8555  8560  8578  8579  8589
     8595  8601  8602  8604  8613  8617  8621  8624  8634  8644  8648  8650  8651  8652  8655  8658  8659  8662  8666  8672  8673
     8677  8681  8683  8688  8693  8695  8699  8701  8708  8709  8715  8720  8735  8738  8744  8747  8753  8757  8760  8778  8780
     8782  8786  8789  8791  8793  8795  8802  8803  8804  8813  8818  8829  8830  8833  8838  8841  8846  8850  8854  8856  8857
     8862  8863  8864  8868  8869  8870  8872
140  Poor quality pastures          8376  8382  8388  8405  8415  8432  8436  8444  8456  8460  8461  8468  8488  8502  8504  8507  8511
     8516  8528  8540  8560  8562  8578  8589  8624  8644  8660  8747  8780  8782  8786  8826  8830  8837  8838  8853  9652
141  Meadows   8386  8391  8396  8397  8400  8403  8405  8412  8416  8432  8442  8463  8477  8498  8503  8528  8540  8544  8550
     8555  8562  8578  8585  8613  8626  8659  8666  8678  8680  8683  8688  8693  8694  8695  8698  8700  8714  8733  8760  8778
     8780  8782  8791  8795  8796  8802  8803  8813  8818  8830  8833  8850  8853  8863  8864  8867
142  Irrigation and water meadows         8379  8404  8441  8465  8468  8509  8516  8581  8651  8680  8698  8764  8773  8783  8802  8856
     8868
143  Marsh grassland  8434  8463  8489  8515  8579  8650  8660  8706  8780  8791  8829
144  Parks     8375  8722  8738  8804
145  Accommodation land    8372
146  Cattle breeding  8374  8379  8386  8389  8394  8396  8400  8415  8416  8419  8429  8444  8463  8509  8524  8535  8539  8540
     8545  8551  8555  8563  8567  8590  8594  8595  8597  8603  8626  8659  8660  8700  8711  8722  8771  8783  8791  8847  8852
     8853  8856  8866  8870
147  Cattle fattening  8394  8405  8463  8489  8496  8544  8606  8611  8613  8614  8617  8619  8621  8622  8626  8629  8634  8636
     8639  8644  8645  8649  8658  8661  8662  8665  8666  8672  8674  8678  8680  8681  8683  8688  8694  8699  8701  8706  8708
     8720  8724  8741  8745  8753  8756  8765  8774  8780  8784  8791  8818  8833  8849  8854  8857  8862  8864  8867
148  Dairying  8371  8373  8374  8375  8376  8377  8379  8386  8388  8389  8391  8396  8397  8400  8404  8405  8415  8416  8419
     8423  8424  8429  8432  8433  8434  8435  8444  8446  8447  8453  8454  8456  8457  8462  8463  8466  8467  8468  8478  8489
     8494  8498  8507  8508  8514  8516  8524  8533  8535  8540  8542  8544  8547  8548  8558  8560  8563  8572  8573  8589  8590
     8595  8597  8599  8602  8603  8604  8605  8607  8610  8611  8617  8619  8621  8622  8624  8626  8629  8635  8645  8646  8647
     8648  8649  8655  8656  8658  8659  8660  8661  8662  8664  8665  8666  8672  8674  8677  8680  8681  8683  8685  8688  8693
     8694  8696  8699  8706  8708  8713  8714  8720  8722  8735  8744  8745  8747  8752  8755  8756  8786  8791  8793  8795  8804
     8812  8813  8818  8819  8827  8830  8831  8833  8837  8841  8844  8845  8846  8847  8849  8850  8852  8854  8861  8863  8864
     8866  8870
149  Cow keeping      8409  8412  8578  8659
150  Sheep breeding   8386  8394  8400  8403  8404  8432  8444  8453  8461  8477  8486  8496  8498  8507  8508  8509  8516  8528
     8540  8548  8550  8551  8565  8567  8605  8612  8626  8640  8651  8661  8672  8673  8677  8678  8695  8698  8700  8711  8715
     8720  8751  8752  8753  8758  8760  8764  8771  8773  8782  8783  8787  8795  8806  8807  8819  8821  8826  8833  8846  8853
     8856  8857  8862  8866  8869  9652
151  Sheep fattening  8394  8424  8461  8462  8463  8548  8565  8594  8612  8648  8652  8680  8681  8757  8762  8778  8841  8845
     8872
152  Droving          8463  8489  8791
153  Horses    8693  8783  8853
155  Oxen      8400  8404  8463  8478  8500  8508  8509  8540  8550  8614  8636  8666  8687  8718  8738  8807  8831  8872
157  Rabbits          8433  8501  8866
158  Deer      8501  8587
159  Animal diseases  8388  8400  8605  8607  8813
160  Straw     8534  8853
161  Hay       8372  8374  8379  8387  8394  8396  8397  8400  8402  8412  8442  8480  8509  8551  8585  8592  8678  8680  8685  8708
     8714  8737  8741  8752  8758  8760  8771  8780  8783  8802  8812  8833  8867  8868
163  Stall or yard feeding  8585
164  Milk      8403
165  Butter    8372  8402
166  Cheese    8402  8849
169  Good orchards    8382  8394  8465  8477  8666  8695  8798  8854
171  Fruits    8380  8382  8394  8428  8477
172  Market gardens   8405  8409  8412  8639  8659  8670  8695  8799
173  Allotments       8495  8695
178  Hops      8514  8703
179  Flax and hemp    8428  8496  8496  8544  8544  8614  8631  8636  8691  8757  8757  8758  8760  8760
180  Dyestuffs        8394
181  Reeds and oziers       8751
182  Teasels   8394  8428
```

Staffordshire

1	Tithe-free district	9236	9294	9299	9304	9307	9330	9345	9347	9354	9390	9399	9401	9439	9454	9471	9477	9512	9533	
2	History of tithe payment	9487																		
3	Tithe practices and agriculture		9290	9339	9424	9432	9455													
4	Exemptions from tithe	9237	9240	9245	9247	9254	9255	9259	9261	9262	9263	9274	9281	9282	9287	9289	9303	9312		
	9313	9320	9335	9338	9339	9341	9352	9357	9368	9373	9378	9380	9383	9388	9389	9392	9397	9402	9404	9408	9410
	9412	9412	9413	9415	9416	9418	9422	9423	9429	9430	9431	9444	9445	9460	9461	9473	9479	9485	9489	9514	9516
	9519	9521	9530	9532	9556																
5	Tithe in kind	9230	9245	9262	9300	9306	9311	9314	9339	9349	9364	9369	9421	9428	9431	9434	9437	9474	9489	9504
	9508	9509	9540																		
6	Compositions	9229	9232	9237	9239	9249	9254	9255	9256	9259	9262	9271	9272	9273	9274	9276	9280	9288	9290	9291
	9300	9311	9320	9325	9332	9348	9349	9368	9369	9376	9380	9382	9386	9397	9408	9425	9432	9435	9448	9457	9473
	9474	9492	9504	9520	9538	9550															
7	Moduses	8531	9229	9230	9232	9240	9241	9245	9248	9249	9252	9257	9260	9263	9265	9273	9275	9277	9282	9286
	9289	9290	9290	9293	9295	9298	9302	9303	9308	9309	9311	9314	9316	9321	9323	9324	9325	9326	9329	9335	9336
	9338	9339	9346	9348	9349	9352	9356	9364	9366	9368	9369	9370	9373	9374	9376	9377	9381	9388	9389	9398	9403
	9405	9408	9410	9411	9421	9422	9424	9425	9427	9428	9430	9431	9435	9436	9437	9438	9441	9444	9448	9451	9455
	9465	9466	9470	9475	9480	9485	9486	9487	9488	9494	9496	9501	9502	9503	9508	9509	9511	9521	9526	9528	9530
	9531	9540	9543	9553	9554																
8	Glebe	9232	9517																		
9	Local topographic descriptions		9275	9335	9341	9377	9411	9433	9437	9515	9530	9544									
10	Regional topographic descriptions	9237	9242	9248	9260	9275	9286	9308	9310	9338	9341	9400	9403	9417	9430	9431	9432			
	9469	9497	9509	9531																	
11	Village morphology	9250	9319	9333	9379	9445	9528	9530	9540	9549	9560									
12	Church	9275	9498																		
13	Country houses and ornamental gardens		9379	9379	9406	9486	9544													
15	Cottages and cottage gardens		9319	9375	9433																
16	Field boundaries	9286	9393																		
18	Small, irregular closes	9237	9441	9497																	
21	Coppice	9424																			
22	Plantations	9319	9379	9424	9433	9465	9515	9551													
24	Productive woodland		9335	9433																	
25	Poor woodland	9377	9379	9468																	
26	Commons	9379	9450	9450	9480	9519															
27	Furze, gorse and heathlands		9256	9298	9335	9363	9379	9424	9424	9450	9450	9544									
28	Moorland	9237	9257	9374	9447																
31	Wasteland	9257	9324	9393																	
32	Climatic hazards	9257	9302	9374	9451	9459	9497	9517	9545												
34	Land requires drainage	9241	9257	9302	9310	9341	9353	9364	9365	9383	9424	9429	9444	9450	9489	9498	9530			
35	Land liable to flood	9250	9375	9410	9433	9453	9528													
36	Productive soil	8531	9237	9245	9246	9256	9268	9275	9277	9284	9286	9306	9314	9318	9319	9339	9355	9365	9367
	9370	9375	9379	9383	9406	9421	9433	9434	9436	9445	9453	9459	9486	9491	9497	9519	9531	9539	9540	9544	9545
	9554	9557																			
37	Poor soil	8531	9237	9242	9246	9256	9257	9258	9277	9286	9298	9333	9335	9339	9341	9353	9363	9365	9371	9379
	9383	9394	9410	9414	9429	9447	9453	9459	9461	9515	9528	9539	9545	9547	9551						
38	Heavy (clay) soil	9230	9232	9233	9237	9238	9241	9242	9243	9244	9245	9246	9248	9250	9257	9258	9267	9268	9277
	9281	9290	9302	9305	9306	9310	9314	9319	9324	9333	9337	9338	9339	9341	9342	9346	9352	9353
	9355	9357	9364	9365	9370	9371	9374	9375	9377	9385	9393	9395	9400	9410	9412	9417	9421	9424	9428	9429	9430
	9431	9432	9433	9434	9437	9441	9444	9447	9450	9451	9452	9453	9455	9461	9464	9465	9466	9468	9469	9485	9486
	9489	9497	9508	9509	9515	9519	9526	9528	9530	9532	9539	9545	9549	9554	9557	9560					
39	Loamy (turnip) soil	9232	9258	9260	9268	9277	9284	9286	9306	9314	9319	9336	9339	9346	9355	9358	9367	9370	9375
	9383	9385	9395	9396	9400	9421	9428	9433	9436	9441	9447	9451	9452	9455	9461	9465	9486	9489	9491	9497	9532
	9539	9544	9557	9560																	
40	Light soil	8531	9230	9233	9238	9243	9250	9258	9267	9286	9290	9305	9324	9342	9362	9379	9381	9396	9403	9411
	9413	9437	9450	9459	9464	9480	9486	9494	9497	9518	9532	9545	9557	9560							
41	Several varieties of soil	9233	9237	9241	9243	9246	9260	9277	9290	9302	9335	9339	9352	9365	9370	9375	9379	9395
	9424	9428	9433	9441	9452	9530															
43	Sand or gravel	9233	9235	9237	9241	9242	9243	9245	9246	9250	9256	9257	9267	9277	9281	9284	9290	9298	9302
	9306	9310	9314	9318	9324	9335	9338	9341	9352	9353	9363	9364	9370	9379	9381	9383	9394	9410	9413	9414	9424
	9428	9429	9430	9434	9441	9445	9450	9453	9459	9464	9466	9468	9480	9489	9491	9494	9497	9498	9508	9509	9518
	9526	9532	9545	9547	9551																
44	Peat	9235	9257	9298	9341	9410	9429	9430	9466	9497											
46	Good local roads	9233	9235	9238	9260	9275	9284	9286	9319	9338	9385	9403	9441	9450	9458	9461	9486	9526		
47	Poor local roads	9281	9355	9469																	
48	Turnpike and main roads	9277	9341	9394	9395	9414	9434	9437	9445	9452	9458	9465	9469	9494	9498	9531	9532	9547
	9551	9554	9560																		
51	Canals	9241	9277	9338	9451	9455	9540														
52	Railways	9277	9557																		
53	Markets accessible	9233	9238	9275	9286	9290	9318	9355	9379	9381	9411	9433	9447	9458	9461	9465	9517	9519	9530
	9551																				
55	Provincial markets	9453	9528																		
57	Fairs	9517	9528																		
58	Market prices	9318	9333																		
59	Landowners and their estates	9246	9246	9277	9344	9352	9353	9395	9400	9400	9406	9452	9485	9486	9539					
60	Land occupiers	9238	9257	9344	9353	9417	9421	9468	9517	9530											
61	Farm size	9232	9379	9459																	
64	Common grazing	9519																			
65	Lammas and other common rights		9338																		
66	Rents	8531	9232	9233	9237	9241	9256	9260	9298	9302	9305	9324	9338	9339	9342	9362	9365	9367	9383	9410	9424
	9433	9451	9459	9464	9466	9468	9491	9519	9526	9528	9540										
67	Urban influences on value of land	9379	9530																		
70	Enclosure or improvement of waste		9237	9257	9277	9337	9377													
71	Enclosure of commons	9235	9277	9309	9311	9323	9409	9456												
72	Enclosure of open fields	9236	9485	9487																	
76	Conversion of arable to pasture	9233	9455																		
82	Drainage channels and ditches	9286																			
84	Ridge-and-furrow	9444																			
85	Underdrainage	9238	9277	9421	9441																
86	Tile drains	9353	9450																		
89	Lime	9277	9333																		
92	Dung	9290	9318	9333	9445	9465	9530	9551													
100	Oil dust, unspecified fertilisers or manures		9458	9551																	
101	General comments on crop rotations		9280	9284	9318	9319	9370	9417	9437	9465	9489	9532									
102	Irregular rotations	9237	9257	9318	9333	9450	9451	9515	9545												
103	3-course rotation	9245	9281	9302	9314	9346	9352	9364	9434	9468	9486	9508	9509	9557							
104	4-course rotation	8531	9235	9241	9242	9243	9245	9248	9256	9258	9260	9268	9275	9277	9281	9298	9305	9306	9308

Staffordshire contd.

		9310	9314	9318	9324	9335	9339	9342	9352	9358	9362	9363	9364	9383	9395	9396	9406	9410	9411	9424	9428	9429
		9432	9434	9441	9447	9450	9452	9453	9455	9459	9461	9464	9465	9466	9468	9486	9491	9497	9498	9508	9509	9526
		9528	9530	9539	9544																	
105	5-course rotation		9242	9243	9244	9258	9267	9268	9277	9284	9306	9324	9337	9338	9339	9344	9353	9355	9357	9363
		9365	9377	9379	9395	9412	9413	9414	9431	9437	9441	9447	9450	9455	9458	9465	9469	9480	9485	9494	9497	9498
		9517	9519	9531	9540	9547	9549	9551	9554													
106	6-course rotation	9230	9232	9370	9375	9394	9414	9433	9444	9518												
107	7-course rotation	9375	9433																			
108	8-10-course rotation	9319																				
110	Wheat	9286	9314	9318	9363	9374																
112	Oats	9374	9451																			
113	Rye or meslin		9235	9363	9413																	
114	Corn yields	8531	9229	9237	9241	9280	9281	9290	9298	9302	9314	9324	9342	9346	9365	9367	9374	9383	9413	9421
		9424	9430	9455	9464	9466	9491	9517	9528													
115	Beans	9232	9233	9241	9245	9281	9305	9310	9314	9337	9338	9352	9357	9385	9412	9417	9424	9430	9431	9432	9434
		9444	9464	9475	9485	9489	9518	9519	9528	9532	9557	9560										
116	Peas	9277	9434	9475	9545																	
123	Clover	8531	9230	9235	9238	9241	9243	9248	9258	9260	9267	9275	9277	9281	9286	9302	9306	9308	9310	9314	9319
		9335	9338	9339	9342	9352	9353	9355	9357	9358	9363	9364	9365	9374	9375	9381	9383	9385	9394	9395	9396	9412
		9413	9414	9421	9424	9429	9430	9431	9432	9434	9436	9437	9447	9451	9452	9455	9458	9464	9465	9480	9485	9489
		9494	9497	9498	9508	9509	9517	9518	9519	9528	9532	9544	9547	9549	9551	9557	9560					
125	Trefoil	9243																				
126	Tares and vetches		9353	9451	9455	9526																
129	Turnips	8531	9230	9233	9235	9237	9241	9242	9243	9245	9256	9258	9260	9267	9268	9277	9281	9284	9286	9298
		9305	9306	9310	9314	9318	9319	9324	9338	9339	9342	9352	9353	9355	9358	9362	9363	9364	9365	9367	9375	9379
		9383	9395	9396	9400	9403	9406	9410	9413	9414	9417	9421	9424	9429	9430	9431	9433	9434	9436	9447	9450	9451	9452
		9453	9455	9458	9459	9459	9461	9464	9465	9466	9468	9475	9480	9486	9489	9491	9494	9497	9498	9508	9509	9517
		9518	9526	9526	9530	9532	9539	9540	9544	9547	9549	9551	9560									
131	Swedes		9385																			
132	Potatoes	9237	9245	9248	9256	9256	9257	9302	9310	9318	9379	9381	9405	9410	9421	9429	9430	9431	9434	9447
		9451	9489	9508	9509	9532																
133	Bare fallows	8531	9230	9232	9237	9241	9242	9244	9245	9248	9256	9257	9258	9267	9268	9277	9281	9298	9302	9305	9306
		9308	9310	9314	9319	9324	9337	9339	9342	9344	9346	9352	9353	9357	9365	9375	9383	9385	9395	9400	9403	9412
		9417	9421	9428	9429	9430	9431	9432	9433	9434	9437	9441	9444	9447	9450	9451	9452	9455	9464	9465	9466	9468
		9469	9486	9489	9497	9508	9509	9518	9526	9528	9530	9532	9539	9554	9557							
134	High farming	9230	9260	9275	9277	9306	9314	9318	9337	9352	9357	9367	9379	9385		9406	9412	9433	9434	9458	9459
		9465	9485	9528																		
135	Low farming	9268	9333	9353	9417	9444	9515	9530	9549													
136	Remarks on the absence of turnips			9381	9412	9554																
138	Recent increase in productivity		9245	9277	9339	9353	9364	9395	9458	9465	9532	9551										
139	Good quality pastures			8531	9237	9243	9248	9250	9268	9286	9314	9319	9335	9337	9339	9341	9344	9355	9357	9362
		9367	9371	9374	9375	9377	9379	9381	9394	9405	9410	9411	9412	9428	9433	9436	9437	9461	9486	9515	9528	9531
		9544	9557	9560																		
140	Poor quality pastures			8531	9341	9363	9379	9515	9549													
141	Meadows	9243	9250	9344	9346	9362	9367	9371	9375	9379	9410	9411	9433	9450	9453	9468	9498	9519	9528	9557
		9560																				
142	Irrigation and water meadows			9235	9246	9277	9319															
144	Parks	9237	9406	9424	9486																	
145	Accommodation land		9519																			
146	Cattle breeding		8531	9298	9302	9324	9342	9363	9365	9383	9410	9424	9461	9464	9491	9517						
147	Cattle fattening	9235	9237	9245	9310	9338	9341	9346	9385	9421	9424	9430	9431	9434	9453	9461	9466	9508	9509
		9517	9528	9530	9532	9557																
148	Dairying	8531	9232	9235	9237	9241	9244	9245	9248	9250	9256	9257	9275	9298	9302	9305	9308	9310	9319	9324
		9335	9337	9338	9341	9344	9357	9365	9371	9374	9375	9377	9381	9383	9385	9394	9410	9411	9421	9424	9430
		9431	9433	9434	9437	9445	9451	9461	9464	9466	9468	9469	9486	9489	9491	9508	9509	9515	9517	9526	9528	9530
		9532	9540	9544	9557	9560																
150	Sheep breeding	9232	9235	9241	9260	9298	9302	9324	9338	9363	9365	9374	9383	9410	9424	9459	9461	9464
		9466	9485	9491	9517	9526	9530	9539	9540	9557												
151	Sheep fattening	9310	9338	9385	9461	9528																
153	Horses	9517	9530																			
154	Pigs	9375	9433																			
158	Deer	9237	9424																			
161	Hay	9243	9257	9367	9411	9412	9428	9433														
164	Milk	9381	9445	9530																		
166	Cheese	9235	9237	9248	9257	9260	9275	9310	9335	9337	9357	9363	9377	9434	9451	9468	9485	9486	9489	9508	9509
169	Good orchards	9237	9319																			
171	Fruits	9237	9237																			
172	Market gardens	9256	9379	9445																		
174	Cabbages		9451																			
181	Reeds and oziers	9341	9410	9433	9475	9517																

Suffolk

1	Tithe-free district	6217	9563	9576	9696	9707	9728	9742	9743	9748	9771	9779	9790	9795	9826	9829	9831	9832	9833
		9836	9888	9940	9970	9989	10007	10074											
2	History of tithe payment	9649	9657	9876	9963	10005													
3	Tithe practices and agriculture		10040																
4	Exemptions from tithe	9575	9596	9603	9619	9642	9660	9675	9701	9784	9837	9862	9863	9865	9904	9914	9924	9935
		9936	9938	9944	9948	9968	9982	9992	9996	10000	10010	10023	10024	10027	10030	10034	10055	10061	10070
5	Tithe in kind	9745	9793	9802	9810	9865	9889	10040	10049	10058									
6	Compositions	9567	9568	9580	9587	9605	9613	9619	9621	9627	9628	9632	9633	9634	9635	9641	9642	9648	9649	9650
		9654	9666	9672	9674	9677	9678	9686	9691	9697	9701	9715	9722	9738	9745	9751	9764	9765	9774	9778	9802
		9813	9814	9815	9821	9830	9835	9837	9842	9876	9895	9896	9897	9903	9924	9931	9934	9938	9963	9974	9984	9985
		9991	9992	9997	9998	9999	10005	10008	10009	10017	10029	10032	10034	10044	10046	10047	10049	10050	10051	10052	10056	10062
		10066	10070	10077	10078														
7	Moduses	9561	9593	9613	9619	9644	9648	9677	9693	9698	9746	9793	9796	9812	9814	9815	9841	9860	9879	9893
		9908	9922	9925	9930	9935	9944	9950	9955	9959	9963	9964	9968	9972	9977	9988	9996	10004	10005	10015	10034	10046
		10062	10065																
8	Glebe	9580	9655	9691	9719	9751	9876	9893	9897	9903	9934	9974	9999	10001	10016	10023	10046	10047	10049	10070
9	Local topographic descriptions		9629	9750	9773	9801	9862	9883	9889	9911	9917	9928	9943	9950	10082				
10	Regional topographic descriptions	9562	9666	9681	9683	9689	9721	9726	9741	9759	9869	9889	9930	9939	9957	9976	9997
		10002	10012	10015	10016	10020	10033	10042	10072	10079									
11	Village morphology	9562	9573	9574	9599	9631	9692	9723	9775	9811	9827	9971	9977	10068	10069				
12	Church	9584	9598	9629	9645	9692	9754	9759	9760	9798	9852	9859	9862	9883	9887	9914	9916	9927	9950	9951

614

Suffolk contd.

9953 9957 9967 9979 9986 9995 10023 10033 10060 10068

13 Country houses and ornamental gardens 9561 9586 9618 9629 9694 9711 9713 9736 9747 9797 9801 9811 9819 9869 9977 9979 10073 10082

14 Farm houses and buildings 9562 9595 9606 9616 9663 9689 9726 9960

15 Cottages and cottage gardens 9590 9616 9616 9694 9713 9780 9789 9811 9819 9845 9857 9977 9995 10013 10072

16 Field boundaries 9564 9598 9645 9692 9718 9760 9791 9798 9811 9883 9883 9889 9905 10018 10071

17 Open fields 9573 9727 9754 9889

18 Small, irregular closes 9680 9718 9720 9769 9773 9791 9811 9847 9939 10000 10018 10071

19 Large, regular fields 9612 9811 9983 10013

20 Hedgerow timber 9773 9791

21 Coppice 9573 9590 9592 9604 9622 9625 9630 9656 9667 9668 9676 9692 9694 9702 9704 9706 9726 9732 9744 9773 9796 9857 9870 9893 9909 9912 9917 9923 9932 9977 9980 9988 10000 10003 10018 10035

22 Plantations 9561 9579 9595 9597 9607 9616 9618 9626 9656 9669 9676 9681 9685 9692 9724 9725 9729 9732 9735 9744 9760 9789 9811 9812 9841 9848 9857 9870 9871 9893 9909 9917 9959 9977 9983 9994 10021 10045 10071 10072 14827

23 Woodland management 9914 9977

24 Productive woodland 9562 9569 9604 9626 9645 9653 9805 9810 9857 9868 9994 10023 10045

25 Poor woodland 9583 9589 9600 9618 9622 9631 9637 9655 9667 9676 9680 9713 9732 9768 9870 9947 9971 9988 10003 10073 10080

26 Commons 9614 9614 9718 9729 9752 9796 9811 9871 9871 9874 9912 9936 9944 9955 9960 9990

27 Furze, gorse and heathlands 9572 9573 9573 9597 9612 9614 9626 9637 9694 9708 9724 9727 9735 9752 9767 9767 9825 9827 9868 9873 9873 9889 9889 9892 9928 9933 9968 9977 9983 9983 9990 10013 10016 10021 10025 10025 10043 10071 10072 10072 14827

30 Fens 9799

31 Wasteland 9955

32 Climatic hazards 9569 9572 9577 9578 9591 9597 9598 9612 9614 9639 9676 9705 9731 9735 9736 9750 9757 9762 9782 9804 9806 9827 9844 9852 9862 9869 9874 9878 9881 9882 9905 9907 9915 9920 9926 9929 9933 9943 9955 9978 9994 10016 10025 10041 10053 10061 10064 10069 10076 14827

33 Excessively steep land 9892

34 Land requires drainage 9592 9596 9603 9612 9622 9631 9655 9668 9706 9709 9713 9718 9746 9755 9788 9799 9841 9858 9875 9879 9886 9890 9898 9898 9902 9918 9923 9936 9942 9946 9951 9971 9978 9995 10016 10048 10054 10068 10072

35 Land liable to flood 9569 9593 9595 9600 9607 9625 9647 9657 9683 9685 9708 9732 9752 9753 9787 9804 9812 9820 9893 9909 9922 9939 9956 9977 9988

36 Productive soil 9562 9564 9574 9578 9598 9601 9602 9625 9629 9630 9639 9644 9645 9646 9653 9655 9662 9663 9670 9679 9681 9690 9705 9711 9731 9734 9747 9750 9766 9769 9780 9785 9788 9797 9801 9810 9822 9825 9834 9851 9854 9862 9878 9900 9908 9911 9919 9922 9929 9944 9966 9968 9977 9978 9979 9990 10013 10014 10019 10023 10024 10036 10048 10054 10058 10061 10064 10068 10073 10075 10076 10079 10080 10081

37 Poor soil 9572 9598 9601 9602 9603 9608 9614 9615 9622 9625 9626 9645 9663 9664 9666 9683 9685 9705 9708 9710 9711 9712 9725 9731 9732 9754 9769 9772 9773 9775 9780 9781 9788 9789 9791 9800 9801 9818 9827 9834 9847 9850 9852 9854 9862 9862 9868 9873 9879 9890 9893 9899 9909 9918 9919 9922 9926 9929 9933 9937 9968 9971 9977 9983 9984 9988 10003 10013 10019 10031 10043 10048 10059 10061 10072 10080 14827

38 Heavy (clay) soil 9561 9562 9565 9566 9569 9570 9573 9574 9577 9579 9581 9582 9583 9589 9590 9591 9592 9593 9595 9596 9598 9599 9600 9604 9606 9608 9609 9610 9612 9616 9617 9623 9630 9631 9638 9639 9644 9646 9647 9655 9656 9661 9663 9664 9668 9676 9680 9682 9684 9687 9688 9690 9692 9698 9699 9702 9704 9705 9706 9709 9710 9713 9716 9717 9718 9719 9720 9721 9723 9729 9736 9739 9740 9741 9746 9747 9749 9755 9757 9758 9759 9760 9761 9765 9766 9767 9768 9769 9770 9772 9775 9776 9780 9781 9782 9784 9785 9792 9796 9797 9798 9799 9800 9804 9805 9806 9810 9811 9812 9824 9841 9844 9847 9848 9857 9858 9859 9860 9863 9865 9866 9867 9870 9872 9874 9875 9878 9879 9881 9882 9883 9885 9886 9887 9889 9893 9894 9898 9899 9900 9902 9912 9914 9915 9916 9918 9919 9921 9922 9923 9925 9926 9927 9930 9932 9936 9937 9942 9943 9944 9946 9949 9950 9951 9952 9957 9958 9959 9960 9964 9966 9967 9971 9972 9973 9975 9978 9979 9980 9982 9984 9986 9987 9994 9995 9997 10000 10002 10003 10004 10006 10010 10011 10012 10013 10016 10018 10020 10021 10024 10030 10033 10035 10037 10038 10039 10040 10041 10042 10048 10054 10055 10057 10058 10059 10060 10061 10063 10064 10065 10067 10068 10073 10075 10076 10079 10080 10082

39 Loamy (turnip) soil 9564 9569 9570 9573 9574 9578 9579 9581 9589 9590 9591 9592 9595 9597 9599 9607 9609 9610 9618 9622 9625 9629 9631 9637 9644 9647 9653 9657 9662 9664 9667 9669 9670 9676 9679 9680 9681 9684 9689 9692 9694 9702 9704 9706 9709 9710 9711 9713 9717 9723 9726 9729 9731 9732 9735 9744 9753 9757 9758 9760 9761 9766 9767 9768 9769 9770 9773 9776 9782 9787 9789 9792 9796 9797 9801 9803 9804 9806 9811 9812 9847 9868 9869 9871 9872 9877 9882 9893 9899 9906 9909 9917 9922 9929 9937 9939 9942 9945 9948 9950 9952 9953 9959 9967 9973 9975 9980 9982 9984 9988 9994 10000 10002 10014 10016 10018 10021 10022 10023 10025 10030 10040 10042 10048 10057 10064 10069 10073 10076 10079 10081 10082

40 Light soil 9564 9569 9578 9581 9592 9596 9597 9607 9614 9645 9694 9698 9706 9712 9731 9757 9762 9769 9770 9788 9791 9806 9825 9827 9852 9857 9862 9868 9869 9872 9892 9894 9898 9899 9901 9908 9917 9920 9929 9933 9939 9943 9945 9947 9959 9977 9982 9983 9984 9987 9994 10000 10016 10025 10039 10040 10064 10069 10071 10072 10073 10076

41 Several varieties of soil 9615 9616 9647 9804 9805 9811 9812 9844 9845 9849 9862 9868 9871 9872 9883 9890 9899 9909 9921 9922 9929 9942 9955 9968 9979 9982 10000 10011 10021 10025 10027 10030 10040 10048 10057 10073 10079

42 Chalk 9573 9593 9676 9689 9754 9889 9930 9957 10011 10060

43 Sand or gravel 9565 9566 9570 9572 9573 9574 9579 9584 9586 9589 9595 9600 9601 9603 9610 9612 9616 9618 9622 9625 9626 9629 9637 9638 9640 9644 9647 9653 9656 9657 9667 9669 9676 9680 9683 9685 9689 9692 9694 9723 9725 9726 9727 9732 9735 9744 9750 9752 9759 9760 9761 9765 9767 9769 9773 9780 9787 9789 9799 9801 9804 9805 9809 9811 9812 9820 9822 9834 9843 9854 9859 9862 9863 9865 9867 9870 9871 9872 9873 9877 9879 9889 9892 9907 9909 9916 9917 9922 9930 9954 9956 9972 9973 9983 9988 10000 10002 10011 10012 10016 10019 10021 10025 10030 10033 10036 10037 10043 10045 10048 10053 10054 10057 10063 10065 10067 10068 10079 14827

45 Fields remote from farms 10016 10035 10064 10065

46 Good local roads 9562 9565 9566 9569 9663 9705 9723 9724 9753 9762 9765 9811 9865 9867 9885 9900 9966 9972 9983 10016 10043 10054 10063

47 Poor local roads 9788 9792

48 Turnpike and main roads 9586 9590 9596 9608 9615 9655 9684 9692 9716 9724 9732 9792 9868 9869 9901 9937 9949 9973 9975 10000 10003 10012 10021 10022 10036 10039 10059 10076 10079 10082

50 Water carriage 9574 9577 9578 9581 9592 9597 9612 9626 9647 9680 9683 9735 9736 9762 9770 9804 9828 9849 9862 9872 9920 9929 9955 10014 10027 10048 10064 10069 10071

53 Markets accessible 9569 9577 9603 9612 9614 9647 9655 9662 9680 9684 9692 9724 9732 9736 9750 9752 9762 9765 9770 9776 9804 9811 9812 9828 9834 9865 9867 9879 9943 9948 9959 9967 9975 10003 10027 10041 10054 10059 10063 10073

54 Markets inaccessible 9582 9772 9887 9900 9905 9921 9972 10045 10057

55 Provincial markets 9566 9578 9582 9612 9827 9943 9990 9997 10016 10041 10069 10073

56 London market 9566 9577 9760 9765 9770 9805 9929 9943 9955 10014 10041 10073

57 Fairs 9827 9899

58 Market prices 9876 10031 10054

59 Landowners and their estates 9586 9597 9598 9602 9616 9631 9661 9719 9736 9750 9760 9797 9852 9862 9926 9926 9942 9953 10002 10027 10031 10053 10072 10073

60 Land occupiers 9581 9590 9603 9662 9664 9689 9724 9755 9791 9811 9828 9852 9862 9869 9942 9943 9943 9973 9982 10031 10039 10068 10072

61 Farm size 9581 9584 9597 9598 9607 9614 9630 9682 9720 9754 9755 9757 9759 9770 9773 9852 9859 9887 9914 9916 9922 9927 9933 9943 9951 9953 9957 9973 9983 9995 10043 10060

Suffolk contd.

62	Leases	9664	9762	9946	9972	9982	10059	10069												
63	Farm implements			10040	10040															
64	Common grazing			9569	9705	9796	9936	10027												
65	Lammas and other common rights						9874	9889	9990											
66	Rents	9572	9581	9727	9804	9827	9890	9930	10068											
68	Rates	9747	9914																	
69	Farm labour and wages				9926															
70	Enclosure or improvement of waste					9694	9702	9762	9818	9854	9933	10072								
71	Enclosure of commons			9809	9847	9870	9930	9933	9945	9956	9977									
72	Enclosure of open fields			9822	9906	10023														
74	Occasional ploughing of grassland			9572	9983	10031														
75	Conversion of grass to arable				9694	9702	9983	9984	10061											
77	Paring and burning		9657																	
81	Marsh drainage			9581	9607	9847	9961	9968												
82	Drainage channels and ditches			9564	9709	9798	9920	9961												
85	Underdrainage		9562	9564	9566	9569	9570	9574	9577	9581	9582	9583	9597	9599	9604	9639	9645	9662	9663	9664
	9668	9676	9684	9705	9709	9711	9716	9719	9734	9736	9749	9755	9757	9761	9766	9770	9776	9797	9798	9804	9806
	9810	9844	9849	9857	9860	9862	9866	9868	9874	9875	9878	9885	9886	9890	9899	9900	9912	9915	9918	9923	9926
	9932	9942	9943	9950	9956	9959	9967	9973	9975	9978	9982	9994	9997	10003	10040	10041	10048	10057	10058	10061	10064
	10073	10076																			
86	Tile drains		9662	9875	10041	10073															
87	Marl	9694	9822	10072																	
88	Chalk	9822																			
92	Dung	9574	9577	9581	9615	9692	9725	9749	9750	9752	9762	9770	9776	9804	9806	9827	9828	9844	9878	9886	9899
	9905	9915	9942	9943	9951	9967	9982	10012	10014	10038	10040	10059	10069	10073							
94	Fish	9647	9850																		
95	Bones	10025	10057	10059																	
98	Rape cake		10059																		
99	Chemical fertilisers			9647	10057																
100	Oil dust, unspecified fertilisers or manures					9612	9828	9844	9869	9929	9959	9990	10040								
101	General comments on crop rotations				9645	9692	9848	9990	10024	10068	10069										
102	Irregular rotations		9818	9883	10031																
103	3-course rotation		9573	9889																	
104	4-course rotation		9561	9562	9564	9565	9566	9569	9570	9572	9573	9574	9577	9578	9579	9581	9582	9583	9584	9586
	9590	9591	9592	9593	9595	9596	9597	9598	9599	9600	9601	9602	9604	9606	9608	9612	9614	9615	9617	9618	9623
	9626	9629	9631	9636	9637	9639	9640	9644	9645	9646	9647	9653	9655	9657	9662	9663	9664	9666	9669	9670	9676
	9679	9681	9682	9684	9685	9687	9688	9689	9690	9692	9698	9699	9702	9704	9705	9709	9711	9713	9716	9717	9718
	9719	9720	9721	9722	9723	9729	9731	9734	9735	9736	9738	9740	9746	9749	9753	9754	9755	9757	9759	9760	9761
	9762	9765	9766	9768	9769	9770	9772	9776	9780	9782	9784	9788	9789	9796	9797	9798	9799	9800	9803	9804	9805
	9806	9809	9810	9811	9820	9822	9825	9828	9834	9841	9843	9844	9847	9848	9849	9850	9851	9852	9854	9858	9859
	9860	9862	9863	9865	9866	9867	9868	9869	9870	9871	9872	9873	9874	9875	9878	9879	9885	9886	9887	9892	9893
	9898	9900	9901	9904	9905	9907	9908	9909	9912	9914	9915	9916	9918	9920	9922	9923	9925	9926	9927	9929	9930
	9932	9933	9937	9939	9943	9944	9945	9946	9948	9949	9950	9951	9952	9955	9956	9957	9958	9959	9960	9964	9966
	9967	9971	9972	9973	9975	9976	9977	9979	9980	9982	9983	9984	9987	9988	9990	9994	9995	9997	10000	10004	10006
	10012	10013	10014	10015	10016	10020	10021	10022	10023	10024	10025	10027	10030	10033	10036	10037	10038	10040	10041	10042	10045
	10048	10053	10057	10058	10059	10060	10061	10063	10064	10065	10067	10068	10069	10073	10075	10076	10081	14827			
105	5-course rotation		9724	9725	9827	10043															
106	6-course rotation		9645																		
110	Wheat	9598	9639	9662	9731	9886	9912	9960	10064												
111	Barley	9662	9765	9902	9929	10022	10041														
112	Oats	9852	9902	9948	10031	10057															
113	Rye or meslin		9572	9597	9712	9724	9760	9805	9806	9818	9827	9852	9854	9868	9869	9883	9889	9929	9933	9983
	10016	10031	10043	10072	10076																
114	Corn yields		9722	9725	9822	9827	9876	9955	9974	10005	10013	10049	10075								
115	Beans	9561	9564	9569	9577	9593	9598	9599	9617	9630	9631	9638	9664	9670	9676	9684	9688	9704	9718	9719	9720
	9723	9734	9736	9740	9746	9761	9766	9782	9858	9862	9867	9893	9899	9902	9904	9916	9922	9925	9932	9936	9964
	9995	10006	10014	10021	10033	10037	10038	10042	10067	10081											
116	Peas	9569	9597	9598	9599	9638	9663	9719	9734	9736	9738	9869	9904	9990	9994	10037	10038	10067			
117	Rape	9984																			
118	Coleseed		9577	9869	9878																
122	Unspecified grass seeds			9875	9886																
123	Clover	9561	9562	9564	9569	9574	9577	9581	9582	9593	9597	9598	9599	9601	9612	9614	9617	9623	9630	9637	9638
	9639	9662	9663	9664	9669	9676	9679	9684	9688	9689	9698	9704	9709	9718	9719	9720	9723	9734	9736	9738	9740
	9746	9749	9753	9754	9755	9757	9761	9762	9766	9770	9776	9782	9797	9804	9820	9827	9828	9844	9851	9858	9860
	9862	9866	9868	9869	9872	9874	9878	9885	9886	9893	9898	9899	9902	9904	9912	9915	9916	9920	9925	9926	9929
	9930	9932	9936	9942	9944	9948	9950	9953	9955	9959	9960	9964	9967	9972	9973	9975	9978	9990	9994	9995	9997
	10004	10004	10006	10021	10025	10033	10037	10038	10040	10041	10048	10057	10059	10064	10064	10065	10067	10073	10076	10081	
124	Sainfoin		9572	9694	9869																
125	Trefoil	9564	9569	9574	9577	9581	9597	9599	9614	9639	9662	9664	9684	9709	9736	9749	9755	9757	9761	9762	9766
	9770	9776	9804	9827	9828	9844	9868	9869	9874	9878	9898	9899	9902	9920	9926	9929	9948	9950	9959	9967	9973
	9990	9994	9997	10025	10041	10048	10059	10073													
126	Tares and vetches		9565	9569	9581	9582	9598	9603	9612	9638	9662	9663	9664	9679	9684	9709	9746	9749	9755	9757
	9760	9761	9770	9776	9788	9797	9806	9851	9858	9874	9878	9883	9886	9904	9915	9919	9925	9926	9943	9946	9967
	9973	9975	9978	9982	9994	10033	10040	10041	10057	10059	10061	10069	10073								
129	Turnips	9562	9564	9565	9566	9569	9572	9573	9574	9577	9578	9581	9582	9583	9584	9589	9593	9596	9597	9599
	9602	9603	9607	9614	9625	9631	9637	9638	9639	9644	9645	9646	9653	9655	9662	9663	9664	9666	9669	9670	9676
	9679	9682	9684	9688	9689	9698	9709	9717	9719	9724	9729	9736	9746	9753	9754	9755	9757	9758	9759	9761
	9762	9766	9768	9769	9770	9776	9788	9797	9798	9799	9804	9805	9806	9811	9844	9849	9852	9859	9860	9862	9863
	9866	9867	9869	9872	9874	9878	9879	9883	9885	9887	9889	9890	9899	9900	9904	9912	9914	9915	9916	9918	9919
	9920	9922	9926	9927	9929	9930	9933	9936	9942	9943	9944	9946	9949	9951	9952	9953	9959	9960	9964	
	9967	9973	9975	9978	9979	9982	9988	9990	9994	9995	10013	10016	10021	10022	10023	10025	10031	10033	10036	10037	10040
	10041	10045	10048	10054	10057	10058	10059	10061	10063	10064	10065	10067	10068	10069	10071	10073	10076	10081	10082		
130	Mangolds	9564	9565	9569	9577	9581	9582	9603	9612	9662	9663	9664	9682	9684	9702	9705	9709	9719	9723	9736
	9749	9757	9761	9762	9770	9797	9806	9844	9849	9860	9867	9872	9874	9878	9879	9885	9887	9900	9912	9914	9915
	9920	9925	9926	9927	9929	9930	9936	9946	9959	9967	9973	9978	9982	9984	9994	10012	10040	10041	10048	10058	10059
	10060	10061	10063	10073	10081	10082															
131	Swedes	9887	10025	10069																	
132	Potatoes	9828	9961																		
133	Bare fallows		9561	9564	9565	9566	9569	9573	9578	9581	9583	9593	9596	9598	9600	9602	9603	9604	9608	9617	9638
	9645	9646	9655	9664	9676	9679	9684	9698	9704	9718	9719	9720	9723	9729	9736	9740	9746	9749	9757	9761	9766
	9768	9776	9782	9799	9804	9805	9811	9844	9858	9867	9874	9878	9879	9882	9890	9899	9902	9912			
	9918	9919	9922	9923	9925	9926	9932	9942	9946	9948	9952	9957	9959	9964	9967	9973	9975	9980	9994	9995	10004
	10006	10013	10021	10033	10037	10038	10040	10041	10042	10057	10058	10059	10060	10061	10065	10073	10081				
134	High farming		9562	9579	9647	9664	9705	9750	9791	9797	9802	9825	9849	9850	9869	9892	9961	9977	9983	10013	10014
	10022	10023	10040	10061																	

Suffolk contd.

135	Low farming	9598	9949	9971	9977	10016													
136	Remarks on the absence of turnips					9598	9600	9604	9606	9608	9617	9668	9705	9784	9848	9923	10006	10035	10038 10042
137	Remarks on pests and crop diseases					9683	9722	9882	9902	9912									
138	Recent increase in productivity			9918		9976													
139	Good quality pastures			9589	9599	9600	9601	9623	9630	9663	9676	9690	9699	9702	9705	9706	9746	9767	9768 9769
	9770 9789 9796 9797 9804 9810 9811 9824 9827 9858 9863 9877 9881 9898 9908 9927 9928 9937 9939 9952 9968																		
	9984 9988 9994 10021 10023 10024 10053 10054 10061 10064 10071 10079 10081 10082																		
140	Poor quality pastures 9566 9581 9586 9590 9596 9600 9601 9603 9604 9606 9607 9609 9625 9647 9655 9661 9669																		
	9681 9682 9683 9694 9720 9736 9736 9757 9758 9769 9773 9776 9781 9782 9784 9787 9796 9809 9848 9849																		
	9850 9858 9859 9860 9866 9868 9872 9886 9889 9893 9894 9902 9907 9915 9918 9929 9947 9951 9956 9959 9961																		
	9968 9971 9975 9984 9986 9987 9994 10000 10002 10003 10006 10011 10018 10021 10025 10025 10031 10035 10039 10041 10048																		
	10073 10080 10081																		
141	Meadows 9564 9566 9574 9579 9592 9596 9609 9610 9616 9622 9623 9625 9626 9637 9638 9644 9653 9656 9661																		
	9667 9668 9680 9681 9682 9684 9687 9690 9694 9702 9704 9705 9710 9713 9718 9729 9732 9735 9744 9769 9782																		
	9789 9791 9798 9806 9812 9848 9851 9852 9881 9889 9893 9911 9912 9919 9920 9922 9927 9932 9961 9977 9994																		
	10000 10003 10016 10021 10024 10039 10043 10048 10057 10064 10067 10068 10080 10082																		
142	Irrigation and water meadows 9562 9666 9945 10018																		
143	Marsh grassland 9570 9574 9578 9581 9586 9595 9597 9601 9607 9625 9647 9657 9669 9683 9684 9685 9726 9731																		
	9752 9753 9773 9787 9820 9847 9850 9851 9854 9904 9909 9919 9920 9929 9952 9953 9963 9968 10015 10027 10043																		
	10048 10073																		
144	Parks 9586 9589 9597 9598 9609 9616 9618 9622 9667 9668 9676 9683 9694 9711 9726 9727 9736 9744 9760 9784																		
	9788 9789 9797 9801 9811 9812 9819 9868 9869 9892 9899 9937 9959 9968 10015 10071 10073																		
145	Accommodation land 9834																		
146	Cattle breeding 9564 9684 9692 9719 9770 9956 10076																		
147	Cattle fattening 9574 9577 9578 9581 9582 9597 9599 9612 9664 9684 9749 9752 9757 9760 9761 9762 9766 9770																		
	9776 9797 9803 9860 9869 9874 9878 9898 9899 9920 9930 9959 9967 10014 10048 10057 10061 10073 10076																		
148	Dairying 9574 9581 9597 9603 9688 9755 9819 9828 9867 9918 9925 9930 9943 9961 9982 10031 10043 10063																		
150	Sheep breeding 9569 9574 9577 9586 9597 9612 9614 9626 9639 9683 9688 9689 9708 9712 9724 9725 9736 9757																		
	9760 9797 9804 9806 9827 9852 9869 9920 9933 9953 9955 9975 9983 10016 10031 10031 10040 10041 10043 10048 10063																		
	10076																		
151	Sheep fattening 9569 9578 9582 9599 9612 9662 9709 9719 9749 9757 9761 9762 9766 9770 9776 9797 9866 9875																		
	9899 9912 9915 9943 9950 9967 9973 9978 9994 10041 10061 10069 10073																		
153	Horses 9720 9755 9797 9881 9902 9912 9951 9953 9975 10025 10031 10061																		
154	Pigs 9755 9926																		
155	Oxen 10043 10063																		
156	Poultry 9569 9912 10076																		
157	Rabbits 9618 9983 10031 10072																		
158	Deer 9616 9669 9724 9868 9869 9928 9968 10071 10072 10073																		
159	Animal diseases 9849 9890																		
160	Straw 9647 9772 9915 9978 9997 10041 10048 10069 10073																		
161	Hay 9562 9564 9569 9574 9577 9578 9582 9583 9596 9599 9601 9606 9614 9637 9639 9639 9662 9664 9684 9718																		
	9729 9739 9749 9750 9757 9761 9762 9766 9770 9772 9776 9782 9797 9798 9806 9811 9854 9857 9866 9868 9872																		
	9875 9878 9881 9885 9886 9898 9899 9902 9909 9912 9915 9920 9929 9936 9942 9948 9949 9950 9955 9959 9967																		
	9973 9984 9994 9997 10031 10040 10041 10045 10048 10057 10058 10059 10064 10069 10073 10076																		
162	Manufactured feedstuffs (cake etc.) 9574 9577 9577 9599 9612 9664 9736 9749 9757 9760 9761 9762 9770 9797 9797																		
	9827 9844 9849 9860 9866 9872 9874 9878 9886 9899 9920 9943 9959 9967 9973 9973 9990 10040 10057 10061 10073																		
	10076																		
163	Stall or yard feeding 9564 9578 9582 9664 9684 9709 9749 9761 9766 9776 9844 9849 9866 9867 9872 9874 9878 9885																		
	9886 9899 9912 9918 9920 9926 9929 9930 9943 9946 9959 9967 9994 10041 10048 10057 10059																		
164	Milk 9982																		
165	Butter 9885 10068																		
166	Cheese 9885 9918 10068																		
167	Wool 9708																		
169	Good orchards 9811 9819 9977																		
170	Poor orchards 9956																		
171	Fruits 9917 9977																		
172	Market gardens 9595 9956 10069																		
174	Cabbages 9663 9705 9869 10048 10081																		
175	Carrots 9612 9822 9920 10025 10069																		
178	Hops 9569 9759																		
181	Reeds and oziers 9630 9847																		

Surrey

1	Tithe-free district 10094 10131 10168 10169 10201 10205 13558 14811 14812 14828																		
2	History of tithe payment 10182 10212																		
4	Exemptions from tithe 10083 10102 10110 10117 10120 10122 10126 10127 10132 10134 10145 10146 10152 10156 10162 10164 10165																		
	10170 10173 10179 10185 10193 10195 10196 10200 10206 10209 10216 10217																		
5	Tithe in kind 10092 10097 10120 10127 10132 10143 10161 10164 10203 10214 13560																		
6	Compositions 10087 10097 10120 10124 10125 10129 10130 10134 10135 10137 10148 10151 10156 10158 10164 10172 10178 10179 10180																		
	10183 10186 10187 10188 10194 10198 10202 10203 10204 10206 10207 10208 10209 10211 10213 10214 10217 13557 13561 13566 14810																		
7	Moduses 10128 10156 10217																		
9	Local topographic descriptions 10084 10085 10089 10092 10099 10104 10106 10110 10119 10126 10136 10145 10147 10163 10165 10173																		
	10174 10216																		
10	Regional topographic descriptions 10140 10149 10185 10188 10192																		
11	Village morphology 10091 10105 10112 10127 10142 10166 10210																		
12	Church 10085 10092 10136 10145 10165 10173 10177 10185 10210 10216 10218																		
13	Country houses and ornamental gardens 10085 10089 10092 10116 10126 10127 10143 10143 10163 10166 10166 10195 10218 13554 13560																		
16	Field boundaries 10086 10102 10110 10112 10132 10152 10170																		
17	Open fields 10091 10092 10119 10143																		
18	Small, irregular closes 10086 10120																		
19	Large, regular fields 10149																		
20	Hedgerow timber 10132 10170																		
21	Coppice 10084 10085 10098 10119 10140 10188																		
22	Plantations 10084 10104 10112 10118 10127 10133 10139 10147 10165 10182 10218																		
23	Woodland management 10140 10165 10190																		
24	Productive woodland 10085 10118 10133 10218																		
25	Poor woodland 10098 10102 10105																		
26	Commons 10083 10084 10093 10104 10105 10119 10128 10139 10175 10177 10177 10188 10199 10185 10185 10188 10199 10218																		
27	Furze, gorse and heathlands 10083 10084 10085 10093 10104 10105 10120 10123 10139 10166 10177 10185 10188 10199 10218																		
31	Wasteland 10136 10140																		
32	Climatic hazards 10085 10110 10139 10147 10162 10167 10184 10215																		
33	Excessively steep land 10084 10085 10105 10112 10119 10133 10140																		
34	Land requires drainage 10086 10093 10096 10099 10100 10106 10119 10126 10132 10139 10149 10161 10170 10193 10215 10218																		

Surrey contd.

35	Land liable to flood	10139 10218
36	Productive soil	10090 10091 10092 10096 10127 10128 10139 10140 10154 10174 10175 10188 10192 10196 10200
37	Poor soil	10083 10084 10085 10091 10093 10096 10098 10102 10105 10109 10112 10116 10119 10120 10127 10128 10133 10136 10139 10140 10146 10147 10170 10175 10177 10188 10192 10193 10195 10199 10215 10216 13560
38	Heavy (clay) soil	10083 10084 10086 10089 10093 10096 10098 10099 10100 10102 10104 10105 10106 10107 10109 10112 10116 10118 10119 10120 10121 10126 10127 10128 10132 10133 10136 10138 10139 10140 10141 10145 10146 10149 10152 10154 10161 10162 10163 10165 10166 10170 10173 10174 10175 10184 10185 10189 10192 10193 10195 10196 10199 10210 10215 10215 10216 13560
39	Loamy (turnip) soil	10084 10089 10099 10102 10112 10123 10132 10139 10140 10152 10154 10185 10188 10196 10215 13554
40	Light soil	10084 10085 10091 10092 10093 10104 10112 10117 10119 10123 10145 10154 10167 10188 10192 10195 10218
41	Several varieties of soil	10083 10093 10098
42	Chalk	10083 10098 10107 10112 10116 10118 10119 10126 10140 10141 10162 10163 10165 10174 10184 10185 10188 10189 10192 10216
43	Sand or gravel	10083 10085 10089 10090 10091 10096 10098 10099 10104 10107 10112 10116 10118 10120 10123 10126 10127 10128 10133 10136 10138 10139 10141 10143 10145 10146 10154 10162 10165 10167 10174 10175 10177 10184 10185 10188 10192 10195 10200 10210 10215 10216 10218 13554 13560
44	Peat	10177
46	Good local roads	10102 10107 10118 10126 10149 10152 10162 10165
47	Poor local roads	10086 10100 10105 10110 10170 10188 10199
48	Turnpike and main roads	10086 10099 10105 10107 10112 10116 10120 10126 10139 10140 10161 10163 10165 10166 10195 10200 10218
51	Canals	13559
52	Railways	10112 10154 10163 10167 10193 10195
53	Markets accessible	10154 10161 10162
55	Provincial markets	10107 10118 10120 10132 10152 10175
56	London market	10091 10123 10127 10140 10161 13560
58	Market prices	10123 10127 10167 10174
59	Landowners and their estates	10085 10102 10116 10218 10218
60	Land occupiers	10085 10092 10126 10128 10141 10165
61	Farm size	10128 10136 10140 10145 10173 10174 10177 10184 10185 10216
64	Common grazing	10097 10106 10119
65	Lammas and other common rights	10105 10119 10139 10188
66	Rents	10102 10127 10152 10170 10215
67	Urban influences on value of land	10091
68	Rates	10120 10136 10145 10173 10174 10177 10185 10216
70	Enclosure or improvement of waste	10109
71	Enclosure of commons	10122 10153
72	Enclosure of open fields	10108 10117 10196
77	Paring and burning	10109
85	Underdrainage	10120
89	Lime	10102
92	Dung	10123 10161
101	General comments on crop rotations	10100 10143 10161
102	Irregular rotations	10112 10116 10162 13554 13560
103	3-course rotation	10092 10107 10112 10163 10199 10216
104	4-course rotation	10084 10085 10086 10089 10092 10093 10096 10098 10099 10102 10106 10107 10110 10112 10116 10117 10118 10119 10121 10123 10126 10127 10128 10132 10136 10139 10140 10142 10143 10145 10146 10149 10152 10154 10162 10163 10165 10173 10174 10175 10177 10185 10189 10193 10196 10200 10210 10215 10216 10218
105	5-course rotation	10089 10104 10110 10120 10123 10132 10133 10147 10173
113	Rye or meslin	10085 10118 10127 10128 10139 10143 10167 10175 10177
114	Corn yields	10105 10125
115	Beans	10085 10100 10106 10109 10110 10112 10116 10120 10127 10136 10145 10162 10170 10173 10192 10196 10215 10216
116	Peas	10085 10096 10106 10110 10120 10127 10128 10132 10143 10167 10215
123	Clover	10085 10089 10096 10099 10100 10102 10105 10106 10107 10109 10112 10116 10117 10119 10121 10126 10127 10133 10136 10138 10140 10142 10143 10145 10147 10149 10152 10154 10162 10165 10170 10174 10175 10177 10184 10185 10192 10193 10196 10199 10215 10216 10218 13560
124	Sainfoin	10105 10107 10112 10116 10133 10154 10163 10165 10184
125	Trefoil	10102 10116 10218
126	Tares and vetches	10084 10085 10100 10102 10110 10112 10119 10133 10136 10140 10149 10166 10167 10175 10192 13560
127	Lucerne	10147
129	Turnips	10084 10089 10093 10096 10098 10099 10105 10107 10110 10112 10116 10117 10118 10119 10120 10123 10126 10127 10128 10133 10136 10140 10141 10142 10143 10145 10146 10147 10152 10154 10162 10163 10165 10166 10167 10173 10174 10175 10177 10184 10185 10189 10192 10196 10200 10210 10215 10216
130	Mangolds	10100 10140 10143 10192 10200
131	Swedes	10143 10200
132	Potatoes	10091 10106 10107 10143 10167 10195 10215 13560
133	Bare fallows	10085 10086 10096 10098 10099 10100 10102 10105 10106 10109 10110 10112 10116 10118 10119 10120 10121 10126 10128 10132 10133 10136 10138 10140 10146 10149 10162 10163 10166 10170 10173 10174 10175 10184 10185 10189 10192 10193 10199 10210 10215 10216 10218
134	High farming	10091 10092 10127 10133 10139
135	Low farming	10109 10112 10140 10147 10192 10218
136	Remarks on the absence of turnips	10106 10193
139	Good quality pastures	10084 10090 10098 10110 10127 10152 10163 10196 10200 10218
140	Poor quality pastures	10084 10093 10098 10100 10104 10105 10109 10112 10123 10126 10128 10139 10140 10141 10146 10163 10170 10189 10193
141	Meadows	10090 10098 10104 10110 10127 10128 10139 10140 10141 10146 10152 10154 10163 10165 10167 10175 10184 10188 10189 10196 10200 10218
142	Irrigation and water meadows	10163 10218
144	Parks	10116 10127 10139 10140 10165 10175 10182
146	Cattle breeding	10118 10128
147	Cattle fattening	10120 10128 10140 10161
148	Dairying	10143 10195 13560
149	Cow keeping	13560
150	Sheep breeding	10089 10128 10139 10162 10189 10195
151	Sheep fattening	10107 10118 10126 10128 10141 10143 10184
153	Horses	10110 10143
158	Deer	10182
160	Straw	10123 10127 10161
161	Hay	10084 10086 10099 10102 10105 10107 10110 10117 10119 10127 10140 10141 10143 10154 10161 10193 10200 10210
163	Stall or yard feeding	10139 10143
164	Milk	10143
172	Market gardens	10091 10166 10167 10192 10195 13557
174	Cabbages	10167
175	Carrots	10118 10128
176	Onions	10167
177	Other vegetables	10167
178	Hops	10118 10121 10128 10134 10136 10142 10174 10185 10193 10215
181	Reeds and oziers	10167 10196

Sussex

1	Tithe-free district	10280 10281 10282 10284 10356 10394 10478 10493
2	History of tithe payment	10325 10399 10400 10429 10466 10473 13562
3	Tithe practices and agriculture	10320 10428
4	Exemptions from tithe	10219 10221 10224 10226 10227 10230 10237 10239 10246 10253 10257 10262 10269 10270 10272 10285 10288 10289 10291 10292 10295 10298 10299 10308 10318 10320 10321 10323 10327 10335 10336 10349 10352 10354 10362 10363 10366 10367 10373 10375 10383 10390 10400 10403 10410 10411 10422 10425 10427 10429 10433 10440 10457 10463 10468 10476 10482 10485 10490 10491 10495 10496 10498 10502 10505 10507 10508 10510 10512 10514 10515 10520 10522 10524 10526 10527 10528 10529 10530 10531
5	Tithe in kind	10333 10344 10393 10422 10424 10471
6	Compositions	10220 10221 10223 10230 10231 10232 10233 10234 10236 10247 10258 10262 10265 10278 10286 10290 10294 10302 10303 10306 10308 10317 10319 10321 10323 10327 10348 10350 10362 10363 10365 10371 10375 10378 10383 10411 10414 10416 10424 10429 10436 10449 10457 10468 10476 10490 10497 10510 10515 10521 10527 14802 14819
7	Moduses	10222 10227 10238 10241 10247 10256 10262 10269 10274 10294 10321 10325 10348 10352 10362 10365 10383 10385 10400 10403 10429 10440 10450 10457 10469 10495 10498 10511 10526 10528 10530 14813
9	Local topographic descriptions	10353 10379 10392 10434 10448 10475
11	Village morphology	10243 10353 10358 10373 10434
12	Church	10289
13	Country houses and ornamental gardens	10293 10406 10434 10469 10475 10483
14	Farm houses and buildings	10305 10305
15	Cottages and cottage gardens	10305 10477 10485 10491 10533
16	Field boundaries	10344 10422 10450 10462
17	Open fields	10305 10425
18	Small, irregular closes	10344 10450 10462
20	Hedgerow timber	10450
21	Coppice	10248 10250 10289 10296 10374 10380 10425 10492 10501 10504 10511 10513 10518 10530
22	Plantations	10289 10293 10299 10425 10455 10520
24	Productive woodland	10235 10248 10250 10270 10300 10352 10358 10373 10379 10380 10381 10403 10405 10406 10420 10431 10452 10458 10483 10492 10496 10507 10523 10524 10530 10532
25	Poor woodland	10289 10296 10299 10311 10333 10335 10358 10374 10379 10440 10462 10469 10492 10503 10507
26	Commons	10311 10320 10333 10335 10353 10434 10469 10491
27	Furze, gorse and heathlands	10289 10293 10299 10305 10311 10320 10320 10325 10325 10366 10434 10469 10485 10504 10504 10520 10520
32	Climatic hazards	10324 10326 10345 10451 10475 10520
33	Excessively steep land	10289 10311 10324 10419 10426 10485
34	Land requires drainage	10263 10269 10320 10329 10345 10377 10381 10484 10485 10487
35	Land liable to flood	10259 10268 10270 10300 10305 10328 10342 10344 10345 10349 10364 10384 10401 10431 10434 10440 10461 10472 10496 10520 14817
36	Productive soil	10227 10243 10259 10266 10268 10269 10287 10291 10295 10297 10305 10313 10316 10329 10333 10340 10342 10345 10349 10353 10384 10385 10389 10393 10401 10412 10419 10421 10425 10431 10434 10440 10443 10450 10455 10477 10484 10485 10486 10487 10489 10491 10495 10496 10502 10504 10511 10513 10518 10520 10522 10533 14817
37	Poor soil	10232 10235 10239 10242 10246 10263 10269 10274 10291 10296 10297 10299 10305 10311 10316 10320 10326 10333 10343 10344 10349 10353 10405 10419 10420 10427 10431 10440 10450 10454 10458 10477 10484 10485 10491 10495 10498 10504 10505 10520 10531 10532
38	Heavy (clay) soil	10219 10232 10235 10237 10240 10242 10244 10246 10248 10254 10257 10259 10263 10267 10268 10269 10270 10271 10272 10273 10274 10285 10288 10291 10292 10298 10299 10300 10307 10309 10310 10312 10318 10320 10329 10333 10335 10339 10340 10341 10343 10344 10345 10347 10349 10349 10352 10353 10357 10358 10361 10365 10366 10367 10368 10370 10372 10373 10376 10377 10379 10380 10381 10384 10390 10403 10405 10415 10418 10419 10420 10431 10434 10437 10438 10439 10440 10441 10442 10445 10446 10450 10452 10454 10458 10460 10462 10472 10477 10482 10484 10487 10488 10492 10495 10498 10501 10502 10505 10507 10508 10511 10512 10513 10517 10519 10522 10523 10524 10525 10528 10529 10530 10531 10532 14817
39	Loamy (turnip) soil	10219 10227 10237 10243 10248 10250 10259 10261 10267 10269 10287 10288 10292 10295 10309 10313 10316 10328 10329 10334 10338 10340 10342 10345 10346 10349 10353 10359 10364 10373 10374 10376 10389 10393 10401 10412 10417 10425 10427 10438 10443 10445 10455 10456 10461 10477 10481 10484 10485 10486 10489 10491 10492 10495 10496 10498 10512 10520 10522 10523 10533
40	Light soil	10239 10244 10263 10285 10289 10307 10312 10332 10397 10406 10409 10427 10434 10446 10450 10460 10477 10481 10491 10502 10503 10524
41	Several varieties of soil	10227 10242 10246 10250 10256 10260 10263 10269 10340 10341 10353 10357 10379 10434 10442 10445 10446 10492 10498 10499 10501 10507 10508 10513 10520 10530 14817
42	Chalk	10242 10244 10261 10268 10269 10272 10291 10296 10305 10307 10309 10312 10314 10326 10330 10338 10339 10340 10341 10353 10357 10360 10389 10392 10397 10406 10409 10418 10419 10426 10427 10437 10439 10441 10442 10444 10446 10448 10451 10469 10475 10477 10483 10484 10485 10488 10499 10504 10522 10525 10530 14817
43	Sand or gravel	10232 10242 10246 10256 10257 10260 10263 10267 10270 10271 10288 10289 10291 10293 10295 10300 10313 10320 10324 10330 10332 10335 10341 10345 10347 10354 10357 10358 10361 10364 10372 10379 10403 10415 10417 10420 10427 10440 10445 10450 10461 10462 10481 10482 10485 10487 10491 10496 10498 10499 10501 10502 10507 10508 10513 10519 10520 10525 10529 10530 10531 10532
44	Peat	10342 10357 10434
46	Good local roads	10295 10329 10381 10392 10412 10418 10431 10442 10446 10448 10452 10483 10533
47	Poor local roads	10242 10248 10434 10450 10477 10508
48	Turnpike and main roads	10235 10269 10270 10274 10299 10370 10373 10377 10403 10419 10420 10421 10431 10437 10440 10442 10450 10452 10462 10469 10477 10498 10499 10501 10502 10504 10513
50	Water carriage	10244 10268 10305 10412 10418 10421 10502
52	Railways	10235 10291 10370 10373 10437 10442
53	Markets accessible	10232 10254 10271 10295 10326 10343 10347 10357 10368 10370 10376 10384 10393 10415 10425 10426 10427 10435 10438 10441 10442 10446 10448 10455 10469 10488 10496 10498 10501 10502 10507 10511 10513 10518 10519 10528 10531 10532
54	Markets inaccessible	10318
55	Provincial markets	10263 10343 10358 10370 10373 10426 10450 10505 10533
58	Market prices	10268
59	Landowners and their estates	10305 10342 10406 10469 10520 13562
60	Land occupiers	10305 10320 10520
61	Farm size	10263 10320 10342 10477 10507
64	Common grazing	10320
65	Lammas and other common rights	10491
66	Rents	10320 10333 10481 10504
67	Urban influences on value of land	10355 10421 10442
68	Rates	10466 10480
70	Enclosure or improvement of waste	10242
71	Enclosure of commons	10221 10383
82	Drainage channels and ditches	10422
85	Underdrainage	10416
88	Chalk	10419
89	Lime	10450
92	Dung	10370 10426 10450
101	General comments on crop rotations	10242 10245 10310 10326 10335 10339 10374
102	Irregular rotations	10239 10355 10507
103	3-course rotation	10261 10273 10307 10330 10335 10339 10359 10372 10382 10393 10415 10427 10440 10455 10499 10511 10512 10522 10525
104	4-course rotation	10219 10227 10232 10235 10237 10240 10242 10250 10254 10257 10260 10261 10266 10267 10270 10271 10285 10288

619

Sussex contd.

10291 10293 10295 10298 10300 10305 10309 10312 10314 10320 10326 10330 10332 10334 10335 10338 10341 10342 10344 10354 10357 10358 10361 10366 10367 10368 10372 10390 10392 10393 10409 10415 10427 10437 10439 10440 10443 10444 10445 10448 10451 10475 10477 10482 10486 10489 10491 10496 10499 10505 10507 10511 10512 10517 10518 10519 10528 10529 10531

105	5-course rotation	10274 10326 10339 10437 10444 10451 10462 10499 10531
106	6-course rotation	10243 10254 10307 10314 10444 10533
113	Rye or meslin	10311 10370
114	Corn yields	10342
115	Beans	10243 10245 10256 10259 10285 10297 10310 10318 10345 10367 10374 10376 10380 10384 10390 10425 10450 10455 10462 10487 10495 10502 10508 10511 10512 10525 10531 10533
116	Peas	10256 10259 10261 10285 10297 10345 10367 10376 10380 10385 10443 10455 10508 10512 10529 10533
117	Rape	10244 10254 10261 10296 10297 10305 10307 10313 10314 10316 10324 10360 10406 10419 10427 10437 10444 10469 10472 10483 10484 10488 10499 10513 10516 14817
118	Coleseed	10311
123	Clover	10305 10318 10365 10440 10477 10484 10491 10516 10520 10533
124	Sainfoin	10296 10297 10305 10307 10406 10426 10451
126	Tares and vetches	10219 10227 10243 10245 10257 10259 10272 10273 10298 10305 10313 10316 10318 10324 10335 10340 10349 10366 10367 10370 10374 10390 10415 10419 10438 10448 10450 10455 10461 10472 10484 10486 10489 10505 10508 10516 10523 10528 10529 10530 10533
127	Lucerne	10305 10451
129	Turnips	10219 10227 10237 10239 10243 10244 10248 10250 10254 10257 10259 10260 10261 10266 10268 10269 10288 10292 10295 10296 10297 10305 10307 10313 10314 10316 10318 10320 10320 10324 10326 10335 10340 10342 10345 10354 10355 10358 10360 10370 10373 10374 10376 10385 10403 10406 10419 10421 10425 10427 10437 10440 10443 10444 10446 10450 10455 10469 10472 10482 10483 10484 10486 10487 10488 10489 10491 10492 10495 10496 10498 10499 10501 10504 10505 10507 10511 10513 10518 10520 10523 10525 10529 10530 10531 10533 14817
132	Potatoes	10358 10450 10502 10507 10523
133	Bare fallows	10219 10227 10235 10239 10240 10244 10248 10256 10259 10267 10269 10270 10272 10273 10274 10285 10285 10288 10296 10297 10298 10299 10300 10307 10310 10318 10335 10340 10344 10345 10349 10352 10358 10366 10367 10373 10374 10376 10380 10381 10384 10390 10403 10406 10415 10419 10425 10437 10438 10440 10441 10444 10446 10450 10462 10469 10477 10483 10492 10495 10498 10499 10501 10502 10503 10504 10505 10507 10508 10511 10512 10513 10516 10519 10523 10524 10525 10528 10529 10530 10531 10532 14817
134	High farming	10248 10268 10324 10345 10353 10364 10381 10425 10485 10495 10507 10533
137	Remarks on pests and crop diseases	10333
138	Recent increase in productivity	10416
139	Good quality pastures	10244 10246 10259 10268 10292 10295 10299 10311 10313 10316 10329 10333 10340 10342 10346 10353 10365 10370 10373 10376 10380 10384 10412 10415 10418 10421 10431 10434 10435 10438 10448 10456 10460 10462 10472 10477 10485 10487 10491 10496 10501 10502 10520 14817
140	Poor quality pastures	10235 10246 10256 10268 10270 10272 10274 10296 10299 10305 10311 10313 10329 10342 10344 10349 10353 10359 10364 10380 10401 10406 10409 10418 10431 10434 10485 10499 10501 10504 10530 14817
141	Meadows	10311 10313 10328 10342 10344 10355 10365 10373 10462 10485 10513 10520
142	Irrigation and water meadows	10392
143	Marsh grassland	10305 10347 10364 10477
144	Parks	10274 10358 10406 10434 10462 10469 10475 10491 10520
146	Cattle breeding	10244 10270 10345 10358 10373 10377 10380 10418 10441 10454 10456 10458 10460 10523
147	Cattle fattening	10235 10292 10295 10373 10380 10412 10418 10425 10456 10460 10472
148	Dairying	10316 10370 10437 10472
150	Sheep breeding	10244 10268 10296 10297 10305 10316 10324 10329 10333 10345 10358 10360 10373 10376 10380 10397 10409 10418 10419 10420 10426 10437 10438 10441 10456 10461 10469 10472 10483 10488 10503 10513 14817
151	Sheep fattening	10259 10270 10292 10373 10377 10412 10425 10456 10523
153	Horses	10299 10437 10472
154	Pigs	10305
155	Oxen	10437 10472
156	Poultry	10305
158	Deer	10462 10475
160	Straw	10426
161	Hay	10365 10462
164	Milk	10316 10370 10426 10437
165	Butter	10316
169	Good orchards	10477 10533
170	Poor orchards	10311 10335 10485
171	Fruits	10311 10462 10485
172	Market gardens	10370 10389 10434 10501
178	Hops	10246 10257 10263 10267 10269 10271 10272 10285 10335 10345 10352 10366 10367 10380 10411 10415 10431 10438 10450 10458 10501 10502 10505 10508 10512 10517 10519 10524 10528 10532

Warwickshire

1	Tithe-free district	10544 10545 10556 10564 10566 10574 10576 10583 10587 10589 10591 10593 10596 10598 10600 10604 10609 10617 10626 10630 10635 10638 10643 10660 10665 10666 10667 10669 10670 10671 10674 10681 10687 10688 10693 10694 10706 10707 10711 10712 10714 10716 10717 10719 10724 10732 10748 10752 10753 10755 10758 10759 10764 10765 10775 10776 10779
2	History of tithe payment	10538 10546 10547 10568 10578 10580 10592 10599 10602 10616 10629 10633 10637 10661 10685 10697 10701 10708 10728 10729 10745 10769 10773
3	Tithe practices and agriculture	10721
4	Exemptions from tithe	10542 10547 10559 10561 10570 10572 10577 10578 10580 10605 10610 10613 10620 10622 10623 10629 10636 10639 10644 10655 10656 10657 10663 10675 10677 10680 10682 10686 10698 10703 10704 10708 10718 10722 10726 10727 10730 10731 10733 10735 10739 10751 10760 10778
5	Tithe in kind	10615 10640 10678
6	Compositions	10538 10542 10547 10554 10555 10559 10568 10570 10577 10585 10592 10610 10615 10621 10623 10631 10636 10640 10645 10655 10680 10704 10705 10727 10760
7	Moduses	10544 10546 10547 10549 10559 10575 10577 10593 10605 10613 10615 10619 10622 10631 10633 10636 10639 10644 10645 10649 10652 10655 10668 10677 10680 10685 10698 10700 10701 10702 10704 10705 10708 10713 10718 10721 10721 10728 10739 10760 10761 10767
8	Glebe	10560 10562 10590 10592 10689 10708 10710
9	Local topographic descriptions	10536 10540 10594 10605 10613 10658
10	Regional topographic descriptions	10722
11	Village morphology	10560 10586 10658 10673 10709 10737 10747 10750 10762 10778
12	Church	10618 10647 10658 10689 10691 10709 10723 10725 10740 10750
13	Country houses and ornamental gardens	10605 10648 10683 10690 10726 10737
14	Farm houses and buildings	10594 10658 10709 10720
15	Cottages and cottage gardens	10536 10538 10605 10625 10641 10642 10653 10654 10683 10696 10722 10723 10771 10778
16	Field boundaries	10605 10721 10723
17	Open fields	10536 10761 10762 10770 10771
18	Small, irregular closes	10594 10624 10721 10737
19	Large, regular fields	10658
20	Hedgerow timber	10658

Warwickshire contd.

21	Coppice	10594 10696
22	Plantations	10560 10563 10624 10654 10747 10778
23	Woodland management	10535 10618 10642 10647 10689 10690 10691 10718 10720 10740
24	Productive woodland	10536 10538 10605 10648 10718 10750
25	Poor woodland	10623 10778
26	Commons	10536 10538 10594 10653 10737 10770 10771 10771
27	Furze, gorse and heathlands	10560 10586 10594 10733
32	Climatic hazards	10540 10584 10586
33	Excessively steep land	10594 10641 10642 10653 10696
34	Land requires drainage	10538 10586 10722 10749 10770 10771
35	Land liable to flood	10641 10646
36	Productive soil	10535 10543 10586 10618 10625 10646 10654 10658 10659 10663 10682 10689 10691 10696 10702 10709 10713 10720 10721 10742 10747 10750
37	Poor soil	10538 10560 10586 10594 10642 10658 10675 10689 10690 10696 10720 10721 10722 10737 10750 10778
38	Heavy (clay) soil	10535 10536 10538 10557 10560 10563 10578 10584 10586 10594 10603 10606 10612 10618 10625 10628 10632 10641 10642 10646 10647 10653 10654 10659 10662 10673 10683 10689 10690 10691 10696 10697 10702 10709 10715 10720 10721 10722 10723 10737 10740 10742 10747 10749 10750 10751 10762 10766 10770 10771 10778
39	Loamy (turnip) soil	10536 10540 10573 10578 10584 10606 10632 10642 10648 10658 10663 10673 10691 10702 10715 10721 10743 10747 10751
40	Light soil	10658 10689 10740
41	Several varieties of soil	10558 10560 10563 10586 10605 10613 10651 10721 10726
43	Sand or gravel	10538 10551 10557 10560 10563 10594 10618 10632 10646 10647 10651 10653 10659 10673 10697 10715 10721 10723 10737 10770
44	Peat	10721
45	Fields remote from farms	10641
46	Good local roads	10536 10563 10673 10726 10747
47	Poor local roads	10594 10653 10662 10721 10723 10737
48	Turnpike and main roads	10557 10558 10702 10709 10715
50	Water carriage	10651 10702
51	Canals	10653
52	Railways	10603
53	Markets accessible	10560 10605 10606 10613 10632 10646 10651 10663 10696 10702 10713 10721 10725 10726
54	Markets inaccessible	10662
55	Provincial markets	10563 10641
59	Landowners and their estates	10538 10586 10590 10613 10622 10623 10632 10636 10640 10689 10705 10723 10751 10766 10778
60	Land occupiers	10586 10606 10696 10737 10742 10747 10766
61	Farm size	10535 10578 10618 10632 10647 10659 10689 10691 10709 10721 10722 10723 10725 10740
62	Leases	10722
65	Lammas and other common rights	10594 10725
66	Rents	10594 10673 10743
67	Urban influences on value of land	10560
68	Rates	10535
69	Farm labour and wages	10594
70	Enclosure or improvement of waste	10623
72	Enclosure of open fields	10578 10594 10624 10770
75	Conversion of grass to arable	10646 10721
76	Conversion of arable to pasture	10547 10709
85	Underdrainage	10557 10594 10612 10651 10662 10751
89	Lime	10653 10723
92	Dung	10702 10721 10725
101	General comments on crop rotations	10606 10612 10708 10718 10737 10742 10766
102	Irregular rotations	10536 10538 10557 10584 10612 10647 10653 10696 10709 10715 10723 10737 10766
103	3-course rotation	10557 10648
104	4-course rotation	10535 10536 10543 10573 10618 10628 10646 10648 10658 10673 10704 10713 10742 10770 10771
105	5-course rotation	10551 10557 10558 10594 10647 10659 10663 10684 10689 10742 10743 10749
106	6-course rotation	10535 10540 10563 10603 10625 10658 10663 10683 10691 10704 10722 10740 10747 10762
108	8-10-course rotation	10718
111	Barley	10540 10557 10663
112	Oats	10540 10647
113	Rye or meslin	10560
114	Corn yields	10547 10560 10594 10640 10658 10704 10750
115	Beans	10535 10540 10646
116	Peas	10540
123	Clover	10646 10673 10689 10691 10718
126	Tares and vetches	10558 10628 10658
129	Turnips	10535 10536 10538 10540 10543 10551 10557 10558 10563 10578 10628 10646 10653 10689 10691 10709 10726 10747 10762
132	Potatoes	10584 10632
133	Bare fallows	10536 10557 10558 10563 10628 10646 10683 10747 10749 10762
134	High farming	10536 10578 10662 10663 10721 10747
135	Low farming	10538 10578 10605 10612 10632 10641 10651 10653 10720 10737 10742 10770 10771 10778
136	Remarks on the absence of turnips	10586 10750
139	Good quality pastures	10535 10551 10560 10563 10573 10586 10603 10605 10624 10625 10641 10646 10647 10648 10654 10659 10668 10682 10690 10696 10718 10723 10725 10726 10737 10743 10761 10762
140	Poor quality pastures	10538 10540 10578 10612 10625 10628 10646 10653 10654 10682 10690 10720 10721 10737 10747 10750 10751 10761 10778
141	Meadows	10536 10538 10557 10560 10563 10586 10720 10722 10723 10726 10747 10761
142	Irrigation and water meadows	10618 10647 .10696 10709 10747 10762
144	Parks	10605 10624 10648 10673 10683 10726 10778
145	Accommodation land	10632
146	Cattle breeding	10606 10628 10673 10709
147	Cattle fattening	10551 10606 10709 10715 10743
148	Dairying	10551 10578 10594 10606 10632 10641 10646 10653 10668 10673 10682 10690 10696 10709 10715 10721 10722 10723 10737 10743 10770
150	Sheep breeding	10551 10628 10673 10715 10726 10770
151	Sheep fattening	10658 10673
154	Pigs	10605 10696 10771
155	Oxen	10673
156	Poultry	10696 10771
157	Rabbits	10720
158	Deer	10720
159	Animal diseases	10658
161	Hay	10560 10606 10618 10632 10646 10709 10722 10761
169	Good orchards	10536 10538 10594 10641 10696 10720 10722
171	Fruits	10641

Westmorland

1	Tithe-free district	10793 10805 10822 10830 10833 10845 10855 10860 10873
2	History of tithe payment	10792 10797
3	Tithe practices and agriculture	10781 10784
4	Exemptions from tithe	10785 10786 10787 10792 10794 10799 10802 10804 10813 10819 10825 10828 10829 10831 10836 10852 10854 10865 10867 10871 10875
5	Tithe in kind	10784 10786 10787 10790 10795 10799 10814 10816 10834 10835 10840 10847 10850 10851 10853 10857 10866 10869 10870 10871
6	Compositions	10785 10792 10801 10804 10825
7	Moduses	10781 10782 10784 10785 10801 10804 10811 10812 10814 10829 10832 10835 10842 10848 10850 10863 10870 10871 10875 10876 10878
9	Local topographic descriptions	10787 10813 10816 10828 10871
10	Regional topographic descriptions	10786 10814 10821 10828 10857 10862 10867
11	Village morphology	10834
13	Country houses and ornamental gardens	10828 10857
14	Farm houses and buildings	10844
16	Field boundaries	10784
18	Small, irregular closes	10789 10812 10844 10851 10861 10869 10876 10877
19	Large, regular fields	10817 10851 10861 10877
20	Hedgerow timber	10865
21	Coppice	10871
24	Productive woodland	10865
26	Commons	10784 10786 10787 10812 10844 10856 10857 10870
27	Furze, gorse and heathlands	10787
28	Moorland	10813 10818
31	Wasteland	10870
32	Climatic hazards	10782 10787 10799 10813 10818 10828 10844 10851 10853 10861 10877
33	Excessively steep land	10782 10787
34	Land requires drainage	10787 10791 10796 10812 10818 10853
36	Productive soil	10786 10787 10790 10795 10799 10843 10862 10868 10871 10877
37	Poor soil	10790 10799 10853 10862 10865 10868 10869
38	Heavy (clay) soil	10799 10821 10851 10865 10869 10876
39	Loamy (turnip) soil	10786 10795 10817 10861 10876
40	Light soil	10788 10876
41	Several varieties of soil	10841 10844
43	Sand or gravel	10790 10799 10812 10821 10843 10844 10877
44	Peat	10790 10799 10818 10844
46	Good local roads	10799 10817 10844 10851 10869
47	Poor local roads	10787 10812 10861 10876 10877
48	Turnpike and main roads	10844 10868 10877
53	Markets accessible	10799 10877
54	Markets inaccessible	10787
58	Market prices	10814
59	Landowners and their estates	10781 10816 10817 10851 10865
60	Land occupiers	10851
61	Farm size	10784 10789
63	Farm implements	10816
66	Rents	10788
67	Urban influences on value of land	10781
68	Rates	10802
70	Enclosure or improvement of waste	10784 10865 10868
71	Enclosure of commons	10784 10802 10819 10828 10853 10854 10865 10871 10875
77	Paring and burning	10865
79	Subsoil ploughing	10816
89	Lime	10784
92	Dung	10868
101	General comments on crop rotations	10786 10787 10812 10814 10843 10851 10856 10865 10868 10876
102	Irregular rotations	10851
103	3-course rotation	10788 10821 10846
104	4-course rotation	10788 10795 10813 10843
105	5-course rotation	10817 10844 10861 10868 10877
106	6-course rotation	10868 10869
111	Barley	10782 10787
112	Oats	10782 10787 10861
123	Clover	10786 10795 10817
129	Turnips	10786 10795 10812 10817 10821 10843 10844 10846 10851 10856 10861 10868 10876 10877
132	Potatoes	10786 10814 10817 10821 10834 10843 10846 10856 10861 10868 10876
133	Bare fallows	10786 10812 10817 10821 10846 10851 10861 10869 10876 10877
134	High farming	10816
135	Low farming	10818 10841
138	Recent increase in productivity	10865
139	Good quality pastures	10781 10782 10787 10789 10803 10818 10853 10871
140	Poor quality pastures	10812 10816 10818 10836 10851 10861 10877
141	Meadows	10782 10814 10836 10857
144	Parks	10817
146	Cattle breeding	10784 10818 10843 10856 10871
148	Dairying	10834 10843 10856 10871
150	Sheep breeding	10781 10782 10784 10787 10788 10791 10796 10803 10814 10816 10821 10834 10835 10840 10843 10846 10856 10857 10868 10870 10871
151	Sheep fattening	10814 10868
152	Droving	10868
153	Horses	10781 10831
161	Hay	10781 10787 10814 10818 10836 10840 10857 10868
164	Milk	10784 10834 10856 10871
165	Butter	10784 10834 10843 10856 10871
166	Cheese	10843
167	Wool	10814 10840 10870

Wiltshire

1	Tithe-free district	10883 10890 10893 10904 10941 10946 10949 10952 10967 10970 10994 10996 11024 11034 11041 11043 11045 11046 11049 11063 11098 11105 11108 11110 11114 11115 11122 11124 11131 11132 11146 11147 11152 11157 11158 11165 11179 11202
2	History of tithe payment	10934 10972 11053 11106
3	Tithe practices and agriculture	11142
4	Exemptions from tithe	10881 10898 10899 10905 10907 10919 10922 10925 10929 10931 10936 10944 10950 10951 10955 10973 10975

Wiltshire contd.

      10976 10978 10979 10982 10998 11000 11012 11020 11022 11029 11031 11053 11057 11058 11068 11069 11071 11078 11080 11084 11086 11087 11090 11091 11093 11099 11104 11106 11120 11133 11137 11140 11142 11151 11160 11161 11166 11167 11168 11172 11184 11185 11195 11203 11211

5 Tithe in kind   10888 10897 10934 10945 10947 10954 10959 10985 10988 11069 11078 11085 11103 11190
6 Compositions   10882 10888 10907 10911 10920 10934 10937 10943 10944 10950 10965 10975 10979 10980 10983 11005 11032 11035 11038 11074 11086 11087 11094 11103 11130 11153 11170 11185 11188 11192 11193 11194 11204
7 Moduses   10880 10881 10884 10895 10907 10917 10920 10922 10956 10962 10971 10976 10978 10987 11000 11014 11026 11029 11036 11050 11057 11070 11079 11084 11088 11091 11099 11109 11136 11142 11145 11154 11164 11168 11173 11176 11190 11204 11211
8 Glebe   11093
9 Local topographic descriptions   11050
10 Regional topographic descriptions   11210
17 Open fields   11004 11070
20 Hedgerow timber   10881 10886 10891 10892 10894 10896 10897 10899 10900 10901 10903 10905 10906 10909 10913 10917 10919 10921 10923 10925 10926 10929 10930 10932 10939 10940 10958 10960 10962 10968 10971 10974 10977 10980 10982 10985 10986 10989 10990 10991 10997 10998 11007 11009 11010 11011 11013 11014 11017 11018 11019 11021 11023 11026 11027 11029 11030 11031 11037 11050 11054 11056 11059 11060 11062 11064 11065 11066 11068 11069 11070 11071 11073 11075 11076 11080 11082 11083 11085 11088 11095 11096 11099 11100 11101 11102 11104 11107 11113 11117 11119 11123 11125 11126 11135 11136 11137 11138 11139 11142 11143 11144 11145 11149 11154 11155 11159 11162 11163 11167 11171 11173 11174 11175 11177 11178 11180 11181 11182 11183 11187 11189 11191 11195 11196 11197 11198 11200 11206 11208 11209 11212
21 Coppice   10894 10897 10900 10903 10905 10909 10917 10919 10923 10929 10935 10948 10960 10962 10971 10977 10985 10986 10990 10991 10993 10997 11007 11009 11010 11011 11014 11019 11023 11025 11030 11037 11051 11054 11056 11059 11060 11062 11065 11066 11070 11073 11075 11076 11080 11088 11095 11096 11100 11102 11107 11119 11123 11126 11135 11139 11144 11155 11159 11167 11169 11171 11175 11178 11182 11186 11195 11197 11198 11205 11208 11210 11212
22 Plantations   11002 11009 11013 11071 11082 11085 11100 11102 11186
25 Poor woodland   11016 11120
26 Commons   10947 10981 10993 11010 11018 11025 11051 11059 11085 11089 11120 11139 11154 11178 11186 11186 11200
27 Furze, gorse and heathlands   11054 11178
32 Climatic hazards   10884 10962 11025
33 Excessively steep land   11210
34 Land requires drainage   11067 11071
36 Productive soil   10884 10925 10984 10995 11050 11052 11183
37 Poor soil   10921 11016 11052 11070 11169 11210
38 Heavy (clay) soil   10881 10884 10886 10894 10896 10897 10900 10903 10905 10913 10917 10919 10921 10930 10932 10935 10939 10940 10958 10960 10962 10971 10980 10982 10984 10991 10997 10998 11010 11014 11016 11017 11018 11019 11023 11029 11030 11031 11037 11044 11050 11051 11052 11059 11064 11065 11066 11067 11070 11073 11075 11076 11080 11082 11085 11088 11096 11100 11101 11107 11117 11119 11120 11123 11125 11135 11137 11138 11139 11142 11143 11149 11163 11164 11167 11173 11174 11175 11176 11183 11186 11187 11191 11206 11208 11209 11212
39 Loamy (turnip) soil   10886 10899 10909 10930 10932 10995 11013 11023 11026 11027 11062 11068 11089 11136 11163 11173 11178 11192 11198
40 Light soil   10881 10892 10905 10906 10913 10917 10919 10923 10925 10940 10962 10980 10985 10986 10989 10990 10997 11011 11017 11019 11021 11026 11037 11039 11073 11075 11080 11093 11096 11099 11101 11113 11125 11142 11143 11144 11145 11149 11161 11173 11176 11186 11191 11195 11206 11208 11210 11213
41 Several varieties of soil   10929 11016 11050 11186
42 Chalk   10879 10884 10891 10896 10897 10899 10909 10910 10925 10926 10947 10948 10954 10955 10962 10968 10971 10974 10981 10985 10992 10993 10995 10998 11002 11004 11007 11008 11009 11010 11016 11018 11023 11025 11029 11030 11039 11044 11050 11051 11056 11064 11068 11069 11071 11089 11093 11095 11099 11111 11116 11117 11119 11126 11128 11139 11154 11155 11162 11164 11169 11171 11175 11178 11180 11181 11182 11187 11192 11196 11198 11200 11201 11203 11205 11209 11212 11353
43 Sand or gravel   10896 10897 10900 10901 10903 10923 10925 10929 10939 10940 10958 10968 10971 10977 10981 10984 10990 10995 10997 11002 11004 11009 11010 11014 11016 11018 11023 11029 11042 11052 11054 11059 11060 11062 11064 11065 11068 11070 11071 11080 11082 11083 11085 11088 11089 11093 11095 11096 11099 11102 11104 11111 11117 11120 11123 11125 11126 11137 11138 11139 11144 11155 11159 11164 11167 11173 11174 11177 11178 11181 11183 11187 11189 11195 11196 11197 11201 11203 11206 11209
44 Peat   10901 10909 11016 11064 11082 11102 11155 11178 11196 11206
46 Good local roads   10995 11210
48 Turnpike and main roads   10962
53 Markets accessible   10925 10929 10995 11145
55 Provincial markets   10925
59 Landowners and their estates   10891 11128 11204
60 Land occupiers   10988
61 Farm size   10891
62 Leases   11093
64 Common grazing   11086 11093
66 Rents   10879 11016 11090 11210
68 Rates   11195
69 Farm labour and wages   10987
70 Enclosure or improvement of waste   11041 11093 11130
71 Enclosure of commons   10929 10936 11027 11148
72 Enclosure of open fields   10897 10906 10978 10992 10993 11091 11158 11164 11185
92 Dung   10925
101 General comments on crop rotations   10914 10925 11052 11076 11099 11104 11145 11154
102 Irregular rotations   10901 11104 11120
103 3-course rotation   10884 10894 10899 10913 10921 10928 10930 10932 10940 10958 10971 10980 10982 11018 11025 11029 11030 11031 11059 11060 11083 11121 11125 11135 11137 11139 11163 11177 11183 11191 11192 11197 11198 11208 11209 11212
104 4-course rotation   10879 10881 10884 10886 10891 10896 10897 10899 10900 10903 10905 10906 10909 10913 10917 10919 10923 10925 10926 10929 10939 10947 10955 10958 10960 10962 10968 10981 10985 10986 10987 10990 10991 10992 10993 10995 10997 10998 11002 11004 11007 11009 11010 11011 11013 11014 11016 11017 11018 11019 11021 11023 11026 11027 11037 11039 11044 11050 11054 11056 11062 11064 11065 11066 11068 11069 11070 11071 11075 11080 11082 11083 11085 11088 11089 11090 11093 11095 11096 11100 11102 11104 11107 11111 11116 11117 11123 11126 11128 11138 11144 11154 11159 11162 11164 11167 11171 11173 11174 11176 11180 11181 11182 11186 11187 11192 11195 11196 11200 11203 11205 11206 11209
105 5-course rotation   10879 10884 10892 10910 10925 10935 10947 10948 10954 10962 10974 10977 10981 10985 10989 11008 11016 11050 11051 11059 11068 11080 11089 11101 11104 11136 11139 11143 11145 11155 11161 11175 11178 11183 11201 11210 11353
106 6-course rotation   10980 11010 11050 11113 11145 11149
107 7-course rotation   11050
113 Rye or meslin   10914 11104 11186
114 Corn yields   10879 10894 10897 10900 10901 10903 10905 10906 10909 10910 10917 10919 10921 10923 10925 10926 10930 10935 10939 10940 10954 10955 10960 10971 10974 10977 10982 10986 10987 10990 10991 10992 10993 11002 11004 11007 11008 11009 11010 11011 11013 11014 11017 11018 11019 11023 11026 11027 11029 11030 11032 11037 11044 11051 11052 11054 11056 11059 11060 11062 11064 11065 11066 11068 11069 11070 11071 11073 11074 11075 11076 11080 11082 11083 11088 11095 11096 11097 11100 11101 11102 11107 11109 11111 11112 11116 11117 11119 11123 11125 11128 11129 11135 11136 11137 11138 11139 11143 11144 11149 11155 11159 11162 11163 11164 11167 11169 11171 11175 11176 11177 11178 11180 11181 11182 11183 11187 11191 11196 11197 11198 11200 11201 11203 11205 11208 11209 11210 11212 11213 11353
115 Beans   10884 10894 10901 10913 10928 10958 10971 10980 11025 11030 11067 11076 11083 11121 11176 11191 11192 11206 11212 11213
116 Peas   10901 11213
117 Rape   10914
123 Clover   10879 10884 10886 10892 10896 10897 10900 10901 10903 10909 10910 10913 10917 10919 10923 10925 10926 10928 10930 10935 10939 10940 10948 10954 10960 10968 10971 10974 10977 10980 10985 10986 10989 10990 10991 10992 10993 10995 11002 11004 11007

Wiltshire contd.

		11008	11009	11010	11013	11014	11017	11018	11021	11023	11025	11026	11027	11029	11037	11039	11044	11050	11051	11052	11054	11056
		11059	11062	11064	11066	11067	11068	11069	11070	11071	11073	11075	11082	11083	11088	11090	11095	11096	11097	11100	11101	11102
		11107	11111	11113	11116	11117	11119	11123	11125	11126	11128	11129	11136	11138	11139	11143	11144	11149	11154	11155	11159	11161
		11162	11163	11164	11167	11169	11171	11174	11175	11178	11180	11181	11182	11186	11187	11191	11192	11196	11197	11198	11200	11201
		11203	11205	11209	11210	11212	11213	11353
124	Sainfoin	10884	10914	10980	10995	11104	11113	11161	11169	11192	11213
126	Tares and vetches	10914	10958	11104	11138	11206
129	Turnips	10884	10891	10901	10913	10914	10925	10926	10929	10980	10989	10998	11021	11050	11056	11090	11099	11104	11113	11117
		11145	11154	11161	11169	11174	11186	11192	11206	11210
131	Swedes	10928	11154
132	Potatoes	10884	10958	10988	10995	10995	11050	11104	11145	11213
133	Bare fallows	10913	10928	10980	10982	11030	11121	11176	11186
135	Low farming	11142
139	Good quality pastures	10925	11093
140	Poor quality pastures	10921	11071	11186
141	Meadows	11126
142	Irrigation and water meadows	10901	10925	10992	10993	11013	11044	11056	11064	11093
144	Parks	10984	10990	11195
147	Cattle fattening	11176
148	Dairying	10929	11042	11052
150	Sheep breeding	10891	10929	10998	11071	11145	11176
151	Sheep fattening	10960	11176
155	Oxen	10929
158	Deer	11195
161	Hay	11016	11042	11052
170	Poor orchards	10891
171	Fruits	10891
172	Market gardens	11123
181	Reeds and oziers	10974	11013

Worcestershire

1	Tithe-free district	11217	11226	11227	11231	11239	11245	11247	11249	11250	11255	11259	11267	11273	11279	11281	11288	11289	11291
		11292	11294	11296	11299	11302	11306	11307	11309	11312	11314	11317	11340	11345	11355	11356	11361	11362	11364	11366	11371	11373
		11375	11377	11378	11393	11396	11400	11401	11413	11417	11420
2	History of tithe payment	11260
3	Tithe practices and agriculture	11288	11289	11347	11350	11351
4	Exemptions from tithe	11220	11224	11225	11234	11238	11240	11246	11252	11253	11256	11257	11269	11278	11284	11285	11287	11293
		11298	11315	11319	11321	11326	11332	11333	11336	11339	11342	11344	11347	11348	11350	11352	11359	11360	11363	11365	11367	11368
		11370	11388	11389	11392	11397	11398	11402	11407	11408	11414	11416	11419	11421	11422
5	Tithe in kind	11234	11251	11359	11412
6	Compositions	11216	11219	11221	11222	11225	11228	11230	11234	11236	11240	11241	11242	11256	11270	11271	11272	11274	11280	11282
		11284	11285	11286	11298	11327	11333	11339	11344	11348	11350	11356	11357	11358	11359	11360	11363	11365	11367	11368	11372	11374
		11379	11380	11381	11386	11389	11390	11391	11392	11395	11398	11402	11404	11408	11409	11411	11419	11421	11422
7	Moduses	11221	11225	11232	11234	11240	11272	11280	11284	11286	11295	11297	11308	11322	11325	11337	11343	11347	11349	11365
		11372	11374	11382	11392	11395	11403	11405	11408	11416
8	Glebe	11271	11282	11284	11372	11402
9	Local topographic descriptions	11394
10	Regional topographic descriptions	11394
11	Village morphology	11300	11351
19	Large, regular fields	11311
20	Hedgerow timber	11214	11215	11218	11220	11223	11224	11232	11237	11243	11248	11251	11252	11254	11257	11258	11264	11265	11268
		11271	11275	11276	11277	11278	11283	11287	11290	11293	11295	11300	11301	11303	11304	11305	11308	11310	11311	11313	11315	11316
		11318	11320	11321	11322	11323	11324	11325	11326	11329	11330	11334	11335	11336	11337	11338	11341	11342	11343	11346	11347	11349
		11352	11354	11369	11370	11376	11382	11383	11384	11385	11387	11388	11394	11397	11403	11405	11406	11407	11410	11412	11414	11415
		11416
21	Coppice	11220	11243	11248	11265	11268	11271	11287	11290	11297	11320	11321	11322	11329	11349	11354	11369	11370	11391	11394
		11405	11415
22	Plantations	11258	11382
24	Productive woodland	11352
25	Poor woodland	11347	11351
26	Commons	11336
32	Climatic hazards	11288
33	Excessively steep land	11220	11323	11394
34	Land requires drainage	11301	11336	11376	11383
36	Productive soil	11223	11264	11268	11308	11313	11326	11337	11352
37	Poor soil	11218	11220	11223	11224	11264	11275	11297	11323	11343	11351	11394	11412
38	Heavy (clay) soil	11214	11215	11218	11220	11224	11232	11243	11251	11252	11257	11258	11264	11265	11271	11275	11276	11278	11283
		11287	11290	11293	11295	11297	11300	11301	11303	11304	11305	11310	11311	11315	11316	11320	11321	11322	11323	11324	11325	11326
		11329	11330	11334	11335	11336	11337	11338	11341	11342	11346	11349	11351	11369	11370	11383	11384	11387	11388	11389	11394
		11397	11403	11405	11406	11407	11410	11412	11414	11415	11416
39	Loamy (turnip) soil	11215	11258	11264	11265	11268	11275	11277	11287	11293	11297	11308	11310	11337	11347	11354	11370	11387	11388
		11389	11416
40	Light soil	11215	11252	11257	11268	11293	11300	11305	11311	11313	11341	11343	11376	11403
41	Several varieties of soil	11276	11323	11336
42	Chalk	11334
43	Sand or gravel	11214	11223	11243	11251	11252	11254	11276	11277	11278	11290	11295	11297	11300	11305	11315	11316	11318	11323
		11324	11325	11329	11335	11336	11347	11352	11369	11382	11385	11397	11403	11407	11410	11415	11416
44	Peat	11243
46	Good local roads	11264	11310
47	Poor local roads	11215	11301	11329
48	Turnpike and main roads	11264
53	Markets accessible	11256	11256	11264	11276	11277	11310	11311	11347	11407
54	Markets inaccessible	11215	11329
55	Provincial markets	11288	11289	11347
58	Market prices	11282
59	Landowners and their estates	11311
60	Land occupiers	11394
61	Farm size	11305
65	Lammas and other common rights	11339
70	Enclosure or improvement of waste	11351	11386	11418
71	Enclosure of commons	11254	11386
72	Enclosure of open fields	11227	11307	11331	11365	11422
75	Conversion of grass to arable	11389

Worcestershire contd.

76	Conversion of arable to pasture	11389
85	Underdrainage	11301 11310
92	Dung	11256
101	General comments on crop rotations	11275 11293 11311 11316 11321 11376 11382 11383 11407
103	3-course rotation	11218 11220 11237 11248 11251 11252 11257 11258 11283 11295 11303 11304 11320 11325 11329 11334 11335 11336 11337 11338 11346 11354 11369 11376 11382 11384 11385 11387 11397 11405 11406
104	4-course rotation	11214 11215 11220 11223 11232 11243 11251 11252 11254 11264 11265 11268 11287 11290 11293 11295 11297 11300 11304 11305 11308 11310 11311 11315 11316 11318 11322 11324 11325 11329 11334 11336 11337 11341 11342 11343 11347 11349 11351 11352 11369 11370 11382 11384 11385 11387 11388 11389 11394 11397 11403 11405 11410 11412 11415 11416
105	5-course rotation	11215 11224 11258 11264 11276 11277 11278 11315 11323 11325 11330 11335 11343 11346 11385 11389 11410 11412 11414
106	6-course rotation	11257 11268 11278 11301 11326 11412
107	7-course rotation	11389
111	Barley 11220 11305	
113	Rye or meslin	11297
114	Corn yields	11256 11282 11282 11305 11389 11405 11409 11414
115	Beans	11215 11218 11232 11237 11248 11251 11252 11256 11257 11258 11264 11275 11276 11278 11283 11287 11295 11300 11301 11303 11304 11310 11311 11315 11316 11320 11321 11322 11323 11324 11325 11326 11329 11330 11335 11336 11337 11341 11342 11343 11347 11349 11354 11369 11382 11383 11384 11385 11387 11389 11394 11397 11403 11406 11409 11410 11412 11414
116	Peas	11218 11251 11268 11278 11303 11325 11338 11343 11387 11389 11409
123	Clover	11232 11257 11268 11278 11293 11308 11311 11315 11316 11318 11321 11322 11325 11329 11330 11334 11337 11341 11369 11376 11383 11384 11385 11387 11389 11397 11403 11407 11409 11412 11416
126	Tares and vetches	11251 11256 11268 11330 11382 11403 11406
129	Turnips	11220 11223 11251 11252 11254 11256 11258 11268 11276 11282 11293 11295 11297 11305 11308 11311 11315 11316 11318 11325 11329 11334 11336 11337 11341 11341 11343 11347 11352 11369 11376 11382 11385 11388 11389 11397 11409 11410 11416
132	Potatoes	11256 11282 11343 11407
133	Bare fallows	11214 11215 11218 11220 11232 11251 11252 11256 11257 11258 11264 11275 11276 11278 11283 11293 11295 11300 11301 11303 11304 11305 11310 11315 11316 11320 11321 11322 11323 11325 11326 11330 11334 11335 11336 11337 11338 11341 11342 11343 11347 11349 11351 11369 11376 11382 11383 11384 11385 11387 11388 11389 11394 11397 11403 11406 11407 11409 11410 11412 11414 11416
135	Low farming 11275 11389	
139	Good quality pastures	11215 11351
140	Poor quality pastures	11310 11351
141	Meadows	11351
148	Dairying	11215 11347 11351
150	Sheep breeding	11215 11223 11243 11297
151	Sheep fattening	11297
153	Horses 11220 11301	
154	Pigs 11282	
169	Good orchards	11288 11289
172	Market gardens	11288 11289 11330 11350
174	Cabbages	11350
175	Carrots	11350
177	Other vegetables	11350
178	Hops	11218 11223 11271 11282 11283 11295 11322 11325 11329 11330 11338 11354 11370 11376 11379 11380 11382 11384 11387 11394 11398 11399
181	Reeds and oziers	11347 11390

York City and Ainsty

1	Tithe-free district	11426 11427 11428 11429 11443 11448
2	History of tithe payment	11426
4	Exemptions from tithe	11423 11431 11433 11440
5	Tithe in kind	11425 11432
6	Compositions 11455	
7	Moduses	11430 11432 11440 11453 11458 11807
10	Regional topographic descriptions	11455
17	Open fields	11437
34	Land requires drainage	11451
35	Land liable to flood	11425 11451 11456
36	Productive soil	11432 11438 11455
37	Poor soil	11438 11455
38	Heavy (clay) soil	11425 11432 11438 11440 11451 11455
39	Loamy (turnip) soil	11432
40	Light soil	11438
43	Sand or gravel	11440
50	Water carriage	11425
52	Railways	11437
53	Markets accessible	11425 11451
67	Urban influences on value of land	11438
72	Enclosure of open fields	11429 11443 11456
92	Dung 11440 11451	
101	General comments on crop rotations	11432
103	3-course rotation	11438 11440 11451
104	4-course rotation	11437 11455
106	6-course rotation	11437
114	Corn yields	11440
115	Beans	11425 11432 11437 11440
123	Clover 11425 11437	
129	Turnips	11432 11437 11438 11455
132	Potatoes	11437 11451
133	Bare fallows	11425 11432 11437 11438 11440 11451 11455
139	Good quality pastures	11432 11440 11451
140	Poor quality pastures	11451
141	Meadows	11425 11451
145	Accommodation land	11438
146	Cattle breeding	11432
148	Dairying	11455
161	Hay 11456	

Yorkshire, East Riding

1	Tithe-free district	11460 11466 11471 11475 11476 11482 11483 11491 11493 11495 11496 11507 11508 11515 11516 11517 11528 11533

625

Yorkshire, East Riding contd.

```
              11536 11537 11539 11540 11545 11546 11547 11551 11553 11556 11558 11561 11562 11564 11568 11573 11574 11576 11579 11582 11584
              11589 11593 11597 11601 11607 11610 11613 11614 11624 11627 11629 11638 11642 11646 11647 11651 11655 11656 11659 11661 11662
              11663 11664 11668 11670 11671 11678 11679 11682 11693 11699 11700 11707 11708 11712 11713 11714 11717 11718 11721 11722 11725
              11728 11729 11737 11741 11742 11745 11746 11749 11765 11766 11770 11777 11779 11780 11782 11783 11785 11789 11790 11791 11801
              11803 11804 11805 11806 11911 12612 13563
```

2 History of tithe payment   11486 11487 11488 11771
3 Tithe practices and agriculture   11462 11521 11604 11665 11680 11692 11772 11781 11798
4 Exemptions from tithe   11469 11472 11478 11481 11485 11490 11492 11498 11501 11504 11505 11509 11514 11523 11524 11525 11526
   11527 11529 11541 11543 11550 11554 11557 11559 11565 11567 11580 11581 11585 11590 11591 11602 11609 11616 11617 11618 11619
   11622 11631 11631 11641 11644 11648 11666 11674 11675 11677 11681 11687 11688 11696 11697 11702 11703 11716 11724 11727 11730
   11734 11736 11738 11739 11744 11751 11753 11754 11755 11758 11759 11767 11769 11771 11778 11781 11784 11788 11797 11822 12518
5 Tithe in kind   11462 11474 11477 11492 11497 11580 11592 11649 11654 11669 11674 11692 11701 11704 11727
6 Compositions   11459 11492 11504 11534 11549 11609 11635 11637 11649 11652 11657 11731 11798
7 Moduses   11486 11499 11506 11522 11535 11550 11560 11596 11598 11602 11603 11606 11616 11621 11633 11635 11667 11697 11701
   11709 11724 11731 11740 11744 11774 11788
8 Glebe   11686 11771
10 Regional topographic descriptions   11514 11603 11604 11611 11633 11657
11 Village morphology   11751
13 Country houses and ornamental gardens   11706
15 Cottages and cottage gardens   11751
17 Open fields   11499 11577 11611 11612 11631 11665 11683 11727 11764
19 Large, regular fields   11557 11756
22 Plantations   11557 11751
25 Poor woodland   11751
26 Commons   11462
27 Furze, gorse and heathlands   11751
31 Wasteland   11462 11557
32 Climatic hazards   11505 11557 11592 11683 11727 11756 11799
34 Land requires drainage   11513 11519 11530 11560 11595 11595 11596 11602 11611 11612 11653 11686 11691 11706 11723 11727 11751
   11751 11763 11764 11772
35 Land liable to flood   11630 11669
36 Productive soil   11462 11469 11484 11497 11505 11513 11519 11525 11526 11550 11557 11621 11630 11643 11676 11683 11688 11706
   11716 11774 11787 11798
37 Poor soil   11497 11498 11505 11513 11525 11526 11530 11550 11559 11596 11602 11630 11631 11645 11653 11675 11680 11691 11744
   11751 11764 11772 11798
38 Heavy (clay) soil   11469 11484 11494 11497 11498 11499 11505 11513 11514 11519 11521 11526 11527 11535 11557 11559 11566 11594
   11595 11602 11603 11618 11621 11630 11631 11633 11639 11643 11657 11665 11669 11675 11676 11680 11683 11683 11691 11705 11716
   11723 11744 11751 11755 11764 11798 11799
39 Loamy (turnip) soil   11462 11484 11505 11513 11514 11519 11526 11604 11605 11611 11630 11639 11643 11676 11688 11692 11720 11727
   11735 11744 11752 11755 11774 11784
40 Light soil   11592 11633 11657 11675 11705 11724 11727 11744 11772
41 Several varieties of soil   11519 11530 11535 11550 11560 11604 11631 11633 11676
42 Chalk   11494 11513 11557 11577 11625 11645 11672 11716 11756 11787
43 Sand or gravel   11462 11498 11505 11513 11521 11525 11530 11550 11557 11559 11595 11602 11605 11630 11633 11653 11716 11724
   11744 11751 11756 11763 11764 11772
44 Peat   11560 11764
46 Good local roads   11755 11799
47 Poor local roads   11499 11513 11557 11577 11653 11691 11756
48 Turnpike and main roads   11605 11764
51 Canals   11530 11543
53 Markets accessible   11513 11550 11611 11723 11755 11799
54 Markets inaccessible   11691 11756
55 Provincial markets   11469 11535
59 Landowners and their estates   11521 11560 11604 11625 11639 11653 11680 11706 11772 11772 11772 11774
60 Land occupiers   11527 11691 11723
61 Farm size   11653
66 Rents   11484 11497 11498 11530 11535 11596 11602 11645 11675 11676 11724 11763
68 Rates   11462
70 Enclosure or improvement of waste   11527 11751
72 Enclosure of open fields   11514 11525 11531 11554 11558 11625 11635 11643 11697 11711 11779
75 Conversion of grass to arable   11595
76 Conversion of arable to pasture   11692
78 Warping   11497 11566
80 Reclaiming and embanking   11749
85 Underdrainage   11706
87 Marl   11602
92 Dung   11527 11550
95 Bones   11625 11643 11787
101 General comments on crop rotations   11497 11665 11669 11680 11691 11705 11727 11755 11764
102 Irregular rotations   11527 11680 11681 11727
103 3-course rotation   11484 11497 11521 11535 11559 11611 11618 11621 11643 11665 11669 11680 11705 11798
104 4-course rotation   11469 11498 11499 11513 11514 11521 11525 11526 11557 11594 11596 11604 11605 11633 11645 11672 11675 11683
    11688 11692 11716 11720 11724 11735 11744 11752 11756 11784 11799
105 5-course rotation   11462 11513 11514 11519 11525 11530 11535 11557 11592 11605 11639 11643 11657 11752
106 6-course rotation   11526
107 7-course rotation   11557
112 Oats   11557
113 Rye or meslin   11462 11513 11525 11602 11612 11744 11751
114 Corn yields   11474 11514 11596 11599 11602 11612 11619 11625 11636 11643 11654 11683 11686 11764
115 Beans   11469 11484 11497 11513 11514 11521 11527 11535 11557 11559 11612 11621 11630 11631 11633 11643 11665 11669 11675 11683
    11691 11705 11724 11752 11755 11798 11799
116 Peas   11605 11724 11755
117 Rape   11560 11602 11764
118 Coleseed   11525 11630 11727
123 Clover   11497 11526 11602 11605 11611 11612 11653 11669 11691 11692 11727 11755 11764 11799
126 Tares and vetches   11484
129 Turnips   11462 11484 11494 11498 11513 11514 11519 11521 11525 11526 11527 11530 11535 11543 11550 11557 11592 11594 11602
    11604 11605 11612 11625 11633 11639 11643 11645 11672 11675 11630 11681 11688 11691 11705 11716 11720 11727 11744 11752 11755
    11756 11764 11784 11787
131 Swedes   11787
132 Potatoes   11527 11543 11605 11611 11612 11630 11630 11675 11630 11681 11727 11764
133 Bare fallows   11462 11469 11484 11497 11513 11514 11519 11521 11526 11527 11535 11550 11557 11559 11594 11595 11596 11602 11604
    11605 11611 11612 11625 11630 11631 11633 11653 11665 11669 11675 11680 11683 11688 11691 11692 11705 11720 11727 11735
    11752 11755 11764 11798 11799
134 High farming   11521 11543 11645 11676 11688 11723 11752 11763

Yorkshire, East Riding contd.

135 Low farming   11462 11513 11612 11631 11653 11691 11751 11772
136 Remarks on the absence of turnips   11577
138 Recent increase in productivity   11592 11625 11643 11751
139 Good quality pastures   11526 11535 11543 11557 11566 11621 11676 11692 11752 11755
140 Poor quality pastures   11513 11526 11566 11602 11612 11705 11727 11751
141 Meadows   11680
144 Parks   11706 11724
146 Cattle breeding   11469 11499 11513 11676 11680
147 Cattle fattening   11543 11680
148 Dairying   11513 11526 11543 11680 11716 11724 11744
150 Sheep breeding   11469 11498 11526 11543 11672 11676 11716 11724 11744 11784 11787
151 Sheep fattening   11557 11645 11784
153 Horses   11526
157 Rabbits   11530 11592 11625 11772
159 Animal diseases   11621 11669 11723
160 Straw   11557
161 Hay   11705
162 Manufactured feedstuffs (cake etc.)   11557
165 Butter   11744
166 Cheese   11744
172 Market gardens   11535
179 Flax and hemp   11596 11630 11727

Yorkshire, North Riding

1 Tithe-free district   11811 11816 11824 11834 11840 11842 11852 11877 11890 11902 11937 11944 11946 11947 11962 11970 11973 11975 11977 11979 12007 12011 12013 12014 12023 12033 12034 12045 12053 12064 12081 12082 12084 12086 12089 12106 12119 12125 12126 12140 12141 12149 12179 12191 12193 12200 12211 12213 12221 12227 12244 12253 12269 12272 12283 12285 12288 12289 12299 12304 12308
2 History of tithe payment   11839 11938 11966 11972 12009 12013 12014 12019 12194 12306
3 Tithe practices and agriculture   11860 11871 11891 11894 11914 12134 12294 12627
4 Exemptions from tithe   11814 11818 11819 11828 11837 11843 11845 11851 11855 11859 11860 11864 11868 11869 11873 11876 11879 11880 11883 11884 11886 11891 11897 11906 11909 11913 11915 11922 11924 11938 11943 11945 11958 11993 11998 12006 12008 12015 12019 12022 12028 12032 12035 12038 12040 12042 12048 12054 12059 12065 12072 12076 12078 12090 12092 12097 12105 12107 12109 12115 12117 12118 12120 12128 12131 12144 12151 12152 12161 12165 12172 12180 12186 12187 12192 12194 12199 12202 12205 12207 12215 12218 12230 12232 12234 12235 12236 12237 12240 12246 12251 12257 12258 12271 12275 12284 12292 12297 12300 12303 12311 12313 12314 12315
5 Tithe in kind   11827 11835 11839 11865 11897 11901 11927 11931 12027 12056 12072 12074 12077 12225 12251 12267 12271 12300 12301
6 Compositions   11815 11829 11835 11846 11849 11853 11862 11863 11875 11876 11886 11889 11895 11897 11898 11905 11907 11910 11929 11931 11941 11971 11972 11974 11976 11978 11981 11984 11991 12004 12006 12010 12012 12016 12027 12028 12030 12031 12042 12043 12046 12051 12058 12059 12060 12062 12063 12072 12073 12076 12077 12088 12090 12092 12095 12096 12097 12100 12102 12112 12129 12131 12134 12138 12142 12148 12158 12159 12167 12174 12186 12187 12189 12198 12219 12223 12224 12225 12231 12235 12236 12237 12243 12247 12248 12249 12251 12255 12259 12260 12262 12271 12275 12276 12278 12281 12292 12295 12297 12305 12310 12313 12749 12850
7 Moduses   11823 11828 11829 11830 11831 11837 11839 11841 11844 11850 11851 11853 11856 11858 11861 11862 11863 11865 11867 11868 11871 11876 11879 11885 11887 11888 11892 11899 11910 11912 11913 11914 11919 11920 11922 11925 11926 11928 11943 11949 11955 11963 11964 11971 11978 11992 11993 11995 11996 11999 12018 12022 12025 12026 12029 12030 12039 12046 12049 12051 12056 12058 12059 12060 12068 12072 12073 12074 12076 12077 12087 12092 12109 12115 12118 12120 12121 12122 12124 12125 12127 12128 12129 12134 12136 12137 12142 12144 12146 12147 12150 12156 12159 12164 12170 12180 12182 12183 12187 12196 12206 12208 12215 12218 12220 12222 12232 12237 12248 12251 12259 12262 12279 12281 12286 12290 12300 12301 12309 12315 12749
8 Glebe   11819 11922 12059 12105 12123 12156 12159 12165 12188 12208 12243 12247 12249 12251 12265 12291 12292 12301 12850
9 Local topographic descriptions   11808 11809 11825 11831 11848 11851 11856 11864 11871 11874 11915 11945 11989 11994 12001 12057 12078 12104 12110 12145 12153 12154 12175 12177 12196 12205 12210 12214 12216 12217 12228 12250 12280 12291 12293 12294 12312 12317 12367 14822
10 Regional topographic descriptions   11809 11825 11867 11869 11901 11920 11921 11933 11939 11951 11958 11967 12009 12021 12022 12032 12036 12040 12041 12043 12044 12057 12066 12078 12092 12109 12111 12116 12150 12160 12195 12202 12216 12230 12238 12239 12251 12263 12307 12317 12319 12367 12738 14822
13 Country houses and ornamental gardens   11916 11958 12025 12098 12110 12312 12738
16 Field boundaries   11808 11851 12154
17 Open fields   11961 12017 12142
18 Small, irregular closes   11912 12146 12154 12195 12205 12206 12265
19 Large, regular fields   11961 12067
21 Coppice   12196
22 Plantations   11954 11958 11994 12136 12216
24 Productive woodland   11851
25 Poor woodland   11893
26 Commons   11808 11831 11879 11939 11952 12008 12010 12041 12057 12072 12099 12165 12175 12195 12261 12278 12317 12367
27 Furze, gorse and heathlands   11827 11831 11837 11939 12010 12029 12115 12307 12317
28 Moorland   11808 11827 11831 11862 11864 11879 11887 11914 11940 11945 11951 11964 11967 11983 11988 11994 12000 12001 12005 12009 12029 12041 12044 12071 12072 12083 12085 12098 12099 12107 12115 12130 12142 12153 12165 12175 12182 12195 12209 12215 12241 12294 12319 12367
32 Climatic hazards   11851 11854 11857 11864 11912 11915 11945 11948 11980 11983 11989 11999 12005 12009 12029 12037 12047 12055 12065 12067 12078 12092 12115 12116 12130 12136 12145 12146 12153 12160 12163 12175 12195 12239 12242 12266 12282 12294 12317 12367
33 Excessively steep land   11867 11887 11916 11994 12000 12005 12036 12050 12072 12085 12115 12171 12175 12195 12225 12243 12280 12294 12367
34 Land requires drainage   11831 11857 11864 11870 11912 11930 11933 11935 11948 11957 11961 11999 12010 12021 12091 12145 12162 12202 12203 12205 12216 12217 12282
35 Land liable to flood   11855 11869 11933 12022 12146 12170 12202 12217 12228 12250
36 Productive soil   11808 11812 11835 11837 11845 11851 11854 11860 11878 11891 11893 11894 11896 11915 11916 11921 11950 11951 11967 11969 11993 12000 12001 12003 12005 12010 12025 12029 12037 12054 12055 12065 12067 12071 12072 12078 12085 12092 12093 12094 12098 12100 12103 12104 12107 12110 12111 12117 12118 12121 12129 12132 12133 12135 12137 12143 12153 12157 12162 12163 12170 12172 12175 12180 12190 12197 12205 12210 12229 12238 12243 12245 12254 12263 12265 12267 12268 12270 12273 12293 12294 12312 12648 12666
37 Poor soil   11837 11857 11870 11871 11879 11893 11894 11914 11917 11918 11919 11930 11934 11939 11964 11967 11983 11988 11999 12000 12001 12005 12008 12010 12012 12029 12036 12040 12041 12055 12066 12067 12085 12092 12093 12099 12104 12107 12115 12117 12118 12121 12130 12143 12163 12170 12175 12177 12182 12190 12205 12217 12229 12252 12265 12266 12268 12273 12277 12287 12291 12315
38 Heavy (clay) soil   11812 11818 11825 11827 11835 11845 11848 11851 11855 11857 11866 11867 11870 11871 11874 11878 11891 11893 11896 11901 11912 11915 11916 11917 11918 11919 11921 11930 11933 11934 11935 11939 11945 11948 11954 11957 11958 11967 11980 11993 11997 12000 12009 12015 12020 12022 12025 12032 12037 12040 12041 12044 12047 12050 12055 12057 12061 12066 12067 12070 12083 12085 12088 12091 12093 12104 12109 12113 12116 12117 12118 12135 12136 12139 12143 12144 12145 12146 12154 12160 12162 12163 12165 12166 12168 12170 12172 12178 12184 12190 12196 12197 12202 12203 12205 12206 12209 12214 12217 12229 12238 12239 12243 12252 12254 12260 12263 12265 12266 12268 12270 12273 12277 12280 12282 12287 12291 12293 12296 12302 12315

Yorkshire, North Riding contd.

		12627 12738 14822
39	Loamy (turnip) soil	11808 11809 11835 11848 11860 11866 11869 11874 11878 11884 11893 11896 11935 11950 11954 11955 11957 11967 12009 12010 12017 12020 12025 12061 12067 12070 12083 12092 12094 12098 12103 12104 12110 12111 12113 12117 12118 12129 12134 12136 12157 12165 12166 12190 12197 12206 12210 12228 12230 12238 12245 12260 12263 12268 12270 12287 12294 12367 12648 12738 14822
40	Light soil	11827 11867 11874 11935 11945 11961 11988 12000 12001 12005 12009 12050 12085 12098 12134 12153 12160 12202 12214 12225 12242 12267 12317 12627 12648 12666
41	Several varieties of soil	11818 11848 11851 11879 11903 11915 11935 11940 11952 11953 11954 11958 12009 12020 12022 12041 12067 12091 12099 12205 12214 12241 12251 12273 12280 12319 12627
43	Sand or gravel	11808 11809 11812 11818 11825 11851 11878 11879 11896 11903 11915 11916 11945 11951 11954 11967 11993 11999 12009 12010 12037 12041 12054 12061 12067 12075 12091 12099 12110 12114 12116 12117 12121 12133 12143 12144 12145 12146 12153 12154 12162 12163 12171 12175 12178 12205 12241 12242 12254 12265 12280 12282 12293 12296 12312 12317 12318
44	Peat	11812 11818 11903 11935 12067 12098 12121 12146 12170 12265 12266
45	Fields remote from farms	11879 12099
46	Good local roads	11871 12055 12067 12206 12238 12265
47	Poor local roads	11857 11912 11916 11948 11954 12047 12098 12116 12136 12146 12153 12195 12205 12265 12294
48	Turnpike and main roads	11854 11893 11958 12113 12154 12206 12245 12302
50	Water carriage	12010
52	Railways	11855
53	Markets accessible	11896 11957 12055 12098 12111 12114 12145 12154 12238 12265 12282 12293
54	Markets inaccessible	12047 12146
55	Provincial markets	11989 12001 12184 12265 12271
57	Fairs	12113
58	Market prices	11912 11971 12167 12223
59	Landowners and their estates	11831 11845 11860 11893 11985 11988 12025 12067 12075 12094 12098 12118 12175 12198 12263 12312 12318 12738
60	Land occupiers	11845 11848 11893 11983 11989 12098 12121 12121 12175 12175 12206 12267 12291 12319
61	Farm size	11827 11893 11915 12012 12116 12315
62	Leases	11845 11935 11989 12009 12094 12206 12217 12266 12293 12302
63	Farm implements	12000
64	Common grazing	11808 11827
65	Lammas and other common rights	12072
66	Rents	11808 11818 11827 11835 11845 11864 11866 11874 11903 11919 11934 11945 11989 11993 11997 11999 12000 12010 12012 12050 12070 12072 12085 12093 12098 12104 12110 12111 12113 12117 12118 12133 12166 12168 12170 12175 12180 12196 12205 12214 12225 12251 12252 12260 12265 12268 12270 12273 12277 12280 12291 12293 12312 12367 12648
67	Urban influences on value of land	12113 12121
68	Rates	11831
70	Enclosure or improvement of waste	12071 12666
71	Enclosure of commons	11983 12008 12041 12047 12121 12133 12182 12241 12250 12367
72	Enclosure of open fields	12627
74	Occasional ploughing of grassland	11857
75	Conversion of grass to arable	11916 11923 12302
79	Subsoil ploughing	11857
80	Reclaiming and embanking	11930 11993 12098 12265
85	Underdrainage	11867 11912 11930 12003 12100 12129 12139 12190 12196 12235 12238 12265
86	Tile drains	11855 12093
89	Lime	11808 12003 12024 12093 12107 12293
92	Dung	11983 12139 12196
95	Bones	12005 12094
99	Chemical fertilisers	12217
101	General comments on crop rotations	11867 11871 11916 11920 11940 11951 11957 11961 11993 12040 12044 12072 12110 12118 12196 12203
102	Irregular rotations	11857 11953 11954 11993 11999 12005 12009 12113 12282 12315
103	3-course rotation	11825 11835 11845 11848 11857 11866 11867 11869 11874 11878 11884 11891 11894 11901 11912 11916 11917 11918 11919 11920 11921 11930 11933 11948 11957 11969 11980 11997 12009 12012 12015 12020 12047 12050 12057 12066 12067 12070 12085 12088 12103 12104 12107 12113 12115 12116 12132 12139 12154 12160 12163 12165 12166 12170 12190 12203 12205 12206 12209 12214 12229 12239 12252 12254 12266 12268 12273 12277 12282 12287 12302 12319 12367 12627 12738
104	4-course rotation	11812 11818 11825 11827 11845 11848 11851 11857 11860 11866 11869 11874 11878 11891 11903 11915 11916 11921 11934 11935 11940 11945 11950 11954 11957 11969 11999 12000 12001 12005 12009 12010 12017 12020 12022 12037 12038 12050 12054 12065 12067 12071 12072 12075 12078 12083 12092 12094 12098 12104 12110 12111 12114 12117 12118 12121 12133 12135 12137 12139 12144 12150 12153 12154 12157 12160 12163 12166 12171 12172 12175 12184 12190 12196 12197 12202 12205 12210 12225 12228 12230 12243 12245 12252 12263 12265 12266 12267 12268 12270 12277 12280 12282 12287 12291 12294 12302 12307 12312 12317 12367 12627 12648 12666 12738
105	5-course rotation	11827 11835 11871 11896 11940 11988 12000 12009 12010 12036 12057 12070 12072 12083 12092 12132 12146 12153 12165 12195 12225 12243 12280 12293 12296 12302
106	6-course rotation	11827 11954 11993 12146
110	Wheat	12177 12238
111	Barley	11827 11983 12205 12238 12268
112	Oats	11983 12072 12098 12107 12130 12153
114	Corn yields	11827 11912 11916 11929 11948 11999 12024 12030 12038 12050 12052 12056 12066 12067 12100 12104 12110 12116 12117 12118 12133 12154 12167 12170 12196 12218 12223 12225 12259 12265 12268 12293
115	Beans	11825 11835 11848 11866 11867 11871 11874 11884 11891 11901 11920 11921 11954 11961 12000 12012 12015 12017 12020 12032 12052 12067 12070 12085 12088 12135 12137 12154 12166 12168 12190 12203 12205 12206 12209 12214 12273 12282 12291 12302 12319 12627
116	Peas	11848
122	Unspecified grass seeds	11980 12254
123	Clover	11848 11860 11869 11912 11954 12000 12010 12017 12032 12054 12066 12070 12083 12085 12113 12114 12116 12135 12137 12139 12146 12154 12184 12190 12202 12203 12205 12206 12243 12260 12265 12266 12267 12296 12627
129	Turnips	11812 11818 11825 11848 11851 11860 11867 11869 11874 11878 11884 11903 11912 11916 11921 11933 11945 11948 11954 11980 11983 11993 11997 12001 12005 12008 12009 12010 12020 12022 12025 12036 12037 12038 12043 12047 12050 12052 12054 12057 12061 12065 12067 12070 12071 12072 12075 12078 12083 12085 12091 12092 12094 12114 12115 12116 12117 12121 12133 12137 12144 12146 12154 12160 12165 12166 12171 12175 12177 12190 12195 12197 12202 12206 12210 12225 12228 12230 12239 12242 12243 12245 12250 12251 12252 12263 12265 12266 12267 12268 12270 12273 12280 12287 12294 12296 12302 12307 12312 12317 12318 12648 12666 12738
132	Potatoes	11818 11935 11945 12043 12050 12072 12091 12121 12144 12175 12206 12241 12250 12251 12252 12293 12294 12318
133	Bare fallows	11825 11835 11845 11848 11857 11866 11867 11869 11871 11874 11878 11891 11891 11894 11901 11912 11916 11917 11918 11919 11920 11921 11930 11933 11934 11954 11957 11993 11997 12000 12001 12010 12012 12015 12017 12020 12022 12037 12038 12040 12057 12061 12065 12066 12067 12070 12072 12078 12083 12085 12088 12103 12109 12113 12115 12116 12121 12135 12139 12146 12160 12166 12171 12177 12190 12195 12202 12203 12205 12206 12209 12214 12225 12230 12239 12241 12243 12254 12263 12266 12273 12277 12282 12287 12302 12307 12312 12318 12319 12627 12738
134	High farming	11845 11891 12094 12100 12267 12293
135	Low farming	11831 11851 11893 11894 11916 11918 11954 11955 11983 12005 12015 12047 12055 12139 12190 12302
136	Remarks on the absence of turnips	11919 11920 11939 12009 12088 12178 12217 12291
137	Remarks on pests and crop diseases	12154 12296
138	Recent increase in productivity	11988

Yorkshire, North Riding contd.

139	Good quality pastures	11845 11856 11871 11878 11894 11914 11915 11917 11930 11951 11967 11980 11989 12003 12017 12025 12037 12040 12052 12054 12057 12061 12078 12083 12091 12103 12111 12113 12121 12127 12132 12137 12157 12162 12165 12168 12172 12177 12178 12202 12203 12216 12228 12239 12242 12250 12251 12261 12307
140	Poor quality pastures	11870 11894 11917 11918 11945 11948 11964 11969 11980 12003 12072 12078 12099 12130 12132 12154 12182 12196 12239 12241 12307 12738
141	Meadows	11917 11930 11951 11983 11989 12025 12037 12091 12103 12111 12127 12143 12163 12178 12228
144	Parks	12025 12178 12207 12241 12281
145	Accommodation land	12113 12121
146	Cattle breeding	11818 11848 11866 11874 11878 11887 11915 11919 11934 11989 11993 12001 12012 12043 12055 12071 12072 12088 12098 12170 12214 12251 12261 12291 12312 12367 12648
147	Cattle fattening	11808 11812 11915 11935 11983 11993 12043 12065 12072 12088 12113 12117 12121 12170 12268 12293
148	Dairying	11808 11818 11837 11866 11874 11914 11919 11921 11934 11948 12001 12012 12043 12088 12117 12121 12170 12175 12205 12214 12261 12268 12312 12648
150	Sheep breeding	11812 11827 11837 11848 11856 11866 11874 11878 11884 11887 11914 11915 11964 12001 12005 12029 12050 12057 12071 12072 12098 12107 12118 12121 12127 12170 12175 12182 12214 12251 12261 12268 12291 12312 12367 12648
151	Sheep fattening	11808 11809 11993 12055 12098 12143 12205 12261 12648 12666
152	Droving	12113
153	Horses	11934 12012 12088 12107 12121 12205 12367
154	Pigs	11945 12012 12043 12088 12104
156	Poultry	12005 12012 12043 12088 12104
158	Deer	11808 12136 12153
159	Animal diseases	11827 11939 12044 12055
160	Straw	11912 11983
161	Hay	11864 11871 11878 11912 11920 12037 12061 12066 12091 12107 12111 12130 12144 12160 12162 12242 12265
163	Stall or yard feeding	11983
164	Milk	12251
165	Butter	11808 11887 11915 11989 12001 12175 12291 12312
166	Cheese	11887 11914 11915 12175 12312
167	Wool	11831 11887 11935 11945 11989
172	Market gardens	12202
175	Carrots	12251

Yorkshire, West Riding

1	Tithe-free district	11449 11464 12322 12332 12334 12341 12342 12343 12345 12347 12348 12357 12361 12365 12366 12370 12376 12382 12395 12402 12420 12423 12426 12438 12441 12443 12446 12452 12458 12472 12488 12490 12493 12499 12505 12506 12508 12512 12513 12540 12541 12561 12569 12571 12572 12576 12597 12600 12601 12607 12610 12614 12629 12636 12641 12647 12661 12665 12687 12706 12713 12717 12718 12719 12737 12750 12751 12756 12760 12763 12765 12791 12803 12804 12809 12813 12824 12834 12844 12866 12872 12878 12883 12897 12905 12916 12929 12931 12939 12943 12946 12952 12954 13564 14820 14832
2	History of tithe payment	12325 12336 12339 12387 12433 12451 12468 12630 12694 12795 12876 12955
3	Tithe practices and agriculture	12323 12386 12413 12429 12487 12502 12638 12686 12734 12787 12802 12817 12856 12865 12891 12915 12925 12934
4	Exemptions from tithe	8431 11900 12169 12321 12324 12325 12328 12346 12355 12358 12359 12369 12372 12374 12377 12388 12389 12392 12399 12422 12425 12427 12430 12431 12442 12445 12447 12467 12475 12482 12485 12492 12498 12501 12509 12519 12520 12522 12523 12525 12533 12534 12535 12538 12542 12545 12555 12558 12563 12565 12577 12582 12611 12623 12625 12630 12638 12639 12645 12646 12649 12654 12658 12659 12660 12662 12668 12671 12672 12673 12674 12676 12690 12695 12696 12700 12705 12708 12710 12715 12723 12726 12727 12731 12739 12740 12741 12747 12749 12755 12757 12764 12771 12777 12778 12780 12784 12787 12788 12789 12790 12792 12799 12800 12802 12805 12814 12817 12817 12818 12826 12827 12829 12830 12832 12835 12836 12843 12848 12851 12855 12856 12862 12863 12877 12884 12886 12892 12893 12895 12901 12902 12906 12907 12908 12909 12919 12921 12922 12923 12930 12932 12934 12935 12936 12942 12944 12951 12956 12957 12958 14834
5	Tithe in kind	12263 12323 12354 12360 12371 12408 12416 12430 12436 12454 12457 12534 12549 12587 12618 12622 12637 12650 12680 12686 12700 12736 12741 12755 12757 12797 12802 12805 12816 12827 12835 12843 12875 12882 12898 12957
6	Compositions	12320 12321 12324 12331 12336 12356 12362 12371 12408 12429 12432 12435 12436 12442 12450 12455 12456 12462 12474 12475 12480 12484 12487 12489 12494 12497 12498 12503 12511 12519 12523 12527 12530 12534 12538 12543 12550 12553 12556 12558 12559 12560 12584 12590 12598 12615 12616 12618 12625 12630 12632 12633 12653 12659 12670 12673 12675 12679 12680 12684 12700 12704 12733 12734 12746 12755 12762 12770 12772 12775 12782 12792 12793 12797 12815 12816 12818 12841 12860 12876 12879 12885 12887 12895 12899 12919 12941 12947 12949 12950 12951 14834
7	Moduses	8431 12321 12324 12333 12336 12346 12351 12354 12360 12372 12375 12378 12379 12384 12386 12387 12394 12397 12401 12408 12419 12428 12434 12435 12442 12445 12448 12457 12459 12461 12462 12475 12477 12480 12481 12484 12485 12494 12495 12501 12504 12509 12514 12517 12527 12528 12533 12538 12543 12545 12547 12550 12551 12554 12556 12557 12559 12562 12563 12568 12577 12584 12586 12593 12595 12596 12602 12613 12619 12624 12625 12628 12630 12632 12633 12634 12638 12652 12653 12654 12662 12669 12670 12671 12673 12677 12678 12680 12684 12692 12693 12694 12695 12696 12697 12698 12701 12702 12703 12705 12711 12715 12720 12721 12727 12730 12732 12744 12755 12759 12764 12768 12769 12770 12772 12778 12779 12784 12786 12788 12789 12792 12793 12794 12797 12798 12800 12801 12811 12815 12816 12820 12822 12823 12825 12826 12832 12833 12841 12848 12858 12859 12860 12865 12870 12874 12877 12881 12884 12885 12886 12887 12892 12896 12899 12901 12903 12907 12908 12909 12911 12912 12926 12932 12940 12941 12947 12949 12951 12953 12955 12956 12958 12959 14834
8	Glebe	12559 12784 12816 12932
9	Local topographic descriptions	12387 12567 12574 12609 12639
10	Regional topographic descriptions	12360 12384 12392 12431 12463 12501 12507 12509 12521 12525 12536 12552 12556 12565 12570 12589 12624 12644 12656 12667 12681 12685 12731 12732 12741 12766 12814 12836 12900 12953
11	Village morphology	12444 12707 12875 12930 12959
13	Country houses and ornamental gardens	12428 12528 12539 12594 12734 12798 12957
14	Farm houses and buildings	12374
15	Cottages and cottage gardens	12444
16	Field boundaries	12567 12700
17	Open fields	12410 12805 12868
18	Small, irregular closes	12444 12618 12692 12869 12892
19	Large, regular fields	12340 12350 12781 12851 12953
22	Plantations	12364 12528 12640
26	Commons	12354 12380 12388 12482 12482 12501 12532 12549 12565 12639 12707 12781 12781 12802 12868 12868 12915 12927
27	Furze, gorse and heathlands	12482 12533 12604 12898
28	Moorland	12323 12353 12375 12377 12388 12396 12401 12429 12431 12440 12480 12521 12532 12549 12587 12599 12609 12631 12638 12655 12667 12832 12856 12858 12859 12962
29	Mosses	12882
31	Wasteland	12359 12835
32	Climatic hazards	12350 12359 12373 12379 12411 12467 12482 12507 12570 12574 12587 12677 12686 12699 12768 12781 12783 12827 12842 12882 12915 12928 12934 12960
33	Excessively steep land	12330 12380 12411 12485 12567 12575 12594 12644 12656 12685 12692 12766 12781 12817 12962
34	Land requires drainage	12330 12360 12364 12496 12501 12570 12609 12617 12623 12650 12699 12700 12734 12784 12801 12805 12836 12851 12865 12875 12888 12902 12917 12925 12934 12945
35	Land liable to flood	12359 12364 12373 12429 12473 12476 12516 12555 12556 12570 12640 12644 12699 12707 12794 12827 12860 12892 12914 12915 12930 12953
36	Productive soil	12323 12329 12340 12352 12355 12358 12359 12374 12380 12384 12391 12393 12416 12425 12431 12444 12469 12470 12476 12478 12479 12491 12502 12509 12520 12525 12536 12539 12555 12567 12573 12583 12587 12588 12617 12638 12639 12644 12655

Yorkshire, West Riding contd.

      12667 12671 12681 12682 12685 12689 12699 12700 12707 12708 12710 12714 12732 12734 12742 12745 12775 12776 12783 12784 12789 12794 12798 12807 12814 12816 12835 12842 12851 12860 12868 12869 12882 12892 12898 12900 12902 12915 12927 12930 12937 12953 12957

37   Poor soil   12330 12351 12355 12360 12364 12368 12373 12375 12377 12386 12388 12391 12401 12431 12467 12470 12476 12479 12485 12495 12502 12516 12520 12532 12539 12552 12570 12573 12583 12587 12622 12631 12639 12644 12655 12667 12668 12671 12672 12672 12676 12682 12692 12699 12700 12714 12731 12734 12742 12784 12798 12816 12835 12836 12847 12851 12858 12859 12862 12863 12869 12882 12917 12930 12937 12948 12957 12962

38   Heavy (clay) soil 12323 12330 12337 12340 12344 12350 12355 12359 12360 12364 12368 12379 12384 12386 12391 12392 12409 12413 12418 12422 12431 12453 12454 12467 12469 12470 12473 12478 12478 12479 12495 12496 12500 12502 12507 12520 12528 12529 12539 12546 12552 12555 12565 12583 12587 12594 12598 12599 12617 12622 12623 12624 12639 12640 12650 12656 12664 12668 12671 12672 12686 12692 12699 12700 12707 12714 12731 12734 12736 12741 12742 12745 12749 12766 12767 12768 12776 12783 12784 12787 12789 12790 12801 12805 12816 12817 12835 12836 12842 12847 12851 12862 12863 12865 12875 12877 12882 12891 12892 12898 12900 12902 12906 12914 12915 12925 12930 12934 12937 12948 12953

39   Loamy (turnip) soil 12323 12340 12350 12355 12358 12364 12374 12409 12410 12422 12465 12473 12479 12496 12500 12515 12536 12546 12555 12583 12587 12588 12623 12624 12640 12655 12656 12671 12681 12692 12699 12740 12742 12749 12766 12783 12784 12801 12807 12827 12877 12898 12900 12902 12906 12914 12928 12930 12934 12937 12953 12957

40   Light soil   12379 12384 12392 12393 12413 12431 12467 12473 12500 12507 12537 12617 12650 12668 12686 12692 12707 12784 12816 12817 12842 12847 12851 12898

41   Several varieties of soil 12359 12360 12387 12396 12409 12411 12440 12502 12507 12515 12528 12539 12552 12583 12639 12664 12671 12787 12835 12856 12877 12898 12902 12945 12959

43   Sand or gravel 12355 12359 12373 12379 12453 12467 12473 12478 12491 12500 12502 12516 12529 12587 12594 12609 12639 12640 12650 12656 12672 12699 12787 12789 12790 12805 12829 12835 12847 12882 12898 12917 12953 12957 12960

44   Peat 12409 12507 12549 12570 12587 12592 12768 12787 12835 12882 12898

45   Fields remote from farms 12682 12776

46   Good local roads 12340 12350 12351 12440 12465 12491 12500 12507 12515 12599 12640 12682 12685 12692 12768 12776 12789 12827 12829 12851 12869 12882 12928 12934 12957

47   Poor local roads 12337 12410 12422 12444 12507 12570 12609 12623 12740 12953

48   Turnpike and main roads 12360 12373 12480 12516 12537 12549 12640 12699 12700 12714 12740 12776 12801 12860 12875 12928 12948 12957

50   Water carriage 12510 12570 12609 12640 12882

51   Canals 12337 12374 12707 12869

52   Railways 12337 12350 12368 12917

53   Markets accessible 12368 12440 12453 12465 12469 12507 12528 12570 12583 12640 12685 12686 12700 12707 12745 12766 12776 12783 12789 12829 12842 12871 12934 12937

55   Provincial markets 12340 12500 12640 12668 12677 12685 12776 12789 12842 12860 12871 12892 12928

56   London market 12502 12560 12871

58   Market prices 12368 12428 12479 12494 12774

59   Landowners and their estates 12478 12528 12539 12650 12671 12677 12734 12757 12787 12807 12957 12960

60   Land occupiers 12323 12425 12431 12444 12454 12473 12476 12480 12496 12520 12618 12639 12644 12686 12734 12767 12783 12805 12807 12865 12915 12960

61   Farm size 12323 12375 12409 12463 12476 12480 12529 12555 12559 12567 12570 12622 12639 12677 12736 12802 12860 12865 12869 12875 12882

62   Leases 12677 12734

63   Farm implements 12639

64   Common grazing 12917

65   Lammas and other common rights 12882 12917

66   Rents 12323 12330 12337 12416 12428 12429 12431 12453 12467 12470 12479 12480 12501 12509 12529 12539 12546 12552 12555 12556 12570 12583 12598 12639 12664 12671 12672 12676 12699 12700 12701 12714 12734 12745 12787 12790 12798 12807 12816 12832 12847 12860 12863 12898 12915 12962

67   Urban influences on value of land 12598 12639 12775 12783 12789 12842 12962

68   Rates 12453 12469 12677

70   Enclosure or improvement of waste 12363 12538 12639 12639 12654 12655 12665 12756 12760 12798 12798 12835 12898 12917

71   Enclosure of commons 12372 12532 12644 12654 12665 12677 12734 12746 12756 12760 12816 12817 12858 12859 12897 12917

72   Enclosure of open fields 12332 12446 12639 12661 12665 12714 12760 12944

75   Conversion of grass to arable 12359 12510

76   Conversion of arable to pasture 12487 12495 12537 12559 12622 12631 12644 12699 12734 12934

78   Warping 12510 12560 12570 12835 12871

80   Reclaiming and embanking 12500 12587 12639 12882

81   Marsh drainage 12587 12882

82   Drainage channels and ditches 12510 12570 12699

85   Underdrainage 12495 12699 12817 12875 12906

89   Lime 12525

92   Dung 12352 12393 12411 12453 12469 12485 12502 12622 12685 12636 12700 12710 12745 12789 12869 12871 12891 12962

95   Bones 12700 12960

98   Rape cake 12473 12865 12934

100 Oil dust, unspecified fertilisers or manures 12609

101 General comments on crop rotations 12337 12350 12364 12478 12536 12567 12570 12639 12650 12655 12685 12700 12714 12749 12783 12794 12814 12832 12835 12863 12865 12868 12875 12898

102 Irregular rotations 12359 12379 12444 12478 12485 12570 12592 12622 12798 12829 12934

103 3-course rotation 12330 12337 12360 12392 12396 12409 12454 12473 12478 12495 12570 12583 12623 12650 12656 12676 12686 12699 12700 12710 12714 12736 12741 12742 12789 12794 12800 12835 12836 12863 12877 12902 12917 12948

104 4-course rotation 12329 12337 12340 12352 12355 12358 12360 12364 12368 12374 12384 12391 12396 12410 12413 12416 12422 12425 12440 12463 12465 12470 12473 12478 12479 12491 12495 12496 12500 12510 12515 12520 12529 12539 12546 12552 12555 12565 12583 12587 12588 12594 12617 12622 12623 12624 12639 12640 12655 12664 12668 12671 12672 12686 12689 12692 12699 12700 12707 12708 12714 12740 12749 12766 12775 12776 12784 12789 12790 12794 12805 12827 12829 12835 12836 12842 12851 12856 12863 12868 12869 12877 12882 12892 12900 12902 12906 12915 12917 12927 12928 12930 12934 12957 12960 12962

105 5-course rotation 12351 12373 12500 12507 12516 12536 12587 12644 12682 12741 12816 12829 12860 12865 12934 12960

106 6-course rotation 12500 12814 12934

108 8-10-course rotation 12476

110 Wheat 12359 12373 12431 12453 12882

111 Barley 12491

112 Oats 12379 12431 12453 12509 12532

113 Rye or meslin 12351 12373 12516 12587

114 Corn yields 12330 12360 12401 12411 12416 12442 12463 12487 12495 12542 12699 12700 12731 12733 12792 12871

115 Beans 12364 12422 12470 12478 12487 12496 12502 12510 12520 12525 12583 12623 12624 12650 12686 12692 12699 12700 12707 12734 12741 12776 12794 12801 12805 12816 12817 12835 12836 12842 12851 12865 12877 12882 12892 12902 12915 12925 12930 12934 12937 12948 12953 12959 12960

116 Peas 12500 12817 12960

117 Rape 12362 12425 12960

118 Coleseed 12362 12794

123 Clover 12360 12422 12478 12487 12491 12510 12525 12528 12529 12539 12552 12570 12583 12587 12623 12639 12644 12650 12664 12672 12686 12689 12699 12707 12708 12736 12749 12776 12790 12801 12816 12817 12842 12847 12851 12863 12868 12871 12877 12891 12892 12900 12906 12914 12930 12934 12937 12953 12959 12960 12962

124 Sainfoin 12692

127 Lucerne 12410

Yorkshire, West Riding contd.

129 Turnips 12323 12329 12337 12355 12358 12360 12362 12364 12368 12373 12374 12379 12384 12388 12392 12411 12414 12422 12425
  12440 12444 12465 12467 12470 12473 12478 12479 12480 12487 12491 12496 12500 12507 12515 12516 12520 12525 12528 12529 12530
  12537 12539 12546 12552 12555 12556 12565 12567 12583 12587 12588 12594 12598 12609 12617 12622 12623 12624 12639 12644 12650
  12655 12656 12664 12667 12668 12671 12672 12681 12682 12685 12686 12689 12692 12699 12700 12701 12707 12710 12714 12731 12734
  12741 12745 12749 12766 12767 12776 12783 12784 12787 12789 12790 12794 12801 12805 12807 12814 12816 12817 12829 12830 12835
  12836 12842 12847 12851 12856 12860 12863 12865 12868 12869 12875 12877 12882 12900 12902 12906 12914 12917 12928 12930 12934
  12937 12957 12959 12960
131 Swedes 12410
132 Potatoes 12323 12337 12355 12362 12368 12373 12379 12388 12414 12422 12444 12478 12479 12480 12502 12510 12528 12529 12532
  12555 12556 12560 12567 12570 12574 12583 12594 12598 12644 12655 12667 12677 12685 12686 12699 12701 12714 12731 12734 12742
  12766 12767 12783 12789 12790 12794 12801 12807 12829 12835 12858 12859 12860 12865 12868 12869 12871 12917 12934 12937 12962
133 Bare fallows 12329 12350 12355 12358 12360 12364 12368 12375 12379 12384 12392 12411 12422 12440 12454 12470 12473 12478 12479
  12487 12496 12507 12510 12515 12516 12520 12525 12528 12529 12536 12546 12552 12565 12570 12583 12587 12588 12594 12598 12617
  12622 12623 12624 12631 12638 12639 12650 12655 12656 12667 12672 12676 12686 12689 12692 12699 12700 12707 12710 12714 12734
  12736 12741 12742 12745 12749 12766 12775 12776 12783 12784 12787 12789 12790 12794 12805 12807 12814 12816 12830 12835 12836
  12842 12847 12856 12863 12865 12868 12869 12871 12877 12882 12891 12887 12892 12902 12906 12914 12915 12917 12925 12927 12930 12934
  12937 12948 12953 12959 12960 12962
134 High farming 12352 12374 12411 12425 12431 12463 12515 12681 12685
135 Low farming 12351 12392 12473 12480 12515 12573 12650 12668 12734 12767 12801 12817 12882 12898
136 Remarks on the absence of turnips 12454 12573 12676 12862 12915
137 Remarks on pests and crop diseases 12623
138 Recent increase in productivity 12495
139 Good quality pastures 12323 12329 12337 12374 12375 12391 12393 12396 12422 12429 12453 12480 12482 12496 12500 12501 12510
  12525 12536 12537 12539 12549 12555 12556 12567 12573 12574 12575 12589 12599 12604 12639 12640 12655 12683 12699 12700 12707
  12741 12768 12781 12784 12789 12790 12814 12830 12832 12875 12914
140 Poor quality pastures 12355 12359 12364 12374 12392 12425 12429 12453 12473 12480 12482 12521 12532 12549 12592 12599 12604
  12655 12667 12692 12699 12700 12742 12768 12781 12801 12858 12859 12860 12945
141 Meadows 12373 12377 12388 12393 12429 12473 12491 12496 12500 12515 12532 12555 12573 12574 12575 12589 12598 12631 12639
  12644 12671 12683 12707 12741 12742 12768 12790 12794 12832 12858 12859 12860 12914 12928
142 Irrigation and water meadows 12500
143 Marsh grassland 12915 12945
144 Parks 12465 12734 12862 12902 12957
145 Accommodation land 12344 12373 12414 12556 12594 12842 12860 12875
146 Cattle breeding 12364 12374 12379 12428 12429 12440 12465 12491 12509 12520 12539 12549 12552 12556 12575 12583 12587 12589
  12592 12599 12640 12644 12656 12672 12683 12701 12707 12740 12805 12827 12830 12832 12860 12863 12900 12917 12957
147 Cattle fattening 12411 12428 12501 12509 12552 12555 12556 12640 12644 12664 12672 12699 12701 12707 12714 12732 12740 12789
  12790 12832 12860 12875 12882 12898 12915
148 Dairying 12323 12330 12344 12368 12387 12409 12416 12429 12463 12480 12501 12509 12520 12529 12539 12546 12549 12552 12556
  12575 12583 12589 12592 12631 12639 12644 12650 12656 12664 12668 12672 12677 12683 12685 12701 12732 12789 12790 12802 12805
  12807 12827 12830 12832 12847 12860 12863 12865 12875 12882 12900
149 Cow keeping 12414 12594 12766 12860
150 Sheep breeding 12323 12337 12364 12374 12388 12401 12409 12411 12428 12429 12463 12465 12470 12482 12491 12501 12509 12510
  12515 12516 12537 12539 12549 12552 12570 12573 12575 12583 12589 12599 12604 12639 12640 12644 12650 12664 12671 12672 12683
  12699 12701 12707 12732 12734 12740 12768 12798 12802 12827 12832 12847 12858 12859 12860 12863 12898 12900 12915 12917 12957
  12960
151 Sheep fattening 12428 12429 12479 12491 12520 12555 12583 12671 12714 12790 12807 12957
152 Droving 12860 12875
153 Horses 12323 12387 12525 12537 12539 12552 12587 12592 12622 12664 12671 12685 12714 12790 12798 12863 12865 12898 12900 12915
  12917
154 Pigs 12479
155 Oxen 12740
156 Poultry 12480 12917
158 Deer 12851 12862
159 Animal diseases 12521 12699
160 Straw 12379 12465 12574 12937
161 Hay 12329 12344 12368 12377 12388 12393 12422 12429 12440 12465 12500 12529 12556 12573 12594 12644 12650 12685 12742 12814
  12830 12858 12859 12953
164 Milk 12480 12631 12677 12860 12875
165 Butter 12480 12549 12701
166 Cheese 12549 12701
167 Wool 12428 12494
169 Good orchards 12640
172 Market gardens 12631 12686 12766
174 Cabbages 12350
179 Flax and hemp 12570 12794
182 Teasels 12362 12520 12671

Anglesey

1 Tithe-free district 13821 13841
2 History of tithe payment 13821 13889
4 Exemptions from tithe 13825 13826 13828 13837 13849 13873 13881 13889
5 Tithe in kind 13885
6 Compositions 13833 13836 13838 13842 13850 13861 13863 13875 13876 13877 13878 13882 13883 13884 13885 13887 13889 13890 13891
  13893
7 Moduses 13817 13819 13820 13822 13828 13829 13833 13836 13838 13842 13853 13855 13862 13865 13866 13867 13871 13873 13875
  13876 13882 13883 13884 13885 13887 13888 13889 13890 13893
8 Glebe 13829 13831 13836 13841 13847 13849 13855 13871 13877 13881 13882 13888 13894 13896
9 Local topographic descriptions 13818 13828 13849 13859 13860 13871
10 Regional topographic descriptions 13839 13846 13851 13859
11 Village morphology 13860
12 Church 13818 13820 13822 13831 13839 13848 13851 13855 13857 13862 13869
13 Country houses and ornamental gardens 13892
14 Farm houses and buildings 13822 13822
20 Hedgerow timber 13828 13835 13837 13845 13847 13849 13857 13858 13860 13886 13894 13895
22 Plantations 13820 13828 13837 13853 13857 13858 13860 13864 13873 13895
23 Woodland management 13852
26 Commons 13851 13851 13896
29 Mosses 13822
31 Wasteland 13822 13823 13831 13832 13846 13847 13857 13860 13871 13875 13891 13892 13896
32 Climatic hazards 13832 13848 13851 13858 13859 13869 13881 13886 13892
34 Land requires drainage 13818 13825 13830 13846 13852 13869
36 Productive soil 13827 13831 13839 13847 13853 13854 13855 13856 13858 13859 13860 13864 13873 13886 13891
37 Poor soil 13818 13820 13825 13826 13827 13828 13830 13832 13837 13840 13843 13845 13846 13851 13853 13864 13871 13881 13888

Anglesey contd.

```
       13886 13894 13896
 38  Heavy (clay) soil    13823 13825 13827 13830 13835 13840 13855 13858 13862 13864 13869 13871 13888 13894
 39  Loamy (turnip) soil  13822
 40  Light soil    13820 13823 13826 13827 13828 13832 13835 13839 13845 13847 13849 13851 13854 13856 13858 13860 13862 13864 13869
      13881 13886 13892 13895
 41  Several varieties of soil    13818 13839 13845 13853 13857 13862 13886 13894
 43  Sand or gravel    13842 13845 13848 13849 13852 13856 13857 13869 13877 13882 13888 13891 13892 13894
 44  Peat    13825 13828 13830 13840 13864 13888 13892
 46  Good local roads    13873
 47  Poor local roads    13846 13848 13852 13862 13869 13881 13888 13894
 48  Turnpike and main roads    13827 13828
 50  Water carriage    13833 13845 13849 13858 13886 13894
 53  Markets accessible    13827 13847 13857 13864 13891
 54  Markets inaccessible    13846 13858 13894
 55  Provincial markets    13847 13851 13858 13859 13860 13862 13886 13895
 59  Landowners and their estates    13823 13825
 60  Land occupiers    13842
 61  Farm size    13823 13842
 63  Farm implements    13843
 66  Rents    13819 13878
 67  Urban influences on value of land    13878
 71  Enclosure of commons    13827
 77  Paring and burning    13827 13843 13896
 80  Reclaiming and embanking    13858 13894
 89  Lime    13818 13820 13825 13827 13830 13832 13840 13845 13848 13849 13855 13858 13864 13873 13886 13888 13891 13892 13894 13896
 90  Seasand    13817 13828 13832 13845 13856 13858 13886 13894
 92  Dung    13832
 93  Seaweed    13817 13828 13842 13845 13856
101  General comments on crop rotations    13820 13825 13827 13830 13831 13832 13835 13837 13839 13840 13842 13845 13847 13848 13851
      13852 13854 13855 13857 13858 13859 13862 13864 13869 13871 13873 13881 13886 13888 13891 13892 13894 13895 13896
102  Irregular rotations    13837 13846 13877 13886
104  4-course rotation    13842
105  5-course rotation    13853
106  6-course rotation    13849 13853
107  7-course rotation    13822 13823
111  Barley    13847
114  Corn yields    13833 13843 13865
129  Turnips    13822 13823 13825 13826 13827 13832 13836 13837 13840 13845 13846 13848 13849 13850 13851 13852 13854 13855 13856
      13860 13862 13863 13864 13866 13867 13869 13873 13875 13881 13883 13886 13888 13889 13890 13891 13892 13894 13896
132  Potatoes    13817 13818 13819 13820 13822 13823 13825 13826 13827 13828 13830 13831 13832 13833 13835 13836 13837 13839
      13840 13842 13843 13845 13846 13847 13847 13848 13849 13850 13851 13852 13853 13854 13855 13856 13857 13859 13860 13862 13863
      13864 13866 13867 13869 13871 13873 13875 13881 13883 13886 13888 13889 13890 13891 13892 13894 13895 13896
133  Bare fallows    13827 13832 13832 13837 13840 13840 13846 13847 13849 13851 13852 13854 13855 13860 13864 13867 13869 13875 13883
      13886 13888 13890 13891 13892 13894 13896
134  High farming    13820 13845 13856
135  Low farming    13835 13859 13895
137  Remarks on pests and crop diseases    13852 13859 13869 13892
139  Good quality pastures    13839 13847
140  Poor quality pastures    13818 13822 13830 13832 13842 13849 13857 13888 13894 13895
143  Marsh grassland    13853 13864
146  Cattle breeding    13825 13852
148  Dairying    13819
153  Horses    13819
154  Pigs    13825 13837 13852 13894 13895
159  Animal diseases    13853
161  Hay    13893
165  Butter    13895
```

Brecon

```
  1  Tithe-free district    13904 13905 13974
  4  Exemptions from tithe    13906 13919 13925 13927 13928 13948 13963 13966 13969
  5  Tithe in kind    13941
  6  Compositions    13909 13938 13941 13950
  7  Moduses    13874 13906 13912 13914 13915 13924 13927 13933 13948 13957 13958 13960 13961 13964 13965 13970 13971 13976 13977
      13978
  9  Local topographic descriptions    13927 13928 13931
 20  Hedgerow timber    13874 13899 13906 13910 13913 13919 13921 13922 13925 13927 13929 13930 13932 13933 13941 13948 13953 13958
      13963 13965 13966 13969 13971
 22  Plantations    13948 13956 13966 13971
 24  Productive woodland    13919 13939
 25  Poor woodland    13927
 26  Commons    13964
 28  Moorland    13964
 32  Climatic hazards    13931
 33  Excessively steep land    13903 13920 13923 13931 13957 13962 13964
 34  Land requires drainage    13901 13910 13917 13964 13978
 36  Productive soil    13915 13919 13920 13924 13931 13941 13943 13947 13953 13965 13979
 37  Poor soil    13899 13921 13941 13947 13960 13962 13979
 38  Heavy (clay) soil    13901 13902 13906 13912 13913 13914 13916 13917 13925 13929 13930 13935 13937 13940 13948 13958 13960 13963
      13966 13967 13969 13972 13978
 39  Loamy (turnip) soil    13926 13943 13947 13953 13959 13964 13971 13975 13979
 40  Light soil    13874 13899 13901 13902 13903 13908 13910 13913 13915 13916 13920 13922 13924 13931 13932 13941 13943 13947 13949
      13953 13955 13957 13959 13961 13964 13965 13966 13969 13975 13977 13979
 41  Several varieties of soil    13975
 43  Sand or gravel    13902 13903 13907 13908 13910 13919 13922 13924 13925 13926 13927 13929 13933 13935 13937 13939 13940 13949
      13953 13958 13962 13963 13969 13970 13971 13972 13975 13977
 44  Peat    13916 13927 13933 13963 13964 13970 13971 13976 13977 13978
 45  Fields remote from farms    13920 13923 13931 13957 13962
 46  Good local roads    13975
 47  Poor local roads    13931
 48  Turnpike and main roads    13943
 51  Canals    13943
 53  Markets accessible    13943 13975
```

Brecon contd.

54	Markets inaccessible	13962 13964
65	Lammas and other common rights	13912
67	Urban influences on value of land	13959
101	General comments on crop rotations	13874 13898 13910 13925 13929 13956 13958 13959 13963 13965 13969
102	Irregular rotations	13943
104	4-course rotation	13908 13914 13922 13926 13935 13939 13941 13943 13947 13960 13967 13979
105	5-course rotation	13903 13906 13912 13913 13914 13915 13935 13937 13962 13964 13976
106	6-course rotation	13899 13902 13907 13912 13919 13922 13926 13940 13948 13949 13966 13967
107	7-course rotation	13919 13921 13931 13932 13953 13957 13961 13972 13977
108	8-10-course rotation	13874 13916 13917 13920 13921 13924 13927 13930 13932 13933 13953 13955 13960 13975 13979
109	More than 10-course rotation	13933 13947 13970 13971 13978
114	Corn yields	13909 13918 13919 13928 13938 13941 13950 13952 13968
116	Peas	13909 13936 13938 13950 13965
123	Clover	13874 13906 13910 13913 13918 13921 13922 13925 13927 13929 13930 13933 13936 13938 13941 13948 13950 13958 13963 13965 13966 13969 13971 13978
129	Turnips	13909 13910 13913 13918 13919 13922 13929 13936 13938 13941 13948 13950 13956 13959 13965 13968
132	Potatoes	13909 13918 13922 13936 13938 13950 13952 13968
133	Bare fallows	13874 13906 13910 13913 13916 13919 13921 13925 13927 13929 13930 13932 13933 13948 13953 13956 13958 13966 13969 13971 13978
139	Good quality pastures	13898 13957
140	Poor quality pastures	13957 13965 13978
141	Meadows	13965
150	Sheep breeding	13874
153	Horses	13929
161	Hay	13909 13918 13928 13938 13950 13952 13968
169	Good orchards	13909
172	Market gardens	13906 13921 13932 13948 13958 13963 13966 13971

Caernarvonshire

1	Tithe-free district	14089 14094
2	History of tithe payment	14090
3	Tithe practices and agriculture	14132 14158
4	Exemptions from tithe	14117 14126 14136 14155
5	Tithe in kind	14142
6	Compositions	14088 14090 14143
7	Moduses	13870 14091 14093 14095 14096 14098 14099 14100 14101 14102 14104 14105 14110 14111 14111 14113 14114 14117 14118 14119 14120 14121 14123 14124 14125 14126 14127 14128 14129 14130 14131 14132 14136 14137 14140 14142 14144 14145 14146 14148 14149 14151 14153 14155 14158 14159
8	Glebe	14095 14129 14132
9	Local topographic descriptions	14095 14097 14107 14113 14124 14155 14159 14270
10	Regional topographic descriptions	14131 14158
11	Village morphology	14093 14107 14127 14129 14150 14152 14270
12	Church	14093 14099 14105 14125 14130 14150 14154
13	Country houses and ornamental gardens	14125
16	Field boundaries	14122 14122 14153
20	Hedgerow timber	13870 14092 14093 14098 14100 14105 14112 14114 14117 14125 14127 14129 14132 14137 14140 14142 14145 14158 14270
22	Plantations	14096 14097 14098 14105 14107 14110 14113 14117 14119 14123 14129 14138 14145 14151 14153 14159 14270
24	Productive woodland	14095 14098
27	Furze, gorse and heathlands	14091 14151
28	Moorland	14135
31	Wasteland	13870 14093
32	Climatic hazards	14091 14096 14122 14135 14147 14147
33	Excessively steep land	14095 14110 14113 14118 14152
36	Productive soil	14117 14126 14129 14132 14133 14136 14139 14145 14147 14149
37	Poor soil	13870 14091 14095 14097 14099 14101 14103 14112 14113 14114 14117 14118 14119 14129 14138 14142 14145 14152 14155 14157 14158 14159
38	Heavy (clay) soil	13870 14091 14098 14099 14101 14105 14107 14110 14112 14113 14114 14118 14119 14126 14131 14132 14133 14136 14142 14149 14151 14153 14155 14157 14158 14159 14160
39	Loamy (turnip) soil	14115 14120 14123 14137 14139 14146 14147 14150
40	Light soil	13870 14091 14093 14096 14097 14098 14101 14103 14105 14119 14125 14126 14129 14130 14131 14132 14136 14141 14142 14145 14149 14153 14155 14157 14270
41	Several varieties of soil	14138
43	Sand or gravel	13870 14091 14092 14095 14096 14098 14103 14105 14112 14113 14114 14115 14118 14125 14127 14129 14133 14135 14136 14137 14138 14141 14142 14143 14154 14157 14160
44	Peat	13870 14112 14117 14123 14125 14140 14141 14145 14153 14159 14160 14270
46	Good local roads	14133 14140
47	Poor local roads	13870 14095 14101 14112 14138 14147 14153 14155 14270
48	Turnpike and main roads	14095 14110 14118 14133
49	Roads recently improved	14154
50	Water carriage	14091 14158
52	Railways	14123
53	Markets accessible	14120 14132 14133 14135
54	Markets inaccessible	14099 14101 14118 14152
55	Provincial markets	14132 14153
58	Market prices	13870 14124 14132 14133
59	Landowners and their estates	14097 14125
61	Farm size	14121
67	Urban influences on value of land	14133
70	Enclosure or improvement of waste	14160
81	Marsh drainage	14160
89	Lime	13870 14091 14095 14098 14100 14114 14119 14122 14140 14142 14147 14149 14150 14153 14155 14157 14158 14159 14270
90	Seasand	14157
92	Dung	14136 14145 14147 14149
93	Seaweed	14091 14150 14157 14159
101	General comments on crop rotations	13870 14092 14096 14097 14098 14099 14100 14105 14112 14114 14117 14118 14119 14123 14125 14126 14127 14129 14131 14132 14135 14136 14137 14140 14142 14145 14151 14153 14155 14158 14270
102	Irregular rotations	14091 14093 14112 14135 14140
104	4-course rotation	14115
105	5-course rotation	14113 14133
106	6-course rotation	14138 14141 14143 14150
107	7-course rotation	14103 14154 14160
108	8-10-course rotation	14101 14107 14120 14139 14146 14147

Caernarvonshire contd.

- 109 More than 10-course rotation   14130 14157 14159
- 110 Wheat   14100 14149
- 111 Barley   14100 14149 14150
- 112 Oats   14100 14149
- 113 Rye or meslin   14157
- 114 Corn yields   14096
- 123 Clover   14105 14137
- 126 Tares and vetches   14155
- 129 Turnips   14091 14098 14100 14104 14111 14114 14119 14124 14126 14127 14129 14136 14137 14140 14142 14151 14153 14155 14270
- 132 Potatoes   13870 14091 14093 14096 14098 14099 14100 14102 14104 14105 14111 14112 14114 14117 14119 14121 14123 14124 14125 14126 14127 14129 14131 14132 14136 14137 14140 14142 14145 14149 14151 14153 14155 14158 14270
- 133 Bare fallows   14091 14098 14099 14114 14124 14127 14129 14137 14140 14149 14151
- 134 High farming   14133
- 135 Low farming   14091 14093 14103 14107 14110 14114 14131 14157 14159
- 136 Remarks on the absence of turnips   14131
- 138 Recent increase in productivity   14103 14107
- 139 Good quality pastures   14129 14140 14145 14147 14158
- 140 Poor quality pastures   13870 14091 14096 14097 14101 14105 14110 14112 14117 14118 14119 14125 14130 14131 14140 14145 14153 14158 14159
- 141 Meadows   14096 14132
- 143 Marsh grassland   14160
- 146 Cattle breeding   13870 14123
- 148 Dairying   13870 14124 14143
- 150 Sheep breeding   14105 14123
- 153 Horses 14112
- 154 Pigs   14100 14132
- 161 Hay   13870 14102 14111 14112 14117 14121 14123 14125 14126 14132 14136 14149 14151 14158
- 165 Butter   14123 14124 14133 14138 14157
- 166 Cheese 14123

Cardiganshire

- 2 History of tithe payment   14016
- 4 Exemptions from tithe   13989 14016 14024 14025 14035 14048
- 5 Tithe in kind   14028
- 6 Compositions   13994 13998 14016 14018 14022 14028 14040 14042 14045
- 7 Moduses   13868 13872 13981 13986 13989 13990 13992 13994 14013 14014 14026 14030 14045 14050
- 19 Large, regular fields   13872
- 20 Hedgerow timber   13980 13981 13982 13986 13992 13997 14003 14009 14013 14015 14020 14024 14025 14028 14031 14035 14041 14049
- 21 Coppice   14022 14023
- 22 Plantations   14023
- 23 Woodland management   14022 14023
- 24 Productive woodland   14022
- 26 Commons   13982
- 27 Furze, gorse and heathlands   14051
- 33 Excessively steep land   13985 13996 14001 14004 14030
- 34 Land requires drainage   13989 14013 14024 14031 14046
- 36 Productive soil   13872 13992 14005 14007 14015 14024 14050
- 37 Poor soil   13985 13992 13996 14005 14006 14024 14039 14046
- 38 Heavy (clay) soil   13872 13982 14003 14005 14007 14009 14013 14014 14020 14021 14025 14027 14029 14031 14035 14037 14038 14039 14044 14047 14049 14050 14051
- 39 Loamy (turnip) soil   13992 14005 14011 14014 14019 14024 14037 14048
- 40 Light soil   13872 13983 13985 13986 13988 13991 13996 14001 14005 14009 14012 14013 14015 14017 14020 14024 14025 14026 14028 14030 14033 14041 14042 14044 14046 14047 14048 14049 14050 14051
- 41 Several varieties of soil   13872 13986 14024 14046
- 43 Sand or gravel   13980 13983 13989 13996 13997 14000 14004 14005 14012 14014 14017 14026 14028 14031 14035 14043
- 44 Peat   13872 13982 13995 14011 14024 14027 14031 14035 14037 14039
- 53 Markets accessible   14028 14051
- 66 Rents   13986 14006 14028
- 81 Marsh drainage   14023
- 93 Seaweed   13872
- 101 General comments on crop rotations   13980 13981 13982 13986 13991 13992 13995 14009 14013 14024 14028 14031 14033 14039 14047
- 102 Irregular rotations   14004 14006
- 106 6-course rotation   14037 14038
- 107 7-course rotation   13988 14011 14015 14026 14035
- 108 8-10-course rotation   13872 13983 13989 13997 14000 14003 14005 14009 14015 14020 14025 14026 14027 14029 14030 14035 14041 14043 14044 14049 14050
- 109 More than 10-course rotation   14042 14044 14046 14051
- 111 Barley   13872
- 114 Corn yields   13987 13990 13994 13999 14006 14008 14018 14045
- 116 Peas   13989 13994 14008 14018 14025 14033 14043
- 123 Clover   13868 13872 13982 13986 13989 13992 13994 13997 13998 14000 14008 14009 14015 14018 14020 14024 14028 14031 14035 14039 14041 14043 14045 14049 14051
- 129 Turnips   14008
- 132 Potatoes   13872 13980 13986 13990 13992 13994 13995 13997 13998 14000 14008 14009 14013 14018 14031 14033 14039 14041 14046 14047 14049
- 133 Bare fallows   14003 14009 14051
- 135 Low farming   13993
- 136 Remarks on the absence of turnips   14047
- 143 Marsh grassland   13989
- 150 Sheep breeding   14040
- 153 Horses   14040
- 154 Pigs   14040
- 161 Hay   13868 13994 13998 14008 14018 14026 14045 14048

Carmarthenshire

- 2 History of tithe payment   14061
- 3 Tithe practices and agriculture   14196
- 4 Exemptions from tithe   14052 14056 14061 14084 14085 14162 14168 14169 14172 14173 14181 14186 14189 14190 14191 14194 14198 14821
- 5 Tithe in kind   14056 14069 14199
- 6 Compositions   14061 14081 14082 14173 14177 14178 14179 14184 14185 14186 14187 14199

Carmarthenshire contd.

7	Moduses	14053 14055 14056 14062 14063 14065 14067 14068 14070 14072 14076 14078 14080 14081 14082 14084 14087 14161 14162 14163 14172 14173 14179 14181 14183 14187 14190 14191 14194 14196 14198 14199 14201 14202 14203 14204 14205 14206 14821
9	Local topographic descriptions	14172 14176
10	Regional topographic descriptions	14065 14074 14174
13	Country houses and ornamental gardens	14172
17	Open fields	14083
18	Small, irregular closes	14053 14070 14081 14087 14161 14169 14170 14193
20	Hedgerow timber	14052 14054 14057 14059 14062 14063 14065 14067 14068 14070 14076 14079 14081 14082 14083 14084 14087 14161 14162 14163 14170 14171 14172 14174 14175 14176 14180 14189 14190 14191 14193 14194 14196 14197 14201 14202 14203 14204 14206 14821
21	Coppice	14056 14178
27	Furze, gorse and heathlands	14176 14176
31	Wasteland	14062
32	Climatic hazards	14176 14186
33	Excessively steep land	14174 14178
34	Land requires drainage	14065 14068 14079 14161 14172 14194 14206
36	Productive soil	14052 14054 14067 14069 14074 14082 14166 14171 14180 14191 14202 14206
37	Poor soil	14082 14174 14176 14180 14183 14197 14200 14202 14206
38	Heavy (clay) soil	14053 14055 14059 14062 14063 14066 14067 14068 14069 14071 14072 14075 14076 14079 14080 14081 14082 14083 14085 14171 14172 14180 14194 14195 14196 14197 14200 14202 14204 14206
39	Loamy (turnip) soil	14064 14069 14162 14163 14180 14196 14201 14202
40	Light soil	14053 14054 14057 14062 14063 14065 14066 14068 14070 14071 14074 14076 14077 14078 14079 14081 14082 14083 14087 14161 14162 14163 14166 14170 14171 14172 14174 14180 14188 14189 14193 14195 14195 14196 14201 14203 14206 14821
41	Several varieties of soil	14074 14084 14087 14172 14195 14196 14206
43	Sand or gravel	14053 14054 14063 14075 14083 14084 14085 14087 14174 14175 14190 14195 14196 14201 14202 14203
44	Peat	14062 14063 14064 14065 14067 14075 14080 14083 14163 14174 14191 14197 14204 14206
45	Fields remote from farms	14162
46	Good local roads	14196 14201
47	Poor local roads	14070 14161 14170 14172 14174 14178 14183 14193 14201 14206
50	Water carriage	14081
53	Markets accessible	14078 14081
54	Markets inaccessible	14068 14087 14172 14174 14178
58	Market prices	14061 14081
59	Landowners and their estates	14189 14193
60	Land occupiers	14178
61	Farm size	14053 14070 14087
66	Rents	14074 14083 14195 14196
71	Enclosure of commons	14179
77	Paring and burning	14174 14183
89	Lime	14174
100	Oil dust, unspecified fertilisers or manures	14083
101	General comments on crop rotations	14063 14070 14074 14079 14081 14082 14162 14163 14166 14174 14179 14180 14183 14185 14188 14194 14196 14200 14201 14203
102	Irregular rotations	14183
106	6-course rotation	14055 14189
107	7-course rotation	14185 14189 14821
108	8-10-course rotation	14052 14053 14054 14057 14059 14064 14065 14067 14068 14076 14080 14084 14161 14172 14185 14190 14191 14202 14203 14204 14206 14821
109	More than 10-course rotation	14059 14062 14065 14068 14069 14071 14072 14075 14076 14077 14082 14083 14084 14085 14087 14170 14171 14172 14174 14175 14182 14193 14197 14202 14204 14821
110	Wheat	14176 14183
111	Barley	14183
112	Oats	14176
114	Corn yields	14056 14058 14086 14165 14169 14171 14177 14178 14179 14181 14185 14186 14192 14198 14200 14205
115	Beans	14186
123	Clover	14052 14054 14057 14058 14059 14062 14067 14070 14079 14082 14084 14085 14087 14161 14171 14172 14174 14175 14177 14178 14180 14185 14189 14190 14192 14193 14194 14196 14198 14202 14204 14205 14206 14821
129	Turnips	14163 14166 14185 14186 14189 14192
130	Mangolds	14186
132	Potatoes	14058 14061 14081 14084 14163 14165 14169 14177 14178 14180 14185 14186 14190 14192 14194 14198 14205
133	Bare fallows	14067 14077 14085 14175 14180 14185 14190 14194 14821
134	High farming	14189
135	Low farming	14188
136	Remarks on the absence of turnips	14174
139	Good quality pastures	14068 14087 14166 14180 14196 14202
140	Poor quality pastures	14068 14172 14196
141	Meadows	14081
143	Marsh grassland	14179
144	Parks	14193
146	Cattle breeding	14165 14174
148	Dairying	14062 14161
150	Sheep breeding	14084 14179 14185
161	Hay	14058 14165 14169 14178 14179 14185 14192 14198 14205
164	Milk	14169
174	Cabbages	14081

Denbighshire

2	History of tithe payment	14225
3	Tithe practices and agriculture	14255 14284
4	Exemptions from tithe	14207 14208 14212 14213 14217 14227 14235 14247 14248 14252 14269 14278 14282 14289 14292 14297 14299 14303 14306 14307 14312
5	Tithe in kind	14225 14240 14312
6	Compositions	14218 14225 14229 14240 14255 14258 14262 14264 14280 14283 14310 14311
7	Moduses	14208 14214 14215 14216 14217 14219 14225 14227 14228 14240 14246 14247 14248 14256 14262 14264 14271 14278 14288 14289 14293 14301 14302 14306 14311 14312
8	Glebe	14225 14229
9	Local topographic descriptions	14216 14227 14228 14230 14232 14258 14268 14271 14272 14273 14274 14282 14284 14287 14289 14299 14307 14308 14309
10	Regional topographic descriptions	14227 14259 14298 14305
11	Village morphology	14282
12	Church	14215 14234 14238 14247 14266 14299
13	Country houses and ornamental gardens	14216 14246 14248
16	Field boundaries	14281

Denbighshire contd.

18	Small, irregular closes	14283 14309
20	Hedgerow timber	14106 14134 14207 14208 14209 14210 14211 14212 14213 14214 14215 14216 14217 14219 14220 14221 14222 14223 14226 14228 14230 14231 14232 14233 14234 14235 14236 14237 14238 14239 14241 14242 14243 14244 14245 14246 14247 14248 14249 14251 14252 14254 14257 14259 14261 14265 14266 14267 14268 14269 14271 14272 14273 14274 14275 14276 14277 14278 14279 14281 14282 14284 14285 14286 14287 14288 14289 14290 14291 14292 14294 14295 14296 14297 14298 14299 14300 14301 14302 14303 14304 14305 14306 14307 14308 14309 14312
21	Coppice	14294 14309
22	Plantations	14210 14217 14238 14246 14247 14253 14261 14269 14276 14282 14287 14289 14290 14291 14297 14299 14302
24	Productive woodland	14248 14289
26	Commons	14214 14217 14238
27	Furze, gorse and heathlands	14258 14275 14297
28	Moorland	14250 14258 14284
31	Wasteland	14226 14227 14281
32	Climatic hazards	14134 14210 14216 14220 14228 14238 14254 14258 14265 14268 14273 14283 14286 14309
33	Excessively steep land	14254 14274 14284
34	Land requires drainage	14226
35	Land liable to flood	14255 14277 14300
36	Productive soil	14106 14134 14207 14214 14216 14234 14238 14246 14247 14248 14261 14265 14266 14267 14268 14272 14274 14276 14278 14279 14281 14282 14285 14286 14287 14288 14289 14290 14291 14292 14298 14302 14308
37	Poor soil	14106 14217 14226 14230 14231 14232 14252 14253 14269 14271 14278 14279 14282 14289 14290 14291 14294 14296 14297 14299 14306 14307 14308
38	Heavy (clay) soil	14208 14211 14212 14213 14214 14222 14223 14226 14227 14232 14233 14234 14236 14237 14239 14242 14243 14244 14245 14246 14248 14257 14265 14271 14276 14281 14285 14287 14289 14290 14291 14295 14297 14299 14300 14301 14302 14304 14308
39	Loamy (turnip) soil	14134 14209 14211 14233 14261 14265 14268 14278 14281 14282 14286 14288 14301 14305 14312
40	Light soil	14106 14207 14208 14214 14215 14217 14230 14232 14234 14238 14239 14253 14254 14259 14266 14267 14269 14271 14272 14273 14274 14275 14277 14282 14284 14285 14287 14288 14289 14290 14291 14294 14308 14309
41	Several varieties of soil	14208 14232 14238 14278 14289
43	Sand or gravel	14134 14207 14210 14216 14219 14220 14221 14226 14227 14228 14230 14235 14241 14243 14244 14245 14249 14251 14254 14257 14265 14267 14268 14272 14273 14274 14275 14276 14277 14277 14281 14284 14288 14289 14294 14295 14296 14298 14301 14302 14303 14305 14308 14309 14312
44	Peat	14232 14253 14258 14259 14278 14281 14282 14289 14294 14297 14299 14306 14307
46	Good local roads	14134 14208 14209 14227 14228 14248 14265 14267 14268 14274 14279 14284 14286 14288 14289 14302 14305 14308 14309
47	Poor local roads	14217 14230 14232 14252 14254 14258 14273 14284 14294 14299 14306 14307
48	Turnpike and main roads	14275
50	Water carriage	14208 14255 14261
51	Canals	14227 14274 14308 14309
53	Markets accessible	14134 14214 14233 14265 14266 14268 14274 14275 14279 14308 14309
54	Markets inaccessible	14217 14273 14284 14299
55	Provincial markets	14208 14227 14255 14267 14302 14306
58	Market prices	14265
59	Landowners and their estates	14212 14216 14252
60	Land occupiers	14226 14275 14291
61	Farm size	14238 14250
65	Lammas and other common rights	14214 14258
66	Rents	14286
68	Rates	14281
69	Farm labour and wages	14238
70	Enclosure or improvement of waste	14271 14281 14289
71	Enclosure of commons	14271 14272 14282
72	Enclosure of open fields	14227
77	Paring and burning	14252 14284
89	Lime	14207 14208 14209 14210 14212 14213 14215 14220 14228 14231 14238 14247 14261 14265 14266 14267 14268 14271 14273 14274 14275 14276 14277 14278 14279 14284 14286 14287 14288 14291 14292 14294 14297 14298 14302 14305 14306 14309
92	Dung	14220 14248 14305
101	General comments on crop rotations	14106 14134 14207 14210 14211 14212 14214 14216 14217 14219 14220 14222 14223 14224 14227 14228 14230 14231 14232 14234 14236 14237 14238 14239 14241 14242 14243 14244 14245 14246 14247 14248 14251 14252 14253 14254 14257 14259 14260 14261 14265 14266 14267 14268 14269 14271 14272 14273 14274 14275 14276 14277 14278 14279 14281 14282 14284 14285 14286 14287 14288 14289 14290 14291 14292 14294 14295 14296 14297 14299 14301 14302 14304 14305 14306 14308 14309 14312
102	Irregular rotations	14285
104	4-course rotation	14227 14235 14300 14303
105	5-course rotation	14207 14227
106	6-course rotation	14224 14272
107	7-course rotation	14224
108	8-10-course rotation	14307
111	Barley	14134 14265 14269
112	Oats	14273 14306 14307
114	Corn yields	14227 14246
115	Beans	14211 14212 14221 14222 14223 14237 14248 14255 14257 14292 14300 14304
116	Peas	14106 14134 14211 14212 14221 14222 14223 14232 14234 14237 14243 14249 14251 14255 14257 14261 14267 14268 14272 14276 14277 14287 14290 14300 14304 14308 14309
123	Clover	14214 14224 14233 14235 14242 14255 14260 14267 14271 14276 14279 14286 14287 14292
126	Tares and vetches	14212 14213 14265
129	Turnips	14106 14134 14207 14208 14209 14210 14212 14213 14214 14215 14216 14217 14219 14220 14224 14226 14227 14228 14230 14231 14232 14233 14234 14235 14238 14239 14241 14242 14244 14245 14246 14247 14248 14253 14254 14255 14259 14261 14265 14266 14267 14268 14269 14271 14272 14273 14274 14275 14276 14277 14278 14279 14281 14282 14284 14285 14286 14287 14288 14289 14290 14291 14292 14294 14295 14296 14297 14298 14299 14302 14303 14305 14306 14307 14308 14309 14312
132	Potatoes	14106 14134 14207 14208 14209 14210 14211 14212 14213 14214 14215 14216 14217 14218 14219 14220 14221 14222 14223 14228 14230 14231 14232 14233 14234 14235 14236 14237 14238 14239 14241 14242 14243 14244 14246 14247 14248 14249 14251 14252 14253 14254 14255 14257 14258 14259 14260 14261 14265 14266 14267 14268 14269 14271 14272 14273 14274 14275 14276 14277 14278 14279 14281 14282 14284 14285 14286 14287 14288 14289 14290 14291 14292 14294 14295 14296 14297 14298 14299 14300 14302 14303 14304 14305 14306 14307 14308 14309
133	Bare fallows	14134 14207 14208 14209 14211 14212 14213 14215 14216 14223 14226 14228 14230 14233 14236 14237 14238 14239 14241 14243 14244 14246 14247 14248 14249 14251 14254 14255 14257 14259 14265 14267 14268 14271 14272 14273 14274 14275 14277 14278 14281 14285 14286 14287 14288 14291 14292 14294 14295 14296 14297 14298 14299 14300 14304 14308 14309
134	High farming	14209
135	Low farming	14234
139	Good quality pastures	14207 14214 14246 14248 14261 14276 14279 14302 14305
140	Poor quality pastures	14215 14232 14247 14252 14259 14275 14279 14281 14284 14290 14306
141	Meadows	14255 14271 14275 14277 14281
142	Irrigation and water meadows	14268
144	Parks	14210 14211 14248
146	Cattle breeding	14258 14271 14284
148	Dairying	14271

Denbighshire contd.

150	Sheep breeding	14228 14230 14232 14235 14241 14258 14259
151	Sheep fattening	14306
160	Straw	14233
161	Hay	14209 14210 14216 14233 14272 14279 14285 14287 14300
165	Butter	14208 14209 14214 14279 14291
166	Cheese	14209 14214 14227 14279
172	Market gardens	14255

Flintshire

1	Tithe-free district	14325
4	Exemptions from tithe	14315 14320 14322 14332 14333 14343 14345 14351 14353
5	Tithe in kind	14315 14316
6	Compositions	14316 14317 14319 14323 14328 14334 14348 14351 14354
7	Moduses	14314 14315 14316 14318 14319 14321 14323 14326 14328 14329 14330 14331 14335 14336 14337 14340 14341 14342 14343 14345 14347 14348 14350 14351 14352 14353 14354
8	Glebe	14328 14338
9	Local topographic descriptions	14320 14330 14340
10	Regional topographic descriptions	14326 14353
13	Country houses and ornamental gardens	14315
20	Hedgerow timber	14314 14315 14318 14320 14322 14324 14325 14326 14329 14330 14331 14332 14333 14335 14336 14337 14340 14341 14342 14343 14345 14349 14350 14352
21	Coppice	14317
22	Plantations	14315 14320 14322 14324 14332 14333 14354
26	Commons	14330
27	Furze, gorse and heathlands	14328 14342
32	Climatic hazards	14328 14336 14338 14349 14353
33	Excessively steep land	14326
35	Land liable to flood	14323 14353
36	Productive soil	14315 14320 14322 14324 14325 14327 14330 14333 14335 14336 14340 14341 14345 14347
37	Poor soil	14324 14327 14335 14336 14349
38	Heavy (clay) soil	14315 14320 14322 14323 14324 14326 14327 14329 14333 14335 14343 14344 14345 14346 14350 14352 14353
39	Loamy (turnip) soil	14314 14325 14327 14330 14338 14341 14347
40	Light soil	14320 14324 14336 14336 14339 14347
43	Sand or gravel	14318 14324 14325 14330 14331 14332 14333 14335 14336 14337 14338 14339 14340 14341 14342 14343 14345 14346 14347 14349 14350
44	Peat	14318 14336
46	Good local roads	14325 14326 14330 14335 14336 14338 14340 14341 14343 14345 14347 14353
50	Water carriage	14347
52	Railways	14336
53	Markets accessible	14326 14330 14336 14338 14340 14341 14343 14345 14349
55	Provincial markets	14325 14330 14338
59	Landowners and their estates	14315 14324 14332 14332 14353
66	Rents	14313 14324 14325 14343 14353
69	Farm labour and wages	14330
71	Enclosure of commons	14318 14322 14327 14341
74	Occasional ploughing of grassland	14343 14349
76	Conversion of arable to pasture	14353
80	Reclaiming and embanking	14332
87	Marl	14335
89	Lime	14320 14326 14330 14332 14338 14343 14347 14349
101	General comments on crop rotations	14314 14318 14320 14324 14325 14329 14330 14331 14333 14335 14337 14338 14339 14340 14341 14342 14343 14344 14346 14347 14349 14350 14352
102	Irregular rotations	14353
105	5-course rotation	14315 14327 14345 14353
106	6-course rotation	14315
107	7-course rotation	14313
108	8-10-course rotation	14322
111	Barley	14320
113	Rye or meslin	14335
114	Corn yields	14353
115	Beans	14315 14324 14332 14333 14336 14338 14345 14347
116	Peas	14315 14324 14325 14328 14335 14336 14337 14345 14347
123	Clover	14313 14315 14324 14332 14333 14336 14338 14339 14344 14345 14346 14347 14353
126	Tares and vetches	14315 14345 14347
129	Turnips	14314 14315 14318 14319 14320 14322 14324 14325 14328 14329 14330 14331 14332 14333 14335 14336 14338 14339 14340 14341 14342 14343 14345 14346 14347 14349 14350 14352 14354
132	Potatoes	14314 14315 14318 14319 14320 14322 14324 14325 14328 14329 14330 14331 14332 14333 14335 14336 14337 14338 14339 14340 14341 14342 14343 14345 14347 14349 14350 14352 14354
133	Bare fallows	14314 14315 14318 14320 14322 14324 14325 14329 14330 14331 14333 14335 14336 14337 14338 14340 14341 14343 14344 14345 14346 14347 14349 14350 14352 14353
139	Good quality pastures	14313 14332 14333 14336 14345 14347
140	Poor quality pastures	14313 14323 14324
144	Parks	14332
150	Sheep breeding	14353
151	Sheep fattening	14315
161	Hay	14328 14332 14333
165	Butter	14345
166	Cheese	14343

Glamorgan

1	Tithe-free district	14359 14369 14393 14441 14452 14479
2	History of tithe payment	14396
4	Exemptions from tithe	14361 14433 14435 14437 14454 14459 14474 14482 14489
5	Tithe in kind	14430 14440 14454 14464 14475
6	Compositions	14356 14366 14367 14376 14395 14408 14410 14411 14412 14423 14426 14433 14442 14453 14454 14456 14457 14464 14468 14475 14482 14483 14489
7	Moduses	14356 14358 14360 14365 14368 14375 14379 14390 14391 14394 14397 14401 14408 14409 14414 14417 14419 14422 14428 14430 14431 14434 14435 14438 14443 14446 14448 14454 14455 14461 14463 14468 14469 14474 14476 14480 14481 14482 14486 14490
10	Regional topographic descriptions	14419
19	Large, regular fields	14440
20	Hedgerow timber	14358 14360 14361 14370 14379 14397 14401 14402 14406 14417 14435 14438 14443 14448 14449 14450 14458 14461

Glamorgan contd.

		14469 14471 14474 14475 14478 14484 14485
26	Commons	14361 14417
32	Climatic hazards	14424
34	Land requires drainage	14364 14379 14405 14417 14420 14435 14481
36	Productive soil	14370 14402 14435 14451 14455
37	Poor soil	14381 14397 14417 14420 14450 14469 14478 14481
38	Heavy (clay) soil	14358 14361 14364 14365 14370 14374 14377 14379 14381 14382 14384 14400 14401 14402 14405 14407 14413 14417 14419 14420 14432 14434 14435 14438 14443 14446 14448 14451 14455 14459 14463 14471 14475 14476 14485
39	Loamy (turnip) soil	14374 14438 14449 14480
40	Light soil	14360 14362 14370 14377 14381 14382 14394 14417 14419 14420 14424 14439 14446 14450 14459 14461 14473 14475
41	Several varieties of soil	14419 14420 14435 14455
43	Sand or gravel	14362 14365 14379 14406 14432 14434 14449 14455 14458 14467 14469 14473 14474 14476 14478 14484 14485
44	Peat	14434 14446 14459 14478
46	Good local roads	14475
47	Poor local roads	14377 14424
48	Turnpike and main roads	14377 14381
53	Markets accessible	14461 14481
54	Markets inaccessible	14424
66	Rents	14471 14475
67	Urban influences on value of land	14377 14381 14481
89	Lime	14448
101	General comments on crop rotations	14358 14361 14370 14379 14426 14440 14443 14448 14458 14459 14471 14474 14480
102	Irregular rotations	14481
103	3-course rotation	14360 14451 14455 14467
104	4-course rotation	14360 14365 14374 14384 14401 14405 14406 14432 14450 14451 14455 14476 14485
105	5-course rotation	14402 14413 14459 14473 14476
106	6-course rotation	14394 14400 14406 14484
107	7-course rotation	14406 14417 14461 14463 14475 14484
108	8-10-course rotation	14377 14382 14397 14417 14434 14435 14438 14439 14461 14469
109	More than 10-course rotation	14435 14438 14446 14469 14478
114	Corn yields	14363 14364 14366 14367 14376 14383 14390 14391 14395 14408 14409 14410 14411 14412 14414 14415 14416 14422 14423 14424 14426 14430 14433 14440 14442 14453 14456 14457 14464 14468 14480 14482 14483 14486 14487 14488 14489 14490 14491
115	Beans	14408
123	Clover	14358 14360 14363 14364 14366 14367 14370 14383 14384 14390 14397 14401 14402 14406 14410 14412 14415 14417 14422 14423 14424 14426 14430 14433 14435 14440 14442 14453 14456 14457 14458 14461 14464 14468 14469 14471 14474 14475 14478 14480 14483 14484 14487 14488 14491
129	Turnips	14360 14364 14366 14367 14370 14384 14390 14391 14395 14402 14406 14412 14414 14423 14430 14433 14440 14442 14449 14450 14451 14453 14468 14480 14485 14487 14488 14490 14491
132	Potatoes	14363 14364 14366 14367 14375 14376 14383 14390 14391 14395 14411 14412 14414 14415 14423 14424 14430 14433 14442 14453 14456 14457 14458 14459 14468 14475 14487 14488 14489 14490 14491
133	Bare fallows	14358 14361 14379 14401 14406 14417 14426 14435 14438 14443 14448 14449 14450 14459 14461 14471 14474 14475 14478 14484 14485
135	Low farming	14379
136	Remarks on the absence of turnips	14379
138	Recent increase in productivity	14451
139	Good quality pastures	14360 14450
140	Poor quality pastures	14430 14481
141	Meadows	14430
143	Marsh grassland	14360
145	Accommodation land	14377 14481
146	Cattle breeding	14397
150	Sheep breeding	14480
155	Oxen	14367
161	Hay	14363 14364 14366 14367 14375 14376 14383 14390 14391 14395 14410 14412 14414 14415 14416 14423 14424 14426 14430 14433 14440 14442 14453 14456 14457 14461 14464 14468 14480 14483 14487 14488 14489 14491
165	Butter	14399
166	Cheese	14399
172	Market gardens	14449 14450

Merionethshire

4	Exemptions from tithe	14500 14503 14507 14507 14510 14513 14517
6	Compositions	14496 14512 14513 14518
7	Moduses	14492 14493 14495 14496 14498 14499 14500 14502 14503 14505 14506 14508 14509 14510 14511 14512 14514 14515 14516 14517 14519 14520 14521 14522 14523 14525
8	Glebe	14505 14507 14523
9	Local topographic descriptions	14492 14493 14494 14499 14500 14506 14508 14510 14515 14516 14519 14520 14521 14523 14525
11	Village morphology	14492 14493 14506 14524
12	Church	14501 14524
13	Country houses and ornamental gardens	14492 14492 14503
15	Cottages and cottage gardens	14493 14493
17	Open fields	14502
20	Hedgerow timber	14492 14494 14495 14499 14500 14501 14503 14505 14506 14507 14508 14509 14510 14515 14516 14517 14519 14520 14521 14522 14524 14525
22	Plantations	14500 14501 14503 14507 14517
25	Poor woodland	14505
27	Furze, gorse and heathlands	14497 14522 14525
28	Moorland	14525
31	Wasteland	14501 14503
32	Climatic hazards	14492 14493 14494 14497 14499 14505 14508 14509 14516 14519 14520 14522 14523
33	Excessively steep land	14492 14525
34	Land requires drainage	14497 14515
35	Land liable to flood	14497
36	Productive soil	14494 14499 14501 14503 14506 14510 14525
37	Poor soil	14497 14500 14501 14510 14516 14517 14525
38	Heavy (clay) soil	14507 14510 14516 14517
39	Loamy (turnip) soil	14494 14522
40	Light soil	14492 14495 14499 14501 14503 14505 14506 14508 14515 14516 14520 14521 14522 14523 14524 14525
43	Sand or gravel	14492 14494 14495 14497 14499 14500 14505 14506 14507 14508 14509 14510 14515 14516 14517 14519 14520 14521 14522 14523 14525
44	Peat	14492 14499 14500 14506 14510 14515 14516 14517 14520 14522 14523
46	Good local roads	14494 14501 14505 14508 14509 14525
47	Poor local roads	14500 14503 14506 14509 14517 14519 14521 14523 14524
48	Turnpike and main roads	14521

Merionethshire contd.

50	Water carriage	14492 14505 14507 14519 14520 14521
52	Railways	14493
53	Markets accessible	14520 14525
54	Markets inaccessible	14500 14505 14506 14523
55	Provincial markets	14495 14508
58	Market prices	14495 14500 14503 14506 14521 14525
60	Land occupiers	14523
61	Farm size	14498
65	Lammas and other common rights	14506
70	Enclosure or improvement of waste	14504
77	Paring and burning	14520
89	Lime	14494 14500 14501 14503 14505 14507 14508 14510 14516 14517 14519 14520 14521 14522 14525
92	Dung	14517
93	Seaweed	14509
101	General comments on crop rotations	14492 14494 14495 14499 14500 14501 14503 14505 14506 14507 14508 14509 14510 14515 14516 14517 14519 14520 14521 14522 14523 14524
110	Wheat	14492 14509 14524
111	Barley	14509
112	Oats	14492
113	Rye or meslin	14492 14495 14506 14519 14520
126	Tares and vetches	14501
129	Turnips	14493 14495 14495 14499 14501 14505 14508 14510 14511 14514 14515 14516 14520 14522 14524
132	Potatoes	14492 14493 14495 14499 14500 14501 14503 14505 14506 14507 14508 14509 14510 14511 14514 14515 14516 14517 14519 14520 14521 14522 14523 14524 14525
133	Bare fallows	14495 14499 14501 14505 14506 14508 14509 14515 14516 14519 14520 14522 14523
135	Low farming	14524
136	Remarks on the absence of turnips	14519
137	Remarks on pests and crop diseases	14523
139	Good quality pastures	14508 14509
140	Poor quality pastures	14497 14500 14507 14517
141	Meadows	14499 14506 14508 14517 14519 14520 14521 14522
143	Marsh grassland	14497 14520 14522
146	Cattle breeding	14495 14506 14517 14519 14522 14523
147	Cattle fattening	14504
148	Dairying	14506 14523
150	Sheep breeding	14495 14506 14517 14519 14520 14521 14523
151	Sheep fattening	14504
152	Droving	14521
153	Horses	14493
154	Pigs	14495 14509
161	Hay	14499 14500 14507 14511 14516 14517 14520
162	Manufactured feedstuffs (cake etc.)	14522 14523
165	Butter	14495
167	Wool	14506
173	Allotments	14493

Montgomeryshire

1	Tithe-free district	14542
2	History of tithe payment	14578
4	Exemptions from tithe	14529 14530 14531 14532 14533 14538 14539 14543 14546 14547 14548 14550 14551 14553 14554 14557 14558 14560 14563 14567 14568 14580 14591 14592 14594 14595 14599 14601
5	Tithe in kind	14555 14559 14569 14573 14598
6	Compositions	14527 14534 14541 14555 14559 14584 14593
7	Moduses	14528 14529 14530 14531 14532 14533 14534 14535 14536 14537 14538 14539 14540 14541 14543 14544 14545 14546 14547 14548 14550 14552 14553 14554 14555 14558 14559 14560 14561 14562 14563 14564 14565 14566 14567 14569 14570 14571 14574 14575 14576 14577 14578 14579 14580 14581 14582 14585 14588 14591 14592 14594 14595 14596 14597 14598 14599 14600 14601
8	Glebe	14558 14584
9	Local topographic descriptions	14537 14558 14560 14563 14566 14570 14571 14574 14575 14585 14589 14592 14597
10	Regional topographic descriptions	14535 14538 14580
11	Village morphology	14530 14543 14547 14571 14592
12	Church	14589
15	Cottages and cottage gardens	14580
18	Small, irregular closes	14597
20	Hedgerow timber	14526 14528 14529 14530 14531 14533 14535 14536 14537 14538 14539 14540 14542 14543 14544 14545 14546 14547 14548 14549 14550 14551 14552 14554 14556 14558 14560 14561 14562 14563 14565 14566 14567 14568 14570 14571 14574 14575 14579 14580 14581 14582 14585 14589 14590 14591 14592 14594 14595 14596 14597 14599 14600 14601
21	Coppice	14570 14597
22	Plantations	14530 14531 14532 14546 14547 14548 14554 14556 14558 14562 14563 14567 14570 14571 14579 14580 14592 14595 14599
23	Woodland management	14563
31	Wasteland	14567
32	Climatic hazards	14529 14536 14537 14538 14544 14549 14560 14561 14564 14565 14566 14568 14569 14570 14571 14574 14575 14583 14594
33	Excessively steep land	14526 14540 14546 14549 14551
34	Land requires drainage	14529 14560 14585 14595
35	Land liable to flood	14540 14601
36	Productive soil	14526 14531 14533 14547 14549 14558 14561 14568 14570 14572 14574 14581 14583 14589 14590 14592 14594 14601
37	Poor soil	14526 14529 14532 14533 14536 14538 14539 14544 14546 14548 14551 14552 14554 14558 14562 14563 14567 14568 14571 14585 14590 14591 14592 14595 14601
38	Heavy (clay) soil	14528 14529 14531 14533 14536 14539 14540 14543 14546 14548 14550 14560 14561 14562 14565 14567 14568 14569 14580 14581 14582 14590 14591 14593 14594 14595 14596 14599 14600
39	Loamy (turnip) soil	14526 14537 14558 14561 14574 14583
40	Light soil	14528 14530 14531 14533 14536 14537 14538 14539 14545 14546 14547 14548 14549 14551 14552 14556 14558 14561 14562 14563 14565 14566 14568 14569 14570 14571 14572 14574 14575 14579 14585 14589 14590 14591 14594 14597 14601
41	Several varieties of soil	14533 14572
43	Sand or gravel	14526 14531 14537 14540 14542 14544 14545 14549 14552 14556 14558 14560 14561 14565 14566 14570 14574 14575 14583 14596 14597 14600
44	Peat	14552 14556 14567 14571 14575 14585 14589
46	Good local roads	14526 14530 14537 14543 14561 14562 14566 14568 14570 14574 14580 14583 14589 14592 14597 14599
47	Poor local roads	14535 14539 14546 14552 14565 14571 14585 14595 14596
48	Turnpike and main roads	14531 14543 14544 14575 14594
50	Water carriage	14537 14579
51	Canals	14548 14561 14583 14592
53	Markets accessible	14526 14535 14540 14543 14544 14561 14562 14574
54	Markets inaccessible	14552

639

Montgomeryshire contd.

55	Provincial markets	14537 14567 14585 14594
58	Market prices	14585
59	Landowners and their estates	14542 14547
61	Farm size	14565
63	Farm implements	14569
66	Rents	14550 14563 14587 14590 14593
70	Enclosure or improvement of waste	14530 14585
80	Reclaiming and embanking	14594
85	Underdrainage	14565 14594
89	Lime	14529 14532 14535 14537 14539 14540 14543 14544 14546 14556 14560 14561 14562 14563 14565 14566 14568 14570 14571 14574 14575 14579 14580 14583 14585 14589 14591 14592 14594 14597 14599
92	Dung	14526 14579
101	General comments on crop rotations	14526 14528 14529 14530 14531 14532 14533 14535 14535 14536 14537 14538 14539 14540 14542 14543 14544 14546 14547 14549 14550 14551 14552 14554 14556 14558 14560 14561 14562 14563 14566 14567 14568 14569 14569 14570 14572 14574 14575 14580 14583 14585 14587 14589 14591 14592 14594 14595 14597 14599 14600 14601
102	Irregular rotations	14538 14545 14571
110	Wheat	14536 14565
111	Barley	14529 14543 14560
112	Oats	14560 14585
113	Rye or meslin	14566
115	Beans	14591 14593
116	Peas	14528 14530 14531 14532 14535 14536 14539 14543 14546 14561 14563 14569 14570 14574 14575 14580 14583 14590 14591 14592 14593 14594 14596 14599 14601
123	Clover	14530 14535 14536 14539 14543 14547 14548 14550 14551 14552 14558 14572 14580 14581 14582 14591 14594 14600
126	Tares and vetches	14530 14546 14548 14551 14580 14592 14594 14599
129	Turnips	14526 14528 14530 14531 14532 14533 14535 14536 14537 14538 14539 14543 14546 14547 14548 14549 14550 14551 14552 14554 14556 14558 14560 14561 14562 14563 14565 14566 14567 14568 14569 14570 14574 14575 14576 14577 14578 14580 14581 14583 14585 14589 14590 14592 14593 14594 14595 14597 14599 14601
132	Potatoes	14526 14528 14529 14530 14531 14532 14533 14535 14536 14537 14538 14539 14542 14543 14544 14546 14547 14548 14549 14550 14551 14552 14554 14556 14558 14560 14561 14562 14563 14565 14566 14567 14568 14569 14570 14571 14574 14575 14576 14577 14578 14579 14580 14581 14583 14585 14589 14590 14591 14592 14593 14594 14595 14596 14597 14599 14601
133	Bare fallows	14529 14530 14531 14532 14533 14535 14536 14537 14538 14539 14542 14543 14544 14546 14548 14549 14550 14552 14554 14560 14561 14562 14563 14566 14567 14568 14569 14571 14574 14575 14580 14582 14583 14585 14590 14591 14592 14593 14594 14595 14596 14597 14599 14600 14601
135	Low farming	14526 14572 14587
139	Good quality pastures	14530 14531 14543 14546 14550 14558 14568 14569 14580 14599 14601
140	Poor quality pastures	14531 14548 14550 14551 14568 14571 14579 14591 14599 14601
141	Meadows	14531 14540 14543 14548 14571 14574 14580 14595
146	Cattle breeding	14530 14549 14567
148	Dairying	14549 14594
150	Sheep breeding	14549 14552 14567
151	Sheep fattening	14560 14585
154	Pigs	14585
161	Hay	14526 14529 14531 14532 14535 14538 14539 14540 14543 14546 14547 14548 14550 14551 14552 14555 14556 14558 14561 14562 14565 14567 14568 14574 14578 14579 14582 14583 14585 14590 14591 14592 14594 14596 14599 14600 14601
165	Butter	14530 14567 14585
167	Wool	14537
169	Good orchards	14580
172	Market gardens	14576

Pembrokeshire

1	Tithe-free district	14613 14621 14643 14784 14801
2	History of tithe payment	14614 14781
3	Tithe practices and agriculture	14663
4	Exemptions from tithe	14605 14619 14623 14636 14637 14645 14654 14657 14658 14660 14670 14676 14677 14681 14690 14696 14699 14702 14704 14706 14723
5	Tithe in kind	14622 14626 14663 14672 14704 14775 14794
6	Compositions	14602 14604 14606 14608 14609 14614 14622 14625 14630 14641 14645 14652 14663 14679 14689 14691 14704 14705 14716 14776 14781 14782 14783 14790 14794
7	Moduses	14634 14650 14654 14657 14659 14660 14662 14668 14683 14697 14704 14722
9	Local topographic descriptions	14664 14682 14687 14697 14700
10	Regional topographic descriptions	14639
12	Church	14664 14682
20	Hedgerow timber	14605 14607 14610 14612 14615 14617 14619 14623 14624 14627 14628 14631 14634 14636 14638 14639 14644 14646 14647 14650 14651 14654 14655 14656 14657 14658 14660 14666 14668 14670 14678 14681 14683 14684 14685 14688 14692 14694 14699 14702 14703 14706 14708 14714 14717 14718 14721 14723
21	Coppice	14669
22	Plantations	14682 14693 14711
25	Poor woodland	14778 14793
26	Commons	14626 14694
27	Furze, gorse and heathlands	14698 14713
31	Wasteland	14628
32	Climatic hazards	14617 14664 14668 14669 14687 14697
33	Excessively steep land	14682
34	Land requires drainage	14615 14635 14659 14674 14684 14706 14793
36	Productive soil	14605 14615 14620 14626 14639 14644 14647 14649 14650 14657 14688 14710 14711 14792 14798
37	Poor soil	14605 14620 14635 14657 14664 14668 14678 14682 14686 14687 14688 14697 14698 14700 14713 14788 14792 14793
38	Heavy (clay) soil	14607 14610 14619 14620 14623 14624 14627 14634 14640 14648 14651 14653 14656 14658 14660 14668 14670 14674 14678 14683 14684 14685 14686 14692 14693 14694 14699 14702 14703 14706 14709 14714 14720 14722 14723 14779 14780 14787 14789 14791 14792 14793 14796
39	Loamy (turnip) soil	14611 14626 14634 14639 14647 14648 14650 14654 14682 14702 14710 14711 14718 14778 14798
40	Light soil	14607 14610 14611 14612 14615 14617 14619 14620 14626 14627 14628 14631 14633 14636 14638 14644 14646 14650 14654 14655 14657 14658 14659 14661 14664 14668 14669 14674 14678 14681 14683 14684 14686 14687 14688 14693 14694 14697 14699 14700 14706 14708 14709 14711 14717 14718 14722 14723 14787 14789 14792 14793 14796
41	Several varieties of soil	14615 14651 14653 14656 14657 14689 14722 14787
43	Sand or gravel	14636 14638 14640 14674 14676 14721 14785 14787 14788
44	Peat	14653 14659 14664 14668 14669 14674 14681 14682 14686 14687 14697 14702 14717 14785 14788 14791
47	Poor local roads	14671 14682 14789
50	Water carriage	14655
53	Markets accessible	14628 14644 14716
54	Markets inaccessible	14646 14668 14671
57	Fairs	14677
58	Market prices	14782

Pembrokeshire contd.

59	Landowners and their estates	14603 14716 14787
60	Land occupiers	14650 14688
61	Farm size	14677
62	Leases 14616 14677	
64	Common grazing	14631 14661 14694
66	Rents	14612 14633 14635 14639 14667 14668 14675 14678 14688 14693 14696 14709 14713
67	Urban influences on value of land	14644 14711
71	Enclosure of commons	14668 14707
76	Conversion of arable to pasture	14663 14688
77	Paring and burning	14713
85	Underdrainage	14655
89	Lime 14682	
90	Seasand	14626
92	Dung 14644 14656	
100	Oil dust, unspecified fertilisers or manures	14687
101	General comments on crop rotations	14605 14615 14623 14626 14627 14646 14649 14650 14665 14675 14676 14682 14694 14697 14698 14699 14708 14709 14710 14711 14713 14720 14722 14777 14782 14787 14789
102	Irregular rotations	14626 14789
104	4-course rotation	14714
106	6-course rotation	14658 14714
107	7-course rotation	14792
108	8-10-course rotation	14611 14615 14626 14634 14639 14646 14648 14649 14654 14655 14657 14658 14664 14667 14669 14674 14678 14681 14683 14686 14687 14688 14692 14693 14694 14699 14700 14702 14703 14710 14711 14713 14723 14778 14779
109	More than 10-course rotation	14607 14610 14612 14619 14620 14623 14624 14626 14627 14628 14631 14633 14635 14636 14638 14640 14644 14647 14650 14651 14653 14656 14657 14659 14660 14666 14667 14668 14670 14674 14678 14681 14683 14684 14685 14689 14692 14693 14700 14702 14706 14708 14717 14718 14721 14777 14785 14788 14789 14793 14796 14798
110	Wheat 14684	
111	Barley 14713	
112	Oats 14682 14713	
114	Corn yields	14603 14604 14606 14608 14609 14616 14622 14624 14630 14641 14645 14663 14671 14672 14673 14677 14679 14680 14689 14691 14704 14705 14707 14712 14715 14716 14719 14724 14775 14776 14782 14783 14790 14797
116	Peas 14628 14704	
122	Unspecified grass seeds	14617
123	Clover	14604 14606 14608 14610 14615 14617 14619 14622 14623 14626 14628 14630 14633 14634 14636 14640 14644 14645 14646 14647 14648 14651 14652 14653 14655 14658 14659 14661 14663 14664 14665 14666 14668 14669 14670 14671 14672 14673 14674 14675 14676 14678 14679 14683 14684 14685 14686 14687 14688 14689 14691 14692 14693 14697 14698 14700 14702 14703 14706 14707 14708 14709 14710 14711 14714 14716 14718 14719 14722 14723 14724 14775 14776 14781 14782 14790 14797
129	Turnips	14604 14615 14617 14622 14650 14652 14653 14656 14663 14673 14676 14703 14704 14705 14711 14712 14714 14716 14719 14722 14775 14781 14782
132	Potatoes	14604 14606 14608 14609 14616 14622 14627 14630 14652 14656 14659 14661 14663 14671 14672 14673 14676 14679 14680 14681 14682 14686 14691 14702 14704 14705 14707 14712 14715 14716 14717 14719 14720 14724 14775 14776 14781 14782 14790
133	Bare fallows	14607 14608 14612 14617 14619 14626 14628 14634 14638 14640 14644 14647 14650 14651 14654 14656 14658 14659 14661 14666 14670 14676 14683 14685 14688 14689 14692 14693 14702 14703 14708 14711 14714 14718 14721 14722 14723
135	Low farming	14650 14708 14713
137	Remarks on pests and crop diseases	14684 14708 14796
139	Good quality pastures	14659 14723 14777
140	Poor quality pastures	14659 14674 14682 14700
141	Meadows 14723	
145	Accommodation land	14649 14711
146	Cattle breeding	14682
148	Dairying 14682	
150	Sheep breeding	14631
160	Straw 14790	
161	Hay 14678	
165	Butter 14616	
166	Cheese 14616	
167	Wool 14704	

Radnorshire

2	History of tithe payment	14730 14762 14769
4	Exemptions from tithe	14731 14737 14741 14760 14767 14771
5	Tithe in kind 14762	
6	Compositions	14726 14738 14746 14747 14749 14756 14762 14763 14765 14766 14767 14768 14769 14770 14772
7	Moduses	14727 14728 14736 14738 14740 14748 14767
9	Local topographic descriptions	14730 14731
15	Cottages and cottage gardens	14762
20	Hedgerow timber	14725 14727 14728 14729 14731 14732 14733 14736 14737 14740 14741 14742 14743 14744 14745 14750 14752 14753 14754 14757 14758 14759 14760 14761 14771 14786 14799 14800
21	Coppice	14738 14743 14764 14767 14795
26	Commons	14734 14738 14799
27	Furze, gorse and heathlands	14741 14741
34	Land requires drainage	14732 14736 14738 14741 14758 14800
36	Productive soil	14733 14745 14757
37	Poor soil	14727 14734 14736
38	Heavy (clay) soil	14725 14729 14731 14733 14738 14740 14750 14752 14761 14771 14786 14800
39	Loamy (turnip) soil	14729 14743 14757
40	Light soil	14725 14727 14731 14732 14733 14736 14737 14738 14742 14744 14745 14754 14757 14758 14759 14760 14799
43	Sand or gravel	14728 14729 14731 14741 14742 14743 14753 14760 14771 14786
44	Peat 14741	
47	Poor local roads	14733 14738 14745
53	Markets accessible	14731
54	Markets inaccessible	14799
64	Common grazing	14730
66	Rents 14734	
67	Urban influences on value of land	14799
68	Rates 14764	
72	Enclosure of open fields	14730
101	General comments on crop rotations	14732 14734 14737 14741 14742 14745 14746 14748 14749 14754 14755 14756 14759 14765 14768 14771
104	4-course rotation	14738 14740 14743 14752
105	5-course rotation	14731 14740 14761
106	6-course rotation	14728 14729 14731 14732 14737 14744 14757 14761 14800
107	7-course rotation	14729 14732 14740 14750 14760 14771 14800

Radnorshire contd.

108	8-10-course rotation	14725 14733 14736 14750 14753 14758 14800
109	More than 10-course rotation	14727 14736 14786 14799 14800
113	Rye or meslin	14746 14747
114	Corn yields	14726 14743 14755 14756 14763 14764 14765 14766 14770 14772
116	Peas	14731 14746 14747 14764 14770 14771
123	Clover	14725 14727 14728 14729 14733 14736 14737 14738 14740 14741 14744 14745 14748 14750 14754 14755 14756 14757 14758 14759 14761 14763 14764 14765 14771 14786 14795 14799 14800
126	Tares and vetches	14731
129	Turnips	14726 14728 14729 14731 14734 14735 14737 14742 14746 14748 14757 14763 14764 14765 14767 14768 14770 14771 14772 14786 14795
132	Potatoes	14726 14734 14735 14746 14747 14748 14755 14756 14763 14764 14765 14767 14768 14770 14772 14795 14799
133	Bare fallows	14727 14729 14731 14733 14736 14737 14740 14742 14744 14745 14750 14752 14753 14759 14761 14764 14786
139	Good quality pastures	14745
146	Cattle breeding	14758
150	Sheep breeding	14799
152	Droving	14730
153	Horses	14741
160	Straw	14766 14767
167	Wool	14799
170	Poor orchards	14767

EPILOGUE

The companion volume to this book, Hugh Prince's and my *The tithe surveys of England and Wales* is written as a handbook to the tithe surveys and discusses first, the nature of tithes, the process of tithe commutation and the characteristics of tithe surveys. The second part of that book is a review of the ways tithe surveys have been used by historians and historical geographers as sources of historical evidence. In this *Atlas and index* the source material in tithe files has been indexed and much of the quantitative data which they contain has been abstracted and presented at scales from that of the individual tithe district, through aggregations of these data in county tables, to maps and tables for the whole of England and Wales. The characteristics of the tithe files of each county and some flavour of the wealth of qualitative information which they contain is provided in a set of county essays. Further data are held in computer files deposited in the E.S.R.C. Survey Archive.

Maps have been used as a principal means of communicating both quantities and distributions, and these, in association with the series of tables and extracts from assistant commissioners' and local tithe agents' reports, provide a sketch outline of the nature of English and, to a lesser extent, Welsh rural landscapes and farming systems at the opening of Queen Victoria's reign. This synchronous and partial picture is but one step towards fully understanding nineteenth-century rural environments and economies. All these materials are now part of the public domain and are offered freely for further analyses in the hope that these will provide us with a yet firmer datum against which earlier and later changes can be measured and with which international comparisons can be drawn.

Appendix Data held in E.S.R.C. Survey Archive, University of Essex

All the numerical and indexing data as transcribed in the Public Record Office and in their original, unprocessed state are held in machine-readable form in the Economic and Social Research Council's Survey Archive. They are stored on a nine-track magnetic tape and consist of 45,520 records of eighty character length recorded at a density of 1600 bpi. Copies of the files may be obtained on application to the Director, E.S.R.C. Survey Archive, University of Essex, Wivenhoe Park, Colchester, Essex CO4 3SQ. In total the data files contain some 1.8 million items, coded as described below.

Data for each of the 14,829 tithe districts are contained on a minimum of three and a maximum of six records of eighty columns each. All numerical data are recorded as right-justified integer numbers.

Record 1

Cols. 1–2
County reference number. Counties are those recognised by the Tithe Commission and the numbers are identical to those used by the Tithe Redemption Commission, viz.:

1	Bedfordshire	24	Northamptonshire
2	Berkshire	25	Northumberland
3	Buckinghamshire	26	Nottinghamshire
4	Cambridgeshire	27	Oxfordshire
5	Cheshire	28	Rutland
6	Cornwall	29	Shropshire
7	Cumberland	30	Somerset
8	Derbyshire	31	Hampshire (Southampton)
9	Devon	32	Staffordshire
10	Dorset	33	Suffolk
11	Durham	34	Surrey
12	Essex	35	Sussex
13	Gloucestershire	36	Warwickshire
14	Herefordshire	37	Westmorland
15	Hertfordshire	38	Wiltshire
16	Huntingdonshire	39	Worcestershire
17	Kent	40	York City and Ainsty
18	Lancashire	41	Yorkshire, East Riding
19	Leicestershire	42	Yorkshire, North Riding
20	Lincolnshire	43	Yorkshire, West Riding
21	Middlesex	44	Anglesey
22	Monmouthshire	45	Brecon
23	Norfolk	46	Cardiganshire

47 Carmarthenshire
48 Carnarvonshire
49 Denbighshire
50 Flintshire
51 Glamorgan

52 Merionethshire
53 Montgomeryshire
54 Pembrokeshire
55 Radnorshire

Cols. 3–7
Tithe district reference number as it appears in the P.R.O. catalogue.

Cols. 8–33
Tithe district name. Spellings as on the cover page of the tithe file; first twenty-five characters of the name only.

Cols. 34–5
Category of tithe district, whether parish, township, etc., according to the following codes:

B	Borough	BP	Borough and Parish
C	Chapelry	EP	Extra-parochial place
D	District	ID	Tithe district
H	Hamlet	MH	Manor and hamlet
I	Tithing	MR	Manor and lordship
L	Liberty	PC	Parochial chapelry
M	Manor	PD	Parish and district
P	Parish	PH	Parish and hamlet
R	Lordship	PI	Parish and tithing
T	Township	PP	Part of a place
V	Village	TD	Township and district
		TH	Township and hamlet
		UP	United parishes

Col. 36
Format of report on agreement for tithe commutation.
1   'arable' type
2   'pastoral' type
blank no report

Cols. 37–41
Total acreage for which land use data are enumerated (usually this is the titheable acreage but frequently acreages of tithe free land are also enumerated).

Col. 42
Completeness/representativeness of the data according to the following codes:
0 no indication of whether whole district enumerated
1 all district titheable, all land enumerated
2 all district titheable, all land not enumerated
3 exempt categories of land in the district, but acreage specified
4 exempt categories of land in the district, but acreage not specified
5 exempt categories of land in the district, but no indication of whether included
6 exempt estates covering less than 10 per cent of a district, included in area enumerated
7 exempt estates covering less than 10 per cent of a district, but not enumerated
8 exempt estates covering more than 10 per cent of a district and not enumerated

Col. 43
blank

Col. 44
Blank or 1 to indicate that xerox/microfilm extracts from the documents are held at University of Exeter.

Cols. 45–9
arable acreage

Cols. 50–4
grassland acreage

Cols. 55–9
woodland acreage

Cols. 60–2
orchards acreage

Cols. 63–5
hops acreage

Cols. 66–8
gardens acreage

Cols. 69–72
wheat acreage

Cols. 73–4
wheat yield in bushels/acre

Cols. 75–8
barley acreage

Cols. 79–80
barley yield in bushels/acre

Record 2

Cols. 1–7
as record 1

Cols. 8–11
oats acreage

Cols. 12–13
oats yield in bushels/acre

Cols. 14–17
peas and beans acreage

Cols. 18–19
peas and beans yield in bushels/acre

Cols. 20–3
acreage of bare fallow

Cols. 24–7
clover and seeds acreage

Cols. 28–9
yield of clover and seeds in cwts/acre

Cols. 30–3
acreage of turnips

Cols. 34–5
yield of turnips in £s/acre

Cols. 36–7
yield of pasture in shillings/acre

Cols. 38–9
yield of meadow in cwts/acre

Cols. 40–1
yield of hops in cwts/acre

Cols. 42–3
yield of orchards in £s/acre

Cols. 44–5
yield of gardens in £s/acre

Cols. 46–7
yield of wood in shillings/acre

Cols. 48–51
number of cows

Cols. 52–5
number of bullocks

Cols. 56–8
number of horses

Cols. 59–63
number of sheep

Cols. 64–5
rental of arable in shillings/acre

Cols. 66–7
rental of pasture in shillings/acre

Cols. 68–80
blank

Record 3

Cols. 1–7
as for records 1 and 2

Cols. 8–9
date of report on tithe agreements if one in file;
38 – 1838
39 – 1839
40 – 1840
41 – 1841
etc.

Cols. 10–24
Either:
name of assistant commissioner/local tithe agent
or:

Cols. 10–12
numerical code for name of assistant commissioner/local tithe agent

1 T. S. Woolley
2 T. S. Woolley Junior
3 J. Townsend
4 F. Browne Browne
5 H. W. Meteyard
6 R. Kynaston
7 J. Pickering
8 W. Heard
9 J. M. Mathew
10 R. B. Phillipson
11 H. Pilkington
12 J. J. Rawlinson
13 E. Greathed
14 T. Sudworth
15 T. Martin
16 J. Holder
17 T. Turner
18 A. Jackson
19 H. Dixon
20 J. Penny
21 J. S. D. Selby
22 A. O. Baker
23 C. Osborn
24 J. Farncombe
25 T. C. Parr
26 T. Phippard
27 T. P. Hilder
28 J. Jerwood
29 F. Leigh
30 R. Page
31 C. Pym
32 J. Coldridge
33 A. Owen
34 G. Louis
35 W. Glasson
36 W. Richards
37 J. Johnes
38 W. Downes
39 J. Fenton
40 T. Hoskins

41 J. D. Merest	55 T. J. Tatham
42 H. B. Gunning	56 M. Sayer
43 ? Mears	57 G. Ashdown
44 T. Sutton	58 C. Warner
45 A. Biddell	59 G. C. Symons
46 C. Howard	60 R. Atkinson
47 G. Bolls	61 J. Smalepiece
48 J. S. Penleaze	62 J. Smith
49 R. Hart	63 T. Neve
50 J. B. Neal	64 J. Hodsen
51 J. West	65 C. Wilson
52 N. S. Meryweather	66 E. Y. Hancock
53 J. Milner	67 H. Gilbert
54 H. Jemmett	

Cols. 25–30
acreage of common

Cols. 31–80
Index to contents of tithe file, numerical codes as integers separated by commas. End of index is marked by /.

Records 4, 5, 6

Cols. 1–7
as records 1, 2, 3

Cols. 8–80
index codes are continued on these cards if necessary

These code headings identify the original set of 250 subject index headings before redundant headings were eliminated and those only occasionally used combined to form the set of 182 as in the published index above. Now that the index is published it is considered unlikely that future workers will wish to consult the original, untransformed version in the Archive and so the codes are not listed here. A typescript code book is held by E.S.R.C. Survey Archive who will supply a copy on request.

References

Adams, I. H. 1976. *Agrarian landscape terms, a glossary for historical geography*. London, Institute of British Geographers Special Publication No. 9.

Allison, R. 1966. The changing landscape of south-west Essex from 1600 to 1850. University of London Ph.D. thesis.

Burrell, E. D. R. 1960. An historical geography of the Sandlings of Suffolk 1600 to 1850. University of London M.Sc. thesis.

Caird, J. 1852. *English agriculture in 1850–51*. London, Longman, Brown, Green and Longman, 2nd edition.

Cameron, L. G. 1941. *Hertfordshire*. Report of the Land Utilisation Survey of Great Britain, part 80.

Carpenter, Aileen M. 1964. Changes in the agricultural geography of the south Hertfordshire plateau, 1750–1888. University of London M.A. thesis.

Chambers, J. D., and Mingay, G. E. 1966. *The agricultural revolution, 1750–1880*. London, Batsford.

Chapman, J. 1961. Changing agriculture and the moorland edge in the North York Moors, 1750–1960. University of London M.A. thesis.

1973. Agriculture and the 'waste' in Monmouthshire from 1750 to the present day. University of London Ph.D. thesis.

Chiplen, R. F. J. 1969. The rural landscape of the Blackmore Vale c. 1840. University of Exeter M.A. thesis.

Cobbett, W. 1912. *Rural rides*. London, Dent, Everyman edition, Vol. 1.

Collins, E. J. T. 1975. Dietary change and cereal consumption in Britain in the nineteenth century. *Agricultural History Review*, 23, pp. 97–115.

Cox, E. A. 1963. An agricultural geography of Essex c. 1840. University of London M.A. thesis.

Cox, E. A., and Dittmer, B. R. 1965. The tithe files of the mid-nineteenth century. *Agricultural History Review*, 13, pp. 1–16.

Cunningham, G. L. 1974. The changing landscape of the Dorset heathlands since 1700. University of London Ph.D. thesis.

Darby, H. C. (ed.) 1936. *An historical geography of England before A.D. 1800*. Cambridge, Cambridge University Press.

1960. An historical geography of England twenty years after. *Geographical Journal*, 126, pp. 147–59.

(ed.) 1973. *A new historical geography of England*. Cambridge, Cambridge University Press.

Deane, Phyllis, and Cole, W. A. 1967. *British economic growth 1668–1959*. Cambridge, Cambridge University Press, 2nd edition.

Dicks, T. R. B. 1964. The south-western peninsulas of England and Wales: studies in agricultural geography, 1550–1900. University of Wales Ph.D. thesis.

Dittmer, B. R. 1963. An agricultural geography of northwest Wiltshire, 1773–1840. University of London M.A. thesis.

Dodd, J. P. 1976. Norfolk agriculture in 1853–4. *Norfolk Archaeology*, 36, pp. 253–64.
   1979a. Hampshire agriculture in the mid-nineteenth century. *Proceedings of the Hampshire Field Club and Archaeological Society*, 35, pp. 239–60.
   1979b. Gloucestershire agriculture 1801–1854. *Transactions of the Bristol and Gloucestershire Archaeological Society*, 97, pp. 101–16.
   1979c. The West Riding crop returns for 1854. *Yorkshire Archaeological Journal*, 51, pp. 117–29.
   1980. Herefordshire agriculture in the mid-nineteenth century. *Transactions of the Woolhope Naturalists Field Club*, 43, pp. 203–22.
   1982. Wiltshire agriculture in 1854 – the value of the Board of Trade returns. *Southern History*, 4, pp. 145–65.
Edwards, J. W. 1963. Enclosure and agricultural improvement in the Vale of Clwyd, 1750–1875. University of London M.A. thesis.
Evans, E. J. 1976. *The contentious tithe. The tithe problem and English agriculture, 1750–1850*. London, Routledge and Kegan Paul.
Frost, M. J. 1964. The changing land use in the upper basin of the river Mole. University of London M.Sc. thesis.
Gramolt, D. W. 1961. The coastal marshland of east Essex between the seventeenth and mid-nineteenth centuries. University of London M.A. thesis.
Grigg, D. B. 1966. *The agricultural revolution in south Lincolnshire*. Cambridge, Cambridge University Press.
Harley, J. B. 1973. England *circa* 1850. In Darby (ed.) (1973).
Harris, A. 1961. *The rural landscape of the East Riding of Yorkshire, 1750–1850, a study in historical geography*. London, Oxford University Press.
Hartley, F. D. 1953. The agricultural geography of the Chilterns *c.* 1840. University of London M.A. thesis.
Harvey, D. W. 1961. Aspects of agricultural and rural change in Kent, 1800–1900. University of Cambridge Ph.D. thesis.
   1963. Locational change in the Kentish hop industry and the analysis of land use patterns. *Transactions of the Institute of British Geographers*, 33, pp. 123–44.
   1964. Fruit growing in Kent in the nineteenth century. *Archaeologia Cantiana*, 79, pp. 95–108.
Healy, M. J. R., and Jones, E. L. 1962. Wheat yields in England, 1815–59. *Journal of the Royal Statistical Society*, 125, pp. 574–9.
Henderson, H. C. K. 1936. Our changing agriculture: the distribution of land in the Adur Basin, Sussex, from 1780 to 1931. *Journal of the Ministry of Agriculture*, 43, pp. 625–33.
   1941. Changes in land utilisation in Derbyshire 1837–1937. In A. H. Harris, *Derbyshire*. Report of the Land Utilisation Survey of Great Britain, part 63, pp. 71–4.
Holt, Harriet M. E. 1984. Assistant commissioners and local agents: their role in tithe commutation, 1836–1854. *Agricultural History Review*, 32, pp. 189–200.
   1985. Upland farming in northern England *c.* 1840–*c.* 1870. University of Exeter Ph.D. thesis.
Holt, Harriet M. E., and Kain, R. J. P. 1982. Land use and farming in Suffolk about 1840. *Proceedings of the Suffolk Institute of Archaeology and History*, 34, pp. 123–39.
Jarvis, J. B. 1946. Changes in land use in south-east Denbighshire. In E. J. Howell, *North Wales*. Report on the Land Utilisation Survey of Great Britain, parts 41–3, pp. 734–43.
Kain, R. J. P. 1973. The land of Kent in the middle of the nineteenth century. University of London Ph.D. thesis.
   1974a. The tithe commutation surveys. *Archaeologia Cantiana*, 89, pp. 101–18.
   1974b. Contemporary opinion concerning the possible conversion of pasture to arable after tithe commutation. *Cantium*, 6, pp. 77–9.
   1975. Tithe surveys and landownership. *Journal of Historical Geography*, 1, pp. 39–48.
   1979a. Compiling an atlas of agriculture in England and Wales from the tithe surveys. *Geographical Journal*, 145, pp. 225–41.

1979b. Tithe as an index of pre-industrial agricultural production. *Agricultural History Review*, 27, pp. 73–81.

1984. The tithe files of mid-nineteenth century England and Wales. In M. A. Reed (ed.), *Discovering past landscapes*. London, Croom Helm, 1984, pp. 56–84.

Kain, R. J. P., and Holt, Harriet M. E. 1981. Agriculture and land use in Cornwall *circa* 1840. *Southern History*, 3, pp. 139–81.

1983. Farming in Cheshire *circa* 1840: some evidence from the tithe files. *Transactions of the Lancashire and Cheshire Antiquarian Society*, 82, pp. 22–57.

Kain, R. J. P., and Prince, H. C. 1985. *The tithe surveys of England and Wales*. Cambridge, Cambridge University Press.

May, J., and Wells, S. F. 1942. *Montgomeryshire*. Report of the Land Utilisation Survey of Great Britain, part 36.

Mitchell, P. K. 1965. West Cleveland land use, *c.* 1550–1850. University of Durham Ph.D. thesis.

Mosby, J. E. G. 1938. *Norfolk*. Report of the Land Utilisation Survey of Great Britain, part 70.

Naish, M. C. 1961. The agricultural landscape of the Hampshire chalklands, 1700–1840. University of London M.A. thesis.

Orwin, Christabel S., and Whetham, Edith H. 1964. *History of British agriculture 1846–1914*. London, Longman.

Parton, A. G. 1973. Town and country in Surrey *c.* 1800–1870: a study in historical geography. University of Hull Ph.D. thesis.

Perry, P. J. 1981. High farming in Victorian Britain, prospect and retrospect. *Agricultural History*, 55, pp. 156–66.

Phillips, A. D. M. 1973. A study of farming practices and soil types in Staffordshire around 1840. *North Staffordshire Journal of Field Studies*, 13, pp. 27–52.

1976. Agricultural land use, soils and the Nottinghamshire tithe surveys *circa* 1840. *East Midland Geographer*, 6, pp. 284–301.

1979. Agricultural land use and the Herefordshire tithe surveys, *circa* 1840. *Transactions of the Woolhope Naturalists Field Club*, 43, pp. 54–61.

Porter, Regina E. 1974. Agricultural change in Cheshire during the nineteenth century. University of Liverpool Ph.D. thesis.

Postgate, M. R. 1961. Historical geography of the Breckland, 1600–1850. University of London M.A. thesis.

Powell, J. M. 1962. An economic geography of Montgomeryshire in the nineteenth century. University of Liverpool M.A. thesis.

1969. Tithe surveys and schedules: some Montgomeryshire examples. *Journal of the National Library of Wales*, 16, pp. 87–96.

Prothero, R. E. (Lord Ernle) 1961. *English farming past and present*. London, Heinemann and Frank Cass, 6th edition.

Sandell, R. E. (ed.) 1975. *Abstracts of Wiltshire tithe apportionments*. Devizes, Wiltshire Record Society.

Shave, D. W. 1941. The distribution of arable land in the upper Wey basin in 1840, 1870, and 1939. In L. D. Stamp and E. C. Willatts, *Surrey*. Report of the Land Utilisation Survey of Great Britain, part 81, pp. 392–7.

Sill, M. 1982. East Durham: mining colonisation and the genesis of the colliery landscape, 1770–1851. University of Durham, Ph.D. thesis.

Turner, M. 1981. Arable in England and Wales: estimates from the 1801 crop return. *Journal of Historical Geography*, 7, pp. 291–302.

Waugh, T. C. 1977. *GIMMS reference manual*. Inter-University/Research Council Report No. 30.

Willatts, E. C. 1933. Changes in land utilization in the south-west of the London Basin, 1840–1932. *Geographical Journal*, 82, pp. 515–28.

1937. *Middlesex and the London region*. Report of the Land Utilisation Survey of Great Britain, part 79.

Lightning Source UK Ltd.
Milton Keynes UK

177801UK00001B/1/P